A COMMENTARY ON JUDGES

16th–17th Century Facsimile Editions

A Commentary on JUDGES

Richard Rogers

THE BANNER OF TRUTH TRUST

THE BANNER OF TRUTH TRUST
3 Murrayfield Road, Edinburgh EH12 6EL
P.O. Box 621, Carlisle, Pennsylvania 17013, USA
*
First Published 1615
This Facsimile Reprint first published 1983
ISBN 0 85151 377 8

Printed in Great Britain
at the University Press, Oxford
by Eric Buckley
Printer to the University

A COMMENTARY VPON THE WHOLE BOOKE OF IVDGES.

PREACHED FIRST AND DELIVERED IN SVNDRIE LECTVRES; SINCE collected, and diligently peruſed, and now publiſhed.

For the benefit generally of all ſuch as deſire to grow in faith and Repentance, and eſpecially of them, who would more cleerely vnderſtand and make vſe of the worthie examples of the Saints, recorded in diuine hiſtory.

PENNED BY RICHARD ROGERS PREACHER of Gods word at *Wetherſfield* in *Eſſex*.

HEBR. 12.1.

Wherefore ſeeing we are compaſſed with ſo great a cloud of witneſſes, let vs caſt off euery thing that preſſeth downe, &c.

Whatſoeuer is written, was written for our inſtruction, that wee through conſolation of the Scriptures might haue hope.

LONDON,

Imprinted by FELIX KYNGSTON for *Thomas Man*, and are to be ſold at his ſhop in Pater-noſter Row, at the ſigne of the Talbot. 1615.

TO THE RIGHT HONOVRABLE, SIR

EDVVARD COKE KNIGHT, LORD chiefe Iustice of England, and one of his Maiesties most Honorable priuie Counsel: R.R. wisheth all blessing internall, externall, and eternall, from God our Father through Christ Iesus.

RIght Honourable, as it hath alway befallen the best both Diuine and Humane lawes to be peruerted by common profanenes and lewd custome: so may it be verified in all other things of like precious nature, that they could neuer escape the taint of humane errour and abuse. Witnesse the institution of the holy feast of Shiloh mentioned in this booke: which though first was chiefly vsed as a memoriall of Gods benefits, yet in processe of time grew to extreme abuse, and gaue occasion to the vnlawful stealing of the virgins in their dances. Nay, witnesse euen this approueable custome of Dedicating bookes: which though it hath been long taken vp and continued for good and respectiue reasons: yet hath it been of old the practise of heretikes, and still is of vnworthy writers to conueigh the poison of their books into the inferiour sort, by stiling and gracing them with the names of remarkable personages.

Religion and Christianitie, the ministerie of the Word, and the Profession thereof, are things in name and nature, of the highest value: howbeit, as the fairest apple to the worme, so are these exposed to the treble corruption of error, infidelitie, and hypocrisie. Semblably, the writings of Diuine argument (whether vpon Scripture, as this, or Treatises consonant thereto) are of singular vse in the Church: yet neuer free from the malignitie of some men. Especially such as who either out of their curiositie can endure nothing which clawes not their leprous humor: or through their carelesnes, professe either to meddle with no mans writings at all, or without putting difference to embrace good and bad with equall affection.

For the two former of these three, (I meane the vngraciously nice, and the gracelesly sensuall:) this I must say, that since the Scriptures themselues (the most solemne of all other both for matter and stile) cannot rellish with them: I despaire that my writings should procure their appetite. Yea peraduenture this worke of mine will displease their daintie eyes and fingers, by the very bignes, and so preiudice their further handling. These therfore (if their disease be incorrigible) I professe not my selfe a cooke, for to dresse their diet; but rather leaue them to feede vpon the chalke and morter of their vnsauourie Pamphlets, while others nourish their minds with more wholesome meate: and send them to the trough and akornes, since they refuse Angels food. For the latter sort, (since there is more hope to correct their error, then the others vice) I pray to God, that with their generall willingnes to reade, he would giue them an vnderstanding heart, to discerne aright of things that differ: that the holy eye of their iudgement may be, like a Musicall eare in the distinguishing of sounds, and like the fining pot of the Goldsmith, in seuering the gold from drosse, or his touchstone in discouering of mettals. Also my hope is, that such as buy new bookes of all sorts, may happily light vpon this, among others: which if they shall doe, I wish them no worse, then that the gaine they reape, and the taste they get from this, may disgrace and distaste with them, all fruitlesse and offensiue authors.

Pardon me (right Honourable) if I haue been ouer bold, in aduenturing to publish these poore labours, and thrust them vnder your patronage. I haue not sinisterly aimed at the Poets marke, who wisheth all writers, to set a glosse vpon their worke by a glorious entrance: But partly to shroud my selfe in God vnder your authoritie, against the tempest and violence of all

χρῆ προσώπον τηλαυγὲς. Pind.

vniust

vniust censurers (such as I named before:) and partly (yet chiefly) to commend the diligent perusall of this booke to all religious or indifferent Readers, by your Honours example: perswading my selfe, that you will not more willingly become patrone to the writer, then a patterne of the things contained in the writing it selfe. And, as by Gods ordinance, the oyle of Consecration was first powred vpon the head of *Aaron*, yet Psal.133.2.
staied not there, but ranne downe thence vpon his beard, and to the nethermost skirts of his clothing: so, I iudged this order no whit preposterous, if first I presumed to powre this oyle (fetcht out of the Lords Tabernacle) vpon your Honours head: that so from you (as the sweet showres trickling downe from the hill to the valley) the fragrancie and fruite hereof might descend lower vnto meaner persons.

Among sundrie other bookes of holy writ, which, in the course of my Ministerie, these fourtie yeeres past, God hath assisted me to explane and go through with my Audience; I haue (for some causes) chosen this, to leaue as a poore pledge and memoriall to Gods Church of my fidelitie, paines, and loue. And, though I respected also the good and request of my owne Congregation herein, into whose hearts I desire doubly to fasten the naile of wholesome instruction (which soone slippeth out): yet seeing my time is short, and my voyce cannot reach beyond her vsuall limits, I haue endeuoured with my pen to draw a long and a wearisome line, that the other defect might be supplied: looking vp to him for a requitall, who hath promised not to conceale the labour of our loue. Heb.6.10.

I haue (Right Honourable) purposely altered the course of my writing, which formerly I haue vsed in my Treatise. As *Elisha* the Prophet put his hands vpon the King of Israel his 2.King.13.16.
hand, when hee bad him shoote: so, when wee vndertake the handling of Scripture, the holy Ghost allowes vs not to say all wee can inuent, but requires vs to put our hands in his hands, and to applie our selues more strictly vnto his drift, then in Tractates of our owne, wherein generally our scope and libertie is more large. Yet as the text hath led me, I haue held my selfe to these two markes: The one more generall to build

vp

vp the Chriſtian Reader in faith and good life: To the which end as I haue alreadie written a large Diſcourſe, (if it haue yet come to your Honours hands) containing grounds and directions for the more eaſie practiſing and growing in them both; ſo now in this I haue annexed liuely examples out of the Scriptures to illuſtrate thoſe precepts: the naturall repugnancie whereof to fleſh and blood might otherwiſe breake out into gainſaying the Art it ſelfe and the practiſe thereof. The other, particular: to ſhew to the diligent Reader, what vſe the hiſtoricall examples of the old Teſtament (eſpecially) doe afford vs: a matter in this our contemplatiue but cold age, little reſpected, and leſſe vnderſtood.

The which (ſuch as it is) I haue boldly preſented vnto your Lordſhip vpon a three-fold conſideration. The firſt this: God who hath made you a principall member in this great bodie of our land, both in gifts perſonall and publique, hath iuſtly proportioned a principall place of employment for you aboue others. Your complements of Nature, Art, Experience, he hath (I doubt not) accompliſhed with ſauing grace. Your pietie towards God, teſtified by your reuerend hearing his word, and reflecting it ſelfe in loue vpon his Miniſterie: your ſage and well menaged gouernment of ciuill affaires: your learning bewraied by your iudicious and aſſiduous reading of Schollers bookes, and fauouring their authors: all theſe argue ſtrongly, that though Poperie, ignorance, iniuſtice and euill manners could well forgo you, yet the Church, the Common-wealth and literature could ill want you. And the ſame God who hath thus enriched you, hath crowned his gifts in you, ſo that while you liue, your Name is bleſſed, and at the end of this life, you ſhall not dye vndeſired. Why hath the Almightie thus graced you? Doubtleſſe not for your ſelfe onely, but to this end, that as the Sunbeames drawing vp the ſweet vapours from the earth, ſuffer them to fall vpon their thirſtie mother againe, with a doubly fruitfull influence: ſo Gods talents meaſured out largely vnto you, might entirely returne their honour vnto the giuer with ouerplus. The veſſell that is full, and runneth ouer, hath for it ſelfe, and bedeweth the earth alſo

which

which is neere it. And seeing the greatest goodnesse of the best creature cannot reach so high as God himselfe: therefore hee expects that you drop it vpon this lower region of Saints who excell in vertue; yea vpon his Church and Gospell, (whereto he hath by letter of Attorney made ouer all such debts) to the promoting and aduancing whereof, the aduantage of your Honour and authoritie (besides your other gifts) is chiefly to be employed. Giue me leaue then (I beseech) to improue that common interest, which our Mother the Church claimeth in you, for the vndertaking of this my writing. You are chiefe among the sonnes of wisedome, which *is iustified of all her children.*

Psalme 16.2.

Math.11.19.

Secondly, your Lordship knoweth well, that the Church and Common-wealth are friendly neighbours, each bordering vpon other, both compast with one wall, and both yeelding mutuall aids & defences each to other. As outward peace could hardly be setled, except humane lawes enioyed the brotherly assistance of the spirituall sword: (which is a law present when no other is, euen to the conscience) So the ministery of the word should not so much preuaile as it doth, (little though it do in comparison) except the pleasant dewes of Hermon did refresh the barren mountaines of Zion, I meane, except the ciuill sword of iustice did backe and authorize the same against them, who profanely cōtemne the word, as the smartles stroke of a leaden edge. The due obseruation whereof (right Honorable) hath caused me to offer you this gift, that so I (one of the meanest) might thankfully acknowledge in the behalfe of the whole Church, that vnder his Maiesty she hath obtained much quietnesse through you, and that many things are worthily done to this nation by your prouidence, (as sometime that euill man but not euill Orator said to a person and in a case farre vnlike:) which I haue therefore vttered in your eare, not only for that your Honour is well able to digest your owne felicity and merit, but that I might exhort you to excell your selfe in time to come, and to bring forth most fruite in your age: remembring that it is as hard a thing to stand to the reparations of some house, as to build it out of the ground: and it hath euer

Eadem sunt Ecclesiæ & Ciuitis mœnia.

So *Moller* and others morralize that in Psalm.133.3.

πάντῃ πανταχοῦ ἀποδεχόμεθα. Actes 24.2.

καταπέψαι τὸν ὄλβον. Pind.

bin iustly questionable whether the purchase, or preseruing of vertue be the more difficult. Sure it is that the Prologue and Scene of your life hitherto worthily carried, promise to the beholders a close deseruing rare applause.

Lastly, your place and name seemed to claime this Dedication. The booke I write vpon conteines the most famous history of the renowned Iudges of ancient Israel. And God hath set your Honour in the chiefe seat of iustice, euen made you (vnder his Maiestie our highest Iudge) the principall Iudge in our English Israel. Besides, the argument of the booke (if it please your Honour to take a view of it) doth as peculierly concerne you, the presidents of these Worthies well deseruing your imitation. As that Romane Captaine beholding the images of his victorious ancestors, found himselfe enflamed with earnest zeale of equalling or surpassing them: so, I doubt not but the laying open of these Iewish Captaines in their liuely colours, will rauish your religious spirit, with the loue and emulation of their graces. And here (ere I finish) suffer me to recommend vnto your Honour, two of the most heroicall vertues in these Gouernours. The one, their inuincible courage,
Iosh.1.2. (the Epitome of a Christian Magistrates worthines) though they liued in the most forlorne times, and dissolute, wherein the Idolatries and iniquities of Israel, seemed to striue with her captiuities and calamities, and whether man sinning or God reuenging should get the vpper hand. A manifest token of the immediate warrantise of these Iudges from heauen; enabling and encouraging them with so incredible fortitude and successe. The other (last named, but in nature first) is their ad-
Heb.11. throughout. mirable faith: which as the Author to the Hebrwes could not silence in that thicke clowd of witnesses, so thereby he impor-
Heb.10.37. teth, that is generally the life whereby all Christians liue; and especially the fortresse, yea armour of proofe for the Magistrate. Not onely the sword of the Lord in the hands of *Gedeon, Barak, Jphtah*, and *Samson* (mentioned in this booke) to fight with against their forreine enemies: but also a singular both offensiue and defensiue weapon, for your Honour first, and then for your inferiors in place of gouernment, against the

intestine aduersaries (no lesse hurtfull) of God, his Gospell, and our common peace. For this sword rusteth not, nor looseth her edge with time. In the desire of this happy blessing vpon these my poore trauels, I most humbly recommend my selfe and seruice to your Lordship, and your Honours person and weightie affaires to the protection and direction of the Almightie. From my poore house at *Wethersfield* in *Essex*. Ianuary 20. 1615. resting

Your Honours most humbly deuoted in the Lord,

RICHARD ROGERS Minister of the Gospell.

LECTVRES OR SERMONS VPON THE WHOLE BOOKE of IVDGES: and first, the entrance into them.

I Confesse, it is no small matter for a man to take vpon him to set foorth Lectures or Sermons of any part of the word of God, especially of an whole booke thereof: and the rather for that it is a matter of much greater difficultie and danger so to doe, then to preach them (seeing for mine owne part, I would easilier be brought to preach three Sermons, then to set foorth or penne one:) and besides, we see that learned men (I speake of many) who might for their excellent gifts profit many, and doe the Church much good, are hardly drawne thereto. I leaue their reasons to themselues: perhaps they thinke it a needlesse worke to set foorth more bookes. For mine owne part, I knowing that many would reade little, if there were not new bookes set foorth, I thinke it to good purpose to labour in that kinde: especially when the things set foorth are for the quickening vp of the present drowsie age. And so I testifie my iudgement by my writings, that I am of another minde: not for that I would dissent from learned men, or seeke glorie and praise by this my practise, when (to speake as the truth is) I confesse freely, that as I come many degrees behinde them in gifts for that purpose: so I would not take vpon me this exercise of writing, vnlesse I were led to it by waightie reasons: but in the simplicitie of my heart I speake it, that I set my selfe to this worke, as I can haue time and leisure from my publike imployment in my Ministerie, and other priuate duties, euen to keepe my selfe from danger in this euill world, as idlenesse, too much tampering in the world, and such like needlesse and hurtfull businesse, as well as for the desire I haue to benefit any other hereby: and besides, I thinke it better to benefit the Church while wee liue, being but a short time, (other may rise vp after to perfit such beginnings) then to burie our gifts vtterly, and so to depriue it altogether of the same by death.

Reasons of this my attempt.

Also I see that euery age of men hath sundrie troubles annexed to it (the old as well as the young) and occasions are offered of sinning and offending God many waies by one occasion or other, which are not thought of before they come. In so much as when the danger of youth and of the former yeeres of our life is passed with inward peace, and without any grosse and iust offence to others (which yet to doe is few mens cases, and rarely obtained, and not without much striuing and watching to enter in at the straight gate:) yet the diuell so much the more enuieth our credit in the Church, and the comfort we haue from God, in such an estate, especially the Ministers: and therefore hee doth the more bend his force against such, that hee may in their latter end disgrace them by winding them into some reprochfull and foule offences: that so he may (as much as in him lieth) make their former vertues and part of life, to be ridiculous and of no account.

And therefore, as I am not ashamed to confesse, that I haue receiued wonderfull

cause

cause of thanksgiuing to God, for his so great bountie and fauour towards me (the most vnworthie) in my younger yeeres, to keepe me from the infection of the time, and sins of the age wherein I haue liued, (yet God be mercifull to my many slips and infirmities) so I am not (I say) ashamed to confesse, that I feare in this my declining age, hasting apace to the graue (as with griefe of heart I haue seene in many) that I may possibly, yea and that full easily, be drawne to an vnprofitable, earthly, idle, and dead course of life, and thereby, to greater offending of God, and blemishing of my profession and Ministerie, vnlesse I should labour to preuent it by some set labour and study, and so to hold fast that which I haue receiued of the Lord: and that is, by the occupying and vsing the gifts which he hath giuen me, as in this kinde of studie, namely
2.Pet.3.17. *of writing, I may: and also if I should not endeuour to grow forward in grace, experience, and in the knowledge of our Lord Iesus Christ, (from the which a man may be easily hindred by the error of the wicked) rather then to looke what I haue done heretofore, I might easily flatter my selfe thereby, and so (at least) stand at a stay: or (which is worse) goe backe, and so lose my part of happinesse with them that continue to the end. For I make chiefe account of that, hauing it not in fruition as yet, but by hope onely: and I know it may easily and many waies be hindred and staied, as Satan can handle the matter, and as I see many goe to worke. And for this cause I desire to be occupied vntill the Lord come, and in this manner, hauing more then one foote in the graue. And to the end I may tye my selfe to liue the freer from dangerous falles and offences, while I am here a stranger and absent from home, and therefore I say, I haue set my selfe to this kinde of worke, as being not able through debilitie of body, and lamenes, to trauaile abroad, and helpe other neighbours, more then at home, by preaching, as I haue done since I first began (where my labour was desired:) and by conferring much, as occasion was offered, as I vsed in health to doe. And if any laugh at this which I haue said of my fearing my selfe, as thinking it meere folly, I cannot doe with it, neither am moued for their so censuring me: but I tell them this, that while they feare not their frailtie also but count it foolishnes, they hast apace to vtter miserie.*

Now for taking this booke in hand, to set out my Sermons vpon it, which I haue before preached, though I haue gone ouer, in the course of my Ministerie, many other besides this: I take this booke in hand, not as making comparison betwixt it and other bookes of Scripture: but partly seeing no Lectures or Sermons are set out vpon it, that I know, to giue light and helpe to such as need it: and partly at the earnest desire of those that heard my Sermons on it: and if I may know and perceiue my labours in this to be thought worth the setting foorth, I would be willing, as much as in me lieth, to doe the like in some other booke. In this worke, beside the people, who are not brought vp in learning, who may see that their whole life may be directed hereby and may much profit by it, so I intended also in it to benefit Students and Preachers, who are not yet experienced: nor best furnished with matter for the edifying of the hearers: so that beside the fruite they may reape hereby in common with the people; so they may learne how to make vse of the historicall part of the Bible, and learne to draw doctrine and instruction out of the examples thereof, fit for the people (and that out of the bad as well as the good) euen as well as out of other Scripture: which all haue not learned to doe, neither haue attained vnto: and therefore doe oft times offer violence to the Scriptures, by making allegories of them, and so wresting them to another sense then the holy Ghost hath made of them; without which manner of handling them, they can draw none or little matter out of the most examples in the

stories

ſtories of them: and ſo beſide that their doctrine is not ſoundly gathered, ſo they giue too fearefull ſuſpition to the ignorant, that ſuch parts of the Scripture are barraine and drie, while they doe by ſuch ſhifts, and yet indirect, ſo hardly draw matter and doctrine out of them, when yet it is certaine and cleere, that they are full of ſound inſtruction.

But to come to my purpoſe, I will now ſet downe ſome generall things before I enter into the text, which may giue ſome light to the better vnderſtanding of the whole book: ſuch as I gather partly, by obſeruing & laying together that which I read in it, (comparing one thing with another:) and partly out of that learned and reuerend Father Maſter Peter Martyr, *whoſe workes neither the moſt priuate men can vnderſtand, nor many Miniſters, though they may vnderſtand them, can come by, neither if they can, ſhall they finde there, that which ſhall be much for their ſimpler hearers benefit.*

And firſt let the reader marke, how this booke agreeth with all the former, from Geneſis to the end of Ioſhua, *and what is the ſumme of them and this. Concerning the booke of Geneſis, after mention is made (in the beginning of it) of the creation of the world, and the generations to the flood: it doth afterward ſhew, how God choſe his people out of* Abraham *and his poſteritie, and how they were ſent into Egypt to auoid the famine. In Exodus theſe things are the principall: how the people of God multiplied and increaſed in the land of Egypt, till there roſe a King who cruelly oppreſſed and vexed them ſore: and how they were deliuered out of the bondage, which they were in there, by* Moſes: *and how they had lawes giuen them, to gouerne them. And this laſt point is the ſumme of Leuiticus alſo. The booke of Numbers declareth their diuers reſting places in the deſert, and their goings forward toward the land of Canaan. In Deuteronomy,* Moſes *being to depart out of this world, and to leaue the people, doth moſt faithfully repeate the law to the generation which came after the former, and which then liued, I meane, to the poſteritie of* Abraham. *Then came* Ioſhua *and led the people into the promiſed land, and diuided the land of the Amorites and Canaanites, which partly was ſubdued and gotten out of their hands, and partly remained to be conquered: he (I ſay) diuided it amongſt the twelue tribes, according to the commandement of God, after he had brought them ouer Iordan, ſlaine many of the Kings of Canaan, and poſſeſſed their cities and grounds in that countrey. This is the ſumme and contents of the booke of* Ioſhua. *After his death, (to come to our purpoſe) the Lord gouerned his people the Hebrewes, being placed in that land, by iudges: whom to that end he indued with excellent gifts, and by them deliuered and kept the people out of the hands of their enemies, who as yet did all the daies of the Iudges remaine in great numbers to vex them.*

But to vnderſtand better the meaning of the word [Iudges] a materiall point in this booke to be vnderſtood, though to iudge ſignifie to know the caſes of ſuch as contend, and be at variance, and to giue ſentence of iudgement betwixt men: yet theſe Iudges mentioned in this booke, had not that office, neither were called Iudges in that reſpect. But (as the word ſignifieth alſo, to reuenge and to redeeme out of bondage) thus did thoſe Iudges deliuer and redeeme the people, as in this booke is at large declared. (I ſpeake not of Samuel, *who is ſaid after, to iudge them alſo, by deciding* 1.Sam.7.6. and 15. *controuerſies and ciuill cauſes) But theſe Iudges had that office aſſigned them of God, to deliuer the people (as I haue ſaid) out of their enemies hands, and ſo to iudge them: and therefore were called by that name of Iudges, and this booke that intreateth of them and their acts throughout, is called,* The booke of Iudges.

And

The Entrance into the booke.

And briefly to lay out the ſtate and condition that theſe people, the Hebrewes, then liued in: whereby the office of the Iudges may the better be vnderſtood: they hauing not yet conquered the land, were occupied (as at their firſt entrance into it, and after Ioſhuas death a while) in ſubduing it, and their enemies: but afterward they ſuffered them to remaine, and become tributaries to them, and were thereby (as God ſaw it meete, and as need required) in great perill and miſerie by them, and then, becauſe they were his people, leſt they ſhould haue been vtterly deſtroyed, theſe Iudges were raiſed vp by him, without the election of men, to reſcue and deliuer them. But afterward when they were at reſt, and peace, God gouerned them not by thoſe Iudges: (therefore Iphtah, when he was deſired, would not raigne ouer them) neither had they authoritie ouer them: but he vſed the help of ſome other excellent perſons, fit by their vertues and gifts for that purpoſe, and they ruled the people: but the Iudges (as I ſaid) were ſtirred vp by the Lord, in great dangers, brought vpon them by their enemies, to be helpers and deliuerers vnto them, and to keepe them in peace afterward, while they liued. So that theſe Iudges were not choſen by ſucceſsion, as Kings: neither by the voyces of the people, but were raiſed vp by God (as wee haue heard) indifferently, as well out of one tribe as another: and how meane and vnfit ſoeuer they were before, for that purpoſe: God did furniſh them by and by after he had ſtirred them vp, with moſt excellent gifts for that end, to the which he appointed them. And it went farre better with the people while they were vnder them, then it did afterward, when they would needs haue a King to raigne ouer them. For they did alwaies deliuer the people of Iſrael out of the calamitie with which they were oppreſſed: whereas their Kings did ſometimes waſte them, and bring them into captiuitie, and were (the moſt part of them) Idolaters.

And although vnder the Iudges, the people were ſomtimes oppreſſed grieuouſly by ſtrangers, and eſpecially vnder Samſon by the Philiſtims (for why? we muſt know, their horrible ſinnes deſerued it, and prouoked God to deale with them in that manner:) yet they were neuer led into captiuitie while they liued with them. Againe, there were few of the Kings good men, in Iſrael, not one: the Iudges (for the moſt part) were all ſuch. A good teſtimonie whereof, we haue in the Epiſtle to the Hebrewes: where we thus reade of the commendation of them: The time would be too ſhort for me to ſpeake of Gedeon, Barak, Iphtah, and Samſon: theſe the holy Ghoſt commendeth. And though ſome of them (as men) did ſometime fall, yet we are to thinke they returned and roſe vp againe: ſeeing the Scripture (as I remember) doth neuer condemne them. So that in reſpect of them, and by their helpe, (if the people could haue ſeene it and made benefit of it) we may ſay, they liued in a golden age.

Now whereas it is not ſo apparantly to be ſeene, that this booke doth ſet foorth Chriſt vnto vs, in all the commendations of theſe Iudges: (who yet is the end of all bookes of Scripture) to ſuch as demaund about it, I anſwere: that Chriſt is not cleerely ſet foorth in any of thoſe bookes of the old Teſtament firſt written: but darkly, and by types and figures, as God ſaw it meete for thoſe ages: and ſo wee are to thinke of this booke, where the deliuerances from ſo great enemies, as are mentioned herein, are types of that great deliuerance and redemption of men wrought by Chriſt, out of the iawes of the diuell. And let the commending of ſundrie of thoſe Iudges by the holy Ghoſt ſatisfie vs, that they could not haue been good men, nor haue liued by faith, as they were ſaid to haue done, if they had not beleeued in Chriſt, and been ſanctified thereby. Beſides, what authoritie ſhall we giue to the old Teſtament, if they who

are

are commended in it, to haue been men of God, as diuers Kings and Prophets, with many other, did not liue and walke by faith, (seeing it is not expressely set downe) without which they could not please God?

Now the summe of this booke is thus much: first, a declaration generally, of the estate of the religion and manner of worshipping God, which these Israelites vsed in their Common-wealth from the death of Ioshua *to* Eli *the Priest, (for the storie of* Ruth *containes things done in the daies of the Iudges, Ruth* 1.1.*) and more particularly this booke layeth out their sinnes, and Gods calling them out of them by sundrie warnings and iudgements, vnto repentance, with many fearefull examples of their reuolting and turning backe againe: whereby may bee seene how corrupt they were both in religion and manners: and this booke is a liuely glasse (if we well consider it) of this our age.*

The parts of the booke are three. The first setteth downe the slouthfulnesse of the Tribes in executing the commandements of God against their enemies, and the punishment threatned for it, Chap. 1. *and* 2. *and their slouthfulnesse is illustrated by the contrarie course of* Iudah *and* Simeon *(who were forward to goe against them) as in Chapter* 1. *to verse* 21. *is to be seene. The second part is from the* 2. *chapter to the* 17. *which treateth of the Iudges, and their great actes, according to occasions offered, who in their due time were raised vp. The third part is from chapter* 17. *to the end: and setteth foorth some odious and monstrous acts committed in those confused times, when there was no ordinarie Gouernour: and therewithall, the punishments which followed.*

The author of this booke is vnknowne, but yet the booke is canonicall, and authorized also by the new Testament. The time of the actes of it, from the death of Ioshua *to* Eli *the high Priest, is gathered to be about* 300, *yeeres. The end of this booke (as shall better appeare in the particular handling of it) is to instruct and perswade vs, in this latter age of the world, to carry our selues vprightly, and in a streight and well ordred course, both in prosperitie and aduersitie: I meane, to hold the feare of God in both, and to keep hope and patience in and through out this our pilgrimage, with prayer and repentance: which if we do, God will be no lesse with vs, then he was with the good people mentioned herein.*

The order which I purpose to obserue in the Lectures vpon this booke, is first to giue the short summe of the Chapters: then to deuide euery Chapter into parts, for the better distinguishing the points thereof, that they may be better vnderstood, and more clearely seene into: thirdly, I giue the sense of the verses more fully, and lay forth the doctrine with the reasons, and vse thereof, though for the most part, they be not alwaies expressely set downe, which manner of handling the diuerse histories of this booke (as also I thinke the same of our preaching out of all other Scriptures) namely, that after the meaning and sense, apt and fit instruction should bee drawne out, with the application to the present state, need, and vse of the hearers, plainely and pithily as may be for their best edifying I hold meetest to be vsed.

And I would to God, that there were consent giuen therto of al Preachers, and that this course were aimed at: I wish that euery one did not follow his owne priuate course who hath neuer learned any good way or order of preaching. Whereby it commeth to passe, that some fill their Sermons with the froth of their owne braines, or the bare authorities of men, and least proofe is brought out of the Scriptures: Also some preach darkely to the little benefiting of the hearers, not to mention all which were endlesse.

And

And although for many other things I leaue the consideration therof to my reuerend and learned brethren, yet in this I hope without ostentation, and arrogating ought to my selfe, I may be allowed to speake: in regard of the long time which I haue spent in studying, learning, and practising (as I haue been able) the holie exercise of preaching. And now to end these my Lectures, this I say: that beside the varietie of much good therein contained, there are some points to good purpose, occasioned touching faith, and repentance: and sundrie directions giuen how to seeke the Lord when we haue slipped, and how to beare trouble aright.

Thus much I thought good to say before I enter into the seuerall Sermons, euen to this end, that some good light may be giuen, as to him that marketh duly it may appeare. Now I will proceed to the text it selfe.

THE FIRST SERMON VPON THE FIRST CHAPTER OF THE BOOKE OF IVDGES.

VERS. 1. *And it came to paſſe after that* Ioſhua *was dead, that the children of Iſrael asked the Lord, ſaying: who ſhall goe vp for vs againſt the Canaanites, to fight firſt againſt them?*

VERS. 2. *And the Lord ſaid,* Iudah *ſhall goe vp: behold I haue giuen the land into his hands.*

IN this Chapter two things are chiefly contained, (to ſet downe the ſumme of the Chapter and parts of it together:) The firſt is the commendation of the tribe of *Iudah,* to the 21. verſe: (the cauſe we ſhall heare afterward.) The ſecond is the ſetting downe of the ſinne of the tribes that are mentioned after, in that they ſlothfully ſuffered the Canaanites to liue by them, and did not expell them, and that is to the end of the Chapter. *Iudah* is commended in a double manner: firſt for the actes they did now at this time after *Ioſuahs* death, and they are to the eight verſe: and then for that which that tribe had done before his death in the reſt of the verſes to the 21. *The ſumme and parts of this Chapter.*

The firſt part of the Chapter.

To come to the meaning of the firſt 7. verſes, ſeeing they lie together, after the death of *Ioſhua,* who had bin their guide and had gone before them, *The meaning of the 7 firſt verſes* the children of Iſrael ſaw that they muſt make warre with the forraine nations: for vnto that day the whole land though it was promiſed and deuided amongſt them, was not yet wonne by them, nor conquered, but in the lot and inheritance of euery tribe there were the Canaanites their enemies ſtill dwelling and remaining. And ſeeing they knew they muſt be driuen out by force and ſtrong hand, as God had commanded; therefore they doubted not, whether they ſhould goe out againſt them to warre or no: but which tribe ſhould firſt begin, and goe before, and gouerne the reſt. And the thing was of ſuch waight, that they went to the Lord about it, and asked of him by the high Prieſt before the propitiatory and Mercy ſeat, as the manner then was in doubtfull caſes, which of their tribes ſhould begin the battaile. Exod. 28. 30.
And ſo they had an anſwere from him to their ſatisfaction, who ſhould goe vp before them, and in that their attempt, God proſpered them, for he had

promiſed

promised so to do. And *Iudah* sought helpe of *Simeon* his brother and neighbour tribe, who consented readily so to doe: and they prospered in that their attempt, and had victory ouer the Canaanites, as is set downe; together with the destruction of *Adonibezek* their King. Thus much for the meaning of these 7. verses in some generall manner.

Now we haue the meaning of these verses, it remaineth that we drawe from thence such instructions as are afoarded vs out of them, beginning with these two former here set downe: and first out of the first verse. In that this people was now constrained to looke about them, and (now *Ioshua* was dead) to doe that themselues for their peace and quiet, which hee was wont to doe for them: wee are taught, that when chiefe & speciall persons are taken away, who were wont to beare the burden for many other, then they who were left behinde, must put forth themselues, and take the more paine, and be put to greater plondges then they were before. Oh it is a great ease, if men could consider it aright, when they haue others to beare the brunt for them, while they them selues may as it were, sit in peace: while our Sauiour Christ was conuersant with his disciples on earth, he sheilded them, prouided for them euery way, and bare off the blowes from their shoulders. As when the Pharisies cauilled with them, (whereby they might easily haue bin discouraged) he tooke their part, they being too weake, and defended them. So he said to *Peter* a litle before his ascention: *When thou wast young thou girdest thy selfe, and wentest whither thou wouldest: but when thou art old, another shall girde thee, and leade thee whither thou wouldest not.* When Kings gouerne wisely and conscionably, the people sit vnder their vine and figtree, as it was said they did, that liued in the dayes of *Salomon*, when hee had about him *Nathan* the Prophet, *Zadok* the Priest, *Benaiah* a most worthy Counseller, with such like. Also when people are setled vnder faithfull and able teachers, who watch for their soules, they liue (as it were) in a corner of heauen, (if they can see) who obediently sit at their feete to heare them. And so I may say of children, who haue their prouident and godly parents to regard their welfare, they know not what sorrow and trouble meane: for the glory of children are their fathers. And of other inferiours, while they haue their good friends and gouernours about them, who seeth not, that they be priuiledged and prouided for aboue others: but when all these faile, then beginneth the woe and sorrow of all those, whom they leaue behinde them: which in the vnwelcome parting of couples in mariage, (the husband from the wife, or she from her husband, where true loue was betwixt them, is daily seene and proued, to the deepe sorrow of the longest liuer of both.

Doct. 1. in verse. 1.

Note.

Matth. 9. 11. 12

Ioh. 21. 18.

1. King. 4. 25.

Al this which I haue said, should whet on such as are so backed by others, to weigh the great goodnes of God in giuing them such helpes, and to yeild them due reuerence, loue, and obedience in the Lord, and to be more carefully giuen to euery good worke, while they haue so great incouragements. But because the inioying of such is made so common a matter, and a thing of no great reioycing while they liue with them: (for according to the prouerbe, we best know what a good thing is worth when wee feele the want of it) therefore it were good for them to suppose oft times, and to put the case, that such worthy helpes and friends are taken from them, and what they should then doe being left without them; for as the vine wanting his

raile

raile to prop it vp, runneth on the ground and waxeth wilde and vnfruitfull: *A simile.*
so inferiours being destitute of their godly superiours, waxe degenerate, and grow out of kinde, lying open to mischiefe as *Saul* did after *Samuels* death. 1.Sam.28.15.
But to speake the truth (the more is the pitie) this is rare and hardly to bee found, that such take any great good by those helpes while they inioy them, (vnlesse it be in things temporary, for their ease, maintenance, and seeking Note.
of liberty to the flesh,) neither when they forgoe them, haue grace to bewaile the losse of them in any other respect then that which is earthly: neither doe they looke to stand vp as they ought (in the want and roome of them) with care and confidence to become lightes and good examples, and to keepe themselues from euill, as they were kept some of them (no doubt) by their good friends before. Such prouide ill for themselues, seeing as it was with this people of Israel heere, when *Ioshua* was dead, that they had a great losse, and were constrained now to looke better about them then they needed to doe before, euen so they hauing now the like befalne them, must now take the burden on themselues, which was borne by others for them before. The which being so, men should make this vse of such changes, to *Vse* 1.
prouide and learne to want their good helpes and friends before hand, and arme themselues as *Iob* did, to looke for their change, when they see they must needs forgoe them. They should also acknowledge daily with hearty thankes to God, what a benefit they haue of them, while they inioy them, *Vse* 2.
and doe all good that they may by the helpe of them. Which they cannot doe, but they must of necessitie feele the losse of them, to be very great, and see that they must now lay their shoulders to the burden, and therefore labour to be the fitter to beare and vndergoe it, and to want them, who were wont to stand them in so great stead. This as it is wholesome direction and aduice to such as haue their helpers and friends as yet remaining with them: so it is easie to see euery where, what calamities they sustaine, who made no such vse of them, while they comfortably inioyed them. For the which purpose, this I adde, and so I end this point: oh how sweetly and to their good liking haue many liued, when they had others to beare their burdens for them: as husbands, wiues, subiects, children, neighbours, and other by their friends: in which benefits they who inioyed kindely and aright, there is no doubt, but that (which is the chiefest of all) they haue therewith, that God is their friend also: but seeing many depend onely on them in a carnall manner, and on their liuing still with them, and rest not on God; therefore their proppes faile them, and their desolation commeth vpon them, as the enemy vpon an vnarmed man.

More particularly, we are taught here by their example, who sought to *Doct.* 2.
God in their doubtes for counsell and resolution, that in all our doubtfull cases, (which are not fewe) partly touching our estate towards God, and partly particular duties and actions of our speciall callings and conditions of life: while we remaine here on earth: we should consult with and aske counsell of God for our resolution, in such manner as he hath taught vs: and in no wise to conceale and bury our wants and defects that trouble vs, or passe by the sinnes that cleaue to vs, or other difficulties in our dealings and businesse that oppresse vs; for so we prouide ill for our selues, euen to liue in ignorance and sorrow (with other inconueniences annexed thereunto) for

euer after. And yet when we seeke answere and resolution, wee must not thinke, that we are inioyned of God to doe it in the same particular manner that these did, by the high Priest, for that might be thought a great trouble to vs, seeing there is none in these daies to aske counsell for vs: but we must know, that we haue *Moses*, the Prophets and Apostles: and (by the helpe of them) the Ministers of God, Pastors and Teachers, to bring vs Gods message and minde out of his word, and thereby to instruct vs. And wee
Act.17.11. our selues, as occasion serueth, are to search the Scriptures, and answere our owne doubts thereby, and settle our estate to God ward, as *Dauid* did in the
Psal.43.5. Psalmes oft, and namely where he saith: *Why art thou heauy (O my soule) and why art thou so troubled within mee? Still trust in God, and praise him which is the*
Psal.119.9. *best of all.* And againe: whereby shall (a man yea) a yong man (who doth more hardly ouercome his passions) denie his way, that so hee may proue himselfe blessed? he answeres out of the Scripture, *euen by taking heed thereto as Gods word teacheth.* Thus I say, we are to search the Scriptures by hearing and reading them, which doe reueale Gods will vnto vs, or consult with the men and brethren whom the holy Ghost hath set ouer vs to that ende.

Note. But this is the misery of this age, nothing is to be called into question among vs: we thinke we haue all knowledge, and doubt of nothing, no, not in the waightiest matters: why so, I pray you? is it because we be diligent and carefull to learne, and daily to search into our selues and into the word to see what is a misse, that we neede no helpe of other? Nay, that is fewe mens care, the most are no such: but they chiefly are desirous to enquire further what the good will of God is toward them, who haue most profited thereby already, and so ought other to doe: who if they were not both carelesse how they liued, and so obserue no want in themselues: and drowsie or wandring when they heare, it could not be, but where there is an ordinary ministery, they should grow much in setlednesse and sound knowledge: whereas we see, strangers who are not taught at home, but resort where sound teaching is, they I say, though they know as much as other, are more inquisitiue and desirous to be answered in their doubts, then such as haue the daily meanes at hand whereby they might be resolued. It were to be reioyced for very much, if hearers of the Gospell did frequent the houses of Preachers, as they do Physitians to enquire of their bodily health: then there were some hope that they looked to liue for euer, as they desire to liue long heere in bodily health, though that can be but for a very short season. But those daies are gone, which yet I in my time haue seene, when in the places, which I meane, both men women and seruants would rise early to dispatch their businesse on the Lecture day, to the end they might repaire thither, and inquire of God in the congregation, and would be as ready to take good priuatly also by questions to very good purpose, and necessary, when they might. A bout maintenance and bodily prouision, how many questions (I pray you) are moued before one dayes or weekes worke bee brought to an end? and is any so ignorant, that he knoweth not, that he that mindeth his way to eternall life, hath many causes in the day and weeke, to aske of himselfe by secret questioning, whether all be well with him concerning his account making to God? But there are few or no doubts about

such

ſuch matters as doe greatly trouble vs now a daies, wee run on at ſixe and ſeuen as the blinde man caſts his ſtaffe, not looking before vs, that we might be ſafely guided. But what commeth of ſuch raſh proceeding without conſulting with God, by that one example in the booke of Numbers may ſuffi- Numb.14.45.
ciently appeare, when certaine of the people of Iſrael would needs goe vp to fight with the Amalekites and Canaanites of their owne head, not ſent by the Lord: for they came out againſt them and deſtroyed them.

There is another fault committed in this kind, though, I am perſwaded, not with ſo bad a mind: but ſeeing it is not without great danger I will giue warning about it. And that is, when men do feele many doubts to ariſe, by reaſon of their ſinnes, and ſore trouble of conſcience: but yet through feare leſt they ſhould not haue an anſwere to their liking, or for ſhame, leſt they ſhould bewray their ignorance, and ſecrets, and ſo bee reproched and mocked for the ſame, they do conceale them, till ſorrow deuoure them for not opening their mindes about them, euen as water pent in, burſteth out vio- Note.
lently and doth much hurt, which in time hauing been let foorth and vented, might haue auoided it. What had become of the people in the booke of the Actes of the Apoſtles, when they were pricked at their hearts, as with the point of a ſword, if they had not come to the Apoſtles, and made their complaint, ſaying: *Men and brethren, what ſhall we doe?* and yet they had Act.2.37.
ſtrong temptations not to open their griefe to them, becauſe they had much prouoked them before, and railed on them. Therefore if any be troubled, as theſe were with doubts, eſpecially in their conſcience, and bee in great ſtraights and vnquietneſſe, through feare of Gods diſpleaſure and wrath, if they cannot with their owne knowledge put away their trouble of mind, let them inquire of the *men and brethren*, whom they are well perſwaded off, for reſolution and comfort, as they did: who, as they haue been inſtruments of God to pricke and wound them, ſo are they alſo to helpe to eaſe them: and they need not feare (God hauing promiſed) but that they ſhall find reſt to their ſoules, how impoſſible ſoeuer it ſeemed to them to bee ſo. And this be ſaid of the firſt verſe.

In this next it is manifeſt, that God gaue them an anſwer from the Propi- Verſe 2.
tiatory or Mercy-ſeate: which they receiued by the high Prieſt: for ſo hee vſed to doe, and it was one of the ordinarie meanes, whereby God ſpake to them in thoſe daies. And he did not onely ſo, whereby they were ſatisfied, (their queſtion being anſwered:) but he alſo incouraged them to goe to the worke he ſet them about, promiſing them the victorie in that warre againſt the Canaanites, ſaying: *I haue giuen their land into the hands of Iudah*, who ſhall goe before the reſt in attempting the warre againſt them.

Out of the which words witneſſing ſo gracious an anſwere to them from God, we may clearely ſee, that our ſeeking to God in our doubts and neceſſities, is not in vaine, neither is the labour loſt in ſo doing. For we are to know and be perſwaded, that God anſwereth his in their ſuites and demands, and indeed otherwiſe it were a deadly diſcomfort, and would diſcourage vs much from the well doing of dutie, as it maketh (we ſee) the wicked at their wits end, when they being in great danger, can haue no helpe from God, as we reade it was with *Saul*; who, when he ſought to God and asked counſell of him, to ſerue his owne turne thereby againſt the Philiſtims, rather then to

please him,and hee answered him not; hee in depth of sorrow complained and cried out,saying: *The Lord hath forsaken mee, and answereth me no more, neither by Prophets,nor by dreames.* But blessed be his name,he dealeth not so with his: neither let this trouble them, (for so they will say) that although God answered this people of Israel here,when they sought to him, yet hee doth not so to vs now: for they are to know,that it is his promise to vs,in all
1.Ioh.5.14. that we aske of him according to his will,to grant it,as well as here hee answered to them in that they asked. Therefore in the Psalme he saith.*Call on*
Psal.50.15. *me in the time of trouble,and I will heare thee,and thou shalt glorifie me:* which agreeth with the words of our Sauiour vttered to all his; *Aske,and it shall be*
Matth.7.7. *giuen you: seeke and ye shall finde.*

So that it is certaine,that euery child of God, that maketh his mone,and thus poureth out his complaint to him,shall be heard, which should not a little whet vs on, and animate vs *to draw neere to God:* wee hauing so sure a
Iam.4.8. word of promise,*that he will draw neere to vs.* For in seeking to a mortall man in our distresse,though he be little aboue vs,we know how readily & chearefully we goe about it,when we are perswaded of a good answer, and when we doubt not of his kind and louing affection toward vs: and on the contrarie, how hardly wee are drawne to sue to one,that is alienated from vs. And seeing the care thus standeth betwixt God and vs,that the oftener we come to him,the more welcome wee are, (for this is as true as the former speech) seeing such are most inward with him,and beloued of him,as *Abraham,Moses* and *Dauid,*who of others repaired oftest to him, and receiued most of him; I say,seeing it is thus betwixt God and vs,how lamentable is it, and to be bewailed,that this is not more common for men to repaire to God? who if they could marke it,may easily perceiue, that while they neglect to doe so, they increase their trouble, and get nothing. But seeing I am entred vpon this matter,I thinke it not amisse,to shew, how three sorts offend about this. The common sort wholly neglect and omit prayer altogether: the first thinking that though they pray not,they shall speed as well, and haue as good lucke (for so they terme it) as others shall: boldly affirming,that they see no good come of it,they: and yet in their distresse they thinke they should pray: but then they hauing neither will nor skill thereto,in stead thereof, do curse and rage for that they are not helped and deliuered: though some of them
Pro.1.20. do vtter words in their passion,the Lord heares them not,as we read, Pro.1. For it is all one as if they vttered none. And though they cannot pray to God, yet they make their complaints, and moane to euery man that they haue acquaintance with,and that will heare them. And for them to breake their minds to them that cannot helpe them,when yet they would so gladly finde helpe,and to passe by him in whom there is present and sure helpe to be found,what folly? nay,what madnesse is it? for (to say the truth) God is not sought vnto in any sort of such,no,not when all other shifts faile: (as I haue said.) But to speake of the second sort,who being professors,a forwarder sort in religion then the former,these should pray,and that in faith, confidence,and repentance with comfort, as well as in desire of obtaining the things which they want,with patient waiting Gods leisure, but euen they seeke not to God in this manner,which yet is the onely right way of praying,that he teacheth vs,or alloweth in vs. For prayers made to him without

these

these properties, are but a bare noise of words, vaine repetitions, and idle Matth.6.7.
speeches, which God abhorreth: neither may such looke to receiue any thing, as S. *Iames* saith: *Ye aske and obtaine not, because ye aske amisse.* Iam.4.3.

And when they see they receiue not the things they aske, euen they as well as the other who are further off, doe gather, and imagin, though falselie and vniustly, that prayer doth no good, and that it is but lost labour, seeing they are not heard in theirs, when they pray amisse, and so they waxe more slacke and negligent therein, as the other omit it altogether. And the lesse maruell it is, seeing euen good Christians (to come to the third sort) who go farre beyond both, do so forget themselues ofttimes, and are so deluded by the diuell, that euen they omit zealous and feruent praying, and fall to pray coldly, deadly: so many vaine deluzions, and alurements stand vp in their way to vnsettle them, and misty clouds of trouble to discourage them. And while it is thus with them, and while the flesh iustleth against all that good is (they not resisting it in time) it commeth to passe, that euen they who haue Gal.5.17.
learned to pray aright, and haue oft and vsually done so: do yet soone decline, sometime and before they bee aware, fall to pray more by custome Matth.6.57.
and course, then hartily and aright. For we are not to be ignorant of this, that we are as wel vndermined and slily deceiued by the malice and subtilty of the diuell and our euill hearts, about our prayers to corrupt and hinder Luk.18.1.
them, as we are in our liues to breake out and be offensiue therein. And we ought to marke our declinings and decay in the one, as well as our coldnes and deadnes in the other: for pray well and liue well, and contrary. For want of the which, it goeth so ill with vs as it doth, that we walke oft times Note.
heauisy, and cannot say that God heareth vs, as it is heere said of this people, that God answered them: for euen after we haue prayed, yet we are not satisfied, neither rest we by faith perswaded that God will heare vs: which yet is one of the chiefest fruites of prayer. And thus much of Gods answere to them.

But yet further we are to marke, that he did not barely answere them, as he might haue done, and haue said onely, *Let Iudah goe vp:* that shall be mine answere to you: but he addeth to it a gracious incouragement, which was more then they demanded, saying: *I haue giuen the land into his hands:* Commonly men in their suites to their betters, aske more then they looke for: thinking by that meanes to obtaine somewhat answerable to their expectation. But God giues more then is asked, or thought needfull. The which dealing of his doth adde yet greater hartening and incouraging of vs to prayer, when we see that he oftentimes promiseth and giueth more to vs then we looked for: as the deare Saints of God haue found in their time. *Ioseph* whose feete were pinned in the stockes, prayed that he might be deli- Psal.109.18.
uered out of prison, whereinto he was thrust at the suite of his whorish mi- Gen.39.19.20.
stris, for not consenting to her vnchast request: but God not onely deliue- Gen.41.14.
red him, but brought him out with great honour.

Esther prayed against the spitefull attempt of *Haman*, and that she and her Esther.7.10.
people, which were also Gods people, might be preserued from the deadly snare, which he had laid for their liues. But what did the Lord? He not onely saued them, but vtterly destroyed, and cut cleane off, in a most shamefull and reprochfull manner, both *Haman* and all his seede. So, the woman of Esther.9.10.

Mat.15.22. Canaan asked of Christ helpe for her daughter possessed with a diuell: but
Luk.15.22. he granted vnto her, beside that she asked, euen what she would. And wee know, that when the prodigall sonne, in his penurie and miserie, being glad to refresh himselfe, and fill his bellie with swines food, desired that he might be receiued, but as a seruant into his fathers house: and he was entertained, and taken in as a sonne, and nothing of the costliest apparell, and daintiest food was thought too good for him.

And whereto tend all these examples, but to incourage vs, to acquaint our selues with God, by seeking to know his will, and by oft and earnest repairing to him: assuring our selues, that wee shall not onely obtaine of him that which we come for in our prayers, but oft times much more, according
Heb.11.6. to that in the Epistle to the Hebrewes: *He that commeth to God, let him know that he is a plentiful rewarder of them that seeke him.* And he hath no experience of Gods louing kindnesse, who knoweth not, neither hath found this himselfe: for doe we aske all particular benefits euery day, which we inioy? no, nor one of many. But we should leade a poore life, maimed, as a body wanting fingers, eyes, tongue, &c. if wee receiued not more oft times then we aske. But to omit other things too long to stand vpon, who hath not had proofe of this, (a matter of greater waight) that whereas sometime, in the anguish and heauinesse of his soule for feare of the wrath of God, iustly prouoked by his sinnes against him, hee would haue thought it happinesse not to haue bin at all, but especially in liuing heere, to haue bin freed from feare of condemnation: who (I say) hath not proofe of this in himselfe, that hee hath yet liued to see by good and infallible euidence, beside that which hee desired) himselfe to be made assured of eternall glory? so true it is that God giueth his, more then they could aske or thinke: because they aske in the name and mediation of the sonne, whose merit and intercession is infinite.

So likewise we haue oft times bin in the depth of other calamities: and seeking to God for helpe therein, we haue not onely found deliuerance, but therewith blessings vnlooked for, to our great admiration and comfort. And if God hath not giuen vs our desire that way, yet, least he should seeme any way to come short of his promise, he hath suffered the crosse to remaine, till he hath made vs see, and therefore to say, that it hath turned to a farre greater benefit to vs, then if he had presently deliuered vs out of it, or (which is more) then if he had neuer laid it vpon vs at all: so true it is that God giueth his more then they could looke for in asking, or thinke to receiue. This should vphold vs against grudging, when at other times wee thinke God
Reuel.3.18. deales too sparingly, and shortens vs of our desires. But wee are blinde in obseruing these things, because we want the eye salue of faith, which onely can make vs see it to be thus.

But, before I leaue this verse, another thing heere is worthy to be mar-
Hebr.2.6. ked, that he doth not onely incourage vs to seeke to him earnestly, by the like large offer which he made here to this people: but here withall, he gi-
Psal.1.3. ueth vs sufficient incouragement to the worke, that he setteth vs about. As he doth here to the tribe of Iudah: *Thou* (saith he) *shalt fight my battels against mine enemies, and thou among others shalt goe about this worke: and though this were enough to harten thee to it, in that I command thee; yet know this for thy better incouragement, that I will be with thee, assisting and blessing thee, yea and I will also*

giue

giue thee the victory, by deliuering them into thy hands. And for better certainty to them, he telleth them, that he hath done it already, when yet it was to do. To teach vs, that if God speake the word, it should be counted all one of vs, as if he had done the deed. Much like to this is that in Hebrwes 6. Where God is denied to do as ill masters doe, that is, to take no knowledge of their seruants worke: no, he is not forgetfull of his seruants labours, nor vniust to leaue them vnrewarded, but telleth them before; that he will deale liberally with them. Hebr. 6. 10. Hebr. 2. 6.

Men promise much and performe little: yea many are so vniust, that they set other about their worke, but they are neuer willing to pay them their hire, and to come to a reckoning, because they are well content to defraud them of their due, and to take their labour, in a manner for nothing. But God is a liberall pay-master, he promiseth afore hand more then we can looke for: euen to make vs able and fit for the worke, that so it may not bee toilesome nor tedious vnto vs: beside the reward that he giueth afterwards: euen as he did to *Iosuah* before, when he should leade the people at the first into the land of Canaan: hee not onely promised him the whole land, but added therewith, *I will be with thee, I will not leaue nor forsake thee.* Ios. 1. 5.

And this being duly considered and belieued, were the strongest motiue to set vs forward cheerefully, not onely in those duties and workes of our callings, which doe cause some delight, and are ioyned with some profit: but also in other, which require much toile and haue nothing to incourage vs, but this, that God commands vs, and would haue vs goe to worke otherwise, and namely, both the Magistrate and Minister to do those great works required of them, with that cheerfulnes and readines, that I haue mentioned: yea the husbandman and the artificer, after the same manner to set vpon their workes inioyned them, and so likewise euen seruants, doore keepers, and hewers of wood, and drawers of water, which are the basest seruices, and meanest of other callings, as also the keepers of sheepe and swine, to be so occupied in their callings, that as long as they know they are in the condition in which they should liue and serue God, and that he will bee with them and blesse them therein, they may abide in the same with comfort, resting vpon his prouidence, and trusting in his promise, that they shall reape the fruit of it assuredly. Iohn 4. 34. Psal. 84. 12.

And the same I would say of women, in their places and condition, and the worke that they are occupied about, in bruing, baking, sowing, spinning, and such like huswifery but that I should stay to long. The which behauiour so heauenly in their earthly businesse, would better become them, (a man would thinke) and should be desired and sought for of them, if they were wise: that so they might liue cheerefully and peaceably: it would better become them (I say) then the life which now they leade, which for the most part, is led distrustfully, vnquietly, in fretting, raging, and earthly mindednes, &c. And all because they trust not in God for successe, neither belieue that he will be with them to direct and helpe them, as also to giue a good end to their labours, though they do not alwayes attaine the outward profit which they seeke: God prouiding better for them, euen in that hardnes, (as they count it) that their contentation and patience, shall be a grea- Deutr. 12. 7.

ter

ter blessing to them, then if they had inioyed all the commodity that might haue bin looked for of them.

Oh wofull people, who like not their labours and worke, which God allotteth and appointeth to them: but take in hand what they thinke good, and therein promise to themselues, as the worldly men did who are mentioned in Saint *James*, namely, what gaine they shall haue without the promise of God: and therefore, if they be disappointed, they could finde in their hearts to contend with God, for not yeelding their hope and desire vnto them, for though they will not bee directed by him, what and how they should do: yet they will quarrell and dispute with him, if they faile of that they looke for: for what else are their secret murmurings and frettings; but against him in their disappointments? Thus we see how ill they prouide for themselues, who take not the worke they goe about from God, that so they might also prosper therein: but they are wise, and shall not repent it, who, as *Iudah* heere did, desire God to teach them what his good pleasure is, to haue them to do: for therein they are sure that it shall goe well with them, whatsoeuer they take in hand. In which respect *Dauid* wished the meanest place in Gods house, that is to say, where he ruleth: rather then the greatest and highest elsewhere. Wel shewing by his example, that the poore who in their simplicitie can make the like choice, may liue farre more sweetly and peaceably, then the mightiest which refuse to learne so to do: and that *Salomon* ment, when he said: *A dish of greene hearbs with peace, is better then a stalled oxe with strife.*

Iam.4.13.

Psal.84.12.

Note.

Obiection. But from this and such like places it is obiected, that God dealt farre better with that people, then he doth in these daies with vs. For they in a particular doubt or trouble might goe and aske counsell of God, and he gaue them an answere againe thereto: which if he did grant to vs in like manner; then (they say) we had good cause in deede why we should serue God, as readily and ioyfully, as they did: but we haue no such libertie to aske in that manner: nor the like prerogatiue in his answering vs againe.

Answere. To the which I say, that this liberty was granted them in one respect, (which diminisheth nothing of Gods fauour to vs) and this it is: That people of Israel had a promise of God, that their common wealth should in some sort abide vnto Christs comming. For the which cause, when they were in great ieopardy to be rooted out by enemies, God gaue them leaue thus to aske of him what they should do, and he resolued and satisfied them according to the promise which he had made them, to wit, that they should not be driuen out of the land: whereby they knew, that those troubles should not be (as they feared) their vtter ouerthrow. And as for their captiuity afterwards, it was but for a season, and they were at the appointed time, restored againe, and returned into their owne land. Now what great prerogatiue had they by such answeres from God about that particular, more then an earthly benefit? They had this temporary blessing which they needed: we as we haue it not, so we stand in no need of it. But we haue farre greater then they had, as the meanes of our saluation farre more cleerely brought to light, and this is the greatest of all benefits. And seeing wee haue many bookes of holy Scripture which they had not, especially when these things were done, which now are spoken of: as the Prophets and the new Testament; wee

Psal.126.1.

may

may well allow them somewhat, which we want. And for praying to God, either about and for things heauenly or earthly, we haue farre more easie accesse to God, then they had, this one thing excepted, that they had this one liberty granted them, (as I haue said.) And it would aswell appeare by the fruit of our prayers, if we were zealous, and oft, and constant therein with vprightnes of heart in the vse of that liberty of praying, as God hath allowed and taught vs to doe. But it followeth in the third verse. Rom.12.12. compared with Iam.5.16.

THE SECOND SERMON VPON THE FIRST CHAPTER OF THE BOOKE OF IVDGES. Vers. 3.4.

VERS. 3. *And* Iudah *said vnto* Simeon *his brother, come vp with me into my lott, that we may fight against the Canaanites, and I will goe with thee into thy lot; and* Simeon *went with him.*

ALthough God had promised to deliuer the Canaanites into the hands of *Iudah*, yet it was not to the end they should sitte idle; and waite for it: but that they being so well incouraged, should vse such helpe thereto, as was at hand, and such whereby they might bring it to passe. And because the tribe of *Simeon* his brother had his possessions mixed with, and lying among the fields of *Iudah*; therefore they called him to helpe them, and they two mutually assisted one the other. So that there neere dwelling and neighbourhood caused them to defend one the other. From their practise and example, iustified by the Scripture, we learne two lessons: First, that although God hath promised any blessing to vs of his owne free goodnes, yet it is no let to our faith to vse all good meanes that he offereth vs, for the effecting of the same: but rather we ought to doe so, as *Iudah* here did, for as they were to ioyne both Gods promise and prouidence together in this action of warre; so are we bound to doe in al actions of peace; I meane to beleeue the one and serue the other, as we haue seene. And we should tempt God if we doe otherwise. *The sense.* Doct. vers. 3.

And so we are commanded to doe: When God promised helpe in the Psalme, yet he willeth all his to waite for it by meanes vsing, fitte and like to bring it to passe: For thus he saith; *commit thy way to me and be thou doing good, and I will bring it to passe.* Therefore *Dauid*, when God had stablished the kingdome in his hands by promise, yet in the treason of *Absalom* his sonne, he did not onely prouide for himselfe to saue his life, and keepe the kingdome to himselfe by flying, but he vsed also the helpe of *Hushai* the Arkite, and the sonnes of the Priestes *Ionathan* and *Ahimaaz*, to frustrate the attempts of *Absolom*. Psal.37.3.5. 2.Sam.15.&16. 34.

And when *Paul* had receiued answere from God by an Angell, that there should Act.27.30.

should not one of them that were in the shippe with him, lose their life in that dangerous voyage and sore tempest; yet afterwards, when the mariners would haue gone out of the shippe; *Paul* said to the Centurion, *Except these*
Pro.20.4. *abide in the shippe, ye cannot be safe.* Therefore *Salomon* saith, *that the slothfull who will not worke in Sommer shall starue in Winter. Dauid*, though anoynted King in *Sauls* stead, yet did so much the more cherefully vse meanes to attaine it, by how much he was secured of the issue by promise: Euen so wee (except God should reueale his meaning to be otherwise, that is to helpe without meanes) are bound to doe in all actions both spirituall and temporall: neither can we haue peace otherwise, whither we enioy our desire or not. This doctrine we haue great cause to learne and marke well, for both in matters of this life, and also concerning our saluation, we must be guided by it. If in sicknes, pouerty, or any other bodily distresse wee feele cause to complaine; then with our prayer of faith vse we the helpe of the Physition; labour we diligently in our calling, and vse we all other good meanes, as we haue occasion, and as godlines will suffer, to obtaine and come by that helpe which we want, and God hath promised. So in the trouble of minde, wherein we haue large promises of Gods vpholding and comforting vs, re-
Act.2.37. paire we to the *men and brethren*, who as they are skilfull to wound, so are they also to heale; and God who hath promised, will thereby, and by the like meanes, send deliuerance.

And here slacknes and negligence are much to be taken heed of, then the which there is no greater bane, if we by faith waite for the promise: yet there is another extremity to be auoided, as wel as the neglecting of meanes, and that is, that we ascribe not so much to them, that we tie God thereto, so that if we vse them, we imagine we cannot faile of the helpe we desire. In one of these two extremities, wicked men are continually holden, that either they vse no meanes, (as they that hearing God hath elected to saluation those whom he will saue; conclude, that if they be elected, they shall be saued, howsoeuer they liue, whereas God hath prædestinated the meanes, as well as decreed the ende:) or if they vse meanes, they attribute all to them, and nothing to God: as they who glory of their great wealth, which by their wisedome and trauaile they haue gotten, which is to sacrifice to their nets. And thus much of the first point.

Doct.2. The second thing that we haue to learne of these men of Iudah, is that as they vsed the helpe of their next neighbour *Simeon* (as they might more
Rom.12.10.20. commodiously doe then those who were farther off: so it is to instruct vs,
Luk.10.34.35. that there should be loue and a readines to helpe one another, as neede requireth among neighbours, and not an vnkinde refusing mutually to be aiding one another, as though we could liue alone on earth, because sometimes we haue no neede one of another; and as though Christs charge were so little to be regarded of louing one another. The reasons why wee ought to haue a great care of this dutie is, (besides Christs commandement) first, seeing one time or other all stand in need of the helpe and gifts one of another. I to day, and thou to morrow, and God hath dealt with the societies of men as with the members of the bodie; giuing to euery member a distinct facultie, that they might all agree to the good of the whole, seeing that none could well be spared without blemish. Secondly,

neighbours

neighbours are set neere in habitation, to the end they should bee neerely knit together in affection,and be readier to helpe,then they who are farther off.

The benefit of this,though it be greatest in trouble; yet it is in all times amiable and full of comfort. It is preserued by due and daily meeting in the publike assemblies at the preaching of the word, prayer and the vse of the Sacraments: also priuately,as they may conueniently,by good commu- Heb. 10.24.25.
nication,and by kind greetings,salutations. and auoiding all wronging one another,and discourtesies,in word, deede or countenance. Whereto they Note.
who will not be subiect,and that readily,knowing that they nourish and vphold neighbourhood and loue thereby, they shew that they are willing to breake off this knot. It is hindred by selfe-loue,whiles euery man regardeth himselfe onely,or for the most part: and especially where men are more frowardly and churlishly disposed, who had neede oft to remember the words of our Sauiour,saying,*Hereby shall all men know that ye are my disciples,* Iohn 13.35.
if ye loue one another.

But I cannot tell how it commeth to passe, that one man is a wolfe and lion to another,(yea,euen such as dwell together neerer then in one towne,) by his *Nabal*-like churlishnes,and blockish, if not mischieuous,behauiour: who when they should also the more neerely be linked together,doe thereby take occasion to be sooner wearie one of another; to contend also, and fall out for small trifles,as there shal not want matter sundrie waies,if men be not carefull to preuent the same. Wherein yet this is worse; that such as are euer at iarre with one or other that dwell neere them,or with them, doe couer their sinne by answering,they agree well enough with others who are farre from them. Whereas it were monstrous if we deserued bad report among them who know vs not. For who seeth not that it is an easie matter to bee at peace with strangers, with whom a man hath no dealings,neither commeth oft in their company? But the Apostle teacheth, that we should fetch testimonie of our Christian behauiour and good conscience, not so much from them that are a farre off,where we seldome come;but from them especially,with whom wee dwell and conuerse vsually and deale: for thus he saith to the Corinthians amongst whom he had liued; *This is our reioy-* 2.Cor.1.12.
cing,the testimony of our conscience, that in simplicitie and godly purenesse wee haue had our conuersation in the world,and most of all toward you.

And to draw to an end in this point also, it should be throughly resolued to euery good Christian,not to grieue and offend the meanest that he liueth with,either by priuat contention,or iniuring them,or by any other reproch- Note.
full behauiour;but to liue peaceably with them,so much as in him lieth,and Rom.12.18.
to looke carefully that he do so,and offer them friendly and good measure; that so he may stop the mouthes of the ill disposed, and haue interest in the other: such persons when God shal visit them,to bring them on to Christian religion,and exhort them, and so to haue hope to bring them to repentance,and thereby to inioy the fruit of such wise,kind, and peaceable liuing with them,in loue and inward comfort, which passeth vnderstanding. But yet if any will needs breake off from vs, because wee will not haue *fellowship* Ephes.5.11.
with them in the vnfruitfull workes of darknesse,and *walke after the same excesse of* 1.Pet.4.4.
riot that they doe; here we must remember,that we must *ioyne speech with ho-* Heb.12.14.

linesse,and no further. And (though it grieue vs) forgoe that agreement, which we cannot lawfully hold: and wee should be comforted in this,that we haue sought it as much as in vs lieth.

Thus as I haue shewed Gods people how to keepe neighbourhood and loue one with another,that they may beware of strãgers,which neuer doth good: so I will giue a watchword to the vnruly and disobedient,of their grosse and common contentions and iarres,with such as they liue among, wishing them to consider, how wearisome they make their liues and displeasing,and therefore to studie to liue quietly,and not to be companions in euill with them,to thinke thus, that if Gods deare seruants sometime disagree,and liue vnkindly,for that they haue no more grace;(though they haue some;)then much more they should begin to auoid and mislike all such their vncharitablenesse,and other ill parts of their liues who haue no grace;
Galath.5.15. and that speedily; *lest if they bite one another,they be consumed one of another.* I deny not,but they haue shew of neighbourly fellowship,among them, but it is most chiefly in wickednesse, wherein many ioyne easily together; but as concerning friendship, they are inconstant and hollow, and are onely friends while they haue that which they would haue,and no longer,nor no further. And this of them briefly and by the way. And now seeing I haue said; I will adde a word to another sort, and that is this: that if the neerest in place and kindred,should bee most neere in affection, (as the very law of nature teacheth,and all will acknowledge) how much more then the married couples? In whom to see this band of loue broken,it is not only strange, but monstrous. And let this shame all such to heare this, seeing that which hath before been spoken in reproofe of others, who offend this way, shall most of all condemne them. It followeth in the next verse.

Vers.4. *And Iuda went vp, and the Lord deliuered the Canaanites, and the Perezites into their hands,and they slew of them in Bezek,ten thousand men.*

Iudah,as he was commanded of God,so he did: for so it is said here, *hee went vp,&c.*so that as he counselled with the Lord,what he should doe;euen so,when hee knew his mind,he was as ready to obey.This condemneth the rash zeale of many,who are as readie to aske and goe to the word, and pray in the congregation after their manner, as the best: but they consider not why they doe so;as though they thought God were pleased with such halfe seruice as they vse,much like to *Saul* who was forward to sacrifice, thinking God to be highly pleased therewith:but as for the obeying the commandement of God in destroying the Amalekites,he was farre from it,he did it by
1.Sam.15.22. halues,so that the Prophet *Samuel* was faine to say to him, *Hath God as great pleasure in burnt sacrifice, as that his voice should be obeyed? Behold,to obey is better then sacrifice; and to hearken is better then the fat of rams.* So to make a shew of much forwardnesse,and to haue no heart nor readinesse to doe as men pre-
Matth.7.21. tend; and to say,*Lord,Lord*,and not to bee willing to doe his will, is abomi-
Psalm.50.16. nation to the Lord. For *he loueth truth in the inward parts:* he saith, *Oh that*
Psalm.51.6. *there were an hart in this people, to keepe all my commandements alwaies, that it*
Deut.5.29. *might goe well with them.* God cannot abide that men should shew more then is in them; which also his seruant *Paul* abhorred to doe, as we reade in that place

place to the Corinthians,saying:I would haue none thinke otherwise of me then they see in me. Thus we see,what vse we ought to make of this example of *Iudah*,that is,to giue God this honour, that as wee pray and resort to him te know his will,so we be as ready to indeuour to doe it; and to seeke to be faithfull and true seruants vnto him,rather then to be so accounted,for it shall otherwise be little to our comfort. This of *Iudahs* obeying,now let vs see what the Lord did to him. 2.Cor.10.6.

We haue heard of the promise made to thē by God of subduing the Canaanites; now it is shewed how he performed it, in this, that the men of *Iudah* slew 10000.men of them, & of another people that ioyned with them, namely,the Perezites,which were also of the 7. cursed nations. (And heere this victorie is briefly set down,but the maner how it was gotten, is more at large laid forth in the verses following). The rest of them (seeing their armie was very great) it is to be thought, fled away,out of whom their King was taken and caught.. By this the Lords keeping of promise with *Iudah*, we see it prooued,which was before affirmed, that God hauing spoke the word once,it is as much as if hee had done the deed, his word and deed are both one. Which,in so great matters especially as he promiseth,is worthie to be regarded. For we may say now of our selues,as the Prophet said of former times; *Our fathers hoped in him,and were not disappointed: they put their trust in him,and were not confounded.* This, when wee see how hardly it is found in men to keepe their promise,and that they cannot bee trusted of their word, though they promise; yea,and bind it with an oath, no, though they be depended on in waightie cases; this (I say) should make vs to thinke our estate twice happie,who may be allowed to rest and put our affiance in God,without feare of being disappointed in the greatest matters. *Doct.*2. Psalm.22.5.

For if wee can but wait patiently, wee may bee sure it shall come to passe which he hath promised; yea,till heauen and earth perish, one iot or tittle of that which he hath spoken,shall not faile,but be fulfilled. What comfort ought this to bring to all beleeuing Christians, who haue promises made them by him of temporary deliuerances,and benefits, and of eternall happinesse? Oh what were wanting here, if there were faith to beleeue them? Besides,whereas it is one of the greatest griefes of Gods people to see vile men prosper in their wickednesse,and to flourish as the greene bay tree,and to haue more pleasure,honor,and wealth, then they could looke for,whereby they seeme to men,to be here placed in an immortalitie; yet seeing it is certaine they shall come to naught,and to destruction, who abide in that estate,for the mouth of the Lord hath spoken it, what patience and contentment should this bee to the faithfull, to remaine constant in their hope and well doing,though they haue many discouragements? and to wait with patience a little while,seeing he that will come, will come,and not tarrie.But this point is often taught,therefore it shall suffice to haue said this of it: only applie wee this truth to the bad in Gods threatnings, as the promise hath been applied to the beleeuers,that if he threaten them,and they stand it out with him, he will surely pay them home, as he dealt with *Nebuchadnezzar* and others. Matth.5.17. Note. Psal.73.13. Psal.1.last. 2.Pet.3.9. Heb.10. Dan.4.31.32.

Now for Gods deliuering the Canaanites into their hands, wee must know,that this was done without all iniustice and seuerity,(which some wil *Doct.*3.

be ready enough to thinke otherwise of) though there be no mention here made of their desertes and transgressions: but it is manifest in the Scriptures, that they were most grieuous. And that appeares by the Lords owne words in the booke of Genesis: where, when hee would shew a reason, why hee would hold the posteritie of *Abraham* so long a season in Egypt, before they came into the land of promise, he makes it to be this, namely, for that *the sins*

Genes.15.16. *of the Canaanites were not then come to the ful*, which time then was not, but now was fulfilled and come to passe, and therefore they were now iustly punished; *Abrahams* seed being long before this, brought out of the Egyptian bondage. Now as the sinne of the Canaanites was growne ripe and knowne to God to be come a great height, though it be not here set downe; (yea, though it be not manifest to all that read the storie) and yet cleare enough, as I haue said, and therefore they suffered and were punished most iustly: so we that heare this must be perswaded, that God dealeth most righteously in all his visitations and iudgements, though men do not alwaies see the cause.

Genes.4.13. Which we haue great need well to learne; seeing we are readie with *Cain* to to charge God with rigour and hard dealing, by the smallest occasion, when (yet) we neither haue argument to vphold vs, and we might haue learned of

Iob 9.3. *Iob*, that *there is no disputing with God*; (and if he gaue vs nothing at all, yet he should owe vs nothing, we are indebted to him for all that we haue.)

Psalm.51.6. This *Dauid* confessed, when the Lord corrected him: and whereas he might haue been thought to haue dealt too hardly with him, reproouing him so sharpely, and sending so heauie a message to him, as he did by the

2.Sam.12.7. &c. Prophet *Nathan*, yet *Dauid* himselfe confesseth his fault to haue been so heinous, and his sinne so great, that God did shew mercie in correcting him, ra-

Psalm.51.4. ther then seueritie; and added this, that hee should alwaies be iustified, and found righteous, howsoeuer men should iudge of him. This, though men dare not in words denie, if they should be asked what their opinion is, concerning it: yet when God taketh them seuerally in hand, and that his rods

Note. be vpon themselues, rare are they, that shall then be of that mind, and so confesse to him, or before men, especially if their afflictions bee long, or smarty, that yet the Lord is iust, & his dealings are righteous: but rather they crie out impatiently, that they are handled as no other men be, and that they would they had any other afflictiō vpon thē in stead of that which they suffer. And if they be exhorted to patience, they ask with the wicked king *Ieboram*, how

2.King.6.33. can they *attend on God any longer*, in their so great calamities; whereas he ha-uing a mercifull respect of vs, regardeth, what wee are fit to beare, and mo-

1.Cor.10.13. derateth his chastisements accordingly, and promising that *he will lay no more on vs then he will make vs able to goe vnder*; it is (most certainly) our great sin, when we labor not to containe our selues meekly, and to see so much amisse (as ful easily we may) in our euill hearts and liues, as that we may say alwaies in his sorest correcting of vs, the Lord is righteous, and euer to bee praised.

Secondly, this should teach vs, not to take part with the wicked, in moning and pitying them for that he so pursueth them, when wee see the hand of God vpon them, but rather iustifie God, nay, giue thanks vnto him for his iust dealing with them: and although we wish their saluation, yet wee may reioyce in their punishment, euen as mourne for their impunity, when they prouoke them. Especially if we know them enemies to the Church, seeing then

then we iudge not before the time,and wee know *it is iust with God to render tribulation to all that haue troubled his*: but when the estate of the afflicted is vnknowne to vs,although we may be assured that God is iust, yet wee must not condemne them,but leaue him to God. 2.Thes.1.6.

Now to speake a little of the Canaanites,because they escaped long, being so great offenders,yet in that they were met withall at last,it teacheth vs; that as *God will not alwaies suffer his rods to lie on the backe of the righteous*, so neither will he suffer the wicked to escape and goe vnpunished,but he will bee reuenged on them in his due time,yea and that quickly, whereas they (yet) thinke the cleane contrary, and imagine, that if they bee not punished as soone as they haue trespassed,they shall neuer come to any reckoning; and therefore they merrily promise themselues,and say, *Doubtlesse the bitternesse of death is passed*;and thinke that God will neither doe euill nor good: Nay, they begin to applaud themselues in their wicked doings,as wee may see in the Psalme: where the Lord himselfe chargeth them for it. *Doct.*4. Psal.125.3. Luk.18.8. 1.Sam.15.32. Psal.50.21.

Therefore this and the like Scripture commeth in fit season to be vrged vpon all such, that though they *cry, peace, peace*,and cast the remembrance of punishment behind their backes, yet God will set it before their faces, yea and make them smart, as if they were stung with adders and hornets; their sinne will most certainely finde them out. *Haman*, after all his cruelty and malice, was powred out against Gods people with great ioy, notwithstanding also the Kings countenancing and backing of him therein, had yet a snare set for him at a sumptuous banquet,and by the prayers of the faithfull, receiued iust punishment for his doings, when he little looked for any such matter. *Iezabell* being suffered to goe forward in her murthers, and spirituall whoredomes along time, not sparing the Lords faithfull Prophet *Elias*,but threatned death to him also,when she was in the middest of her pride,braying boldly against the Lords auenger *Iehu*, comming to doe execution vpon her, was cast downe out at the window by her owne Eunuches in great disgrace; her braines being squashed against the stones, till she was made dogges meate and doung, for all her former glory. 1.Thes.5.3. Ester.7.10. 2.King.9.30.31. &c.

The same I might say of infinite other who scorned to heare of any thing, or iudgement to be comming against them; who yet were made as vnlike to the persons they were before in their iollitie,as if they had neuer bin they, (as the rich man in the Gospell, and the Epicure) euen as if one should see a goodly palace with all the rich furniture thereof, to be burned vnto ashes. But alas,what is our speaking of such things to a new generation,risen vp after them, as farre gone as they in their iniquities, yea adding to them also other sinnes both strange and fearefull: Are any made wise by former examples, though they come not short of them in their abominations? (that I say no more) but they haue one thing or other to wash away the remembrance of such workes of God, or to tush at them who tell them that they shall be like them in their punishments. And if they bee scared at any time with feare of Gods iudgements it is with them, but as it is with theeues, when there is hue and crie after them, then they giue in, but if it bee past, they peepe out of their holes, and fall to their trade a fresh,til they be found out and taken: and so doe these. Luk.12.20. Luk.16.22.23. *A Simile.*

But I will turne away from this kinde of people, as fearing that I doe but

lose my labour about them, I will bestow my words where I haue more hope to preuaile, and doe good by them. I am not ignorant that right worthy and good Christians doe sometime fall into this disease; and are rocked a sleepe with them before mentioned, in some particular falles: that when they haue found sweetnes in some baites of sinne, and haue so farre forgot themselues, that they are snared by the deceitfulnes thereof, they haue begun to thinke that it is good being for them there, and to continue still in so doing, and they are loath to be diseased, they loue not to thinke for the time (behold to what point the best may easily be brought) that God will come
Matth.25.5. against them for their so being disguised. This is more then with the fiue
Cant.5.1. wise virgins to begin to nodde; nay it is with the Church in the Canticles, *to fall a sleepe*: doubtlesse, this is as dangerous an estate for godly Christians, as it is vnbeseeming them.

But what of this some (perhaps) will say? what doth the punishment of the Canaanites concerne these? I answere, it concernes them very much. For though they are not seated nor saped in sinne as they, and their like, of whom I haue spoken already: and therefore are not in danger to be punished like to them, yet is their sinne great, for that they haue bin tenderly regarded of the Lord, and haue set this loue more sweet then the hony combe; and haue been aduanced to honour, (greater then Princes) to be sonnes and
Psal.109.106. daughters, to the Lord almighty, yea and they haue sworne with *Dauid*, and therefore should performe it, to keepe his righteous iudgements: now then, for them to looke backe onely to Sodome, and to giue place to their euill lusts, but so farre, as to take liking of, and please themselues in any vnfruitfull workes of darkenes, so as they could be content still to solace themselues therein, it is in them periury; against God treachery, and in it selfe, sinne, for such persons to commit, most fearefull and horrible.

And if they espie it not betimes, which they ought to haue preuented and
Note. shunned at the first entrance into it, God will rouse them out of it to their cost, with terror and abashment, especially if they haue fallen so oftentimes, and haue experience, what woe it hath brought them in times past before they could rise vp againe: and in what a torment and hell they lay, before they could returne. And yet I would haue no man take me thus, as though I thought, that a man truly conuerted to God, can alwaies be in one, and
Note. the same state of libertie to serue God, or holde the same measure of grace
Rom.7.19. at all times, or as though he might not possibly, yea easily, through his euill heart, (which in great part remaineth lusting after euill, and rebellious a-
Psal.30.6.7. gainst God) as though he might not (I say) be easily carried after the euill, which at an other time he wholly abhorreth, and hath victory ouer. I doe not deny but this may be, and is with the best; but to nourish these ill desires, and to delight in them, and so to be in danger to commit the sinne, which hath drawen the heart to bee made drunken with it, whether it be whoredome, reuenge; vniust dealing, &c. (for so it may come to passe) this I say, changeth his sweet life into sowernes, and (to shew the danger of such boldnes further) it doth vtterly disguise him; and make him and his profession rediculus.

And to let him see what this will grow to, hee may further vnderstand that God dealeth with such, after this manner; that first, he suffereth them

to be vnsetled in their course, so that they serue God awkly and vntowardly, (as he goeth to worke, that vseth dull edged instruments) they cannot pray, nor walke roundly and cheerefully in their calling, but are full of vnquietnes, with much grudge of conscience, and a very tast of hell, which to continue many houres, or dayes, is yet an heauier burden, and greater bondage. Note.
And yet if they relent not, when they be vnsetled, and when they see themselues thus far out of the way of godlines; a greater danger is like to follow, that is, that they shall be hardened, and so, farre from repentance, and then they fall from euill to worse, till they breaking into other open offences bee met withall and requited, with sundry open and shamefull punishments. This is the Lords manner of dealing with his owne, euen as he dealeth with the vngodly, first to warne them secretly by the accusation of their conscience: and if that doe them no good to call them backe; then he casteth them into bodily or visible iudgement. And so the best ende they haue of Rom.6.21.
their bad doings, is to goe backe with shame and sorrow, whereas they might haue shunned both, and haue liued in peace and with comfort.

Which being duly considered, hath made mee oft to maruell, that men Ier.31.18.19.
whom I know to be very carelesse, can yet bee so quiet. Me thinks where much sinne is committed, and such as the persons cannot be ignorant of it, when they haue done it, they should not put it vp so cleanely, and sleepe vpon it so easily, but that it ought to trouble them, euen as the stomacke ouercharged, seeketh to be vnburdened. So (I say) I thinke they should haue but Note.
small peace within, when so much may bee seene to bee amisse without; for let them set as faire a face on their bad doings, as they can; yet can they not be the whole men that they goe for, and God wil not be mocked, they must cast vp their vnsauorie gorge, and clense their harts and hands from euill be- Iames 4.8.
fore God will accept, and take knowledge of them for his. For if the conscience, being tender, and like the apple of the eie, can suffer no violence; how can they loade it with so great a burden of knowne sinnes, but they must needs cause it to cry out, if they doe not with true repentance seeke to God for mercie to ease it? For a penitent soule cannot feele the least violence to be offered to the conscience by sinne committed, but it crieth out to be cured; and therefore, they who giue greater cause, cannot bee in good case, when they set it light, hauing so sore offended. And thus much by occasion of the Canaanites sinne: It followeth.

THE THIRD SERMON VPON THE FIRST CHAPTER OF THE BOOKE OF IVDGES.

Vers.5. *And they found Adonibezek in Bezek: and they fought against him, and slew the Canaanites and the Perezites.*

Vers.6. *And Adonibezek fled, and they pursued after him, and and caught him, cut off the thumbes of his hands and of his feet.*

Vers.7. *And Adonibezek said, Seuenty Kings hauing the thumbes of their hands, and of their feete cut off, gathered [bread] vnder my table: as I haue done, so God hath rewarded me. So they brought him to Ierusalem, and there he died.*

The sense. TO make entrance into these verses which I haue read, yee haue heard how God gaue victorie: now it is shewed more particularly, how the victorie before mentioned, was gotten, the place being set downe where the battel was fought, that is, in Bezek: and the King of the people is mentioned, who was *Adonibezek*, who fled in the battell, as being too weake, but was taken, and handled, as is set downe in the text, to wit, hee had the thumbes of his hands and feete cut off. Whether the men of Iuda knew that he had so dealt with other, or no, or whether the Lord directed them so to doe, without knowing any such thing, it is not expressed, but he himselfe confessed that hee had done so to others, and that God had requited him with the like. That which was said of the Canaanites punishment, that it was inflicted vpon them when their sin was growne ripe, may as truly be said of their King, as by his owne confession may be gathered: but hauing spoken of that point alreadie, I omit to say any more of it.

Vers.5. *Doct.* But seeing this *Adonibezek*, being taken as he fled, had his thumbs cut off, as he had cut off others before; out of these verses let vs first note this, that God measures out to men, euen as they measure and mete to others: according to the words of our Sauiour, *With what measure ye mete, shall bee measured out to you againe.* (Matth.7.1.) So that, as we haue done to other, so shall we be dealt with. The Lord confirmes this truth, where he saith, *He that sheddeth mans blood, by man shall his blood be shed.* (Genes.9.6.) Which was rightly verified in *Haman*, and that in many points: For first, as he accused Gods people vniustly, so he was charged, and that by the King himselfe, where yet he was not guilty: and he was condemned without solemne iudgement, seeing he had done so to others; (Note.) and when he was handled most reprochfully and adiudged to most shamefull punishment, yet there was none that pitied him: (a wonderfull thing to be spoken of one, that had been in so great fauor with the King) and why this? euen because he had been pitilesse towards other, that it might be verified which was then true, and afterward written, *Iudgement shall bee mercilesse* (Iames 2.13.)

to

to him that ſheweth no mercy. Why was he hanged, and that vpon the gallows, that he had ſet vp for godly *Mordecay?* I ſay ſtil, euen that the ſcripture might be fulfilled euery way, that as he had done, ſo it might be done to him again: for in that hee purpoſed to doe it, it was done alreadie in Gods account. Eſter.7.10.

Now that wee may bring this neerer to our ſelues; many among vs complaine, how they be wronged in their dealings with men; they are euill ſpoken of, ſlandred, railed vpon, (they ſay) and many other waies abuſed. And they thinke they receiue very hard meaſure at mens hands hereby; they maruell at it, and complaine, that none are vſed as they be: but what blindnes is it, that couereth there eies? For doe not all that liue with them, know, at leaſt, their owne conſciences can tell them, that they haue dealt euen ſo with other, and thereby haue giuen cauſe to be ſo dealt withall, againe? But oh blind ſelfe-loue, that cannot ſee that, which all other doe ſee I meane, which thinkes that tolerable in ones ſelfe, which yet hee accuſeth and condemneth in another, and ſeeth not the iuſt iudgement of God vpon himſelfe by other mens wronging him, which hee himſelfe by his iuſt deſerts, hath brought vpon his owne head. Note.

Hereof it is, that if we thus tell them, (which is the very truth) that their ſinne hath found them out, they haue no eares to heare vs: and if we warne the like offenders, before their puniſhment commeth, that God wil after the ſame manner be auenged of them, yet they will not beleeue vs, till hee viſit them in ſome ſuch heauie manner indeed, and then (with *Iosephs* brethren) they begin to ſay: *We remember our ſinne this day*, that euen as other haue done to vs, ſo wee haue done to other before: and as this cruell King *Adonibezek* ſayd here, *Seuentie Kings thumbs, haue I cut off, &c: as I haue done; ſo God hath rewarded me.* And this men ſhall come to either in Gods fauour, to their amendment, or in his diſpleaſure to their hardning, and confuſion. And therfore it were wiſedome to confeſſe it in time, while wee may bee taught and told of it: for all mens conſciences will crie out to them that it is true, that they haue by word or deed iniuried other, before they haue receiued ſuch meaſure themſelues: but if they had not in that kind, and particular manner offended, yet they are ſure, they haue done it, ſome other way; ſo that they haue iuſt cauſe, if they wel waigh it, and looke to Gods hand therein to beare all ſuch indignities (as they count them) as are offered them, both with meekeneſſe and contentedly. And were it not that God dealt thus with men, they would neuer acknowledge nor diſlike the ſinne which they are guiltie of: but ſuffer it to lie ſecret in them, and worke them a miſchiefe. Whereas yet it being ferreted out by ſuch iudgements of God, they cannot but confeſſe it, eſpecially when they bee in any great feare, and danger of death. And for vs who are now warned, if wee haue had our part in this ſin, that with the common ſort wee haue ſmitten others with our tongue, or wronged, or intended euill any way againſt them, learne wee with great regard, to put a ſpeedy end thereto by repentance; leſt God awake and preuent vs by ſome ſuch like iudgement againe, as we haue cauſed to other, and to this end put wee theſe two leſſons in practiſe, neither in heart, word or deed, offer we any hard or vnequall meaſure to any man: and if any offer it to vs, if it be poſſible, that it may be without our great hurt, let vs quietly and meekely paſſe by it, and make no great matter of it, for the time ſhall come wherein Geneſ.42.21. Note. Rom.12.21.

wherein we ſhall wiſh wee had done ſo, and not haue laid that ſo neere our heart, which might more eaſily haue been paſſed by of vs.

Verſ.7.Doct. But in ſaying, *God hath rewarded him*, it is to be noted, that he an heathen Idolater, could ſee ſo farre, as to aſcribe to God his affliction. Whereby we may ſee, that very bad men doe acknowledge God to be the ſtriker and puniſher of them. But where ſhould he learne it? for though it did him no good, to acknowledge it, yet it is that, which many who haue been baptized, doe not come to, but curſe and ban, rage and fret in their afflictions, crying out of their ill fortune, as they call it, ſo farre are they from reſting in the iuſtice of God, and to ſay, hee hath done righteouſly. Alſo as they aſcribe to chance and fortune their calamities, ſo doe they runne for helpe to Witches and Sorcerers, when they be oppreſſed with them, which is greatly to the conuicting of them. For why ſhould not they much more ſee the hand of God when they are viſited: if Heathens haue ſeene ſo farre, as to aſcribe to God their troubles, and to confeſſe their ſinne, as this *Adonibezek* did here.
Pſalm.95.10. This not onely checketh ſuch as I haue mentioned, but laieth hard to their charge alſo, that make ſome ſhew of goodneſſe, who yet doe harden their hearts vnder their afflictions, and will not know Gods waies, though they ſee well enough that they ſuffer for their euill deeds, neither will relent, nor feare his iudgements, though they cannot deny, that they are due to them for their deſerts. More particularly, ſuch as this Heathen King was, ſhall riſe in iudgement againſt ſuch profeſſors, as will not ſee their crueltie, vnmercifulneſſe, their vncleanneſſe, which they nouriſh in themſelues; their oppreſſions alſo and iniuries they doe to their neighbours, though they bee moſt clearely laid before them.

When yet *Pharaoh* and other ſuch, haue (eſpecially when Gods hand was
Exod.9.27. heauie vpon them) acknowledged that the Lord had done it. For euen the wickedeſt mans owne conſcience ſometimes accuſeth him, that hee doth euil: and ought not theſe much more, we haue farre greater light; to tremble when they haue ſo groſſely offended, & ſay, *Againſt thee, againſt thee (O Lord) we haue done this euill?* And eſpecially; when they know what danger they be in thereby, and what heauie plagues hang ouer their heads for the ſame. Although ſuch muſt goe further then ſo, euen to tell it to themſelues, that God will not be at one with them, vnleſſe they acknowledge their faults alſo, and ſubmit themſelues to him, as his word teacheth, howſoeuer it ſhall pleaſe him to correct them; and withall, to reſolue, in all conditions of their liues whatſoeuer, to indeuour, and be readie to obey him.

*Doct.*2. Alſo this ſhould teach vs, when we receiue indignities at mens hands, yet
2.Sam.16.10. to looke to God, who ſet them a work againſt vs, as *Dauid* ſaid of *Shemei*, and not as the dog doth, to catch the ſtone, and leaue the ſmiter. And though they haue wronged vs willingly, yet if wee conſidered, that the Lord did it, we ſhould the leſſe be mooued or offended with the inſtrument: whereas we on the other ſide, beate our braines, and ſtraine our ſelues, al that we can, to purſue them, and ſeeke to be reuenged on them, whom yet the Lord will ſufficiently puniſh for the wrong they haue done. For example, wee are ſo out of quiet for a word ſpoken againſt vs, as if it were treaſon. when in the meane while, we doe not once thinke, how we haue prouoked the Lord, to ſtirre vp ſuch ill perſons againſt vs. *Adonibezek* (we ſee here) would not aſcribe

ſcribe it to the Iſraelites,but ſaith,it was God that did thus vnto him.

Furthermore here,by this that we heare his crueltie, thus laid out by his *Doct.3.*
owne mouth,that he had played the tyrant againſt many,and thoſe no meaner perſons then Kings,to cut off the thumbs of their hands and feete, and not to ſome few of them,but euen ſeuentie perſons; wee ſee what a raging furie this vice of crueltie is,and to what depth of euil it carrieth men,that do not wiſely conſider the fouleneſſe and ſhamefulneſſe of it. For whereas one man ſhould be ſociable with another,yea with ſtrangers,if occaſion be offered,(ſeeing euery one is our neighbour,) this crueltie cutteth of all fellow- Luk.10.37.
ſhip,nay all libertie of inioying ſuch benefits of peace,goods,or the like. So that the cruel man is farre worſe then the thiefe,who(yet)is odious,and driuen frõ habitation with men in their free dwelling houſes, into a loathſome priſon among brutiſh companions. For he,vnleſſe he be cruell alſo, is content to take a ſhare in his goods,whom he robbeth;but the cruell man is not content with a ſhare,but if his might be ſutable to his mind,he will haue all, at one time or other,that is his whom he purſueth,yea he wil thruſt him out of houſe and home,yea,and out of the world alſo, before he can be ſatiſfied.
Caine,a little after the corrupt eſtate of things entred into the world, was a Geneſ.4.8.
patterne of cruel ones,who when he had no cauſe giuen him by *Abel* his innocent brother,of hard handling him;yet becauſe he was accepted of God, and himſelf not,did not hate him only without a cauſe,but which was moſt vnnatural and monſtrous in him,roſe vp againſt him,and ſlue him.*Pharaoh,* Exod.5.9.
when he had almoſt tyred the poore people of God,who were ſtrangers in his land,with burdens and toile aſmuch as they could beare; yet was not ſatisfied therewith,but made their burthen farre greater,til their life was more vnwelcome then death it ſelfe,that his crueltie might be manifeſt to all. *Haman* ſo exceeded herein,that it was too little to take the goods of Gods peo- Eſter.7.4.
ple from them,and to hold them bondmen, vnleſſe hee might haue their liues alſo. And what ſhould I ſpeake of *Iezabel,*who being a woman,exceeded men who were cruell alſo? And of *Rehoboams* cruell handling his ſubiects,as his ſtorie declareth, and of *Ioſephs* brethren, who conſented to ſell him into a far countrey, whence he might neuer returne to trouble them,as they hoped,but further,the moſt of them agreed to take away his life alſo, and yet if they had killed him,euen they themſelues had loſt their liues alſo in the famine that God ſent afterwards. they being preſerued by *Ioſeph* among all other men.

Theſe might make crueltie odious to vs. But many that heare this of it, deſire to know what manner of thing it is,that rageth after this ſort, and like the flaming fire,deuoureth and deſtroyeth, where it commeth. Their demand is godly, and I will briefly ſatisfie it. That they may therefore ceaſe maruelling, that this fury, crueltie I meane, bringeth ſuch ſtrange effects forth,they may know,that it is a vile and vitious habit or cuſtome, whereby men are carried to do things both harſh and hard,and that beyond all courſe and compaſſe of reaſon. Now where men are thus ſet vpon their will,to deale with other,and are led to it without reaſon, much more without religion,there how can they chuſe, but to bee rigorouſly handled, and cruellie delt with,who fall into their hands? Which maketh the cruell man to bee hated of all: For ſuch are barbarous and vnciuell,as if they had ſucked the

Dragons

Dragons in the desert,and their hearts so bound with the sinewes of iron, that they spoile them whom they pursue, as raging raine and tempest rendeth the trees, and destroyeth the fruites, and they are no more mooued with the life of a man,then if a dogge had fallen before them. And therefore no maruell,that *Dauid* hauing his choice of plagues presented to him, made a present exception to his owne nature and kind, fearing and knowing the crueltie of men; saying: let me not fall into the hands of man. This the Heathen *Seneca* saw,when he said; Thou art deceiued, if thou giuest credit to the lookes of those that meet thee. They haue the faces of men,the minds of wild beasts. If he spake this of man in generall,what would he haue said particularly of the cruell man? with whom this speech is as common; [burne,kill,cut,Poison young,old,men,women, brethren, kindred,] as to eate their meate. Whosoeuer doe but crosse them with a mistaken word,or wrie countenance, it is but a word and a blow with them, and though they murther vpon light occasions,and haue no gaine by their death, they haue inough in that they take pleasure in it. But whither might a man goe in this argument? I will giue an instance in lower matters of this kind.

Hereof it is,that if one neighbour bee trespassed by another,in his corne or other commodities,by cattell,or any other way, though it bee without any fault of him that hath done the trespasse, the other is readie in rage and furie to seeke reuenge,by laming and hurting the cattell; which hee would doe to the owner,(like *Lamech*) if he durst,or will with spite and railing and exacting at his hands sixe times the valew of the damage and detriment that he sustained,though if he annoy the other in a worse manner,he yet maketh nothing of it,but will shift it of. This is a cruell part,in things of so little valew vnto a neighbour: What would hee doe (thinke wee) or he that is like minded to him,in matters of waight, and to a stranger? and so much the more,I may call such dealing crueltie, seeing it is offered by such an one as trespasseth another time in a farre worse manner himselfe. The like may be said of cruell Landlords,Masters,Guardians,Stepmothers,&c. which measure not them whom they offend against, by themselues. For though there be diuers degrees in the many kinds of this foule vice of crueltie,yet we must know,that the least and lowest is vnseemely in a man and odious.

Indeed it is more noisome and furious, if it bee accompanied with
Prou.27.4. enuy, therefore *Salomon* saith, *Who can stand before enuy?* for the enuious are obstinate, and cannot bee reconciled. Therefore whatsoeuer
Prou.12.10. measure be offered by such,it is certaine,that it shall be hard inough,seeing *their very mercies are crueltie.* What remaineth then for such persons to doe, to the end they may (if it be possible) cast of this crueltie,as a most filthie and loathsome garment,but this? that they giue themselues no rest,til it become as odious and loathsome to them,as it is to other, which is not hard for him to obtaine,that will be perswaded to looke into the odiousnesse of it: that when he hath found it,he may fall downe at the Lords feete for mercie to couer the foulenesse of it,and forgiue it; and that being beleeued, imbrace
Act.16.30. gentlenesse and mercie,and kindnesse toward others,in stead of rigor. Like the Iaylor in the Actes: who,though he had vsedg reat crueltie against *Paul* and *Silas*,yet when hee repented, did wash their wounds most louingly, which before scourging of them,he had made in their bodies,and set meate be-

before them in his houſe moſt cheaerfully,whom he had before thruſt hungry into the inward priſon moſt cruelly. Alſo let it teach vs,both to pray that wee bee not giuen ouer into the hands of vnreaſonable and vnconſcionable men, who are as abſurd as cruell in their malice. As the Apoſtle willeth the people to pray, 2.Theſ.3.and to giue thanks that wee haue been either kept from being a pray to ſuch deuourers, or mercifully ſnatcht out of their iawes,as a coſtly garment out of the fire. 2.Theſ.3.2.

But to paſſe from this,let vs weigh that he had vſed this crueltie vpon ſeuentie Kings: ſo that he was not ſatiſfied,by ten or twentie times continuing his cruelty toward ſo many,no nor three times twentie and more; and would haue done the ſame many hundred times more, if hee had not been cut off,and ſo hindred,as God in much mercie prouideth that ſuch doings ſhall haue an end. And by it we may learne,that when men haue entred into a bad courſe,it is neuer time for them to leaue and come out of it, eſpecially,if they haue benefit thereby, and take liking and delight therein; and moſt of all,if with profit and delight it be growne into a cuſtome with them. *Simon Magus* had a long time bewitched Samaria with his ſorceries, euen almoſt the whole citie: and neuer went about to deſiſt from that practiſe, till he was,againſt his will,broken off by the preaching of *Phillip*. *Demetrius* the Siluer-Smith had done the like in another kind,in the citie of the Epheſians,deceiuing the people along time for his owne gaine, in making ſiluer ſhrines or temples for the Idol *Diana*. *Doct.*4. Acts 8.9.&c. Actes 19.24.

And this is ſo true,that if a man do but fall into any particular ſinne,once or twice,he is readier to commit it twenty times,then once to be think himſelfe about breaking it off. As if it be by making of a lie, and falſe ſwearing, deceiuing,breaking the Sabbath, picking and ſtealing, or the like bad tempering and needleſſe medling any other way. In *Peter* this may bee ſeene, who neuer went ſo farre, as to intend and purpoſe any euill, but being demanded a queſtion only on the ſudden,which hee looked not for, whither he were Chriſts diſciple, denied the truth, but through feare, againſt his conſcience,and hauing once ſo done,being asked the ſame the ſecond time, did ſo againe; and the third time being prouoked ſo, denied it with an oath and a curſing of himſelfe,if he knew the man. *Iehoſophat* could not be warned to forbeare fellowſhip with *Ahab* and his ſonne *Iehoram*, hauing once ſuffered himſelfe to take pleaſure therein,though he had a ſharpe warning of it,and ſmarted alſo for the ſame. And *Sampſon* for the loue of a Philiſtine woman,ſuffering her vnlawfully to moue queſtion to him about that which tended to the looſing of his life,and the graces of God in him, which were moſt precious; becauſe he cut her not off, neither ſtaied her at the firſt, but anſwered her,which he ſhould not haue done, though he ment not to tell her the ſecret that ſhe asked,yet he anſwered and trifled with her ſo long in needleſſe and dangerous talke,that at laſt,through importunitie ſhe got that which ſhe ſought,and which hee neuer ment ſhee ſhould obtaine, till hee found,when it was to late) what it is to yeeld and giue place to euill,though but once or twice. Note. Mark.14.17.

For as the breaking out of waters by cutting the banck that holdeth them in,is the ouerflowing of much ground,and ſpoileth it: ſo the making of a breach in the conſcience,and the yeelding and giuing place to euill but *A ſimile.* Note.

a little,layeth open a man to much bondage and anoyance thereby, ſo that he goeth on,as on that runneth a pace from the top of an high and ſteepe downe-hill,who is not able to ſtay till he come to the bottome. This truth
Prou.23.27. which is verified in ſo many things,*Salomon* hath moſt liuely exemplified in one : ſaying,An harlot is a deepe graue,and a narrow pit: which he that falleth into,can hardly get out of to eſcape ? And therefore to come to make vſe of this which hath been ſaid,wee are to know, that the counſell and rule that the Phyſition giueth for the preſeruing of health, namely, that wee ſhould reſiſt the beginnings of danger ; and ſo we ſhall be free from the euill that would follow,the ſame is meete for all ſuch to bee followed, as deſire to inioy their ſpirituall health,and that their ſoules may feare well, and that is, that they take great heed,when they be firſt inticed by the deceitfulneſſe of ſinne,that they reſiſt ſtrongly before delight be kindled, and dally not with that which they are tempted with ; leſt they bee alſo hardned : which if they doe,they ſhall,by purging out that corruption, finde the fruit of that holy
Matth.26.41. counſell and promiſe in the Goſpell, *Watch and pray, ſo ſhall yee not fall into*
Gen.39.12. *temptation.* Oh,if ſome could haue done it,when with *Ioſeph* they haue been
Note. inticed,and could haue ſhaken of the leaudneſſe of their euil hearts; at what eaſe,and in what freedome might they haue walked, who haue, by giuing place to their luſts, and not kurbing them vp in due time ; brought themſelues into a loathſome ſtate of life,and to a continuall bondage ? And this confutes them,who being reprooued for ſinne, excuſe themſelues like children,that it was the firſt time : or,that they went not ſo farre, but they could
Pſalm.51.5. eaſily deſiſt.As they that dally with, women or maydens by vnchaſe ſpeech, behauiour,or euill thoughts,of whom many fall by degrees to commit folly,nay filthineſſe, becauſe they reſiſted not dalliance,and nipt not that curſed fruit in the bloſſome.

Now that which remaineth in this verſe is a queſtion to good purpoſe : and that is,why the Iſraelites did not kill this tyrant *Adonibezek* out of hand, but reſerue him to this bondage,and to die ſo ? The anſwere is,God giuing them commandement, not to ſpare the Canaanites, and hee hauing been more cruell then ſome other ; God(to bee ſure)inclined their hearts to doe ſo,both that he might haue the meaſure that hee had offered other, and alſo that it might be knowne,that hee died not in warre, which had been ſome glory to him ; it being vnmeet,that ſo cruell a perſon ſhould haue ſo honeſt a death. Another queſtion may bee this concerning himſelfe why this tyrant,when he had ſo ſhamefully defaced and diſmembred ſo many Kings, yet why he would haue them to feed vnder his table. There is no doubt, but that he did it, to remember and ſhew the glory of his victories, and while they were made to feede ſo baſely vnder his feet, as dogges to gather that which fel from his board,it was to ſatisfie his proud and vaine glorious humor therewith,as well pleaſing to him,as if his eares had been filled with muſicke. By the firſt,namely,that fact of the Iſraelites ; we may learne that it is meet that monſtrous doings & vilanies, with the perſons who wrought them,ſhould be made odious according to the deſert of them. As murtherers of Princes,the Lords annointed,to bee put to the extreameſt torments before their fearefull death. As we haue been certified of the exquiſit tortures that were lately executed in France vpon a popiſh and baſe fellow, which imbrued his hands in the blood of his Soueraigne. So wilfull and common murtherers to be hanged vp in chaines to the view of all, for the vnnaturall killing of their neighbour or companion. And so it is meete, that other malefactors should be dealt withall according to their wicked waies, and according to the commandement of God, that euil may be taken away from the land, as it was said of *Ioab*. Our lawes haue well prouided for many such: and if it pleased our Gouernours to thinke well of it, that Atheists, Blasphemers and Adulterers might haue their share among the rest according to their deserts, the case would bee much better with vs by many degrees at this day. And this be said by occasion of the first question. 1.King.2.31.

From the second, and the answer of *Adonibezek* glorying in his crueltie and subduing so many Kings vnder him for his pleasure, (as the Philistines when they listed, called in *Sampson* out of the prison, his eies being put out, to make them passe-time;) it giues occasion to vs to consider the excessiue pride, lust and other badnesse of people, (this present age not being behind any of the former therein) that when God hath brought them out of their swadling cloutes, after they came naked into the world, wherein they were like to haue miscarried a thousand times before they were able to runne about, being so shiftlesse and vnable to helpe themselues, (that I say no more in this place of their misery besides) yet they are no sooner out of the shell (as we vse to say) nor come to mans estate, but they shew themselues to the world as plaiers on the stage, no lesse disguised in their stomacks, behauiour, and qualities, then many of them be in their apparell. And especially if they be great and borne to any thing, it is admirable to see, what profanenesse, licentiousnesse, riot, gaming, and such like intemperance is euery where to be seene in them: who for their owne pleasure, care not how they dominere ouer their inferiours who are vnder them, and ripen them apace who are about them, in all kinde of euill. For what else, (for the most part,) is to bee learned in such seruice? and how they seeke to match their equals in any Italienate fashions and disguised carriage of themselues, and to desire to rise vp to the higher places of their betters, chiefly to this end, that they may haue more libertie to doe euill: that as this tyrant tooke pleasure in his kind, in the sins which he liked, (which yet was no admirable thing in him who was an Heathen Idolater) euen so doe men in this age, (who liuing vnder the Gospel, should blush to heare it) not seeke what pleaseth God, who hath set them vp; but their owne pleasure. And it is so vsuall and common among many of the greater sort, that it is taken vp among the meaner also; in so much, that many of them degenerate from their profession thereby, and become little better then brutish: but a greater number of them (to bee sure) doe little honour it in their liues, which I say rather to comfort and incourage them, who haue no fellowship with them in their vnfruitefull works of darkenesse, then in hope to doe good to many of the other offenders.

THE FOVRTH SERMON VPON THE FIRST CHAPTER OF THE BOOKE OF IVDGES.

VERS. 8. *Now the children of Iudah had fought against Ierusalem, and had taken it, and smitten it with the edge of the sword, and had set the citie on fire.*

VERS. 9. *Afterward also the children of Iudah went downe to fight against the Canaanites that dwelt in the mountaine, and toward the South, and in the low countrie.*

VERS. 10. *And Iudah went against the Canaanites that dwelt in Hebron, which Hebron before time was called Kiriath-Arbah: and they slew Sheshai, and Ahiman, and Talmai.*

VERS. 11. *And from thence hee went to the inhabitants of Debir: and the name of Debir in old time was Kiriath-Sepher.*

The sense.

THese verses and the other that follow to the 17.verse, are repeated out of the book of *Ioshua*, chiefly out of the 15.chapter, and are brought hither to this end, that we may vnderstand that the Tribe of *Iudah* possessed Ierusalem, while *Ioshua* was yet aliue, and therefore they might the easilier and better bring *Adonibezek* thither prisoner. And the things that are here repeated out of *Ioshua*, are partly these, in the foure verses which I haue now read, namely, the taking of Ierusalem, Hebron and Debir, and their fighting against the Canaanits that dwelt in the mountaines; and partly those things following afterward to the 16.verse, as shall be shewed when I come vnto them. And that they are here repeated, is manifest hereby, for that it is declared in that Chapter of *Ioshua*, that the King of Ierusalem was then taken, and was brought into the hands of the people of God, and that the children of *Iudah* dwelt there with the Iebusites. In the 17.verse, the holy storie returneth to set downe what *Iudah* and *Simeon* did further at this time, as he began to declare before from verse 4. to the 8. That which concerneth Hebron and Debir shall be set downe in their place.

Doct. generally out of all these verses.

Now this repetition out of the booke of *Ioshua* here brought in, vnto the 17.verse, (for the 16. is a short interlaced story of the Kenites) this repetition (I say) is here brought in, lest the Reader should be troubled, as though the same things which are mentioned here, had been now done after the death of *Ioshua*, which are set downe there to haue been in his life time. And this is done that there might be no stumbling nor offence thereat, we may therfore note out of all these verses in generall, the great care that the holy Ghost had in setting downe the Scriptures, freeing them from errour, and making one to agree with the other: so that if men were able to discerne, they might euer see it to be so. It is true indeed, that many things in them are hard to be vnderstood,

vnderstood,*which the wicked peruert*,as S.*Peter* saith, *to their owne destruction:* 2.Pet.3.16.
but where care is ioyned with gifts of knowledge,(which gifts some attaine See Pro 30.5.
to,) there may bee seene a most sweet agreement betwixt them, and no one Psalm.12.6.
either to iarre with another,or any one to be friuelous,or absurd,as some are
bold to affirme,but *seuen times tried in the fire*,and,*pure and holy*,as the Psalmist Psalm.19.8.
saith: and therefore to all good vses of knowledge, and confuting of error, 2.Tim.3.16.
or practise in life,and comfort,profitable. For though all Scripture is not a- Rom.15.4.
like,but some plaine and some obscure; yet,first,they are plainest which are more necessarie for faith and life; and, they that haue obscuritie in them, serue to exercise and sharpen our vnderstanding rather, and to prouoke an appetie,in vs to diligence and care for attaining the true meaning of them, then to driue vs from in reading them. To the shame of Popery,this that I haue said is to be marked,for the professors thereof doe challenge them for their difficultie and hardnesse,so as they are not to be suffered in the hands of the common people,whom if they withheld not from the true vnfolding of them,they might reape great profit by reading them.

Also to the iust reproofe of many,both Atheists,and other not much differing from them,this is to be noted; for they, that is the Atheists,scoffe at the Scriptures,and bouldly iustle against *Moses* and Christ: these,who are the prophane,as bouldly,and yet blindly, reason, dispute, and quarrell against some particular Scriptures,which they vnderstand not,as if they were
competent iudges,as that in the Psalme,*Moab is my washpot, ouer Edome will I* Psalm.108.9.
cast my shooe, which yet is (as they would see and acknowledge, if they were not more bold and rash,then wise and skilfull) to very good purposes, as setting downe Gods threatning of iudgements against his enemies; as also that of *Samsons* tying foxes tailes together with firebrands, to spoile the Philistimes corne; with such like also they raile against the doctrine of predestination,and the sinne against the holy Ghost. But not counting them worth the answering,I conclude: seeing the Lord hath left the Scriptures so pure and free from all error,(the matters in them being so profitable and heauenly,)I conclude(I say) that if we desire to liue comfortably by the benefit of them; let them bee our treasure, while the world trample them vn-
derfoot, yea, and let our meditation and delight bee so much the more in Psalm.1.2.
them,and that continually. And this bee noted out of all these verses generally,to the 17.in that they are a repetition out of *Ioshua*.

Now more particularly,in that so worthy things were done by this Tribe Doct.vers.8.
before,and that therefore they were chosen now, rather then any of the other Tribes to guide the rest,seeing that they were wisest and faithfullest in Gods matters,as appeareth by the mentioning of these great actes,done by them; let it teach vs this; that such as are wisest and faithfullest,ought to bee vsed and placed in the chiefe roomes of the seruice of God,aboue the rest.So
Paul was endued with excellent gifts,*and counted faithfull, before God put him* 1.Tim.1.12.
in his seruice,and then he imployed him in the most waightie businesse. So Iosh.2.14.
Ioshua sent faithfull spies,to view the land of Canaan. This thing had such
force in the heathen Kings,as in *Pharaoh*,that hee preferred *Ioseph* aboue all Genes.41.40.
the chiefe Nobles of the land,though he was but a stranger? saying, where shall we find a man like this man fitted for this worke? and in the Kings of
Babylon,that they committed the great and waighty matters of the King- Genes.41.

Dan.3.30. & 6.2. dome to *Daniel*,and the three Children,because they saw, that the spirit of God was in them to doe well aboue others. So *Abraham* trusted *Eliezer* his seruant,in that waighty matter of the marriage of his sonne *Isaac*, hauing none like him : yea, *Ahab* himselfe made *Obadiah* (a worthy man) Steward of his houshold,though hee had inough of other beside. The holy Ghost 2.Sam.23. makes mention at large,of those Worthies which *Dauid*(for their good seruice in the warres against the enemies of the Lord) exalted to the highest roomes next him.So did *Iehoiada*.Hence it is,that the Wise man saith, *Wo to* Eccles.10.16. &c. *that land,whose Princes are children*,and being not fit for any gouernment,rise vp earely to drink strong drink. Yea *Salomon* being put to his choice, desired 1.King.3.9. *an vnderstanding heart,wisely to goe in and out before the people*. And such ought Masters of families,Magistrates and Gouernours in Townes to be,as well as Ministers. And this order God hath set and taught vs, in commending and commanding faithfulnes and diligence(which are excellent vertues,)in seruāts,who yet are the meanest persons,therby teaching vs, much more to prefer these gifts in them who are vsed and imploied in higher callings and places, and so much the more,if wisdome be ioyned with them. And these qualities *Iethro* required in such magistrates as should be chosen; and the like Exod.18.21. 1.Tim.3.2. *Paul* required in such as are called to the ministry, besides other like furniture : which giueth vs great cause of mourning,when wee see the contrary : and of reioycing,where these vertues are to bee seene and found in them, who are put in trust. And such should executors of willes, and schoolemasters be,into whose hands men are constrained to put their children,and goods ; and comprimitters of cases betwixt neighbours, should be like vnto 1.Sam.26.21. them,who are trusted with much oftentimes. And this honour,honest and faithfull men haue with many,that in iudging of matters, they will, if their case be good,desire to haue such to giue their sentence, and iudgement for them in their doubtfull causes rather then others,though they set not greatly by religion themselues. And this ought to incourage vs all, to labour for Gods graces,seeing they make a man stand before the honorable : though money, fauour, or other respects are the chiefe gifts which most obtaine great places by.

Now whereas a doubt may arise here, where it is said, that *Iudah* had taken Ierusalem,how it appeares to haue been so, seeing it is not expresly set

Obiection. *Answere.* downe in *Ioshua*,chap.10. To that I answere, though it bee not plainely so said, yet it may well bee vnderstood, by the things that are written there : namely,that the King of Ierusalem was taken and put to death, and that *Iudah* dwelt in the citie,and could not cast out the Iebusits that dwelt therein. By which,I say,it appeareth, that the citie was then taken, although it was not as yet wholly possessed, and so did they slay the inhabitants, and set the Doct out of ver.8.9.10. city on fire. Here by the occasion of the destroying of these cities,Ierusalem, Hebron,Debir,and others many, let vs consider the desolation that God sendeth vpon goodly places,and the inhabitants thereof, when his hand is against them, and when hee is purposed to blow vpon them, and to set them, as it were, on the stage to the view of the world. Yea doubtlesse,when he pleaseth to take the iudgement into his hand, all the beautie and glorie of the world must vanish at his presence, and the gloriousest solemnities and monuments come to vtter decay. And to put vs in mind hereof, of,is this written and ſet downe, to ſhew vs the changeable eſtate of the flouriſhingeſt proſperitie of fleſh. The which a man would thinke, that ſhould behold them in their beauty and time of their glory, that the enioyers thereof,did liue in a paradice and petty heauen, euen here vpon earth: whereas,when God hath blowne vpon them, they are more deſolate then the winter,and like to an houſe waſte and ruinous. When *Nabuchadnezzar* and the foole in the Goſpell prided themſelues, the one in his great Babell, the other in his abundance,ſuddenly comes a voice to both of them: to the one, *Thy Kingdome is departed from thee:* and to the other, *O foole, this night ſhall they take thy ſoule from thee.* For wee muſt know, that as there is a time to flouriſh,ſo is there a time to fade,a time to bee borne, and ſo to grow vp,and a time alſo to die. Therefore when the diſciples,much like the fooliſh people of the world,looking vpon the goodly buildings of the Temple, began to haue them in admiration,ſaying: *Behold, Maſter, what goodly buildings are here*; he making ſmall account of their ſpeeches,anſwered them fitly in this manner: *I ſay vnto you,there ſhall not a ſtone remaine on a ſtone* of all that yee ſee ſo coſtly and beautifull. Where are all the great perſons become, that poſſeſſed the earth not long agone,with all the glory thereof? They that made others afraid with their very countenance and looke, behold, they may bee troad vpon by the meaneſt, that were abuſed by them? As *Dauid* ſaith, *I haue ſeene an end of all perfection:* which *Salomon* his ſonne prooued by clearer experience,ſaying of all; *Vanitie of vanities.* Of feaſting and banqueting, to ſpeake a word,how well pleaſing and welcome ſo euer it bee, yet how harſhly and fearefully it endeth many times, let *Balſhazzars* example teach vs. As for fauour and beautie,another of the precious things of this world, whatſoeuer it promiſeth in outward ſhew, how can the glory thereof bee more baſely ſpoken of,then we ſee,and in few yeeres find it to be,and in the Prouerbs,it is ſaid to be in theſe words: *Fauour is deceitfull,and beauty is a vaine thing.*

Dan.4.28. Luke 12.20. Mark.13.1. Pſalm.119.96. Eccleſ.1.1. Dan.5.6. Prou.31.30.

Note. The ſame may be ſaid of al other things, that are precious vnder the ſun, as ſolemne marriages, inheritances, aduancements, with ſuch like, they all fade,as doth the flower. Now was their time come here mentioned, to bee brought to deſtruction,and the time of thoſe that remaine is comming apace,euen as the fall of the leafe in due ſeaſon. And they that carrie their hearts moſt high, muſt remember that this day is not farre off,though it ſhal be a day of lamentation and woe,to them that haue their delight here. For oh death how vnwelcome art thou to a man that hath laid vp no better treaſure then tranſitory? And yet what is leſſe thought on? but as the Pſalmiſt ſaith,the children that ſee all this,approoue of their fathers courſe, and follow it. The twelue daies,as the time of the natiuitie, commonly paſſed in reuell rout,a liuely picture of this ſhort and painted Paradiſe, as they count it,in many great houſes,where their play and belly-cheere is ſoone and ſodainly at an end,with more ſorrow then their pleaſure was in the middeſt of their enioying of it. Pſalm.49.14.

And therefore, who can thinke of the madneſſe of the world without mourning? but oh that there were many to bewaile it. To ſee the carking and caring,the deceiuing,the couſonage that is almoſt euery where, and all to clime vp to this hill of promotion and libertie ſeeking, to liue as

Note. men liſt, in whoring, in drunkenneſſe, in play, and ſuch like paſſing the time, and yet when they are come to the top, they muſt by and by bee throwne downe againe with greater violence and ſhame. But if the change it ſelfe be ſo vnwelcome, then much more, whē it cōmeth vpon them both ſuddenly See Pſal.73.19. and fearefully. So that the vileſt would not change their eſtate for theirs, whom erſt they admired. But, ſay ſome, ye trouble vs with telling vs theſe things, ſhew vs as well, how we may remedy them. I anſwere to ſuch as feare the changes, that I haue ſpoken of, and are troubled to heare of them; feare Pſalm.112. God, and ye ſhall not need to feare the comming of theſe, whenſoeuer they Note. ſhall befall you; elſe that which you feare, ſhal come vpon you euen to vtter deſolation. And whereas many demand, if we, who ſo diſgrace the vngodly practiſe of the world, and are out of loue with it, are not ſubiect to changes alſo, as well as others; as from wealthy to want, from health to ſickneſſe, till death doe follow. I ſay this to them who haue laid vp their treaſure in heauen, it is the welcomeſt day to thinke of going hence, whatſoeuer they leaue behind them, and they haue ſo valued the tranſitorie and momentany pleaſures of this life, that they are willing and deſirous to forſake them all, if they were all theirs, for that which there they hope to enioy. In which reſpect, is that ſpoken by the Preacher, *The day of death is better then the day of birth.* But Eccleſ.7.3. to proceed.

Verſ.9.10. The holy ſtory mentioneth further both generally in this verſe, how *Iudah* had fought againſt the Canaanites that dwelt in the mountaine, and toward the South, and in the low country, and more particularly againſt them that dwelt in Hebron, and ſo, diſcribeth that citie by another name that was Ioſh.15.13. giuen it in former times, that is, Kiriath-arba, or the citie of one *Arba*, who was a Giant, and the father of *Anak*, which *Anak* hauing three ſonnes, *Sheſhau*, *Ahimau*, and *Talmai*, *Iudah* ſlew them there. Theſe Anakims ſo called of their father, were mighty, tall and ſtrong, as appeareth by many other 1.Sam.17.7. Scriptures, ſo by that which deſcribeth *Goliah* of Gath, by the ſhaft of his ſpeare, that it was like a weauers beame, and that, which ſpeaketh of the ſpies that went to view the land of Canaan; who returning, feared the people Num.13.34. with the report of their ſtature, ſaying, *that they themſelues were but as graſſehoppers to them.* Theſe giantlike men therefore, and thoſe which were about and vnder them, being taken away, what a benefit muſt it needes bee to the children of Iſrael? Now though theſe were properly called Anakims and Giants, and that their kind and poſteritie remaine not now to vexe faithfull Chriſtians, as they did then Gods Church, yet as there haue been many kinds of enemies, ſo there are, and alwaies ſhall be, which ſhall doe the ſame to the people of God, being cruell and ſcornefull contemners of the humble and innocent, that they did to the Iſraelites: who make their liues vnpleaſant, with grieuous burdens, which they lay vpon them, and deadly feare that they hold them in, and if they take not their life away from them alſo, yet they make it weariſome to them, ſo that many of them deuoure themſelues, theſe therefore may well be called Giants.

When therefore God ſhal weaken ſuch Anakims, and abate their power, Eſter.8.16. or take them away, when they cannot bee reclaimed and brought to repentance, it muſt be counted the ſingular mercy of God. For the world is full of ſuch, in whom the prouerb is verified, that might ouercommeth right.

When

When men who haue power,authoritie,and wealth, so deale and liue with others,that they hold them in continuall slauery and feare. Thus *Pharaoh* was a Giant,and as the sonne of *Anak* to *Iosephs* posteritie, laying burthens vpon them,which they could not beare,and not thinking he had oppressed them enough by doing so,added yet more vnto them also. And thus they play the parts of giants,which grind the faces of the poore,to whom sound reason,euen the commandement of God, diswading them from it, is vtterly vnsauorie,and crauing of pity at their hands,is in vaine.

This is apparent in sutes and controuersies, betwixt the mightie and the meane,the one eating vp the other, as if they were bread. So such as are set in place to chase away wickednesse,receiuing and deuouring gifts out of the hands of the guilty,and lion-like roaring against the innocent,and so sucking aduantage out of them,and liuing by the sinnes of the people,are very Giants,and no better then Anakims. All such and the like aggrieuances, are to be groned vnder,by the godly in the eares of the Lord. And they who are deliuered from such burdens, haue great cause with reioycing, to praise God,as the people did, when they were brought back out of the captiuitie, saying: *Our mouth was full of laughter,and our tongue filled with ioy*.But of this Psalm.126.2.
enough,because I haue spoken of the like point before,in vers.7.

Now to goe forward in the story, it is said, that *Iudah* had not rested in Vers.7. Iosh.10.26.
these destructions of the Canaanites, and of many other mentioned in the booke of *Ioshua*,but proceeded further to take Debir,another citie scituated by Hebron,but more of this in the next verse. And in the meane season,here it is to be considered,how vnwearied *Iudah* is said to haue been in the worke of the Lord,euen in procuring the destruction of his enemies, the Canaanites,with *Ioshua* while hee liued, who was the chiefe guide of the rest. For this diligence of theirs, in going from one peece of this worke to another, should be a notable incouragement to all that are seruants to God in any worke that he sets them about,that they should not doe it negligently, nor stand at a stay after good beginnings, as though they had done sufficiently alreadie. They must not repeat their labours and cumbats which are past,as though they had done enough, but looke to those which are to come: as the Apostle teacheth in the Epistle to the Philippians. And this is carefully Philip.3.13.
to be regarded,whether it be in performing outward duties,as these men of *Iuda* did,or inward,as in resisting temptations,patient bearing of afflictions, and the like; they should alwaies be vnwearied in the worke of the Lord. For to this end God hath promised strength by the armour of a Christian.

And thus it is meet for al such to grow from strength to strength,and from faith to faith, (as God hath giuen commandement,) and to verifie that which is written by *Salomon*; *the righteous shineth as the light vnto the perfit day*. Rom.1.17.
As plants when the be rooted in good ground doe burnish and spread their Prou.4.18.
branches,and bring foorth fruite plentifully. And such must know,that it is Note.
a sore discouragement to the weaker Christians,when they shall see dampes and deadnesse in the ancienter professors, who haue been sometimes prouokers and stirrers vp of others to the duties of godlinesse. A great blemish, doubtlesse,it is in them who may iustly be charged to doe so. For beside other inconueniences, this is one, that it beateth a strong conceit into the hearts

hearts of the weake,that they find not that liking in Gods seruice that they are told of,and promised in the word of God which they heare. As if God were not to be trusted in setting forth so large offers and priuiledges therein: or as though he were wearie of weldoing to his: the which to affirme is rancke blasphemie. They should all so know,such I meane,as God hath put in his seruice, that they ought now after long continuance therein, and in his house,to bee as fathers to procure and seeke the good of the weaker sort of their brethren,and to haue great care that none become faint by their ex-
2.Pet.3.17. ample; but therefore to shine as lights, *and grow daily in grace, and in the knowledge of our Lord Iesus.* Oh it is comely for others to behold, and their owne glory,to see that they follow the Lord stil directing and going before
Iosh.14.8. them,as they did at any time past. Like *Caleb*,who fortie and fiue yeere after the Lord had set him about his work, as one of the two,who were counted more faithfull then the rest,was as strong and fit for it,as hee had been so many yeeres before. I know it is a rare thing,partly seeing few liue so long; partly seeing many waxe soone wearie of well doing, and either haue not meanes to set them forward,or else haue no desire to vse them with that delight which once they did; beside their many discouragements; it is there-
Note. fore(I say)a rare thing to see men faithfull and constant for any long time, in goodnesse. But so much the more commendable it is,where it may bee
Gal.4.18. found: oh,it is a good thing alwaies to be constant in a good matter. I deny
Matth.25.5. not but the best may easily,and doe,with the wise virgins begin to nod, and
Cant.5.2. with the Church in the Canticles fall a sleepe; but therefore is it the needfuller for them to be quickned vp by Gods promises, and other incourage-
Reu.2.7. ments,as where he saith,*To him that ouercommeth will I giue the tree of life*, that
Matth.26.41. is,euerlasting life,and such like. And also to quicken vp themselues,as I haue said,by diligent,watching and feruent prayer,&c. that they perish not with the wicked of the world,while they liue among them.

For they know that by faithfulnesse and constancie therein.they grow at last to perseuerance,and to a good end of their conflicting daies: and that they must depart from many ill actions and bad companies, which other make themselues merry with all. But if such shal begin to think that their reward here,and in the life to come,wil not be answerable to the losse of their
Matth.19.29. pleasure that they forgoe,(which reward (yet) is *an hundreth fold more euen in this life*, beside happinesse afterwards) let them cast their account before they begin: but if they feare nothing but their owne weakenesse, let them
Psalm.27.1. not be discouraged,God will be their strength;let them *cast their care on him,*
1.Pet.5.7. *and he will care for them.* Thus by this which I haue said of this matter,it may easily be seene,that they take the right course to happinesse,who with these men of *Iuda*,hold out constantly and vnwearied in well doing,notwithstanding all discouragements,temptations and opposition to the contrary.

THE

THE FIFTH SERMON VPON THE FIRST CHAPTER OF THE BOOKE OF IVDGES.

VERS. 12. *And Caleb said, he that smiteth Kiriah-Sepher, and taketh it, euen to him will I giue Acsah my daughter to wife.*

VERS. 13. *And Othniel, the sonne of Kenaz, Calebs younger broother tooke it, to whom he gaue Acsah his daughter to wife.*

VERS. 14. *And when she came to him to aske of her father a field, and she lighted off her asse, and Caleb said vnto her, What wilt thou?*

VERS. 15. *And she answered him, Giue me a blessing, for thou hast giuen me a South country, giue me also springs of water. And Caleb gaue her the springs aboue, and the springs beneath.*

THis citie Debir, it is said, was in times past called Kiriah-sepher: that is, the citie of one *Sepher*, to put a difference betwixt that and some other of that name. And it is said here, that *Caleb* seeing more difficultie to winne this city, offered a reward to him that would set vpon it. But I must againe put the Reader in mind, that these things mentioned from the 8. verse to the 17. were done in the daies of *Ioshua*, and are but repeated here, to commend the faithfulnes, and care of this Tribe of *Iuda*: and as they were done then, so the subduing of this city is ascribed to *Ioshua*, in Iosh. 10. because he was their chiefe guide, and gouernour in all these warres, though *Caleb* offered a reward to him that winne it, because it was his inheritance, and *Othniel* here mentioned was the person that tooke it, and enioyed the reward. This be said for the meaning of these two verses, and for reconciling this place with that which I cited out of *Ioshua*. *The sense of the vers. 12. 13.* Ioshua 10. 38.

Now for the benefit which wee are to reape from hence, it is manifold; first by this, that there was more difficultie and danger in the winning of this citie then other; it giueth vs to learne and to marke, that in going about the duties of our particular callings, (as this warring against these cities of the Canaanites was theirs) we must not thinke it strange, if some part of our life, and at sometime, be more incumbred then other parts, and at other times: and that we should not be discouraged, nor disquieted, when we see it to be so, euen these good seruants of God did find it so in some part of their work, more then in some other: and yet they did not for all that breake it off, but wisely bethinke themselues, how to ouercome the difficultie of it, by more then ordinarie paines, and care, when the businesse required it. The like may be said of the religious duties of our generall callings, both concerning the first, and second Table, there is not alwaies that confidence, ioy, cheerefulnesse, diligence, and feruency in the vse of priuate meanes, or fruitfulnesse *Doct. 1.* Psalm. 30. 6. Psal. 42. 4. 5. Note.

in

in doing good to others: we find these come off with much difficultie sometime, in respect of others. And this commeth not to passe by chance, as neither it did to them, (as men vse to say) but by the prouidence of God, who most wisely disposeth so of it, that it may not oftentimes be so with vs, that we haue hard successe, lest we should be discouraged, and also lest we should not bring our worke to any good point, but (as they say) our labour should be lost, and in vaine, and nothing should goe forward; as if in husbanding the ground by sowing, reaping, and all other worke belonging to it, the weather should alwaies be dropping.

And although it be not often so, yet hee seeth it conuenient that sometime men should find it so, I meane hardnesse, to bring their worke to passe, and some difficultie about it, though they haue skill in it, to the end they may haue proofe of their patience at such times, and bee thankfull to God when it falleth not out so oftentimes, but that they haue good successe for the most part. And also that they may learne experience against other like times, to be contented, when it shall so fall out againe, that so they may shew
Note. one euen tender in their life (as much as may bee) and in euery part of it, some equalitie, in care, contentment, cheerefulnesse, hope, and patience, and not to to bee carried into extremities, as many are, by the occasions that are offered, and that come to passe daily. And this ought to guide all men in their callings, and in the actions of their liues, that, as well when things go against them, as when they goe with them, they may in al estates be thankful,
Iob.1.21. (as we reade holy *Iob* was) especially, seeing they know, that God ordereth both good successe, and also the contrary to the good of his.

The husbandman is hindred sometime by the rainy weather: but yet so, as he hath his seasons free from it, to doe his businesse in. The Artificer is troubled about putting away his wares, and the falling of the price, so that he cannot alwaies make his aduantage of them, as ordinarily he doth, for the maintaining of himselfe, and his charge. But God changeth those times, so that they doe not alwaies keepe at one stay. The good minister is sometime troubled about the carelesnesse, and prophanenesse of his people, and is grieued for the ill successe that he seeth on his labours, but God giueth him incouragement againe, that some doe regard his ministery, and receiue the Gospell to their amendment, and saluation. Besides the diligentest labourers in preaching are oft to seeke of necessarie helpes for this life; and more then their due they rarely find and seldome meet with, (what need soeuer they haue) if they get that truly paid them; the ministery being in so little account with men of the world, of which sort the greatest number is. So women in their places haue many crossings of them by their husbands, seruants, and about children. and matters of familie, beside other vnlooked for
2.King.6.33. accidents and troubles, which we see doe cause many of them, who are not seasoned with grace, and sauing knowledge, to bee exceedingly impatient, disquiet, and out of order. Therefore if they, who are religious should not vnder the like crosses be better gouerned, though they enioy many comforts in the married estate, they should euer, and anon bee out of frame, and vnquiet, and in no sort enioy the benefit of that estate, as God hath allowed them to doe, as too many can testifie.

In more particular manner I might shew the disapointments that al sorts of

of people meet with and haue. As the labouring man for his part,is not behind the rest,in finding much hardnesse,by meanes of his poore estate, and the great prices of necessarie things at sometimes especially: but I should be too long,if I should stand vpon particulars. To these when wee adde other disapointments and crosses, as ill debters, sutes in the law,losse of friends, who were vpholders of them,while they liued, diseases and sicknes, with a thousand more,which cannot be remembred: all may see there arise many things in all conditions and dealings,to make some part of mens liues hardlier passed in peace and quietnes to their good liking,though they haue, for the most part,good successe,and do vsually labour with some ease,as I haue said. And why doe I set downe all this about the matter in hand? but that we may see the wisdome and mercy of God herein,who mixeth both together,because if all our life should be smoothly carried, and easily passed, we should be made thereby vnfit for our change,especially for great trials,when they come;and so likewise,if it should be for the most part tedious and troublesome,there should be nothing (in a manner) but wearinesse and discomfort. And therefore all sorts should seeke to be in Gods fauour, that so they may also bee vnder his gouernment in both estates, and that while they are so,they may daily keepe so; and that aboue all other things, which estate of life onely hath the promise of blessing in euery calling and condition, and where it is wanting, all confusion (for the most part) breaketh in amongst men,that they be not only vnquiet in their troubles, and doe most vncomfortably,go vnder difficulties;but also when they enioy any more freedome and prosperitie,they be euen in their best estate,vnprofitable,if not offensiue and troublesome. And if it seeme strange to any, that God thus disposeth of mens trauels and dealings,that the successe be vncertaine,let them looke to the end why he doth so,before set downe; and namely, if they be much troubled,for that many casualties fall out in their liues,they must know,that if it were otherwise,they would keepe no compasse,and therefore God seeth 1.Pet.1.7.
it meet sometime that it should be so.

But another thing to be noted here in *Caleb,* is this: that when hee saw it *Doct.*2.
required courage,as well as skill,to aduenture and set vpon this citie,for the destroying of Gods enemies that were in it,as hee was commanded,promiseth his daughter to him that would set vpon it. This was no small matter that he offered,but marke why? as I haue shewed,all may see hee did shew this forwardnesse to the rooting out of Gods enemies. And it teacheth,that Matth.5.12.13.
for the Lords sake,we ought to doe much,and yet count it no great matter that we doe. To aduance his name,and helpe to set vp his true worship,and the sincere preaching of the Gospell,the ouerthrowing of his enemies, and for such like seruice of his,euery man ought to be ready and willing to be a- Heb.10.33.
based in his countenance,weakened in his wealth, and sustaine much hard- Note.
ship,if need be. *Dauid* may be brought in here,and set in none of the meanest roomes,for that which he did in this behalfe. For beside that there was none in his time,that honoured God more then hee did in the louing, frequenting,and longing after his being in the Lords house, and the place where his honour dwelleth: so hee bare reproch as mighty as hee was,and that willingly for his zeale toward God: for when he brought the Arke of God with shouting,and sound of trumpet into the citie of *Dauid,*dancing before

2 Sam.6.16. before it, *Michael, Sauls* daughter, looked out at the window, and dispised him, as thinking it too base a thing for a King to doe so: but he answered, it
Ester.4 16. was before the Lord, and that he would yet, for his sake, be more vile. So *Ester*, for bringing the people of God out of desolation, and vtter rooting out,
Exod.32.32. put her life in danger, saying, *If I perish, I perish.* So *Moses* and *Paul* desired
Rom.9.3. rather to perish, then the people of God should be forsaken, and so God his glory be empeached.

And why should they not, all these, (I meane) and other such, as well as they, euen Kings and Queenes lay downe their Crownes at his feet, and aduance him, who hath honoured them aboue others? And much more wee, how are meane and inferiours, should think our selues happie if we may bee imployed by him, or if any thing that we haue might doe him seruice. Ac-
Marke 1.31. cording to that which is written, Mark. 1. *He that loueth father or mother, more then me? is not worthie of me.* And it is true indeed, that wee should loue nothing so well, but we should forgoe it for the Lords cause; therefore when
Prou.23.26. he saith, *Giue me thine heart (my sonne,)* we should reioyce that he will aske and take any thing that we haue, and yeeld it him with all readinesse. But for ought I see, I may iustly complaine, and say: wee are like those children, which hauing gotten what they can at their fathers hand, cast him off, and flourish boldly with that which they haue gotten of him. So to speake what I thinke, as I see with mine owne eies, when God hath inriched men with his manifold blessings, there is not one of many that considereth it, of
1.Cor.4.7. whom he hath receiued all that he inioyeth; but glorieth of that which is not his owne, and setteth out himselfe with anothers goods, as though hee owed nothing to him, of whom he receiued him.

And yet, to aggrauate our sin, I must needs adde one thing, I am perswaded, (greatly to our shame and conuiction) that many in the Papacie, who shal neuer haue reward for it, are brought (through error) to do many things and giue much, in a superstitious zeale to this end, that they may bee saued. But if they doe that which God neuer required at their hands, and therfore amisse; ought not we, who haue learned better, to do readily that which we are commanded, especially our reward being certaine? If they doe it to merit that which they shall neuer attaine; ought not we much more, to doe the duties which we are commanded, who belieue that we haue the best things freely promised, I meane eternall life, which also in due time shall bee giuen vs of God, and that of his meere mercie, and bountie? And if *Caleb* would giue his daughter, should not wee much more giue some part of our substance to feede the hungry, and to helpe cloath the naked, when we may yet reserue sufficient for our selues besides? Whereas the truth is, that all is too little that wee can doe to good vses, that wee might honour God: (as *Caleb* here could affoord him the best thing that they had) and yet all is of vs thought to much (when it is but little) that we doe this way, lest wee should hinder our selues.

*Doct.*3. And to end this verse, this *Caleb* being a godly man, and as well renowned and approoued for his grace, as for his greatnesse; in saying, that hee
Deut.7.3. would giue his daughter to wife, sheweth, that hee had well learned *Moses* doctrine, in whose daies he liued, and namely in this point, (as he had in many other) that children are not to dispose of their owne marriage, but the father.

ther. To whom,though many haue lost their honour that way,as being vnfitter to make choice,then their children themselues; yet God hath giuen them this libertie,that if they do no good with it,they may be conuicted by it,who for their place and yeeres,should be fitter to make the match in good sort,then the children,who for the most part are caried, not so much by religion, and good aduisednesse,as by will, and rash heate to make their owne choice: and therefore it is ofttimes iustly requited by God,who ought chiefly to be obeyed in that action,that to make their sinne the better appeare, their match is as soone repented of, many times,as it is inioyed.

Moses therfore,who was Gods mouth to the people, was commanded by him to teach this,that the parents had authoritie in prouiding marriages for their children: for thus he saith,*Thou shalt not giue thy daughter to the sonne of the Canaanite,nor take his daughter to thy sonne.* And therefore we reade that *Sampson* gaue this honour to his father and mother, for the granting of their consent in his marriage,(as many other did the like)for thus he saith: *I saw a woman,and she pleaseth me well,now therefore giue me her to wife,* And *Paul* comming long after *Moses*, agreed with him, as being both faithfull seruants to their Master; he teacheth that this dutie belongeth to the father,saying: *He that giueth his daughter in marriage,doth well,* signifying who should giue her. Although I speake not this, as though they might force their children to what marriages they list;but to giue their consent,and aduice must bee had, with some speciall and iust cause shewed(if it be expedient,) when,and why they may not. So that this being cleare,it doth the more bewray the boldnesse,wilfulnes,and disobedience of many children,who would be thought wise enough to know their duties,who yet doe not meanely grieue their parents,but also prouide ill for themselues, in making their matches at their own pleasures: who,beside,that they bring in one little better,then a Canaanite ofttimes at least,a waspe,an hagge,or otherwise, badly qualified into, and amongst a good kindred,so they themselues seldome agree, and especially if the one partie draw any thing neerer to God,then the other.

Iudges 14.2.

1.Cor.7.38.

Hereof it commeth to passe, I will not say onely, but doubtlesse in great part, that there are so many disordered, and offensiue, matches and marriages, and the persons so wearisome one to the other, that they must either be parted by other,or they will part themselues; or if they cannot,yet they doe little better: for dwelling both in one house,yet,they may not(many times) meete, but be parted at bed and board, and they must haue them that are of another house, to set them together; whereby, it may bee easily gathered, what manner of Christian and sociable life they enioy together; and what fruite they reape of iustling a side the commandement of God about their comming together. But it is not my purpose to shew the annoiances that be in all vnlawfull marriages, I doe but poynt at some,which fall out, yea, and come oft,and ordinarily, where Gods ordinance and commandement is reiected, as when the children make their owne marriages without their parents,or against them.

But seeing occasion may be taken here, of mouing a question or two, I will stand a little vpon these two verses for the satisfying the doubts that are raised: and make vse thereof afterward. It is therefore obiected here, whither *Caleb* did aduisedly, and whither he was to be commended for this offering Vers.12.13. *Obiection* 1.

fering of his daughter to him that ſhould winne Debir: for what knew he, whether he might lawfully keepe promiſe with the partie, ſuch an one, as he
2 might haue been? Alſo it is obiected, that he who did winne it, was thought to be too neare a kinde to him, *Othniel* by name, being ſaid to be his younger brother, ſo that he might not lawfully take her to wife. Theſe things there-
Anſwere 1. fore require an anſwere. To the firſt, that wee are chiefely to looke to this, namely, the commendation of *Caleb*, that he would offer ſo largely for the deſtroying of Gods enemies, according to Gods commandement, and this the holy Ghoſt intended to declare, and not that we ſhould make queſtion,
1.Cor.13.5. whether he did it rightly and lawfully, or no. For as *charitie is not ſuſpitious*,
Ioſh.14.11. ſo he being ſo rarely commended for his pietie, and obedience to God, it becommeth not vs to iudge him for that, which we cannot accuſe him of, neither can any ſuch thing be gathered againſt him out of the text. It is true, he offered his daughter vpon the condition mentioned, and there is no more ſet downe in what manner, or with what reſpects; but he did it ſo, as he was commended for it, neither is he charged to haue done it raſhly: what hath any man therefore to doe to challenge him for it? But if they can proue him to haue done raſhly (which they ſhall neuer be able to doe, ſeeing the holy Ghoſt commendeth him for it) then it is not denied, but that it was his ſinne.

The vſe of this anſwer. Now, if any vrge this againſt him, to take libertie thereby for dealing raſhly, and without due conſideration in waightie caſes, or in the caſe of marriage, particularly, affirming that they doe but as *Caleb* did, and they aduenture it, either in their owne, or in making of their childrens marriages, with ſuch perſons whoſe conuerſation they doe not know; Let them ſeeke a better defence for their doings, then the example of *Caleb*; for beſides, that we muſt liue by rules, and not by examples; ſo neither can they draw any ſuch liberty from his practiſe. But whatſoeuer may bee ſaid to haue been done by any good man concerning this matter, it skilleth not, we haue a
1.Cor.7.39. commandement to marry in the Lord. And as for them, that ſeek to defend their matches, which haue ſlightly bin made, wherein God hath had either ſmall or no hand: he hath ſufficiently branded, and ſet his marke vpon them, that as they haue not been gone about, nor finiſhed by his allowance and direction, ſo they are not by him alowed, (though mariage otherwiſe bee honourable,) and therefore not beautified with the ſweete ſociableneſſe and other commodities, which he hath annexed to thoſe marriages, which he approueth. But I will ſpeake more at large of this matter, when I ſhall haue more direct occaſion offered. That which I haue ſaid of raſh marriages, I may ſay, and ſo take me) of all vnaduiſed and inconſiderate actions and attempts whatſoeuer, that as men can haue no authoritie for the taking them in hand, from *Calebs* example, no neither haue from the Scriptures in any place; euen ſo, and thereafter ſhall their gaineſayings be by them, who will needs goe to worke in that manner.

Anſwere 2. To the next obiection, that he gaue his daughter through his raſh offer to one of his owne fleſh, who could not marrie her by the law of God, being his brother, and therfore vncle to her: to this I ſay that, he was not his younger brother, to whom hee gaue her, I meane *Othniel*, but his kinſeman, and the leaſt euery way among his brethren, the children of his father, both in

yeeres,

yeeres,authority,and wealth. But yee will obiect, that the text calleth him his brother: I answer, that Christs kinsmen were called his brethren, and yet were not so; and all Diuines almost grant,that *Marie*,the mother of our Sauiour had no more children then Christ only;and therfore they expound those places,Mat.13.& 12.of his kinsmen and kinswomen.And that this the Hebrew word,here vsed, אח which properly signifieth a naturall brother, is put as vsually for a kinseman also, and the posteritie of brethren, the Scripture is cleare, and plentifull in shewing it. Reade for Example, Leuit.25. where the word *brethren* signifieth the children of brethren: *Ouer your brethren,the children of Israel, ye shall not rule one ouer another with crueltie.* And numb.32. shall your brethren the children of Israel goe to warre,and ye tarrie here? In both places,by brethren,the Scripture meaneth the posteritie and children of the 12.sonnes of *Iacob*, and so many other Scriptures doe. And so to returne,if this *Othniel* and *Achsah* had been within the degrees forbidden,that he might not haue married her, but it had been against the commandement of God,who doubteth,but that hee would haue been better aduised,and that hee meant not in offering her to doe any thing that should offend God? I say therefore if either *Othniel*,or any other winning the citie,could not lawfully haue married her, *Caleb* would haue supplied his offer some other way to the contentment of the partie.

Matth.13.55. and 12.46.

Leuit.25.46.

Numb.32.6.

And vpon the answer to the question,I say much like as vpon the answer of the former question, as the matter requireth, and giueth occasion. Let none gather from this speech of *Caleb*, that it is lawfull to marrie within degrees forbidden,as though *Caleb* had made such a marriage for his daughter. And although he were called his kinsman,yet seeing it is not said, he was his brothers,or sisters sonne, therefore I haue no necessarie occasion offered to answere the question, whether Cosin Germans may marrie together: but yet seeing I haue thus spoken of it,I therefore signifie my iudgement agreeing with such as I haue read and conferred with, and that is this, that although the word of God doe not expressely forbid it, yet seeing it prohibiteth those degrees that be further off,it is of great probabilitie, that Christi- should more then in a common manner consider and examine for what weightie and speciall causes they doe imbrace,and not abstaine from such marriages. And me thinkes he hath giuen some watchword thereof vnto vs in this,that the life of many couples so marrying together,hath been found tedious,and accompanied with mutual dislikes betwixt the parties,when no reason could be seene thereof beside that,and for proofe hereof,it hath been acknowledged,that to haue been the cause thereof. For my part, when the question hath been propounded to mee about such marriages, I haue (as I know the practise of many my betters to haue been) I haue (I say) disswaded from them for inconueniences, not as vnlawfull: and so I leaue this point. But to returne to *Caleb*,although he had maried his daughter within degrees forbidden, yet it had giuen no libertie to vs to doe so, neither to doe any thing else,that is vnlawfull,or forbidden by the word of God,forasmuch as we haue our direction there,what we may do,either in matters of marriage, or in any thing else whatsoeuer. And therefore wee ought little to regard examples,that leade any other way. And thus these obiections being answered,I will proceed in th story.

Vers.12. Deut.1. And first that it is said here that *Othniel*, being a valiant man, took the citie Debir, notwithstanding that the difficulties to win it were very great, by this wee see, that besides this verifieth the prouerb which is heere spoken of him, *that a mans gift preferreth him*, (as the like may be said of *Ioseph, Daniel*, and others) and that all men should seeke for the gifts of God, which they may attaine, to honour the giuer, who preferreth them thereby: I say, besides that,
1.Cron.4.10. we may learne that *Othniel* being religious, and his prayers being most faithfully made to God, as we reade in the Chronacles, so that God heard them, and yet he tooke incouragement by the offer of *Caleb* to set vpon that great worke; we may (I say) learne, that euen godly men may take, and vse the benefit of such incouragements, as are lawfully offered them to the going about any worke that God commandeth them. It is true indeed, that euen his bare word alone ought to put life into vs, and quicken vs to our duties, and much more, because there is a promise of blessing annexed to the obey-
Psalm.19.11. ing of euery commandement of his, yea a great promise of reward: but yet,
Gal.5.17. seeing we are weake, because of the flesh that striueth against the spirit in vs, therefore we haue need of all helpes and furtherance that may whet vs on. And therefore, though it was the dutie of *Othniel* to set against the enemies of God, as the rest of the Israelites were bound to doe, yet there is no doubt, but he was much more earnestly set on by this incouragement. So, it is the dutie of euery faithfull minister of God to preach the Gospel diligently and
John.21.16. willingly, euen for the commandement of Christ, *If thou louest mee, feede my lambes, and my sheepe*: yet if the Lord blesse his labours plentifully, and the people minister to him, readily, so that hee bee sufficiently prouided for, no man doubteth, but that hee shall doe his dutie much better, as seeing thereby that hee is (as good reason why hee should so bee) highly and well regarded. So a Christian man that laboureth with his hands in the calling God hath set him, ought to bee occupied therein willingly, and for conscience sake; but if God blesse him with good successe, he shall goe about the duties of it farre more chearefully, and in better sort. In all things we find it thus. If the Gospell be soundly and diligently preached, all ought to be ready to heare it, but if magistrates themselues bee forward that way, and cause others by their authoritie to doe the same, so that they see the Gospel be had in good account, shall it not (thinke we) quicken euen the best much more then they should otherwise be? not that these meaner incouragemẽts should most preuaile with men, but the Lords commandement; yet that shall the better doe it, when these also be added, to helpe our weakenes. But to looke to these principally, while the chiefe is neglected, that is a thing meerely preposterous, and the next way to pul downe al right maner of going about our duties, what shewes thereof soeuer men wil make, and how commonly so euer the the greatest part offend this way. And yet God seeing the infirmitie of his people, and their vntowardnesse to godly duties, and how hardly they are brought to the well discharging of them by his bare commandement, hath drawne them on by fit rewards, promises, and incouragements. For who doubteth, that the deare seruants of God are much heartned and helped forward thereby? and yet Gods charge (as I haue said) ought most to preuaile with them, though hypocrites and time-seruers doe make their greatest account of them, other, little setting by this in the meane while,

while,till God open their eies to repent, or till they bee hardned. For what one of a thousand in any calling or condition would labour and trauell euen for the necessarie helpes to this life, by the vertue of the bare commandement[thou shalt labour]if gaine and profit came not in thereby?

To proceed,*Othniel* being the meanest in his fathers house, and yet *Caleb* keeping promise with him,in giuing his daughter to him; it commendeth his faithfulnes in that he did not winde out dishonestly from making good his word,as men vse to doe; euen as hee is set forth, and praised in many other respects before. To be praised of men,or to praise a mans selfe is matter of small reioycing, *but he, whom the Lord praiseth is blessed*; as *Iob* was, seeing God himselfe spake of him thus to Satan, *Hast thou not considered my seruant Iob,that he feareth God,and departeth from euill.* And so he commended *Zacharie* and *Elizabeth*,and *Cornelius*.But to come more particularly to that which he is commended for here, I meane his faithfulnesse in keeping his promise, and that in so great a matter; and when he had that which he would at *Othniels* hands;how many(thinke we)shall be found that wil doe so?but winde out from standing to their word, dishonestly, and with subtill distinctions, wranglings,and wrestings of the matter,and other setting downe their meanings then they had,when they promised, especially if it bee for their owne benefit and aduantages? Oh,it is lamentable euery where to behold it, so that the innocent (who are for the most part of the poorer sort) goe commonly by the hardest; and yet, let vs know in the meane while,that God will take part with the wronged and oppressed, and therefore let vs beware of it. But the world is come to this, that there is no hold of the most mens word: no,nor of their wrighting neither,if by any meanes,it may be shifted off,and denied. Which caused *Salomon* to cry out, saying: *Euery man will boast of his owne goodnesse, but where shall wee find a faithfull man?* It is a vertue that God requireth to be in him,whom hee will put in his seruice,I meane faithfulnesse,as *Paul* sheweth of himselfe,that he was counted faithfull,and then put in his seruice. And wee in our earthly dealings, what other good parts soeuer we find in our seruants,yet we are glad to forgoe them all,if we cannot haue them faithfull,and trustie to vs. And so vnfaithfulnesse on the contrary,is so disliked and hated euen of those who are faultie in it themselues,though blind through selfeloue in seeing it, that they who can no way hide it,but that it breaketh forth in thẽ to be seene openly, are brought into vtter discredit by it. And euen so,if others,who as commonly offend in it,but can more cleanely conuay, and hide it with setting a faire face on it, were brought to light,as they are,who cannot so easily couer it,they should (doubtlesse)be in little account,how many so euer they be who are tainted with it. *Gehezay*, *Iudas*, *Ananias*,with *Saphira* his wife,and *Simon Magus*, who gaue shew of faithfulnesse, after hee heard *Philip* preach, these with many such do testifie,how this faithfulnes is iustled aside,and reiected. But happie was *Nathaniel,a true Israelite,in whom there was no guile*,who then did reioyce for it, and now doth inioy the fruit of it in heauen, while the staine,and reproch of the other mentioned,will neuer be put out. And so(to conclude) must they all shew this faithfulnesse, who desire to enter into the Lords Tabernacle,and consequently truly performe that which they haue lawfully promised,as in the Psalme is plainely shewed. And but for the auoiding of

[Margin notes: Doct.2. — 2.Cor.10.18. — Iob.1.8. — Luke 1 6. — Acts 10.2. — Prou.20.7. — 1.Tim.1.12. — Note. — Iohn 1.47. — Psalm.15.4.]

tediousnes,it might further be laid out more at large. For,as I haue said somwhat to the disgracing of this sin of vnfaithfulnes in general,& in deceiuing one another by breaking promise,so it is much more odious when it is practized vnder pretence of religion: I meane, while men shall professe with their mouthes to feare God,and yet denie the power thereof in their liues, as some of them did,of whom I haue spoke before.

Verse 14.15. Now to shew *Calebs* liberality to *Othniel*,it is shewed,that as he had giuen his daughter to him; so hee gaue him a liberall and rich dowry with her, which we vnderstand to haue been so by her owne words; when she said to her father,thou hast giuen me a countrey: and this he did, that it might bee seene that he gaue her freely to him,as he had promised to doe: for hee was a great Prince,and *Othniel* was of the same Tribe. Moreouer,(to shew the the libertie that children haue allowed them of God,)it is said here,that she desired other ground of her father,(as she had mooued her husband before to doe,with springs of water fit for their vse, seeing that was dry ground, which he had giuen her. And she tooke the fittest oppertunitie to request it, when she hauing gone to abide and dwell with her husband, and they both had(in all likelihood)viewed the ground,after that,she returning to her father,who came to meet her,she cast her selfe from her asse,that she might do reuerence, and her dutie to her father, and then shee made this petition to him. This be said for the clearing and better vnderstanding of these two verses. This story,though briefe,doth giue good light to vs both about one dutie of parents in marrying their children, to wit,to prouide for them,and as they may conueniently also of and about the liberties of the children againe,when they are bestowed in marriage,namely,that they may make request for necessaries,if there haue been neglect thereof before.

And first, concerning parents, seeing *Caleb* gaue possessions with his daughter at her marriage, according to his greatnesse; euen possessions of ground,which had not bin lawfull for him to haue done,but that the young couple were both of the same Tribe,it teacheth that parents at the putting of their children (which haue been obedient to them) from their charge,at their marriage,should as sufficiently prouide for them as they may, and as it may stand with other conueniences. They should not seeke and desire to please them in marriage without their charge,for many inconueniences goe

Genes. 25.5.6. Ioshua 14.& 15.16.&17. therewith: as *Abraham* gaue portions to *Isaac*,and *Ishmael*,and the Lord declared to vs in the story of diuiding the land of Canaan, that hee was well pleased with this,that prouision should be made for posteritie,one generation after another. Neither could societies be otherwise maintained among men in good sort,nor children be bestowed in fit and due time in marriage, whereby very great hurt and detriment must needs fall out,both to Church and commonwealth.

But herein I meane in parents prouiding for their children, (as farre as my knowledge reacheth) there is for the most part, no great fault to bee found: although indeed,there are some vnnaturall and hard harted men, from whom little or nothing can be wrong,(though ability faile them not) till they must leaue their goods to bee scrambled for by their children with much strife and contention seeing they could neuer bee brought to dispose of them in any reasonable sort while they liued. But to leaue these, and

come

come againe to the other, their fault is twofold otherwise, though the most of them be not to be charged this way, as I haue said. The one is, that they get much of their wealth by ill meanes, which they leaue richly to their children at their death, or bestow it as they please vpon them in their life. The other is, that they oft put all out of their owne hands into their childrens, to preferre them in marriage, and setting them vp so high, they bring themselues as low. These two euils are very common, and require good looking to, for the amending of them. For the first, it is a sweet comming in of their goods to them which they wring from others by oppression, extorsion, violence, or fraud; it is (I say) sweet in the comming in, but as bitter it shall bee, (to the full) at the going out.

The Lord hath set vs our bounds, that wee should in no wise offer others that measure, which we are vnwilling should be offered to vs againe, which rule, though I am perswaded that Preachers may teare their tongues to the stumpes, before they shall bring many to be guided by, yet some (I hope) wil submit themselues vnto it. But in all dealings, there are so many waies found out to vphold mens estates, or to augment them, and the greatest pretence is for their children, that they will heare nothing, if it be spoken to perswade to equitie, and innocency which make the practisers thereof bold as a Lion, and to the trying of their doings, whither they be good or no. Math. 7.1.12. Prou.28.1.

Such, and so many kinds of deceiuings, and cruell dealings there are practised, as by Executors in detaining the goods committed to their fidelity, to be put to good vses; such rackings of mens rents, that they neuer regard how the tenant with all his toile may, in any poore sort, be maintained; but they are forced by necessitie to leaue their farmes, and some to run cleane away. Such exactions in their loanes, till they fill the prisons with them, who cannot pay their vnreasonable demands, whereas they should looke for no benefit thereby, but that only which might stand with the benefit of them that vse and imploy the stocke. And to giue a taste of the rest by these, who are occupied in greater dealings, (for who can recken vp all) to come to smaller matters, who almost deales iustly in them? But ioynting there is one of another in two penny dealings (as pinching in measures and waights to get a groat or a shilling or in the whole bargaine, with the like, so that such gaine is more sweete to them, then all the rest, which they may lawfully take for their commodities, as it is in the Prouerb, *stollen* things, though they be but *waters are sweet*. But by this, conceiue of the rest. This shal suffice to say of the first sinne of parents about prouiding for their children; that I say nothing of the great hurt they doe themselues hereby: for while they are thus greedily set to seeke commoditie for their children, they bereaue themselues of knowledge and grace: yea, and they waxe very sloathfull and negligent in vsing the meanes to increase both; and that also beside the omitting the doing of good to others. By this meanes leauing no blessing, (as *Caleb* did) but a curse to their posteritie, who must pay the shot full dearely, for all those commings in of vnrighteous Mammon. Better it is to be the beast, then the child of such parents. Prou.9.17.

The second fault of parents followeth, that is, to put themselues out of all, euen house and home, (as they say) and that for the preferring of their children to great mariages, (little else being respected of them) wherein, though they

they deale ill in the former to the loading and burdening of their consciences, yet in this latter, they prouide most vnwisely for themselues, and their bodily estate and maintainance, and thereby it must needs goe the worse with their soules. True it is indeed, their children gaine wel by the bargaine, (if all other things be sutable in their match, as religion in both parties, and good liking betwixt them, for that very cause, that they be both heires of the promise) but what wisdome is that in the parents, to depriue themselues and many poore neighbours, of the benefit, which they might, and by good right ought to haue inioyed by keeping their estate, especially the greatest part of it in their owne hands, and to thrust their heads vnder their childrens wings; to lift vp them, and pluck downe themselues, when yet, for the most part, their children are very vnfit for it? But be they as they may be, I meane fit enough to vse that estate, yet they hauing once obtained a right in al, and being put into possession thereof, how vnmeet is it that the parents must be beholding to them for that which they haue to liue with all? And yet, that shall be with grudging enough yeelded vnto them, especially after a while. For they deale with them as flatterers do with their benefactors, when they haue sucked what they can, then vnthankfully they cast them off, and turne them ouer perke, nay, more then that, if their parents haue kept any thing in their owne hands to relieue themselues, some children are neuer well, till they haue, vnder some colourable shew of reason, wound euen that from them into their owne hands: or if they cannot, then their death is longed for, that so they may haue all. So that their old age is tedious, and irksome to them, wherein they should looke for most kindnesse and quietnes at their childrens hands, and the greatest respect and regard to be had of them.

For their occupyings; I deny not, but when age hath made them vnfit for labour, or ouerseeing their commodities, it may be conuenient to yeeld them into their childrens hands, those I meane, which in all respects shall be thought meetest for the same; but vpon good conditions, yet, that their parents may be well dealt with by them, and keepe the chiefe hold in their owne hands for the time. And these two dangers being wisely auoided by
1.Tim.5.8. parents, I freely affirme, that they ought to prouide for their children, as I haue said, when they bestow them in marriage, wherein (yet) this must bee obserued of them, that they straine themselues the further to do them good, and more good, as they haue shewed themselues most obedient to them in the Lord, and most humble, and are qualified with other good fruites of religion. And this be said of the parents prouiding for their children, at the putting of them forth to marriage, by occasion of *Calebs* so doing to his daughter. Now followeth the other point in this short story, that is, the libertie, which the children haue at that time, to make request for themselues to their parents: But I will here cut off, as hauing been ouer long.

THE

THE SIXTH SERMON VPON THE FIRST CHAPTER OF THE BOOKE OF IVDGES.

NOw to goe forward in the story where I left concerning *Caleb* and *Acsah* his daughter, wee are here to consider what *Acsah, Calebs* daughter said to her father when he met her, as we haue heard what he himselfe her father did to her, when he gaue her to *Othniel* in marriage. She (it is said here) when she came first to her husband, moued him to aske of her father a field; but whither he was loath and refused, or whither he tarried too long, she lighted off her asse and made the request to her father her selfe, he giuing her oportunitie by asking of her, what she desired; for it seemes, hee saw, shee came to some such end, then she besought him, that as he had giuen her drie ground without water, so he would giue her springs of water to it, for her bounds were great and large; and she requesting this of him, he gaue them vnto her contentation. Now from hence we may learne (as I said,) besides the reuerence she shewed to her father in lighting from her beast, what the libertie of children is when they are bestowed in marriage, and that is this: Vers.14.15. *The opening of them.* *Doct.*

They may desire of their parents, as their abilitie will giue leaue, such things as they see to be needful for them in their place, to the honest supply of their wants, if their parents haue neglected, or not seene, and remembred it; seeing they are to looke to it, and none are fitter nor meeter to helpe them. For through want of necessaries, there is much discouragement ofttimes to young beginners, and the parents are to prouide and lay vp for the children. 2.Cor.12.14. But whilest it is allowed them to desire things needfull and meet of them, it is not fit for them in a stout and stately maner to require it, and so to forget themselues, but in humilitie to request it. Neither is it fit for them to serue their owne turne in what they list, for the setting vp their owne countenance, or to pluck from others, who are as wel to be regarded as they; (which yet is too common,) that euery one is for himselfe, and doth not consider another by himselfe. This, I say, must be taken heed off, lest it raise disagreement and hard thoughts betwixt them and their brethren. As for her demand, the text plainly sheweth, that it was very needful that she asked, though her father had granted out her portion before: for wee know in those drie and South Countries what need there was of water. And we see that her request being so reasonable, her father neuer stood about it, but yeelded to her freely and liberally, euen springs in the vpper and nether grounds. In like manner parents should doe to their children according to their abilitie, as I haue said before.

It followeth.

VERS. 16. *And the children of Keny, Moses father in law, went vp out of the*

the city of Palme trees with the children of Iuda, into the wildernesse of Iuda, that lyeth in the South of Arad, and went and dwelt among the people.

The sense. WE haue heard of *Caleb, Othniel* and *Acsah*. Now to proceed in the Chapter, there is added here in this next verse interlaced betwixt the former, and the next following a briefe mention of the Kenites, the posteritie of *Keni Moses* father in law, how they came downe with the Tribe of *Iuda*, at the time when they destroyed Hebron and Debir, and they dwelt by them in tents. For *Hobab*, the sonne of *Keni* and his retinue, being perswaded

Numb.10.29. by *Moses* (when the children of Israel were in the wildernesse going toward the land of Canaan) to goe with them hee promising them, that as the Lord had said to him, he would doe them good; so he (I meane *Moses*) would likewise make them partakers thereof. Hereupon some of these Kenites went with him and the children of Israel, and were guides to them in the wildernesse, the way that they went; and these Kenites came ouer Iordan with Israel, and abode with the Tribe of *Beniamin* at Iericho, the citie of Palm-trees, and from thence they came and abode with the men of *Iuda*, after they had woon the forementioned citie, and other thereby. And the story recordeth that these went and liued with the people of Israel, to be better instructed in the right manner of worshipping God, as they had by their predecessors

Doct. made beginnings therin before. This dwelling of the Kenites with the people of God, and in leauing their owne countrey, for the ioyning thēselues to them, as it highly commendeth them, so it teacheth, that it is behouefull for vs, and our dutie, and much to our benefit, to ioyne our selues, (as wee may haue oportunitie,) to the godly and their fellowship. These Kenites, if they had done as the most doe, they had been ignorant of the law of God, and so had lyen in darknesse, and had not knowne the Lord, their hope and happinesse, but they more regarding to seeke true knowledge, and therefore leauing their owne countrie, and being much kindled and incouraged thereby with the loue of Gods promises, they prospered among the people of God.

Note. And so, I say, wee ought to seeke and ioyne our selues in acquaintance with the religious and godly, who liue by faith and hope, such as maketh not ashamed. For though wee liue not among the Heathen, yet wee liue for the most part among Papists, Atheists, blind and prophane Worldlings: whose conuersation and example wee are easily infected by, and made like vnto

1.Cor.6.11. them. *I wrote to you* (saith Saint *Paul*) *that ye company not*, that is, that ye haue no fellowship *with fornicators*, drunckards, extorsioners, Idolaters, railers, and

1.Cor.15.33. such like, for we know, that *euill words corrupt good manners*. So that, although we cannot but liue where such be, as Israel did with the Egyptians: yet we are bound, euen in our ciuill contracts and dealings with them, (which wee cannot chuse but haue, and vse with them sometime;) to beware, that wee be not drawne to meere societie with them, lest we learne their manners, or at least wincke at them, and beare with them, of the which wee should shew our vtter dislike; seeing we know, that two cannot walke together, but they must be of one mind, and yet wee must not scorne or disdaine the worst or

Note. meanest of them, but liue among them in al innocencie, humility, and good carriage of our selues, lest we harden them; but rather that wee may wait patiently, to see if God at any time will giue them repentance.

And

And if the company and neere acquaintance with the godly be so precious, then beware lest *we forsake our fellowship, as the manner of some is*, but make Heb.10.25.
we much of such, and let our *delight be*, (as *Dauid* said his was,) *in the Saints* Psalm.16.3.
that are on the earth, and in such as excell in vertue. And such as dwell among them, and haue dealings with them, as neighbours that are neere seated together, must needs in some sort haue; let them take heed, that through commonnesse of liuing with them, they waxe not wearie of this blessing, as wee easily are brought to be, and so we be easily alienated from them by testinesse and conceits, as too many are) euen by small occasions, and for very trifles; when we haue yet learned, one to beare anothers burthen: and religion teacheth vs to make especiall account of, and in any wise to seeke peace with them, and insue and follow after it, though it flie from vs, that by so doing, Heb 12.14.
all may say, we be the very disciples of Christ indeed, for that we so loue one John 3.35.
another. Thus let them doe good and take good mutually together euery way as they can. But to whom are good people commonly daintiest? euen to such as dwel a farre off from them: God declaring thereby, that they who dwell by them, are blind in not discerning and seeing what such a benefit is worth, and therefore that they prouoke God to giue them their habitation, and to send them among such as they themselues be, that is, vnquiet, and froward people, yea and worse then so, I meane prophane & skorners, that they may thereby the better know what godly friendship is worth, who, if they had been wise, would haue kept themselues well, while they were well, that is, in better company. I haue seene in my time, some that tooke a pritch a- Note.
gainst such as feared God, and were truly religious, and in their distempered heate, and ouerhastie dislike and wearinesse of their fellowship, though they were farre better then themselues, (thus are men caried of their sections rashly, wilfully, and in passion:) in this their heate (I say) they would needs resolue to remoue their dwelling, and when they had made choice of it to their owne liking, when no perswasions might stay them from it, they were so handled by strangers that knew not God nor their duties, and so vexed and crossed among them, that they cried out one to another, *Wo is me that I am* Psalm.120.5.
constrained to dwell in Meshec, meaning, that they were then so troubled with them that had no pitty nor regard of them, that they with shame confesse then, and cry out, that godly neighbours are a treasure, and wished with much losse to dwell by them againe.

This example of the Kenites should further teach vs, that though it is both *Doct.2.*
lawfull and meete to regard maintenance, yet we ought to respect chiefly in remoouing our dwellings, the true knowledge of God, which now is to be attained of vs by a sound ministery, and that is seldome without some whose companie is to bee desired, and whose acquaintance may make our liues sweet and ioyfull. As *Ruth* the Moabitesse did therefore follow her mother Ruth.1.16.
in law *Naomi* into the holy land, out of her owne country, and could not be plucked from her by all the prerogatiues thereof, her kindred, acquaintance and such like. It was the commendation of strangers, as we oft reade in the Ester 8.17.
Scriptures, that when they saw Gods blessing vpon the Iewes, they turned Zach.8.23.
to their religion, and said with *Ruth* to *Naomi, thy God shall be our God:* whereas we see that the most sort are rather content to part with some good commoditie, then they would dwell among Gods people, thinking it a bondage

1.Peter 4.4. to liue with such as will not run to the same excesse of riot with them. Commonly when men change their dwellings they respect some sinister end thereof, as profit, or the fulfilling of their lusts, and let religion goe where it will. But, to passe from these, such a mind should they haue, as *Ruth* and the like had, that trauell into farre countries to see them, that they might with
1.King.10.1. Matth.12.42. the Queene of the South, seeke the wisdome of God to guide them, as well as to see the countries, or reape commodities and pleasures there, or else it is out of question, that they shall bring home the vaine fashion, with the rude and heathenish manners thereof, to the tainting of other, and their owne vtter vndoing, as by too wofull experience we see at this day. To returne from trauellers to the other, and though I confesse that men in their remoouing their dwelling may, yea, and must regard their commoditie; yet not that only, but withall they should with *Abraham*, set vp an alter, that is, retaine Gods true worship, and see how it may be vpholden where they shall become.

VERS. 17. *But Iuda went with Simeon his brother, and they slew the Canaanites, that inhabited Zephath, and vtterly destroyed it, and called the name of the city Hormah.*

18. *Also Iuda tooke Azzah with the coastes thereof, and Ashkelon with the coastes thereof, and Ekron with the coastes thereof.*

19. *And the Lord was with Iudah, and he possessed the mountaines: for hee could not driue out the Inhabitants of the valleyes, because they had chariots of iron.*

The sense. NOw this 16. verse of the Kenites being spoken of, we are come to an end of the long repetition of the actes of *Iudah*, done in the time *Ioshua*, mentioned frō the 8. verse to this 16. which was, as we heard interlaced, and here the holy Ghost returneth to *Simeon* and *Iudah*, and proceedeth in these two verses, to set downe other actes of theirs after *Ioshuahs* death, as he began to doe in the beginning of this chapter vnto the 8. verse, and sheweth how they destroyed another city of the Canaanites Zephath by name: and that they tooke more cityes besides which were after, as by their names here sett downe, we know, possessed of the Philistines. Now it is to be noted, that they wasted some of the cityes vtterly by fire, as Hazor and Iericho, and so they delt with this here mentioned. Zephath: whereas they inhabited others of them. Why they delt so with this, it is not sett downe, but they did as they were commanded. We are sure it was, that God might shew his kindnesse to Israel, when some of them were vtterly subuerted, where greatest danger was to be feared: and to testifie his seueritie and his iustice to such of his enemies; and therefore it is not for any to crie out of it as crueltie, which the righteous God saw meet to be done.

Doct, vers.17. And by this we must learne, that though wee bee forbidden to hate the persons of our enemies, yet when wee bee set by the Lord to execute iudgement vpon them, our eie must not spare them, vnder the colour of charitie or compassion, for their propernesse, manhood, or any other foolish respect; Neither may we do the worke of the Lord negligently. Thus *Ioshua*, though
Ioshua 7.25. he pitied the state of *Achan*, yet plainely tels him, *In as much as thou hast troubled vs, the Lord shall trouble thee this, &c.* Thus the Lord punished *Saul* seuerelie

ly for ſparing *Agag*,and *Ahab* for ſo dealing with **Benhadad,** ſaying,*Thy life ſhall goe for his.* And therefore we muſt be well aſſured of Gods commandement,when we goe about any ſuch thing,againſt ſuch perſons as bee leaud, ſtubburne and willfull. This commandement of God is to be extended not onely againſt all traiterous enemies of the Church,but alſo againſt that rauening and roguiſh progeny of ſpoilers of the peace and gouernment,and hauocke makers of the commonwealth, as murtherers, &c. And therefore confuteth the curſed practiſe of Ieſuites, who,if they be not as yet practizers in that kind themſelues,doe yet by all meanes labour to extenuate the odious facts and treacheries of their complices by falſe reports: and traducing the iuſt proceedings of Chriſtian Princes, and the execution of their lawes for the reſtraining of ſuch monſters,by infamous libels,and the like. But we muſt here take great heed alſo, that we colour not our cruell and vncharitable actions with a pretence of zeale to God,and yet giue place to our affections,vnder a colour of ſeeking the glory of God: which may eaſily be done, as the Apoſtles did,calling for fire from heauen vpon the Samaritans, when they would not receiue Chriſt into their citie: but wee muſt know, that all men being our neighbours,wee muſt bee enemies to none. For the which cauſe *Dauid* prayed for his owne enemies,as namely for *Saul,* when yet hee prayed againſt Gods enemies,hauing alſo good warrant to doe ſo. And *Moſes* being the meekeſt of other in his owne caſe; yet againſt *Corah* and his companie who were the enemies of God,how earneſtly did hee deale, pronouncing that the earth ſhould open,and ſwallow them vp aliue for their rebellion. And *Paul,*who teacheth vs *to ouercome euill with good,* doe yet pray feruently againſt the falſe teachers, ſaying to the Galathians, in great compaſſion towards them,*I would to God,that they were cut off, which doe diſquiet you.* So that as we heare they did,it behoueth vs to beare our owne iniuries and indignities committed againſt vs with all meekneſſe,and to deale mildly in our owne matters,but in the Lords farre otherwiſe.

1.Sam.15.23. 1.King.20.42. Luke 9.54. Luk.10.29.30.&c. Pſal.69.22.&c. Numb.16.30. Rom.12.laſt. Gal.5.12.

And where it is demanded,whether may the godly pray againſt Tyrants, by whom the true worſhip of God is hindred; I anſwere, that againſt their tyrannie and cruell doings we ought to pray, but not againſt their perſons, who may poſſibly repent. For the Lord not hauing reuealed to vs, that for all their wickedneſſe,they haue yet committed the vnpardonable ſin, therefore what good meaning ſo euer wee haue therein, wee are not allowed to pray for their confuſion. But if God once make knowne his mind to be ſuch as he will haue them deſtroyed,or not to be prayed for, then we muſt both approoue of it,and execute it accordingly: and yet ſo, that as they are men we pitie them,as our Sauiour denouncing againſt the people of Ieruſalem, ſhortly after to bee deſtroyed, yet wept in beholding the miſerie that was comming vpon them.

Luke 19.42.

In this next verſe,it is ſhewed that *Iuda* yet preuailed further, and woon other cities named in the text, which yet, in the 3. chapter of this booke,are ſaid to haue been in the hands of the Philiſtines,as they were alſo long after. For the people of Iſrael oft prouoked the Lord, and ſo loſt againe ſome part of that which they had won,euen as it was like now to bee,that for their ſin they loſt theſe cities which they had before inioyed. In the 19. verſe it is ſaid, that *Iuda* poſſeſſed the mountaines alſo; and to the end that nothing might be

The ſenſe verſe 18.19.

be ascribed to the men, namely, to them of *Iudah*, and to *Simeon*, for *Simeon* had entred into couenant to ioyne with them their brethren in these warres, and so did here (though *Iuda*, who was appointed thereto, be onely named) to the end (I say) that nothing may be ascribed to them, it is expresly added,

Doct. ver. 18.19 that the Lord was with them in those their great enterprizes. To teach vs by whose might they preuailed, and what was the cause that they did so, euen this, seeing God was with them. And all men wil grant as much, that if God be with a man he shall prosper, and none shall be against him, to do him hurt, as the Apostle writeth. And there is sufficient reason of it. For who shall re-

Rom. 8.31. sist him? or if he say the word, who shall call it backe? Now we are to know, that God is not with any man idle or weake, but mighty, as he saith himselfe

2. Cron. 16.9. to *Asa* by the Prophet: *The Lord looketh downe from heauen to see who is weake, that he may be strong with him.* But to the end so worthie a point as this is, may throughly doe vs good, we must vnderstand that to haue God with vs, so as we may rest surely perswaded that he is so, and inioy his presence constantly while we liue, (which is a treasure vnualuable and vnknowne to the world, it is required of vs by God, that we first haue him for our God; and be truly reconciled to him by our Lord Iesus Christ: for then he will neuer leaue vs,

Iosh. 1.8. neither forsake vs, but safely keepe vs to the resurrection day: but otherwise, except God be thus made ours, and we vnited to him by faith, which howsoeuer it should be done, cannot here be more set downe, what portion of wealth, wisdome, &c. we haue out of that communion with him, it is accursed. And further we are to know, that God may bee with men in some sort, as by his power and bodily helpe, and at some time, and yet not be with them to their effectuall comfort and alwaies. These are great matters, and duly to be considered of vs, for he may be with the wicked, so as he was with *Ahab*, when he gaue the great hoastes of *Benhadad* into his hands: yea, and that which is more, hee may bee, and is present with the vnbeleeuers in the congregation, when he inlightneth them to vnderstand that which is soundly taught, and to take liking of the same. But this is by his power onely, but

Luke 1.28. not by his effectuall grace and fauour; as he was with *Mary*, who being freely beloued of God, he was also with her: and his being with her, made her blessed and ioyful: and if he be thus with vs, he wil both spiritually grace vs,

Iudges 6.12. and also bodily blesse vs, as shall be expedient for vs, euen as hee did *Gedeon*, when he was said to be with him. And this, to the end we may not deceiue our selues, it behoueth vs to marke, for our singular and continuall comfort: and therefore let men giue all their diligence to make their saluation sure, and to come into the fauour of God, that so they may abide therein, then

2. Pet. 1.5. will he be with them to guide, keepe and comfort them: and otherwise, they

Iohn 15.10. may haue God with them (I deny not) sometime, as I haue said, though hee owe not euen that to them, but so (yet) they may be miserable and vnhappie still, but in a better manner hee was here with *Iuda*, both before and at the time here mentioned; also he declared the same by giuing their enemies into their hands. This confuteth the conceit of such as measure Gods being with them by his raising them in wealth, or giuing them their desires. As

Iudges 17. last. *Micah* an Idolator applauded himselfe as beloued by God, because hee gaue him a Leuite to be his priest, whereas he giueth many wicked men their desires in wrath, when yet he denieth to his owne, theirs in fauour. And this is

that,

that,which we haue to make profit of,out of the words before mentioned, that *Iudah* prospered,seeing God was with him.

We haue heard that they ouercame the inhabitants of the hill countrey, seeing God was with them. Now in the same verse it is added, that they did not ouercome the inhabitants of the valleies, seeing they had charriots of iron. And hereby this vnbeliefe of theirs began their sorrow and miseries, which the other tribes followed them in, to the end of the Chapter. The common translation is, *they could not driue them out:* but it is not so in the Hebrew: the better translation addeth another word, namely, that they went not about it. Neither of both is out of the originall, but that seemeth to bee the sense, for it is otherwise vnperfit. For it is thus there, *they did not to driue them out,* which is to be supplied, *they went not about to doe it.* Whither of both soeuer it was, that they did not either go about it, it was their fault: or whither we take it thus, that they could not, euen that was their fault also. For God promised, that although they had chariots of iron, yet hee would deliuer them into their hands, then they failed in beleeuing Gods promise; and so they going from God by vnbeliefe; God likewise went from them: so that God being with them, and they beleeuing him, they ouercame them them that dwelt on the mountaines; but they not beleeuing God, as he had promised in Iosua 17. seeing they had iron chariots, therfore they did not ouercome them in the vallyes. Therefore, howsoeuer we take it, there was a fault in the men of *Iuda.* For though it may be obiected, that God would not giue them victory ouer the one as well as ouer the other; I answere, that is true, but that was through their fault, that they beleeue not that his word, as he had promised. Vers.19. *The sense.* Iosua 17.18.

So that the doctrine which we are taught from hence, is this, that though God bestow many good blessings vpon vs, while we beleeue in him, hauing promised it, euen as he did here on *Iuda,* and so long, hee shewes himselfe to be with vs: yet if wee giue in, and withdraw our selues through vnbeliefe, and belieued not his promises, he will faile vs in other blessings, and deny vs them. A most worthy truth, and much to be regarded of vs. For so it is now with vs, as it was then with the men of *Iuda.* So saith our Sauiour to the man that brought his son to be healed that had a dumbe spirit, *If thou canst beleeue, all things are possible to him that belieueth,* meaning thereby, that all things that are agreeable to the will of God shall be granted to him that beleeueth: for faith seeketh nothing that is contrary to his will, or not reueiled in his word. So saith Saint *Iames; If any man want wisdome, let him aske of God, who giueth to all plentifully, and casteth no man in the teeth: but let him aske in faith, and wauer not:* and so speaketh the Scripture throughout. And to bind this more sure, the Lord himselfe saith to the Hebrewes; *If any man withdraw himselfe, my soule shall haue no pleasure in him:* that is, if he beleeue not. *Doct.1.* Marke 9.23. Iames 1.6. Heb.10.38.

Excellent is that saying of the Lord to this purpose in the Chronicles: The Æthiopians and the Lubims, were they not a great people? yet because thou diddest rest vpon me, I deliuered them into thy hands: but now thou hast done foolishly in relying on the King of Syria, and not on the Lord, therefore hee leaueth thee to thy selfe to beleeue, and so driuen and disswaded from the contrary. Yet this causeth mee oft to maruell, that wee being so incouraged, neither the vnbeleeuers 2.Chro.16.7.9.

doe hast or long and thirst for faith, as though it were little worth, neither can other who yet should bee most readie, bee brought to waite daily and
Note. constantly to grow in this grace of beleeuing: neither doe, although they haue obtained alreadie to belieue; for al that, nourish faith as they are taught,
Col.2.7. that so they may abound therein with thanks-giuing. And much it is to be lamented, that seeing God is not with vs, to blesse and beautifie vs otherwise; we should for all that neglect so great good, as we might get thereby, and rather with others, follow fancie and reason, sloath and example, and that is, to beleeue no more then we see. Oh wofull vnbeleefe, that fillest our liues with so many fretting sorrowes and deadly discomforts! True it is, that many to make their fault small, doe answer, that the people that liued before the comming of Christ, might much easier beleeue then wee now, because they
Ioshua 6. reade in the stories such examples, not onely of *Abraham*, but also of *Ioshua* and many of the people in the destroying of Iericho to haue done so. And
Ioshua 3.15. the Priests aduenturing to set their feet on the waters, beleeuing that they should giue place to them to go ouer them on dry foot, as God had promised; with many other like. But they are grossely deceiued who thinke so, euen as much as they, who will say that in the dawning morning light a man may see as clearely, as at noonetide. For who is ignorant of this, that the mystery of faith is nothing so clearely reuealed in the old Testament, no, not by many degrees, as it is in the new? So that although some of the chiefe fathers, (who were to goe before the people, and bee lights to them, as *Moses*, *Noah*, *Abraham*, and others, receiued inlightning of God, more and in greater measure then we doe in these daies; yet the Church consisting of the common people at this time, hath cause a great deale more to beleeue, and farre more easily may imbrace the promises,) by the ordinary meanes they they haue, (I say not what God may do,) and so liue by faith more easily, I say, then they did or could doe. But this is our sinne, that we search not into our selues so much, as to see whither it be so; neither if we find it to be otherwise, are we grieued for it, or seeke to amend it. But there will be occasion offered to speake more largely of this matter in many places of this booke, therefore I will here containe my selfe.

But one thing more here, by so good occasion, I will note about faith, worthy our remembrance and regard, and that is this: that though the Tribe of *Iuda* beleeued the Lord and his promises in one thing, and did therfore valiantly, I meane in expelling the Canaanites that dwelt in the hill countries, and the Lord was with them accordingly: yet in another thing they did not beleeue, namely, that God would expel the enemies that dwelt in the valleyes, because they had iron chariots, and therefore they went not about it, neither did they obtaine any such thing of God. Whereby we see,
Doct.2. that we may possibly beleeue one promise, and yet not another: and (which is no great maruell) wee may beleeue when the case is more easie, and the
Note. thing which is promised is of lesse difficultie to obtaine, (as here it was with them) then when it is otherwise. Euen so, we may beleeue at one time, and yet not at another. The reason of both is, seeing wee are fickle and inconstant, therefore wee fleet and change in time, and wee are also timerous by meanes whereof it commeth to passe, that although we may be brought to belieue a thing of lesse moment, or which in former time we haue belieued;

yet

yet at some other time, and in another thing, where in we haue no experience, and which striketh vs with greater feare, there we faint and giue ouer. The vse of this is: that we accustome aquaint, and bend our selues, when we haue giuen credit in some things to God, that we may do the same in other; and if we find it otherwise, then that we take knowledge of our weakenesse, and thinke our strength in beleeuing not to be very great. And therefore we thus seeing our wants therein, are not to please our selues and rest in that which we haue done, but looke to that which is yet to be done of vs: and as Saint *Iames* speaketh of patience, that it *should haue her perfit worke,* so faith must haue her perfit worke also. That thus wee may goe a degree further, as the Apostle willeth the Colossians, namely, *to abound in faith.* Which cannot bee without thankes giuing to God, and much ioy to our selues. Note. Iames 1.4. Colos. 2.7. Rom. 15.13.

VERS. 20. *And they gaue Hebron to Caleb, as Moses had said, and he expelled thence the three sonnes of Anake.* Verse 20.

THis giuing Hebron to *Caleb* is repeated, for it had been giuen to *Caleb* by *Moses* before; (as it is said in the booke of *Ioshua*) and now the warres of the Tribe of *Iuda* being set downe, the chiefe captaine whereof, *Caleb* was, this is againe spoken of. And it is said, that to him this citie, with the coasts thereof was giuen, namely, by *Ioshua*, as God had appointed in Deutronomie. That which is the chiefe matter here of giuing Hebron to *Caleb,* as it was before promised, and he was not holden backe, no, nor deferred, nor defeated of it; teacheth, that wee ought in no wise to detaine any mans due from him, though it bee in our power to doe it; nor to withhold reward from him that hath deserued it. Gods will is, that euery man inioy his owne (as wee would ours) which he hath bestowed vpon him. And this being so sharpely reprooued by Saint *Iames,* in masters towards their seruants, withholding their due from them, doth much more challenge them, who in waightier cases haue wrought vnrighteousnesse against any. Thus hee writeth, *Behold the hire of the labourers which haue reaped your fields* (*which is of you kept backe by fraud*) *crieth, and the cries of them that haue reaped, are entred into the eares of the Lord of hostes.* It hath been a pollicie vsed by gouernors, to promise great rewards to such as shall bewray dangerous practises of traitors, or find out open malefactors, or performe good seruice against the enemies of the Church and their countrey, which if they be not regarded and rewarded accordingly, how shall the hands of men be strengthened and they incouraged to doe these duties? Iosh. 14.13. Deut. 1.36. *Doct.* 1. Iames 5.4.

Ahashuerosh an Heathen King, when he had been deliuered from the treason that two of his seruants intended against him, and that by *Mordecay,* who detected it, as soone as he vnderstood (after it had been forgotten a time) that he had not been rewarded for his faithfull seruice, he did in most ample maner command, and saw it effected, that he should be rewarded. So *Belshazzar* did to *Daniel,* for his faithfull seruice, and *Pharaoh* to *Ioseph* in an admirable manner. Much more that which is a mans owne is to be restored, or pay him at the due time; as by the executor, the borrower, or any other who by right ought to doe it. But euen among Christians the neglect hereof, and the shifting Ester 6.10. *Compare Dan.* 5. 7. *with* 29.

shifting of many, contrary to couenant, oath, promise and bond, calleth their
Psalm.15.4. profession into question among such as would gladly conceiue better of
them. But God meetes with such iustly: for neither are they trusted in
their health, nor yet pitied in their distresse, but beare a marke of their vntrustines, and vnfaithfull dealing vnto the day of their repentance, or to their graue. And therfore they who are put in trust, and defeate the orphan, or other to whō it is due; as also those banckrupts, who inrich themselues with the goods of other men, and then giue it out, that they are not able to pay, though they haue it in their power to do it, or disable thēselues by their vnthriftines & carelesnes; and all such as hold from men that due that belongs to them, shal feele Gods anger as bitter, as masters shal, who detaine & hold backe their seruants wages. But they doe no better who will claime it before it is due, or else will bee displeased, and will prouoke to sute, although they know no iust cause: for that which is sought in such a case, I meane before it be due, is to be obtained either by intreaty (if it may bee yeelded) or by agreement and composition: but the rule before mentioned, bindeth only to lawfull, not irreligious promises.

Doct.2. As for that which is here said in this 20. verse, that *Caleb* expelled out of Hebron the three sonnes of *Anak*, vnderstand, that they are those three who are mentioned in the 10. verse, *Sheshai, Ahiman* and *Talmai*: where the driuing of them out is ascribed to *Iuda* in the general, which in this verse is particularly said to haue been done by *Caleb*, who was chiefe in the worke. For the doctrine to be gathered hence, reade verse. 10.

THE SEVENTH SERMON VPON THE FIRST CHAPTER OF THE BOOKE OF IVDGES.

The second part of the Chapter.

VERS. 21. *But the children of Beniamin did not cast out the Iebuzites, that inhabited Ierusalem; therefore the Iebuzites dwell with the children of Beniamin in Ierusalem vnto this day.*

The sense of vers.21. NOw followeth the second part of the chapter, which laieth out the beginning of the calamities of the people of Israel, as to the end of the chapter may bee seene, namely, that all the Tribes suffered the nations, who were their enemies, to remaine among them, contrary to the commandement of God in the booke of Numbers: for thus
Num.33.52.55. he saith, *When ye are come ouer Iordan, into the land of Canaan, ye shall driue out all the inhabitants of the land before you.* And a little after; *If*

ye will not driue out the inhabitants of the land before you, then those whom ye let remaine of them, shall be prickes in your eies, and thornes in your sides, and shall vex you in the land wherein you dwell. The first of the Tribes that is said to haue suffered the Canaanites to remaine in their coasts (that excepted that wee heard of *Iuda* in vers. 19.) and did not cast them out, was *Beniamin*, which was neere to *Iuda*. And although it be said in *Ioshua*, that the Tribe of *Iuda* could not cast out the Iebuzites that inhabited Ierusalem, but burnt some peece of the citie; yet there it is said they dwelt with them therein: so it is said here of *Beniamin*, seeing that citie of the Iebusites was a part of it in the lot of them, and part in the lot of *Iuda*, that they dwelt also with *Beniamin* still, and were not cast out till the time of *Dauid*; but they of *Beniamin* built it againe, after *Iuda* had burnt it. Ioshua 15.63. 2.Sam.5.8.

Now seeing they had a precise commandement from God to expell the Iebusites, thence it was their sinne that they did it not: the least that they may be charged with, was slouth and negligence, and the seeking of their owne ease, which to doe in things forbiden, is most dangerous. Doct. vers. 21.

By this then we see the euil that sloathfulnesse and ease seeking bringeth, to wit this: that it selfe holdeth a man from obeying God, though there should be nothing else to doe it. And that is when, for the ease and pleasure which is taken therein, men dull the edge of courage and forewardnesse to good duties, which was in them before: such an one is the slouthfull, whose words are these; A lion is in the way, meaning thereby, that hee cannot labour, euen as a man in a sweet slumber is most vnwilling to be awaked. This slouth is a sweet poyson: keepe from it he that can, but he that doth not, it will slea him, as *Salomon* saith; As the common sluggard doth loath and shun labour, and therefore loueth to bee doing any trifling thing, rather then to worke, and be well occupied, so doth hee that is slow in the duties of Gods seruice; he lets them passe and omits the opportunity of doing them, which ought much to be regarded. For as *a word spoken in season*, is much worth, *euen like apples of gold and pictures of siluer*, euen so is an act or deed done in due time, as namely among other, that wise and godly courage of *Ester* shewed in due season in going to the King, for the preseruing and sauing her owne life and her peoples from the traine that *Hamon* had laid for them in season. Oh, euen so is forewardnes and readinesse to goe about the worke and businesse that God inioyneth vs in euery condition of life. But there are extremities on both sides: There are some that fall to their worke, but looke after nothing else, whereas all should be first sanctified to God themselues first, that then their workes may be accepted of him. Others would seeme, and be taken for godly; but they are carelesse and slacke in following the works of their callings, nay they condemne the prouident and diligent, as worldly and miserable muckwormes. Both these are extreames to bee auoided of Christians, by ioyning both callings together, I meane religion and labour. But for this sloath (to say a little more of it) if wee take not great heed, the best of Gods seruants may soone be drawne to it, and no way sooner, then if we begin to waxe wearie of well doing in our generall or particular calling, and suffer our selues to be plucked from our stedfastnesse therein, by the error of the wicked, and to be caught and snared with the deceitfulnes of sin: for so we are rocked a sleepe ere we be aware, in which case it shall be no easie Prou. 22.13. Prou. 1. last. Prou. 25.11. 2. Peter 3.17. Heb. 3.13.

sie matter to awake,or bring our selues backe againe into our former good course. And so shall we liue vnprofitable,fit onely to consume and wast the good benefits of God. Oh ! what a death it is to a sloathfull person to be vrged to the duty that he hath cast off,and hath now no pleasure in,nor ability vnto? (as to a Minister to preach in his old age,who looked not after it in his youth?) to the which estate he hath brought himselfe;euẽ as a ruinous house falleth downe altogether; when it is let go to decay for want of repairing in time.For the remedying of the which mischiefe,in al that are annoyed with it,I see no better direction,then that which our Sauior hath giuen vs in these words,when he saith; *occupie till I come.* Whereby he meaneth not only the worke of our calling,but also that euery one that will prosper,should vse his talent, euen such gifts as God hath bestowed vpon him; as knowledge, wealth,time,grace,and such like, to the doing of good with them, and not to bury them vnprofitably in the earth. For beside that the fruit of idlenesse is pouertie,theft,beggery,&c. God also loueth and blesseth the painefull and diligent; and thus if we be carefull,after Gods direction,to bee well occupied,wee shall bee free as from other euils,so from this danger of sloath. The like counsell to that which our Sauiour giueth, is that of Saint *Paul* to the Ephesians,that they *redeeme the time:* that is, buy it out of the hands of idlenesse,vnprofitablenesse and euill: and then employ it faithfully to necessarie vses and ends. And the rather,because so much pretious time is already spent in vaine,let that which remaineth be better passed to recouer our losse. The life of a Christian can least of all other stand with idlenes. It is without respect of the particular calling, as husbandry, marchandize, or other trading,full of diligent heed taking,that the conscience may be kept pure and good: but much more (al may see) when labour in these is adioyned to the other: therefore the punishment of the sloath is not small, but as the Wise man teacheth. *The idle mans backe shall be clothed with ragges,* and his belly pinched and starued for want of food, and by this wee may guesse what his soules diet shall be. It followeth.

Luk.19.13. Ephes.5.16. Prou.23.21. &6.11.&20.4.

VERS. 22. *They also that were of the house of Ioseph went vp to Bethel, and the Lord was with them.*

VERS. 23. *And the house of Ioseph caused to view Bethel (and the name of the citie before time was Luz.)*

VERS. 24. *And the spies saw a man come out of the citie,and they said vnto him,shew vs (we pray thee) the way into the citie,and we will shew thee mercy.*

VERS. 25. *And when he had shewed them the way into the citie,they smote the citie with the edge of the sword: but they let the man and all house depart.*

VERS. 26. *Then the man went into the land of the Hittites,and built a citie, and called the name of it Luz,which is the name thereof vnto this day.*

The sense of these verses.

NOw after the mentioning of the Tribe of *Iuda* and *Beniamin,* and what they did,it is in order set downe what the other Tribes did,to wit,how they suffered,and did not expell the Canaanites neither. And yet the house of *Ioseph* is exempted,which comprehends the Tribe of *Ephraim* and *Manasse* together. First therefore it is declared what those two ioyntly together did,to vers.27.in the words of the text here set downe, and then,what they did seuerally,to verse 30. That which is said of them ioyntly together,is to

their

their commendation,that they went against Bethel, which fell to their lot, and the Lord with them to incourage and strengthen them, so that they feared and tried which way they might most easily take it. (Now the name of this citie had in times past been called Luz,as we reade in Genesis,but *Ia-cob* as he went to Padan Aram from the wrath of his brother *Esau*, resting there,and the Lord appearing to him, and comforting him,called the place Bethel,that is,the house of the mightie God.) But to goe forward,they that were sent about that businesse, namely, the Tribe of *Ioseph*, seeing a man to come out of the citie, asked of him in which part of it they might set vpon it,and on which side was their going out and comming into it, (for thereby it appeareth that they had shut it vp for feare of Israel, and that they had left but some secret way for their necessarie vse to goe out and in thereby,) and they promising the man largely, hee shewed the way to them, and they en-tred and slue the inhabitants,and tooke it,and sent the man away wel rewar-ded, or rather (as it was indeed) he banished himselfe from them into ano-ther countrey, and was so wealthy,that hee was able to build another city, and called it by that name,Luz. Genes.28.19.

This worke of the house of *Ioseph* which they went about;namely,to take this citie Bethel,(which was before in the deuision of the land of Canaan giuen to them,) as God had inioyned them, doth liuely set before our eies, as in a glasse,the dutie of all Gods people,that is to say, readily to goe about and set vpon the worke that God hath appointed them and laid vpon them, yea and this is to be done, whatsoeuer lets and discouragements may stand vp in the way to hinder them. For hath not he commanded them? And is not he able to remooue those impediments,rather then they shal hinder his worke in the hands of his seruants? which they beleeuing,are to go forward, and commit the successe to him that hath promised to bring them through all difficulties which might hold them backe. For otherwise, if wee looke not to God by faith,but what let is in the way, and be hindred thereby; we shall cast the commandement of God behind our backe,and do as they who obserue the wind,and therfore sowe not;and looke too much to the clouds, and therefore reape not; and so for feare of inconueniences we shal let passe necessarie duties. Againe,when we thriue and haue good successe, we blesse God,and are merry;but if we be crossed, we curse & disguise our selues with impatience. Whereas it ought to be enough to vs,that God hath brought it to passe either thus,or otherwise. And beside the authoritie hee hath o-uer vs,his bountifull rewarding of vs in his seruice,ought to incourage vs to adresse our selues to all such worke: and not onely so,but further, seeing he commandeth and would haue vs doe it,as it may be most for our owne ease, that is,willingly,readily,chearefully; for the Lord loueth that, in all his ser-uice;as he loueth a chearefull giuer. And we know (for our owne parts) that men go awkly and vntowardly about that work which they take in hand vn-willingly. And we are all to learne of our Sauiour, who hath giuen vs exam-ple herein,saying, that his meate and drinke was to do his Fathers will. Ioshua 16.2. Doct. out of vers. 22.23. Note. Eccles. 11.4. Deut. 28.47. 2. Cor. 9.7. Iohn 4.34.

Besides,we are made,redeemed & set here to that very end,to *serue the Lord in holinesse and righteousnes without feare all the daies of our life*,and not to please our selues,how hard soeuer the worke is,that is to be done of vs. And that is our life, ioy, and comfort, no other course of walking is life but death: no Luke 1.74.75.

other

other is sauory,or soundly ioyfull. And this should bee thus in all callings and conditions,as with Magistrates,Ministers,Husbandmen,Artificers,Masters of families and others,who doe (I denie not) many things required of them by God,but not one worke as another; neither that ioyfully which they doe,and as if it were the worke that God hath set them about; for then they should doe it readily,but for their bellies, and in other carnall respects. For why? they can indeed do them no otherwise, because they do not first know themselues to bee the Lords redeemed ones, that so they may easily obtaine other things at his hands. But I would that euen they who are so, did goe about that which they doe by Gods commandement chearefully, and with delight for the Lords sake; then should there many excrements be cut off from the infinite actions which are done in our liues, and with so much sinne remooued; many plagues and annoiances should bee auoided from mens liues also. But alas,the most professors are not acquainted with going to worke in Gods seruice after this manner,neither find any sauour in this Christian course: but respect onely their owne commoditie, and that they may bee without feare of want and penury; and the most doe worse, that is, spend their precious time in idlenesse, play, and vaine pleasures at least: and as for seeking first Gods kingdome to be vnder his gouernment,and to rest on him for other things by lawfull labour and meanes vsing,it is one of the hardest things for them to fasten on: though God hath yet promised that such onely shall bee blessed. But of this somewhat hath been said before.

It is further added in this verse,that while the house of *Ioseph* went vp against Bethel,the Lord was with them,which seeing it is here added, I will say somewhat of it,though I haue spoken thereof before by another occasion. Now this house of *Ioseph*, thus going about the worke that God had commanded them,is said to haue God with them in their worke; for so hee had promised. Which teacheth,that this assurance we haue from him,that if we attempt ought by his commandement,he hath set his seale to it,that we shall haue successe and prosper in our worke. So was it said to *Ioshua* in his
Iosh.1.5. first going against the Canaanites, *I will be with thee,* and hee belieued and prospered euen so,these and the like promises of God being belieued of vs, are our comfort,and thereby wee learne experience how to doe the like for the time to come,in what worke soeuer the Lord shal imploy vs. This would make men vse their callings not so as they should bee burdens to them,but recreation,going merrily to their work as they may with Gods good allowance,and leauing it of with fitnesse to other good duties, as prayer, reading, singing,meditating,&c. If this were beleeued,men should be free from the plodding and distracting cares of the vngodly, who make their liues wearisome by distrust of Gods prouidence,fearing they shall begge ere they dye, &c. and from the moyling and toyling labor of such as tire themselues with
Eccles.5.18. their callings. For God giues rest to his beloued,as *Dauid* saith, Psalm.127.2. And from this temporary rest,he will in due time,translate them to eternall rest. All which I say, not onely to the denouncing sharpely and heauily against the common professors of the Gospell,who will beleeue God no further then they see him; but also to the iust reproouing of those, who haue obtained of him to beleeue in deed,that they shall haue eternall life, and yet

in

their particular trials, in which they are taught to depend vpon him, and to cleaue to his promises made and granted out vnto them to that very end, that they should doe so, they yet stagger and doubt, as if they had neuer had faith. He that desireth to heare more of Gods being with his, let him reade that which hath been said on verse 19. Note.

This place Bethel being so called, that is, the house of the mightie God, because the Lord appeared to *Iacob* there, whereas it had in times past been called by another name, it very well teacheth (seeing nothing is set downe in vaine in the Scriptures but to good vse) that it is commendable, as occasion is offered, to giue conuenient and meet names, such as may instruct in some good thing, drawne from some good example, or putting vs in mind of duties either to God or men. As God gaue the name by the Angell vnto our Sauiour, calling him Iesus. Some care not what name they giue to their children, of most notorious persons, as counting it their credit that they may be like them: resembling herein the Idolatrous King of Babel his Eunuchs, who purposely altered the names of *Daniel* and his fellowes, in token that they should renounce the true God and his seruice, and embrace the contrarie. Some giue such names to them, as the rehearsing of them, causeth laughter. Vers. 23. Genes. 28. 19. Dan. 1. 7.

Which is vnseemely, seeing the name is giuen in the assemblie of the faithfull, and in the presence of God, and when they are to bee entred into the Church of God. We doe not place religion in names or titles: yet neuerthelesse a wise and godly choice in this matter may be had, that the names giuen, may be in stead of instructions to the parties named. In the apparrelling of our bodies in comely maner, we will haue care that the very shoe, which is the least matter, be decently put on, and sutable to other partes of our attire: so there being required a proportion in all our actions, this one is not to be neglected. Therefore in the old Testament, the names were giuen either according to the euent of things, about the time of the birth of the child, as *Moses* called one of his sonnes *Gershom*, that is, *stranger*, because hee was then a stranger in another land: or their names were borrowed from their holy predecessors, to put them in mind to follow their steppes, or some such like respects they had in giuing them. Now let vs heare of the spies. Exod. 2. 22.

In this verse, where it is said that the spies met this man comming out of the citie (for what cause he went it is not expressed;) somewhat is to be noted by occasion of the man, and somewhat from the spies. By the man first, going in his simplicity, out of the city, (whither to saue his life, or vpon some other necessarie occasion,) meeting with these spies, and falling into such a streight thereby, that either he must loose his life, or betray the citie, (for the spies said to him, shew vs the way into the citie, and we will shew thee mercie.) We may see what streights and difficulties we meet with, be subiect to, and in danger of, in this life: for that perill which we neither feare nor once thinke of, may befall vs, euen to the hazarding of our liues, much more of our vndoing, or the losse of the best of Gods blessings that we inioy, as wife, children, goods, &c. In the story of the French Massacres we reade, that by the popish faction, a whole assemblie of Protestants were slaine at the Sermon. The Shunamites child went into the field in the morning well, but Vers. 24 25. *Doct.* 1. 2. King. 4. 20.

2.King.4.1. died at noone. The widow of one of the children of the Prophets, who liued in good estate for a great part of her husbands time, yet through the debt he was in at his death, shee was brought into that streight, that her two sons must bee sold to pay the debt, and carried away from her, perhaps to bee brought vp by Idolators in an idolatrous land; and she knew no other for a time, though God prouided better for her. *Iob* his children in the middest
Iob 1.18.19. & 2 7. of their merry makings, were destroyed by the fall of the house, and he himselfe lost all at once, and his bodie was filled with scabbes and sores. Samaria
2.King.6.25. was besieged, and the danger so great, that the king therof was resolued, and looked for no other, but that he and all that hee had, must be at the pleasure
Lam.1.12. of another man. And Ierusalem was so ouerwhelmed with griefes, that she was driuen to complaine, that no sorrow was like her sorrow: when yet before she had been the beauty of the whole world. These difficulties, as I haue said, with many other both mentioned in Scripture, and seene in experience, may fall out in our liues, so that we shall be driuen to crie out euery one of his owne burdens, what shall I doe? yea, and it may bee an innocent mans case, to be brought into such straits, and his, who is godly, and he shal not be able to auoid it till God send helpe. As for the wicked, such streights come vpon them, as an armed man vpon a naked.

Now seeing God hath such vantage of vs thereby, and that throughout this present life, & may most iustly inflict them vpon vs, (that I say no more)
Vse 1. oh what cause haue we to make precious vse hereof? for the which cause in so necessary a matter, I thinke good to set downe some vses thereof to the Reader: And first this is one, that we should euery day (which is a part of our iourney home) as oft as wee find it so, acknowledge with admiration, Gods goodnesse in that he spareth and freeth vs from such streights, and not only so, but also from so many great calamities and casualties as we are kept from, and much more, if our life bee freed from smaller afflictions also, but most of all if we be loaden with his benefits. Which I speake to the iust re-
Psalme 68.19. proofe of such as hauing their part in all these, yet passe ouer all blockishlie and vnthankfully, but if some crosse befals them, then they break out against
Vse 2. God impatiently and brutishly. Secondly, make we this vse of it, that seeing we are all subiect hereto, and by our iust deserts bee alwaies in danger and feare to be thus abased; therfore to be humbled, and prepare our selues daily
Vse 3. Note. Luke 9.23. for them, and as *Iob* did, to looke for our change. Thirdly, we haue little need to trouble our selues with an ill conscience any manner of way, and so to procure needles sorrow, if wee be daily in danger of so great vexations. And
Vse 4. lastly, set we little by the best things here, they being subiect to a thousand changes, but lay we vp treasure for our selues, that shall neuer fade nor be taken from vs. And to them that obiect vpon this, that seeing we may fall into so many and great streights, what prerogatiue haue the righteous, and what shall they doe, liuing in such an estate as well as other? I say, let them
Deut.5.29. trust in God and feare him, that so it may be well with them, as he hath promised it shall, and so doing, he will keepe many such calamities from them, and giue them deliuerance out of many such difficulties; and turne those that abide vpon them, to their singular benefit and good, or receiue them
Psalm.3.25. vnto glory, when others in the meane while shall be at their wits end with the strangenesse of their plagues, or, which is much worse, bee cast into hell.

This

This we haue to learne by occasion of the man: Now of the spies.

The spies offered him kindnesse, if he would shew them the way into the citie: in that they dealt kindly with him, rather then roughly and cruelly, seeking such a matter at his hands, they did as became them. But hee being one of the cursed nations, how could they (ye wil aske) promise him mercy? for though they did so to *Rahab* before, yet she turned to their religion: and so did the Gibeonites serue them as bondmen, and imbraced their religion also. But no such thing can be said of this man, for hee went vnto the Hittites, out of the seuen cursed nations, and dwelt there. I answere: we must interpret the lawes of God against the Canaanites, and concerning the rooting them out, by mitigating them with this equity, that if they made peace with Israel, they should not roote them out. And this appeares by that which is written in *Iosbua*, that these nations were rooted out, seeing none of them saue the Gibeonites, made peace with the Hebrewes.

Doct.2. *Obiection.* *Answere.* Iosh.11.19.

And this being so, teacheth all men to deale euen with the bad kindly, and to be harmelesse toward them. And though they be of them who haue deserued punishment (as this man of the citie Bethel might by as good right haue been put to the sword as the rest in the citie, vntil he yeelded himselfe) yet for as much as they be in misery they are to bee pitied, vnlesse their facts be horrible and beyond the course of common trespasses, in which case they must be punished by authoritie accordingly: for in so dealing with them, there is hope that their harts may be mollified, and they in time be brought to repentance: whereas by rigor and rough handling of them they will (questionlesse) be hardened. And if they fall into the Magistrates hand, and must needs for their fault bee put to death; it is enough that they haue that inflicted vpon them which is their due, though they bee not pursued with crueltie also. *Ioshuas* dealing with *Achan*, who yet for his trespasse must bee put to death, may be a paterne for all men, to teach them to auoid crueltie, and to shew kindnesse and mercie to such as bee in miserie. Thus hee saith, when his sinne was found out against him, *My sonne giue glory to the God of Israel, and make thy confession to him, and shew me now what thou hast done.* And as *Ioshuas* example, for his louing dealing toward the offender *Achan*, is to be highly commended: so the contrary is as odious in the Preists and Iewes: for when they had gotten that which they sought at *Pilats* hands, to haue our Sauiour, against all law, to be condemned, they were not content with that, but most cruelly and despitefully handled him with mocks, and taunts, and all disgrace that might be: But it was as good as might be looked for at their hands.

Iosh.7.19.

But while I am minding this matter of dealing kindly and mercifully with the afflicted, it commeth to my remembrance, among many other things iustly to be bewailed, how lamentable the estate of malefactors is in some places at least in this land: as they are miserable throughout their whole life, so especially at their death they are most of all, seeing that, after they be condemned, that they goe to execution without any meanes to bring them to conscience of their wicked liues, feare of the iudgement to come, and to some knowledge and hope of eternall life: whereas, if it pleased those which are in authoritie, some fit Minister of God might be appointed to take them in hand after they be adiudged to die. I will not say what good might be done to the poore prisoners thereby. But for mine owne part, when I was young, and able to trauell, I did that dutie my selfe ofttimes in compassion of their misery, and saw blessing on my labours; and the word which I preached to them, in that little time which they had to prepare themselues, I saw it (I say) to be apparantly blessed of God, to my great contentment and comfort, and good hope of them. I remember well, that at sundry times, that though I was but a stranger to them, yet after that I had through Gods blessing brought them to see their damnable and miserable estate by means of their sin, and had shewed them, that euen then they were nearest mercie, I was receiued of them with great liking, especially after they had tasted of the glad tidings of the Gospell to quiet and comfort their heauie hearts. Yea, I may truly say, as I did clearely see, I was to them more then their owne father could haue been vnto them, for the message brought vnto them.

And beside this that I haue said of them, the like meditation vnto this, I had of the estate of many people in the land, who run as swiftly to hell as the other; through ignorance (most falsely called the mother of deuotion, but rather the mother of all mischiefe and confusion) also prophanenesse, and other grosse sinnes, though not so lyable to the law of man to bee punished as the other. These are also without a Minister that is able and willing to leade them a better way: who, if they had such meanes as might conuert them to God, and that they who are such good instruments, might bee incouraged and backed in their labouring to reclaime them, they should haue cause to giue God great thanks, and the persons also, by whom they be so well instructed and comforted. But if I should here bewaile all such also, as being taught yet are little the better; as I cannot chuse but pittie them, seeing the Gospell is hidden from them, and therfore they dying so, shal most certainely perish; I say, if I should bewaile these, how far should my complaint reach? I shut vp this point therfore, cōcluding thus, Oh that there were not so much hardnes of heart in many Ministers and others, who might helpe this, wishing that they had a little of the compassion that was in our Sauiour, as the Euangelist
Matth.9.last. recordeth, when he saw the people dispersed, as sheep without a shepheard. And againe, Oh that we could deale pitifully, kindly, and louingly with the miserable and the afflicted; and that all the gentlest meanes were vsed to reclaime offenders, of whom there is hope, such as are as this man of Bethel was, in great distresse, which is not done but very rarely, and therfore is there much hardnesse of heart, in those to whom it is neglected, and wilfulnesse, that carrieth them to all profanenesse and impenitencie.

Doct.3.ver.24. And thus (to returne to the spies againe) seeing it hath been proued that they did not vnlawfully in sauing this Bethelite aliue, the most that can bee said of their so doing, could be but an inconuenience (seeing he gaue no token that he turned to their religion,) for ought that we can see) and yet this was a smaller inconuenience then if they had killed him, and so to haue been put to their shifts how to haue found the secret way that led into the citie: this also teacheth vs a good point, that when wee see in attempting of our lawfull businesse and labors, that some inconuenience must needs be borne, that which is lesser of two, if it be without sinne, is to be gone vnder: that so we may auoid that which is greater. For want of which consideration, and

due

due regard of that which I ſay, while men ſtand at the ſmaller, to auoid that, they runne into a greater, if not into ſinne it ſelfe. As in many inſtances it may be ſhewed; and this among other, may bee one. Many a man will not make others priuie to ſome of his dealings, being ſuch as may bring him in good commodie: and this he forbeares to doe, onely for that he would not haue the commoditie and benefit that he reapeth thereby, to be knowne to any other, which were not ſo great an inconuenience, if it were knowne to ſome faithfull friend. And what falles out in the meane while thereby? euen this, which is much greater: that for want of skill how to vſe that dealing or trafficke aright, and in the beſt manner (which by the helpe of ſome wiſe friend he might haue learned) hee loſeth a great part of his commoditie, which he might haue inioyed; yea, and thereby falles to offend God by impatience and murmuring, when he ſeeth that he commeth ſhort of his expectation and hope. So many a man falling vpon theeues, in a deſperate mood, refuſeth to yeeld his money, though he be vnable to reſiſt, and ſo loſeth both money and life too. And ſo doe many refuſe, through ſtomacke, to agree with their obſtinate aduerſary, becauſe they are loth to loſe and forgoe any thing. Whereas by ſtanding out with him to the vtmoſt, they forgoe not a little, but ten times the value.

Much like to that which many do about their bodily health. They doubt at leaſt, if they know not alſo, that ſome ſore diſeaſe is breeding in them, yet will they not conſult with ſome experienced Phyſition. And why? I ſay, to auoid ſome inconuenience, as the taking of phiſick, which is nothing pleaſant to them, or to ſaue charges, or becauſe they would not loſe any time in following their profits. And what falles out thereby in the meane while? euen this, that a greater inconuenience meeteth them: ſo that for the auoiding of that which was but ſmall, they loſe both profit, and life alſo. This thing is the more to bee regarded, becauſe wee ſee by experience that commodities are ſo mixed with diſcommodities, that in things indifferent, the one goeth not without the other. This is true, as in all comforts of this life, ſo particularly in marriage: and that as well in going about it, as liuing in it. For the firſt, many to auoid the troubles of the married eſtate, which is the ſmaller; are put to many inconueniences; as to liue in vnquietneſſe and diſcontentment, and by vnſetledneſſe in a ſingle eſtate to fall to fornication, (that I ſay no more) which will prooue to be farre greater. Many againe reſolues by marrying, (if they can make themſelues great thereby) to ſhunne a meane and low eſtate in pouertie, and thinke, if they can doe ſo, they ſhall be void of trouble, and yet while they looke no further, they weary themſelues with many more ſore and dangerouſer troubles; though mariage be lawful, yet ſuch an attempting of it, is not good. Againe, by this rule among married couples, the one partie ſhould yeeld to the other without too much rigor and auſteritie, or contending in a thing indifferent: the husband in giuing libertie to the wife to ſpeak when there is cauſe; to viſit friends; to take vſe of ſome commodities to her owne behoofe and benefit, rather then to denie them, becauſe they feare ſome inconuenience may come thereby; when yet it is certaine, there ſhall farre greater be ſeene to fall out by doing otherwiſe. And ſo in all other dealings: if all inconueniences cannot bee ſhunned, yet let vs be ſure, by labour, prayer and godly wiſdome, to auoide the hardeſt.

And one ſpeciall good vſe of this doctrine, is, that we take heed, we bee not too ready to iudge our neighbour for bearing with ſome inconueniences, (as we are too forward and too ready to doe) when they muſt doe it to free themſelues of greater; and in ſo doing we condemne our ſelues, ſeeing wee our ſelues are ſubiect to the ſame doctrine alſo. For what haue wee to doe to iudge our brother in ſuch a caſe; who if he haue ſuſtained an inconuenience, wee may well thinke, he hath done it, to him a greater. This alſo condemneth them, who, if they bee a little croſſed with ſome hard accident, do by and by grow deſperate, and make the rent greater by their raſhneſſe and impatience, &c. ſcorning to ſtoope to the neceſſity which God hath laid vpon them, and not wiſely declining extremity. Though they cannot auoide the inconuenience befalne them, yet they ſhould ſhunne the ſinne of murmuring which is greater, for elſe they beare the burthen of both. But I cannot goe through this ſtorie at this time; I will therefore here cut off.

THE EIGHTH SERMON VPON THE FIRST CHAPTER OF THE BOOKE OF IVDGES.

Verſ. 25. *A queſtion.* IT followeth further about this Bethlite, (for it is to good purpoſe) to enquire heere, whether this man did well in betraying the city, and what is lawfull in the like caſe. For as concerning the ſpies, no queſtion is to be made of their drawing the man to it, whether they did well or no;
Anſwere for it was their worke aſſigned them of God to deſtroy thoſe nations, and therefore to vſe the meanes in going about it. So was it alſo lawfull for him to do it, they ſignifying to him what Gods wil was in that behalfe. But whether the man beleeued that, and therfore whether he did it in faith, or to ſaue his life, and his friends and goods, it is vncertaine. The firſt is more poſſible, then probable, to haue been the cauſe that drew him to doe it; but the laſt is moſt likely; yet wee may not determine which, except the Lord went before vs: therefore according thereto was his act good and commendable in him, or otherwiſe.
Doct. ve. ſ. 25. Now for vs, the caſe ſtandeth farre otherwiſe, then it did with him. For it is not lawfull for vs to yeeld to any ſuch thing as he did, in betraying the city, but odious and horrible. The Lord Ieſus ſpeaking of the like matter, as a thing moſt monſtrous to attempt or goe about. He ſaith, *many ſhall hate and*
Matth. 24. 10. *betray one another*: a fearefull thing to heare, much more for one to doe it to a whole City.

Nay all bitter violence and cruelty is odious in vs one towards another, ſimply, and without all reſpects; much more when it ſhal be done for gaine or or preferment. No, neither is it any way tolerable for the sauing of ones owne life. We must in all these cases, haue our discharges and warrant from God, for that which we doe; as *Rahab* had for hiding the spies: which wee hauing Scriptures most clearely to direct vs in all our actions, no such thing, from what example soeuer, is to be followed of vs in these daies. Neither is the fact of *Iael* in killing *Sisera*, nor the Israelites borrowing and carrying away of the Egyptians treasures, any thing to imbolden vs to doe the like: she doing it against Gods enemies the Canaanites; they doing that which they did by the Lords appointment. In a word, to doe any euill that good may come of it, is odious.

Iosh.6.25. Iudg.5.24. Exod.12.35.

Lastly, out of these two verses it is good for vs to marke, in that this poore Bethlite was the instrument of taking the city; what poore meanes and helpes God oftentimes ministreth, for the effecting of that which hee commandeth to be done; yea though the worke be great, and the means weake and vnlikely to bring such a matter to passe, it skilleth not. Both these things may be seene, both in stirring vp and preparing that sillie woman in *Ioshuas* time, to receiue & lodge the spies, whom he sent to view Iericho before they tooke it, as also by blowing trumpets of Rammes hornes, and by compassing of the city Iericho seuen times, to make the walles of it to fall downe. Who seeth not that these were poore engins to batter walles? and also to giue this Bethlite into the hands of these spies, that they might by his helpe easily take the city? For when God will haue a worke to be brought to passe, he appointeth the meanes also for the same purpose; which being alwaies knowne to him, but seldome to vs ordinarily, till we meet with them (not by chance, but by his will and appointment) it doth often take heart from vs, and much dismay vs from cheerefull going about that which wee are commanded, so weake is our faith, when with vnbeleeuing *Thomas* wee doe not see and behold with bodily eyes the meanes which are yet sufficient and at hand through Gods promise.

Doct.2. Iosh 6.16.&c.

So much the more it behoueth vs to be well acquainted with that which is taught vs heere: for it is a singular encouragement to vs, (wee being so weake) when we haue an hard labour laid vpon vs, and we see no meanes to bring it to passe, to know (yet) that God will prouide helpe, though wee see not how; as he did prouide a sacrifice for *Abraham* to offer in stead of *Isaac*. Indeed, if he should deale with vs as *Pharaoh* did with the Israelites (who enioyned them an hard taske, and great worke. but yet they must make shift how to effect it, (which was impossible for them to doe) then it were no maruell if we were pensiue, and at our wits end what to doe. But (God be thanked) if we can beleeue him, that he will make it easie, and prouide accordingly; most cheerefully may we be occupied, from day to day, in all that by Gods Commandement we set our hand vnto. This caused the Apostle *Paul* to be so diligent and vnwearied in bringing so many nations by his preaching, to embrace the Gospell, and saluation thereby; when yet there were so many and great discouragements in his way.

Gen.22.8. Act.from 13. to 21.chap.

This caused those worthy seruants of God, *Zorobabell*, *Ezra*, and *Nehemiah*, not onely to returne into Iudea; but to build both the city vp againe, being greatly ruinated; and euen the walles thereof, and also the Temple; when hauing commandement from God so to doe, they beleeued that hee

Nehem.2.17.

would shew them how, and bee with them, to inable them, though wee are not ignorant, how many blocks and maine enemies there were in their way to hinder them. And wee haue no other stay to looke for the promised saluation, but this, that hee that hath commanded vs to liue by faith, and waite by hope, will finde meanes to bring it to passe, although we see little how, many times; in so much that we oft feare and doubt, it being the waightiest
1.Pet.4.18. case of all other; euen as Saint *Peter* also saith, *that the righteous are scarcely saued*. And euen so, the labouring man, and the Artificer could neuer bee vpholden to follow their calling with any peace, if they should looke onely how hardly they are like to bee maintaine, and should not stay themselues by faith, that God will prouide for them, they themselues not being negligent. And be this the stay of vs all, in our hardest condition wherein wee be set by God, that hee will bring vs through, though wee see not how, and that also in good sort, because he hath promised.

Vers.26. Now it remaineth, that we see how well this man was rewarded that did helpe forward Gods people in their worke, to the destroying of his enemies, by shewing them the way into the city, though it bee not set downe with what mind he did it. Thus they dealt with him: they did not onely set him free, and his whole family, from the destruction that lighted vpon the other citizens; but they did also suffer him to carrie away his wealth: yea and so greatly enriched him, that he was able to goe build a citie. And by this wee see, that such as bee helpers and friends to Gods people, neuer
Iosh.6.24. loose their reward: as *Rahabs* example and the Kenites doe most cleerely
1.Sam.15.6. proue & declare. A notable encouragement both to Gods people, to know that the Lord so careth for them, that hee will cause many, euen of the wic-
Prou.16.7. ked, to be friends to them, and helpefull: and it is no lesse comfort to them that are so affected to them, they may bee sure they shall not lose their labour, but be well rewarded. And so much the more wee ought to bee quickened by this doctrine, seeing Gods people haue many and strong enemies in this world, and they themselues are weake and soone discouraged. And this is a great refreshing to them, when they haue promise of such helpes, as whereby their burthen is made easie. And the Lord hath said much in his word to the encouragement of both; and therefore the Psalmist speaking
Psal.122.6. of Ierusalem Gods people, saith. Let them prosper that loue thee. And to *Abraham* the father of beleeuers (which alike is spoken to all that are beleeuers, as *Abraham* was) thus he saith; *I will blesse them that blesse thee,*
Gen.12.3. *and curse them that curse thee*. So that as *Ahab* was spared, insomuch that the plague threatned came not in his daies, but in his sonnes, because he repented, and yet it was but outwardly, wherein hee gaue but a bare shew of it, euen so, they that doe to his people any good, though it bee but in an outward action, as this Bethlite did heere to the Lords people, shall not lose their reward.

It is true indeed, that this but temporary for the most part, which they receiue, as the helpe that they minister to them is so: but besides that it is much that God will regard them at all, who are not faithfull to him (for they might feare rather the contrary, that he would pursue them as his enemies) because they be not repentant: besides this (I say) they get acquain-
Note. tance with the godly hereby oftimes, whereby they be in hope, that they shall

ſhall learne their religion, and follow their conuerſation, which if they ſo like and approue of, that they loue them the better for it, then do they gaine exceedingly by it indeed, I meane by that friendſhip that they ſhew them. For then they come within the compaſſe of a better bleſſing, and are partakers of a greater promiſe, euen that in the Goſpell; *Whoſoeuer receiueth a Prophet, in the name of a Prophet, ſhall receiue a Prophets reward: and he that receiueth a righteous man, in the name of a righteous man,* (that is, for his goodneſſe, and becauſe he is a good man) *ſhall haue the reward of a righteous man alſo.* Matth.10.41.

This ought for iuſt cauſe to aſtoniſh and terrifie them who are profeſſed enemies to them becauſe they walke vprightly, and hate none more deadly; 1.Ioh 2.12.
according to the prouerbe; The righteous is an abomination to the wicked. Prou.29 27.

This ought alſo to draw the hearts of the common ſort who profeſſe religion, better to regard Gods people, and not to bee more brutiſh then the Heſt.8.17.
heathen nations who feared Iſrael, ſeeing they ſaw God was with them, yea and let them while they liue among them obſerue their example, and profit by them, as they in the Acts.9.31. Act.9.31.
If they will ſay they know not who they are; I anſwere, that they ſpeake vntruly; for in the time of their owne affliction and miſery, they can diſcerne and doe know them, and will aske for them; although at other times they are thought of them to bee too preciſe and deuout, and call them Scripture-men in contempt; yea euen ſuch as againſt whom they will ſet themſelues: to theſe therefore, if they will ſhew that they be wiſe indeed, let them adioyne themſelues, and make much of them, till they verifie the Scripture; the Lambe and the Lion ſhall Eſa.11.
feed together: for if God in their trouble and abaſement haue giuen them vnderſtanding and diſcretion to know them, and afterward they make no more reckoning nor account of them; they cannot bee ignorant that they haue done wickedly, and are able to ſee what they doe in caſting them off. And let them be ſure, that their ſin will find them out in time, and the Lord Numb.30.
will caſt off them, for that they haue dealt ſo with them. But much more if they or others begin to ſmite them with their tongue, and to kicke at them, and diſgrace them. This bee ſaid of the houſe of *Ioſeph* ioyntly. It followeth in the text.

VERS. 27. *Neither did Manaſſes deſtroy Bethſhean with her townes, nor Taanach with her townes, nor the inhabitants of Dor with her townes, nor the inhabitants of Ibleam with her townes, nor the inhabitants of Megiddo with her townes, but the Canaanites dwelt ſtill in that land.*

28. *Neuertheleſſe when Iſrael was ſtrong, they put the Caananites to tribute, and expelled them not wholly.*

29. *Likewiſe Ephraim expelled not the Canaanites that dwelt in Gezer, but the Canaanites dwelt in Gezer among them.*

30. *Neither did Zebulon expell the Canaanites that dwelt in Kitron, nor the inhabitants of Nahalol, but the Canaanites dwelt among them and became tributaries.*

31. *Neither did Aſher caſt out the inhabitants of Accho, nor the inhabitants of Zidon, nor of Ahlab, nor of Ach-zib, nor of Helbah, nor of Aphik, nor of Rehob.*

32. *But the Aſherites dwelt among the Canaanites the inhabitants of the land: for they did not driue them out.*

33. Nei-

33. *Neither did Napthali driue out the inhabitants of Beth-shemesh; nor the inhabitants of Bethanath, but dwelt among the Canaanites the inhabitants of the land: neuerthelesse the inhabitants of Beth-shemesh and Bethanah became tributaries vnto them.*

The sense. IN these verses the holy story layeth out the sinne of the other Israelites beside *Beniamin*, for that they cast not out, nor destroyed not those Canaanites which dwelt in their seuerall lots, according to the commandement of God, but onely made them tributaries to them. And before all the rest the tribe of *Manasse* is reckoned to haue done so. But whereas it is said in *Ioshua*, that this tribe did then so, that is, make them tributaries then: it is not so to be vnderstood, but that is said there by an anticipation; that is, by setting downe that before, which came to passe afterward. For that was afterward to come to passe, that is, at this time heere mentioned, which was after *Ioshuas* death. For in the daies of *Ioshua*, and of the Elders that liued with him, the people contained themselues, and did their duties in resisting their enemies, by his worthy conducting and going before them. And by this their departing from the commandement of the Lord, which for a time they obeyed, we see how they declined in a short time and waxed weary of obeying.

Iosh.17.12.

Iosh.24.31.

Doct. Out of all these verses in generall. The which, and namely in so many of them, teacheth, how ready men are to leaue and forsake a good course, although they haue hardly, and with much adoe, been brought to embrace and fasten vpon it; which much concerneth vs to marke. For we are easily deceiued about this, and thinke both of our selues and others, that if we beginne to dislike, and turne away from some grosse and common faults that wee were wont to commit; then the worst is past with vs, and that wee ought iustly to bee reckoned among the godly; whereas it is nothing so, but we be yet, for all that, farre off. For a farre greater matter is required to the endeuour effectuall calling to repentance may be approued of God, and be found indeed, as in other places I haue shewed, how we ought to try and search into our selues, and cannot now stand about it.

Note.

Luk.14.31.
Lam.3.40.

But although wee were truly turned to God, and had, as these, obeyed God for a time with a good heart, yet ought we to feare danger, in respect of our owne frailty, and according to the present occasion, when wee see to what point these tribes came, for all they had followed the Lord commendably for a time, in beginning to cast out the nations as they were commanded. And the reason of this, to wit, that wee should thus carefully looke to our selues, is this, that we are reformed but in part, and that in small part: in which respect yet, because we haue receiued some grace, we are able thereby to desire and goe about to doe God some seruice, and specially at some time; namely, while we be watchfull to hold vnder our rebellious passions, assisted by grace: but what then? For wee hauing a sea of corruption euer flowing in vs, and our owne concupiscence beside outward obiects enticing vs a contrary way; it must be drained and purged out daily, by little and little, and not bee let alone in vs, lest it should choake and drowne the grace that we haue receiued; which if it be, wee become impotent by and by, so that wee doe not onely cease to obey, but wee are carried rather as with a

Note.

streame

ſtreame to any euill that we be tempted to; and namely, to this one heere mentioned that ouertooke theſe tribes; that is,to be wearie of well doing: and ſo much the rather,ſeeing there are ſo many allurements and occaſions in euery place to prouoke vs and ſet vs forward.

And although we are not without helpe,nor naked in the middeſt of all theſe ſtormes, yet if wee know not theſe things; yea and if alſo wee doe not reſiſt carefully ſuch euill as I haue mentioned; neither ſtriue to nouriſh ſuch ſparkles of grace as are kindled in vs,our hearts being ſet wholly hereupon, as the waightieſt thing that we haue to deale in; what maruell is it, though wee fall from the goodneſſe that was wrought and begun in vs, and ſo become others then we were before? Which I ſpeake not as though we muſt do nothing but watch and reſiſt ſome one or few inticements which would (I grant) ſoone waxe tedious to vs; neither is that impoſed vpon vs by God, but we are to know, that while we bee aiming at one good thing or other,our worke goeth well forward, ſo as wee doe wiſely labour to diſcerne among good things, what the beſt is,and moſt neceſſary to bee done for the time, and what ſinne and corruption is moſt to bee reſiſted. Thus I haue ſtood ſomewhat long in this point,to ſhew how eaſily we may poſſibly fall from our ſtedfaſtneſſe in a good courſe, and what care ſhould bee in vs againſt the contrary; which I entred into (as ye may remember) by ſo good an occaſion of the coldneſſe and declining of the tribes from the knowne commandement. Note.

Now I will goe forward, as my purpoſe was, to ſhew ſomewhat more particularly,how we vſe to decline, and breake off good beginnings; euen as theſe tribes did,who began well to execute Gods commandement for a ſeaſon,in rooting out his enemies,but went not forward. And this let vs ſee in ſome ſort, both in our ſelues and alſo toward others. For the firſt, we cannot bee ignorant that many of vs of good hope haue ſometimes carefully ſearched into our ſelues,to finde out ſuch corruptions of our hearts as haue Lam.3.40. brought our whole liues out of frame: and therein wee haue done God good ſeruice; and when wee haue found them out, as careleſneſſe, ſlothfulneſſe, vncleane deſires,and worldlineſſe,&c. we haue had them in the chaſe, Note. and hunted them, with diſgracing them, watching and praying heartily a- Matth.26.41. gainſt them for a time. This alſo hath been another peece of good ſeruice done vnto the Lord: but our not being alwaies alike forward,but neglecting care (as through corruption and vntowardneſſe it will ſoone come to paſſe) and the vſe of good meanes, or our feruency therein. Oh how haue wee drooped and hanged the wing; yea and if more ſpeedy heed hath not been taken,how neare haue we been brought to this bondage, to bee well content to let theſe and ſuch like our ſinnes to be quiet in vs, without any great purſuit, or offering of any great violence to them, till they haue recouered ſome ſtrength in vs againe, and preuailed, and begun in moſt vnſeemely manner to maſter vs,and bring forth noiſome fruit, euen like themſelues; as the Canaanites did grow ſtrong and mighty againſt Iſrael,when they were not held downe as God required,but ſuffered to liue and be let alone?

But to proceed no further in this,if theſe noiſome weeds be not plucked vp, how can good ſeed bring forth her fruit, (for all may eaſily ſee what followeth, ſeeing the roofe muſt needs totter if the ground-ſels bee pluckt away)

away) therefore if we slothfully suffer our selues to grow to this point, who seeth not that we offend God as sore, and as grieuously prouoke him to displeasure by such disobedience, as these tribes did by making a league with the Canaanites, and not expelling them as they began, and should still haue done? For the transgression is alike in both, and that of one and the same commandements, while they ought to haue rooted out persons out of the land, and we sinnes out of our hearts and liues. Thus I haue shewed how like we are to the Canaanites in suffering sinnes in our selues, which should haue been rooted out rather: now let vs also see it in some particular manner how we be too like them in our dealings toward others.

For euen as they failed in suffering the Canaanites to remaine amongst them, and did not expell them; so doe wee suffer them who are little better then Canaanites in their behauiour and manners to abide therein, till they corrupt and taint them that dwell among them; as if an infection were dispersed round about to poyson mens bodies. The people of Israel set themselues to seeke their owne quietnesse and ease (though they broke the commandement of God) in letting the Canaanites liue still, and abide in the land. And to this point things are come in our daies, that whatsoeuer God command to bee done, and good and wholesome lawes enioyne against many fowle sinnes, yet if the executing of them require labour and any cost, and it bring any toyle and trouble, and hinder mens ease and profit; behold, *a Lion is in the way*; they will not at all take them in hand; or if they haue begun, they soone waxe wearie of the worke, and giue it ouer (neuer enioying Gods promise to harten them to the obeying of his commandements, but yeelding to their owne corrupt reason) so that there is little rooting out of grieuous disorders and lewdnesse of life, in towne, countrie, or familie: as whoring, drunkennesse, gaming, ill companies, and such like: and as little pursuing of the persons that disguise themselues therewith, either in Church or Common-wealth. And this was a greater fault in these tribes to let the Canaanites remaine, and not expell them; because they were strong enough to haue done it; and stronger by much then they on whom they should haue executed Gods charge: for so it is said, verse 28. *When Israel waxed strong*, yet did they not expell them wholly, but onely put them to tribute. So this aggrauateth the sinne of our time, forasmuch as God hath giuen authority into mens hands to remoue such disorders, and greater gifts of knowledge and ability to ouermatch such euils as he would haue to bee rooted out, and yet there wanteth zeale, and courage to goe about it. And though things shall neuer bee brought to that perfection that were to be wished, yet much might be done that is vtterly neglected. This be said and noted out of all the verses in generall, and of all the tribes mentioned therein.

A simile.

Prou.22.13.

Note.

Vers.27.28.39. Now more particularly, somewhat is to bee said of Manasse and Ephraim: who did not alike behaue themselues when they were seuered, as when they were ioyned together: then they went the one with the other roundly to the worke, and prospered: but now they being diuided, they were backward and slothfull, and so let the Canaanites grow and multiply. That which I will obserue heere is this: That we looke heedfully to this, that we make much of godly society, and labour to enioy it therefore, and to take all the

Doct. Out of vers.27. 28.compared with the former, from vers. 22.to27.

the good that we may by it. For wee haue much encouragement thereby, whatsoeuer good wee goe about, wherein it may bee vsed. For as the Wise man saith; *Two are better then one; if one lie alone, how should he be warme?* And so many good persons being ioyned together in a good worke, (like fire-brands in a chimney, that giue a glowing heate when they are laid together, when one alone soone goeth out) one is refreshed, helped, hartened, and comforted by the other; according to the kind of worke which they take in hand: and so one alone is much weakened, made heauie, and soone discouraged. As *Moses* his hands failed against *Amalek*, till *Aaron* and *Hur* propped them vp. But *Moses* and *Aaron*, *Caleb* and *Ioshuah*, *Dauid* and *Ionathan*, and so much more many together, as their employment required, who doubteth but that they did much more roundly and readily dispatch the worke appointed them of God, then if they had been disioyned and asunder? Therefore doubtlesse, where both, if there bee no more, or many are sound hearted in seuerall to God and his worship, and like minded and vpright hearted each to other, the Lord is doubly honoured, the Gospell graced, euen in the eyes of the wicked; the aduersarie stronglier resisted by their vnited force; besides the strengthening one the others hands in the way to happinesse.

Eccles.4.11.

A simile.

And therefore the publike assemblies of the faithfull haue great force to quicken and to comfort the people of God, in the seeing the faces of one another, all being present together to meet the Lord there; farre otherwise then one alone can finde it, though he be well minded also, and enioyeth no such benefit of the ministry at all, vnlesse it can be no otherwise. Euen so Christian fellowship in priuate betwixt the people of God, for their mutuall edifying and comfort, as they haue opportunity to enioy it, is many waies gainefull. And though solitarinesse hath also her kinde and sweet vse; and though there is a time to be alone, when a man desireth it, who is fit to vse it; yet to be tied to it, or (which is worse) to bee in bad company euery while, it is such an vncomfortable estate, that if it were not for imployment in their particular calling, wherein they may bestow their chiefe time, they should make their life meerely tedious and wearisome. Therfore I maruell, that godly fellowship and acquaintance is no more sought and made account of; nor the communion of Saints (which is but one fruit of the Gospell) in no heartier and greater request, nor no better vse made of it where it is enioyned; but broken off among some, by euery light and small conceit, teatch, or sinister report and slander, and by such like occasions. And seeing I haue spoken this of fellowship, one thing I haue thought good to adde, and that is: if it bee possible let a wise Christian bee neuer to seeke of some one faithfull friend at the least, to whom he may breake his minde in all doubtfull cases, and communicate with him about necessary matters, and who may be to him as an eye to watch ouer him, and as another him-selfe to comfort him.

Note.

Note.

Let this suffice to shew what a benefit Christian society and godly fellowship is many waies, to them that can rightly vse it; according to the words of the Psalmist, *Behold how good and pleasant a thing it is, brethren to dwel together in vnity:* and what danger and discouragements there arise in the priuate condition; where no helpe by Christian communion of neighbors

Psal.133.

is enioyned; and therfore what heed is to be taken therin that such a band be not broken where it is, and where none is, that it be speedily (as may be) sought and procured: that for want of aduice, fellowship and good company, so many waies requisite, men be not plunged into depth of troubles, both in matters of soule, and in things of this life; many of the which might easily haue been auoided.

Now it followeth, which I will deferre to the next Sermon.

THE NINTH SERMON VPON THE FIRST AND SECOND CHAPTERS OF THE BOOKE OF IVDGES.

VERS. 30. *Neither did Zebulon expell,* &c. as before to vers. 34.

VERS. 34. *And the Ammorites draue the children of Dan into the mountaine, so that they suffered them not to come downe to the valley.*

VERS. 35. *And the Ammorites dwelt still in Mount Heres in Aijlon, and in Shaalbim, and when the hand of Iosephs family preuailed, they became tributaries.*

VERS. 36. *And the coast of the Amorites was from Maaleh-akeabim, euen from Selah, and vpward.*

Vers. 30. NOw it followeth. From this 30. verse, to the 34. the holy Story setteth downe particularly, how the tribes of *Zebulon, Ashur* and *Naphtali,* did euen as the other tribes before mentioned, of *Beniamin, Manasse,* and *Ephraim*; that they let those Canaanites liue still among them, and did only put them to tribute. Wherein to see the agreement that was in this sinne betwixt them and the other, it is worthy the noting, and may bee of singular vse vnto vs. For they did as if they had consented together, one to doe as the other did, (whereas they could (yet) but heare one of an others doing) they did (I say) euen as the other before mentioned, for their ease and quiet, make leagues with the Canaanites, contrary to that which God commanded them. Which sheweth vs, that it is the lesse maruell that we see it so in our age, and that it hath been so from age to age, that there is agreement in sinne among all estates, yea in the same sinne, as if they did mutually resolue to ioyne therein. For *Paul* speaking of grosse sinnes which should raigne in the world, in the latter age after Christ, tels vs, that the times, that is, the people in the seuerall ages, should be tainted therewith. And as it was in the daies of *Lot,* so shall it bee in the ages following; they did eate and drinke, and marrie; that is, they made them their paradise. And as they haue done, and liued in former times, so they doe, and will doe, still. And as they sought their felicity,

Doct. 1. 2. Tim. 3. 1. Matth. 24. 37.

felicity and hearts desire heere in some transitorie things; as in gathering wealth, hunting after vaine pleasures, and seeking of promotion: euen so, this doe many at this day, who professe the Gospell, and yet this is the estate of the ciuiler sort; there are greater abominations then these: the way of truth they haue not knowne; the feare of God hath not been before their eyes; but is this done in one place as in another, yee will aske, as the sinne heere spoken of, was alike spread throughout the tribes? I answere; neuer more then at this day. Therefore when the meaner sort receiued not the word with fruit, I turned (saith the Ppophet *Ieremy*) to the mighty, to the learned, to the Priest, &c. as declaring that hee looked to finde it otherwise Ier.4.
there; but behold, all were alike.

So is it said by our Sauiour, *as it was in the daies of Noah, so shall it bee at the comming of the sonne of man*, and (as he saith) in the latter age, whereof this in which we liue is a part, *they did then eat and drink, marrie, and giue in marriage*, (these were things what they did then most minde and set their hearts on, and knew nothing of any danger) *till the flood came and tooke them all away.* And what doe men now, or haue done in our remembrance in the former daies, but euen so, and the same things? What pleasure haue men, saue in eating and drinking, and following after their delights? and as the tribes did, for their ease and pleasure commit sinne, euery one his owne way: so what doe men, but euery one that which doth best serue his owne turne. What effectuall and sauing knowledge of God is there to be found, saue only heere and there in a few persons? and generally the Gospell is a mysterie, Note.
and the pearle in it is hidden from one, as from another, though *it bee hidden* 2.Cor.4.3.
from none but from them that shall perish. What excessiue and vnsatiable seeking after the worlds good is there, as in other ages? what bold prophaning of the Lords Sabbaths, when yet he hath plainely charged vs the contrary, saying: Remember yee keepe them holy? And what should I further set downe other agreements betwixt men in their liues and practise, whether we compare our daies with the former, or in the same daies one man with another? And yet one would thinke that the examples of former times should teach the latter wisedome. That seeing they who now liue may behold, how they haue been taken away, and that oft times in the middest of their delights, and could keepe themselues from death no more then others; therefore it ought worthily to cause them to looke further, and to prepare a better, and a more enduring inheritance against they must goe hence. But to grow to an end; seeing it is so that the world is like it selfe, and the sinnes of it haue entertainment alike for the most part, with one as with another, I will shew the cause of it why it is so, and teach the vse of it before I end. (For besides the diuels malice, who ruleth alike in the hearts of the children of darknes, & draweth them to the same euils, in the most places) Gal.5.19.
besides this, I say, all men are corrupted in their harts, imaginations, and desires: they all loue euill, and loath that which I good. Wherby it commeth Gen.6.5.
to passe, that the sins that one embraceth, an other delighteth in also; hauing no ability nor will to resist or turne from them, but drinketh them vp, as the fish doth water. And there is nothing able to make it otherwise but one: and that is the grace of regeneration & new birth, which changeth a man, & giues him a new hart and will, whereby he disliketh the former inclination

and disposition that led and caried him amisse before. And hereby the deceitfulnesse of his sinfull heart being found out, he groweth to be out of loue and liking with the desires which came from it, and consequently from the uill words and actions that proceeded from it; and both mindeth and doth the contrary things. Thus hee is, as wee see, turned into an other course of life, different from the men of the world. But because few light on this change, and this grace entreth not into many; but is resisted rather, and that in a deadly manner, euen when by sound preaching it is offered vnto them; therefore they abide in the same estate wherein they were before, so that they are not subiect to the grace that should guide them, neither indeed can be. Thus it commeth to passe, that few being new borne, the most agree in the same euill, to the which (the heart being alike disposed vnto it) they are carried.

Note.

And whereas it will (perhaps) be obiected, that the good nature that is in many, more then in some others, and good education doe put difference betwixt men, as well as sanctification, and the changing of the nature of man; be it knowne vnto them, that the best nature is poysoned, and enclined to all sinne, and hath the seede thereof: and the best education, being not seasoned with religion, can but worke ciuility in a man; or (at the most) restraine him from some outward and open wickednesse; it cannot giue him a new heart, neither therefore make him a new creature. And I conclude with the vse of this doctrine, that all such as desire to be better guided then naturall men can be, must seriously labour to be acquainted with their hearts, searching out by the Law of God, the depth of falshood and euill that is in them, which is great and much: and (as they are taught) bewaile it, as that which bringeth forth fruit vnto death, till they obtaine pardon thereof, and of their other sinnes: with the which grace they receiue will and strength, though weakely, to liue well, and to please God; yea and for the obtaining of all these, let them attend to sincere preaching, not by fits, but ordinarily and constantly as they may, and so God will draw them out of the puddle in which other lie still, and worke that grace in them, whereby they shall be reformed to the image of Christ their head, and to the similitude of the members of his body, which are all vniformely gouerned by the same spirit, which worketh alike fruits in all. And this is the onely way to come by it.

Note. Ier.17.9. Gal.5.22. Iam.3.17.

Doct.2. But another thing is to be noted by these tribes beside, (which I haue said already, and that is, seeing they could not chuse but heare one of another what they did) how one was led by the example of the other. For though one easily agree with another in euill (as I haue said before) yet I cannot tell how it commeth to passe, that when wee haue example also from others of any bad course, we are much more easily riueted into it thereby. Nay this example so much preuaileth, that although wee haue Gods commandement neuer so plaine to the contrary, with threates annexed thereto, wee boldly breake through it, and not onely affect and commit the same, as in the former doctrine I said wee doe; but wee beare it downe before vs, as it were a streame. It could not easily haue been thought that this people of Israel, one tribe after another, could (there being so many of them) haue sought their owne ease, in making peace with the other nations, hauing receiued

ceiued so straite a commandement that they should expell them: and yet they did so handle the matter among them, that it was as it were vtterly forgotten among them, and they grew to bee confirmed in a contrary course. But when one tribe had broke the ice to another in breaking through the commandement, it became as a matter that lay dead, few looked after it. So it would hardly haue been thought, that *Saphira* could haue been brought to consent to the holding backe of that summe of money which was consecrated to so good and holy an vse; which was by making a lye, and standing stifly in it; but when she knew her husbands mind, and had him to goe before her therein, so that he made no matter to commit such a trespasse, shee was emboldened to doe it also by his example.

Likewise, who would haue said that well nigh the whole city of Samaria should haue been drawne to receiue *Simon Magus* his sorceries? but after that some had begun, and there was none to reproue and shame them for it, the rest fell to it, hauing such examples before them. And a man would wonder to see how such cleare & streight charges as God hath giuen to men, of departing from iniquitie, and of not *following the multitude to doe euill*, should Exod.23.2.
be so troden vnder foot, and cast behinde mens backs. Ministers are commanded as they loue Christ, they should feed his sheepe, and his lambes: Ioh.21.15.
the people, that they should giue all diligence to make their calling and election sure: young men not boldly take their pleasure, and spend their youth licentiously: old men, that they should be patternes to the young in good life, &c. 2.Pet.1.10. Eccles.11.9.
But as if God might be mocked, hell agreed withall, and as if the Scriptures that straitely vrge these things, were an old wiues fable, so they are regarded. For what one of many, either Minister maketh euer the more conscience of zealous and diligent preaching; or how many of the other sorts feare the commandement to depart from euill? It is enough to them that they haue others to goe before them in the euils which they doe. For euen as sheepe and beasts follow the formost ranke, whithersoeuer it leade them, euen so these like beasts doe. Thus by the seede of ill example sinne encreaseth, and iniquitie aboundeth in all places, till at length a confusion of all things follow, in offices, duties, and estates both in Church and Common-wealth. And the rather, if men see such goe before them in euill as seeme to haue excellency in any gifts, whereby they can maintaine their sinnes; as by wealth, learning, authority, or any such like. In which respect the sinne of the tribe of Iudah was the greater, in that they beleeued not that God would enable them to cast *out the inhabitants of the valleyes*, seeing they had chariots of iron, and so they becomming examples to their brethren therein; and being the chiefest, though they had done commendably in expelling many other of them; therfore the rest of the tribes thought their sinne more tolerable, and made the lesse of it, though they yet had not so good a pretence for their doings as Iudah had. But to returne to our selues, we are to know, that it is great boldnesse to follow bad examples, the damnation of such sleepeth not. Let not men bee deceiued, God hath all these things and such like registred and writen, not with inke and paper, (for then there were hope that in time they might bee worne out) but in his remembrance, which neuer faileth. If *Paul* wish that men follow not his example (so rare a patterne of piety) further then hee followes Christ; what

shall they haue to answere, who looke no further then to this, that they see others doe so, how odious soeuer their doings are? Let that serue vs for doctrine concerning examples, forasmuch as they that leade and towle vs on by their example, cannot helpe vs to beare our punishment, when their own shall be intolerable to them, seeing company shall not ease the torments of the damned in hell; howsoeuer heere they could ioyne hand in hand to commit their sinne with pleasure and consent. And let vs bee so farre from following others in their doings, further then they follow the rule that should guide vs all, that our owne light may so shine before men, that they may blesse God for vs, and learne of vs. So shall wee shew our selues wiser then these tribes, whose sinne we haue seene laid open vnto vs, and bee well fenced against all danger by ill examples. The last verses in this chapter now follow

VERS. 34. *And the Amorites droue the children of Dan into the mountaine; so that they suffered them not to come downe to the valley.*
35. *And the Amorites dwelt still in mount Heres, in Aijalon, and in Shaalbim, and when the hand of Iosephs familie preuailed, they became tributaries.*
36. *And the coast of the Amorites was from Maale-Akrabbim, euen from Selah and vpward.*

The summe. NOw in the shutting vp of the chapter, the holy story bringeth in the tribe of Dan, shewing that these Danites had not the liberty that the other tribes had: for they yet had strength to expell the Canaanites that were in their lot, and did not: these were couped vp in a narrow roome vnto the mountaines, and yet were not suffered to possesse them neither: but they were not permitted at all to dwell in the vallies, but their enemies had them out, and kept a great part of their possessions in their hands by force. So that we see that the negligence of the other tribes in suffering the forbidden nations to remaine and waxe strong; caused these their brethren to be wronged, and to go without their due which God had allotted them: For if they had kept their enemies out, they might haue been able now to helpe this tribe of Dan: who if the house of *Ioseph* had not done more then the rest, they had been left almost without habitation.

Doct. And by this we may see, that mens sinnes doe not only redound to their owne hurt, but also to the hurt of others. Whereas none are hurt, neither themselues, by those that feare to offend God, and be carefull to do their duties, but they may receiue great benefit thereby. But the other hurt many, as well as themselues. As wee see bad parents, what woe they hoard vp for their vnhappy children, as *Ahab*, and the like. What they do to themselues, this place giues no occasion to shew directly, but by consequent, but how other feare the worse by them. And the same may bee seene in many particulars among vs also, both touching body and soule. As first, how many soules doth an ignorant, idle or scandalous Minister destroy and cause to perish? How many good people doth an vngodly Magistrate grieue, discourage, and make faint in good duties, and flesh the vngodly? as *Salomon* saith; *When the righteous are in authority, the people reioyce; but when the wicked beareth rule, the people sigh.* The riotous, ill company keepers, and such

Prou.29.2.

as

as giue ill counsell,how many doe they spoile? as in the Epistle to the Corinthians we reade; where it is said, *Euill words corrupt good manners.* And what discredit to the godly,and to the Gospell it selfe, hypocrites who professe it,doe bring,Saint *Paul* declareth,speaking thus to the Iewes; *Thou that teachest another,and teachest not thy selfe,* causest the name of God to bee euill spoken of: so that both when the Gospell is truly preached, and also practised of some,yet both are ill spoken of by the wicked, because of the offence that hypocrites giue. And generally the wicked are the causes of mischiefe and punishment from God, vpon the places where they liue; causing the earth to mourne,and be wearie of the inhabitants,yea Gods children are of the worse for their neighbourhood, not onely while they gather infection by them to their soules; but they smart bodily also with them, and by them oftentimes in a publike calamity which their wicked liues haue caused. 1.Cor.15.33. Rom.2.21.24.

Further to giue briefly some instances of this also, in the hurts that wicked men do to others in things of this life (for it would be too long to shew it at large) what doth the gamester,spendthrift, and the slothfull person, but bring all to naught,and vndoe his familie,as well as bring himselfe to beggerie? What doth the oppressor and the vsurer, in exacting that which is agreed vpon(how hardly soeuer it can be yeelded) but fleece the borrower, till he makes his skinne to grow to his bones for want of flesh? How many cormorant-like rich men doe the like in other kindes, imposing rents vpon their poore tenants, which constraine them to labour for them onely, in prouiding their due against their day, and cannot maintaine themselues so well as seruants may and ought to be? whereas God alloweth them to liue, and bee well maintained by their labour? And other defraud the labourer of his wages,or pay what they list; and yet Saint *Iames* saith, *Their cry is entred into the eares of the Lord of hosts.* Oh! it cannot be expressed, what are the discommodities and annoiances,which the sinnes of men,and their wicked liues,doe cause and bring vpon others as well as themselues(as the the tribes heere wrought woe to their neighbors these Danites) seeing all the plagues and mischiefes which are euery where to be found,are to bee imputed vnto them,to verifie that which is written; *Woe be to the world,because of her iniquities.* And this be said of the tribe of Dan and of all the rest. Iam 5.4.

Now there remaineth a question to be answered,and so I end the whole chapter. And the question is this; seeing the tribes dwelt with the Canaanites,and tooke tribute of them,whether it bee lawfull for a godly man to dwell and bee conuersant with the vngodly,as Papists,&c? I answere, that seeing Christ kept company with the publicans and great sinners; and seeing Saint *Paul* would not giue leaue to a beleeuing wife to depart from an vnbeleeuing husband, if hee will dwell with her; therefore it is not simply vnlawfull to dwell with such: but if the godly be well setled in sound knowledge,and strong in faith,so as they be not tied to communicate with them in their false worship of God,they may: but yet with certaine cautions. As first this,that in companying with them,they intend and endeauour to perswade them to sound religion, and that to this end they shew themselues kinde and gentle,the better to draw them on. But if they be in feare and danger to be drawne themselues,they ought to cut off such fellowship. *An Obiect. Out of these verses of the second part.* *The Answ.* Math.9.10. 1.Cor.7.13. *Certaine cautions to be obserued in companying with Papists,&c.* 1

The second thing that they must take heede of, is; that they liue vnre- 2

proueably and without iust blame among them: for otherwise they shall
3 do them hurt,and harden them,rather then doe them the least good. Thirdly, they may not in the least matter vnder any colour of friendship mixe themselues with them,either in their false opinions,or in worshiping God; no not although they should hope thereby to draw them on the easier to embrace Christ: as many hypocriticall professors doe, and thereby couer their voluptuousnesse, couetousnesse, and prophanenesse; who should rather remember this,that they may not do euill,that good may come of it.
4 Lastly, they must take heede that they seeke not their owne profit at their hands by companying with thē;nor to take their pleasure in gaming & play with them,whereby they bewraying their weakenesse(as impatience,greedinesse of gaine,wrangling,or being immoderate in spending the time therein) they should set them further backe from imbracing the Gospell. Therefore,if these cautions be not regarded,and also if wee haue no hope to win them,wee must craue pardon, and leaue them to God; hauing no more to doe with them in that familiar manner, further then of necessity which may possibly bee,either on our part, or on theirs; (as if their neede should bee great, and they had no other way to bee relieued by, then by vs, or if our liues should be preserued by them: In which case we ought to be very warie,lest we be intangled by them. Also we may company with them, if we bee linked to them by the bond of nature; as they being our parents,brethren,kinsfolke,or in ciuill respect,as being our magistrates,masters,&c. But as for putting children to schoole with teachers that be of that religion, it is no way fit nor lawfull, seeing by their gifts of learning,they may so draw an high conceite of them from the children,that they may the easier distill and drop poyson into them by their corrupt religion. And this for answere to the question,and withall an end of the whole chapter.

THE SECOND CHAPTER.

VERS. 1. *And an Angell of the Lord came vp from Gilgal to Bochim, and said, I made you goe vp out of Egypt, and haue brought you vnto the land which I had sworne vnto your fathers, and said, I will neuer breake my couenant with you.*

2. *Ye also shall make no couenant with the inhabitants of this land, but shall breake downe their altars: but yee haue not obeyed my voice. Why haue yee done this?*

3. *Wherefore I said also, I will not cast them out before you, but they shall bee as thornes vnto your sides,and their gods shall be your destruction.*

4. *And when the Angell of the Lord spake these words vnto all the children of Israel,the people lift vp their voice and wept.*

5. *(Therefore they called that place Bochim) and offered sacrifices there vnto the Lord.*

The summe of the Chapter.

WE haue heard in the first chapter the notable victories of Israel ouer the nations,while they obeyed the word of God; and also the sin of many of them in suffering the Canaanites to liue. Now it followeth, how the Lord of his goodnesse reproued them for the same, by the messenger

ger that preached to them; and the fruit that followed thereof. And afterward, vnto the end of this chapter, the holy Story ſetteth downe the ſumme of almoſt the whole booke; namely to the 17. chapter; taking occaſion to doe this from the acts of former times: beginning at the things which were done before *Ioſhuas* death. The ſumme of all the reſt of this chapter from verſe 6. is thus much: *Ioſhua* a little before his death, hauing called the people together, and giuen them their charge (as appeareth in chapter 23. and 24. of that booke) that they ſhould beware of Idolatry, and feare the Lord, after that, he ſent the people away, and died: in whoſe daies, and in the daies of the elders that liued after him, the people obeyed his charge, as it is to bee ſeene in this chapter, from the 6. to the 11. verſe. But after that, it is ſhewed how the next generation that aroſe after them, declined from that good courſe: and ſo did the ages that followed them, one was like another, throughout this booke vnto the 17. chap. and here with it is declared, how God dealt with them. And that in few words was thus; they fell to prouoke God by Idolatrie and other ſins: then the Lord was diſpleaſed with them for it, and deliuered them into their enemies hands: after that they cryed to the Lord, and he raiſed them vp Iudges, or deliuerers of them; yet they obeyed not euen them, which cauſed him to be againe offended with them, and to threaten them as is to be ſeene to the end of this chapter. And this is declared and laid out by the diuers examples of the people, throughout all this booke, vnto the 17. chapter, according to the generall diuiſion made of the whole booke in the beginning. Ioſh.24.

According to the meaning now ſet downe, the parts of this chapter follow, which are two: The firſt, is a calling of the tribes that had offended, to repentance, to verſ.6. The other, is the ſetting downe of the eſtate of the people after *Ioſhuas* death, and Gods dealing with them vnder the Iudges, throughout theſe 15. next chapters, vnto the 17. and this is to the end of this chapter. *The parts two.*

I will leaue the laſt part to the due place, wherein it is to bee conſidered, and examine the firſt as order requireth. And heere in this firſt part we may ſee theſe two things: A reproofe of the people by the Angell, to verſe 4. and the effect that followed thereon; that is, the peoples repentance, to the ſixth verſe: ſo that in the firſt part of this chapter is ſhewed, how the people had prouoked God already by not driuing the nations out, after their firſt entrance, and the death of *Ioſhua*: as wee haue heard in the former chapter: and that they were brought to repentance. In the ſecond part is declared, how another generation that knew not the Lord did much worſe: for they not onely made couenants with the Canaanites as the other did, who were brought to repentance; but alſo ſerued all manner of Idols, and prouoked the Lord thereby. To begin therefore with the former branch of the firſt part, that is, their reproofe, the meſſenger that was ſent to them, (to make it more forcible to pricke their conſciences) firſt rehearſeth the benefits which God had beſtowed vpon them, which ought rather to haue drawne them to obedience. And this he doth in the firſt verſe, as ye may ſee: then he ſetteth downe the faults for which hee reproueth them. One, that they made leagues with the Canaanites, contrary to Gods commandement; the other, that they had not caſt downe their Alters; and he expoſtulateth with *The ſumme of the firſt 3. verſes.*

them

them for the ſame,ſaying,*why haue ye done this*,contrary to the charge which the Lord gaue you? in the 2.verſ.And laſtly,he threateneth them,that their diſobedience ſhould be to their great puniſhment, ſaying; I will not driue them out,but they ſhall bee prickes in your ſides,and their gods ſhall bee a ſnare vnto you,and this in the 3. verſe. Now it remaineth to ſpeake more particularly of theſe in order. But before I come to ſpeake of the meſſage, I will ſay a little of the meſſenger.

Of the firſt verſe perticularly. The word Meſſenger, or *Angel,* ſignifieth ſometime a created nature without a body,(as Hebr.1. Angels are called *miniſtring ſpirits*) and theſe aſſumed ſome forme at Gods commandement for the time then being, the better to accompliſh their office,as Geneſ.18. Sometime this word ſignifieth any other meſſenger that God ſendeth to execute his will: as Reuel.2. and 3. where by the Angell, is ment the miniſter that was ſent to them, a meſſenger from God. And whether of theſe ſoeuer is ment heere,it maketh no matter,and it being not particularly expreſſed in the text, it is ſufficient for vs, that wee know it was a miſſenger ſent of God; and therefore ſufficiently authorized: and of thoſe to whom he was ſent, one who ought to be reuerently receiued and beleeued. And let it teach vs,that God alwaies vſed the miniſtry of his ſeruants to reueale,as it hath ſeemed good vnto him, and to declare his will vnto men; either about the generall couenant of grace and promiſe of ſaluation, or about any other particular thing as hee ſaw cauſe; and this he did whether they were Patriarkes, Angels,Prophets, or Apoſtles,by whom he did it in ages paſt,or (as he doth now) other miniſters of the Goſpell, as Paſtours and Teachers, whom he vſeth at this day to reueale his will vnto the people. The which declaration of his will by them out of his word from time to time, as it highly commendeth his great kindneſſe to theſe to whom he ſent thoſe his meſſengers, (ſeeing wee know hee hath not done it at all people in any age) ſo it teacheth vs (as others that were before vs, it did the like) that wee are bound to heare them,in all that the Lord ſhall ſay to vs by them.

Heb.1.14. Gen.18.2. Doct.1. Out of verſ.1. Heb.1.1. Act.10.33.

Matth.10.40. According to that which our Sauiour himſelfe ſaith, *He that heareth you, heareth me,and he that deſpiſeth you, deſpiſeth me.* And ſo much more wee are to heare them,and receiue their meſſage with all readineſſe,ſeeing as it hath been glorious in all ages, ſo it is moſt of all in this latter age; wherein is reuealed to vs, that all things hath been performed by our Sauiour which appertaine to mans happineſſe, and which were in ages paſt onely foretold; and therefore they may much more fully and clearely bee made knowne to the hearers now,if the meſſenges who ſhould bring the tidings,be faithfull and able to doe their meſſage. In which caſe wee muſt receiue them as the Lord himſelfe, and the word which they preach, *not as the word of man, but (as it is in deed) the word of God*; that ſo it may worke in vs effectually,as phyſicke in a corrupt body,both to make vs ſicke,and to recouer and heale vs againe; God hauing prouided,that in what eſtate ſoeuer the people be, euery one ſhould receiue his portion, by the right diuiding of the word vnto them. And the ordinarineſſe of their meſſage, ſhould not make either their miniſtery the leſſe ſet by: but rather wee ſhould haue them in ſo much the more eſtimation, and admire therein the vnſpeakeable prouidence of God and loue of our Lord Ieſus, who (as hee ſendeth vs not to extraordinary meanes)

1.Theſ.4.8. Gal.4.14. 1.Theſ.2.13. Eſa.50.4.

meanes) so yet he hath promised the ordinary vnto his Church, euen to the end of the world: as in the Epistle to the Ephesians is to be seene. Ephes.4.11.

Which being duly considered, doth bewray the wofull and lamentable estate of the most hearers (though they are in most fearcful estate that heare not) who euen where the word is preached with power and authority, haue it in small account and reuerence. And what should the Lord doe more vnto them, hauing thus offered his dainties vnto them? and yet they are so ful stomacked, that they finde no sauour nor pleasure in them. They giue themselues leaue, so to wallow in their sensualities, and to take their fill of earthly delights, that they finde no sauour in his heauenly delicates: yea and yet some of them are such, as heretofore haue heard with ioy; yea and a man might haue thought, they would haue pluckt out their eyes for them that brought the glad tidings vnto them, now are waxen full, and count them their enemies for telling them the truth; and some thinke themselues within a few weekes, able to teach their teachers: as other haue turned their zeale into luke warmenesse, their reuerence into contempt, conceitednesse, worldlines, and deprauing of the Scriptures. And so like fooles, while they loath this wholesome and sweete Manna of the word of life, which is the approued truth of God: they relish fantasies, and haue great taste and delight in dreames and lies: insomuch as that if any would faine himselfe to come from the dead, and affirme, that he brings them newes from thence for any sound knowledge or faith that they haue, they are ready to receiue them. Oh people infatuated and bewitched (as *Paul* saith to the Galathians) seeking, as one that runneth vpon a swords point, their owne destruction. But of these enough.

Hos.6.4. Matth.11.17. Note. Gal.3.1.

THE TENTH SERMON ON THE SECOND CHAPTER OF THE BOOKE OF IVDGES, on the same text. vers. 1.

NOw further let vs marke, that the Lord sending his messenger to the people heere did (after they had fallen from his couenant that hee made with them) to moue them to repentance (as in these 3. verses is to be seene.) And heere let vs marke (I say) how God is faine to preuent them by this messenger, while they lay in their sins, before they could accuse themselues, and complaine, saying once among themselues; *What haue we done?* and so to seeke recouery. They were fit to be more and more hardened, and to runne on still, yea to couer their sinnes as *Adam*, and flee from God as *Ionas*, and to sit downe vpon them and hide them, as *Rahel* vpon *Labans* Idols; but to bethinke themselues, what they should do to come out

The further laying open of this verse. Gen.3.10. Iob 31.33. Gen.31.34.

out of their ſinnes, and ſo to helpe themſelues out of danger thereby, they
2.Sam.12.7. were vtterly to ſeeke, and altogether vnfit. They may bee likened to *Dauid*, who hauing lien long in two fearefull ſinnes, was ſo farre from repenting of them, that *Nathan* was faine to leaue off parables, and to ſpeake plainely be-
Mat.26.74.75. fore he could conceiue him. And to *Peter*, who hauing denied his maſter, had no power to riſe out of his ſinne, till the Lord Ieſus looked backe vpon him, by the which watchword, *Peter* called to minde, together with the the cocks crowing, the words which Ieſus had ſpoken to him; to wit, that he ſhould denie him, and then he went out and wept bitterly.

Doct.2. And by this wee may ſee, what a dangerous thing ſinne is; I meane not onely the committing of it, which one would thinke were feareful enough, but for that afterward they are not able to riſe out of it, but lie ſtill in it (when yet men thinke they can repent of it at their pleaſure) and when they liſt, though it trouble the conſcience, as raw fleſh doth the ſtomacke: but they are hardened in it for a time, eſpecially ſoone after the committing of it, ſo that they cannot at all humble their hearts, and bewaile their ſinne to God. And if they come to themſelues again after a time, yet it is by Gods preuenting of them, as I haue ſaid; and while he renueth his grace in them, as relenting and remorſe for it, and the renouncing of it, and crauing of pardon. Thereby indeed they are inabled to repent, and ſo to returne to their former workes. But this is not (wee ſee) any power in them, for they are not able to bring their hearts thereto, nor to doe any ſuch thing of themſelues. And yet I ſay more, that many times when they haue fallen, they doe not attaine this grace neither; before God brings them to heare by preaching, or by affliction calleth them to a deeper conſideration, or by ſome ſuch like meanes bringeth their ſinne to light, and into diſgrace with them; as to theſe people hee did heere at Bochim; and then it may bee they ſtay their courſe and returne.

But now let this be well weighed herein, what a diſtraction and diſquietneſſe it hath been to them all this while, to lie bound as it were with the chaines of their ſins, as they haue been, that they cannot helpe themſelues; and to bee ſo bereaued of the graces of God, as faith, hope, ioy in the holy Ghoſt, feare of offending, and ſuch like; that they lie dead in them, as if they
Note. had no part in them, and they hauing no vſe of them to ſtrengthen them to any good doing, although they be in themſelues profitable to all holy vſes; whereas in the meane while, who would loſe his ſweet communion with God, if he bee wiſe enough to conſider what I ſay; though it ſhould neuer be brought againſt them? no though it were but for an houre or a day, with the comforts belonging thereto? which yet theſe whom I haue ſpoken of, when they haue ſinned againſt their knowledge, doe depriue themſelues of, whole moneths and yeeres. And why doe they thus? If they ſuſtained all this, as from their triall from God, their patience were commendable; or if it were poſſible to honour him thereby, it were ſome commendation to them: but when it is for the hauing of their owne will amiſſe, and for the enioying the pleaſures of ſinne for a ſhort ſeaſon, oh how lamentable is it to
Note. thinke? So that this wiſedome ſhall well beſeeme the ſeruants of God, to giue all diligence to keepe well, while they are well, and in no wiſe to haue their teeth ſet on edge with the deceiueable baites of ſinne, which the world

ſo

so greedily runneth after, forasmuch as they shall see how deare it shall cost them; and yet let them know this, that such shall not bee onely void of the forementioned graces, but they shall also smart through many punishments. And now if it be so hard for them to come to repentance when they haue fallen, who yet before had enioyed that gift soundly: how much further off are they, who neuer haue part in it at all? neither are like to haue, euen as wee see by daily experience (how fearefull an estate is that to liue in) vnlesse they wait on God diligently in the ordinance of preaching to attaine it.

Now wee haue heard how God was faine to prouoke them to repentance, before they could set themselues toward it: It followeth to see by what reason he vrged them to it, after I haue said a little of the places heere mentioned, Gilgal was a citie in the plain of Iordan, not farre from Iericho, from this Gilgal the messenger is said to haue come. And Bochim is a place neare adioyning to it, in which this message was done to the people of Israel, who had by their sins caused it. It was not called Bochim before, but had the name giuen by occasion of that which fell out there, that is, the weeping of the people, when their sinnes were brought to their remembrance; for so the word Bochim signifieth, namely, *weeping*. At this place therefore (to returne to the purpose) the Lord told them of their disobedience, and beginneth to make it odious to them by rehearsing his benefits great and many: as if hee should say, what cause haue I giuen you to deale thus vnthankefully and disobediently with me. Hath my kindnesse been thus requited of you, that you returne me euill for my good will? *Doct.3. Out of vers.1.*

Heere as in sundry other places wee may see what effects the benefits of God doe commonly worke in men; and that is, forgetfulnesse of them, and vnthankfulnesse for them, and a meane account making of them; also boldnesse in seeking of carnall liberty thereby (vnto the which we are so readily caried, and to prouoke God much more then if they had neuer enioyed them; little remembring that the Lord giues them a watchword, that they should rather looke in all things to be thankefull. Iustly therefore was this people heere chalenged for their vnthankefulnesse. This was the cause why they were warned before, that they should take heed when they were come into the land of promise, and should there possesse *great and goodly cities, which they builded not, and houses full of all manner of goods, which they filled not; and wels which they digged not; vineyards, and Oliue trees, which they planted not; and when they had eaten and should be full, they were warned* (I say) *that they should beware, they forgot not the Lord, which brought them out of the land of Egypt*, &c. signifying vnto them, that wealth and ease would goe nigh to make them to forget Gods mercies, by which they were deliuered out of their miseries. By which wee see the peruersenesse of our depraued nature, which turnes the wholesomest food into poyson, as the corrupt stomacke doth the daintiest meates. We abhorre him who hauing receiued freely good turnes, and benefits, forgetteth his benefactor when hee is promoted, &c. yet it is certaine that men are the worse for Gods benefits, and are more bold in sinning against him, by the abundance of his earthly and common blessings. So *Dauid* confesseth, that *before he was afflicted hee went astray*: so that his benefits (wee see) did him not so much good as his chastisements. And so *Ieremy*

1. Thess.5.19.

Deut.6.10. 11.12.

Deut.32 compare from v.9. onward to vers.19.

Psal.119.67.

Ieremy said,that he was *as an vntamed calfe,* till God corrected him. Wofull experience teacheth, how rare the man is who may truly say otherwise? to wit,that benefits knit his heart neerely to God,before he bee taught it by affliction. And yet we must know, that neither that of it owne nature draweth men to loue and obey God any more then his benefits; but as God worketh that grace,,of his especiall fauour; without which our whole life is meere disobedience, I say, further then his grace guideth vs, and keepeth vs within compasse in both estates. Common blessings and generall we thinke and say, belong to others as well as to vs; and as for speciall and priuate, while we reape and feele them,we say,[Blessed be God] but wee are not for
Luk.17. the most part,knit to him in dutie euer the more. The tenne leapers being cleansed, returned not to giue thankes, saue one. And hee to whom tenne thousand talents were remitted,shewes this fruit of his thankefulnesse,that
Mat.18.28. he caught his fellow by the throat who owed him an hundred pence, bidding him pay that he owed. And why this? For the heart of man naturally is puffed vp with prosperity, and vaine estimation of himselfe, and hee prideth in that which will be his ouerthrow and waxeth hardened,and is so far off from humility, and meane thinking of himselfe, that all may perceiue (who can rightly iudge) that it maketh him prouder, and more scornefull, yea vtterly vnlike him he should be,and disguised: and yet to become great and get much in this vale of misery, while things of greatest price are not asked after,how eagerly doe men runne after it,as fish follow the baite with greedinesse: nay they laugh all such to scorne that find fault with them for so doing,and who doe not follow them in that excesse,and let better things passe by them as little worth? yea and yet this doe they,who lawfully come by wealth and promotion, and to whom the Lord giueth prosperity without any indirect or vnlawfull meanes: euen such (I say) doe offend in the like manner of excesse and greedinesse, and fall into the same danger thereby that the others doe,who attaine to it by shifting, and against conscience.

Obiect. What then, some (perhaps) will say,it is lawfull for vs to enioy the earthly benefits of God? And againe,are there none that rightly vse prosperity and

Answ. plenty? I answere, God forbid; for men may, and some doe much more good thereby to others especially, then vnder the crosse, and in aduersitie. But this is rare: for a contrary mischiefe rather in prosperity befalleth men,

What maketh prosperity to be abused. and that is,that (for the most part) they suspect not,neither feare any danger: no not when they grosly forget themselues,and abuse their prosperity,when
1 yet it hangeth ouer their heads,and is most hardly auoided. Moreouer,nei-
2 ther doe they obserue themselues,lest they should become drunken with it, neither search into themselues to finde out how they offend thereby. Both which are necessary for a man in prosperity to doe, yea and to vse to doe so daily,for the cutting off the dangers that may otherwise ensue therby. And
Note. yet as the best practises against this and other sinnes,yea though they be neuer so conscionably and reuerently put in vre, doe by little and little grow common,and lose their strength; so therefore besides both these, a Christi-
3 Iob 14.14. an man must oft with *Iob,* tell it seriously to himselfe,that he must looke for his change, and say,it will not alwaies be summer; and thereby cracke the pride of life, and abase the excesse of carnall delight, which prosperity will
4 otherwise ful soone raise vp in him most dangerously. And last of all,if God continue

continue his daies of health and welfare, so that smartie crosses be kept from him, let him crosse his naughty and vnruly affections, and those especially by which he is most like to offend, and be in danger, chasing them away by feruent prayer against them, and grow in fruitfulnesse thereby, as he who receiued fiue talents, brought fiue more, which he had gained thereby. And these things being duely obserued, as being those which be most necessary, I will not doubt to affirme, that the man who doth so, shall vse prosperity well, and be profitable many waies thereby, which yet of another man that doth not so, I cannot warrant: nay, I dare be bold to say hee shall not. But seeing the godly doe rarely thus, by this Iudge, how the world vseth prosperity, if the godly so hardly vse it well. Luk.19.18. Mat.25.20.

Another thing is worthie to bee marked heere, where the Lord moueth the people to repentance, by rehearsing his benefits bestowed vpon them, and that is this: that of all reasons, this ought most to preuaile with Gods seruants, to disswade them from their sinnes which they haue fallen into, and to raise them out of them, or to preuent the committing of the like, this (I say) ought most to preuaile with them, euen the often remembrance and due consideration of Gods benefits, though with griefe it may bee spoken, this aduice preuailes too little. This reason God vsed heere, and the people were conuicted thereby, and yeelded, and confessed themselues guilty: For why? the loue of God constrained them, which hauing been before shead plentifully into their hearts. Now when they heard this sharpe and iust reproofe, and that from God himselfe by his messenger, they saw clearly their sinne, and namely their vnthankfulnesse, how they had forgot Gods benefits, and trod vnder foote his louing kindnesse, it being the most precious of all other things, which went neare them, they knowing that hee had done so many & great good things for them; and this, with the remembring of his benefits in some perticular manner, as they heard them repeated, caused them to cast vp their vnsauoury gorge, and so to returne from their deceiueable and damnable offences, & to imbrace againe the mercies of the Lord, who was their first husband. And with this putting the people in remembrance of his many and great benefits, God doth draw them on oft in other places to feare him. As when hee saith in Deuteronomie, I thy God haue blessed thee in all that thy heart could desire. Thus in another place also hee calling the people to repentance, whom he compareth to a vine, and labouring to draw them from their ingratitude, putteth them in mind, that he had planted them being his Church, in a place most plentifull and abundant. This caused *Dauid* euermore to haue Gods mercies in great remembrance, and to set his benefits before his eyes, that hee might shame himselfe for his sinne passed, and by all meanes seeke to come out of it. And therefore in the psalme 103. he as though hee had not been thankfull (when yet he excelled all men therein) quickeneth vp himselfe thereto, saying; *Praise thou the Lord, O my soule, and all that is within thee praise his holy name.* And in the 51. Psalme; to perswade himselfe to repentance, hee saith, that his mercies are great, and that there were in him multitudes of compassions. Other reasons, drawne from the dreadfull feare of Gods iudgements, may (I confesse) terrifie for the time the hearts of Gods people, and hold them in awe, as it were by violence: but they worke not kindly to bring them to dutie

Doct.4. Out of vers.1. 2.Cor.5.14. Rom.5.5. Deut.28. Esa.5.2. Psal.103.2. Psal.51.1.

with cheerefulnesse, though they may stay them from further euill for the time, till forcibler perswasions come. But when all is said that can be, it is the loue of God that constraineth men that they should liue to God, not to themselues. And yet I will not say that this reason shall alwaies preuaile with vs, although where it doth not, wee may well conclude, that wee are much out of order, and haue grosly forgot our selues.

2.Cor.5.14. Note. *The first benefit bestowed on them.*

Doct.5. In vers.1.

Now I come to the particular benefits which hee bestowed vpon them, forbearing to repeate them euery one together, seeing they may bee read in the text, for times sake, but one after another as they lie in order. The first is, that he had brought them out of Egypt, which was a countrie which was wholly infected with superstition and idolatry; and therefore most dangerous to dwell in. And what a benefit was it then for them to bee deliuered from thence, euen as from Rome; or in another respect, from Sodome? For there they must haue been corrupted with the pestilent contagion of their idolatrie, beside the most heauie burthens and bondage, with which both they were, and still also they must haue been pressed with, if they had remained there. Hence it is, that almost euery where in the Scripture, where mention is made of Gods goodnesse to Israel, this their deliuerance out of Egypt is most commonly reckoned as the principall, because without it all other blessings had been as nothing. Therefore let vs also know, that it is a singuler mercy of God, to be freed from the false worship of God, and idolatry, if I should say no more; but especially when there is ioyned with that a deliuerance from bodily troubles also. A benefit, whereof many thousands in this land are partakers, which their fellow brethren in other nations, being as Israel was in Egypt, Iuda in Babylon oppressed with idolatry, would thinke they obtained an vnualuable benefit, if they might haue freedome from it. And so they may well thinke: For oh what a liberty is it both to soule and body? and yet we may haue it with farre more ease then they had it; that is, without trauell or iourney.

Ezek.20.7.8.

And although they cannot value it in any sort according to the worth of it, who haue neuer felt the burthen of a troubled conscience, and bodily vexations; yet wee that haue, though they bee nothing so grieuous as they had; we (I say) are euery day (that we rise out of our beds to doe our necessarie businesse) to confesse this maruellous worke of God for our deliuerance. And yet I deny not, but that other benefits of God are to bee sought for also; as the enioying of the sincere preaching of the Gospell to the further welfare of our soules, and things necessary for this present life, that so there may want no encouragement to Gods seruice. But howsoeuer the Lord should denie vs the one, I meane plentie for our bodies, which yet for many yeers he hath most gratiously yeelded and granted vs: yet we should contend for the other, I meane sound and sauing knowledge by an happie and sound ministery, by all meanes, if possibly wee may enioy it. Which I speake to the iust reproofe of all such as doe onely regard their outward estate in the world, little or nothing looking after the benefit of true happinesse by their soules welfare: forecasting altogether to plant themselues ther, whither the hope of earthly commodities doth leade them. And though the townes, families, and kindreds be neuer so prophane and superstitious, to the which they make hast, yet that they little regard; but so as

Note.

commodity and honour may be gotten (as their common queſtion is, may we looke for any good there?) they will dwell, there they will liue and dei, Pſal.4.7.
and there they will match and leaue their children to remaine after them. But as from holding them from the infection of Popery, or labouring to ſhield them vnder a ſetled good miniſtery, and ſo to minde and ſeeke their ſaluation, it is no part of their thought. Nay there bee thouſands in this land that luſt after the ſeruitude of Popiſh Egypt againe; earneſtly deſiring that day (which God turne away) the Lord forgiue it them, (as our Sauiour prayed for them that crucified him) they know not what they do. So farre are they from thankfulneſſe for their freedome, that they are voluntary ſlaues vnder that *Pharaoh* of Rome, euen in their owne countrey.

But to returne, and ſo to draw to an end, let it be counted of vs a rare and ſingular mercy of God, to be free from great calamities, and extremities both of ſoule and body, as theſe Iſraelites were, who were deliuered out of Egypt, and the bondage thereof. And by occaſion of this which I ſay, this I further adde, that ſuch as liue void of grieuous paines and diſeaſes, (as well as Egyptian bondage) which others, yea and thoſe many of Gods deare children are vnder, as the ſtone, collicke, gowts, vlcers, gripings, and ſuch like; alſo ſuch as be not in vtter penury and want, nor yoked with vnquiet, vnkind and ſupeſtitious companions in marriage, nor with vnmercifull Note.
land-lords, and cruell ouerſeers and gouernours (which doe make their life weariſome to them, and conſume all their cheerefulneſſe and comfort, as as the moth eateth vp the beauty of a garment) let all ſuch (I ſay) beare their other pettie and ſmall diſcommodities, troubles, and viſitations, patiently and contentedly, and bee highly thankfull for that they are deliuered from farre greater: yea and let them acknowledge, that if with freedome from theſe and the like, they hold ſound peace with God, and bee free from the ſtings of an euill conſcience alſo, that they enioy a peece of a paradiſe, though in a meane condition: and let them pitie thoſe which are in ſuch depths of griefe, that their feruent prayes may moue the Lord to pity them alſo: and let them that be free from them, reſolue with themſelues and endeauour to vſe their liberty and health to all poſſible good doing. And yet let this bee knowne alſo, that where God layeth theſe great burthens vpon ſome of his, hee giueth them the greater grace to goe meekely vnder them. And let vs beware, leſt through our ſecurity and negligence God may iuſt- Note.
ly vpbraid vs with his benefits (as heere he doth Iſrael) that hauing elbowroome and liberty to ſerue God in our places and callings, without any to diſturbe vs, or hold vs vnder, we enbondage our ſelues by an ill conſcience, looſeneſſe, ſecurity, earthlineſſe, and the like euils, by which our life ſhould be as irkſome as in Egypt, or Babell.

The ſecond benefit heere mentioned, that God beſtowed vpon them, *Doc.6.in ver.1 The ſecond benefit.*
was, that he brought them into the fruitful land in which they dwelt, which was a farre greater matter then the former; as ſhewing them plainly that he thought it not enough to deliuer them out of bondage, except hee filled them with good things alſo. He had done much for them if hee had onely deliuered them out of that fearefull bondage, though hee had left them in the wilderneſſe; but to bring them alſo into that fruitfull land, and to giue

it to them, oh admirable kindnesse! Behold then heere the great bountifulnesse of God, that hee can as well and willingly giue abundance to his children, as keep them out of great troubles. He is not therby wasted nor diminished in his blessings, by giuing them out & liberally bestowing them; being a fountain of riches neuer drawne dry. So he said to the posterity of
Psal.81.13. his people: Oh that Israel would haue hearkened to me, and haue walked in my waies; I would soone haue brought downe their ememies: I would haue fed them with the fat of wheat, and with honey out of the rocke. Neither neede we thinke that he standeth at it to giue vs these, whose honour it is to bestow great things; and hath already giuen vs the greatest of all; euen
Rom.8.32. his owne sonne; and therefore can much more afford vs these smaller benefits also. As we know that he did giue great riches to *Abraham, Isaac, Iob,* and to other his faithfull seruants, whom he loued dearely. And wee in this land haue good proofe hereof, in that (with deliuerance from bondage) we haue the Gospell, peace, gouernment, plentie, and such like. And more particularly, we in this land haue cause to admire the goodnesse of God, in deliuering vs from the cursed practises of those Iesuites & Locusts, whom that beast hath sent forth to destroy vs, Prince, Nobles, Magistrates, Ministers: and to root out Church and policie among vs, and bring in darkenesse and confusion againe. Wee owe (doubtlesse) as great thankes to God for these mercies (and specially in the late Treason) as Israel did for their freedome out of Egypt, and the ouerthrow of *Pharaoh* when he pursued them.

Obiection. Now then to this common obiection, why God doth not enrich so his faithfull ones in this latter age? (which obiection many are readier to put forth questions, then to take any adswere to it) for (say they) though men of the world haue great substance, and swim in wealth and riches; yet Gods people are seldome so; but are held downe with pouerty and wants; in so much as one is hardly able to relieue another; and thereby also (they say) they doe the lesse good in bringing on, and perswading to religion, seeing they whom they goe about to perswade, doe feare that their God loueth them not whom they serue, seeing hee bestoweth not wealth vpon them, as he doth vpon others who are not for the most part, especially in some places, religious at all: also they feare that if they themselues should bee religious, euen they should become poore also. This (I say) troubles many, them therefore I answere after this manner.

Answere 1. To doe them good, hee is ready to bestow riches vpon them, and better things also. As he said to *Ieroboam*, when of a seruant he made him a King:
1.King.14. *If this had not been enough, I would* (saith hee) *haue giuen thee more:* If then to him a bad man hee would haue giuen more, if hee had vsed that well; then who doubteth but that he would be liberally handed to his deare children, if it were for their good? But otherwise (indeed) hee thinketh them better
Iam.4.2. held backe then bestowed; as he answered by Saint *Iames*, when they asked, they obtained not, because they asked amisse; that is, to bestow the things they asked, vpon their lusts: but if they might haue bettered by them, hee would haue liberally giuen vnto them. And as he answered *Paul*, when hee gaue him not that which hee asked (and yet that which he asked was a bet-
2.Cor.12.9. ter thing then riches) *my grace is sufficient for thee:* so in denying them to his faithfull seruants, he giueth his grace, which worketh contentment in them,

and thereby though their outward estate bee weake, hee yet euen in that, keepes them from the noisome euils of the dayes they liue in, that I say no more. And further to answere them, they must hold this for a truth, that euery mans estate wherein God setteth him (I say not that which hee by his sinne hath brought vpon him) is best for him, as we in the Lords prayer are well taught, when wee are directed to aske our daily bread; euen such successe in our estate, poore or rich, as our heauenly father seeth best for vs, euen that is *our daily bread*, with the which we must be contented.

Answ. 2.

Petic. 4.

And yet this is further to be added, that hee that hath meate, drinke, and apparell, he is not to bee counted poore, when indeed the wealthiest hath no more, neither is better satisfied with that which he hath then such an one being gratious: and as for the superfluity that he hath, which is counted his glory, how commonly doe we see it to become his bane? And where is the man that is not the worse for his wealth, it being *his strong hold*, which maketh him bolder to sinne, that way that he is most carried by his sensuality, much more then the poore man dare do. And though God setteth vp some, it is for their triall, and for the maintaining of all estates, & preseruing of fellowship in the Church and Common wealth. And as for the godly, they should not want wealth, but that it is for the most part, vsed of many euen of them, to snare and entangle them in this deceiueable world; which as the beast that is caught by the hornes in the bushes and briers; and as a man with bolts on his heeles is holden from running: so doth it hold them back from running apace to the heauenly life.

Pro. 18. 11.

Neither let this trouble any, that while most of the godly want, our fathers vnder the law, and before the comming of Christ, had great wealth and possessions; and yet were godly and saued; and therefore if God loued vs, he would as well bestow them vpon vs now: for wee must know that his outward seruice then was more costly then now it is, which required more wealth: and moreouer they had one vse of their riches, which we haue not that by these earthly things, God did figure out to them things heauenly; as by the earthly Canaan, hee did the heauenly Ierusalem: for when that earthly countrey was promised our fathers, they enioyed it not, but liued strangers in it, but they in those promises looked further, that is, for a better, which they enioyed. This that hath been said may fully answere the question. I couclude therefore, that God can freely and willingly bestow liberall portions vpon his faithfull seruants, as well as keepe them out of great calamities, if he see it to be best for them when their estate is weake: and seeing it were not like to be good for them to enioy, which he thinkes not good to giue them, let them the more contentedly labour to be without it.

Heb. 11. 13.

Now followeth the third benefit heere mentioned, and that he had promised that hee would neuer breake couenant with them. Heere the Lord may seeme to giue them great aduantage: for if hee binde himselfe thus to them, they being such as did oft times (as they are charged heere to haue done) breake their couenant toward him, it may seeme that hee is tied to them, that he shall neuer breake his couenant with them, seeing he hath promised so vnto them whatsoeuer they doe, or howsoeuer they breake theirs, or behaue themselues toward him. Then the which what is more absurd? For the answering of this therefore, and for the vnderstanding these words

The third benefit, the laying out of it.

Obiect.

Answ.

of the verse, two things are to be considered: One is, of what couenant hee speaketh, when he saith, he had granted this vnto them, that he would neuer breake it. The other, whether hee spake this simply, or vpon a condition; namely, if they should obey him. These two being answered, will make the matter cleare.

Now for the first, wee are to know, that by the couenant heere mentioned, hee neither meaneth the particular couenant which hee entreth into
Gen.17.1. with the faithfull, *to be their God all-sufficient* for euer (for that hee will neuer
Ioh.13.1. goe from, but *whom he loueth*, as he loued them ere they loued him, so *to the end he loueth them*,) neither doth he meane the generall couenant of sending
Rom.3.3. Christ to redeeme the world: for the vnbeleefe of man could not make that promise of God frustrate, and of none effect: but he meaneth the couenant of enioying the land peaceably, into which hee brought them, with all the commodities therein. Now that couenant was made with them conditionally, if they should be obedient to him. And this is the other thing, which I said was one of the two, which serueth for the better vnderstanding of this speech; where he saith by his messenger, that hee had made a couenant with them, which hee would neuer breake; and that was, if they should endeauour to walke with him, hee would continue them in that good land which hee had giuen them, and blesse them therein; otherwise he would bee free from his promise, and hee would cast them out after long bearing their disobedience, and punish them sundry waies in the meane sea-
Deut.28. son. And euen so he did to them, seeing they kept not couenant with him as he required of them, and which he bound them to, as in the next verse is to be seene. And this for the clearing of the forementioned doubt.

Doct.7.in ver.1. This point being thus determined, doth minister this heauenly instruction to vs, that if we did faithfully, and with a good hart set our selues to obey the Lord, and yet I meane no otherwise, then as may of vs be performed, he would doe great things for vs euen in this world: he would feede vs with good things, euen with the bread of wheat, and that the finest, as hee saith in
Psal.81.16. the Psalme; and other earthly blessings answerable: and would not suffer the proud to domineere ouer his inheritance, but soone bring them down. And yet wee must know, that if his owne people shall sinne against him,
Psal.89.31. he will correct them with the rod, and often withdraw from them the sweet fruit of his fauour, and the light of his countenance, which was wont to refresh and comfort their soules: so that euen the priuiledges which issue from this couenant, may in great part, and for a great while lie drowned in them and be to seeke, as ioy, peace, confidence in prayer, with such like, and their
See Doct. on vers.5. temporary benefits vtterly lost. Oh therefore notwithstanding many large and great and worthie promises be made to vs, yet when wee doe not labour to be faithfull in our couenant, but take our liberty amisse, euery one his way, as he thinkes good: behold, our sinnes depriue vs of many blessings
Ier.5.25. which we might haue enioyed, *and hold many good things from vs*, as *Ieremie* saith, and bring many euils vpon vs: and euen so the Prophet *Esay* witnes-
Leuit 26. seth, though *the Lords hand is not shortened that he cannot saue, neither is his eare*
Esa.59.1. *heauie, that it cannot heare, yet your iniquities* (saith he) *haue separated betwixt you and your God, and your sinnes haue hid his face from you, that hee will not heare.* So
Note. that if these things be rightly weighed, it may truly be said, what we will not suffer

ſuffer the Lord to doe vs good,nor to fill vs with his bleſſings,as hee is ready to doe; euen we our ſelues, becauſe wee will not ceaſe to prouoke him. And this is liuely laid out by the Prophet *Amos*, where he ſaith, that it rained vpon one peece of ground,and not vpon another: and wherefore was it,but for the ſinne of thoſe that poſſeſſe it? contrary to our blind reaſon, who looke (as *Sampſon* did) that it ſhould alway goe well with vs, howſoeuer we deale with God,or defraud him of his due, breaking couenant with him. Amos 4.7. Iudg.16.

If this be ſo, then our Sauiour agreeth well with it; who ſaith, *The meeke ſhall inherite the earth*: for that which they haue, ſhall bee ſweeter to them, then great riches of the vngodly; and it ſhall multiply alſo when God ſeeth good. So that it might make one to maruell to ſee them who are counted Gods people, many times to run ſo greedily after the world,and the vaine allurements of it, in ſuch wiſe, that they go backe in grace as faſt, as though Gods caring for them were nothing like their owne; and as though they had forgotten that he promiſeth ſufficient wealth to a godly life, godlineſſe hauing the promiſes of things both earthly and heauenly; and yet ſo it is with them,that he who can catch faſteſt,imagines he ſhall ſpeed beſt: when all may ſee that they who ſeeke to be guided by God,haue beſt ſucceſſe and bleſſing, others going without it. But whereas they obiect, that they are richeſt for the moſt part who ſauour no goodneſſe; that ought to trouble no man,for full ſoone ſhall the riches of iniquity,and thoſe riches that cauſe it,right ſoone (I ſay) ſhall they betake them to their wings, and leaue the reconing behinde to bee made, by them who haue ill gotten and ſpent them, which ſhall be little to their liking: for know we this, that they are neuer to be counted bleſſings,without the grace of vſing them aright. Matth.5.5. 1.Tim.4.8.

THE ELEVENTH SERMON CONTINVED VPON THE SAME TEXT, Verſ. 2.3.

VERS. 2. *Ye ſhall make no couenant with the inhabitants of this land*, &c.

THe ſecond verſe now followeth, wherein the couenant in the behalfe of the people, is ſet downe, as it is on Gods behalfe in the former verſe. For a couenant is betwixt two parties at the leaſt. The points of their couenant are theſe two; one,that they ſhould make no league with the inhabitants of the land; the other,that they ſhould breake their altars downe. Then hee findeth fault with them, not for Idolatry wee ſee, (which as yet they had not fallen to) but for the not keeping of their couenant. And hauing clearly conuinced them,he expoſtulateth with them, and asketh them why they had done ſo, as if hee had been ready to heare their excuſe, Verſ.2.3. *The ſenſe. The couenant of the people with the Lord.*

excuse,if they could alleage any; if not,their sinne must needs be the greater. After this hee proceedeth to shew the punishments that should bee inflicted on them: and they were three. The first, that hee would not expell these nations for them: and what then? The other two arose from that: for it followed then, that they should abide still in the land, to the great hurt and annoyance of the of Israelites who dwelt there. And the two waies,as I haue said: first,that they should be as thornes to pricke them,and put them to paine: the other,they should be as snares, in which they should be taken,and caught with their sinnes: and when they should afterward fal to their Idolatry, they should most grieuously be punished.

These things being thus set downe, wee may obserue these foure things in these two verses: first their couenant with God: secondly, the conuicting them by the Angell, of breaking it: thirdly, the Lords expostulating
Doct.1. with them for it: fourthly, the punishment threatened for it. Concerning the first,in this that the people was bound to couenant with God, as he did with them, learne all of vs, that if wee will looke for benefit by Gods couenant made with vs,we must enter into couenant with him, and looke to bee faithfull in keeping it with him: which I speake not as though wee may claime any thing by due desert thereby, but that wee may know that God hath so appointed,and we ought to performe it accordingly. And though
Ier.31.31. God maketh promise here but of earthly benefits,yet in other places he couenanteth with his,to giue them heauenly also; as pardon of their sins, and life eternall,and he will most surely keepe promise in both. So although the godly are bound heere onely to some particular duties, yet in the generall couenant, they are vrged both to beleeue those things which God promiseth them,and also to walke before God continually in their whole course, wherein yet their failings are not reckoned against them, which by frailty they offend in: but if any will boldly tempt God, being carelesse in looking to their couenant; let such know that God will not bee mocked, their sinne will finde them out. And so vnderstand it of particular couenants, such as this was that God made heere with this people. If hee promise to blesse them in their marriage,earthly affaires and businesse, with such like,if they bee faithfull therein, as they couenant; then if they faile,and bee false-hearted,God is free from his word and promise.

Doct.2. The next thing in the couenant is, that God in forbidding them fellowship with those nations,and commanding them to pull downe their altars, on which they were wont to offer to their false gods,did thereby cut off occasion from them of committing Idolatry: teaching vs thereby, that if we will auoide the occasions of euill,we shall also be kept from the euils themselues, yea grosse sinnes; as idolatry, drunkennesse, adultery and the like, though we be very prone to commit them. And yet on the contrary, if we will not shunne the occasions of them,and the meanes that leade to them, we shall vndoubtedly fall into them. Take one for example,the most common of the rest. If we bee foolishly and vnbeseeming our profession snared with some woman, as hauing been caught by her eye lids, and taken with that which is precious in her; we must,to auoid the fowle and shamefull sin
Iob 31.5. of adultery; first with chast *Iob*,to make a firme couenant not to looke vpon her: secondly,neither talke of her,nor with her,whereby wee might easily nourish

nourish wicked lust and desires. And thirdly, come we not in her company if it may be, as godly *Ioseph* refused to doe, or at least looke wee not after her, Gen 39.10. neither let our thoughts linger nor carrie vs that way, but by feruent prayer be chased away farre from her, and then there is no feare of committing the sinne, or of falling into any further danger, for the word of the Lord hath spoken it. So I might say, many a man might haue eschewed murther, if hee could haue withdrawne his heart from wrath and reuenge; and so might many haue auoided oppression, and miserlinesse, if they could haue snibbed the first straying concupiscence and their vnlawfull desires after another mans commodity.

I propound these instances among the rest (not hauing time to speake of all, or many,) for that the diuell spiteth the seruants of God, and seeketh more specially these waies to bring his malice to passe, casting a blindnesse vpon them, that they shall hardly see, no not when they be in great danger, Note. till they be fallen into it, by being taken with the baite that he laid for them. Yea wofull experience hath made vs to see this to be too true: and they who haue broken out of this snare, know with what difficulty they haue escaped; and as for the common sort, who shew no great religion in their liues, there are few of them but are brought to shame, if opportunity serue, some of these waies, or be made to hang downe their heads by reason of guilty consciences; Note. and such mischiefe both the one and the other might haue auoided, and namely vncleannesse one of the foulest, if they could haue been perswaded to shunne the occasions thereof, in keeping out of the company of such as by whom they become besotted and impotent; and also if they could walke soberly in their particular callings by them, as hauing nothing to doe with them. So that we may see what good they get by their dalying, vnseasonable companying, and loose talking which they vse with women, which yet is one of the chiefe delights that the ciuill sort of men doe take, and yet they would thinke they should haue great wrong offered them, if they should be warned of it.

But to come more particulerly to this couenant which the heads of Israel must keepe toward the Lord, of casting downe their alters, and of hauing *Doct.3.* no fellowship with the Canaanites, they affoord a seuerall lesson. By the first that I mentioned, this may bee learned, that Christian Magistrates are by their authority to pull downe all Idols, and abolish superstition both Deut 7.5. of the infidels and heretickes, and the occasions of Idolatry, and to purge their dominions and iurisdictions from such drosse and abominations. (*Hezekiah* brake downe the brasen serpent being abused, and called it *Nehushton*, 2.King.18.4. that is, a peece of brasse.) And so much the rather, seeing Gods worship is simple and vncompounded, and hee that addeth thereto any superstitious ceremony, tainteth the substance as much as lieth in him. And all Christians ought to doe the same in their priuate houses, and places subiect to them, as their fields, farmes, Chappels, &c. And yet let them take heed, that they attempt not to doe so out of their callings, or in other mens houses, or other places where they haue no authority to meddle, vpon any deuotion or good intent (as they cal it) either to honor God, or benefit others, or though it were to winne the Idolaters themselues. For that course is not onely not ordained of God, to winne the Idolaters to sound religion, but also forbid-

den:

den: and other meanes, as the preaching of the word, conference, &c. are appointed to root the same out of mens hearts, and to turn them from such blind deuotion. The other may bee tearmed zeale, but vnaduised, corrupt and sinfull; neither of an wise Christian to be vsed. And this bee noted by occasion of the one part of the peoples couenant: namely, that they must pull downe their alters.

Doct.4. The other, to wit, that they should haue no fellowship with them, I haue spoken of before, chap 1. vers. last, saue onely that I spake not particularly of making marriages with Idolaters; which yet followeth by good and necessary consequent. For if a priuate Christian fearing God, may haue no familiar conuersing with such, then much lesse in marriage making with them, which is the nearest fellowship of all other. And so I briefly conclude

Deut.7.3. with the charge giuen by the Lord in Deuteronomie, *Yee shall make no marriages with them, neither giue thy daughter to his sonne, nor take his daughter to thy sonne.*

Doct.5. Now the messenger of God hauing told the people of the couenant which they were bound to, he shewes them their sinne, that they had broke their couenant; and conuicteth them of it saying: *ye haue not obeyed.* Which being so spoken to them, they could not deny it. And this Scripture teacheth, that men ought to bee conuinced of their sinne by the word of God, and to haue them so proued to be iust prouocations of God, which yet they liue in, as that they may not bee able to denie them; and all to the end they may the easilier be brought to repentance, and not onely told in preaching what is sinne, which I grant must be done; but as farre as may bee, they are to bee charged as guilty who are so: and to bee vrged as they haue giuen cause, so farre as that they may be pricked in their consciences, vnlesse their hearts be flintv, and so to say from their hearts, we haue sinned. And this is one principall point in preaching to be aimed at by Gods commandement

2.Tim.4.2. to *Timothy*, where it is said, *preach the word, in season and out of season, rebuke, conuince, and exhort with all lenity:* and this conuincing is most auaileable, (through Gods blessing) among other meanes to awake the drowsie conscience, and so to quiet and reforme it. This is that which our Sauiour fore-

Act.2.37. Ioh.16.8. telleth vs in Saint *Iohns* Gospell, that the spirit of God, that is, the power of the word inspired by the holy Ghost, and preached by his Apostles and Ministers after his resurrection, should conuince the world of sinne. So we reade in the second of the Acts, that *Peter* proued against the Iewes, and conuicted them in their consciences that they had crucified the Lord of glory who consented thereto. And it is said immediately following there, when they heard it, they were pricked in their hearts. Thus when *Dauid*

2.Sam.12. could easily yeeld to the truth generally set downe to him by *Nathan*, but could goe no further; namely, to see himselfe faulty, whose sinne reached to the heauens, the Prophet *Nathan* conuinced him, and told him, saying; *thou art the man* that hath dealt so cruelly and wickedly; and then hee could say,

2.Sam.24. 16.17. *I haue sinned.* So in Sam. 24. when God had shewed *Dauid* his sinnes, in numbring the people, he repented and yeelded. vers. 17.

Thus *Paul* dealt with the Romans, when he sought throughly to make odious to them their former ill course, *What fruit had yee* (saith hee) *in those things whereof ye are now ashamed?* their consciences bare them witnesse that they

that they had none. And as this kind of dealing with the people in our preaching is most profitable, and like to doe most good, so it is one of the hardest matters, namely, to rouze vp the conscience, and to conuince it. Profitable I say it is, for that if it be awaked and pricked, it cannot but acknowledge the sinne in all likelihood, and bleed and so relent for it, and craue pardon, and abandon it, which is the direct way whereby the holy Ghost guideth men to saluation: but if any be drowsie and sleepy conscienced, so that they be not moued by hearing any reproofes, or doe striue against the light of their owne conscience, being conuinced which is more, or wax hardened, which is worst of all, and a most vnkind abusing of that gratious worke of God in them: I bewaile their case, for they not onely receiue not any benefit thereby, but doe waxe worse, and so depart from God, so as they seldome returne to him againe (for the most of them) of which sort *Iudas* was, and some others. And yet these shifts men will vse when they are conuicted: for either they are not pricked, or struggle against it and seeke to shift it off; or else they are hardened by the deceitfulnesse of sinne; all which ought most carefully to be taken heed of. Note. Heb.3.12.

To returne therfore, it is profitable for the hearers to be oftentimes conuinced, and otherwise our ministery doth them little good, but so it is also hard to winde in with them, and to pierce their hearts, as I said; I meane to bring the hearers to this point, that they shall cry out and say, euery one for his owne part, I haue sinned. For concerning the ministers, who should bee one speciall meanes to doe it: they, for the most part abstaine from this worke altogether; either winding vp all in obscurity, that they are not vnderstood, or at least contenting themselues with the bare propounding of the truth, without applying it to the conscience, or discouering the corruption of the heart, that so the hearer may not escape. This worke they leaue to the peoples discretion. And alas they are so farre from working the word vpon themselues, that they haue many starting holes and excuses for their sinnes, and extenuate them, and alleage their owne infirmities, and other mens examples, so that though they be stricken by our preaching as with an arrow, yet they be harnessed and bumbaced in such wise, that they will shift off the blow, and not bee wounded thereby, but rather will follow their owne euill courses the more, and harden their hearts still, who may well set the best side outward (I denie not) and for a while carrie a faire shew, as though all were well with them, but God knoweth their harts, and let them be sure that their sinne shall find them out, and it shall not goe well with them in the end. The vse of this is, that we so looke to our selues in the whole carriage of our liues, that we feare not what may be said to vs, or brought against vs (so verifying the prouerbe, the righteous is bold as a Lion) and the rather seeing wee haue *iudged our selues, that wee may not bee iudged of the Lord*; and haue kept our consciences pure and good, to the end we may not feare conuincing of them, (for the word of God can offer no violence to them who offer it first to themselues) especially for any wilfull offending: but yet if for all this we be found too light, and in some things worthy to be blamed, (as who can looke so narrowly about himselfe but he may be iustly charged) or if wee breake out amisse, then our dutie is to desire that the word may challenge vs euen for that: and being conuinced of it, let vs wil- Note. Numb.32.23. Prou.28.1. 1.Cor.11.31. Note.

lingly and readily yeeld, wherby we shall free our selues from the iust blame of blockish, sleepy, of secure and obstinate hearers.

Doct.6. But now I passe from this conuincing of them by the messenger of God, to the expostulating with them for the breach of their couenant, saying: *Why haue ye done this?* As if he should say in the person of God to them, if ye can shew any reason why yee may doe thus, I giue you leaue, come forth, and make your answere: but the people answered not a word, in token that they held themselues guilty. This teacheth that God is equall and righteous in his proceedings, yea euen toward those who haue prouoked him: as he saith in the like case by his Prophet, to those that were the poste-
Esa.1.18. rity of this people heere mentioned, *come and let vs reason together,* &c. Hee
Note. doth not as men do, who will smite them who haue done them wrong before they shall know why; and are neuer willing to come to good conditions with them, how tractable soeuer they might finde them. These are indeed cruell and vnmercifull men, who will not offer any indifferency; the Lord (I say) dealeth not so; but offers to them who haue dealt trecherously and broken couenant with them; that if they can alleage any sound reason for their doings, yea euen from himselfe, as that hee hath dealt hardly with them, and hath been void of compassion to them, hee will heare them, and
Ier.12.1. giue them leaue to plead their owne cause. Which aduantage hee giuing
Psal.51. them, he doth stop all mouthes and is iustified himselfe, in all his words and workes.

Which makes greatly for the conuicting of all such as say like them in E-
Ezek.18.25. zechiel, *the Lords waies are vnequall,* and that he could haue kept them from such falles and dangerous estates thereby, as come vpon them. Where yet who seeth not, that hee hath set double hedge and ditch betwixt them and their sinnes; nay rather brazen wals, to the end they might not come neere
Note. nor commit them. Hee hath (to speake plainely) sent his Prophets among
Gen.2.17. them, to forbid and threaten them, euen as hee did to *Adam,* if hee should reach out his hand, and eate of the forbidden tree. Hee allureth and seeketh
Luk.15. to win them, and perswadeth them to imbrace the good way, and not to come neare the way of death and punishment; euen as hee seeketh them who are lost, but few of them will heare and come: so that he may say, what shall I doe more for this people: yea he may as well say to them, as hee did to the people by *Hosea* the Prophet, when he said; *O Ephraim, what shall I doe*
Hos.6.4. *vnto thee? O Iuda, how shall I entreate thee?* So that if any harden their hearts
See Iob 39. in such manner, to charge God for their sinnes, from which yet by no per-
37.38. swasions nor reasons they could bee reclaimed: nay for the maintaining wherof they haue shewed themselues rebellious and obstinate: know they, that while this Scripture and such other shall remaine to witnesse against them, they shall neuer bee able to finde the smallest ease by such cauiling, whereby they doe but as it were by patching new with old, make the rent worse.

And by this we may see, that we were not best to trust to our owne ima-
Iob 31.33. ginations, nor to follow our owne waies: neither to deale as *Adam,* to excuse our selues; nor to be like to them in the Gospell, who when they were bidden to the marriage, sent their answere as it pleased them, but so as it lit-
Luk.14.18. tle became them; for thereby wee wade but the deeper into danger, and beare

beare away more blowes, as it may bee ſaid of them that ſtriue againſt his chaſtiſements. For euery tongue that ſhal contend with him in iudgement he ſhall condemne. And this we may ſee if wee liſt, in that fearefull example of him that hid his talent in the earth, which he was commanded to put to vſe, and occupie it. Hee thought hee had reaſon enough to ſay for his defence, that hee knew him to bee an hard man of whom hee receiued it; and therefore would be ſure to returne him his owne againe. But what anſwere heard he? euen this, *Take the vnprofitable ſeruant, and caſt him into vtter darkeneſſe, there ſhall be weeping and gnaſhing of teeth.* Therefore we ſee by this, as alſo by our text, in that the people had nothing to anſwere, when a reaſon was demanded of them why they had done ſo; that when men haue followed their owne ſwinge, in ſinning as they haue deſired, they ſhall neuer bee able to anſwere any thing in their owne defence ſoundly, nor iuſtly; but to the further encreaſe of their ſinne, as I haue ſaid already, but ſhall bee tongue tied: wherupon it followeth, that which I haue proued, that the Lord hath ſo good right when he dealeth againſt ſinners, that entring into iudgement with them, hee feareth not to giue them all vantages that they thinke will ſerue their turnes: but in the end they ſhall ſee that they do but make themſelues thereby the more guilty. For by theſe meanes in giuing this people liberty to anſwere what they could, their ſinne was the more aggrauated againſt them, they hauing not ſo much as any colour to defend themſelues. And this being ſo, let vs learne hereby not to yeeld onely by ſilence, but to be humbled alſo and relent; and proceed on to true repentance: yea, let vs beware that wee haue no controuerſies with the Lord, by being bold to offend and prouoke him; thinking (though fooliſhly and falſly) to make a good end: for be we ſure we ſhall neuer make our part good againſt him: neither let vs ſinne in hope; for when wee are threatened puniſhment for the ſame, or when we ſhall be arraigned, we ſhall eaſily be found guilty, and the Lord ſhall be iuſtified, and then all our faire ſhewes muſt vaniſh, leauing vs in the briers. Eſa. 54. 17. Mat. 25. 30.

Thus we haue heard the people reproued for their ſin: now the threatning of the puniſhment followeth, which is ſharpe and ſore; and is ſet down in three points. The firſt is, that God would not expell their enemies, as hee had vpon condition promiſed: the ſecond, that their remaining ſtill in the land ſhould be as thornes in their ſides: the third, their gods ſhould bee as a ſnare to catch them in, to their deſtruction. Verſ. 3. *The ſenſe.*

And for the firſt of theſe puniſhments, namely, that God ſhould not expell the Canaanites, it is well to bee weighed what he meant by it, that wee may the better ſee what a puniſhment it was: Now his meaning in thus ſpeaking was this: for as much as yee haue not ſtood to your couenant to driue the nations out, but haue ſuffered them to remaine there ſtill; neither will I ſtand to mine, which was but conditionally made with you: ſo that wheras I promiſed to be with you, and ſtrengthen you, and to expell them for you as I haue begun to doe, now I will doe ſo no more. And what will follow of that? euen this, that if I doe it not, you ſhall not be able to doe it of your ſelues; for ye are too weake, as ye haue good proofe. And yet if they be not caſt out, they ſhall remaine to your deſtruction. This the Lord meant by ſaying that he would not caſt them out. *The firſt puniſhment.*

*Doct.*1. This first punishment teacheth vs this; that when we remoue not annoiances while we may, we shall not be able afterward, when we would. Now
Note. our greatest annoiances are euery mans speciall sinnes, euen as this one, their breaking off couenant with the Lord, was theirs. And when wee see some of the speciallest of these our sinnes, and what eye sores they be to vs, while our hearts goe after them, and what trouble and sorrow they bring with them to vs; and yet wee cast them not from vs, but still retaine them; it shall come to passe afterwards, that they shall get such strength in vs, that we shall not be able to depart and come out from them, no not then when wee would. For they shall so winde themselues into vs, and so draw our delights after them, especially through long lying in them vncontrolled, that wee shall become drunken with them, and besotted, so as wee shall be vtterly impotent, and not by our prayers or other meanes (if we vse any) be able to preuaile against them.

Note. Nay I say more, when God shall visit vs with sicknesse or otherwise, or when his word hath in speciall manner wounded our consciences, and feared vs with his displeasure for them; yet euen then wee shall not be able to breake off from them, and come out of loue with them; they haue so strongly and forcibly drawne vs after them, euen as an husband, a naturall man vpon his death-bed can hardly depart from the wife of his youth, whom he hath dearely loued. And if (as in that case it comes sometimes to passe) if, I say wee doe crie out of such sinnes in the anguish of our consciences, or when we thinke we shall die, (as such afflictions will search deepe, and (perhaps) constraine vs to vtter in our extremity and paine, some confessions of them, and dislikings, and to make purposes, while God holds vs (as it
Note. were) on the racke with promise and protestation, neuer to returne to them any more; yet it shall appeare, that euen those promises are but wrung from vs by force and feare, as *Sauls* confession was, when hee heard hee should lose his kingdome. For when Gods heauie hand shall once bee off, from wringing and paining either our minds or bodies, wee shall bee ready to runne to our old byas againe, as *Ahab* did after his rash and hasty putting on sackcloth, and to imbrace those and the like sins, with as great liking (that I say no more) as we did before.

Behold therefore what a bondage it is to bee deluded by, and ouercome of such base commanders, and what iniurie we doe our selues, when we fall into league with any speciall sinnes; and why doe wee not throughly and hartily dislike and set against them while they be as it were in the bud, and as yet but newly sprung vp in vs, and in their first alluring of vs? yea rather why did we not rather keep thē out at the first, so that they might haue had no such power ouer vs? For there is hope in the beginning of our acquaintance with them, to withstand and shake them off, if wee would set our selues to the purpose to doe it; namely, as the word of God teacheth vs, that is, with diligence and vprightnesse, knowing that wee should not lose our labour. Whereas if wee giue place to tentations, and foolish allurements, and doe not wisely and seriously withstand the beginnings thereof, wee bee not only in danger to become slaues to them afterward, and vnable to chase them away when we would, as I haue said; but also to prostitute our selues
Rom.13.13. to many other which are their companions, till wee finde that which this people

people found heere in expelling the Canaanites,that we cannot possibly be rid of them; or if some few doe,yet it is with exceeding difficulty. So that they are wise who giue not vp their members as weapons of sinne, but by faith set themselues to mortifie it betimes, after they haue attained sound hope to be saued: knowing that otherwise the strong man Satan will hold and keepe possession, if a stronger then hee come not, euen the Lord himselfe by his power to driue him out. Rom.6.13.

And yet if this bee well begun and attempted of vs, I thinke this caueat or watchword not vnprofitable, but necessary, that although wee haue got the vpper hand,and cast out the vncleane spirit,yet if we shall suffer (by our carelesnesse and sloth) this good worke to slake and to bee broken off, our enemie will make another assault vpon vs, and gather strength to recouer his possession againe. For though he be once driuen out, yet hee imbarkes himselfe (if he can get in againe,as he laboureth to doe) and stronglier keepeth the hold with double force and courage; nay seuen fold more then at the first he did, and then what will the end bee, all may see; to wit, though not worse then in the beginning, as it is with him,who did but goe about it,but did it not in deed, yet with exceeding difficulty and perill,though hee had expelled him before.

From hence it is, that many at this day, and those also of the forwarder sort,haue no courage in them to roote out sinne in their townes and families, seeing they entertaine the same in themselues. And if they attempt any such thing, yet they doe it but faintly,and soone leaue it off. And hereof it is, that numbers neuer grow to any great ripenesse in religion, I meane the practise of it,neither doe euer come to see the tenth part of the fruit of it in the comfort that it bringeth, because they are not wise to chase away those common sinnes, to the which they doe most lie open, nor doe but dallie with them,and neuer oppose themselues against them any thing hartily,especially any long time together. So that many liue in whoredome, in malice,in oppression,deceiuing,and the rest (for the most part) who are kept from reprochfull euils, yet liue but a dead and vncomfortable life, seeing they doe not resist offers to sinne, when they haue any made to them, as *Gedeon* did the kingdome, but seeke and hunt after them rather: and such a life hath small force in it to perswade others to repentance. And this of the first punishment. Note.

THE TWELFTH SERMON ON THE SECOND CHAPTER OF THE BOOKE OF IVDGES.

The ſecond puniſhment. NOw to proceed. The ſecond puniſhment threatned, to wit, that they ſhould bee thornes in their ſides, is next to bee weighed. Oh how fearefull is this? For what is more irkeſome, then continually, night and day, lying or going, to haue thornes pricking our fleſh? which muſt needs breed griefe vpon griefe, and ſorrow vpon ſorrow. And this came to paſſe afterward vnto this people of Iſrael, who were oft brought, as is manifeſt in this booke, and in the Scriptures following, to ſin after ſinne, and puniſhment vpon puniſhment, for ſuffering the Canaanites and Idolaters to liue amongſt them, and the Lord to bee prouoked, and the land defiled thereby. *Doct.2.* And in the large laying out of this puniſhment vpon the people of Iſrael, let it teach vs, that fellowſhip and familiarity with ſuch, and with prophane perſons will pricke our conſciences, as thornes our fleſh, *Note.* when wee muſt oft remember, that wee haue thereby not onely allowed them in their bad ſpeeches and examples, againſt our knowledge and conſcience, which will pricke and vexe vs afterwards if there bee any true feare of God in vs: but alſo, that we our ſelues be tainted by their fellowſhip, and not dulled onely in grace and gifts. But of this before.

This doctrine may alſo more generally be applied to all ſinnes which we ſhall ſuffer to lurke and lie in vs, they are as thornes in our fleſh afterwards. Howſoeuer in the committing of them, they be as ſweet and pleaſant baits, yet after, they become as choakes and bitter vomiting vnto vs. We may not thinke that their ending will bee as their beginning at the committing of them: when *Adam* ſhould eate the fruit forbidden, oh how the Serpent *Note. Gen.3.6.* baited it with pleaſantneſſe to the taſt, beautifulnes to the eye, but vnſpeakeable benefit to his fond perſwaſion, for that it ſhould bring with it the knowledge of good and euill, to make them like vnto God himſelfe. But when it was taſted of them, what gall or wormewood was euer like bitter vnto it? *2.Sam.11.2.* what thornes, did pricke the heart of *Dauid*, after that hee had been deceiued and ouercome with the bait that the diuell had laid to catch him withall? *Pſal.51.2.* what thornes, I ſay, did pricke him after, as in that Pſalme made by him doth liuely and plentifully appeare, and in ſome other which lay out his ſorrow, ſhame, anguiſh, doubting, and fearing that hee had loſt all grace, by hauing his deſire in committing of that ſinne. And it is the beſt that can bee ſaid of thoſe, who (hauing hauing had warnings and charges giuen them, to tie vp their vnruly affections, and outragious luſts, and not to dallie with the

the ſinnes that they haue been allured by) haue yet been ſo farre from regarding ſuch inſtructions, that they haue giuen ouer themſelues vnto theſe defilements. They haue, I ſay, found them thornes, as *Dauid* did, though few of them haue euer had the thorne plucked out of their fleſh, to diſquiet them no more, as he had; I meane to bee brought to ſound and kind repentance, as he was.

The third puniſhment was, that their gods ſhould bee ſnares vnto them. 3
A ſnare we know is ſet to take and catch the bird or conie vnawares, that ſo it may be killed at the pleaſure of him that ſet it. And ſo hee ſhewes them, that they not foreſeeing wiſely, that their not rooting theſe nations out, would proue a ioyning with them in the worſhipping of their gods, and ſo would become their deſtruction; for their ſo fooliſhly running into the ſnare, he ſhewes them, I ſay, that they ſhould be taken therein, and fall thereby, and by other noiſome ſinnes, into the hands of the Lord, who would ſcourge them grieuouſly, one generation after another, till they ſhould periſh out of that good land. And euen ſo it came to paſſe, and they found all true that was told them: for to thoſe enemies to whom they had moſt wickedly ioyned themſelues in league; they were often in ſubiection and bondage, and thereby ſpoiled of all their goods, liberties, and bleſſings, and afterward caſt out of the land among the Babylonians and Aſſyrians.

And by this wee may ſee, that by idolatrous and wicked company keeping wee haue ſnares ſet for vs, to bring vs in fellowſhip with them in their fowleſt ſinnes. For ſo the Lord hath ſaid, if wee will conuerſe and haue fellowſhip with them, by making of marriages, and eating with them, wee ſhall alſo fall to their faſhions, and partake with them in their ſinnes as this people did. For great is the force of friendſhip, to draw vs to that which wee neuer intended; nay againſt which we reſolued to keepe our ſelues. And who is ſtrong enough among vs to withſtand all the allurements & perſwaſions of carnall friends (wee being oft in their company) who haue ſo many waies to draw and allure vs, but that one time or other he ſhall bee conſtrained to yeeld, or if he ſhould not, how can he beare al the diſlikes, frownings, diſpleaſures, and hard handlings, with the which hee ſhall bee ſet vpon and purſued? And we ſee as much: and the remedie is, to refraine their companies and neare fellowſhip with them altogether; and yet although we do ſo, and thereby bee free from danger on that ſide, yet wee muſt know, that without as great care had to keepe our liues free from all other offences, wee ſhall ſome other way lie open to ſome of them, whereby as great danger is like to enſue. And by this gather, that wee ſhould neither bee idle nor vnprofitable in the acknowledgement of Chriſt, if wee ſeeke to proſper. But ſeeing we behold the practiſe and vnwearied labour of the bad and popiſh ſort, to winne men to their vngodly courſe, this one thing I muſt adde more particularly: Let vs that profeſſe our ſelues Chriſtians, be aſhamed to bee ſo careleſſe and ſlothfull in the companies where we come, to draw and moue men to faith and repentance, and to ſtirre vp better perſons to loue and to good workes, and through ſelfe loue ſo to pleaſe our ſelues in rotten talke as we doe. And this be ſaid of the puniſhments.

[Exod.23.32. — Note. — 2.Tim.3.5. — 1.Theſ.5.11. — Heb.10.24.]

Now I haue ſet downe the words of Gods meſſenger, whereby hee ſought to turne the people from their ſinnes, vnto God by repeating his benefits, *Obiect.*

nefits, and by reproofes and threats. I should heere haue ended with his speech, but that I see an occasion of propounding an obiection and doubt, will be taken from hence. For which cause I will set it downe and answere it, before I goe to any new matter. The obiection is this, seeing the messenger of God mouing them to repentance, doth with his reprouing and conuicting them, make no mention of faith, it may seeme that faith was not of such price then as it is now, no mention being made of it, or if it were, that the people might be driuen to desperation rather, then brought to repentance, being not encouraged to beleeue the pardon of their sin, as well

Answ. as to forsake it. To the which I answere; first, that they could not be moued to repentance, if they had not had with all encouragement & perswasion to beleeue: for though hee name not faith expresly, yet seeing repentance and that cannot be separated, neither could repentance therefore be vrged vpon them without it. Secondly, I say, this people did repent, as it is cleere by the text; therefore they also beleeued. And thirdly, the messenger repeating Gods promises to them; what doth he but finde fault with them for not beleeuing the same before? I conclude therefore, that hee moued them to beleeue, which is the chiefe thing in our turning to God. And so let all bee perswaded, though it bee not alwaies expressed, euen as it was said to the

Act 16.31.34. Iaylor, when hee asked what hee should doe to bee saued; beleeue in the

Heb.11.6. Lord Iesus. And as without faith it is impossible to please God; so let it bee looked vnto principally, that we rise vp, and lie downe, and walke accompa-

1.Ioh.5.4. Vers.4.5. nied with that, for so we shall resist the tentations, allurements, and discouragements, with other difficulties of this life.

The sense. This being thus answered, now I proceed to the second point in this first part of the chapter, and that is the fruit of the sermon that the people reaped by it, which was repentance, and that is set downe in these two verses, not in expresse words, but by signes thereof, and those are set downe to bee three. The first was, that *they lifted vp their voice*; the second, *they wept*; the third, *they offered sacrifice*. By the lifting vp of their voice, wee can conceiue no other thing, but that they heartily confessed their sinnes, and cried out of them, which they heard to haue been reproued by Gods messenger, and craued pardon of them, accusing themselues. They being guided therein by God, as the Prophet *Hosea* in his time taught the people, that in repenting they should take to them words, as well as to haue a good heart. By their weeping, they signified deepe griefe conceiued for displeasing God, and prouoking his wrath against them. And their weeping was so great, that the place took the name thereof, and was called *Bochim*, that is, a place of weepers, and by their sacrifice they declared their faith, that their sinne was pardoned. For the sacrifices were shadowes of Christs death; and they in offering them, beleeued as the fathers of those times did, they constantly beleeued (I say) that all their sinnes were forgiuen by the death of Christ, resembled by the offering of them. To the which also there is no doubt, but

Hos.14.3. that they added thankes, as the Lord directed the people in *Hosea* to doe in the repentance which hee required of them; which also was resembled by their peaceofferings.

Now to examine these things more perticularly, this doctrine of repentance which heere occasion is offered to speake of, I will the briefier passe

ouer

ouer, seeing I haue spoken largely of it in other Sermons, though not in this booke, saue onely so farre as the words require somewhat to bee said. And first, seeing the hearing of that sermon did worke so good things in the people, I meane many of them, and bring forth such fruit, wee are taught not onely to pray the Lord of the haruest to send such labourers into the haruest, as may bee able and fit to bring home the Lords haruest; but also what we should doe when wee heare such diuine sermons, and doctrine as this was which the messenger of God heere preached vnto them, which do vrge our consciences by laying out our sinnes: for all doctrine is not of that argument. I grant we ought by all doctrine to be moued, according to that which wee heare, and as occasion is offered, either to griefe or to comfort: but when wee are more specially taught the doctrine of repentance, wee should follow the example of these heere mentioned, who cried out of their sinnes, and mourned deepely, and craued pardon. And likewise of other that did the same; as the people that came after these, when they heard *Samuel* reprouing them, lamented after God; and they who are mentioned in the booke of the Acts, at *Peters* sermon, *were pricked in their hearts*, and sought comfort. So (I say) should wee doe, I meane, both such as haue repented already, to renue it, and such also as are yet to enter vpon it. And it is fearefull when these fruits may be seene in them and others, that so many among vs, hearing the like sermons, can goe vntouched in their consciences. and with drie eyes or harts: for though these be not sufficient, yet with faith they are commendable.

Doc vers.4. and 5.

1.Sam.12.1.

Act.2.37.

Secondly, and more principally heere, as this people lifted vp their voice and wept, when they were reproued for the abuse of Gods benefits, and for breaking of their couenant, by Gods messenger: so among all other good instructions (which are infinite) we should be greatly moued and sore grieued, when wee shall heare that wee are iustly charged by preaching, for the like faults; as for the ill vsing of the blessings which God hath bestowed vpon vs, and for breaking the couenant which wee haue made with him, because these two ought to be so thorowly minded of vs daily, that wee should giue no iust cause to be rebuked for the neglecting of either of them. For what doe we in our liues commendably, if these two bee wanting, and neglected of vs, I meane if we doe not bind our selues by couenant, to bee more fruitfull in dutie, and more cheerefully to go about the same, while we see Gods benefits continued to vs, whereby he doth (as it were) hire vs thereunto? And secondly, if we make not new couenants with him from time to time to walke constantl in our vprightnesse, rather then to deserue iust rebuke for breaking and looking loosely to the old? But if wee haue due regard of both these, from time to time, wee shall both keepe all other parts of our liues within compasse the better, and also we shall not need to feare that we can sustaine any sharpe reproofe iustly, (which is euer vnwelcome to flesh) for the same.

Doct.2.

Note.

But yet further, to say somewhat more perticularly of these three signes of their repentance; we must know, that the inward graces which are testified by the outward signes thereof heere set downe, are rather to be sought of vs in our repentance, as relenting and melting of the heart for offending God, humiliation, faith, and the like; then the outward signes themselues;

the

the last especially, as the offering of sacrifice, both expiatorie, to seeke forgiuenesse of sinnes, and eucharisticall, representing their thankes, which were meerely ceremoniall, and proper to the Iewes; therefore not now to be vsed of vs; and yet in them laudable, this ceremony being then in vse to expresse their faith and beleeuing in Christ, and their thankesgiuing, as we doe simply offer to God both, and without them. This be said of their offering sacrifice first, though mentioned last. The other two, of lifting vp their voice, and weeping, are alwaies to bee aimed at in our repentance, but can-
Note. not alwaies be attained, neither are therefore of necessity to bee vrged, nei-
*Doct.*3. ther to be rested in if we haue them. For the first of them; namely, the lifting vp the voice in prayer and confession of sin, and accusing of our selues, it is required by the Prophet *Osea*, of such as could shew it: for in vrging the
Hos. 14.2. people at that time to repent, saying, *O Israel, returne to the Lord thy God*, hee addeth: *take vnto you words, and say vnto him, take away all iniquity and receiue vs graciously, and we will offer the calues of our lips*, &c. But all cannot expresse their minds in words; as namely, the ignorant, especially some of them, and some in the bitternes of their hearts powre out their prayers without words
1.Sam. 1.13. at some time, as *Anna* did. Therefore if it may be, and that also it be most expedient (as if it may be an helpe to quicken vs in feruency) the voice is to be lifted vp, but not alwaies of necessity to be inioyned.

*Doct.*4. Now concerning weeping, which they also heere are said to haue adioyned, it being a further degree of sorrow then many can attaine vnto, it is not of necessity to bee imposed vpon vs, (as I haue said) as though repentance could not be without it: though where it can be, and accompanieth repentance, it doth more deepely search into the heart, satisfie the party so moued, and quiet the mind, which was before troubled and vnsetled. This I haue thought good to say of their outward signes of repentance. And seeing they were set downe to testifie the same in the people, therefore all may see that this repentance must be euer found in vs, whether any of the signes bee
The summe of repentance briefly. present or no. And the points thereof are these; that the heart bee deepely pricked for sinne, that it bewaile the same, as purposing neuer to turne to it or the like againe: which is all that can bee for the present time, and that
*Doct.*5. there bee yet for all this aggrauating of the sinne, a beleeuing according to the promise of God, that it is all freely remitted by God through Christ, which more or lesse quieteth the heart: and if that beleeuing be there, it wil purge it from dead workes also afterward, and keepe it from sinning any more, in such manner as it did in former times, the heart and whole man being sanctified already through beleeuing. And this is the substance of repentance, which we are to practise by the example of this people, as also of
Ier. 31.18. Hos. 14.2 3. many other in the Scripture; as in *Ieremy*, *Hosea*, and diuers other.

Obiect. But heere may a doubt arise about the repentance of the people, that it may seeme not to haue been such as it hath bin set downe to be. For if they repented at this time, why did they not bring forth fruits of amendment? whereof this was one, yea a chiefe one; to wit, that they should after this, haue rooted out the idolatrous Canaanites, they being now so sharpely reproued for that they had not done it before, but rather made leagues with them, when yet that making of peace with them, was one of the chiefe sins that was laid to their charge? and in all sound repentance, the sins bewailed,

acknow-

acknowledged,and repented of,must needs be amended (wee know) in the persons. For answere hereto, it is to bee thought,that the Lord held backe strength and courage from them, so that they could not fight against them, prosperously,as they had done in the daies of *Ioshua*. And this he did,to the end they might beare that as a mark of their sin and disobedience. For God, according to his accustomed maner,did receiue them into his fauor, when they repented : but hee did not by and by restore againe to them the other particular gifts, which for their iust deserts hee had taken from them ; as strength of body, and courage of minde, they hauing both been abused of them before,neither necessary to saluation. *Answ.*

Which thing is most needfull for vs to marke for our great benefit : For euen so he dealeth at this day,as he did in former times, and with that people. So hee dealt with our first parents after their fall : for though they repented,and were receiued againe into fauour, yet the euils and discommodities which they brought vpon themselues and mankind, did not the Lord take away ; neither was that quiet and sweet abode of theirs in Paradise, enioyed of them at any time after. So *Sampson* lost the gift of his bodily strength for a time, after hee had so greatly displeased God ; which I might say of many other,to wit,that they lost the vse of such graces as before they enioyed. And so doubtlesse,such as after a commendable profession of the Gospell,when they had before been truly conuerted to God by faith and repentance, did fall againe to their old sinnes,or to drowsinesse and coldnes in his seruice ; such, I say, haue found and receiued the like measure at his hands,as most cleare experience hath been hereof in this late deceased generation,and in some who still remaine of them ; whose first zeale and loue which they had at their first receiuing the Gospell, being after slaked, hath neuer after been as it was, recouered. For though they haue seene their falles,and repented, and obtained mercy, yet the Lord hath left a marke of that their sinne behind, both to minister and people, so that they haue rarely recouered their former zeale, the one in feruent preaching, and care taking ouer the people, the other in cheerefull profession, vprightnesse of heart,and holy walking ; but haue limped in some sort afterwards, and they doe come short of the grace they had before ; the which the Lord hath suffered to put them in remembrance of that their sin ; euen as a man hauing fallen from an high beame or tree, and broken his bones, though hee get them set together againe,so that they may serue the turne in some sort,yet he neuer feeles them perfectly cured, but euer painfull and lame afterward, or much impaired. Note. Note. *A simile.*

And to adde one instance more ; such as after they truly repented haue fallen into adultery, or any such hainous crime, though they haue risen againe out of it,and giuen good testimony thereof, although they come to be truly perswaded,that it is forgiuen them,yet what vnquietnesse doe they oft finde within themselues, what shame and holding downe of the head doth it cause outwardly before men, whereby they are much appalled and held backe,in respect of that they might haue been, from good doing : besides,how many of the louers of the truth are strong enough to receiue them as they did before,(though it be their sinne that they doe not) and as freely to communicate with them euery way ; but are much estranged from them, Note.

and

and hardly conceiue of them, whereby it may bee seene, that their credit is much impaired thereby among men, although they bee still in fauour with God, as *Dauid* and others were. The which the Lord in his prouidence doth to them, and such like, to keepe them in awe, who are so ready to breake out againe, and that all may see how God detesteth sinne, euen in his owne, and also that hee may thereby stir vp more serious repentance, and constant holding on in that course, and that they bee not led away from it by the errour of the wicked, in such as are brought into the right way already.

That which hath been said of this point, (that I may teach a further vse of it) ought to prouoke al such as by the grace of God are kept from such reprochfull sinnes, to yeeld continuall thankes to God for it, (which it is to be feared, is much neglected) as well as for other benefits, which giue them iust cause to doe the same. But if any lie in knowne and offensiue crimes, and yet

Note. can cnnningly keepe them from mens eyes, and looke no further; let such know they are worse then the worst I haue spoken of, whose sins yet haue broken out before men. And seeing the best may fall possibly, and that dangerously, and so doing are sure that their sinne will finde them out, and that they shall smart accordingly; let the other much more thinke that God will vnskirt and vnuizor them to their shame, in his good time, and let the best count it no lost nor needlesse care to keepe themselues well while they are well, I meane, free from notorious and knowne sinnes, and let them endeauour to giue good example without wearinesse, that so they may bee free from such fearefull offences. And this be said of the peoples repentance.

Doct. 6. To all the former instructions out of these two verses, this I adde, that if the bitter weeping of the people there, caused the place to take the name from thence, so that to this day it is retained, and is called a place of weeping: and further, we see how long the remembrance of it is kept for many yeeres after: then it doth strongly commend to vs, what care we should haue while we liue, to possesse the generations comming after vs, of good examples giuen by vs among them that liue with vs, which may doe good when we are gone: either Ministers by their diligent and feruent preaching, and godly liuing; or the people in more then ordinary receiuing the message of the Gospell with thanksgiuing, and other commendable fruits following. The place of such inhabitants, whether it receiue a name from such things done there, as this *Bochim* did heere, or no, it is not so materiall. But this is to bee thought, that the remembrance of such good things done them, might harten and encourage many that shall come after them, not in that place onely, but also in many other, to follow such examples. But whether they doe or no, this is too true; that no vile actions shall bee done to leade the people from God and goodnes, no disorder, I meane vnruly behauiour, and reuell rout keeping; but their example shall bee taken vp (to be sure) not onely of them that haue seene them; but also of them who shall come after them, hauing heard of them, and be made customes, if not petty lawes among themselues, as the custome of spending the twelue daies at the Natiuity, &c. doth too truly testifie. And thus I end.

THE

THE THIRTEENTH SERMON ON THE BOOKE OF IVDGES.

The second part of the Chapter.

VERS. 6. *Now when Ioshua had sent the people away, the children of Israel went euery man into his inheritance to possesse the land.*

7. *And the people had serued the Lord all the daies of Ioshua, and all the daies of the elders that outliued Ioshua; which had seene all the great workes of the Lord that he had done for Israel.*

8. *But Ioshua the sonne of Nun, the seruant of the Lord died, when hee was an hundred and tenne yeeres old.*

9. *And they buried him in the coasts of his inheritance, in Timnah-heres in mount Ephraim, on the north side of mount Gaash.*

10. *And so all that generation was gathered vnto their fathers, and another generation arose after them which neither knew the Lord, nor yet his workes which he had done for Israel.*

11. *Then the children of Israel did wickedly in the sight of the Lord, & serued Baalim.*

12. *And forsooke the Lord God of their fathers, which brought them out of the land of Egypt, and followed other Gods, euen the gods of the people that were round about them, and bowed vnto them, and prouoked the Lord to anger.*

13. *So they forsooke the Lord and serued Baal and Ashteroth.*

NOw followeth the second part of the chapter to the end; which also containeth the summe of the rest of the second part of the booke vnto the 17. chapter, and setteth downe the estate of the children of Israel vnto the death of *Sampson*, and that was after this manner. 1. The people prouoked God by their sinnes. 2. God punished them for them, and that by other nations. 3. He raised vp Iudges to them: and 4. When they cried vnto him deliuered them. 5. After that they brake forth and fell to Idolatry againe. And this was their estate all the time that passed till the acts mentioned in the 17. chapter, as is shewed by perticular examples through all the chapters before that, beginning in the third. But if any see reason not to consent that these verses in this second part of this chapter doe lay forth the summe of the second part of the booke in generall, it maketh no great matter. He must yet grant, that in them is set downe the estate of the people generally at the time after *Ioshuas* death, who knew not the Lord: and in the chapters following, more perticularly; vnto the *The sense.*

seuenteenth chapter. The distinct matters in this second part of the chapter are these fiue now mentioned. 1. Their sinne. 2. Their punishment. 3. Their crying to God. 4. Deliuerance. 5. Their reuolting. The first of them was their sinne, the which is set downe from the eleuenth verse to the fourteenth, with the occasion that they tooke to fall in that manner, and that is from the sixth verse to the eleuenth. And the occasion was the death of *Ioshua*, and other good gouernours heere mentioned, that outliued him: for though in their time the people serued the Lord, as heere it is said, yet after them arose another generation that knew not the Lord, and then they forsooke him. Of these now as it followes in order.

And first let vs consider what is said of *Ioshua*, then of the people, and lastly of them both. Of *Ioshua* first in his life, and so come to his death; then of the people after his death. In that it is said of him that he had sent the people away to their inheritance, before he died; as it is recorded, Iosh. 24. it causeth a question to bee moued, why hee had called them together before his death; that appeareth in the chapter mentioned now, throughout vnto the

Iosh.24.28. 28. verse: and it was to this end, to rehearse Gods benefits to them, and to exhort them to serue the Lord, and this was a little before his death, at which time also he renewed a couenant betwixt the Lord and the people: the like to which we reade that *Iehoida* did betwixt the Lord, and *Ioash* the

2.King.11.17. King And so did *Nehemiah*, *Iosiah* and other, whose rare & godly example is

*Doct.*1. set forth most clearly and liuely, to be a patterne to all Christian magistrates,

In vers.6. euen the highest, how they should count it their greatest honour to honour the Lord among the people, and cause them to doe so likewise; to aduance his true worship also, and therefore to see true and sound doctrine taught and not to suffer superstition, nor false opinions to bee thrust vpon the Church: and to prouide, as neare as may be, that the people may know, that they doe not require these things of them for fashion, but in sincerity; and

Heb.11.6. that seeing the Lord is a plentifull rewarder of them that seeke him: therefore they must not thinke themselues discharged, in that they prouide for the outward peace of the people only (wherein yet they doe very commendably) but that they may liue godly also; because vnder God they are the

Custodes vtriusque tabulæ. maintainers and preseruers of both tables. And the best that they can yeeld the Lord for aduancing them is, to serue him in feare themselues, and *kisse*

Psal.2.11. *the sonne*, and prouide that others may doe so, and that without disturbance, by them that are corrupt in their religion, and profane. And thus they are to goe before them zealously, and faithfully in their owne practise, as this

Iosh.24.15. noble man *Ioshua* heere did, professing it openly that hee would doe so, say-

Deut.17.19. ing, whatsoeuer other doe, *I and my house will serue the Lord.* And that then and now these things might the better bee done, the Lord commandeth in

Deut.34.11. Deuteronomie, that the highest in authority should be studious in the book of God. All the forementioned things did *Moses*, who gouerned the people before *Ioshua*: who both are to bee followed in their religious course; because experience hath alwaies taught vs, that if the chiefe rulers bee zealous and religious, the inferiours will embrace piety and godlinesse likewise; at least, not be against it. And contrariwise: but if they should not, yet the people must themselues walke with God.

*Doct.*2. And thus did *Ioshua* send the people away, as it is said in the text, and with gracious

gracious words exhorted them, and ſpake to them when hee was readie to die; as in the forementioned chapter of *Ioſhua* appeareth, that hee might leaue his laſt words ſo fruitfull among them, that their print might remaine in them after his death, euen as it did. And ſeeing he ſent them away in this manner, wee ſhould know, that it becommeth meaner perſons much more to do ſo; I meane, to giue exhortation to their children, ſeruants, and neighbours, if they haue freedome from paine, which often times hindreth right good men, and this is the beſt memoriall that they can leaue behinde them at their death. There ſhould be a wiſe putting of the houſe in order, & a ſetting of mens eſtates at a ſtay before death come, as *Hezechiah* was willed by the Lord to doe; a chiefe part whereof is this giuing of exhortation: and this ſhould be; both that the minde of the viſited partie may bee eaſed and at quiet, and to preuent all trouble among thoſe that remaine behinde. For if this be not done before ſickneſſe) as commonly it is neglected, it had need to be then gone about with all ſpeed. But whiles this dutie ought to bee performed, of vſing good ſpeech to the ſtanders by, how many are there who are ſcarce able or willing to take direction themſelues, when they lie vpon their death bed? ſo farre are they from bequeathing gracious counſell and exhortation to others, and all becauſe they ſought no ſuch matter in the daies of their peace, health, and liberty, nor deſired that their family ſhould. And this bee ſaid of *Ioſhua*; now of the people, according to the diuiſion made before, in the entring into this verſe. They being now ſent away, went euery man to his inheritance, as it had been before diuided to them by *Ioſhua*, and ſo reſted at home in peace, after their many hard battailes and troubles. Thus the Lord dealeth with his people, that for a time they finde hardneſſe, and afterward deliuerance and peace; as after a ſtorme commeth faire weather. Thus *heauineſſe endures for a night, but ioy commeth in the morning*. We all ſhunne trouble, and it is of it ſelfe grieuous and vnwelcome; but herein we are much faulty, that as tedious as it is, few of vs lay to auoide it aright, by eſchewing the ſinnes that cauſe it: but rather bring it vpon our ſelues by our raſh attempts, and other wilfull, careleſſe, and bad doings; whereas we might be free from many troubles, if wee could take counſell of God in our matters, and ſtoope to his gouernment. And for example, it may be ſaid, wee prize not outward peace (to liue ſafely and quietly in our houſes) at any high reckoning, in which eſtate yet wee might doe much good; but we trifle out our precious time at leaſt, if we bee not worſe occupied; whereby, when wee raiſe trouble againſt our ſelues, wee take not the beſt way commonly to goe through it cheerefully, and meekely committing our way to God wholly, by doing all the good we can, and ſo waite vpon him patiently, for a good iſſue.

2 King. 20. 1.

Doct. 3.

Pſal. 30. 5.

Pſal. 37. 3.

Now after the people were ſaid to bee ſent away, it is further ſaid, that they ſerued God while *Ioſhua* and other godly gouernours liued. Oh therefore how happy a thing it is to enioy ſuch? For much helpe, encouragement and eaſe the inferiours haue by them (they bearing the burthen off from the ſholders of the other being more weake and vnfit thereto) who if they were not they muſt beare it themſelues. For when the people haue by their meanes the Goſpell purely preached, and liue ſafely vnder their vine and figge tree, as they did in the daies of *Salomon*, with the liberty to ex-

Verſ. 7.

Doct. 1.

See more of this in chap. 1. ver. 1. Doct. 1.

1. King. 9.

change and vtter their commodities and wares,little doe they weigh it, for the most part,what a benefit it is,who doe commonly enioy these blessings by the kinde,wise,and religious care of their gouernours.So to come lower euen among our selues, they who liue vnder inferiour guides,as people of the meaner sort vnder godly headburrowes and guides in their townes,
Note. who haue great encouragement to Christian duty by them, together with good example,rather then checkes taunts,and discouragement (which many feele in bad townes) oh how sweet a liberty doe they enioy that can prize it aright? what a furtherance to godlinesse? So to be in a religious and well ordered familie,where God and his true seruice is chiefly regarded,it is a corner of heauen in respect of other houses, though there want not in them many bodily comforts.

And if such a thing bee set downe heere of the people to their commendation and their gouernours also,and for vs to behold and thinke vpon,that while such liued together, the one was well guided by the other, and God religiously serued of both; then let all such as enioy the benefit of good and Christian gouernment, in house, or out of house, especially in both, fall downe before the Lord,and acknowledge it to his great praise,and the binding of themselues vnto him. and pray earnestly that they may giue good testimonie of it,by seeking to be setled in the feare of God, and to grow vp in faith,knowledge,and grace thereby. I know it is no common thing either to finde the one or the other, but where any are vnder the authority and wing of godly guides,let them make account that it is their summer season,
Note. not like the winter snuffes and brunts. And as for such as fauour not good dwellings, but rather shunne them, as *Esau* did good marriages, I deny not but they may hold vp their head with the highest, and beare out matters with the bigest, and shift to get a share in the pleasures of sinne for a season; but they are as farre from true happines as they are from spirituall and sound comfort,though few haue eares to heare it, till they smart by it. Now further,for people that liue vnder a good ministry,(to say a little of them,*Moses* his being among the people,doth wofully prognosticate, vnto what a passe they are like to grow, if they had elbow roome. For though none might liue happilier then they, yet who (for the most part) doe lesse looke after it? for as they in *Moses* absence from them but fortie daies, made themselues a calfe to worship: euen so the people are so brutish in these daies,and disordered, euen while their faithfull pastors liue with them, that the greatest part of them,take no good by them: what did I say? nay they liue most offensiuely vnder them. A signe of a wofull condemnation ready to come vpon them,all may see it is in their so doing, for louing darkenesse,
Ioh.3.19. in the cleare light of the Gospell more then it. And though some of them who are more subtill doe carrie the matter more closely, yet they are restrained by necessity or shame, not reformed by grace, and the power of the word. And let others who are not so bad,and yet not brought to true repentance,let them (I say) make better vse of such helpes while they enioy them, as they did in the Acts of the Apostles, and especially let them see that all bee well betwixt God and them; yea and let them get furniture of grace to vphold them afterward also, lest too late they lament, that they tooke no
1.Sam.28.11. good by them, and bewaile the want of them (as *Saul* did *Samuel*) when

when there is no helpe.

But heere in as much as we see these people held out in Gods seruice but for a time,and that was, while they had good gouernours and ouerseers liuing with them: it auaileth much therefore to obserue in our selues what it is that maketh vs embrace religion, and what is the chiefest thing that causeth vs to hold on the same. (A worthie point for all to learne, and namely such as pretend they loue the Gospell) it much concerneth vs (I say) to know and be assured whether it be fauour of men,commodity,credit,example, or other outward respect, which moueth vs to professe any thing more zealously then some other doe, or whether for conscience sake, in that God commandeth vs so to doe,and for the fauour and sweetnesse that wee finde therein, and in the Gospell which wee heare. For euen thereafter shal our welfare,prosperity,and perseuerance be. For if wee haue tasted how good the Lord is, and haue found that hundred fold that is promised, and verefied in vs which is written in the Psalme, that *a day in Gods house is better to vs then a thousand else where*; then we may know that wee haue builded vpon a rocke,and our building shall stand,and till we meet with a better booty then that,and may serue a better master then the Lord is (which shall neuer be) wee will keepe close to him, and count his seruice to bee perfect freedome. And to such as demand of vs whether wee will continue and hold on in a godly course,or goe backe,as Christ demanded of his Disciples, we shall be able to answere with *Peter: whither shall wee goe?* wee are in the way to eternall life,and we will not change our Christian course for any other. Otherwise it is not enough to boast of our loue to God, and to say [Lord, Lord] when yet we will take no paines throughly to gage our harts and to see our affection well ordered, that so good life may follow.

Doct.2. Mat.19.29. Psal.84.11. Match.7.24. Ioh.6.68.

Now while the holy Ghost speaketh of the people, how they followed the Lord all the daies of *Iosbua,* and the godly elders; hee stayeth a while about them,giuing them this testimony, *that they had seene the workes of God which he had done among them:* meaning that they had not barely looked vpon them but obserued,and (as *Mary* did the words of the Angell) had laid them vp in their hearts to consider them. For what profited it then otherwise to see them? For there is no doubt, but that there were many more aliue at that time, who had seene the miracles and great workes which the Lord had wrought in placing them in Canaan; but they were not worth the naming, seeing they had not also made vse of them; but these had seen them in another manner, so that they acknowledged the Lords power and goodnesse toward them thereby; declaring that to be the cause of their constant seruing of God, and cleauing to him, euen because they had seene them. And it is no lesse (doubtlesse) then a great cause of the godlinesse of them that haue any in them; namely, that they are such as haue seene and weighed Gods wonderfull acts, as his mercy and gracious working by the power of the Gospell in themselues or other; as also for that they haue had proofe of his mighty vpholding of thẽ in a good course against all aduersary power of the prince of darkenes,and his band. In like manner this hath hartened them to duty not a little,for that as they haue seen it alwaies to go well with them while they feared the Lord, and departed from euill; so they haue seene the heauie hand of God to haue been against others, that

Doct.3. Luk.1.38. Luk.2.51. Note.

haue peruerted their waies, & followed a bad course; so that although they haue prospered heere for a season, yet when God in his due time hath blowne vpon their visored felicity, they haue wanzed away in his displea-
Eccles.7.15.17. sure. This *Salomon* commendeth to vs in his example, who professeth that it was his practise to behold and consider all things (not impertinent matters as a busie bodie, but profitable) and especially the courses and issues of the righteous and wicked. By which meanes hee attained to great experience and wisedome, both to guide himselfe and others. Euen as his father *Dauid* did also; saying, that he was made wiser then the ancient, because he considered such things. But this meditating of Gods wonderfull workes; and namely this one, the greatest of other, how he hath appointed to saue some from vtter perdition, and letteth others goe on in their sinnes, though it be a strong motiue to draw men to God, yet (with griefe it may be spoken) it is vtterly wanting among most men. Their hearts are set on follie and vanity. He that hath liued to see many laid in graue, hath scarce a thought that hee shall follow, and goe the way that all haue gone before him in. As for that
Luk.13.3. they heare, that *except they repent they shall all perish*, although they know their hearts are hardened, so that they neither can repent nor haue the least desire after it; yet they crie peace, peace, as though all were safe. So that it may now iustly be complained of, which *Salomon* hath long agoe bewrayed, that
Prou.17.24. the fooles eyes are in euery corner of the world; meaning that they are busying themselues any way needlesly, and amisse; but as for things out of the
2.Pet.1.9. world or aboue it, that is (as Saint *Peter* speaketh) a farre off, their eyes are sore and pur-blind, they cannot looke after them; and as the Prophet spea-
Ier.4.22. keth, they are wise to doe euill; but to doe well, they haue no knowledge. The Lord himselfe bewaileth this brutishnes in men, that like vnreasonable creatures they minde onely that which is present, and before their eyes; but
Deut.32.29. oh (saith hee) *that my people were wise, and did consider their end.* For that is wisdome indeed, which seeing the most doe want, therefore they neuer enioy the thousand part of sweet liuing heere, as they might doe.

Vers.8. Now the holy story hauing spoken of the workes which *Ioshua* and the people did in his life, maketh mention of his death, as that which followeth, when all the actions of life are ended. And therefore *Dauid*, when hee was
1.King.2.2. departing hence, said; *I goe the way of all the world.* As wee haue therefore heard much of the actions of our life; so let vs heare somewhat of death, as
*Doct.*1. the text giueth vs leaue and occasion. And in that we heare that he died the seruant of the Lord, as hee had long liued, and had done so many worthie things in his life (death and departure hence being so solemne a thing as it is) we should bee much moued, not onely to thinke vpon the end of all
Psal.37.37. flesh, but especially of our owne death, and to prepare for it aboue all things, and to learne to die; that so wee might with him, die the seruants of God. Which though to a naturall man it be impossible, yet the Lord maketh it tolerable, yea easie, and a welcome thing, to all such as haue first learned to liue well heere, or at least are fit to die. For perseuerance in good life, meeteth with a good death, and ioyfully embraceth it: in which respect *Salo-*
Eccles.7.2. *mon* saith, *that the day of death is better then the day of birth*, as being the entrance into life. And therefore the text saith, *Ioshua the seruant of the Lord died:* noting that his death was not as the death of euery common man, but a blessed

blessed death, and a rest from the worke of the Lord, in which hee had been faithfull in his life; and therfore now looking for his reward, from the Lord a bountifull paymaister, death was welcome to him. As it is reported of an ancient Father of the Church, that being 80. yeeres old, and being then to bid farewell to his friends, said; Thus long haue I serued the Lord, and now it grieueth mee not to die; for I haue a good master, thereby meaning that death was far more welcome to him then life; euen as that day is to a faithfull seruant, wherein he is to receiue liberall wages for his long seruice, then all the daies are that went before. And thus S. *Paul* speaketh of *Dauid*, that *when he had serued his time, he slept*: meaning that hee rested from his labours in body, while his soule returned to God who gaue it. And when we haue learned, and fitted our selues to die, then the hearing of death, and the beholding it in other, is a fit meane to quicken vs to the looking after it our selues, and to further and confirme vs in readinesse to die well; considering deepely of it and of our owne mortality with it. And it much helpeth to thinke vpon the infinite thousands mentioned in the Scriptures (who haue been taken hence by death) and namely, the rolles of Kings, such as haue been more noble and memorable persons, who seemed to haue an eternity heere, by their dignity, pompe, and prerogatiues aboue other men, as also among our selues more neerely to hearken after, and thinke vpon the death of such as wee haue knowne or liued with; oh it doth not a little helpe to cracke the pride of life in vs, and to prepare for death. All which in fit seasons and vpon good consideration, being set before our eyes, are singuler meanes to fasten this meditation vpon vs, that wee also may willingly and readily giue place to death: and this shall much easilier and the better bee, while by our reioycing that we haue in Christ Iesus our Lord wee die daily before death doe come. By meanes whereof, as it is vncertaine, when we see any to die among vs, who shall bee next; so euery one should put forward himselfe, as the Apostle did in a case not vnlike, being told by their master *that one of them should betray him*; euery one asked for himselfe, saying, *is it I master?* Euen so (I say) we ought to resolue, euery one for himselfe, that he may be the next, that so death may the better be prouided for. And let this serue by this occasion, for a meditation of death.

Heb.11.6. Eccles.12.7. Act.13.36. 1.Cor.15.53. Matth.26.22.

His old age being an hundred and ten yeeres, are reckoned as an honour to him, that being so commended for his godlinesse, hee liued so long. To whom *Moses* and *Caleb* may bee added, full of yeeres and grace. Doubtlesse it is no lesse to a man seruing God so religiously, so long a time. For it is not an honour bestowed vpon all, to become fathers and worthies, in the Church for their long continuance in grace, when we see the loue of so many to waxe cold, and a farre greater number to bee reprochfull in their age. But gray haires are a comely ornement, *when they are found in the way of righteousnesse.* For although it bee happinesse for the people of God to die betimes seeing to bee with Christ is best of all, yet to liue long heere, (if God may be honoured by vs in our life, is an high honour also another way, euen by doing much good. And so *Dauid* confessed, saying, If I may liue to keepe thy word (for thereby God is glorified) I shall count it a great bountie vnto me. Which reason *Dauid* and *Hezekiah* vsed, desiring life to this end, saying, *The liuing, the liuing shall praise thee,* Esa.38.19. And in the Psal.

Doct.2. Prou.16.31. Phil.1.23. Psal.119.17. Esa.38.19.

Psal.6.5. None can worship thee in the graue. This,a man would thinke, should stir vp all that haue made good beginnings in Christian life, to long after perseuerance therein, yea though they liue vnto old age, and that they may bee experienced and well seene in the waies of God, that so they may declare
1.Ioh.2.14. them to others. Which as it is rare, and few mens cases to doe; so it is their honour that doe it,and their benefit who enioy it. I speake this to the shame of such as doe by small occasions depart from good beginnings, and in the pride of their hearts,and contempt of other, take conceits against their brethren,who hold constantly the profession of their hope,and breake off their fellowship with them,directly contrary to the word of God, or some other
Heb.10.25. way depart from a good course; so that few such doe hold out to the end in their good beginnings, but lose that honour that *Iosbua* had,who in his old age died as he had long liued; to wit,the seruant of the Almighty,then
Heb.1.7. the which title,the Angels had no greater honour.

Vers.9. It is further added of *Iosbua,* that he was buried in his owne inheritance, which was in mount Ephraim,in the place mentioned in the text, and that without superstition. Now concerning buriall wee are to know,that God hath appointed that it should bee for the honest and decent couering of the body,vntill the resurrection day; and that the bodies of the faithfull should bee as it were, laid vp in the earth, in hope of their honour at the last day; though many righteous persons haue by the cruelty of their enemies especially, been denied this liberty of buriall, which is the comliest manner of bestowing them, but it hindred not their happinesse. Beside, the bodies of God children, for that they bee the temples of the holy Ghost, ought (if it may be) decently to be buried,and not to be cast forth into the fields. And
Ier.22.19. it was a kind of a curse to *Iehoiakim, to be buried like an asse* But to say no more of this,yet about buriall I adde one thing. that whereas it goeth against the edge with men and women, that their bodies should so bee abased at that time,as to be wrapped and wound vp, and laid in graue, some of them hauing liued sumptuously,and daintily heere before,and therefore costly cloathed,and in fine apparell; they must know,that this mortality and corruption must,by Gods ordinance bee put off, before immortality and glory can be put on, and that this abasement,together with the laying of them by the walles,in the vtmost and meanest roomes, which were wont to haue their abode in the costliest and seemeliest places, as also the homely laying forth
Note. of them by meane people, they themselues in their life time hauing had company with the wealthier and better sort: this I say, with all other abasements and disgrace, serueth to this end, euen to abate and pull downe the pride of men that is in them, and to cause them to esteeme meanely of their bodies,in their flourishingest estate,which they haue too much pampered, and gloried in,by setting out of them so vainely. It is a fit cooling and check for such as haue so abused them, to see in the vsage of other mens,what shall be done to their owne. As for other who haue glorified God in their bodies, and vsed them as meet instruments of their soules to make them fitter to serue God, they knowing that their graue is made (by the graue of Christ) a sweet bed for their bodies to sleepe in, till by the power of his resurection,they shall rise to partake eternall life with their soules; and that it is not as a prison or dungeon to locke them vp in,till the resurrection of condemnation,

demnation, as whereto the wicked are reserued: they (I say) knowing this, are not dismaied but comforted in thinking of this. And further, they hauing learned that it is appointed that all shall once die, and that such abasement of their bodies must bee, before they enioy immortality and glory, they I say, doe both submit themselues willingly thereunto while they liue heere, rather then take a pride in their bodies, as too many doe (yea euen in their haire) and they bewaile the sinne rather which hath brought such reproch, and farre greater misery then that vpon men, and with our Sauiour, despise the shame that is set before them, and beare contentedly such reproch, in certaine hope of the glory which they are going to. Heb.9 last. 1.Cor.15. Note. Heb.12.2.

To this which I haue said of burial, one thing more let vs consider: that seeing *Ioshuas* buriall is onely spoken of simply and barely (without any addition) which also yee shall reade of the Kings and great persons burials in their histories: it is worth the considering, what superstition the Prelates of Rome haue brought into this ceremonie of buriall, as they haue done about all other pieces of their religion; partly to blindfold poore soules, in making them to thinke, that their dead shall fare the better for their trumpery (when yet they doe but deceiue and feed them with false comforts) and partly while they seeke their owne, and their shauelings gaine thereby; but both for the aduancing of their superstitious religion. In perticular, some of these abuses are, that there must bee prayers made for their soules, ringing, to helpe them the sooner out of Purgatorie, burying them neere the high alter, with candles burning vpon their toombes; and diuers other such superstitious orders whereby they perswade the ignorant, that God is as busie in making prouision for them in heauen, as they are in heaping and vsing much trumperie about their buriall heere on earth. And this of buriall, and so of the rest for this time. *Doct.2.* Note.

THE FOVRTEENTH SERMON ON THE SECOND CHAPTER OF THE BOOKE OF IVDGES.

AFter the holy story hath spoken of the life and death of *Ioshua*, it proceedeth to shew what the people did after his death, and makes two sorts of them. The one were they, who about that time died: the other they who being another and new generation liued after them, when the good elders were dead and thereby tooke occasion to fall to wickednesse. Of the first it is said, that they were gathered to their fathers, meaning they died: and those were they that were left aliue, a young seminarie in the wildernesse, and came into the land of Canaan, with *Caleb* and *Ioshua*; these I say, who then came lustie and young into the land, were now full of yeers, and died. The phrase Vers.10. *The sense.*

of

of ſpeech heere vſed, that they were gathered to their fathers, is oft vſed in the Scriptures, to ſignifie thereby that they died; and the reaſon why they that died were ſaid to be gathered to their fathers was this: ſeeing both their bodies were buried in the earth with theirs, and their ſoules were ioyned to theirs, according as they were good or bad.

Doct. And in that theſe were gathered to their fathers, now that they had liued out the age of men, which euen then was threeſcore and tenne; or at the moſt foureſcore, and that with much wearineſſe, wee ſee that they who liue to the vtmoſt of their yeeres cannot paſſe threeſcore, or a few more, with any fitneſſe to be imployed profitably in any calling (without which, life is

Pſal.90.10. but burthenſome) and ſo *Moſes* ſaith in his time; therefore how neceſſary is it that the precious time which is allotted vs to liue heere ſhould bee employed to the beſt vſes by vs, who profeſſe that wee liue to that very end eſpecially, conſidering how few attaine euen to theſe yeeres; and how much time is of neceſſity to bee beſtowed in eating, and reſt taking, that I ſay nothing of many other auokements, and beſide both how faſt & ſuddenly our end commeth. The which I ſay, not onely for that I ſee how men lengthen out their liues endleſly, in their owne fooliſh reckoning; ſtretching them on the tenters, and ſaying, they may liue yet 30. 40. 50. yeeres longer: and therupon, how vainely & badly the cōmon ſort do ſpend their time (whom I haue little hope to perſwade to do better) but for that many of good report doe nothing carefully redeeme their precious time from either endleſſe and needleſſe buſying their mindes about the commodities of this life, or trifling it out little better then idly (if not as the other doe) ſo that they can giue ſmall good account of the well paſſing of it; as that good man *He-*

2 King 20.3. *zekiah* did. 2.King.20.3. and as the Apoſtle commandeth to the Epheſians,
Epheſ.5.16. without which the ſo paſſing of it ſhall bee reckoned among their other
Luk 19.24. ſinnes.

Doct.2. This be ſaid of that generation that died; now of that which liued, and tooke occaſion to doe wickedly when their forefathers were dead. This people it is ſaid heere, knew not the Lord; that is, effectually; neither therefore acknowledged him, nor they knew not his workes; that is, as we heard before, made no vſe of them, neither profited by them, without which the bare knowledge of them was nothing. A deſcription therefore ye ſee heere ſet downe of an euill people, to wit, that they were ſuch as neither knew God, nor his workes. And no maruell; for if they who did both, I meane the former generation, of whom I haue ſpoken, did ſee that which they did by the meanes of good teaching and example, it is no ſtrange thing, that theſe did neither of both, who had not theſe good helpes which the other had: It is not poſſible for ſuch comming out of darkeneſſe, to walke before God in reuerence and cheerefulneſſe. For how ſhould men come to vnderſtand myſteries, as the ſauing knowledge of God in Chriſt is, and the effectuall knowledge of his great workes, to bee brought to his feare by them, and ſo to doe more then they that only ſay, Lord, Lord, and do not the will of the Lord; how (I ſay) ſhould they come to ſuch knowledge, vnleſſe they ſhould be plainely taught, and haue ſome to breake the ice to them, in following and practiſing it, and ſo in giuing good example to them? Therfore in places where both are wanting, ſuch perſons as I ſpeake of, are not to bee

ſought,

ſought,vnleſſe they enioy both,by the benefit of other places, being deſtitute of them in their owne habitation : which is ſufficient to moue all ſuch of vs as enioy better helpes,to mourne for the deſolation of thoſe that want them : as we cannot chuſe,if we haue the ſpirit of our Sauiour, who pitied ſuch as they were ; and to entreat the Lord to ſupply their wants. And further,this bewraies the vnhappineſſe of all ſuch as doe not heartily ſeeke after both, but are content to liue without them ; I meane the getting of the knowledge of God,and Chriſt,to the certainty of ſaluation,Ioh. 17. and alſo to liue with ſuch, as neere as may bee, who may bee ſhining lights to them,vnto ſanctification of life. Mat.9.36. Ioh.17.3.

This laſt ſort of the people affordeth alſo an other leſſon vnto vs, that the latter generations are for the moſt part backwardeſt in goodneſſe,and more declining from it, then the former. It was no wonder if it were ſo in theſe that wanted the meanes,for it is ſo,euen where they are enioyed. Wee ſee how thoſe plants and flowers that were rare a few yeeres agoe, grow now in euery garden ; for one getteth them of another ; ſo ſinne growes by tradition and example, and daily encreaſeth, each age adding ſome new, till they come to the full meaſure. And though commonly old things decay and waxe worſe,yet old *Adam* the older,the ſtronger. Sinne hath his ages of growth for as the world growes older, ſo ſinners multiply who trading in ſinne,doe ſtill exceed the former age in all kind of leaudneſſe ; and one conſenting with the other in exalting follie, whether wee conſider number of perſons (equall compariſon being made) or the fouleneſſe, or boldneſſe in ſinne,wee muſt looke that the latter daies will bee worſer. The pride,couetouſneſſe,and drunkenneſſe of our preſent age was not ſeene in our forefathers dayes as now : nay (which is monſtrous) not in the middeſt of Poperie, although this extenuateth not their other ſinne, for euen they in ſubtilty and ill conſcience exceed their former ages alſo. There is now more knowledge indeed where long teaching hath been,but becauſe men receiue not the truth in loue and ſincerity, God accurſeth it with barrenneſſe. Honeſt ſimplicity,which is not tainted with craft and ſubtilty,and therefore fitter to receiue the print of the Goſpell, is iuſled out, by ſuch as are (for the moſt part) riſen vp more prophane and filthie ; more ſcornfull alſo and hardlier perſwaded to goodneſſe then the former generations. And though this may bee found true in the generall eſtate of all (as toward the end of the world,and in the latter daies our Sauiour foretold it ſhould be ſo) that iniquitie ſhould abound,and haue the vpper hand : yet in perticular generations one after another, it may alſo be ſeene to bee ſo ; that if the Goſpell bee planted in a nation countrey, or towne, and bee continued from one age to another, though the meanes be like,yet the latter generation ſhall come behinde the forme,in feruencie,diligence,and euery way in yeelding fruit of the Goſpell commendably in reſpect of it ; they will verifie the prouerbe, New things are dainty,and old loathſome. *Doct.3.* *A ſimile.* Note. Mat.24.12.

For I cannot tell how it commeth to paſſe, that yee muſt grow glutted with the word,and wearie and aſhamed in ſome ſort of the godly zeale and forwardneſſe that they haue ſeene in others of former times. They will receiue the Goſpell,as other haue done,but they thinke it more then needeth, to ſtoope to the ſimplicity of it, and to bee zealous patternes to other in

practiſing

practising the perticular doctrine of it, in one point, as well as in another; but seeke to take more liberty then they are willing to examine vpon what good grounds they doe it: neither will they bee forward in going one before another in mercifulnesse, in iustice, and in seeking to punish notorious faults in their families and townes, and in the like good example giuing, and thereby discourage them, who else were like to come forward, if there were not laid such blocks in their way. So that we had need to stirre vp our selues by the examples of them that haue gone before vs commendably, rather then to please our selues in that which we doe, and to rest therein without contending, and striuing to doe better. For who is ignorant that such an estate cannot be good? And if wee will bee aduised, let vs know that our reward shall bee great, if wee honour the Lord with greatest forwardnesse
Psal.19. in religious duties, when iniquitie aboundeth in the world, and when the loue of many shall waxe cold.

Vers.11. *The sense.* Now I haue shewed the occasion of this peoples sinne, namely, that their good gouernours were dead; their sinne it selfe now followeth in these 3. next verses: and that in this manner: first generally, then perticularly. In this verse thus; that they did euill in the sight of the Lord, and that they fell to Idolatry. Heere to stay a little, till I passe to the other two verses: the euill which they did (most certainly) displeased the Lord in a most grieuous manner. As by the same word heere vsed, the like is meant in other places, where it is said, that the Kings of Israel did that which was euill in the sight of the Lord. And so on the contrary, those things which were good in the
1.King.16.2.27. eyes of the Lord, as the acts of many of the Kings of Iuda were; they were
2.King.18.3. said to please him highly. But when God hath giuen vs many encouragements to his seruice, and yet we regard not to bee the better by them, what maruell if hee abhorre such doings, and make open exclamation against
Doct. them, as he doth heere, when both hee hath set hedge and ditch to hold vs from committing them, and also hath giuen vs many causes of doing better, both by teaching vs, and by other his manifold benefits, and also looketh for it at our hands that we should doe so?

So that although the sinne of this people was manifest to the view of the world, as well as before God; yet if it had been secret and hid from men, it had been euill in the sight of the Lord: euen so I say of our selues, if wee minde not Gods matters and seruice chiefly, but walke loosely, and hollowly, we shall iustly be challenged to doe that which he cannot abide, howsoeuer men find no fault in vs. For though there be degrees in sinne, and one is more grieuous then another, yet they that set not their hearts wholly to seeke the Lord, with a great care to please him in all things, euen they doe that which is euill in his eyes, seeing the eyes of the Lord search narrowly, and spie that which men see not; Therefore what may be said to the liues of the greatest number, and yet some of them, such as reproue others, and are not in many of their doings to be charged iustly by any, yet when they bee not vpright in heart, and faithfull to God in one thing as well as in another, yet (while they be not so bad as other) they doe euill in his sight. For see-
Rom.2.last. ing not they whom man, but whom God approueth are praiseworthy; they
Luk.1.6. therfore shall haue this still and euer against them, that they did euill in the eyes of the Lord if he commend them not, as he did *Iob*, saying thus, they

are vpright, feare God, and depart from euill; which if it were well thought on, there should smal cause be found, why they who are tender conscienced, and feare to doe euill, should be so scornfully and spitefully railed vpon, and disgraced by the men of the world, for that they dare not be so loose in their liues as other are, shewing thereby that they can abide none but such as do euill in the sight of the Lord. And this of the eleuenth verse. Iob 2.3.

For of the word [*Baal*] I will speake in the next verse together, with other of like sort. But first in this twelfth verse the holy story saith, that they forsooke the Lord, who yet was the God of their fathers, and had brought them out of the bondage of Egypt. This as it was more then to displease God in some particular actions (for it was a leauing of the true worshiping of God, which is the fountaine of well doing dutie in our life:) so it is aggrauated by the fauour and benefits heere mentioned; to wit, what God had done for them: and further, the greatnesse of their sinne may bee laid out more fully by comparing it with *Peters* answere to our Sauiour. For when he saw some of his hearers to depart from him, vpon no iust cause, but onely a bare conceit; and he asked *Peter*, if they and the rest of his fellow Apostles also would depart from him; hee answered, saying, *Lord whither should we goe? thou hast the words of eternall life.* As if hee should say, that they hauing found them so good and bountifull to them already, and hauing such hope still of greater good from him hereafter, as they knew not where to finde the like, it should haue been absurd for them to depart from him as the other Disciples did. Vers 12. *The sense.* Ioh. 6.68.

And to speake the truth, who can say any lesse? And so might this people well haue answered, and so they ought to haue said also, euen as *Peter* did. But it was farre from them, because some of them had neuer cleaued to the Lord in truth before, nor trusted in him, but walked hollowly and vnfaithfully towards him, though now they did much worse. And by them we may see to what a fearefull estate they may grow, to what depth of sinne they may fall, who embrace not religion conscionably, euen for the worthinesse and excellency thereof, and for the good they haue, or ought to haue gotten by it, and for the loue they should beare to God, who hath loued them first; but rather began to professe in a passion, or in some other outward and mutable respects; such (I say) may be like in time to depart from God altogether, and then in what other state are they, but without God in the world? For when mens hearts become hardened once by the deceitfulnesse of sinne, they doe next after that grow worse, and so depart from the liuing God, as it is written in the Epistle to the Hebrues. Now as I haue spoke of these who were but outward professors, when they were at the best, how they did wickedly in the sight of the Lord; so there being some better among them who did so likewise. We may further note hereby, that though we beginne wel as some of these did, in the true renouncing of euil, yet we not holding on faithfully and carefully, by considering duely Gods goodnesse toward vs, and zealously embracing good meanes, we may easily, and by little and little, yea and shall also together goe backe, euen as these did: but of the reuolting of such I haue spoken a little before. *Doct.* Heb. 3.12.

Now therefore it followeth. I will shew how this people fell to Idolatry, euen to worship Baal and Ashtaroth, and such other Idols as the people and Vers. 11. 12. 13. *The sense.*

nations serued, who dwelt about them: but first what is ment by these names of the Idols heere named. *Baal* signifieth a patrone or helper, as they tooke the Idoll *Baal* to be. *Ashteroth* was the God of the Sidonians, an Idoll which in the forme of a sheepe was worshipped. And by the word *Baalim* heere, is meant all manner of Idols, such as were worshipped among them. To this point the people of Israel were now come, that seeing they would not expell those idolatrous nations while they might; neither continued to serue the Lord, as they ought to haue done; behold, they themselues now departed from him also, and fell to idolatrie with them. Where, besides that we may learne, that when we auoide not the occasions of sinne,
Doct. vers. 11. 12. 13. 14. we cannot looke to auoide the committing of the sinne it selfe, of the which I haue spoke in the former chapter; we may further see, that after men once forsake the Lord, and his waies that haue been made knowne vnto them, they fall to most lothsome sinnes, euen to most grosse and fowle Idolatry: yea and there is no end of such abominations with them, if God restraine them not.

Euen so the Lord complaineth in *Ieremie*, saying: *My people haue commit-*
Ier. 2. 13. *ted two euils, for they haue forsaken me the fountaine of liuing waters, and haue digged to themselues pits that will hold no water.* It would neuer haue been thought, that people so well prouided to liue happily, as these were by their manifold encouragements (euen as wee haue seene our selues in our time many to haue been among vs) it would neuer (I say) haue been thought that such could grow to be so monstrous and prophane, that none might seeme to goe beyond them therein: Euen so it may bee said; and to apply this to our selues, oh, if men could see what God hath done for them in these daies, when hee hath granted them to liue in the daies wherein the Gospell hath shewed most cleare light, and made manifest the way to eternall life, to them who sat in darkenesse, and when heerewith he hath giuen peace and abundance of earthly commodities also, &c. Oh (I say) that they could in this their time see these things? how happy might they haue been thereby? but they are hidden from them. Now therefore when for all these they haue yet followed their owne hearts desire, and the course of such as know not God; we may say on the other side, oh how iustly may it bee complained of, to their no lesse shame then misery?

Doct. 2. Now if any desire to know what Idolatry is, and what is meant by that they were said to commit it; let them know this for answere to both: Idolatrie is a worshipping of Idols; and hath two parts, outward and and when wee giue that to them which is proper to God, in either of these inward: wee commit idolatry. The inward, when wee trust in, pray, giue thankes, or subiect our selues vnto them, whatsoeuer in heauen or earth, or in the water vnder it. The externall is; when wee manifest our affections to them by any outward things, as bowing the knee, vailing the cap, prostrating our selues to them, or in vsing any other ceremony appointed by God for his owne seruice. Now whereas this being vrged to the Idolaters of our time, I meane the Popes votaries: their answere is, that they giue not honour or worship to the Image, or that which they giue reuerence to; be it stocke, or whatsoeuer, but onely to God and Christ himselfe in the Image; let them heare to their shame what Saint *Paul* saith to the Corinths,the Image or Idoll is nothing saith hee: that is to say,God is not in it,or vnder it,whom they say they serue in them, and that hee is represented in such images: and what do they worship then but the creature? Whereby wee may truly gather, and all that list, may cleerely see that their bowing to them,and prostrating themselues before them,is grosse Idolatry, whatsoeuer they pretend, as they haue been oft and learnedly answered. The same may be said of their offerings, burning of lights, their going on pilgrimage to the Saints departed, and such like. Now as for their miracles, they are false and wrought by Satan,which God doth suffer for two causes: one to try his, whether they will goe from God thereby; the other to punish themselues and other wicked ones, by beleeuing lies. And as for *Cornelius* bowing to *Peter,* and *Iohn* to the Angell, they did not take them for God, and yet because they went too farre, they were forbidden by them. 1.Cor.8.4. 2.Thes.2.9.

But yet in these verses, let vs note a thing or two more. For seeing this people saw and heard that God allowed their fathers worshipping of him; as *Abrahams, Iacobs, Moses* and others, and yet they followed not their example,it made their sinne greater: For our fathers, such as the holy Ghost heere meaneth,are to be followed; namely,*Moses* and the Prophets; as *Paul* in the 24. of the Acts affirmed, that he in seruing God, *worshipped the God of his fathers,* and followed them therein. Such fathers if the Papists would follow,when they boast that they haue the fathers on their side, all controuersies about matters in question betwixt them and vs: as transubstantiation,reall presence,adoration of Sacraments,and such like; would soone be at an end. And let vs see that we retaine the true seruing of God,that those our holy fathers did,seeing with such seruice we haue heard God to be pleased. Doct.3. Act 24. Act.24.14.

And further note,in that the miracles of Egypt are repeated, and applyed heere to this generation,which yet were done long before, as though they had been brought out of Egypt themselues, being not yet borne: and this was to the end that they should profit and be moued by them as wel as their fathers; note (I say) that the miracles and workes of God in times past wrought by the Prophets,our Sauiour,and the Apostles,ought to serue for our benefit,and we ought to haue vse of them, as well as they before vs, in whose daies they were wrought, although we saw them not done: whereupon this is set downe, *that whatsoeuer things are written, are written for our learning,* both that we should,among all other vses of them, bee confirmed in the doctrine of the word, and also looke for no more proofe of it by other miracles to be wrought in euery age following. And if we be resolued of the truth of this,let vs see that we be guided by it also. And this be said of the sinne of the generation that rose after the death of the good elders: now of their punishment. Doct.4. Rom.15.4.

And the wrath of the Lord was hot against Israel, and hee deliuered them into the hands of spoilers,that spoiled them: and he sold them into the hands of their enemies round about them, so that they could no longer stand before their enemies. Vers.14.

Whithersoeuer they went out, the hand of the Lord was sore against them, as the Lord had said,and as the Lord had sworne vnto them; so he punished them sore. Vers.15.

We haue heard of the first point of the foure, in this second part of the chapter; namely,of the sinne of the people. The next point followeth (as I said before,) of the punishment, with the which the Lord pursued them *The sense.*

for it,which was two fold: the first was,the anger of God conceiued against them for it,the second the fruit of it. And that is set downe heere to be partly the spoiling them of their goods, and partly bondage to their enemies; and more generally,that Gods hand was against them,so that they were not able to stand before them; by meanes wherof they were in anguish and straits, not knowing what to do. Behold how their estate was changed,yea and that so soone, after they turned away from the Lord : euen so shall all finde it. But come we to the particulars.

When therefore it is said heere,that God was angry with them, we must not so take it, as though God were subiect to passions as men are, as either
1.Sam.15.30. anger or repentance,&c. but such speeches are vsed, and now this one, of Gods anger, to the end our faults may appeare the more grieuous, in that they are said to prouoke him who is so hardly moued. Againe, to our capacity they are vttered, to giue vs to vnderstand, that God doth and will doe the same things that men, being angry for faults committed against them, will doe; that is, be reuenged vpon the offenders: and yet hee is free from passion. What are we then to think,when we heare that God is angry? to set light by it,as the most do; when yet we heare that he is not led by passions?
Doct.vers.14. no,but to be troubled for it, because we cannot but feare that God will doe the same to vs, that an angry man, being offended, will doe to such as prouoke him. For why? are we stronger then he? or thinke we that we shall eschew and decline danger? when yet in his anger he is compared to a Lion, who seeketh his prey? No doubtlesse; for his wrath is assisted with power,
Psal.18.8. and with presence. And therefore it is said in the Psalme, *If his anger bee kindled,the earth is moued,and the foundations, of the hils are shaken.* And againe, *If*
Psal.2.last. *his anger be kindled but a little, happie are they that trust in him.* Which places, with many other such, doe liuely shew the danger of them that prouoke him; and that as he is angry iustly, so his anger is (without respect of persons) or parciality declared against all sorts without exception,that prouoke him: the greatest shall as well smart as the meanest, as the text there importeth.

But the vse of this is,seeing God is prouoked by our sins, that we should beware that we offend him not in the common manner as men doe, in the prophaning of his Sabbaths,his word and Sacraments,in slander, lying,dissembling,incontinency,and vnchastnesse of body and minde,in deceiuing, oppressing,and a thousand waies more: and especially we must looke that we liue not in vnbeleefe,which is disobedience in an high degree, euen to
1.Thes.1.8. the Gospell; for which *Paul* saith, the wrath of God is reuealed from hea-
Ioh.3.last. uen. But if wee haue fallen into any such, the next heed to bee taken of vs is,not to sleepe vpon them,but tremble,for that we know Gods wrath is
Ephes.5.6. kindled against vs, and who knoweth whether vengeance may come forth and take hold of vs,before our hearts relent, and before wee meet him with repentance? *When the Lion roreth all the beasts of the forrest quake*; and is it not time for vs to doe the like,when the mighty Lion of the tribe of *Iudah* is moued? And if it be meet that euen the children of God be held in awe, by considering that he their God is a iealous God,yea a consuming fire; and againe,if they cannot but tremble to behold him in displeasure sometime, with his enemies,as well as they see him in his smiling countenance toward his

his owne people; how much more should they tremble, when it is their owne case, and when they themselues are the persons vpon whom hee frowneth? And if the Princes wrath be death, as we see it is by *Ahashuerosh*, Hest.7.7.
when he was inflamed against *Haman*; how dangerous is the estate of them who most iustly haue stirred vp the Lord against them? For which cause our Sauiour saith; *Feare not him who can but destroy the body: but feare him that* Mat.10.28.
can cast body and soule into hell: I say feare him? So that the man lying in known sinne, not repenting, is the man of misery, if hee could see it, howsoeuer hee sooth vp himselfe, or be soothed by other, for the mouth of the Lord hath spoken it. And I haue wondred oft, that so many offending, as are knowne daily to doe, and that willingly and loosely, yea and with boldnesse; and that they being in so great danger thereby of sundry punishments euery Note.
day; I haue wondred (say) that so few make hast to rid themselues out of that fearefull condition; and especially they seeing so many to smart from time to time for the same and the like sinnes that swarme in them: and yet further, to giue too apparant tokens by their impenitency, that it will be infinitely worse with them, when they bee gone hence. Thus much for this time.

THE FIFTEENTH SERMON VPON THE BOOKE OF IVDGES, THE REST OF THE fourteenth and the fifteenth verses, a part of the former text, and on these *verses following.*

VERS. 15. *Whithersoeuer they went out*, &c.

16. *Notwithstanding the Lord raised vp Iudges, which deliuered them out of the hands of their oppressors.*

17. *But yet they would not obey their Iudges; for they went a whoring after other gods, and worshipped them, and turned quickly out of the way wherein their fathers walked, obeying the Commandements of the Lord, they did not so.*

18. *And when the Lord raised them vp Iudges, the Lord was with the Iudge, and deliuered them out of the hand of their enemies all the daies of the Iudge (for the Lord had compassion of their gronings, because of them that oppressed them and tormented them.)*

OF Gods anger and the feare therof, being the first punishment, we haue heard. Now followeth the next, which is the effect of it. For they who are angry, consult and deuise, how they may reuenge themselues vpon such as haue offended them: the like is set out heere in the Lord: the effect of whose anger is set downe, first to be the spoiling of their goods, and then the bondage

dage they came in to their enemies, which was farre greater. And these are the sorer because God dealt not with them himselfe, but gaue them ouer to men, yea cruell men, such as *Dauid* desired he might not fall into their hands, because there was no mercy with them. But to say somewhat of the former of these two; to such as be in prosperity, we know that the losse of wealth is found by experience, and taken of men to bee one of the hardest iudgements that doe befall them; the reason is, for that they loue their money and goods almost if not altogether as well as their liues. And yet a great punishment is this which they sustaine by them, that when the Lord hath giuen them as blessings, they lose the right vse of the, for and through their foolishnesse and sinne, and cause that for the most part they become curses to them. And God in his wisedome doth send such penalties oft times among many other vnto them, as it is said heere, hee gaue them into the hands of spoilers. But this was yet farre worse, when they must goe vnder it, and yet neuer consider by whom, and why they were thus punished. Behold in this people, the extreame follie of sinners at this day; who though their hearts are set vpon their wealth and commodities, yet neuer bethinke themselues to be freed from the danger of Gods wrath, which often wasteth

Note. them to nothing. Know we therfore, that if we decay in our goods, by bar-

Pennie-wise. Pound-foolish. rennesse of the ground, or vnseasonablenesse of the weather, by debt, suretiship, or by any other such like, and especially by mispending them; know we (I say) we haue a warning thereby, sent vs of God, for some ill parts of

Deut.28.15.33 life, as it is said in Deuteronomie, If thou wilt not obey the voice of the Lord thy God, then the fruit of thy land, and all thy labour shall a people that thou knowest not, eate: and the heauen that is ouer thee shall be brasse, and the earth vnder thee, iron.

Deut.28.51. And againe, *A nation that is of a fierce countenance shall eate the fruit of thy cattell, and he shall leaue thee neither wheate, wine, nor oyle, neither shalt thou prosper in*

Vers.29. *thy waies.* By all which, and this which is in the text, that they heere were spoiled of their goods, as it should make vs carefull to preuent euen his iudgement among many other, by vpright walking with God, and harmelesse liuing among men, how foolish and precise soeuer that course of life

Gen.17.1. seeme to many: so when wee haue gone out of the good way, and fallen from that obedience which we haue couenanted to yeeld vnto God, and sustaine such losse thereby, aboue all things let vs seeke to finde out the cause

Ier.8.4. Mich 7.7. Ioh.5.14. thereof, and that speedily, as *Ieremy* requireth, and beare our losse because we haue sinned; and sinne no more lest a worse thing befall vs. And let vs not count it our hard fortune, (as foolish men tearme it, for there is none) when wee are so wasted in our goods, neither please wee our selues in condemning and charging the second cause thereof, whereby we are spoiled of them; for whatsoeuer be the instrument of our losse or vndoing, sure it is, that the Lord is the effecter and worker of it. And therefore it is said in Deuteronomie, of this and all other his fearfull iudgements, after that hee hath sent them, when it shall be demanded, wherefore hath the Lord done this?

Deut.29.25. how fierce is his great wrath? they shall answere, because they haue forsaken the couenant of the Lord God of their fathers, therfore hath the Lords wrath waxed hot against this people, to bring vpon it euery curse that is written in this booke.

And the same doctrine that I haue taught of the spoiling of mens goods, that it is a fruit of the wrath of God for their sin, (this being excepted, that the Lord may impouerish his people (who feare him) in fauour and mercy) The same I may as fitly and truly say of the bringing of them into seruitude and bondage vnto vile and cruell persons: but let the one bee vnderstood by the other, seeing I speake of this in another place. But I will further obserue another thing heere, that seeing it is said that they were led into bondage after they were spoiled of their goods, and so smarted by both, we may note how God so dealeth with the disobedient oft times, euen as hee did heere with these, that as their sins go not alone, so neither doe their punishments. So that God dealeth with such as offend him not one way, but many; as he did puinsh *Achan*, both with shame, and with paine: so *Pharaoh* was visited with terrours, and with bodily plagues also: euen so now many are pursued with crosses in their goods, reproch in their name, and in their body with paine and diseases. And this he doth, that men may know they shall pay deare for their stolne pleasures, how sweet soeuer they bee to them in their fond account, and that so both together may hold them backe from prouoking him. For as *Esay* saith, one iudgement shall not serue the turne, if men struggle and fight against it, and stand out with God, when hee smiteth gently, his hand will bee stretcht out still; and looke what the former hath not done, the latter shall make good. As wee reade in *Ioel*, that fruit which one plague consumed not, another did, till an vtter riddance follow of all. But men bite vpon the bridle, and curse their lucke, but look not into themselues: so when God strippeth men of their goods, and then casteth them into bondage, as hee did deale with them heere; or when hee doth the like to vs, that one iudgement come in the necke of another to vs, I thinke it may bee said truly without respect of damnation, that wee haue paid deare for stolne pleasures, and our bold taking of our liberties amisse. And seeing I haue not spoken particularly of going into seruitude, and our nation hath not knowne what it meaneth, nor how sharpe a scourge it is; yet seeing many fall into it by Turke and Spanyard, who haue little feared it; therefore I wish them to reade of it in Deuteronomie: secondly, to consider of it by the estate of the people of Israel in Egypt: and lastly, to lay it out, and set a view of it before their eyes, by the Popish and cruell tyrannizing ouer our soules heere in our owne land in the daies of Queene *Mary*, when we could enioy no liberty of the word and Sacraments, but our brethren who refused their Idoll-seruice and false worship, were tortured and tormented by the bloody persecutors: and what may men looke for then at the hands of strangers? And this to be said of bondage.

Doct. 3. Note. Esa 9. last vers. Ioel 1.3. Deut. 28.48. 49.50.

Now further, in that it is added in generall in the text, that they could not stand before their enemies; for being so weakened by them in goods, number, and strength, what maruell? Let this be obserued, that God vseth his and our enemies against vs his children, when we prouoke him by our sins: as hee vsed *Nabuchadnezzar* against Ierusalem, and *Senacherib* and others. Not that God putteth new poison and malice into them, who had nothing else in them before; but that hee iustly suffereth and letteth them alone (without any bridling or restraining them) to vomit vp their venome, and their cankered hatred, and letteth them loose to Satan. Whereby this among

Doct. 4. Note.

mong many other things may bee learned, how vncertaine the comfort is that ſome take in this, that the Papiſts (they hope) ſhall neuer preuaile againſt the Proteſtants,nor Popery euer yoke them any more. Yes,if God be diſpleaſed with them,he may plague them that way, by raiſing them vp as enemies againſt them,as eaſily as hee did heere the Canaanites againſt Iſrael; and if they were without feare that way, hee may and can meet with them after ſundry other ſorts, little to their comfort, as they may ſee daily it their ſinnes be not remoued out of his ſight: ſo that as the Prophet ſpea-
Amos 5.19. keth,it ſhall be with them,as if though they eſcape the Lion,a Beare ſhould meet them: or went into the houſe,and leaned his hand on the wall, and a ſerpent bite him.

Doct.5. By this which wee haue heard of the puniſhment of this people, it appeares that they had load enough vpon them,as one would thinke, and yet, as though there had not bin enough ſaid of the hand of God againſt them, the holy Ghoſt addeth heere, *that whitherſoeuer they went forth,the hand of the Lord was againſt them*; as if it ſhould bee ſaid, whatſoeuer they tooke in hand or went about,it proſpered not, but they were croſſed therein; whereas of
Pſal.1.3. the godly,we reade in the firſt Pſalme,the contrary to be ſaid and ſet down. The like is ſpoken by the Prophet *Azaria* to the people of Iuda,in the ſecõd
2.Chron.15.6. booke of Chronicles. This though it be not ſeene of many, nor marked of the diſobedient,and therefore not complained of,yet their miſery therefore is the greater,ſeeing they goe on brutiſhly, *as the foole to the ſtocks, and the oxe*
Pro.7.23. *to the ſlaughter, till a dart pierce through their liuer*. But ſome feele and perceiue it, when God being angry with them, his hand is againſt them, as experience witneſſeth (though he deale not now ſo much nor apparantly againſt his enemies in bodily as ſpirituall plagues) for doe not many loden with ſorrow and miſery crie out,that God fighteth againſt them,though there be no outward puniſhments to bee ſeene vpon them? and that they neither proſper nor enioy any inward peace, but are weariſome to themſelues, curſing their lot,and wiſhing themſelues out of the world; nay laying violent hands vpon themſelues,for very anguiſh of heart and madneſſe: thinking (falſely) ſo to eſcape their miſery. And how heauie a thing is that, (thinke wee) eſpecially when they know not how to remedy it? And as it is thus with them, euen ſo Gods hand is euer with his faithfull ſeruants in all their
Pſal 91 11. waies which God hath ſet them in. They are *like the tree planted by the riuers*
Pſal.1 3. *of waters,that bringeth forth fruit in due ſeaſon: and whatſoeuer they do it ſhall proſper*. Indeed this is the leſſe ſeene to be, becauſe they finde it ſo hard a thing for them, in the middeſt of ſo many diſcouragements, to continue in their vprightneſſe as we may ſee who marke it; but they are oft vnſetled and broken off by the burthen of the fleſh from their innocency, or elſe are forced with much adoe to recouer themſelues being fallen, and are in great heauineſſe thereby. But while God vpholdeth them by his grace,hee doth alſo make them well liking,and to proſper,yea in their weakeſt eſtate, in reſpect of other,and to recouer.

Doct.6. And whereas it is added, that this purſuing of them by the Lord in all that they ſet their hand vnto, was *as he had ſworne to them*, it is to teach vs, that it could be no otherwiſe: ſeeing God ſpeaketh nothing in vaine,much
1.Sam.15.29. leſſe if he ſweare to it,according to *Samuels* words, the ſtrength of Iſrael will

not lie. One iot or tittle of his word cannot faile. It is farre more firme then the law of the Medes and Persians, which yet altered not. So that if the Lord speake the word or sweare (except it be conditionally) whether it be a threatening to such as prouoke him, or a promise of any good things to such as trust in him, it shall most certainly come to passe, what attempts soeuer there be to the contrary, as is daily to be seene. And therefore it is to be wondred at, that men are so little moued thereby; but for all his threats, go forward in their bad course, till the euill threatened doe come vpon them, and cause them to crie out; euen as Gods seruants also doe smart, when his promises being certaine, are for all that, not beleeued of them. But this matter is oft occasioned. And this bee said of the peoples sinne, and of their punishment. It followeth now in the text. Mat. 5.17.

VERS. 16. *Notwithstanding the Lord raised vp Iudges, which deliuered them out of the hands of their oppressors.*

17 *But yet they would not obey their Iudges; for they went a whoring after other gods and worshipped them, and turned quickly out of the way wherein their fathers walked, obeying the Commandements of the Lord, they did not so.*

18. *And when the Lord had raised them vp Iudges, the Lord was with the Iudges, and deliuered them out of the hand of their enemies, all the daies of the Iudge: for the Lord had compassion of their gronings, because of them that oppressed them and tormented them.*

NOw follow the other things which I mentioned before in the sixth verse in laying out the points of this second part of the chapter, and that is, how the Lord raised them vp deliuerers in their oppressions when they cried vnto him, who were called Iudges. This cannot bee vnderstood of any one time, seeing he sent not many Iudges at once among them, in any time of their affliction. Therefore hee sheweth heere to the end of the chapter, what was the condition of the people of Israel, and the changes and diuerse courses that they were, in the time of the Iudges. In few words it was thus: when they cried to the Lord in their oppressions, he pitied their grones, and raised them vp Iudges, which were deliuerers of them, as I said, and he was with them to blesse them, and yet they turned away from him againe for all that, and so he was prouoked to go against them afresh, as is set downe in the latter end of this chapter, & in some of the verses that follow. *The sense.*

And first, in that it is said in the eighteenth verse (for these three verses are to bee ioyned and read together) that they groned to the Lord vnder their oppressions, who saw nothing amisse in themselues before; it must teach vs, that calamities will search and stirre vs vp to griefe, and to make our mone to God for very anguish of heart, how carelesse and iollie soeuer wee haue been before, when wee boldly prouoked him, and when wee haue been so carelesse and headstrong, as that nothing could serue to plucke downe our stomackes, yet sore troubles haue broken our hearts, as if we neuer had been otherwise. Therefore when his word will not preuaile, the Lord is faine euen to maister men by strong hand, that at least hee may tame them by violence, if he cannot bow them to repentance: euen as men handle horses and such beasts as they cannot rule; they cast them, and keepe them vnder by binding them, that so they may worke their pleasure on them. The wilde Verse 18. *Doct.* Note.

Asse

Iob 33.15. Asse must be taken in her moneths, when she cannot resist: and this course the Lord is driuen to take with vs, to wit, to make our hearts to smart, and to loade them with sorrowes, or else there would bee no rule with vs: thus I say he is faine to take vs downe. According to that which is said in the Psal. Psal.78.34. *When he smote them, they sought him, yea they sought him early: Pharaoh* himselfe when he felt the smart of the plagues of Egypt, sought for *Moses* to pray for him to the Lord. Long it is before men are fitted and framed to heare See Hos.6.1. compared with cap.5.13.14. the Lord speake vnto them: but being bitten with sorrow, they are glad to cling to him. But alas what commeth of the most of these his corrections and sharp dealings with such? Nay, for that I can say no more but this, that the most of them doe but bow for the time, as a bulrush with the winde, their goodnesse being as the morning dew, and so it goeth away, and they cry out onely while the rod is held ouer them, and afterward they returne againe to their old byas.

And so did these heere, and so doe many seeke the Lord for a time, and yet turne aside againe as a broken bow. But if such as be thus cast downe (as these were) when God afflicteth them, so that one would think they would neuer lift vp their bristles against him any more; if these I say doe yet waxe bold, and kicke vp their heele against him, what shall we thinke of them who relent not at all for their euill doings, no nor for Gods heauie hand vpon them, but harden their harts, as the dog which biteth the staffe that beateth them? What then, yee will aske is to bee done; if groning vnder mens burthens of sinne and punishment haue no good effect? All the remedy heere is this, that men in such cases finding out their sins, doe also seriously consider of the foulenesse of them, and the woe that they bring with them, and so tread them also vnder their feet, and beleeue better things to bee comming from God toward them, euen mercy and forgiuenesse, which onely are able to crush their sinnes in peeces afterwards, as well as to make them kindly and truly acknowledged and cried out of, while the smart taketh hold of them. This be noted of their groning.

Vers.16.18. Now behold what the Lord did when they did thus complaine and cry out; he had compassion on them, and raised them vp Iudges, that should deliuer them out of the hands of their oppressors and spoilers, and he did so, and was with them; and it repented him that he had so suffered them to be oppressed. He doth oft as he did to *Ahab*, pitty sinners, when they smarting for their faults cry out of them: but he doth not receiue them to mercy, except they truly forsake them; which I say for our instruction, that wee may know that the Lord is easily to be entreated of vs, waiting indeed our repentance. And when we do but giue signes of disliking our sinnes for the time, Note. he stayeth his heauie hand from pursuing vs: what would hee doe, thinke we, if we came home to him with all our hearts? But so we must know on Note. the other side, that hee in so dealing with vs, heapeth hot coles vpon our heads, add maketh vs vnexcuseable, when wee hauing such faire encouragement at his hands, shall yet keepe a loofe from him, and shew vnfaithfulnes, when we haue made couenants with him of amendment.

Vers.17. But heere commeth in their misery, as in this verse is to bee seene, that when he did all this to them that heere is set downe, yet for all his pitying them, and shewing so great kindnesse toward them, yet their Iudges, who could

called them from Idolatry, were not heard nor regarded of them. They considered not what a benefit it was to enioy such, although they cried in the anguish of heart for helpe in trouble. Now in that this was a common thing with them after their deliuerances, thus vnthankfully to deale with the Lord, in not obeying their Iudges; for so they are charged heere to haue done: and in the chapters following is to be seene that they did so: by this briefly let vs learne, that men are rarely the better for their deliuerances out of their troubles, howsoeuer they crie to God in the middest of them. Whereas a man would thinke it should be the thing most regarded of them, and they should be oft in considering both how irkesome and vncomfortable it was to them, when they lay in affliction; as in paine of body, by sicknesse or disease, or in pursuit by enemies, or in any other distresse: also what a gracious liberty it was, and what ease to them, when they were deliuered yea and with all this they should yeeld rare thankesgiuing to God for the same; especially seeing it is the end of all deliuerance, euen the greatest, and withall this, that we may serue the Lord euer after without feare. Luk.1.74.

Againe, another thing is not to bee omitted in this verse, that in stead of hearkening to, and obeying God and their Iudges, they fell againe directly to Idolatry, and so forsooke the God of their fathers; and most brutishly bowed themselues to their Idols which were but blocks, and could doe nothing for them. A deceiueable pleasure they tooke therein (as mans nature is very prone to serue God after a grosse and false manner) yea and the holy story sheweth, that they did quickly fall to this, and turne out of the way; to teach vs how soone a well ordered course, and good things are forgotten and laid aside. This as it may bee obserued, in this people, that they soone waxed wearie of their good beginnings; so also it is apparant in others that come after them; who though they haue good example before their eyes, to goe before them therein, yet they are soone carried another way; especially when the chiefe persons are gone, who delighted in well doing. And yet further to lay out their sinne, it is set forth by an apt and fit similitude of fornication, euen as holinesse to God is in the Scripture oft times compared to chastnesse in marriage.

For as the whoremonger is drunken and besotted with his lewd companions, so that he can regard no counsell, neither can see it to be his discredit, to be linked in with such an one: neither is moued with the wasting of his goods which is caused thereby: euen so the spirituall whoremonger, which is the Idolater, is as blind as his Idoll, and cannot bee disswaded from it; but an Image and Crucifix ouerswayeth him, when the worshipping of God in spirit and truth is tedious, and vtterly vnsauoury to him. The reason of all this which I haue said of him, and of all such at this day, who aggrauate their sin in the like manner, is this; that men regard nothing but their ease & vain pleasure, & haue no consciences to performe their promises & vowes made to God in the time of their affliction. Againe, they being either void of faith vtterly; or hauing receiued some small measure of it, and being slow & negligent in the meanes vsing daily and duly, whereby it should be confirmed; they hauing also others to ioyne & keepe company with them in doing as they do, it easily commeth to passe, that they so soone decline, and their promise which they made to God of repentance, doth vanish like the sparkles. Note.

THE

THE SIXTEENTH SERMON VPON THE SECOND CHAPTER OF THE BOOKE OF IVDGES. Verſ. 19. 20. 21.

VERS. 19. *Yet when the Iudge was dead, they returned and did worſe then their fathers, in following other gods to ſerue them, and worſhip them; they ceaſed not from their owne inuentions, nor from their rebellious way.*

20. *Wherefore the wrath of the Lord was kindled againſt Iſrael, and he ſaid, becauſe this people hath tranſgreſſed my couenant, which I commanded their fathers. and hath not obeyed my voice;*

21. *Therfore will I no more caſt out before them any of the nations which Ioſhua left when he died.*

22. *That through them I may proue Iſrael, whether they will keepe the way of the Lord to walke therein, as their fathers kept it, or not.*

23. *So the Lord left thoſe nations, and droue them not out immediately, neither deliuered them into the hand of Ioſhua.*

Verſ. 19. NOw followeth the laſt branch of this ſecond part of the chapter; that is to ſay, that when the Iudge died, the people did worſe then their fathers, (as is ſet downe in this verſe,) whereupon the wrath of God was kindled againſt them, as appeareth in the twentieth verſe, and then the fruit of it, namely, Gods puniſhing of them is ſet downe in verſe 21. and the end why he did ſo, in the 22. that was, to proue them, and therefore it is ſaid in the laſt verſe, that God left the enemies in the land ſtill in *Ioſhuas* time, and did not caſt them out. Now of theſe as they lie in order.

The clearing of the text. That it ſhould bee thus with this people as in this verſe it is ſaid, it is no leſſe lamentable then wonderfull. For when God had pitied them, (they groning to him) and ſent them Iudges, who ſhould deliuer them out of their oppreſſions, and they likewiſe did deliuer them indeed: after that bleſſing, who would not haue ſaid that they would haue proued a rare people in thankes and obedience vnto God? Now therefore, in that they turned another way when the Iudge was dead, who was ſent to deliuer them, and kept not their couenant which they had made with God, but rebelled againſt him, what trecherie was this? And to that end is their ſinne aggrauated in this verſe, to wit, that they did worſe then their fathers, but following their owne inuentions and euill waies. *Doct. verſ. 19.* By all which it is to be gathered, what light-headedneſſe and inconſtancy is in men, who haue ſometime made earneſt profeſſion of amendment; alſo what lewdneſſe accompanieth the ſame, to ſet it on worke. Heereupon it is, that all good exerciſes of prayer,

prayer, and purposes of good life are soone forgotten, and worne out of memory with many. A simple minded man would thinke, that where there hath been so much knowledge in people, and shew of good conscience going with it, as that they both doe cause confession of sinne, and accusation of themselues, with breaking forth into solemne protestation and couenants of turning to God with all their heart; he would thinke (I say) that if after ten or twelue yeeres absence from them, he should returne againe; that hee should finde rare profiting in the Christian trade; at least much forwardnes in knowledge and in all good duties, and they so setled therein, that they could not be remoued any more from them. Note.

But as people much to bee lamented! they who might looke for such a thing, shall be like rather to finde it farre otherwise, and much worse, as wee see heere it was with these. And in stead of growing in knowledge and grace, at least of setlednesse and stedfastnesse in their good beginnings, they shall be found reuolters from the same rather; as it goeth with men now adaies, and to haue deuised with themselues, or consulted with others about new waies and courses of life, cleane contrary. Some to fall in with Papist and sectaries, other to bee drawne to whoredome and vncleannesse; and the greatest part into depth of worldlinesse, sutes, vncharitable contentions, and the like: which though it be fearefull to heare of, yet it is common, and easie to be found, euen while good exercises of preaching and some good neighbourhood continue, and bee enioyed of them: and therefore how much more shall this be found where such good meanes are wanting? Oh if goodnesse preuaile not with them, and haue not the vpper hand, yea if it be not loued aboue all other things, and in price aboue them, and diligence vsed daily in the practise of good duties, all shewes of the best beginnings will soone turne to the contrary. And good reason it is, that where men professe godlinesse, which is the greatest riches, *and hath the promises of this life and of the life to come*, good reason (I say) that there they should not be ashamed, to seeke by all meanes to aduance and honour it, to the end that all may know the worthinesse and price of it; and that it is not without reward euen in this world. Which while few regard to doe, they are worthily put to reproch and shame. 1. Tim. 6. 6. & 4. 8.

But heere, beside that which hath been said (a good occasion being offered out of all these verses together) wee may gather a good direction for a great part of our life, and that as well before affliction come, as in the time of it, and after deliuerance out of it. Before it come, and while God giueth vs leaue to serue him with cheerefulnesse (which is a sweet portion in this life) we should greatly labour to keepe well, while we are well, and not doe as this people did here, to wit, prouoke God to punish vs for sinning against him as the world doth, negligently or wittingly. Secondly, if we haue, for al our heed taking, broken out against conscience, (which without good heed taking, may full easily be) we should cry to God after our fall, & from vnder our burthen, not tarrying till we be driuen to it by extremity, as these heere were: and further when we cry to him, wee should wait patiently, (and the rather because we haue by our sinne prouoked him against vs) till God deliuer vs. Thirdly, seeing he will most certainly helpe, being thus sought to, let vs beleeue and be perswaded, that hee will heare vs graciously, as wee see Doct. *Out of all these verses together.* 1 2 Note. 3 Psal. 50. 15.

heere he did them, who yet were great offenders, and thus let vs strengthen
4 and inable our selues to this patience with confidence. Fourthly, when wee be deliuered, let vs afterward oft remember & consider in what an vncomfortable estate we were before, and how good and gracious the Lord hath been to vs, to bring vs out of such aduersity, and with daily thankes cleaue to
Psal.89.31. him yet more neerely then before; and in no wise prouoke him by renewing our sinnes, as these did heere, which were monstrous, and to our owne cost (be we well assured) it shall be. And thus if we be carefull to doe, it shall
5 goe well with vs, and good daies shall we see, as may be looked for in so bad
Deut.5.30. a world; and such as haue their thousands of gold, shall not bee able to buy
Note. and purchase with all their abundance.

Vers.10. But to passe to the next verse. I hauing spoken of the reuolt of this people in the former verse, (beside the direction which by occasion I set downe there,) the holy story goeth on heere to shew what the Lord did to this people thus turning from their good beginnings, after the death of the Iudge; He was sore displeased with them, and his anger was kindled against
Doct. them. Here to say the same that I did there of Gods anger, were but a needlesse thing. That which I note of it heere, is this; that as before hath been seene, so through the whole book it appeareth, that it is vsuall with the Lord to doe thus; namely, when men sinne, to be angry; that is, to do as men will, when they be angry, for otherwise wee haue heard that neither anger, repenting, nor any such affection, or change is in the Lord. And is it not meet that God should thus deale with vs thinke we, when we are so ready by euery occasion to prouoke him? For if this held vs not in awe, we should, euen we who are his owne oft times breake out as the common sort do (the flesh being wearie of penting in) whereas the loue of God (I grant) should bee
2.Cor.5.14. sufficient to constraine vs to our duties. And what a thing were it, that God should alwaies bee angry with a man? doubtlesse if any one could bee perswaded that he were so affected to him, not onely his whole life should bee in daily and deadly vnquietnesse; but he should also be ouerwhelmed with the thought of it, and driuen to desperation. And yet we may know by that which hath been said, that God hath iust cause to doe no lesse, but to let his anger burne as fire against such as prouoke him. But indeed hee oft deferres the declaration of his wrath, giuing men time and liberty thereby to repent, and doth not once shew it many times, when hee is often prouoked. Hereof it is, that when God being iustly displeased, and yet men doe not in in the meane while repent and turne to him, humbly seeking mercy; that hee doth afterward declare by his manifold or sore reuenges, that hee was long before prouoked to anger, and iustly offended with them. But this is wisely to bee marked of vs, that though his owne people sinne, (*as there is*
1.King 8.46. *none that sinneth not*) to wit, by ouersight, infirmity, vnauoidable ignorance,
Note. and such like; whereas hee doth not by and by, suffer his anger to breake
Psal.130.3. forth, the reason is this: he hath said himselfe, that he wil not looke straightly what is done amisse of them: and beside, when they see that they haue fallen so, they rise againe, and this they do daily and ordinarily returning to him againe, & cast themselues down in true humiliation before him, in the meditation & application of the work of their redeemer Christ, and so the Lord is pacified with them againe. Therefore such as are wise, will bee most

carefull

carefull to keepe away occasions of Gods displeasure; seeing the Lords anger is a consuming fire, and while that is prouided against, men may possesse their soules with peace, and may goe out and in with him daily, with good liking and comfort, thus much of Gods being angry againe, now of the punishment that followed vpon it. Heb.12.29.

God being thus displeased with them, seeing they had so shamefully transgressed and broken the couenant that he made with their fathers; *therefore hee will no more* (hee said) *cast out any of the nations that Ioshua left behinde.* For although Israel was oft deliuered out of the hands of sundry of them by their Iudges; by whom also many of them were slaine, yet they were not vtterly rooted out, but their posterity sprung vp againe afterward, and multiplied in the land, to the great disquieting, vexing and annoying of his people. This I say was the punishment: And how sore it was, may bee thought by this, that these nations were left among them to their destruction; as in verse 3. we haue seene, where wee heard the same punishment threatened by the Angell to them at Bochim. But then they repented, and there is no doubt, but God accepted it, as hee promised. But this was more grieuous, that afterwards their posterity did worse then they. For they there were reproued, and threatened, for making couenants with the Canaanites: these for falling flatly to Idolatry with them. Heere, besides that wee may see that for the most part, men waxe worse and worse, and the good decline, and the bad decay and wanze away in their sinnes, as may bee seene by the example of these compared with that we reade in the second verse; wee may further learne againe, as in verse 3. we heard, that God will be discharged of his couenant towards men, in and concerning the outward benefits of this life, if they stand not to their couenants which they haue made with him. Vers.21.

And if they bee his owne people, hee will punish their offences with the rod, and their iniquitie with strokes; though hee take not his mercy vtterly from them: and if they be other, he will much more leaue them helpelesse, and to shift for themselues, so as they fal into depth of euill, who might haue thriued and prospered through his blessings. Yea and they might haue bin in good hope to haue embraced his couenant of grace and mercy also: as many are brought by Gods temporary benefits to seeke after spirituall, so might these haue done also. Therefore, little doe men know, what vexation they they bring vpon themselues, when they waxe carelesse in their couenants keeping which they haue entred into with God; (as the leauing of some grosse sinne, or the forsaking of ill company, worldlinesse, or such like offences;) and so forgetting themselues, fall to them againe afterward. They shall surely runne on from euill to worse that deale so with God, and from smaller punishments to greater iudgements, so little cause they shall haue to reioyce, for glory of their winnings thereby. Psal.89.31.

So that beside other manifold punishments which cannot bee reckoned vp, they that breake couenant with the Lord, shall alwaies haue some speciall eye sores left to vexe them, as these nations were to Israel. And as this worthily layeth forth the forementioned punishment, in vers. 15. *that the hand of the Lord was sore vpon this people of his*; euen so wee shall finde it who are vnfaithfull to him in our couenants, as that either stubborne and disobedient children (none of the least plagues) shall rise vp to make our liues

Prou. wearisome to vs, which (as *Salomon* saith) *shall be as corruption to our bones*, and that many waies; as in wasting our goods riotously, and with harlots, and vnthriftinesse, or by imbracing popery, and otherwise by waxing prophane. Or we shall be crossed by vnkinde, spitefull and vnquiet neighbours; who with sutes, brawlings, and sundry disagreements, shall make our best pleasures to be turned into bitternesse and wormewood: or we shall be plagued
Note. with seruants, who shall consume vs, and bring reproch and vexation vnto vs, by defiling our houses, or working vs some other annoiance: so likewise with vnfaithfull and scandalous Ministers, sutes, or controuersies, so that by one or other of these, or such like, wee shall haue no comfort in any thing; beside the many diseases, as collicke, stone, burning agues, consumption; for which wee shall bee constrained to cry out, and say, wee haue no pleasure in our liues. And yet a greater punishment then all these, wee shall not know, when these plagues be vpon vs, that they are for our vnfaithfulnesse in our couenant, (though more or lesse, it is the case of the most that professe the Gospell, thus to forget our selues) which thing yet (in great griefe I vtter it) is to be seene in many, that when Gods hand is sore against them, yet they know not why it is so, namely for their sinnes, to the end they might amend.

Vers. 22. & 23. In this verse the end is set downe, why God would not cast out the Canaanites: to wit, to proue them whether they would keepe the way of the Lord; (and therefore it is said in the next verse, that he left, and did not deliuer them into the hands of *Ioshua*: and if they did obey the Lord in fighting against them, and making no leagues with them, but follow and do as their good forefathers had done, then they might reape the fruit therof, I meane, the Lords promise; to wit, that he would be with them to assist them, to enioy the land to their hearts desire: If they should do otherwise; then they should declare thereby that their strength was neuer great, if they fainted
Prou. 24. 10. being tried; and beside, they must beare the burthen that should light on them.

Doct. vers. 22. And by this we may learne, that God hath this end in afflicting his, that they may haue exercise of his graces in them; as patience, faith, hope, and such like, that being found furnished therwith, they might giue God praise, and they themselues might reioyce: and that they might be humbled, if the contrary should be. And this we ought to be resolued of in all our troubles, euen when we cannot finde out in our selues any particular sin, for which
Note. the Lord afflicteth vs. So that wee bee farre wide, and offer our selues great iniurie, when we doe not resolue of this, that in Gods afflicting vs, he tryeth vs, that so we may behaue our selues accordingly. The same may bee said, if heresies spring vp among vs, that God tryeth vs what we will doe: as Saint
1. Cor. 11. 19. *Paul* saith, *There must bee heresies euen among you, that they who are approued*,
Reuel. 13. 10. that is, of sound religion and godlinesse, through long experience, *may bee knowne*. It should teach vs, seeing God doth so, alwaies to haue our hearts carefully set vpon it, and to tell it oft to our selues, that whatsoeuer bayts of
Note. sinne are set before vs (as a cup of pleasant wine well coloured, yet mixed with poyson) wee should not meddle with, nor reach out our hand thereto, and how bold and busie soeuer we behold other to bee in snatching greedily at them, and to deuoure them; yet we may not bee enticed with them,

nor looke on them; for why? God doth trie vs thereby what strength of grace is in vs, to resist and turne from them; and as for them that doe most readily embrace them, they shall soone vomit vp their sweet morsels with bitternesse.

Now to adde this last verse with the former 22. whereas it is said, that Vers.23. God did not deliuer all the nations into the hands of *Ioshua*, as he did some, and could as well haue brought vnder all the rest; it further teacheth vs, to haue an eye to Gods workes, what things he doth, and to resolue our selues, that he seeth alwaies good reason thereof: and follow we his direction, and he will leade vs to see as much. It is a good grace in vs, if we can iustifie him in all that he doth, and to say with the people in the Gospell, he hath done all things well. And yet it is so, whether we affirme it or no. But seeing wee are grauelled and amazed at many of his workes, not seeing any reason in them, but we are rather ready to reason against them, and rebell; [as when he crosseth vs in our attempts aud doings, and that not once, but often, nor in one thing, but in many, and that apparantly, and more then in ordinary manner, about our goods and bargaines, health, and the like] heere therefore I say, humbly to submit our selues to that which he doth, though it bee no other then we pray daily to doe [thy will bee done of vs] oh it is a thing well beseeming vs, and yet but our duty. And thus wee should say; (if that goe not with our liking which God doth) hee could haue done otherwise, as heere hee could haue cast out the Canaanites in *Ioshuas* daies: but as hee left them to try the people; so he aduisedly letteth things alone to proue vs how wise, confident, and obedient we will bee therein. Hee could giue learning without study, and deliuerance out of trouble by and by, or withhold it altogether, that it should not take hold of vs, but he doth not, neither seeth it best so to do, to the end we may frame our selues to his good pleasure, and in euery part of our life bee subiect to him. And this bee said of the second part of the chapter, and of all the branches drawne out of the same, and so of the whole chapter. It followeth in the next.

THE SEVENTEENTH SERMON ON THE THIRD CHAPTER OF THE BOOKE OF IVDGES.

VERS. 1. *These now are the nations which the Lord left, that hee might proue Israel by them, euen as many of Israel as had not knowne all the warres of Canaan.*

2. *Onely to make the generations of the children of Israel, to know, and to teach them warre, which doubtlesse their predecessors knew not.*

3. *Fiue Princes of the Philistines, and all the Canaanites, and the Zidonians, and the Hiuites that dwelt in mount Lebanon, from mount Baal-hermon vntill one come to Hamath.*

4. *And these remained to proue Israel by them, to wit, whether they would obey the Commandements of the Lord, which he commanded their fathers by the hand of Moses.*

5. *And the children of Israel dwelt among the Canaanites, the Hittites, and the Amorites, and the Perizzites, and the Heuites, and the Iebusites.*

6. *And they tooke their daughters to be their wiues, and gaue their daughters to their sons, and serued their gods.*

The summe of the chapter, and parts 2.

THe summe and parts in generall of this Chapter may be fitly set downe together: for in the first sixe verses is shewed, why God left the nations in the land, and which those nations were. In the rest of the Chapter there are three defections or fallings away from God in the people of Israel mentioned, and three plagues sent vpon them for the same, and a threefold deliuerance by three seuerall Judges. And thus the holy story beginneth to set downe the state of the people, as was said in the former Chapter.

The first part of the Chapter.

The meaning of the foure first verses.

ANd first why these nations were left still in the land, two reasons are set downe: one in the first and fourth verse, and that was to proue them: the other in the first and second verse, and that was, to make them know warre; not meaning thereby to make them skilfull warriours, (though necessity draue them to that, when they saw they must trust to their skill) but to let them see what it was to bee put to their shifts, and to fight with weapons, who had neuer been wont to doe so, neither their fathers, seeing the Lord had in the former warres with their enemies, extraordinarily fought for them without their owne labour and skill.

To

To come to the first reason generally set downe in the first verse,and particularly in the fourth,I haue spoken of it in the former chapter, and the last two verses: It is heere repeated to beate it into them deepely; and to make them thoroughly perswaded thereof, that they might then, (and so wee now) bend all the force of our hearts to looke well about vs, how we beare our troubles meekely and patiently,depending vpon God for a good issue: which dutie he most certainly looketh for at our hands, as throughout the Scripture he teacheth and admonisheth vs to doe; and wee cannot but bee much disquieted by our afflictions,if wee doe otherwise, notwithstanding that our corrupt nature doe carrie vs much to rebell against the same. This is that which we haue to learne by the repeating of those words in this verse, namely that it is said, God left the nations in the land to trie the people of Israel, and to trie them in this, whether they would keepe his commandements or no. Doct.vers.1. and 4. Psal.37.3. Psal.50.15.

Moreouer,we must marke that which is set downe here in this first verse: that the Lord is said to haue held these nations still in the land, which was to the exceeding sore vexing of his people: to teach vs, that the raizing,remaining, or remouing of troubles, they are all of the Lord, and by his appointing; euen by his will, and of his wise disposing, whether wee respect the whole Church, or any part or member of it: and they come not by chance, or a mans ill fortune, as the ignorant people speake, (neither is there any such thing) but as the Lord himselfe saith in the Prophet *Amos, there is no euill in the city*, that is,no trouble, *but I the Lord haue sent it*. And if it were otherwise,the best people, as the worst are, should (by their afflictions) be at their wits end. Wee may not therefore rest our selues in the second causes,neither vexe our selues about them (as we doe too oft) which is a spurning against the Lord,but patiently beare them: seeing that whatsoeuer the instrument bee, it is certaine, the Lord is the ouer-ruling cause,howsoeuer it is euident, that oft times wee cause and bring them our selues: and therefore we ought to bend our selues in all earnest manner, to patience: and so much the rather, seeing hee further certifieth vs,that hee doth all for the best to such as feare him: so that wee doe but encrease our sorrow,who by impatience encrease our sinne; and therefore prouoke we not him,from whom all trouble commeth, and who through his Almighty power can cast into hell also, but feare wee to doe euill in his sight euermore,that wee may auoid both,and ascribe vnto him our deliuerances also, that seeing all such deliuerances are from the Lord, hee may haue his due praise from vs. Doct.2.in vers.1. Amos.3.3. Note. Note.

In the end of this verse and the second,where it is said,*that God left the nations still in the land,that he might teach this generation of Israel, warre,which neither they, nor their fathers had in times past knowne:* which is another reason, why those nations were not driuen out; this is the more cleare meaning of it. When the Lord by trying them,had found (though he was neuer ignorant what they would doe) and made manifest the impiety and idolatry of the people of Israel to themselues: he tooke away from them their strength in war,and withheld his aide from them, which hee had in times past giuen to them,and to their fathers in battell with their enemies,so that now when they went to warre by their owne power, the Lord withholding his from Vers.1.2. *The sense.*

 them,

them, they knew what warre meant, which before they knew not, when the Lord had fought for them: for then hee gaue them strength, and terrified their enemies and weakened them, and gaue good successe to the Israelites, but now he left them to shift for themselues: and therefore wee see what is meant by this (*that they had not knowne warre*) when as yet they had not broken their couenant with God, for he had fought for them. They knew not then what it meant to goe to warre, for the Lord had fought for them, but now they did begin to learne.

Doct. ver. 1. and 2. And heere we may see, that when by Gods kindnes and many comforts ministred by him, we cannot be kept in compasse, nor be brought to cleaue to him with all our hearts, hee will take another course with vs to bring vs thereto: for hee will acquaint vs with wants, trouble and sorrow, as hee did this people heere, to see if they can bring vs thereto: and yet such is his loue to vs, if they preuaile with vs, and worke kindly vpon vs to bring vs to repentance, he will returne to vs againe graciously, and continue still his former bounties toward vs. Iosh. 6. 14. 17. When *Ioshua*, and the good generation in his daies truly serued the Lord, they were preserued from their enemies, and knew not what war meant, the Lord himselfe fought for thē, while they did little more many times then looke on. And in our first parents we may cleerely see this to be exemplified: while they yet liued in innocency, and were vpheld with the grace of God, they neither knew nor felt any euill: but when Gen. 3. 7. they had disobeyed by eating of the forbidden fruit, they began to know what good and euil meant. In like manner, children, while in their younger yeeres they haue been subiect and obedient to their parents, they are tenderly handled, and haue all things with ease prouided for them: but when they grow vp rude and stout, and for that, are put forth to their shifts, they come to know what hardnesse meanes (who before were not acquainted therewith) by the rough handling of strangers.

And let it be well thought of by vs, for euen so God dealeth with vs, if Note. we can by his mercies be drawne to dutie, he is ready to bestow them plentifully vpon vs, hee thinketh nothing too good for vs, so as wee need not know the sorrowes and vexations that are in the world, in comparison of that which many thousands doe feele, and smart by them. But if we will follow the common course of others, to be like to them in euill, we shall soone know that it was no meane benefit to be so sheltred by the Lord, as we were before; and namely, that shall be, when wee begin to feele his heauie hand Note. against vs. And wee in this towne, and heereabout haue seene, while wee haue made it our chiefe delight, to follow the Lord, not regarding the examples and multitudes of bad and irreligious persons (who dwell among vs) to be withdrawne by them, we that haue done so, wee haue seene, I say, Gods exceeding goodnesse toward vs (I speake to his praise) and desire I may neuer see the contrary. And in comparison of the world, I meane, the ignorant and prophane sort, who desire not to be acquainted with the Lord and his waies, it may truly bee said, that wee haue seene many good daies, when our chiefe care hath been to liue vnder his gouernment; and when wee haue failed at some time more then at others, and through frailty forgotten our selues, hee hath mercifully quickened and brought vs backe againe: so that (for the most part) wee haue not knowne what the sorrowes

of

of the world meane. And our worst daies haue been, when we haue forgot our selues,and forsaken the good and right way, and walked or stepped aside into by-waies,then he hath taught vs (by wofull experience) what sorrowes and vexations meane. For example: when we haue in the simplicity of our hearts ioyned in the sweet doctrine of the Gospell preached vnto vs, and haue minded it chiefly as our best treasure; and when wee haue as well feared to offend the Lord in those things which haue liked vs best, prouoking one another to loue and to good workes, oh how hath hee made vs to prosper? and when hath he frowned vpon vs,but when we haue peruerted our waies. Note.

In this verse the nations are reckoned whom the Lord would haue to remaine in the land, among whom his people the Israelites must dwell: reade them in the text. By this that they must dwell with these wicked nations, wee are taught, that it is one of the punishments among many other, which our diuers kinds of sinne draw vpon vs, that euen because of them we must sometime dwell with the wicked: for though all must haue to do with them,(or else they must goe out of the world) yet this that I now speak of, is another matter. *Dauid* dwelt among the haters of peace out of the holy land: as for the Church of Pergamus, whose habitation was where Satans throne was; that was Gods triall to them. But the dwelling of Israel in Babylon, and their fathers before them among the Egyptians: and the dwelling of these heere mentioned among the Philistims, Canaanites, and Heuites: these habitations (I say) were Gods punishments and curses,euen the fruit of their deserts and grieuous sinnes: who vexed them many waies, as if Hornets should haue stung them: and because such dwellings are brought vpon men by their owne prouokings of God, and that sundry waies; therefore beside the smart that they sustaine by them through outward troubles, they haue this added thereunto, that they cannot meekely and quietly beare them, for the wound that they haue made in their conscience by their knowne sinnes, which is most grieuous vnto them, seeing they must and cannot but remember,that they iustly sustaine them. One example of our time I will alleage of two persons, a yeoman and his wife (I might bring many) These two dwelling among sundry good neighbours and religions, because they were not like minded to them, because they distasted the Gospell,tooke a sore pritch against them, without any iust cause giuen them,and therupon in wilfulnes remoued their dwelling from them. Their going away was to enioy better neighbours, and to bring in the world,and the commodities thereof the faster. But (to be short) seeing yee will long (no doubt) to heare the end; so it was,that they enioyed not that which they sought and went for; for their wealth wasted, and their neighbours,who had neuer known what it ment,neither had learned to vse them neighbourly,dealt roughly with them, and sore vexed and wearied them: vpon this, the Lord visited them both, with great sicknesse, euen both of them together. And then they had leisure to bethinke themselues of the change they had made,and especially with what minde they had done it: and then the crying out of their doings in this behalfe,and that they did (as it fell out) in the presence of some of them, whom they had first dwelt among, being sent for, by them vpon occasion though they dwelt more

Vers.8.5. Doct. 1.Cor.5.10. Psal.120.5.6.

then twentie miles distant from them; not sparing to charge themselues deepely, and to shew their great repentance for their rashnesse and wilfulnesse in their remouing euen to them. So the man died there, the woman in a maruellous manner bewailing her offence, which was compounded of many, and this from day to day. In which time it fell out that I was an eye and an eare witnesse of much more then I say: Shee by little recouered so farre, as shee might bee carried from thence, and so shee returned to her first dwelling (no friend could perswade her to the contrary) but neuer recouered her health; but within a while after died at her owne house, acknowledging and bewailing her sin to her neighbors that visited her, bearing the shame of it meekely and with contentment. This example I thought not to be out of season to make mention of, by so good an occasion; to admonish some to make better reckoning of good neighbourhood, who are too ready vpon a tetch taken, to ease themselues with thinking to recouer their dwellings. Besides, let vs not be secure about this, to dwel we care not where, nor in what places soeuer, (because some can doe no otherwise, but it is laid vpon them to bee yeelded to of them, by meere necessity) for though it bee Gods triall to some of them, and other haue it, as their iust punishment, yet make wee account of Christian and peaceable habitation as more then a common benefit. And yet such must know also, that they must keepe themselues vnstained among the wicked and ill disposed, and haue no fellowship with their vnfruitfull workes of darkenesse, but groane vnder their burthen to God, that he may ease them of it in time, and seeke to supply their want in some other place by the publike meanes (if they want them) as they may. But let other if they can, be free from the company and neere dwelling of such as are prophane, noisome, and spitefull, enioy their freedome rather, as
1.Cor.7.21. Saint *Paul* saith of seruants: if it be their lot to be so, let them be contented, but if they can be free, let them vse it rather. And that not onely for the hurt that they may easily get there; but let their delight also bee in the saints which are on the earth, and their fellowship with such as excell in vertue,
Psal.16.3. for the manifold good that they may reape by them. But heere an end of this matter.

Vers.3.5. *An Obiect.* Now before I goe from the third verse, which I haue ioyned with the fifth; to shew that Israel dwelt among the nations, this doubt is to bee answered, namely, how it can bee affirmed, that the cities of the Philistims are said not to haue been possessed of the Israelites, I meane Ekron, Askelon, and Gaza, but to be at the time heere mentioned, in the Philistims hands: seeing in the first chapter of this booke, vers. 18. it is said, that they were taken and
Answ. enioyed with their borders, of *Iuda* and *Simeon* in warre made with them. To the which it is answered, that they were indeed at that time taken by them; but now after that, they were not in the possession of them, but for the sinnes of Israel, their strength was abated, and the Philistims power was confirmed. Whereby without any difficulty it came to passe, that they recouered them againe.

Doct. vers.3.5. By the which it may bee obserued, what changes and alterations sin worketh, (God in his prouidence so appointing) for by their sinne this came to passe. By eating the forbidden fruit, what an alteration was wrought in the estate of our first parents, that they lost their honour, their holines, and their happinesse

happinesse in one moment of time, and were brought to the contrary, euen to vtter misery. And *Dauid* for that one sinne with *Bathsheba* the wife of *Vriah*, what a breach made he of the most sweet peace of conscience, which hee before enioyed, beside the changes that it wrought in this life, by many punishments, and in his posterity also? Psal.51.8.

The like is wel knowne of *Sampson, Salomon*, and many other of the Lords people. That we may see that he spareth not his owne, if they prouoke him, as he saith in the Psalme; *If mine owne children breake my lawes, I will punish euen their sin with the rod*, &c. And are they exempt in this age who sin in the like manner? How are many of them plagued for breaking couenant with God, in committing some reprochfull sinne; as adultery, deceit, spite, and reuenge, oppression or wrong, grosse worldlinesse, forsaking their constant course in a godly life, and their zealous worshipping of him? These, I say, and such like iniquities (for so cunningly can the diuell handle the matter, that they may all possibly fasten vpon them) what changes (thinke wee) doe they bring to passe? as sorrow for ioy, feare in stead of godly courage and confidence, shame for credit and good report, with many such like? This is foretold in Deuteronomie 28. a chapter to this purpose, worthie to bee often read ouer, because it containeth a prophesie of all the euils which were inflicted vpon this people in their times, for their apostacy and backsliding from God. If a man be absent but seuen yeeres from his acquaintance, Oh, how will they say, hee is changed? But this is nothing to the change that sinne worketh. Yea and not only the forementioned sinnes, which are grosse among men, doe worke these great changes in their liues; but also those which are grosse in the eyes of the Lord, euen they do the like: as the minding, delighting in, and attempting the forementioned sinnes, or the like, though it bee but vnder-hand (as they say) and not effected nor committed, what alterations doe these worke in a man also? And beside their other punishments which change and disfigure them, the often buffeting of the conscience (which is some taste of hell) doth also as hornets torment them. What doth idlenesse of minde worke, and the wandring after other loathsome lusts and desires? also a slight following of mens callings, and much more the grosse neglecting of them (wherein yet faithfully and diligently to be occupied is a piece of Paradise) what do these (I say) and such like bring to passe, but vnwelcome changes, decay, and wasting of their estate with bondage, and disguisednesse, which they bring themselues into, in such wise, that they haue not the benefit of the Christian life themselues, and they are afraid through an euill conscience, to reproue sinne in other; and if they should, yet are they not regarded in that which they say: for they haue dishonoured the Lord, and hee hath taken their honour from them, that their words shall not bee set by: So that I may truly say, their sin hath brought many changes into their liues, and they neuer almost recouer the comfort of their former daies, (for I speake of such as haue knowne better) since they vnhappily lost it. I haue but shewed in some sort what changes sinne worketh in Gods people.

Psal.89.31.

Note.

Deut.28.16. to the end.

Note.

Note.

And seeing it is lesse doubted of, that it doth much more in the liues of them who were neuer well gouerned: I will not make the like discourse of the effects that it worketh in them, but shut vp briefly that which I meane to

say

say thereof. And to speake the truth,as sinne swarmeth, rageth, and getteth the vpper hand in them,so it maketh strip and wast where it goeth, and hauoke of all that good is,where any apparance was of it in them,as the vnseasonable frost or East wind doth of the tender blossomes in the spring: and the like it doth worke in their estates and liues that commit it,by bringing in punishment and iudgements of God thicke and three-fold. As by whoredome and riot, the wasting of body and goods; by drunkennesse, diseases; by quarrelling and vncharitablenesse, sutes; and losse of their sweet peace in neighbourhood; by pride,stoutnesse and statelinesse a fall; yea ruine and vtter misery. Examples are infinite: as in the destruction of Babel for their insolency against God; the swallowing vp of *Chorah* for his rebellion may be seene: also in the drowning of *Pharaoh* for mocking of God so oft: to the young man the threatening of iudgement for his iollity: the rich mans going to hell for taking his pleasure heere: in all these (I say) with a great number more, this is to bee seene, what woe sinne hath wrought to the committers of it: and it would much more in Scripture and experience at this day appeare,if men were not wittingly blind in beholding it; as also but that God hath had a regard to maintaine and preserue society among men; for which cause,many wicked ones are spared for a time. And this be said of the changes that sinne worketh,which I haue said by occasion of the Israelites losing and yeelding againe the cities of the Philistims, with the priuiledges thereto belonging, into their hands because of their sinne.

Note. Numb.16.31. Exod.14.28. Eccles.11.9. Luk.16.

Vers.6. The sense.

Whereas it was said before,vers.1. and 4. that those nations were left to try Israel,whether they would obey the commandements of the Lord;here it is set downe how they carried themselues in the triall: namely, that they made marriages with them,and serued their gods; they had no power to resist and doe otherwise. And by this we may see,with what danger wee liue among Idolaters and wicked men: for in that it is said heere, that they ioyned in marriage together,which was specially forbidden them in Deuteronomie, it is that which the Lord did foresay would come to passe thereby. And he forbad them such mariages principally for this cause,seeing he foresaw and knew that by vnequall matching together, his worship would bee greatly impaired,if not turned into the contrary. For godly and religious persons are often alienated by the parties contrarily minded vnto them, from the true God; as in *Salomons* example (so wise a man) is to bee seene: who was exceedingly corrupted, and builded places for strange Gods to worship them in,being inticed thereto by strange women,whom he loued. And our age hath sustained most grieuous shipwracke of conscience and goodnesse,in that many therein haue ioyned in marriage with Papists, and other prophane hellish Atheists: For when they haue by their familiarity together,made marriages with them; what remaineth, but that they,as these did heere,doe turne to their religion also, and serue in the manner that they doe? But of this before,chap.2. vers.2.

Doct. Deut.7.3.4.

THE

THE EIGHTEENTH SERMON VPON THE THIRD CHAPTER OF THE BOOKE OF IVDGES.

The second part of the Chapter.

VERS. 7. *So the children of Israel did wickedly in the sight of the Lord, and forgat the Lord their God, and serued Baalim and Asheroth.*

8. *Therefore the wrath of the Lord was kindled against Israel; and he sold them into the hand of Cushan rishathaim King of Aram-naharaim, and the children of Israel serued Cushan-rishathaim eight yeeres.*

9. *And when the children of Israel cried vnto the Lord, the Lord stirred vp a sauiour to the children of Israel, and he saued them, euen Othniel the sonne of Kenaz Calebs younger brother.*

10. *And the spirit of the Lord came vpon him, and hee iudged Israel, and went out to warre; and the Lord deliuered Cushan rishathaim King of Aram into his hand, and his hand preuailed against Cushan-rishathaim.*

11. *So the land had rest fortie yeeres, and Othniel the sonne of Kenaz died.*

NOw I hauing shewed how God tried his by people dwelling among the idolatrous nations, what they would do, and we hauing seene also what they did, to wit, that they made marriages with them, and serued their gods, both which haue bin set downe in the first part of this chapter: I will now proceed to the second part, and come to the three examples therein set downe by the holy Ghost; and heerein I will speake chiefly of these things therein, to wit, of the sinne, punishment, repentance and deliuerance of the people, and how they turned away againe from the Lord afterwards. The first example is to the twelfth verse: the second to the 31. verse: the third, to the end. The first hath these foure things to bee considered; one is the peoples reuolting from God, in this verse: another, the punishment brought vpon them for it in the eighth verse: the third, the peoples crying to God vnder it, vers. 9: and the fourth, the Lords sending helpe in the rest, vnto the 12. verse; with the fruit that followed.

Their sinne is set downe, first generally, that they did euill in the sight of the Lord; and then more particularly, that they forgot him, and fell to Idolatry. Heere I giue this watchword to the reader, that seeing I shall in this booke often meet with things that I haue already spoken of, at least, that there are diuerse things mentioned oft and sundry times heerein; therfore I will not goe ouer them againe, as oft as I meete with them, being the same

ſpecially in the ſame manner,which were but a wearying of the reader with repeating one thing oft: but I will note and chiefly follow ſuch things, as beſide them are occaſioned there. All the things in this verſe are ſuch: I will therefore doe as I haue ſaid, and referre the reader for the reſt, to that which hath been ſaid of them before. Their ſinne ſet downe in generall, that they durſt offend God ſecretly,and do that which was euill in his ſight: and that they forgot the Lord,and remembred not his kindneſſe, and many benefits; and their Idolatry and worſhipping the gods of the nations,which aroſe of the two former: theſe things(I ſay) duly conſidered of vs,do teach this worthie point; to wit,how men breake out into groſſe and foule ſinnes, by the forgetting of Gods goodneſſe toward them, and the taking of boldneſſe to ſinne againſt him, in doing that which is any way euill in his eyes. And ſo by the contrary; the direct way to liue godly, and to bee free from reprochfull ſinnes,is to feare to do any thing amiſſe in the ſight of the Lord
Note. in ſecret, and to keepe in mind his benefits, by daily recording them with feruent and hearty thankes. For if the child be drawne to a naturall loue and ioying in the parents, and ſo to bee afraid to diſpleaſe them, ſeeing they make much of it,and giue it all good things: what maruell is it if the Lords benefits,which are renued vpon vs euery morning,being duly recorded of
Lam.3.23. vs,ſhould draw vs to delight in him,and make our ſongs of him;alſo that we being ready to doe his will,and afraid to offend him in ſecret, what maruell (I ſay) if we ſhould abhore to diſhonour him openly? And if elder children endued with grace,will be faithfull to their parents in their abſence, and ſo ſhunne boldneſſe in offending them in preſence: who doubteth, but that if we feare to offend our God in ſecret,we ſhall ſhunne open and greater offences alſo? So by the contrary this is cleere, that if we grow to this point, that we dare doe that which is euill in Gods eyes,and to forget him, and his vnſpeakeable kindneſſe, though wee commit not by and by the groſeſt and moſt odius things,yet it will not be long before wee breake out euen groſly, wax bold alſo, and worke that which is odious in the ſight of men.

Whereas we ought euer to haue before vs Gods bounty and kindneſſe in ſuch wiſe,that they may be barres in our waies,to keepe vs euen from ſmal offences,that ſo the groſer ſinnes may much more bee kept from vs. And ſo
Pſal.51.4. *Dauid* affirmeth,that if he had not been bold to ſinne againſt God in ſecret, he had neuer broke out ſhamefully before men. We know the diuell is cal-
Gen.3.1. led a ſerpent; which word ſignifieth properly a creeper,becauſe his proper-
Note. ty is, by little and little creepe and winde into vs,to withdraw our hearts from vprightneſſe and conſtancy therein; alſo to cauſe that Gods benefits ſhall be more meanely accounted off of vs: and then boldneſſe in ſinne will creepe vpon vs eaſily, and after that wee ſhall not feare the attempting of great and grieuous ſinnes alſo. It is our wiſedome therefore to conſider Gods goodneſſe to bee ſo great, and the ſame ſo continued to vs daily (as who ſhall but meanely obſerue and weigh the ſame,but he muſt needs confeſſe as much) that we ſhould be afraid and aſhamed to offend and diſpleaſe him, through negligence much more by forgetting our ſelues in both to ſin openly and wilfully. This be ſaid of their ſinne. The puniſhment followes.

Verſ 8. *The ſenſe.* For this the Lord was ſore diſpleaſed with them, and what maruell? ſo many ſinnes being wrapped vp together,as we haue heard. And hee raiſed

vp

vp againſt them this King of Aram heere named, who held them in bondage eight yeeres. Heere it plainly appeareth, that when God is prouoked, hee will bee reuenged: (as wee haue ſeene in the former chapter) and not winke at vs, as we are giuen to thinke. And this is not a matter that falles out now and then (as we ſay) but ordinarily, and that vpon countries, townes, families, as well as perſons, accordingly as the occaſion is offered. And yet he ſheweth it not alwaies immediately; as wee ſee in deferring his puniſhment to the old world an hundred and twentie yeeres, after he was diſpleaſed with them. So he ſent a famine in *Dauids* time on the Iſraelites, for ſinne committed before by *Saul*, in ſlaying the Gibeonites. But though he ſometime deferre, it is to bring the offenders to repentance, as the Aopſtle ſaith to the Romans. And if that come not, he wil in deferring, doe as he that draweth his bow deepely, that the ſtroke may be the more deadly. And yet oftentimes he deferreth not, as in *Corah, Ananias*, and *Saphira*, and others is to bee ſeene. And when men commit knowne ſinnes, they may make their reckoning, that one of theſe waies God will meet with them early or late, the leaſt of them both will be deadly and vnwelcome. *Doct.* *Pſal.50.21.* *Gen.6.3.* *Rom.2.4.*

Now then the caſe ſtanding thus, and wee knowing how vnwelcome and weariſome his puniſhments are; we ſee what we haue to doe; that is to ſay, to beware that wee prouoke not God, by following the deuices and deſires of our wicked hearts, aud ſo grow hardened through the deceitfulneſſe of ſinne. Oh therefore that wee ſhould be ſo bold and ready to offend, who yet blanke ſo ſoone, and are ſo ſore diſmaid, yea when there ſhall but ſome ſmall correction be laid vpon vs! Oh that neither examples of other, nor our owne experience can make vs wiſe to preuent and auoid ſo many and great iudgements, as are drawne vpon vs daily by needleſſe follie, or wilfull offending! And ſecondly, if we haue already falen, what ſhould bee more looked after, then ſpeedily to remember from whence we bee fallen, and to caſt vp our gorge, and repent, leſt the Lord come vpon vs vnprouided. And as for ſuch as at the hearing of this dare obiect againe, that they beleeue that no ſuch thing ſhall befall them: for they haue (they ſay) done as much as I ſpeake of, and yet they are ſafe to this houre, and haue eſcaped puniſhment: I ſay of them, what haue I to doe with them? I tremble to heare of their brutiſh and bold inſencibleneſſe. They are as one aſleepe in the maſt of a ſhip in great danger, but they feare nothing: and as one neare death by ſickneſſe, but being ſenſeleſſe, feeleth no paine; and as *Naball* a groſſe ſinner, but regarded nothing that was ſaid to him, till he knew he muſt die, and then he was as a ſtone or or blocke, onely breathing. The puniſhment of ſuch as boaſt, that they are ſafe for all their ſinning, and haue eſcaped all danger, puniſhment, (although it be not ſeene of many, nor of themſelues) is yet far more grieuous then if it were ſeene with eyes, that it is the ſpirit of ſlumber, or an hardened heart, which is of all other the greateſt puniſhment. *Note.*

Thus we haue heard that God was diſpleaſed with them; and therefore vengeance could not be farre off, but muſt follow, and now it is ſhewed in what manner that was executed. Gods puniſhing them at this time, was eight yeers embondaging them vnder an heathen and idolatrous King, who might command them what he would, and lay vpon them burthens at his pleaſure. And what the curteſie of ſtrangers was, wee may ſee in Deutero- *Another point in this verſ. 8.* *The ſenſe.*

Deut.28.50. nomy; namely such, as that they should not regard the person of the old, nor haue compassion on the young: and such courtesie as *Benhadad* shewed to *Ahab*, and yet it was before hee was in bondage to him, and when hee did but besiege him and his chiefe city, and had onely some likelihood to subdue him, which hope of his, yet was frustrated also. For this it was, & thus 1.King.20.6. he sent him word: *Thy siluer and thy gold is mine, thy women and thy faire children are mine: Or else I will send my seruants to thee by to morrow this time, & they shall search thy house, and the houses of thy seruants, and whatsoeuer is pleasant in thine eyes, they shall take it in their hands and bring it away.* This was the courtesie which *Benhadad* shewed, when he was but in besieging Israel: but these were heere subdued to *Cushan-rishathaim*, and already in his hands, yea and that for eight yeeres, which time vnder such bondage was (we may be sure) thought a long time.

Doct.2. Now we that heare it may iudge, whether they paied not deare for their liberties, that they tooke in sinning: the chiefe of the which was Idolatry. There is no doubt, (considering that which heere we reade) but that the Idolatry, and other sinne which was so pleasant to them in their prosperity, was as bitter to them now in their bondage which it brought them into, neither could it pluck them out of it. But by this let vs learne, what woe and misery men sustaine and bring vpon themselues for a little stolne liberty, and to speake as the truth is, onely for hauing their will: but let none looke to finde sinne afterward, to be, as while it is in committing. Eight yeeres sore bondage, with the discommodities and irksomenesse that accompany it, for a little liberty to liue at their pleasure? And what excellencie or superabounding sweetnesse (thinke wee) and delight might that be which cost them so deare, and which they enioyed so short a time? Alas it was but the pleasing of their humour in falling downe before a stocke or a stone. And Note. such are their delights at this day; transitorie, vaine, and soone flitting away, if not filthy also; for which they pay so deare, that they debarre themselues of all sound and true comfort for them heere, that I say nothing how they prouide for themselues hereafter, beside other annoyances that they meete Gen.19.24. withall. Sodome and Gomer for a whole city, *Zimry* and *Cosby* for particular persons, the former to bee destroyed with fire and brimstone for their fil- Numb.25.8. thy pleasures; the latter to be thrust thorough in their tent, as they were about their vncleannesse. What was their gaine, if it be laid with their losse? and for them that haue been thought to haue sped better in their matches by the like doings, they cannot be reckoned vp, nor found in the Scriptures, nor yet in experience. So that we might be wise, if we did well weigh it, to auoide the sinne, that so we might auoid the punishment also.

Vers.9. The third thing noted in this first example of this people, is their seeking to God; and that in faith and repentance. For when sorrow pinched them by reason of their grieuous bondage, and they saw all helpe of man failed them, they fled to God, acknowledging, that they had now proued by wofull experience, that the worshipping of strange gods had done them little good, my meaning is, they had thereby, and by their other sinnes, brought those calamities vpon themselues. And this their crying to God, was not the action of one man, or family, but of the body of the people in generall: and some among them (no doubt) did it soundly and vnfainedly: & therefore

fore they repented,though it bee not so expresly set downe, as in some places; and so we must vnderstand this that is said of them heere. It is laid out by this word *crying*,as the holy Ghost in the first of *Samuel*,7. doth set down 1.Sam.7.1.
the repentance of the people after the like manner; namely,by their lamenting after God; and in other places the same is done either by some signe, or by some fruit of it; so heere by crying. As if it should be said,that by this they testified their sorrow for displeasing God, their beleeuing of pardon, purpose of amendment, and their feruent prayer and confession of their sin, as all these are required by the Lord in true repentance, in *Hosea*, 14. And Hos.14.2.3.
this is the fruit of calamity in the elect,or rather of Gods goodnesse towards them,whereby he calleth them to himselfe by affliction.

This place,though briefly,yet pithily,teacheth all Gods people what to doe, when they haue prouoked God to afflict them for their sinnes: and that is this; they should after the thinking vpon both, seriously cry vnto God, and call vpon him assoone as they shall bee able; and this is to draw neare to him,as the people in *Iames* are directed to doe. And this I teach by Iam.4.7.
so good occasion heere offered, because though men bee for the most part, secure and carelesse; yet if their sinnes bee once brought to mind, and laid before them in any deepe and dreadfull manner; they are in another extremity, as in feare and terrour, doubting that God will not heare them though they pray: for this is their disposition in that time through tentation, when they haue prouoked God, to bee alienated and turned from him by dreadfull feare and vnbeliefe, to whom they were wont while they walked vprightly to haue accesse by prayer before. *Adam*,after his sinne, was Gen.3.
afraid of Gods voice, (wherein yet before he reioyced) and did hide himselfe in the thicket for feare of it. So *Dauid* cryeth and complaineth when Psal.119.25.
hee felt his sinne, that his soule cleaued to the dust; meaning that for very griefe hee was almost brought to the graue; and againe, that hee was in Psal.130.1.
the depth of trouble,as not seeing for the time how to get out of it. This anguish he felt in his soule,though he was deare in the eyes of the Lord. And the 51. Psalme testifieth how hee was wrapt in sorrow, as if his bones had been broken, thinking for the time, that hee had lost all grace of the spirit. Psal.51.8.
And no lesse cleerely doth this appeare in *Ionas*, after that the Lord had pursued him for his sinne, when in the bellie of the fish he cried thus: I said, I Ionas 2.4.
am cast away out of thy sight, the waters compassed mee about vnto the soule. So I may say of Gods best seruants,when they haue seene the horror of his wrath against them, for some sinne that wounded them, they haue been dismaied, and almost past hope, and brought to fainting for the time. And by this wee may see, that the secure and carelesse people who (wee know are not behinde other in sinning,are in a contrary extremity. But to returne to the other,if Gods seruants apprehend his wrath,and then fal into the tentation of the diuell, who can cunningly deceiue them, in making it seeme greater then it is,to be kindled against them,they are cast downe, as it were with a deadly blow: and thus (I say doe all in that case, till God put away feare from them. And seeing these two are contrary; to wit,to bee turned from God by feare and vnbeliefe,and to returne and come home neare vnto him againe by faith; and seeing they meet so neare together in one person, so that one of them oft times immediately succeedeth the other;

therefore all poſſible ſpeed and care is to bee vſed, that when feare, through the accuſation of the conſcience taketh place, faith ſhould be at hand to ex-
Ioh.9.31. pell and ouercome it. But againe to obiect further, it is ſaid, *God heareth not ſinners,* and therefore hee will not (they ſay) heare them crying vnto them.
2.Sam.12.13. But to this I anſwere, that when men repent, he heareth them, as wee ſee in *Dauid, Peter,* and other. And ſuch need not be diſcouraged from comming to him, but take hope aſſuredly that hee will heare them. Indeed they that dare not come and humble themſelues to him after their offence, and ſo ſtand firme in their hearts; or other that doe call vpon him, yet for all that doe it in ſhew rather then in faith and repentance, they (I ſay) doe all one, as if they did not cry to God at all. They therefore who haue learned that God will certainely ſmite and puniſh, if they ſinne; let them alſo learne, what they muſt doe, and how they muſt ſeeke to the Lord when hee puniſheth, as theſe men did heere, taking heed of the extremities before mentioned. If they deſire to turne away Gods wrath from them; then cry they to him alſo in ſeeing their ſinne, and laying it neare their hearts; and if they relent and turne from it, let them beleeue that his anger is alſo turned away from them, they vnfainedly purpoſing amendment of life, and looking duly to it afterwards: but more happie are they who looke warily about them, that they prouoke him not at all, but dutifully and conſtantly hold on their Chriſtian courſe. And this of their crying to God, the third point.

*Doct.*2. The fourth thing in this firſt example now followeth; to wit, of their deliuerance, in this and the next two verſes: wherein conſider theſe foure things: firſt, God raiſed them vp *Othniel* to be their deliuerer: then ſecondly, how he furniſhed him thereto: and thirdly, how hee gaue his aduerſary into his hands: and fourthly, what followed thereof. *Othniel* is deſcribed heere to be the ſame man, of whom wee heard in the firſt chapter, and who
Iudg.1.18. won the city Debir. He is called a ſauiour, becauſe he ſaued Iſrael out of the hands of their great aduerſary *Cuſhan,* that had held them long in bondage: by which deliuerance they had good teſtimony, that Gods diſpleaſure was turned away from them. The Lords thus ſpeedy turning vnto them vpon their repentance, is marueilous, but yet agreeable to that which is ſpoken of him in the Scripture; namely, that hee is *ſlow to wrath, and very readie to for-*
Ioel 2.12. *giue.* And it is to teach vs that, which wee are hardly brought to beleeue, namely, that he is moſt ready to remit and to remoue his puniſhments, yea when we haue prouoked him thereto by our ſins, if it repent vs. When *Dauid* confeſſed his ſin, the Prophet *Nathan* being ſent of God to moue him to repentance, and vnderſtood by his confeſſion, that he did ſo; anſwered him
2.Sam.12. immediately, *thy ſinnes are forgiuen thee.* So the poſterity of this people heere mentioned, when God had ſent vpon them a ſtrange iudgement in their
1.Sam.12.19.20. wheat harueſt, euen thunder and raine, that they might thereby perceiue and ſee, that their wickedneſſe was great in asking a King, contrary to Gods commandement, who had forbidden them ſo to doe: and the people had giuen teſtimony of their repentance, in deſiring *Samuel* to pray for them, and confeſſing that ſinne in asking a King, and their other ſinnes; hee an-
1.Sam.12.22. ſwered; *Feare not, the Lord will not forſake his people for his great names ſake, becauſe it hath pleaſed the Lord to make you his people, and I will not ceaſe to pray for you, but I will ſhew you the good and right way.*

And the whole Scripture throughout is full of examples,that tend to the ſame end. So that it may boldly and truly bee ſaid,the Lord is gracious,and of great kindleſſe,and repenteth him of the euill that hee had brought vpon his. So that it remaines,that this heauenly Scripture lie not by vs vnoccupi- Exod.34.6.
ed,and without fruit and vſe. But ſeeing wee doe oft forget the Lord, and thereby doe that which is euill in his eyes (oh fickle and inconſtant people that we are) wee ſhould not ſleepe in our ſinne, but repaire to this remedie to rend our hearts rather then our garments, and neuer to thinke our ſelues Ioel 2.13.
well till we haue recouered our loſſe,and by faith, ſee that wee are receiued into fauour with him againe; for hee waiteth for this our humiliation, and it ſhall neuer come before him in vaine and be fruſtrate,but he will moſt certainly accept of it,and as for vs we ought neuer to be quiet, till wee doe ſo. And wonderfull it is,and to our great detriment,that the way being ſo open to Gods mercy,and louing kindneſſe, euen to them that ſtand in need of it while they ſmart for their prouocations of him, it is (I ſay) to bee wondred at,that ſo few take benefit by it, yea and that aſſoone as they haue offended, Note.
they haſt not to returne to him againe,but wander in vnbeleefe, and hardneſſe of heart, till they bee driuen to it by meere neceſſity to bow and cry vnto God.

And the more wee bewray our blockiſhneſſe herein, in that wee bee ſo hardly brought vpon our knees,when we haue ſinned againſt God,wee are to know (for I thought it meet to vtter it) that there are no knots nor difficulties in this doctrine,namely, that God will be found when hee is ſought vnto,and will heare when he is prayed to. It is a moſt cleere and well approued truth,and none faile of helpe, but ſuch as doe not either heartily ſeeke it, if they know how, or elſe ſuch as are ignorant how to doe it. And that which I haue ſaid of repenting and returning to God,when wee ſee ſome ſpeciall fault committed,either by negligence or wilfulneſſe; to wit,that we ſhould in ſolemne manner thus cry vnto God,as we haue been taught,euen ſo we ought to doe,though there be no apparant wilfulneſſe ſeene, in our daily ſlips and infirmities, to offer vp to God daily our ſutable repentance for the ſame,that ſo we may bee no time, or not long in the leaſt manner eſtranged,no, nor abſent from God, but continually goe in and out before him through the day,and ſo all our life long, which is our Paradiſe and felicity in this world. And this be ſaid of the firſt ,of the three examples, as occaſion hath been offered, to the tenth verſe.

THE NINETEENTH SERMON ON THE THIRD CHAPTER OF THE BOOKE OF IVDGES.

Verſ.10. WE haue heard how God raiſed vp a ſauiour or deliuerer to the people of Iſrael when they cried to him in their oppreſſion, euen *Othniel*: now it is ſhewed, how he fitted and furniſhed him for ſo great a worke. And that was thus: *Othniel* being a priuate man, and one of the meaneſt of his fathers houſe, only ſomwhat enriched by his marrying of *Ackſah, Calebs* daughter, and a man of ſome courage, was the perſon whom the Lord ſtirred vp for this purpoſe. And he being further off then many other from ability hereunto, it is ſaid, that the Lord gaue him his ſpirit, meaning the fruits of his ſpirit; as knowledge and iudgement to vnderſtand the matters of God, and his will; which are things moſt requiſite for a gouernour, and he gaue him alſo encreaſe of courage, ſtrength and wiſedome for warre, and beſides them all, certified him by his ſpirit that he was called of God to ſuch a ſeruice. Now all things being thus appointed by God, he, as it is ſaid heere, iudged Iſrael, that is, hee executed his office, in taking vpon him the protection of his people; wherein the Lord being with him, hee reſcued them out of bondage to liberty againe, and gouerned them, and reſtored the pure worſhip of God among them: and more particularly concerning the ſubduing of the aduerſary of Iſrael, it is ſaid, that the Lord ſtrengthened him againſt him, that *Cuſhan-ruſhathaim* I meane, and gaue him into his hands.

Doct. And this cleerely teacheth vs, that all gifts of the ſpirit, and all excellent effects thereof, they are none of ours, they are the Lords, he giueth and diſtributeth them at his pleaſure, as we ſee heere, that it was the ſpirit of the Lord that came vpon *Othniel*, whereby hee brought to paſſe the great things that he did. And whatſoeuer is of any note in man for price and excellency, it is all of God, and commeth from his meere bounty. Alas there is no bird ſtripped of her feathers more bare and naked, then man in himſelfe, is void of goodneſſe: for what hath he that he hath not receiued? Inſomuch as all that he hath to glory of is his ſinne. A moſt holy and approued truth, which giueth God his due, and layeth out man in his colours, that hee is nothing elſe, if he robbe not God of his honour, and pranke not vp himſelfe in his gifts, he is nothing elſe (I ſay) but naked, poore, and a mirrour of miſery. *Saul* the King of Iſrael, when he wrought ſo great a deliuerance for Iſrael againſt the Ammonites: *Moſes* and *Ioſhua* in the mighty preuailing for them againſt the Heathen nations, and that in ſpite of all their teeth, who were the

Note. / Iam.1.17.

proudeſt

proudest of them; yea and *Salomon* in all his royalties, what had they to commend & set out themselues withall, but the gifts which God furnished them with? How doe numbers iet vp and downe, vaunting themselues, who hauing some gifts giuen them of God, but to a farre other end then they vse them for, namely to honour him, and not themselues; doe neuer thinke of any such matter, but dare more boldly sin against him, then otherwise they durst doe, and all because hee hath bestowed some gifts vpon them, as personage, beautie, strength, wealth; euen as one should strippe a poore body out of his ragges, and put costly and comely apparel vpon him.

For though men be but earth and wormes meate, yet how doe they set vp themselues, some for their high aduancement, some for their riches, which yet are but borrowed; and other for their painted sheath, till they take all honour (that they can) from God? yea as if they were petty Gods themselues, and he onely to bee called God of them. Oh admirable pride, blindnesse, and forgetfulnes in flesh! and oh as great patience and long suffering in God, that he can beare it at their hands! And yet for all that I haue said I denie not, but hee can afford them these his gifts and farre greater, if they could giue him his due thereby, and vse them to set forth his goodnesse by them, as were meete. The same I might say of learning, and all other gifts of God, they are the Lords, and bestowed at his pleasure, not to puffe them vp that haue them, but that in loue and humility they should vse them for 1.Cor.13.1.
the good of others. And much more then his supernaturall gifts of the spirit, as godly zeale, care to please God, and such like ought to be vsed to the same ends.

Point 2.

Now to proceed, when God had giuen his spirit to *Othniel*, it is said, *Hee iudged Israel*; that is, he did as a valiant captaine, pull them out of seruitude, and take the yoke of bondage from their necks, and restore to them the true worship of God, and gouerne them, and so the land had rest. All this, with such like befell them, when Gods anger was turned away from them, at the repentance of the people. In their bondage and misery, who would haue said, that it could easily, or in short time haue been remoued? especially, that such a change might haue been seene? But this teacheth, that when Gods *Doct.2.*
anger is remoued from a people or person, all things goe well there, punishments are turned into blessings, and great heauinesse into ioy and comfort. Euen as a cloudie, darke, and tempestuous day is forgotten, when the cleare *A simile.*
and faire sunshine ouerspreadeth and beautifieth the earth: and like as when two great men who by their strife and contention disquieted all, are againe made friends, and reconciled; for then the people in that towne reioyce, and hold vp their countenance. So it is said heere of this people, that they hauing been brought into such extremity for eight yeeres, God sent this *Othniel* a deliuerer and a Iudge, to whom he gaue courage and wisedome, so that he brought their enemies into subiection, and the people had rest and deliuerance. By all these signes of his fauour, God declared that his anger was remoued. And euen so, we shall see good daies, if we take heed that God be not prouoked to anger by vs: and though his anger be kindled, yet if we cry and grone to him vnder our burthen, lift vp our hearts and beleeue that he will be mercifull vnto vs, (as most certainly he will) and turne away his wrath and displeasure from vs: for in his fauour is life, and when his louing counte-

countenance ſhineth vpon vs, all other things ſhall turne to vs for the beſt. And the Lord doth either remoue outward puniſhments from vs, or elſe vphold vs ſo with his grace to beare them patiently and meekely, that they ſhall be no burthens,but matter of comfort vnto vs. Oh that we ſhould not be ſo wiſe as to preuent this one thing,namely,that the wrath of God might be kept from our ſoules,while the body ſhall want no looking to, that I ſay no more,yea and the meaneſt haue both care and skill,when the tempeſtuous and vnſeaſonable weather commeth, to ſhroud themſelues from it, and beware that it doe not annoy them.

Note.

But further heere, in that both eſtates of this people are ſet downe together,as their bondage with their freedome, their reſt with their trouble,the time of the one,with the time of the other; the holy Ghoſt (I ſay) in ſetting downe both together,doth teach vs to conſider of both,in the like caſe, the one as well as the other, and by the grieuouſneſſe of the calamity to meditate thus: Oh what ſhould wee haue done, if wee had ſo long continued in the eſtate that they were in; wee, I ſay, who by the mercy of God haue enioyed much peace,with plenty of commodities: if enemies euen ſtrangers had brought vs into ſubiection to them,how ſhould we haue borne the burthen? So likewiſe by our deliuerance from them, wee ſhould meditate of Gods goodneſſe to vs after trouble,and from enemies, and to bethinke vs, (which too ſeldome is done of vs) what a great fauour of God it is vnto vs, when paine, penurie, or the like are taken from vs, and to prize the ſame at an high reckoning. And he that deſireth to ſtirre vp himſelfe to true thankfulneſſe to God for ſuch a change and deliuerance will doe thus,as hee ſeeth good cauſe, and hee ſhall in beſt manner performe it,by ſuppoſing in our beſt eſtate,that the contrary would be very diſtaſtfull,painfull, and irkſome vnto vs,and yet might haue oppreſſed vs, which yet being through his exceeding goodneſſe paſſed away from vs, behold now light and ioy is come in the place of it. For as the light is the more eſteemed by our being in the darke; and faire weather is the more welcome to vs, after tempeſtuous and vnſeaſonable times: euen ſo is the conſidering of ſore troubles lately oppreſſing vs,an eſpeciall meane to bring proſperity into an high reckoning with vs; which a man would ſay, wee had need to doe, who ſhall obſerue,how ſoone we make it a common thing,and little worth, or rather abuſe it to our owne great hurt and detriment.

Note.

A Simile.

Verſ.11. Concerning the time of the peoples reſt vnder *Othniel*,euen fortie yeers, I take it to be the true meaning of the ſtory, and agreeable to the originall, howſoeuer the interpreters differ about it, the beſt tranſlation maketh for it. But in the ſtory of *Ehud*, verſ.30. more (if God will) ſhall be ſaid of it,where the vſe of it ſhall be alſo added. So *Othniel* hauing ſerued his time, was gathered to his fathers,as we are to looke and waite for the ſame, after the like ſeruice in our places. And this of the firſt example of the three before mentioned.

Verſ. 12. *Then the children of Iſrael againe committed wickedneſſe in the ſight of the Lord; and the Lord ſtrengthened Eglon King of Moab againſt Iſrael,becauſe they had committed wickedneſſe before the Lord.*

13. *And he gathered vnto him the children of Ammon,and Amalek,and went and ſmote Iſrael,and they poſſeſſed the city of Palme trees*

14. *So*

14. *So the children of Israel serued Eglon King of Moab eighteene yeeres.*

Now followeth the second: The summe whereof is this, that the people of Israel prouoked God to anger againe by their sinnes, when *Othniel* was dead. And God strengthened the King of Moab against them, with other most wicked confederates; who oppressing them sore a long time, they cried to the Lord as they had done before, and hee stirred vp another sauiour, one *Ehud*, who deliuered them out of their grieuous bondage. According to this briefe laying out of the story, the parts may be discerned to be foure, as in the former. Which being easie to bee perceiued, I will not stand to set them downe, but speake of them as they lie in order. vers.12. *The summe and parts 4. to the 31. verse.*

The first thing heere to be noted, is, that the people againe wrought euill in the sight of the Lord, as they had done before. And this shewes that they broke out further then they did, while *Othniel* liued, or else nothing should haue been said more then before in his daies, during whose time though they be not commended, yet neither are they discommended. Therefore to say nothing of either, seeing I haue no ground for it, let that be obserued whereof the text giueth iust occasion how prone and ready we are to break out, assoone as we haue any opportunity. Oh the flesh is soone wearie of pending in. While we are well fenced against falles by good teaching and company, I must needs say, all is much the better with vs, and we be the easilier kept from great offences. Heere in this land especially, where wee haue the purity of the Gospel, and of the true worship of God established among vs, (for it is grosse indeed to fall from a good course, while that is present) and also while godly Magistrates are with vs to encourage vs, as it was with them while *Othniel* liued. But for all this, (as grosse as it is) when men will let loose themselues with the times to the sinnes thereof, and such helpes faile them, as I haue spoken of, what care soeuer hath been among them of honouring God in former times, they are soone carried away, euery man as he is disposed, by his owne corruption one to some sinne, and another to another. And yet where all the forementioned outward helpes be, we being easily brought to make common things of them, the false heart will be ready to breake out, and fasten delight in some sinfull pleasure or other, if it be not strongly held in by grace, as by a bridle. Doct. vers.12. Note.

Whereas we should rather grow vp stedfast in our hope, curbing vp our vnmortified affections, that so we might be vnoffensiue in our Christian course, and the better be able to helpe to shelter other weake brethren from being ouercome and led away by strong tentations, rather then our selues (who haue tasted how good and bountifull the Lord is) to be plunged into the depth of them, by what occasions soeuer to their great offence. I haue oft lamented, and still doe, the lamentable case, and wofull estate of such, who are easily and readily deceiued with the baits of sinne, when I see to what shamefull shiftings and bondage they bring themselues, by their yeelding thereto, who might haue walked at great liberty toward God, and with much comfort in their life. But we must confesse, that this should be much better done on euery side, if diligent teaching were ioyned with good example in the chiefe, to giue light and encouragement to the meaner sort, and godly Magistrates, according to their duties, encouraging the good, and ready to keepe vnder the bad and disobedient. But oh that many of both

sorts

ſorts were not diſcouragers. And yet without reſpect thereof, euery particular perſon ſhould looke to his owne waies, not promiſing himſelfe ſuch helpes in this euill world to be euer at hand. This be ſaid of the peoples prouoking of God againe, and of their breaking out, after the death of *Othniel.* Of other things which might be noted heere, hauing already been ſpoken of, I will forbeare to ſay any more, both in this place, and throughout the booke.

The ſecond point in verſ. 12. The ſenſe. The puniſhment which God inflicted vpon the people for their renued ſinnes, which is the ſecond thing in this example, followeth in this and the next two verſes: and it was this; that the King of Moab, and other who aſſiſted him, held them in bondage eighteene yeeres; and tooke Iericho, which was called the city of Palme trees, and ſet aide there, the more to oppreſſe Iſrael, ſeeing it was by the paſſage ouer Iordan toward Moab. Where we ſee againe, that if we ſhall waxe bold to ſinne againſt the Lord, hee will ſmite, as we haue heard, come it ſooner, or come it later. But in that hee is ſaid here to ſtrengthen Moab, and as it were to furniſh him againſt his owne people (the wicked Idolaters againſt his true worſhippers) onely for breaking forth now at this time heere mentioned, to offend the Lord more then commonly; it may ſeeme ſomewhat ſtrange. For theſe Ammonites and A-

Doct. malekites were moſt vile enemies of God, and groſſe Idolaters. But he will haue vs to know this, that he doth often puniſh his owne people, by them that are worſe then they. And as we ſee he ſendeth theſe curſed nations vpon them, ſo we need not doubt but that hee can and will ſend the very Papiſts, (as little as many looſe Proteſtants feare it) to vexe vs, if we prouoke him, euen as he hath done heretofore, when the ſinne of men, and their knowledge was leſſer then now it is. And ſo the Lord ſpeaketh in Deutero-

Deut. 32. 21. nomie, *Becauſe ye haue prouoked me by that which is no God, I will prouoke you by them, whom ye haue deſpiſed as no people.* It is as harſh a thing to ſuffer by the meanes of ſuch as be worſe then our ſelues, as it is for the child to be beaten by the ſeruant. But God will ſuffer them, partly becauſe hee knowes that to be the way to abate men, partly becauſe their enemies will ſet it on to the purpoſe when they are let looſe to hurt them, through the malice that is in them; euen as their father the diuell doth when he can. But God would haue his owne learne by the ſmart which they ſuſtaine by their trouble, that their ſinne is farre more odious then they account it, yea then theirs, who whip them, becauſe they haue been taught to know the Lord, and couenanted to ſerue him, but the other are ſtrangers, who are vnacquainted with his waies. And all this is well to be marked, becauſe this errour ſticketh faſt and deepe in the minds of ſome, that wee need not feare the Papiſts, Spaniards, Ieſuites, or any ſuch Heretikes, becauſe we profeſſe the true religion that they hate, and worſhip Chriſt Ieſus whom they diſhonour. And therefore hauing a good cauſe, they ſay, why ſhould we feare, God will fight for vs. I anſwere, they muſt haue with their good cauſe, a good conſcience alſo: for elſe they may as truly ſay, that God will not ſuffer a good man and true, to be robbed of a theefe, or hurt by a witch, which Scripture and expe-

Iob 1. 2. rience doth ſufficiently confute: but as God exerciſed holy *Iob* by the diuel, the head: ſo he doth other of his deare ones by witches and other wicked people, which are his members: and that hee ſuffereth (as hee ſeeth cauſe) worſe

worse people then his owne to domineere ouer them: the Egyptians tyrannie ouer Israel, the Canaanites cruelty, and the examples of other nations in this booke against Gods people after both; with the experience of all ages are sufficient to testifie.

That is cleare enough, but let vs further see the reason thereof, and Gods meaning therein. For he doth not punish his owne people by the wicked, his enemies, because they are in better account with him then they: neither to put them in hope that they shall goe vnpunished in the end, because hee vseth their seruice (as he did Satan against *Iob,* to try him,) but because hee will hereby manifest how great a sinne it is to abuse, and liue vnworthy the Gospell; therefore he beginneth first to visit his owne people, and oft times euen by them. But afterwards, as *Amos* saith, he *will visit Damascus, Moab, and Ammon, and make them drinke of the dregs*: for if hee doe this to a greene tree, in comparison of them, how much more will he do it to the withered? And as the Lord will be auenged of his enemies, so after hee hath corrected his owne he will againe returne to them. Therefore the Church is brought in by the Prophet *Micha* to say thus: *Reioyce not ouer mee, O mine enemie, for though I fall yet shall I rise againe*: as the Prophet speaks, meaning that the Lord would finde a time, both to take corrections of them, and yet to be pitifull to them againe; euen as the father will burne the rod when the child relenteth, and promiseth amendment. And this, if the wicked will not see that he chastizeth euen his owne, hauing sinned against his knowne truth, but once (as it were) and therefore hee will much more haue a day for them, to pay them to the full for their manifold and long continued rebellions: if they (I say) will not regard it, let Gods seruants profit by it euery way, both they who are iustly visited for their sinnes, and also they who are more free; who know that hee doth vse to begin iudgement with his owne house, that they may thereby returne vnto him.

Amos

Miah.7.7.

1.Pet.4.17.

Besides that which hath been said of these nations, how the Lord strengthened them against Israel; so wee may further note heere how they were confederate together against Gods people: wherby we may further learne, how the wicked who can seldome agree together betwixt themselues, (for their leagues are soone broken) can yet easily ioyne together to vexe Gods people. And thus these three nations did consent in one to smite them. Euen as we reade that *Herod* and *Pilate,* which had been enemies one to the other, were made friends by ioyning both against Christ. As two dogs that fight each with other for a bone, yet both ioyne in biting the passenger. Or as theeues who consent to rob the true man, though they cannot agree in diuiding the spoile: for in that they disagree each from other, it is because they want the true band of vnion: but in that they consent, it comes from their mutuall hatred of vertue, and feare lest their owne kingdome should be ouerthrowne. And we finde it as true in these our daies, that they who cannot brooke one another, but haue sharpe contentions and broyles betwixt themselues, can yet with free consent, band themselues against Gods seruants. Which, (to leaue them to repent for it if God giue them grace) one would thinke should make vs cling and cleaue fast vnto the Lord, that yet we may haue him on our sides, and to stand with vs against them, whensoeuer they shall strengthen one another to molest and oppresse vs; and also

Vers.13.

A Simile.

to maintaine our Christian amity with our brethren the more strongly, by breaking off contentions, which easily arise, lest the children of this world condemne vs.

Vers.14. *The sense.* The punishment is bondage, and as the former generation was to the King of Aram, so now they were in bondage to the Moabites: the time that it continued, was more then double in respect of the former, euen eighteene yeeres. The people that now were brought into bondage, though they were neither all that were in the former calamity, nor they only, yet the rest who were growne vp at this time, had seene the workes of God, and receiued the religion of their fathers; and therefore they smarted iustly with the rest, with whom they had sinned. *Doct.* By them both wee learne, that they prouide ill for themselues, who make slight vse of Gods former corrections for sinne, and that thereby they bring and pull downe vpon themselues greater iudgements. Ioh.5.14. As Christ said to the man that was healed, *Goe thy way and sinne no more, lest a worse thing befall thee.* Leuit.26.18. So he threatened in Leuiticus, that if they did not amend by the former punishments, hee would adde seuen times more. And did not *Pharaoh* finde it, who for his mocking of God, and hardening his heart against him, when he confessed that God had been iust in sending vpon him so grieuous iudgements at the first, prouoked him to send many more vpon him afterwards?

And we at this day, who haue had deliuerance from trouble, which our sinnes procured and brought vpon vs, haue too good proofe of this that I Note. say: that we smart more by the after sinnes, and those which we renue daily, then by the former: euen as a renued wound is more smartie and dangerous. And stands it not with the righteous iudgement of God, that it should be so? Is it meet that we should tempt God in such a manner, and that wee should not beare the marke of it about vs in our flesh, or in our consciences? And so we doe. For to say nothing of those who sinne more willingly, in whom this is more clearely verified, it appeareth in the weaker sort of Gods children euidently, who sinne but of negligence and some carelesnesse ra- Note. ther then wittingly, that they smart also for the same. For beside their outward crosses, their oft doubtings also of their saluation, whereof yet they haue had assurance before: and by many great feares they haue oft times, that all is not well with them to Godward: the which (for the most part) do come of the slight and slender vse that they make of their deliuerance from their first feare and trouble of minde which they sustained. And it would much more appeare in many others, that their latter troubles which they beare, and by which they smart; for their latter and new prouokings of God are farre more grieuous then the former, and they farre hardlier recouer out of them, if they did not burie the remembrance of them, and willingly forget them, through the hardening of their hearts: when yet if they could consider aright of it, euen that is the greatest punishment of all. And although they rise out of it againe in time afterwards, yet it is done confusedly; or if they see their sinne and repent of it, it is after a good space, and so, much time hath at the least been lost, or vnprofitably passed ouer by them.

2 And whereas this punishment that was cast vpon them, was bondage to a forraine nation, both cruel and idolatrous; Oh it was a yoke most vnwel-

come:

come: and so we are to account of it, whensoeuer, and whomsoeuer of vs it shall fall vpon. Subiection in children to parents; in seruants to masters; in subiects to Prince, is naturall and kind. But no such thing is bondage to strangers, but fearefull and tedious, as we haue heard oft times, when some persons heere among vs haue been taken by the Turkes, yea and Dunkirks, into what wofull state they haue been brought. And although God hath mercifully perswaded our nation it selfe from it; yet we know in what danger we haue been, especially to the Spaniard; and namely in that yeere, 1588. And let vs not be senselesse in hearing this, or carelesse: for if these reuoltings in the better sort, and prophanenesse (with many particular sinnes) in the common sort, continue, if the Lord punish vs not, with that one kind, we may be sure that some one or other shall be in the roome of it; yea and if we be not blind in beholding it, the plague and dearth hath already seazed vpon many thousands, whatsoeuer be behind to arrest such as remaine. Note.

Vers. 15. *But when the chilbren of Israel cried vnto the Lord, the Lord stirred vp a sauiour to them, Ehud the sonne of Gera, the sonne of Iemini, a man lame of his right hand: and the children of Israel sent a present by him to Eglon King of Moab.*

The third point and fourth in this second example follow, namely, the cry of the people, testifying their repentance, and the Lords mercy, who pitying them, sent them another like *Othniel,* who should deliuer them. The man is named and described in the text. He first slue the King of Moab, and after, ten thousand men of his, strong and good warriours, and so deliuered Israel out of bondage. This followeth in the story, but it was necessary for me to mention it heere, seeing otherwise, this sending of a present by him to the King of Moab, which the people of Israel are in this verse said to haue done, should haue been hard to vnderstand, to what end it is set downe: whereas the sending of it to him by the men of Israell, was the meane of killing the King of Moab, and the pretence that they had to couer their intent. But more of this afterwards, as the words of the text when I come to them, shall offer occasion. But now let vs handle the points that are in this verse, as they lie in order, and as for this time we shall be able. *The sense.*

First, it is said that the people cryed to the Lord from vnder their sore bondage, wherewith they were oppressed. And had it not been better for them to haue been without it, and to haue serued the Lord with comfort, as they did while *Othniel* liued with them? so should they not haue needed to cry. How this their crying was a signe of their repentance, I haue largely shewed in the former example, vers. 9. and that may serue for both. But that which I will note now from their crying, is this; that the best end of our pleasures of sinne, is howling and crying; which though it did heere accompany repentance, (as seldome it doth) yet is it painful, but without it, dreadfull and deadly: neither doe many meet with that (as I said) though too many haue their part in this. For the times that follow sinne, when it is done and ended, are not like the time in which it is committed: they full of smart and sorrow, this taken vp in deceiueable pleasure. Doct. vers. 15. Note.

Consider this all you that are giuen to your appetite, and will haue your pleasure, where ye can come by it, howsoeuer the Lord forbids it, and how deare soeuer it cost you. If ye may end with crying (which yet they can ill away with, who hunt after vaine pleasure, I meane, that which is compani- Note.

on to repentance) ye haue infinitely to thanke God for it: but who can assure you that ye shall speed so well, and haue so good an end thereof? who may iustly feare (an hundred to one) that painfull crying, which maketh way to perpetuall howling and gnashing of teeth. As your sinnes haue been great, so shall your cries be great, saith the Lord; as namely he doth by *Abraham* to the rich man: *Sonne, in thy life time thou enioyedst thy pleasure, but now*
Luk.16.25. *thou art tormented.* Is not this lamentable, when we might liue comfortably, enioying our health, peace, liberty, and welfare with Gods good liking? But oh wofull it is, that none of his benefits, how precious soeuer, are commonly accounted of vs according to their value; to wit, thankfully, nor vsed soberly and aright, but so as we are inforced to cry out at the last (at least we haue cause so to doe) of our abusing of them. For there cannot a iot or tit-
Eccles.11.9. tle of Gods word fall to the ground, who saith, Reioyce O young man in thy youth, and let thine heart cheere thee in the daies of thy youth, and walke in the waies of thy heart, and in the sight of thine eyes, but know that for these things he will bring thee to iudgement. But I cannot goe through this whole verse at this time. But thus much of this third point beside that which I haue spoken of it elsewhere.

THE TWENTIETH SERMON ON THE THIRD CHAPTER OF THE BOOKE OF IVDGES.

Now followeth the fourth point in this example, and that is; how God had mercy on the people when they cried vnto him, and gaue them another deliuerer, this *Ehud* by
Doct.2. in vers.15. name, of the family of *Iemini*, which pertained to the tribe of *Beniamin*, and lame on his right hand. And by this, as it appeares that Gods hand is not shortened in raising vp one deliuerer after another; so we may see how good and kinde the Lord is, in hearing the cries and grones of his people, and that often times; euen againe and againe, when they make their complaint vnto him. And this hee doth as well in the daily pardoning of our infirmities which are innumerable, (for who can reckon them?) as also in such falles as are more grieuous, if it repent vs from our heart, as he willeth vs to doe in
Hos.14.1.2. *Hosea.* Which doctrine is warily to be receiued, for wee are ready to fall into extremities on both sides. For some doubt and feare that God will not receiue them againe, though they returne to him, remembring their former shamefull and wilfull transgression: but that errour of theirs must be amended. Other are ready, when they heare of Gods receiuing sinners gracious-
Note. ly, and that againe and againe (they lamenting after him,) they are ready (I say) to thinke that they shall easily bee forgiuen, without any remorse or pricke

pricke of conscience for their sinne: which is a grosse abusing of Gods patience and his readinesse to receiue sinners, who haue offended: and differeth not much from them, who say, [*Let vs sinne, that grace may abound.*] The middle way betwixt both is safest to goe in: to wit, not to cast away their confidence, when they vnfainedly turne to God, and yet not to take or arrogate to themselues the beleeuing of pardon, while they continue bold in sinning, without broken and relenting hearts. Note.

And this lesson being learned of vs, as God teacheth it, and hath himselfe giuen example vnto vs, is a sound and certaine rule to guide vs toward our neighbours who haue offended vs: that is to say, that as he embraceth and forgiueth sinners returning vnto him; so we should not bee cruell or hard-hearted toward them, but readily to receiue them, when they submit themselues. According to that which our Sauiour answered to *Peter*, when he asked him, how oft he should forgiue his brother, *vnto seuen times?* he answered him, *I say not vnto seuen times, but seuenty times seuen.* We ought therefore to forgiue them: but what? not the transgression of Gods law, for we cannot doe that, *for none can forgiue sinne but God.* But the wrong and iniurie done vnto vs, and the euill minde they beare toward vs, (I say) that wee ought (as we professe in the fifth petition) to remit. As for satisfaction, if he haue taken away our goods, we may, in the remitting that, doe, as the repentance and ability of the partie shall giue occasion: and so I say of the punishment which he hath deserued, if he haue hurt vs in our body, name, or otherwise; yet if it bee expedient, and that wee sustaine not any great detriment thereby, we may remit it. But yet in some case, though we forgiue the wrong, yet wee may vrge the partie that is culpable, to satisfaction and punishment, according to the law of God, and the nation where wee liue; lest men should be emboldened to sinne thereby: yea and sometime wee who are wronged, ought so to doe necessarily: otherwise we should sin against God, and the Common-wealth. And thus *Achan* by *Iosua*, and the theefe on the crosse, were iustly punished and put to death, for why? both Gods law and mans had else been broken. This I haue said of this matter, there being some difficulty about it, that we may see what wee are bound to remit vnto our neighbour, and how farre. Mat.18.21. Mat.9.3. Note. Iosh.7.25. Luk.23.41.

An other thing in this verse is, that this *Ehud*, who was giuen them as a deliuerer, is said to haue bin lame, but in what part of his body? euen on his right hand, that member which might worst be missed, especially in a valiant captaine and man of war, as he was, and now called to shew his strength and skil, wherin we can say no lesse, but that God doth that which is strange and maruellous in our eyes. For he sheweth vs hereby, that he when it pleaseth him, (and that is most commonly) vseth weake meanes to effect and bring great matters to passe, that his glory may be more easily seene, and giuen vnto him: yet flesh and carnall reason will not yeeld easily thereunto. But for proofe of the doctrine, looke what base and weake instruments the Lord vsed to vexe a mighty King (I meane *Pharaoh*) namely, Frogs, Lice, Locusts, & such like. So *Ionathan* & his armor-bearer slew many of the Philistims: *Dauid Goliah*. In the Prophet *Ioels* time, how did the Lord plague the drunkards, and the sinners of the land, who were so iolly, hauing the fruits of the earth in plentifull manner to serue their turne, as though there Doct.3.

had been none that could haue resisted them, how did he (I say) plague the the stoutest and the mightiest of them by the like weake meanes, spoiling thereby the fruits of the earth, without the which their iollity must fall to the ground? Thus the Prophet speaketh: *Heare ye this, O Elders, and hearken all ye inhabitants of the world; whether such a thing hath been in your daies, or in the daies of your fathers: That which is left of the Palmer worme, hath the Grashopper eaten, and the residue of the Grashopper, hath the Canker worme eaten, and the residue of the Canker worme, hath the Caterpiller eaten.* And to see the mighty hand of God in other matters, which farre exceede these, (for God can and doth this often, but this ought not to cause vs therefore to bee slight in meanes vsing to serue his prouidence,) How did hee by his Apostles, who were simple men, and of no great account in the world, yet how did hee by their ministery and weake preaching, (as it was accounted) subdue the proud and stately world to the obedience of the Gospel? Euen *Paul*, but one man, how many cities, yea countries did he bring from darkenesse to light, and from the power of Satan, vnto God; insomuch as whole Asia was filled with his doctrine, and both Iewes and Grecians heard the word of the Lord. And so in our daies hee hath perswaded many to become true Christians by the ministery and labours of them, who are of small reputation in the world.

Ioel 1.3.

Act. 19.10.

And why he bringeth to light such excellent tidings of the kingdome of glory, by so weake meanes; Saint *Paul* sheweth the reason in these words; *We haue this treasure in earthen vessels* (saith he) *that the excellency of that power might be of God, and not of vs.* Therfore despise not the weake, by whom God worketh; neither let such discourage themselues, who by the grace of humility, meeknesse, loue, and such like, with their small gifts, shall edifie and build vp the Church of Christ, when the knowledge in the bare letter, of such as are thereby puffed vp, shall doe little good. And as it is in the ministery, so shall it be seene in the people, that true godlinesse accompanying the knowledge of Christ, though ridiculous among men, shall do much in perswading and drawing many to the loue of the Gospell, and fellowship therein; which as it is the greatest, so it is (doubtlesse) the rarest thing that is to be seene among the people. As in the example of the woman of Samaria is to be seene, who brought her neighbours to Christ, being conuerted her selfe: yea and this may bee seene still at this day, that euen priuate persons truly religious, shall with their humility, diligence, and loue, doe much more good then they who haue variety of knowledge and vtterance, being destitute of those graces, though they bee little accounted of. The vse of all that I haue said of this point is, that we haue the works of God (how meanely soeuer accounted of) and specially his worke of grace in men, that wee haue them (I say) in most high reuerence, in comparison of the gloriousest acts of men. And this of the foure points in this story, from the 12. verse; namely, 1. the reuolting of the people from God: 2. the Lords punishing them: 3. their crying to God: and 4. his sending a deliuerer to them. And thus much of this matter.

1. Cor. 4.7.

1. Cor. 13.1.2.

The sence of that which remaineth in the 15. verse.

But these foure things in this second story thus ended, there remaineth somewhat in this verse, that hath not yet been spoken of, and much in the whole chapter by occasion of the last point, I meane of *Ehuds* deliuering them; with which I will proceed; and first with that part of this 15. verse that

that remaineth. The words are these: [*And the children of Israel sent a present by him to Eglon King of Moab.*] Heere, if this trouble any, that the largest part of this story remaineth behinde vnhandled, and wherefore it should bee so, seeing the foure materiall points or parts of the chapter haue (as wee haue seene) been handled already: I answere; all that is behinde to the 31. verse, doth issue and grow out, and by occasion of the last point of the 4. namely, of the deliuerer whom God raised vp to the people, I meane *Ehud*, and is set downe to illustrate and amplifie the deliuerance of the people, as shall appeare, euen how God deliuered them from the bondage of the Moabites, and gaue them rest. The person being this *Ehud*, as hath been said, the story shewes how hee wrought this their deliuerance; and it was thus: first, by slaying the King of Moab himselfe, which reacheth to the 27. verse: then by killing ten thousand of the men of Moab, which is to the 30. verse; after the which followeth the subduing of the Moabites, and the deliuerance and rest of the people, to the 31. Now of the first of these in the first place; namely, of killing the King. For the laying forth of the which wee are to consider, first, the things that went before it, namely, by what meanes hee wrought such a great worke, and they are set downe to the 21. verse: then the act it selfe, which is to the 23. and the things that followed, to the 27. The things that went before it, as the meanes to worke it by, were the double going or iourney of *Ehud* to the King of Moab: the first when hee deliuered the present to him onely: to the nineteenth verse: the last, when he did the act it selfe, to the 21: In his first iourney to him, note these three things: one, the occasion of it, that was, a carrying of a present to him: the second, his furnishing himselfe to do the deed, with a short and sharpe dagger: then the deliuering of the present. Thus the storie being set downe at large in the text, I haue laid it forth in the seuerall parts of it, so farre as in this place is expedient for the better vnderstanding of the reader. Now let vs go through them all in order. And first, whereas it is said in the latter end of this 15. verse, *That the children of Israel sent a present by Ehud to the King of Moab*, for so it was indeed, as the word in Hebrew מנחה signifieth, and not tribute: this (as I said) was the occasion by which he went to him: so by this present, the King of Moab was blindfolded, that hee might not suspect any such matter afterward, to bee intended by *Ehud*, when hee attempted and went about the fact indeed. For though it was lawfull for him and the Israelites to goe about to kill him, yet it was nothing meet, that they should by any vndiscreetnesse, giue him occasion to suspect it. And by this which was allowed in them, we may see, that it is lawful and not displeasing to God, for a good man being in danger or displeasure with another, and namely a superiour, to remoue it (if he can) by a gift or present. I know presents may be lawfully sent in other respects, namely, to shew thankfulnesse for kindnesse receiued: and I know also that a gift somtime is sent to the helping forward of a bad matter, and for the corrupting of iudgement, which is most odious; neither of both these is meant heere. But to get fauour, and namely, with our betters, by such meanes, when we know no other to bee like to preuaile, there is nothing against it, but that wee may serue Gods prouidence that way, for the remouing of displeasure. And so did our father *Iacob* seeke to put away the wrath of his brother *Esau*, and to procure his fauour. And although

Doct. 4. in vers. 15.

Gen. 32. 13.

although he who receiueth it,doth oftentimes offend therein, for that hee should yeeld fauour without it, yet for the giuer wee know what *Salomon* saith; *A gift in secret pacifieth wrath.* And it doth as well pull downe the heart of him that sendeth it,as mollifie him that receiueth it, which is farre better then that both,or either of them should rankle and bee inflamed, each against the other. And this may suffice to haue been said of this matter, and so of the whole 15. verse.

Vers. 16. *And Ehud made him a dagger with two edges, of a cubit length, and he did gird it vnder his raiment vpon his right thigh.*

17. *And he presented the gift vnto Eglon King of Moab, and Eglon was a vny fat man.*

18. *And when he had now presented the present, he sent away the people that bare the present.*

19. *But he turned againe from the quarries that were by Gilgal, and said, I haue a secret errand to thee O King, who said, keepe silence, and all that stood about him went out from him.*

20. *Then Ehud came to him (and he sat alone in a sommer parlor which he had) and Ehud said, I haue a message to thee from God. Then he arose out of his throne.*

E*Hud*, whom God had giuen to the people for a deliuerer, was by the consent of them,chosen to goe with the present to the King of Moab, and he knowing that he was to deliuer the people out of his hands, did thus goe about it;namely,to prouide him a sharpe dagger for more speedy expedition thereof, and girded the same vnder his right thigh, that there might be the lesse suspition of that he intended. For though the danger could not be but very great,and he notwithstanding he doubted not of good successe from God,yet he cast with himselfe how many and great the perils were in going about it,that he might the wiselier auoid them. I confesse, that this act that they intended to doe,namely to kill the King of Moab secretly, and thus to prouide for it, and to couer it by the present that hee offered him, I confesse (I say) that if God had not called him to it, and set him about it, it had been an action (in many respects) odious,and highly to be condemned. But God raising him vp to such an end, hee was approued of him therein, and that was his encouragement and emboldening, that God had called him to accomplish that worke.

Doct. in vers. 15. and 16. And heere note from that which I haue now said, that this is that which must encourage vs in the difficultest matters; that we in taking thē in hand, are set a worke by God,and do know,that he is pleased with the things that we goe about: this (I say) is that which we must be perswaded of,that wee haue him with vs, to the end wee may cheerefully goe through with them. Looke wee carefully to this, and wee shall prosper,and make we it our common practise in our affaires,and we shall throughout see good daies. But if we haue no allowance from him in doubtfull cases,and much more in such as haue apparant shew of euill,we may not enterprize them any more then *Ehud* might heere without his warrant. And where wee haue no commandement for that which we take in hand, as in a thing that is indifferent, let vs know our liberty, and that wee doe that which wee are perswaded doth please

please God best, and so wee shall haue peace in that wee goe about. But how little this is regarded, and how men take in hand the things which they doe of their owne head, and to their owne liking, and how ill successe they haue in such of their actions, as it is lamentable to behold it; so I refer the reader that is desirous to know more of it, to chap. 1. vers. 19. 22. where I haue said more of it. This be said of the first thing of the three, in sending the present.

In this second of the three things, in that he went so well appointed; let vs marke, that when *Ehud* was sure of good successe in this great worke, and that God would be with him, hee was not idle nor carelesse, but had greater regard how to goe about in the best manner, furnishing himselfe, and prouiding this weapon for the purpose. Wherein againe wee must learne, that it behoueth vs to vse all good meanes, as diligence, prouidence, and wisdome, for the well bringing to passe euen of those things wherein God hath promised good successe, and to bee with vs. Yea and further to doe them with readinesse and cheerfulnesse, as we see we haue good cause, being so wel encouraged. And so all may see, and we our selues may know that we goe not to worke as men of the world doe: I meane coldly and deadly, onely for the hope of profit, pleasure, or such like whetting vs on, which are the motiues and perswasions that earthly minded and worldly men haue in doing their busines. And what a grace and blessing is that, in our earthly businesse and common workes, that wee may bee so heauenly minded in them? for much more we may looke and hope to be well assisted, as the workes which wee goe about, are more heauenly. But thou maiest reade more of this, Chapter 1. verse. 4. Doct. in vers. 16.

The third thing of the three now followeth, which was the presenting of the gift, in carying and offering this present to *Eglon* the King of Moab, (which seemed, to such as heare of it, no matter commendable, that *Ehud* should kill him vnder pretence of kindnesse) yet hee intending a further matter thereby, then he shewed, to wit, the deliuering of Gods people by killing him their enemie, it was not onely lawfull, but also praise worthy in him. And this act of his teacheth, that when we doe such things as are not of best note, nor most commendable in the eyes of men, such as this of *Ehud* seemed, yet lawfull & allowed of God, we should (if it may be) intend some further and better thing thereby, as *Ehud* here did. And although it haue no effect for the present time; I meane, that good which we purpose and aime at, yet to wait opportunity to bring it so to passe. But this wil be better vnderstood by laying it out in particulars. As for example; if a man be in the company of a bad person, which in it selfe is no credit to him, (& yet it is not vnlawfull) or if a man giue almes to a poore man who hath no goodnes in him, (which may be thought of some to be a maintaining of him,) in both these cases and the like, he that I speake of, ought to haue a further reach and meaning, that is, a desire and endeauour to do the parties good; as to admonish and reproue as there shall be cause seene, or exhort & seeke to draw them (as he shall see best opportunity) to repentance; and thereby to stay all from taking offence thereat. And so I say of all such actions: *Hester*, as we reade, bad *Haman*, the enemie of Gods people to a banquet. It was like to sauour ill to the godly that should heare of it: but at his first comming thither, vers. 16. 17. Doct. 2. Hest. 5. 5.

though

though she spake nothing against *Haman* to the King, yet at the second banquet shee obtained deliuerance to Gods people, who were appointed by *Haman* to bee slaine: and beside that shee procured is ouerthrow. To both which, she made way by bidding him to the first banquet, and entended it,
Mat.9.10. though she made no shew then of any such thing. So our Sauiour did eate
Luk.19.7. and drinke with the publicans and sinners. It was hardly thought off by the Pharisies: but he sought their conuersion by it. Therefore in such actions as haue not the best shew of goodnesse (to the end we may bring no violence to our consciences, nor disquiet to the godly, and the better allo to stop the mouthes of others) it shall bee meete for vs to aime at and intend better things then are seene at the first shew. But then it may bee truly said on the contrary, that they who doe things in shew, scarce honest, as to haunt suspicious places, and the company of those who are of ill note and name, and yet meane worse then is seene, namely to practise whoredome, and fall to
Note. drunkennesse and ill rule, it may (I say) truly bee affirmed, that such are vile persons, and very bad indeed. And most of all they who will shew signes of goodnesse, as of loue by friendly familiarity, sobriety and religion, and yet spite vs and our holy profession behinde our backes, and carrie themselues leaudly, are of all other the worst. But to returne, the like we see in *Iehu*, who although he seemed cruell to the view of the world in murthering the house
2.King.10. of *Ahab*, yet hauing an eye to the calling of God, went through it with courage, which was to be commended. But heere must bee a caueat obserued, that is, that no man presume by these examples to enterprize such like matters without warrant from God, alleaging for himselfe that his end is good and profitable: this is to go to worke of our own head, yea to call euill good, and to doe euill, that good may come of it. As in a mans priuate case to take vpon him to reuenge his owne wrong, which belongs to the Magistrate. For as the Lord warrants a man by the sincerity of his intention, to goe forward, when the thing is lawfull (as we see in that act of the two tribes and an
Iosh.22.30. halfe building an altar) so when we haue no word to beare vs out, we runne into the lapse and offend against the expresse prohibition of the Scriptures,
Mat.6.10. which is, [Thou shalt not do thine owne will,] whereas that it is written, we
Petic.3. 1.Thes.5. should auoide all appearance of euill. It is not vnlawfull simply for a good man to bee in the company of one that is euill; but this excuseth not him, who obserueth no circumstances herein, but shall associate himselfe with such as are of bad note, in gaming, drinking, or haunting of suspected places (as I haue said) although he abuse the extraordinary fact of *Hester*, and the example of our Sauiour, or pretend (as some will) the good of the party.

But as *Ehud* was appointed to present the gift to the King of Moab, so it is said heere hee did: which wee know was a great honour and credit vnto him. And he was worthie of it, who did afterward aduenture so great danger with it. So God alloweth to them that serue him in high places, and performe great duties in Church and Common-wealth, hee alloweth them much credit, honour, and dignitie. And for the one as Princes and noble persons, such as *Dauid*, was, *Salomon*, *Hezechia*, and *Iosia*, with *Moses*, *Ioshua* and others, haue enioyed the same, in respect of some that were as great as they, but not as godly: Euen so it is with vs: For they that truly honour and fauour learning, and good ministers, and make much of them that feare the

the Lord; resisting and opposing the common aduersary; they are highly honoured of the Church of God: and so it is also in the ministery: for (as the Apostle saith) they that rule well, are worthie of double honour: If they 1.Tim.5.
labour painfully and faithfully in the word, and goe before their flocke, as Ioh.10.
good sheepheards, and so rule and guide them by both, and by other censures, as occasion shall be offered, they worthily enioy loue and reuerence, with the fruit of both, as credit, and maintenance. And good reason there is why it should be so with both: for the one laboureth and watcheth directly for the peoples soules: the other, in their kinde and place, for the maintenance of their peace, liues, and goods. And that which I say of these I may say proportionably of meaner persons, and lower places: that as they doe seruice to God in their liues, places and employments; so are they of greater account, and more set by, (and well worthy) then other who doe not so. For their care, faithfulnesse, and trauell for the honour of God is much; and the Lord hath promised to honour them who honour him, and to leaue the other without honour. And so it was heere, that *Ehud* had great honour in that he was appointed to deliuer the Present to *Eglon* the King of Moab: And who worthier then he? For beside his other many worthy acts that he did for the peoples peace and deliuerance: who among them all would haue aduentured their liues for the rest? Of whom it may bee said, as *Pharaoh* said of *Ioseph:* when he directed him how to prouide in the seuen yeeres Gen 41.38.
of plenty, for the seuen yeeres of famine, a wise man that should bee fit for that businesse; *Pharaoh* said to his seruants, where shall wee finde a man of vnderstanding like this? let him bee set ouer the land of Egypt about this worke.

Heere the holy Story setting this downe, that *Ehud* presented the gift to Doct.2.in
Eglon, addeth this, that he was a very fat man, which may seeme to be vttered to no end, seeing it is neither set downe to his commendation, nor to his discommendation; but this is mentioned, that we may see a reason of that which is in the 22. verse. And as it is not commended or discommended in him; so by occasion heereof, this I will say, that fatnesse of body is to bee thought of, as a thing neither with a man nor against him in it selfe. For some are more disposed thereto naturally then other, though they haue both one diet, and alike kinde of easie life; euen as we see how one tree waxeth great and tall in the same soyle, where another is both small and low, as one Oke in comparison of another. But where men are naturally apt thereto, good keeping doth set one forward. And therefore no maruell that it is so with such as liue deliciously, eating and drinking, and vsing other liberty at their pleasure. But this may not bee spoken without vse and profit: this let vs learne, that such, either Ministers or other as giue ouer themselues, and let the bridle loose to excesse in eating, drinking, sleeping, playing, idlenesse, ease, and such like, and get fat that way, may little reioyce in it, and shall wish that they had by labour in their callings, and other good meanes, taken themselues downe, as *Paul* chastized his body, or at least haue good testimony that they haue not growne to that point through their owne sinne; Tit.1.12.
therefore that prouerbe is vsed by *Paul* against the *Cretians*, out of *Epimenides*, *The Cretians are alway liers, euill beasts, slow bellies or Epicures.* And their commendation shall be no greater, who in the profession of the Gospell, fat themselues

themſelues through idleneſſe, ſloth, eaſe ſeeking, and ſhunning labour in their callings. And this of *Ehuds* firſt going to *Eglon* to deliuer the Preſent.

The ſumme of verſ.18,19,20. The ſecond followeth, in which he ſlue him. Wherein we may obſerue, firſt his conueighing home of the men that came with him, and brought the Preſent (which he deliuered) that they might be out of perill, when he ſhould doe that worke of God, ſo full of difficulty and danger. Secondly, how he came backe againe to *Eglon*, telling him he had a ſecret errand and meſſage to him, and this was to remoue the company which attended on the King, from the place of his preſence. Thirdly, when hee had obtained that, hee repeated his words, adding this, that his meſſage was from God, that ſo the King might attend to it with more reuerence (as hee did, and in token thereof ſtood vp,) and that he might the leſſe ſuſpect any danger, and *Ehud* might haue aduantage thereby, the more eaſily to diſpatch him. Thus

Verſ.18. much is in theſe three verſes. Concerning the firſt, of ſending away the people vnto the quarries, a place where ſtones were digged vp, neare to Gilgal, a city of the Iſraelites neare Iordan. In that he followed them after the preſent was deliuered, till they were paſt danger, he reſpected many things; and namely, that he might bee freer from care of them, as alſo leſt their tarying ſtill whiles he went about that worke, might haue been a meanes of bewraying it; and further he was loth to bring any more into danger then hee muſt needs. All theſe reaſons moued him to ſend the people away, and tended to

Doct.verſ.18. the quiet and peace of his conſcience. And his example herein ought to bee our inſtruction; that wee may learne to goe about waighty matters with all poſſible deepe and due conſideration, wiſedome, and warineſſe, as *Ehud* heere did. And if we be not ſufficient of our ſelues hereunto, then take wee aduice of thoſe that be wiſer then we. For the which purpoſe *Salomon* ſaith,

Prou.15.22. *Without counſell thoughts come to naught, but in the multitude of counſellors, there is ſtedfaſtneſſe.* So we muſt bee ſure that ſpeciall care bee vſed, as I haue ſaid, that when great and waighty buſineſſe is impoſed vpon vs, all poſſible regard be had to ſee it well brought to paſſe, and gone about.

This leſſon being ill learned of *Peter*, Chriſts beloued Apoſtle, may warne vs, by the exceeding danger that befell him thereby, to put it better in practiſe. For when Chriſt told him of a moſt waighty matter; namely, that hee ſhould denie him: *Peter* moſt ſleightly regarded it, anſwering raſhly with-

Luk.22.32. out conſideration, that he ſo little feared that which Chriſt told him of, that he was ready to goe to priſon, and to death with him: and ſo reſting in his bold anſwere, and deceiueable confidence that he had of his owne ſtrength, for want of aduiſed deliberation, he fell into the ſinne that his Maſter foretold him off, and by a very ſmall occaſion, denied him indeed: and ſo his example is ſet downe and left to vs, to learne wiſedome thereby. *Moſes* did otherwiſe and farre better: for when he was told that he muſt be ſent to *Pha-*

Exod.3.13. *raoh* by the Lord to doe his meſſage vnto him, which ſeemed to him ouer difficult and waighty, yet conſidering thereof aduiſedly, when he ſaw it was impoſed vpon him by the Lord, hee ſtouped to it, fitted himſelfe for it accordingly, and well diſcharged it, and proſpered. And let theſe two examples bee duely weighed and regarded of vs, though contrary the one to the other: and the more vrge vs to practiſe this doctrine: and otherwiſe let vs

not

not maruell that we thriue not in our waighty attempts,if God be not reuerently harkened vnto in his watchword and warnings, and (as it is most meet) duely attended vpon of vs. And this for the generall. Now particularly let this teach vs,that in doing those actions, which specially tend to the glory of God,we haue an eye also to the good of our brother. Let vs carrie our selues so in our zeale toward God, that in the meane season wee neglect not dutie toward men, neither cause our loue towards our brethren to bee called into question. This is to build in heauen,and pull downe as fast vpon earth. *Ehud* heere did farre otherwise. It was highly commendable in *Paul*, Act.26.29.
and became him well,that he desired King *Agrippas* conuersion, without enioyning him with that benefit,his owne bands. And it becommeth vs to be so wisely feruent in Gods cause,that yet wee would not willingly hazard the safety, liberty, credit, wealth and welfare of others,by our zeale and suffering for it : nay rather, (if there be cause) redeeme their freedome by our owne damage and detriment. Many are of this preposterous opinion, that because they thinke themselues strong enough to vndergoe trouble and reproch for the Gospell,and a good cause; therefore they looke that all other zealous persons should doe so too, and are ready to censure them sharpely who are not as they themselues seeme to be, not regarding their weaknesse (who not finding themselues fit to beare the burthen, should bee pitied in that behalfe) or else they thinke that it is a discredit to their good cause, to suffer for it alone : and thus they winde them into a dangerous snare with themselues by drawing them to promise and vndertake that which they be vnfit for. Whereas we reade that some of the ancient, and some of our late Martyrs,who wisely and charitably tendring the peace and good of their weake brethren, resolued to beare the brunt themselues, and counselled them to prouide for their conscience,by flight from persecution, if they felt not themselues fit to goe vnder it. For the rest,looke in the next Sermon.

THE ONE AND TWENTIETH SERMON WHICH IS THE FIFTH ON THE THIRD CHAPTER of the booke of IVDGES.

OF *Ehud* it followeth still of his conueying away the men when the Present was deliuered, that all inconuenience might bee auoided on both parts : of whom let vs learne, not onely to bee warie that wee bewray not secrets vndiscreetly to any (which hee wisely preuented by sending them away) and therefore much more not to many: But also as he did,so let vs doe; it agreeing with the rule of charity,namely,that if danger,trouble, or sorrow must needs ensue and follow by doing such things which wee goe about, and must needs take in hand, yet let our care be that the trouble bee no more to Doct 2.in vers 18.

any then it must needs be, nor the danger or heauines take hold of no more then must of necessity haue their part therein. As *Ehud* saw the burthen lay vpon him, hee might if hee would, haue laid it vpon other beside himselfe, but that in no wise hee would doe, but sent the rest of the company home, that they might be out of danger. Which thing I well remember our Sauiour also most carefully practised, and that with no lesse tender loue and kindnesse toward his weake Disciples. For when the Priests and Iewes with their band of souldiers came to apprehend and take him, they telling him, when he demanded of them whom they sought, that they sought him: hee
Ioh.18.8. answered them, *If ye seeke me, let these* (meaning his Disciples) *goe their way*: and the reason of that speech was, that they might escape danger.

Much like to both these examples, was the doing of the Shunamite in the second booke of the Kings. For when her child was dead, which the Prophet *Elisha* obtained of God for her, shee hauing none before, and shee
2.King.4.21.22. knowing and beleeuing, that it should be restored to life againe vnto her; when she had talked with the Prophet, and made her mone and complaint vnto him, which shee saw shee might doe, and yet returne home againe the same day: what did shee, thinke wee? Surely this, shee locked vp the dead child in the Prophets chamber, (which shee had perswaded her husband to build for him in their owne habitation, to rest at, when hee passed by) and made his death knowne to none, lest trouble and sorrow should thereby haue been caused to the whole family, and neighbours thereabout, and by faith had the child restored aliue vnto her againe. The griefe and care for it must needs light on her, and she sustained it her selfe, and would haue no other to sorrow for it, or be troubled about it. But our sinne about this thing is great, that when wee might with a little trouble to our selues, free and
Note. ease many other, yet wee raise and procure it to other also: yea and wee bee not satisfied, vnlesse they smart as well as we. So farre are we off from regarding other, and from seeking their peace, who would liue peaceably by vs. As for example, it is commonly to be seene, how many rough and boysterous husbands grieue and disquiet both wife and family, by their loud and vnbeseeming as well as vnseasonable complaints and outcryings, (whereby they disquiet the whole family) for some ouersight which they espy; yea they haue oft times no cause at all to doe so; or at least if they had any iust cause to be grieued, yet a little patience and bearing with the trespassers (as the cause requireth) and sober and kinde telling them of it, might haue done farre more good, and haue kept the whole family quiet. The same I may say of the wife, if she be giuen to waspishnesse, and bee shrewish, hot, and wrathfull, who thereby troubleth both husband and the whole house: and this accusation reacheth yet further; euen to the spitefull and malicious, who are not onely oft iarring, and at strife with their neighbours vpon small or no occasions, but are ready to sue them at the law for euery trifle, and so trouble both them, and themselues also. Whereas the vertuous Queene *He-*
Hest.4.16. *ster* beholding how shee was the onely hope and helpe vnder God of the Churches deliuerance from *Hamans* plot and deuising to wast and destroy it vtterly; tooke vpon her the going about it, though it was with most likely perill of her life, and that without the hurt of any one beside; saying in so doubtfull a case, If I perish, I perish. Yea *Saul* himselfe, who yet had no commenda-

mendation through the ſtory for vprightneſſe and goodneſſe, would not ſuffer any of the murmurers and repiners againſt his entring in, to bee puniſhed at his firſt comming to his kingdome, as ſome would haue had it, but choſe rather to put vp the diſgrace, ſaying: there ſhall no man die this day; for to day the Lord hath ſaued Iſrael. And this by occaſion of *Ehuds* ſending the people away that went with him, being the firſt of the three things mentioned, to be contained in theſe 3. verſes. 1.Sam.11.13.

Now followeth the ſecond thing, to wit, of *Ehuds* ſecond going to *Eglon*, and what he ſaid. Hee returned in haſt from the place neere Gilgal in the land of Iſrael, whither hee had conducted the people, which could not bee farre from the place where King *Eglon* lay: for hee hauing brought the Iſraelites into ſubiection to him; it is cleere thot he lay neere their borders, the better to ſee them kept vnder: and he comming to him, told him hee had a meſſage which was of ſecreſie to doe vnto him. Whereat the King required him to ſtay the vttering of it, till the company ſtanding by, were commanded out of the place. For hee hauing ſo lately receiued a preſent at his hand, had no ſuſpition of any trechery to be intended by him. The company being gone, *Ehud* was admitted to come neare vnto him. And telling him that his meſſage was from God, hee ſtood vp to doe reuerence at that name: and ſo by this meanes he had the way made more eaſie for him, and the better opportunitie to doe the worke he went about. Verſ.19. 20. *The ſenſe.*

And in theſe two verſes we may ſee, conſidering that the Lord called *Ehud* to this worke, for the deſtroying of that his peoples enemy, and to deliuer them out of his hands, (for elſe it had been a moſt bloody and trecherous act) we may ſee (I ſay) the courage and confidence that was in him, to aduenture that great danger that hee did, by going about to kill *Eglon* the King: who, if before his attempt he had been detected and found out, had been put (who doubteth?) to moſt extreme tortures among enemies, and no friend of his ſtanding by or in preſence. And what had hee to vphold himſelfe by, in that great difficulty and fearfull danger, but his truſt in God, and confidence, that hee who laid that worke vpon him, would bring him well through it? And yet how hard a thing it was for him, who ſeeth not, if he will rightly conſider it, in that difficulty and great ſtraite that hee was in, to beleeue that God would make way for him, and enable him to ſuch a worke, all likelihoode thereof being taken away. And this teacheth vs, what the nature of faith & confidence is, wherſoeuer, and in whomſoeuer it is to be found: that they looke not vpon things that are ſeene, which may work deadly diſcouragement and anguiſh: but vpon that which is not ſeene with mortal eye, and that is Gods power and willingneſſe ready at hand to helpe vs forward, and to encourage vs (to waite for the accompliſhing of that which we beleeue and looke for) in our greateſt need. Doct.verſ.19. 2.Cor.4.24. Note.

This it was that animated and ſtrengthened *Ehud* to attempt this dangerous worke. And this faith and confidence hartened and emboldened the Prieſts, when the Lord by *Ioſhua* commanded them for their paſſing into the land of Canaan, to ſet their feet on the water, to goe ouer the riuer Iordan, (how vnlikely ſoeuer it was) their beleeuing (I ſay) the Lord by the mouth of *Ioſhua*, that a way ſhould be made for them to paſſe through ſafely, as on dry land, euen that it was that hartened them to doe it, who yet in ſo Ioſh.3.13.14.

doing, must of necessity haue been drowned by mans reason and iudgement. And this faith made *Peter* bold to pronounce to the lame and diseased, euen while they lay visited, to pronounce (I say) in the hearing of all
Act.3.6. and 9.34. that stood by, when he saw no likelihood thereof appeare: *Iesus Christ maketh you whole, arise and walke.* For hee beleeued Christ who had said to him that he should worke a miracle, whensoeuer it was expedient, and that faith made him bold to say so: whereas if that had not been immediately done indeed, which he foresaid should come to passe, that the parties should bee healed; he should haue been vtterly discredited, and laughed to scorne, and cast out from mens company, as a deceiuer.

This faith made the holy Martyrs yeeld their bodies to the fire, for the
Note. defence of Gods truth, while they beleeued, not onely that they should bee receiued after into glory; but also that God would strengthen them for the present time to endure the flame. And this it is that inableth vs to suffer the hardnesse which wee willingly sustaine throughout our liues, euen this, that we trust and rest perswaded, that God will bring vs well through it, and
Act.21.13. afterwards receiue vs into his eternall kingdome. Which caused Saint *Paul* to vtter these words: *Why weepe ye thus, and rend my heart? for I am resolued and ready not to bee bound onely, but also to die at Ierusalem for the name of the Lord Ie-*
1.Tim.4.10. *sus:* and euen so he taught, writing to *Timothy*; *Therefore we suffer because we beleeue in the liuing God, who is the sauiour of all, but especially of them that beleeue.* And this of *Ehud* in these two verses, and of his words spoken to the King. and as for such as aske why he deluded the King with a lie, while hee went about to kill him, seeing hee vttered no message to him at all; when yet hee told him hee had a message from God vnto him: to them I answere; the word which is translated message or errand, doth not onely signifie a word or message by mouth, but also a thing or deed, such as that was which he did vnto him; for he was sent from God to kill him, euen as among the Latines, *Verbum & res. Quid hoc verbi est? Quid hoc rei est?* both are one.

The vnfolding of the latter part of vers.19. and of the 20. Now followeth the third thing, and that is in this 20. verse, namely, of *Ehuds* last words to the King immediately before he killed him, and of *Eglons* behauiour thereat, as it is heere set downe, let vs consider: of which, this I say; In that he should so simply hearken to, and beleeue him, admit him into his secret parlour, and that *Ehud* being a stranger, should neither be suspected, nor searched (as the manner is, and great reason was for it) before hee should haue accesse to the King, and that none of all the Kings attendants should aduise such a matter, that hee should not bee suffered to stand on his feet before the King, which was more suspitious,) but rather commanded to bee vpon his knees before him, and then that hee should cause his owne company to goe out of the place, and leaue them two onely together; but especially to let *Ehud* depart, before they saw all to be wel: These (I say) and such like, if the Lord had not blinded, and cast a myst before them, could neuer haue passed as they did. And we may say, it was much like that which
1.Sam.26.15. we reade of *Abner*, captaine of *Sauls* hoast, and all his men; to wit, that when he imagined that *Dauid* pursued him, and sought his life, and should therefore haue more specially watched and attended the Kings person, then at other times; yet that euen then all the armie should be asleepe together where they lay; in so much that *Dauid* challenged *Abner* for it; was it not admirable?

rable? For it could not haue been so in any reason, except God had cast a sleepe vpon them, to the end that *Dauids* integrity and innocency toward *Saul*, might be knowne, when there was seene no other way to shew it, and all saw (that would) how he might haue killed *Saul*.

And hereby let vs learne, that when God will haue any worke wrought, or any thing brought to passe for his glory, the good of his Church, or destruction of his enemies, he hauing many waies to bring it to passe, will effect it through infinite difficulties, without our troubling our selues about it. For his prouidence alway ministreth to, and makes way for his purpose till it be executed. *Dauid* was so coped in by *Saul* at one time, that there seemed no hope of escape: but then the Lord whistled him away, and set him about other businesse. What lets and discouragements (thinke wee) had *Noah* to hold him from that great worke of building the Arke to the preseruing of the world, and the Church of God? I will leaue it to the consideration of the reader, rather then spend the time in laying it forth. In the bringing to passe Gods promise to *Ioseph* in his dreame, what a long time was it before it was effected? euen well nigh twentie yeeres: and how vnlike, and in the meane while, how many difficulties were raised and set in the way to the frustrating of it? as the malice and enuie of his brethren, some of them intending and seeking to kill him, but all the company consenting that he should be sold to strangers a farre off, from whence they thought he should neuer haue bin any more seen of them, neither his dreames come to passe: and then his imprisonment also after all, by the false accusation of his whorish mistrisse: who would not haue said, that by the meanes of all these, he should haue been vtterly depriued of the benefit of the promises which God had made to him? But could they preuaile? was any iot of Gods word made voide, so that it came not to passe?

Doct in vers. 19. & 20. — 1. Sam. 23. 27. — Gen. 6. 13. 14. — Gen. 37. 21. 22. — Gen. 42. 21.

And was all the cruell malice of *Haman* easily auoided in plotting the destruction of all the Iewes Gods people: the day thereof being appointed, the King perswaded by him to let all be as hee would haue it, and no friend to them, (but they were as sheep appointed to be slaine) but they that were in as great danger themselues, that is to say, *Hester* and *Mardocai*: and when shee the Queene, who was all their hope vnder God, should goe about to helpe them out of the danger, she brought her selfe thereby into the present perill of her life. And yet because it could not be possible that the Church of God should be ouerthrowne, did not he most strangely deliuer it? But to let passe examples in Scripture; euen thus the Lord hath and doth vphold his Church heere and there for a time against all enemies and lets, and will doe, till he hath accomplished, and made vp his number. And when wee see that he continueth his fauour more specially to any place or people, through many trials, let vs say, the Lord hath done great and maruellous things for them, and they had need to acknowledge his kindnesse, and profit by it more then in common manner, lest their account be harder to be made then other mens. And to come to shew it more particularly, and so to conclude this point; if euery priuate person whom this concerneth, could weigh through what difficulties, (as tentations and discouragements,) God hath brought him to hold and keepe faith and a good conscience, both in the beginning, middle part of his combate and conflicting daies, and more speci-

Hest. 7. 50. — Note.

ally when he hath well nigh runne his race,and finished his course with ioy;
Note, oh what thankes would he render to the Lord for it? For all such may well remember how oft they haue said within themselues, that they shall neuer be stablished and perseuere to the end,and that the promise of heauen made to them,is too good to be true. And yet God hath so mixed his power with their weakenesse, and so vpheld them beyond their expectation, that hee hath brought them safely through all that they feared. Oh I cannot sufficiently magnifie and commend this goodnesse of the Lord, and withall, the glorious worke of faith,and what wonders they effect! and yet little known or asked after. But seeing the arme of the Lord is no more shortened now, then in times past,but he doth great things for them that beleeue at this day;
Psal.37.3. let vs also learne *Dauids* lesson : *Commit thy way to the Lord* (saith he) *and beleeue that he will effect it*, and he will doe it in deed,without any needlesse and
2.King.7.2. indirect trouble,or fretting care of thine : but if we beleeue not, I deny not
Hest.4.14. but that we may see (as *Elisha* told the Prince of Israel, and *Mordicai Hester*) Gods promises performed to others which hee made, as the vnbeleeuing Prince did,but we shall haue no part therein our selues, nor cause of sound reioycing thereat,in as much as we had no exercise of our faith in beleeuing them. Therefore this worthily deserueth at the hands of all the children of God (to whom the fruit of this doctrine hath in any measure been granted, and who haue any proofe of their faith at al,that at least they yeeld the Lord thus much ; that as they bee thankfull (yea euen with admiration) to consider how hee hath brought matters to passe for them beyond hope : so that they arme themselues to beleeue still, and that more assuredly that God is able and willing to make way for them in all their desires,or distresses,without which yet they shal lose the benefit of this his power and loue. But more of this,as occasion shall be offered.

Doct.vers.20. As for *Eglons* rising vp at the mention of God, as though hee had reuerenced him, (for this is the next thing that followeth in the text) howsoeuer they vsed to doe so at that time who were but heathen Kings, as *Baalam* before, when *Balak* then King of Moab,came to him, and his Princes with him,to aske what Gods answere was to him, *Baalam* (I say) then spake thus vnto him : Arise *Balak* to heare Gods voice, and to giue reuerence to it. Concerning his rising vp (I say at the naming of God (that wee may make some good vse of it, wee are sure it serueth to conuince Atheists, and prophane ones,who are farre from yeelding any. But if yee will say, what reuerence was that which they gaue,seeing they were Idolaters,and did it at the naming of God,whether it were the true God *Iehouah*, or any other, I say, sufficient to condemne these. But some make shewes of reuerence when in truth they offer disgrace. So we reade of the Pharisies,that when it was pro-
Ioh.9.24. ued to them by the blind man,that Christ had opened his eyes, which they could not abide to heare, they would not take knowledge of it ; but as though they might boldly and freely detract from him whom they hated, (so that they gaue words of honour to God) bewrayed their hypocrisie, who would seeme holy, and therefore said ; *giue glory to God,wee know that this man is a sinner:* and so bewrayed that they had no religion,when yet they would seeme to goe before others therein : seeing this is true, that hee that honoureth not the sonne, neither doth hee honour the father. Let all this then,

then,both ſerue to ſhame all brutiſh and prophane perſons,(who yet are in the viſible Church) who aſcribe not ſo much to the word preached,neither regard the meſſage of God, with ſo much reuerence as this heathen *Eglon* did; who in token thereof ſtood vp when *Ehud* told him that he had a meſſage for him from God. But to leaue theſe,let it bee a watchword to vs that profeſſe the true worſhip of God,that we pleaſe not our ſelues in the worke wrought; I meane in giuing outward and bodily worſhip to God, and in calling him father; ſeeing neither they who draw neare to him with bodies onely,doe pleaſe him; neither all that ſay, Lord, Lord, ſhall enter into the kingdome of heauen,but he that doth the wil of the father that is in heauen: and againe, ſeeing it is written, that all who call on the name of the Lord, muſt depart from iniquity: let vs regard that duly, without which wee ſhall haue no more to commend vs to God,then this Heathen King had. But of this enough before,cap. 1. verſ.4. It followeth.

Mat.15.9. Mat.7.21. 2.Tim.2.19.

Verſ. 21. *And Ehud put forth his left hand, and tooke the dagger from his right thigh,and thruſt it into his belly.*

22. *So that the haft went in after the blade,and the fat cloſed about the blade,ſo that he could not draw the dagger out of his belly,but the dirt came out.*

The ſenſe and doctrine of theſe two verſes.

OF *Ehuds* intent and preparation to kill *Eglon* King of Moab, wee haue heard: now followeth the execution of it. For as *Iael* was ſtrengthened by God,to deſtroy and kill *Sicera*,captaine of *Iabin* King of Canaan; ſo the Lord ſtrengthened *Ehud* heere, to bring downe *Eglon* King of Moab, that Iſrael his people who cried vnto him, might bee deliuered out of the bondage that he had brought them into. And thus God in a moment tooke away the life and honour of him both together,by one deadly blow? wherin hee would ſhew vs the wofull eſtate of thoſe, who haue nothing but in this world, to what end they may come euen heere, they know not how ſoone and ſuddenly, beſide the irkeſome deſolation that ſhall meet with them when they goe hence. Oh the baſe and lothſome death that God would haue him brought vnto, and yet in his flouriſhing eſtate, ſo far from likelihood of any change or decay at all! If wee regard any thing,wee will conſider this: examples are infinite. Thus *Belſhazzar* and *Herod* were taken downe in the middeſt of their iollity. Adde to theſe, *Nabal* for the vncomfortableneſſe of his death, with *Zimri* that burned himſelfe, to burne the Kings pallace in Tirza, and ſo died; and with *Ioaſh* the King of Iuda, who was ſlaine of his ſeruants,and *Iezabel*, whoſe blood was without compaſſion daſhed againſt the ſtones. Euen ſo, doe wee not daily ſee the flouriſhing eſtates of men turned to moſt deſolate decay? in ſo much as they bee iuſtly reproued for making them their Paradiſe; and that by the words of our Sauiour [are theſe the things ye looke after?] and alſo when hee bewailed them, for that they died without hope. And heere by ſo fit an occaſion as is offered by *Ehuds* killing of *Eglon* this King of Moab: I thinke it not vnfit in this place, (though in a word,and by way of execration) to note and bring to the remembrance of the Reader, the curſed practiſe of Ieſuites in murthering, and bringing vntimely death vpon the Lords annointed, Kings and Princes, vnder the colour of their

Doct.in verſ.21. 1.Sam.25.37.38. 1.King.16.19. 2.King.12.20. Luk.21.6. Luk.19.41.

heresie (as they call it) or lest they should incurre some way the Popes displeasure for not doing so; as though they would helpe the Lord to cut off such as flourish and prosper. And the rather I mention them, because they defend themselues by this fact of *Ehud*, and such like, most impudently and absurdly, to couer their horrible treasons and murthers. The two last Kings of France were thus handled, and the facts with the doers highly extolled by these that hartened them on thereto. Oh villaine intolerable! whereby, as by their persecuting the Gospell, they most liuely shew themselues to bee vtter aduersaries to Christ, and to bee most neare akind to them who commit the sinne against which we should not pray, that cannot bee forgiuen. But to leaue them whom God alloweth not to bee instruments of such bloody acts and trecheries, let vs returne to the persons before mentioned, who liued heere in pleasures of sinne for a season, and were without God in the world, and soone perished miserably.

These with many other mentioned in the Scriptures, and in later Chronicles (for I speake of the chiefe and greatest persons, seeing they doe most moue affection,) so highly aduanced in this world, and yet so soone and suddenly spoiled and bereaued of all their honour and excellency (as I haue said) and to change it with a base death, and a worse estate afterwards; doe liuely set before our eyes the misery of all such, as looke no further, then after brauerie, iollity, vaine pleasure, and large possessions, which they can neither keepe, when their deadly blow is giuen them, and when their dreadfull woe commeth, so that they might bee any comforts to them; nor lose and part from them (if they haue any time to thinke thereof) without deadly dislike, and most bitter vexation. So that it may worthily warne all such as be of high degree, and much more vs that are inferiour persons; and therefore ought first to stoope to consider of, and prouide for our ende, that when we must depart hence, (which time is most vncertaine) we may bee prepared to die happily, and prouide to be receiued into heauenly habitations. For wee see what a pitifull and dangerous thing it is to rest vpon that which we enioy heere, as wealth, pompe, young yeeres, or any other earthly prosperity. The Lord scatters men in the imaginations of their hearts. He sweepes downe their warped thoughts, as copwebs with beezome. It had been well with *Eglon*, and such as hee was, (all that heare of him will say) if he had enioyed nothing; and much better if hee had been nothing. Note. Euen thus the hand of God is against all his enemies, and when the day of reckoning commeth, they perish. It is reported (in the history of that time) that an Emperour of Rome, *Adrian* by name, when hee should die, and leaue all his iollity, being suddenly stricken with great terrour, vsed these words: *Oh my poore wandring sillie soule, which hast been long a companion and guest of my body, what shall hereafter become of thee, or whither wilt thou goe? Thou hast been iollie, merrie, and full of sporting and pleasures, but now thou must goe where there is no such matter, forlorne, desolate, and forsaken.* Behold in this great man, the wofull apprehension and fearefull presage of the woe to come, euen while he liued: the which doubtlesse seazing vpon the mighty and glorious (when no outward thing can comfort them) should flaight and terrifie al sorts and degrees of men from resting vpon any earthly props, wanting Gods fauour for their chiefe stay and refuge.

Melanct. in Adriano.

And

And heere in laying out the fearefull manner of killing *Eglon*, occasion being offered to make mention of that which was lothsome to the eare; in that it was vttered in more seemly termes and words: we may learne how warily wee should speake of things more vnseemely, or which are more harsh in the hearing; and follow the holy Ghost in our termes, namely, to vtter that (which might else offend the eares of the most) in more seemely and honest words. So the action of the marriage bed is vsually expressed by the holy Ghost in most chast and seemely words. As it is said of *Dauid*, when *Abishag* the Shunamite was brought vnto him to minister to him, though she cherished him, and lay in his bosome in his extreme age, that he might get heate by her, it is said in modest words, *that the King knew her not*: so *Mary, how can this be, seeing I knew not a man?* Such are the termes vsed by the holy Ghost, of discouering the shame and couering the nakednesse of *Noah* our father, as *Shem* and *Iaphet* did. And although education and good manners teach vs modesty, yet grace must teach the language of Canaan, whereof this is a part. The Lord commanded Israel to couer their excrements with their paddle, because hee walked among them: and so ought we to behaue our selues, especially Preachers must beware of brode, vnseemely, and offensiue speech in this kinde, because they are to vtter the will of God, in the most seemely and reuerent phrase and manner. And diuers other such might bee brought forth, but that I would not bee long in this matter, where fewer words may serue. Which is to the iust reproofe of many in our time, who as they are rude and brutish in their behauiour, so haue they as beastly and filthy tongues to vtter their mindes by, in too vnseemely manner, as they know who are their companions, and like vnto them. And this of *Ehuds* killing *Eglon*.

Doct. in vers. 22.

1. King. 1. 4.

Luk. 1. 34.

Deut. 23, 12, 13. 14.

THE

THE TWENTIE TWO SERMON ON THE THIRD CHAPTER OF THE BOOKE OF IVDGES.

VERS. 23. *Then Ehud got him out into the porch, and shut the dores of the parlour vpon him, and locked them.*

24. *And when he was gone out, his seruants came, who seeing that the doores of the parlour were locked, they said; surely hee doth his easement in his sommer parlour.*

25. *And they tarried till they were ashamed: and seeing he opened not the doores of the parlour, they tooke the key and opened them, and behold their Lord was fallen dead on the earth.*

26. *So Ehud escaped (while they tarried) and was passed the quarries, and escaped to Seirah.*

NOw of the things that followed this action, and pertained to it, according to the diuision made in the end of the fifteenth verse: they are set downe in these foure verses, and tend all to this end, to shew how God made way for *Ehuds* safe escaping. And therefore first note we somewhat generally, and then more particularly afterward. For his comming forth, in that none of the Kings seruants were at hand to goe into the Kings parlour presently, or if they were there attending, yet that they should be so negligent and forgetfull to goe in forthwith, but to tarrie till *Ehud* might be gone past all danger, it was as I said of his going about it, so ordered by God, that all might say, thus hee would haue it, and then we know, that none can withstand or resist it. To teach vs the same so that although a man would thinke, that there might be many waies to ouerthrow and frustrate Gods purpose, yet none of them shal stand, for why? there is no counsell against the Lord. Who would not haue thought, but that *Pharaoh* might haue kept the people of Israel still in his land, and that none could haue brought such a mighty people) euen many hundred thousands) out of it against his will? But yet behold, seeing God would deliuer them, it was not he, nor all his chariots, no nor all the Kings in the world, if they had ioyned with him, that could haue hindred it.

Prou.

Exod.12.41.

It might likewise haue been thought an easie matter for King *Ahab* and *Iezabel*, full of spite and cruelty, with all their strength, friends, and retinue, whom they might haue commanded and set about it, to roote out and take out of the way, the poore Prophet of God *Elias*, which they desired most earnestly to haue done: but seeing God would preserue him to honour his name, it was in vaine for them to attempt or goe about it. So for *Paul*, one sillie

1.King.19.1.2.

seely Apostle to conquer so great a part of the world by the preaching of the Gospell, which it had vtterly reiected, how admirable a thing was it? seeing it is manifest, that the malitious Iewes resisted, and came against him in all places: but who might withstand God, when he would haue it so? For in that one city at Corinth, he bad him go forward in preaching, and faint not, where he had much people; adding this for encouragement thereto, that none should be able to hinder it. And let vs in these daies be wise by so many faire warnings. It cannot be that one of Gods faithfull shall perish, therefore let vs not smite at such, with tongue nor hand as hee loueth: hee will fight for them, and curse them that curse his, and they shall repent it, if not too late, that they went about to hurt them. But of this I spake before in the former Sermon, though not in the same words, nor making the same vse thereof: therefore thus much briefly of these verses in generall.

Act.18.9.10.11

Note.

Gen.11.35.

Now that it is said in this verse, that *Ehud*, when he had done this worke vpon Gods enemy, came forth neither in feare, nor any great haste, in any disguised manner, but as though hee had done nothing worthy suspition, neither gaue any token of a guilty conscience, but as one that had serued God in that worke. It liuely setteth before our eyes the peaceable fruit of an excusing and quiet conscience. Behold the like in *Iael*, the wife of *Heber*, who hauing slaine *Sisera*, whereas any other doing such an act of his owne head with a murthering mind in such a matter, could hardly haue auoided it, but he should haue bewrayed himselfe easily and palpably: as is to bee seene in *Iudas* betraying his master, who cried out of his owne fact, saying; I haue sinned in betraying the innocent blood. And it may teach vs how greatly the quiet and excusing conscience of the innocent and righteous man differeth from the guilty and accusing conscience of the vngodly. And it agreeth with the words of the Wise man, who saith; *The righteous is bold as a Lion, but the wicked fleeth, when no man pursueth him.* The ground of this his peace, was the discharge of that duty which the Lord imposed vpon him, in this extraordinary case, the which otherwise had been abominable parricide. And although this viperous brood of Iesuites pretend the like dispensation from their pettie god the Pope, and thereupon harden their hearts, and set an impudent face vpon the matter, as if they had no wound or terrour of conscience: yet the truth is, their ground being naught, the cause of this boldnesse is shamelesnesse, impudency, and want of conscience at all, if they be not wounded. Hell can onely terrifie these helhounds, for God they feare not, and they haue hardened their faces (as it seemeth) to regard no man. Where we may see a double benefit that the godly reape and enioy by hauing allowance and warrant from God for the duties they doe: to wit, inward quietnesse of mind, and strength and courage thereby to beare any outward danger or trouble, if need should bee, and both the contraries to pursue and take hold of the other, that is, an hellish minde toward God, and terrour and dread though they bite it in, in regard of the world, or an hardened heart which is worse then both.

Doct. of vers.23.

Iudg.4.22.

Mat.27.4.

Prou.28.1.

As for those which waited on the King, they did foolishly: they should haue cast the hardest, when *Ehud* came forth of the parlour, and haue stayed him, and not haue kept out so long, and haue made such delay as they did: for delaies are dangerous where the matter is weighty, in which they are vsed.

Vers.24.25. *The clearing of them.*

sed. And they being thought so wise that the keeping of their Lord and master was committed to them: they failed greatly and grosly in their duty; and therefore they reaped the fruit thereof, when after their long tarying,
Doct vers. 24.25. they came in at the last and found him slaine. This is that which delay breedeth in all things, (not in their doings onely) and the more danger, the greater the things are, as I haue said. Thus *Baanah* and *Rechab* by the negligence of the Kings officers, slew him on his bed. And as this teacheth euery priuate man to be diligent and warie about the duties that belong to his function and calling, to preuent losse and damage; so especially it commendeth vigilancie and circumspection in al such, as through whose hands great matters of state and gouernment doe passe, that neither by their carelesnes, conniuence, or other sinister respects, they suffer that mischiefe to grow vpon Church and Common-wealth, which by their prouidence might in season be preuented ere it bee helpelesse. The fit season therefore is to bee taken, in earthly businesse and our common affaires, as this was heere by *Ehud*: wee must vse the opportunity; reape the corne when it calleth for the sickle, and strike the iron while it is hot: so our market must be made, while a good peniworth may be had.
Eccles. 5. Doe all thou hast to doe with diligence, while the day lasteth: the night will come, when in such workes cannot be done. Remember the rich man, who being in hell in torments, was denied a drop of cold water, because hee auoided them not while he enioyed plenty. So *Haman*
Luk. 16.25. made request for his life too late. And by their slacknesse and delay we may
2. Cor. 6.2. much more be warned in the weighty affaires that concerne our happines, to take the fit season: that is, to seeke the Lord while he may bee found, and
Esa. 55.6.
Eccles. 12.1. not driue off from day to day, but to remember our maker in the daies of
Psal. 95.8. our youth, and to day, while wee heare his voice, not to harden our hearts, but imbrace his message both in the Law and promises of God by faith vnto saluation. The seruants that kept not *Saul*, but slept in great danger, were
1. Sam. 26.16. accessaries (as *Dauid* tels *Abner* in *Sauls* case) though they betrayed him not: euen so the carelesse delayer to get faith and repentance, shall perish, as
Luk. 13.3.
Psal 50 16. he that hates to be reformed. The fiue foolish Virgins knocked to be let in,
Mat. 25. 11.12. when the doore was shut. Euen so in all particular actions of our life, looke we before all other things to keepe our conscience pure and good. To the like purpose much might bee said. And this by occasion of the seruants delay, and their astonishment, when they saw how it fell out to them thereby.

Doct. vers. 26. *Ehud* reaped the benefit of this their delay, for while they thus draue off and lost the time in which they should haue carefully attended vpon their Lord, hee escaped out of their hands, and wound out of all danger, hee passing the quarries, which it seemeth were places betwixt Gilgall of the Israelites, and the Moabites, which before he could get beyond, he was not past danger: and so comming to Seirah, a place heere mentioned in the borders of Israel, further off from danger, he was in safety. And thus wee see againe, that they who are wise and speedy in their businesse, doe thriue and prosper, when they who delay the time, doe apparantly sit in their owne light, and worke their owne sorrow and annoyance, as wee haue heard: euen as he who hauing foolishly refused a good bargaine, which might haue been for for the benefit and maintenance both of him and his long after, mourneth and

and dispaireth of the like offer and opportunity. The diligent hand maketh rich, and he that watereth shall also haue raine. Cursed is hee that doth the Lords businesse negligently. The people in *Iohn Baptists* time receiued the word with greedinesse, happie was hee that could enter first into the kingdome of God, and they that make no hast doe neuer come thither. And yet they that striue to enter in at the straite gate shall bee receiued into glory: when other shall seeke to enter afterward (too late) and shall not bee able. And therfore the Apostle tels vs, that such as can redeeme the time, are wise men; the foolish beleeue euery thing, and so driue off, and are taken in the snare. Thus wee see the wise take the opportunity, and bring their matters thereby to a good passe. But for all that I haue said of speedinesse, yet vnderstand me thus: that rashnesse is as farre from commendation, as driuing off the time, and delay. Thus much of *Ehuds* first worke in killing the chiefe enemie of Gods people, that *Eglon* the King; which was a great meane of their deliuerance and rest.

Mat.11.

Compare vers. 16. with the 15. of Ephes.5.

Vers. 27. *And when he came home, he blew a trumpet in mount Ephraim, and the children of Israel went downe with him from the mountaine, and hee went before them.*

28. *Then said he vnto them, follow mee, for the Lord hath deliuered your enemies, euen Moab, into your hands. So they went downe after him, and tooke the passages of Iordan toward Moab, and suffered not a man to passe ouer.*

29. *And they slue of the Moabites the same time about ten thousand men, all fed men, and all warriors; and there escaped not a man.*

30. *So Moab was subdued that day vnder the hand of Israel, and the land had rest fourscore yeeres.*

THe second meane of Israels deliuerance followeth; and that was, the cutting off of ten thousand of the valiant men of Moab, which was the other good helpe toward their deliuerance beside the killing of the King, which now followeth to the ending and making vp of this Story, to vers.31. But first it is shewed what *Ehud* did to the bringing of this to passe. The things that *Ehud* went about, whereby so many of the Moabites were slaine and Israel was deliuered, were these three: first, as hee was a valiant man, so he comming to the place heere mentioned, Seirah by name, (it was not Seir in Idumea, but neare to mount Ephraim in the land of Canaan, as was said before) hee did not leaue the worke vnperfect, which hee had begun in killing the King of Moab, but 1. with a trumpet he called together the men of Ephraim, and by his authority stirred them vp to warre: and 2. to encourage them the better therto, he assured them from God of the victorie: and 3. with this, they tooke vp and beset the foords of Iordan, where the Moabites passed ouer too and fro out of Israel into the land of Moab: and by this meanes they stayed such of them as were on that side the riuer, that they could not escape and goe ouer, and those that came out of the land of Moab ouer the riuer to rescue their fellowes, and pursue Israel, they slew also, till ten thousand men of good courage were cut off. And this if they had not done, the Moabites being so inraged against them for that which was done to their King, they had made spoile and hauocke of them, whereas

Vers.27. *The sense and summe of these 4. verses.*

now they subdued them,and obtained a long time of rest themselues. Thus much for the clearing of these 4. verses.

The meaning of vers.27. particularly. Now of that which we are to learne out of them. *Ehud* did not delay,as we see,for that had bin full of danger,but now while the Moabites through astonishment at that which was befallen them, could not by and by see and determine what was best to be done,he plied it, and went to worke, as wee haue heard. It is as hard a matter to vse an opportunity wisely,and pursue the occasion effectually when it is offered, as it is at first to get and take it. But *Ehud* lost no time,but followed it hard : and as he had escaped while the seruants delayed; so now hee gathers his army together, while the Moabites (being amazed with terrour) were fit by passing to and fro to bee pursued, and discomfited. *Doct.* And as this doth shew how vnwearied wee ought to be in those actions that tend to the glory of God, the good of the Church,and the confusion of the enemies thereof; so, more generally it teacheth vs, when we haue made a good beginning in any thing,that we should not bee slacke in going forward,and following it : but as *Ehud* heere did,wisely and carefully labour to bring our worke vnto an end. It is a thing much more common to begin well, then to goe forward so, whether wee vnderstand it generally, to make a beginning in Christianity, or in any particular part thereof,it is most true. For the formost, many of vs come to professe the Gospell indeed, and imbrace it commendably, by hearing it ioyfully, in conuersing with Gods people kindly, & in forsaking many parts of our former bad liues. *Note.* But when wee should hold on in this good manner to search *Iudg.19.* further into our selues,to finde out our ranke corruptions, and to purge our selues of them,and to be grounded in our most holy faith, and stablished as we may attaine to,we waxe soone weare,and begin to stand at a stay, and so we lose all our labour that we haue bestowed already,and frustrate the work that was well begun.

And so to say the same of particulars, it is well seene, that many attempt sundry good actions commendably; as the labouring for a good Minister, and the drawing of the people to godly society and loue in a towne, and to haue an eye to the vnruly: other begin good exercises and orders in their family, and namely, prayer morning and euening; and some vse good meanes for the well ordering,and good gouerning of their liues,and labour to roote out particular abuses out of them,and to entertaine grace and good duties,and many such like I might mention. But I cannot tell how it commeth to passe,that as if they thought these good things should last but for a while,or as though they would hold in good plight without meanes (wherin they shew that they are not well grounded, though they did well for a season) so they goe to worke, and what with discouragements and crosses on the one side, and allurements and prouocations on the other side, they faint and breake off: whereas that should not bee, till the worke were brought to a good end, that so they might goe forward in other duties in like manner. Neither should wee looke to the things past,what good wee *Phil.3.13.14.* haue done more then other, to become lesse carefull thereby in going forward; but what remaineth yet to bee done till wee haue brought our good attempts to passe; and one good duty should follow after another,vntill we haue finished our course with ioy. Wee must remember that the Merchant

went

went and bought the pearle when hee had found it: and the wise Virgins kept oyle in their lampes. And heere it were to good purpose to thinke of *Ehuds* vnwearied care and labour, till he had brought all to a good end, and of such other as did the like; and to consider with our selues (as hee and such did) how all that hath been done of vs in such cases, should bee but in vaine; and beside, great danger and detriment must needs come vpon vs, if wee should (as too many doe) breake off in the mid way. Oh what doe men lose heereby: euen beside all their labour, the fruit of it also. But of this we haue occasion to speake often elsewhere. Mat.13.42. Mat.25.4.

Further, in that it is said that he hartened them on against the Moabites, assuring them that the Lord had deliuered them into their hands, and that he drew them after him, and they did as he willed them; wee see the worth of a good guide, what he may doe with those which he is set ouer, and how much, strong and well grounded perswasions preuaile, where they be vsed in season and good manner, God blessing them as hee hath promised. Heathen Captaines haue done much with their souldiers, and Princes and lawmakers with their subiects: who yet (we know) could neither certifie them of the things they promised, and encouraged them to hope for, neither if they could; were the things of any other sort or kinde, then temporary. Now then how much more are they like to preuaile with men, who both bring infallible promises from God, and also of things which please him (as *Ehud* heere doth) and they doe not onely glad the hearts of the persons therewith, in as much as they vnderstand thereby that God will blesse them heere abundantly, and also that their reward is great in heauen. Note.

As the Lord spoke to *Iosbua* saying: *Bee valiant and of good courage, for I haue giuen the whole country of the Canaanites into thy hands:* so spake *Ehud* heere vnto the men of Ephraim in the name of God, and by his authority. And these are the perswasions that are like to preuaile, I say not with the faithfull onely: but (if any may bee) these are of force to moue euen other also. Not that they can be throughly perswaded thereof without faith, but for that they doe very much moue their minds, and the rather by the example of better then themselues, and also they doe cause them the more to enquire into such things, and how they should bee done, till they grow acquainted with them, that so they may in time beleeue and so doe them in faith also. And let this which I say bee better considered in two things: the one in the promises of eternall life, the other in those which belong to this present life. Iosh.1.3.

For the first, when God shall by some faithfull messenger of his, assure the hungring soule, and the man of an afflicted spirit, of pardon of his sinnes, and eternall life, and that he shall vndoubtedly enioy them, requiring this withall, that he giue credit therto, and beleeue the same; how greatly (think we) do they moue and preuaile with him, as we see Christs words did with *Zachee*, and *Pauls* with the Iailor, and with many other? And for the second likewise, I meane the temporary promises of this present life (as this was one, that *Ehud* heere offered and set before the people) as the promise of blessing and good successe to such as obey God, by walking diligently in their particular calling, and the promise of a good end and issue out of trouble to them which commit their way to God, and are well occupied vnder Luk.19.8.9. Act.16.33. Note.

it in the meane season: to these, I say, how forcible are such promises, and what power haue they to vphold the hearts of such, in a comfortable expectation of the things promised? whereas without them, nothing could doe the same. Oh therfore what good may a godly Minister do in both (euen as other superiours also, especially being men indued with the gifts of the spirit) if he continue in loue to put the poore people daily in remembrance of these things, in the middest of the manifold changes of this life? And therefore as God shall impart to any man in the ministery or otherwise; more light, wisedome, experience, and grace, either in beleeuing or obeying, the more must hee apply himselfe to enlighten, aduise, and strengthen those whom God hath set him ouer for that purpose; knowing that it is not euery mans case, to be able to minister vnto himselfe or other, aduice or direction, (though it were much to be desired) especially in a matter of difficulty, and in a doubt of conscience, or in tentation, or vnder the crosse. *Peter* therefore
Luk. 22. 31. is betrusted with this office, to confirme his brethren, as a man of a thousand,
Psal. 51. 13. as *Dauid*, Psal. 51. vndertooke it, who had himselfe first well learned it, and was the better able to performe it to other. Neither let any man thinke it a disgrace to himselfe thus to see, and walke, by the eyes, and vpon the feet of others. It is a mans wisedome, and a great portion from God, to receiue direction by such meanes. Heere I will stay.

THE TVVENTIE THREE SERMON ON THE THIRD CHAPTER OF THE BOOKE OF IVDGES.

Vers. 29. 30. *The sense.*

NOw to goe forward; the valiant warriours of Ephraim being encouraged thus by *Ehud*, and other helpe being called together therewith, as we haue heard, and they keeping the passages to and fro, betwixt Israel on their owne side, and Moab on the other side of Iordan, they killed all the Moabites that offered themselues to stirre and be helpers in that time of their great calamity and abasement, wherein they had lost their King: these (I say) whom *Ehud* drew together, so bestirred themselues, that ten thousand of the best warriours of the Moabites were put to the sword. Thus they of Moab were weakened, and *Ehud* and the people of Israel did more and more preuaile. By all this we see that as there is a time of affliction and calamity to the people of God (as it had
Doct. vers. 29. 30. beene heere to Israel) and that is, when they haue prouoked God, and their sinnes haue made them naked before the Lord, that is to say, destitute and
Exod. 32. 25. voide of the grace and helpe of God, (as it is said of their fathers when they had made a Calfe in Exodus) as I say, there is such a time; so there is a time againe of deliuerance and ioy, and that is, when the people rise out of their sinne

sinne penitently, and seeke the Lord with their whole heart, then hee most graciously returneth to them againe, in whose fauour is life.

And this comfortable estate may wee enioy from time to time, to haue the Lords louing countenance to shine vpon vs, far more delightfull to our soule, then the fairest and sweetest weather can bee to the creatures of the earth, if we can like to preferre it, as it is the best before all other: and we hauing obtained grace to doe so, if we shall goe a step further, and can thinke it our best wisedome to continue in so doing, wee shall abide in Gods fauour also, and keepe our selues well when we are wel, which is the happinesse that can in this life be enioyed. The Lord doth not stint and tie vs to times, in which only we may haue peace with him, and see good daies; but he would that wee should liue in safety vnder his protection all the day long: and so from time to time, that we may haue proofe how good and bountifull hee is. But we are waily and inconstant, and abuse his lenity and kindnesse toward vs, when hee not onely holdeth many troubles and sorrowes from vs, but also lodeth vs with the benefits of health, and welfare, inward and outward, and that also while others smart and are in heauinesse.

Note.

Ioh.15.10.

Deut.33.12.

Note.
Psal.68.19.

Wee deale with him, as pampered horses, and children much made of, who right soone waxe loose and wanton, And wee cause the Lord to turne our good and ioyfull daies into glooming and sorrowfull times: as through the stories of the booke of God doth euery where appeare, that many after good beginnings did so though little to their comfort. Oh how soone did this people mentioned in this booke, and their fathers, as wee reade in Deuteronomy, with sundry other generations following, as the stories doe testifie, kicke vp their heele against the Lord, when hee did yet feede them with the fat of wheat, and make them drinke of the sweet. And this reuolting worketh such a change in our best states and seasons, as causeth to complain and cry. Let it therefore cause vs to bee resolued vpon this, and that in due and good consideration, so that wee may constantly hold the same: to wit, that if wee desire to see good daies heere, and enioy long life with the Lord hereafter: that (I say) wee flie euill, and follow that which is good: and heerein let vs see that wee deale not hollowly with the Lord: and if by occasion we slip or fall, and forget our selues (as this people heere did, vers.7.) yet let vs take heede that we harden not our hearts, and so lie still, but beare our punishment contentedly, because we haue sinned, and make speed to turne againe to the Lord our first husband, who will receiue vs graciously: and as he hath smitten vs, so he will heale vs; and as hee did before comfort vs, so he will restore ioy and gladnesse to vs, as in time past. And this being done daily in the smaller slips, shall the easilier be gone about in greater fals, and shall also be a meane to keepe vs from them. Yea doubtlesse the Lord will doe great things for vs; and as hee abased the enemies of this people, the Moabites heere, so will hee bring the wicked vnder vs, and leaue them afflicted and scourged in our roome.

Deut.32.15.

1.Pet.3.11.

Note.

Mica.7.7.

Prou.

Now followeth the third and last thing mentioned in this latter part of the story, and that is, rest after, for a good while.

Vers.30.
The vnfolding of it.

This long time of peace the Lord granted them, and could willingly affoord it them, and it is all one to him to giue a long time thereto, as a short. And as it was a great blessing, so it was more then was promised. Indeed the

the Lord said, that he would giue Moab into their hands, and the people enioyed that (as a fruit of their faith) which laid hold on Gods promise. But besides, he lengthened out the time of their rest, further then hee promised them. To teach vs that God neuer commeth short or behinde hand with vs
Doct. vers. 30. in performing his promises, but giueth vs good measure, heaped vp, and
Luk. 6. 38. running ouer; and thereby sheweth that hee is liberall and bountifull toward vs. And this is his vsuall manner of dealing with his, to giue more then they aske or looke to receiue; for hee giueth more then hee himselfe promiseth. The prodigall child asked, that hee might be receiued but as an
Luk. 15. 19. 22. &c. hired seruant, but his father, who resembled the Lord in kindnesse, receiued him for his sonne, and declared it by entertaining him gladly, with all things
Mat 15. 22. 28. agreeing therto. So the woman of Canaan came to Christ for helpe for her daughter; but he not onely granted her that, but also bad her take what she would. Euen as father *Iacob*, who feared that hee should neuer see *Iosephs*
Gen 37. 33. 34. compared with 48. 11. face, thinking he had been deuoured of some wild beast, did yet see his childrens children.

This if it were beleeued, were able to make our liues comfortable. For to say the truth, all our welfare is according to our faith, and yet the Lord giueth farre aboue that which we can beleeue. Therefore this ought to en-
Note. courage vs, to labour to giue him credit in all that we see he imposeth vpon vs, and requireth of vs, in that wee vnderstand and see, and rest perswaded that he will haue vs to goe about it. For we may know, that our reward shall be exceeding great in so doing. Let vs instance this in two or three particulars, and we shall finde the same that other haue done before vs. If we marke it, we may perceiue, that when we haue somtime in our afflictions besought the Lord but for some ease and mitigation of the force of them, whether sicknesse, paine, disease, or any such like, he hath deliuered vs altogether, and besides, blessed vs abundantly. And so to shew it in any other particular, when great sorrow hath been rising toward vs, he hath oft times turned our sorrow into ioy. And euen so, as long-continued peace was to this people vnlooked for, when their very deliuerance from subiection to the Moabites, would haue been ful welcome, though it had been but for a short time, that they might haue had but some breathing from their bondage: so the Lord dealeth with vs, that whereas in some of our troubles, we haue feared as *He-*
Note. *zechiah* did, that wee should neuer see light, nor good daies any more; yet
Esa. 38. 11. the Lord of his exceeding goodnesse hath restored vs to our former sweet liberties for a long time after. But oh what might be said of this argument? Although we must also know, that hee seeth reason sometime, and that for good cause, to hold vs off and deferre vs. But more of this in Chap. 1. ver. 2. And heere an end of this story.

Vers. 31. *And after him was Shamgar the sonne of Anath, which slew of the Philistims sixe hundred men with an oxe goade, and he also deliuered Israel.*

THis short story of *Shamgar*, is the third and last story mentioned in this chapter of the Israelites deliuerance, by an other Iudge. But who this *Shamger* was, or of what tribe hee came, the Scripture doth not set downe. But it appeareth, that when they had enioyed long peace vnder *Ehud*, after his

his death, the Philiſtims began to vexe and oppreſſe them, and then the Lord ſtirred vp this *Shamgar* to defend them, that they might not againe be brought into bondage as they had bin before. And among other of their victories which were many, this one is brought in, as moſt admirable, though it be but briefly mentioned. For a great number, euen hundreds to be ſlaine by one man, and he vſing ſo weake an inſtrument, and the whole nation of the people to bee preſerued thereby from ſo fierce enemies, what is in this whole booke ſpoken of, of the like kind, to be ſo ſtrange and admirable? vnleſſe it be the like act of *Sampſon*.

Wherein we may ſee, that euery ſlight thing may be a weapon of warre for Gods people, when hee will ſay, it ſhall preuaile: and that it is not the number of men, nor the meanes, that God regardeth when hee will get the victory. Therefore *Dauids* ſmall and ſmooth ſtones to throw in his ſling, 1.Sam.17.
were ſufficient furniture and armour to ſley the Philiſtims champion *Goli-* 40.49.
ah: and *Sampſon* with the iaw bone of an Aſſe ſlew a thouſand men: and Iudg.15.15.
Iael with a bare naile, killed *Siſera*, that valiant captaine of *Iabin* King of Canaan. And ſo great an act did this *Shamgar*, by ſo weak an inſtrument, when the Lord pleaſed to giue the victory. And this truth ſhould wee ſee verified as clearely as euer they did, if we would hold this ſure and conſtant, that wee are his, and deare vnto him: ſecondly, when we feele our outward oppreſſions and diſcouragements, or our inward infirmities, feares, and tentations, if then (I ſay) wee did not looke how weake wee our ſelues are, and vnfit to wade through them all, and beare them, forgetting Gods power, which ſer- 1.Sam.30.6.
ueth for the vſe and comfort of his weake ſeruants, and to be made knowne in their infirmities: euen ſo wee ſee *Dauid* did, namely in his ſore diſtreſſe, 2.Chron.12.9.
comfort himſelfe in being wearied with *Sauls* purſuing of him. And yet what a grace that was in him, we may ſee by this, that hee being at an other time, and forgetting himſelfe, in a ſore combat, brake out thus, and in his raſhneſſe ſaid, *I ſhall one time or other fall by Saul*: But wee ſhould looke how 1.Sam.27.1.
ſtrong the Lord is who loueth vs: who alſo lookes downe from heauen, to ſee who are weake, that he may be ſtrong with them. For indeed when wee 2.Chron.16.9.
ſee our owne impotency, this ſhould lift vp our heart, and cauſe vs to reach out our hand to Gods mercy, which is in a readineſſe for vs. So that if he be able to helpe vs, that ſhould bee enough for vs, how vnable ſoeuer wee bee to beare the burthen our ſelues. So wee haue learned to beleeue, and to Pſal.27.1.
ſpeake, *The Lord is my light and ſaluation, whom ſhall I feare? the Lord is the ſtrength of my life, of whom ſhall I be afraid?* Remember wee alſo what the A- Phil.4.13.
poſtle ſaid: *I am able to doe all things through him that maketh me able.* And a- 2.Cor.12.10.
gaine, *I will reioyce in mine infirmities: for when I am weake, then am I ſtrong*: euen ſo we not fainting in our many troubles, but by faith drawing and deriuing Gods power vnto vs, as we haue good leaue to do, yea as we are commanded by himſelfe to doe, we may reſt quiet, for God will not diſappoint vs, and in that reſpect the Apoſtle *Iames* willeth vs to bee greatlieſt comforted, when we fall into diuerſe tentations, that ſo our faith may be tried to be found (and that is better then gold) bringing patience with it. And yet if Iam 1.3.
the Lord be not with vs, nor wee cling not to him by faith, no munition or warlike furniture when it is needed, nor the ſtrongeſt nor ſureſt helpe in time of peace ſhall be able to doe vs any good. Therefore neither could the walles

Iosh.6.2. walles of Iericho preserue the city when God went against it, nor *Goliahs* sword defend him, but turne against him; nor *Pharaohs* Chariots get victorie for him, but faile him when the Lord would not go with them. And

Psal.33.16. therefore euen as it is said in the Psalme, that a King is not saued by the multitude of an host, neither is the mighty deliuered by his great strength; so an horse is but a vaine helpe to saue a man. And so wee may say of all creatures. If the Lord be at peace with vs, they are on our sides, to stand with vs; but if he frowne vpon vs, they shall be against vs. Lo such a thing it is to bee in league and fauour with him, that all shall turne to the best vnto vs thereby; yea euen the fiercenesse of our enemies: the heauens, the earth, the creatures shall be all at one with them, who are in couenant with him, who is the Lord of them. But I will proceed in the next chapter.

THE FOVRTH CHAPTER OF THE booke of IVDGES.

Vers. 1. *And the children of Israel began againe to doe wickedly in the sight of the Lord when Ehud was dead.*

2. *And the Lord sold them into the hand of Iabin King of Canaan that raigned in Hazor, whose chiefe captaine was called Sisera, which dwelt in Harosheth of the Gentiles.*

3. *Then the children of Israel cried vnto the Lord, for he had nine hundred Chariots of iron, and twentie yeeres he had vexed the children of Israel very sore.*

4. *And at that time Debora a Prophetesse, the wife of Lapidoth iudged Israel.*

5. *And this Debora dwelt vnder a Palme tree betweene Rama and mount Ephraim, and the people of Israel came vp to her for iudgement.*

The summe and parts of the chapter 4. IN this Chapter is set downe another falling of the children of Israel from God, and Gods correcting of them: their repentance also: and lastly his deliuering of them by *Debora, Barak*, and *Iael*. The first of these is in the first verse, the next in the second verse, their repentance in the third: and their deliuerance in all the rest of the verses, to the end of the chapter.

The first part of the Chapter.

In that this relapse of theirs was said to be after *Ehud* was dead, as though *Shamgar* had not been betwixt both, it was most likely it was for that, hee was but a very short time a deliuerer vnto them. But yet he was after *Ehud* a deliuerer of the people, though but for a short time, as appeareth in the last verse of the former chapter.

Vers.1. For the first of the foure things, I meane the sinne of the people of Israel, which againe they committed (for so it is said heere, *that they did againe that which was euill in the sight of the Lord*) vnderstand it of them who had seene the former deliuerance, and also of their posterity who enioyed the blessing. Of the phrase or manner of speech vttered by the holy Ghost, to wit, that they did euill in the sight of the Lord; I will not speake any more, hauing handled it twice before. But of their sinne let vs consider. And that is, that

that they abused their long enioyed peace and rest vnder *Ehud*. The summe of it is,that they did leaue the right way of seruing God,and encreased their sinne sundry waies. And this is indeed the disposition and common pra- Doct.vers.1. ctise of men, who are not led and gouerned by Gods grace, that they are not the better for their prosperity, but much worse: for by aduersity they are held downe,and disabled from much sinne,and so are restrained at least; so that,as the way is shut vp to them from thence by affliction,so their appetite is much abated thereby also. But in liberty, peace, and abundance of Gods benefits,they are more easily led on, and enticed, and so the was is set open to them, and they doe as readily walke in it; and being vngouerned, they are soone let loose. And we must know,that it is not thus with the wicked onely, but euen with such as haue been sometime vnder Gods direction,that euen they are ready to forget themselues,yea and the most doe, and waxing bold, breake out by meanes of their prosperitie after the same manner.

And so it fell out with *Dauid* himselfe, who when hee had subdued his enemies vnder him almost on euery side,euen to his hearts desire,he fell most dangerously to the great prouoking of God. And *Iehosaphat*, otherwise a 2.Sam.11.4. godly King, when hee was lifted vp and made drunke as it were,with the company and fellowship of wicked *Ahab*, did sore forget himselfe,so that he was faine to be reproued for it of the Lord by his Prophet. A lamentable case, that when they bee so sore oppressed either by enemies,or other 2.Chro.19.2. crosses,that their life waxeth wearisome to them, and their distressed estate causeth all that looke on them to pity them: and when the Lord shall in that misery of theirs haue compassion of them,and set them at large,it is a lamentable case (I say) that they should become so grosly vnthankfull, forget their late aduersity,and as soone in a manner as God hath enlarged them by his benefits, that they should thus vnnaturally (as I may say) disguise themselues,euen as if they would set themselues to grieue the Lord for his gladding and comforting of them. This may (I thinke) bee a watchword to vs,to take heed how we vse our prosperity, and to teach vs to make small hast to be made great in the world by Gods preferments, great wealth and Note. commodities,vnlesse we lay faster hold of grace wherby we may vse them rightly; that is, to bee humble vnder them, and thereby forward and fruitfull in doing the good that we may. Let vs then take heed seriously,that wee count it not happie in it selfe to liue delicately for a season; from whence it commeth through our corrupt nature, that wee contemne others,giue our selues to vanity,pleasures,wantonnesse,and delights, and some of vs also to profit seeking and gaine,though neuer so filthy and grosse,as our chiefe treasure,whereby godlinesse decayes, and the vse, at least the power of all good meanes.

But what should wee doe (yee will aske) when God giueth vs such a wealthie and a comfortable outward estate? I say we should be *rich in good* 1.Tim.6.12. *workes*, and doe workes to necessarie vses. Oh, men so well prouided for, Tit.3.8. what good might bee done to their owne soules, and to the soules and bodies of their brethren. But to this point (alas) things are now come,that we may say with griefe, that few haue any mind to vse their liberties aright,or (almost) to doe any good. And this being duly considered, should cause our

our wondrings to cease, why so few godly Christians enioy any great portion of outward blessings in comparison, (for it is so) euen because the Lord prouideth a better thing for them, when hee giueth them a mediocritie in them all, as of maintenance, of credit, account and fauour with their betters, and mixeth each houre of sunshine with an other of cloudy and vnpleasing weather; and all to keepe their affections from growing too ranke, and intemperate, and to containe them within their bounds in that condition, which is best for them, and fittest to serue the Lord in, without loathing or wearinesse. The earth which is too strong and lusty, runneth vp into weede and stalke, but the well tilled and compassed, bringeth forth a plentifull crop. And rare is the man, whose fruites are not more gratious and constant in a moderate estate, then in a mighty, which caused the wise man to say; Neither to much, Lord, neither too little, for I shall runne into the extreame of vnthankfulnesse or discontentment. Doubtlesse, if as prosperity groweth, so piety encreased withall, and the loue of the giuer waxed stronger, as his gifts are multiplyed, and waxe greater, and God would not stint men as hee doth. But it is cleare, men can beare no excesse or abundance in this kinde, without notorious defect or decay in godly duties: outward welfare of body (like the splene) causeth a leanenesse and euil-fauourednesse of soule, as most men vse the matter. But this be said of the first of the foure things contained in this Chapter; namely, of their sinne.

Note.

A simile.

Pro.30.8.

THE TWENTY FOVRE SERON VPON THE FOVTRH CHAPTER OF THE BOOKE OF IVDGES.

The second part of the Chapter.

Vers.2. OF the first thing of the foure contained in this chapter we haue heard. Now followeth the second, and that is their punishment, who so prouoked the Lord: namely, that he gaue them ouer to an other aduersary, more fierce and furious then the former: that was one *Iabin* King of Canaan, that raigned in Hazor: But ye may obiect, that such an one in all respects was slaine by *Ioshua*, much aboue an hundred yeeres agoe. For thus wee reade in the booke of *Ioshua*; *At that time Ioshua returned and tooke Hazor, and burnt it, and smote the King thereof*, to wit, *Iabin, with the edge of the sword: for Hazor before time had been the head city of all those kingdomes.* I answere, it was so indeed, and now another of that name and kindred, was risen vp, and had builded the city againe, and now being growne strong and populous, preuailed against Israel, and held them in the greater bondage; and for this cause, euen that he might be reuenged vpō them for his predecessor, whom their fathers, *Ioshua* and

Obiect.

Iosh.11.10.

Answ.

and others, had wasted and slaine, and they did therefore oppresse them much the sorer. This I thought good to say for the clearing of this difficulty. Now to proceed: This *Iabin* King of Canaan is further described by his chiefe captaine, which was *Sisera*, a great warrier, and terrible. Whereby we may know, that the ease of the Israelites was restlesse seruitude, and the hope of their deliuerance desperate.

Now by this new calamity thus brought vpon this people, (to omit that which I said of the punishment in the former examples) where a man would not haue looked for it, we may obserue and see, that when all things seeme quiet and peaceable to vs, and when we think that we are safe on euery side, so that no hurt can befall vs, yet if the Lord haue a controuersie with vs, hee doth in a maruellous manner raise vp some great trouble against vs: yea and that as it were, out of the sparckles of former afflictions, (when we suspect none) as hee did heere, which were thought to haue been quenched long agoe, he bringeth a fire and flame, as it were, to burne and consume vs. So that when men thinke all to bee sure, God raiseth vp vexations that way where one would not looke for them. The *Amalekites*, when they had taken *Ziclag*, lay drunken and wallowing like beasts, fearing no danger, and were suddenly come vpon and slaine. So the Apostle saith, *When men cry peace, and that all things are safe, then shall sudden destruction come vpon them, when they are not aware, like the trauell vpon a woman with child, and they shall not bee able to auoide it.* Doct. vers. 2. 1. Sam. 30. 16. 1. Thes. 5. 3.

Thus God seeth it good to tame and taw the licentiousnesse and pride of men, and (that which is maruellous to say) if hee should not doe so, there were no liuing for vs one by another. The best in towne and country, would kicke vp their heele; yea and notwithstanding hee thus pluck downe the pride of one or other euery day, yet such as are spared bee neuer the better. The long visitation with plague, which hath swept away many thousands, what are the most part the better for it? The irreligious boldnesse of many in this age, if they bee in fauour with their betters (whose breath yet is in their nostrels) or if they haue but wealth aboue the common sort, nay if it be but bare health, how doe they abuse it? how little doth good teaching, or the diuerse examples of Gods iudgements vpon sundry others, preuaile with them? And why? because (while they feele them not, the day of reckoning is put farre off, and we dreame that we haue a priuiledge aboue all others, till the effect confute vs. The casting downe of Babell, the drowning of *Pharaoh* and his army, the thrusting through of *Zimri* and *Cosby* in their tent, the swallowing vp of *Chorah* and his company into the earth, with thousands more in ages past, and now all cut off in fearefull maner, for their seuerall rebellions against the Lord (lamentable to speake) what little abatement of sinne (yet) for all this, doe they worke in the most? nay are they not worse and worse who liue in these latter daies, and haue heard or seene the iudgements of the former times? Therefore let such of vs as cannot but confesse, that God hath done much more for vs, watch and beware, lest for the like loosenesse and bolddesse found in vs, the Lord awake vs; and if hee seaze not vpon vs with the same plagues, as he did on these; yet (seeing his quiuer is full of arrowes of all sorts, that is with all kinds of iudgements) he will reserue some for vs, as he hath done to others before vs, and come vpon Note.

on vs suddenly in the like manner.

The opening of the latter part of vers.2. Now this *Iabin* had for the chiefe captaine of his armie, *Sisera* heere named, who is said to haue his abode in Harosheth of the Gentiles, so called, for that it was a countrey full of woods: (for so the word signifieth) whereto, as vnto a most safe and well fenced place, the Canaanites who were Gentiles, did fly, and repaire, and dwelt safely therein; when so many of them had been slaine in *Ioshuas* daies, and there they remained, grew vp, and strengthened themselues, vnto the time that is heere mentioned. Thus they growing vp, and not being cut off, as God commanded the people of Israel to doe, we see now what a vexation euen this one generation of the Canaanites in that corner of the land, were vnto them, beside many other in diuers other parts of it.

Doct.2.in vers.2. And by this we see what mischiefe and woe wee prouide for our selues, (euen such as cannot bee knowne till they come) and all this through our neglecting duties commended (as this people of Israel heere did) and suffering euill persons and their foule vices, to grow vp, in and among vs, which we might easily in time haue subdued and brought vnder. I say, the suffering of them, which wee haue been full willing to nourish, and could bee brought to offer no violence vnto them, haue caused sorrow vpon sorrow, and most wearisome and vncomfortable daies vnto vs: which when they were come, we would haue bought of with much cost, and could not. Thus

Note. anger, impatience, wrath, vncharitablenesse, reuenge, teachines, frowardnes, lewd lusts, and vncleane desires, with many other like, though wee haue thought them not worthie of rebuke, neither could bee brought to deface, and disgrace them, no not to our owne selues, that so they might haue been ouercome and weakened in vs; ; euen these haue mastered vs, and waxen strong in vs, which is enough to disfigure the godly life in vs, and to marre the beauty of our profession; besides that these ingender in vs, and bring forth litters of open and outward sinnes, (al may easily know what I meane) farre more shamefull and monstrous then themselues.

The third part of the Chapter.

Vers.3. NOw followeth the third thing in this Story, namely, the repentance of the people, set forth as in the former chapter, by crying. The reasons thereof are added, and they are two; the one, because this *Sisera* had nine hundred iron Chariots, wherwith by continuall egresse and regresse he had vexed them sore: the other, that he had done thus to them twentie yeeres. Of this crying, signifying their repentance, I haue spoke before, and also of the repentance which their fathers offered, when God afflicted them. That which is to be considered heere, not spoken of before by the like occasion, is this:

Doct. That where it is said, they were twenty yeeres in bondage, before they repented and turned to God; we may behold the monstrous and poysoned

Note. disposition of our nature, which will not stoope nor bow to the Lord in true humiliation, vntil it be driuen by maine and force, euen till we be shut out euery where else. As wee see in children of a stubborne nature it is neither a checke, nor a rod will breake their stomacks: nay it is not a few stripes that

that will make them cry out, and when by rougher handling of them, they be forced to roare, it is but for very sullennes; til they see there is no remedy but that they must receiue correction for their euill doings, and then the multitude of strokes. and the smart they feele breakes their hearts at length, and makes them yeeld: and euen so it is with vs, who should bee much wiser: whereas if wee should but step aside a little from our Christian course, we ought with the like willingnesse of mind by which we strayed, returne and rise vp againe. For so the Prophet *Ieremy* complaineth; *Doth a man fall, and not rise againe; or goe out of the way, and not returne?* And if this rebelliousnesse and bad disposition were in the wicked onely, it were lesse to bee maruelled at, but let it be well considered, and it shall be found in such as haue sometime serued God in truth; who if they lose the hold that they had, and haue suffered the wicked flesh, that is, their sinfull nature, to get the vpper hand in them againe; oh how hardly is it put out of possession againe? So that as the diuels said to our Sauiour Christ, *thou art come to torment vs before the time.* So it is euer too soone, and very imprisonment to the wicked flesh, to be brought vnder the Lords wing againe, and to put on his yoke, though it be easie as it is said to be. Ier.8.6. Mat.8.29.

This is the cause why licentious dissolutenesse is in so great account at this day in all sorts, and so dimme light shineth out of them who should bee lights to other. And if it should be demanded, how Gods people can keepe so long from vnder his gouernment, and are so loth to returne againe vnder it: I answere, partly confused knowledge, ignorance and forgetfulnes how to returne (if they were euer well grounded at all) is one cause; and partly the lothnesse and vntowardnesse of the flesh to bee pent in, seeking liberty rather amisse, euen that is the other. And thus while men haue any shelter how rotten and helpelesse soeuer it be, they flie from God. But for as much as when no shifts will serue, they must returne againe to the Lord their first husband, as it is said in *Hosea,* let all that bee wise, with all speed returne to him, and make godlinesse (as it is indeed) the greatest riches and chiefe stay, seeing that is alwaies and onely comfortable. As it is the Psalme: *A day is better therein, then a thousand elsewhere.* And seeing wee in miseries and troubles do as this people heere did, often fall a sighing and sorrowing, yea murmuring and fretting, and yet turne not to God, nor from our sinne; but bite on the bridle of our punishment, and yet at last we must bee brought to it for all our vnwillingnesse; therefore as we should take heed that we keepe the profession of our hope firmely, while wee may; so yet when wee haue fallen, let vs not despaire, no nor yet delay to turne to God with the soonest, as I haue said. Hos.2.7. 1.Tim.6.6. Psal.84.11.

Againe, by this people many may learne good. They were held vnder and pursued by him that had nine hundred Chariots of iron, alwaies going out and in among them, to vexe and oppresse them on euery side. A plague great enough one would thinke, for euen *the mercies of such are cruell.* And yet this was not the worst that befell them, for God was also against them, and had sold them into their hands: and now while it was thus with them in so great misery, what should they doe? and yet which is more, twentie yeeres to be in this estate, how should they be able to abide it? By the fearefull example of these, and yet some of them belonging to God, it is good for *The vnfolding of the other part of vers.3.* Prou.12.10.

vs to take occasion to consider the estate of them, who are vnder sundry sore and great calamities, the Lord sending them for their rebellions and grieuous prouokings of him, and himselfe frowning vpon them, who should haue been their comfort in their troubles. Oh how should it grieue vs to behold it? For when they are in perplexity and vexation, by men or otherwise, and then haue God against them also; this commeth neare the saying,
Ecclef.4.10. *Woe to him that is alone.* Herein *Dauid* shewed himselfe wise: for when hee heard Gods message from the Lord, concerning the chusing of his punish-
1.Sam.24.14. ment; he answered; *Let me fall into the hands of the Lord, and not of men:* The reason was, because he knew himselfe to haue repented, and therefore that in iudgement the Lord would remember mercy. But oh how terrible a thing is it to fall into the hands of God being our enemie; or into the hands of men, when he hath giuen vs vp to their pleasure, to be handled as wee deserue? Euery affliction is sharpe and heauy, when God makes it so, by setting an edge vpon it, and by pressing downe the conscience vnder the loade of his wrath. Consider some particulars: for example. The pouerty and penurie of many thousands, and the same as poore in knowledge of God, and
Note. grace. Others in marriage vnquiet, thrusting one another out of doores, children crying about them, the neighbours disquieted among them, all going to hauocke in family, and God in the meane time also an enemie to them, what an heauie calamitie is this to behold? Others to bee taken cap-
Iudg.16.21. tiues by forren enemies; as *Sampson* put to grinde, or (which is worse) to the gallies; and which is worst of all) to haue no God to flie to in this their distresse, which yet is the case of many, who haue held their heads full high, and were also farre enough in their owne conceit, from such an estate, oh how wofull is it? And if the sore diseased, sicke and pained persons should bee added to these, with other miserable ones, and yet without God in the world; all these thus to bee distressed, which I haue mentioned, with such like, almost without number, oh how lamentable is it to thinke on? And whereas some of these bee Gods children, they must know, that if they will doe as his enemies, he will make them somewhat like them, in bearing the marke of it: so that as the wicked flie from God, and hate him for smiting them for their sin: so his owne children hauing likewise prouoked him, shall oftentimes make but slow hast to him, through an ill conscience telling them that they are not welcome, till they come in another manner; to wit, in vnfained repentance. All this I haue spoken to a double end; one, to perswade all to labour aboue all things to make God their friend, that is, by seeking to be reconciled to him, that thus in their troubles they may haue a refuge to fly to for comfort. The other is, to moue such as are free from both kinds of miseries, to pitie them that are vnder both; and to consider, that seeing they may goe in and out before the Lord without feare, both in their daily course of life, and also in their suites, &c. therefore they should deadly abhorre sinne themselues, which onely makes them feare his power and iustice, and that as much as euer they reioyced in his fauour, and so doing, mourne for them whose misery I haue mentioned, that are in an estate both dreadfull and damnable. And this be said of the first three parts of this chapter, out of these three verses, to wit, of the sinne of the people, of their punishment, and of their repentance.

The

The fourth part of the Chapter.

THe fourth part of this story followeth, of Gods deliuerance of them out of the hands of *Sisera:* and this vnto the end of the chapter; and that deliuerance was wrought, as I said before, by the helpe & ministery chiefly of the three persons mentioned afterwards in this chapter, *Debora, Barak,* and *Iael. Debora*, though a woman, was stirred vp by the Lord to iudge Israel, that is, to declare the will of God, in that time of extreame calamity, vnto the people; to answere their doubts, what they should doe, and to bee the chiefe meane of their deliuerance, by counsell giuing, and encouraging of *Barak* and the rest. *Barak* was he that should leade the army, and pursue the enemies, and with a small armie of the people to ouercome and destroy them: and *Iael* killing the great captaine of their enemies, I meane *Sisera*, with her owne hands, had her due commendation among the rest, all were diuersly employed, and yet each of them helping forward the execution of Gods iustice and charge vpon that huge armie of the Canaanites, and for his peoples deliuerance. This bee said in generall of the whole worke that followeth, spoken of in this chapter. Now I will goe to the particulars, verse by verse. *Vers. 4. The summe in generall to the end.*

And to begin with *Debora* to verse 14. and to see what she did. First, the holy Story describeth her in this verse and the next. Secondly, it is said the children of Israel came vp to her for iudgement, vers. 5. And thirdly, it is shewed what she said to *Barak*, hauing sent for him, vers. 6.7. then how shee answered *Barak*, when she saw him not forward, vers. 9. and last of all, how she encouraged him to the battell, after they had prepared themselues on both sides to it, as is shewed to verse 14. She is described, first by the extraordinarie place that she was set in, to wit, that shee was a Prophetesse: secondly, by her condition of mariage, that shee was the wife of *Lapidoth:* thirdly, by her calling, that she iudged Israel: and fourthly, by her dwelling, vnder a Palme tree, betweene Ramath and Bethel, in mount Ephraim. And by this woman, and the other two persons before mentioned (as I haue said) God gaue a new and great deliuerance vnto his people out of their twentie yeeres bondage, vnder that *Iabin* King of Canaan. And this vnspeakeable goodnes of the Lord in passing by their so great and foule indignities so oft times wrought and committed against him, doth yet better and better confirme vs in that which we haue been taught before, that the Lord is so tenderly affected to his people, that hee cannot turne away his eare from their prayers and grones vnder their heauie burthens, but pitie and deliuer them. No, as the Prophet saith, if a mother should forget and bee hardhearted to her owne child, yet the Lord cannot bee so to his, which doth iustly lay to their charge the wilfulnesse and stifneckednesse that is in many, and heape hote coles vpon their heads, seeing that when they may haue ease and helpe in their oppressions and miseries for the asking of it and praying for it, without their further charge and trouble, they cannot bring their hearts to it, but chuse rather wilfully and frowardly to lie still in their sorrowes, then to humble their hearts, and seeke after God for deliuerance. And as God is kinde to his, so he setteth out himselfe to be so, to the end he may harten and *Doct. Out of all the verses following in generall.* *Esa. 49.15.*

embolden vs to beleeue the same, wee being in our greatest need most hardly perswaded so to doe, through the great vnbeleefe that is in vs. Also he sheweth such compassion to vs in another respect, euen that wee should also learne to shew the like goodnesse and kindnesse to our brethren in their calamities, that we may so much the better resemble him. But of this before. Heere I will end.

THE TWVENTIE FIVE SERMON ON THE FOVTRH CHAPTER OF THE BOOKE OF IVDGES.

Doct. 1. in vers. 4.

NOw to proceed: besides that which wee haue heard, wee may note hereby what weake and vnlikely meanes God deliuereth, when it pleaseth him. For as before hee raised vp *Ehud*, a man lame of his right hand, to deliuer his people, and after him *Shamgar*, who had no other weapon then an an oxes goade thereto; so now he vsed a woman, (for shee was the wife of one *Lapidoth*) as his instrument, to the effecting of so great a worke as the ouerthrow of that *Iabin* was. To shew, that his power is not tied to valiant and mighty men, lest his glory should be giuen to them also; nor to strength and forces, though hee allow them to be vsed, and yet not trusted in, but to this, that wee put confidence in him, who is our strong rocke against our strongest enemies: as Prouerbs

Iam. 5. 16. 18. 10. and to our prayers which auaile much with him, if they bee feruent.

2. Chron. 20. And this he requireth straitely to be beleeued of vs. And so hee vseth to doe also in the deliuerance of his peoples soules out of the bondage of Satan and hell. For by meane men, and those that bee of no great note for their wealth or preferment, hee subdueth the hearts of the mighty, piercing and breaking them with the powerfull force of their preaching, (if they wil lend their eares to heare them) that so the excellent gift of faith may be wrought

2. Cor. 4. 7. in them, he so *putting heauenly treasure in earthen vessels*, to that end and purpose; and that all may say to his praise when they see it, that it is hee that worketh, and whose the power is, though sillie man bee vsed by him as his instruments.

Of Deboras calling that she was a Prophetesse. Doct. 2. in vers. 4.

This woman, as God vsed her to deliuer his people, so she was also endued with the spirit of prophesie, to reueale the will of God to them, and to answere their doubts. For which cause it is said in the next verse, that the people came vp to her for counsell and iudgement: For it is thought, that their oppression by that *Iabin* was so great, that the people of Israel could not haue ordinary Iudges. Now though it was rare to haue women Prophetesses, yet now and then God stirred vp such, as *Miriam* the sister of *Moses*,

2. King. 22. 14. *Hanna* the mother of *Samuel*; and *Hulda* in the daies of *Iosias* the King: and in

in the new Testament,as *Anna* the daughter of *Phanuel,* and the 4. daughters of *Philip,* in the booke of the Acts recorded. And it is not vnlike, that some of these women that were indued with the spirit of prophesie, did instruct and teach the people,declaring to them those things which God had reuealed vnto them,seeing the gifts of God are not giuen to bee buried,but to be vsed for the edifying of the Church in publike and priuate. And for proofe of this which I say,we are to know, that prophesying is not onely taken for the foretelling of things to come,but for making knowne the will of God in matters of saluation,and to both ends God vsed women sometimes, though now he forbid them. (As for those forged,or diabolicall shee saints and Prophetesses,of whom the Church of Rome boasteth, we ascribe as much credit to them, as the dreames of Monkes deserue.) Therefore wee must also heere take heed,that wee bring not that into example which the Lord hath wrought extraordinarily,when it hath pleased him: For wee are tied by *Pauls* rule,set downe to the Corinthians, to wit, that women keepe silence in the congregation. He addeth a reason, because they must bee subiect to their husbands. But the teachers office is to haue authority ouer those which are taught by them, and to gouerne them also as well as to instruct them,which is not permitted to the wife ouer her husband, neither ouer other men. But seeing the Lord in these latter times vseth not commonly extraordinary instruments as he did in former daies; especially vnlesse he furnish them also with extraordinary gifts, but ordinary: therefore wee are to admire and reuerence his goodnesse in both: and the vse hereof is, that as it is our bounden duty to praise God highly, for that hee hath stirred vp some in all ages to be lights and helps,in and for the good of his Church,yea and extraordinary,as we see heere,in the want of other,so (to come home to our selues) while he prouideth ordinary helpes and meanes for vs in these daies to the building vp of the same, his Church among vs, it behoueth vs that both we receiue them with all due reuerence,making right vse of them; and that none presume to set vp themselues extraordinarily, as many of these separatists do without gifts answerable,although God hath done so somtime, and fitted them for the same, and granted that priuiledge to his, when it hath seemed good vnto him.

Luk.2.36. Act.21.9. 1.Cor.14.34. 1.Cor.14.34. 1.Thes.5.20. Heb.13.17.

Now further to proceed, this which is said of the marriage of *Debora*, being a Prophetesse, can teach vs no lesse then this, that they who haue attended on God in the ministery in former times, whether men or women,or such as doe it at this day,are not despised of God for their married estate,but counted of him faithfull, and put in his seruice, as this *Debora* was: which though there is no cause to make question of, (seeing they who teach other the whole counsell of God,and so by consequent, how to vse the married estate aright, a man would thinke should much more bee fit to vse it in the best manner themselues) yet I say so, for that the Romish prelacie, who snatch at euery occasion to raile on the Ministers of the Gospell, (and so they doe because of their marriage,) doe what they can most spitefully and iniuriously to bring the faithfull Preachers into an odious account with all men. And they haue thought this a meet matter in them to barke at, vnder a pretence that the marriage bed,(for they thinke better of the whorish bed) can no way stand with such an holy calling as the ministery is; which being

Of Deboras married estate. Doct.2. in vers.4.

Heb.13.4. Gods ordinance for all states of men to enioy, were shamefull in them to spurne against, though they themselues liued most chast, seeing while they goe about to disgrace the persons, they fight against the ordinance of God, yea and that which is highly commended of him: but much more reprochfull and odious it is in them so to doe, seeing the same deuout persons, (as they would bee counted) are, and that many of them, as is well knowne, grosse whoremongers themselues, (that I say no worse) and such as liue in filthie vncleannes, though Priests by their calling. But for further proofe of this truth, I meane the mariage of Ministers to be lawfull, seeing I haue begun to speake of it, this I will adde: that the examples of the Ministerie vnder the Law, as well as their practise at the comming of Christ, and after in the Apostles times, doe maintaine and iustifie it: yea and since those times, the Church of God for many hundred yeeres, (till *Gregories* and *Siricius* times, who were Popes of Rome) doe proue and testifie the same. The Prophets first, as [a] *Obed, Hanany*, and other: the [b] Leuites, as *Mattaina* and his predecessors; and [c] for Priests, *Aaron, Eliazer* and their posteritie, all vnder the Law married, declare that they are by malice blinded who condemne mariage in the Ministerie. And for the latter times in the new Testament, *Zacharie* and *Elizabeth* so liued in their mariage, to wit, iust before God, and walking in all his commandements, as had been impossible for them to do, if their condition of life had bin vnlawfull. And for the Apostles, *Peter* himselfe was married, to goe no further. This by the occasion offered, I haue spoken as briefly as I could. And let them that serue God in the Ministerie, preach Christ Iesus diligently, and endeuour faithfully to be vnoffensiue in conscience toward God, and in their liues toward men, and they shall not need to feare such Scorpions, for their sting is plucked out from doing them any hurt. And if the vncleannes and lewd liues of some persons in the Ministerie, gaue no more occasion to the aduersaries of insulting, (which yet is the fact and sin of some persons, and not any blot in the calling) then that some do take the benefit of the ordinance of God, in that they are married; many Ministers might sit without red cheeks and a glowing conscience, and the aduersarie with shame hold his peace, without any triumphing And let this also that hath been said, check and controle that relique of Poperie, that still hangs about many of the people, in the Ministery, who verily thinke them worthy and good Ministers who leade a single life, without any other respect, whereas mariage is nothing, and singlenes, yea virginity are nothing of themselues, but a pure spirit in a body vndefiled in both, which some of these little regard.

[a] 2.Chro.15.1.
[b] 2 Chro.16 14
[c] Exod.29.4.
Luke 1.6.

Verse 5. *Of Deboras dwelling.*

The next thing in the describing of *Debora*, is, the setting downe of her dwelling, that it was vnder a Palme tree in Mount Ephraim, and the naming of her husband, being (no doubt) a man of good note then, though to vs vnknowne; these things, I say, seeing nothing is set downe in vaine in the holy Story, had (as it may seeme) more vse in that time, then wee now can see: which I may truly say of many other things therein contained, which should somewhat satisfie the reader, when hee seeth not so much in some places, as he doth in another. And yet the holy Ghost sets downe many circumstances oftentimes, as for the fuller credit of the historie, especially where it else might seeme questionable, as the time, places, names, &c. so to

giue

giue more light to the thing handled. Onely let this content vs, that, as a dwelling was allowed her, though she being a Prophetesse, was married, and perhaps of some note, it being expressely spoken of, and set downe: so it may serue to assure vs that God doth the same to such at this day as are in the same condition, seruing him with honest and good hearts in the Ministerie; I meane hee alloweth them a place to liue in, to their good contentment, euen such as hee seeth fittest for them: though the Popish Clergie, and some other also, count them vnmeete to liue at all, but rather worthie to be rooted out of the earth. But of this thus much. Doct. vers. 5.

Now it is further said here, that the children of Israel went vp for iudgement to her, I meane *Debora*; who by the spirit of prophecie, answered their doubts, and determined of their controuersies, and declared to them the will of God; by all which, they might the better doe the duties that concerned them. Where we are to consider the louing kindnes of the Lord, as to them, that they might euen then in their oppression by the King of Canaan, haue one to answere their doubts that troubled them; so in other ages, and much more in this of ours, that he hath prouided, that such as make question of any thing that troubleth them, may be answered and satisfied. If that which she did, being but one person, and a woman, was to be accounted a singular fauour of God (as who can deny it?) what a mercie of God is this to vs, that we haue solemne and publike assemblies, not in one place of the land, but in many, (and but for the sinne of some persons, should haue them throughout in all places) to teach the will of God, that all who are not wilfull, or negligent, may learne to know the Lord, from the greatest to the least, and also the things that belong to their peace? Thus when (I say) we may priuatly vnburthen our selues of any doubtfull and dangerous opinions, or trouble of conscience (as wee may, God be thanked) and that many waies; oh what a priuiledge is it? These things ought so much the more to moue vs to be in admiration at the loue of God the giuer, because in false religion and worshipping of God, (as in the Papacie) there is no such thing to be looked for, or enioyed: for their seruing of God, is compact of fancies, dreames, and lies, the inuentions of men, as a dunghill is full of filthines and drosse. And as for the relieuing the conscience of any such as are distressed and disquieted, there is as much comfort ministred to them either out of *Parsons* Directorie, or out of the Meditations of Frier *Granatensis*, (which yet sauour most of all the rest, of any pietie) as the poore traytor *Iudas* found at the hand of the Priests, when he complaining and crying out, that he had sinned in betraying the innocent blood, answered, after the vnmercifull manner of such as they were [looke thou to that] as if they should haue said (though they set him a worke) shift for thy selfe: that is the comfort thou shalt haue of vs. But to returne: Though God hath euery way prouided well for vs to be instructed soundly, and graciously relieued and comforted, (as I haue said) yet it is to be lamented, that many of vs are glutted with the good meanes that wee haue, and suffer them to lie by vs, as it were a rusting. And euen thereafter is the good fruite that we bring foorth in our liues thereby. Doct. 2. in vers. 5.

Verſ.6. *Then ſhe ſent and called Barak the ſonne of Abinoam out of Kedeſh of Naphtali, and ſaid vnto him, Hath not the Lord God of Iſrael commanded, ſaying, Goe and draw toward Mount Tabor, and take with thee ten thouſand men of the children of Naphtali, and of the children of Zebulon?*

Verſ.7. *And I will draw vnto thee, to the riuer Kiſhon, Siſera the Captaine of Iabins armie, with his charets and his multitude, and will deliuer them into thine hand.*

Verſ.8. *And Barak ſaid vnto her, If thou wilt goe with me, I will goe, but if thou wilt not goe with me, I will not goe.*

Verſ.9. *Then ſhe anſwered, I will ſurely goe with thee, but this iourney that thou takeſt, ſhall not be for thine honour: for the Lord ſhall ſell Siſera into the hands of a woman. And Debora aroſe, and went with Barak to Kedeſh.*

The meaning of theſe foure verſes,

NOw we haue heard the deſcription of *Debora*, and what ſhe was: it followeth how ſhe went to worke in this great buſineſſe of the Lord againſt *Iabin*. She therefore as God commanded, ſent to *Barak*, as he is here deſcribed in the text, the ſonne of *Abinoam*, that hee ſhould goe and furniſh himſelfe with tenne thouſand men, and aſſured him, that God would giue him victorie ouer *Siſera*, the Captaine of *Iabins* armie, and ouer all his multitude. *Barak* at firſt feared, but after beleeued, and went forward to the worke: and ſeeing he was afraid through vnbeliefe, therefore he refuſed to goe without her; for the which ſhe found fault with him, and told him God would puniſh it, ſo that he ſhould not haue that honour, which otherwiſe he ſhould haue had. And after that, *Barak* and *Debora* went to Kedeſh together. Thus much for the meaning of theſe foure verſes. Now of both theſe *Debora* and *Barak* in order. Firſt of the meſſage in the ſixth and ſeuenth verſes: then of that which followed vpon it, in the other two following.

More particularly of the ſixth and ſeuenth verſes.

Of *Debora* firſt, the holy Storie ſetteth downe this, that ſhe ſent the meſſage of God to *Barak*, adding thereto the promiſe of victorie; both which I ioyne together, ſeeing wee may more cleerely ſee that which wee haue to learne thereby. And out of both points of her ſpeech, namely the commandement of God to *Barak*, and his promiſe of good ſucceſſe; this ioyntly I giue the reader to marke, that theſe two things are the principall motiues and reaſons to perſwade, and that are to leade vs in the moſt of our actions, (to the end, we may rightly effect and bring them to paſſe) namely the commandement of God, and his promiſe of bleſsing. I ſay, in the moſt of our actions, not all; for as much as ſome of them are free and indifferent to be done, or left vndone of vs, and in them we are thus to be guided; namely, that we vſe that part of our libertie in things indifferent, which we ſhall by due conſideration find to tend moſt to the glorie of God, our owne inward peace, and the edifying or leaſt offence of Gods people. Otherwiſe (as I haue ſaid) in things forbidden or commanded by God, let vs take our direction accordingly, as we haue heard, and harten on our ſelues to ſhunne that which is forbidden, or to obey the contrary, being incouraged by the promiſe of bleſſing annexed to both. And this is a moſt bleſſed and comfortable direction to all Gods ſeruants at this day, and ſhall be likewiſe to the end of the world.

Doct.1.in verſ.6.and 7.

What are the principall reaſons that are to leade vs in the moſt of our actions.

And

And it is that which hath carried our fathers forth in their most difficult workes and parts of their liues. *Moses* in going to *Pharaoh*, to fetch the people of Israel out of their grieuous bondage, which *Pharaoh* would not agree to, what encouragement had hee hereto? verily euen this, that God said to him, goe, for haue not I commanded thee? And againe, I will be with thee to bring it to passe. And the same was *Ioshuas* authority, and the hartening of him to the guiding of the same people into the land of promise, and in rooting the idolatrous nations out of it, euen the word of the Lord, he speaking thus vnto him: *Arise, goe ouer this Iordan, thou and all this people, vnto the land which I giue them: as I was with Moses, so I will bee with thee; I will not leaue thee, neither forsake thee.* And this was *Pauls* vpholding and stay, as throughout all the places whither he went preaching; so at Corinth, where hee was in great danger. For thus the Lord said to him by a vision in the night; *Feare not Paul, but speake, and hold not thy peace; for I am with thee, and no man shall lay hands on thee to hurt thee, for I haue much people in this city.* And the same I may say of many other.

Exod 3.11.12.

Iosh.1.25.

Act.18.9.

And by the same commandement and promise of God, wee are guided still, who prosper and like well in our life, and no other waies. And this is that life of faith, which is so highly commended in the Scriptures, when it is said, *the iust shall liue by faith.* And are not wee subiect to the same discouragements, and the like that they were in ages past? that so we may see wee haue the same need to bee strongly vpholden, and soundly encouraged, as they were? But though it be not to bee doubted of, but that many doe see this, and haue learned thus to be guided in their actions (for they only liue comfortably) so it is as much to bee lamented, how infinite persons know not that there is any such easie and plaine way to guide them; no, neither can they bee brought from being led by their carnall reason, and prophane custome, in the actions of their life, neither can bee brought to stoop and submit themselues to any such gouernment, as God hath seene best: by meanes whereof they going about them, as it liketh them best, not looking what God requireth; if they doe a good thing, or what he promiseth, therfore they doe it not so as he is pleased therewith; to wit, because hee commandeth it, much lesse to that end, and with such a mind as it should bee done with, eucouraged by his promise. Therefore they haue many plagues in their liues by following their owne desires and waies; and when it falleth out better with them, that they prosper in the world, yet haue they no sound comfort in any thing that they doe. Apply this to all affaires in mens callings.

Note.

Heb.10.38.

Note.

Note.

Therfore I will say this one thing to thee, whosoeuer thou art that wouldest liue comfortably. Try the working of this doctrine in thee: looke but one weeke to thy calling faithfully, to discharge the duties of it consciona-bly; and so farre as thou hast knowledge, endeauour to obey all other commandements of God; and be firmely perswaded of the promise of God to thee, that thou art safe in so walking. For he hath annexed a promise of blessing to the obeying of euery commandement: yea and that an hundred fold more then thou forgoest thereby. Thou wilt aske, how shalt thou know that God doth reward thee so? I answere, bee thou iudge thy selfe, if he deale not so with thee. For example, let this be the case: Thou wilt say, if

Note.

if thou wert not tied so strictly to obey God,thou couldest take thy pleasure in merrie company, or benefit thy selfe as other men doe, to gaine and get commodity, whereas now thou being tied to make conscience, darest not doe so,but must lose and forgo much thereby. I heare thee; now heare thou me likewise. Thou confessest that the profit and pleasure thou forgoest by obeying God,is vnlawfull,and against conscience; for otherwise, who holdeth thee from it? Now put the case,that when thou hast so gotten it, God vrge and cause thy conscience to prick thee,and thou beest wounded therein, which stingeth worse then Hornets; for so God doth one time or other make mens sinne smart and sting the committers of it,in most painfull sort, or (which is worse) leaues them hardened. If thou knowest what this meaneth, or beleeuest that which I say to thee, what wouldest thou not giue to be healed of this intolerable paine? Euen all that thou hast,how much soeuer it be. For that is a signe to thee of losing thy soule vtterly, if thou persist therein: and *what shall it profit a man to winne the whole world and lose his soule?* Thou fishest with a golden hooke, which being lost, is not recompensed by all thou catchest therewith. Now answere mee, haddest thou not been voide and rid of this terrour and tast of hell, if thou haddest auoided and resisted thy sinne? Mightest thou not haue been quiet and merrie, as other of Gods seruants be,if thou haddest obeyed the Lord? Then tell me, would not that thy mirth and quietnesse haue been an hundred fold better, and more welcome to thee then thy profit & pleasure, which hath brought thee this hellish torment of conscience? this wound and sting which taketh away all delight from thee,so that for deliuerance out of it,thou wouldest giue all that thou hast? Therefore know, that God will giue an hundred fold more profit,ease,& pleasure to thee,euen in this life,if thou obeyest him, or doest any thing for his sake, ouer thou shalt find by making thy best gaine of thy sinne. But I must remember my selfe, for I haue bin long in this point. Only this I adde,that it is to bee bewailed, that this heauenly wisedome so little entreth into men,nor preuaileth with them. Alas they haue no leisure to thinke of the reckoning,being in the middest of their iollity.

Note. Mat.16.26. Mat.19.29. Note.

Doct.vers.7. It is also worthy our noting, that while *Sisera* was in his flourishing, and iollity,the Lord threatens to take him downe,and to bring him low. I will, saith the Lord to *Barak,* draw vnto thee the chiefe captaine of *Iabins* army, and his chariots,and whole host, to the riuer Kishon, and deliuer him into thine hand. Oh! how fearefull then is the estate of Gods enemies, euen such as are euill workers,and set against Gods people, that in the middest of their pompe and pride,the Lord hath taken their names (though in another manner,and to another end then the names of Recusants are taken) to answere it,euen that he may be reuenged on them? And hath not this been a common vse with such? with *Chorah, Naball, Iezabell,* and many others; that while they walked heere on the earth at liberty, their destruction was told from heauen to bee at hand? and they summoned to appeare to their arraignment? and if some of them then did not, neither now many doe know before it commeth, neither once dreame of any such thing, nor feare it: yet seeing it is euer comming,(and hauing threatened it) and so it hangeth as a sword point continually ouer their head; oh how vncomfortable is it to thinke vpon? Oh therefore be we alwaies vnder his wing and abide we

Ecclesf.11.1.

in his loue,that so we may be euer out of horrour and feare, that God doth not marke vs for his enemies. Which miserable condition the vnbeleeuers are alwaies in,vnlesse they be hardened,which is far worse, as I said before: for if his anger be kindled but a little (as it is euer toward them a great deale) happie are they that feare him. I would not therefore bee a bad person,if there were any way to shun it,euen for this cause,whereas yet all the terrors heere,are but a glimps of those that follow afterwards. And contrarily,why should not the godly be content to beare some hardnesse heere, seeing they are freed from the greatest terrours (if they know their liberties) both heere and heereafter? But somewhat like this I spake of in *Eglons* example before. Psal.2.12. Note.

Now I should proceed to speake of *Barak,* hauing begun with *Debora,* and said of her that which is occasioned by the text: but I should haue no time thereto in this sermon; therefore an end heere.

THE TWENTIE SIXE SERMON ON THE FOVRTH CHAPTER OF THE BOOKE OF IVDGES.

WE haue heard of *Deboras* message to *Barak,* in the two former verses. Now followeth *Baraks* answere to her message in this eighth verse. *If* (saith hee) *thou wilt goe with me, I will goe, else not.* This answere of his seemes to yeeld little to Gods commandement, sent to him by *Deboras* ministery, neither to ascribe any thing to Gods promise,and therefore shewes how he profited not by those two strong peswasions to leade to duty, mentioned before, but proues that hee ascribed more to her presence, then to Gods promise: which,what could it be lesse,then a great blemish in him, as may bee seene by his amending his fault afterwards? Whose faith is so highly renounced among the worthies, in the epistle to the Hebrues? Beside, she was offended with him, for his so answering, and therefore it was (doubtlesse) infidelity in him. If it bee asked, why then is hee afterward so highly commended for his faith? I answere, that when the message came first to him,the thing enioyned him from God by *Deboras* message, seemed to be most full of difficulty. For he was commanded to make commotion, and to rebell against him that was King ouer them, to wit, this *Iabin,* who was very great and mighty; he was also charged to gather an armie of men together, though hee was but a priuate man himselfe. These things therefore for him to take in hand, and that against such a fierce and strong captaine as *Sisera* was,it made him afraid to set vpon such a worke, and especially,while he was vnexperienced in so great a triall and difficulty,and this was the Vers.8. Heb.11.32.

the cauſe why hee could not beleeue, except ſhee went with him,that God would deliuer him with his men of warre into his hand.

But afterward weighing better the commandement of God, and his promiſe,God by his ſpirit aſſiſting him,hee beleeued the words of *Debora*, and obeyed,and ſo obtained the victory by faith,as it is ſaid in the forementioned place to the Hebrues. And how vſually this falleth out, and com-
How ſoone faith is quailed. meth to paſſe,euen to the godly,that at the firſt they doe ſtagger and doubt, and beleeue not by and by, and that through the ſtrong reliques of the old *Adam*, there is no man of God but hath proofe; and yet for all that, after-
Note. ward they being ſtrengthened by the ſpirit of God, recouer themſelues againe,and beleeue confidently. This is apparent in *Dauid*,euen after he had
Pſal.51.2.10. beleeued,ſaying, *O Lord, waſh mee throughly,cleanſe me, for I am wholly filthy:* And againe,*Create in me a new ſpirit*; as if the old had been vtterly loſt. Alſo
Exod 3.11. compared with 10.26. in *Moſes*, when he was firſt commanded to goe to *Pharaoh*,how fearefull he was at the hearing of the meſſage, and how hee ſhrunke backe: but after-
Note. ward,how boldly did he execute the ſame, and deliuer it vnto him? Euen ſo the beſt of vs,when we heare of the death of our deare friends,or of great loſſes that are befallen vs; alſo at the beginning of great ſickneſſe and paine arreſting vs,oh how doe we faint,and diſtruſt that we ſhall neuer ſubmit our
Pſal.37.3. ſelues,and yeeld obediently to them (though God command vs ſtraitly to doe ſo) while wee caſt both our eyes on the burthen and croſſe; that is, on
1.Cor.4.laſt. the the things that are ſeene,as the Apoſtle ſpeaketh, and while wee are not yet come to our ſelues to looke vp to God with confidence, and to things not ſeene,but eternall. But when we weigh how they come from him that loueth vs,and therefore cannot intend our hurt; we then ſubmit our ſelues to God,and ſtay vpon him for grace to go vnder all, and waite patiently for a good iſſue. And becauſe our hearts ariſe oft times againſt our brethren, when we ſee theſe weakeneſſes in them, and begin to iudge and thinke too hardly of them for the ſame, the Lord therefore letteth vs ſometimes ſee the ſame or other ſuch in our ſelues,that ſo wee may learne to beare with the infirmities of them.

Gal.6.1. And when wee haue experience of this, it cauſeth vs to bewaile tenderly the weakneſſes that we ſee in our brethren, and with the ſpirit of meekneſſe helpe to hold them vp, rather then by and by to cenſure them ouer ſharply for the ſame. And it is to be deepely bewailed,to ſee how farre off many are from duty in this behalfe, (though otherwiſe religious,and ſuch as loue the truth frō their herts)are ouercome with deadly cōceits againſt their brethrē
Note. when they ſee they haue fallen by infirmity,& are ſtrongly incenſed againſt them,& leaue thē to themſelues,neuer telling them of it kindly,as if they ſee thē ouercome of impatience,teaſtineſſe, anger, or if their zeale & feruency in ſeruing God be ſlaked,& abated, or that they be offenſiuely taken vp of, and carried away with the world. Theſe and the like (I confeſſe) are iuſt cauſes to raiſe griefe in vs,and are much to be diſliked of vs,when we eſpy them in ſuch as be well thought of by vs,and they are blemiſhes in them not to be borne with or allowed: but yet for all that, when wee ſhall ſee ſuch things in them,wee muſt beware that wee cenſure them not too hardly, (for who hath giuen vs authority to iudge them?) crying out vncharitably,that there is no religion in them. For though it cannot bee denied,but that the diuell hath

hath, by watching his opportunitie, got aduantage ouer them; yet they being not vntractable, but only deceiued in their so offending, and yet in other parts of their liues they holding their care to please God, and labouring to keepe a good conscience; we must not for some one such weaknes, fall by and by to such hard iudging of them, and to depart from them (which is vtterly against charitie and dutie) but to think, that there being so many snares to intangle men, it may easily enough be so with them, as wee may see it to be with our selues (if we be not blinded with selfeloue) in the like trials, for that we doe not, without special grace, and heed taking, auoid the like falles. And therfore we must hope that they may, yea and shal (no doubt) through Gods helpe, arise, and grow in good sort out of them againe.

And yet I doe not speake this as though I would iustifie such offences in the liues of Gods people, or as though I went about to salue them vp with gentle words, (for I know, that where such breaches are suffered to passe in the liues of them who are otherwise religious, they doe much hurt to other by example, and to themselues by quenching the spirit in them, specially if they be defended and continued long in, vnconfessed, and renounced, that they may be forgiuen them) but yet we that behold them, must wisely shun extremities in iudging of them, on the one side, as well as on the other; as I haue said, and no more condemne the persons, then we allow the sins. And as for the common professors, who when they see such, frailties appeare in the forwarder sort of Christians, begin to please themselues therein, and to condemne all other good parts in them, I say to them, if they stumble thereat, and they themselues walke on in their grossenes, they shall in time see themselues guiltie of farre greater and more horrible sinnes; or if they still goe forward in condemning and insulting ouer them, they shall doe it to their owne confusion. And this by occasion of *Baraks* distrust.

More particularly also let *Baraks* answere in clinging so to *Debora*, teach Gods people this wisdome, not ouer-much to giue place to their affections, euen in things lawful, but to submit themselues to the will of God, and pray for strength to rest therein. It seemed a very equall and commendable request in *Barak*, to desire the companie, aduice, and direction of *Debora*: and so it was in the generall: but when hee saw it was Gods will hee should depend immediatly vpon him for successe, he saw againe that it was his weaknes so much to depend vpon her presence. And although it is so commendable a thing for men to cleaue to the Ministery and assistance of their faithfull guides, while they continue among them, yet if any espieth his owne weakenes and childishnes in this, that he cleaueth too neere vnto them, as thinking that without them hee shall miscarrie, and cannot bee vpholden without them, let him checke himselfe, and labour for such strength of knowledge and faith, as may inable him to go vpon his owne feete, and liue by his owne faith, depending directly vpon Gods promise of vholding and preseruing him in the middest of his discouragements, feares, and weaknes, without such meanes, if he may not enioy them. But while some with *Barak* ascribe too much to the Minister of God, it is too true, that many despising and nothing regarding the ministerie of men, grow shiftles and shameles, being as farre from hope of happinesse, as they are voide of grace and goodnesse.

Doct. 1. in vers. 8.

V Now

Now followeth the ſpeech of *Debora* to *Barak*, when he made the fore-
Verſe 9. mentioned anſwere vnto her, to wit, that he would not goe, vnleſſe ſhe went with him. And this ſhe ſaid: I will go with thee, but it ſhall not be for thine honour. Wherein ſhe findeth fault with him, and tels him, that hee ſhould ſuffer the puniſhment of his infidelitie, while the glorie which he might otherwiſe haue had thereby, ſhould be giuen to a woman, meaning *Iael*, and not in the leaſt part to her ſelfe: whereby ſomewhat may be noted, both generally and particularly. For the firſt, we may learne that which may do
Doct. verſ. 9. vs much good; to wit, that God will puniſh vs ſome way for our vnbeliefe. For wee ſee, that God doth not put vp at mens hands, this and ſuch other ſinnes, as I named in the former verſe; eſpecially, when they come more of
Note. knowledge then of frailtie, and when we ſee that we doe amiſſe, and yet through blind ſelfeloue, we will not finde fault with our ſelues for the ſame, but extenuate or hide our ſinne, God therefore ſpared not *Zacharias* for his
Luke 1. 8. vnbeliefe, though otherwiſe a righteous man, but made him dumbe for a ſeaſon. And he telleth vs all as much in the Pſalme, where he ſaith, *If mine*
Pſal. 89. 31. *owne children breake my ſtatutes, and keepe not my commandements, I will viſite their tranſgreſſion with the rod, and their iniquitie with ſtrokes; although I will not take my louing kindneſſe from them.* The like is to be ſeene in *Moſes*, who becauſe he diſtruſted the Lord in ſmiting the rocke, bare the ſcarre thereof to his death, being denied entrance into the land of Canaan. So *Ioaſh* for di-
2. King. 13. ſtruſting *Eliſhas* meſſage, and ſmiting the earth but thrice, was rebuked by the Prophet, who would not haue found fault with him, if he had not bidden him ſmite it oftner. Thou ſhouldeſt (ſaith he) haue ſmitten fiue or ſixe times, and ſo thou ſhouldeſt vtterly haue deſtroyed *Aram*, but now thou ſhalt foile them but thrice; and ſo they ſhall get ſtrength againe to reuenge themſelues. And euen ſo doe ſuch both feele and finde, who regard not what the Lord ſaith vnto them, neither giue credit to his word, and much more all ſuch, as giue the bridle more groſſely to their vnruly paſſions. And this ſhould (a man would thinke) both cauſe vs all to ſhunne ſuch boldnes with God, as will prouoke him to make vs ſmart for the ſame: and alſo, it ſhould make vs beare the more with the infirmities of our brethren, for as much as wee ſee God correcteth them for the ſame, and ſhall wee alſo adde ſorrow to their ſorrow, when wee ought rather to haue compaſſion on them, and pitie them? This be noted in generall.

Doct. 2. in verſ. 9. Now more particularly, ſeeing *Barak* was puniſhed with loſing the glorie, which he ſhould haue had but for his vnbeliefe, this teacheth vs, that glorie, and good name & report, is reckoned among the good things that a godly perſon may deſire and be glad to enioy: nay, it is that which hee ſhould enſue, becauſe it is a token of Gods approbation, if his people report well of vs: ſeeing they are taught by the ſame ſpirit, to diſcerne who are like
3. Ioh. 12. them. Therefore *Iohn*, by a probable argument, proueth *Demetrius* to be a good man, becauſe of his good report. It is to bee lamented, that all they whom God alloweth, doe not deſire this alſo, and deſerue it by the fruites of their loue toward his Church: For it is the note of an arrogant and diſſolute perſon, to ſcorne the good opinion that his brethren conceiue of him. Euen as precious oyntments are knowne by their ſmell, ſo is a godlie Chriſtian by the ſauour of his good name, eſpecially in the place where he dwelleth,

dwelleth,as being best knowne there. Indeed,the principall care should be to giue the Lord his due praise, for else we beguile and deceiue men in causing them to thinke well of vs,and much more we doe dangerously deceiue our selues: but that being well regarded and looked vnto,in the next place let our care be that the Church of God may giue vs allowance, and see iust cause to report well of vs. As it is said of *Zacharie* and his wife,that both they were iust before God,and toward men vnreproueable,and therfore of good report. So *Cornelius* had a good name among the Iewes. Now glorie or good name, is a certaine good opinion and estimation conceiued of a man for his well doing. For those things which good men doe vertuously and well, doe purchase commendation and glorie vnto them. The end to the which which we ought to vse and direct this good report,is this,namely the aduancing of the name of God,and also to giue good example to other of following vs: and as the ends are both good, so is that good also, by the which they are procured. Therefore although a good name bee not to bee sought for it selfe, as though that were the thing wee chiefly intended, and rested in, and no other, yet it is not to be despised, for those ends which I haue mentioned,namely,the glorifying of God, and the edification of our brethren. Luke 1.6. Act.10.22.

Now to end this verse, let this be briefly added,that *Debora* yeelding to, and helping the weaknes of *Barak* in going with him,teacheth vs thus to regard,helpe,and incourage our weake brethren,by counsell,trauaile, and example. Doct.3.in vers.9.

Vers.10. *And Barak called Zebulun and Naphtali to* Kedesh, *and hee went vp on his feete with tenne thousand men,and Debora went vp with him.*

Vers.11. *Now Heber the Kenite,which was of the children of Hobab,the father in law of Moses, was departed from the Kenites, and pitched his tent vntill the plaine of Zaanaim,which is by Kedesh,*

Vers.12. *Then they shewed Sisera,that Barak the sonne of Abinoam,was gone vp to Mount Tabor.*

Vers.13. *And Sisera called for all his charets, euen nine hundred charets of yron,and all the people that were with him, from Harosheth of the Gentiles vnto the riuer Kishon.*

IN these foure verses,the holy Ghost sheweth,how they did on both sides prepare their armies,both *Barak* and *Sisera*. He accompanied with *Debora* at Kedesh, gathered together ten thousand men out of the tribes of *Naphtali* and *Zebulun* to Mount Tabor, which of the writers is called also Ithaberins,not farre off from Kedesh, for they went on foote. The place is neere to the borders of Asher,Naphtali and Zebulon. And this mount hath neere it,the riuer Kishon, where the Prophet *Elias* killed the priests of *Baall*. And note, for the better vnderstanding of the story,that al the places mentioned, to wit,Kedesh,the plaine of Zaanaim,mount Tabor, were all neere ioyning together,and to the riuer Kishon. This of *Barak*. *Sisera* hearing of this preparation of *Barak*, did also make ready his armie, which is not mentioned here,saue his nine hundred charets of yron: but *Iosephus* saith,he had thirtie thousand footmen,tenne thousand horsemen of the Canaanites, and three thousand other charets. But howsoeuer it was, sure it is, that hee made a mightie preparation, and therewith he came to this riuer Kishon. And this of the preparation on both sides, mentioned in these foure verses And with both there is a briefe storie put in, of the dwelling of *Heber* the Kenite, the sonne of *Hobab*, *Moses* father in law, that he had pitched his Tabernacle, and was by Gods prouidence come to dwel nigh the riuer Kishon, and in a part of the border of Kedesh. But why this is brought in, shall appeare better afterwa d in vers. 18.

The chiefe thing in this verse to bee noted, is the faith wherein all these agreed and consented, which are here spoken of and mentioned, I meane *Barak* and his armie, with *Debora*. For they tooke in hand a most hard work against so fierce a Captaine, as *Sisera* was; so well prouided and appointed by *Iabin*, who was King ouer the Canaanites. And who would not haue said, that their preparation against the Israelites, must needs in the reason of man, haue wrought an vtter ouerthrow of them? As sure it is, if they had been ouercome, as they were an handfull, and few to many; and weake also, but their enemies strong; they had bin most cruelly and barbarously handled by them. But notwithstanding all this, when they were perswaded, that as they were set on worke by God, so in his power they went about it, and tooke it in hand; not casting their eyes vpon the difficulties and disparagements, that were in the way against them, for God (they beleeued)
Doct. vers. 10. would stand with them, and giue them the victorie. And this indeede is the
Ioh. 14. 1. right propertie of faith thus to doe, to look vp to God, who hath commanded that which we take in hand, and promised blessing thereto. By this and
Heb. 11. 8. by no other meanes, *Abraham* the father of beleeuers, forsooke his owne countrey, and went whither God sent him, from all his kindred, not knowing what he should finde in the place whither he went. And *Moses* chose
Heb. 11. 24. rather to suffer affliction with the people of God in the wildernesse, then to enioy the pleasures of sinne for a season in the house of *Pharaos* daughter,
Ios. 6. 20. which the Scripture saith he did by faith. And thus did the walles of Iericho fall downe, as God had promised, at the seuenth daies end, the people beleeuing it should be so, and compassing them about all that time, with the blowing trumpets of rammes hornes, as God had commanded. And this is it, which we should intend, and looke to doe in all that we goe about. This
A commendation of faith. faith, for which also these worthie persons are by name commended in the eleuenth to the Hebrewes, is able to carrie vs, as well as euer it did them, through all difficulties, while we haue an eye to the charge giuen vs, and the promised reward, although we see nothing with bodily eyes, but that which is against vs, and matter of discouragement. For so the Apostle S. *Iohn* saith,
1. Ioh. 5. 4. *that this faith ouercommeth the world*, euen all the difficulties that are in it. This faith, when it is once setled on the great promise of saluation, is afterward the fitter to apprehend and lay hold on these temporarie promises of this life, about the which (it being a Iewell of inualuable price) if we were occupied and exercised with so constant a care, as wee are about matters of lesse waight, (if not needlesse and vnprofitable) we should be able to say much of the benefit that commeth by it, and haue neere acquaintance with God by the helpe of this our faith. But seeing I haue spoken of this matter before, I will bee the briefer in it, though wee cannot heare too often of it,

from

from good ground of the word, as occasion is offered.

But whiles I am thus in commending of *Bararks* faith, me thinkes I heare some obiecting, that the last thing spoken of him in the ninth verse, was his vnbeleefe; how is hee therefore say they, so suddenly brought to such a change? I answere, that though *Barak* had been hindred before by vnbeleefe, yet afterward hee recouered himselfe, as wee see heere; and that was when God had giuen him better consideration of the charge enioyned him, and promise made vnto him. So if we haue failed in beleeuing through the difficulty that wee see, or by rashnesse, yet let vs weigh Gods promise more duly, and so beleeue more hartily, and be better stayed by good consideration. And to that end let none sit downe like a tyred person, and giue ouer his hold and hope, saying; I see this is too good and precious for mee to enioy, for I should neuer be able to beleeue it, &c. Not so; but then let thy want encrease thy thirst, as *Dauids* did, Psal. 51. and desire to bee enlarged, Psal.51.2.3. and pray, Lord helpe my vnbeleefe. And remember that weakenesse may be forgiuen, where there is striuing against it; but wilfulnesse, or preposterous and inuincible vnbeleefe is damnable; for God lookes to bee credited Ioh.3.16. vpon his word, promise, and oath, besides the many experiments which we haue, if not of our selues, yet of other men; who of weake became strong. And as God bare with *Baraks* infirmity heere, in yeelding to him, that *Debora* should goe with him: so he will tender and helpe our weake faith, and that many more waies then we can see, and all to encourage vs. Thus much be said of this.

THE TVVENTIE SEAVEN SERMON ON THE FOVRTH CHAPTER OF THE booke of IVDGES.

NOw further, let vs note in this verse by the ioynt agreement of all these heere mentioned; I meane *Debora*, Doct.2. in vers.10. *Barak*, and the ten thousand of *Zebulun* and *Nephtali*, (especially it being so needful that they should so consent together) how good and worthie a thing it is for the seruants of God to ioyne and bee like minded in good things; though it doe not directly tend to their owne profit and earthly benefit, or not so much as to the common good & behoofe of al the people, or many, (as here it did,) but to a town or family, the commendation of this gift of free consent together in many good people is clearely to be seene in the Apostles, and those that kept company with them; of whom it is said, that they were altogether of one mind: which caused Saint *Paul* to make so earnest a request to the Philippians to remoue from them contention and pride; whereby this con- Act.2.10.

ſent and agreement is eaſily broken. For wee know it is no eaſie matter for many to ioyne and agree together, and that by reaſon of ſo much contrariety as is in mens minds, and for that one is ſo ready to croſſe and withſtand an other, eſpecially in good things, through Satan by his ſubtill and malitious policy working therewith, who gaineth much by their diſtraction and diſagreement, as in *Paul* and *Barnabas* may be ſeene. It is therfore to be ſought & laboured for alwaies, by the loue and wiſedome of godly teachers, who by their doctrine, perſwaſions, and good example, doe much helpe heereto. Thus had *Debora* and *Barak* preuailed with theſe ten thouſand, that they drew them to this worke ioyntly, as if they had been but two perſons. Oh, agreement in good things, what is like it, either in beauty or delight, as the
Pſal.133.1. Pſalmiſt ſpeaketh, *Behold how good and pleaſant a thing it is, for men to dwell together in godly vnity?* And experience teacheth the ſame. For there, many vniting their force of courage and wiſdome in one, they doe eaſily reſiſt the common enemy, and (which is harder) their owne corrupt paſſions and rebellious nature, the which to what euill and miſchiefe it carryeth them, the infinite broyles, ſutes, quarrels and controuerſies of almoſt all places do too truly teſtifie. Such are they who in louing and kind agreement betwixt themſelues, doe ſubmit themſelues to the word of God, whereby they become meeke and humble, and ſo they eaſily conſent to that which is good. The want of this godly agreement, and the contrary readineſſe in men to breake out one againſt another, hath oft cauſed mee to bewaile, (for who ſeeth not great cauſe ſo to do) the boyſterous and fierce contentions of many, and thoſe not onely of the common ſort, who are for the moſt part rude and ignorant, but of them alſo who are to be counted brethren, and yet doe ſo readily let looſe their hearts to bitter contentions and raſh iudgings of their brethren, if they doe not worſe: and yet (which is greater madneſſe) this is for a ſmall cauſe (as if they doe but diſſent in opinion and iudgement one from another in things indifferent, wherein both follow the light of their knowledge,) whereby they giue too great teſtimony, that they little know themſelues aright, and that they haue full ſlightly ſearched into themſelues, to ſee their many ranke corruptions of ſelfe loue, priuie pride, frowardneſſe, impatience, vncharitableneſſe and ſuch like, that ſwarme and beare ſway in them; and that they beſtow ſmall coſt vpon themſelues, nor time to find fault with their owne doings, (to wit, how farre they are off from the rule of charity,) that ſo they may become humble and peaceably minded toward others. Nay, (which is worſe) they hold their vnchriſtian conceits and iudgings of their brethren, ſo ſtrongly and wilfully, that they verifie the prouerbe, making their bitter contentions with them like the bars of a palace, that cannot bee broken: and like cities ſtrong and well fenced,
Prou.18.19. that cannot eaſily bee beaten downe. This is farre from godly agreement, and conſequently from that harty louing together, which ſhould bee like a
Eccleſ.4.12. threefold cord, that is not eaſily broken, which our Sauiour ſaith is a ſure token that they in whom it is, are his very Diſciples indeed. As for agree-
Ioh.13.35. Pſal.2.1.2. ment in euill, ſuch as theirs was in the Pſalme, it is as hurtfull and odious, as
Prou.11.21. it is common: but *though hand ioyne in hand, the wicked ſhall not eſcape vnpuniſhed*; and ſo I leaue them, adding this; where there is no agreement in euill, there leſſe is committed. And therefore wee had need to pray the Lord

to

to send a spirit of diuision among such, as that was betwixt the Pharisies and Sadduces, that so much mischiefe may be preuented rather then stablished. And this of the preparation of that *Debora* and *Barak* made.

Now followeth, (before I come to *Sisera*) a short story of *Heber* the husband of *Iael*, put in by the way, to wit, that he (being of the posterity of *Hobab, Moses* father in law, who remoued from his kindred and brethren, as we saw in cap. 1. vers. 16.) was come to this Kedesh to dwell, where *Barak* assembled his men of warre. To the which place God by his prouidence directing him, sent him, as appeares afterward in vers. 17. that thereby hee might, as he did by *Iael Hebers* wife, cut off this great enemie *Sisera*. By which we may learne a right profitable lesson. That while we goe on heere in our simplicity in this earthly dwelling to serue Gods prouidence, as his word leadeth vs, God will in our most casuall actions direct, regard, & blesse vs so, that in time we shall see it to be so, though we knew not before what should come to passe. *Heber* remoued his dwelling from his kindred, not in hatred to them, but as he saw it most conuenient for him, though (it is true) he intended not thereby the destruction of *Sisera*, neither came there any such thing into his mind; but the Lord purposed it, and appointed that by this meanes of his comming to dwell there, it should be brought to passe: *Heber* onely considering, and aduisedly bethinking himselfe what was best for him to do about the setling of his dwelling, and seeking to liue among Gods people, and looking no further.

Vers. 11. *The vnfolding of it.*

Doct. vers. 11.

So by the selling of *Ioseph* into a strange countrey, a thing in likelihood tending to his vndoing, yet it is manifest, as hee told his brethren, that God sent him before, to preserue them and their posterity aliue, and not they. So when *Iacob* was sent away by *Rebecca*, his mother, to Padan Aram, to auoide the wrath of his brother *Esau*, the cause was good, but hee went, vncertaine what should befall him in a strange land; and therefore hee thought, and vowed, if he might haue bread to eate, and clothes to put on, and that God would be with him, and keepe him in his iourney, that then he should be his God, meaning that he should bee more strongly confirmed in so counting him. Therefore God, who guided his iourney, blessed him greatly, so that when he returned, hee remembred Gods benefits which hee had since that, bestowed on him, saying: *I came ouer this Iordan with my staffe*; that is, poore, and without all prouision, *but now haue I gotten two bands.* So when *Moses* married *Iethros* daughter, liuing obscurely in the wildernesse, and suffering affliction with the people of God, who would haue thought that any good should haue come thereby? And yet beside his admirable deliuering of the Israelites out of *Pharaohs* bandage, he was also a meane to draw *Iethros* posterity to religion, and the true worship of God thereby. Euen so, offer we our selues vnder Gods gouernment, and all things shall bee in time, directed by him to a good end, though we see it not by and by; yet wee shall; so as wee may be bold to say it, for he will bring it so to passe. For it is to bee knowne, that while we wander heere on earth, yet we are not in darkenesse, as others are; neither are we cast off as Orphans and left desolate, but God careth for vs his faithfull ones, otherwise then he doth for the rest of the world.

Gen. 45. 8. Gen. 28. 20. Gen. 32. 10. 1. Pet. 3. 2. 1. Tim. 4. 10.

And it being so with vs, though wee see not the mind and purpose of God toward vs in particulars at the first, and what will fall out through the

course of our liues, yet wee are sure that his speciall prouidence watcheth ouer vs for our good; so that we need not doubt but that God directeth all things to that end. This is a wonderfull stay to all beleeuing people; and without faith, sound knowledge, and vse thereof, all Gods doings are strange to vs, both before we see the issue of them, and sometime afterward also, and namely his crosses and afflictions: but as they are distasted of vs, and vtterly vnwelcome, so are his benefits neuer receiued of vs in good sort, and to the right end; namely, to make vs trust in him more firmely, and cleaue to him more constantly, whereas we should be much more moued hereby, to
Rom.5.4. commit the successe of all vnto him, till our experience haue brought the hope that shall not make vs ashamed. For there need bee no doubt but that
Prou.6.22. he watcheth for vs thus clinging to him, when we sleepe, and vpholdeth vs while wee walke, and proposeth good towards vs, euen then when wee see no likelihood thereof. And while it is thus with vs, it is not vnprofitable to consider, how ill it goeth with those, who rest vpon blind fortune (as they call it) and goe on in the strength of their carnall wisedome, looking for great matters, but all in vaine, they being little or nothing acquainted with Gods prouidence. Lamentable it is to see how such are tossed, vexed, and vnsetled with cares and sorrowes, and that not only in their most vncertaine and doubtfull affaires, but also in those which are more sure and certaine, as they thinke and imagine.

Doct.2. Besides, it is not vnprofitable for vs to marke another thing in this short story, and that is this: that seeing this *Heber* remoued, and had his dwelling apart from the rest of his brethren the Kenites, vpon good consideration, (for otherwise the holy story would haue found fault with it,) the rest of
Iudg.1.16. them departing from Iericho, and dwelling with the tribe of Iuda in their borders, (as we heard in chap.1.) in that, I say, *Heber* did thus, who yet, as is cleare by the story, did not offend God therein, wee see it is not vnlawfull for the people of God to settle their dwellings apart from their neighbours and kindred, & brethren in profession; but it may fal out to be meet for them to do so: for God hath not appointed that all the faithfull should dwel together; neither can it be sometime for sundry considerations and respects: as we reade that *Abraham* and *Lot*, by reason of the great abundance of cattell that they both had, and for want of pasture, departed one from another: euen as before when their posterity grew and multiplied in one familie, they married, and were dispersed into diuerse. And many other things doe cause that. Indeed if wee may dwell together with Gods people, in the places of best choice, it is not to be neglected, but desired hartily (for many shall be hindred from it by necessity) and if that liberty may bee enioyed of vs, let vs make a pretious reckoning of it, and set our selues to liue together kindly, profitably, and peaceably, which too many regard not to doe, but if it cannot bee without great inconuenience, let vs not striue against God, for we gaine nothing thereby, and what know we what God hath appointed to be done by vs in another place? It may bee wee may bring some to God by our remouing, and bee seated among such as shall bee like our selues, or may by our good conuersation which they shall see, be turned vnto vs. Which two things we should principally aime at, and endeauour vnto when we must change and remoue our dwelling.

Now

Now it followeth that after this short degression (as we haue heard how Barak prepared and furnished himselfe to warre, so it was told Sisera what he had done) and that hee prepared his army likewise when hee heard that Barak had done so. His power what it was, I meane, how great and feareful, I haue shewed already. That which we haue heere principally to note, in addressing himselfe to the battel, is the difference betwixt him on the one side, and Debora and Barak with their few thousands on the other. They both prepared themselues to warre we see, but these went about it by Gods commandement; hee in the pride of his owne heart, and without God. They trusted in the promise of God for victory, he in his owne strength, and great army. They went against Gods enemies, he against Gods friends, yea against God himselfe. Whereby we may see that it much auaileth to haue a good cause to maintaine, and to haue God to goe with vs therein, as many examples in Scripture testifie of the warres of godly Kings with idolaters. A good cause is the defence of the Gospell, and the true worship of God by a Christian Prince, against such as would force him to Poperie, or any other false worship, by open warre: also the maintaining of his owne dominion, bounds, or right in great and waighty matters, or recouering them being vniustly detained from him. A Christian Prince in these and such like cases may make warre, and command his people against the enemie: and so I may say of the like. But to leaue this instance and to lay out this doctrine in another, more familiar to the common sort; it is manifest where the like is to be found among vs who are in peace, to wit, that we haue a good cause, and our controuersies with the bad, it is manifest, I say, that the one sort hath great encouragement by the goodnesse of his cause, to follow it rather then the other, who hath none at all, but much against him. For where all these encouragements are, or the most which Barak had, and of which I haue spoken; they are to animate men to their duties; so I will not say, what successe and blessing particularly shall follow them who vse them, but they shall most certainly reape great fruit thereby, and abundantly one way or other: and therefore good reason that such should doe the Lords worke diligently: and contrariwise, the other, if they could bee made to consider what they goe about, in following a bad matter, they should neuer dare be bold to proceed as they doe, to wit, as Sisera did to defend an ill cause, but they would feare to goe forward, and desist from their attempts. Good and bad goe to worke both alike (as these heere did) for outward preparation, but not in a like manner, nor with the like minde, nor to the like end. And although Sisera had not wilfully, in the pride of his heart, gone against Israel because they were Gods people (as Pharaoh did) and although hee bee not properly to be charged for not consulting with God, or weighing the cause in going against Gods people; (for alas he was an Heathen, and therefore ignorant of such matters) yet to speake the best that may be said of him, hee trusted in chariots, horses, souldiers, and munition; thereby purposing with maine force to reduce the rebellious Israelites, as hee counted them, to the yoake of obedience, and knew also that they were Gods people. But it was indeed no wonder that he tooke this course, being a cursed Canaanite, such an one as he was. But to leaue him, and to come nearer our selues; is it not admirable, that among vs who are of the visible Church, there should bee found

Vers. 12.13.

Note.

Doct. vers. 12.13.

found some, that in their enterprises, life and dealings, maintaine an euill cause one against the other, as *Barak* and *Sisera* did? for what though their actions both ciuill in religious exercises be the same, and that in outward respect there appeare little or no difference in some of them? yet so prophane and vnconscionable many of them are, that they hold the righteous an abomination, and deface, as the Pharisies did Christs, their best actions, and will see no difference betwixt their owne and the others. And to please themselues, thus they say of them; Tush, as precise as they seeme: they doe but as we; they follow their trades, buy, sell, eate, drinke, marrie, &c. and we do as they, reade, pray, heare the word, receiue the Sacrament, &c. what
Mat.24.40. oddes therefore betwixt vs? yes: for why? shall not two be in the field, or at the mill, and yet the one receiued, the other forsaken? and the one a reprobate, the other chosen? Surely as they differ in their ends, so they differ in the meanes vsing that leade thereto: and though they differ not in dying, for the outward manner) yet they differ in this, that one dieth happily, the other miserably: and so they doe in their affections differ, as in their
Psal.4.7.8. desires, hope, encouragements, and successes. The one asketh, *who will shew vs any good?* The other prayeth, *O Lord lift vp the light of thy countenance vpon vs,* for it is more to vs then all abundance. And in this light both of knowledge for direction, and of grace for assistance thereto. The godly man walketh looking at the promise in all his lawfull attempts, knowing also that the
Psal.84.13. Lord, who is his light to guide him, will bee his defence also, to vphold, prosper and blesse him. The other walkes in darkenesse, being led by erronious opinion, sense, example, nature, and sometimes shame, feare, and proud confidence in himselfe; and therefore goeth through many dangers, smarts, sorrowes, whether he be crossed, or whether he haue his desire. Hee reeleth also and stumbleth, as the Egyptians did, when darkenesse did ouerspread them, while the Israelites walked in safety, at liberty. In a word, the one serueth God, the other the diuell: the one is cheerefull, patient, confident: the other of a contrary minde and carriage. Therefore let euery man who desireth to be approued of God, judge himselfe, and as for others, both such as I haue spoken of, and they who doe the same actions with them, though wee know not with what mind, let vs conceiue the best, so farre as in charity we may, of them; but yet let vs suspend our sentence and allowance of them, till after longer triall, and further knowledge of, and acquaintance with them. And consider yee that reade this what I say, and the Lord giue you vnderstanding. For in that which I haue said of the wicked incensed against the righteous, (their deeds being good, but their owne euill) consisteth a great difference betwixt a true Christian and a counterfait; as to him that will lay both sorts together with good consideration, shall appeare. And of this Scripture heere an end.

THE TVVENTY EIGHT SERMON ON THE FOVTRH CHAPTER OF THE BOOKE OF IVDGES.

Vers.14. *Then Debora said vnto Barak, Vp: for this is the day that the Lord hath deliuered Sisera into thine hand. is not the Lord gone out before thee? So Barak went downe from mount Tabor, and tenne thousand men after him.*

Vers.15. *And the Lord destroyed Sisera, and all his charets, and all his host with the edge of the sword before Barak, so that Sisera lighted downe of his charet, and fled away on his feete.*

Vers.16. *But Barak pursued after the charets, and after the host vnto Harosheth of the Gentiles: and all the host of Sisera fell on the edge of the sword: there was not a man left.*

WE haue heard in the former verses how both sides, *Barak* I meane, and *Sisera*, addressed themselues to battell: in these (to come more neerely to the intent of this fourth part) is shewed, whose the victorie was, namely *Baraks*: and how? verily *Debora* incouraging and assuring him, that euen the same day wherein she spake it should bee obtained and gotten; and he beleeuing it, went downe with his men of warre, (few though they were) and he meeting *Sisera* with his bands at mount Tabor, (no more is said of the matter) they were destroyed both charets and horsemen, not a man was left, but either drowned in the riuer Kishon that was there by, or slaine there at mount Tabor, or pursued (as the charets and horsemen were) and so put to the sword, and *Sisera* himselfe was driuen to flie away on his feete, but in vaine. Oh the wonderfull deliuerance that God gaue vnto his people that day! *The summe of these three verses.*

This here set downe, is the third speech that *Debora* vsed to *Barak*, and that at mount Tabor: and though the last, yet not the least, but mightie, forceable, and in due season. For it appeareth by the text, that when *Barak* saw *Siseras* huge army, he was dismaied, and therfore sought the fittest place about mount Tabor, and the surest, to shrowd himselfe in, from the violence and rage of *Sisera*. Which fainting of his, she perceiuing, called him backe, and stirred him vp to fight, by her words and perswasions, saying, No power of man how great and fearfull soeuer, shall be able to hinder thee from obtaining the victorie, which the Lord hath purposed to giue thee this day. At which speech of hers hee was animated, and tooke heart, and went to the battell, and, as we haue heard, preuailed. *Verse 14. The vnfolding of vers.14.*

And here is most notably set downe one meanes whereby the power of faith is strengthened, and whereby it is wonderfully drawne to contemne and *Doct.*

and ſet light by all diſcouragements, and breake thorow them, the leaſt whereof without it, would bee ready to ſet a man at his wits end. And that was here *Deboras* heartning perſwaſion to *Barak* (as Gods voyce) to animate him. And therefore it much auaileth to heare Gods promiſes oft times by the publike Miniſterie, and effectually publiſhed and fitly applied vnto vs in the fitteſt manner that may bee, and in ſickneſſe, temptation, and other times of fainting, when a man is much weakened and diſmaied, to haue, as *Barak* had here by *Debora*, ſuch forcible and liuely quicknings: but beſt of all, if a man be able himſelfe to doe that dutie to himſelfe, and by the prayer of faith to ſtrengthen himſelfe in ſuch time of need. Oh! there are many ebbings and faintings in our liues, euen after good ſtrength and refreſhing: we haue ſometime good patience and hope vnder our croſſes, but another time wee feare the greatnes of them, that they will ſwallow vs vp, eſpecially if they be more then common. Againe, wee ſometime purſue a ſinne, and haue it in the chace, and preuaile ouer it, which hath ſore laid at vs, and wound in with vs very farre, to draw liking and conſent from vs vnto it: and ſometime it carrieth vs with maine force after it.

Note.

And what is it that hath relieued vs at ſuch times? Truly euen this, if we haue been able to beleeue that God will ſtrengthen vs againſt it, and that he hath promiſed ſo to doe, and if alſo by prayer not fained, wee haue ſet our faith a worke, though it hath lien as almoſt dead before; euen thus we grow to weaken the liking of that ſinne in vs: as for feare of danger or ſhame of the world, they are but dull edged tooles to cut off the head of ſuch a monſter. And although wee be brought oft times to that point as to doubt, yet we ſhould alſo ſtriue by our faith in our prayers againſt it, and it ſhall not be in vaine to doe ſo. And the ſame wee ſhould doe in our feare before affliction commeth, and in our heauines for it, when it is come. For they that know any thing of the eſtate of a Chriſtian, know this; that he is many times in great feare of falling into ſome ſinne, yea and perhaps, that which is foule and odious, though it be not vſually ſo: Now if we doe not call to minde, that God hath promiſed ſtrength againſt all ſuch aduerſarie power, and that by the weapons of our warfare, (which are not carnall, but ſpirituall) wee ſhall be able to beate downe ſuch ſtrong holds; and if with the prayer of faith (as need requireth) we ſet not our ſelues ſo to doe, we ſhall ſoone perceiue that we loſe ground, and grow weake, as *Barak* did for a while; who yet was ſtrengthened againe by *Debora*, ſo that hee did moſt valiantly afterwards, in ſo much that he was renowned among the Worthies, and reported to haue obtained the victorie by faith; for at the hearing of *Deboras* words he went downe from mount Tabor with his men neere to the riuer Kiſhon againſt *Siſera*. This of the incouragement by *Debora*, and the fruite of it *Barak*.

Verſe 15.16. Now it followeth that the Lord gaue *Barak* victorie, the rare and marueilous victorie, ouer his and Gods enemies. For the Lord waſted the huge armie of *Siſera*, howbeit, by the fighting of *Barak* and his men againſt them. And ſuch of them as haſted in their flight toward Haroſheth of the Gentiles for ſafetie, (from whence they came) they were ouer taken alſo and put to the ſword, ſo that none eſcaped. And *Siſera* was driuen (ſo great the ſlaughter was, and the battell ſo ſore) to forſake his charet wherein hee rode, and to

eſcape

escape on foote, if it might be, among the common souldiers. Now it is to be considered by what meanes this great victorie was gotten : tenne thousand vnexperienced souldiers going against so many thousands of horsemen, and footmen, and yron charets. The Lord (it is said) gaue *Barak* the victorie; which no man doubteth of, seeing he is all in all: It is an harder question, how *Barak* obtained it of God : and that was by faith, after that *Barak* got strength and courage againe by *Deboras* perswasions, she her selfe being constant in faith all the while: for then, and not before, he went down from mount Tabor with his men to meete *Sisera*, being before afraid, looking downe from thence vpon the huge armie that he saw. This was *Barak* his armour of proofe to defend him, euen his faith. And if this cannot bee cleerely enough seene in this storie, fetch more cleere proofe of that which I say, from another scripture. Thus writeth the author of the Epistle to the Hebrewes, after he had set downe the faith of sundrie persons, as *Abraham*, *Moses*, and other; he addeth : *What shall I more say of Gedeon, Barak, &c. who waxed valiant in battell,* and by faith turned to flight the armies of the aliants. Heb.11.32.

And by this wee may see againe the mightie force and power of faith, where it is firme and strong, what great things it bringeth to passe. It is no marueile though it be said by the Apostle, that *faith ouercommeth the world,* euen all and the greatest difficulties therein. For what hardnes doth any man goe thorow in his whole life like vnto this here mentioned, and ouercome it also, vnlesse it be thus, euen by the helpe and power of faith ? which is no more then to giue credit to God in that which he speaketh, when wee see no such thing, nor likelihood of it, but rather of the contrary many times with our bodily eyes. Euen thus hath God magnified his word in all ages, when men haue found euery part of it true by faith, and by this it hath pleased him to make men see his vnspeakable kindnesse, while they beleeue the promise in which he offereth it vnto them. By this faith we also at this day haue sure hold of forgiuenes and eternall life, euen so many as are wearie of sinne, and thirst for both, and that because we iudge him faithfull that hath promised, and by this we are perswaded of a good end of our daies, because God hath said it, to all in whom he hath made a good beginning thereof. So saith the Apostle, faithfull is he that calleth you, who will also doe it. So that all things are possible, how vnlikely soeuer, to him that beleeueth. This is the cause why some more esteeme and price this faith then gold that perisheth : and declare, that they cannot doe too much to come by & retaine it, euen while they bee laughed to scorne of the wicked world, who think it meere foolishnes to doe so, as *Noah* the preacher of righteousnesse was in his time, while he beleeuing that an vniuersall flood should come, prepared the Arke. But herein I might wade infinitly, and this I confesse, that howsoeuer I forbeare to speake of the most of other things twice; yet of this I professe to speake as oft as I shall haue occasion, the thing it selfe being so excellent, so necessarie, and yet so difficult, to see thorowly into. I only now require, that we may weigh the power and truth of Gods word, to the end we may stay our selues vpon it. The word of a man whom wee count faithfull, doth much perswade vs in great difficulties, and quickeneth vs if hee bring vs good tidings, when we were before in great heauinesse. When *Beniamin*

Doct. 1.Ioh.5.4. Note. Note. Phil.1.6. 1.Thes.5.24.

iamin came with this ioyfull tidings to his father *Iacob* full of heauinesse: *Io-*
Gen.45.26. *seph thy sonne is yet aliue, and is ruler ouer all Egypt*; the heart of *Iacob* reuiued. If it be so by giuing credit to a man; what confidence and ioy is it like to worke, if we beleeue a glad tidings which may bee of many things sent vs from God? Doubtlesse, hereby our weake knees are strengthened, and our sorrowfull hearts are comforted more then can be expressed. I wish therefore that vnto vs concerning faith, that which S. *Iames* did of patience, to wit, *that it may haue her perfect worke*, so should wee be sure to want nothing that is good.

The next thing after the victorie ouer *Siseras* armie, is to see the extremity that he himselfe, the leader and chiefe captaine of it, was brought vnto: for he was faine to leaue his charet which was his defence, and to shift for himselfe on foote among the common souldiers, that he might saue his life if it were possible. This, I say, remaineth in this 15. verse to be added. And here, as in fittest place, I think good to note this, because of the former doctrine, (one contrary cleering the other): that as *Barak* and *Debora* did by faith so great things, by so small and weake meanes: so *Sisera* wanting this (as being of the heathen Canaanites, how could he so much as taste of it?) was for all his wisedome, policie, and power, wasted, put to flight, and al his troupe and
Psal 33 17. band brought to destruction. Here was verified that saying, *an horse is but a vaine thing to saue a man*: Likewise another scripture that saith, *Some put their*
Psal.20.7. *trust in charets, and some in horses, but we will remember the name of the Lord our God: They are brought downe and fallen, but we are risen and stand vpright*. And therefore (to referre the reader to gather the infinite annoyances of vnbeliefe, and therewith the great benefits of faith out of the former doctrine) I
Heb.11.6. will conclude that as *without faith it is impossible to please God*, so God being against all which are destitute of it, and an enemie to them, how can they looke to stand against him, but to fall and bee confounded? And this they finde daily one or other of them, though it be little marked, and it is soone forgotten, (another generation rising vp in their roome) who know not the workes of God, and yet they haue their time also set them, wherein they shall finde the like. For if this be true in the greene tree, how much more in
1.Pet.4.18. the withered? If through vnbeliefe, euen the righteousest finde it a matter of such difficultie to be saued, before they attaine it, what shall become of him that is an vnbeleeuer altogether? And further, if particular defects in
Numb 21.12. faith cost *Moses* and *Barak* disaduantage and dishonour, what shall the end of such be as neuer had any? Surely the wrath of God abideth vpon them:
Iohn 3 36. and so shall doe for euer, and shew it selfe in a farre more terrible manner, if they haste not after it, and so, as that they attaine it, Ioh.3.

Doct.2. And here another thing is to be marked, that when God doth not blesse, but blow vpon mens furniture & furtherances, and taketh part against thē, euen these things which were armour and defence to them before, they cast them away as burthens and impediments. As *Sisera* here was driuen to leaue his charet now that he was so pursued of his enemies, which yet had been, and was counted, as his house of defence vnto him. For God will haue
Note. vs know, that his fauour is toward all his, as the pleasant sunshine to the earth and the creatures therein, which maketh all pleasant and beautifull, and if that should cease to shine, the earth with all that is therein, should

stinke

ſtinke and come to naught. Euen ſo, if God turne away his louing countenance from a man, and frowne vpon him, all that was precious to him before, is vnpleaſant, euen as the moth conſumeth the beautie of a garment, as it was ſaid of Ieruſalem, when God was diſpleaſed, that all her pleaſant things were matters of ſighing and ſorrow vnto her. Whence is it, that many a man of great poſſeſſions, can yet finde no fauour nor relliſh in them, eſpecially if any affliction or trouble be vpon him? Why is the heart ſo locked vp, that it cannot ioy in any commoditie? in wife, children, wealth, fauour? Will ye know the reaſon? becauſe firſt, outward things are ſo farre ſweete as the Lord ſweetneth them, and otherwiſe the enioyers thereof find no taſte nor ſweetnes in them; no, they haue no vſe of them. If God be not a mans portion, all other portions are enioyned without his loue, and ſo turne to gall and bitterneſſe. As *Nabals* wealth, *Achitophel* his wiſedome, *Hamans* fauour. For when *Ahaſhueroſh* abandoned *Haman*, what ſtead did his wife, friends, or former fauour ſtand him in? The wrath of the King blaſted all theſe, as the froſt or Eaſt winde doth the tender buds. *Nabals* heart was as a ſtone, when he preſaged the euent that followed. *Achitophels* wiſedome was that which brake his necke. Againe, the wicked force themſelues to finde a deceiuable ſweetneſſe in theſe tranſitorie things without God: therefore he iuſtly depriues them thereof, and turnes them out of kinde, ſo that although hee hath ſuffered them for a while to flouriſh, and take their pleaſure in them, yet when they haue long ſurfetted of them, they poyſon them, yea and in ſhort time alſo, as he ſeeth good.

Lamen.1.10.

Pſal.119.59.

The vſe of this is, that wee account the fauour of God all in all to vs, and further then wee haue that ſhining vpon vs, glorie not in any earthly prerogatiue, as honour, beautie, wealth, or whatſoeuer elſe. For many of the vaine people of the world doe finde to their coſt by wofull experience, that when they haue ſpent their whole life and precious time to get them, (I may truly ſay alſo, they haue loſt heauen for them) yet they finde (I ſay) with what vexation they enioy them, though they would make others beleeue, that they are as a paradiſe vnto them: But to bee ſure they cannot keepe them, when God will pluck them from them, as we ſee both by the two rich men in the Goſpell, and by daily experience: and that is enough for wiſe men to proue how little there is in them. And this by occaſion of *Siſeras* loſing all.

Luke 12.20.

Luke 16.23.

Verſ. 17. *Howbeit Siſera fled away on his feet, to the tent of Iael the wife of Heber the Kenite: (for peace was betweene Iabin the King of Hazor, and betweene the houſe of Heber the Kenite.)*

18. *And Iael went out to meet Siſera, and ſaid vnto him, turne in my Lord, turne in to me, feare not. And when he had turned in vnto her tent, ſhee couered him with a mantell.*

19. *And he ſaid vnto her, giue me, I pray thee, a little water to drinke, for I am thirſtie: and ſhee opened a bottell of milke, and gaue him drinke, and couered him.*

20. *Againe, he ſaid vnto her, ſtand in the doore of the tent, and when any man doth come and enquire of thee, ſaying; Is any man heere? thou ſhalt ſay, nay.*

21. *Then Iael Hebers wife tooke a naile of the tent, and tooke an hammer in her*

hand, and went softly to him, and smote the naile into his temples, and fastened it into the ground, (for he was fast asleepe and wearie) and so he died.

The opening of these verses. WE haue heard how by *Debora* and *Barak* the battell was prospered, as in this fourth part of the chapter hath been noted: now it followeth how a full end was put to it by *Iael.* To whose tent *Sisera* fled, as the fittest refuge for shelter, it being neere the place where the battell was, and peace being betwixt *Iabin* the King of Canaan, and *Heber* her husband. The things principall in these 5. verses, are three. One how *Sisera* fled thither, in the seuenteenth verse. The second, by what meanes his death was brought on, in the next three. The third, that it was by her effected, in the 21. And this story doth shew, why that is set downe in the eleuenth verse, where I referred the Reader to this place, to wit, that *Heber* the husband of *Iael*, came and dwelt in the plaine of Zaanaim by Kedesh, apart from his brethren, euen to this end, though he intended it not, yet by Gods appointment and prouidence, that *Sisera* might haue his deadly wound and blow there. And by *Siseras* flying on foote to *Iaels* tent for succour and shelter, we see another difficulty that this *Sisera* was driuen to, beside the ill successe that he had in the fight; and withall we may obserue, to what shifts and extremities wicked men though they bee great & mighty persons may be brought: for they who could command a whole country, may be constrained to hide their head in a priuate tent and corner. And they who haue gloried as Lords of all store and plenty may come to this, that they may be glad of a draught of milke or water to saue their liues. To *Ahab* King of Israel this word was sent by *Benhadad* who besieged him, that all his siluer and other precious things were his, whereto *Ahab* answered, it is true (O King) thine they are. And the same *Benhadad* so boasting and braging ouer him, was afterward himselfe brought to this point, and that by the same *Ahab*, that hee loosing in two battels, as good as two hundred and fiftie thousand men, beside chariots and horses, he was driuen to flie on horse-backe into a secret chamber, and yet euen there to be in great feare of his life also. And so in other stories it is reported of *Darius* the Persian King, that being in flight pursued by his enemies, and in a great thirst passed by a Lake, out of which hee tooke vp puddle water, and hauing drunke it out of his hands, protested hee neuer dranke sweeter in his life.

(Margin: Doct verf.17. Note. 1.King 20.3.)

Now if such mighty ones may for their sinnes bee driuen to such straites and shifts, then meane persons much more are easily and soone depriued of all that they haue, and that many waies. Therefore if wee be wise who now liue, or they who shall come after vs, howsoeuer wee enioy much, wee will learne, as wee haue oft been, and heere are taught, *not to put our trust in vncertaine riches, but in the liuing God*; neither to be high minded, but humble and lowly (knowing to what changes we be subiect) in which estate there is no danger. And in that wee miscarrie not daily, with the silly worme that is trod on, and with the beast slaughtered, that fed euen now at the pasture, it is onely Gods forbearing vs.

(Margin: 1.Tim.6.17.)

In that it is said that *Heber* had peace with *Iabin*, the Scripture sets not downe how and in what manner it was: therefore by occasion of this their peace, about which, or the like, seeing some might moue a question; for answere

ſwere and our inſtruction this may be ſaid, that if there were conditions betwixt them, (*Iabin* and *Heber* I meane) about limits and bounds of ground, how farre they ſhould reach, or what hee ſhould pay for the ſame, or ſuch like, they were lawfull: but if they had been for the ioyning with him againſt his enemies, without reſpect, (which was not ſo) then their peace had not been good, nor to bee allowed. According to this that I ſay, let our inſtruction be. For if a ciuill league be betwixt the true worſhippers of God and Idolaters, about keeping and enioying that which is ſeuerally their, ſafely and quietly, that is not to be diſliked: for the godly while they be heere, deſire not to dwell alone in the world, neither can they chuſe (they know) but they muſt haue dealings with the men that liue in it: and againe, they are commanded by the Apoſtle, *that they ſhould, as much as in them lyeth, haue peace with all men.* Rom.12.12. And ſo moſt Chriſtian Emperours haue had peace with the barbarous people that were ſtrangers to true religion, and ſo did the people of Iſraell with the nations which were neare adioyned to them, (except the ſeuen that were accurſed) for the Lord did not command them to make warre with the reſt that dwelt about them.

But if they ſhould vrge the religious people to ioyne their aide with them in making warre with them againſt other nations which are Gods people, that in no wiſe is to be yeelded vnto. For it went ill with *Iehoſaphat*, for going to warre in league with *Ahab* againſt Ramath in Gilead. As alſo for ioyning in fellowſhip with *Ieheram* his ſonne, when hee ſent ſhips with him into Tarſis: for a tempeſt ariſing at Ezion Gabar, his ſhips were broken. Compare 1.King.22. 48 49 with 2.Chron.35. 36.37. So *Aſa* King of Iuda ſent ſiluer and gold to *Benhadad* King of Aram, to help him againſt *Baaſha* King of Iſrael, but hee was reproued for it of the Lord. 2.Chron.16.3. And ſo (no doubt) it is lawfull for Chriſtian Princes to confederate with not onely Chriſtian, but Popiſh or Heathen in ciuill caſes, as for the better ſecurity of their dominions, maintenance of peace, and thoſe commodities which follow thereupon, as traffique, &c. but to hold correſpondence with them in religion, or to profeſſe themſelues friends to their friends, whom God curſeth; or enemies to their enemies that were to doe as they in the Pſalme, that banded themſelues together, whom God will ſcatter. 2.Chron. 19.2. Pſal.2.1.2. Now that which I haue ſaid of leagues made betwixt nations, or one man, (as *Heber* was) with a King, namely, *Iabin* King of Canaan, the ſame I ſay of one priuate perſon with another, liuing together: And that is briefly this: that a godly Chriſtian may liue in peace with the wicked, and vſe him in ciuill caſes to buy and ſell, and borrow, and lend, as it may conueniently bee done betwixt them; but this muſt alwaies be prouided for, that he ioyne not with him in his ſinne, neither that hee haue any fellowſhip with him in falſe worſhip. Heb.12.14.

Verſ.18. Hitherto of *Siſera* his going on foot to the houſe of *Iael*; now it is ſhewed how ſhe vſed meanes to bring him to his death: firſt, as is mentioned in this verſe. For ſhee went to meet him, and drew him in by faire and alluring words, and bids him not feare. Heereby (there is no doubt) hee was more throughly perſwaded, that hee ſhould bee ſafe there. But this was a traine to draw him to further danger, as we ſee by that which followeth, ver.21. And all this duely conſidered, with other things which ſhee did, mentioned in the text, causeth queſtion to bee made, whether *Iael* did well or no, in thus

deceiuing him. But that question is easily answered. For shee doing it to an enemy, not hers, but Gods; one that all Gods people ought, by vertue of his commandement to haue rooted out as they were able; in a word, a chiefe
Iudg.5.24. Canaanite, and shee blessed and praised of God for that which shee did. By all this I thinke, it is cleare shee offended not at least in the substance of the action. But this hath been answered before, by the like occasion in *Ehuds* example. But for vs who haue not the like commandement (except the ciuill Magistrate, and the lawfull executioner,) wee haue in no wise, liberty to follow her example, but to sticke fast to the rule that teacheth vs, to walke toward all men in vprightnesse, and all good simplicity and innocency, giuing vnto the worst their due.

THE TWENTIE NINE SERMON ON THE FOVRTH CHAPTER OF THE BOOKE OF IVDGES.

Vers.19.20.21. IT followeth of *Sisera*, who being very dry with trauelling on foote, and inward griefe heating him, desiring somewhat wherewith to quench his thirst, and shee gaue him liberally milke to drinke, which was fittest to bring him asleepe. But when he had well drunke, he forgets not the danger he was in, while such as passed by might be ready to aske after him there; and therefore hee diligently instructeth her to be carefull euery way for his preseruation and safety. By the giuing him drinke that he might fall asleepe, and so she might the more conueniently dispatch him by so good an opportunity, she shewed her readines to help cut off Gods enemies, and therin as wel to serue him as his Church,
Doct. vers. 19.20.21. which well appeareth in these three verses: and this thing in generall, wee all are bound to follow her in, though not in that particular manner.

Luk.16.8. For as God commended the vniust steward, for that he had done wisely in making prouision for himselfe, when he was put out of his stewardship; although he condemned his particular fact, in that he sought it by falshood and fraud: so is our godly care to helpe the members of the Church, and to resist the enemies of it, both are very commendable in vs, though we must beware of all vnlawfull meanes vsing, which tend thereto. Thus as *Debora*, *Barak*, and *Iael* wrought a wonderfull deliuerance for Gods people; so they who haue place and authority put in their hands by God, are bound to doe for the safety of the whole Church, if they will proue themselues faithfull and zealous. And priuate persons whose power cannot reach farre, ought to doe the same toward particular members of the Church, and that part of it where they dwell, so farre as they shall be able.

Of *Iaels* readinesse to cut off Gods enemy *Sisera*, and of her faithfulnesse

wee haue heard: now further in this 19. and 20. verſes is ſhewed how God Verſ.19.20.
did cauſe him to truſt *Iael*, and to put confidence in her for the hiding and
keeping him from his enemies. And as he did in this; when he purpoſeth e-
uill againſt wicked men, he commonly blindfoldeth them, takes away pro-
uidence and counſell from them, and ſuffereth them to chuſe that courſe to
follow in their liues and actions, which proues the vnhappieſt to them, euen
worſe oft times then their greateſt enemie could take againſt them; as I may
ſay of *Pharaoh* in his wilfull ventering on the ſea to follow after Iſrael: what Exod.14.28.
enemy could ſo much haue hurt him, as he did himſelfe. So that a wicked
man is neuer ſure of peace and ſafety when he is at the beſt; for the Lord is
able to defeate him firſt and laſt, euen many waies: for why? there is no
peace to the vngodly, as the Prophet ſaith; neither is there any counſell a- Eſa.57.21.
gainſt the Lord *Iehouah*. Againe, as hee truſted in her, ſo the Lord made her
deceiue and diſappoint him. Both which doe confirme vs in that which
hath now been ſaid, and teach vs, that when it pleaſeth him, hee leaueth the
wicked deſtitute of all helpe, and fruſtrate of their hope of ſucceſſe, or that
they put in their friends, yea and further, hee will make all his creatures to
worke againſt them. Which he doth, to ſignifie to them, that hee is againſt
them alſo. Which though hee teſtifie to them before by his word, which
ſaith, *the wicked are an abomination vnto the Lord*; and againe, the workers of i- Prou.1.5.9.
niquity doth hee abhorre; yet he ſeeing that his word is caſt behinde their Luk.13.27.
backes, doth therefore as it were, ſpeake to them by his creatures, and that as
ſenſibly (to ſuch as can iudge) as hee did to *Baalam*, in opening the mouth Note this. Numb.22.28.
of the dumbe Aſſe, and cauſing it to ſpeak to him, when he (ſeeking the wa-
ges of iniquity) would not haue heard the Lord ſpeake to him, nor enclined
his heart to obey him.

Thus doth God deale with vile and vnconſcionable men, that he will ſet
(as I ſay) not their friends onely, but euen the hoſt of heauen, and the crea-
tures of the earth againſt them. Thus *Saul*, when he had forſaked the Lord, 1.Sam.19.12.
could neither haue his daughter faithfull vnto him, to ſend *Dauid* his ene- 1.Sam.28.15.
mie to him, neither could he haue any Prophet of God to ſpeake to him in
his greateſt neceſſity and ſtraits, as his own words do teſtifie, he complaining
thus; I am in diſtreſſe, for God is departed from mee, and ſpeaketh no more
to me by Prophets, &c. Neither could *Senacherib* haue his ſonnes truſty to 2.King.19.37.
him, but was ſlaine of them, by whom he ought by nature to haue been de-
fended: yea and they did it in the Temple, while hee was worſhiping *Ni-
ſhroch* his god, in whom hee truſted, and looked alwaies for helpe from him,
and notwithſtanding he preferred him before the true and liuing God; yet
euen then he was diſappointed. Thus *Ammon* alſo and *Iezabel* were not ſe- 2.King.21.23.
cure from their owne ſeruants. And if it bee thus done to the mighty; how 2.King.9.33.
much more then to the meane, who haue leſſe helpe to ſtand by him? And
not onely their beſt helpes faile and deceiue them, but, as I ſaid, all things
are againſt them. Thus haileſtones helped Gods people to deſtroy their e-
nemies the Canaanites: *The Lord* (ſaith the holy ſtory) *caſt downe great ſtones* Ioſh.10.11.
*from heauen vpon them, and there were more that died of the haileſtones, then they
whom the children of Iſrael ſlue with the ſword.* So the waters, euen the riuer Ki-
ſhon deuoured this hoſt of *Siſera*. So *Abimelech* was ſlaine with a piece of a Iudg.9.53.
milſtone. *Abſalon* by an oke catching hold of his long haire, (his ornament) 2.Sam.18.9.

Numb 16. 31 32. 1.King. 20.30. *Chorah* swallowed vp of the earth. So a wall fel vpon seuen and twenty thousand *Aramites* that escaped the battell.

Iosh. 10.12. The Sunne also stood still in the middest of the heauen, and hasted not to goe downe for a whole day: and this was to the end it might the longer giue light, and bee an helpe to *Iosbua* and the people to auenge their enemies. And (to adde this one thing to the former,) I affirme, that there are not the meanest nor basest creatures, but they are harnessed as men of war, to fight in the Lords cause, and at his commandement, against the wicked, Exod. 8. and 9. & 10. chap. as the many plagues cast vpon *Pharaoh*, I meane the lice, flies, grashoppers, and the like, euen they (I say) may testifie. So that in this one respect, in that neither the friends of the wicked shall be faithfull to them, when God will otherwise haue it; and namely when they are vnfaithfull to him, but that he himselfe and his creature shall be armed against them, what can bee said lesse then this, euen woe be vnto them. But infinite are the other plagues that hang ouer them, and doe oft times meete with, and take hold of them: besides that they are euery houre in danger, when some kind of fearefull death or other shall sweepe them away to carrie them to their last and vttermost ruine. So that, as I note some of the wofull iudgements that hang ouer them, or be already vpon them; so if there were many more particulars set downe as they might bee, with the intolerable and most terrible paines of Note. the damned, one would thinke there were small cause, why any should flock to their company, or long and desire to be of them, and to taste of their dainties. And yet they are at this day, (which is so much the more to bee bewailed,) as the sand of the sea, and swarme in all places; that for my part (I say) when I cannot but know it to be so, and thinke vpon it, and what little hope Ier. 9.1. there is to reclaime the most of them; *Oh that mine eyes were a fountaine of teares, that I might weepe bitterly for the woe and losse of so many people.* If it seeme Rom. 9 27. Mat. 20.16. strange which hath been said of the multitudes of them that shall perish, the mouth of the Lord hath spoken it. Though Israel bee as the sand of the sea, yet but a remnant shall be saued. And although I censure not men by the mischances as they are called, that befall them (but are indeed the iust iudgements of God vpon them) sithence neither all wicked men are thus punished, nor all thus handled are wicked men: yet seeing this is the lot of the vngodly, and the portion of their cup which their wicked life hath brought vpon them, let none of them ease their stomacks by charging God, neither wash off all with crying out of their hard fortune and hap, as they count it; their onely hope (if any be) is to beleeue and bewaile it. Neither let the godly call into question the prouident care of their louing father, because they see that oftentimes these casualties and calamities betide them, but cleaue more firmely to the promises and the whole truth of the word, beleeuing that (seeing they are at amity and peace with the Lord) hee can make all creatures instruments of their good; and not onely their friends faithfull to them, both in heauen and earth; yea their very enemies to bee at one with them, and more trustie to them, then they are one to another. And if God thus tender their whole person, then their soules be pretious in Mat. 4.6. his eyes, and their bodies (no man doubteth) are also regarded of him, and both are safe vnder his protection.

An Obiect. **But now to speake a little of *Iaels* faithfulnesse, though a like point to this hath**

hath been handled, yet her action in alluring *Sisera* into her tent (with promise that he should be safe there, and bidding him not feare,) and yet murthering him afterward so cruelly (as it seemeth) this (I say) beside that I haue said of it, is thought to be so farre from the trustinesse which should bee in them, who vndertake the safety of those whom they receiue into their houses, that it is counted rather barbarous cruelty & trechery. And the more to vrge an answere hereunto, it is obiected, that it hath alwaies been as well the care as the credit of such as take strangers into their custodie, to see thē safely kept in their houses from annoyance and danger. *Iure hospitij*, as we say, that is, by the right due to them by those that receiue them. The example of *Lot* is alleaged, who for the defence of those strangers that turned in vnto him, offered much inconuenience to himselfe, and his daughters, that hee might free the strangers whom he receiued, from iniurie. The like is said of the care of that old man (mentioned hereafter in this booke) to the Leuite and his concubine, whom he had receiued as strangers into his house. Hereupon and by the like, it is concluded, that as it were by an vniuersall law, the promises that are made to strangers for their safety, should bee inuiolably kept. The very Barbarians shewed much kindnes in a like case, as wee reade in the booke of the Acts to *Paul* and his company entertaining them kindly, yea and did more also then that vnto them, for they laded them with necessaries at their departing.

Gen. 19.8. Iudg 19.23. Act. 28.10.

To all that hath been said of faithfulnesse to bee shewed to such as it is promised to, as *Iael* did: I answere, that I am of the same mind, that it ought to be so; and the Scripture doth straitely vrge the same. But yet wee must know, that no bands of familiarity and equity are so neerely ioyned together, and so iust, but that if God for causes best knowne to him, command otherwise, they are to bee broken. And so it may seeme to bee of this act of *Iael*. For seeing the Lord had now cursed, and commanded to be destroyed, these Canaanites, and *Sisera* their captaine, therefore neither shee nor any other might heere take vpon them to saue or spare them, but doe to them as God directed them, and so she did. Thus the Leuites followed and obeyed *Moses* in killing their friends and kindred, who had committed idolatry with the Calfe which they had made, and pleased God highly in so doing. In this respect, and by vertue of this commandement of God, *Abraham* went about to kill his sonne: and they that thinke foolish pitie ought to be shewed contrary to the word of God, let them remember what befell the King of Israel, who when hee had spared *Benhadad* the King of Aram, contrary to the word of God, was reproued by the Prophet at the cōmandement of God, in these words; *Because thou hast let goe out of thy hands a man whom I appointed to die, thy life shall goe for his life.* And therefore to returne to *Iael*, forasmuch as I see, that the Lord was the only gouernour of this worke, and commended her for it, in the next chapter, by *Debora*, yea pronounced her blessed, when the action of killing *Sisera* is spoken of; therefore I conclude, that she being certainly perswaded of Gods wil in that which she did, and commanded of God so to doe; her deceiuing of his hope, was no more sinne in her, then *Abrahams* attempt to kill his sonne was, or the Leuites sleying of their kindred for their idolatry. And this for answering the question. The doctrine hath been taught already, that wee haue no authority to follow

Answ. Exod. 32.27. 1. King. 20. 42. *The vse of the answere.*

follow her example, but the word, wherby our actions must be guided as by a rule, and by no example without it. Thus wee haue seene (as I said in the beginning of the chapter) that the Lord by *Barak, Debora*, and *Iael*, subdued *Sisera* with his huge armie.

It followeth:

Vers.22. *And behold, as Barak pursued after Sisera, Iael came out to meete him, and said, Come, and I will shew thee the man whom thou seekest, and when he came into her tent, behold Sisera lay dead, and the naile in his temples.*

Vers.23. *So God brought downe Iabin the King of Canaan that day before the children of Israel.*

Vers.24. *And the hand of the children of Israel prospered, and preuailed against Iabin the King of Canaan, vntill they had destroyed Iabin King of Canaan.*

The sense of these 3. verses. NOw it is shewed, how *Iael* came out to meete *Barak*, who not finding *Sisera* among those who were slaine, followed after him; and she told him what she had done vnto him, and thus she preuented *Barak*, lest hee should wearie himselfe with seeking him, and bee grieued when he found him not, and hee came into her tent, and found it so. And by *Baraks* pursuing him, it appeareth that *Sisera* was not deceiued in that hee feared it, and warned *Iael* to preuent it. Likewise it appeareth here, that the Lord deliuered his people out of the hands of *Iabin*, and destroied him. Here let vs note two or three things, and so come to an end of the whole chapter. And first, *Doct.* though *Iael* must imbrace and hold peace with *Iabin*, yet wee see her heart went not with him, neither did she like his crueltie and oppression of Gods people, but sought to turne it away, and she reioyced to see the people of God to preuaile, and to helpe them all that she could, as *Nehemiah* and *Ester* did, vsing their fauour they found with Kings, to this end. It teacheth, *Doct. vers. 22. 23.* that the godly doe giue good testimonie how they dislike it, when the wicked rule, and haue all in their hands: as *Iael* did here, by her worthie helping to beate downe *Iabins* and *Siseras* power. For (as *Salomon* saith) when they beare rule, the people sigh. And contrarily, what ioy they haue, when God *Prou. 29. 2.* giues them godly guides, and makes them to prosper, such as *Moses* and *Iosua* were, with other, who did more aduance the Lord and his true worship, as it became them, then they did themselues. And so it is in meaner estates, that we haue great cause to praise God, when he feebleth and disgraceth the vngodly, and prospereth the enterprises of his seruants, in any place of superioritie and gouernment, and so in meaner conditions. And let all such as are vnder them, glorifie God by bringing foorth much fruite, when they *Iohn 15. 9.* enioy such liberties, and let them feruently intreate (for much good may be done in such times) the Lord when it is otherwise, to change it: remem- *Psal. 122. 62.* bring that which is written in the Psalme: *Pray for the peace of Ierusalem, they shall prosper that loue thee, I will procure thy peace, &c.*

Doct. 2 out of all these verses. Further we may learne, that as *Barak* pursuing *Sisera*, as he was commanded, obtained a great blessing of God; so shall all that incline their hearts to *Psal. 19. 11.* follow the commandements of God with a pure heart. For it is the fruit of Gods promise, and he is not pleased, if wee walking wisely and diligently in our calling, doe not beleeue the same. For through vnbeleefe, wee depriue

God

God of his honour, and our selues of our owne due, which hee hath freely and graciously bequeathed vs. But contrarily, by giuing credit to God, and walking in a good course, (as frailtie will permit) we may in reuerence, and yet in confidence, looke surely for blessing, either outward with other, or at the least, the inward ioy of a good conscience, that is as continuall feasting, which is alwaies a companion in such a case. And therefore great pitie it is that wee should through our owne folly, at any time, depriue our selues of such a benefit. And especially this blessing wee may enioy by faithfull discharging of our duties, that as *Barak* here heard by *Iael* the good tidings concerning *Sisera* that she had slaine him; euen so, much good shall wee reape by the members of the Church to the gladding of our hearts: It is one of the fruites of well doing, which followeth it, as the shadow doth the bodie: as good report, and successe in things, and incouragement to goe forward. Whereas if our waies be crooked, and euill in the sight of the Lord, wee may looke for no better in places where we come, but to heare of that which will sting vs, as the coales of Iuniper. And from hence are many of the cries and complaints that we heare: for mens ill doings are rung about their eares, with reproch, threatnings of them, and such like, as doe make them take little ioy in their liues. So on the contrarie, many shall bee the comforts of them that doe well. And as *Iael* here did not a little glad the heart of *Barak*, by telling him of the death of *Sisera* the chiefe enemie of Gods people, while hee pursued after him; so it is the part and dutie of all Gods people to bring ioy and gladnesse to their brethren, as they are able, and to keepe sorrow and griefe from them by all meanes, as occasion shall be offered. And this should be one speciall fruite of the communion and fellowship of Gods seruants here on earth. But in as much as for all *Barak* pursuing of *Sisera*, yet he slew him not himselfe, but *Iael*. Here *Barak* saw the Doct.3.
word of God liuely verified, which *Debora* had spoken of vnto him before in the 9. verse, to wit, that the honour of that victorie should not go to him, but to a woman, as we see it did to *Iael*. And euen so, if we marke, we shall as cleerely see the same, when we haue offended against the Lord, that one or other chastisement shall meete with vs, and seaze vpon vs, and if it be not with vs after we haue sinned, as if an arrow should pearce thorow our liuer, Prou.7.23.
for the sorrow wee conceiue for it, be wee well assured it is behinde and to come, and in the meane while, or one time or other, wee shall carrie some marke of our disobedience, as *Barak* did here, for that was the word of the Lord that it should be so, as *Debora* said, I will goe with thee, but the honour of the victorie shall not be thine: as hath been noted before with the vse thereof.

Lastly, we may see by this subduing of *Sisera*, and destroying his mightie Doct.vers.24.
armie, how easily the Lord can breake the forces of his enemies, and pull downe, and turne away their wrath and rage from his people, (as a man would turne the riuers of waters, which way he listeth) or cut off their persons from the earth; and if it were not so, what good man could liue by them? And what a comfort that may be to Gods people, in that the Lord cuts off their enemies in due season, is not hard to conceiue, when we consider what a scourge and plague one man oft times is to another, being inraged and incensed, euen a wolfe, nay a diuell. But waight a little, and behold,

In

in time, the arrow of Gods deliuerance to his, and shame and confusion vpon his impenitent and implacable enemies, except (as is rather to bee desired) he change their hearts. But of this more largely before vers. 15. Thus much for this chapter: I will end this Sermon with the beginning of the next.

THE FIFTH CHAPTER ON THE Booke of IVDGES.

Vers. 1. *Then sang Debora and Barak the sonne of Abinoam, the same day, saying;*

Vers. 2. *Praise ye the Lord, for the reuenging of Israel, and for the people that offered themselues willingly.*

Vers. 3. *Heare ye Kings, hearken ye Princes, I, euen I, will sing vnto the Lord, I will sing praise to the Lord God of Israel.*

The summe and parts of this Chapter. THe summe of this Chapter is a praising of God by *Debora* and *Barak*, after the victorie.

The parts of it are three: the first is, one point of their song consisting in offering praises to God, to vers. 14. The second laieth out the goodnesse of God to Israel sundrie waies in this battell, and namely three: first, she bringeth in them that did helpe in it, to vers. 19. by occasion whereof, mention is made of such as did not helpe. Secondly, she sheweth how vnprosperously it fell out against the Canaanites in the battell, to vers. 23. Thirdly, the hinderers of the victorie from Israel, are cursed, and *Iael* that did helpe to get it them, is pronounced blessed, to vers. 28. The third part of the chapter sheweth how in their song they mocked the boasting of *Siseras* friends, to vers. 31. and so as an addition thereto, they shut vp the song with a prayer in the 31. verse.

The first part of the Chapter.

NOw to leaue the two last parts, to bee considered of in their due place, I come to the first, and that is their song, which containeth three things. The first that is in their song, is this; that they exhort the Israelites to praise God with them for those that offered themselues willingly to the battell, in the two first verses; and the Kings and gouernours, that were strangers, to heare what they said, and that is in the third verse. In the second part, and next verses following, they set downe the Lords mercies long before powred out on their fathers, and now lately to them in the deliuerance of his people, to the eighth verse, and exhort them to praise God who inioyed the commodities that came by the victory, to the twelfth verse. The third thing is, that *Debora* stirreth vp her selfe againe to sing praise to God, and *Barak* to the triumph, vers. 12. 13.

Doct. vers. 1. Now to begin with the first and second verses, wherein they exhort Israel to praise God with them, before they begin the song: for they enioyed the benefit of deliuerance, as well as they that got the victorie: It teacheth, that all such as receiue Gods benefits, doe owe this dutie of praise to him, and

and that the heart and the tongue, if it may be, ought to goe together in that action. The Lord looketh for it, and the Church hath alwaies practised it, Luke 17.17.
though not in a like manner. As *Moses* and *Miriam* did full solemnely at the Exod.15.1.
drowning of *Pharaoh* and his charets: so the women for the many victories that God granted to Israel, came foorth singing in this manner: *Saul hath killed his thousand, and Dauid his tenne thousand.* Likewise *Ezechias* after his 1.Sam.18.6.
recouerie, with *Anna* the mother of *Samuel*, and many other. And it was Isai.38.9.&c.
the vse and practise of Gods seruants to penne their songs, and often to repeate them, to quicken the memoriall of Gods benefits and his kindnes, in their owne and the hearts of other, and to knit themselues more neerely to him by this part of his seruice performed in Christ Iesus, according to his will.

Agreeable to this is the exhortation of the Apostle, *In all things be thankfull:* 1.Thess.5.18.
for as *Gods mercies are renued euery morning*, so good reason, that our Lamen.3.23.
thankes should be also. And as it is acceptable to God, so it is no small benefit that redoundeth thereby to our selues, for it drieth vp the bitternes that is readie to rise vp in vs by occasion of Gods afflicting vs, and crucifieth and scattereth such like poysons as lie lurking in our hearts; thankfulnesse, I say, Note.
chaseth them away, and suffereth them to haue no place there. Indeede it is proper to Gods people to offer to him this dutie, euen as it is said, *in Sion is God praised*, the hypocrites (as the Pharisie, who glosingly vttered these Psal.65.1.
words, *Lord I thanke thee, that I am not as other men*) they cannot praise him, Luke 18.11.
but the consent of mindes and hearts sanctified, as the sweete harmonie in Note.
musicke, this onely can doe it, and teach others the skill to doe it also. As therefore the thankes of most men (wanting the feeling of Gods loue and blessings) is meere dissimulation and taking Gods name in vaine: so it is much to be lamented, that the better sort (whom it would become so well) stirre themselues vp so little and slowly hereto. For thanksgiuing, as confession and supplication, should be seasoned and accompanied with feruencie, as a companion: which amplifieth and (as *Debora* here did) makes songs of the blessings which others passe ouer in silence: besides the affection it selfe, which is inlarged in a more then common manner, especially being quickned (as she here was) by some new or rare testimonie of Gods loue, either bodily or spirituall mercies, or deliuerances from euill of both sorts. But here we may say, Plenty makes vs barren: for though we haue so much cause of thankes, that we can looke on no side, but wee may see many: in so much as we be bound to shew it in things, yet most men know neither how to begin, nor to make an end. The daily benefit of health, recouerie out of diseases, protection from dangerous casualties, peace of land, and peace in familie, posteritie, thriuing in the world, credit, our haruests and commodities, nay our Sabbath and Communion, in the Gospell and the fruites of it; who (may it be thought) makes his daily song of these, adding hereto personall benefits, which euery one receiueth in his owne person. Many mens prayers consist of suite and request making to God, without any thankes either adioyned or following, as in the nine lepers is to be seene; others giue thankes in words, but they want wings to lift them vp to heauen, I meane, faith, feruencie and loue. And the best thinke it enough to mumble a little inward thankes, and that sometimes, for some blessings: but who is the man

of many, that makes his thankes breake out into songs? Songs are more then common praises. Christians should haue two bookes, in the one to record their faults and falles; in the other to register Gods benefits: both should serue to set them a worke in confession and thankes. For thankes neuer goe alone without other graces: A thankfull heart is patient also, humble, faithfull, conscionable, dutifull: by thanksgiuing we quicken vp our faith, zeale, feare of God, and renue our couenants daily: for how can wee dishonour him, when we professe our selues to be infinitly beholding to? This, besides that it iustleth out iangling, contention, and ill spending the time; so it drieth vp the froth of our euill hearts, fretting, discontentment, impatience, hardnesse of heart, and all of the same kinde, as I haue said. In a word, he that praiseth God aright, worships him aright, as we see in the Psalme: and so to say much in one word, he that is thankfull is a good Christian. Oh then let vs looke better to this, and make amends for our arrearages herein. For hee that lookes wee should bee thankfull for affliction, as that holy man *Iob* was, much more (a man would thinke) lookes that it should be so for blessings, which most iustly by many degrees do more chalenge it. Let euery one that of the Israel of God say, The mercies of the Lord continue for euer. Let it not seeme tedious to recount old mercies, both the greatest of redemption, and the lesser of preseruation: yea helpe we our selues forward mutually, as *Barak* and *Debora* here did sing in consort. Doubtlesse an vnthankfull life, is a sottish, hellish life, ouergrowne with all that naught is, and therefore lothsome to a Christian. He that saith, I would I could doe euery duty as well as this of thankes, is a foole, not knowing what he saith, he prates like a Parrot. Thankfulnesse is not without godlinesse. But I cannot well proceed further at this time.

[Margin: Note. — Psal. 50. 23. — Note.]

THE THIRTIETH SERMON ON THE FIFTH CHAPTER OF THE BOOKE OF IVDGES.

[Margin: Doct. 2. in vers. 1.]

WE haue heard largely of thanksgiuing in the former sermon with the causes, manner and necessity thereof; now beside the action of thanksgiuing, which I haue spoken of, the circumstance of time is also to bee marked; that is to say, that they did it the same day: for so it is set downe in the holy story: *then sang Debora and Barak the same day*. This teacheth vs not to make delay in any good thing, but vse the opportunity in due season, and so for this duty of giuing thankes. And while the occasion offered of so doing is fresh and in remembrance, the mind feedeth the affection with more plentifull matter, that it may be stirred vp more feruently to performe

forme that dutie: whereas in time things grow stale and are forgotten; yea and that quickly: so that wee had need to take the vantage against our bad memories, and blockish hearts, by such meanes. And although ordinarily we should performe this dutie, three times a day in solemne manner; namely in the morning, euening, and at noone tide, yet otherwise beside that, as God shall giue vs occasion by more then common benefits and deliuerances, we should prouoke our selues hereunto; and namely, as Saint *Iames* saith, when one is merrie or disposed to ioy, let him not suffer that affection to vanish, but expresse and vtter it to God in singing praises. And so afterward we ought to continue the memory of his infinite mercies throughout our whole life, and to this end write them, (we that can) that whereas they grow to a multitude in time, and all cannot alwaies be remembred, as were to bee wished in some sort; yet at least wise, when wee reade them ouer, wee may readily renue (as we shall see cause) our thankes to God for them. But great is mens blockishnesse, as I haue said, and endlesse wandring by swarmes of cogitations after other things, which hinder this, wherby they see not cause hereof; and when they doe, yet their slothfulnesse is such, that they delay and deferre to pay this due to God, till their appetite be gone, and afterward lets and hinderances comming in the way breake it off, so that they cannot performe it. And this be said of thankes. Psal 55 17. Note.

In the second verse shee shewes why God should bee praised: one cause was, for that he had been auenged of his enemies in the behalfe of the people, and for their sakes: for though hee had long vsed them as executioners of wrath against his disobedient people, yet now their sinne was come to the top, and his peoples sin was repented of; therfore their turne was come about now to be brought to punishment. Another cause of their thankes for the people Zebulun and Naphtali, who had willingly offered themselues to follow *Barak* against *Sisera*, although hee had no authority ouer them before. Both these are expressed in this verse, in these words; Praise ye the Lord, for auenging of Israel, and for the people that offered themselues willingly. Heereby wee learne, first, that God is the reuenger of the iniuries and wrongs of his people, euen as hee himselfe saith; *Vengeance is mine, and I will repay saith the Lord*: yea, *hee will doe it in his due time, and that right soone*: for so he saith, and we had need to marke it. If, saith he, the vnrighteous Iudge will doe right to the poore widow, lest shee troubling him with oft suing vnto him, should at last weary him: shall not God auenge his elect which cry day and night vnto him, yea though it bee long? I tell you hee will auenge them quickly, and recompence tribulation to them that trouble his, as the Apostle speaketh. Waite we therefore, hee hath not forgotten himselfe; but as the Wise man saith, *If thou seest the oppression of the poore, there is a greater then the oppressor*. But though there might much more be said of this point to the like purpose, yet who beleeueth these things? according to the words of our Sauiour, *When the sonne of man commeth, shall he finde faith on the earth?* teaching vs, how hardly men should beleeue, though hee gaue therein a fearefull watchword thereof, to all that should come after, which should make vs the better to looke to it: so this complaint may as iustly bee made still at this day, that wee are dull and slow of heart to beleeue this and such other truths as were vttered to vs by the Prophets and Apostles. Vers. 2. Doct vers. 2. Rom. 12. 19. Luk. 18. 7. 2. Thes. 1. 6. Eccles. 5. 7. Luk. 18. 8. Luk. 24. 25.

Apostles. But that is our woe and misery; for why should wee not rest quietly, while the Lord takes part with vs that are his children, and giues vs so faire and strong encouragement?

Doct. 2. in vers. 2. But let vs passe to the next point in this verse. The other thing in this verse is this, that the people should praise God for those that offered themselues readily and willingly to pursue Gods enemies, which teacheth, that such as doe the worke of God, should goe about it willingly

2. Cor. 9. 7. and cherefully. For as *he loueth a chearefull giuer*, so he doth a cheerefull doer of that which he commands: and contrarily, *Cursed is he that doth the Lords*

Ier. 48. 2. *businesse negligently*. It is therefore highly to bee reioyced in, and God much to be praised for it, where men are forward in Gods matters, and where the

Note. waightier and more excellent they bee, the more courage and delight men haue in the taking of them in hand. Among the which I reckon the preaching of the Gospell and the profession of it, with the duties of our particular callings, and such like, wherin to be forward & cheerful, as people be in hay and haruest, & in going to markets and faires; it honoureth God highly, and all such as behold it, ought to praise God heartily for giuing such gifts to men, as are rarely to be seene among them: for they that doe so, shew plainly that they looke for a reward from God, when they can goe roundly and readily about businesse, which other men so aukely goe about. For the most part men be too forward and ready to leaud company keeping, and to the sins of the time, and other workes of the flesh; but when they should obey the Lord, or bee set about any good worke, especially, whereof no profit is like to redound to them, they goe most aukely and vntowardly about it; euen as the euill debter, who is to do worke to his creditour to pay him. And therefore fearefull and grieuous is the sinne of those loose liuers, who if any bee forwarder and zealouser in Gods matters then other, in duty doing to him ward, them they mocke and discourage, who yet sinne grieuously, in that they be not companions with them. But of this the lesse, because I haue spoken of it in the former chapter. Thus much of this verse.

Vers. 3. Now in the next, in calling Princes and great persons to harken, as they doe in this verse; it is to teach them to know from whence their victories and all greatnes come, and to ascribe them to the Lord, according to Christs words in the prayer, [thine (O father) is kingdome, power, and glory for euer:] as for them, there is not the least iot of the praise thereof due to them, God honours them, in that he will make them his instruments therein, and furnish them with any gifts to that purpose, I meane, to doe him seruice. And yet as though they were of absolute power of themselues, forgetting the Lord that aduanced them, they ascribe their great acts and victories to

2. King. 19. 36. 1. King 20. 3. themselues: as *Senacherib* against *Hezechia*, and *Benhadad* against *Ahab*; yea and this they did both of them, before they had got the victory, and did not tarrie till they had conquered their enemies, and then crow ouer them, (which yet had been their great sinne) and prided themselues in that they had done, as *Nabuchadnezzar* in his Babell; and therefore they were put to shame, both of them most worthily, being themselues brought vnder in a manner fit for such braggers, as would thrust the Lord out from helping them; nay rather they challenged euen him, and opposed themselues against him, as is to be seene in the story of both. And therefore in one battell *Benhadad*

hadad lost an hundred and seuen and twentie thousand men, so that hee and his, euen a few that were left with him, were constrained to flie; and in the other battell, wherein very many of his men were slaine, hee was brought to greater shame and abacement, as his last refuge; to wit, his seruants to goe to the King of Israel with ropes about their necks, to entreate for their liues. And as for *Senacherib*, the Angell of the Lord slue an hundred foure score and fiue thousand of them in one night: and such successe, at least in the end haue all such, as are like to them. Hence it is that the Scripture (for the further bewraying the pride and vanity of such) vseth these phrases; *The Lord smote Beniamin before Israel. The Lord fought for Israel.* And againe, stand still and behold the saluation of the Lord, &c. And among other names the Lord is called, *strong in battell,* and the Lord of hosts. And surely if a sparrow fall not to the ground without his wil, neither is the lot without his disposition; much more doe the euents and hazards of warre depend vpon his prouidence, being oft times matters of as great weight, as the alteration of kingdomes and estates come to. Now if Princes must know their victories and honour are giuen them of God; then much more we inferiours ought to learne it well, that we are beggers, and haue nothing; nay wee are worse then nought, rather then that wee haue ought to glory of, as it would soone appeare, if we could be brought to consider aright of it, euen what infection is in vs to taint and poyson all our actions; or if the Lord should but thrust at vs for our euill deeds, but euen (as it were) with his little finger.

2.King.19.35.

Exod.14.13.

Besides, in this verse *Debora* declareth that shee will, yea (repeating her words) that she will praise the Lord; whereby it appeareth shee called *Barak* to it her selfe, and sheweth, that shee was so liuely quickened and stirred vp with the feeling of Gods goodnesse declared vnto them, that she would doe that dutie, if no other did. For as the whole Church of God fared the better for this victory; so she acknowledged her selfe a part, to haue receiued great benefit thereby also; and therefore as she was formost in the onset, so is shee first in thankesgiuing, and put not off the duty to the rest of the people, but rather goes before other therein. And indued so God worketh in his oft times, that his seruants are so rauished with thinking vpon his louing kindnesse, that they cannot bee satisfied with prayer and praise giuing to God in publike among other, but they must doe it also by themselues alone, as *Dauid* saith; I wil praise God in the congregation, and I wil praise him in secret: and they are so bent vnto it, that if other should not, yet they themselues, & as many as they can prouoke, will do it, as the noble man *Iosua* said; If al run to idolatry, I and mine will serue the Lord. And if we consider it well, how few weigh Gods goodnesse in publike blessings, (as in the late discouerie of the treason) although many praise God openly for fashion, and in ceremony, we shall find it no more then needeth, to practise this duty alone by our selues apart, as we reade of the tribes oft times, as well as among others; else would not our Sauiour haue willed vs to goe alone, euery one by himselfe into his chamber to pray, as *Isaac* also did in the fields, how little soeuer many be acquainted therewith; and therefore finde the lesse benefit by the prayers and thankesgiuing, which they make with others (they being in great likelihood made but in hypocrisie) or which others make for them. Euery mans owne soule best knowes what cause hee hath of thankes, better then

Doct.2.

Note.

Iosh.24.15.

Mat 6.6.
Gen.24.63.

then others, and accordingly let him professe it, though there bee not many which will be brought to it. And of *Deboras* first words in the song wherein shee stirred vp the Israelites to praise God, and the reasons why, thus much be said.

Vers. 4. *Lord, when thou wentest out of Seir, when thou departed out of the field of Edom, the earth trembled, and the heauens rained, the clouds also dropped water.*

5. *The mountaines melted before the Lord, as did that Sinai before the Lord God of Israel.*

6. *In the daies of Shamgar the son of Anath, in the daies of Iael, the high waies were vnoccupied, and the trauellers walked through by-waies.*

7. *The townes were not inhabited: they decayed, I say, in Israel, till I Debora came vp, who rose vp a mother in Israel.*

The summe of these verses, and more particularly the fourth and fifth verses.

IN the first of these two verses, which also containe the beginning of their song, *Debora* setteth downe the Lords great mercy in one example to her forefathers the people of Israel, which had been shewed long before: in the latter two, shee maketh mention of his goodnesse toward them at that very time present. In the great deliuerance mentioned in the former chapter, but more particularly to speake of both, and to begin with the first in the fourth and fifth verses, we are to know, that this story mentioned by her, containeth the acts that were done by the Lord, after he brought the people of Israel beyond mount Seir, when Israel (38. yeeres after their going out of Egypt into the desert) were come neare to the land of Canaan: namely, how wonderfully the Lord tooke part with his people there, and ioyned himselfe vnto them against their enemies. For he going with them in a pillar of fire and a cloud, did terrifie their enemies the Ammorites in such wise, that though the Israelites were vnexperienced in warre, and strangers there, and were weake and vnfit also for such worke, yet their enemies could not resist them: and not onely so, but she saith, that the Lord cast such a feare vpon them, as if the earth had trembled, and great stormes and tempests had been cast downe from the clouds, and as if the mountaines had melted, and been shaken. By these allegoricall speeches she describeth the feare that was smitten into the Amorites at Israels comming neare them, when the Lord brought them out of Egypt. And further shee addeth to the same end, that euen as mount Sinai (for so it must bee vnderstood, though the word (like as) bee not expressed) at the Lords comming downe vpon it, was shaken and moued; so did the nations at the comming of Israel feare, and were terrified.

And in laying out Gods kindnesse thus towards her fathers long before shewed to them, as commonly this is reckoned to be one, that he brought
Iosh.24.2.&c. Iudg.2.1. them out of Ægypt thorow the fearefull wildernesse to Canaan, in many other places of the Scripture: her meaning is, to declare that hee shewed not this fauour now of late onely to them who liued at that time, but of old and
Doct. vers. 4.& 5. long agoe also to his people in former ages, as they stood in need of his aide diuersly, and that for their sakes also. And if wee obserue the Scriptures, (which are a glasse of Gods administration and gouerning of his Church) wee

we shall see that there is little mention made of other nations of the earth, or their affaires, but the bent of them is wholly (as it were with a streight line) directed to the Churches vse and benefit, as either to punish or blesse them for his people sake. To this his Church all his workes of loue, mercie, iustice, wisedome, prouidence, are referred: for though God be the Sauiour of all, yet especially of the faithfull in his Church. From whence wee are to learne, that God hath in all ages bin bountifull and gracious to his Church, as well as now; euen to our forefathers in their daies, and so from age to age as it is written, his mercie endureth for euer. For it hath been deare to him, as the spouse or bride to the Bridegrome. And his loue hath been more hot then fire that cannot be quenched with much water. And to this end, hee hath been so affected to it, that it might know that he loueth it: as hee saith in Exodus: *If ye will diligently attend to my voice, and keepe my couenant, ye shall be my chiefe treasure in all the earth, though all the earth be mine.* A doctrine most needfull to be made vse of among vs, seeing his people be as deare to him now, as in any age past, and he did neuer so cleerely testifie his loue to his Church in any generation heretofore since Christ, or before, as hee hath done to this. Exod. 19.5.

And if it were beleeued, and wee throughly perswaded of it, there were nothing like to draw vs more neerely to Christ, nor to set our hearts and delight vpon him, then the oft and due meditation and thinking on it: whether we speake of those who are in Christ alreadie, or of such as lie yet in vnbeliefe, to draw and perswade them. For these should be better incouraged by many degrees more then they be now, to labour to taste how good the Lord is: and they who haue alreadie begun, should breake through all lets and difficulties (which doe much hold them backe) farre more easily then now they doe, to be vnited more neerely vnto him their head. Whereas it may be spoken with griefe, that in stead hereof, many professing well, euen where Gods loue is made knowne, doe cleaue to the pleasures of sin, profits and preferments, howsoeuer come by, rather then to striue to enter in at the streight gate: and the best are too backward, considering that if we haue any treasure in heauen, our hearts must needs be there also set on heauenly things: but they who mind earthly things aboue other, which should be all in all with them, and doe as seldome thinke rightly of either of both, and yet would be thought to doe otherwise, are no beautie but a blemish to the Christian life. Oh how lamentable is it then, that so many still remaine! (as the old world out of the Arke, and the latter world out of the Common-wealth of Israel) so these euen as aliants from the Church. For though all crie, The Church, The Church, because they heare there is no mercie, blessing, or saluation out of the Church; yet as if Baptisme were sufficient, they seeke not the priuiledges of the Church; effectuall calling, faith, charitie and sanctification, and the fruites thereof; and therefore they are still little better then the scumme and offscouring of the common band of the wicked; who hauing no title, no promise, no God, no hope, but are out of Gods precinct and gouernment: and therefore wee may say of these, The Church is wanting in the Church. All Gods mercie, and whatsoeuer is excellent in him, are out of their reach; no such priuiledges appertaine vnto them, because they are not separated from the wicked, whom the soule of the

Doct.2. the Lord abhorreth. Againe, in that God made the enemies afraid of his people at their comming thither, it was his great loue toward them to honour them so highly among those who contemned and hated them: and if hee had not so fauoured and taken part with them, they had been vtterly discouraged, and ouerwhelmed by them. And he would teach vs thereby, that though his children be basely esteemed, and contemptible among the prophane worldlings, who are busily set to follow their pleasures and profits, scorning religion as too base for them, yet he makes them oft afraid of them, when it pleaseth him, and their consciences doe accuse them, that seeing their own waies are euill, and that the others good, & do please him, that they shall come to iudgement, when the other shall lift vp their heads and
Mark.6.20. reioyce. Therefore it is said, that *Herod feared Iohn* Baptist, and when he had beheaded him, yet hearing that Christs fame was great a little after, hee was afraid that he had been *Iohn*, and that he was risen againe from the dead, to be reuenged of him. So when the iudgement of God fell vpon *Ananias*
Acts 5.11.12. and *Saphira* for their dissembling, and the people saw that God did honour his Apostles, and magnifie their ministerie among many, it is said that great feare came vpon the wicked, who knew that they liued not after the Apostles doctrine, neither liked their course: insomuch, as they durst not through an accusing conscience, ioyne themselues to them whom God honoured, for feare least they should haue been brought foorth openly, and bewrayed by some iudgement of God, for their halting, as *Ananias* was. So *Felix*
Acts 24.25. though he were *Pauls* Iudge, yet trembled, and was afraid, when hee heard him boldly to preach of iustice and temperance, meete for his place, but farre from him, and of the iudgement to come; and yet *Paul* himselfe was then without all feare thereof. *Sehon* and *Og* trembled, and were afraid, to see the high hand and outstretched arme of the Lord, wherewith Israel was carried.

It was not for naught, that the Lord expostulated so with the man who
Matth.22.12. came among those that were bidden to the feast, not hauing on his wedding garment: saying vnto him, What doest thou here without it? for the man was euen speechlesse, and could not for feare and astonishment vtter his words. The Lord will haue all such to know, that the companie of his faithfull people is not for the prophane, and for scorners; by the which example, and many other such, he hath (as it were) put a bridle in the mouthes of many, that though they despise Gods people, yet they shall not be without feare of them: and therfore he cast the dread of his people vpon them,
Note. as here it is said. And hath it not been seene in the late persecution of the Protestants in this land in the time of Poperie, which some yet aliue can testifie to be true, that many of the persecutors were more terrified in hearing their answers to them, and beholding the boldnes and courage that was in them, then the Martyrs themselues were terrified by their sentence of death read and pronounced against them. And be we no lesse assured of this, that many ill disposed people, who would wish that there were neither God, nor iudgement, nor any better liuers then themselues, yet they are constrained oft times to say, the godly life is best, and yet fret to see it in the practisers of it, being void of it themselues. Oh therefore, happie is the people whose God is the Lord *Iehoua*, and blessed are they that haue him for their King.

And let this vphold, content, and delight all such, though they seeme to be the vilest and most miserable of all other, God will not forget their longing to be dissolued, and to be with him, and know they, while they doe so, their worst day in the week shall be farre better, then the others best in the yeere. And howle ye despisers, and tremble and vanish away, for that ye see, great is their portion, whom ye hate, with the Almightie, and your selues cast out of his fauour and habitation; and euen so in your aduersitie & day of Gods visiting you (as *Diues* in hell had sense thereof) ye doe acknowledge it. The old world scoffed at *Noah* his building the Arke, till the flood came, and then his former preaching terrified them. In like manner, I say, if we walked in our innocencie with vprightnes and reuerence among men, the Lord would worke astonishment in the wicked and reprobates, and the very godlinesse of his people should conuince and amase the beholders and contemners, as *Pharaos* troopes were, when they said, *The Lord fighteth against vs for Israel.*

Act.13.41.

Exod.14.25.

The next verses I referre to be handled in the next Sermon.

THE THIRTIE ONE SERMON ON THE FIFTH CHAPTER OF THE BOOKE OF IVDGES.

verſ.6.7. *The more cleere meaning of the.*

NOw (to goe forward) these two next verses are the sixth and seuenth: wherein is set downe their late receiued fauour of God, as in the two former verses, his loue of old to their fathers hath been spoken of. In these two, to the end that this their deliuerance by the Lord may be seene to be the greater, and his loue to them, she laieth out the desolation that they were in before the victorie, that one contrarie might the better be seene by the other. The holy Ghost therefore sheweth, in what afflicted state the Church of God was by reason of their sinne, and that from the death of *Ehud* till *Debora* got the full victorie. For though *Shamger* and *Iael* did worthily and valiantly in their place, yet Israel was sore oppressed after the death of the one, and before the great act of the other; so as passage by the high waies, traffique, iudgement, and habitation in their villages, were intercepted vntill now: and Israel was constrained to keepe themselues in strong and well fenced Cities, vnlesse they would become a prey to the Canaanites. And this oppression continued by *Iabin*, till *Debora* was raised vp by God, and till her gouernment began. Of *Iael* we reade not of any great thing that she did before, neither is it like that she had done any, because she had peace with *Iabin*, and *Sisera* also fled to her as to a trustie friend, and therefore it is like that she is named with *Shamger* for honour sake, because she shee liued in these troublesome and dangerous times, and because shee did one worthy peece of seruice afterwards.

Doct. And heere by these calamities of the people of Israel, and the desolation that they had been in, when all good liberties and pleasant things were taken from them, it is right worthie our consideration, to thinke what a fauour of God it is, that together with the true preaching of the Gospell, all the forementioned commodities are enioyed of vs; namely, outward peace in the land, and that we may *dwell safely vnder our vine and figge tree*, and may eate of the fat, and drinke of the sweet, that wee may safely trauell and passe throughout all places and countries of this dominion, by the protection of good lawes, and that we haue exchange of our commodities with the benefit of good neighbourhood, and husbandry, to the preseruation of our liues, and the maintaining of our families, &c. All these this people had been depriued of; whereas the want of any of them would soone driue vs to complaine heauily, and cry out. Oh we do little consider how deepely, yea how infinitely wee are bound to to the Lord for these liberties, and for the great good wee may reape and enioy thereby. And yet these many good things which the Lord hath vsually bestowed vpon vs, and daily doth, (blessed bee his holy name therefore) wee thinke because all the land enioyeth them as well as our selues, wee owe no speciall duty of acknowledging them, more then we see the most doe, which is not worth the speaking of; nay we looke for them by due and good right; and which is worst of all) many do spend them wastfully, and to the maintaining and encreasing of diuers sinnes among them, which we durst not do if wealth and quietnesse were wanting: so truly the Wise man speaketh of one of them; [the rich mans riches are his strong city, and as an high wall in his imagination. And in a word, we haue so little leisure to thinke of God his goodnesse, that by abusing his benefits wee hast to bring vpon our selues the same misery which these were in, vnder, and especially after this *Shamgar*, and before God stirred vp this *Debora* among them.

1.King.4.25. Nehem.8.10. Note. Prou.18.11.

Oh, how doe we prouoke our good God to cast vs into some sore calamities, as they heere were in, that we might cry to him by feeling the smart thereof, as some daily doe, whom God would haue to bee examples to the rest, lest many should tast of their diet? but fearefull it is for all this, to see how few are the better for all the iudgements of God that bee vpon themselues, or that they behold others for the same sinnes which they both commit boldly, but runne on till their course come to suffer (yet) worse and heauier things at Gods hands for them. But while wee cannot amend it in others, let vs bewaile it in them, which is a right property of true loue; praying also for them, and for our owne parts; let this example of these their calamities, so many and grieuous as haue been spoken of, cause vs to account of Gods goodnesse so highly, in withholding them from vs, that they may make vs fruitfull thereby in euery good worke, especially seeing wee haue many other good encouragements thereto: and also for that when wee want them, we say wee can doe little good without them. But now in that shee addeth, *Till I, euen I Debora arose*] we must take it farre otherwise then it soundeth; not ascribing her words to a passion of womanish impotencie and boasting, much lesse to a contempt of *Barak*, who was the instrument of the

The clearing of the next part of the verse.

the victorie, as well as her selfe; but to the heauenly exaltation of her spirit, lifted vp pathetically to praise the Lord for the great deliuerance wrought by her: as we see the like in *Dauid*, in the Psalmes; *Paul*, and others. And this deliuerance being wrought by *Debora*, teacheth, that al the forementioned calamities, being remoued from the people, by her their gouernour at that time, it teacheth I say, what great things the Lord worketh by the Magistrate and gouernour, as he did by her, shee being at that time the same to the people, euen their Iudge in Israel. But indeed this is done especially when they are zealous for Gods matters, and doe their duties in their places, and haue the spirit and affection of her, euen to be mother like vnto the people, who as shee gaue counsell to her inferiours, as a mother to her children, being a Prophetesse, and deliuered them from their enemies, being their Iudge: So they being set ouer them, as guides and Magistrates, should bee vnto them who are committed to their charge, euen like minded to her, to wit, to haue care that they may be taught, though they be themselues no Prophets, by such as are furnished of God to that purpose: and with a motherly care to protect them from iniurie and wrong, and to turne the edge of the sword against their enemies. And thus much of Gods mercies of old, and lately shewed on his people, as in these 4. verses hath been declared. But it followeth. *Doct.2.*

Vers. 8. *They chose new gods, then was warre in the gates. Was there a shield or speare seene among the forty thousands of Israel?*

9. *Mine heart is set on the gouernours of Israel, and on them that are willing among the people, praise ye the Lord.*

10. *Speake ye that ride on white Asses, ye that dwell by Middin, and that walke by the way.*

11. *For the wife of the archers appeased among the drawers of water: there shall they rehearse the righteousnesse of the Lord, his righteousnesse towards his townes: then did the people of the Lord goe downe to the gates.*

THe holy story hauing set downe the peoples deliuerance out of their great calamity and oppression from *Siseras* army, goeth on in this eighth verse, and sheweth the cause why they were cast vpon them, and that was for their idolatry, by meanes whereof (it is said) they had no heart to take vp weapon, no not any of them throughout all the tribes, against their enemies. In the next three verses, all sorts are stirred vp and called to praise God, that tooke benefit by the victory and deliuerance, as shall bee particularly shewed, when I shall come vnto them by the order of the text. Now to begin with the eighth verse, *Barak* and *Debora* vtter this in this part of their song, that then the warre began to oppresse the Iewes, and the enemies to besiege their cities and gates, where they held their Iudgement seates, when they had turned to idolatry: so that this was the cause of their grieuous punishment. *The sense of the eighth verse.* *The summe in generall of the other three.*

By the which we may see how greatly God is displeased with men, when they will runne after the sins that they haue been forewarned of, and commanded to take heede of; (euen the sinnes which his soule abhorreth) as Israel had oft times been admonished of this Idolatry. The Lord will not *Doct in vers.8.*

put

put it vp at their hands. And who can denie, but that it standeth with most sound reason, that when men, who are but vile wormes, shall thus boldly kicke vp their heele against their maker, they should smart for it, and not be suffered to commit such insolencie against him vnpunished? And therfore he gaue vs examples hereof in the Apostate Angels, *which kept not their place* that he set them in, and therefore that he threw them downe for their disobedience: and in our first parents whom hee draue out of Paradise, when they hauing so great liberty, as they might haue eaten of any fruit in the garden except one tree; yet counted all little, in respect of that which was forbidden them, and stood on thornes, till they had cast behinde them the commandement of God, and eaten of that forbidden fruit also. Now if God spared not the Angels, and our first parents, who were innocent before that their fall, what may other offenders looke for? whose sinnes are as the haires of our head in number?

Iude 6.

Gen. 3. 24.

Note.

And in that he dealeth not thus with wilfull transgressors at this day, it is not for that he should be vniust or carnall in so doing, but he beareth much with them, as all may easily see, and is patient toward them, to this end that he may thereby bring them to repentance; which if any abuse, they pay for all their boldnesse in the end; in so much that hee who speedeth best, shall haue small cause to brag of his winnings. And yet he shoaleth out some one of an hundred, heere and there, (not many indeed in comparison of those who haue offended in that kind) whom he striketh by and by with deadly blowes, and setteth him on the stage, to publish, as it were, by his wofull example to all the rest; (though he bare longer with some other, for the cause before alleaged, what he might doe to them, yea and in perfect iustice execute vpon them. And therefore let all that are wise take warning, while they hold a good course, to continue it, and they that are out of it, hast speedily vnto it: and let none tempt God boldly, to doe that which he forbiddeth, for he will not be mocked, they shall pay deare for their so doing. And yet though God spare them from outward warre and iudgements for a time, yet as the Prophet *Esay* speaketh, that there is no peace to the vngodly; so they may be sure they shall haue warre with him in their minds. And let all praise God, to whom he giueth an heart to shunne the euill and sinnes of the time in which they liue. And for the idolatry of the Church of Rome, I may say most of the Papists doe wilfully and malitiously erre against the truth; and some for their pompe and bellie, and many doe it of meere superstition, and blind deuotion, and custome, as they receiued it of their forefathers; seeing they that least offend therein among the rest, doe put Christ out of office in their seruice they giue him, and honour him as their King, but with a crowne of thornes, and a scepter of a reed in his hand; bee it knowne vnto them, that their damnation sleepeth not, their woe is at hand: And that they may partly gather by the vncomfortable, yea fearefull death of many Papists and great masters, and maintainers of popery who for all the boldnes in their life time, whereby they beare out matters; yet when they must die, some cry out they are vndone, other cry out of their religion: and but for the hardnesse of their hearts, it would be seene in more of them. And no maruell, seeing they try not their estate what it is? This being obserued, that the greatest offenders among them shall smart most. But yet this

Rom. 2. 4.
2. Pet 3. 9.

Note.

this I will say, that for all their deuotion and fast cleauing to the Church of Rome, if it please God, that if they might bee brought to heare the sermons of learned and religious preachers, and to admit of their conferences, many of them would renounce that trumpery, as standing vpon rotten props, and embrace the truth of the Gospell stablished so strongly.

And further, in that it is said that they could not take vp a weapon against their enemies; no, they had no heart to handle shield or speare, because of their sinne, as idolatry, and other enormities; it plainely shewes, that mens *Doct.2.* sinne turneth euery thing out of course against them, and contrary to the nature, vse and end, for the which it is created and appointed of God: euen as this people durst not take weapon in hand to fight for their liues, their consciences accusing them, that God would be against them. Wherefore is the weapon ordained, but for a mans defence against his enemie? and why hath God giuen courage to man, but that at such a time, I meane of warre, and other necessity, it might be put to vse? But behold heere was neither of both imployed or set a worke, any more then if they had not beene at all. When *Achan* had troubled Israel, by taking the execrable thing, the Lord tels *Ioshua*, that therefore they could not stand before their enemies. How Iosh.7.12. much more if they themselues had sinned? Oh mens sinnes turneth plenty Note. into want, courage into timerousnesse, and fainting of heart; and light into 1.King.13.4. darkenesse, and all out of kind. Behold what it did in *Ieroboam*; when hee stretched out his arme against the Prophet of God, for reprouing him for his idolatry at Bethel, his arme was immediately withered and dried vp, that he could not draw it in againe. So *Gehazi* when he had taken most wicked- 2.King.5.25. ly both money and raiment of *Naaman* the Syrian, pretending his masters sending him for it, and after his returne had answered his master *Elisha* with a lie; maruellous it is to say, and against nature and any sound reason in mans iudgement, what came vpon him, euen a leprosie forthwith, so that he went out a leaper as white as snow. And the band of Priests, Iewes, Ioh.18.6. and souldiers, that came into the garden to apprehend and take our Sauiour Christ, so boldly and trecherously, yet suddenly they went backe like drunken men, and fell to the ground astonished, and vnfitted vtterly, for such a purpose as to lay hold of him, and that at one word spoken by our Sauiour and yet not in terrifying manner, as he might haue done, saying: he was the man whom they sought. So that in seeking him, they were both lusty and ready to lay hold of him, yet when they had found him, they could doe nothing to him: for their sinne had taken their power and ability from them. For who is able to reckon vp how many waies God hath to visit, astonish, and terrifie men for their sinne? Therefore among other punishments in Deuteronomy threatened, this is one, a trembling heart, a sorrowfull mind, Deut.28.65. and feare both day and night. And if the Lord should not handle some thus, other would not bee afraid, but would abuse his Maiesty, yea and faithfull people also much more grosly would tempt God, then now they dare doe, though euen now many doe it too boldly, when they forget themselues. But Hypocrites goe verie farre in sinning boldly, as other doe who are like them; therefore many are apalled among vs, some hauing their wit and reason taken from them; some become foolish, some madde men; other Note.

against nature, laying violent hands vpon themselues; their seuerall sinnes doe (though no reason of man seeth it) doe (I say) driue them to it. This is another fruit to be ioyned to the former, which sinne bringeth forth. True it is indeed, the Lord dealeth not thus in kind with all sinners: nay wee see how impudent and brasen faced most bee in their leaud courses, and set vp their bristles against the ordinance of God. But though their foreheads bee of brasse, yet their hearts be glassie, their consciences (if they would yeeld) are as water powred forth: they haue not the true Lion like courage and boldnesse which in their iollity they would haue all thinke that they haue, but sin hath infeebled them, they cannot abide the force and sting of their conscience, but fall downe coward-like, when it smiteth them: neither can their sinne abide the hand of God, which as it is euer readie to be reached foorth against them; so when it is so indeed, they are soone dismaied, as *Nabal* was, when he heard he should dye. True it is, they set a good face vpon the matter openly, bragging and bracing, as I haue said: but when their conscience and they goe to it hand to hand (as it doth but seldome) then in their necessitie it is with them, as if an armed man were vpon them; their white liuerd hearts doe vtterly faile them. And yet where is he, that by such checkes of the word, and his conscience, and the feare of many arrestings of him from God, doth once complaine and crie out of his estate, and so seekes strength and recouerie out of it, by faith, peace, and confidence, with the true detestation of his sin, which like a Witch so inchaunteth and disableth him of all courage and boldnesse, and turnes him into a very coward and weakling? Now in that men doe not perceiue this, as they might easily do, their blindfolding of themselues, and hardning of their hearts, is the cause thereof.

Verse 9.10.11. *The laying open of these verses.* Now *Debora* turneth her selfe to diuers kinds of men, and distinguisheth them one from another, exhorting them all, as she her selfe did, to praise and magnifie God. This I will lay open more plainly, it being somewhat hard otherwise for some readers to vnderstand, and discerne the same. And first in this verse she beginneth with the chiefe of the armies, and those that offered themselues willingly to the battell. In the next verse, she speaketh to the rich Merchants that rode on costly beasts, that were, as hee calleth them, white Asses, and such as sat in iudgement. And thirdly in this same verse also, she speaketh to all meaner persons that trauailed on foote, seeing there was now libertie for them to passe to and fro in the high waies, she moueth these (I say) to magnifie God: Euen all sorts of people who went out and in by the gates of the citie for their businesse, profit, pleasure, or any other necessarie vse. In the second verse, she nameth the very boyes and girles, who could not safely goe out to draw water, without danger of the archers, who lay in waite secretly to shoote at them, and so put them in perill and ieopardie of their liues, or to be sore wounded; these might now (she saith) fetch their water without feare of hurt. Then she calleth to them who dwelt in villages and vnwalled townes (their danger hauing been very great, so as they were driuen away from their houses) telling them that they might now returne home againe, and dwel in them quietly as in times past: and last of all, she speakes to those who were wont to meete in the gates of the

the citie,that is,in the open places for iudgement. All theſe ſhe moues to praiſe the Lord, for that he had now, by that one deliuerance and victorie, ſet them all at libertie,and in peace.

Now to make our profit of theſe verſes,and more particularly to examine them,and to begin with the ninth; whereas ſhe ſaith in this verſe, that her heart was ſet on the gouernours of Iſrael, or (which is all one) her heart was toward them to prouoke them: meaning, the cauſe was ſo great why they ſhould praiſe God, that ſhe could not chuſe but ſpeake to them: as if ſhe ſhould ſay, ſhe deſired moſt earneſtly that the chiefe of the armie, and the gouernours and captaines thereof, and great men, ſhould praiſe God: the reaſon was, becauſe they, with her and *Barak*, were the chiefe in that buſineſſe, and they going before them, the other ſhould the eaſiler be drawne by their example to follow. And it liuely teacheth, and ſetteth before the chief doers in ſuch martiall affaires, alſo the wealthie, and heads in ſocieties, that they ought to be the firſt in giuing good example, both of praiſing God, and in other commendable parts of Chriſtian dutie. For why? The greateſt haue a greater portion in Gods bleſſing and deliuerance, then the meaner haue: I meane, they enioy much, and haue much to loſe, and therefore they owe much while they enioy all in peace. And ſecondly, it is a goodly ſight to behold Captaines in warre, and Gouernours and Magiſtrates in peace; and more particularly (to deſcend lower, and to come neerer the Commons) Headboroughs in townes, and the fathers of families, to be lights in religion and holy practiſe, to the reſt, and examples in the ſeruice of God: and the inferiours to follow, euen as the flocke followeth the bell-weather: for they are both ſoone diſcouraged by their backwardnes, and haue need of ſetting forward, as by incouragement and good example they are eaſily brought to be. Doct.verſ.9.

Therefore the Lord in giuing charge to all by their families, that they ſhould remember to keepe holy the Sabbath; beginneth with the gouernour thereof, ſaying, firſt thou ſhalt doe it; then hee goeth forward to the ſonne, daughter, and ſeruant: Euen ſo on the contrary, and much more, when the greateſt perſons goe before the reſt in ill example, we ſee how readily they follow. So wee reade, that the Prieſts, Leuites, and guides of the people were the chiefe and firſt in taking to them and their ſonnes, ſtrange wiues of the Amorites and Canaanites, againſt the commandement of God, and then many of the people followed them therein, when they were returned out of the captiuitie. Euen ſo wee might ſee it throughout, if I ſhould alleage many examples. And ſo God be thanked, in ſome ſort wee ſee, that where the chiefe men in any ſocietie, be forward in ſeeking knowledge, and be zealous in flying euill, and reſiſting it, as their places will giue leaue; and in following a good courſe, their care and labour is not in vaine, but to good purpoſe: but where the guides of other, as their Miniſters, maſters of families, and chiefe in townes, are prophane, lewd, ill company keepers, idle, gameſters, make-bates, contentious and ſlanderers, there yee may bee ſure to finde them that are led by them, and that depend vpon them, to be ſutable. But otherwiſe, if they ſee that the winde blowes againſt them, then they hang downe the head, and are nipt in the bloſſome, and containe themſelues. And here ſee a note of difference betwixt the godly and the *Command.4.* *Ezra.9.2.*

 lewd.

Iosu.24.15. lewd. The one, with *Ioshua*, vndertaketh for himselfe and his, they will serue the Lord. The other, like those Pharisies, are not onely ill disposed themselues, but doe also pull backe, and pluck downe, with them, as many as they can, from the best orders and companies. And while men must liue with such, rare is he, who (in such a case) is a law to himselfe, and can keepe his resolution, rather to serue God alone, then to giue ouer for want of companie. But if any be better disposed then other among them, they must fetch their light from other places, for the most part, or else bee in danger in the companie they come into, to lose that little they haue, and to be led into darknesse.

The opening of the other part of the verse, and the Doct.2. Now *Debora* hauing spoken of the chiefe, doth by that occasion descend to name and mention the meaner sort of the armie, to wit, the two tribes of *Naphtali* and *Zabulon*, who were willing to take that worke in hand against the Canaanites, and were easily drawne to put to their helpe, as appeareth chapt.4.10. They therefore being so forward in so good a cause, and thereby reaping so happie a fruite of their labour, that is, victorie ouer their enemies, euen they (I say) lose not their due commendation, but are brought in here by *Debora*, as the woman in the Gospell who powred ointment on our Sauiour, of whom he said this: *Wheresoeuer the Gospell should be preached, that which she had done to him, should be spoken of.* So the people that honoured God in this worke, are praised by her: which was also to their comfort. *Dauid* saith of seafaring men, that they could best speake of Gods wonders in the deepe: so these being eye witnesses, nay, instruments, and helpers forward of this deliuerance, might best (by experience) speake of the goodnes of God therein, and so (no doubt) did honour him for it, and therfore God would honour them, by regestring their memorie: euen so there is nothing lost, that we doe at Gods commandement, and for his sake, he is a plentifull paimaster and rewarder. But in that both chiefe and meane, were to praise God for the victorie, she calleth thē to a renouncing of their owne strength, or boasting of their owne arme, which possibly they might haue done, and

Heb.2.6. Doct.3. in vers.9. to ascribe all to God: as indeed she might well; for what were a few of two of the meanest tribes of *Zabulon* and *Naphtali* able to doe against the entire forces and mightie armie of *Iabin?* euen so, they that are forward in Gods businesse, vnlesse they grossely forget themselues, they are readie to honour and praise him, which cannot be without their owne comfort. For these two agree well together, that where there is readinesse to obey God, there is the like in praising him, and abasing of our selues, and that also accompanied with ioy of heart. And as it was heere with *Debora*, so she sought to haue it with them: and the same we see in *Dauid*, when hee being aduised by *Abigail*, not to shed innocent blood, he being easily perswaded by her counsell to forbeare, did so, and after it praised God highly, and arrogated naught to himselfe for following her aduice, when she had so wisely and in so good season ministred it vnto him; and that (wee may be sure) was not without his owne reioycing. Oh it well becommeth vs to bee forward in Gods matters, and yet not to be proud for our so doing: and there can come no worse end thereof, then thankes to God, who hath vsed vs as his instruments, and comfort to our selues: as wee may truly say, who doe more thankfully and ioyfully partake the Word and Sacraments, then they who

haue

haue with most profit receiued the Gospell,and are most zealous welwillers to religion? whereas the slothfull,and they who are vntoward thereto, neither finde any tast or sauour therein, but are most diligent to promote ill causes,they shall in stead of the prerogatiues of the other,haue (as they iustly deserue) reproch,vexation, and other punishments of God, euen in this life. Therefore let all in humility bee carefull and ready to bee imployed in Gods busines and seruice,and not to arrogate ought to themselues; for that is the onely sweet life,and to be desired: and herein is our heauenly father glorified,if we bring forth much fruit.

In this verse she speakes vnto the rich and wealthy, who for honour sake, Ioh.15.9.
and the rule they had ouer the people did ride on costly beasts, as we reade Vers.10.
in chapter 10.4. and 12. verse.14. These whether they liued by their lands *The meaning of*
and reuenues, or by their traffique and merchandise, for as much as they *the first part of*
were hindred by the enemies from enioying their commodities, and their *this verse,with*
passage had been cut off both by sea and land,and now they might freely en- *the Doct.1.*
ioy the same againe: they therefore were to come forth (she said) and giue thankes to God for that great enlargement and liberty. And thus wee see, the Lord will not haue the duty of praise hudled vp in grosse, as though a word for fashion might serue the turne; but in perticular, he will haue all sorts (as they feele his benefits sweet and comfortable to them diuersly) so to make new amplifications, and hearty repetitions of his goodnesse, that so all ioyning in a consort together,the musicke may be the sweeter,and his praise may be the fuller. For no one condition of people could possibly haue laid forth the benefit of their deliuerance,and the commodity of this their liberty and peace restored to them in any manner as all sorts might together: the Merchant could record his owne priuiledge that hee enioyed thereby,better then the husbandman; and so euery one in his seuerall place more then in anothers. But what was this in respect of that which she requireth;namely,that all stand forth in it together? And to take occasion to shew in this one worke of God,what a goodly thing it was for all sorts of people to praise God then,ioyntly together for their deliuerance and victory; who doth not conceiue what an heauenly sight it were if the like might be seene throughout in the congregation, for the renued benefits of God,whereby wee liue and are made ioyfull? I say, if with heart and voice wee did thus praise God, as well for them, as for those that are past, what a goodly sight were it? As it was by *Moses* and *Miriam*, and with the men and women, for the ouerthrow of *Pharaoh*: the like was, for the deliuerance of the Church in *Hesters* time; and in some of our solemne praising of God, we may see it so among vs. But oh then, what a solemne and triumphant sight shall that be,when the Lords glory shall bee sung and sounded forth in his heauenly kingdome,by Angels and Archangels, Patriarches,Prophets,and Apostles, Martyrs, Saints, and all that blessed company; I say, what a solemne sight
shall that bee? The very thinking that such a thing shall bee, is the greatest Note.
comfort that can be heere enioyed,and next vnto that celestiall ioy it selfe: of the which we would not be depriued, if wee were wise,nor lose our part therein (by musing often on it,) for all that is transitorie and vanishing,what so euer account they make of it who know no better.

But to returne now to the rich and great men whom *Debora* in this verse Doct.2.in vers.10.

 moueth

moueth to praise God, by this let all the rich and such as enioy wealth and great commodities doe the same, and acknowledge what a benefit it is to them, whether they bee great Merchants, to buy and vtter their wares, for their maintenance, and encrease of their wealth, which could not bee, but must needs faile, if that lay dead; or liberty of trauelling safely, and of free contracts were hindred, and whether they be otherwise great in riches and reuenewes; let them doe this likewise; and the greater persons they bee in either kind, the more let them seeke to excell themselues in this duty of praising God, and they being forward in that, they may be inabled to doe more good workes to necessary vses. By which we may also see, that God alloweth wealthy men to occupie and prosper in their calling; for why? he commandeth them to walke in their callings till he come; and teacheth, that the
Prou.10.4. diligent hand maketh rich: and there need bee no question made of that, for the Lord allowes that men should encrease rather then diminish that which they haue, both to auoide burthensomnesse, and for the supply of others, so as they practise godlinesse therewith, as equity, truth, sincerity, innocency, patience, & such like. The which they haue good incouragement to do, when they haue both liberty to follow their courses of dealing, and al-
1.Tim.4.8. so seeing godlines hath the promises of this present life, and of that which is to come. And if it were so that men were debarred of traffique, and the vse of their calling, as these rich men here mentioned had been, what an heauie crosse were that, seeing there is no other way, but to spend vpon the stocke till all be wasted? & that is soone done, where it is not renued: alas, how shall the family be maintained, & all charges defraid, if the freedome of gathering in mens commodities and dealings bee taken from them? Doe wee not see that the weather, or a little sicknesse, disabling a man to worke, causeth complaining? how much more when the liberty is wholly interdicted? But yet if God doe somtime blesse, men may not looke to haue alwaies one and the same course of thriuing and prospering. But howsoeuer it bee, let all bee highly thankfull, for that they may vse the benefit of traffique, or other improuing of their commodities, as these now did, and let them be fruitfull in well-doing, as they would readily promise to bee, if they were againe vnder the crosse, and ioyfull in the vse of preaching and Sacraments, with other duties; which is the true praise that God expecteth. But as for such as depriue themselues of the benefit thereof by their owne default, they haue much to answere for. Such are idle persons, and ill husbands, as we call them, and such, as, if the Lord somewhat alter the course of their takings and gaines, and they come short therof, ouer they did somtime before, they fret and complaine that their trades be naught, & that they shall be vndone: and much like to them are they, who hauing got by their trades well, conceale their estates, & faine themselues bankerupts, to defeat others of their goods; or such other as cast the burthen vpon their thriftlesnes and improuidence vpon their trades, dealings, or blind-fortune, forgetting how God had somtimes blessed them therein before. Therefore let vs know (whatsoeuer the bad practises of men are) that it is a great fauour of God, that people may haue free recourse to markets and faires, and other like places of buying and selling commodities, euen as the want thereof is a sore punishment, when people neither know where they should vtter their commodities, nor

buy

buy them whereof they ſtand in need: in both which conſiſted their maintenance, as was ſaid before. And yet lamentable it is to ſee, what abuſe the corrupt cuſtome of our time hath brought this liberty vnto. For many doe not onely ſteale away Gods due, I meane the Sabbath, to doe their worldly buſineſſe on; but there are other, whoſe common trade and practiſe it is (in a more prophane manner,) to harbour theeues, to receiue ſtollen wares, to entertaine drunkards, to become bauds to adulterers, and to ſpend that day leaud, and vnſeemely meetings and match-makings, ſtage-playes, and other reuell rout; and all vnder the honeſt colour of exchanging commodities, and maintaining their charge. So that in ſtead thereof, men and women ſet to ſale their good name, chaſtity ſobriety, and whatſoeuer elſe ſhould bee pretious to the godly.

Now vnto theſe before mentioned, of greater wealth and place, whereas ſome thinke, that in the next words ſhee ſpeaketh to men of meaner ſtate, *The opening of another part of verſ.10. and Doct.3.* ſuch as is ſaid here [dwelt by Middin] a place they ſay, where they met more vſually for a Mart or exchange of their wares, which place being before intercepted by the enemies, and now free for all to haue recourſe to it, and paſſe too and fro by the high waies, ſhee exhorts them that repaired thither to praiſe the Lord. This opinion of theirs is gainſaid by the pureſt tranſlations, and beſide, one thing ſhould bee vnderſtood in both places, to wit, of traffique and merchandiſe, if it were ſo. But the word [Middin] is not to be taken heere for the proper name of a place where wares were ſold; but the words [dwelling by Middin] are to bee tranſlated thus; [ſitting in iudgement.] As if ſhe ſhould ſay, let men of authority and rich lawyers, who may now ſit in iudgement about ciuill cauſes, let ſuch praiſe the Lord, becauſe they may now doe it ſafely. It is the honour, credit, peace and benefit of Magiſtrates and learned counſellors, as alſo the welfare of the people, that places of iudgement and iuſtice be frequented and vpholden: as we ſee heere in England in our Terme times at Weſtminſter, and out of Terme in other places, where equity and right are maintained, and wrong and iniurie puniſhed. Oh it is a time full of deſolation, when through famine, plague, or any infection, ſuch places muſt lie vnoccupied in the times when they ſhould be frequented and ſet a worke in deciding cauſes, helping the innocent to his right, and weeding out of euill doers. Whereby we may gather how heauy times thoſe were, when iudgement ceaſed, and the open places where iuſtice was miniſtred, were laid waſt, and left voide. And therfore we reade in the former chapter, that the people could not enioy that liberty of publike iudgement ſeates, but they were driuen to go priuately to *Debora* for iudgement, not dwelling ſumptuouſly in palace or caſtle, famous in that reſpect, *Iudg.4.5.* or honourable, but obſcure vnder a Palme tree. Now therfore as they when they might againe boldly and freely ſit in iudgement, are heere called to praiſe God for it: So ſuch perſons with vs enioying ſuch priuiledges, ought to call themſelues duely and daily to zealous thankeſgiuing, with ſuch other duties as accompany the ſame, yea their whole life ſhould ſauour thereof. And they ſhall haue much to anſwere to God who do otherwiſe. As for the people, what duty they owe for enioying this benefit, I will ſhew by a fitter occaſion in the next verſe.

But to let theſe goe of whom I haue ſpoke in this verſe, becauſe *Debora* *Doct.4. in verſ.10.* heere

heere ſpeaketh alſo to all ſuch as went, and walked by the way; this ſhould cauſe all ſuch as goe to and fro about their buſineſſe, pleaſure, or other neceſſarie vſes, as trauellers, to praiſe God highly for ſuch liberties, ſeeing a little before that, the high waies lay vnoccupied: and to ſpeake of the benefit thereof one to another to his praiſe, and not to trauell to and fro in rude, prophane, and looſe manner, gabling like wild geeſe in vnciuill and rude ſort; as though they enioyed ſuch liberties to offend God by them. And much more ought their behauiour and communication to bee ſober and Chriſtian like, when they goe to the houſe of God, to bee edified by the word, prayer, and Sacraments, and alſo when they returne home againe, and in a word, to walke harmeleſſe in all places; which behauiour is much out of vſe in this land, and yet (God bee thanked) not altogether in ſome places. But heere an end for this time.

THE THIRTIE TWO SERMON ON THE FIFTH CHAPTER OF THE BOOKE OF IVDGES.

Verſ. 11. NOw to proceed with the reſt that I haue begun withall, heere *Debora* ſpeaketh to the ſeruants, that in going forth to draw water for their neceſſary vſe, were not free from the archers, who ſhot at them, and put them to much paine, trouble, and danger, or feare at leaſt thereby. Where we ſee, that as they who are in the meaneſt places of ſeruice, are not to bee ſuffered to enioy their liberty to liue idly, but to be imployed and occupied, (as *Dauid*, when he was young kept his fathers ſheep) and ſet to worke, that they may be maintained thereby: (and ſuch ought to be thankfull when they may goe to it in peace:) ſo they are to bee admitted alſo, and taken into the number of them that worſhip God in the aſſembly, and therefore ought duly to bee brought thither by their gouernours, and taught there to know him. Euen ſuch as cut wood and draw water, the very droyles in houſes, (as they are called) who doe the moſt ſeruile workes: and therefore in ſome countries, ſuch as keepe ſwine, ſheepe, and cattell, which is more baſe then to ſerue them onely, euen theſe I ſay, being of them who are redeemed by the precious blood of Chriſt, as well as other, ſhould be taught to honour God aright, and to liue vnder his gouernment, and therefore not ſuffered to liue brutiſhly, as in ſome places they doe, but be brought forth by their parents or rulers, into the congregation of the faithfull, to learne thoſe things that concerne their happineſſe and peace: this being preſuppoſed, that there they ſhall be taught. Which I ſpeake to the ſhame of ſuch maſters, and gouernours, as neuer regard any ſuch matter, neither conſider that they owe that education to them, for the

[Margin: 1. Sam. 16. 11. — beside "much paine…"; Note. — beside "moſt ſeruile workes"]

ſeruice

seruice they doe them, and the vse they make of them, and most of all, that they owe it them, by the band with which they are tyed to it by Gods commandement: whereas the life of such is as miserable for their soule, as they vnder the Turkes gallies for their bodies: yea euen as asses who spend the day in toyle, and then are thrust at night into emptie stables; so are they sent after their tedious and brutish seruice, vnto their wofull home, and at last to hell, as a heauie recompence of their labour. Fie therefore vpon such tyrants. And yet if some masters in conscience of the commandement, doe (for some it may be doe) giue them more libertie to goe to the assemblie to worship God; yet oft times another euill is in the way, that when they come there, they haue nothing taught them, so that by one meanes or other, all that list may see they die miserably: of which sort, oh that the number were not too great. Thus much of these.

The next sort spoken to in this verse, are they, who dwelling in villages and vnwalled townes, were left desolate, and driuen from their habitations, and they laid waste, rifled, robbed, and left ruinous by the enemies: this to be the meaning of the second point in this verse, appeareth cleerely by the best translation; these she saith, might now safely returne to their habitations and townes, and make vp their ruines and breaches, and dwell in them againe as before. They were therefore to acknowledge the goodnesse of God with the rest, who yet beside the driuing them from their owne home, were also much impouerished, and sustained great losse, beside feare and trouble thereby. And this (besides the dutie of thanks for our safe and conuenient dwelling and harbour) should teach vs all to bee highly contented, and patiently to beare our impaired and decaied estate, when by Gods prouidence, without our fault and negligence, it falleth out to be so, seeing we cannot be ignorant, that Gods people haue had their part in such aduersities before vs: also losses by fire, water, or any other spoyling or wasting of our goods, when small likelihood could be seene thereof before. For these things fall out, and the like changes, where and when God will, for the sinne of men, as cousonage, deceit, securitie, hypocrisie, wilfull ignorance, worldlinesse, idlenesse, delicacie, excesse, &c. (which God curseth sometimes with beggerie) rash trustings, suretiship, &c. and they should beare their punishments, because they haue sinned: and after their repentance, when God hath staied the plague, they should thankfully, and without murmuring, receiue the remnants of their commodities, if any remaine to them: as wee reade the men of *Beniamin* did; and not desperatly and impatiently to leaue all at sixe and seuen, because they see themselues disabled from euer recouering their former estate: which is a signe of a proud heart, refusing and scorning to stoope to the Lords hand and visitation, as *Iob* himselfe did, whose losse yet (we know) was exceeding great. But oh the madnes of men, who when they being occupied about their commodities, are crossed in them, contrarie to their expectation, they are at their wits end, when the Lord hath taken but that which he lent them. They dreame of an eternitie here, and when they haue well feathered their nest, (as they say) they thinke they are well for many yeeres: oh death how vnwelcome art thou to such? nay the smallest losses doe cause them to rage and crie out. The Lord therefore seeing this, pulleth from one here, and from another there, to acquaint all

The opening of the next point in vers. 11

Doct. 2. in vers. 11.

Mich. 7. 7.

Iudg. 21. 23.

Iob 1. 21.

Note.

with

with changes, and teacheth them thereby, that if there remaine but somewhat to them, of the plentie which they sometime enioyed, so that they haue not vnthriftily wasted it themselues, they should be thankfull, as these here are willed to be, who full gladly came againe to their ruinous dwellings, from the which they had been driuen by the force of their enemies. And they whose hearts cannot bow to yeeld to their afflictions meekely and patiently, but doe rebelliously and brutishly harden them against God for his iust corrections, shall gaine this thereby, to haue them with *Iudas* broken in peeces with his mallets of terror and despaire, to their vtter confusion. Oh, full little doe such know themselues, by spurning against God,
Lamen.3.22. to kicke (as it were) against pricks. It is Gods mercie (as the Prophet saith) that they are not consumed: much more then, to giue them breathing, being, and liuing, and therefore they should humbly receiue Gods corrections.

The last sort that she calleth to praise God, were they that came together in the gates of their cities, where their iudgement seates were appointed to be. These meetings had ceased, and had been broken off, through the preuailing of their enemies, and now by their deliuerance were frequented againe. What a punishment that was, and how great a calamity to the Common wealth, to haue execution of law and iustice left off, and laid downe, tending so necessarily to the safegard of mens estates, or to the maintaining thereof; by the cutting off of malefactors, and the doers of iniurie, as robbers, and such like; how great a plague that was, I say, they well know, who are not ignorant, that the whole safetie (in a manner) of the Commonwealth, is maintained and vpholden by such due execution of law and
Doct.3.in vers.11. iudgement. And for this benefit (that I may come from them to our selues) all that liue in the Church and Common-wealth with peace and welfare, haue cause to magnifie Gods exceeding goodnesse in that one respect. For hereby they liue safe and quiet in their houses, they enioy their goods and commodities, and that which is the greatest of all other, they may the better haue libertie and the benefit of true seruing of God, which maketh all the rest of their liberties sauourie. And this with the other particular commodities which are enioyed of vs hereby, is to bee acknowledged to bee great and bountifull, the rather for that such common blessings vsually enioyed, are seldome reckoned of vs to be thanke worthie. And among those who went out and in at the gates, we may vnderstand all other, who either passed through, for their profit, pleasure, or for any other necessarie vse and cause, which libertie all may conceiue how great it was, and therefore both they then, and we now who enioy the same libertie, must hold our selues infinitly bound to praise God in this behalfe.

And now we haue heard how *Debora* hath called all sorts to the praising of God, and that euen for such benefits as are in little account with vs, no nor thought of, how great they be, let it warne vs of one common fault, that we be more mindfull hereafter of Gods goodnesse, in his ministring to our vse, the daily benefits which he bestoweth on vs for this present life, then we are wont to be: as the sunne-shine and the raine; the peaceable following of our callings within doores and without; the vttering and exchange of our commodities; our safe dwelling from danger of enemies, and the benefit

nefit of mill and market. And what shall I say else? as for our freedome from forrain enemies, and our trauel without danger, from place to place, with other that are innumerable: which though we haue thē in great part in common with the vnreasonable creatures, yet without them we know our life should be deadly wearisome to vs, yea none at al. I say it is certaine that these common blessings, and many other such are not acknowledged of numbers through the seuen yeers together, which should bee remembred (one or other of them, I meane) oft times euery day: which if it ought to be in these common benefits now mentioned, (which yet are but transitory;) then what cause had the Apostle, in respect of all together, which serue for his life, and that which is to come, to charge vs *in all things to bee thankfull?* And 1.Thes.5.19. by this that all sorts are heere spoken to by the Prophetesse; it teacheth that all sorts of men, and particular persons among them, are to know that they must answere to God for themselues about thankes, euen as elsewhere euery man is commanded to walke in his particular calling, and the duties thereof. For so saith the Apostle in the first epistle to the Corinthians; Let euery man abide in the same vocation wherein hee was called. But it followeth 1.Cor.7.20. in the text.

Vers. 12. *Vp Debora, vp, arise and sing a song: arise Barak, and leade thy captiuity captiue, thou sonne of Abinoam.*

13. *For they that remaine, haue dominion ouer the mighty of the people: the Lord hath giuen me dominion ouer the strong.*

NOw that *Debora* hath called all the people of Israel to thankesgiuing for the victorie, in the three former verses, shee stirreth vp her selfe in this twelfth verse by an elegant figure, that other might bee whetted on by her example to doe the same. And she calleth *Barak* to triumph, and with a certaine pompe to make a shew of his enemies captiuity and conquest: which was to the great honor of God, when all might vnderstand, that the Canaanites were for the most part slaine, and they that remained aliue, were prisoners to the Hebrues, who were most like a little before to be chopped to pieces of them & other of Gods enemies. In the 13. verse she amplifieth the victorie by another comparison of the conquerers, with those who were conquered: these hauing been valiant, wise, and well prouided: but that they ouercame them; namely, the Israelites were but as a remnant, and yet base and contemptible. This is the summe of these two verses. *The sense of these two verse.12.13.*

Out of her prouoking of her selfe to praise God, as if shee had been much behinde in that dutie, when yet she had been commendable therein, as wee haue heard, and had also vrged other thereto; wee may see that this hath been the manner and course of Gods people, to thinke they could neuer do enough in praising God, when they haue entred seriously into consideration of his goodnesse, but euer thought themselues cold and backward in respect of that they ought to haue been. Doubtlesse the due weighing of the cause, made her stil to see more and more into Gods admirable kindnes, till she was ashamed of her vnthankfulnesse. But some will say, all cannot be as *Debora* was: it is well if we can be thankfull when we be prouoked by others, they say, and by good meanes, as by the word, &c. To which I answere, Doct. 1. out of vers.12.

swere, It is cleare indeed, wee come behinde her in the duty; but is there not enough to moue vs to be equall to her, yea to excell her therein? Shee is thus thankfull for the victorie, wee haue no need nor cause to fight: shee praiseth God for peace recouered with the hazard and danger of ten thousand men, we enioy ours without putting it into question: shee, for bodily blessing, we haue infinite to the maintenance of health and welfare, then the which what could shee haue more for this present life? besides many that are spirituall to season the other, and yet wee come short of her in thankfulnesse neuerthelesse. And that which I haue said of *Debora*, the same we may see in *Dauid, Anna*, and others. Hee in the Psalme, hauing none equall to him in the performing of that duty, affirming that hee would doe it three times, nay seuen times a day, and that hee would doe it openly in the congregation, and priuately by himselfe; yet as though hee had much forgot himselfe, and had waxen dull, and been behind other therein, hee quickeneth vp himselfe to it, saying; *O my soule, praise thou the Lord, and al that is within me, praise his holy name.* Hee stirreth vp himselfe, wee see, to bee feruenter, when yet he was very forward before. Which I speake not, as if both he and other Gods best seruants and most feruent, did not feele oftentimes a kind of sleepy deadnesse in them to good duties, and remissenesse of spirit creeping vpon them, (as it is certaine they doe, seeing they carry that corruption about them, which will oft cause a wearinesse in them of well doing for the time,) but they hauing a greater power of grace working in them to subdue it, they gather vp and stirre themselues againe by such occasion, to more earnestnesse, and so finde themselues refreshed (by a new meditation of their slacknesse) with double courage to set vpon their duties. And to that end they helpe and sharpen on themselues, as *Dauid* and *Debora* did; and sometime are supported by other, as we see *Moses* his weake hands were faine to be holden vp by *Aaron* and *Hur* against *Amalek*. By this we see a manifest difference betwixt them and the wicked: who though (as they say) they like well of prayer, and hearing, and of thankesgiuing: yet they professe they cannot endure nor away with such continuall seruice; affirming where that is vrged that men shall neuer haue done. For as they who beleeue how greatly they are beholding to God for his goodnesse, do charge themselues with their vnthankfulnesse, euen when they are forwarder then the most; considering they are then but vnprofitable seruants: so the other are ready to post it off to others, as testifying thereby, that they be more beholding to God then they hold themselues to be, and thinke euery little to bee enough that they are to doe to God, yea and that a word and away may serue the turne; euen very froth it is that they offer to him, a mocking, no sacrifice: the heart neuer enclining (for it cannot) to any such thing.

Psal.103.1. *Exod.17.12.* *Rom.8.7.*

The clearing of the next part of the verse.

Another thing in this verse is concerning *Barak*, and that is, that hee should in a shew, and with solemne pomp set out the conquest and victorie which God had giuen them ouer their enemies. Which though after the victory in warre, it was vsed to bee done by the Heathens ouer such as they conquered, to the priding of themselues, and the vttermost disgrace of them that were subdued; yet this was (we see) spoken by the Prophetesse, to the end that God might haue honour therby; for one end she propounded, both of his act, and of her owne; and that was, the giuing of honour to the

the Lord. For the seeking of a mans owne glory, is no glory, but a taking it from God, and a prouoking of him thereby. Nay, where men would thinke that it as a due desert to them; yet euen there let them beware that they take it not; but let vs all acknowledge Gods goodnesse with thankfulnesse, for that he will vse our seruice to the honouring of his name. But to flesh and pride our selues in the yoking and subduing of our enemies, this were no better then the act of *Adonibezek*, who most cruelly cut off the thumbs of the hands and feet of seuenty Kings, and made them as dogs, to eat bread vnder his table, that hee might glorie in their extreme reproch and shame. This act of triumph was common to the people of God with the Heathen, but not done in so prophane and common a manner. And as it hath been in war, so the like in some sort we see at this day in the time of peace, that tehre are of al sorts who hauing sutes and controuersies depending betwixt them, get the day of their aduersary, and doe bring the one the other to a meane and poore estate; I speake of such as contend lawfully, and hauing a good cause, and right on their side, they preuaile by order of iustice one against the other, and doe in a certaine manner triumph thereby. But what then? In all this the one beareth as hee is more graciously seasoned then another, a lowly mind, and remembreth (though he haue the better hand, and other wealth beside,) whence hee came, who set him vp, and why; that is, not to glory foolishly of his welfare ouer his aduersary, but to be thankfull to God, and therefore is moderate and sober in the vse of all such liberties, and more fruitfull in doing good. The other vseth them to pride himselfe, to scorne others, to boast of his successe, and to be more impudent, prophane, and lawlesse. Both these triumph ouer their aduersary; but the one in good manner as not glorying that he hath gotten the victorie of himselfe, or by his owne strength, the other most vnbeseemingly, being a slaue, and pesant to his vnbridled lusts, and glorying in the pride of life. Prou.25.27. Doct.2.in vers.12.

The reason of honouring God by them both, *Debóra* and *Barak* I meane, is set downe by her in this verse; and that was, seeing the Lord had wrought wonderfully for them, and giuen many men, euen an huge army, into the hands of a few; and valiant and noble warriers he had caused to be subdued by them, that were but weake and meane. And though shee ascribe it in the first part of the verse, vnto the persons; yet that we may know that she ment them to be but the instruments onely appointed by God to get the victory, therefore in the latter part of the verse, she maketh the Lord the cause of it, saying, that he made them able to obtaine, and so to preuaile ouer them. Vers.13.

And so we (dearely beloued) when the like falleth out to vs, that God by small meanes worketh great things for vs, let vs learne before to be ready to see and acknowledge it. For example, when the Lord shall asswage the extremities of his seruants, either in paine, sicknesse, feare of vtter vndoing, or in the cruelty of their enemies, whereas none saw how they might bee like to recouer themselues any more; as when all helpe and hope by manward is past; when he (I say) shal then shew his helpe, that was not in any likelihood to haue been looked for, is it not time to behold his great goodnesse and wonder at it with due praises? His preuenting of that notorious Gunpowder-treason, with the remouall of many great enemies of his people, when death onely was like to haue done it (God knoweth when) and that in Note.

our remembrance,since the entering in of our late deceised Queene of blessed memorie,and the Kings Maiesty, (whom God inable to tread them vnder his feet) what thankes doe these worthily require of vs?

Moreouer, to see the fruit of this Gospell, which is for the most part so contemptible in the world; what great things it doth in subduing the stony hearts of many vnto the power of it,and in changing them, (though for the great cumpasse of the land,and the long time that it hath bin preached, we may and ought to lament, that it hath preuailed with no more, yet that grace that the sincere preaching of it hath wrought in many thousands,is to be remembred, thought vpon, and acknowledged, to Gods eternall praise. Euen as in all ages God hath done wonderfully, I meane, great things by small meanes; as in casting downe the walles of Iericho by seuen daies compassing it with blowing trumpets of Rammes hornes. Also his inabling *Gedeon* with three hundred men to ouerthrow an armie of the Midianites, who as grashoppers couered the face of the earth. And *Dauid* with his sling to conquer great *Goliah*. But I must heere cut off, seeing the verses following are many,and must be handled together.

THE THIRTIE THREE SERMON ON THE FIFTH CHAPTER OF THE BOOKE OF IVDGES.

The second part of the Chapter.

Vers. 14. *Of Ephraim their roote arose against Amalek: and after thee, Beniamin,against thy people,O Amalek: of Machir came rulers, and of Zebulon they that handle the pen of the writer.*

15. *And the Princes of Issachar were with Debora, and Ishachar, and also Barak: he was sent on his feet in the valley: for the diuisions of Reuben were great thoughts of heart.*

16. *Why abodest thou among the sheepfolds to heare the bleatings of the flockes? for the diuisions of Reuben were great thoughts of heart.*

17. *Gilead abode beyond Iordan: and why doth Dan remaine in ships? Ashur sat on the sea shore,and tarried in his decayed places*

18. *But the people of Zebulun and Naphthali haue ieoparded their liues vnto the death in the high places of the field.*

The sense of vers. 14.

THis is the first point of the second part of the chapter, in these words of the text to the 19. verse: which second part was diuided into three: as is to bee seene in the first entrance into the chapter. In the first, they are brought in to the song first, and commended by *Debora,* that did helpe in the warre, in the 14. and part of the fifteenth verse, and by occasion of them, they are mentioned next,and their

their slothfulnesse is reproued, who being of the tribes, did not helpe in the battell; which is done in part of the fifteenth verse, the 16. and 17. and after shee commendeth *Zebulun* and *Naphthali*, for that they had ieoparded their liues for their brethren, and this in the eighteenth verse. This to be the meaning of these verses, all may see that will throughly looke into it. But yet it must be acknowledged, that there is difficulty in some of them.

This therfore I will cleare as I am able, and labour to remoue the doubts which may be raised to trouble the Reader. To the which end wee must remember that which was before said, that *Debora* first speaketh of them in this second part of the chapter, which did helpe in the warre. And shee beginneth with *Ephraim*, And whereas some expound it that this root of *Ephraim* that rose against *Amalek* was *Iosbua*; and by *Beniamin*, in that they vnderstand him that should fight against them afterward; that is to say, *Saul*, who did so indeed. It is true, that both these are said to haue gone against *Amalek*, but what is that to this purpose? For heere in this part of the song, *Debora* signifieth who they were that fought against the Canaanites at that time. Therefore it is rather likely, that by the root of *Ephraim* she could not meane *Iosbua*, who was dead long before; but she meaneth her selfe, being one that was a chiefe person in that tribe: for it appeareth, that shee was an Ephramite, and it is said that she iudged Israel, *dwelling vnder a Palme tree between Ramath and Bethel in mount Ephraim.* And sure it is, that by her charge and authority the battell was taken in hand. But then ye will obiect, that the warre heere mentioned is said to haue been against *Amalek*, not the Canaanites: I grant it, but by a figuratiue speech; in *Amalek* we are to vnderstand the Canaanites also. And thus much for answering this first doubt out of these words, [*Of Ephraim their roote arose against Amalek.*]

The next is out of the words which follow immediately in the same verse, which are these; [*and after thee, Beniamin fought against thee O Amalek.*] Heere vnderstand this word (*Amalek*) as before. But that by *Beniamin* here, we should vnderstand *Saul*, being of that tribe, there is no sense in it, *Saul* being yet vnborne; but certaine of the tribe of *Beniamin*: for it appeareth by these words in the text, that some of the tribe of *Beniamin* also adioyned themselues to *Debora*, from the first beginning of the battell, though (it is to be thought) they were but few in comparison. The other words in this 14. verse haue this meaning; as these first [*out of Machir came rulers*] that is, out of them heere named of *Machir*, which was a noble family in the halfe tribe of *Manasses*, there came certaine worthy men to helpe in the battell. The last words of the verse, which are these, [*Out of Zebulun there came they that handle the pen of the writer,*] they haue this meaning; that the learned and skilful Lawyers, who were exercised in handling the pen, did helpe as they might fitliest be employed and vsed, whether by weapon or by counsell. The first part of the fifteenth verse concerning *Issachar*, hath this sense: that this tribe is highly commended, both for that they that were chiefe in it consented to *Debora*, and also, for that they did in their place, as *Barak* did in his: for as he was sent to mount Tabor, so it seemeth that the Princes of *Isbachar* were sent into the valley with their footmen, and in the perill and ieopardy of the Israelites by their enemies, they did set vpon them with great courage, and behaued themselues valiantly, and therefore they are highly commended.

The meaning of vers. 15. and 16.

Thus she hauing mentioned them that helped in the battell, she turneth, by occasion of them, to those that did not helpe, beginning in this 15. verse with the tribe of *Ruben*. That tribe is reproued, for that it held backe to the great griefe of their brethren, from fighting among them, and for that they did not in so great danger come foorth to helpe them. This tribe dwelt beyond Iorden in the fat pastures, and as it appeareth, for their too much minding, and care of their cattell, and their commoditie thereby, they neglected the care of the Common-wealth. And in that it is said, that there were great thoughts of heart for the Reubenites diuiding themselues from their brethren, whether the meaning of the words be, that these thoughts were great and loftie in them, that scorned to goe at *Deboras* commandement, being but a woman; or whether they were thoughts of wondring and lamenting in their brethren, for that they came not as well as others, to helpe them in the battell; the repetition of the words doth giue more warrant for to take them in this latter sense, as a lamentation: as if it should be said, Oh that *Reuben* should not come ouer Iorden to helpe as the most of the other tribes did: oh, it was wondred at, and much to be lamented. And besides, to charge that tribe to be proud and insolent, is more then wee may or ought to doe vpon an vncertaine ground, for it requireth good proofe for the auouching of that.

Reuben (that is the Reubenites that came of him) is here described by their calling and trade, that they were keepers of cattell, and the places that they dwelt in, namely among goodly pastures. And where it is added, *Why sattest thou among the sheepfolds to heare the bleating of the flockes?* it is so to be taken, as if the Reubenites abode and remained still with their cattell, for all the danger that was: and did declare thereby that they did set more by them, then they did pitie their brethren, by going to helpe them. In the 17.

The meaning of verse 17. verse, Gilead is in like manner complained of, they abode still in their dwelling place beyond Iorden, as the Reubenites did, dwelling neere vnto them; while their brethren the Israelites were in great ieopardie, fighting with

Obiect. their enemies. But here commeth another great doubt to be answered, that seeing *Machir*, a noble familie in the tribe of *Manasse*, was said before, to come to helpe their brethren, and they possessed Gilead: I say if Gilead bee commended before to come, why is it here reproued for not comming?

Answ. This doubt is answered thus: *Manasse* had two sonnes, *Machir* and *Iair*, of whom came two great families, both which possessed Gilead. Therefore those Gileadites which came of *Machir*, could not bee they who are reproued, for they came to helpe; but the familie of *Iair*, who also dwelt in Gilead, for they came not.

The next that are reproued here, are they of the tribe of *Dan*. Who are not reproued simply for trauailing in ships vpon the sea, but they are blamed here for remaining in ships. Now at that time (whether they did so to shelter themselues thereby from their enemies on the sea, or for their trafique, and did not rather goe out of them, and helpe the rest) they were worthie to be found fault with, for their so doing. For what though they were striken with such a feare, when they heard of the armies of their enemies? that was their sinne, that they hasted not to the rest, against their enemies to assist them, but that they put themselues in ships, that so they might passe

and

and escape from them, or follow their owne priuate businesse: which was a thing vtterly vnbeseeming them, they were therefore worthily and iustly reproued for it, as I haue said.

The last tribe that is found-fault with, is the tribe of *Asher*, who excuse themselues for being absent from their brethren; partly for that they dwelt farre off, and partly for that their townes and cities were ruinous, and not well fenced, and therefore they said, they tarried at home, lest their enemies might haue taken occasion by their absence to spoile them, which they saw they might easily haue done. And there is no doubt, but that it was grieuous to these tribes to be thus rebuked; the which the holy Ghost would haue to be done, partly for their owne cause that they might see in what great fault they were by not going to helpe their brethren, how lightly soeuer they accounted of it, and also that they might repent for it: and partly in respect of others, which I will shew when I come to the doctrine. And this be said of the tribes commended and reproued, except the two tribes of *Zebulon* and *Naphtali*, who did more specially ieopard their liues for their brethren, as it followeth in the next verse.

Here she commendeth them both in an high manner (though some chiefe men in the tribe of *Zebulon* she had praised before, and that for their forwardnes against Gods enemies, in so great perill, as we haue heard, they were in. For it was a ridiculous thing in the iudgement of men, for such a small number as they were, to goe against such huge armies, and all as valiant souldiers addressed in warlike furniture, by whom they might haue been swept away in lesse then an houre; but they preferred God and his word before their owne liues. By the high places mentioned here, the mount Tabor is signified, on which they were appointed to stand to behold the multitude of the Canaanites, and yet they not flying away from them, but marching toward them, their faith appeared to bee so much the greater, and therefore they are thus commended. Thus much for the meaning of these fiue verses. *The sense of verse 18.*

Now I haue cleered that which was needfull to be made plaine in this storie, there being some difficultie therein; the next thing is, that we seeke a further benefit by it. And first by them who are commended for yeelding their helpe in that great worke of the Lord, as *Ephraim, Beniamin* and *Ishaker*, mentioned in the 14. and 15. verses; we may see, that such as doe set themselues to further Gods people, or his seruice, shall not be vnrecompensed, nor forgotten; as these are here regestred to their praise, neither is any to thinke, that the labour and trauell so bestowed, is in vaine. And whereas some obiect, That now the Scriptures are finished, and therefore no man can looke for the same particular reward that these enioyed; I meane, to be Chronicled in the monuments thereof: yet let them know, that if they be faithfull and constant to the end, the Lord hath written their names in another booke, farre more durable, euen the booke of remembrance, wherein he writeth the workes of the Saints, that he may both here, and for euer reward them, and honour them before men Angels. For though it be vsuall with men to doe as the Butler did to *Ioseph*, I meane to let goe vnrewarded many kindnesses and duties done to them by their neighbours, yet God who is lesse bound to the best, by any due of desert, but only of his free pro- Doct. of verse 14. 15. *Obiect.* *Answ.* Matth. 25. 34.

mise and gracious fauour, he, I say, will not doe so: for why? if one offer but
Mich.1.42. a cup of cold water vnto any, in the name of a Disciple, that is, because he is so, the Lord will not leaue him vnrewarded. Therefore when the woman in
Mark.14.9. the Gospell had powred ointment on the head of our Sauiour, he said, that wheresoeuer the Gospell should be preached, that act of hers should bee remembred and spoken of. Much more they who shall honour God more fruitfully and faithfully, may assure themselues, that great is their reward
Matth.19.29. from him: for hee that shall forsake any thing for his sake, shall receiue an hundred fold for it, euen in this life, besides the happinesse that abideth him in the life to come.

Oh therefore the blockishnes and vnbeliefe of the greatest part euen of Christendome, who desiring to enioy good daies while they liue here, doe in no carefull manner take the way thereto; but shift as the baddest sort do, to take their part in the sinfull pleasures of this life. By meanes whereof, though they thinke themselues on the surer hand, and to play the part of wise men; yet in truth they neuer finde the quiet and sweete fruite of the Gospell, which yet many of them professe; nor euer attaine the happie life, here or after, that they looke for.

Oh, things present doe so dazle their eyes with their deceiueable beauty, and their hearts are so hollow, inconstant and vnfaithfull, that if they be tickled with loue and liking of any thing that pleaseth their humour, how dishonest, yea and filthie soeuer it be, they are drawne after it, as the silly fish with the bait. So that it is no maruaile, that few doe beleeue that their labour in the Lord shall be rewarded; by chusing rather to abide affliction,
Malach.3.14. then to embrace the short pleasures of sinne. Oh the number is great of them that follow the deuices and desires of their owne wicked hearts, vpbraiding the godly with the small gaine they get by their zealous profession of religion. Indeed it is a thing impossible for an vnbeleeuer, to see either the vnfruitfulnes of his owne estate, or the gaine of the contrarie: as wee see by them in Malach.3. who aske in plaine termes, If it be not in vaine to serue God, and what profit commeth thereby, &c. But this ought not to trouble the righteous, as we see in the 16. verse of the same chapter: but if through
Psal.73.13. frailtie they slip into that temptation, as *Dauid* did, Psal.73. let them doe as he did, vers.17. enter into the Sanctuarie of God, and change their opinion. But as fast as one seeth another taken away, and for all the fearefull manner of the death of some of them, who haue liued as if they feared neither hell nor iudgement day; yet what one of an hundred remaining behinde still, is brought any thing neerer to a Christian life thereby?

Doct.2.in vers.14.15. Now more particularly by these of *Machir* or *Manasses, Zebulon*, and *Issachar*, which were chiefe men in the tribes, and yet forward and readie to ioyne with the rest against Gods enemies; wee learne, that as the mightiest and wealthiest should not come behind others in any part of Gods seruice, but put foorth themselues before them, as these here did: so they that doe not so, must see that they shall haue reproch for their negligence and sloth, as the other shall be renowned of God himselfe, as wee see here these be: which were enough to put heart and courage into that sort of men particularly, if sinne haue not plucked it out. But of this I speake in other places by occasion, and therefore I say no more now.

Now

Now *Debora* passeth from these whom she commended, and turneth to the other whom she discommendeth, in these verses. Whereby we may see how great the reproch of thē is, who do not helpe in Gods house, to set forward his worke, and to ioyne with his seruants therein. For such do not only discourage their brethren, and let the worke lie raw and vnperfect; but they flesh their aduersaries, and God knoweth whether they would not also turne on their sides, if they should be tryed. Wherein it is not amisse to obserue the plaine dealing of the holy Ghost in this narration: for as he ingenuously yeeldeth testimony of praise to the well deseruing: so hee conceileth not the shame of the carelesse and slothfull, but rebukes them without respect of persons. Which dealing, as it sheweth what course he will take in that solemne day, wherin he will iudge the world with equity: so it should driue all fooles out of these conceits, whereby they beguile themselues saying; tush, God will doe neither good nor euill; and that hee will not smite them, but they shall escape better then others, &c. which was the errour of them who (till they found the contrary) would neuer be perswaded but their estate was good, saying, Lord, Lord, &c. as though thereby they should haue entred into his kingdome. And as this is true in the generall, so is it in particulars, both bodily and spirituall. For though in the corrupt practise of this wicked world, we see euery one is for himselfe, as the prouerbe speaketh; posting off the regard of the needy to others: yet if we enter into the Lords sanctuary, and looke what is required by his word, wee shall finde it odious, vnnaturall, and highly displeasing in the sight of God, that there is not compassion in one to another, and care in one ouer another, as equity and band of duty requireth; that as they should warme the hearts of their brethren with relieuing them readily in their bodily necessities and dangers; so should they comfort their soules likewise with holy instruction and spirituall refreshing, as by good occasion and opportunity they may. And as these should haue done it in warre, so ought we as well in peace. This dutie owe superiours, either in nature, age, place or gifts, to the inferiours, to backe, encourage and instruct them: equals, to each other, to admonish, comfort, visit, and support, or restore one the other in meekenesse as there shall be cause. This is not the Ministers duty alone, but of others; which if it were practised, wee might say indeed that great is the benefit of Christian fellowship; whereas now men looke vpon one another, as if they knew them not, and had as lieue haue their roome as their company. But what other is to bee looked for, while Gods ordinances, (whereby hee hath prouided that this duty of caring one for another, shall bee nourished) are contemned and set at naught? But yet for all this, I would not thus bee vnderstood, as though men ought to breake off and leaue their lawfull callings to seeke (as some say they do) occasions to be doing of good, by conference, &c. as some idle and phantasticall persons are glad to pretend such things, to the end they may liue idely, and be held within no bounds: but yet (as it may fall out) when they are called more necessarily to some speciall duties of visiting one another in sicknesse, or eating and drinking together, for the time, vpon some such waighty and iust occasion they may. But otherwise they are, and that with faithfulnesse and diligence, to attend vpon their lawfull vocation, vnlesse with their conference and good communication and Vers. 15. 16. 17.

ſuch like doing of God, they may do the duties of their callings alſo; which in trauelling and iourneying together about their buſineſſe, they may. And this be gathered from the reproofe of all the tribes in generall, mentioned in theſe three verſes.

2 But now let vs marke ſomewhat out of them more perticularly. For of *Reuben* and *Gilead* it is expreſly ſaid, that they neglected this duty for their owne profit, and that they were more bent to the ſeeking of that, then to lend their helpe where they owe it. This was found fault withall in them:
Luk.14.18. euen as our Sauiour found the like fault with them, who were inuited by him vnto another duty, euen to the great ſupper, as theſe were to fight againſt Gods enemies, they excuſing their abſence for their owne priuate aduantage, euery one his way: one had hired a farme, another had bought oxen, and he muſt euen then go trie them; and another had married a wife; to whom may bee added the third ſort of hearers mentioned by our Sauiour, whoſe ſinne was of the ſame kind, whom the cares of the world, and thornes of riches choke, ſo that the ſeed ſowne in them brings forth no
Mat.13.22. good fruit. This worldly minde and ſloth in men to preferre their owne profit before Gods buſineſſe, far more waighty; God in no wiſe can abide. And yet a common ſinne it is, and not in the worſt ſort of profeſſors onely; (as we ſee in *Martha*, who loſt the beſt part, when Chriſt was at her houſe, and that by cumbring her ſelfe needleſly) who for their owne priuate commodity neglect and paſſe by duties to God and their brethren, and thoſe very waighty: for while they puddle for earthly pearles, they forgoe the peerleſſe pearle of faith and regeneration, being, (if they could ſee it) farre more gaineful then their beſt merchandiſe, and by infinite degrees excelling them all. And let vs all take heede, ſeeing commonly it ſo falleth out, that he who is wittingly careleſſe in ſome duties, is not very forward in other, how waighty ſoeuer, that it be not ſo with vs, that while we aime at heauen, more then ſome other, we be not waighed downe, as it were, with bolts vpon our heeles, to the depth of earthlineſſe, and ſo make our dwelling vnder the earth; in perpetuall darkneſſe.

And this by the occaſion of the ſin in theſe two tribes, bewailed by *Debora*, ſpeaking in her ſong of one of them thus; *for the diuiſion of Ruben*, in that he diuided himſelfe from his brethren, *there were great thoughts of heart*, that is, much maruelling and lamenting for his ſo doing. Of the other thus: *Gilead remained beyond Iordan*; as if ſhe ſhould ſay, euen then, when their brethren were fighting with their enemies, they of Gilead ſat ſtill at home, whom yet the buſineſſe concerned as much as themſelues that lamented it. And was not that then very lamentable? And as I haue ſpoken of this one ſinne, the ſame may be ſaid of the reſt how much to bee bewailed they are, and namely, theſe more neere akind. Euen ſo it is, when good men to theſe, as techineſſe or conceits, or any other ſiniſter corruptions to ſeparate men from their brethren, and thereby to make them backward in helping forward the good things which otherwiſe might bee, as in keeping the vnruly in order, and within compaſſe; or helping to bring in a ſound and good miniſtery, or any other commendable thing, by their care and induſtry. Oh how it ſhould grieue vs when wee ſee them backward in any good thing, who ſhould bee forward. Indeed when the diuell hath ſo fare wound in

with

with men, as to diuide them from their brethren, they stand stifly in defence of their doing (so little doth it greeue them) but it pierceth the hearts of the godly, in respect both of the wrong done to themselues, & the scandall offered to others; as also because they deserue thereby, that their former forwardnesse and fruits should bee called into question. *Demas* made light of his going from *Paul*: but hee writes mournfully of it to *Timothy*, in this manner: *Demas* hath forsaken me, and hath imbraced, that is to say, hee resteth in this present world. And no maruell; for the truth is, the better a mans properties be, the more lamentable are his personall blemishes. Euen as when a man comely, and of very good shape in all other parts very personable of body, hath a wooden leg, or some other grosse disfiguring of him, all men obserue it with commiseration and pity. 2.Tim.4.10.

Now of *Dan* seuerally she complaineth, for that they of that tribe fled away for feare of the enemies, from their dwelling places, if not also for their worldly profit, as *Reuben* and the other did, as we haue heard in the exposition of this verse. So that as these did another way, and in another respect deserue blame, as wee see, namely, for their feare of their enemies, whereas they should haue rather vnderstood, that it behoued them to haue taken part with their brethren: so the ill fauourednesse (if it could bee seene with the eye and the vnseemelinesse of it in them,) teacheth what a slauish affection this feare and timerousnesse is, and what a burthen to Gods seruants, when their faith is damped, and hindred by it, that it cannot haue the proper worke; that is, to harten and encourage them to bee forward and zealous in the worke of the Lord, but shiftingly to prouide for themselues. And therefore in the Reuelation, this spirituall fearefulnesse is threatened as seuerely as adultery and murther; and therefore (doubtlesse) is no lesse then a great blemish. This, I say, is in men a shamefull sinne, to be content that other shall beare the brunt, and themselues goe free. Such shall smart and be wounded deeply, when the other shall reioyce. Howbeit this I will adde, that as this fearefulnesse comming from a false heart, destitute of the loue of God and faith, is damnable disobedience to God, and trechery to men: so yet because it may through infirmity cleaue to a right good seruant of God (for we must wisely discerne of the cause from whence it ariseth,) therefore we must not count alike of both: as we haue good warning by *Peters* example, who of meere frailty feared to confesse his master, but by and by he went by himselfe, and wept bitterly for it: whereas they whose feare riseth of falshood and meere carnall respects onely seeke grosly to auoide danger, but relent not after for their sinne: therefore we must bewaile both, but pity them that haue been ouercome through frailty, and commend their estate to God, to giue them more strength and courage, and not daring be bold to censure them so farre as to say, that *Christ will denie them before his father*; for they are as farre from falshood and malice, as they are from resolution and Christian magnanimity, yea and much further; and let vs rather that thinke we stand, beware that we fall not. Doct.vers.17. Reuel.21.8.

Now after all these, she speaketh of the men of Ashur, who excused their not comming forth to helpe against their enemies, by meanes of their weak defences at home, and their farre distance: but howsoeuer they thought they had good reason for their absence, we see that they are also reproued by the Doct.2.in vers.17.

the spirit of God in *Debora.* To teach vs, that it shall little boot vs to make defences for our sinne, and that wee cannot hide it from God, and that hee looketh for another thing at our hands, that wee should not refuse to obey his word, no, though it be with some danger. Which if we refuse to do, as these are heere dispraised, and sharpely reproued for not so doing; so we in the day of iudgement shall be not onely put to shame and rebuke with irrecouerable losse for our slight gaine by our excuse making; but also we shall be cast from Gods presence for euer. Thus wee haue heard how shee hath commended the tribes that did fight against the enemies, and dispraised those that refused, and hath said nothing of *Iuda, Simeon, Leui,* and *Gad*; and therfore neither haue I any thing to say of them, who must haue my ground of all that I speake, from the word. And that which remaineth in this first point of the second part, is of the two tribes, *Zebulun* and *Naphtali:* who in the middest of the earthlinesse, feare and pretences of their brethren, did (as wee haue heard in the exposition of this verse) put their liues in danger by

Doct. vers. 18. fighting with the enemies. Of whom although I haue spoken sufficiently before, yet this I adde, that if the cause so require, we should be ready to giue

1. Ioh. 3. 16. our liues for the brethren. Which Saint *Iohn* meant, when he said, *wee ought to lay downe our liues for the brethren, euen as our sauiour did, leauing vs an example.* And as this case falles out seldome, so yet when it doth, we ought not to be to seeke of this readinesse, and willing minde to do this seruice for them,

Note. considering that we are neuer like to yeeld our liues in better maner, vnlesse it be for the Lords cause and Gospell directly, which is in a manner all one. And why not? when we see that some will be ready to doe so for some benefactor of theirs, who hath been bountifull toward them. As S. *Paul* saith,

Rom. 5. 7. *for a good* or bountifull *man, perhaps some will die.* Now if wee ought to hold our liues on this condition, that beside the many casualties whereto they are subiect, they ought also to bee ready to bee offered at the pleasure of God with all things else that we enioy with them, wee may see, that it is no wise part to be wedded to that which wee haue heere lent vs heere below, nor to our liues themselues, as we are (and the rather, for that our Sauiour professeth, that he who will saue his life, shall lose it) prising them at so high a reckoning as wee doe; namely, to count them as our paradise; which is the chiefe cause that we doe so dote vpon them, and also that we do so meanely esteeme and make account of the life to come, as that our hearts do little long after it. And to conclude, by the opposition of these forementioned tribes, let vs learne wisedome, and iudge righteous iudgement. Let vs marke the repugnant example of both sorts of men, the zealous according to knowledge on the one side, and the carelesse on the other: also their actions their affections, and their reward, obseruing how the Lord honoureth, encourageth and recompenseth the one with the loue of his people, & maine blessings: and how he brandeth the other with a blacke cole of infancy and shame: that as we like or abhorre their portion) so we may like the grace of the one, and abhorre the practise of the other. It followeth.

THE THIRTY FOVRE SERMON ON THE FIFTH CHAPTER OF THE BOOKE OF IVDGES.

Verſ.19. *The Kings came and fought, then fought the Kings of Canaan in Taanach by the waters of Megiddo: they receiued no gaine of money.*

Verſ.20. *They fought from heauen, euen the ſtarres in their courſes fought againſt Siſera.*

Verſ.21. *The riuer Kiſhon ſwept them away, that ancient riuer, the riuer Kiſhon. O my ſoule thou haſt marched valiantly.*

Verſ.22. *Then were the horſe hoofes broken with the beating together of their mightie men.*

IN theſe words is contained the ſecond point or branch of the ſecond part of the chapter, wherein *Debora* ſetteth downe the manner of the battell on the behalfe of the enemies, namely, that they came ſolemnely to fight, and well prouided; accompanied with Kings, both of Canaan and other countries, to furniſh and adorne the armies: and yet for all that, they fought vnproſperouſly and vnhappily, and had very hard ſucceſſe. For the Lord fought againſt them from heauen; the riuers and waters ſwallowed them vp, and ſwept them away: and their horſes were vnhoofed. Now when they were fought againſt all theſe waies, they were ſcattered & fell before Iſrael, in wonderfull manner, for all the multitude & ſhew of them. This vnproſperous fighting of theirs, is ſet down by her, firſt generally in the 19. verſe, & then more particularly in the next three; as ſhall appeare when we come to them. In the 19. verſe thus; by a figure whereby (not without a bitter vpbraiding of them) ſhe intimateth more then ſhe expreſſeth. *They receiued no gaine of money*: nay, they loſt all, and Iſrael enioyed a rich ſpoile. The like figure is vſed in the Pſalme: *A broken heart thou wilt not deſpiſe*, that is, Thou wilt make great account of it. The phraſe it ſelfe, as we vſe it, (for it is a nipping ſcoffe) is as much, as if ſhe had ſaid, they might put the gaines in their eyes, &c.

The ſenſe of theſe foure verſes.

Pſal.51.17.

In this verſe alſo ſhe ſheweth the pompe and multitude of the enemies, and how they filled all the plaine betwixt mount Tabor, and the townes of Taanach and Megiddo, euen to their riuers running by them, which were called by the ſame names; this (I ſay) *Debora* doth as well declare, as how ill they ſped, namely, that they got not that which they ſought and looked for, I meane, the ouerthrow and ſpoile of the Iſraelites: nay rather, they were miſerably ſpoiled and deſtroyed themſelues. By the which, two things may be noted: One, that wee may ſee the glorie of wicked men, floriſhing like the

Verſe 19.

the greene bay tree. I ſay, of wicked men, (for otherwiſe, I grant, godly perſons may be honourable and great) and we may ſee alſo that this their glo-
Pſal.37.35. rie reacheth, as it were, to the very cloudes, as wee reade in the Pſalme: yea and that in the time of warre, as here, which yet can in no wiſe ſhew it, as the times of peace may: yea, and that for their glorie they may be ſholed with Princes, and be almoſt companions with Kings: theſe, I ſay, and ſuch like, we may poſſibly ſee, as terrors to daunt and grieue vs; for the aduancement of them, is heauineſſe and matter of hanging downe the head to the righteous. And what of this, you may ſay, when this may bee ſeene? and why ſhall it be thus? Surely, that Gods people may not haue their eyes dazeled with their pompe and glorie, when they ſhall ſee them pulled from it; but that they may hereby be weaned and eſtranged the more, from the dangerous and poyſoned baites that would hurt them, as they haue done the other, but by faith ſee their downfall euen in the middeſt of their glorie, and while they to their hearts deſire enioy all outward things, and all becauſe they are the Lords ranke enemies. Secondly, that they may cleaue to God more faithfully, and alſo waite more conſtantly to ſee the glorie of ſuch turned to ſhame, if they preuent it not by repentance. And let this be the vſe of this firſt thing vnto vs.

2 The ſecond that I note here is this, (according to that in the Prouerbs)
Prou.12.27. *that the wicked doe not alwaies roſte that which they get in hunting*: that is, they doe not alwaies attaine to that, which they promiſe themſelues in the earneſt deſire of their hearts; and whereof they haue great likelihood, as well as hope: but God cutteth them off from it, to their great vexation and diſappointment: yea, and the godly ſhall ſee it, and triumph, as *Debora* did here, and Iſrael ouer *Pharao*. For though that be true, that they are fatted here, and haue more then they might looke for, (which yet they haue but to their deſtruction) yet, that the righteous may not enuie them, but ſee that the Lord takes their part againſt them, and leſt the proud themſelues ſhould thinke there is no God that ſeeth them, they are croſſed in their purpoſes, and many times when they hope for that which they would moſt willingly
2.King.6.12. enioy, the Lord fruſtrateth and mocketh them, as he did the King of Aram, when all his ſecret plots and purpoſes againſt the King of Iſrael, were bewraied to him by the Prophet *Eliſha*, and hee ſheweth them thereby, that they haue him not alwaies at their commandement: as neither can they goe about any of their attempts, without his ſufferance. That it may be verified, that (when none elſe can) yet euen then *God reſiſteth the proud*. And as the Lord thus matcheth and diſappointeth them, when it ſeemeth good to him, in their common dealings, that they attaine not that which they aime at, and looke for; ſo eſpecially when they fight againſt God, and play the giants againſt heauen like *Nebuchadnezzar*: and when their inſolencie vttereth it ſelfe againſt the poore Church of God, (as many of them chuſe this as the fitteſt obiect to vomit their poyſon vpon) then the Lord in an anſwerable manner riſeth vp and ſcatters them; lookes downe from heauen, and laughs them to ſcorne, and ſcatters them: for why? they banded themſelues againſt his annointed.

For example ſake, though the Scripture be full of ſuch, let theſe two at
Gen.11.4. this time ſuffice. The one is of them that would build a citie that ſhould

reach

reach vp to heauen,to get them a name, the Lord set himselfe against them, cast downe their building,and called the name thereof Babell,that is,confusion. For what a pride was in them, and to what had it been like to haue growne, if God had let them alone,and suffered their worke to goe forward? The other example is of *Haman*,who being so inward with the king, and aduanced by him,when he looked yet to rise higher, he was, vnlooked for,cast downe from all his dignitie, when his shame was made sutable to his glorie. And thus (as it fared here with *Sisera*) in stead of great successes and increasings of their purposes and dignities,they are not defeated thereof only,but are faine to lose that which they enioyed before; the Lord making their ambition, the next meane of their ouerthrow. So God deales with many; of whom,some rising out of the dunghill to great wealth and honour, not only are ioynted otherwise oftentimes, but when they want nothing but life and length of daies,to enioy their florishing estate still, behold,euen that way he meeteth with them,and by death, somtime reprochfull enough, but to be sure, with paine and woe enough, besides that after their going hence, hee cuts them off from all their iolitie, as it were,at one blow. And who,fearing God,might haue liued by them,if they could haue prolonged their daies? Ester 7.10. Note.

This be said of the 19.verse,and in generall of their ill prospering against Israel,in their fighting: now more particularly, *Debora* sheweth in this verse, that euen from heauen,that is,from the higher region of the aire,the starres and planets raised the raine and the winde in their faces,yea the haile and tempests to fight against *Sisera*, so that thereby God shewed himselfe to be against him,all his preparation and furniture of charets, horses and men seruing him to no purpose,but disappointing him. This teacheth vs,that when God will both heauen and earth,and the powers of both, shall fight against Gods enemies, euen as all the plagues written in the booke of God,doe at his commandement, seaze vpon, and torment them. So the haile from aboue slew Gods enemies,and the Sunne stood still to that end: so frosts and floods, plague and famine, with other such, haue in our time fought against them from God. I haue handled this point more largely before, I will onely answere one obiection in this place. It is obiected, that the godly sustaine the forementioned iudgements and the like,as well as the wicked: therefore when shall wee be able to proue and say, the Lord in laies them vpon his enemies, as if he aimed at that alone? For *Iob* had his sheepe and seruants burnt vp and deuoured by fire from heauen, as if Satan would thereby haue perswaded him,that God himselfe made warre with him from thence: his body was also smitten with sore byles,from the sole of his foote vnto the crowne of his head,and he tooke a potsheard to scrape him I answere,that God sendeth these and the like to his children,as trials, or corrections to heale them of some dangerous disease, as pride, loosenes, worldlinesse,&c. but to his enemies, as scourges for their wicked liues, to begin their hellish torments here; and as this euer true, so if their sinnes be manifest, wee may so iudge of the particular offenders that he meaneth no lesse toward them, and that without any feare of iniurying them, vnlesse they repent. Verse 20. Doct. vers.20. Leuit 26 19. Exod.14.28. Iosh.10.11.12. *Obiect.* Iob 1.16. *Answ.*

The next particular assistant to Israel, that is said to haue fought against Verse 21.

Sisera, was the riuer Kishon: which though it was not vsually deep, yet now the waters rose higher, and ouerflowed the bankes, and was spred out further: and because both the armies met there by, therefore it is described by her, the riuer of mettings, namely of both the armies, for the word is better translated so, then as some doe translate it *the ancient riuer*, and by an elegant repetition of the word, sheweth that it drowned and carried away many of the enemies, euen as the dust and other filthinesse is swept out of an house with a broome. Not that all were slaine that way, which could not be, when the men were many, and the place not large, but that many flying, were there destroyed. And this being a thing neither feared of the enemies, nor made reckoning of by Gods people, doth worthily teach vs, that when we walke vprightly with God, he causeth many things to lend their helpe to vs, which wee neuer thought of, nor looked for; and not onely persons to be kinde to vs, but also other commodities, comforts, and incouragements to meete with vs: yea the very places where we dwell, and whither we come. And the very same things which haue been fatall and deadly enemies to others, to be helpfull, and as it were, made friendly vnto vs.

Iacob thus being faithfull to the Lord, hee inriched him greatly, ouer hee euer looked for, or saw likelihood of, but rather of the contrary: and so dealt he with his father *Isaac* before him, being among strangers in the land. And
Note. so he prouideth for many of his deare seruants, who comming strangers to a place, where it was little likely to get, either grace, knowledge, or other commodities, he hath yet by giuing them honest and good hearts, blessed them otherwise, with loue and fauour of the best, with a sweete life, inward peace, growing in goodnesse, fruite of prayers and other holy labours, with contentment, and such like; that it may for euer worthily perswade all to get
1. Tim. 1. 12. into Gods seruice, and to be vpright hearted toward him, seeing godlinesse bringeth so many and great commodities. But of this I spake somewhat before also. But on the contrary it may be said, that when men seeke not the Lord with all their heart, neither be carefull that their waies may please him; they not only prosper not long, (which yet they were as like to attaine to as the most) but they lose euen that which they had, and are tossed about with many calamities, and with this, as the greatest of all, that when God frowneth vpon them, they beleeue it not: the danger whereof may easily be gathered by the drunkard, in the Prouerbs; who was stricken, he said, for his
Prou. 23. 35. sinne and the fruites of it, whoredome and such like, but hee was not sicke; he was beaten, but hee knew not, therefore he would follow his sinne yet still.

2 The speech vttered by *Debora*, [*O my soule thou hast marched valiantly*] or, as it is in the Hebrew, O my soule thou hast *trod downe strength*, namely of the enemies, which we know was very great. If wee take it in the first sense, she triumpheth in a generall manner through the courage and furtherance that God gaue her: if in the latter it is the same, but more particularly she speaketh to her soule reioycingly, that she had trode vnder foote might and strength, seeing God had armed her with power against so great enemies, as if she should say, that therefore she need to feare the power of none hereafter, God being still with her. Both affoord this worthie instruction, that when wee haue seene that God hath giuen vs great deliuerance while wee

trusted

trusted in him,as she heere did, wee should for euer after promise our selues 2.Chron.16.8.
that hee will doe the like to vs still, seeking to him in the like manner,that so Note.
we may harten our selues to beleeue it. This agreeth with Saint *Pauls* do- Rom.5.4.
ctrine, that *experience bringeth hope*: and with his practise, saying, God hath 2.Cor.1.10.
deliuered vs, doth deliuer vs, in whom wee trust that yet hereafter also,hee will deliuer vs. And doublesse this experience is the proper fruit which faith bringeth forth, without which what were our life? wee are not freed from all affliction, because we haue escaped one: but we remaine still subiect to the same, or the like: and what shall it boot vs to haue been ouercommers in the one,if we be foiled by another, (as we may easily be,euen by a lesser, without this armour) through vnbeleefe, when before through faith wee ouercame a greater. Surely, no more then it should haue booted *Dauid* to haue killed the Beare,if he had been slaine by the Lion, or the Philistim. And therefore learne hence,that though we ought to beleeue in him for his promise sake; yet we much better doe it (or ought to doe) when we haue a pawne lying by vs, I meane experience of the truth of it: but hard is the case of them who haue neither of both.

The third thing that made the Canaanites fight vnprosperously against Vers.22.
Israel, was the breaking of their horse hoofes with the oft beating together of the mighty. The horse hoofes are naturally most sound and strong,so that they be not easily cleft asunder, nor broken: but they ranne heere with such violence in that skirmish to saue themselues, and so smote one against another,that they broke their hoofes. In which case wee know, that they could neither sit their horses to pursue their enemies; neither shift for themselues by flying. This most liuely teacheth vs, that no man should trust in his owne strength,nor in the strength of an horse, in charrets, or in riches,no not in Princes power,nor in any earthly thing whatsoeuer. It is as easie for the Lord now to leaue men, and disappoint them in their vaine confidence of young yeeres,great wealth, hope of long life, or such like, as it was to plucke off *Pharaohs* chariot wheeles,and heere to breake the horses hoofes of the Canaanites, and so to bring vpon them destruction thereby. Thus we haue heard in this second branch of this second part of this chapter,how hard and ill successe the Canaanites had in this battell.

Vers. 23. *Curse ye Meroz (said the Angell of the Lord) curse the inhabitants thereof; because they came not to the helpe of the Lord, to the helpe of the Lord against the mighty.*

24. *Iael the wife of Heber the Kenite shall be blessed aboue other women, blessed shall she be aboue women dwelling in tents.*

25. *He asked water,and she gaue him milke, she brought forth butter in a lordly dish.*

26. *She put her hand to the naile, and her right hand to the workemans hammer: with the hammer smote she Sisera, she smote off his head,after she had wounded and pierced his temples.*

27. *He bowed him downe at her feete, hee fell downe, and lay still at her feet,hee bowed him downe,and fell: and when he had sunke downe, he lay there dead.*

The sense of these 5. verses. IN these verses and this part of the song followeth the third and last branch of the second part of the chapter; wherein *Debora* first setteth downe the wrath of God against such as refused to helpe in the worke of the Lord, as were the Merozites; and that shee doth in this 23. verse. And then she declareth the fauour of God toward them that helped therein, (besides those who were in the battell) as *Iael*, and this she doth in the other 4. verses. More particularly in this 23. verse she calleth all in her song to curse this city with her; for that it being neare the place where the battell was, yet the inhabitants thereof refused to helpe their brethren, being called thereto, and requested. The other tribes before mentioned had some kind of excusing themselues, neither were desired, though they knew of it; but these beheld and yet would not set hand to helpe; therefore they are thus dealt with. But seeing it might be thought to come of stomacke and reuenge, that shee pronounced such sharpe threats against them; therefore she saith, the Angell of God bad her sing so.

Vers. 23. And thereafter we are to learne what we may doe about cursing: that it is in no sort lawfull for vs to curse any man, for to satisfie our owne reuenging mindes. For when we deale in our owne matters, we must loue our enemies; and as our Sauiour teacheth, *blesse them that curse vs*: but if God at any time shew that hee will haue any to bee destroyed, they who know his will, they are to approue the same. This is the harder to learne, because that corruption which lurketh in vs, and is chained vp from notorious breaking out willingly, seeking the opportunity and pretence of zeale to shrowde it selfe vnder; euen as a secret traitor seeing the dore open which leadeth to the Princes chamber, dare not goe in alone, but waiteth till some of the nobles or guard passeth in, and in that company he cunningly conueyeth himselfe to worke mischiefe. Pray we for grace therefore to watch the dore of our lips, through which many good words of blessing passe: and let vs beware that no cursed speech passe by also, vnder what colour soeuer. And thus did *Dauid*, directed by God, and other of the faithful, who cursed Gods enemies, as in the Psalme: who yet as they were, did otherwise in kind affection, and the same not euill, bewaile them. As *Samuel*, and *Ieremy*, and our Sauiour, did bewaile and weepe for the destruction of wicked men; wherin we haue no doubt but they pleased God. Now to such as demand what they shall doe to them who vexe the godly, and rage against the Gospell? the answere is, that we are to pray God to change their minds, or to weaken their power, that they may not be able to doe the euill they would: and if this be not granted, then wee must craue strength to beare that which wee must goe vnder.

Mat 5.44.

Iam. 3.10.11.

Psal. 109.6. &c.

And heere wee must further learne, on the contrary, by the example of these of Meroz, to obey God, calling vs to any duty, as they did, who followed *Debora* and *Barak*; and to helpe those that are in want and need; especially if they follow their calling, contrary to that which these men of Meroz, and the people of Peniel and Succoth, in the seuenth chapter did, who denied to refresh *Gedeon* & his men, as they pursued his enemies and theirs. But if these were pitifully handled, and the men of Meroz cursed for not helping their brethren; what thinke we shall be done to them, who not onely helpe not the seruants of Christ, but vexe, grieue and oppresse them? And if no other thing can disswade them from such a course, yet let this; that they themselues are euer like daily to bee taken hence by death: then shall they come to their accounts, as they see on euery side many to be, who were as vnlike as they; and while they remaine here, they shall haue God against them, who hath professed that hee will bee an enemy to those that are enemies to his. And this of *Meroz* briefly, for in so long a worke I am vnwilling to repeate the same thing often. Note.

Now she calleth all Gods people to blesse and wish well to *Iael*, as one blessed among other women of her linage and kindred, who dwelt in tents, as the Kenites did; and repeateth the words for more force. Thus the Lord would haue her commended vnto all posteritie, to the rouzing vp of other, who are slack and backward in all good things, that when they shall see that God doth so highly account of the readinesse of some in his businesse, other may be quickned to the same care in well doing. For were this deeply imprinted in mens hearts, and throughly perswaded to the, and often thought of, that God knoweth their workes, and is a plentifull rewarder of all that seeke to please him, they would be much more forward, euery one in the things which are commanded him. But of this I haue spoke also by occasion offered, before. Verse 24. Heb. 11. 6.

Here *Debora* commendeth the wisedome of *Iael*, but such as proceeded from faith in her, that she called *Sisera* into her tent, and couered him, and gaue him drinke fit to cast him into a sleepe. And in that it is said, *she gaue him butter* also *in a lordly dish*; it is likely that she offered food to him, that he might drinke the more liberally. By all these she made way the more easily for that she afterward brought to passe. By this example we are taught to be wise and circumspect in the things we goe about. For though it be requisite that they bee lawfull, yet if wee bee not circumspect, and doe not forecast inconueniences, and to doe them in season, and fit time, good manner, and to the right end, there may much griefe, discommodity, and inconuenience follow, which will much disquiet vs: and through rashnes and improuidence, wee may bring that to an ill end, which yet was lawfully taken in hand of vs. As if men will embrace religion, yet they walke loosly and lightly. *Rebecca* when she saw that *Iacob* her deare sonne was deadly hated of his brother *Esau*, and that hee sought opportunitie to kill him; did not onely keepe him out of the way (for so he might one time or other haue had his will of him as *Cain* had of his brother *Abel*) but auoided many dangers at once, by sending him into a far countrey to her fathers house (from whence she came) to dwell there (though it was hard for her to forbeare the sight of him any long time) euen with her brother *Laban* in Padam Aram. And why? she knew that in that space the wrath of his brother would be abated, as she also said. A wise part therefore it was in her, in that weightie matter. And the wisedome of *Abigall* in preseruing her house, which the foolishnes of *Nabal* had otherwise destroyed, was as commendable. And such wisedome to preserue our liues, goods, credit, grace, and inward peace therewith to preuent dangers, and auoide many needlesse troubles, is a great furtherance to liue well, and to make our liues more fruitful to other, and comfortable to our selues. Onely take wee heed that we ascribe naught to our wit, and that we perke not aboue that which is meete: but in all humilitie Verse 25. Gen. 27. 43. 1. Sam. 25. 28. Note.

ſerue we Gods prouidence,and ſo we ſhall finde it no ſmall benefit to be free from careleſneſſe, raſhnes, and fooliſhnes, which throughout our life cauſe much euill and griefe,which are vnwelcome. About this ſee more in chapter 3.15.

Verſe 26. *The ſenſe.* *Debora* here addeth to the wiſedome of *Iael*, her courage and fortitude. For was it not a point of courage for a woman to ſet vpon ſo valiant a Captaine,as *Siſera* was? and to take the naile in one hand,and the hammer in the other, (it ſeemeth other weapons were not at hand) and to aduenture to ſtrike them into the temples of his head,as he lay? For what though he was aſleepe? might hee not at the firſt blow haue ſtarted and riſen vp with the paine,and ſo haue ouerthrowne her in his rage, and that a great deale more likely then to haue receiued his deadly wound at her hand? The very forme therefore, and being of this fortitude, was no manniſhnes, or ſtoutnes of courage by nature,(for of that we can ſay nothing) but only faith.

The ſenſe of verſe 27. And in this laſt verſe of this third point, in this ſecond part of the chapter; when hee was almoſt ſlaine, *Debora* ſetteth downe certaine motions, which appeare in ſuch as haue their deadly blow by violent death. For he being ſo wounded, his body through extremitie of paine, bowed twice or thrice. For he went about to riſe: but hauing no ſtrength, he fell downe againe,and lay miſerably at the feete of *Iael*. And thus God brought proud *Siſera* to ſhame,and to a fearfull end, though ſo valiant a Captaine, and that by the hand of a woman.

Now what ſhall wee ſay to this? Surely it teacheth,that when God will doe ſome great thing by any,he will alſo fit and inable them thereunto. E-
1.Sam.10.9. uen *Saul* himſelfe had an heart giuen him furniſhed with gifts for gouern-
Exod.3.11. & 10.26. ment,when God had once called him. *Moſes* when hee ſhould be ſent to *Pharao*,to carrie the people of Iſrael out of Egypt, how did hee complaine and diſable himſelfe? but when God had furniſhed him, hee waxed bold.
Luke 1.35. The Virgin Mary,when word was brought her, that ſhe ſhould be the mother of our Sauiour,anſwered with aſtoniſhment;*How can this thing be,ſeeing I know not a man?* But when it was told her by the Angell, *the holy Ghoſt ſhall come vpon thee,and the power of the moſt high ſhall ouerſhadow thee: therefore alſo that holy thing that ſhall be borne of thee,ſhall be called the ſonne of God; Then Mary ſaid,Behold the ſeruant of the Lord,be it vnto me according to thy word.*

The examples are infinite, that may be brought to this purpoſe. But I will containe my ſelfe, adding onely this one,how ſhould the Apoſtles,being poore fiſhermen,doe ſo great a worke,as to ſubdue the greateſt part of the world to their doctrine? which was as if a man would haue vndertaken to tame the wilde beaſts in the wilderneſſe: But by Chriſts ſending them the moſt powerfull gifts of the holy Ghoſt; as the confirming of their faith, the increaſe of knowledge, courage in paines taking,and to withſtand their enemies,the gift of tongues,and of working miracles, wee ſee it came ſo to paſſe. And though ſuch things be not wrought in theſe daies,as neither is it neceſſarie that ſuch ſhould now be wrought; yet many of the ordinarie workes which God will haue to be done by his, in this latter age, are great and not to be paſſed ouer ſlightly.

For how vnlike a thing is it,for a priuate man or woman, who haue no other outward gifts of God, to ſpeake of, but onely this, that they can reade the

the Scriptures in their owne language; how vnlike is it, I ſay, that ſuch li-
uing among people of moſt prophane and bad behauiour, ſhould not bee Note.
tainted with them, and defiled by them; as he that toucheth pitch? Nay,
that they being baited, diſgraced, and ſcorned of them, (as they are in many
places) ſhould not faint and be diſcouraged by them, and driuen from their
hope, and profeſſion of it, but that they ſhould walke on in the vprightnes
of their hearts, and innocencie of their hands, ſo farre and ſo long, till their
light ſo ſhining, doth lighten ſome of theſe which hated them, who ſat long
in darknes, and cauſe them to embrace that conuerſation, to the which they
had been ſuch deadly enemies before; this (I ſay) is a thing to be wondred
at, euen as to ſee the *lambe and the lion to feede together.* And yet (God bee Eſay 11.6.
bleſſed) ſo it is at this day, in ſome places, and ſo it hath bin in former times,
that when mens waies haue pleaſed the Lord, he hath cauſed not only their Prou. 16.7.
very enemies to be at one with them, but alſo their very hearts to be intirely
knit to them. Yea many ſillie perſons, ſo furniſhed with grace by God, haue
forced great ones to wiſh from their hearts, for all their wealth and power,
that they were like to them.

And yet this is more, that a Miniſter of the Goſpell, who is to challenge
them openly that keepe not the commandements of Ieſus, and in his name Reuel. 12.17.
to rebuke and threaten the workers of iniquitie (though all this is, of the lo- Iohn 16.8.
uing and kinde Preacher, done to ſaue their ſoules, by turning them from 1. Tim. 4.16.
their euill waies;) that ſuch a Miniſter, I ſay, who is not only hated for his
good will, and *counted their enemie for telling them the truth*; but alſo accuſed Gal. 4.16.
by them, purſued alſo, and not ſuffered to be quiet among them; yet ſhould
conſtantly hold out his labours, with a life vnoffenſiue, what a work of God
(thinke we) is that in him? who were like to continue ſo gracious a courſe
in the middeſt of ſo many diſcouragements (whereof I haue mentioned
but a few;) if the Lord ſhould not giue them faith to beleeue, that of their
loue to him, they ſhould feed his lambes and his ſheep, and that in ſo doing, Ioh. 21.15.
they aſſure themſelues they ſhall be plentifully rewarded? and to this end
that he will giue them ſhoulders, I meane courage to beare their ſo great a Heb. 11.6.
burthen? Theſe are no ſmall things, which yet God worketh among vs, that
we may ſee he regardeth vs, as he did ſome in former times.

The other and laſt thing to be noted in this ſecond part, is of *Siſera*; that Verſ. 27.
the Lord pulled him downe, and caſt him from his ſo great honour and va-
liantnes. For as it was a great abaſement for ſuch a *Nimrod* to be driuen to
ſo great a ſtreight, as to lurke in another mans houſe, not daring to peere
foorth (as the ſillie bird beaten into the buſh by the hawke) ſo it was yet
farre baſer to fall by the hand and at the feete of a woman. Let vs learne, that
the Lord bringeth to naught the high and haughtie, and that to their vtter Doct. verſ. 3.27.
ſhame, who were ſo great and proud. It is no ſtrange thing in the Scriptures
to finde it thus, though fooles wonder at it, who will learne no inſtruction
by it. The Lord caſteth the mightie from their ſeate. Witneſſe *Abimilech*,
who in his deſperate mood, being ſtriken on the head with a milſtone by a Iudg. 9.54.
woman, called his page, and bid him to runne him through, leſt it ſhould be
ſaid, *A woman ſlew him.* And yet that which was ſaid of him, was reprochfull
enough, to wit, that a baſe page ſlew him: and agreeth well with the point
in hand. Thus *Abſolon*, who had ſtomacke to riſe againſt his father, ſo kinde

2 Sam.18.15. to him, was brought to a base and reprochful death, very fit for such an one, being thrust through by *Ioabs* common souldiers. And *Iezabel*, scorning God and his Prophets, was, according to the fore telling of the Lord, made
2.King.9.37. dogges meate, and dung vpon the earth, being throwne out of the window from her royall palace. The proud and stout Iewes, who railed on *Peter*,
Acts 2.37. calling him despitefully, *a drunken man*, were so terrified with their sin, that they were glad to seeke to be comforted euen by him, whom they had scorned. And well is it with them, whose pride the Lord resisteth in mercie for their good, as hee did *Pauls*, by appalling him first, and then sending him to poore *Ananias*, who being his comforter now, had been a prey for him, if God had not preuented it. For the rest whom I haue mentioned (they excepted also in the second of the Acts) the other, I say, were resisted to their
1.Cor.1.21. cost and vtter vndoing. And so by the foolishnes of preaching (as it pleaseth the world to call it) and an humble submitting of themselues to his holy doctrine, they that are saued must attaine; but as that generation of vipers, the Pharisies, were glad to come to *Iohns* ministerie, if so be they tooke any
1.Pet.5.7. good by it. Be we therefore humble and meeke, they who are graced, are they that finde fauour with him; but as for the proud, he resisteth them, and setteth himselfe against them, till they be confounded (if they so abide) and be brought to naught. And therefore let the scorners and enemies taunt and mocke the simple professors of the truth, like Edomites, they shall one day wish they had been like them, and iudge them more happie then themselues, as *Diues*, for all his superfluitie, did wish that he might haue had, not the estate of *Lazarus*, (which he saw no hope to attaine) but the thousand part of it, euen that he might dip his finger in cold water, and quench his thirst; which yet might not be granted him. And therefore, let vs but stay a while, and containe our selues, and wee shall see these boasters and contemners, (if they will needs hold on their course) wee shall see them (I say) swept away, and they shall be no more: so little cause shall we see of hauing our teeth water after their dainties. They are wise, who can in the iolitie and prosperitie of the enemies of the Church, see their ouerthrow by faith,
Psal.73.18,19. and count their florishing and bragges to be but vaine crakes. And thus much be said of the second part of the Chapter.

THE

THE THIRTIE FIVE SERMON ON THE FIFTH CHAPTER OF THE BOOKE OF IVDGES.

The third part of the Chapter.

Verſ.28. *The mother of Siſera looked out at a window, and cried through the latteſſe; Why is his charet ſo long a comming? why tarrie the wheeles of his charets,&c.*

Verſ.29. *Her wiſe Ladies anſwered her, yea, ſhe anſwered her ſelfe with her owne words.*

Verſ.30. *Haue they not gotten, and they diuide the ſpoile? euery man hath a maide or two, Siſera hath a prey of diuers coloured garments; a prey of ſundrie colours made of needle worke on both ſides, for the chiefe of the ſpoile.*

Verſ.31. *So let all thine enemies periſh, O Lord, but they that loue him, ſhall be as the Sunne when he ariſeth in his might. And the land had reſt fortie yeeres.*

IN theſe words is contained the third and laſt part of the ſong of *Debora*, and ſo of the Chapter, and hath two members: in the firſt, ſhe bringeth in the boaſtings of the women that were enemies to Gods people, and *Siſeras* deare friends, and derides them, in the firſt three verſes. In the laſt member, ſhe oppoſeth a propheticall prayer againſt their boaſtings, wiſhing therein to the remainder of Gods enemies, deſtruction; and to the Iſraelites, all increaſe of good things: and that increaſe ſhe laieth out by a compariſon of the Sunne from the riſing to the noone tide; euen ſuch ſhe wiſheth it to be. More particularly, to come to the firſt point, ſhe ſaith, that *Siſeras* mother was looking out, and longing for her ſonnes retune, with his great ſpoile and bootie, fearing yet the hardeſt, becauſe he tarried ſo long, till ſhe was anſwered by her Ladies, and ſo anſwered her ſelfe; that he was buſie in diuiding the ſpoile. *The ſenſe of all theſe verſes.* *Of the 28. particularly.*

This place laieth out the exceeding care that parents haue of the welfare of their children, and the thought they take for them in any likelihood of danger, they being betwixt hope and feare about them: and if they be long out of ſight, they are much penſiue for them, and troubled within themſelues, eſpecially if they be in any perill. The which (ſetting apart the odious fact of *Siſera*) was commendable in his mother, and according to the rule of nature, to hope and long for his proſperous returne, and to feare the contrarie. So *Saul*, that was after King of Iſrael, knew his fathers affection to be ſo tender ouer him, that when he was ſent to ſeeke his aſſes, and tarried long, not finding; he haſted home, leſt his father ſhould turne the care of recouering the aſſes into care for his ſonne. And *Iob*, though in a farre better reſpect, *Doct. verſe 28.* *1.Sam.9.5.* *2.Sam.18 33.* *1.Sam.9.5.*

spect, feared, euen when his sonnes feasted together for increase of loue, lest they should offend God. So *Dauid* in his charge to *Ioab*, abounding in this tender loue toward his sonne *Absolon*; when hee made warre against him, did streightly command him to intreate him gently: And S. *Paul* teacheth,
1.Tim.5.8. that we should haue care of our owne; which well becommeth all, and the contrarie is vnnaturall: whether wee respect their neglect of their bodily maintenance, and so leauing them to sinke or swimme, when yet they may relieue them, or their soules welfare and saluation, by neglecting or denying them holy instruction & education in the waies of the Lord; by meanes whereof, they are left as a prey to the lewd and bad, by their wicked companie and example; which is farre worse then bodily penurie and miserie, though who knoweth not, that it is wofull to be brought vp idle, and without a lawfull trade of life, destitute of necessaries. Of both vnderstand that
Prou.22.6. of *Salomon*; Teach a childe, &c else he may teach thee on the gallowes. But
2.Tim.3.3. ἄστοργοι. as there is a sinne in the defect, that is, vnnaturalnes in parents to their children, not to be allowed, no not so much as that of *Siseras* mother, which I last of all mentioned; so there is in the excesse, another sinne that is farre more common then that; as when parents are too fond ouer their children, and cannot abstaine from shewing affection toward them, and that without discretion, to wit, to the vnruly, disobedient, and subtill and wilfull; as well as to the simple, timerous, tractable, and religious; whereby they giue them occasion, nay they incourage them to abuse them boldly, saucily, and with small respect, and to winde them which way they list. Thus *Dauid* by *Adoniah*, and *Ely* by his sonnes found it, and smarted for it accordingly. Whereas men should hold their children in a godly awe, and keepe them within compasse, by authoritie, which God hath giuen them ouer them; and yet not in rigour, neither voide of parentlike kindnesse. For want of which re-
Note. gard had by parents toward their children, on both sides great inconuenience falleth out; that some are handled and oppressed with vnseasonable seueritie, who deserue it not; and other are cockered with too much indulgence and lenitie, till they be made much the worse for it. And not much vnlike to this last mentioned affection in parents, is this, or rather a branch of it; that some of them, through a deceiuable humour, deale out their loue to their children vnequally, when yet by the cariage of themselues it is equally deserued, affecting the one for some outward respect, or priuate conceit; as *Isaac* did *Esau*, and *Dauid Absolon*, who thought there was not such another to be found.

There is yet another error in parents toward their children, who are too farre carried in affection to them, and that is, that because it is permitted vnto them, nay commanded, to prouided for them; therefore they runne into most troublesome and pensiue care to prouide for them, and thereby fall into most noisome temptations & snares of the diuell to benefit them, whereas they ought to haue well learned this lesson before, that for all their affection toward them, they should not offend God for their sakes, nor neglect or lose any grace, neither leaue any worke of charitie and mercie vndone, nor ieopard their owne saluation by wounding their conscience any manner of way for them: They should consider, that it is ill pitie towards their children, which makes them impious against God, and iniurious against man,

man, and moſt of all againſt themſelues: nay rather, what torment ſhall it not be to their conſciences, vnleſſe it be worſe, to remember that they haue increaſed their childrens portions with the complaints of the poore, or through their worldlineſſe, and they muſt now goe and ſuſtaine endleſſe woe for it. Note.

But while I thus ſpeake, it ought of children to be marked, that this affection of the parents, if it were but according to nature rectified, and ſanctified in them toward their children, (though it did not weaken their eſtate for their preferment, (as I haue noted out of the fact of *Calebs* endowing his daughter) ought to be a ſufficient motiue and perſwaſion to them their children, euer to ſhew all reuerence, obedience, and thankfulnes to them; though many parents, and mothers eſpecially, who can moſt hardly bee brought to keepe within their bounds toward their children, may after they come to yeeres of diſcretion, iuſtly complaine, that the more they haue ſhewed their loue to them, the leſſe they are ſet by, and regarded of them. Oh what I haue obſerued and ſeene in this which I now ſpeake of, and that not in one or two? but another occaſion may be giuen to ſay more of it in another place. And this of *Siſeras* mothers affection to him.

Of *Siſeras* mothers ſpeech we haue heard, much longing for his returne: Now it followeth in this verſe, how the other Ladies, among whom his wife was thought to be, anſwered her, and that in ſuch wiſe, as appeareth in the text, that ſhe being ſorrowful, was ready to take comfort by their words; euen as all that be in heauineſſe (which is vnwelcome of it ſelfe) would willingly, and are eaſily brought to deſire comfort, yea though it be not miniſtred to them from any good ground, nor aright. And the ſumme of their comfort was this; that there was no doubt nor queſtion to be made, but that *Siſera* had got the victorie ouer his enemies: and that his tariance was, as in ſuch caſes it falleth out, for the diſtributing of the bootie and ſpoile which was taken therein, to euery one according to his labour, condition, and worthineſſe: which (ſaid they) being much and of great value, after ſo noble a conqueſt, it could not in a ſhort time be diſpatched. This was the conceit and falſe perſwaſion of the Ladies, wherein they reſted, and did comfort themſelues for all that his long tariance. And it ſetteth a worthie inſtructiō before vs: namely, how readie people are to be carried away with vaine conceits and vngrounded hopes of comfort, and how eaſily they deceiue themſelues therewith: whereas they ſhould looke that they haue good warrant for that wherein they take comfort. For elſe what other thing is it, then as the common prouerbe ſpeaketh, namely a building of caſtles in the ayre? Euen as hee that dreameth ſleeping, or imagineth waking, that the thing which hee deſireth, ſhall euen ſo come to paſſe as hee would haue it. What is more fooliſh then to pleaſe ones ſelfe in thinking, that he may finde ſuch a maſſe of gold, and be aduanced to ſuch and ſuch honour, and thereupon to take pleaſure in promiſing himſelfe what a pleaſant life hee will leade. Verſe 29.30. *The meaning.* Doct. verſ. 29.

And is this fooliſhnes thus to deceiue a mans ſelfe? Then how much greater wiſedome is it, or what better ground hath it, which the wiſe men of the world (as they are called) doe make their common practiſe? who yet doe ſcorne the fanſies and dreames of the other, who haue naught? And that

that is this: They reckon how long they shall liue in the estate they are in, and hope to come to better. They make account what great bargaines they shall haue, and what great gainings and commings in: how plentifull increase their corne, cattell, and other commodities shall bring foorth. Others in another kinde, euen about that which best liketh their humour, doe seriously beate their braines, how they may be reuenged vpon them whom they deadly hate, and what meanes and waies they will vse to bring them low, and haue their will of them. Another sort resolue how merrie they will be with their mates and companions, in drinking, whoring, and in their sundrie kindes of play and pastime: whereas many times they are cut off from their hope before, and when it is come, it lasteth not. All these and such like, as *Agag* (who merrily promised himselfe, that al feare of death was past, when it was at hand) what warrant haue they of these their conceits and fond delusions, and dangerous dreames? When S. *Iames* mocketh one sort of them, saying; *Goe to, ye that say, to morrow we will goe to such a place, &c.* And againe, *Salomon* challengeth all sorts of them, asking them why they boast of to morow, when they cannot tell what may fall out ere to morow, in such a changeable world as this is, and what alterations may come before? as they that obserue may see daily, to the iust condemning of all such for meere fooles, that rest vpon such brused reedes, and broken holds, and yet goe for the only wise men.

Note.

Iames 4.13.

Prou. 27.1.

How many haue made their account all these waies that I haue mentioned, to haue their will fulfilled? and to vexe Gods people at the heart, threatning to roote them out, as *Haman* did the Iewes; who yet haue themselues been, before their reckoning was accomplished and brought to passe, ouerthrowne and laid in the dust? For do such as are but wormes, looke to haue the Lord at commandement? and to appoint him how hee shall rule the world, dispose of things, and serue their turnes? And yet as absurd a thing as this is, what one among many is ashamed of his boldnes and folly, or as if he were wearie of it, and repented, doth take a better course, and seeketh to haue warrant and good assurance of that which he comforteth himselfe in? or how many other take example by them to be any whit the wiser?

Note.

But for better sight into the folly of these men: and to make it appeare to be more grosse, let vs put the case, that these future ioyes of theirs were not vncertaine, as they are of all seene and found to be, but that they were sure to enioy all their pleasures, profits, and iolities that they make account of, and that also as long as sense and strength would suffer; what had they gotten? Must they not soone be forced with old *Barzillai* for very age to giue ouer, and to say, Can we discerne betwixt good and euill? haue we any taste in that we eate, or in that wee drinke? can wee heare any more the voyce of singing men and women? But although these are dangerous errors (as who can say lesse of them?) yet they are but (as we say) particuler aberrations in their actions, whiles many of them haue been taught, and doe professe to be better gouerned: whereas there is another kind of conceitednes, to wit, of erroneous iudgement, no lesse common, but farre more dangerous, because it directly concerneth the hope of eternal life, which they are content to fixe on mens opinions, renouncing the pure word of God for their light and direction; whose liues cannot possibly please God, when they haue no faith

2.Sam.19.35.

faith to beleeue in his promises. Such is the vnsauourie and damnable doctrine of Rome, whose light is darknesse, and their best comforts are deadly and strong errors, and blasphemous delusions.

Others there are, who through meere ignorance, suffer themselues to be led into a fooles paradise, conceiuing strangely of their good case they are in, because of their false perswasion, that God is mercifull; and that they are none of the worst sort: God (they trow) neuer made them to damne them: they meane well (they say) and heare, pray, receiue the Sacrament, loue honestie, with a thousand such worne reasons. And yet error is so strong, (especially in this kinde) that euery man cleaueth to his conceit, and as the prouerbe is, wee easily beleeue that, which wee would haue so: whereas, God knoweth, the end of this hope is shame. The mother of *Sisera* was neuer more notably disappointed of her hope and expectation, then these fooles shall be, when they looke for the effect thereof, as the spiders web, which is swept downe in a moment.

But to returne to that from which I a little digressed, I meane, of mens putting their confidence in things changeable and transitorie, in as much as all this which I haue spoken of, vanish in a short time; so what wisedome is it to hunt after such things, as children doe after a butterflye? and to make them their felicitie, as if God had appointed no better things to be attained and come by? Nay further, seeing they must giue an account of these their doings, which they shall neuer be able to doe, to their comfort, of one among a thousand; what wisedome is this to be counted, when they must for their pleasures of sinne, which they enioyed so little a while, when they must (I say) heare the sentence pronounced vpon them, Depart ye that were louers of pleasures more then of God, to endlesse woe, where weeping and gnashing of teeth shall be, who would needes preferre a short and small folly, before happinesse eternall.

Note.

Luke 13.47.
2.Tim.3.4.

Therefore let vs learne first, to ground our opinion out of the word, and be sure wee can well iustifie our hopes and conceits: and reioyce in these things that will stand by vs, and whereof we haue good warrant from Gods owne mouth: which cannot deceiue vs, nor frustrate our hope. And if yee aske, what this reioycing is that I meane; I answere, this: to know that our names are written in heauen: and to endeuour to haue alwaies a good conscience both before God and men: to haue ioy in the holy Ghost, and to be perswaded that a crowne of glorie is laid vp for vs, when wee shall once lay downe this tabernacle of our body, and shall haue finished this our course in this manner. In a word, our ioy ought to be in the Lord, and in his alsufficiencie. And let this be to vs in stead of the boastings that other make here, of their vaine, vncertaine, and deceiuable hope, and ioy, as this was of these heathen and prophane Ladies, who might haue waited and hoped for *Siseras* ioyfull returne, till their eyes had fallen out of their heads, before they could haue enioyed that which they looked for, but as farre from it then, as at the first.

Luke 10.20.
Act 23.1.
2.Cor.1.12.
2 Cor.5.1.

More particularly in this 30. verse, *Debora* being a Propheteffe, laieth out in her song how the Ladies did descant of the diuiding of the spoile, in these two points, that besides their goods, euery souldier got a maide or two, but *Sisera* had precious things, namely, garments of diuers colours wrought by

Verse 30.
Doct.

the needle, which were very costly. By the first, that they must needs so immodestly and vnchastly breake foorth, (as *Debora* saith they did) speaking of the common souldiers, that euery one got a maide or two at his pleasure, which if it were so, was vnmeete talke for women to haue in their mouthes, it sheweth, where there is no true knowledge of God and his word, there whoredome is but a pastime and may-game, a matter to laugh at euen among women as well as men; yea euen in the aged themselues (who should goe before others in sobrietie) we shall behold yet, a delight to speake of, see, and heare vncleane actions and reports, euen as other weightie matters are also lightly set by of them. Which is the lesse marueile that it was so with them, when euen where the Gospell is preached, it may be seene to be so. In so much, that they may praise God highly, who haue receiued light and conscience to make difference betwixt good and euill, and to abhorre and haue in detestation this vngracious and rotten kinde of speech not beseeming Christians, and all such cursed workes of darknesse; which to doe, is farre off from them who liue in darknesse, and walke in vnbeliefe.

But these Ladies ascribe to *Sisera* the costliest and best things, as we haue heard. Where besides that wee see, that they and all such deceiued themselues in their erroneous conceits, as hath been shewed before; so wee may
Note. see what are the things which be in best account with the ignorant and vnbeleeuers, and they are iolitie, earthly glorie, and things costly and precious in the estimation of men. As for thankes to God, of whom they receiue all, and for making heauen their treasure and portion, it is no such matter as they are acquainted with, or doe (almost) dreame of. Which is still to teach Gods seruants how great their portion is, who haue not the things of greatest price in this world, their rest and treasure, but things durable and eternall: but more of this before.

Verse 31. Now by this acclamation with ioy, *Debora* concludes her song, praying, that as *Sisera* triumphed, so might al Gods enemies: meaning, that as he was destroyed, so all like enemies of God might be: and on the contrarie, that all who loue the Lord may not only be preserued, but multiplied and beautified with all good things, euen as the Sunne groweth in his beautie to the noonetide. Where first, in that *Sisera* was shamefully slaine, and returned no more home with victorie, as his mother also did feare as much, let vs learne, that the euill which the wicked feare, shall light vpon them. Their feares are many, as both the Scripture testifieth, that feare shall be vpon
Psal. 32.10. them on euery side, euen as their sorrowes also are many. And whereas I
Obiect. noted before, that they doe please themselues greatly in their hope of the best things, some may thinke I contradict my selfe, in saying they are afraid,
Answ. and fearfull: I answere, they may haue both; feare, I meane, and hope, at diuers times, and yet neither of them good, but hope deceiuable, and feare troublesome. Beside, wicked persons are not all of the same kinde, and feare is seene most in them who are least euill: but boldnes is in the worser sort:
1. Ioh. 4. 18. all wicked men incline to feare properly and naturally; for it is a companion to sinne, ignorance, and vnbeliefe, but they hope and presume wilfully, and labour to expell feare, which though in great part they doe indeede, yet because no violent thing is continuall, therefore oft times they mistrust, and feare, and suspition of trouble comes in place againe. And we may see, that

that list to marke it, that it is so, as in *Balaam*, who wishing that hee might haue died the death of the righteous, feared that he should not doe so. The same I may say of many other: For why? they running deep in debt with God, their conscience accuseth them, that they shall one time or other be called to their vnwelcome account, and so, the thing that they feare, shall come vpon them. And yet will they not come to agreement with God, by iudging themselues, that so they may not bee iudged of him, but bee free from all feare (as frailtie will permit) of his iudgement, and therefore refusing so to doe, their feare iustly falleth vpon them. Numb.23.10. 1.Cor.11.31.

The saying of *Salomon* proueth that they haue many feares, where hee saith, *the wicked flieth when no man pursueth him*: that is, through feare. And that may be seene to haue possessed the very Pharisies (who yet bare it out most boldly before men) by the words of *Nicodemus*, bewraying his fellow Pharisies ill conscience through feare, saying to Christ, *We know that thou art a teacher sent of God,* and acknowledge thy great miracles: as if hee should haue added this, though wee will not be knowne of any such thing before men, yet thus it is with vs, when wee meete and talke of thee together, and are afraid. But some will aske, What then shall we doe to such? shall we aduise them to shake off their feares, and plucke vp their hearts against them? Doubtlesse no: this were to fight against their conscience, and to make it impudent and hardned (which is much worse) whereas it did before but accuse them: but if they cannot preuent such feare by remouing the cause thereof, which is their sinne, let them next to that be perswaded to repent for it. We reade of the third Captaine that came to *Elias*, that beholding his two fellowes deuoured with fire from heauen for doing their message to the Prophet so imperiously and boldly, he came to him in all submisnes, and entreated him to come downe to the King. Euen so, to come to our selues, aske thy conscience what makes thee feare? If thou findest that the Lord hath a controuersie with thee, and (that depending) and that thou canst not be quiet, goe and seeke agreement with him, as the Captaine did; it is but a follie to stand out with the Lord: for if thy conscience accuse thee, he is greater, as knowing much more against thee. If thou canst come to the Lord, and say, in the truth of thine heart; O Lord, I feare lest my sinne should bring some sudden destruction vpon me: I haue no peace within, nor without, because of it, and thy displeasure for it; I goe continually in hazard of some fruite thereof, besides that which is eternall: therefore, say (O Lord) humble me, and cause me to feare sinne, and not the punishment only: turne my terror into broken heartednesse for sin, and so bring peace and quietnes againe into my soule. Doe thus, I say, and thy feares shall vanish; otherwise, who shall pitie thee in them, if thou pitiest not thy selfe, in taking the way to remoue them? And to this purpose, I aske, did not the Priests in the Gospell meete with that which they feared, when Christ, whom they would needs crucifie, that they might be rid of him, rose againe? to bring a greater feare vpon them at the last then at the first? And as they would in no wise feare, when th eir sinne was at the highest, and yet we see they were constrained to feare; so there is no doubt, but that there are some hardned, which doe what they can, to put feare away from them, *hauing their consciences seared with an hot iron, whose damnation* (yet) *sleepeth not*, neither shal they Prou.28.1. Ioh.3.2. 2.King 1.14. 1.Ioh.3 20.

escape feare, but it will seaze vpon them, when they would not. And wheras it may be said, the godly are much afraid sometime as well as other; I answere, it is true: but that tendeth to a good end; as if they haue taken libertie amisse, or rather stolne it, to breake out of the good and righteous way which they had couenanted to walke in, they cannot but bee afraid, when they come againe to themselues; but it is for that they see they haue offended their mercifull father, therefore they cannot be quiet, till they bee in fauour againe with him. And let the other know, that euen so and much more must they do, to wit, in their falles, feare; and take no rest nor peace to themselues before that: else, when their time commeth, that which they feare, shall also fall vpon them: but if they consider duly of their estate, and while they may, and before the time of their trouble come, turne their feet againe into the way of Gods testimonies, God will burie all the indignities which
Hos. 14 3. they haue wrought against him, and will receiue them graciously.

2 In the first branch of her propheticall prayer, that, not her enemies, but Gods, might be as *Sisera*, she hauing warrant so to pray, did as became her, and so shall all wee doe, who shall doe so, vpon so good a ground and warrant: but otherwise take we heed that wee pray not against any, what faire pretence soeuer wee haue to doe so: for as God hath reclaimed very bad ones, so what know wee whom he may call home among vs? But of this I haue spoken.

3 For the other part of *Deboras* prayer, that the louers of God may prosper in the abundance of all good things, and grow therein, as the Sunne doth in his strength to the noonetide, let it bee noted, that this is prayed for to them that loue the Lord; and onely to them, as the blessing in the second Commandement is to them that loue him, who testifie that they doe so, by keeping his commandements. And this prayer being made in faith, obtaines as much, as is asked in it. And therefore when she prayeth for it, it is all one, as if she had affirmed, that it shall be so: namely, that they which loue the Lord shall want nothing that is good. And so *Dauid* saith, who had good
Psal. 23. 1. experience of it, that the Lord withholdeth no good thing from such as
Psal 84 13. keepe their hearts pure and good: which none can doe, but they that loue him. Yea and marke further that she saith, they shall grow therein euen from strength to strength as the Sunne doth, euen to his full beautie. So speaketh *Salomon* in the Prouerbs: The way of the righteous shineth as the light,
Prou. 4. 18. that shineth more and more vnto the perfit day: signifying thereby, that
Luke 2. 52. the godly herein resemble the Lord Iesus, who himselfe increased in strength of body with addition of grace, and fauour with God and men: and so they also increase daily in knowledge and grace, vntill they bee ioyned to Christ their head, and see the Lord in the Sion of his holinesse.

Behold then here a singular priuiledge, which the louers of God doe enioy: that while they looke carefully and constantly to preserue and vphold the loue of God in them, euen thereby they grow in grace and knowledge of God, and of Christ; and they come to haue more neere acquaintance with them, and haue proofe of their fatherly kindnes toward them, and so haue stronger hope, that it shall yet be better with them afterward: for their obedience passed, yeeldeth them more courage and strength to go forward in their good course. Now if we did consider the miserable courses of many ny,who for want of this gracious gouernment of God,runne into all kinde of ſinne,and fearefull puniſhments,(for the wicked waxe worſe and worſe) and how ſome euen of Gods deare ſeruants by their very declinings and careleſnes, for a ſmall time,ſee many ill daies,how ſhould we make account of this precious libertie, bequeathed vnto vs in this behalfe? For ſuch as looke to the maintaining of the loue of God in them, and the nouriſhing Note. of it by thankfull acknowledging of his euer flowing kindneſſe toward them,(I ſpeake a great thing) neede to feare no worſe eſtate to Godward then they haue enioyed alreadie : but euery day to looke for better and better,both greater faith,and better obedience; which cannot be wanting to Note. vs,but when we are wanting to our ſelues, and failing in our loue to God: and yet I meane no perfectiō of it,which cannot be in any,but more vſe of ſinceritie and feruencie in Gods ſeruice, euen ſuch as hath alreadie been in them. But he that liſteth to reade more of this growing in grace of my ſetting downe,may reade the twelfth chapter of the ſixth treatiſe of my book. In the meane ſeaſon, let this ſpeech of *Debora*, make ſuch to looke better about them, who are farre from this thriuing and growth in grace, or the fruite of it,if they deſire to be in honour and fauour with God. And if they be voide of them,let them know,that the cauſe thereof is,that they loue not God, whatſoeuer they pretend to the contrarie; and without that, what welfare can there be to the ſoule? It cannot proſper,but rather decaieth as a man that is ſicke of a deſperate diſeaſe, and growes worſe and worſe, till vtter conſumption and death it ſelfe doe follow. Therefore it is a worke of no ſmall weight to trie our ſelues whether we loue God: it will quite the coſt abundantly. If we can once get that, wee are on the thriuing hand, no feare but wee ſhall doe well: and then wee giue good proofe thereof,when wee loue,and deſire well to the brethren,when nothing is too deare for himſelf, and where there is ſtill an earneſt thirſting after both: (as all things that grow haue an appetite of growth) theſe (I ſay) with more then a common care of honouring God in the place we liue in, a daily longing home, with vprightnes and conſtancie; are euidences of our loue to God that cannot deceiue. And this affection (be wee well aſſured) will breake out where it is,by ſuch fruite as I haue mentioned,as *Iosephs* did vnto his brethren. Gen.45.1

4 To this ſong of *Debora*, the holy ſtorie addeth this, that God gaue his people by and after this victorie, fortie yeeres reſt and quietnes. A great bleſſing: euen ſo we all know what a benefit any great deliuerance is,out of paine,ſickneſſe,priſon, bondage,penurie,or the like miſerie,eſpecially when it is for long continuance? But how much more then, the ſweete peace of conſcience that paſſeth vnderſtanding, and ioy in the holy Ghoſt, and that for long continuance, after the trouble of minde and feare of damnation, which was ſometime? But of this alſo elſewhere ſomewhat hath been ſaid.

THE THIRTIE SIXE SERMON ON THE SIXTH CHAPTER OF THE BOOKE OF IVDGES.

Vers.1. *Afterward the children of Israel committed wickednesse in the sight of the Lord, and the Lord gaue them into the hands of Midian seuen yeeres.*

Vers.2. *And the hand of Midian preuailed against Israel: and because of the Midianites, the children of Israel made them dennes in the mountaines, and caues, and strong holds.*

Vers.3. *When Israel had sowne, then came vp the Midianites, the Amalekites, and they of the East, and came vpon them,*

Vers.4. *And camped by them, and destroyed the fruite of the earth, euen till thou come vnto Azzah, and left no foode for Israel, neither sheepe, nor oxe, nor asse.*

Vers.5. *For they went vp, and their cattell, and came with their tents, as Grashoppers in multitude, so that they and their camels were without number; and they came into the land to destroy it.*

Vers.6. *So was Israel exceedingly impouerished by the Midianites: therefore the children of Israel cried vnto the Lord.*

The summe and parts of this Chapter are 4.

IN this Chapter, it is shewed, how Israel againe prouoked the Lord by their wickednesse, vers.1. And how the Lord punished them by the Midianites, to vers.6. Then that they cried vnto the Lord, and he reproued them, to vers.11. And lastly, how he called *Gedeon* and prepared him to deliuer them; and this is to the end of the Chapter.

The first part of the Chapter.

The summe of the first part.

TO begin with their sinne, it appeares that they did grieuously prouoke the Lord, as they had sometime before done, as in the third and fourth Chapters it appeares, where their punishment was likewise a long time continued vpon them. But yet after the death of *Debora* and *Barak*, the valiant deliuerers of them out of the hands of the Canaanites, they did againe depart from the good course wherein they had liued before, and fell againe to idolatrie, and other sinnes. This be said of their sinne, as may be gathered out of the first verse, and the 25.

With the which to begin, for our further benefit, the instruction that we are to take out of from hence, is this; That seeing in all the stories before set downe, as well as this, of the punishing of Israel, they begin thus: The children of Israel did againe that which was euill in the sight of the Lord: seeing

ing (I say) it is thus, we may learne, that it is naturally ingrafted in the heart of man, that though there bee holy affections kindled in it by some good meanes, yet in time they dye, and wane away; and in stead of them, the heart is carried againe to the euill, that it most desireth. And it being thus with them that haue some goodnesse and beginnings of faith in them, what are all the faire shewes of hypocrites, when they be at the best, but a morning dew? So that though men may (perhaps) serue God for a while, Hos. 6.4.
in a good manner; yet they are gone from it before wee be aware, waxing wearie and prouoking God afresh; this ficklenes and inconstancie are so deeply rooted in them, and thereupon it falleth out, that they are carried away by the error of the wicked, and inticements of the world, from a good course; to be fashioned like other men, though it be very grosse and absurd which they fall to.

A great reason hereof is this, that the best are renewed but in part, and much corruptiō remaineth to be purged out of thē, which requireth the taking vp of their thoughts and care; which it is meet they should take knowledge of, that so they may see that they haue worke enough, (and haue little Note.
cause to be idle and waxe wearie of it, I meane (beside many other duties) of crossing aud subduing the euill of their hearts; especially, seeing their reward is so great in so doing. And yet with griefe it may be said, that in all ages, both persons and Churches little considering this, haue fallen to this course that I now complaine of. As they in the Psalme, *who started aside like a* Psal. 78.35.
broken bow. The people in Exodus did the like; who in the absence of *Moses* from them, but a few daies, fell most shamefully to idolatrie. So the peo Exod. 32.6.
ple mentioned in S. *Iohn*, who counted *Iohn* Baptist *a burning light, and for a* Ioh. 5.35.
time reioyced in him: whereby yee may gather, it was but for a time. These with many, too long to be stood vpon, doe shew, how soone men decline from a good course.

And wel it were with vs in this latter age, if we looked better to our selues then they did: but as well persons and families, as almost whole townes, wanze and waxe cold in their seruing of God; who yet were sometime of the forwarder sort of professors, a few God reserueth who desire to keepe their first loue to the Gospell, and their brethren, that they may be a seed in Note.
euery corner of the land almost, to teach the generations to come, (if the world continue) to feare the Lord aright, hee hauing appointed a remnant to remaine, and a Church, though small, vnto the worlds end. Which being so, teacheth the best of vs, what need we haue to desire to enioy the best meanes, and namely the sincere preaching of the Gospell, whereby we may grow on in grace and knowledge of Christ, and cleaue neerely to him: considering how oft wee haue been by Gods gracious working in vs, reuiued and refreshed thereby: and how dead in good duties wee are, and vnprofitable (our consciences being Iudges) without them. And it is well, if here by this, we winde out of all poisoned baites that are laid for vs.

And this of the first of the foure parts of the Chapter I haue spoken in this former part of this verse, and somewhat also before in other Chapters, that is, of the peoples sinne.

The second part of the Chapter.

NOw it followes, the second, that is, of the punishment that followed their sinne,and how they cried to the Lord vnder it,in these sixe verses. Their punishment was seuen yeeres oppression by the Midianites, as in this verse is to be seene,and the manner of their oppressing them,is set downe in the fiue verses following. And for their oppression by the Midianites, let it teach vs,that it was iust because they had sinned. For God scourgeth men iustly,and not without their due desert: *Man suffereth for his sinne*,as the Prophet *Ieremy* saith: So that if any should thinke they are hardly handled, being punished of God, let them proue themselues without sinne, or else let them hold their peace. Nay,I will yeeld more then so to them,let them be able but to proue this,that they haue only offended through infirmitie,and not rather wilfully,and of knowledge,and they shall either be freed altogether from great vexations in their liues; or else they shall freely and without constraint confesse,that God hath dealt iustly,yea mercifully,in so visiting of them,rather then that he hath done them any wrong. Thus much for this,and that God will punish, when men prouoke him by their transgressions,as we may here learne,I haue in other places shewed.

Verse 1. Doct.2.in vers.1. Lamen.3.40.

Verse 2. *The sense.*

The manner of the Midianites oppressing the people of Israel, was the spoiling them of their victuall,namely corne and cattell, for the space of seuen yeeres,without which they could not liue. Their corne they destroied, when they had sowen their fields. And they were driuen to make them cabins in the hollow places of the earth, vnder the hils and rocks,where they had holes and creuises to let in light,to defend themselues from them: and in the fields and lower parts of the earth they made them dennes and darke places,not fit for habitation,but in which they might safely lay their goods and substance,to hide them from the Midianites. They made also high towers and strong,from which they might see a farre off, which could not be beaten down easily: and these shifts they were faine to make. For their enemies were as grashoppers on the face of the earth, and their camels and other beasts,to destroy the fruites of the Israelites,were almost without number. What these Midianites were, and of what stocke they came, it is not necessarie to inquire,seeing it is not set downe,though some writers say that they had their beginnings thus: that one of *Abrahams* sonnes which he begat of his wife *Ketura*,builded a citie beyond Arabia in the South,in the desert of the now called Saracens, and called the name of it Midian, or Madian, and the people of it were called Midianites,or Madianites,and were supposed to be they of whom the Kenites came. These brought with them the Amalakites,and men of the East to helpe them.

Deut.28.33. Esay 17.10.11.

This was a grieuous and sore affliction, to be thus driuen to extremities for want of food. And yet no other then was long before threatned (among many other) to come vpon them for their apostacie and idolatrie. For what though we heare of no consuming of the people of Israel in battell; yet, beside that it could not be, but that many of them were slaine by so long and violent assaulting them, so what death is more cruell then by liuing, to be famished?

famished? and what miserie in this life greater, then to be to seeke of foode, where it can hardly be come by, and yet that which is to bee reserued, and had, is scarcely fit to preserue life? Here therefore by the contrary wee may see, what a benefit of God this is, when in a land, and in cities, townes and villages, all people may be fed fit for their condition, when there is no inuasion of forraine enemies to spoile and destroy the fruits of the earth, whereby the inhabitants are preserued: nor any famine, by any other iudgement of God; and when there is no iust cause of complaining in our streetes. We know in the great famines that are mentioned in the Scriptures, yea and in smaller famines in our owne remembrance, what crying and lamentations there haue been. In the daies of *Abraham*, *Isaac*, and chiefly of *Iacob*, when they were forced to send into Egypt for corne. Gen.42.2. In the time of *Elimelek* and *Naomi*, when they were driuen from their dwelling in Bethelem Iuda, to goe and soiourne in the land of *Moab*, for want of food: Ruth 1.1. and after in the daies of *Ioram* King of Israel, when the men had no other way to preserue their liues, but by eating that which was against nature, yea and yet they could hardly come by it; 2.King.6.25. and when the women did eate their own children, as also in the last besieging of Ierusalem by the Romans.

And to what end speake I this, but that we should lift vp our hearts, and more feruently, and oft be thankfull to God for this one benefit of plentie? although who seeth not, that it is indeed but one of many, yea of infinite other, which wee receiue? And why doth God this? Euen to the end men may follow their callings, diligently and conscionably, with cheerefulnes; Doct. vers. 2, 3, 4, 5. and with the same minde walke in the feare of the Lord continually. And therefore the euill example in life, that in the abundance of Gods earthly blessings doth flow euery where, in drunkennesse, and all lasciuiousnes, doth draw vpon men greater plagues, then wants and famine are, and that is, leanenes of soule, blindnes, vnbeliefe, hardnesse of heart, and impenitencie: which if we had the spirit of the Prophets, wee should deeply bewaile. But to leaue such, I adde this, that for the quickning vp of the best, it were fit for them, Note. when they grow to a meane and common esteeming of these benefits of God, to suppose with themselues, and put the case that they were in want and penurie, euen in the state of this people of God by the oppression of the Midianites, or the like: As that when they haue sowne their seede, it should be spoyled before their faces, so that they should not eate of it, and that the prouision which they haue made for their liues, should be carried away by enemies, or taken from them, and they famished for want of it: it would make them better to value and prize such benefits, and yeeld to the Lord a more holy and fruitfull vse of them. Whereas commonly men doe not so, till they be driuen to it by wants, and decay in their substance, then they can say; Oh what plentie of Gods benefits we once enioyed?

Another thing in these verses is to be marked, that we bring double vexation vpon our selues by sinning against the Lord, Doct. 2. and by seeking to haue our will, against the word of God. The one is this, the affliction that is sent vpon vs for sinne, as here the stirring vp of the Midianites against the people of Israel for their transgression; or any other, as losse of their goods, diseases, ieopardie of their liues, &c. The other vexation, is that which proceedeth from the former: and that is of many sorts, as may be liuely seene in this present

sent storie,and namely in these verses. For what toile,time,and cost, beside the disquietnes that went therewith, were they driuen to bestow (that I may include much in few words) to defend,or to saue themselues from the vtmost hurt and danger, which was wrought and intended against them? what shifts were they faine to make to preserue their liues, and saue their goods out of their enemies hands? which yet when they had done what they could,they were not able to doe.

If they had been only hurt by them in their cattell,corne,and other commodities, and had sustained that onely for their punishment,it had been a
Note. deare paying for their pleasure,that they took in their sinne; but when they were in this bondage,that they could doe nothing else but watch and ward for their liues, and to build and botch, digge and delue, and beate their braines to deuise, how to hide their commodities from them, what sorrow vpon sorrow, and one vnquietnes vpon another did they heape vpon their heads, till they lost all the welfare of their liues in a manner, and made them more wearisome and vnwelcome then death it selfe? Is this the fruite of sinne,and the good that it bringeth to the committers thereof? And yet if I should lay out the fruit of the sinne of *Cain, Esau, Absolon*, and other, who could not be staied from the committing of it; what better thing could I say of it,or what better fruite could I proue it yeeldeth to the committers of it?

So that as the baite is pleasant which the poore fish biteth at, but it being caught by the hooke,bringeth paine,torture,and wearying of it selfe to saue the life: so is it with him that will needes taste of the pleasure of sinne, as I haue said. And if this be the great good that it intendeth against such as follow one kinde or other of it with tooth and naile, who also lie sucking to draw pleasure out of it,as a childe doth by the breast,then let them all be taken and condemned for fooles, who are masters in that profession, and are vpholders of that trade and occupation. Yea let them bee reckoned in the
Prou.14.15. number of them, of whom the prouerbe speaketh, *The foole beleeueth euery*
Prou.1.22. *thing*. And againe, *O ye fooles, how long will ye loue foolishnesse?* For why? they haue chosen a way that seemeth pleasant, but the issues thereof are the way of death. They doe most certainly take more paine to goe to hell, then the righteous doth to heauen. And as their reuolting brought vpon them this miserie,so let all those who haue falsified their promise, and broken their solemne couenant to God of seeking more zeale, greater fruitfulnes, watchfulnes and care,let them (I say) also feare that their euill conscience wil draw vpon them one accusation and trouble after another, and that the further they decline, the greater sorrow they bring vpon themselues. Some haue been brought to that point, that they haue made question whether they might lay violent hands vpon themselues,to auoid the terror of minde.

Doct.3. Further also obserue here,what shifts they chuse to make,rather then they would seeke to God by humiliation and repentance,for release. They loue their freedome well, who hauing their citie besieged by the enemie,till extreame famine compell them to eate dogges, cats, and such vermine, as is noisome to nature, yet chuse to endure such difficulties, rather then yeeld. And so doubtlesse, they loue their lusts well, who suffer themselues to bee made such slaues and drudges to them (as these here were) rather then they would

would abandon them, and returne to the Lord with vnfained renouncing of them. Alas, they must leaue them with shame and double repentance at length, when they haue wearied themselues as these did: but till their owne rod hath made them smart, who may tell them of the vnfruitfulnes of their toilesome trade? Toilesome I may truly say; both considering with what great adoe they bring their sinne to ripenes and perfection; and then what shifts they vndergo to winde themselues out of the woe and miserie, which (in stead of fruite) their sinne brings vpon them? It is a good piece of the life of an adulterer, first to compasse and fulfill his vncleane lusts: and when he hath done, to couer and keepe himselfe from shame, and to make faire weather of it againe. And so the thriftlesse spend-good, what adoe makes he to scrape together somwhat to maintaine his riotous humour? and when he is brought to beggerie, then he must cast about him afresh, how hee may defray that, and auoid the gallowes, or a base and wretched life. In a word, it is true which *Salomon* saith in Ecclesiastes; *To the sinner God giueth paine:* he Eccles.2.26. giues him sowre sauce to his sweete meate, painfull seruice to his sweet lusts. And yet without Gods speciall goodnesse neither of these shall preuaile with a lewd person to pull him from the loue and liking of them, though they cost him so deare, and though he beare and bring foorth with paine, and the sweate of his face. There will be found an *Hiel* to build Iericho, though hee knew it will cost him and his neuer so dearly. Therefore they are happie whom God hath entertained into his house, and holds them vnder his gouernment: because neither is his word tedious to them, nor his Matth.11.last. commandements grieuous while they are doing them: and as for any trouble which can befall them after for their so doing, first know that it can not sting them being borne for a good cause, and they shall goe vnder it without disquiet, be vpholden in it by grace, and after count it great ioy in that they suffered.

The people of Israel, we haue heard in the former verses, did kindly shew Verse 6. in their doings, the nature and disposition of sinful and wicked persons, who little trust to God in their troubles, they forgot him, and did flie for succour and refuge to earthly helpes and staies; as towers, dennes, and other munition and defence, forsaking him; but the holy storie sheweth in this verse, that none of them all preuailed, neither did they preserue them. And although by their shifting they saued their liues, and got and saued that foode which with much adoe kept them from staruing; yet who seeth not the miserie, which, for all that, they indured in extreame pouertie, bondage and feare? Euen so, wee must know, that it is not enough for wicked persons to beware of their enemies, and to fence themselues from the common troubles of the world; but first of all, and chiefly they should preserue themselues from the wrath of God; which while like fooles they doe not, they preuenting and auoiding the same, they seldome escape, nor be free from the other. Therefore the Lord in the prophecie of *Habakkuk*, laugheth to Habak 2.5.6. scorne such made defences of men. And in *Obedia* the Lord saith to such; Obediah 3.4. *Thou that dwellest in the clefts of the rocks, whose habitatiō is high, that saist in thine heart, who shall bring me downe to the ground; though thou exalt thy selfe as the Eagle, and make thy nest among the starres, yet euen thence will I bring thee downe, saith the Lord.*

They

They doe not ſee that God hath a thouſand waies to fight againſt them: and that he who plucked off *Pharaos* charet wheeles, and broke the horſes hoofes of *Siſera*; who drew vp the great Lord *Haman* to the gallowes; that tooke heart from the Ammonites and Moabites, that in ſtead of fighting againſt Iudah, they fell vpon and ſlew one another; and weakened *Zenacherib* ſo, that he ſlew by an Angell in one night, an hundred, foure ſcore, and fiue thouſand of his armie; they doe not ſee, I ſay, that he who did thus ſhew his might againſt theſe mightie ones, and many waies beſide, hath done the like; can alſo fruſtrate their attempts and hope in theſe daies alſo. The ſpirit of ſlumber is caſt vpon them, and blindneſſe hath taken hold of them, that they cannot ſee and beleeue, that the like iudgements ſhall not meete with them, till they haue felt and ſmarted by them.

Exod.14.25. Iudg.5.22. Eſter 7.10. 2.Chro.20.22. 2.King.19.35.

Therefore let men make peace with God firſt, and turne from their ſins, that he may alſo turne from his fierce wrath: or elſe when they make their reckoning of peace, and proſperitie, length of daies and deliuerance from their enemies, and other troubles, the contrary euils fall vpon them; and if not preſently, yet they are at hand, and alwaies iuſtly to be feared, before they come. Oh what proofe haue wee ſeene of that which I ſay, as former ages haue done alſo? How many might haue done well, and proſpered, if they had been more carefull to be reconciled to God, then to leane to their owne deceitfull dreames, by a vaine hoping, that life ſhould ſtill haue been granted them, the which, while it laſted, they were as they thought, in paradiſe: but for all their welfare were ſoone cut off from all. And the reaſon is, that men goe to worke without God, they neither ſeeke his fauour, nor direction from him, either in their actions or afflictions: and therefore their enterpriſes are either croſſed, or elſe curſed in the vſe and enioying of them: and as for their troubles, they are to ſeeke either how to abide them, or to get out of them in a good manner. Thus a wicked man is vnhappie both waies, whether hee proſper or no: for either hee feares a change, or elſe his feare commeth vpon him, as an armed man. Therefore when I conſider this, I thinke the beleeuing Chriſtian twice happie, euen when he is iudged miſerable by men of the world, becauſe hee hath choſe the good part with *Mary*, and hath ſought to haue God on his ſide, who doth not only keepe fearefull iudgements from his, being a ſure defence in time of need, but maketh that portion which they enioy, a ſweete and ſauourie bleſſing vnto them; and yet they haue farre greater riches then thoſe. Thus much of their puniſhment, in the ſecond part of the Chapter.

Note.

The third part of the Chapter.

Doct.2. in verſ.6.

THe third followeth in this ſixth verſe, namely, that the people repented, and turned to God: which as was ſaid before, is teſtified, and declared by a ſigne thereof, which is crying. And here, not to inſiſt vpon the ſame things, which in other places I haue done, that which I wil note from hence is this, that ſeeing they now ſought to him at laſt, who ſhould haue been their firſt refuge, we may note another point of vnthriftineſſe, and fooliſh dealing in the men of this world; That when they will needes goe trie maſteries in their neceſſitie and calamities, by truſting to broken holds, and vaine

vaine helpes of their owne deuising, and smart for it, as I haue said; then at last with shame they must be faine to sue and repaire to God. And what if he will not receiue then? as it falleth out sometimes to bee so, as in the Pro-
uerbs, [Because you would not heare when I called, ye shall crie, and not be Prou.1.20.
heard] Whither goe they then? But if he doe, what a farre fetched iourney
haue they taken before, yea full of vexation and wearisome, besides that Note.
they haue lost all their former labour? I conclude therefore, with this ad-
uice and warning to such as haue eares to heare; *Seeke the Lord while he may* Esay 55.6.
be found, and driue not off from day to day, lest he come suddenly and there be none to turne away his heauy wrath from you: and in the meane while, happie are they who doe so. For they in so doing shall not doe as this people did here, flie to rocks, hide themselues in caues of the earth, and build towers to be safe from their enemies, as these did here from the Midianites,
which yet did not safely keepe and defend them, but they flie to the safe Prou.18.10.
rocke and tower of defence; as the wise man calleth it; I meane, to the name of the Lord, euen the Lord of hostes, who is a most strong place of refuge, the righteous flie thither and are saued.

THE THIRTIE SEVEN SERMON ON THE SIXTH CHAPTER OF THE BOOKE OF IVDGES.

Vers.7. *And when the children of Israel cried vnto the Lord, because of the Midianites,*

Vers.8. *The Lord sent vnto the children of Israel a Prophet, who said vnto them, Thus saith the Lord God of Israel; I haue brought you vp from Egypt, and haue brought you out of the house of bondage,*

Vers.9. *And I haue deliuered you out of the hands of the Egyptians, and out of the hand of all that oppressed you, and haue cast them out before you, and giuen you their land.*

Vers.10. *And I said vnto you, I am the Lord your God: feare not the Gods of the Amorites, in whose land you dwell: but you haue not obeyed my voyce.*

NOw whether they cried to the Lord, first through anguish Verse 7.8.9.10.
of heart, which was caused in them by the force of their calamities; but was neither pleasing to God, neither could obtaine any thing of him, vnlesse it had come from faith: (which is very probable) or whether before their crying, the Lord sent the man of God here mentioned, vnto them, it cannot certainly be said; but sure it is, God of his great mercie to them, sent a Prophet to preach to them, and to bring them to true repentance, speaking to them much like the messenger that

Iudg.2.3. was ſent to their fathers before at Bochim. For he repeates Gods benefits to them, as the other did, and deliuerances, and chargeth them with diſobedience alſo.

Verſe 7.8. Out of theſe words wee may ſee, it is a fit time for preaching to worke, when men are inwardly ſtung with ſmart of their afflictions, as it appeareth theſe were, when the man of God was ſent to preach vnto them; for then men will ſuffer themſelues more eaſily to be reproued for their ſinnes, and

*Doct.*1. will accuſe themſelues, as they ſee cauſe; and the word is receiued into their hearts more readily: whereas they are otherwiſe moſt commonly hardned, and hate to be reproued. And yet further then men come prepared to our daily and ordinarie preaching, it profiteth them nothing. The danger is this, that they are like to quench the ſpirit after, and to dull the edge of ſuch good beginnings of grace in them, which will moſt certainly come to paſſe, if they be not carefull to ſtirre them vp daily. Men while they haue elbow roome, thinke that the preacher, yea God himſelfe muſt be beholding to them for their hearing: but when God hath them cooped in a narrow compaſſe, his roddes being held ouer them, then the Preacher is welcome, yea ſought to earneſtly, and God is plied with confeſſions and prayers. We ſee it, though with griefe, and haue too great experience of it, in the practiſe of the ſecure and irreligious ſort, who though they mind not God all the yeere long, yet fall to prayer and deuotion when ſome great thundring, lightning, and tempeſt doth aſtoniſh them, and when the likelihood of death is vpon them. His word they heare daily without any great reuerence, but his terrible workes, ſeene and felt, though but ſeldome, make them hide themſelues in corners for feare. By whoſe example we ſee, what need the Lord hath to bore eares into our ſoules, by terror, and amaſing iudgements, as *Iob*

Iob 33.16. ſpeakes, chap. 33. becauſe his word is wound about mens fingers, and made but as the confuſed noiſe of many waters, and as a ſound beating the aire, going in at one eare and out as faſt at the other. Let not ſuch boaſt themſelues as are ſpared, except they applie themſelues to the hearing of Gods voyce by the Miniſter, who can skill to doe his meſſage with more regard and earneſtnes: for either the more is behind, if they belong to God, and they muſt haue ſomewhat to quicken their appetite thereto, and to make it ſinke deeply into their hearts, and worke vpon them powerfully for their good; or elſe woe be vnto them, the Lord in all likelihood hath caſt them off, and taketh no pleaſure in them, and greatly it is to be feared that when affliction ſhall come vpon them, yet by reaſon of that their former vnbeliefe and contempt of inſtruction, they ſhall doe them little good. The thing that they ſhould doe is this: when the Lord laieth his hand vpon them, let them examine themſelues, touching their affection to the word, and how little they were moued by it in the time of their health & proſperitie, and ſo they may eaſily finde, that their blockiſhneſſe, and careleſſe or vnprofitable hearing; their deadnes, fulnes of ſtomacke, and ſuch like, with earthlineſſe, wearineſſe, wandring, drowzineſſe, &c. haue cauſed the Lord to ſend ſuch

Note. trials vpon them (be they inward or outward) as might grinde off their flat and blunt edge, and ſet on a ſharper and keener vpon them: that with deſire and meeknes they may embrace the word, and finde it ſauourie to their taſte, till it haue wrought vpon them as it ought, that is, euen to caſt them

into

into the mould of it. And this let such know, that if their afflictions tame them not, nor meeken their spirits vnder the hand of God, but that they fight against him, as *Pharao* did, and will not see and vse well this season which is offered them, that if they be deliuered once againe out of them, they may haue sound preaching in all high reuerence; let them know (I say) that their case is wofull and desperate. For as the Lord saith in the like case by his Prophet; O people how shall I intreate thee? or what shall I doe vnto thee? So he may say vnto them: for he hath no other physicke, then his word, mercies, and chastisements. If none of all them can breake the heart, there is no helpe, nor hope, that if he should vse extraordinary courses (which they are not to looke for) that hee should preuaile any more with them, then he did with the Priests, who going against their consciences in bringing Christ to his death, were no more moued with his resurrection. Therefore they are wisest, who put not the Lord to this extremitie, but hearken to him when he speaketh, and offereth them faire, by the voyce of his messengers: and deferre not till affliction, as a second warning, be sent vnto them: lest then also, they be found alike vnprouided, and being hardned, lest God should not vouchsafe them that mercie to mollifie & soften them: as (the truth is) they who tempt him so farre by presumption, doe not easily recouer themselues, though God doe visit them by his corrections, or iudgements, but rather (for the most part) go further from him, and increase their rebellion. Hos.6.4.

But whether these men cried out being forced thereto by their many and sore afflictions or no, this is sure, that when the man of God had deliuered his message to them, and had shewed them their vnthankfulnes to God for their many deliuerances, and had conuicted them of their disobedience, they did then crie out in token of their great griefe for their offending God, as their fathers before had done. Here (not to repeate the same things which I noted before out of the like words vttered at Bochim) this is to be marked, that the Lord here sent his messenger, as he did there, to call the people to consideration of themselues, and their doings, and we see what need they had thereof. All generations declare what they are, and to what wrack and ruine they come, who are not helped, and that in due time and season, with this wholesome instruction from God; that the righteous smiting them they may not fall into the hands of the vngodly, to be rung about by them to their vtter shame and reproch, and so fall into the iawes of the diuell, to be vndone without recouerie. And when the Lord dealeth so graciously with any, as that they may enioy this benefit of sound teaching, let them beware that they harden not their hearts at the hearing of it, (the oftner they heare the happier it is for them) but with meekenes receiue it, that it may bring foorth fruite in them plentifully, euen to eternall life. Doct.2. Psal.341.5.

The Prophet, who was sent vnto them, puts them first in minde of Gods benefits, and many deliuerances from their enemies. The next thing here to be considered of vs out of these words in the 8. and 9. verses, beside that which we haue heard by the like occasion, is this; that we record and keepe a memoriall (as they here should haue done, and were reproued for not doing) of our deliuerances out of trouble and calamitie, in which we saw, that we might, yea must haue lien ouerwhelmed and drowned, if the Lord had Verse 8.9.

 not

not in good time brought vs out of them. These deliuerances, I say, out of bondage, prison, sicknesse, paine of body, and anguish and torment of conscience, and the like; and how oft they haue been enioyed of vs, and how comfortable and welcome vnto vs; ought to be daily remembred and acknowledged with heartie praises to God, as well as his benefits. Hee who marketh them, shall finde them many and great, beside those that are common, so that he may truly say, God hath deliuered from meny deaths. And because of the peoples forgetfulnes, in the former ages, we see how oft they were put in minde of this one deliuerance out of the bondage of Egypt. Therefore the Prophet *Dauid*, and other holy Penmen of the Psalmes, in the behalfe of the people, doe so often call to minde, and sometimes with admiration and astonishment, Gods former deliuerances, as the whole 124. Psalme witnesseth thus: *If the Lord had not been on our side (may Israel say) when men rose vp against vs, they had swallowed vs vp quick, the waters had ouerwhelmed vs, &c.* Oh our forgetfulnesses of the like kindnesse of God, it is enough to accuse to Godward, though wee had no other sinnes, seeing wee
Note. cannot be ignorant into what dangers, and depths of sorrow we haue sometime been plunged, when wee lay crying and complaining, and (perhaps) praying also vnder the burthen of them, that it would not haue bin thought that we could euer haue forgot the Lords kindnesse, if he should euer haue brought vs out of them: and yet when he hath done so, yea againe and a-
Gen.40.23. gaine done so, we haue with *Pharaos* Butler, and the nine leapers, forgot all. Whereas we haue learned, that many yeeres after, euen as long as wee reape the benefit of such deliuerances, yea euen till death, we should praise God for the same, according to that which was taught our fathers in the Psalme:
Psal 118 2. *Let Israel now say* (that is, long after their deliuerance) *that God is gracious, and that his mercie endureth for euer.* Now I haue spoke but of thankes for deliuerance out of trouble, to the which, if we adde his benefits (which are innumerable) what can be required of vs lesse then this, that in all things, and
1.Thess.19. alwaies wee should be thankfull? And this bewraies the blockishnesse of such, who being vrged to giue thankes, aske wherefore? what haue wee receiued more then others? we enioy but our part, in common blessings, as the most doe, &c. As if thankfulnes were some extraordinarie dutie, lying onely vpon some few persons, rarely fauoured of God. No, the Lord requires no more of thee, then he doth of them who are equall to thee, nay inferiour to thee in benefits. But thou like the swine, takest all that commeth, not regarding what, or whence, so thy turne be serued: and thus deuourest many blessings, through thy brutishnesse, which a godly Christian would make matter of daily praise; and inlarge the greatnesse of them, by musing both how vnworthie he is of the least, and how ill it should goe with him, if he were but in the case of such as want them. If the Lord should exercise such vnthankfull blockes with the diseases, which many deare seruants of his suffer, the paines of Colique, Strangurie, Burning feuers, the Stone, and giue them their portion in penury, cleanenes of teeth, nakednes, sicknes, &c. they would then cease extenuating Gods benefits, or cōparing themselues with such as are inriched with greater then themselues: yea, they would then thinke that freedome from chastisements, were great cause of thankes,
Prou.27.7. though they wanted many blessings. But to the full stomacke, the hony combe

combe is not ſweete. Others thinke this dutie diſcharged, if they haue their tongues tipt with formall words of bleſſing and thankes; though their hearts, and loue be ſet vpon the bleſſing, and not on the beſtower of it, and therefore out of the ſame fountaine commeth bitter as well as ſweete; they curſe God as eaſily when the leaſt thing croſſeth them, as they bleſſe him while hee pleaſeth their humour, by ſeaſonable weather, plentifull crops, good ſucceſſe in their affaires, &c. whereby they bewray that their thankes are but the froth of prophane perſons, and comming from their luſts being ſatisfied, euen as their prayers alſo did in their troubles and extremities, as Saint *Iames* ſpeakes. And a third ſort there are, better then the former, who Iames 4.3.
yet cannot be brought to ſeaſon their whole life with this thankſgiuing, as *Paul* requireth: neither yet thinke themſelues worthie of reproofe, for vnthankfulneſſe. They ſay, they hope it is neither lying nor whoring, nor wronging, &c. which they ſuffer for, when they are afflicted: and as for this that they be not alwaies thankfull, what ſinne will we make it? they cannot repeate (they ſay) the ſame words ſo often. For anſwere, I ſay: vnthankfulnes (indeed) is no direct ſinne againſt man, but it is farre greater; for it is an high degree of wrong offered to God, and neuer goeth without an heart and life tainted with many lothſome euils & corruptions. Therfore, let not theſe examples be rules for Gods people to follow: let their whole life be an honouring of God by thankſgiuing: and as they only can do it, becauſe they are beholding to his Maieſtie for farre greater fauours, then ſtrangers; ſo let them both in their prayers, and otherwiſe in their vſuall practiſe, entertaine this dutie alſo, as a daily companion, as a token that they do not vſe Gods bleſſings to boldnes, looſenes, wantonnes, or any other licentiouſnes, but get ſtrength againſt them; ſo that all their life may fare the better for their thankfulnes, and other ſuch good meanes, as indeed a thankfull man, weigh it aright, is the onely good Chriſtian; and the life that is voide of it, goeth with much diſobedience, as we ſhall ſee in the next doctrine.

In this tenth verſe the man of God telleth them, that the Lord charged Verſ.10.
them, that they ſhould not ſerue the gods of the Amorites, and yet they did. So that their obedience was like their thankes; they neglected that, ſo they did this. There ſhall need no proofe, that we are too like them in both. Our liues witneſſe it: but, O wretched people wee, who receiuing a charge from him, who hath done vs all the good that we could neuer haue deſired, and is all in all to vs; yet as though we were tyed to him by no bond of dutie, we refuſe to be ſubiect and obedient to him in things he commands vs. The heathen Centurion could ſay, *I haue ſouldiers vnder me, and I ſay to one,* Matth.8.9.
goe, and he goeth; and to another, come, and he commeth: and to my ſeruant, doe this, and he doth it: And we, who haue ſolemnely couenanted with the Lord, and haue been (as I may ſay) hired with bleſſings to ſerue him; wee turne our backes vpon him, and with his owne benefits we ſtrengthen our ſelues to grieue him, in the breach of his Sabbaths: in the leauing off, or cold vſe of our prayers; in vncharitablenes, reuenge, and the breach of other particuler commandements, which is not to be ſuffered.

THE FOVRTH PART OF THE Chapter.

Verſ. 11. *And the Angell of the Lord came and ſate vnder the oake which was in Ophrah, that pertained vnto Ioaſh the father of the Ezrites, and his ſonne Gedeon threſhed wheate by the wine preſſe, to hide it from the Midianites.*

Verſ. 12. *Then the Angell of the Lord appeared vnto him, and ſaid vnto him; The Lord is with thee, thou valiant man.*

Verſ. 13. *To whom Gedeon anſwered: Ah my Lord, if the Lord be with vs, why then is all come vpon vs, and where be all his miracles which our fathers told vs of, and ſaid, Did not the Lord bring vs out of Egypt? but now the Lord hath forſaken vs, and deliuered vs into the hands of the Midianites.*

Verſ. 14. *And the Lord looked vpon him, and ſaid; Goe in this thy might, and thou ſhalt ſaue Iſrael out of the hands of the Midianites: haue not I ſent thee?*

Verſ. 15. *And he anſwered him; Ah my Lord, whereby ſhall I ſaue Iſrael? Behold, my father is poore in Manaſſeth, and I am the leaſt in my fathers houſe.*

Verſ. 16. *Then the Lord ſaid vnto him: I will therefore be with thee, and thou ſhalt ſmite the Midianites as one man.*

NOw wee haue heard the third part of the Chapter, that they turned to the Lord by the reproofe of the man of God, which though it bee not expreſſed, appeareth by this, that God ſent them tidings of deliuerance. The fourth part followeth, wherein the victorie ouer the Midianites is promiſed. This promiſe is amplified foure waies. Firſt, by naming the perſon, who ſhould deliuer them; that is, *Gedeon*, to verſe 17. The next, by granting him a ſigne, whereby hee might know who hee was that ſpake to him, to verſ. 25. The third was a charge of caſting downe Idolatrie, giuen to him by the Lord, to verſ. 33. Laſtly, how *Gedeon* attempted warre after the Idolatrie was deſtroyed, God granting him a double ſigne, whereby he might know that he ſhould haue the victorie, and this to the end of the Chapter. Thus much be ſaid in generall of this fourth part of the Chapter.

The ſenſe to verſe 17. The particuler branches follow: the firſt is, that *Gedeon* ſhould deliuer Iſrael out of the hands of the Midianites. For the declaration of the which foure points are alſo to be conſidered. Firſt, the Angels appearing to *Gedeon*, and ſaluting of him comfortably, to verſe 13. The ſecond is, *Gedeons* ſorrowfull anſwering of him, to verſe 14. Thirdly, the Angels words to remoue his heauineſſe, ſaying, hee ſhould deliuer Iſrael, to the 15. And laſtly, when *Gedeon* ſaw not how it could be done by him, the Angel told him, and ſatisfied him, to the 17. Now let vs looke into theſe verſes more neerely. It is ſaid in

Verſe 11. 12. this 11. verſe, that the Angel of the Lord came after the peoples repentance, and ſate vnder an oake in that place Ophrah, where *Ioaſh* dwelt, who was of the familie of *Abiezer* in the tribe of *Manaſſe*, and the father of *Gedeon*. This Angell was the ſonne of God, (as verſe 13 proueth) appearing to him in the ſhape of a man, and ſaluting him thus, *The Lord is with thee, thou valiant man*; as it ſhall well appeare, by the courage that God will giue thee in the waightie affaires that follow. Now *Gedeon* was thraſhing corne, to hide it from

from the Midianites,that he might preserue his life thereby,and the liues of thofe that were his. And this fpeech the Angel had to *Gedeon*,before he told him that he fhould deliuer the people out of the hands of the Midianites.

Out of this 11.verfe,note diuers things,and firft this: that men of wealth and place,as *Gedeon* was, in fo meane a tribe, though hee was fpoiled of the neceffarie helpes of maintaining his life, as the moft of the reft alfo were, fuch men(I fay) fhould not refufe labour,as husbandrie,or any other of honeft fort. *Gedeon* had feruants,and yet he thrafhed the corne himfelfe. And it is a thing which we reade to haue been not onely practifed of him, but of the old fathers mentioned in the Scriptures;as in all other writers,that what time they had free either from religious or ciuill affaires,they imployed it about cattell and corne. For they would not fpend the precious time in eating,drinking,play,or idleneffe,which they abhorred, euen as the religiouser, yea and the ciuiller fort of our Gentrie alfo doe. For they take vpon them honeft imployments. The one fort, after reading diuine bookes and Chronicles, and ftatutes, whereby they may benefit both themfelues and others, with the knowledge of Gods law and mans: the other, after they haue read of matters to helpe gouerne and doe good in the Commonwealth,(although they little looke after religion) will haue recourfe to husbandrie. Doct. out of verf. 11.

Such, namely of the firft fort, were *Abraham, Ifaac, Iacob* and others, as *Gedeon* here, whofe father *Ioafh* was in fome authoritie among the people, yet his fonne contemned not the practife of husbandrie, which is and may be fpoken to the iuft charging of many in our age, who if they bee borne worfhipfully, thinke it too bafe, how meane foeuer their wealth be, either to fet and appoint to themfelues any times for reading, or to haue any skill in that honeft ftate of husbandrie, faue onely to take their rents and liue of them; which yet were more commendable in them, if they did not confume the reft of their time in idleneffe, paftime, or worfe. Whereas tillage, keeping of cattell, planting in their fields, and grafting with fuch like imployments,are both delectable,gainfull,and honeft, and fuch as chace away many needleffe charges, and much ill company, (which is a great wafter) and the ill fpending of the time in fuch vaine exercifes as they delight in. And if it be not allowed to men of worfhip to paffe their time in fuch manner,but that euen they muft occupie their talent, till the Lord come, and Luke 19.13. not paffe the time in flefhly eafe taking, play, idleneffe,and other like prophane behauiour, much leffe is it tollerable in meaner perfons to be ill imployed. But befide this,feeing by fo fit an occafion I am lead to fpeake,I will therefore fay a little (and that not vnprofitable) of this common fort of people. For the moft part,(fetting afide the skumme of townes, I meane, the vnthriftie and riotous,and the godleffe poore,who liue vpon the fweate of others) this I may fay,that they take paine enough, and a man fhall not need to fpend much time in perfwading them to worke: but this is hardly beaten into them, to obferue the due manner of working, or the end why, or the ground whereupon. The motiue is penurie,the end couetoufneffe, and the manner brutifh. They want, and would haue to defray the hard world, or to beftow vpon their lufts, and to maintaine themfelues in pride of life: but neither worke they becaufe they thinke it is a fin to be idle, nor becaufe they looke for any other fruite of their labour, saue the bringing in of the peny. They see not whose commandement it is, that they should labour, Genes. 3. therefore they goe through it with vexation, discontentment, distrust, endlesse carking, and tying God to their girdle, to giue what successe they desire: which if they get, they take it for granted, that he loueth them: if not, they storme. *To the impure, all things are impure*, and so are their callings: they doe the workes of them commonly, not to shunne noysome lusts, temptation, and the fruites of sloth: nor to serue Gods prouidence, neither to sharpen and fit themselues thereby to religious exercises, and to good duties, nor to auoide offensiue burthening of others, nor to doe good and relieue them that want, &c. and so to obey God in all: nay, to speake the truth, when they are in their shops, at markets, in their fields, they are far from setting God before their eyes: much lesse doe they beleeue that God is with them there, to blesse them in their worke, as well as when they are occupied in duties meerely religious. Sinister ends and causes doe compell the most to yeeld some obedience to Gods commandement; but, doubtlesse, if all were now men of worth, and might liue of themselues, we should haue few workers. As we see by their words, saying, Oh such a man is happie! Why? because he need not worke, nor toyle as we doe, but liue easily, and enioy the world at will. And by this they bewray that they could bee content to doe so too, if necessitie vrged them not to doe otherwise. Therefore, their labour is as displeasing to God, as their idlenesse, in a manner, as they vse it. A wofull thing, and not without the curse of God vpon such as will not learne a better direction: that whereas some goe about their worke in faith, beleeuing that because they are Gods beloued, therefore God will giue them rest, blessing and successe: others rise earely, sit vp late, drudge and droile, eate the bread of care, and drinke the water of affliction; yet either they thriue not, or at least, they are as much to seeke of soule-prouision, I meane grace and hope of saluation, at the end of their wearisome life, as at the beginning: whereas it shoud haue been their first work, after they came to yeeres of discretion. Which should teach vs wisedome, and not to giue God a short and formal pittance of seruice, when we be at Church on the Sabbath; but seeing that great worke is to seeke with the most, therefore to giue all their diligence thereto, that is, to make their saluation sure; that all the sixe daies we may wholly giue vp our selues to other affaires, without so much as minding God, or godlinesse. For the Lord will haue vs serue him religiously, as well in actions ciuill, not religious, (of their owne nature) as holy: and this is the scope of his third Commandement, which tieth the seruice of God to euery part of our liues in our common course of liuing, as well as the second doth, to religious duties: and therefore must be extended to our particuler callings, as being the greatest part of our time, and wherein our liues are most taken vp. But I will proceede in the next Sermon, and here an end. Now to proceed where I left.

Gen. 3. 19.

Tit. 1. 15.

Psal. 127. 1.

THE

THE THIRTIE EIGHT SERMON ON THE SIXTH CHAPTER OF THE BOOKE OF IVDGES.

WHile *Gedeon* was thus hard at worke and labouring, the Angell came and ſpake comfortably vnto him, as if he had bin praying, or in the like exerciſe; and not to terrifie him. To teach vs, that our buſineſſe and works of our callings are no lets to vs frō hauing cōmunion and fellowſhip with God, neither doe hinder his preſence and comfortable being with vs. And the ſame may be ſaid of our callings themſelues ordained by him, bee they meane and baſe, or waightie. Therefore the Lord was with *Iacob* in his journey, and in the way when hee was going from his brother *Eſaus* wrath and rage. And ſo hee made the Goſpell effectuall in *Lydia* by *Pauls* preaching, ſhe being then a ſeller of purple, and rich, and not yet truly conuerted to God. And the Lord bleſſed the two tribes in their calling, and habitation, ſaying: Reioyce *Zebulon* in thy goings out, [that is, in thy proſperous voiages on the ſeas] and thou *Iſhachar* in thy dwelling in tents, meaning in thy quiet keeping at home about thy traffique and buſineſſe.

Doct.2. in verſ.11.

Gen.28.[illegible]

And by this which I haue ſaid, let vs marke; that if it be not long of our ſelues, our lawfull callings and buſineſſe are no hindrances of vs from the ſeruing of God holily and religiouſly, (as ſome thinke they be) but that from them we may goe to prayer or the like exerciſe, in good manner, euen as wee may from theſe to them. Although I may truly ſay this, that for not well learning it, few can ioyne theſe wiſely and rightly together, becauſe their affections and delights are ſet too egerly towards that which ſauers of the earth and of gaine; which is the cauſe that meaſure is not commonly kept therin. *Dauid*, ſaying, that he had rather be a doore-keeper in the houſe of the Lord, then to dwell in the tents of the vngodly, (which he would not haue ſaid, if mens attendance vpon the baſeſt worke in their lawful callings, had been an hindrance to them from Gods ſeruice) may by his words ſtay and comfort many weake Chriſtians, who thinke that they are much letted from the duties of godlineſſe, euen by the very vſing of their callings, becauſe they be not ſpirituall, as prayer and the like exerciſes are. But to end this, let the vſe of that which hath been ſaid, be thus much vnto vs, that wee euer labour to be ſo innocent, & well gouerned in al our earthly buſineſſe, and workes of our calling, that we may not driue the Lord from vs, but haue him alwaies with vs by the ſpirit of truth, direction, and comfort, as we haue heard he hath been with other (and was here with *Gedeon*) in their earthly affaires, for that is the vſing of them aright, and in their kinde.

Note.

Note.

The

The next thing in this verse is this, that though the Lord sent his Angell to *Gedeon* for his owne reliefe and comfort, and also the peoples, yet wee see this was not done, till they were brought neere to extremitie: all helpe of man was past: and they had no other refuge vnder God, but to prouide for themselues by flying from their dwellings to saue their liues. As for example, *Gedeon*, whose father was in some authoritie, and therefore none of the poorest, yet was at this point, euen thrashing a little corne, by the aide and nourishment wherof, he and his might flie from the Midianites, as farre as that lasted to carrie them.

By this we learne, that God seeth it expedient in his wisdome, sometime to leaue the godly long vnder the crosse, and not to put an end to their troubles by and by, as ordinarily he vseth to doe: according to that which is said
Psal. 30.5. in the Psalme; *Heauinesse may endure for a night, but ioy commeth in the mor-*
Heb. 10 37. *ning*. And againe, *He that commeth, will come, and not tarrie*. But he knoweth
Hos. 6.4. well, that when he vseth so to doe, wee commonly conceiue hope thereby, that our affliction (be it sicknesse, disease, losse, or any such) will not hold vs long; and therefore our deuotion is more short and cold; and we in so do-
Note. ing, neither honour God, nor haue any proofe of our faith and patience, neither experience, another time after, how to beare our trouble aright: For the which cause, the Lord sometime disappointeth our false hope, and putteth vs to greater plunges, by holding vs longer in our affliction, to the end we may search our selues deeplier, and we may be more throughly touched with the feeling of our sinnes, and rebellions; and so turne to him in faith and amendment.

For this cause the Lord holdeth vs sometime on the racke the longer, as in paine, sicknesse, or penurie; as also bondage to such as haue superioritie ouer vs, and vse it to our great disquiet and wearying of vs, and we pray and long to be deliuered, but the Lord seemeth not to heare vs pray, but letteth the burthen remaine still vpon vs. Wherefore, thinke we, doth he so? when
Lament. 3.39. he professeth, that he afflicteth not willingly, neither delighteth therein, and yet we lie in paine and griefe. I answere, the Lord seeth wee be not yet tamed and humbled sufficiently, great hath the pride of our hearts been, our inconstancie, vnfaithfulnesse, vncharitablenes also, with other sinnes, and our mindes are set on the world excessiuely, and wandring after our diuers lusts. And we are like to returne to these courses againe, if we were set at libertie, as soone as we desire: therefore doth he seeke to weane vs from these and the like, by continuing such vnwelcome crosses vpon vs.

So wee are for the same causes depriued oft times of our deare companion in mariage, which is a great part of death it selfe; or driuen from our owne habitation into the fearefull prison, which taketh much from the delight of liuing; yea, and we are tried with sudden dearth, as oft times by excessiue raine and wet; sometime by drouth: as *Gedeon* here was in as hard a case, being driuen to flie from his owne dwelling, in a manner famished. In these & the like, God leaueth his seruants, for the causes which I haue mentioned: and also to the end that his deliuerance and ease giuing after them all, may be the more precious when it commeth, hauing been so long desired: and thirdly, to this end he holdeth his roddes the longer ouer vs, that patience may haue her perfect worke in vs, and himselfe haue the whole

praise.

praise. An example of this which hath been said, wee haue in *Ioshua* 7. where Ioshua 7.5.
the people hauing promise of Gods assistance, went against the men of Ai, not making question but they should speed as well as they had done before at Iericho. But loe, on the sudden they were smitten before their enemies. This astonisht them, till the Lord tels *Ioshua* the cause: Ye looke, saith the Lord, it should be with ye as at other times, but I see cause of the contrarie. Looke well into the matter, and ye shall find that there is sacriledge among ye, and therefore ye cannot stand before your enemies. So that though they were doing the worke of God, yet because there was found in them this infection, it made the Lord to crosse their hopes, that so they might purge out their sinne, and goe about the worke in a better manner. Many wonder why the Lord laieth them long vpon their sicke beds, whereas if they had their health, they say they should worship him in publike and priuate with more cheerefulnes. Wheras the Lord aimeth at a further matter, and would purge out their coldnes, hypocrisie, carelesnesse, and other sinnes accompanying them euen in their good duties, that so they may returne thereto with more reuerence, and conscience. We reade that *Paul* after his great lifting vp into heauen, was buffeted with vnwelcome temptations: which though hee prayed that he might be rid of, yet the Lord suspended his helpe, that *Paul* might be humbled, and fitted to vse his knowledge the more fruitfully.

Now followeth the salutation of the Angell; *the Lord is with thee, thou valiant man.* If we marke the ebbe and low estate of *Gedeon* (as we haue heard) Verse 12.
it was wonderfull to heare this newes brought him, that the Lord was with Note.
him, as it was lamentable to see in what distresse he was, when hee heard the words of this message vttered to him. For it was as much as if the Angel had said, the Lord loueth thee, as one of his deare ones, and he is with thee euen now to comfort and preserue thee, euen in this thy oppression, and therfore none shall be against thee to hurt thee. This was much to be said in such a time of calamitie, to such an afflicted person. And yet, wee must know, that it yeeldeth to vs the like instruction. That euen in great outward troubles, and inward disquietnes of minde, when a body would thinke that God, and all good men were our aduersaries; yet in all this is God with vs whom he hath made a couenant with, yea he loueth and careth for vs, as deare and precious vnto him, euen as Christ Iesus the sonne of his loue was, though without beautie among men, and as a withered branch, despised, Esay 53. Esay 53.2.
Therefore the spouse in the Canticles saith, *I am blacke, but comely O ye daughters, &c.* meaning, that the Lord Iesus her husband esteemed no whit lesse Cant.1.4.
of her, neither was she any whit lesse amiable in his eye, being tanned in the sunne, then when she was in her perfect beautie. Indeede, the sinne which causeth the Lord to afflict, is odious: but the affliction it selfe argueth, that he makes much of vs, because thereby he would purge out of vs that which he misliketh, which affliction when it hath wrought kindly, the Lord can soone change our hew, and restore our former beautie, as *Iobs* example witnesseth.

The reason is this, he hauing once testified his loue freely vnto vs before, at our effectuall calling, and shedding it plentifully into our hearts by the Rom.5.5.
holy Ghost, saying to our soules, I am your saluation, and your exceeding great reward, and your God allsufficient: and binding vs to beleeue the Gen.17.1.
same;

same; he remaineth like himselfe, and changeth not; and therefore hee requireth that wee should doe the same, that is, by faith hold it fast in our perswasion, that he doth so And this is more, that the Lord is so affected to vs in the depth of our afflictions, as if we were freed from them all, and were in the middest of all prosperitie, which is hardly beleeued for the time while
Iudg. 19. the crosse oppresseth vs. The vse of this is, that we labour aboue all things to
1. Ioh. 5. 4. be builded vp in our most holy faith, that as by it wee ouercome other difficulties in the world, so we may thereby ouercome this feare and doubt also in the middest of our calamities; namely, that in our tribulations wee may not shrinke backe from this perswasion, that for all these, yet God is with vs,
Psal 73. 1. according to that which the holy man saith in the Psalme; *yet God is good to Israel, euen to all that are of an vpright heart*, though in outward shew it might
Psal. 130. 1. seeme otherwise. And againe, *Out of the deepe* [he meant of sorrowes] *he cried vnto the Lord, and he heard*, and deliuered *him*. And to make one point of two, the same vse we ought to make of the other words of the Angell, in calling him valiant man; which was true, because God said it, yet to *Gedeon* vnlikely to be so, and yet he found it afterwards to be so. Let it teach vs, to giue God his due, namely, that he be beleeued in al that he saith; yea that he saith vnto vs, though we be not able to see nor feele so much for the present time,
Note. as neither *Gedeon* did. A point worthie to be marked, seeing where God giueth good testimonie of his fauour, or reuealeth his will in any thing, we are not as readie to ioyne with him, for the most part; but doe faint and doubt, because wee see not with bodily eyes (as *Thomas* desired to doe) the thing promised, as we would. And whereas this troubleth many, that the wicked take occasion hereby to despise them, when they see that God seemeth not to regard them, while hee so abaseth them: let such know, that their mistaking of the matter, & their false surmising of Gods good meaning to them, shall not hurt them, if they fixe the eyes of their mindes vpon this, that God is vnchangeable & constant in al his waies, also if they can learne to esteeme of themselues according to that knowledge and inward feeling they haue had of Gods ancient loue and regard of them in times past: and so doing, the more their enemies scorne them, the neerer the Lord is to them, to take away their reproch.

Vers. 13. But this is well and cleerely laid out in the next verse, therfore I will passe to that. It appeareth in this verse, that as neere as God was to *Gedeon*, yet he saw it not: but concludeth, that seeing he and the people of the land were vnder such oppression by the Midianites, that it could not be well with them, neither could he beleeue that God was with him. And he confirmes himselfe therein, by a reason, though of no strength, thus: God was indeed with our fathers (he saith) when he brought them out of Egypt, & wrought many miracles for them, but hee did not so now for him and the people, therefore how could he thinke, said he, that God was with him now. This spake *Gedeon* from an heauie heart, euen then when the Angell was sent directly to him with glad tidings. But let vs further examine his words, and
Doct. make our benefit of them. In saying, the Lord could not be with him while the Midianites so oppressed them, he shewed his great weaknesse, as I said in the former verse, affirming that he could not beleeue, while hee saw it to be so with him. Whereby we may see, how hardly the faithfull can be perswaded,

ſwaded, that the Lord is with them in affliction, how ready ſoeuer they bee to acknowledge it at other times, which I ſpeake not, as though none were: for both the three children caſt into the hoat burning furnace, and *Daniel* into the Lyons denne, haue left moſt worthy teſtimonie of their inuincible faith in their great extremitie, with many other both in ages paſt, and now among vs. But yet in time of calamitie it muſt needs be ſaid, eſpecially if it be long and ſmartie, that our corrupt nature, which is vntoward, and hardly ſuffereth vs to giue credit to Gods promiſes is furtheſt off then from letting vs ſee into them, and beleeue them; and the diuell is readieſt to worke vpon our weakeneſſe at ſuch times, and to take the opportunitie thereof to feare and terrifie vs; and with his fiery darts of vnbeliefe to pierce our hearts, whereby it is with vs, too oft and vſually, as it was here with *Gedeon*, in ſo much that the Lord being euen then neare vs by his promiſes of comfort and incouragements, which were ſufficient to content and ſtay vs, yet wee ſee it not, neither thinke it to be ſo, ſeeing we giue not our ſelues to ſtudie and conſider aright of this point; which diſtruſt of ours is as vnbeſeeming vs, as it is burdenſome to vs. The remedie muſt be that which I ſpake of before, and ſhall haue cauſe to mention it againe, and that is, to reſt vpon the word and promiſe of God, though we ſee not preſent helpe, as Chriſt ſaid to *Martha, Did I not tell thee, thou ſhouldeſt ſee the glorie of God, if thou canſt beleeue?* As for profane perſons who want faith, what wonder, if they meaſure Gods loue by their preſent flouriſhing, and liuing in eaſe, or wealth, and by their enioying of theſe outward things below, whereby their luſts may bee ſatiſfied? And what wonder, if they iudge it impoſſible, in their deepe diſtreſſes and croſſes, that euer they ſhould wade out of them? As wee reade of that Prince of *Iehoram* in Iſrael in a ſore famine, who hearing the Prophets meſſage from God, touching ſuddaine plentie that ſhould bee on the next day, hee ſaid: *Though the Lord would make windowes in Heauen*, to powre downe corne and prouiſion, *yet this thing could not come to paſſe.* What was this elſe, but a bold preſuming in great blindeneſſe of that which hee apprehended not, and a very deriſion of the prophecie? And the like we ſee daily in ſuch brutiſh people, who hearing vs preach this doctrine of depending vpon Gods allſufficiencie by faith, euen in affliction, doe little better then ſcoffe at it; Giue vs wealth, ſay they, and corne and wine, giue vs our fill of meate and drinke and money, and as for faith, take it whoſe will. Therefore while they proſper, they are as merry as *Nabal*, but if God giue them a ſuddaine blow, it ſtrikes them downe flat: they neither haue any armour, to beare off the dint thereof, neither faith to beleeue that it ſhall euer be any better with them, but much worſe. Their euill conſcience makes them feare, that this trouble, or that diſgrace, either ſickneſſe or loſſe, will be their vndoing: and as *Hamans* friends comforted him, ſo they doe themſelues, Heſt. 6. and that was thus, *Thou ſhalt ſurely fall.* And yet in their iollitie who haue ſuch apparance of hope, and ſo great confidence in their eſtate, that it ſhall continue, as they? Better and better they looke for, and feare no change till it come. This I ſay of them: but how vnbeſeeming is it, that a beleeuer ſhould haue ſo much as a tang of this ſtrong vnbeliefe in his deepe ſorrowes? to wit, not onely to wiſh it were otherwiſe, which in ſome ſort is not to be diſalowed, and eagerly to deſire a redreſſe, and impatiently to beare the burthen which

[Margin notes: Dan. 3. 21. — Dan. 6. 16. — Note. — Ioh. 11. 40. — 2. King. 7. 2. — Pſal. 4. 6, 7. — Heſter 6. 13.]

his sinne hath brought vpon him: and not to be little vpholden by this, *that*
1.King.20.23. *God is the God of the vallies as well as the mountaines*; that his loue is the same in trials (if it also appeare not greater) which it was in prosperitie. So vnwelcome is the crosse, and so sweete is the contrarie to the flesh, that men haue no eares to heare of this doctrine, to beleeue that God is neare vnto them; yea euen with them in the middest of their sufferings. For why? They looke onely at this, in my prosperitie God was with me, but now my estate is contrarie, therefore God is absent. And therefore if any man be at hand to promise them health, fauour, or reliefe in their sicknesse, trouble or losse, they lift vp their eyes, and open their eares to that voice, though it come but from a man like themselues; but to God who hath promised, I will bee with thee, I will not leaue thee, nor forsake thee, they cannot bee comforted with that saying, but still looke full heauily, and swearing with *Gedeon* euery one by himselfe: *Oh Lord, if it bee so that thou art with me, how*
Ioshua 1.5. *then is this euill and trouble come vpon me?* Why? Did I euer promise thee (saith he) that no aduersitie should betide thee? Nay rather, haue I not sent this euill, that thou mightest therein haue good proofe of my loue toward thee, in vpholding thee therein? And learne this lesson yet better, that I am ye-
Heb 13.8. sterday and to day, and the same for euer. And this is the more odious in vs, that we doe not onely faile thus in great and searching troubles, such as this was; but euen in smaller also. And yet, which of vs will not be ready to accuse the Israelites (if question be moued of them) for calling for their flesh-pots and garlike, being then in the wildernesse, which sometime they had in Egypt, and for their murmuring, when they had no other foode but Manna, and now and then wanted water: thus our tongues are ready to descant of others, and our censure to goe vpon them; which ill becommeth those that shew by their own fainting vnder lighter crosses, that their strength of faith was but small in the time of their peace, and when they had libertie and freedome from affliction, though then they could say aloude with open mouth, that they knew God, beleeued in him, and loued him.

This be noted of vs, out of *Gedeons* first words in this verse: but now further, in that he was much occupied in remembring and speaking of his forefathers, counting them happie for the myracles which God wrought for them, in respect of himselfe: hereby wee see how common a sinne it is amongst vs, that wee measure our happie estate to God ward, by our present
Ioh.14.2. sense, I meane, by Gods blessings or corrections vpon vs, which who seeth not how an vnequall a rule it is to goe by?

Doct.3. But further let vs marke, that *Gedeon* being much occupied about the prerogatiues of Israel in Egypt, to wit, how God shewed himselfe present to them, in working miracles for their deliuerance as if there had been no other thing done there; and as though hee should say, they were happie, but wee die here for want of helpe: but marke we (I say) this that he speaketh not a word of their bondage, and hardnes, which they suffered there, and in the wildernesse, as well as that they saw his miracles.

And so doe we, if we haue not the peace, prosperitie, welfare, and other prerogatiues that many of Gods seruants haue, and namely of our condition: (by meanes thereof (I say) we thinke he is present with them) but wee
Note. account our selues to be forgotten and neglected of God in comparison of them;

them; when yet wee little know of the wants and sufferings, both outward and inward, of such as we iudge to bee so happie, and God to bee present with: neither doe wee heare of their sorrowfull complaints: and thus wee iudge and speake, because of their present prosperitie which wee see; when yet it is apparent that wee our selues are not destitute of as great blessings some other way. A great infirmitie (doubtlesse) but much greater it is in vs, who haue been taught this oftentimes from many worthie grounds of holy Scripture, that wee should not iudge of our selues by others, seeing wee know not their estate as we doe our owne: for it is certaine, that they haue many great calamities vpon them, euen then when we iudge them to be so happie; and there is no doubt, but that they thinke the same of vs, for some good things they see in vs, which they want, and are voide of, we haue a surer rule to goe by, which cannot deceiue vs, that is this: that the Lord once louing vs, he doth all things for the best to vs. Which if it be so, why forget we that, and measure our estate by other mens. And because wee haue not so vsually the comfort of our faith by present sense and feeling thereof, when yet we dare not denie but we haue other graces of God in vs, and the workes thereof, which are inseparable companions to it, wee doe offend much in this, that wee will both bee readie to iudge, and conclude, that we haue no faith, and will count other happie in respect of our selues, when yet we little know their wants, and complainings thereof, as I said before.

Besides, this sheweth what an enemie our corrupt nature is vnto vs, in the well bearing of our troubles; and how ingenious and skilfull wee are, to catch vp that which should hurt vs, as children doe in handling kniues, or such like, and turne the edge of euery thing against our selues, which being with godly dexterity hādled, might singularly benefit vs. But oh, how slow and dull are we in taking hold vpon any such thing as might stay vs, quiet, resolue, and comfort vs? Rare is that man who hath learned this wisedome, and giueth not place to the diuell, from whose malice it is, that in temptation all things seeme contrarie to that they be, because we looke vpon them with a troubled eye, and through a false glasse. The instance here vsed by *Gedeon*, was meete to haue confirmed his faith, rather then to haue weakned it, if he had taken it aright. For if in their troubles before, and in the wildernesse, the outstretched arme of the Lord saued them, euen miraculously, whose worthinesse yet was as little as his to deserue it; then how could it hence follow, that now it was shortned, and weakned, so that it could not helpe him, but was as present to vphold him? Againe, let men learne wisedom by this, in the vse of example of other men, that by their sides we strike not through the Lord by our vnthankfulnes. *Salomon* saith, *Say not that their daies past are better then the present*, this is follie. Oh, say men, In the daies of our forefathers, what plentie, what seasonable times, what happie liuing there was? Why so? And yet if it had been so, they wanted many things of more precious nature, which we enioy: and had their part in all our crosses too, famines, yet the people were but a few, pestilence, sword, and warre especially; also ill seasons of droughts and wet: vnlesse their murmuring be against God, for multiplying mankinde, what cause haue they else, to open their mouthes and complaine? But our vnthankfulnes for that wee enioy, Eccles.7.12.

 causeth,

causeth vs to be discontented in our selues for that we want, and to grudge against God for partialitie; whereas if we compared things equally, we had ten times more cause of preferring the present condition, taking it with all hardnesse, as it is not to be denied but there is much. And so oft times doe
Prou.22.2.
the poore grudge against the wealthy, or rather against the Lord who made both, as *Salomon* saith. One repines that hee is rather a tenant, then a landlord: an vnderling, rather then a commander; a deformed person, meanly accounted of, behind hand, diseased, rather then as such or such wealthie men, great, personable, honourable, before hand, healthfull. Consider as wel their wants as their endowments; their grace, as their other parts; the vse they make, and the account they must make of them; their troubles also which accompanie them, as well as their gifts and blessings: and so doing, thou shalt see, if not thy selfe equall, (for God is the author of such inequalitie, and that in great wisedome) yet at least not so much inferiour; to bee sure, to haue cause to be more thankfull.

Doct.4.
But this (lastly) is not to be omitted; that *Gedeon* asking for the miracles which their fathers told them of, doth shew, that their fathers had according to the commandement of God, declared to their children the wonderous workes that he had done for them; and it seemeth also, that he had learned by them, to know and beleeue them. So must parents and children doe, the
Psal.78.1.
one should be able to tell, as we see in the Psalme; and the other to hearken to the great workes of God, and not to fables: neither should tales of vaine things be told, as of Robinhood; nor the dregges and fragments of popery, and filthie reports of lewd actions, to corrupt their children; as too many parents doe, and hurt them as much this way as any other, who yet are not a few: but they should cause them to drinke in the water of life, by good instructions. And if parents pleade their owne inabilitie hereto, let them know, that the Ministery of the word is a special meane to supply that want: let them be diligent hearers themselues, and tell the same foorth to other, and stirre vp their children to doe so: that so by liniall descent, the knowledge and feare of God may be deriued to their posteritie; that the Lord and his goodnesse to them, may be had in perpetuall remembrance. And let their children see that they minde Gods matters with no lesse cheerefulnes and regard, then they haue done their worldly affaires: and to this let their parents traine them; for else they will see light at a creuise, and wee know it quickly pricks that will be a thorne. As they be framed vp and manured at first, so their soile will after either beare thornes and briars, or good fruites.

THE

THE THIRTIE NINE SERMON ON THE SIXTH CHAPTER OF THE BOOKE OF IVDGES.

NOw followeth the third point in the diuision of these sixe verses, and that is, the words of the Angell to *Gedeons* sorrowfull answere, thus: Whereas thou saist, that God shewed his power to your fathers in deliuering them by miracles, go thou armed by him with the like power, and thereby deliuer thou Israel out of the hands of the Midianites, and thereby thou shalt know that God is as able to doe great things now, as well as before, yea and that he doth in like maner for his people euen now, as he did in ages past. And to make his words of more authoritie with him, he addeth this interrogation, *Haue not I sent thee?* And we must know, that the calling of the Iudges is so diligently described, that we may vnderstand, that priuate men were not able to take in hand such great workes without authoritie from God, as to gather armies, and to take vp weapons against the mightie: it was a matter of great difficultie and danger, and therefore God authorized them, as here he did *Gedeon*, and so hee did others; that they giuing credit thereto, might be heartned: and therefore he saith, *haue not I sent thee?* And to returne to *Gedeon*; thus the Angel proued that God was with him, if he made him able to deliuer Israel, which to doe was no lesse then to worke a miracle. Vers.14. *The sense.*

By this we all that feare God, are taught; that the times are not so hard, no not when we are in affliction, as we take them to be. For either helpe is neerer to vs, then we are aware, (as it was here with *Gedeon*) or we make our trouble seeme greater then it is in it selfe, by aggrauating it, when yet wee might see, that it either is not so great as it seemes, or might be many waies greater; or we haue greater comforts elsewhere, which were able to asswage our sorrowes, if wee did not ouerwhelme our hearts with immoderate heauinesse, which driueth away all comfort from vs. And therefore when wee are sad and heauy through wants and crosses, this lesson should be well learned before of vs, that for all this the Lord is with vs, and he is good to vs: for euen so haue other our good fathers been before vs perswaded in their afflictions; and though they haue now an end of all such languishing feares, dolefull doubts, and troublesome thoughts; yet in their time they had their part in them as we still haue, and we shall haue an end of them, and rest from them, as they now doe. Note. Note.

There hath no temptations taken vs, but such as appertaine to man: and God is faithfull, who will not suffer vs to be tempted aboue that we be able, 1.Cor.10.13.

but

but will euen giue the issue with the temptation, that wee may be able to beare it. And therfore, as our Sauiour said to his Apostles, when their hearts were troubled beyond measure for his bodily departing from them; *Let* Ioh. 14.1. *not your hearts be troubled; beleeue in God, and beleeue in me, that I can helpe you still*, and will be with you: so should wee doe, that is, not looke with both Note. eyes vpon our afflictions, but with one eye vpon his constant loue and assured promises, yea and settle our hope therein more throughly, by saying (as God commandeth) hath not he bidden vs doe so? euen as the Angell saith to *Gedeon* about conquering the Midianites, *haue not I sent thee?* So the two Disciples that went from Ierusalem to Emaus, when our Sauiour went into their companie in the way, bewraied their vnbeliefe concerning his resurrection that day. This day, they say, hee should haue risen againe, but be- Luke 24.21. cause they heard not of it, they did not think that there was any such thing. But did not our Sauiour shew them their fault, so as they saw it? for they knew that it was euen he who they said should haue risen againe that day. Ioh. 11.39. Of *Mary* and *Martha* the like may be said: who were both beleeuers in Christ, and beloued of him; yet when Christ went about to raise vp *Lazarus*, and to that end asked them where they laid him, did they not shew that they thought it could not be now done, and therefore answered; *Lord, by this time he stinketh, for he hath been dead foure daies:* And yet that they might see their weaknes in beleeuing, Christ raised him vp, which they thought impossible. In all these, and in *Gedeon*, wee may cleerely see our faces as in a glasse. For in a crosse, especially if it bee any thing smartie and sharpe, although we gaue testimonie of our faith before, and that with ioyfulnes; yet now in the triall of vs, how poorely are wee armed to goe through it, and Note. perswaded of the good issue of it? Doe we not hang downe the head and faint, and say within our selues, this crosse will be our vndoing? And againe, it cannot turne to our good, neither could any haue been so vnwelcome to vs. For example, if wee be depriued of our deare companion in mariage, or lose some round summe of money, or be otherwise impaired in our wealth, or vnder some strange paine; doe we say, as in time of peace, in meeknes of spirit, the Lord who loueth vs, hath done this for our good? euen he that cannot suffer the winde to blow vpon vs, hath sent it? Doe we say, It must be thus, and is expedient for vs? It is long first (I feare) and full faintly done, if we doe it at length, and few attaine thereto. And yet, doe wee not see in these and the like, the marueilous hand of God, how hee sendeth light in darknesse, ioy in heauines, and as it were, life in death? Doth not God bring vs through them, otherwise then wee looked for, and doth he not make vs see, and afterward acknowledge, that such affliction was good for vs? Euen as he said to *Gedeon* here, doth the Midianites oppressing of you seeme impossible to be auoided? Behold then, euen thou shalt doe that which seemeth impossible, and shalt subdue and ouercome them. Thus wee see how we should make our profit of this answere.

Vers. 15. *The sense.* *Gedeon* receiuing this answere from the Angell, that he should deliuer Israel, doth now in this fourth point aske of the Angell, by what meanes hee shall do so great a matter. For these words, by diligent considering of them, we find not to be spoken doubtingly, as before, but as inquiring, and asking a question: as if he should say, I doubt not but that shall be done which is promised,

promised, but I aske by what meanes it shall be brought to passe. For hee sheweth that he is not of ability, seeing, he was but of a poore family in the halfe tribe of *Manasseh*, which was also meane, not mighty as some other, and also for that he was the least in his fathers house.

His meaning was, that he maruailes that he should deliuer Israel, seeing he wanted all things which were required to so great a worke. For warre could not be taken in hand by a poore man, and one of a meane condition, such an one as he knew himselfe to be, seeing riches and power, and authority especially, were required thereto. And if it be asked whither *Gedeon* offended in mouing this question, seeing *Sarah*, and *Zachariah* were reproued for the like question asking: I am sure, that so *Abraham* and the Virgin *Mary* asked the like, and were not reproued, as neither *Gedeon* was here; Neither was it the mouing of the question that was found fault with: but the doubtfull minde with which it was moued, and therefore they two doubting, were found fault with, that is, *Zacharias* and *Sarah*; *Abraham* and *Mary* were not; neither therefore *Gedeon*, as appeareth by the answere of the Angell, who reproued him not; but answered his question. Esay 36.5.

And by this we may learne, that as questions moued with doubting of that which the Scripture resolueth vs of, is euill, so to moue questions where we are ignorant, of weighty points which we would be resolued of, is commendable, in all matters that tends to edification, and most of all in and about those which are most necessary; as *Paul* himselfe and the Iailer, before their conuersion, and after they began to looke after their saluation, did so; to wit, asked questions about it. And to be slacke and backward in seeking of resolution, in such cases where we are ignorant, and haue cause to inquire and aske, is in no wise to be liked, but rather threatens great hurt and danger: [whereof more might be said; but occasion hath bin already offered to speake of this duty (of seeking relation in doubtfull cases, both in opinion and conscience) before.] Doct.

The Angell answeres him without rebuking him, and satisfieth him in that which he demanded, (that is, how he should be able to doe such a worke:) saying; howsoeuer in warre ordinarily taken in hand, riches, power and care requisite, yet in this, my power without them, shall suffice: for thou shall saue Israel, not by them, but by my power, because I will be with thee, and by the strength that I will giue thee. And so God answered *Moses* when he sent him to *Pharaoh* to deliuer his people out of Egypt: & to *Iosua* in like manner, when he should lead the children of Israel after him, into the lande of promise. And so *Gedeon* here was satisfied, especially by these words of the Angell, to wit, that he should smite *Midian* as if they were but one man, euen as it was all one, for the Lord to destroy one, as it was tenne hundred thousand. And this came to passe when the Midianites slue one an other. So that in vsing meanes to serue Gods prouidence, we doe well, when we see God his meaning to be, that we should do so: but alway with this caueat, that we take heed of *Asa* his sin, who is said to haue made his Physitians his God, by seeking to them and trusting in them, not seeking God [in them. But let vs euer beware least we grow to that profanenes which we read of in that cursed *Rabshaketh*; I meane, to iustle God out from our enter- Verse 16. *The sense.* Exod.3.12. Iosh.1.5.

prises, saying as he did, *Counsell and strength are for the warre*; and so not to trust in the Lord our God.]

Doct. vers. 16. This speech here vttered by the Angell to *Gedeon*, [*I will be with thee*] the Lord vseth oft times, and not alwaies in the same particuler meaning: sometime it is vnderstood of some outward blessing or deliuerance, as he meant to *Iosbua*, in saying, I will be with thee against thine enemies, and bring thee into the land of promise: sometime of the inward and speciall grace of God, to guide and comfort his withall; as to *Mary*, Luk. 1.28. and sometime both, as to *Iacob* when hee dreamed by the way of Aram, God spake to him, and said to him, *I will be with thee*; meaning it both of his grace that he would giue him to vphold him, and also of other helpe; as in the next words which he addeth there, he doth more particulerly declare, saying; I will keep

Gen. 28.15. thee whither soeuer thou goest; whereby he meaneth, that hee would bee with him to deliuer him from outward enemies till hee should inherit the land which he promised him. The words are to be vnderstood in this place in the first sense, namely of deliuering the Midianites into the hands of *Gedeon*: though I denie not, but *Gedeon* obtained the latter also, as well as the former.

And this should teach vs, that if God haue promised to any of his, who beleeue vnto saluation, his power, protection, and helping hand in any outward troubles, they may and ought to beleeue, that he will doe, as hee hath promised. And as he shewed himselfe to be his, in this manner, so hee will vndoubtedly be with vs in this age, to helpe, deliuer, and giue successe to vs, as he hath alreadie done greater things for vs. But yet, seeing we vse to look too narrowly to Gods outward promises, that if they be not performed to vs to the full, we are readie to complaine; therefore know we this, that if he doe faile in any point of that which wee looke for, his promise being but conditionall, he will supplie all such wants by his grace spirituall, so as wee beleeue: as patience, contentation, and confidence, which are farre more worth then if we enioyed the outward benefit it selfe. For the spirituall includeth temporall, as reason in the soule of man containes the inferiour powers of motion, sense, growth, and life. Sunder not those that God hath

Rom. 8.32. combined together. If hee haue giuen vs his Christ, wee know he hath no greater things to denie vs, and much lesse he will smaller. And doubtlesse, for want of beleeuing the greater, wee faile sometimes of the smaller; and that iustly, as a punishment of our dishonouring God by our distrust.

Doct. 2. Besides this, we may learne here, that the power of God communicated to vs, is sufficient to make vs doe and worke great things, farre aboue our reach and abilitie, in warre or in peace; in persecution, also against sinne, the diuell, or whatsoeuer else: as here, when God promised his power to *Gedeon*, he assured him, that euen he, a weake man, should bee able to subdue a mightie and great people. And when is this might giuen to men? euen when God calleth and appointeth them to any seruice that shal require and stand in need thereof. As now *Gedeon* being called to this ouercomming of the Midianites, he was furnished with the gifts he had not before; as wisedome, courage, strength, and faith in particuler promise of assistance and vi-

Heb. 11.34. ctorie. And therefore by it hee is said to haue been made strong, and of a weake

weake man, valiant in battell. Heb. 11. So hee enabled *Paul* to beleeue the Act. 26. 11.
promiſe of ſtanding by him and bearing him out, at ſundrie times before his enemies: whereby hee wrought ſuch a worke, as none but an Apoſtolicall ſpirit could worke. And euen ſtill the like courage, cheerefulnes, hope, gifts, he giues to ſuch Miniſters of his, whom he meanes to vſe to the great ends mentioned, I meane to bring many to Chriſt, Act. 26. and Epheſ. 4. which Acts 26. 18. Epheſ. 4. 12.
he denieth to them whom he calleth not, and who beleeue not in him. So that they neuer ſhall be able to compaſſe that which the other ſhall.

So had *Moſes*, and the Apoſtles, as their place and occaſions offered, did require. And ſo may and ought wee to be perſwaded, that how vnfit and vnworthie ſoeuer we are and feele our ſelues to be, if the Lord call vs to any eſtate or dutie, he will arme vs againſt all difficulties, toile and tediouſneſſe therein. The Lord doth not lay heauie burthens vpon men, and giue them weake ſhoulders: but dealeth out to euery member his meaſure, according to the vſe and ſeruice which belongs to it: a double ſpirit to *Eliſha* aboue *Eliah*, according to his double neede. Euen as we ſee the gift of ſtrength is giuen to the armes and ſhoulders in mans body, becauſe they ſerue for the ſtrongeſt vſe. And ſo, becauſe he knoweth the difficulties both within and without, which a godly Chriſtian ſhall meete with, therefore he leaues him not to ſinke vnder them, but giues him faith, and enables him by that to ouercome, not one or a few, but the world, that is all. And as our Sauiour 1. Ioh. 5. 4.
ſpeakes, *Hath the Lord ſo clothed the graſſe, the creatures*, and will he not much Matth. 6. 30.
more prouide for his people? So by the like argument, hath God giuen euery creature, euen the beaſts, ſome one gift or other, according to the neede thereof, to it own preſeruation, as ſwiftnes to the ſmall, ſtrength to the great, to ſome one kinde of armour, to ſome another; and ſhall he faile in the neceſſarie furniſhing of his people with that grace, without which they ſhould not be able to attaine the end of their redemption and election? No doubtleſſe. But here is a two-fold obiection: Firſt, many who zealouſly deſire to *Obiect.* 1.
doe good in the Church, or otherwiſe, yet want gifts. Anſw. It is not euery *Anſw.*
mans part to iudge aright of another mans gifts: for gifts which may ſeeme meane to vs, may be mightie through the bleſſing of God concurring to effect great matters. Againe, I ſay, if God giue but ſmall ſufficiencie and gifts, he requireth but a proportioned worke and ſeruice: for he exacts not that vantage of him who hath but one talent, which he doth of another who hath fiue. To the ſecond obiection, that many whoſe gifts are great, *Obiect.* 2.
doe little good. I anſwere: Their ſinne is the greater, but that hinders not *Anſw.*
that doctrine; for though all whom God ſets on worke ſhall bee fitted, yet not contrarily, if he appoint them not to the worke, neither call them to it.

Verſ. 17. *And he anſwered him, I pray thee, if I haue found fauour in thy ſight, then ſhew me a ſigne that thou talkeſt with me.*

Verſ. 18. *Depart not hence, I pray thee, vntill I come vnto thee and bring mine offering, and lay it before thee: and he ſaid, I will tarrie vntill thou come againe.*

Verſ. 19. *Then Gedeon went in, and made ready a Kid, and vnleauened bread of an Ephath of flower, and put the fleſh in a basket, and put the broath in a pot, and brought it out vnto him vnder the oake, and preſented it.*

Verſ. 20. *And the Angell of the Lord ſaid vnto him, Take the fleſh and the vnleauened*

vnleauened bread, and lay them vpon this stone, and powre out the broath, and hee did so.

Vers.21. *Then the Angell of the Lord put foorth the end of the staffe that he held in his hand, and touched the flesh and the vnleauened bread, and there arose fire out of the stone, and consumed the flesh and the vnleauened bread; so the Angell of the Lord departed out of his sight.*

Vers.22. *And when Gedeon perceiued that it was the Angell of the Lord, Gedeon then said; Alas my Lord God, for because I haue seene an Angell of the Lord face to face, I shall dye.*

Vers.23. *And the Lord said vnto him, Peace be vnto thee: feare not, thou shalt not dye.*

Vers.24. *Then Gedeon made an Alter there vnto the Lord, and called it Iehouahshalem: vnto this day it is in Ophrah of the father of the Ezrites.*

Vers.17. *The sense.* Of the first of the foure things mentioned in the 11. verse, to wit, who should deliuer Israel out of the hands of the Midianites (which was *Gedeon*) wee haue heard: now followeth the second, namely of the signe which *Gedeon* asked, by which he might know who he was who talked with him. To proceed therefore, *Gedeon* hauing a promise of so great a matter as the victorie, from the Angell, who spake to him; whom he tooke to be neither Angell nor God, but a man to vtter the words of God vnto him; he desires of him a signe, that he might not be deceiued with a fancie, but might know that he was such an one as could make good his word to him, that is, a man of God, as hee tooke him to be. Here before I goe on further in the storie, I will stay a while by occasion of this speech of *Gedeon*. And let vs know, that which he did, in desiring this of the messenger, was meet for him to doe; for it behoued him to trie the spirits, whether they were of God or no. (2.Cor.10.14.) For an euill spirit can change himselfe into an Angell of light. And this is especially to be done, when any thing is vrged vpon vs that is doubtfull, and which may seeme vnlawfull to be done. For there a man may not easily assent, vnlesse he be perswaded that such a thing is from God. Excellent and commendable are the examples of *Manoah*, *Cornelius*, the men of Beroea, for this wisedome. (Iudg 13 12. Act.10.7. Act.17.12.)

Vers.17. *Doct.* And this is to teach vs, that we ought to haue the like scruple, and make the like question, when any thing doubtfull is vrged vpon vs, that for no mans pleasure, nor by example of any, we be led; but to proue all things by the waights of the Sanctuarie, which is the word of God: that so wee may be satisfied. And if in the mouth of two or three witnesses that bee confirmed which is brought vnto vs, wee are there to rest: and that should be enough to vs; but as for miracles or signes now, that it is the truth which is taught vs, we are not to seeke or aske for any. And the like we are to doe in all our troubles and feares, and not to fetch comfort from conceit, or the spirit without the word, or from any thing else, which is but a false ground. And this wise regard in *Gedeon*, to deale sure in so weightie a case, and not rashly to depend vpon a bare mans word for the effecting of so great a work, as hee knew none but God could enable him vnto: laieth greatly to our charge, who in matters of farre greater weight, doe yet deale farre more loosely and slenderly then he did in this. (Prou.14.15.) The wise man saith, *The foole beleeueth*

ueth euery thing: meaning euery thing, which hee desireth and would faine haue, he beleeueth, and is easily perswaded of it that it is so as he would haue it, though he haue nothing of moment and good ground to shew for it. Among men it is counted a signe of great folly to deale thus rawly in things onely concerning our temporall estate, and to rest vpon euery mans word and report, yea though it be but ambigious and obscurely vttered: and the reason is good, why it is so: they who doe so, giue euery man aduantage to ouerreach, abuse, deceiue, and wrong them, besides the great controuersies and contentions, suites and charge, which they procure to themselues needlesly thereby. But (to speake of weightier matters) what one among many counteth it his folly, to hold his saluation vpon sandie grounds and euidences, as vpon his owne good meanings and desires, vpon the good opinion that others conceiue of him, vpon some slight sorrow for sinne, or confessing of it to God, also vpon his hearing of the word, vpon a blinde hope, or vpon some good yet common fruites of hearing; as good speech, in some places, vpon taking liking of good people, liking the Ministerie, or lending, and giuing some thing to the poore in their distresse: these things are good indeed, and (I am perswaded) found to be in few, but yet these are not to be taken for infallible tokens. Nay, concerning this waightie matter, men are willing to build the hope of their saluation, vpon the bare word of a Minister, though hee neuer saw sound reason for his so speaking, and assuring them thereof, but for that they haue been baptized, and doe liue in the visible Church, neither haue they any thing out of the word of God to quiet and resolue themselues: whereas the triall of a mans state to Godward stands in this, that by the Scripture he can proue himself to be an happy person, because the word hath humbled him, changed him, reformed him, and wrought in him faith in the promise, an earnest longing after that which is promised, and a waiting for it, till it be enioyed without wearinesse, and an heartie desiring that other did so likewise, with such other. But of this much is written.

To proceed further, *Gedeon* now hauing desired a signe for the confirming of his faith, and thinking him to be, as I haue said, a man of God, desired him to stay till hee went and prepared for him, as *Abraham* and other had done in the like case, and while he should refresh himselfe, he purposed to talke further with him about the signe. And the things which he prepared for him, were both fit to be eaten as nourishment, as also to serue for sacrifice, though the word signifieth both a gift, & an offering: but for proofe that *Gedeon* brought not these things foorth to the man of God, (as hee tooke him to be) for sacrifice, but that he might be refreshed by them, hereby it may appeare, that he neither set vp any altar there, as he did afterwards, to offer peace-offerings thereon; (reade verse 24.) neither did hee take the man to be God to consume it with fire. I haue set downe that meaning of the verse, which by weighing both, I take to be the truest. And yet I denie not, but that the Angell vsed that meate, beside the expectation of *Gedeon*, he vsed it (I say) for a sacrifice, as appeareth in the 21. verse, and thereby gaue the signe, which was before asked of him. Both come to one end, for a sacrifice was the signe to *Gedeon*, whether first or last. The things that *Gedeon* brought are named in the 19. verse. According to the setting downe of these things,

Verse 18.19. *The sense.*

things, to wit, that *Gedeon* did, as *Manoah* did, that is; offer refreshing to the messenger, we are to know that the men of God were in former times in so great account with his people, that they were glad that might receiue them, and as the manner then was, to make them stay to eate with them. And *A-*
Gen 18.3. and 19.2. *braham*, as I said, did the like: euen so did *Lot* also, and they lost nothing thereby, as we may reade in the storie of them both. The same did *Gedeon* here, who thought him to be an holy man, and therefore desired him to take some repast with him.

Doct vers. 18. and 19. Heb. 13.1. This hospitality was vsed of the godly to strangers, according to the commandement of God in the Epistle to the Hebrewes, which is this; *Be not forgetfull to intertaine strangers*. For they are sad in heart, and when they are regarded in strange places with kind and heartie welcome, as being commended thither by the Church of God, as it is meete they should, (for how else can they be knowne for such) it is a worthie fruite of loue in them that receiue them, and it maketh glad the hearts of the other, who are receiued of them. Much more (then) ought such kindnesse to be shewed to the faithfull, that are knowne to vs, and are in wants. And they that shut vp their compassion from such, (when the prophane will be too forward that way, to their companions, yea to their dogges) *how dwelleth* (as the Apostle speа-
1. Ioh. 3.17. keth) *the loue of God in them?* Not that hereby I approue of their rashnes, who to auoide vncharitablenes and vnmercifulnes, put no difference betweene such as they harbour, or relieue, which the Apostle precisely war-
Gal. 6.10. neth vs of, in the Galath. 6.10. that we aime especially at them that be of the same houshold and body, whom it most concernes vs to looke to, hauing charge of such poore giuen vs by Christ. Such as obserue not this, light vpon good persons by haphazard, as we say, and for the most part doe cast away their bread vpon the waters. For many glozing hypocrites, with counterfeit faces and letters of testimonie, with some pretence of honestie, doe abuse good people, who repent them often of their forwardnes in receiuing such rangers and locusts, both Ministers and others. For besides their gifts, they haue drawne them by cunning flatterie, to lend them money, or shew them other curtesie answerable, and yet as deceiuers, haue left them in the lurch; to teach them wisedome against afterwards. The like may be said of rash Suretiships, Commendatorie Letters, and the like to such, as of whom we haue no pledge, to vse *Salomons* phrase. Let Christians learne wisedome by this, and not vnder colour of pitie become a prey to such hypocrites, as make benefit to themselues of that their ranging course, and will be readie to recompense them with nought but derision and scorne for their simplicitie. Though, I confesse, it is the safer extreme of the two, and the neerer to charity, to be credulous, then too suspicious of them, as being vnknowne and strangers. But as we learned in the former point, not to trust our selues without good proofe, so (I trow) much lesse others, being not approued.

Vers. 20, 21 In these two verses is declared, how *Gedeon* was rewarded for his kindnes shewed to the man of God, as he tooke him to be: and how he seeking carefully to know the will of God, where it much concerned him, and whereof hee doubted, hee was well satisfied and comforted thereby. For the meate which *Gedeon* brought him, being as the man commanded, laid on a rocke, he by diuine power brought fire out of the rocke, and burnt vp and consu-

med

med the flesh and vnleauened bread. Euen as *Eliah* called fire from heauen, 1.King.18 38
and consumed the burnt offering, to the conuicting of the Baalites. And as he for the cleerer manifesting of the miracle, powred much water vpon the burnt offering before it was consumed; so did the Angell here cause the broth to be powred on the place, to moisten it, where the meate should be consumed, for the better manifesting of the miracle. And the like is said of *Abel*, Heb. 11. that by faith he obtained of God this reall testimonie of Gods approbation, that hee receiued his offering and signified the same, as God vsed to doe, by consuming it, Gen. 4. By the like miraculous burning of it, *Gedeon* was confirmed, that the message which was broght him of his deliuering Israel was true, hee being knowne to bee the Lord *Iehouah*, who brought it. Heb.11.4. with Gen.4.4.

And here let vs learne, first by this earnest seeking of *Gedeon* to know Gods will, in that hee was so answered, and satisfied: that wee neuer seeke to the Lord in vaine in desiring heartily to bee resolued of our doubts, or eased in our consciences. For it is true in the praying for these, as for other things, which the Apostle *Iames* saith, *the prayer of a righteous man auaileth much, if it be feruent*. Oh to depend on God in our difficulties and doubtfull cases, and to vse the best meanes we can with confidence, and with an humble & quiet spirit, how much it aduantageth vs? And contrariwise, we may be troubled long enough, before we shall finde ease, if we either vse any indirect or vnlawfull meanes, or if in the vse of the best we commit not our way to God, and depend vpon him. *Dauid* in the 73. Psalme complaines greatly of a temptation which grew vpon him, and strongly assaulted him, to wit, That because they who feared not God, prospered outwardly more then himself did, therefore his estate was not so good as theirs, nor he beloued of God, so much as they: wherein, if God had not shewed him an issue, he being so vnable for the time to stay himselfe, how had he been wearied and discomforted thereby? But hauing with good aduice weighed the matter in the ballances of the Sanctuarie, laying their and his estates together, what signification giueth he of a satisfied and quiet minde? How cleerely saw he his owne follie in grudging at their poore happinesse, or rather daintie miserie? And so as a man recouered out of a frantike passion, and new come to himselfe, how freely doth he shame himselfe, calling himselfe foole, ignorant, and a beast for his so iudging, and then descry the dangerous condition of the vngodly, as that they were set in slipperie places, for all their florishing? So great is the ioy which Gods people conceiue, when they hauing conflicted long with doubts of minde, or sorrow of heart, either before forgiuenes enioyed, or after; they flee to God, either by prayer, as *Hezekiah* did, or hearing the word, reading, communicating their feares and griefes to such as can quiet them and pacifie their conscience: as the example of *Cornelius* sending to *Peter*, and the Eunuch communicating with *Philip*, who went away reioycing, with sundrie others, doe witnesse? which should be sufficient to incourage them who suffer these sores to fester inwardly through concealing them, and so to preuaile against thẽ, (through their negligence and fainting vnder them) to make their cases knowne in time: for if they can neither by prayer, fasting, hearing, &c. find comfort against their heauinesse, resolution in their doubts, strength against sinnes, direction for particuler duties and

Doct. vers. 20. 21. — Iames 5.16. — Psal.73.13,14. — Note. — Esay 38.2.

the like, their last refuge must be to repaire to them that can doe the part of an *Ananias* to *Paul*, or this Angell to *Gedeon*; I meane, bring to mind somewhat which might speake to the heart of them, and restore them to good health and comfort againe. Which (doubtlesse) during the temptation, they could not feele. But the folly of men, or their bashfulnes, or ignorance is great; who denie themselues the libertie which God alloweth them, and so procure the more sorrow to themselues. I speake of such, as may haue resolution, for seeking: whereas thousands cannot, who full gladly would make their benefit thereof. But here it is time to make an end.

THE FORTIETH SERMON ON THE SIXTH CHAPTER OF THE BOOKE OF IVDGES.

Doct. 2. in vers. 20, 21.

HOW *Gedeon* was answered and satisfied about the signe he asked, wee haue heard: Now note wee further here, what a blessing and reward he obtained of God for his kindnesse and curtesie he shewed to the man, as he thought him to be: whereby wee see how God rewardeth thē that receiue and make account of his true seruants and messengers. *Gedeon*, though he were driuen by the Midianites, euen neere to famine, and sore oppressed by thē, so that the forgoing of a little in that time of need and extremity, was more then a thousand times as much in the time of plen-
Heb. 13. 2. tie; yet euen then he did not withhold his liberalitie from this messenger of God. And what lost he by it? Nay, how infinitly did he gaine? So, *Abraham* doing this dutie, receiued for good men, Angels of God. So, that
1. King. 17. 13. poore widow yeelding her mite to the Prophet of God, that is somewhat, euen of the little that she had, receiued great abundance for it. So, our Sa-
Matth. 10. 42. uiour saith agreeably to this: *Whosoeuer shall giue vnto one of these little ones* [he meant such as beleeued in him, and were in the sight of the world, abiect] *to drinke but a cup of cold water onely, in the name of a Disciple, verely I say vnto you, he shall not lose his reward.* But of this dutie before: this I adde by way of remembrance thereof.

This intertainment is a part of liberalitie, and a fruite of the Spirit. So any refreshing of the hearts of Gods Saints, is a worthie worke, and shall be regarded of God. I acknowledge that men must doe in this, as they may
Philem 7. continue other duties which are imposed vpon them, about their own flesh and familie, but yet they must not vnder that colour be cold and backward in this dutie of loue, neglecting and letting passe such opportunities of doing good as are offered, for vncertainties to come. As for them that waste much vpon lewd companie, play, gaming, whoring, drinking, they shall one day

day know to their cost,what it is to lash out,and spend the good blessings of God in such vnprofitable and hurtfull manner, whereby so many members of Christ might be relieued. But for the intertaining and bestowing of a good part of mens goods in such manner as I here speake of, and commended,as *Gedeon* did, it is to receiue men for their mutuall good and edification,and not to euill and carnal ends. And therfore that Christians,through selfeloue,or worldlinesse should be too fast handed,scantie and nigardly towards other their poore brethren, it sauours of small liking or ioy they haue in their communion of Saints,or fruite of their profession,whatsoeuer loue to God they pretend. For the practise of loue and mercie must approue our godlinesse to be sound,and not frothie. And yet this is apparent,that many a man saueth more by his vpright and conscionable walking and feare of God,(the which before hee made no conscience to mispend vpon his lusts, as many other doe) then would well serue them to allot and applie to good vses. But to returne,when the Angell had thus resolued *Gedeon*,by the signe mentioned,he departed from him; which cleerely sheweth to what end he came vnto him.

Now as it falleth out oft times to Gods seruants,that the end of one trouble is the beginning of another, there ariseth a new trouble to *Gedeon*, after that he was deliuered out of the former doubt & danger. And in the next verse,it is shewed how hee was brought out of it, and in the 24. how hee giueth God thanks for it. His trouble was this, that he had seene an Angell of God,therefore he feared hee should die. And no maruell: for wee shall reade in many places,that the old fathers,when they had seene God (as he might be seene,or an Angel,) were sore terrified,and afraid that they should die. So in this vnperfit speech,(saying, I haue seene an Angell of God] hee ment,as we also must supplie it thus; *I shall die*. So *Iacob* after he awoke,and perceiued the Lord to be present in the place, where he lay, and had dreamed that night; was afraid,and said, The Lord was in this place, and I was not aware: and hauing wrastled with the Angell,thinking that he had been a man,maruelled that he liued.

Vers. 22 23.24. The briefe meaning of them all, and a larger vnfolding of the 22.verse.

Genes.28.16.

So when *Manoah* knew that it was an Angell of the Lord, that had spoken to him,he said to his wife; wee shall surely die, seeing wee haue seene God. So the people said to *Moses* on Mount Sinai, when God came downe,they were so afraid,that they desired *Moses* that he would intreate the Lord to speake no more to them in that manner, lest they should die. The reason of this feare in them, was sinne, that made them, as *Adam*, afraid of Gods voice after he had sinned,which before he reioyced aboue all things,to heare. And thus through the darkenesse which came of sinne, they not being able to abide the light of Gods presence, their consciences draue them to flie from God,who is almighty,and holy and pure, who can abide no vncleannesse,which all mortall men are full of: so that euen they who were not tainted with wilfull sinning against God, esteemed it as present death to haue God present. As the good Prophet *Esay* testifieth, saying: Woe is me,for I am vndone, because mine eies haue seene the Lord of Hoasts. And though he confessed that hee was a man of poluted lippes, for the neerer men come to God,the lesse blemishes and smaller they see in themselues) yet we know that was indued with grace. But this in him and others

Iudges 13.21.

Exodus 19. Deut. 5.25.27.

Gen.4.10.

Esai.6.5.

others came of their iustly troubled conscience, vnsound and vnpure, seeing that God of himselfe by nature, is both the author of life and comfort, and therefore not to be feared: and so was he now in his appearing to *Gedeon* in this place full of mercy and goodnesse, and in many things decclared the same vnto him, though he, when he knew that it was the Lord, was euen (as it were) brought out of himselfe, saying alas, because I haue seene an Angell of the Lord, face to face.

Doct. Vers. 22. This teacheth what high reuerence we ought to haue God in, as oft as we come into his presence, where he hath promised more especially to appeare and be present, namely, in the assemblies of his people; and to bee no otherwise affected, when wee thinke of him, and pray vnto him (but yet without terror) and by consequence euery where, because we haue learned, that he is euery where. And the rather wee should follow the examples of the seruants of God in this their reuerence before God, (and yet learning to resist immoderate feare) because of the contrary lightnesse and boldnesse of many in this point, doe not thinke of God in any sort, as his Highnesse and Maiestie doth require. And yet I speake this euen of such as are not of the worst sort. But as for the prophanenesse and brutishnesse of some, who are in a contrary extremity to *Gedeon*, and to all that walke in reuerence before God, it proceedeth from a farre worse cause then the most imagine, to wit, meere grosse ignorance, or infidelity: as appeareth by their behauiour both in publike place, where God is more specially present, and in priuat, whither they resort for their pleasure and businesse. In the one, they passe the time in sleeping, prating, laughing, gazing about, wandring of mind, and the like vnreuerence: in the other in drunkennesse, wantonnesse, gaming, rotten and cursed speech and behauiour. So that the cause of this extreamitie in these, and or their so great vnreuerence, is no other then I haue said, the least of both which, ignorance I meane, prouoketh them not (we see) to deuotion (though Poperie shamelessely calles it the Mother thereof) but to diuelishnesse, and at length, to desparation. For as here the contrary excesse in *Gedeon* arose from the beholding of God amisse, and the too much obseruing of his glory without his goodnesse: so the not reuerencing of God at all, either in his word or works, is the fruite of meere blindnesse and darkenesse and vnbeliefe. But to returne, as the seruants of God, ought to carrie themselues in all high reuerence, in all places, and specially in his worship by Prayer, the Word and Sacraments; so when we indeuour to doe thus, yet if we deepely thinke and consider of our owne vilenesse and wretchednesse, and of Gods greatnesse and glorious maiestie, out of the flesh and humane nature of Christ, and without applying his sufferings and obedience to vs by faith, we cannot be without danger and sense of swallowing vp, as *Gedeon* and other were. And not only so, but we are oft times ouercome and almost ouerwhelmed, when we doe the best wee can, and thinke of Christ as we are able, we are so easily led and carried by the spirit of bondage and feare. And therefore what may we thinke of the superstition in Poperie, which hath caused in the people such carnall feare of God and slauish terrors and seruile worship; but that it is the bane and poison of infinite thousand people? because it is a doctrine that driueth to dispaire, leading men with horror of Gods wrath, but sheweth them no way to escape it which

will

will ſtand them in any ſtead,iuſtling aſide vnfained faith,which onely knits vs to God through Chriſt,and cauſes vs to pray or draw neere to him,without aſtoniſhment, yea with much comfort. But to leaue them, and to returne to the people of God, I grant that this is through want or weakeneſſe of faith,which I ſaid of them : ſuch want and weakeneſſe is oft times in the beſt of vs,or at leaſt may be,ſo that we are not priuiledged from it. And this argueth our great ſinne and corruption,and that our faith is neuer here perfect, when it is at the beſt.The view,ſenſe & experience hereof,and of feare and frighting,is notably and clearely diſcerned to be in vs,in thunder,lightning,or ſome other apparent danger, when the preſence of Gods glorious Maieſtie preſſeth vs more neerely. And though now we in this latter age of the world,are not to looke for ſuch appearances of Chriſt and Angels in the ſhape of men,but are ſent to *Moſes* and the Prophets,and to ſearch the Scriptures to know that,of and concerning God,which we haue need of, yet in the former and firſt age both of them were; as in the forementioned ex mples of *Abraham,Iacob:*and *Manoah* is to be ſeene: and in that Viſion of *Eſay*,when he ſaw God ſit in a throne,and with him Seraphins crying one to another, *Holy,holy,holy,&c.* The vſe hereof is,that we daily by faith,with reuerence,approch to the throne of grace for forgiueneſſe,and thereby take holy confidence to our ſelues to goe out and in before the Lord in all ſeruice,and to view and conſider his workes of iudgement, without corrupt and terrible feare,and yet without vnſeemely lightneſſe and boldneſſe; for this our good God,is a great God *and a conſuming fire,* Heb.12. And by this temperature,we ſhall be kept from extreamitie on both ſides. For as this eſtate driueth away lightneſſe,ſo we may be aſſured,that we bee in beſt manner freed from the feare of Gods wrath iuſtly deſerued by our ſins, (while we hold faſt our confidence and aſſurance of the pardon thereof,with the continual keeping them vnder, being forgiuen) wherby we ſhal be freed alſo from ſuperſtitious,carnal,and ſuperfluous feare,which,whereſoeuer it is, doth not a little diſtemper the mind,and make it vnfit for dutie. Iohn 14.1.

Luke 16.29. Ioh.5.39. Eſay 6.2,3. Note. Heb.12.29.

Now further beſides this, ſeeing after *Gedeons* doubt anſwered by the Angell,this new trouble aroſe immediately, that he feared hee ſhould haue died by ſeeing the Angell of God; we ſee how one trouble and griefe commeth in the necke of another to Gods ſeruants;who if they ſhould not haue deliuerances accordingly,ſhould faint and not be able to goe vnder them. Euen as we reade of *Iob*,that one meſſage being ended of the loſſe of cattell, another commeth to him of the throwing down of his houſe by the winds, and the killing of his children. And although there be intermiſſion from trouble,God prouiding for his people,that they may not be diſcouraged,as if all ſhould come at once,they muſt needs be;yet their frailtie ſo requiring, he ſeeth it beſt that the rod be held ouer them euery while, and ſometime make them ſmart; and all little inough, to hold them within their bounds. For we may all,euen the beſt,ſay with the Prophet,*before we were afflicted,we went aſtray,* but after we kept thy word.

Doct.2.in Verſe 22. Iob 1.18. 1.Pet.1.6. Note. Pſal.119.67.

The vſe hereof firſt is this,that ſeeing we are ſubiect,and lye open to trouble ſo many waies,wee neſtle not our ſelues here below in any earthly delights,ſo that we be vnwilling to heare of any change, but rather looke for it,and be armed againſt it; and ſo the ſmart that commeth thereby,ſhall not

ſting and aſtoniſh vs,as otherwiſe it will. And ſecondly, ſeeing God ſeeth
1.Pet.1.6. it meete in his wiſdome to exerciſe vs with many afflictions, he ſeeing that we haue need of them,and all to the end that ſo he may the better hold vs vnder; it is moſt abſurd,that we ſhould in any ſort ſeeke to fulfill the luſts of our hearts, whereby wee multiply and bring further trouble vpon our liues.

Doct.3. The other thing therefore which we may note here by *Gedeon*, is this, how ſoone our faith is ouerwhelmed by affliction. For though the Angell prooued it to him, to his good contentment, that he was the man which ſhould deliuer Iſrael out of the oppreſſion of the Midianites; yet as though no ſuch thing had been ſpoken to him, nor beleeued by him, by and by, as ſoone as he perceiued that he was an Angell with whom he ſpake, he thinking before that he was but a man of God,behold how he is troubled afreſh. Although theſe two about which he was troubled,were contraries; to wit, the promiſe of God in the firſt, which hee doubted of; and his feare in this laſt by ſeeing his Angell. In the which to ſtay a while, ſeeing it is the point now in hand; we know he could not deliuer Iſrael,as he was told, and beleeued he ſhould, if he muſt die before the time came. And yet not conſidering what he ſaid; he affirmed reſolutely hee ſhould die, when yet Iſrael was not deliuered: euen ſo are we much dazled and vnſetled by affliction. Much like to *Martha*,when her brother *Lazarus* was dead, and Ieſus was
Ioh.11.22. come thither,ſhe came mourning to him, and ſaid, *Lord, if thou haaſt been here,my brother had not been dead: but now I know alſo*, ſaid ſhe,*that whatſoeuer thou askeſt of God,he will giue it thee*. Wherein ſhe teſtified,that he could,if it pleaſed him, raiſe him vp againe. And yet marke, when Ieſus after that, went to the graue to raiſe him from death, and bad them take away the ſtone,*Martha* ſtood by,forgetting what ſhe had ſaid before, and anſwered Ieſus,as not belieuing that he could be raiſed to life,O Lord, it is too late,*he ſtinketh alreadie,for he hath been dead foure daies.*

And who doth not find it to be true,which I haue ſaid,namely,that faith which is well grounded,and worketh now with comfort by loue, ſhall eaſily be found to languiſh and waxe faint through doubting and feare, if affliction come in the way to trie vs? For why? we are ſo prone to vnbeliefe, that if we doe not at the firſt triall,alwaies ſhew and bewray it,which yet oft times we doe,yea,before the trouble come,when we ſee but a likelihood of it,we ſhall at leaſt doe it,if we be long held vnder the affliction,and eſpecially if it be any great matter; as ſome ſore loſſe,paine, or the like. So that it is not without eſpeciall cauſe,that we are commanded by the Apoſtle,not on-
Col.2.7. ly to bee rooted, but alſo to bee confirmed, and to abound in faith with thankſgiuing. Let vs conſider,to this end, that it is but the fruit of our corruption,thus to feare and doubt,when wee ſhould beleeue, and to reaſon againſt Gods promiſes,affirming that they cannot be performed, when wee ſee likelihood of the contrary; yea though we doe it not with any bad meaning,as neither *Gedeon* did here,yet it is our great ſinne to offer God ſuch diſhonour: let vs ſtriue rather to beate downe our fooliſh feares and paſſions,ſeeing it is moſt like,and we are ſure to ſpeede the worſt thereby,and in that we giue place to our paſſions,we ſhall do it to our coſt,although we repent for it. Our Sauiour ſeeing *Martha* in that ſudden feare and diſtruſt, checkes

checkes her, saying; *Did I not say vnto thee, if thou couldest belieue, thou shouldest see the glory of God?* As if he should say; Looke to my word, looke not to the vnlikelihood. *Manoahs* wife was stronger then *Gedeon* or her husband, in the like case: If God would haue slaine vs (saith she) he would not haue said we should haue a sonne, and so ought *Gedeon* to haue reasoned: God will not kill me now, seeing I must deliuer Israel: for these are contraries, and thus when *Manoahs* wife saw that one of them must needs be false, she rather confuteth her husband then the message of the Angell, and concludeth, doubtlesse we shall liue, and not die, for the word of God is more worth the resting vpon, then our owne conceits. And thus it should bee with vs, that Note. we be not alwaies off and on, now carried with full saile of faith, and by and by cast downe, as if we had neuer been the men, this ficklenesse is vnbeseeming vs. Men wish that it were alwaies alike with them, and yet find the contrary; because they kept not their eie fixed vpon the promise, daily renewing their hold therein stedfastly as at any time before they did; considering, that as the Sun is alway the same, whither it be ouer cast with cloudes, or shine forth clearely, so is *Christ Iesus yesterday, and to day, and the same for euer,* vnchangeable in himselfe, if wee change not our perswasion of him through vnbeliefe.

In this verse it is shewed, that while *Gedeon* was thus perplexed with Vers.23. feare, the Lord comforted him, that hee being free from it, might the better *The sense.* goe about that which was appointed him. For we know what a dangerous hindrance to faith, feare is. And therefore, what hart could hee haue to belieue that hee should worke such a deliuerance, who feared death euery minute of an howre? And the Angell put away his feare, by promising him good successe, and quietnesse of mind, and that he should not dye. This is *Doct.* the great goodnesse of God, that he will not long leaue his faithfull people in pinching feare, and pensiue heauines: but in good time deliuereth them, least they should be too much cast downe and discomforted. And so the Scriptures testifie, that God would not haue people left in troublesome passions; as feare or sorrow, which how troublesome they are, our experience teacheth. *Iosua* was sore troubled, when the people of Israel fell before the Iosh.7.7.10. men of *Ay*, but God soone put him out of it. So likewise the good women in the Gospell were sore afraid, by reason of the earthquake, and the appearing of the Angell, but he bid them not to be afraid, euen as here he saith to Matth.28.5. *Gedeon, Peace be to thee.* Thus it were meet for all poore troubled consciences, to mark diligently how comfortably God speaketh to them, as that they should put away their needlesse ad hurtfull feares and griefes; for the which cause the Lord willeth with a doubling his words, Esay 40.1. that his afflicted people should be comforted: for thus he saith there, as also in many other places; *comfort ye, comfort ye my people.* As if he should say, comfort them Esay 40.1. euen at the heart. And this aduice had so much the more neede to bee receiued of them, because when they begin once to be heauy, they forget that they were euer comforted, and passe their bounds in heauinesse. But when such distempered perturbations arise in vs, and disquiet vs through an euill conscience, and by meanes of some offending God willingly or negligently, which by care we might haue auoided, (in which case wee haue no warrant to take comfort to our selues, neither doth God at any time vse to com-

fort vs therein, here the course that is to be taken, is, that we solemnely prostrate our selues before him, accusing our selues, and bewailing our sinne, with broken hearts for mercy, as well as looke for other deliuerance, and he will returne to vs most graciously, powre oile and wine into our wounds most sauourily, and ease our griefe readily, and all our feare shall be driuen
1.Pet.3.13. away. For if we doe well, who (as Saint *Peter* saith) shall feare vs? *Ezekiah* is a notable example of this, who being in his sicknesse troubled with the feare of vntimely death, whereby he feared iustly that the Church of God might the sooner be infected with idolatrie, being not yet well setled in the true worship of God, nor throughly purged; made an heauie complaint, as
Esay 38.10. appeares Esay 38. not for that hee desired life simplie for it selfe, as for the good of the Church. But going to the Lord by prayer in this perplexitie for recouery, the Lord staid his mind, and sent his Prophet to encourage him both by promise and miracle, and beare him word hee should recouer, and then he goeth vp to the house of the Lord, and makes a solemne thanksgiuing for his recouery. But seeing many, euen of Gods deare ones, doe either not know how to repaire to God in this manner, or if they doe, yet they cannot humble their hearts, therefore they trouble themselues with suffering the sting of an ill conscience to pricke them, which in continuance of time is forgotten, and being not kindly healed, they soone breake out againe, and so they make there life vnprofitable when it is at the best, and till they cast vp that vnsauorie gorge by some great outward affliction, which searcheth
Note. deepe, or by some agonie of mind, whereby they are brought by the helpe of some wise and experienced Minister to true repentance, they come to no better estate.

Vers.24. *The sense.* Now followeth *Gedeons* thanksgiuing, which clearely prooueth that hee receiued comfort, and was well staied by the Angels words vnto him. For whether we take it thus translated, as it is by *Tremelius* [*he builded an altar to the Lord, when he had pronounced peace to him*] or whether thus, as in the Geneua translation it is read, he *builded an altar to the Lord, and called it Iehouah-shalom*, that is, the Lord of peace; I say, in whether soeuer of these we take it, it is a thanks to God, yea and that in solemne manner: for if he called him the Lord of peace who had giuen him double peace, to wit, both in freeing him from his dreadfull doubt first, and afterward also from his feare. And so *Gedeon* leauing that remembrance of his thankful hart there vnto posterity, all may see that it was a solemne thanking of God. And to the same end that tendeth which is said, that he built the altar: it was in token of his thanks, after God had quieted his mind, both about the deliuerance of the Israelites from the rage of the Midianites, and also from his feare by seeing the Angell of God.

Doct. And therefore out of this action of *Gedeons*, we learne to take all good occasions of thanks to God, not onely ordinarily for daily benefits, and priuately by our selues as well as openly; but also as God shall giue vs occasion by such mercies bestowed vpon vs, which are more then ordinarie, as here
Note. he did to *Gedeon*, and before this, to *Moses*, *Ioshua*, *Debora*, and others, and doth oft times to vs in the yeere, and in the seuen yeere, by deliuerances, protection, and vnlooked for mercies and benefits. And further, as hee here did it in a solemne manner, so ought we, as much as in vs lieth: for he left testimony

mony of his thanks, to thoſe who came long after him. But of thankſgiuing I haue ſpoken before.

THE FORTIE ONE SERMON ON THE SIXTH CHAPTER OF THE BOOKE OF IVDGES.

VERS. 25. *And the ſame night the Lord ſaid to him, take thy fathers young*
bullocke, and an other bullocke ſeuen yeeres old, and deſtroy the altar of Baal that thy
father hath, and cut downe the groue that is by it.
26. *And build an altar vnto the Lord thy God vpon the top of this rocke, in a*
plaine place, and take the ſecond bullock, and offer a burnt offering with the wood of
the groue, which thou ſhalt cut downe.
27. *Then Gedeon tooke ten men of his ſeruants, and did as the Lord bad him:*
but becauſe he feared to doe it by day for his fathers houſhold, and the men of the city,
he did it by night.
28. *And when the men of the citie aroſe earely in the morning, behold, the altar*
of Baal was broken, and the groue cut downe, that was by it, and the ſecond bullocke
offered vpon the altar that was made.
29. *Therfore they ſaid one vnto another, who hath done this thing? and when they*
inquired, and asked, they ſaid, Gedeon the ſonne of Ioaſh hath done this thing.
30. *Then the men of the citie ſaid to Ioaſh, bring out thy ſonne that hee may die,*
for hee hath deſtroyed the altar of Baal, and hath alſo cut downe the groue that was
by it.
31. *And Ioaſh ſaid to all that ſtood by him, will ye pleade Baals cauſe? or will yee*
ſaue him? He that will contend for him, let him die yer the morning: if he be God,
let him pleade for himſelfe againſt him that with caſt downe his altar.
32. *And in that day was Gedeon called Ierubaal: that is, let Baal pleade for*
himſelfe, becauſe he hath broken downe his altar.

OF the ſecond branch of the fourth part of the Chapter we haue heard; that is, of *Gedeons* asking of a ſigne: Now followeth the third, containing the charge that God gaue him to the 33 verſe.

For after all this that we haue heard, before he begin the warre, hee is commanded to deſtroy and caſt downe idolatrie, and to ſet vp true religion, and worſhip of God. And this is in theſe words: *Caſt downe the altar of Baal, and cut downe the groue that is by it, and erect another, and offer to God thereon:* which *Gedeon* did accordingly: and this to the 28. verſe. And yet he did this with perill euen of his life, as appeareth verſe 30. but God ſtirred vp *Ioaſh, Gedeons* father, againſt the men of the citie, and deliuered him out of their hands, as we ſee, to the 33. verſe. *The generall ſumme of theſe verſes.*

In this verſe, and in the 26. more particularly, the Lord for the deſtroying of Idolatrie, bids *Gedeon* take his fathers young bullocke, euen the ſecond bullocke *Verſe 25 26. The ſumme of theſe two verſes particularly.*

bullocke which was seuen yeeres old,which had been kept to be offered to *Baal*. In those which were superstitious,that they spared no cost for the seruing of their lusts: but the Lord hindred, and held that sacrifice from *Baal*, commanding the alter to be cast downe,and also the groue that was by it, to be cut downe; for in such places for the pleasantnesse of them,the people vsed,and chose to worship, I meane in such places beset with woods and groaues: such places vnder trees,and on hilles,which they called high places,the fathers also delighted in to offer,before the Lord forbad them,being mooued thereby to the meditation of heauenly things the rather. And the Idolaters did the like vnto their Idols, as these here did in offering to *Baal*, through a superstitious opinion that such places were fittest to stirre vp deuotion. And therefore God commanded them to be cast and cut downe, and their altars to be destroyed. And this did God command *Gedeon* here to doe, and another to bee builded: and that second bullocke that was appointed for *Baal*, to bee offered as a burnt offering to the Lord, with the wood of the groue which was cut downe.

Deut.12.2.3. &c.

Doct.vers.25. 26.&c.

Here for our instruction, out of these two verses, this is worthily to be noted, that when God at that time went about to deliuer Israel from the bondage of the Midianites, hee would yet haue Idolatrie to be first ouerthrowne,lest they should afterward returne to it againe. Teaching vs thereby, that nothing goeth forward happily in the Common-wealth, except good order be taken first for the walfare of the Church,namely, by rooting out,and casting downe Idolatry and superstitious worshipping of God,and ignorance; and a planting and stablishing of the true preaching of the Gospell. Which teacheth both Magistrates what is first to be done of them to the people committed to their gouernment, and also priuate men; that in vaine they shall looke (either the one or the other) to prosper in their liues, I meane, to enioy Gods blessing with cheerefulnes and sound comfort, if God be not with an vpright heart first honoured and serued. But if this be, is it all? No, but euen then let them looke to the manner of their worshipping God also,and namely in hearing,let them take heed how they heare,as Christ teacheth,and that is, by casting away all guile, maliciousnes,&c. and to receiue the word (so as it may be ingrafted in them) with meeknes and teachablenes,as becommeth beleeuers. But more of that in another place.

Luke 8.18. James 1.21.

In the meane while,as I haue said of Idolatrie, so I say of their sinnes; let vs further learne therefore,that as they were commanded to put away Idolatrie,which was their sinne, before they could doe God true seruice any other way; so I say,let vs learne,that before we offer to God any acceptable dutie,we put away our sinne,whatsoeuer it be,that riseth vp in our way, be it neuer so liking and well pleasing to vs: For it doth but choake and smother the graces of God in vs,if there be any,euen as the briars and brambles doe the corne,that it cannot spring vp and prosper. And this rule is to bee obserued of vs both of the first time, when God counteth vs faithfull, and putteth vs in his seruice,and of all times following,when wee haue stepped aside. Thus *Eliah* before he restored the sound worship of God,destroyeth the Baalites: and the same course tooke al the good Kings which reformed the Church,as *Iehoshaphat,Hezekiah,Iosiah*. And the Lord charged the Israelites to destroy and roote out the Canaanites at their first entring vpon their possessions,

1.Tim.1.12.

1.King.18.40.

possessions, as wee haue heard in this booke, and before: foretelling them, that otherwise they would draw them from his true worship. *Iacob* therefore before he went vp to Bethel to worship God, did by his commandement, cause all his houshold and those that were with him, lately come out of Padan Aram from *Laban*, to put away their Idols, and clense themselues, that so they might worship the Lord in good sort and manner. So we must purge out the old leauen, and become a new lumpe, as the Apostle speaketh: For it fareth with vs herein, as with the stomacke: which though it receiue neuer so good meates, yet the bodie prospereth not by them, if it be full of corrupt humours: no more doe we thriue in any good actions wee take in hand, if we goe about them, being fraught and clogged with our sins knowne, or such as are suspected to be in vs, till as most filthie corruption they be purged out. Therefore also Saint *Peter* requireth, *that men put away all maliciousnes and guile*, with such like annoiance first; *and then as new borne babes desire the sincere milke of the word*, that they may grow thereby. Gen.35.1. 1.Cor.5.8. *A similitude.* 1.Pet.2.1.2.

And as a sore or wound in the bodie, though neuer so good salues be laid thereto, is not healed thereby, vnlesse the corruption and hurtfull humours be first drawne out: so is it with vs. So that not onely this is true in the generall reformation of the Church, but also of each particuler member of it, and person. And it is the order which the Lord vseth in the fitting of all his people for his vse: first he mortifieth them, then he quickens them. Neither could our Lord Iesus haue risen againe for our iustification, if he had not first died for our sins and transgression. And let him who would haue found comfort in his doing of dutie, first learne this obedience; to subdue and bring into subiection, his rebellious and euill heart and lusts, with the fruite thereof, and then the other shall proceed roundly, without impediment. For all the good doctrine which God hath ordained to sweeten and refresh the soule with, and to furnish the life, also the helpe and benefit of praier and the Sacraments, they all lose their force, and leaue no fruite in vs behinde them, if wee be loden (euery one) with the foule and loathsome sinnes, in which hee hath liued, and that they bee not purged out by true repentance. *A similitude.* Rom.4.25.

And this is easie to be perceiued and seene, as in persons, so in euery place, towne, Church and house, where the forementioned meanes are vsed. And who among vs that haue any experience, but they haue marked this in many, and neede not be ashamed to say it of themselues, that whatsoeuer rules and good instruction, for the well guiding of our liues, haue bin giuen, and learned of vs, with the benefit of the Sabbath, with prayer, publike or priuate, and such like; they haue come to a small reckoning, and they doe vs little good, if we haue not let out the venome of rancour, spite, desire of reuenge, vncleane lusts, worldlinesse, and the like, that haue been seated and spread in our hearts, and cast vp (as filthie vomit) the noisome fruite thereof, out of our liues.

And it is the cause at this day of so little profiting, and so slender fruites of our preaching, as we complaine of iustly, and inueigh against it bitterly; for that people are at a point, they will doe as they haue done, and retaine the sinnes which in times past they haue walked and delighted in, when yet we haue daily, in the earnestest manner that wee could, disgraced, and made them Note.

them odious, with the most fearful & sharp threats of God adioyned thereto. Yea and contrariwise, if any make right and kinde vse of our Ministerie, who seeth not, that they be those that waxe ashamed of themselues, after they haue seene their faces in the glasse of Gods law, and with *Ephraim* bemoned themselues, & bin confounded, because they did beare the reproch of their youth; when the old rootes haue thus bin decaied, then new sprigs of grace haue sprung out in their roome, and then they haue begun to lament after God. Magistrate, Minister, Master of family, and priuate persons, if they be well aduised, they speake thus, yea, they all finde this to be true.

Iere.31.18.19.

Doct.vers.25. And in this 25. verse, it is further said, as we see, that God appeared here to *Gedeon* in the night, when it might haue seemed that he had been neglected and forgotten, euen then gaue he a weightie charge vnto him: whereby we are taught that God watcheth ouer his to doe them good, when they are sleepie, and minde nothing: as we reade he did to *Samuel*, *Salomon*, and other of his faithfull seruants. For *he that keepeth Israel doth neither slumber nor sleepe*: meaning that he waketh and watcheth continually to keepe his from danger: for the which cause it is said, by the Apostle *Peter*, that his eyes are vpon them, as the mothers vpon the young childe, standing by, to see that it take no hurt. For, as it is in the Psalme; if the Lord keepe not the citie, the watchmen watch but in vaine: but if God take part with his, the strongest enemie shall not be able to hurt them. It is said of *Peter*, Act. 12.6. that while he slept betweene two souldiers in the night, bound with two chaines, the Angell of the Lord came vpon them, and smote *Peter* on the side, so that his chaines fell off, and he was deliuered from *Herod*. See also Psal.4. I will lay me downe and take my rest, for thou (O Lord) vpholdest me. But seeing he keepeth the bad also, and there some (perhaps) will say, therefore it might seeme no great matter, that he keepeth and watcheth ouer the faithfull: but for answere, I say with the Apostle, *God is the sauiour of all men*, that is, from outward troubles, *but especially of the beleeuers*; for he preserueth their soules from euill, vnto saluation. As if he said, he keepeth and saueth his own with a fatherly care and affection, but the wicked, though he keepe them, yet he doth so as a Iudge keepeth aliue euill doers, but vnto their destruction. But of his people that is verified which is written by *Salomon*: He watcheth ouer them, when they sleepe, and communeth with them when they awake, and when they walke he doth gouerne and guide them. And hereupon, in that Gods care is thus ouer his, in the night season, as well as in other parts of their liues, hereupon I say it is, that as they reioyce in the Lord alwaies in all that they set their hand vnto through the day; so they haue this fruite of it in the night also, that they meditate and make their songs of his louing kindnesse, as *Dauid* saith of himselfe, that he would praise God in the night season, when the other haue their terrors, for their bad doings, or imagine euill in their beds to draw vpon them greater and speedier iudgements.

1.Sam.3.4. 1.King.3.5. Psal.121.4. Act.12.6. Psal.4.8. 1.Tim.4.10. Prou.6.22. Psal.119.62.

Doct.2.in vers.25.26. Now further, out of both these verses together note, that as it was not enough for *Gedeon* to ouerthrow the Altar of *Baal*, vnlesse he builded another to the Lord; nor to build one to the Lord, vnlesse he cast downe the Idolatrous Altar: Euen so, it is not enough to shunne euill, except we doe good. And therefore it is not sufficient to be no couetous person, except a man bee mercifull: it is not enough to bee innocent, except a man be also

fruitfull in doing good; for one God is the commander of both. It is a true speech, Negatiues conclude nothing: and here it is especially true. Therefore let all such, as whose goodnesse and outward actions witnesse not for them, suspect that they deceiue themselues in the reforming of the hart. For surely an heart purged, will bee fruitfull. Againe, it is not inough to forsake Poperie, &c. vnlesse the pure Gospell bee imbraced. Let the one abandon the other, as Dagon and the Arke could not stand together. They that make an hotch-potch of both, are an abomination to the Lord. And here we may further learne, that two religions in a land, though the one tolerated onelie, two contray or diuers waies I meane, of worshipping God, can no more stand together, then Christ and Belial. For then the Lord would haue spared *Gedeon* a labour, and only enioyned him to goe about the warre and settle sound religion, letting idolatrie alone. The false religion is the canker of Iosh.7.24.
the true, and as the execrable thing tooke hold vpon the whole substance of *Achan*: so doth this bring a curse vpon the other. Now to returne, whereas the Lord bad the bullocke, dedicated to *Baal*, to be offered as a burnt sacrifice to himselfe: I answer, he is Lord of all, he might turne it to what vse he pleased. But it followeth not, that we, without his commandement, may take vpon vs to iumble together Gods worship, and superstition. For the which cause, as sometime he commanded that the gold and other things vsed in idolatrie, should passe through the fire, and so it might be vsed, so somtime, he commanded, that they should vtterly be destroyed. To returne therfore in a word, to the point. As we see what a blemish it had been in *Gedeon*, if he had done the one part of the charge, and not another, like *Saul* in the 1.Sam.15.
businesse of the Amalakites; so by the way, it teacheth, that God alowes not 15.16.
for seruice, duties done by halues, but that they should be soundly and in one part and point as another indeuored after: neither doth hee allow vs to bee our owne caruers to take what pleaseth vs; and turne the other backe again, which we may see more clearely by the example of one that was guiltie of this fault. Of *Iehu* it is reported, that when he had slaine all the cursed posteritie of *Ahab*, and destroyed the Priests of *Baal* (which was the purging out of false worship in great part) yet whereas the other part of setting vp true worship should haue followed it, the text makes a stop, and sets downe a manifest separation betwixt them thus: *But from the sinnes of Ieroboam the sonne* 2.King.10.29.
of Nebat Iehu departed not; nay more, *nor from their golden Calues in Bethel and Dan.* Why then did he destroy *Baal?* Surely he was carried to it, by a common gift of the holy Ghost, euen feruency in that worke: which made him an instrument for that purpose; but that he did it not with a true detestation of the sinne, it is manifest, for then hee would haue abandoned the other also, and haue restored pure worship in stead of it. This should teach vs, that holy instruction, which is so oft in general commended to vs, when we haue hated to the pit of hell (for so the word signifieth in that place) that which is euill, then neglect not to doe that which is good. Rom.13. nay to cleaue to Rom.13.9.
it as a thing which is cemented, as glasse windowes are, the words are pithy. So saith the Apostle, *Let him that stole steale no more:* yet it is not sufficient, Ephes.4.28.
that a man be not a thiefe; therefore he addeth, *But worke with his hands, and doe the thing that is good,* for that is a good token he is reformed. And commonly in Scripture we shall see this order obserued: that vnto prohibitions

first set downe, there are added commandements of dutie: for though of the two it is the first and hardest, to purge out a corrupt habite and a leaud qualitie: yet it is not all, God will haue it appeare to be so by a new and contrary practise to the former, that the worke may be sound and perfect. Neither doth he command men to clense out their euil, and so keep themselues void, empty and barren of grace: (which were to set vp a neutralitie rather
Heb.13.9. then Christianity) but he wil haue men seasoned with grace, and stablished with it, as it is to the Hebrewes. And he who commandeth vs not to sow among thornes nor weedes, giues vs no libertie to neglect planting, when we haue rooted vp the other.

Doct.2. vers.25. For cutting downe the groues, it was before this time (that *Gedeon* was
Deut.12.3. charged to do it) commanded so by God in Deuteronomy; which argueth, that they were greatly abused, as other waies, so in worshipping strange Gods there. True it is, that the old fathers did before the forbidding thereof, worship God vpon high hils, from whence, they seeing farre off, the varietie of Gods creatures, it was a meanes of good meditations to them, and of more sequestring of their minds from earthlinesse. And we our selues being on high places, and beholding the trees, and other creatures of God a farre off, with the situation of the countries on hilles and vallies, what an admiration at the infinite workes of God commeth into our minds, thereby? we are brought to heauenly meditations, and to ponder Gods power, wisdome and loue to vs. The Idolaters (no doubt) chose those places for the pleasantnesse of them, that thereby, and with the delight they had in the worshipping of their idols, they might be rauished in their superstitious maner; as the Papists in their false and will worship, when they be at their fond deuotion, in the places beset with Crucifixes and other Images, sounds and sonnets, doe imagine and dreame that they bee in a corner not of paradise,
2.Cor.11.14. but of heauen it selfe. Thus can *the diuell transforme himselfe into an Angell of light*.

Doct. 3. in verse 25. And here we may see, that howsoeuer *Gedeon* was accounted of God for his faithfulnesse; yet his father maintained idolatrie; for his were the wood or groue, the altar and the bullock, being implements of their idolatrie. And these the Lord commanded *Gedeon* to remooue and take away, to the end wee may learne, that in purging religion, or in the amending of faults, wee must alwaies begin with our owne families, and nearest kindred; lest otherwise we should shew our selues ridiculous, in seeming to be very forward in
1.Pet.4.17. reproouing and correcting other, while our owne bee neglected and passed
Iosh.24.15. by. Thus God beginneth iudgement at his owne house. Thus did *Iosbua* in his reforming the whole Congregation, professe most worthily, *I and my house will serue the Lord*. And *Ely*, a Iudge also, for not gouerning his house, and staying the outrage of his sonnes, is seuerely threatned. And good reason: for sithence next to our selues (who must first of all be reformed, or els our zeale ill becommeth vs, and argueth hypocrisie) the next, I say, are our kindred and families. Therefore wee must without partialitie first set vpon them, that so it may appeare that we detest sinne heartily, in that we cannot endure it in those whom we loue best: and others may be ashamed to stand out in their owne defence, and feare to offend. For if the father first begin with his children, how shall his seruants looke to escape?

Now

Now it followeth how *Gedeon* did that which God commanded him, Verſ.27.
but ſeeing he appointed him no time when hee ſhould doe it, he therefore *The ſenſe.*
diſpatched it in the night, for feare, leſt if he had done it in the day, he might haue been withſtood by his fathers ſeruants, and the men of the citie; yea, and himſelfe haue been ſlaine. In that he obeyed the Lord, he teſtified his faith: in that hee did it at the beſt aduantage, in the night, hee ſhewed his wiſedome. And though he feared, yet his feare was not ſuch, as it hindred his faith.

In both theſe, *Gedeons* example is our inſtruction: his faith firſt is to bee Doct.verſ.27.
followed of vs, that by meanes of it, wee ſhould not *commune with fleſh and* Gal.1.16.
blood, when God commandeth ought vnto vs, but beare downe all lets that ſtand vp in the way to hinder vs from obeying: as friends, and counſell giuers againſt it, and count them, as Chriſt did *Peter*, when hee diſwaded him Matth.16.23.
from going to Ieruſalem to ſuffer death for his people, hee called him an aduerſarie to him, euen Satan. So muſt all ſtrong rebellion be beaten downe, (that ſtandeth vp in our way) by this weapon of our warfare, which 2.Cor.10.4.
is *not carnall but ſpirituall, and mightie through God, to caſt downe ſtrong holds*; it muſt, I ſay, by this armour of our faith, bee brought into ſubiection. And for example: if feare ſtand vp in the way particularly, to hinder vs, let faith ſtriue with it to caſt it out, which is beſt able of any grace that is in vs, to ouercome and put it by. And thus did *Eſter*, who had no ſtronger weapon then her faith, in as great perill of her owne, and her peoples life, both which with *Gedeon* are ſet forth for the example of al that ſhall come after, to follow them in belieuing. But oh, where are ſuch to be found, who ſhall be readie, (no, though it be in the hazard of the Church) to doe that which theſe did, I meane, to fixe their faith on God; or if any be ſo minded, yet how weaklie and faintly ſhall it be done, and how long ſhall it be in performing? But this hath often been ſpoken of.

And this be ſaid of *Gedeons* faith: now ſomewhat be ſaid likewiſe of his *Doct.2.*
wiſedome. His wiſedome is highly commended in his caſting downe their idolatrie; that ſeeing God ſet not, neither appointed the time when hee ſhould doe it, therefore hee did it in the night, wherein hee might bee freeſt from reſiſtance and danger. Doue-like innocency and obedience to God, Matth.10.16.
muſt be ioyned with the wiſdome of Serpents. In many duties doing wee muſt watch the beſt opportunitie, time and place, vnleſſe the Lord preſcribe them to vs. So did *Sampſon* in the great deſtruction of the Philiſtims, watch Iudg.16.30.
time and place, and tooke opportunitie, when thouſands of them were aſſembled to make themſelues paſſe-time by mocking and laughing at him; then he ſet his ſhoulders to the maine poſtes whereon the houſe ſtood, and caſt it downe vpon the Princes and the reſt, and ſlew thouſands of them.

So it was ſaid of *Dauid*, hee did wiſely, whither ſoeuer hee went out, and 1.Sam.18.5.
God was with him accordingly. And it is a ſingular gift of God in his children to be wiſe in the things they take in hand, that they giue no aduantage to the wicked, nor the diuell; but take the beſt and fitteſt occaſions to bee well occupied, as time and place giue leaue, both in holding their profeſſion generally, and alſo in the doing of other particular duties: that where they ſee inconuenience like to come, they may by wiſe forecaſting, preuent the ſame, and lay their moſt care where greateſt danger is to bee ſeene and fea- Note.
red.

red. Wherein though all attaine not the same and like measure, yet it is well when al labour as they are able, to attaine it. But some marre their good actions with the ill and vnwise manner in which they doe them. As *Iobs* friends did, in seeking to comfort him. The particular instances are infinite. But thinke we of them by this example. For if *Gedeon* had gone about the work inioyned him, rashly or vndiscreetly, in the day time, who seeth not that e-
Iud.5.24. uen his obeying of God in such a mnner had marred all? But *Iael* was blessed
1.Sam.25.34. for her wisdome she shewed to pull downe *Sisera*. And thus *Abigail* by her
Prou.14.1. wisdome deliuered her house, as *Salomon* saith; and the wise woman mentio-
2.Sam 20.16. ned in 2.Sam. who saued a whole citie. The children of this generation teach vs herein. And therefore pray we all for the spirit of wisedome, that we not only doe that which we are commanded, but that we studie to do it in the best sort we can: and yet alwaies shunning as a rock, carnall shifts and policies. But of this the lesse shall serue, being also often enlarged.

THE FORTIE TWO SERMON ON THE SIXTH CHAPTER OF THE BOOKE OF IVDGES.

Vers.28.29.30. *The sense.* WE haue heard of *Gedeons* faith and wisedome about the casting downe of the altar of *Baal*: and wee may see a good reason why he was faine to vse the best and surest meanes for the effecting of it, and for the ouerthrow of their idolatrie. First, seeing it was stablished among them, and had taken roote: therefore all that he could do was little enough to throw it downe. And also for that the people were so superstitiously addicted thereto, and so delighted in it. But let vs now see in what outragious manner the people inquire after the man that had done it: and when they with consent agreed, that it was *Gedeon*, how furiously they sought to haue him put to death.

*Doct.*1. Here many good points may be noted about idolaters, which I will briefie set downe. First this, how deepely idolatrie, superstition, and false worship is rooted in peoples hearts, and ground fast; as is to bee seene in these, and through these stories, and those in the booke of the Kings; as the Philistims blind deuotion to their Dagon, and the peoples fond and mad zeale in maintaining the false worship of *Baal* in *Ahabs* time, their offerings to them, their bowing downe, and praying to them. So that a man might haue as easily plucked their hearts out of their bellies, as to haue disswaded and alienated their loue from them. The reasons are, first, because as sinne, so error is strong, plausible and deceitfull. Secondly, God accurseth all that will
2.Thes.2.10. not hearken to the truth, so that they shall belieue lies, and be bewitched therewith.

therewith. See and consider to this end, Esay 44.19. Thirdly, the worst weeds haue deepest roots, and corrupt customes or opinions, because they agree with mans bad nature, are not easily rooted out; whereas those which are good and commendable, are like precious plants or flowers, which hardly take any roote at all, and may be pluckt vp with two fingers. As at this day the cursed reliques of heathenish and popish fashions, how hardly are they laid downe, looke but to some vaine and foolish customes, and the fond deuotion of the superstitions all the yeere long, in kneeling before stockes and stones, and ye may easily guesse how hard a thing it is to remooue and expel them & the like. *Gamaliel* said of the doctrine of the Apostles; If it be not of God, ye shal not need to oppose it, it wil fal of it self. But we must know that God not working by miracle, as he did then, Satan and his complices will in these daies trie the vttermost, and vse all meanes ere that come to passe: yea as we may see, they grow in experience and pollicie, strength and resolution also, to vphold their rotten building, vntill (as at death (to be sure) it shall) it fall vpon their shoulders. Whereas the true and pure worship of God, what authoritie, credit, or heartie loue doth it find or obtaine at the hands of the most of them who professe it? Nay, they haue soone inough of it, many reuolt and fall from it, and they that retaine it, doe it (for the most part) in a most dead and cold manner. Insomuch, as the diligentest preaching, and earnestest perswasions, doe scarcely preuaile so farre with men as that they get so much as a name of a good religion in the places where they dwell: when yet (if it were so) their zeale is neither grounded vpon knowledge, and if it be in some, yet are they not stablished and setled therein; and yet further, euen of them there are very few that hold constantly in a good conscience, the profession of their hope with ioy vnto their end.

Esay 44.19.

Actes 5.34.

Note.

And although this good conscience bee farre from the idolaters of our time, for it can onely come from faith in Christ, and assurance of his fauour, (whatsoeuer blind zeale and deuotion be in them) yet therein they doe, as I said before, giue and ascribe much to their corrupt religion, and false worship, in cost, in time spending about the same, and feruencie therein, aboue a number of vs to ours. So that if they went vpon good grounds, and had any promise from God for their so doing, they might haue to reioyce aboue many of vs. But they and such of our selues, as I compare with them, in comming short of their zeale, shal speed both alike, while they (I meane the Papists) haue this cast in their teeth, *Who required this at your hands?* And againe, let him that set you on worke, pay you your wages. And to them of our profession, this shall be said; *This people draweth neere to mee with their bodies, but their hearts are farre from me, and therefore in vaine doe such worship me.*

Matth.15.8.

And yet this I will adde, seeing I haue ioyned these popish worshippers with the idolaters of ancient time, affirming them to be like to them in zeale, this I say, I will adde concerning them, that this deuotion is but in few of them in these our daies, like to that which was in thẽ of former ages, though (as they blindfold mens eies) it goe for currant, that they bee all zealous that are of that profession, when yet it is manifest that numbers of them are most subtill and hollow hearted dissemblers and deceiuers. For to grant that some of the ignoranter sort are feruent in their false religion and blind deuotion, yet the most of the rest deceiue the world, and are not so zealous as they

they are wilfull,ſpitefull,and malicious,who doe that which they doe, partly for their belly, and partly (though againſt their conſcience) to vphold their religion by tradition,when they cannot by Scripture: and all to this end,that it may,(as much as in them lieth) be receiued for the truth, rather then that of the Proteſtants, whom they deadly hate and abhorre. As for that they hope to merit by their zeale, which doth the more ſet them forward,it is to bee granted, that they are much whetted on thereby,though they be deceiued: but ſhould not the promiſes of God freely made to vs of all good things,much more animate and harten on vs?

2 Another thing note we here,how ſoone and earneſtly they inquired who ſhould deface their Baal,and ſtrippe him of his ornaments? whereas Gods word may lie vnpreached by many occaſions,long inough,before it be asked where the fault lieth, and complained of, and bewailed; or before the neglect thereof be ſought to be remedied. In Poperie,if a man ſhall ſpeake againſt the maſſe,or their breaden God,or diſpraiſe any, yea the leaſt part of their traſh and trumperie,he ſhall be more cruelly handled then for blaſpheming in the higheſt degree. Which appeares by ſuch as in the time of perſecution in our owne land,attempted zealouſly to deface that idoll, who of all other were put to moſt exquiſite torments.Euen as *Gedeon* here was purſued,and as a moſt hereticall and ſeditious diſturbur,was called for to be put to death,for offering that reproch vnto that baſe idoll *Baal.* Oh,it were an happie time, if men were as zealouſly bent againſt atheiſme, ſuperſtition, idolatrie,adulterie,and ſuch like,as many are zealous for them: and that holy and heauenly things were in that account and requeſt with many,that open and apparent ſinnes are with them. And thus at this day doe the moſt men ſtorme and rage at the Miniſter of God (who is Gods ordinarie inſtrument, as *Gedeon* was the extraordinary) when they ſee that he is not content to dally with them, but in good earneſt ſtriueth to pull them from their ignorance,formall,and could worſhip of God, vncleaneneſſe, or whatſoeuer other ſinne they cleaue vnto; (as theſe did to their idoll *Baal*) and ſerue. The poore man *Gedeon* here had not more adoe to ſaue himſelfe from this furious and eager multitude,then the Miniſter hath (in many places where the Goſpell hath not preuailed) to defend himſelfe from a ſwarme of hornets,which flie about his eares,ready to ſting him (I might rather haue ſaid wild beaſts to deuoure him) by their curſed reprochfull ſlanders and virulent tongues for his caſting their *Baal* to the ground.

Alſo it appeareth,that there were not many there that were as *Gedeon*,vpright hearted men,and ſuch as did openly ſhew their diſlike of idolatrie,becauſe they could ſo eaſily find him out, and light vpon him, as the guiltie partie,as they counted him,with ſo ſlight inquiry.So that he was as eminent for his pietie,as *Saul* for his ſtature,who was taler then all the people, and could not lie hidden. And the odious man of many hee was with them, to whom yet if they could haue ſeene, they were all beholding, and but for whom alſo they had all grone to wracke and had periſhed. And wee ſee, what eie-ſores, and how odious ſome one or few good profeſſors of the Goſpell are to a companie of prophane hickeſcorners, and what a troubleſome life they leade amongſt them:being baited and vexed by them at their pleaſure,and made their laughing ſtocke, as *Sampſon* to the Philiſtims: for whoſe

whose sake (yet) they are suffered by the Lord to liue, that they may come to repentance,being neere inough (by all likelihood) to be vtterly destroyed and to be brought to naught,but for them; as we may reade in the story of Genesis,if there had been but ten righteous men in Sodome,the city had not been consumed. Yet,and though they haue such benefit by them, they sticke not to sweare,that but for them they might liue merrily,and without disturbance. Therefore where God hath prouided better for a people,and muzled the mouthes of such tigers and beares as these,so that they may professe the Gospell without danger, or feare, pursuit, and scorne of their betters) who commonly are the wings to protect the inferiour sort of base and spitefull persons) let such see and acknowledge a great libertie and release, and vse it wisely while they inioy it,as the Churches of Samaria and Iudea, and Galilee did in the booke of the Acts. lest God take from them their props,ornaments and protectors of them, and make them to say (as many doe full heauily) we would gladly be zealous and fruitfull in our profession, (but (alas) we cannot so soone peepe out of the doores,but we are pelted in againe,and beaten back with the frownings,disgraces, and oppositions of such as are mightier then our selues. But of this point more anon. Genes.18.32. Actes 9.31.

Thus farre of the outrage of the people: now of the answere of *Ioah* to them,in the next two verses. For he,as a wise Magistrate,did at the first suppresse and bridle the rage of the people. Now because it was said before, that the ground with the groue,altar and bullock did pertaine to *Ioash*, and were his: it is cleare,that he had also vpheld the idolatrie: how was it then, that he should thus lightly suffer the act of his sonne *Gedeon* to passe vnpunished, (some man perhaps will aske,) and that he should find fault with the people,for seeking to punish the trespasser against *Baal?* I answere,that *Ioash* was certified of the will of God,very likely by *Gedeon* his sonne, as *Sampsons* father was by him,that marriage he sought with the Philistim woman was of the Lord. But howsoeuer it was,hee doth shew that God stirred him vp to be a fauourer of his sonnes doing,for hee doth with three reasons driue the people from their hold,and beates them backe from their purpose and attempt. First,he reprooues them for their boldnesse, for that they being priuate men, did without any calling take vpon them to bee reuengers of *Baals* quarrell,and that contrary to the will of God. And secondly,he threatens them with the feare of Gods iudgement,and that presently. And thirdly,by an Ironicall speech against *Baal* (saying,if he be a God, let him pleade for himselfe) he shameth them,and driues them from their enterprize. And this be said for the laying out of the 31.verse. In the 32.he giues his some a name according to the answere hee had made to the people,and that name was *Ierrubbaal.* Verse 31 32. *The sense.*

And here in generall occasion is offered to consider, how strangely God wrought for *Gedeon*,and against his enemies,beyond al expectation stirring vp *Ioash* to assist and oppose the other. Who would not haue said,that the people would haue borne downe *Gedeon*,they being backed so strongly,and hauing an idolatrous Magistrate on their side? But behold,the Lord turnes his heart as he pleaseth,and makes him stand out in the defense of his sonnes act,whose cruell Iudge he had been more like to bee,to condemne him to death,as these mad people required,and looked for. And wee must thinke Doct. in verse 32.

that it was no ſmall courage to him, to doe thus, though a Magiſtrate. For this concourſe of the people was not ordinary,in a iudiciall manner but mutinous,and not vnlike to that of *Demetrius* in the caſe of *Dianaes* worſhip. But the ſame God,who (when hee ſaw it meet) cauſed *Lyſias*,an Heathen Captaine,to become a Protector of *Paul* againſt the Iewes: and *Paul* himſelfe to be a Preacher of the Goſpel which he had before perſecuted,did this alſo,and his hand is not yet ſhortned from doing the like for the good of his Church,and incouragement of his people, according to that ſaying of the
Prou.16.7. Wiſe man: When a mans waies pleaſe the Lord,he will make his very enemies his friends: and by conſequent,thoſe things which were moſt feared, as being like to worke moſt againſt them,he will make them to worke contrarily,euen to their moſt good and furtherance: and beſides, God turnes the hearts of men,as riuers of water. Examples we haue in *Cyrus* the reſtorer of the Iewes,and the worſhip of God. *Pilates* wife, *Achiſth* to *Dauid*, &c. But this by the way onely.

More particularly,we may ſee in *Ioaſh*, who was before an Idolater,but being inſtructed about the will of God againſt that wickedneſſe,how ſoone hee was able to reſiſt and ſtand againſt it. This teacheth that it is but ignorance and vnbeliefe, that cauſeth many to practiſe and maintaine, either a falſe worſhipping of God,or any like wickedneſſe: though I denie not, but ſome doe worſe,who though they know it to be euill,yet will doe ſo wilfullie. The other are to be better hoped of; who if the Lord vouchſafe them the mercie that he did *Ioaſh*, ſhall ſoone bee changed from their former ill courſe,and abhorre and ſtand againſt that moſt deadly, which before they maintained and practiſed. And therefore a deteſtable ſtate to liue in,is Popery,out of the which they will not ſo much as ſeeke to be brought, by hearing the Goſpell preached,and therefore they lie ſtill therein to their confuſion,with all ſuch as doe like vnto them. Whereas many in other kinds of ſinne,are brought out of it by preaching, and are turned to God by true re-
1.Tim.1.15. pentance. Agreeable whereunto is that of *Paul,I was a perſecutor, blaſphemer, &c. but the Lord had mercie vpon me, becauſe I did it ignorantly.* Noting that one
Ioh.9.41. cauſe why few of his ſect were conuerted,becauſe,as our Sauiour ſaith,*They knew they did euill,therefore their ſinne remained.* This is not to incourage any
Ioh.3.19. to liue in ignorance; for the leaſt puniſhment is condemnation, if men preferre darkneſſe to light,whatſoeuer the cauſe be. But as Chriſt ſaith,in Mat-
Matth.11.20. thew 2. The iudgement of Tyrus and Zidon ſhall bee eaſier then of Corazin and Bethſaidah at the day of Gods comming, for they had repented, if they had been inſtructed. The vſe is,to comfort ſuch as affect to be ignorant, hoping thereby to eſcape Gods wrath: whereas rather they ſhould conſider that their ignorance wil procure it,yea,is a chiefe cauſe of other ſinne which cauſeth it: yea and becauſe that it is eaſie and no hard matter for ſuch as are ſimplie and not wilfully ignorant,to get knowledge and faith,if they would applie themſelues to hearing; therefore ſeeing they perſiſt in their blindnes, they cauſe an inuincible ignorance to grow vpon themſelues,which ſhal be as ſeuerely puniſhed as obſtinate diſobedience and contempt. But let ſuch as God hath mercifully enlightned,conſider and pitie the thouſands that lie
Iohn 14.22. in darkeneſſe,praying God to preuent them with the light,wondering that God ſhould reueal himſelfe to them,rather then to the world.

Alſo

Also we may learne from hence, that when God sheweth mercie to one in a kindred or family, it oft redounds to many of the rest, as when one is raised to promotion, the rest fare the better. So here God reuealing himselfe to *Gedeon*; his father, and so his familie were brought to the knowledge of the true God. The reason whereof is double. First, Gods blessing vpon the seed & stock of the righteous. Secondly, because where God hath wrought graciouslie in some one in a kindred or family, there commonly is wrought a great desire to doe good to the rest, and that in great tendernesse and loue. As *Paul* professeth to the Romans, My hearts desire for Israel is, that he may be saued. And although they doe not alway preuaile (because saluation followeth Gods election, not nature) yet often it doth: and where it is otherwise, the iuster is their condemnation. For proofe of this, our Sauiour Christ himselfe may bee an example, who brought his disciples, and some of his kindred to be religious. And he hath taught vs, that the Gospell is compared to leuin, which spreaddeth further and further. And thus by some one whom God hath well seasoned with grace, many of the rest haue been in like manner made partakers of the same grace with them. A ioyfull sight to behold. I would it were not so in Poperie, that one did draw many: and it were to be wished, that it might be seene to be more common in the receiuing of the Gospell effectually, that the rest of the familie and affinity did so. This, I say, is often seene; though commonly one of a city, and two of a tribe, as the Prophet saith, meaning but a few. Yea, how often is it seene, that a godly *Abigail* is coupled with a *Nabal*, and *Iob* with a foolish *woman*? How truly is it said of many good parents, *Their children are vngratious*, as they tell *Samuel* to his face? yea and of how many parents also, who are badly disposed, that euen their children shall rise vp against them, and condemne them, for that they go before them in knowledge & the feare of God? while they being wedded to their will, take scorne to learne of them; nay, it were well, if they would learne of good teachers, and that they abused not their authoritie to curbe and discourage their children. But as for the third sort, most wofull is their estate, when like father like child, as the head is so is the foote, all ignorant, brutish and vngodly, as *Esay* saith.

Doct.2. Rom.10.1. 1.Sam.8.5.

Now further by *Ioash* his answer, let vs consider some thing, and then by the people, as occasion is offered. In him by the speeches he vsed, note we the properties of a worthie magistrate, to wit, to defend Gods true worship, and to cast downe idolatrie, to oppose himselfe against the seditious and cauillers, and other wicked men, euen vnto death. His countenance, courage and power, beside his affection, ought to be manifested in Magistrates, for the defence and stablishing of all Gods seruice; and so should it be also in meaner men. But the commonnesse of euil, and the strength that it hath got in al places, dulleth the edge of the most of these now a daies. And this slacknesse and coldnesse, in Magistrates is as truly the cause why iniquitie so aboundeth, as any other: so that if euill hauing the vpper hand doe cause both publike officers of iustice, and priuate persons to be more vnable to resist it, and so the more vnwilling to goe about to punish it, they may thanke themselues. *Dauid* professeth of himselfe, that *betimes he would cut off from the house of God, the wicked*: that is, all scorners and maligners of the sound worship and worshippers of God. Oh it were to be wished (& indeed in that we

Doct.3. Vers.31. Matth.24.12. Psalm.101.8.

pray

pray no more earneſtly for ſuch, wee iuſtly complaine) that all gouernours were of *Dauid* his minde, that ſo the reſt might liue vnder their authoritie, an honeſt and quiet life, free from the noiſomnes of ſuch goates as by their hornes and ſtinch peſter the ſheepe, which would faine liue peaceably, and ſerue the Lord by them. For when the common ſort ſee ſwearing, blaſphemie, the contempt of the Sabbath, drunkenneſſe, and other abominations to ſwarme in many places, who ſeeth not that both they dare more boldly doe the ſame, and that they who will not, ſhall be ſcorned and grieued to ſee them?

Doct. 4. We may further note here that ſinne ought to be ſo odious, and in ſo vile account, that we ſhould be much grieued to behold the maintaining of it, and them that will ſtand for it. For now that *Ioaſh* was himſelf armed againſt idolatry, he demaunds if they, the blind people would ſtand for it, and plead for *Baal.* And yet they might haue replied, we plead no more for him, then thou thy ſelfe haſt done, and that very lately, in whoſe groue *Baal* was placed. But now the caſe was altered with *Ioaſh*, euen as it was with *Paul*, when he preached the Goſpell which he had perſecuted before. It is a notable token of repentance, when mens affections and deſires are quite changed from the euill things, which before they could not be drawne from: yea and when they breake out into holy indignation at themſelues and other, for the ſins which they committed againſt God, although they know them forgiuen. And ſurely, an vpright hearted man would thinke that all ſhould abhorre the ſin that he hateth, and it grieueth him to ſee another deceiued and held in the ſnare that he himſelf hath bin holden in: & therfore counts it abſurd that any ſhould maintaine and delight in it: whereas the contrary now a daies may bee ſeene, that hee is diligently marked that will ſtand againſt it: and ſo few there be ſo well minded, that they may ſoone be noted.

2. Cor. 7. 11.

Their ſhamefull boldnes is likewiſe to be marked by the words of *Ioaſh* here, ſaying; *Will ye plead for Baal? he that doth ſo, let him die before the morning.* Who although they ſaw the Magiſtrate againſt them, yet they were ſo blind, that they ſtood in the defence of their idolatrie. And euen ſo we may ſay; Great is the boldnes that is growne vp in this age, while not only they doe the euils openly, which men and women in former ages haue bluſhed for the ſecret doing of the ſame [be it the ſinne of *Zimri* and *Cozby* or the like]: but alſo ſuch dare reuile and raile vpon thoſe who ſpeake againſt their lewd doings. But theſe truly verifie the ſaying, *The wicked men and deceiuers waxe worſe.* And how ſhould it be that in the laſt daies ſhould be ſo perilous times, if as the day of the world groweth neerer to an end, ſo ſinne waxed not more and more out of meaſure ſinfull? And that, both for the number of ſinnes, (for we ſee new additions and faſhions daily) and for the meaſure alſo, I meane the greedines, impudencie and pertinacie of ſinners, who are not aſhamed of their euils, but with the harlot in the Prouerbs, who wipeth her ſelfe as cleane of all her filthineſſe, as if ſhe had been a virgin. Wee ſee whores were growne, by that time, to a degree of boldnes: for *Tamar* was judged an whore by her father, becauſe ſhe had couered her face. But this maske is long agoe pluckt off, not onely from them that bee of her occupation, but the moſt ſpirituall adulterers now a daies, are ſo farre from being aſhamed to ſhew their faces, that they are not thought maſters of their trade,

2. Tim. 3. 13.

Gen. 38. 15.

trade,if they dare not spit in the face of modestie and all reprouers. And what is to be said of the aged,and men in wealth, (who haue somewhat to beare them out) when euen youthes (of both sexes) whose honour should be their blushing, (which euen heathens called the Colour of vertue) are brasen-faced,and inferiours of al sorts take vp that cursed speech,*who is Lord ouer vs?* But oh,who doth not see the Lords marke set vpon them,while by shame, and sorow their bellies ful,with other miseries,they come daily euery one in his course,to a wofull end? Psal 12.4.

Furthermore, it was well answered by *Ioash, Let Baal plead for himselfe:* meaning,if he can, what need you? if he cannot,it were a shame to pleade for such a god, as could not plead his owne cause. As *Elias* also,in the like case,said to the blind people: and so it may be said to all maintainers of Idolatrie,and such like abomination; If the Idols be gods,whom they worship, let them keepe themselues from the fire. And they who will needs thinke their doings to be good in maintaining and reasoning for such stockes, let them waite and see what will be the end thereof, and what will come of them. They were well set a worke to plead for him, who was so farre from helping them in their neede, that hee could not reuenge his owne cause against such as would deface him: and so are all that are like them; such a master he is whom they serue. Doct.5. 1.King.18.

Lastly,out of this verse 31.and the former,in that *Gedeon* seruing God so commendably,as he was commanded,(for which also hee is by name commended as a worthie person, and a beleeuer) was yet called seditious of them that were themselues so indeede, and that therefore hee was counted worthie to die, who yet was the meane whereby the other did liue, note that when the wicked are charged neuer so iustly for their euill doings, yet they euer returne the accusation vpon their accusers. For example, the doctrine of Gods word,and the Preachers thereof,doe by Gods blessing, become the meanes and outward instruments of much good doing,and some turne from their euill waies thereby, but what dissenting is there among the rest for this,when they see it? In such wise, as that they fall commonly to this exclamation, that both teachers and such as follow their doctrine, are troublers of the people, but as for themselues, they haue done no euill. Euen as the Papists crie on the other side, that they are disturbed and disquieted, for that they may not be suffered to serue God, as they would bee glad to doe,nor their Priests to set foorth their pedlary ware to sale,to the ignorant and superstitious,whom they had sometime deceiued,and as their fellowes in many places still doe, no lesse palpably, then *Simon Magus* did the people of Samaria,whom he had with his sorceries bewitched. Doct.6. Heb.11.32.

These will not suffer their Idolatrous worship at any hand to bee ouerthrowne,but say,as the people said to *Ieremy*, We will worship the Queene of heauen,that is, the Moone and other starres: and as the foolish people of Ephesus,who cried out in a mad mood,*Great is Diana of the Ephesians,* when yet who were more vnlike to make tumults and sedition, then they whom they accused,as *Paul* and his companie? So(to leaue these,and to returne to them whom I began with) thus crie the wicked out when their lewd doings bee reproued iustly out of pulpits; Preachers are seditious; they make strife and tumults where they come, and draw people after them, whereas they Ierem.44.19. Acts 19.34.

they were quiet and well enough before: but who are they whom they draw? euen those who forsake their companie, whom I speake of, and leaue off their cursed manners and behauiour, so that they are now depriued of them, therefore now they make their part good against them, crying out that they are seditious. Thus *Elias* was charged to trouble the land, when he taught the true seruice of God, and reproued Idolatrie, but he shewed who were troublers of the land, to all that list to know it, euen such as be not obedient to the commandements of the Lord. But that all may see, that such are not to be charged as troublesome persons, whose preaching bewraieth the bad sort, who are therefore incensed against them, because their euill deedes are brought to light by them; neither they who obey their doctrine, though they bee hated of the greatest part; that saying of our Sauiour teacheth: *I came not to send peace into the earth, but the sword*, and debate. And againe, *I am come to set fire on the earth, and what is my desire if it be alreadie kindled?* So that if ciuill dissension and trouble follow vpon our preaching, and professing, it is the filthie heart of the rebellious sort, out of which that stinch commeth, as out of a dunghill, who can away with no better sauour.

Matth 10.34.
Luke 12.49.

Doct. vers. 32. Now in that *Ioash* called his sonne *Ierubbaal*, [*Baal* shall contend against him] not in reproch, but for a memoriall he did it; which brought the Idol into contempt. So hee was called *Ierubbosheth*, 2. Sam. 11.21. This sheweth, that he was so farre from being ashamed of his owne or his sonnes fact, that he reioyced in it that Idolatrie had the foile by his meanes, as all well minded people should doe the like. But I proceed.

THE FORTIE THREE SERMON ON THE SIXTH CHAPTER OF THE BOOKE OF IVDGES.

Vers. 33. *Then all the Midianites and the Amalekites, and they of the East, gathered together, and pitched in the valley of Izreel.*

34. *But the spirit of the Lord came vpon Gedeon, and he blew a trumpet, and Abiezer was ioyned with him.*

35. *And he sent messengers through all Manasseh, which also was ioyned with him: and he sent messengers to Asher, and to Zabulon, and to Naphtali, and they came vp to meete him.*

The summe of these 3. verses. NOw followeth the last point of the foure in this fourth part of Chapter, as was noted in the 11. verse. In which is shewed, how *Gedeon* (after that the Midianites gathered themselues together) prepared for warre against them; he hauing before destroyed Idolatrie, and set vp the true worship of God: that thus all the people might see, when it was done, how ill it might haue been

vndone

vndone againe,and how profitable it was for them, which *Gedeon* had done so: though we may remember what troubles and stirres were raised against him,before he could bring it to passe.But oh,what a mercie of God was this to them, that the Midianites were held in all this while? who bound their hands and feete till *Gedeon* had brought so worthie a worke to passe, but euen he whom none were able to resist, euen the Lord omnipotent? The summe of these three verses is this: That the Lord gaue occasion to *Gedeon*, by bringing the Midianites, and other assistants to them, into the land, to preuaile against,and get victorie ouer them. For he trusting to the word of God,by which he had been,and that lately,so well strengthened; prepared to goe against them: and the Lord armed him,and he drew helpe together out of the tribes that were neere vnto him,as is to be seene in the text,so that Israel was againe restored in great multitudes.

Thus after all the trouble that *Gedeon* had,both otherwise,and by feare of the Midianites now prouoking the Israelites to battell, and the many hurts that they did thē before, yet God would (we see) haue his true worship set vp,& Idolatrie cast down first,as we haue heard; which the wise men of the world though they had allowed, would yet haue deferred till afterthe victorie. And note we hereby,that it much pleaseth him,ỳ we should not post off the great and waighty cōmandements of his worship & seruice, for our earthly affaires & bodily businesse,though waighty,if there be time enough to discharge them; no nor lay aside the exercises of praier,hearing,reading, and the like,for our owne pleasure. And we our selues may see, that it is very meete and expedient that it should be so: and how cheerefully we may goe about the one, when wee haue well discharged the other: whereas by deferring,we leaue them vndone altogether sometimes, and our appetite is much quailed when we returne to them. As therfore we reade,that as great neede as there was to make all possible speede to rescue the Church in the great distresse it was in at that time, yet that *Hester* sought the Lord by fasting and prayer,before she went to the King,and went after that with great courage to him for helpe,and preuailed. But it is otherwise with vs; for we, for the most part,first serue our selues (what though in doing things that are lawfull?) and seeke our owne profit and pleasure,which is our great sinne: and yet that is not all,but hauing so done, we are also by the least occasion easily brought to omit the Lords due altogether many times (as I haue said) or at least to performe it slackly,coldly,and by halues,so that it were as good vndone.

Doct.vers.33.

Hester 4.16.

This appeareth to be too true in the common courses of men and many of their dealings, and of theirs who are not the worst. And namely in this one: when we haue set an order for praying in our houses, we will not perhaps,as some doe, omit it altogether afterwards: but yet we then,for the most part,meete to performe this dutie to God, when we haue serued our selues,and filled our bellies first, in which case wee be commonly oppressed with drowsinesse and sleepe,which are (a man would think) vtterly vnmeet to accompanie Gods seruice,and therfore little pleasing to him,that it were farre better to dispose of a fitter time for that businesse, and yet other things not to bee left vndone. And wee must take heed both in this which I now

Note.

Hh speake

ſpeake of,and all the like that we take in hand,leſt we giue iuſt ſuſpition that we thinke any thing is good enough for the Lord.

In the publike worſhip of God,the Church hath giuen a better example, that we doe our duties to God before we refreſh our ſelues. *Abrahams* ſeruant hauing but a meſſage of his maſters to doe,did ſo diligently follow the
Gen.24.33. doing and executing of it, that hee would not take his owne neceſſarie repaſt,in his hunger and wearineſſe,till he had faithfully diſcharged that buſineſſe. And *Iehoſaphat* being neerely driuen by the Moabits and Ammonits, did firſt ſeeke the Lord by faſting and prayer,before he would take weapon in hand. And let all marke what he loſt thereby,or whether hee could poſſibly haue found the like helpe and ſo preſent as he did,by all ſpeedie following his buſineſſe, by all policie and power that hee could haue made. And yet I adde this, becauſe I would lay no burthen needleſly on the conſcience of any man,that in neceſſitie,which cannot be auoided,a man may omit the greater dutie for the leſſe,if it could not elſe be done at all, and ſo as opportunitie be watched and taken to doe it afterwards. To conclude about this matter,let this practiſe of *Gedeon* teach vs this rule, to wit, to giue the precedencie alway to thoſe duties which are of beſt price, and withall of greateſt neceſſitie. Now I call that neceſſitie,which not only is commanded,but abſolutly and alwaies,ſo that it is ſinne to neglect and omit it; as to watch, beleeue,repent,&c. they may not be left of, and laid aſide for any cauſe. So to heare the word in ſeaſon and out of ſeaſon,is commanded,as alſo to doe our earthly buſineſſe on the ſixe daies: yet to omit both, at ſome time is no ſin, becauſe they be commanded but for ſome time to be done,& may in ſome caſes and at other times be diſpenſed with & omitted. but the other are euer neceſſarie; as to be humbled for ſin,to beleeue in God,alſo to loue and feare God,and to be patient, & ſome other, with the like duties of the firſt Commandements. Now theſe are abſolute duties, and charged vpon vs generally and alwaies: no buſineſſe may be preferred before theſe whatſoeuer: no delay is to be admitted,no though it be vnder colour of moſt ſerious returning thereto afterward: For where we take libertie to our ſelues in theſe caſes,God curſeth vs, Satan gets ground of vs,and the worke for the which we lay them aſide, is commonly naught worth, when it is done in the beſt manner. And therefore wee ſee that *Felix* pretending that he would heare *Paul* againe at leiſure of thoſe things, which his terrified conſcience durſt heare no longer for that preſent; neuer had leiſure to heare him againe at all,ſeeing he did it not both when he ought and might. For the ſecond ſort of duties: as prayer in familie,priuatly by our ſelues,with the like,although they are not duties of ſo ſimple neceſſitie, that no other actions may euer hinder them; yet let them who haue ſolemnely couenanted with the Lord to vſe them,and ſeene great cauſe thereof, and fruite thereby, beware how they winde out themſelues of this courſe,vpon vnwarranted occaſions: for ſo they ſhall neuer want ſome one or other ſhift to ſalue the matter, till the breach be growne ſo great,that a ſlender patch will not mend it, nay griefe and ſlight repentance ſcarcely will repaire it: as wee ſee a cloſe and ſmooth lid of a frame,if it warpe once, is not eaſily brought to his leuelnes againe. God ſhall teach wiſedome in the caſes of lawfull omiſſion, to ſuch as leane

not so much and so long, to their owne, till they haue laid themselues vnderfoote. But that the chiefest duties, when all things are rightly considered, ought to be (as I haue said) preferred before other, the words of our Sauiour in that patterne of prayer, Matth 6. do clearely shew; where before he mentioneth any petitions tending to the good of soule or body, hee commands vs to aske the things which concerne the glory of God, which stands in the comming of his kingdome, and doing of his will. So that if it were possible, that a good might aske the pardon of sinne, deliuerance from euill, or necessaries to this life, without respect had to this, that God might bee honoured in all these, it were his great sinne so to doe. For the very saluation of a mans soule is to be hazzarded and neglected, (if it might bee) rather then that it should stand in comparison with this, as by *Moses* and *Pauls* request for the peoples forgiuenes and conuersion may appeare. Matth.6.9.10.

Secondly, in this that the Midianites banded themselues against Israel, very like to haue spoiled them both of their liues & goods, as they had almost done before, we should consider to what changes in our estate we be subiect; and that is, euen vnto the loosing of all the good things that God hath inriched vs with, to make our liues comfortable. Oh, when we are in health, peace, abundance, and well married, with the feare of God accompanying them, it is (doubtlesse) a little paradise that wee liue in, as here on earth wee may looke for, and in comparison of that we may see the most to enioy that we liue among) and they are wise who can acknowledge it, to giue God the praise by bringing foorth much fruit. And yet God can affoord vs this and more too, if we could vse it well, and do good with it But seeing men nestle themselues vpon these vncertaine things, (which is little wisdome in them to doe so, but a bold tempting of God;) we see what strange alterations fall out in their liues that their estate changeth from that it was, I say not as other mens, by age, sicknesses, diseases onely, (for to them we are all subiect) but from towardnesse, hope and likelihood of goodnesse, which they had sometime, and therefore they should haue been rooted, and growne forward therein: and such as neuer had any, waxe much worse and worse, and by their afflictions they be much disguized. Doct.2. Note. Iohn 15.9.

For by that time that cruell enemies, domesticall or forraigne, (I meane in the world) haue oppressed them, as both may easily bee: or suites, debt, suretiship, or prison haue molested them (which commonly fall out to be) or the vnrulinesse and disobedience in children, the vnfaithfulnesse and leaudnesse of seruants, and the vnpeaceablenesse and vnappeasablenesse in neighbours and landlords, with great iniuries offered by them, shall vexe them; together with sicknesse and other calamities which meet with them; I say, when some of these, as mothes in a garment, haue eaten into them, the beautie of their estate is decaied, and consumed: in these cases, I say, they are altered and changed, as if they had neuer been the persons. So that as *Elimelech* by famine was constrained to change his dwelling, and good *Dauid* by his owne sonne was almost driuen from his kingdome; euen so, and much more, when sundry of the forementioned waies shall afflict bad men, doe they not shew the vncertaine hold that they haue (and yet they haue no hold of any better) of the things which are in greatest price heere among men, together with the reproches and disgraces that befall them? that I say Note.

nothing of sundry kinds of death to cut them off from all: and are sufficient proofes of that which I say. So that we haue good cause to beare a low saile, euen when we be at the highest, and to thinke we haue little, when we haue the most. And to looke for our change in our prosperitie, and to make heauen our habitation against we go hence, and the earth with the pompe and beautie of it, but as small and vncertaine riches. Indeed all the glory of these things must haue his end: yet commonly where God is not prouoked much, there is no vnseasonable change of mens prosperitie into misery: but a kindly inioying it with Gods good liking: though sometime God afflict thus for other ends, as *Iob*, &c. And because many of Gods deare ones prouoke him to turne their blessings and delight temporall, as in wife, children, goods, beautie, strength, &c. into sorrowes, and punishments, which must be so, or else it would bee worse with them: let them also beware that they breake not out further against him, least by any sinne wilfully committed and not repented of speedily, they cause and procure this to themselues, that they be roughly handled of him, more then commonly, euen like other men, and that particularly by the grosse abuse of these outward things themselues, whereto they are subiect, they bee not deformed and disguized by strange and rare afflictions. God hath all good things in store for his, but he can also soone strip them thereof, as *Ieremie* saith, in the person of the Iewes, euen as hee withholdeth them altogether from some other. And this I thought good to say, though somewhat of this argument hath been said before.

Note.

Lam. 1. 12.

It followeth how God furnished *Gedeon* with gifts of the spirit, both wisdome and courage, whereby, according to that which hee had said to him before [*Goe in this thy power, and thou shalt saue Israel out of the hands of Midian*] he was new fitted for it. Which teacheth, that when God appointeth his seruants to any charge or businesse of his, hee inableth them to goe through it, and ministreth helpe to them accordingly. So *Paul* saith in a farre greater worke then this of *Gedeons*, that God counted him faithfull, and put him in his seruice, after he had appointed him thereunto. So *Saul* when he was chosen King, had gifts giuen him to gouerne, God making him thereby, as the text saith, another man. So the Lord dealeth with those whom hee maketh Ministers of the Gospell, that they shall doe his message to the people faithfully and diligently, and plainely and powerfully; to the iust challenging of them, who boldly take vpon them so waightie a calling as doth concerne the sauing or destroying the soules of men, hauing no furniture of preaching the Gospell soundly and clearely, neither any care to looke that way, nor other grace bestowed vpon them. Now Gods worke is not onely some great seruice, as *Gedeons* to fight, and *Pauls* to preach, and *Moses* to deliuer Israel from Egypt: but euen to liue in the married estate, to walke in a calling publike or priuate, and much more to professe the name of Christ, in what condition soeuer. And when we speake of Gods calling a man to this worke, (I meane not any sensible calling by voice,) as here *Gedeon* extraordinarilie was: but when a man entreth into these estates, functions, or actions by direction and warrant of the lawfulnesse or necessitie thereof, from the word and ordination of the Church. Vsing also the holiest and best meanes to obtaine faith, knowledge, wisdome and conscience to discharge them well: to such I say,

1. Tim. 1. 12.

God

God will not be wanting, although they may thinke that their case is not as *Gedeons*, (and yet they had need bee no weaker in faith, nor lower brought then he was) and that they are but seely priuate persons; yes, God will so blesse them, and prosper their lawfull enterprises, yea though they deeme themselues vnfit to vndertake such workes, or vnable to goe through them: that so as they shall haue cause to blesse the Lord, and wonder at his loue and faithfulnesse to them, when they who goe about the same, to obserue how he assisteth and blesseth them, and on the other side, how they who relie vpon their own head and pollicie, *shall wanze*, come to nothing, and be resisted by him; as we reade of such as being commanded to goe against the Canaanites refused; but, would needs goe fight against them being forbidden, and therefore they were sore discomfited. But of this I haue spoken before. See and reade Num.14. from vers.40. to 45.

Gedeon being thus furnished, was incouraged to go against Gods enemies, and so much the more, seeing he had such successe before by the promise of the Angell. Where note, how well things prosper with vs, and goe forward, when we are certaine, that we be set a worke by the Lord: and more particularly, when we are furnished with faith in his promises for the present, and time to come, and heartned by the experience of Gods helpe in the time past. For it was not for nothing, that the Lord meaning to set him a worke about a greater seruice, gaue him good proofe first, as of his owne weakenes, so of his assistance in the lesser, I meane in the destroying of *Baal*; of which point more hereafter, if God will. Now both these did worke vpon him mightily, and so wee then especially, when with both, our consciences can witnesse to vs, that we haue cast off, and purged out such sinnes wherein we liued before, oh then, I say, we goe on roundly and readily in the duties wee take in hand. And so on the contrary, if we doe but crop them off by a present and slight dislike of them, we shall sensibly and easily feele how awkelie and vntowardly wee goe to worke, as the Israelites against the Beniamites. Cap.20. But of this point often by occasion before. Verse 34 35. Iudg.20.

In blowing the trumpet, to draw and call together the companie that should assist him, marke who were said to follow him to the battell: euen *Abiezer*, meaning the people in his tribe, and of the familie that he was of, that had been so furiously bent and set against him for the ouerthrowing of *Baal*: who also would haue had him put to death for the same; which may bee maruelled at to see them so turned vnto him. But the Lord (no doubt) changed their hearts; and againe, they saw no hurt fell out to *Gedeon* by *Baal*, as the Barbarians to *Paul* by the viper, which they verily looked for. For many doe iudge of the professors of Gods worship, according to the outward blessing and successe, and especially beginners: who yet in time grow to see into the matter better, as they did, Ioh.4. who told the woman, that though they were drawne by her to heare, yet they beleeued then vpon a better ground, as their owne knowledge. But to returne againe; If men that runne after vaine idols, and all other that serue God amisse, and not after his word, would consider, what they get thereby, euen lesse then nothing; and how they are deceiued in that wherein they put their trust; they would seeke further, and serue the Lord onely, and him also according to his word, with an vpright heart, as knowing him to be a bountiful rewarder and Doct.2. Acts.28.4. Note. Ioh.4.42. Heb.11.6.

pay master. Yea and the godly would take more hart to themselues in Gods businesse, if they considered how the Lord causeth many resisters and enemies of them and their goodnesse, to turne to their practise, and cleaue vnto their profession, to worship at their feete, and to serue God with them. A worthie fruit of their innocency, though it procured them but onely a good report, and some generall allowance: but when it draweth others to the heartie intertainment of the truth with them, in the loue thereof, it is much more. But I noted somewhat of this point in *Ioash*, vpon the entrance into the storie, or else where.

Reuel. 3.9.

Vers. 35.

The rest of the Tribes about him, as *Zebulon*, *Asher* and *Naphtali*, followed him. For though the Lord called *Gedeon* onely, yet he could not alone fight against the enemies. For our faith in God doth not exclude the helpe of men, nor the second meanes which may lawfully and conueniently bee inioyed. For Gods seruants are not led by faith to tempt God, but to serue his prouidence, as in wisdome they learne to doe. And this is one especiall cause why God will furnish him whom hee calleth, because hee giueth him grace to seeke assistance from him in all his enterprises, and to serue his prouidence. And so is one bound to helpe another, where need requireth, as the Tribes here did *Gedeon*. Reade more of this Chap. 2. vers. 3.

THE FORTIE FOVRE SERMON ON THE SIXTH AND SEVENTH CHAPTERS OF THE BOOKE OF IVDGES.

VERS. 36. *Then Gedeon said vnto God, If thou wilt saue Israel by mine hand as thou hast said.*

37. *Behold, I put a fleece of wooll in the threshing place: if the dew come on the fleece onely, and it be drie vpon all the earth, then shall I be sure that thou wilt saue Israel by mine hand, as thou hast said.*

38. *And so it was: for he rose vp earely on the morrow, and thrust the fleece together, and wringed the dew out of the fleece, and filled a bowle of water.*

39. *Againe, Gedeon said vnto God, be not angry with me, that I may speake once more: let me prooue once againe, I pray thee, with the fleece: let it now be drie onely vpon the fleece, and let dew be vpon all the ground.*

40. *And God did so that same night: for it was dry vpon the fleece onely, and there was dew on all the ground.*

The sense of these verses.

HOw *Gedeon* prepared to go to the warre against Midian we haue heard in the former 3. verses, in which began the 4. point in the 4. part of the Chapter, according to the diuision made in the eleuenth verse, whereto wee may remember was adioyned his asking of a double signe. And in these words the holy story sheweth,

eth,that he being now furnished of the Lord with gifts, as we haue heard, and hauing gathered his army together,and being gone to meete the enemies,where they had pitched; in these verses(I say)it followeth how he desired of God the first signe; by the which hee might bee confirmed of,and concerning the victorie. The signe he asked was this: that he putting a fleece of wooll on the threashing flore,the dew might come on the fleece onely, and it might be drie vpon all the earth. Wherein he is maruelled at, that for all the promise of God,and confirming of him before,he should doubt,and aske a signe. I answere vpon the due consideration of the thing,that though it may be like inough,that hee was not altogether void of blame,yet hee did not herein tempt God, (as some did who asked a signe of Christs authoritie) but desired onely to haue his faith confirmed thereby, which would otherwise haue wauered. As the man in the Gospell who beleeued, and yet prayed, *Lord helpe mine vnbeliefe*, so did *Gedeon*. Besides, the Lord granted him his request, without any reproouing of him, which it is not like hee would haue done,if *Gedeon* had doubted. Last of all,I am the rather thus perswaded,because he is reckoned in the Epistle to the Hebrewes,among them that were commended for their faith. Mar.9.24. Heb.11.32.

Herein we are to consider of our weakenesse in beleeuing by occasion of *Gedeons* asking a double signe: and of the louing kindnesse of the Lord in pitying vs therein,and bringing vs out of it,euen as he yeelded to him in both. For our selues this may be said,that though wee beleeue Gods promise, yet there ariseth naturally in vs daily and continuall weakenesse of faith; partly by yeelding too much to carnal reason,partly through ineuitable frailty,the flesh fighting against the spirit in vs. And hereof it is, that we are faine to wrastle,and to be in the batiell as it were, and in the cumbat daily to vphold and preserue our weake faith, which otherwise would soone faile and giue ouer, as by experience we haue oft found in other,and our selues. As in the examples of *Peter* comming on the water to Christ, *Martha* in raising *Lazarus*, *Dauid* complaining of his sadnes and heauines of heart,the Disciples in their too much ascribing to Christs bodily presence,and an hundred more in Scriptures doe testifie. Doct in vers. 36.37.38. Note.

And much more may the same be said of our selues: yet while we feare our frailtie against such assaults, as we haue cause daily to doe, and learne to rest on God, as those deare seruants of God did, wee are much staied, and our hearts well eased thereby, in respect of former times. As to say a little in particuler by the contrary: when wee haue obtained of God the gift of beleeuing that we are freed from condemnation,and that wee shall haue eternall life: if we rest there,and looke not daily to reuiue our hearts by hearing the word often,whereby the feeling of Gods fauour is more reuiued and quickned,and also by remembring and applying Gods promises from day to day,and from time to time,and with both,if we labour not also to reioyce therein, that so we may be kept in holy compasse thereby: wee shall be euer flitting; off and on, and stand at an vncertaine stay: And this shall not onely be at our first beleeuing,(which there is least doubt of) but euen after we haue been stablished and setled therein. For at first, assurance is not easily obtained ordinarily,till we haue had some experience of Gods louing kindnesse towards vs,and of our owne vprightnes. Note.

And euen so I may say the same of beleeuing Gods promises in other temporary things: how we shall faint therein, without the forementioned exercise: and more hardly beare our crosses, or goe vnder some paine and sicknesse, or haue victorie ouer some speciall sinne, and mortifie some corruption that hath much preuailed in vs. But if these be pursued earnestly, and the other promises of grace bee oft and vsually recorded, with feruent prayer to God for strength; it is not to be denied, but much fruite shall follow, and we shall sensibly perceiue, that wee get ground of our selues in that behalfe, and grow more neerely acquainted with the minde and will of God, that he will grant vs further to preuaile against such difficulties: and yet if wee grow to thinke that we shall neuer obtaine grace against our corruptions, nor outgrow discouragements, nor well beare our crosses, or finde blessing in our callings, notwithstanding the vse of publike and priuate meanes; yea further if wee doe minde and looke after these things but now and then, and that slightly also; we may well know, that there is no fruit to be expected to come thereof: which is the cause why some, who are not destitute of true faith, are often times (as it were) new to begin in these things, after long going about them.

Now this standing at a stay, and small profiting in the subduing and striuing against vnbeliefe, commeth not barely and altogether of frailtie, when we would gladly preuaile and cannot: but in great part of yeelding to temptation, and occasions drawing vs violently to sinne against our conscience, (which causeth a mans hold vpon the promises to faile exceedingly) or too
Note. much giuing place to carnall reason, which perswadeth that wee neede not giue such attendance to these things; but in the meane while, wee see that we are greatly set backe thereby. So that it is manifest, that without diligent heed taking to the strengthening of our faith, we easily grow to distrust God and his promises. And much more, if we will hearken to such voyces as we shall too oft heare sounding in our eares, that we neede not take such paine, nor haue our heads beaten and occupied about it: whereas all diligence is to be giuen thereto for attaining so excellent a gift, as that is. And most of all, when by willing offendings of God we weaken our selues; which how small need we haue of, we may easily see, when we consider that wee fall to doubting through the vntowardnes of our hearts, without adding further sinne, our faith being fitly compared to fire, which may as well goe out by negligence in adding thereto, as wilfulnes in quenching thereof.

This our sinne in so hardly giuing credit to God, is aggrauated hereby, that if we are to deale with men, about great matters, wee are easily satisfied, and beleeue them, if wee haue their word and writing: which manifesteth too plainly our distrust towards God, from whom nothing is inough to stay vs, vnlesse with *Thomas* we may grossely feele and see that which we desire. Nay I say more, if we be to compasse any matter for our owne pleasure, profit, or preferment, oh how bold and full of courage we be, although we must goe vnder perill, losse, or any such like thing, for obtaining the same: but to suffer any difficultie or danger, so much as to stretch out our faith to beleeue,
Note. or our hope to waite for that which God hath promised, though hee giue vs neuer so great cause and incouragement, by good euidence and testimonie, and by former experience, of others, and our selues, yet wee haue no heart

heart to it. Therefore if we be wise, let vs be much stronglier built vp in the confidence of Gods fauour, and of his promises, take more paines to abide therein, pray and watch against the occasions of vnsetling it, and chaine vp our so great ascribing (as we haue done) to sense and reason. And so doing, we shall see our selues well propped vp and vpholden, though we haue no promise of miracles to doe it, as *Gedeon* had.

Of one of the signes that *Gedeon* asked, wee haue heard: now followeth the other.

When *Gedeon* had desired one signe, that the fleece might be moistened with dew, and the ground drie, now he desired, that when dew was on the earth the fleece might be drie; and to both the signes asking, God yeelded; which he would not haue easily done, if he had not approued it. To teach, that if in our weaknes and timourousnes wee had this wisedome, to repaire to God, and make our mone to him, in feeling our burthen, and to say with confidence, Lord strengthen our faith; we should be staied and eased: and so in all distempers whatsoeuer, we should not be left to our selues, nor forsaken. Which many (as I said) haue not learned to doe, and therefore their whole life is but a conflicting with doubts and feares, rising anew in their mindes, and that endlesly, by the malice of the diuell disquieting and molesting them: and hindring them from that resolution and holy boldnesse which God alloweth and commandeth to be in them. And whereas the enemie buzzeth into them, that it were presumption to hold the promise of forgiuenes and life, otherwise then doubtingly: this fact of *Gedeon* in so earnest and doubled requesting of strength and confirmation from God, should dash and quench it. And so by our proofe of Gods answering our prayers at one time, wee should learne to vse the same meanes againe in a like manner, and as often as neede shall require at another time: knowing, that as it is Gods honour to be beleeued in his promises; so it stands with his good liking, that we often sue to him, to giue vs some cleere insight into them, how they belong to vs, (though wee tye him to no certaine measure) that so we may be staied. Vers. 38. 39. 40.

Neither is it to be omitted, that *Gedeon* in this second suit, commeth with a deprecation of his owne boldnes and importunitie with God, which must be warily vnderstood. For hereby it followes not, that God was angrie, or *Gedeon* was bold in making this request: (for then *Gedeon* had sinned highly in doing that which he knew would anger God) but rather out of a most inward feeling of that vnbleefe which hee desired to be forgiuen, and supplied with confidence: as also in deepe humilitie, considering how great a libertie he had (being but a sillie worme) that he might speake so freely to the Almightie, and be admitted into such familiaritie with his Maiestie; he vttereth this speech full of reuerence, *Be not angrie with thy seruant*; as if hee should say, It is iust with thee to bee displeased with my weaknesse in beleeuing: but (O Lord) pardon that (bee not angrie) and seeing I craue strength against it, (as thou giuest me leaue to doe) let my desire be granted, and my infirmitie couered. And in both the respects named, the Saints of God in Scripture haue euer vsed themselues thus reuerently and humbly, and the Lord so respectiuely, as *Gedeon* here doth. As the example of *Abraham* shewes, praying for *Gedeon*. So wise, and able to vse such a priuiledge, should

should we al seeke to be,that we knowing how base mettle we are,euen dust and wormes,priuiledge,(that I say no more)and yet admitted into the presence of God of glory,we should admire it with humilitie, that he giues vs accesse to him;oh how should it affect vs, yea what reuerence should it draw from vs? Euen as when a poore man comes often to the same friend to borrow money: he comes not saucily and loosely,as if it were a common matter, and for the which he were little beholding to him,but caries thanks and reuerence in his countenance and behauior. But of this story of *Gedeon* before.

3 And this is that which I purposed to say of, and concerning our selues. Now that which I haue to say of the Lord is this: namely, how respectiue he is to his children,and what a ready eare he giueth to our prayers,yea and that particularly in this point,of strengthening our faith. *Gedeon* twise desired a signe to confirme him,and God granted it to him. To shew,that if(as I haue said) we could pray for it,and long for that grace(as precious as it is) it should be granted vs. But we would bee glad to inioy it,but in our weak-

Note. nesse and fainting,we doe not plie God with feruent requests, that we may be setled in beleiuing either that power ouer our speciall sinne shal be giuen vs,or hope and patience to beare some trouble. If we were oft with God in this behalfe, and earnest; wee should finde, that God would furnish vs accordingly, aboue that which wee could looke for. Thus *Abraham, Dauid, Paul* with others,grew strong in faith. And this of the whole chapter.

THE SEVENTH CHAPTER OF THE Booke of IVDGES.

Vers. 1. *Then Ierubbaal (who is Gedeon) rose vp earely,and all the people that were with him,and pitched beside the well of Harod: so that the hoast of the Midianites,was on the North side of them,in the valley by the hill Moreh.*

2. *And the Lord said vnto Gedeon,The people that are with thee are to many for me to giue the Midianites into their hands,lest Israel make their vaunt against mee, and say,My hand hath saued me.*

3. *Now therefore proclaime in the audience of the people, and say, Whosoeuer is timerous or fearefull,let him returne, and depart earely from mount Gilead. And there returned of the people,that were at mount Giliad, two and twentie thousand,so that ten thousand remained.*

4. *And the Lord said vnto Gedeon, The people are yet too many, bring them downe vnto the water,and I will trie them for thee there: and of whom I say to thee, this man shall goe with thee, the same shall goe with thee: and of whomsoeuer I say vnto thee,this man shall not goe with thee,the same shall not goe.*

5. *So he brought downe the people vnto the water. And the Lord said vnto Gedeon. As many as lap the water with their tongues, as a dogge lappeth, them put by themselues: and euery one that shall bow downe his knees to drinke, put apart.*

6. *And the number of them that lapped,by putting their hands to their mouthes, were three hundred men: but all the remnant of the people kneeled downe vpon their knees to drinke water.*

7. *And the Lord said vnto Gedeon, By these three hundred men that lapped, will I saue you, and deliuer the Midianites into thine hand: and let all the other people, goe euery man vnto his place.*
8. *So the people tooke victuals with them, and their trumpets, and he sent all the rest of Israel, euery man to his tent, and retained the three hundred men: and the hoast of Midian was beneath him in a valley.*

THe summe in generall, and parts of the Chapter are first to bee considered, and then a more particular view to be taken of it afterwards: and the summe may be laid out in the parts, which are three. The first, how God made *Gedeon* send all the people, saue three hundred, backe againe, as being too many for the battell, to verse 9. The second, how God assured him againe of the victorie, by a dreame, which one of the enemies had, and by the interpreting of it by another of them in *Gedeons* hearing, and this to the 16. verse. The third is the victorie it selfe ouer them, which God gaue him: and this to the end of the Chapter. *The summe and parts of the Chapter.*

The first part of the Chapter.

TO come to the first part, there is no difficultie in it, for when hee had pitched his army, ready to goe meete the enemies, the Lord caused him to send them all away (excepting three hundred) lest they should giue out, that they had ouercome the Midianites by their owne strength. And those three hundred hee also appointed to him, taking them out of the ten thousand, that remained after the sending of the other two and twenty thousand away. In *Gedeons* drawing neere the enemies with his armie, wee may see how hee was confirmed in his faith that hee should obtaine the victorie, whereabout he had doubted so much before. And although I grant, that it was meet he should be staied by so great meanes as God vsed for that purpose, yet we see that faith commonly failes most, when the triall is greatest, and the danger neerest. Therefore in that he was now heartned and incouraged, when he saw the great number of the Midianites, and he himself was now with his small armie in comparison of theirs, to meete and fight with them: it is cleare, that he was well perswaded of the truth of Gods promise, and that he did cast himselfe confidently thereupon. Thus his faith grew and shewed it selfe apparantly. *The sense of the first part.* *The sense of the first verse, and the doctrine.* Note. Doct. vers. 1.

So should we, when we haue been much laboured with, to belieue by the preaching of the Gospell, and haue our selues also much been occupied in attaining thereto, we should, I say, then look for the fruit thereof. And namely, to haue proofe of our faith indeed, in and about the common difficulties, wherein in times past wee haue bee foiled, and found it almost impossible sometime, or at least very vnlike that we should preuaile by faith, euen there I say, we should looke to haue some strength thereof otherwise then in former times. As for example, when a man seeth his sinnes and the guilt of them, though he be truly humbled for them: euen then to lift vp the hand of faith to heauen, and lay hold on the mercy of God in Christ. Also in time of temptation, to resist temptation, by beleeuing, that God wil giue vs victorie. Againe, when a man must lose goods, and life, and all that hee hath for the

the Gospell, or else to forsake it, then to cleaue fast vnto it, beleeuing that we shall be great gainers thereby. And so, when a man wanteth meat, drink, and apparrell, yet euen then, to acknowledge Gods prouidence, though by weake meanes, and rest in it peaceably. In like manner, hauing long heard the word, and how we should make it profitable to our selues by belieuing it, we should grow to this point, that we should be wearie of our rouing and wandering, of our sleeping, of our discoursing and disputing against that which we like not, being vnpleasant to our flesh, and say with *Samuel: Speake Lord, for now thy seruant heareth,* and is ready to rest in thy will, whither reproouing, commanding, or incouraging: yea and to be vpholden, guided, reformed, or kept within compasse, whither by the terrors, commandements, or promises of it. So ought we in all other parts of dutie to be readie
Note. to say euery one for himselfe, *Lord, now haue I learned how I should worke in my calling, vse my peace and prosperitie, behaue my selfe in secret, and with others, and walke throughout my life innocently and fruitfully, belieuing that I shall not lose the fruit of my labour. And further, I blesse thy name, I am ready to bee put the triall, and am not altogether as in times past, each occasion offered by thy Maiestie is welcome, I am the more incouraged to stoope meekely vnder mine affliction, when I see thou hast sent it, for then I belieue thou art readier to assist mee in bearing it, and that*
Note. *thou wilt giue a good issue out of it: and therefore farre be it from me to be so plunged and amazed at trials, as I haue been, for that were to be euer learning, and neuer come to knowledge, yea it were alway to be a child, going by the helpe of others, and neuer alone, which is the propertie of a changeling.* And thus doing, wee shall find that which the good Martyr found; that when God called him to the stake he endured the fire, though before hee could not endure the flame of a candle to singe so much as his finger. In these, and such like, to haue proofe of our faith, is a thing much to bee reioyced in, and a good signe that our faith groweth, and is strengthened otherwise then it hath been in times past, ac-
Coloss. 2. 7. cording to the saying of the Apostle to the Colossians: *Be rooted and grow in faith, that ye may abound therein.*

And so I might say of many things particularly, as of impatience, anger, wrath, vncleane and vnchast desires, excessiue feare of trouble, conceits, tetchinesse, rash iudging, and many other more: when we haue pursued, and had them in the chace, disliking, condemning, and long time and oft praying against them, we should looke for some victorie ouer them, and by the faith in which we prayed, to rest perswaded, that such meanes shall not bee vsed of vs in vaine: but looke that the rootes of them, which were fast setled in our hearts before, be now loosened in vs, and more and more dailie, and that it shall so appeare euen then, when any new occasion shall bee offered, and when we shall be prouoked to offend by any. This will liuely shew, (though wee shall neuer be vtterly void of the reliques and execrements of our corrupt and rebellious heart,) that our faith is better confirmed in the word that commandeth vs, to purge them out. And this a man would thinke were more to the honour of Christians, then to boast and iangle of their faith, and faile in the triall ridiculously: which is an easie religion to learne, if it might goe for payment. To whom a man might say, *Where is now that tongue of thine, which so lustily bragged of faith?* as *Zebul* said to *Gaal, cap. 9.*

Also

Also we further see here, that though *Gedeon* had the promise of God that he should ouercome the Midianites, yet hee lies not still, but serueth Gods prouidence by furnishing himselfe with a armie good as he could conueniently to goe against them. And so we ought to vse ordinary meanes to bring any worke to passe appointed vs of God, though wee haue the promise of good successe from him, and yet againe on the other side, we should not attribute any thing to them, for that were to detract from God his due. But of this before at large. Doct. 2.

THE FORTIE FIVE SERMON ON THE SEVENTH CHAPTER OF THE BOOKE OF IVDGES.

Now to goe forward where I left, in this verse, God tels *Gedeon*, that the people of his armie were too many to giue the victory vnto, lest they should ascribe it to themselues. This speech of the Lord sheweth, how vnfit wee bee, to haue any great matter committed to vs, or to our trust and gouernment, for wee are most prone to abuse it: and therefore he is faine oft-times to take away many good things from vs, lest they should much hurt vs, though they might (if wee could rightly vse them) turne to our great good, and the benefit of others. This people of Israel, if they had gone altogether to the battell, and got the victory, they would not haue acknowledged God to haue giuen it them, but their owne power and skill, and yet wee know how miserable they were a little before, when *Gedeon* himselfe complained in what distresse they were, and how low they were brought: so that one would thinke, they were vnfit inough to ascribe ought to themselues, and that they ought rather (hauing been brought from such bondage as they had been in before) yea and they might also easily haue seene cause to giue glory to God for it, if they with two and thirtie thousand (especially so many thousands of them being faint-hearted souldiours) had subdued more then an hundred thousand persons. And this is the more odious in this people, because they would haue abhorred such a leaud conceit or quality in themselues while they remained vnder bandage, yea, if they had been asked: *What if by you (being but feeble and few in respect of your enemies:) the Lord would destroy the Midianites, would you not thinke God had fought mightily for you?* Oh they would haue confessed no lesse, but seene that it had been cause of great thanks. True; till the victorie had been gotten: and then who but themselues had foiled the Midianites? So it may be *Saul* and *Ieroboam* while they were vnderlings, would haue counted it a greater priuiledge, and themselues highly indebted to God, if hee would haue bestowed a lesse matter then a kingdome vpon them, but when they had

Vers. 2.

Note.

Lam. 1. 1.

got it,they shewed they were vnable to be made partakers of so great a felicitie: and wee see, that they were not fit to haue so weighty and glorious matters as kingdoms committed vnto them. Euen as wee see, meane and beggarly persons,that neuer knew what belonged to wealth or dignitie, yet if they be raised vnto it,cannot beare it, nay the ground cannot beare them: if they bee set on horsebacke, they ride out of reason, euen till they breake their owne neckes: whereas ingenuous and wel-bred natures can aswell carry themselues in such a condition, (especially if education and grace meet together) as the poorest can in a bace and simple. And surely many of vs can as hardly beare a little wealth, small reuenues, a few hundreds,nay scores,as *Saul* and the other could their kingdomes: though (ere wee had them) we were as lowly and meane in our owne eies,as our fellowes.

Note.

Therefore,as I said,we may see, how soone we abuse Gods benefits,and all such good liberties,as he bestoweth vpon vs,as riches,health,promotion, credit (I would I might not say spirituall gifts also) euen as *Pharaoh* his princely estate and greatnes: the rich man in the Gospell,his wealth: *Herod*, the very praise and commendation that was giuen him by the people. So we that can challenge nothing at Gods hands as due debt to vs, but trouble and sorrow,which is the fruite of our sinne; what a lamentable case is it,that the Lord sparing vs much from sundrie calamities, and furnishing vs with benefits of diuers kinds,to draw vs to know,loue,belieue in him and honour him,that we cannot for al this,so soone inioy any thing that is ought worth, but by and by wee set vp our bristles, wee forget from what a cursed estate, and whence we came,and kick vp our heeles against the Lord: and yet this is easie to bee seene in all estates of men, and kinds of Gods benefits.

Luke 12.19.
Actes 12.23.

So that the Lord if he loue vs,seeth that there is no better way to be taken with vs for our good, then to take away such liberties againe from vs,and to let out our humours,seeing they breed but a pleurisie in vs,or to crosse vs in them,lest they should steale away our hearts from him,and so we driue him to say of his benefits,as he did of this people: *There be too many of them, I must make them fewer*,or else they wil glory of their multitude and greatnes. Euen so we cause the Lord to say of vs,as to *Saul* (a bad person) they haue too much wealth,I must plucke some of it from them: they haue had health too long, I must abridge them of it: they haue had too many of my benefits,as ease, credit,countenance,&c. vnlesse they could vse them better,I must,saith the Lord,of necessitie take them from them. And this is the cause why the Lord holds many of his vnder,that commonly they haue no great matters put into their hands,and are much crossed in those earthly commodities that they loue best,lest they should be the worse for them. And it is rarely seene,that euen they are better by them,then if they had them not. Therefore except God shall bestow vpon vs an humble and wise heart, and well ballanced with grace,to account of these things as they are,to wit,transitory,and soone flitting away,and to valew the heauenly treasure of faith, and a godly life aboue all earthly riches: let vs know that the Lord deales wiselier with vs, then we are aware,in dieting and shortning of vs: and we our selues shall see it as clearely in time (if wee marke it) as these Israelites did, that God hath done vs no wrong in taking somewhat away which we had, or denying vs somewhat which we desire. And as for such as seeke aboue all things to flo-

Note.

rish and haue the world at will, they are not so happie, as they bee counted, especially in their owne reckoning, neither will shew themselues the wisest men in the end: as by this and the like, may bee seene of them that will weigh it.

But to come yet more neere to that which is noted in the text, not onely men abuse Gods benefits other waies, but this one way also, that is, to vaine-glorie, as it is said, that this people here mentioned would haue done: and therefore the holy story addeth it as a reason why the Lord would not haue so many goe to the battell, least they should say, that they had preuailed by their owne might, and so should haue taken Gods honour to themselues. And by this wee learne, why God denieth, and doth not giue vs in our attempts, many, great, or any meanes at all sometime, and if he doe, yet not with any good successe, or at least, not as hee is wont to doe, (although to mans reason there bee likelihood enough, yea very great) because if he should, man would snatch the glorie from him to himselfe. As *Nabuchadnezzar* did when he said: *This is great Babel that I haue built: Zenacherib* that Dan.4.30.
blasphemed the Lord by his Captaine *Rabshakeh:* So *Benhadad* so grosly for- Esai.36.15.
got himselfe in boasting what he would doe, that hee was answered wisely 1.King.20.11.
in this manner, [Let not him that girdeth on his harnesse, boast himselfe, as he that putteth it off] And they to whom S. *James* wrote, how foolishly concluded they before the successe, and bragged of their gaine, before they Iames 4.13.
knew they should haue it? What would they haue done (thinke we) if they had alreadie enioyed it also? And is not this strange, that whereas wee pretend, (if wee might partake such and such blessings) wee would bee much more thankfull and seruiceable for them, the Lord should conuict vs of dissimulation and falsehood, telling vs that we know not our owne hearts, for wee would bee more proud, bold, and vainglorious? So that if the Lord should not bewray to vs, what poison lurkes in vs, we should thinke that he did himselfe great wrong in cutting many short of their desires, who might be like to doe him seruice by enioying them: whereas (alas) he knowes that in so doing, hee loseth no honour himselfe in so dealing with men, nay hee hath much adoe by such meanes to keepe men from destruction, at least from deepe dishonouring of him. But to returne, it is most true, that if God did not denie much to vainglorious persons which they desire, they would neuer giue him his due, but take it to themselues: insomuch as wee see that such doe not onely vaunt of their wealth, birth, strength, and such like, but if they haue onely some good qualitie, as that they be prouident husbands, or will keepe their promise, and pay their due, where it is owing, they glorie thereof, and disgrace other that faile therein, though the most of their other doings may be cast as dung in their faces, to their shame. But giue we vnto God his due: promise we to our selues nothing, but vpon condition if God will: and acknowledge wee him as the giuer, and as one that hath right to dispose of that which he hath giuen vs: and when we are denied successe in that which wee hope to bring to passe, let vs in token that we confesse the Lord may iustly ioynt vs, not fume and fret, raile and curse, and much lesse vtter we so much in words to others, that we thinke we are accursed, when wee see our selues crossed, but beare wee it meekly and patiently: and the

greater our gifts are, which we haue receiued, in more humble, fruitfull, and dutifull manner let vs shew our selues to vse them.

Vers. 3. That *Gedeon* was bidden to send away many of the people, and why; we haue heard: now let vs see who they are that be exempted from the warre, and sent backe, (of which sort there were two and twentie thousand) the text noteth them to bee those that were faint-hearted and timerous, and so Deut. 20.8. had God commanded in Deuteronomy that such should be sent backe, lest they should discourage other. Here this is to be considered; when *Gedeon* their Captaine thought them meet for warre, and God had called them also to that place, and duty, and giuen them gifts for that purpose, though they waxed timerous: in that they through faint-heartednes, and sloth, did not vse and employ their gifts, the shame and sin was theirs, though God sent backe: I speake it for our owne edification and benefit; for if many here were exempted by God from the battell, and yet thought fit and meete by men, doe not well bestow and vse these common gifts of the Spirit, as skill and knowledge in manuary things pertaining to the bodie, and this present life: how much more may we thinke, that about the more excellent gifts of the Spirit, as illumination, and matters belonging to the life to come, men doe deceiue the expectation of those with whom they liue, and be o-Note. ther, I meane farre worse then they goe for? Oh it is true, that there are many persons, who goe in the sight of men for good: yet the Lord doth not account so of them, but exempt them from his militant Church, euen as he shoaleth out a great many of these souldiers, as faint and vnfit for warre, when they should come to fight with their enemies: whom yet *Gedeon* thought meete persons for it, and yet we know, wee are much easilier deceiued in iudging about them, then these. Looke we therefore to it, in a thing by infinite degrees more precious, how God iudgeth of vs: and hang wee 2. Cor. 10. 18. not vpon the opinion of men. For hee is not allowed whom men or ones selfe praiseth, but whom God praiseth. And therefore we are not to account of all that are among vs professing the Gospell, no, though they be not branded with notorious sins, to be sound hearted and good Christians, though we know no other by them, till God make them manifest, as he did these in their kind: Is it for vs to iudge before the time? but howsoeuer men iudge, such as feare God, and depart from euill (as he himselfe commended *Iob* for such an one) it is sure that they only are accepted of him.

More specially to applie this: As the oddes betweene the faint-hearted and valiant souldiers was great, euen three to one: and yet all went about the seruice of God in outward shew: so great disproportion there is (among such as worship God) betweene the lukewarme or indifferent sort of Rom. 2. 28. cōpared with Reu. 3. 16. Christians, and the feruent, heartie, and zealous worshippers. Indeede God doth not inable nor allow vs to seuer the one from the other (so that wee may determine how farre the number of the one exceedes the other) as here he did *Gedeon*: but wofull proofe bewraieth no lesse then I haue said. And yet he that dismissed these white-liuered souldiers from the armie of *Gedeon*, and onely accepted the seruice of these three hundred, whom hee fitted for the purpose with faith and resolution; will also exclude all hollow-hearted, lukewarme, and temporizing Christians from hauing a part among such as

he

he will honour, so farre as that he will not bee honoured by them. I meane not that all Christians should bee martiall men, and fit for the field: but as Gods worke is diuers, so a diuers kinde of spirit hee requireth in them that doe it: in *Gedeons* men, courage and might; in Christians, feruencie and resolution to walke with God. For though wee haue no Midianites to fight withall: yet we haue worse enemies, both within vs and without: and therfore haue need of spirituall magnanimitie to vse spirituall weapons against them. And though we were not warre-faring men, yet in that wee be but waifaring, (as all Christians are both) we had need of feruencie and spirit. For he that in generall commands, Rom.12. *Be feruent, or hot in spirit*; commands the same in prayer, Iam.5. saying, be feruent therein; likewise in hearing, *Be swift to heare*: telling vs that the violent snatch the kingdome to them, &c. and the like affection also we must haue in all duties. Though in deede when dangers and troubles befall men for their profession, then is a speciall occasion offered of expressing what courage is in them: but if wee nourish not that grace daily in other duties, how shall it be at hand when we haue greatest need of it? And this I speake, because I see that the ancient and heauenly fire which once appeared most worthily in many, both in their entrance and progresse of their good course of pietie and a good conscience, is turned to ashes and extinct, or burnes so close and feeble, that it can hardly be discerned: and in stead thereof, either a blockishnes and deadnes is come vpon men, or a faint-hearted remisnesse and indifferencie, as if men cared not greatly whether they professed or no, and (saue for names sake) many could be content to be without it well enough. And as for such, their disgrace is as farre aboue these souldiers of *Gedeon*, as their sinne: for these were onely sent backe: but the other the Lord vomits out of his mouth. Some there are (through Gods goodnesse euen as *Gedeons* three hundred) who looke to the Spirit, (and good cause, for it is the temper of a Christian) but alas how few? Besides that, the diuell in stead of this grace, brought in a franticke sort of furious persons, whose zeale is to depart from the Church.

Rom.12.11. Iames 5.16. Iames.1.19. Matth.11.12. Note.

Now (to returne to the storie) wee haue heard how two and twentie thousand were sent backe, and that there were but ten thousand left to goe against more then an hundred thousand: and yet that the Lord said, that euen they were too many: this teacheth, that he would haue vs to learne, to depend on him without meanes, (if hee see it to be expedient to be so, but not otherwise) and by those which are very weake: and yet he would haue vs to be perswaded, that he regardeth and seeketh our good, euen when hee doth so. But of this before. *Doct.*2.

He said moreouer to *Gedeon*, that hee would trie these ten thousand for him, and shew him who were fit, that he himselfe might see it. For men are dull and dimme eyed to behold Gods secret power and will to doe them good, if he giue them not eyes of faith to behold them. And why should it seeme strange that the Lord should doe more then wee can see? and if wee shall see no likelihood thereof, his power and goodnesse is the more to bee admired and magnified, who sheweth it so manifestly in our weakenesse, euen when men see not how. As who saw, that mightie *Pharaoh*, *Sisera*, and the Midianites here spoken of, were like to be brought to such a downfall as they were? but it was enough that God had said it. And therefore our Verse 4.

Matth.4.4. Sauiour, Matth. 4. tels vs, *Man liueth not by bread onely, but by the word of God:* and in like manner, man thriues not by his wit, prouidence, care onely, but
Psal 127.2. by the blessing of God: No, his rising early, and his late going to bed, and eating the bread of sorrow shall not auaile to maintaine him, if God plucke backe his hand from blessing it. His apparell heates him not of it selfe, but by the power of the word and promise. Indeede the outward meanes men see, taste, and handle, and therefore in a grosse manner rest in them, and discerne no superiour power of God in them, much lesse beleeue, that it can worke without them: so that if meanes faile of health, safetie, and successe, they giue ouer hope: especially if they see that some great outward barre and let stops their way: whereas yet the three children tell the King of Babel, That they beleeue *the God whom they serue can deliuer them, not onely without meanes, but contrarie to meanes.* Doubtlesse in the Scripture wee haue a watchword giuen vs of this sinne, euen in the matters of saluation it selfe. For although none but the seede of *Abraham* ordinarily were elected and saued (though extraordinarily some were) before the comming of Christ: yet they who onely relied vpon these outward meanes, heard this spoken
Matth.3.9. to them: *Say not within your selues, we haue Abraham to our father: for God is able of stones to raise vp children vnto Abraham.* But because men separate (in the matter of happinesse) the true meanes appointed by God from the end they desire: I meane faith, repentance, humiliation, from election and saluation: it is iust with God also to meete with them in kinde, and to separate their carnall ends: I meane wealth, prosperitie and the like, from the meanes which they vse vnlawfully, and to his dishonour.

Doct.2. And further in that *Gedeon* was told, that hee must take none but those whom God appointed, and those hee must take: it teacheth vs that Gods word must direct vs in all our actions both for peace and warre, be the same neuer so meane and base: and that whatsoeuer face wee set on matters, yet if that be not the light to our steps, we walke but in darknesse. Now then, we who take in hand so many things in the day, and so throughout our life,
Col 3 16. how can wee chuse but serue him after our owne fantasies, if wee haue not that light plentifully dwelling in vs to guide vs? Wherein it is no hard thing to see, that God hath much against vs, and that oft times, when we be at the
Psal.130.3. best, seeing no man can tell the errors of his actions and life, or how oft hee
Psal.19.12. offendeth. So that if hee should looke straightly what is done amisse, who should be able to stand before him? Here I will stay for this time.

THE

THE FORTIE SIXE SERMON ON THE SEVENTH CHAPTER OF THE BOOKE OF IVDGES.

Heere the Lord shewes *Gedeon* who they were that should goe with him to the warre, when they were led to the waters, and those were three hundred which lapped water out of their hands: for these were industrious and fit for their businesse more then the other that drunk kneeling downe, who were like to haue been an vnprofitable burden to the rest by their multitude, and might haue giuen aduantage to their enemies by their vnreadinesse and delay, if occasion should haue been offered. And the thing that the Lord teacheth vs hereby is this: that although he wil haue none to trust in themselues, yet he would haue them ingenuous and industrious men, fit for that which they are imployed about, which thing is requisite in all callings and businesse for men to bee willing, diligent, and skilfull about that they professe, and take in hand, that with good conscience all may be performed: so the contrary of Christians is to be auoided, whether minister, magistrate, or priuate person, the husband diligent handed, the wife huswifely: none lazie, idle, carelesse. But of this I spake more in the story of *Othoniel* and *Caleb*, before chap.1. Verse 5.6.

Here the Lord saith, that by those three hundred men, hee would deliuer Israel: which was another strong confirmation of *Gedeons* faith: for by this he was perswaded to obtaine that which hee had already begun to belieue. And this ought to bee well marked of vs, as the thing which wee haue great need off. For who can so stedfastly belieue, as he ought, and hold constant therein? but by daily and continuall meanes, the Lord doth much reuiue and quicken our faith, to hold on our hope and confidence: which two graces wee must haue well setled in vs, and as faith is strengthened in vs, so are these two. The excellencie of hope is seene in the epistle to the Corinths in these words: *God who hath deliuered vs from so great a death, and doth deliuer vs, in him we hope also, that he will deliuer vs.* Verse 7. Note. 2.Cor.1.10.

The Price and worthines of the other, is to be seene clearely in the Epistle to the Hebrewes, thus: *Cast not away your confidence, for it hath great recompence of reward:* these two (faith and confidence) make their whole life sweet and ioyfull, who had them both, as *Dauid* who said of confidence (which is the fruit of faith, *My heart is fixed, I will sing and giue thanks.* The vse hereof, is this, that wee looke well to it, that wee find our part in these by oft hearing, and all manner of repetitions and experience of Gods promises, concerning his fauour from time to time toward vs, and therewith to marke our often Heb.10.32. Note.

faintings, doubts and feares, yea, and that about one and the same action, that we may see cause the better to fortifie our selues against them. But alas few marke any such thing, I meane euen of those, who may take good thereby, (for all are not capable of it) but shrinke at the hearing of any hardnesse comming toward them, and so gather no experience of their faith, hope and confidence against new trials to come: or of their weaknes, but impatiently goe vnder their afflictions, and so are more ready to faint vnder their burdens afterward.

Note.

Vers. 8. *The sense.*

It was Gods great mercy, that these three hundred did so willingly and readily follow and obey *Gedeon*, according to the word of God to him, which they also heard, I grant: but yet had not God perswaded them inwardly besides, they would haue departed with the rest 31700. and would haue both grudged at the liberty of the other, who were dismissed, and haue refused to beare the burden alone, yea they would haue forsaken him, if they had not looked vnto God. Where we should note, that in doing our duties required by God, we must not regard the forwardnesse or backwardnesse of others so much, nor what they doe: but what it is that God looketh for at our hands. Thus *Caleb* and *Iosuah* encouraged the people to goe forward against the Canaanites, not looking at the backwardnesse of the other spies. For as Gods word and authoritie haue inough in them to perswade vs, so if we looke any other way, as to mens example, or to the issue, or our own conceits and discouragements, wee may bee sure they will easily coole and dismay vs. Therefore (I say) the practise of these, discouers a great sinne in many: who if they haue a burden laid vpon them, grudge that any other should be free: but in matters of priuiledge and honour, grudge that any should be their partners. Both these we see exemplified in the Apostles of Christ and the disciples of *Iohn*. The Apostles seeing one casting out of diuels, who was none of their Masters followers: had indignation and complained to our Sauiour. They thought none but Christ and themselues worthy of such an office. So *Iohns* disciples grudged at Christs, because they fasted often, but Christs fasted not. They thought they had wrong in that others were not held to it, as hardly as they. The cause of the former is especially pride and vnthankfulnesse: of the latter either ignorance, or that which is worse, euen boldnesse therewith. And we see that he is a rare person, who can with equanimitie endure that any should excell him in gifts of body, mind, estate, or grace, with the blessings accompanying them. Nay many, of a melancholike and foolish nature, because themselues are giuen to pensiuenes, sadnesse, &c. enuy and censure such as take more libertie in mirth, recreation, company or diet: though (as *Paul* saith) they may both please God, without condemning on another.

Doct.

Numb. 13. 28. 29. 33.

Note.

Note.

This disease of looking narrowly to other what they doe, and not to God what hee requireth of our selues, (for it is a mixture of many humors, selfeloue, curiositie, distrust and others) this disease (I say) wee may see to haue been in *Peter*, who looking to *Iohn*, (to whom Christ said nothing when hee had laid an heauie burden vpon *Peter* himselfe, asked Christ, saying: *Master, what shall this man doe?* The like is to bee seene in them, mentioned in the Gospell, when they saw other more fauourablie dealt with, then themselues said grudgingly, *We haue borne the burthen of the day, &c.* So the elder brother of

John 21. 21.

of the prodigall repined to see him so well entertained. So that there being many as by these we may see, so ill minded this way, we may boldly say, that it is a singular grace of God in all our duties throughout our life, to shew forth indifferency and charitie: as also to regard what God saith to vs, and not to looke to men what they doe.

But where is this to be seene? in a very few: as for example in the Ministers, when Christ saith to them (in speaking to *Peter*) *If thou louest me feed my sheepe and my lambes*, and be diligent therein. If here and there one or a few regard it, yet how do the most cast their charge behind them, and looke at them that take their ease, whatsoeuer their words be that they loue him? So that the force of the word is not so much to draw them, as example to withdraw: magistrates, housholders, husbands, wiues, and all that professe the Gospell, should follow the example of these three hundred in their seuerall estates and callings. But it is so farre off from that, with the most, that if any other, (and specially if he be of their owne condition and degree) shal make conscience of this dutie more then other, he shall be readie to bee shaken vp and reuiled, as one that cannot be content to doe as other doe, when yet all may see in these three hundred how their example is set forth to their perpetuall commendation, in that they went not after the other their brethren, but obeyed the commandement of the Lord, in following after *Gedeon*. And whatsoeuer become of such as are led by the examples of men, and follow their owne deuices, leauing the plaine way, wherein God hath set them, (whose sinne in due time shall find them out) the other shall be knowne by this marke, to be the Lords, that they forsake all by-waies, and depart from euil with *Iob*, to, testifie that they feare him. The example of *Iosbua* is worthy our imitation in this point, who professed for himselfe and his, that they would serue the Lord, let the rest do as they listed. As if he had said, It should be their best way to serue the Lord as himselfe did, if they regarded their owne prosperitie and welfare: but if they were so wilfull, as to forsake their owne mercy, he and his had learned to follow a better Master, and was resolued to consult neither with flesh nor blood, neither cleaue to lying vanities, but make straight steppes to the commandement of God. Indeed if we see others readier then wee, in dutie doing, willinger to beare reproofe, forwarder in well doing, in mercie, loue, meekenesse, zeale, stronger then we, to endure affliction, or any burden which is vnwelcome to flesh: then doe wee as they doe: yet looke we not so much at them, as at Gods will in their obedience. But in euill follow not the multitude: for the most are alwaies worst: and the best differ and varie among themselues: so that except men will goe by a leaden rule, the word of God must bee the eternall and vnchangeable canon of dutie. Which canon when it shall iudge the actions of men either approouing or condemning them, it shall bee but follie for them to run into the croud (as we say) and shroud themselues vnder the couer of others: whose company shall aggrauate rather then extenuate their punishment. But of following examples, I haue said before.

John 21.15. Iob 1.3. Iosbua 24.15. Iona 2.8. Exodus 23.2.

THE

The second part of the Chapter.

Vers. 9. *And the same night the Lord said to him, Arise, get thee downe vnto the hoast: for I haue deliuered it into thy hand.*

10. *But if thou feare to goe downe, then goe thou and Phurah thy seruant down to the hoast.*

11. *And thou shalt hearken what they say, and so shall thy hands be strong to goe downe vnto the hoast. Then went he downe, and Phurach his seruant vnto the outside of the souldiers that were in the hoast.*

12. *And the Midianites and the Amalekites, and all they of the East lay in the valley like grashoppers in multitude, and their Camels were without number, as the sand which is by the sea side for multitude.*

13. *And when Gedeon was come, behold a man told a dreame vnto his neighbour, and said: Behold I dreamed a dreame, and loe, a cake of barly bread tumbled from aboue into the hoast of Midian, and came vnto a tent, and smote it that it fell, and ouerturned it, that the tent fell downe.*

14. *And his fellow answered, and said, this is nothing else saue the sword of Gedeon the sonne of Ioash a man of Israel: for into his hand hath God deliuered Midian and all the hoast.*

15. *When Gedeon heard the dreame told, and the interpretation of the same, hee worshipped, and returned vnto the hoast of Israel, and said, Vp: for the Lord hath deliuered into your hand the hoast of Midian.*

The summe of these verses.

NOw when the Lord had taken away the strength and power of *Gedeon* from him, I meane, his whole armie well nigh, hee knew full well that this would worke mightily vpon his weaknesse, to dismay him: and therefore in this second part of the Chapter it is shewed, how God after this, incouraged him, and prouided to remedie that his weaknesse. And that was in a strange manner done, euen by his enemies. For God bidding him goe downe to the Midianites tents, did there, by a dreame of one of them, and the interpreting of it by another, shew *Gedeon*, that hee should haue the victorie ouer them. Which when hee heard, hee was anew confirmed in his faith concerning the victorie, notwithstanding the small number of men which he had with him.

The sense and doctrine of vers. 9.

Note.

And first here let vs see how God bringeth *Gedeon* neerer and neerer to the brunt and triall: for now he will haue him goe to the very campe of his enemies, which to doe, was to come neerer to danger, then all that had gone before. But so did the Lord also adde new comfort vnto him, as his triall was greater. For hee saith: I will deliuer them into thy hands, though the danger and feare that might be like to arise to thee thereby, may seeme greater now, then it was before. And it may appeare by the next verse, that *Gedeons* feare was greater, and increased: for the Lord saith, *If thou feare to goe downe, &c.* And this sheweth vs, that ordinarily the neerer a triall in any sore affliction that we feele, doth come toward the issue, the more it worketh vpon vs. The reason is, because while affliction is a far off, the sense is not prouoked by the imagination of it so much, as whē it draweth neere, and threatens vs. But then commonly the minde multiplieth the greatnesse of it, by feare.

feare. As the Disciples were not greatly troubled for their Masters departure, till they saw there was no remedie, but they must needes forgoe him. Which teacheth, that when any such feare hangeth ouer vs, we should not onely from the first hearing of it, frame and settle our hearts against sudden distemper, and aggrauating of it by our foolish conceits, to bee patient and willingly subiect to the hand of God therein, and to weigh our owne weaknes, that as wee may wisely beware of fainting, so wee may pray to God for strength: but also daily, and oft continue such exercise, and the neerer the issue, the more feruently, (like to our Sauiour in his agonie and feare, before the comming of *Iudas* and the rest to take him) as feare indeed will then be readie most of all to assault vs. John 14.1.

And if we faint then, we may know our strength was neuer great. For as patience should haue her perfect worke to helpe vs beare affliction vnto the end, when it is come vpon vs: so wee ought to giue patience the perfect worke before it come, in keeping downe painful feare of it, till it come. And by all that hath been said of this matter here, and in the former processe of the historie, we may see, that wee must oft and much be strengthened both against the feare that riseth before the trouble come, and the smart that it causeth when it is come, till the danger be past and ouer. And it is a good signe that affliction when it commeth, shall not much disguise and astonish vs, when we weaken the terror of it after that manner, and by often meditating of the certaintie of our deliuerance there from, and preparing for our affliction accordingly, before it come: otherwise it will come vpon vs as an armed man, against whom there is no resistance. Prou. 24.10. Iames 1.4. Note.

And seeing God fortified *Gedeon* with a new promise of his helpe, euen when he should goe downe to the armie of his enemies, as hee came neerer the perill: so we may learne, that as trouble shall arise to Gods people, euen so shall their comforts also increase. According to that of the Apostle, *God is faithfull, who will not suffer you to be tempted aboue that ye be able, but as your troubles encrease, so shall your consolations*, and hee will giue the issue with the temptation, that ye may be able to beare it. And though it be one and the same word and promise, yet it hath force at one time as well as at another, to strengthen vs, if wee haue faith to lay hold on it. Such is the Lords dealing with vs, to minse our meate for vs, when our diet likes vs not: this cost he is willing to be at: So that we neede not complaine in such manner: Oh this trouble is intollerable; it will draw foorth the heart blood, I shall sinke vnder it, &c. For it is not required of vs to stand by our owne strength, but to deriue it from Christ our head, in whom all the promises of God are ratified. And this in the losse of friends, goods, or life, or in the likelihood thereof, or in any other affliction, is euer a fit remedie to stay vs vp and comfort vs. So that I cannot tell what we would looke for at Gods hands more, vnlesse wee would desire Angels from heauen to certifie vs of his minde, which he alloweth vs not in this age to looke for. But because this hath been oft entreated of before, I spare needlesse repetitions. Doct. 2. in vers. 9. 1. Cor. 10.13. Note.

THE

THE FORTIE SEVENTH SERMON ON THE SEVENTH CHAPTER OF THE BOOKE OF IVDGES.

Verse 10. THere is yet (as the text sheweth vs) another triall of *Gedeons* faith before the victorie: namely to send him to the Midianites only with his boy. Oh how many had there been before? But God will haue vs to know, that (1.Pet.1.7.) the triall of our faith, is much more precious, then the gold that perisheth, and therefore sendeth vs many trials, as he did to him, that although there seeme to be no great matter in them, yet indeede to him that weigheth it aright, it is found to be farre otherwise. (Note.) For both we see thereby, our weaknesse, which we should not otherwise thinke to be such as it is, and by little and little wee grow out of it, and gather experience, and hope against it, which in time are (Rom.5.4.) greatly to our comfort. And surely if *Gedeon* had so many trials in one duty doing, let not vs plead for exemption from many, though we haue alreadie endured some, and although wee can say, others are free, or haue but few in comparison of vs. But to proceed to another point. It is happie for vs, that the Lord, who diets vs with this ordinarie, vndertakes as well to bring vs safely through our trials, ministring as much grace, as affliction, as hee did (Verse 11. *Doct.*) here to *Gedeon*: so that wee rather should say; Since thou giuest shoulders Lord, lay on what burthen thou pleasest, thy will bee done: Rather, I say, then to compare the irksomnes of the trouble, with the pleasure and ease of the contrary: which will make vs wearie of trials, and like the Israelites in the wildernesse, to long and linger after daintines and Quailes.

We see the couetous man is neuer satisfied with gold: but triall serues to bring in a commoditie of greater price, as I said before. Gold can serue but to feede and apparell vs, except wee abuse it to the pride of life, to make vs thinke our selues in a fooles paradise by enioying it: but this serueth to encrease our spirituall treasure, (if we be wise to vse it in kind) both to purge the drosse away which cleaueth to our faith, meeknes, and patience: and to adde to the measure of it also, so that whatsoeuer good thing we enioy, we should neither haue it in the kinde, nor in abundance and store, but through much triall. Therefore rather let vs learne to count it great ioy, (as S. *Iames* (James 1.2.) saith) when many trials fall vpon vs: then snuffe against God, as if we cared (Note.) not how little grace we had, so we might haue ease therewith: as the sluggard in Ecclesiastes, who saith; A morsell with idlenesse is better then plen- (Eccles.4.6.) tie with labour. I confesse indeed, this is an high degree to ioy in affliction, which is so grieuous in it selfe, and not ioyous: a greater matter then to ioy, (I say not in health, riches and prosperitie, which euery foole can doe) but

euen

euen in hearing the word, or obeying it in many particular duties thereof. Howbeit we want not examples of ſuch as haue found ioy in their trials, I ſay in them (for he that lookes for ioy after them, muſt alſo finde ſome in them) I meane by hope: as *Paul* by name, who profeſſeth no leſſe of himſelfe: and *Dauid* with many others. Yea and wee alſo muſt learne to ſay; Lord thou teacheſt me an hard leſſon to account affliction matter of great ioy: but ſeeing thou ſaiſt there is ſweetnes to be gotten out of this bitternes, (as hony out of the carrion of a lion) therfore I will ſtriue to beleeue it: and that I am as precious in thine eyes, and as deare to thee, euen in affliction, as in peace & freedom, and that I ſhall gaine more by it, then by all my iollitie and eaſe, in which I ſhould haue lien ſtinking, if by trials thou hadſt not kept my faith occupied & liuely. For though faith wãts not matter enough to work vpon, euen when we are at the beſt, and freeſt from trials, yet ſuch is our ſottiſhnes, that promiſes ſeeme not ſweete or ſauourie to vs, except we be driuen to ſeek after them by trials & troubles, but then oh how welcome!

Rom. 5. 3.
2. Cor. 12. 10.
Note.

This ſending him to the campe of the Midianites ſo nakedly and vnfurniſhed, what could it promiſe in likelihood and outward ſhew, but deadly danger? But heare the reſt of Gods words to him; Thou ſhalt (ſaith hee) heare what they ſay, and thou ſhalt be confirmed thereby, and after thou ſhalt goe into the hoaſt of the Midianites and feare and diſmay them, till they be vanquiſhed. By this wee ſee, that wee haue great cauſe to beware, that we take not ſome part of Gods word, and leaue the other, leſt wee depriue our ſelues vtterly of the whole, and all benefit thereof: as *Gedeon* (we ſee) had done, if he had taken one part of Gods ſpeech to him, and left the other. And this thing is too commonly offended in, not only by ſubtill Sophiſters, whoſe ſinne is the greater, becauſe they ſinne of knowledge, but alſo by weake Chriſtians: who through feare and want of experience, doe draw againſt themſelues the threats and commandements to wound them, but the promiſes of God (which by his owne appointment are ſet downe to their comfort properly) thoſe (they ſay) belong not to them. So what a corraſiue were it to a Chriſtian, if hearing this, that, *All who will liue holily in Chriſt Ieſus, muſt ſuffer affliction, &c.* he ſhould goe away (as hee in the Goſpell) heauie and ſad, ſaying: This is an hard ſaying, *who then ſhall be ſaued?* But God be thanked if the promiſes be added to the charge, the heart will be well eaſed, and the burthen in great part alaied. And doubtleſſe the diuell himſelfe would wiſh a Chriſtian no greater miſchiefe, then he cauſeth to himſelfe by this ſeparating of thoſe things which God hath ioyned together. But of this point reade more in the former chapter in *Gedeons* reply to the Angell. And there is as great cauſe that we take heed of ſeparating the word of iudgement and puniſhment from the word of precept and commandement, as the promiſe: for as this cauſeth men to ſtumble where they need not, and plungeth them into feare and deadly deſpaire, ſo the other ſtrengthens them as much in their boldneſſe to offend. As wee ſee *Eue*, by diſioyning the puniſhment threatned vpon her eating the fruite, was the more prouoked to attempt the ſinne. Geneſ. 3.

Doct. 2.
2 Tim. 3. 12.
Geneſ. 3. 6.

More particularly we may here ſee, that God doth ſo order things according to his owne good pleaſure and purpoſe, that hee maketh his to finde matter of ioy, where (in ſenſe and reaſon) ſorrow onely and terror can bee found.

Doct. 3.

found. He fetcheth light out of darknesse, sweetnes out of bitternes, and out of trouble peace. For what might *Gedeon* looke for by going to the campe of his enemies so nakedly, but discomfort and hazard of his life at least, if he had not been slaine also, and cut in a thousand pieces? Yet God intended (and so brought to passe) that he and all the people should liue and be comforted, by hearing there that which did cause it. For example, what might
Genes.12.1. *Abraham* haue looked for when the Lord bad him goe from his friends and countrey to a place that he knew not, neither had any thing in it, but was a meere stranger therein? was not that speech of the Lord full of discomfort at the hearing of it? And yet we know, that he obeying him, was not onely furnished there, to be able to maintaine a mightie familie, euen three hundred and eighteene persons, but also his seede grew and was multiplied as the dust of the earth, and he was made the father of all beleeuers that should come after, and of whom after the flesh, Christ should come.

Heb.11.24. The like may be said of *Moses* sending away from the house of *Pharaohs* daughter, where he had been brought vp so daintily, to goe suffer affliction with the people of God in the wildernesse. And yet what a rare instrument did he make him, to worke the greatest deliuerance for his people that euer was heard off to be wrought by a meere man? Euen so, learne and know we,
Note. that the Lord doth oft turne the greatest troubles of his, to their greatest benefit and good, if they waite patiently vpon him, yea he giueth them farre aboue that which they looke for, insomuch as if it were possible for them to be brought euen to hell, this were but to raise them vp vnto heauen, as they who haue any experience can tell: and *Iona* out of the fishes bellie testified in the middest of extremities and anguish; who out of his greatest feares and sorrowes was exalted to greatest hope and reioycing, as his heauenly and admirable zeale in promising to praise God doth aboundantly shew. It
Ionas 2.9. is said also here, that he and *Phurah* his seruant went to the side of the camp: wherein his faith doth liuely shew it selfe, and that he minded and beleeued what God said, rather then that hee feared the danger that he went in. And
Doct.4.in vers.11. this, indeed, is that which I haue so much beat vpon in this story, and in a word, which we should all doe: that is, trust God whom we see not, and not
Note. eie, and looke too narrowly to the lets that are in our way, to feare and draw vs to vnbeliefe: as we read how *Iehosophat* did, not onely himselfe belieeue,
2.Chron.20.15. as he was willed to doe, but with great courage exhorted also his people to doe the same in the sore danger they were in by the Moabites and Ammo-
Iohn 24.1. nites, and was thereby deliuered: and so did our Sauiour to his disciples when they were greatly grieued for his departure, saying: let not your harts be troubled; ye beleeue in God, beleeue also in me.

Verse 12. Now in that it is said that the Midianites, and their helpers lay as grassehoppers on the face of the earth, the meaning is, they were farre and wide spread, for so the word signifieth, Genes.25. meaning that they occupied a
Genes.25.8. great space of ground, and that they were a mightie number. In which sense it is said in *Iosua*, that *Iabin* got an armie, as the sand of the sea. And how could this but astonish *Gedeon* yet againe, when he beheld the multitude of them, but that his faith vpheld him still as before? Where we are againe,
Doct. much like as in the former point, to learne, that such troubles and trials must we suffer and looke for, from which, we can in sense and reason looke for nothing

thing but discomfort and vtter vndoing: and out of the which in the iudgemen of man, we see no way or helpe to get out and be deliuered.

And who of Gods deare children haue not so felt and found it, in one trouble or triall and other, and at one time or other? When God had promised the land of Canaan to his people, yet before they possessed it, when they sent thither to search the land, & to see what it was, and whether the people therein were strong or weake, many or few, they receiued such discouragement by the answere that was brought backe to them, that they had neither helpe nor hope, euer to enioy it. Againe, what was *Dauid* to *Goliah?* or *Sampson* to so many Philistines? Or what was our English Island to the Spanish forces, and to so many nations as haue risen against it in times past, the Pope himselfe being the chiefe setter on? and yet God fought for vs against our enemies. Numb.13.28. 1.Sam.17.50. Iudg.16.30.

And to shew it in another instance, Oh how many thrice happy people, haue yet oft feared and almost said, there is no hope nor helpe for them in God? but resolued with themselues for the time, in their feare and weakenesse, that they could not escape condemnation and vtter abiection from God? yea and they would haue yeelded themselues willingly to the paine of the damned some hundreds of yeeres (such was their desperate estate) so as they might haue been recouered, and saued afterward: as I my selfe haue heard some of them say little lesse in their despaire, who yet (God haue the glory) haue well outgrowne the same, and haue been restored to comfort. Other of Gods deare children after such plunges and deliuerances out of them, haue after met with other trials, which haue been to their sight as the sea, bottomlesse: and haue constrained them for the time, to breake out, and say, that all good daies were gone from them, who yet haue liued to see better then they had euer seene before. What should I speake of particulars, which were infinite? And all such God hath seene good to exercise vs withal, to appall and pull downe the pride of our hearts, (who do so soone forget our selues) but not to dismay vs, seeing, if it be not long of our selues, we may still find redresse of all such feares from aboue. Note.

Now followes the dreame, that one of the Midianites dreamed, and told his fellow, namely, that a barley loafe tumbled into the hoast, and came into a tent, and smote it, that it fell: and the answere of the other, as the interpretation of it, that it was the sword of *Gedeon*, and that God had giuen the Midianites into his hands. This was that dreame and interpretation, which the Lord sent *Gedeon* thither to heare, (for such meanes it pleased him to vse to confirme him yet still:) where first we see, that God gaue diuine dreames to those which were enemies of godlinesse, and to a nation which afflicted his people: as he did to *Pharaoh*, of seuen leane, and seuen fat kine, that were wel liking, and so he did to his Butler and Baker: and after that to *Nebuchadnezzar*, who had led away *Iuda* captiue, aswell as to *Ioseph*, *Iacob*, and other holie men. But this was here more strange, that neither *Ioseph* nor *Daniel*, no Prophet of God, I meane, interpreted the dreame, but a common souldier. Hee gaue then we see, a true dreame, and the interpretation thereof vnto the wicked. But as the Lord gaue *Saul* a new heart, *viz.* of courage and gouernment, and to *Iehu* of zeale, for certaine ends and actions concerning his own glory, and the good of others onely, and those ends being accomplished, the Vers.13.14. *The opening of them.* Doct. out of verse 13 14. Genes.41.1. Genes.40.5. Dan.2.1. 1.Sam.19.23. 2.King.10.11.

gifts

gifts ceased, because they were but common gifts: euen so these two souldiers were made Gods instruments to confirme *Gedeons* faith, and consequently fitted for the purpose: which being performed, they ceased to dreame diuine dreames, or to interpret them diuinely.

By this we see, that he bestoweth excellent gifts and graces vpon the bad, aswell as vpon the good, which gifts either are meerely naturall and ordinarie, or supernaturall and extraordinarie. Naturall and ordinarie, as industriousnesse, wit, policie, strength, for the attaining of learning, skill, wealth, credit, and the wel gouerning and defending of families, subiects and commonwealths. Supernaturall, as enlightning and knowledge by the word, and specially of the law terrifying, and the Gospell generally working a confused ioy and vanishing faith in them. Extraordinarie, as the gift of miracles, tongues, and the like in the infancie of the Church were. These he giueth to many more then hee giueth faith vnto or regeneration, euen as the visible meanes leading thereto, as Baptisme and the Ministerie, are common to both. And why? because the subordinate ends for which these gifts serue, are more generall, then those which the speciall gifts serue for. Therefore we see, that many are well fitted for naturall, ciuill, morall, and (ministerially) spirituall and diuine ends, who yet are no more fit for the maine end of all, I meane for godlinesse and saluation, then if they wanted the other: because the speciall end is not so large and vniuersall, as the common end is. Yea doubtlesse, the wicked are oft times endowed with common gifts in a farre ampler and more glorious manner and measure, then the godlie: the Lord heaping hot coales vpon their heads, and clearing himselfe from the blame of their condemnation: seeing that he who bestowed vpon them so liberally in the one kind, would not haue denied them the other which accompanie saluation, if they had humbled themselues to the seeking after them, and not rested in the outward priuiledges, as they who boasted of the Luke 10.20. Temple, the Temple, whereas in the meane while. *There came from the North, East, and all quarters, and sat downe with Abraham in the kingdome of heauen*, and themselues, who boasted of the Temple, and were the children of the kingdome, Christ saith plainely, were cast out, and excluded. But of all such gifts, we may say, that seeing they are not the peculiar gifts which are proper to Gods owne children, but those that are common to one and other: it may be said to them, as Christ said to the disciples, when they reioyced so greatly that the diuels were subiect to them, and cast out of men by them: *Reioyce not, that the diuels are subiect vnto you, but for that your names are written in heauen:* so they who haue but knowledge of the Scripture, in the letter only, with memory and speech to carry away and vtter it, hearing the same ioyfully sometime, and are but restrained from some outward euils, let them not glory, and rest themselues therein, without sanctification and faith vnfained, that so their reioycing may be sound, and not to be taken from them, else let them feare, lest it be answered them, as it was to them that pleaded their great workes of preaching and miracles: *Depart from me, ye are workers of iniquitie, I know you not.*

2 And therefore it followeth, that the benefit of that dreame redounded to the people of God, and not to them that dreamed and interpreted the same. Euen as the excellent gifts of an vnsanctified person publike or priuate, may possibly

poſſibly doe. Neither can any gifts of God that the vnrighteous haue, profit them to ſaluation. They haue no vſe of their knowledge, they are not the better for their hearing, and prayers, they loſe all their coſt and trauell that they beſtow in ſeruing God: howſoeuer like dumbe pillers they may direct others in the way, not ſtirring themſelues. For they delight not therin, but draw neere him with their bodies, and ſerue him with lip-labor, but their hearts are farre from him; and therefore in vaine doe all ſuch worſhip him. Which ſhould make them looke about more ſeriouſly, till they can proue, that they doe more then ſay, Lord, Lord, but that they endeuour aboue all things to doe the will of the Lord. How much more vaine is it then to truſt in riches, which of all common gifts are commoneſt, and therefore furtheſt from commending the poſſeſſors of them to God. Matth.15.9. Matth.7.21.

3 Laſtly, let vs marke, that God doth his people good by things which are of no reckoning nor account, (when yet the beſt things that the vngodly haue, cannot profit them) as the dreame and interpretation of it, which indeed was an excellent gift: yet in mens account a meane thing, and for all that, as meane as it was, by that did God quicken *Gedeon*, and comfort him. Euen as wee ſee heere, God vſeth the meaneſt things (as men iudge of them) and things that are nothing worth for the welfare of his ſeruants. So God did by the Manna, (an vnlike thing, and of meane account) nouriſh and preſerue the liues of his people: ſo by foure leprous perſons, that were ſhunned and loathed of al, he ſaued all the people, and ſo he ſaued the Prophet aliue and fed him by Rauens: theſe were great matters by baſe and weake meanes. Exod.16.35. 2.King.7.6. 1.King.17.6.

And why this? becauſe, as *Iob* ſaith, euen the ſtones of the field ſhall be in league with thee, and the beaſts thereof at peace with thee. This doctrine ſeemeth after a ſort contrary to the former: to wit, that the wicked may not take comfort in the glorioueſt things concerning this preſent life, and yet the meaneſt things in this world through Gods goodneſſe, ſhall ſerue for the benefit of the godly, but both may ſtand well together. And to ſay a word or two more of this, what is meaner in the account of the Heathen, then water, bread, and wine, being of their owne nature, common creatures, and yet what great matters are wrought by them in Gods people? Iob 5.23.

So to behold and view the creatures and workes of God, which all may doe, what great matter is it thought to be? and yet what ſweet meditation haue Gods ſeruants thereby to their comfort? Lo then, how they are bleſſed in all parts of their liues who feare God; and that they may find in all things; if they ſift and ſearch them throughly, and marke what God promiſeth accordingly. And when all this is ſo, yet in the meane while, there is no peace to the vngodly, neither is any creature at league with them, but may and ſhall (when God will) annoy them. Eſa.48.22.

This was manifeſt in *Iezabel*, whoſe neere attending ſeruants & eunuches caſt her downe headlong on the ſtones out of the window. This is the ſecret hand of God, but not perceiued. And as for that which hath been ſaid before of the dreame, it is not ſaid to the end we ſhould attribute any thing vnto dreames, now common with vs and naturall, although God had ſaid of that dreame, that *Gedeon* ſhould be comforted by it. 2.King.9.33.

THE FORTIE EIGHT SERMON ON THE SEVENTH CHAPTER OF THE BOOKE OF IVDGES.

Vers.15. NOw followeth the fruit of all this, namely, *Gedeons* thankes to God with reuerence, and how he was hereby much reuiued himselfe, and stirred vp his souldiers to be so likewise. Heerein wee may (notwithstanding the imperfections that wee haue heard of him,) clearely see his faith, both in that hee went to the hoast when God willed him, beleeuing that hee should bee comforted thereby, and now the more when hee had surer hope thereof by the interpretation of the dreame, as God had told him before: for hee was now

Note. cheered, and beleeued further. Thus it behoueth vs to grow to beleeue and reioyce in that which sometime wee could not: and that faith in one promise may bring and breed it in another, that so it may be confirmed in vs, as

Colos.2.7. it was in him, that so wee being rooted in faith, wee may, as the Apostle willeth, grow and abound therein with thankesgiuing.

2 And besides, we may learne, that our thankes ought to be renued for benefits as they are daily bestowed vpon vs, (euen as wee made prayers for them before) as well as benefits past. And this is not to bee neglected as a thing little worth, but to bee duly and speedily regarded: euen as all other duties are to be done in their time and season, and not posted off and omitted for euery trifle: for herein *Gedeon* hath giuen vs an example. As soone as he receiued the promise of victory made him of God by the interpretation of the dreame, hee returned beleeuing it, and gaue praise to God for it, and that by and by, and delayed not. But herein we come farre short of him, and also in taking the opportunity to doe all other duties speedily and in season. What time is fitter to record Gods mercies then in the morning, after we be perfectly awake, both in considering our preseruation in the night past from

Lam.3.23. the dangers thereof, and that his goodnesse is renued vpon vs still for the time to come, to guard and blesse vs as in former times: now therfore what time I say is fitter then it, to stirre vs vp both to thankes, and also to renue our suites to the Lord for continuance of his fauour? But who watcheth to take this opportunity hereunto, but letteth it passe rather through sloth, worldli-

Note. nesse, frowardnesse, &c? And the same I may say of our carelesnesse in other things; when we haue both leisure and opportunity to renue our couenants with the Lord, and to bee armed and resolute throughout the day, against euery euill and prouocation to sinne through the day, that so wee might walke at liberty and in peace: yet who regardeth it, but rather trifleth out the time any way, or else doth worse, rather then to set his heart the best way? But of this duty I haue elsewhere spoken more largely.

So

So wee may note the property and force of faith, to wit, to cheere the 3
heart,and to quicken and ſtrengthen it,ſo farre as in the meaſure of it, it layeth hold of that which it receiueth, and is promiſed, as I ſaid before. And laſtly, how experience imboldeneth vs, and cauſeth vs to prouoke others to beleeue,and ſerue the Lord together with our ſelues, and to make them ſtrong, cheerefull, and comfortable alſo: and this is the end of our experience, and the vſe that wee ſhould make of it toward others, and it pleaſeth the Lord well, that wee ſhould doe ſo, as wee ſee *Gedeon* did to his few ſouldiers.

The third part of the Chapter.

Verſ.16. *And hee diuided the three hundred men into three bands,and gaue euery man a trumpet in his hand with emptie pitchers, and lampes within the pitchers.*
17. *And he ſaid vnto them, Looke on me,and doe likewiſe, when I come to the ſide of the hoaſt: euen as I doe,ſo doe you.*
18. *When I blow with a trumpet and all that are with me, blow ye with trumpets alſo,on euery ſide of the hoaſt,and ſay, for the Lord,and for Gedeon.*
19. *So Gedeon and the hundred men that were with him,came vnto the outſide of the hoaſt in the beginning of the middle watch, and they raiſed vp the watchmen, and they blew with their trumpets,and brake the pitchers that were in their hands.*
20. *And the three companies blew with the trumpets,and brake the pitchers,and held their lampes in their left hands, and their trumpets in their right hands to blow withall,and they cried,The ſword of the Lord and of Gedeon.*
21. *And they ſtood euery man in his place round about the hoaſt: and all the hoaſt ranne,and cried,and fled.*
22. *And the three hundred blew with trumpets, and the Lord ſet euery mans ſword vpon his neighbour,and vpon all the hoaſt: ſo the hoaſt fled to Beth-haſhittah in Zererah,and to the border of Abel-meholah vnto Tabbah.*
23. *Then the men of Iſrael being gathered together out of Nephtali, and out of Aſhur,and out of all Manaſſeth purſued after the Midianites.*

The ſence of theſe verſes.

NOw after theſe many trials followeth the iſſue,and that in manner here ſet downe. For firſt *Gedeon* made haſt,and by that meanes came vpon the Midianites, ere they were aware, and deferred not the time, in the middle watch,which was a little after midnight: for ſo it much behoued him to do,to come vpon them in the fearefull time of the night,and in the deep darke,when *Gedeon* and his men could not be ſeene,how few they were. In which his ſo comming, hee willed his men whom hee diuided into three bands, to take emptie pitchers with lampes in them, and trumpets in their hands: that after the blowing of them, and flighting and frighting of the enemies with the ſtrange and vnlooked for noiſe thereof,they might breake the pitchers alſo,by the hearing of the which,it might ſeeme to them that their ſpeares were broken with fighting,and then the lampes ſuddenly appeared,aſtoniſhing the Midianites, and giuing light to themſelues. Thus did he,and his ſouldiers did likewiſe, though that all this which they did,might haue been thought to bee to ſmall purpoſe. But the

effect thereof, by the onely wise and wonderfull gouernment of the Lord, was this, that one of the Midianites slue another, broke their aray and fled
Chap.3.27. away, crying, much like that which was done, chap. 3. And they that were scattered, and not slaine, were pursued by the Israelites, and taken. Now as there are in these verses three things in generall, to wit, the direction that *Gedeon* gaue his men; then their following it; and lastly, the effect that ensued, so let vs consider them in particular.

Doct.vers.15. 16 17. And first to begin with these three verses together, let vs note, that *Gedeons* speed that he made in taking the opportunity and fit season, to doe the things that we haue heard, teacheth all Christians to doe the same: namely, that they take time in euery thing that they go about, while it is seasonable,
Eccles.9.10. for afterwards it will be too late. In time reape and sow, and doe thy businesse, eate in time, sleepe and trauell while it is light, as our Sauiour dire-
Ioh.11.9. cteth, saying: *Are there not twelue houres in the day?* So in all duties of Christianity, in giuing to the poore, doe it in his need, in seeking the Lord, goe a-
Esa.55.6. bout it while he may be found, so in auoiding and forsaking sinne, resist it in the beginning; and helping to punish wickednesse, and preuenting Gods wrath, doe all accordingly, in fit and due season. There was a time, when the
Luk.16.25. rich man might haue succoured *Lazarus*, and that was, while hee lay at his gates: but when *Lazarus* was dead, the time was gone.

So there was a time wherein the fiue foolish Virgins might haue proui-
Matth 25.12. ded oyle for their lampes: that was, before the bridegroome came: but when he was come, and the doore was shut, the time was past. So there is a time in which men may repent, that they may be saued: that is, while God sendeth his messengers to call them; but when they let the season passe in
Eccles.12.1. the daies of their youth: after, when the time of age, sicknesse, and death commeth: a thousand to one if the time be not gone, and that it be not then too late. For beside that there are many things in the way to hinder: this is none of the least, that late repentance is dangerous. Oh what hath been lost by passing by the fit time and season, the lamenting it deepely by our Saui-
Luk.19.42. our in the people of Ierusalem doth shew, when hee said: *O if thou hadest euen knowne at least in this thy day, those things which belong to thy peace, but now are they hid from thine eyes.*

2.Cor.6.2. Therefore Saint *Paul* told the Corinthians, *This is the acceptable time,* (that is, while they might heare him) *this is the day of saluation.* Sutable hereunto
Ephes.5.16. is that of the Apostle, Ephes. 5. *Redeeme the season:* by which exhortation he teacheth, that although no time should bee spent vnprofitably, yet seasons, (which are times hauing some speciall fitnesse in them aboue others, to doe or receiue good in) must more carefully be obserued; yea redeemed, that is, dedicated to holy vse by forgoing somthing pleasing to the flesh, to purchase them. For not onely workes vnlawfull and needlesse, but euen lawfull and in their time, necessary, must giue place to fit seasons: because then God offereth occasion of some spirituall gaine, which at other times cannot bee obtained. As the Sabbath is a season for instruction and edification, one day of seuen: the other sixe haue not, but by occasion, the opportunity which that hath So when God sendeth publike or priuate iudgements vpon the land, or any persons, that is a season of fasting, humiliation, renuing our couenant: and contrariwise speciall blessings and deliuerances are opportuni-

ties

ties of thankſgiuing, and reioycing. In which and all others S. *Iames* tea- Iam.5.13.
cheth vs what to do: *Is any man afflicted? let him pray*: ſo, *is any merrie, let him ſing*: for theſe are occaſions worth the taking, and not alway occurrent: therefore as God diſpoſeth of vs, ſo let vs apply our ſelues, and improue the ſeaſon to the beſt vſe, and ſuffer not our ſelues to vaniſh away, and abuſe it, through our follie and vnſeaſonableneſſe: which ſinne is more common, euen among the better ſort, then they ſuſpect, to ſuffer themſelues to paſſe ouer the beſt occaſions vnfruitfully. Whereas alas, how ſhall they ſpend their whole time well, who ſpend their beſt ſeaſons badly? As wee know, in the morning, both body and mind is in beſt time for meditation, or any fruitfull exerciſe: if that periſh without fruit, how can the whole day after for the moſt part, be otherwiſe then barrenly and weariſomely paſſed? Men worke vpon their trades ordinarily we ſee: but if their trades bee vp, that is, the wares which they make doe take a great price, and are quicker of ſale then at other times: how will they beſtirre themſelues, and ſet euery one on worke whom they can come by, riſing early, going late to bed, and in a word, how vnwearied are they? It is their ſeaſon they ſay. What buſineſſe will not the houſholder lay aſide on the market day? why? that he may vſe that ſeaſon to furniſh himſelfe for the whole weeke with prouiſion? what thinke we? will the Merchant game, play, drinke, ſleepe, or trifle out the ſea- Matth.13.45.
ſon of his merchandiſe, when hee is come to the place of trafficke beyond ſea? No, all muſt yeeld to the ſeaſon, hee neglects his pleaſure to redeeme that. And if we faile in well vſing the ſeaſons which offer themſelues, what likelihood is there, we will ſhew our ſelues wiſe in procuring ſeaſons to our ſelues? As the truth is, an eaſie thing it were to doe, if wee were not vnſauory, and vnwilling to heare of any thing more then ordinary. But ſomewhat to this effect I noted before in *Gedeons* deſtroying Idolatry.

Alſo this carrying of pitchers in their hands, as *Gedeon* willed them to do: Doct.2.
a few vnarmed men, (euen three hundred) againſt ſome hundred thouſand, well prepared ſouldiers, what an vnlikely matter was it, that they ſhould effect any thing thereby? But wee ſee what a wonderfull victory it brought. The like may bee ſaid of *Ioſhuas* compaſſing the walles of Iericho, Ioſh.6.20.
ſeuen daies, with blowing trumpets of Rams hornes: and yet ſeeing the Lord promiſed, and he beleeued it, the walles of the city at the appointed time fell downe. By both wee learne, that though the meanes bee neuer ſo weake, to effect any good at all, yet if God direct vs to them, and promiſe to worke by them, it behoueth vs to looke vp to him, as *Gedeon* heere did, and wee ſhall ſee the power of God in vſing them though they bee weake: for though they ſerue not for one vſe, which carnall reaſon doth onely looke to, yet they ſhall ſerue for another, which God euer intendeth by them.

Euen as heere wee ſee, that although theſe meanes heere vſed by *Gedeon* and his ſouldiers, ſerued not to beate downe and deſtroy their enemies: yet we ſee that they ſerued to terrifie, affright, and ſcatter them, and to ſet one of them againſt another. And yet our carnall reaſon, if wee truſt not to weapons in warre, ſcoffes at our faſting and prayer, by which *Iehoſaphat* got great 2.Chro.20.
victory, and *Heſter* the Queene preuailed againſt that wicked *Haman* in a 3.17.
moſt great difficulty. So preaching is fooliſh to reaſon, and humane wiſ- Heſt.4.16.com-
dome for bringing men to Chriſt. But reade 1.Cor.1. what the Apoſtle pared with
there 7.10.

1.Cor.1.16. there saith, to wit, *That we must become fooles that we may be wise:* while yet the wit of man deuiseth another way, and most fit to deceiue himselfe: as for example, if he be predestinate to saluation, he saith he shall be saued, though he neuer heare sermon. And euen so men speake of watching ouer their liues, praying, and the worshipping of God in their familie, and the like, that they are more then need to be vsed. So they perswade themselues that policie, toile and labour are all in all, to bring Gods blessing vpon them, in all that they set their hands vnto, though the Prophet in the Psalme haue Psal. 127.1. taught the contrary, saying: *Except the Lord build the citie, the labourers toile themselues but in vaine.* But of this hath often been spoken.

Doct. 3. And here we are further to marke the benefit of good example, and how it preuaileth oft times with inferiours: *Gedeon* here bids his souldiers doe, as they saw him doe, so that he went before them. As all heads and superiours should likewise doe, that they may propound their own example in al good duties. Hence it was, that our Sauiour Christ washing his Disciples feete, propounded the same to them to be followed, and that so they might in humilitie serue one another, (as they saw him their Master to serue them) and not to set vp themselues aloft, as they began to do, and aske, which of them Ioh.13.14. should be greatest. And when the inferiour cannot obiect that the superiour doth not so himself as he requireth of the other, in a dutie common to both, it is a worthie thing.

This is to be applied to the reformation of faults, and the doing of dutie, by word or deed, either in familie or otherwise. And therefore it is a sore accusation against such as being to giue light to others, take no heede or care themselues, or very slight care, how they walke, among and in the midst of those, whom they are to giue light vnto. Parents and guides in families, beside that they doe for the most part little reproue the faults and sins of those who are vnder them, vnlesse it be for and about their owne aduantage, haue small care commonly, of their owne behauiour in their sight, but wil braule Note. and scold, contend, and raile, and liue in other ill courses among them. And it were heartily to be wished, that some who are in greater place, and whose authoritie reacheth further then priuate mens, did not commit the same faults, which they are sued vnto to punish in others. Oh how much it were to be desired that the elder and younger might ioyne and accord together in the worke of the Lord: as wee see and approue this mutuall consent and sweete harmonie in *Gedeon* and his souldiers: I say oh that the ancienter in yeeres, gifts, profession and authoritie, (whom it best becommeth and concerneth most) would incourage and hearten forward the younger sort, to Tit.2.4. heare the word, to be zealous against sinne, to be innocent, humble, dutifull, sober, companions of the good, abstainers from ill companie, and in a word to beleeue in the Lord, to cleaue to his promises, to submit themselues to his gouernment in the whole course of their life: saying to them as *Gedeon* here saith, *As ye haue seene me doe, so doe you.* Thus *Dauid* calleth vpon the people, Psal.34.11. *Come, hearken vnto me, my children, and I will teach you the feare of the Lord* by mine owne experience. For thus and thus long haue I serued him, and I repent me not, that I haue spent my life in the worke of so good a Master. Oh how the experience, confidence, cheerefulnes and courage of one aged seruant in Gods house, animates and puts life into many young beginners

and

and hearers, who (alas) though they be zealous, yet are raw and rude, ignorant and vnexpert, and know not what belongs to such a trade and profession: as how many discouragements, feares, baites, offences, prouocations to wearinesse and apostacie they are to meete with, ere their course be finished. And what a commendable thing is it, that the younger nouices will yeeld themselues to their ancients, learne by their instructions, be perswaded by their exhortations, and follow their examples (so farre as they tread in the steps of Christ) with all meeknes and teachablenes, without presidence and conceitednes? Oh if it were thus in townes and places, what an heauenly order should we see in stead of boldnes, prophanenes, and loosenes in all ages and estates? For though there be examples giuen, and followed, yet it is by such as are the diuels trumpeters, who leade others after them to inordinate courses, vncleannes, riot, lying, scorning them that be better then themselues, which indeed are liker *Abimilecks* troope, then *Gedeons*. But as for good examples, where shall we finde them? who looks to this, to liue so in the former part of his life, that he may be a president in the latter? And if some one odde man be found among an hundred, how doe the multitude of inferiours disdaine him, and winde him about their fingers? But of examples I haue also said somewhat before.

Note.

2.Cor.11.1.

Note.

We haue heard what *Gedeon* bad his men doe: now followeth what he bad them say, that was this: [*For the Lord, and Gedeon*] his meaning was, that he would haue them boldly and without feare proclaime and say one to the heartning and incouraging of another: that the victorie should bee the Lords as the author, and *Gedeons* as the instrument. Thus teaching vs, that as wee should bee examples in our liues to other, so wee should in our words exhort and perswade, as occasion shall be offered, to beleeue the promises of God before they be fulfilled, as *Gedeon* did here his souldiers, to beleeue that God would giue them the victorie. Thus did that worthie King *Iehosaphat* stirre vp and incourage his people, the men of Iudah, to beleeue the words of Gods Prophet, which had brought tidings to him of deliuerance from the Ammonites, Moabites, and them of mount Seir.

Doct. vers. 18.

2.Chro. 20.20.

And this hope wee should haue our selues, by long proofe of Gods promise keeping, that wee may thereupon resolue them (so farre as wee can preuaile with them) that there shall not a iot of all that God hath spoken, fall to the ground: but as our fathers trusted in him, and were not confounded, so neither shall they be disappointed nor ashamed, who trust in him to the end of the world. And when wee haue the like incouragement our selues from other, we should no lesse be confirmed and strengthened, that when they can say to vs, heauen and earth shall perish, but one title of Gods promise shall not faile, we may rest and be satisfied. Oh happy are the people, whom the Lord when he commeth, shall finde to haue been thus exercised.

Matth. 5.17.

THE

THE FORTIE NINTH SERMON ON THE SEVENTH AND EIGHTH CHAPTERS OF the booke of IVDGES.

Vers.12,20. NOw further are laid out, after *Gedeons* aduice to his souldiers, and the propounding of his owne example vnto them, his industrious attempt in his going forward to the Midianites campe, and what hee and his men did together in the way thither, and what successe the Lord gaue thereto. The first of these two is set downe in this 19.
Vers.19.20. and 20. verses, the last in the 21. and 22. His companie was diuided into bands, to the end that they might come vpon their enemies on euery side, and amaze the whole campe with sudden feare. Then he chose for his purpose the fittest time of the night, the middle part thereof, when the enemies being in a dead sleepe, were, with that sudden feare, the more throughly astonished. For the noise of the trumpets, with the mightie crie, made by the men, and the breaking of the pitchers, with the light appearing, did not onely astonish them, but likewise so troubled them, they being scarcely awaked out of their sleepe, that they could not conceiue what it should meane, but thought that many and great hoasts were rush-
2.King.7.6.7. ing into their campe, as the Aramites did, into whose camp the lepers came. And the Lord with all this striking them with a kinde of madnesse, they tooke their owne fellow souldiers for their enemies, and so most miserably slew one another, the Ammonites and Moabites stood vp against them of mount Seir to destroy them, though they were their fellow souldiers: as
2.Chro.20.23. we see also in the campe of the Aramites, into which the lepers came.

This kinde of astonishing the enemies by *Gedeon*, who was directed by God therein, is worthie to be noted of vs: to teach vs, what kindes of terrors and vexings of a rebellious people the Lord hath in a readines to feare them, yea and that when men thinke themselues best fensed against them,
Numb.25.8. out of feare of them, and furthest off from falling into them. *Zimri* and
Num.16.32. *Cosbi* were slaine suddenly and fearefully: *Chorah* and his companie were swallowed vp of the earth, when no likelihood could be seene thereof, till it
1.Sam.30.17. came. The men of Ziklag wallowing like beasts on the ground drunken,
Iudg 9 53. were slaine by *Dauid* when they looked not for it. *Abimilek* by a piece of
2.Sam.18.14. a milstone receiued his deadly wound, and *Absolon* hanged by the haire of his head on an oke. Thus I might goe on infinitly. God hath many waies to scourge his enemies, as he hath to deliuer and comfort his people, *There*
Esay 48.22. *is no peace to the vngodly, saith God.* Oh then how fearefull is it to be a wicked
Psalm.2.12. man? for if Gods anger be kindled but a little, how happie are all they that feare him? for if he haue a controuersie with men, and be against them, oh what terrors are euery while like to fall on them, till they be confounded

of

of them? Some will obiect, that for all this, many wicked persons walke securely, and are as merrie and void of feares, as the best of them all. I answer, first although God meetes them not with such bodily feares as here he amazed these heathens withall, yet there is that within them commonly, which euen in the middest of their merriments causeth their hearts to be heauie, and presage no good vnto them at length. This I say of such as are not hardned. And who can expresse the bitter sorrowes and checks and feares which they feele, who carrie an ill conscience about them? which pursues them both sleeping and waking, and not at Church onely, but euen in their callings, companies, feastings, pleasures, when others thinke full little of it, and themselues wish they could make truce for the while therewith, that it might then be furthest off. So that a poore Christian would not willingly change states with them, to haue their greatest glorie, except he might bee free from their troubled conscience: which is like to the hand-writing vpon the wall of that wofull *Belshazzar*. And this is their portion, euen tempest, Dan. 5. 6.
fire, snares, as the Psalmist saith, euen a sauour of hell, before they come there. As for those that haue learned how to strangle their conscience, and smother it, or who are waxen hardned: let them know, that there is no peace belonging to them, though they stop their eare from hearing of terror. And when God shall quicken, and rouze vp their conscience, woe be to them, for it shall roare vpon them as a lion, and yet God is greater. Therefore if any such shall seeke how to be freed from this horror, let them make 1. Ioh. 3. 20. 21.
their peace with God, and so their conscience shall turne to be their friend: but the rest may heare this doctrine, as *Nabal* heard *Abigails* newes, to their confusion.

It further appeareth by the effect what these fearefull meanes wrought, Vers. 21. 22.
which the holy storie setteth downe in this verse, that the whole campe was astonished, feared, cried out, and fled. In which case let no man thinke that these meanes alone, and apart from Gods work, had any great force to feare, especially to hurt the enemies: for what was there in the blowing of the trumpets, the breaking of the pitches, or in their lampes, to the getting of the victorie? But the Lord put to his hand, and helpe, whereby the enemies were daunted, and set beside themselues, or else, all that was done, had been but ridiculous. And he that made *Goliahs* head to be cut off with his owne sword, he wil still blesse the vnlikely meanes (as the world accounteth them, yea and foolish also) of our prayers, sinceritie, patience, hope and the like, to bring great things to passe, yea and faith to ouercome the world, without the which, what are all other things whatsoeuer? Still I say therefore, as I said before, blessed is the people whose God is the Lord *Iehouah*. But of this, occasion hath been offered to speake almost in euery Chapter.

In the 20. verse, in that the people of Israel in their crie and noise that they made, vttered these words [*The sword of the Lord, and of Gedeon*] therein they testifie, that God was the chiefe cause, and *Gedeon* as the instrument appointed to bring that worke to passe. Not as if they would deuide the victory betwixt God and him, (betweene whom there was no comparison) but to signifie, that as God was the chiefe and principall worker, so it pleased him to vse *Gedeon* as his instrument to effect it. The same it behooueth vs to do: ascribe we to God the glory of all the good we doe, yea and of our saluation

Doct. 2. in verse 20 that was omitted in due place.

especially, which we seeke, but know we that as Gods instruments, we are to
Phil.2.12. worke it on in feare and trembling, and to giue all our diligence, as the Apo-
2.Pet.1.10. stle exhorteth, to *make our calling and election sure*. And so in all duties of faith that we performe; acknowledge we, that we receiue all gifts and abilitie to thinke and to doe, that which is good, and our selues to be Gods workemen and labourers, vnworthy to be imployed by him, euen as we see it to bee an honour to be in a Kings seruice. And further by this, let all captious cauillers take their answer, who say, that the people who depend vpon their Ministers, make them their God. Be it knowne to all such, that as they detest such blasphemy, so yet to the shame of all such scorners, they honour them vnder God, as the instruments of their saluation, and acknowledge them, as here *Gedeons* souldiers do him, to be the hand which God putteth the sword of his spirit into, for the conquering not of mens bodies, but their soules, and the bringing into subiection the thoughts of their hearts, yea the whole
2.Cor.10.4. powers of soule and body, to the obedience of Christ. In which respect *Salomon* praies that *Gods Priests may bee clothed with saluation*. And *Paul* doubts
1 Tim.4.16. not to say vnto *Timothy, He should saue himselfe, and others*. For more particular application of this doctrine, reade verse 2. of this Chapter.

Doct. out of all these 4. verses. This victory is remembred and made mention of in the Psalme, where
Psal.83.9. it is said: *Doe to them, as vnto Midian, and as vnto Oreb and Zeeb*. Which teacheth, that this story, and so other in the bookes of canonicall Scripture, is diligently to bee remembred, that wee may haue vse of the diuers good things that are in it, that through the Scriptures wee might get knowledge,
Rom.15.4. experience, consolation and hope: as to pray as *Gedeon* did in danger and distresse, to hope, and waite for the like successe, in our seuerall necessities, which God will as surely doe and performe to vs, as he did here to his people, hauing made the like promises thereof vnto vs, as vnto them. And through the writings of the Euangelists and Apostles, wee shall meet with quotations of Scripture out of the old testament, as it were setting a second edge vpon them, and teaching the reader with what regard and obseruation he is to reade them. As our Sauiour doth in recording the history of *Lots*
Luk 17.32. wife; and in speaking of the prophesie of *Daniel* touching the pollution of the Temple by the abomination of desolation, and diuers such like places:
Matth.24.15. besides the fulfilling of the prophesies of the Messias, and other things to come to passe in the Church ere the second comming of Christ. For to this end, the holy stories are written, as well as the other books of the Scripture,
Rom.15.4. I meane for our instruction, edification and comfort. As *Dauid* mentioneth
Esay 10.26. this story, so doth *Esay*, speaking of *Zenacherib*, *God shall* (saith he) *raise vp a scourge, like that of Midian*. And so it came to passe, as he prophesied, for the whole armie of that King was slaine by God, euen as this of the Midianites.

Vers.23. Now followeth another thing mentioned in this verse, that is, when the most of them were slaine, the Israelites with *Gedeon* pursued and followed after the rest: where note his wisedome in foreseeing and preuenting danger to come. When he had scattered them, they might haue gotten strength againe afterward, and so haue troubled them as before, (as another *Iabin*
Iudg.4.2. King of Canaan arose) which he preuented. And in warre this is meet to be done against the enemies both bodily and spirituall. Satan being throwne
Matth.12.45. out, laboureth, as our Sauiour saith, to enter in againe. This is also necessarie

in

in euery calling,to be prouident to keepe away danger by wants and oppression concerning both body and soule.

It is great wisedome,to follow herein the vniust Steward,namely in prouiding for the time that should come after: and to follow the example of the fiue wise virgins,who so prouided oile for their lamps,that when the other foolish,for want therof,were shut out at the bridegroomes comming, they entred in with him to the wedding. So wee should deale surely to preuent diuel and world,and al offences,that might break out from vs through our owne corruption,and not to be so foolish, as to bring needlesse sorrow vpon our owne heads by neglecting any meanes that might remoue it. Yea and one Christian with another must be faine,and is forced to deale circumspectly,there be so many weakenesses in vs, and shifts to deceiue, lest they breake off their fellowship. Wee see daily to what perfection men haue brought their trades,and how easily they thriue, through carefull marking and remoouing the seuerall inconueniences thereof,and vsing the best prouidence,and all opportunities making for their gaine,which their predecessors knew not. But alas how raw and rude, yea what bunglers are men in the trade of all trades? who beates his braines to attaine to a gift, readinesse and dexteritie therein? Luke 16.8. Matth.25.10. Note.

Who seekes to bring the excellencie thereof into the view of the world, or vpon their owne proofe and experience to teach others, the next and directest way both of being and walking as a Christian? And why? because men are not wise to follow this trade without breakings off,and many onsets and turne-againes: they neither will search out and vse the best meanes which may make them expert,and bring in gaine,nor will learne wisedome to preuent disaduantages, annoyances, temptations, and therefore their worke goes not forward,their skill in this trade comes not to ripenesse. For behold, while they thinke they serue God commendably in some duties which they apply their mind too,there growes in them noisome lusts,vnseene,vnrepented off,and these make them new to begin, and set them so much behind hand againe, that they almost despaire of euer recouering their forwardnesse neglected.

The Beniamites we reade in the 20. of this booke, met their brethren in the field stoutly: but lo, the euill was behind them, and that they were not aware off,till the flame and smoke ascended, and then all their courage was cooled. To teach vs (if we will prosper) to make cleane worke before vs,and leaue not something vndone,through sloath, which will cost vs double and trebble afterward. And if we bee wise, let vs learne with *Gedeon* how to vse and keepe the victorie as well as how to get it: how to clense out that euill which we are prone to,as do some duties which we like; lest according to the prouerbe: He that flieth and escapeth, will returne and fight againe; whereas we might haue slaine him right downe at the first,and been past all danger. Iudges 20.40.

Furthermore,it is to be noted as commendable in *Gedeon*, that when he had gotten the victory, hee was willing that other should haue part of the glory thereof: to wit,these other tribes, *Nephtali*, *Ashur*, and *Manasse*, who yet could helpe but little,comming after *Gedeon* had gotten the victory with great danger. Which example of his, should teach vs to vse the gifts of Doct.2.

 God,

God, not so that we should seeke glory by them, but to desire that other also might exercise and haue vse of their gifts to the benefit of the Church: we of the Ministery especially should doe this; that wee may bee able to say as
Numb.11.29. *Moses* said, *Would to God that all his people could prophesie*: yea and to this end let vs rather in giuing honour, euen striue to goe before each other, yea the meanest, who may soonest and easiliest thinke themselues neglected and despised. Excellent therefore is the practise of Christ and *Iohn Baptist*, who though they were both admired by diuers sorts of people, and that in such wise, that there was carnall emulation betweene the Disciples of both; yet alway they so carried themselues, that the one honoured the other, and both fulfilled all righteousnesse.

Ioh.3.30. Yea *Iohn* in the middest of his flourishing, yet still acknowledged himselfe but the shadow, and Christ the substance; himselfe the herold, and Christ the Prince: *I must decrease* (saith he) *and Christ encrease*. Which example of his, if his successors had as well regarded, Satan had not so soone corrupted the ministery of the Church with schismes and factions, which are but the fruits of pride and arrogancy.

And if we can grow, or cause by our example and gifts, other to grow in grace, let vs not with the Disciples, contend who shall bee chiefe and greatest. But we though we haue these gifts and the like to glorifie the giuer, and to restraine and hold our selues from this vaineglory, yet wee gape for that by Satans deluding of vs (lamentable to behold) so that when wee haue not praise of men, (who should looke for that from God) if (I say) we cannot get that, we leaue off labouring and sit still: and for this very cause, some, as well in the ministery, as the people, doe part and breake off their fellowship one with another. But of this see somwhat before, in the eighth verse of this Chapter.

Vers. 24. *And Gedeon sent messengers to all mount Ephraim, saying, Come downe against the Midianites, and take before them the waters vnto Bethbarah, and Iordan. Then all the men of Ephraim gathered together, and tooke the waters vnto Bethbarah and Iordan.*

25. *And they tooke two Princes of the Midianites, Oreb and Zeeb, and slew Oreb vpon the rocke Oreb, and slew Zeeb at the winepresse of Zeeb, and pursued the Midianites, and brought the heads of Oreb and Zeeb to Gedeon beyond Iordan.*

Vers.24. IN this verse the holy story sheweth, how *Gedeon* sent to all the inhabitants of mount Ephraim to meet with the Midianites, and take vp the passages, where they went ouer the waters, euen to Bethbara or Bethabora, and Iordan. And the men of Ephraim did so. And so hee made them partakers also of the honour of the victory, as he did the other tribes. This is the summe of this verse. And to make our vse of it, it were to be wished, that we in this our age did as these did: that in all ciuil actions religion did guide vs, that where helpe is needed, and required by one of another, that it were likewise willingly and readily performed; as namely in aiding the widowes and fatherlesse, the poore, and the oppressed

And much more it were to be wished, that we were so ioyned together in the Church, that if there were any excellent and profitable matter begun,

that

that we were willing to haue other coadiutors and fellow labourers to the finishing and perfiting of the same: but wee rather oft times (which is greatly to be lamented) and our sinnes iustly deseruing the same, doe hinder one another: whereas both they ought to bee regarded, who haue a good mind to the worke of God, and doe labour in it, (though they bee not equall with some other,) euen for that which God hath inabled them, and which they are fit to doe: and also they in humility should reuerence their elders in gifts and yeeres, and be readier to learne of them, then to pearke ouer them.

Which sinne in the forwarder sort both of Ministers and people, and in the ancienter and younger sort of both, being suffered to grow for want of loue, so that the one doth not his dutie toward the other, hath caused the Lord seuerely to punish it in both, that being diuided, they are thereby feebled, and the good which they did is hindred and crossed; and not only so, but also that is verified which Saint *Paul* writeth to the Galathians, that *one* Galat.5.15.
biting and deuouring another, they be consumed one of another, at least, by a third sort, but yet through their fault and procuring. But of this I haue spoken in the first chapter.

Ephraim tooke two Princes of Midian, *Oreb* and *Zeeb*: whose punish- Vers.25.
ment by the iust iudgement of God was agreeable to their sinne. The one, namely *Oreb*, was slaine on a rocke and mountaine, called by the same name, *Oreb*: where they had constrained the people of God to hide themselues, and where they had sought them to kill them. The other, that is, *Zeeb*, was slaine at the threshing place or winepresse called *Zeeb*: for those places they spoiled of their victuals and famished them. Where it is manifest, that God forgetteth not, neither winketh at the cruelty of his enemies, but in due time and place will pay them home, so that all that will, may see, that God hath not left them vnrecompenced.

And that either with the same punishment as he did *Adonibezek*, or at the same time, as he did *Iudas*, who betraying his master to death, died first himselfe: or as heere he did to *Oreb* and *Zeeb*, euen in the same place where they did the mischiefe: and as among vs the wilfull murtherers suffer, and are made spectacles by hanging in chaines, to all that passe by, neere the place where they committed the murthers: or if none of these waies hee punish them, yet some other such, that may be as a signe to all, that God will be reuenged on such as they be. For why, as the blood of *Abell*, so doth theirs Gen.4.10.
cry for vengeance: woe therefore to bloody persecutors, and cruell persons, for God and their sinne shall find them out. Therefore let them know this that fall into the hands of such, lest they should bee discouraged. And lest we should thinke that these Princes did but fight for themselues against the Israelites, as in warre men doe, reade of their malice and cruelty, in the Psal.83.9.
Psalme 83. But for Gods iust punishing of his enemies, according to their 11.12.
sin, I haue said enough in chapter 1. of this booke.

THE FIFTIETH SERMON ON THE EIGHTH CHAPTER OF THE BOOKE OF IVDGES.

Verſ. 1. *Then the men of Ephraim ſaid vnto him: why haſt thou ſerued vs thus? that thou calledſt vs not when thou wenteſt to fight with the Midianites: and they chode with him ſharpely.*

2. *To whom he ſaid: what haue I now done, in compariſon of you? Is not the gleaning of grapes of Ephraim better then the vintage of Abiezer?*

3. *God hath deliuered into your hands the Princes of Midian, Oreb and Zeeb: and what was I able to doe in compariſon of you? and when he had thus ſpoken their ſpirits abated towards him.*

The ſumme of the chap. and parts 3.

AFter the admirable victory that God gaue to *Gedeon*, as hath been largely ſhewed in the former Chapter, now in this followeth the purſuit of the reſt of the Midianites by *Gedeon*; but firſt another thing by occaſion of that victory, is heere ſet downe; and that is, the Ephraemites quarrelling with him. The ſumme and parts of this Chapter (to ioyne them together as they may well and conueniently be) are theſe: The firſt is, the contention of the Ephramites with *Gedeon*, for not calling them to the warre, to verſe 4. The ſecond point in this Chapter is, that the men of Succoth and Penuel denied victuall to *Gedeon* when hee purſued and followed after the reſt of the enemies, and their puniſhment, together with the putting to death of the two Princes of the Midianites, *Zeba* and *Zalmunna*, to the 22. verſ. The third containeth certaine perticulers concerning *Gedeon*, as the offering of the kingdome to him and his ſonnes by the Iſraelites, and his refuſing it: and of *Gedeons* Ephod, and the danger that came thereby: whereto is to be added the ſinne of Iſrael, to the end of the chapter.

The firſt part of the Chapter.

The ſumme of the 3. firſt verſes.

TO begin with the firſt part, it is ſaid, that the men of Ephraim contended ſore with *Gedeon*, and fell out with him, for that he called them not to the battell againſt the Midianites, as appeareth in the firſt verſe: whereto the milde anſwere of *Gedeon* is to bee marked, which is ſet downe in the ſecond verſe. And thirdly, how they were appeaſed by it, as wee reade in the third. Of theſe let vs heare more perticularly as they lie in order.

Verſ. 1. the vnfolding of it.

And heere firſt, ſome man might thinke it an vnſeaſonable accident that befell *Gedeon* euen in the chiefe ſpring of his glory; I meane, that in the very necke of the victory ſhould come vpon him ſuch a croſſe blow, as to turne the ſolemnity and honour of his great acts, in ſubduing the Midianites into reproch

reproch and abasement. But the most wise God who best knoweth how to keepe his owne children in compasse, and seeth what corruption they carry about them, by meanes whereof they cannot beare any great blessing, or prosperity, without swelling, and pride; he (I say) doth commonly so dispose of them, that with rare and speciall liftings vs, and heightenings of them, either in grace, wealth, honour, and successe, or the like, hee matcheth and mixeth some great coolings and buffetings of them, to keep them from falling dangerously, in so slippery a place as they stand in. Of *Gedeon* we cannot certainly say any thing to his iust reproofe in any grosse manner, but of great infirmities of his wee haue heard; and therefore doubtlesse hee being a man) hee had that in him which might haue puffed him vp vpon so great successe, if God had not by this great and vnwelcome crosse, preuented it. So *Iphta* comming fresh from a great conquest, was suddenly quailed by his onely daughter. And *Iob* in the middest of his flourishing and prosperous estate, heares all at once, of his children and substance destroyed and spoiled. Likewise *Dauid* had few victories, but the Lord sent him a cooler vpon them, the rebellion of *Absolon*, the cursing of *Shemei*, the insurrection of *Sheba*, the death of *Ammon*, the slaughter of *Absolon*; which (doubtlesse) were enough to purge out any superfluous humour which might rise vp in him, and so to keepe him sober, temperate, and within holy compasse. It is not so strange that the Lord should thus physicke his seruants, being already surfeted with excessiue and sinfull abuse of their prosperity: but it is his great mercy that he should so diet them with these potions, that they may preuent surfeting. The reason is, because first it is the wisedome of the same Physitian to giue preseruatiues, as well as purgations. And againe, sinne is easilier kept out from entring, then thrust out of doores being once gotten in: which the Lord foreseeing, rather chooseth with a little hardship to the patient, then by violent and extreame courses, to preuent matter of disease rather then to heale the disease. And the truth is, it is easier for a man to bee dieted then purged: I meane to beare an affliction which commeth before the spirit and conscience is wounded by a sinne, then which followeth sin, as the deserued punishment of it. But for the point in hand, let vs by this first learne, what a leaud nature there is in vs, that wee cannot haue a little health and welfare, but presently we distemper our selues, so that wee must be faine to be physickt, lest wee should endanger our life: I meane, wee can enioy no good blessing, but we forget our selues, and cause the Lord to allay the sweetnesse of it with some bitternesse, except he will suffer vs to be turned quite ouer with it. Againe, when we enioy any blessing, let vs not measure the same by the pleasure and content which it giues our nature, (for euen in that is a sting which will secretly hurt vs) but by the sober, humble, and thankfull affection wherewith wee imbrace the blessing. And let vs know that then onely we enioy it in kind, and entier, otherwise by halues, and scarce that. And when we see that God sauceth our dainties with soure hearbs, let vs be thankfull to him, and say, Lord I had else fed too much of this dish, till I had ouerlaid my stomacke, euen as children, who finding hony, eate too much of it; therefore blessed be thy name, who suffered me not to be sicke of it, rather then if thou shouldest let me alone, then I should bee prouoked to vomiting, which were worse. And this bee noted of the Lords

Note.

Doct. out of vers. 1.

Iudg. 11. 35.

Note.

Note.

ordering the action of these Ephramites, for *Gedeons* good.

The faults of the Ephramites in this first verse, and first their vnthankfulnes. Now yet these Ephramites shew many foule faults in this action of contending with their gouernour and deliuerer of them, as vnthankfulnes, expostulating with him without a cause & then their dissimulation, who faine themselues to haue been willing to haue gone to warre with him, and yet would not, when they might haue done: and when did they this? euen when they saw the danger of the warre to bee past and ouer, and that now honour was giuen to *Gedeon* for that which he had done: whereas they had been as ready (if hee had lost the victory) to haue (much more) cast that in his teeth.

Doct. 2. vers. 1. To prosecute these a little more particularly: their vnthankfulnesse first was great, and the iniurie which hee sustained thereby, who ought to haue been much honoured of them for his industry and labour, and highly accounted off by them for the same: but if so be their vnthankfulnesse was so great towards him in this, what manner of behauiour (thinke wee) would they haue vsed if they had sustained any wrong or violence at his hands, who deale thus vndutifully, nay rudely, and rebelliously with them, and yet hauing receiued so great a deliuerance by his meanes? and so picking matter of quarrell out of a good turne and benefit? But as we may note the vnthankfulnesse of men when yet they haue iust cause to shew the contrary duty, (as may be seene in many, and namely in *Absolon* to his father, whom when hee had deliuered from death iustly deserued, hee sought his fathers life, and to get away his kingdome also from him:) so wee may by this vnkind recompence they gaue to *Gedeon* for the famous act that hee wrought for their ease and peace; wee, I say, who shall gratifie men, may learne our duty thereby, and that is this, that we were not best, neither ought wee to looke for our reward and commendation for well doing any manner of way from men, but to rest in this, that God knoweth our workes, and it is e-
Reuel. 2. 2. nough, that we are sure, that from him we shall receiue our reward: accor-
1. Cor. 15. 58. ding to the words of the Apostle, Be ye stedfast (my beloued brethren) and vnmoueable, alwaies abounding in the worke of the Lord, for as much as ye know that your labour is not in vaine in the Lord.

But as for men, they oft times disgrace that which is well done of vs, and
1. Sam. 17. 28. reuile, yea and hate vs for it: as *Eliab* did *Dauid*, for shewing himselfe forward against Gods enemies the Philistims, and by name their great champion *Goliah*, for the which hee ought to haue been encouraged rather, and highly commended of him. So *Ioseph*, who had preserued the land of Egypt both for the time of the famine, and long afterwards: yet of that King *Pha-*
Exod. 1. 8. *raoh*, who rose vp in the land some yeeres after; of him, I say, *Ioseph* was not knowne nor regarded: for so the text saith, *There came another Pharaoh, who knew not Ioseph*, though his welfare arose by and from him vnder God, as wel as his predecessors that liued before him did. But especially this was verifi-
Luk. 2. 32. ed in our Sauiour Christ, who being the light of the Gentiles, and the glory of his people Israel, was for the vnthankfulnesse of the people, and their spitefull dealing against him, was faine, I say, to answere them thus: *Many*
Ioh. 10. 32. *good workes haue I done among you, for which of them doe you stone me?* In Heathen stories we reade of the strange ingratitude of people to their victorious gouernours, especially Grecian and Romane: one of whom being dead, had

had this vpbraiding epitaph engrauen, *O vnthankfull countrey, thou shalt not so much as haue the honour of my bones.* But that men liuing in the Church should shew such brutish ingratitude, who should beleeue it that sees it not? *Moses*, the conducter of the people out of Egypt, was neuer quiet from the conspiracy and murmurings of them against him. The Prophets and Apo- Matth.23.37.
stles for their painfull prophesyings and trauels in preaching, what reward found they? So these Ephramites, how recompenced they *Gedeon* for his labour and paines? And the other Israelites also, looke in the end of his Iudg 8.35.
story. And so, if the worthy seruants of Christ in the magistracy and ministery, find the like greetings, courtesie, thankfulnesse, at their hands who should be their best fauourers and encouragers against their aduersaries, yea if they find the people whom they gouerne and teach. and vpon whom they bestow their liues and strength (as the candle that giueth light till it die and goe out,) to requite them with small reuerence, lesse countenance Note.
or maintenance, and least of all with any fruit in true piety of their godly care and labour, in season, and out of season bestowed among them: what vse shall they make hereof? Shall they desist from their good beginnings, and giue them ouer to such as may bee like to teach them by fearing them, who would not learne it by loue, to make more account of them? No: but first let them looke vp to God, and acknowledge his iustice in so trying them, and punishing some sinne in them; and then answere themselues as the Prophet *Esay: I haue laboured in vaine* (to manward) *but my reward is with* Esa.40.10. 62.11.
God: and therfore I must not forsake my standing, nor leaue my calling, but hold out with courage and constancie vnto the end, but more fully of this in the story of *Iephta.*

Now then the vse of this is, and so let vs take it, that we bee not discouraged from conscience and constancy in the seruice of God for the discourtesies, and ill dealing of men, for of God we are to looke for our reward. And yet I must say, that without especiall grace, it is hard to doe thus, and to rest contented with this, that God is a plentifull rewarder of all that seeke, and come to him; and withall to beare the indignities that are offered vs of men. Secondly seeing the world dealeth thus vnkindly with Gods seruants, Heb.2.6.
let their brethren that feare God, bee encouragers and comforters of them, that they may hold on in their good course: for they are but men, and therfore they haue need of encouragement, and their weakenesse requireth that they should bee so dealt with. And let all such as liue in their places of Ministers or professors with any freedome this way, much more with a Note.
good liking and mutuall consent or encouragement, bee highly thankfull to God for such vnwonted fauours, and friendly dealings of men with them, as knowing that it is not the portion which the most in the world find or enioy, but a peculiar indulgence and fauour from God, which ought to stirre vp in them astonishment at Gods kindnesse to them therein, and not pride aud insolencie. And for the sin I now speake of, let vs count this vnthankfulnesse, and the taking in ill part the good actions of Gods people, let vs (I say) count it for a bitter fruit of a naughty, proud, and cancred heart, wheresoeuer wee meete with it or behold it, and thereafter let them thinke of themselues, who shew and offer it.

A 2. fault of the Ephramites, to wit, enuie.

Now further note another of the faults of these Ephramites against *Gedeon:*

deon: and that is,that they enuied him for the honour he got by the victory. Whereby though they sustained no hurt, neither were the worse but the better, yet they could not beare it, that *Gedeon* should haue the glory of it: where we may see a foule property of enuie,and what it is. It is a greefe and sadnesse for the prosperity of other: and namely,of such as bee our equals. For the poore man enuieth not the King; hee may bee grieued that he himselfe wanteth such good things as the King hath,but that is not enuie. And by this we may note the difference betweene hatred and malice on the one side,and this enuie on the other: to this end, as wee haue heard of the one, so we may in a word of the other. Hatred therefore is a greefe conceiued against one for some cause,at least,as we thinke; as *Ahab* hated *Micaiah*, because hee did not prophesie good to him, but euill, as he tooke it, and the same appeareth also by the contrary, out of these words in holy Scripture: *They hated me without a cause.*

Enuie,what?

1.King.22.8.

And when I say,enuie is a greefe at our equals for any eminency, or prosperity that they haue aboue vs; I meane such as are in kindred,estate,yeeres, dignity,or in gifts like vs. And the cause of this enuie is not for that wee are troubled as though any hurt or danger were comming towards vs, from them whom we enuie,(for that is another affection, to wit, feare,) but for that through a cankred stomacke we cannot beare it, that such an one as is no better then our selues,should bee lifted vp so high, and commended so farre aboue vs. And is not this a cursed mind in vs,that wee cannot bee willing that another should fare well, we being neuer the worse,and that wee should haue an euill eye at that,for the which we should reioyce? for so *Mary* and *Elizabeth* did mutually reioyce one for the welfare and blessing of God to the other.

Note.

Luk.1.41.42.

And so much the more detestable is this affection, that whereas some other,being partly naturall,nay bee taken in the good part,this is euer euill: for it is a meere corruption,and contrary to loue,for loue enuieth not: and *Paul* more plainely forbiddeth it to the Galathians,where hee also sheweth the cause of it; namely, [*Desire of vaine-glory.*] For so he saith; be not desirous of vaine glory,prouoking one another,enuying one another. Which heere is to be seene in the Ephramites,who desiring the glory of the victory themselues,did enuie *Gedeon* for it. This affection sheweth it selfe in all such things,as we desire to excell in: yea in the best, euen the gifts of the spirit, for therein,we would haue none to be in account aboue vs: as appeareth in them that preached Christ of enuie: and him that repined at his fellow, for that comming at the eleuenth houre, hee had his pennie as well as himselfe.

1.Cor.13 4.

Galat.5.last.

Philip.1.15.

Matth.20.12.

Now though we are not the worse for the prosperity of other, neither doth it diminish any thing from the good of our estate; yet the enuious man thinketh,that the gifts that are in himselfe are darkened and blemished thereby, vnlesse he haue especial grace to abate and mortifie such thoughts. Therefore to aggrauate this sinne,know we,that as the enuious is sad by the prosperity of another, so(which is worse) he is made ioyfull by his disgrace and abasement: as the Pharisies were, in and for the crucifying of our Sauiour,and *Iosephs* brethren,when they had sold him. Yea so cursed an humor is enuie, and so opposite to loue, that whereas hee who loues vnfainedly would

would part euen with the most precious iewell for the sake of that which it loueth: the enuious person would willingly pull out one of his owne eyes, vpon condition he might lose both his, at whom he grudgeth. So that not vnfitly *Pauls* speech of fornication may be applied to enuie: *Other sinnes are without a man:* but the enuious sins against his owne body, and the health and prosperitie thereof: God iustly plaguing it in the kinde, in that whiles it pines at the eminencie of another, it reflecteth and beateth backe the hurt vpon it selfe, and feedeth vpon the most precious spirits of the soule and life, and consumeth them: seldome doing any harme to the other, while it fretteth out the very heart blood and bowels of it selfe. This enuie is remedied by shaming our selues for that wee cannot abide that our brethren should haue and doe good with Gods gifts to other: considering also that thereby we hinder Gods glorie. Also we shall loosen the rootes of this enuie, if we thinke meanely of our selues, and that God is onely wise, who denieth for iust cause, that vnto vs, wherewith he blesseth others. And thirdly, this shall helpe to weaken it, if wee consider that God hath rather deserued infinite thankes of vs, for granting vs other blessings, which those (perhaps) may want, whom in other respects wee enuie, (for it is his great mercie that wee be not consumed) the one wee will not see, the other wee behold too much. Whereas our eye seeth not the worse, because anothers seeth better: how much lesse if in another kinde we see as well? Doth the foote enuie the eye because it seeth, or the eye the foote because it goeth? But of the contrarie vertue I spake before twice, in *Gedeons* souldiers, and *Gedeons* communicating with *Nephtali* and *Ephraim* the victorie. *Lam.3.22.*

A third sinne in them, the sin of their fathers. *Doct.4.*

And because I now speake of the Ephramites, I thinke it not amisse to adde this of them, that their father *Ephraim* the younger being preferred by *Iacob* before the elder brother *Manasse*, the stocke and offspring of them exalted themselues since from age to age, and are noted for it oft times in the historie of the old Testament. As in *Iosuah* we reade: they among other, were discontented with their portion. So in the twelfth of this booke, the posteritie of them contended with *Iphta* for not calling them with him to battell against the Ammonites after he had ouercome them: euen as these Ephramites did here with *Gedeon*. So *Esau* himselfe deadly hating his brother, deriued this sinne to his posteritie the Edomites, so *Ahab* did Idolatrie to the generations that came after him.

And hereby we may learne, what force some blemishes and corruptions in a stocke or kindred haue to infect almost the whole posteritie: God iustly thus punishing the sinnes of the fathers vpon the children to many generations, punishing (I say) sinne with sinne. As for example, if a kindred bee proud, haughty, stomackful, boasters, giuen to adultery, hollownes of heart, flatterie, lying, mocking, stealing; the rest of the same stock, that are not guided by grace, are for the most part, such. Euen as bodily diseases runne in the blood to the posteritie. And as wee see that a noble stocke stained with treason, may easiler be restored in blood ciuilly by the indulgence of the Prince, then reformed naturally and reduced to loyaltie and fidelitie: so the truth is, the most forcible meane of all outward meanes is scarce able to expell this teint: onely grace can doe it: although euen grace it selfe often times can scarce roote it out so, but that some sprigs or other of the old stock will

will appeare, when it is grafted in another stocke.

Their fourth sin, slightnes and subtiltie. *Doct.5.* And yet one thing more note in these Ephramites, namely, the slights, subtilties, doublenes and hollownes that lie hidden in mens hearts, till they haue occasion to shew them, or grace to repent of them. These would now seeme to haue had great iniurie that they were not called to the battell, whereas it was their owne sin that they went not, for they did forbeare for feare of danger, & were willing to stand by (as it were) lying in the winde to waite for the issue. So that if *Gedeon* and their brethren the Israelites that ioyned with him, had lost the day, then all the blame should haue bin laid vpon them by these Ephramites: but now they had got the victorie by Gods direction and blessing, they complaine on the other side, that they had iniurie thēselues, for that they were not (as they said) bidden to helpe in the battell.

Wherein wee may behold deepe subtiltie and hypocrisie, and how farre all such are from simplicitie and plaine dealing, that according to the prouerbe, howsoeuer the world goe, they will saue one, and howsoeuer it fall out, they will prouide for themselues. Such a one was the harlot that pleaded before *Salomon* against her fellow: and they in the twelfth of this book, where *Iphta* being set vpon by the Ammonites, he sought aide at the hands of the men of Ephraim, and they would not help him: and afterward, when he fighting against the Ammonites preuailed ouer them, the Ephramites came to make warre with him, because he called them not to goe with him against them. A sinne now adaies in common practise, namely in bargaines, where gaine is not so certaine, there they play on both hands cunningly: for they will so couenant in generall and doubtfull manner, that if it hit and fall out well, it shal be a bargaine, and they will be readie to challenge and make claime of it, how slightly soeuer the couenant was made: but if it fall out ill, and against them, then they picke a quarrell, and say, they meant not so as the other taketh it.

1.King.3 22. Iudg.12.1,2.

And therefore such will not make their bargaines plaine, nor their couenants sure and certaine, but slightly conclude, as though they agreed in one; and depart one from another, breaking off with such like words: (we shall agree) vpon which vncertaine termes, let no man that loueth his peace, buy, sell, or deale (as this world goeth) except hee be willing to stand to the hardest, and to take all measure that shall be offered him, willingly. In partnership also, there are many secret and subtill deceiuings one of another, when yet all good shewes of equitie shall be seene, and it selfe to the full pretended.

Note.

Like vnto these are all such as promise great friendship to a man, but if they perceiue their betters brooke not the person, but frowne vpon them that shew any kindnesse to him, then they must, in a dishonest manner, finde some fault with him also, and alleage: that they cannot therefore shew him the kindnes, nor doe that for him, that they had promised. Is this to prouide things honest before men? Is not such dealing apparent dishonestie? So in aduersitie and disgrace, right good men shall be iustled to the wall, who yet if they be againe restored to their former estate, and accounted of, and in fauour with their betters, they shall be sought vnto and regarded, as *Iphta* was. In all these and the like, there is this dissembling to be seene, which was in these Ephramites: a manner of dealing contrarie to simplicitie and plainnesse

nesse,and from good Christians, as a maine blemish, nay as a staine, vtterly to be remoued and abandoned. And this is bad enough euen in ciuill dealings; but when it appeares in matter of religion,farre worse,and by infinite degrees to be detested,whether it be shewed toward God or men.I meane, when as in a subtill & politique manner, (not of feare and frailtie, for then it is not so grosse, though euill) men will abstaine, and conceale their affection to the Gospell, till they see whether the time bee like to fauour or frowne vpon them: in the meane while carrying such a darke and ambiguous countenance, that no man can tell what to make of them. And yet he that cannot carrie the matter thus, but plainly bewray his opinion and iudgement,is counted a foole,and shiftlesse person: as indeed hee is to the world-ward, if there were nothing else to be regarded. It is as possible to make a true cognizance for these temporizers,as a coate for the Moone: for they serue their belly,their ambition, their purse,and as these leade them,so they follow: God they serue none,for their religion is onely a stalking horse for them, to play their part the more cunningly till their turne be serued. The same I say of the committing this sin toward men: what is more odious in a man,then when he shall promise,and pretend all loue and faithfulnes to his neighbour, and yet meane and intend no such thing, but practise the contrarie. Note.

Now *Gedeons* milde answere followes to be considered which he maketh to this quarrell and expostulating of the Ephramites with him: who if hee had answered their foolishnes with the like,and had giuen them as good as they brought, what a broile (thinke we) would there haue been betweene them? But in that hee did not defend his doing by answering that hee was strong enough of himselfe, and had no neede of their helpe, which had been like to prouoke them the more against him,neither commended his owne labour, care, and industrie, which they could not willingly haue heard, neither yet did vnuizer them, by telling them, that they quarrelled without a cause against him,who had sought their helpe, nor any way exasperated them; but contrariwise,yeelded as much to them as with truth and good conscience hee might: neither did hee interpret their contentious words to come of bitter enuie, as they gaue him cause, but rather hee hath left a most commendable example of a meeke and patient seruant of God, and respects all these of honest and lawfull emulation; it teacheth right worthie matter and doctrine vnto vs. Verse 2.

Namely, how wee should deale with such as are insolent, contentious, fierie, and such as thinke, though neuer so vntruly, that they haue wrong at our hands. And that is,that in such cases we must be well staied: & see,that we giue men their ful due,to wit,not to crosse,prouoke,and exasperate thē, but rather to seeme not to see the roote of bitternes that breaketh out of them,but to containe our selues till a fitter time,(seeing they are not then in case to be told of it) and we are to make the best of euery thing, asswaging them with gentle answers, especially if we be but their equals or inferiours, and in one word,not to answere a foole according to his foolishnes, that is, to giue as ill measure as he bringeth; lest wee be like him,but to remember that which we are taught in another place of the Prouerbs,namely, that it is a mans glorie to cease from strife, and to consider and alwaies bearing this Doct. Prou. 26. 2.

Prou.16.32. in minde, that he is better that can rule his owne heart, then he that subdueth a citie.

For except we thus giue place to such, many euils are like to follow, and fall out against vs, in Church and Common-wealth, in familie, and in the course of our life, which yet hereby may, and will (no doubt) for the most part, bee auoided, or at leastwise bee smaller and fewer. Therefore let the yonger sort herein learne to yeeld to their elders, and the inferiours to their betters, though they deale not with them as they ought and should, seeing wee see here that *Gedeon* and afterward *Iphta* being superiours, did forbeare to deale with their inferiours, as they might haue done, and were iustly prouoked to doe. Yea, and let one learne and take out this lesson toward another, after the manner that I haue set downe, as husbands, wiues, masters, ser-
Heb.12.14. uants, and other, that peace with holinesse may be preserued among them. And yet who is he that sheweth foorth this meeknesse and wisedome? But (as is to bee seene in the common iarrings and quarrels of men) the most count it their glorie (and boast of it afterward) when their words bee fierce and more stinging then their fellowes, and come out of a furnace seuen times hotter then his? What (saith he) did he thinke I would turne my face for him, or be put downe with words? No, I trow I gaue him the full measure that hee brought, yea tenne for one, I spared him not awhit. Loe, how fooles fome out the froth of their owne shame. Whereas *Salomon* shewes
Prou.19.22. them their faces in a glasse who doe so, when he saith: *An angrie man stirs vp strife, and multiplieth transgression*, Prou.29. It were indeed an honour for a man to depart, and say, I see he was not in frame to be answered with angrie words, I therefore durst not striue to outshoote the diuell (as it were) in his owne bow. That which hee thinkes becommeth him, I count it my reproch, who professe to fight against my corrupt nature. Therefore let the dead burie the dead, I meane, they that be fit for nothing else, let them giue taunt for taunt, and scorne for scorne, (they are free from righteousnesse, and bondmen to their owne lusts) but I haue learned rather to repay good for euill, then euill. But yet this is not so to be taken, as though in all things we ought to yeeld to froward and peeuish persons, but in our owne priuate cases onely, and when we lawfully may, but in no cases or matters that are contrarie to Gods will, or preiuditiall to his honour. As for example, if these Ephramites would haue set vp *Baals* altar againe, it had in no sort been tollerable that *Gedeon* should haue borne it at their hands, much lesse haue yeelded to them, or we in any such thing. And this be noted by his answer.
Galat.2.11. A worthie example whereof wee haue in *Paul*, who resisted *Peter* and gaue him no place in the point of collusion with the Iewes.

Vers.3. Now followeth the fruite of that his meeke and milde answere vnto them, to wit, that their anger was thereby alaied, which agreeth well with that of *Salomon* in the Prouerbs: *A milde answere putteth away anger*: and
Prou.15.1. and 25. againe, *A meeke tongue breaketh bands*. The second blow makes the fray, as the prouerbe saith. The reason thereof is double: First, because wrath wanteth matter to worke vpon, if it be not opposed. Secondly, meeknesse shameth anger, euen as humilitie makes pride to hang downe the head. And he must be some odde man for rage and fiercenes, who is otherwise. Thus *Dauid* by *Abigails* mildnes, was staied from the bloodie attempt which *Nabals*

bals boysterous roughnes prouoked him vnto. Such a grace is this meeknes and mildnes, that Christ pronounceth them blessed that haue them. He wils vs to learne of him to be meeke: who, as the lambe before the shearer, so opened hee not his mouth. Thereby *Abraham* preuailed with *Lot*: and *Moses* so excelled in this vertue, that he was said to be the meekest man vpon earth. Contraries are cured by contraries, as wee know, and Physitians cure not hot agues by inflaming, but by asswaging: the skilfull Fencer doth scape many a blow, and foile his aduersarie by declining and giuing backe, and not by opposing his body or weapon vnto it. Cannon shot batters downe castles and walls, which yeeld not: but rebound from the soft packe of wooll, that giues place and resists not. The lightning passeth by slight and slender obiects, but consumes and deuoures the solid and well compact substances.

Matth.5.5. Matth.11.29. Philip 2.7. Actes 8.32. Numb.12.3. Note.

And so all that haue experience may see, what fruite wee might reape of this yeelding, and what a good name and report (which is better then siluer) it would bring to vs, as by the scripture now cited, appeares, beside many other worthie fruites, if we did regard to practise it. Yea doubtlesse, and by this meanes wee might euen open the mouth of our hottest aduersarie, (when his heate is ouer) to commend vs, and confesse his owne folly, and our great wisedom, in stopping much sinne thereby, and so he might learne meeknes of vs, as *Dauid* blessed *Abigaile*. But now meane and inferiour persons will not stoope an inch, no not to that equanimitie, wherewith great and worthie personages haue been furnished. The wife oft times shall bee found iustly conuicted of the crontrary fault of shrewishnes and snappishnes: the seruant stout and sturdie will giue no place to his master, few will learne this meeknes. Which causeth them to finde the like that they offer to other: euen rough, currish, and vnkinde dealing, which filleth the world with contention and vnquietnes. Whereto I grant there are many prouocations, but we must obey the Lord in this, that wee should shew all meeknes vnto all men. But some will say, That it booteth them not to vse meeknes either in words or deedes toward such as are vnreasonable persons, who the gentlier they be entreated, the more they play vpon the aduantage, and insult ouer others: yea the yeelding to their furie, is the incencing of them, and addeth oile to the flame. I answere: Roughnes towards such bad and base natures is more meete, then kindnes: so a man keepe his measure, and vnder colour of resisting sin in another, disobey not God. Thus *Elisha* willeth the elders to answere *Iehorams* seruant. But if the persons be such as we cannot safely so controll (though lawfully) let vs say with that good Prophet: *The Lord see it and iudge, and the Lord rebuke them.* Assure we our selues, God hath waies enow to hamper and tame such wolues and tygers. *Iulian* vsed to scoffe at the Christians thus, *Oh your Master Iesus of Galilie bids you turne the other cheeke to him that smites you, &c.* but God made him yeeld, and say: *Thou art too hard for me, and hast gotten the vpper hand, O thou Galilean.* And what was the end of him who pluckt his fellow by the throte, and would not heare his meeke plea? Such is the end of all rough, boisterous, and proud spirits. But so much shall suffice for this time.

Prou.15.1. 1.Sam.25.32. Tit.3.2. *Obiect.* *Answ.* 2.King.6.32. Matth.18.28.

THE FIFTIE ONE SERMON ON THE EIGHTH CHAPTER OF THE BOOKE OF IVDGES.

The ſecond part of the Chapter.

Verſ. 4. *And Gedeon came to Iordan to paſſe ouer, hee and the three hundred men that were with him wearie, yet purſuing them.*

5. *And he ſaid to the men of Succoth: Giue I pray you morſels of bread vnto the people that follow mee (for they be wearie) that I may follow after Zebah and Zalmunna Kings of Midian.*

6. *And the Princes of Succoth ſaid: Are the hands of Zebah and Zalmunna, now in thine hands, that we ſhould giue bread vnto thine army?*

7. *Gedeon then ſaid: Therefore when the Lord hath deliuered Zebah and Zalmunna into mine hand, I will teare your fleſh with thornes of the wilderneſſe, and with briers.*

8. *And he went vp from thence to Penuel, and ſpake vnto them likewiſe, and the men of Penuel anſwered him, as the men of Succoth anſwered.*

9. *And he ſaid alſo to the men of Pennuel, when I come againe in peace, I will break downe this tower.*

10. *Now Zebah and Zalmunna were in Karkor, and their hoſts with them, about fifteene thouſand, all that were left of all the hoſts of them of the Eaſt: for there were ſlaine an hundred and twenty thouſand men that drew ſwords.*

11. *And Gedeon went through them that dwelt in Tabernacles on the Eaſt ſide of Nobah and Iogbehah, and ſmote the hoſt; for the hoſt was careleſſe.*

12. *And when Zebah and Zalmunna fled, hee followed after them, and tooke the two Kings of Midian, Zebah and Zalmunna, and diſcomfited all the hoſt.*

13. *So Gedeon the ſonne of Ioaſh returned from battell, the ſunne being yet hie.*

The ſenſe to verſ. 8.

IN this ſecond part of the Chapter, the holy ſtory, (after the former digreſſion of the Ephramites contending with *Gedeon*) proceedeth orderly to ſet downe the end of the battell what it was, namely this: that when the Midianites and they of the Eaſt, had ſlaine one another, the reſt that remained fled away, that is, fifteene thouſand men: and *Gedeon* purſued them ouer Iordan. And his three hundred men being wearie and faint, hauing laboured all night, he comming to Succoth, the city of Succoth, I meane which was in the tribe of Gad, (for there was another place called Succoth in the deſert, mentioned in the *6.* of Numbers,) and of them hee asked ſomewhat to refreſh his ſouldiers. The men of Succoth who ſhould haue helped, and gone with him to purſue the Midianites, being Iſraelites and neighbours, moſt vnkindly

vnkindly denied to giue them their brethren so much as bread, but answered *Gedeon* contemptuously. For the which cause hee threatned them, when he should returne with the victory, which hee nothing doubted of, (and so he tels them) to deale with them thereafter, euen to teare their flesh with the briers of the wildernesse.

Heere in that *Gedeon* followed after these fifteene thousand of the Midianites that escaped, when the greatest number of them were slaine already, he shewed his wisdome and godly care that he had in preuenting euill and danger, that might haue come vpon the people afterward. For those fifteen thousand, if they had been suffered to runne away without his pursuing of them, they might, and (no doubt) would haue renued their power, and haue come against them againe afresh, which yet now *Gedeon* wisely preuented. Which teacheth vs a singular good lesson, that when wee haue well discharged a dutie enioyned vs, as *Gedeon* had done; yet that this is not all; but we ought to labour to hold that which we haue receiued, and wisely as we may, to preuent whatsoeuer might stand vp in our way to frustrate the same, (and so cause vs to lose all our former labour, and the fruit of our hope:) euen as *Gedeon* did heere in pursuing them that were fled of the Midianites. Doct. vers. 4.

The instances wherein this might bee laid out, are innumerable: I will onely alleage two or there briefly. As if a man should enter league of sound friendship with another neuer so strongly and entirely, and in most solemne manner, (as *Dauid* and *Ionathan* did betwixt themselues) whereby one doth repose himselfe and rest vpon the other: yet if they do not renue their couenant of loue oftentimes, as they two did, and confirme and strengthen it, against all that might annoy or breake it off, there wil fal out so many occasions as will weaken, yea and make it vtterly void. Also such reports will be carried to and fro betwixt them, through absence one from another, and such strangenesse will arise thereby, but especially such conceits, tetchines, taking things in ill part, and rash iudgings: that the former kindnesse will be forgotten, and the league which was so soundly made, as if it had neuer been, will be broken off. And let this which I say bee vnderstood of the couenant that is made in marriage it selfe, so farre as these things now mentioned, may fall out therein; so that testimonies of true loue mutually declared, euen betwixt couples, had need to be daily shewed in stead of renuing of their couenant, or else their loue will fall to the ground. 1. Sam. 18. 3.

Also to passe to another instance, if a man (yea let him bee a good man) entring into the affaires of this world, and disliking the bad courses which are taken by men commonly to get wealth, doe purpose against them all, and that heartily, and dislike the same, yet let him not look daily to performe that which he hath purposed, and stand firme therein, let him not watch and pray against all prouocations to the contrary, and disgrace in his owne eyes all vnlawfull courses and dealings which may bring in commodity, and contemne filthie gaine, and feare danger to his soule by his vsuall and many dealings in the world, (yea though they be lawfull) let him not (I say) thus go to worke, and looke to himselfe, he is (without question) like to grow to the same point that the most are at, to wit, to become a worldly minded man, as the most are, and drowne his religion in earthlinesse. Note.

And the ſame I ſay of him, who in his ſicknes hath made many great promiſes to amend his life, (if he recouer) and neuer to liue ſo badly afterward, as he had done before: I ſay, if hee renue not his couenant with the Lord from day to day, remembring and conſidering to whom he made that promiſe, and in what earneſt maner: this man ſhall reuolt from his good mind, and fall to his old byas againe. For though he hath purpoſed with *David*, yea and ſworne; yet ſhall he not with him keepe his righteous iudgements: for he hath neglected his care, and therefore he faileth of his purpoſe. For as he who keepeth not an houſe in reparation, when there is a ſmall breach, muſt be at a pounds charge, where a ſhilling would haue ſerued, if it had bin taken in hand in time: ſo wracke and ruine ſhall befall him in his good purpoſes, who doe not looke daily and carefully to the maintaining of them. And by this that hath been ſaid of the point in hand, we may iudge of all other inſtances, that when we haue done our duties well, as *Gedeon* did heere, yet if we do not with him preuent after dangers, wee loſe the fruit and hope of our former labours. All this that I haue ſaid of this matter is the better to be marked, becauſe ſuch care from thing to thing in our liues, is the vpholding of the practiſe of Chriſtianitie. More of this point I haue ſaid vpon the like occaſion before in chap 7. verſ. 23.

Note. Pſal. 119.106. *A ſimilitude.*

Doct. 2. Another thing here in *Gedeon* is worth the marking, that he followed after the reſt of the Midianites, whereas he might haue bin like to haue neglected that worke, as needfull as it was, and to haue been reuenged vpon the Ephramites, who had ſo vniuſtly prouoked him, (and ſo hee would haue done, no doubt, if he had been an hot and haſtie man, giuen to his appetite) and to follow priuate affection, as moſt men are giuen to doe. But he counted it a ſmaller matter to croſſe his owne corrupt nature, then to leaue the purſuing of the common enemie. Where wee are taught, that if wee may haue peace in the land, (as *Gedeon* ſought by vanquiſhing them that remained of the Midianites and were fled;) for the obtaining of it, we ought by all meanes to maintaine peace priuately at home with our neighbours, yea and gladly take all occaſions to the procuring thereof, as *Gedeon* did with the Ephramites. The reaſon is, for that the maintaining of peace and agreement at home in priuat, requireth neither loſſe of our liues, goods, or religion, but onely of our will and corrupt affections, (or the forgoing of ſome ſmall thing for peace ſake, which we may lawfully yeeld vnto:) and we are not debters to our rebellious nature, but ought to be profeſſed enemies againſt the ſame.

Note. Rom. 8.12.

Againe, while we haue peace abroad, from ciuill and forraine diſſention, Oh what a benefit it is, as we may ſee by that which we reade of in the firſt booke of the Kings, that in the daies of *Salomon*, euery one liued ſafe vnder his vine, and vnder his figtree? As on the contrary, when there is warre or perſecution, Oh what feare and danger is there? what ſpoile of men and goods is there? yea, what hauocke of all things? Therefore I muſt needes ſay vnto you, that cannot loue your enemies, but boile and ſwell one againſt another, and to you that may liue quietly euery day in the weeke, who yet ſcarcely do it one: that you haſte warre vpon your ſelues, yea you long and groane for it, or for ſome other plague, and if the Lord would (as it were) winck to allure you neerer to him, yee your ſelues tempt him to lay load on you:

1. King. 4.25. Note.

you: and to such I say with griefe, you cannot tell what it is to inioy peace, and make vse of it.

Whereas if you did well consider it, yee would seeke, yea and insue after peace, so far as ye might attaine it with holinesse, and by no meanes suffer it to go from you: and ye would not so yeeld to your lusts and carnal affecti- Heb.12.14.
ons, in fauouring, nourishing, and satisfying whereof, ye depriue your selues of the sweete and infinite fruits of common peace. But if this distemper and vnrulinesse be found in a familie, betwixt husband and wife, or other parts of the familie, it is more to be bewailed; what did I say? nay monstrous. Oh what good might be done in this time of peace, as the Churches did find in Act.9.31.
the Acts? And this should we doe, if we were wise: for so God commandeth: *As much as in you lieth, haue peace with all men.* Yea though it cost vs Rom.12.18.
somewhat, as *Abraham* with losse procured it betwixt *Lot* and himselfe. And Genes.13.8.
if any such be vexed by strangers, and disquieted by them, let them consider, that it is iust with God to punish them so, who haue broken peace, yea and despised it with neighbours, kindred, and wife at their owne home.

And in that it is said here, that they laboured til they were faint and wea- *Doct.*2.
rie, we see that the earnest following of our duties will make vs oft times neglect and forget our selues, and our bodily ease, as they did. So the woman of Samaria was so rauished with Christs sweet communication, as ignorant as she was, (when he first met her at the well) yea saucie and scorne- Iohn 4.28.
full, that for the great desire shee had to heare him, she forgat her selfe, and neglected the care of her bodily businesse. And *Abrahams* seruant so min- Genes.24.23.
ded the dutie which was enioyned him of his master, that although hee had need, hauing trauelled farre, yet hee would not eate, till he had dispatched that which he went about. Thus *Peter*, Actes 10. through the heauenly in- Act.19.10.
tention of his mind, ouercame his hunger, so that before any thing could be made readie, he was in a traunce. And so *Paul*, whose watchings and fastings are in other places set downe to haue been so many, did neglect his sleepe and repast at Troas, through that feruency of spirit, which caused him to preach till midnight, and at Ephesus did vsually for three yeeres exhort them in the night, as well as in the day. But aboue all our Sauiour Christ, who through his earnestnesse and zeale, did many times, as in that holy speech and communication with the woman, Ioh.4. forbeare his meate, and forget to eate: alleaging that he had meate to eate which they knew not of. Iohn 4 31.
vers.34.

Euen so our minds being set seriously vpon our duties, as prayer, reading, good company, the following of our calling, &c. we do not at all many times, or very little mind other things belonging to our bodily welfare; and it is our crowne so farre as we can by good occasions remember that with *Gedeon* we haue done so. Indeed in and about play, pleasure, and seeking after the commodities of the world, the case is cleare, that too too many haue swet, and doe continually forget and disguise themselues, so that neither cold, hunger, heate, or vnseasonablenesse can hold them backe, or hinder them. But in Gods matters, as his worship, and in things which tend to our owne saluation, and the hunting and purging out of some speciall sinnes, also in furthering and bringing on one another to faith and good du- Note.

ties,and so seeking how to do most good to the poore members of Christ, Oh how few are to bee found to doe thus? who yet neither spare labour, time,cost,or any thing else about their owne matters: whereas we should bee so taken vp with Gods matters, that our owne, euen lawfull,might bee moderated at least. Thus *Marie* sat at the feete of Christ, and through her attention to his preaching neglected the lesse necessarie work of preparing for him. Now though euery example bee not a law to bind euery man to the like: yet where we see it so agree with the doctrine of the word,as here; such examples must be our instruction,and we may well gather, that there is a singular affection of loue to God, and ioy in his seruice where it is so, which concernes vs much to follow. And much more we may conclude, that when men (in hearing the word,or prayer,&c.) doe so wander,and are so weary,that euery minute is an houre vnto them,and euery houre ten,till al be done,and some wil not endure out the whole time,but depart,to serue their appetite,or follow their worke, these (we may be sure) are little affected with the action: since other things are predominant with them,which will not giue place,euen when the most religious duties are in hand.

The man of trade must looke to this, yea the worshipfull, and all estates that feare God,to the end that of meere conscience they may obey God in
Ioshua 10.9. their seuerall callings and places. Thus *Ioshua* went all night long to helpe the Gibeonites: and *Gedeon* was neither by hunger nor wearinesse held backe from pursuing after the Midianites. The vse hereof is,to warrant our selues that our greatest delight be in seruing the Lord in one part of our life as in another,as in the chiefest to God,so next in the particular duties of our callings painefully in euery estate and degree, and faithfully, and so to take our rest,refreshing,and recreation,which yet should follow and come after these,and not goe before them.

Vers. 5. *Gedeon* being wearie,and his men; asketh but bread of his owne countrey men,for whose peace he pursued the Midianites,as well as for his own: his reason was twofold, one because they were wearie; the other,because they pursued their enemies,for the safetie of Israel Gods people. In this necessity and distresse of theirs,though otherwise they wanted not,we may note,that it may possibly be the case of any of Gods people to be destitute of
Doct. necessaries for this life,& to be brought into streights both by wāt of food, and also by other calamities. *Dauid* in his fleeing from *Saul*,was so distressed (he and his men) for victual,that he was faine to eate of the Shew-bread, which (out of the case of necessitie) was vnlawfull for any saue the Priest to
1. Sam. 21. 3. eate of,as appeareth in Sam. 21. *Ionathan* and the people with him, were euen readie to faint, and yet might not without perill of their life taste so much as a little honey with the top of his speare to saue and preserue life. And if it were but euen so with vs as it was with him and *Gedeon*,that but a whole day or two wee wanted food and reliefe,we should find it (as small a matter as it is thought to be) as much as life is worth. Daily experience sheweth vs the same,that it falleth out both by sea and by land to be the case of many,who yet were of good wealth, and not likely to come into such need and want: and yet so wee see it to come to passe. One reason is, because all things in this present world are changeable, and besides God will correct some this way,and trie others,as he did *Iob*.

The

The vſe hereof is, that wee ſhould not pleaſe our ſelues in any thing of what account ſoeuer it be, neither reſt, depend, or take too much comfort in our outward preſent eſtate, of health, wealth, wit, learning, worſhip, credit, &c. And further, that wee ſhould be ready to helpe ſuch as ſtand in need, (and ſeeke it at our hands) with theſe tranſitory comforts which God hath giuen vs. As our Sauiour ſaith: *Make yee friends of the vnrighteous Mammon, that when ye ſhall want, they may receiue you into euerlaſting habitations.* And not to grudge at it, (as many doe) but to be mercifull and ready thereto with chearefulneſſe: for with what meaſure we meate, ſhall be meaſured to vs againe, and iudgement ſhall bee without mercy to them that ſhew none. And this chiefly ſhould bee done, when the poore want worke, and corne, and ſuch like neceſſaries: remembring how *Nabal* ſped for his churliſhnes. But of this point by the way, ſeeing I ſhall meete with the like againe. Luke 16.10. Phile.7. Matth.7.1. Iam.2.13.

Out of their reaſon in that they were faint with following the Midianites all night, we may note, that the neede that commeth of faintneſſe or labour in any of our brethren, is an honeſt cauſe for them to ſeeke, and aske, and for vs to relieue them, euen as other neceſſitie is, that God laieth vpon them, as ſickneſſe, age, &c. But yet for all this, the want that commeth of idlenes and of liuing without labour, is not ſo to be counted of, as ſhall be further ſhewed in the next point. But the relieuing of them that are poore indeed, is laid vpon vs by the Lord, telling vs, that wee ſhall haue them alwaies among vs, that we may doe good vnto them: and that if wee haue this worlds good, and ſee our brother hath need, and ſhut vp our compaſſion from them, the loue of God dwelleth not in vs. Which words of his, with ſuch like, ſhould be as a mallet to break our hard hearts, who in ſo great need as is to be ſeene in our townes, are little mooued to compaſſion towards the needy. And as God furniſheth vs euery yeere with new ſtore, ſo wee ſhould hold on in mercy ſtill, as long as we remaine among them. Me thinkes we ſhould readilie and willingly giue at Gods commanding, ſeeing he maketh vs able ſo to doe, in whoſe hand and at whoſe pleaſure it is, to take from vs, and giue to them, that ſo wee might bee driuen to ſeeke to them for reliefe, that before ſought it of vs. To the iuſt reproofe of ſuch I ſpeake it, who thinke all too little for a few bellies, not feeling other mens wants, forgetting the fearefull ſentence pronounced againſt them that omitted this mercy and compaſſion, as well as to them that wrought iniquitie: *Goe ye curſed into euerlaſting fire, for I was hungry, and ye gaue me no meate, I was naked, &c.* *The 1. reaſon.* *Doct.2.* Deut.15.11. 1.John 3.17. Matth 25.42.

Out of the other reaſon, that they fought for the ſafety of Iſrael, wee are further taught, that they ought to haue reliefe alſo, (euen as I ſaid before, it is lawfull and honeſt for them to aske it) who haue been imploied againſt Gods enemies and ours, to defend vs from their rage and tyranny. Conſidering that they carry their life in their hands, and are in danger of ſpending their blood in the cauſe of God, and the peace of the land, whileſt wee may ſit quiet at home, and liue free from ſuch feare. So that although the perſons themſelues be leaud, yet in regard of their ſeruice, we ſhould ſee them prouided for: as *Paul* teacheth ſaying: *Doth any man goe on warfare at his owne coſt?* 1.Corinth.9. And it is our ſinne if they haue it not, or if they ſhould be driuen to goe about to begge, and ſo to become rogues, for that is contrary to Gods commandement, who ſaith: *There ſhall be no beggar in Iſrael.* And *The ſecond. Doct.3.* 1.Cor.9.7. 2.Sam.17.27.

as good order is taken to cut off rogueing from place to place, without any certaine habitation, by setting the poore on worke, and ministring to their necessities that which they want, not being able to maintaine their charge by their labour, (which good order of all faithfull Christians is to be vpholden) so it is a great sinne in many, who in stead thereof, doe nourish them that are rogues indeed, notwithstanding it bee straightly commanded, that
2.Thes.3 10. hee who will not labour should not eate: and who will sooner be moued with compassion toward them, then toward their poore neighbours, whose need they behold daily with their eyes. But more of this in the men of Succoths answer.

Vers.6. The answere of the Princes of Succoth heere followeth, with *Gedeons* words to them againe. And it is like that his suite was carried to them, and their answere returned to *Gedeon* by messengers, which sheweth that it was the fault of them, and not the peoples, to answere *Gedeon* after that manner, not only to denie them very bread, but to giue them also rough and scornefull words. And therefore *Gedeon*, not vpon any priuate reuenge, but as one that had authoritie to doe it, (seeing the fault redounded to the hurt of the Common-wealth, and was not committed onely against *Gedeon* and his men) answered, that he would be auenged of them. If they had been wise they would both haue relieued them, and also in so good a cause, if neede had been, haue gone with them. But let vs examine the words: *Are Zeba and Zalmunna in thy hands alreadie?* As if they should haue said, if they were, they would haue giuen them: but that was no thanke to them, but their owne benefit, credit and honour: but seeing they were not in his hands,
Doct.vers.6. they vncourteously and barbarously denied it to them being their brethren, and in subtiltie they did it, lest they being ouercome of the Midianites, they should haue been hardlier dealt withall by the Princes of Midian, hearing that they had relieued their enemies.

And this subtilty ioyned with selfe-loue, are the two strings to mens bow by the which they shoote out the most of their actions as arrowes. For the
Note. good the most doe, it is not done for the commandement nor for conscience sake, but of selfe-loue for their owne priuate benefit, hoping to be gainers thereby, which may be done by the heathens for any religion or feare of God that is in it: or when they hold back the good, which in conscience they ought to doe, of an euill minde they hold it back: as these men of Succoth did; for feare, lest if they should doe it to some, they should fare the worse at the hands of other, as these men of Succoth here did. A like point whereunto, I obserued in the men of Ephraim.

2 And hereby wee may see, what barbarous rudenesse was in these, who yet were brethren and countrimen to the Israelites: that to *Gedeon* their gouernour, by whom they were vpholden in peace, and who now was in the middest of this last worke of pursuing the Midianites, and rescuing of Israel, they should shew themselues so barbarous and voide of all humanitie. Which was as if when the house top is on fire, they in the nether part should lie still, as though the fire could not hurt them: or as if a man standing vpon the onely bough of an high tree, and thereby only kept from danger of falling, should with his hatchet cut it downe, and by the fall of it breake his necke. This rudenesse and irreligiousnes is in many brutish people at this day,

day,who are not onely no helpers in the wants and necessities of Gods peo-ple,either for soule or bodie,but hinderers, yea and gripers of them. Sense-lesse blocks they are, who can neither heare, see, nor sauour any good to-wards any: but as *Nabal,* who not only gaue not any thing to *Dauids* men, but rated them,and railed on them,thereby casting a mist (as it were) vpon his vnmercifulnes,that it might seeme the more tollerable.

And this we may further note here, in that they by their falsehood, sub-tiltie,and dastardlinesse sought to saue their liues, that wee might not mar-ueile,when we see,that some are readie to betray,forsake,yea and lend their helping hand to persecute their natiue Prince,countrey,and brethren, yea and religion it selfe,and all for the broken and shiuered hope of a transitorie life and safetie, which yet they misse also oft times, as is to be seene in that speech of *Mordecai* to *Hester*: *If we remaine in this danger, doest thou looke to be safe?* For why, God reuengeth such falsehood and cowardlinesse, as our Sauiour saith: *He that will saue his life,shall lose it.* The vse hereof is,that though life be sweete,yet it is not to be preserued by subtiltie, falsehood,and prepo-sterous feare, when the Lord will haue it to bee brought into triall,and re-quireth it at our hands. Euen so in all other things, subteltie and dastardli-nesse is to be auoided,and simplicitie and courage is to be practised. Of this more (God willing) after, in the conspiracie of the men of *Schechem* with *Abimilek.* 3 Matth. 10.39. Note.

Now *Gedeon* threatneth the men of *Succoth* for their barbarousnes and boldnes towards him their deliuerer,(as they had iustly deserued) euen to teare their flesh with the thornes of the desert. The which he iustly did, be-ing their Magistrate: for our Sauiour teacheth, that hee who scorneth but his brother or neighbour, is worthie of the highest degree of punishment. And much more this which was committed against the gouernour, might be thus met with, and requited, he not threatning them in wrath, but vpon good consideration. I will deferre speaking of the punishment,till the infli-cting of it be mentioned: but let this be marked, that *Gedeon* did euen then speake of preuailing against *Zeba* and *Zalmunna* without feare, as if he had alreadie subdued them: therefore he saith, *When the Lord hath deliuered them into my hands,* (as not doubting but that he would) *then I will teare their flesh with briers.* Vers.7.

In the meane time here let vs marke, that hee left not off the greatest and most necessarie dutie which must of necessitie presently be done, to wit, the pursuing of the Midianites: for the other,namely,the punishing of the men of *Succoth,* which was to be done also, but might better bee deferred. This wisedome and discretion is to be learned of vs,that of duties to be done of vs,or euils to be auoided, with the danger and punishment that followeth them,that be first done in both,which of necessitie must be first,and yet the other not neglected nor omitted, but in due season regarded also. *Doct.*

Instances may be these,as there bee many other: to visit parents in great sicknesse,which requireth present duty without delay,is to be preferred and performed,rather then to iourney about profit,though lawfull also, which may as well be done another time. Also to preferre hearing of a Sermon before common businesse, if it be not to our greater hurt,&c. And this I say further,that not onely common actions must giue place to seasons,but euen

one

one seaſon to another. In which our beſt rule is, that wee preferre that seaſon, which occaſioneth a worke of preſenteſt vſe: although ſome other dutie of an higher nature offer it ſelfe. Yea and here obſerue, that euen a ciuill ſeaſon may ſometime bee preferred before a religious. As for example, It falles out that a man is offered ſome fauour, and hope of releaſe out of ſome trouble which he is in, or reconciliation with his aduerſarie, (mightier then himſelfe) if he will vſe ſome preſent helpe, which elſe he cannot enioy: or it may be he hath a ſumme of money to pay vpon a ſet day, and that vpon a great forfeiture: or he is ſent vpon an errand of life and death: ſay it be to fetch the Chirurgian to let his maſter or parent blood, being in a deſperate caſe otherwiſe: or is commanded to ſerue the Prince, &c. Againſt theſe commeth ſome other opportunitie, as of hearing the word, of prayer in familie. Theſe bee all neceſſarie in their kinds, and due times, but in no wiſe ought to iuſtle aſide the other, more needfull to bē done at that time, and theſe may be attended vnto, when leiſure from the other will giue leaue: the other are as the tide, which ſtaieth for no man. Therefore we muſt beware, leſt through our ignorance) though cloaked with honeſtie) or neglect, eſpecially wilfull contempt, we leaue the greater for the leſſer. Which cauſeth to the partie ſo offending, ſhame and ſorrow oft times. As, how ſhall he anſwere his follie, who neglecting the Phyſitian in the caſe before ſaid, ſhall thereby finde his wife, father, or maſter, dead, or paſt recouerie? Such caſes may be: and by one wee ſhould meaſure the reſt. *Paul*, vpon this ground,

Act. 20. 16. and 21. 13. omitted the opportunitie of doing good in Aſia, Act. 20. and 21. that hee might goe to Ieruſalem. *Let vs not be ouer much iuſt*, Eccleſ. 7. *He that wringeth*

Prou. 30. 33. *the noſe, forceth blood*, Prou. 30. Now to this I will ioyne a caueat, and that is, That vnder colour of preferring the greater dutie, wee take not occaſion to neglect the ſmaller afterward; which if we doe, wee ſhall bewray our ſelues rather to be ſubtill ſhifters and diſpenſers with our duties, boldly and looſely, then wiſe redeemers of the time. As for example: If the publike worſhip of God fall out vpon the time of our ordinarie priuate worſhip: let this yeeld this to the other: howbeit ſo, that wee readily returne to the priuate againe in his due place and time, and not pretend our diligence one way, to colour our negligence another way. A feaſt is better then an ordinarie: but the feaſt may better be ſpared, then a man ſhould be depriued of his ordinarie, and ſo ſtarue all the weeke after. This I adde, becauſe ſo prepoſterous is our nature, that whereas one dutie ſhould make vs fitter for another, wee rather neglect the one for the other; as hearing for conference, meditation, or prayer. We ſucke poyſon out of ſweetnes, and waxe the more auke and vntoward, yea wearie of priuate, becauſe wee thinke wee haue ſufficiently quit our ſelues in the publike dutie, either of preaching or hearing. In like manner, it is not vnlawfull for a man to preferre the companie of the choice ſeruant of God either one or more (when we may haue the benefit of thē) before our callings, or attending to our families: but to bee carried ſo after this, that we ſhould grow to diſtaſte and neglect our callings, or the duties of Gods priuate ſeruice, is moſt inconuenient, yea argueth that ẏ diuel hath blinded vs with deluſion ſtrongly, either through our ignorance & ſimplicitie, or (which is worſe) becauſe we are weary of the moſt neceſſary dutie for continuance, vnder colour of our zeale for thoſe which fall out ſeldome.

Now

Now as he preferred not the lesse needfull dutie before that which 2
was more needfull, so hee did not leaue it off (I meane the pursuing of the rest of the Midianites) though hee might easily haue been discouraged by the vnthankfulnesse of his brethren, and their scoffing at him, as many would haue done in such a case. For mens vnthankfulnesse and discouraging of vs with scoffes, doth cause vs many times to breake off good beginnings, whereas he was neither by the men of Ephraim, nor by these of Succoth, put out of his course. It should teach vs, when we haue our warrant from God, for that which we goe about, or auoid, then not to regard, or so to regard temptations and discouragements, that we be hindered and broken off from our good course by them. As neither *Elisha* was by mocking, Note.
2. King. 2. nor our Sauiour, or his Apostles by the opposition they found. 2.King 2.25.
Nay rather they were incouraged. For so *Paul* was by the disswasiues of others, Actes 21. and *Dauid* by *Michols* scorne: and wee ought likewise so to Act.21.13.
be, when we see fewest countenance or assist vs; saying as he did, *I will yet be more vile for the Lords sake*, and then our reward shal be more then common. 2.Sam.6.22.
And as for this that we shall be counted medlers, and busi-bodies, I answer: let God be more with vs then men by whose commandement we do meddle, (as they call it,) and be we aduised and perswaded before, what ground we haue, that so we may reape the good and comfortable vse thereof, and receiue the fruite of the promise. And this of the men of Succoth.

THE FIFTIE TWO SERMON ON THE EIGHTH CHAPTER OF THE BOOKE OF IVDGES.

NOw I will goe forward with the rest of the text that re- Vers.8.
maineth, from the eight verse in these words: [*And he went thence to Penuel*] and so forth, as they are to be read before the last Sermon. Here we may see another discouragement and repulse that *Gedeon* sustained by the men of Penuel: for he being with his souldiers faint and weary, was denied bread not only by thẽ of Succoth, as wee haue seene, but by the men of Penuel also, as appeareth in this verse. For to them he went in the faintnes and wearines of himself and his souldiers, and had the repulse: whereby he might easily haue been tempted, and brought to thinke and feare, that God did not approue of his iourney, but did set himselfe against him. For so Note.
we are wont to conclude by the ill successe we haue euen in good attempts, especially when the lets be forcible, many and diuers, and one in the necke of another: as *Iobes* afflictions were, when among hard messages brought to him of other calamities that were befalne him, this was one that the fire

of God was fallen from heauen, and had burnt vp the ſheepe and the ſeruants,as if God had been againſt him. So that we may learne by this, that things ſometime may goe ſo contrary to our deſire,liking,and expectation, and that in duties which God requireth,and will haue to be done of vs,as if he were not with vs,but againſt vs,yea as if hee would croſſe vs in them of ſet purpoſe. Our dutie here is to looke what God bids vs doe,as the man of God ſent from Iuda ſhould haue done, who was drawne by the old Prophet of Bethel contrary to Gods commandement,to eate there. But indeed
1.King.13.19. the caſe is not alway alike,when ſuch difficulties befall vs : for ſometime we may more clearely ſee cauſe thereof, then at other. For it may bee the ſame mans caſe,at one time to doe a good action, yet in an euill and inconuenient manner: and at another time to be well occupied,and take a good thing in hand,and doe it in a good manner : in both kinds it may fall out,that he hath many diſcouragements. If things ſucceed not with him, whē he goeth about them in the beſt manner, that is, the latter of theſe two ; What then? may not the Lord trie his faith and patience,by ſo croſſing him? And in the firſt kind,much more I may ſay,what maruell,if the Lord croſſe him, when he hath done a good thing in a bad manner,to the end he may call himſelfe to a more due examination of himſelfe, and amend that which was amiſſe, ere he take in hand ſuch holy duties?It was Gods wil that the eleuen Tribes
Iudg.20. ſhould fight againſt *Beniamin* : but were they perſons for their true repentance fit for that buſineſſe?yea and for all their zeale they wanting the principall ; to wit,faith ; that God would bee with them, did they not goe to worke amiſſe? was there not great cauſe therefore why the Lord ſhould fight as faſt againſt them (to driue them to repentance for their reuoltings from him)as they fought againſt *Beniamin?* And to teach them that they wanted meekeneſſe, loue and diſcretion to temper their feruent reuenge withall,that ſo they might doe the holy worke of God in an holy manner? Therefore in ſuch a caſe let men be contented,nay glad,if God croſſe them, that they may the better ſpie out what poyſoneth their beſt duties and deſires,as pride,raſhnes,boldneſſe,and learne hereby, meekeneſſe, humilitie, repentance,feare,&c. for God doth iuſtly ſuffer many diſcouragements to be vpon ſuch,(as he did alſo oft times deale ſo with the Iſraelites going vp
Exod.3.19. to Canaan out of Egypt,Exod.3.) that they may ſtay their courſe, in any euill attempts,and proceed more aduiſedly and commendably in their doings. But it falleth out ſometime,as I ſaid before,that ſore and great difficulties ſtand vp in mens way,not vnlike to *Gedeons :* wherein the Lord deales with his,as if he ſending them on a iourney, would make heauen and earth to be againſt them in their trauels, which is greatly to their admiration and aſtoniſhment. As who would haue ſaid that *Dauid* had been choſen of God to be king,when yet the promiſe thereof, was oft renued and confirmed to him,ſeeing his diſcouragements were ſo many and ſtrong that he met with? whereas *Saul* came to his kingdome eaſily & without trouble? And in ſuch caſes, wherein we haue ſo much to diſmay vs,yet Satan is euer at hand alſo, to worke vpon our weakenes,and to ſet vs much more backward;eſpecially when wee ſhall bee brought to thinke, Gods deeds ſeeme contrary to his words and promiſe,as the death of the Shunamites child,which yet had bin giuen her as an vnlooked for bleſſing.

Now

Now when it pleaseth God to trie vs,by seeming to set such barres in our waies,few of vs are wise inough to see, or at least, rightly to consider,why it is thus with vs,and why God suffereth things so to trouble vs:but as though wee had thereby iust cause to complaine of his doing,and to expostulate with him; we begin to doubt how he wil make good his promise to vs,and whether we may go forward in the good course in which we haue begun: yea,and we are impatient (perhaps) or much disquieted at the least,(if we doe not also fret and fume) and so are discouraged from our good beginnings. Whereby we may see our froth rather then faith,which seemed before to bee good substance, and feele the stinch of our vnsauourie hearts, which vpon small occasion cast out such euill smelles. And yet herein wee differ from *Gedeon*,that,as he was found in his discouragements and crosses to be of farre greater courage and confidence then wee; so his triall was in great matters,and ours but in trifles for the most part. Note.

And not onely when wee bee crossed and hindred in good actions we do thus,but if we haue but some one let in our way,as euen in our common businesse,such distemperature,as I haue spoken of,shall possesse vs: or if we haue lost something,though of small valew,yea though it be but only missing and out of the way:or if we be hindred by the weather which is ordinary,or(as oft it falleth out)through our own rashnesse only,as when we do but stumble and hurt our foot against a stone, what should we then bee like to do, if in going about any duty, we should haue so many and great lets in the way,and crossings of vs,as may easily meet with vs,and those also as it were sent from God to resist vs? It is therefore the singular and onely grace of God to inable vs to belieue and bee perswaded, that hee doth oft times such things to trie vs,and that we may shew foorth the grace of faith and patience that is in vs; and therefore we are to hold our peace,seeing he hath done it. And such hinderances and crossings fall out sometimes,when we are going to prayer priuately, or in our familie,or to the hearing of the word preached,or to receiue the sacrament,&c. from which no wise body will say,we should be withdrawne by any pretence, as though wee pleased not God therein,seeing euen in them some lets do rise vp in the way to hinder vs. And the like we may obserue in those discouragements which are from within our selues. For example,when a Minister in his course of preaching,shall find ill measure at the hands of others, whose good he most seeketh,while they see not the purpose of God toward them; (as *Moses* did by the Israelites when he was first sent vnto them, Exod.6.) or if they shall but despise Gods prouidence toward them,as the Pharisees are said to haue done,how (thinke we) is this like to worke vpon him? or (which is more) if he shall feele within himselfe great vnfitnesse, as *Moses* did,Exod.3.and some vnwillingnesse,deadnesse,drousinesse,or want of assistance from God in discharge of the worke of his ministery,(all which are great dampings to a man,who hath vsed the best meanes to furnish himselfe both with knowledge and conscience) and yet euen the best sometimes haue the proofe hereof in themselues. What thoughts (thinke we)are like to arise in him in such a case? Therfore if a man looke not for these, and if he be not resolued before hand,that such quailings of him may fall out, and also if hee be not armed against the temptations which may arise therefrom, it is wonderfull, Note. Exod.6.9. Luke 15.12. Exod.3.10.

how the diuell may weaken his faith, and zeale, and slacken his purpose of diligence in the Lords worke. But on the other side, if in such a case hee be able to stay himselfe by considering that such trials are vsual (more or lesse) to the best seruants and Ministers of God, (and alway haue been) who haue their ebbings aswell as their flowings, (as *Eliah*, *Paul*, yea our Sauiour himselfe had strong discouragements,) what a singular benefit is this? Much more, if he hauing ouercome the first onset, shall in the second place meditate of the end which the Lord hath in abasing him thus, (he being occupied in Gods owne worke) and that is, that hee may teach him humilitie, yea how to flee out of himselfe and depend immediatly vpon the Lord for sufficiencie and assistance; and not trust to his own wit, study, memory, tongue, or gifts, (which others make their onely refuge, and therefore are often disappointed) oh what gaine shall he reape thereby, and say with *Paul*, I am neuer fitter for Gods seruice then when I am lowest in mine owne opinion: hereafter therefore if I boast, I wil boast of mine owne infirmities, as the A-
2.Cor.12.9. postle speaketh, in which the glory of God is most perfected and aduanced.

Vers. 9. *Gedeon* receiuing the like discourtesie and rude answer of the men of Penuel, as he had before of the men of Succoth, doth in like manner threaten them the throwing downe of their tower in which they so much gloried. And this threatning, seeing it was afterward put in execution, was a crosse and discommoditie: which they did needlesly and by their owne sin bring vpon themselues. By which we may see, that many are authors and causers of their owne sorrow and trouble, which need not haue been, and that by their sinne, as stoutnesse, wilfulnesse, stiffeneckednesse, and other vndutifulnesse, and rude behauiour, they doe (I say) bring vnseasonable affliction vpon themselues, euen as these men of Succoth and Penuel here did. Wee know that peace with men, to liue without feare by them, is a great benefit, and soone lost, and hardly recouered, men being wolues and lionlike one to another, especially if they be prouoked, and most of all, when they haue authoritie and superioritie one ouer another, and so may iustly vexe them who shal fal into their hands, by their wicked deserts and leaud behauiour. Ther-
Gal.5.last. fore all should take heed how they prouoke one another in the least maner, as these did here.

But lamentable it is, that the most men make breaches of their peace, and losse of their commodities, by rigour, crueltie, and by an high mind, and proud heart, not bearing the least iniurie, but bending themselues by and by to reuenge, looking for all good measure to bee offered them by others, but yeelding little or no kindnesse againe: which peruersenesse is also euen betwixt many couples in the married estate, which causeth continuall iarring and vnquietnesse, whereas peace (a man would thinke) were fitter to be seene both betwixt them and all other, whom I speake of. Which they are commanded to seeke with all men, as much as in them lieth, yea and to pur-
Heb.12.14. sue and follow it, though it flee from them, yea and to buy peace, though it cost them somewhat, but not to sel it at any hand, much lesse for trifles. Thus
Genes.13.9. *Abraham* bought his peace of *Lot*. And let men learne to this end to know and consider what they are; to the pulling downe of their pecocks feathers, euen earth, earth, earth, and if they bee weighed in an equall ballance, farre worse then nothing. But of this I spake in verse 4. of this Chapter.

Gedeon

Gedeon goeth forward after the rest of the Midianites, and findeth them resting themselues in Carkor which was in the precinct of the Israelites, from whence they hoped to passe after that night, and so to escape. But *Gedeon* came vpon them on the backside of these two cities, Iogbeah in the Tribe of *Gad*, Numb.32. and Nobah in the halfe Tribe of *Manasseh* being hard by, Num.32. And so the two Princes were suddenly stricken with astonishment and feare, and flying were taken, and the hoast smitten and slaine: with whom were many hangbies, as scullions and such like that followed the army. And in that it is said, that hee returned backe with the two Princes when the Sunne was risen, it appeareth that the warre betwixt them was begun in the night, and in the same night was ended.

Vers.10.11.12.13. *The clearing of these verses.*

Numb.32.35. & 32.42.

By this latter victory of *Gedeon*, it is manifest, what great things through Gods blessing are brought to passe by faith, and the diligence, and vnweariednesse of men in their callings. This is the maine point contained in these verses. Whereas delay and sloth (for I put them together to shew what delaies I meane) are alwaies dangerous, euen as here if *Gedeon* had tarried to rest himselfe but one night by the way, hee had lost all his labour, and the fruit of it, to wit, the destroying of these Midianites. So God to the diligent hath promised his blessing, and good successe as *Gedeon* here found it. The men of Succoth and Penuel laughed him to scorne, but hee looked to God, and had an eye to his promise, which was, that he would giue them into his hands: and yet (as we see) he was neuer awhit the bolder to presume therof, without diligent vsing of the meanes. It was as vnlike, (nay much more vnlikely) that *Dauid* should haue smitten downe *Goliah*, that *Noah* should haue saued the world by the Arke: and many other such things to haue bin brought to passe, as the conquering of the Nations by *Ioshua*: but they all, when they belieued God, that he would doe that which he promised, went to worke with great care and diligence to serue Gods prouidence, seeing he wrought by meanes (as he doth still) and so they preuailed, and obtained that which they sought.

Doct. out of all these verses.

1.Sam.17.51. Heb.11.7.

Ioshua 10.&c.

And this was the power of God through faith, they trusting and resting in him through the Mediator to come, so it is no lesse in vs, (for I will briefly apply it againe, though I haue stood largely on this point before, a new occasion being offered) that we outgrow many lets and discouragements by the same our faith, though wee bee priuie that there is otherwise nothing in vs, and that (when sometimes it hath seemed to vs almost impossible) the Lord hath done much for vs, and wrought great things by vs, while wee haue, although but weakely and poorely gone to work, whether we respect our faith, or our labour, which is the fruit of it. And we hauing been diligent to approoue our selues in both; we haue found the truth of that Scripture verified in vs, which saith, that faith ouercommeth the difficulties that are in the world; and haue growne to the contempt of many sinnes, and the subduing of them, in great measure, which had sometime preuailed against vs; and to be better heartned against afflictions, and to get strength of hope by experience for the time to come. But to see how soone *Moses*, *Ioshua*, and *Gedeon* here grew strong in faith, as in a few daies, which we are going about many yeeres, this ought as to humble vs, for that we are so farre behind them, so to incourage vs, looking duly vnto this, how graciouslie God

1.Iohn 5.4.

Note. Rom.5.4.

aſſiſted them. And ſo (to apply this to the Sacrament) we haue communion with God and with Chriſt therein, and are much confirmed thereby in the couenant he hath made with vs, by our diligence and faithfulnes in preparing our ſelues thereto, which they that beleeue not think abſurd, and more then needs, to looke after. And to conclude this point (ſeeing I haue ſhewed the neceſſitie of it, and the euill and hurt that falleth out on the contrary, I meane by looſenes, idleneſſe, and vnbeliefe, in Chriſtians, by many occaſions heretofore) this I adde, that the cauſe of ſo great difference in the degree and meaſure of grace and goodneſſe, which wee obſerue in many profeſſors, is this, that ſome are painfull in hearing, vſing good companie, marking, with their hearts deeply ſet vpon the ſame, remembring, and making vſe of their knowledge, watching thereunto with prayer, &c. whereas others comber thēſelues ſo much with other matters, that there is no roome or leiſure left for theſe. They looke to thriue ſpiritually, whether they take paines or no, ſleeping or working. It is a true ſaying of a Father, fit to be vrged vpon ſuch: *He that made thee without thee, will not ſaue thee without thee.* He will not ſaue thee for thy labours ſake, but by thy labour. They that gathered more Manna then their fellowes, got nothing thereby: but it fareth otherwiſe here: gather much and haue much, labour little and haue little, euen as the Apoſtle ſpeaketh of another thing on the contrary, he that ſoweth ſparingly, ſhall reape ſparingly. As we mete to the Lord, ſo will he meaſure out to vs againe. He that laboureth not, eateth not: but he that laboureth much, enioyeth the fruite thereof: ſome thirtie, ſome ſixtie, ſome an hundred fold: euen as his diligence is. Oh it is ſtrange to ſee how men ſet themſelues to work in earthly buſineſſe, wherein yet they haue no abſolute promiſe of thriuing, becauſe faith the chiefe help is wanting, but here where the Lord hath tyed himſelfe to bleſſe their labour with abundance, men haue no liſt to ſtirre. A mediocritie of wealth contenteth few, and that maketh them ſo endleſſe and reſtleſſe in their deſires and trauailes: but the commonneſt meaſure of grace pleaſeth them beſt, becauſe that is gotten with leaſt trouble. It is fearefull that men ſhould doe ſo much for the fulfilling of their luſts: and ſo little that they might excell in goodneſſe. But their reward is thereafter. And in the meane ſeaſon God puts as great difference betwix ſuch, as there is betweene *Alexander*, *Cæſar* or the like Captaines (who were vnwearied alſo in their conqueſts) and *Gedeon*, or others like, who fought the Lords battels, and laboured therein by faith in his promiſes. Now it followeth.

Note.

Note.

14 *And tooke a ſeruant of the men of Succoth, and enquired of him, and hee wrote to him the Princes of Succoth, and the Elders thereof, euen ſeuentie and ſeuen men.*

15 *And he came vnto the men of Succoth, and ſaid, Behold Zeba and Zalmunna, by whom ye vpbrayed me, ſaying, Are the hands of Zeba and Zalmunna already in thy hands, that we ſhould giue bread vnto thy wearie men?*

16 *Then he tooke the Elders of the citie, and thornes of the wilderneſſe, and briers, and did teare the men of Succoth with them.*

17 *Alſo he brake downe the tower of Pennuel, and ſlew the men of the citie.*

Now

NOw in these verses following it is shewed that when *Gedeon* had taken the Princes of Midian, and was returned to Succoth, he seeks diligently to know the names of the chiefe men and Elders thereof: and he brought and shewed the Princes *Zeba* and *Zalmunna* vnto them: for hee kept them aliue, not to make his boast of them, but that he might shew them that God had deliuered them into his hands, as hee made no doubt thereof before, that so they might be the more ashamed and accused for that which they had done to him and his men, in denying them bread. And thereupon hee did vnto them as he had threatned, for he tare their flesh, to wit, of them of Succoth, with the thornes and briers of the wildernesse: and then ouerthrew the tower of the men of Penuel, and slew the citizens, either because they insulted more arrogantly then the men of Succoth did, or else because they resisted *Gedeon*, trusting in their tower, and so were slaine. Whether they of Succoth died by the paine & punishment, (as it is most like) or whether their flesh was onely torne, and yet life remaining in them, though the storie doth not declare; yet we cannot be ignorant, how sore and extreame the paine was. What kinde of execution was done vpon the men of Penuel themselues in putting them to death, the storie setteth not downe, but as it is sure they were slaine, so it is (not without good probabilitie) that the other were torne to death also. Vers.14.15. 16.17.

Gedeon meeting this young man, causeth him to set downe the names of the chiefe Elders and gouernours of Succoth in writing, (as it might be the names of the Aldermen and citizens) for he would not trust his owne memorie in so waightie a matter. And this hee did, because hee would not flie vpon any in rashnes and anger, and would be sure by that his aduised deliberation, to punish onely those who were guiltie, and those were the ancients of the citie. As *Salomon* also was very attentiue in hearing the cause of the harlots. To teach vs our dutie in this point, that when any fall into our hands to be corrected by vs, wee doe not at any time hastily in an angrie mood, and without due consideration, vse correction, but weigh the cause rightly, and not reuenge our selues, by satisfying our brutish affections vpon the persons: yea and to let them also see iust cause why they be corrected. And in this wee resemble the Lord himselfe, of whom *Abraham* saith, *It is farre from the Iudge of the whole world to destroy the righteous with the wicked.* Genes.18. *The cleering of verse 14.* 1.King.3.23. *Doct.* Genes.18.25.

It is an hard thing to be ruled by the word of God in correcting others, whereas flesh looketh to nothing, but to the will and reuenge of it selfe, and not to the bettering of the partie, and the good example of other, and discharge of a good conscience before God. Therefore S.*Paul* hath giuen a good rule to all by teaching one kind of correcters, namely fathers, that they should not be bitter to their children: euen as *Achan* in a waightie case was wisely handled, and kindly dealt with by *Iosbua* in a matter of life and death, and was regarded in, and concerning his soule, when sore punishment was inflicted vpon his bodie. Sundrie waies doe men shroud this cursed humour, vnder the false habit of zeale or lawfull seueritie: sometime to couer their ambition, as *Iehu* in killing *Ahabs* posteritie; sometime couetousnes, as *Saul* in slaying some of the Amalekites: sometime pride and reuenge, as the Israelites in warring vpon the Beniamites. All of them failed of the ground, Col.3.21. Iosu.7.19.

end, manner or measure in executing the correction: all which being neglected, and not obserued, doth marre the action, be it neuer so lawfull in it selfe and necessarie. As when the offending partie seeth not the cause of his correction, or is cruelly handled by the correcter, who maketh not the end of his correction or punishment to be the sauing of the partie, and to make the sinne odious that he is punished for, and the same an example to other.
Note. And here is iustly condemned the doing of them who say, they cannot correct but in anger, and while their hearts are exasperated against the partie, as if they should say, they can neuer doe it rightly or without sinne, whereas
Ephes. 4. 26. God saith, *Be angrie, but sinne not:* for anger doth nothing well. Although what neede the word of God or the examples of the Saints bee vsed to shame them, whom heathens may shame? Of whom some prescribe rules to such as are angrie, how they may bridle anger from rash outrage: and one among the rest told his seruanr, I had surely beaten thee, but that I was angrie. This doctrine is to be applied to Magistrates, Parents, Schoolemasters, and other superiors, namely step-mothers, and such as haue rule ouer poore orphanes, or any other, whom it little becommeth to excuse their own corruption by the fault or desert of the partie guiltie: who though hee haue but his due, yet the punisher being no fit person to reuenge by his intemperate heate, may deserue a greater punishment at Gods hand, euen of a murtherer (in heart) of his brother. And we see the effect of such seueritie, is to make the partie corrected to contemne it, and waxe desperate, not penitent, which is the peruerting of the right end of correction.

Vers. 15. By *Gedeons* shewing of these Princes to the men of Succoth and Penuel, to their shame and astonishment (who thought they had been farre enough out of their hands, and therefore scoffed at his pursuing and following after them) I say, by this, wee may note how God oft times turneth the taunts, flouts, threatnings, curses, and iniuries which the wicked doe vexe Gods children withall, he turneth them to their owne shame and euill, and to the comfort of his owne people so abused and wronged by them: as here these mocked *Gedeon*, liuing and walking according to the life of faith, and going about the Lords worke carefully: who now hauing ouercome the Midianites thereby, these wicked mockers are put to shame and paine, yea and to death also. And in like manner it fell out to *Shemei* when he had cursed *Dauid*, to *Zenacherib* scorning at *Ezechia*, for trusting in his God, yea and for blaspheming God himselfe, also to the Pharisees who scorned Christ vpon the Crosse, but after his resurrection were abashed, and to *Haman* deadly hating *Mordecai* the faithfull seruant of God. Now if this appeare thus often times euen heere in this world, how much more at the comming of the solemne and great day, when God shall iudge them? For when they see the Lord withdraw himselfe from his people neuer so little, (wherein hee doth no more then he did to his only sonne in whom he was well pleased) or behold them in some disgrace and abasement in the world: then they insult
Psal. 137. 3, 7. and crow ouer them, as the Babylonians and cursed Edomites did ouer the Iewes in captiuitie: but when as beyond expectation, they see them deliuered, yea and that the Lord graceth them, giues them fauour, restores them
Note. to libertie, and blesseth them with many benefits; then I say, they turne their scornes into admiration, and are ashamed of their vnreasonable disgracing them.

them. But further, if (besides this) the Lord shall pluck themselues downe, and humble them by the like afflictions, then they wish themselues in their case euen with the hardest and worst conditions.

So that we haue good cause abundantly to be contented to seeke to liue by faith in the sonne of God, trusting in, and cleauing to him and his word aboue all other things, esteeming our selues farre more rich thereby (euen when wee are counted most foolish and vile of the scornefull world) then they in their florishingest estate and condition: for why? we rest on God, and waite by hope, hauing him on our side, and are not disappointed: they Psalm.20.7.
cast all (as the desperate Dicer) on blinde hope, likelihoods, and haphazard, and so are deceiued of their expectation. They haue a time of boasting and Note.
glorying, which deceiueth them, and maketh them thinke, that their iollitie and prosperitie will last alwaies, when yet it changeth as the weather, and continueth not in one estate, and they haue no wisedome to consider it, or their end which shall be worst of all. Gods people haue a time of mourning, Psal.126.6.
but the end shall be reioycing: as here *Gedeon* bringeth before his vpbraiders *Zeba* and *Zalmunna* with triumph and glorie.

And with this we may also see, that the euill which they either doe not once dreame of, or which they thinke to be farre off from them, and make a mocke of it, is neere vnto them. According to that which the Apostle saith to the Thessalonians, *When men crie peace, peace, then commeth sudden destru-* 1.Thes.5.3.
ction vpon them, euen as the sorrow of a woman at her trauell. Chorah and his companie, *Benadad* with many other are examples hereof. So that there is no heed to be taken how iocond they be, when they be aloft, or haue their hearts desire, neither neede any to be afraid at the beholding of their greatnes, for why euen while it abideth, it is departing, and while it standeth, it is Eccles.5.8.
in falling, for when they be at their best and greatest, there is a greater then they, who is working their ouerthrow. But who is warned by others woe? But of this briefly, because often.

Vers.16.17.
Gedeon hauing well shamed these men of Succoth and Penuel, doth to them now as he had threatned, verse 7. and 9. that is: he tore the flesh of the men of Succoth with thornes, and cast downe the tower of the men of Penuel (euen their strong hold that they gloried in) he cast it downe (I say) to the ground and slew them. And might not both these punishments haue been auoided, thinke we? Yes, and so had been but for their owne sinne: I meane their vndutifulnes, boldnes, stout and sturdie stomacks, and their slinesse, hoping if Midian had preuailed, to haue gained by their vnnaturall dealing with their brethren, denying bread vnto them.

Doct.
Oh therefore how lamentable is it to see, how men bring shame, sorrow, and destruction vpon themselues by their wicked qualities, and bad behauiour, as wilfulnes, proud stomackes, crueltie, currish and vnkinde dealings, and such other, without the which they might haue enioyed their peace and welfare euen to their hearts desire, and good contentment, yea and the Note.
fauour of God also: for it is nothing but mens sin that keepeth many good things from them, and heapeth many contrarie euils vpon them. As *Achan* by stealing, *Dathan* by rebelling against Gods faithfull seruant *Moses*, and *Israel* by oft reuolting from God, and falling from their couenant, whereof this booke is too plaine a proofe against them.

So

So ſome among vs, are vndone by their idlenes, vnthriftineſſe, and needleſſe ſpending, ſome by their vnfaithfulnes, and deceitful dealing, loſe their credit, and being no more truſted, come to naught: ſome by their oppreſſion ſundry waies, are on their death-bed ſo terrified, that whereas by making reſtitution of a ſhilling, noble, or a pounds valew, while it ſhould haue been done, it might haue brought great eaſe to them: they would now in their terror reſtore ten for one, and yet cannot be quieted neither. So ſome for adultrie are brought to ſhame, and to worſe ſhould bee, if they had their due: and other by ſpitefull, malicious, and reuenging ſpirits, make themſelues odious to all, and they procure ſmall ioy to themſelues. And to adde ſomething touching the particular ſinne of theſe men, which was politike ſhifting and ſubtelty in playing the Newters, while the battell depended in an vncertaintie of iſſue: this I ſay, that of all other kind of offenders, theſe ſlie and wily companions are leaſt pitied of men, when the Lord entrappeth them in their owne ſnare. Sooner would a man let looſe a Lion (if he durſt) out of the pit, or the danger wherein it is, then the Foxe: becauſe (beſides the hurtfulneſſe) it hath ſo many ſhifts to conueigh it ſelfe from danger, and is ſo hardly catcht. Who pitieth theſe men of Succoth and Penuel? becauſe they in ſeeking by ſubteltie to preſerue their liues, iuſtly were beaten with their owne rodde, and loſt them. Whereas he who falles into danger either in a good quarrell, or in his ſimplicitie, is either ſaued by God, or pitied in his ruine by men. And is not this a double miſerie, when men are in diſtreſſe, to heare others ſay of them, they are well ſerued? Heathens haue obſerued this cowardly ſubteltie (for who is more ſubtill, then hee that is moſt fearefull) to be euer vnproſperous: and ſeldome euen in forren diſſentions of Kings and States, haue they ſped well, who haue held off, and plaid the ſpectators of other mens ſucceſſe. For whoſoeuer hath got the vpper hand, they haue ſmarted: if they whom they denied to ſuccour, they are made the prey of them whom they forſooke: if the other, yet they ſmart alſo, in that they did onely forbeare for their ſakes, and not actually helpe. So vnnaturall is it counted, in a common calamitie, to betray one enemie to another, or not to helpe when we are able. Which I ſpeake not to excite men to parts taking alway, in other mens iarres: but to ſhew how iuſtly theſe were handled for their craftineſſe, in denying helpe, not to ſtrangers, but their owne captaine. And euen ſo, how odious doth God make Newters and Temporiſers in religion? they are hated of Papiſt and Proteſtant, and are as curſed, as he that is hanged betwixt heauen and earth. Touching the vſe of this, and how to abhorre this ſinne, reade before in the 2. doct. of the 6. verſe.

Note.

And theſe with like puniſhments for the like iniquities, doe not light vpon other that are plaine, vpright, mercifull, and in a word, religiouſly circumſpect in their carriage, and who make conſcience of their waies. I doe not deny, but that the beſt doe oft meete with ſharpe perſecutions, but they are for good cauſes: or elſe their troubles be but fatherly trials and corrections, for their good: ſo S. *Peter* ſaith, *If ye ſuffer for righteouſneſſe ſake, bleſſed are yee:* And againe, *If the will of God be that ye ſuffer, it is better that ye ſuffer for wel-doing then for euill.* So that we ſee, ſuch haue to beare off the ſharpenes and painefulneſſe of their ſufferings, by their reioycing in the Lord, and by the bleſſed eſtate

1. Pet. 3. 14. 17.

estate that they are in: whereas the other haue their punishments, as forerunners of greater, euen here before hand, as the Apostle saith. Indeed full often (I confesse) they shelter themselues to men-ward by their greatnesse, and shift well inough when meane persons go to wracke. According to the prouerbe, *Great men dote, and poore men smart.* But when God (who is higher then they, as *Salomon* saith) calleth thẽ to account, (as being their only competent Iudge, when they haue broken through other iudgements, by fauor, feare or bribes, as great flies breake through cop-webbes) then they meete with their match. As alas who seeth not what waies there are to bring this about? As displeasure of prince, factions and partakings, treacheries challenges, and highnesse of spirits. As our owne English Chronicles for these 2. or 300 yeeres, plentifully witnesse. Now if the Lord spare not great ones, let all fawning flatterers who seeke to such, and willingly offer themselues as instruments of oppression, cruelty and wrong, because they looke to be safe vnder their wings from punishment (as *Ziba* and such like) let such feare I say: for their patrons shall not shelter themselues, howsoeuer they (no doubt) thinke otherwise. And this be said of this point, for the fuller handling of that which I noted vpon the 9. verse to the same purpose.

And here we may more particularly marke by the executing of punishment vpon these chiefe men of the citie, rather then vpon the common citizens, that as the greatest in place and authoritie haue many priuiledges aboue the meaner persons, both in credit, wealth, estimation, and commanding others: so the Lord brings them foorth to the terrour of inferiours, and they lie open to greater danger, hurt and losse thereby, then others doe, and in time it breaketh out and appeareth, if they doe ill behaue themselues in their places. This is a great cause why men who are aboue other, should carrie themselues humbly and not proudly, as too many of them doe: and also looke well to themselues in euery part of their dutie: for a time will come when they shall pay for all, and when their estate shall be such, as the meanest vnder them, would be full loth to be in their roome. And to such I say as *Dauid* in Psalm. 2. *Be wise now therefore, serue the Lord in feare: and kisse the sonne, yee mightie ones, lest he crush you in peeces: Happie then are all they that trust in him, if his wrath be kindled.* Also the inferiors should here learne, not to murmure against them, because they are so farre aboue them, for they sometime goe vnder more sore and heauy punishments, then they themselues doe: yea and though they behaue themselues commendably in their places, yet God oft correcteth them more then some others, lest they should kick vp their heele against him by meanes of their wealth and greatnesse: as it is too common a thing for such to do. So that as God hath his number among all estates both high and low; so he nurtureth them all by afflictions according to his heauenly wisdome, that they may safely in their appointed time be gathered to their fathers. But here being a fit place to make an end, I will stay for this time.

Doct. 2. in vers. 16. 17.

Note.

Psalme 2. 10.

THE

THE FIFTY THREE SERMON ON THE EIGHTH CHAPTER OF THE BOOKE OF IVDGES.

Verſ. 18. *Then ſaid he to Zeba and Zalmunna, What manner of men were they whom ye ſlew at Tabor? And they anſwered, As thou art ſo were they: euery one was like the children of a King.*

19. *And he ſaid, They were my brethren, euen my mothers children: As the Lord liueth, if ye had ſaued their liues, I would not ſlay you.*

20. *Then he ſaid to Iether his firſt borne ſonne, Vp, and ſlay them: but the boy drew not his ſword, for he feared; becauſe he was yet but young.*

21. *Then Zeba and Zalmunna ſaid, Riſe thou, and fall vpon vs: for as the man is, ſo is his ſtrength: And Gedeon aroſe, and ſlew Zeba and Zalmunna, and tooke away the ornaments that were on their Camels necks.*

The ſenſe. NOw after all this was done, it followeth, (according to the diuiſion of the Chapter in the beginning of it) how *Gedeon* executed puniſhment vpon the two Kings of Midian: whom after hee had ſhewed them to the Princes of Succoth and Penuel, hee purpoſed to puniſh. And firſt, ſeeing they were great men, he ſhewed courteſie to them, in entring ſpeech with them, though hee needed not ſo to haue done. And he asked what manner of men they were, whom they ſlew at mount Tabor: they anſwered, they were like him, and ſo goodly and well fauoured, as if they had been a Kings ſonnes. Whereby it appeareth, that *Gedeon* was a man of ſingular fauour and perſon. When thoſe men were ſlaine the ſtorie ſetteth not downe, but ſeeing the Midianites inuaded the land of Iſrael in the harueſt time euery yeere, it was like that then they did it. He anſwered, if they had not killed them, he would haue ſaued them aliue. And he commanded his eldeſt ſonne to fall vpon them, but he durſt not, being yet young: and they likewiſe ſcorned that, and bad him doe it himſelfe. So *Gedeon* did it.

This enquiring into the act before mentioned by *Gedeon*, was, that they might ſee, that they iuſtly ſuffered. For, notwithſtanding this, he might and ought to haue put them to death, for that God had appointed them thereto, being grieuous enemies of the Church: and the killing of the other two princes *Oreb* and *Zeb* (who yet ſlew not his brethren) is commended in *Pſalme 83.2.* the Pſalme; therefore he ought to haue ſlaine them euen for that cauſe. This ſpeech of his therfore, that he would not haue killed them, but for that they ſlew his brethren, though pitifull, yet was ſudden and paſſionate, and cannot be iuſtified. So that howſoeuer they might haue pleaded for themſelues otherwiſe: ſure it is their mouthes were ſtopped that they could aske no fa-

uour,

uour, in this respect seeing they had slaine his brethren: and his enquiring into that action was commendable in him, if he had proceeded no further, nor so diepely engaged himselfe by oath.

This is one thing that is here to bee noted, that as *Gedeon* did it is meete, that all who are to be punished, should see iust cause thereof, by examining them, and to cleare other, who haue been suspected: as was done by *Iosbua* at the commandement of God to *Achan*, and so the innocent shall haue no cause to complaine. It is good therfore in respect of them, that they may not feare, they shall bee pursued without cause: and also let the guiltie see, how they shall be dealt with, to wit, that they shall be brought to shame and punishment openlie. But here partialitie must be farre off, and anger, and al euill affection remooued. **Doct. vers. 18.**

And this is to be specially considered of all such as shall execute punishment vpon malefactors, or vse correction towards seruants, children, or such like. And as for such, whose sinnes are manifest to themselues or other, and yet not punishable by mans law, God will meet with them, and come against them in his good time, their own consciences giuing them to vnderstand, that they doe that which is wicked in his sight, and that they shall bee iudged for it, if they speedily repent not. But of this I haue spoken more largely in his enquiring of the Elders of Succoth, as touching their fact in slaying them at Tabor in their iollitie, more (God willing) shall bee said in the next replie of *Gedeon*.

Their answer, that they were goodly men, as if they had been the sonnes of a King, doth teach vs, that many for all their outward prerogatiues that they haue aboue other men, in fauour, birth, manhood, or honour and wealth, yet haue no hold of them, yea rather, they are depriued of them in an houre, though they hoped and pleased themselues in looking for the continuance of them for many yeeres, as may be seene in these that slew and were slaine. So was *Sisera* soone cut off, and *Eglon*, *IeZabel* and many others. For they lie open to many more dangers, then meaner persons, especially being wicked, as I haue said. All that are wise therefore, will beware how they please themselues, or rest in any earthly thing here below, but vse it soberly for their owne and the good of others; being like in this changeable world, to change also, and that daily, and their pompe and glory to turne to vanitie: and in the middest of all painted felicitie of this world, happy is he onely, who glorieth and reioyceth in the Lord. Which doctrine (I confesse) is often iterated, but when I consider the great necessitie thereof, and how contrary the most mens practise is thereto: I conclude, that it is the wisdome of the Spirit of God to giue occasion of the same almost in euery sentence, sometime and oft in some chapter, to the end that the commonnesse of the sin might bee somewhat checked by the often repeating and reproouing therof. And so it becommeth them that are wise to iudge, and prepare their appetite where the holy Ghost hath prouided sauoury meate and instruction, and not to be wearie of hearing, where he is not wearie of teaching. **Doct. 2.**

And here (as the fittest place) let vs behold these desperate Princes, how they are brought forth to their answere for a fact which they little dreamt they should euer heare of againe, or answer too: namely, for killing *of those men whom they slew at mount Tabor*. Tush, they in their iollitie had put them to the ſword, with the reſt of the company, no reſpect had of perſons (nay it is like the rather, becauſe they ſeemed to bee of note and worth) and all to make boaſt of their gallant ſpirits, victorious, braue, and proud ſtomacks: not vnlike to him, whoſe glory it was to cut off the thumbes of ſeuentie Princes, and put them like dogges vnder his bord to gather crummes. As touching the abuſe of mens proſperitie I haue oft ſpoken, and of the right vſe thereof: but here one word (more particularly) let me adde to warne men, how they ought to demeane themſelues in their places, when by reaſon either of their great ſucceſſe, vnlooked for preferment, or what other occaſion ſoeuer their corrupt fleſh might take to forget themſelues: I ſay, let men beware what they do in their iolly, luſty, or merry moodes, when they thinke they haue the world in a ſling, and none may controll them: euen then, I ſay, let them controll themſelues, and take heed leſt any inſolent, diſdainefull, cruell, iniurious, words or deeds, breake out of the ſuperfluitie of their pride and brauerie: which hereafter either God or man might bring forth againſt them, when they ſhall bee abaſed and in meaner condition. Which counſell I giue not to them who are in theſe pangs, (for I know it little bootes to tell a drunken man, *You haue done that in your drunkenneſſe which you will repent of being ſober*) but to arme men both againſt all ſuch vnlawfull occaſions, as the moſt ſeeke after, to the end they may vtter this ſtomack of theirs, as gaming, drinking, challenges, quarrels, contentions and ſuites of law, &c. as alſo againſt the corrupt abuſe euen of lawfull bleſſings, which (if a man be not very warie) will tickle and pricke him forward at one time or other, to ſome odious carriage of himſelfe, which afterward may be remembred againſt him to his reproach, loſſe and ſhame, yea ruine, as heere we ſee in theſe. Euen Heathens haue prudently obſerued this, *That a wiſe man will carrie himſelfe no otherwiſe being proſperous, then as one who conſidereth, that one day he may be miſerable.* And indeed ſuch iolly fellowes had need of this warrant euen to man-ward, that they ſhall neuer fall nor decay in their eſtate; ſeeing that elſe, who ſeeth not what fruite they reape of their ſcorne and pride, to wit, that being vnderfoot all men reioyce in their ruine, and make them their paſtime, few or none pitying them, or taking their part: whereas others are lamented and relieued in their miſerie. Who pitieth *Herod* eaten vp with wormes, becauſe he would ſo proudly exceed the bounds of man, and be counted a God? *Haman* was hanged vpon the gallowes: who readeth it not with ioy, rather then is grieued at it? becauſe (while hee was aloft) he made himſelfe the terrour of the Church for his crueltie? How ſhould *Iob* haue anſwered it in his affliction, if hee had vſurped ouer his vnderlings, being in proſperitie? When *Dauid* ſent meſſengers to *Hanun* to comfort him, he cuts off their garments by the middle, and ſhaues them, and ſo ſends them backe to their Maſter. But the time came, when hee repented him of that iolly defiance. Tuſh, ſaith *Sheba*, who is *Dauid*, and who is the ſonne of *Iſhai*? Who is *Abimelech* ſaid *Gaal*? A baſe fellow, I defie and ſcorne him and his: but ſoone after, he wiſht that vnſaid againe, and ſo did the other. And thus of theſe now mentioned, together with *Adonibezek*, and them of Succoth and Penuel, let this ſuffice that hath been ſaid. Therefore as for all deſperate and prophane wretches (whom nothing but the halter, or ſtabbing, or ſuch like deſerued plague of God befalling them, will perſwade

Iudg. 1. 7.

3. Doct. ver. 18.

Note.

Iob 31. 13. 14.

2. Sam. 10. 4.

2. Sam. 20. 1.

Iudg. 9. 28.

perswade the truth hereof) let them goe as they are. But let all Gods people (who are to looke at God aswell as men) beware especially, that they forget not themselues this way: but walke humbly, with due weighing their owne vilenesse, and the changeablenesse of all things here below; else euen they may fall, as *Ezechia* did. Esay 39.6.

As *Gedeon* did heere, so it is lawfull for vs to prosecute our brethrens wrongs, as murther, yea it is meet so to doe, as in the booke of Numbers appeareth, and this, not onely in a priuat respect for that we are their flesh (in which kindnesse is to be shewed to them) but also, (and much more) in the publike behalfe of Church and Commonwealth: both which it much concerneth, that sinne be not vnpunished. This the Lord requireth, as by *Salomons* words may bee gathered, which hee spake of *Ioab*, saying: let him bee slaine, that euill may be remoued, and wee may not bee guilty of the innocent blood, which he hath shed. But to returne to the point in hand, as it is good to reioyce with our friends, and liue together with them for our mutuall good: so is it also a token of our vnfained loue toward them, to pursue their wrongs being dead. And this were highly commendable if it were done according to Gods law. But as it is commonly gone about, I meane, so that flesh and blood with carnall reason doe rule, as it highly displeaseth God, so likewise it marres the action, as in the next point shall appeare. And namely to pursue any for them, when they suffer for their deserts, as the most doe: or when they be hurt by them, with whom they were companions in euill: and therfore iustly suffer at the hands of one another: although the Magistrate is to punish the offendor euen in that case also: as when drunkards or quarrellers shed the blood of each other. And as the Lord himselfe hath put a difference betwixt casuall or vnwilling killing, and wilfull murther: as appeareth by his appointing in each Tribe, cities of refuge, for the safegard of the innocent: so he is farre from iustifying any such cruell pitie, as this, to spare the guiltie murtherer: but will himselfe as well plague them, that shall seeke to stop the due course of iustice against such, as also find out the murtherer himselfe, (notwithstanding the secresie wherewith much villanie is cloaked) at one time or other. *An eye for an eye, a tooth for a tooth, and he who sheddeth blood, his blood shall be shed.* For the blood of the slaine crieth strongly in the eares of the Lord, as that of *Abel,* and as the widow, who by her importunitie compelled the Iudge to heare, and doe her iustice of her aduersarie. And this further condemneth the deadly reuenge which is betweene many, not persons onely, but families and kindreds also, who vpon such murthers, band themselues, and take parts each against other irreconciliably, more fit for Pagans indeed then Christians, who should be ioyned together in loue, rather then diuide themselues into sworne brotherhoods in mischiefe, like those two, *Simeon* and *Leui.* Lastly, it bewraieth the leaudnesse of the Romish pretended pitie and mercifulnesse (not in protecting the guiltlesse,) but in sauing the vilest malefactors from the hand of the lawfull Magistrate, whom God hath appointed to be the terror of ill doers, and not the mocke and may-game of such shauelings. For if they being pursued, can get into those Temples (or rather dennes) of theeues, they are rescued (as in Sanctuaries) for feare of law and punishment.

[Margin notes: Doct. vers. 19. — Numb. 35.31. — 1. Kings 2.31. — Ioshua 20.2. — Exod. 21.24. — Luke 18.5.]

Againe, in that *Gedeon* saith, and sweareth to it, that hee would not haue 2

killed them,if they had saued his brethren aliue,who ought to haue done it, for pursuing the people of God, (neither had he authoritie to saue them, though hee had to destroy them:) and the Holy-ghost commendeth the act: it teacheth,that it is a very hard matter to doe good actions aright, but that they will one way or other be blemished and obscured: euen as *Iephtahs*
Iudg 11.30. courage & constancy in warring against the Ammonites was much dashed by his vnseasonable & rash vow. And so particularly through our hastines, boldnes,blindnes,or the like corrupt humours,many good actions do lose their beautie. Which thing as it is with great regard to bee looked to of vs, so it teacheth,that we must not cleaue to al the examples of Gods seruants, without respect and difference,nor follow them,because they did them,but
1.Cor.11.1. examine their grounds,and how they did them,following them only so far as they haue obeyed the Lord: for therein onely they are presidents for vs to follow,where their doings are examples agreeable to the rule that should guide vs: for that is to be looked vnto which is Gods, not mens. And further it should teach vs more specially, to examine our actions,the manner, end,affections and minde wherewith they be done; which is the thing that I doe here aime at to lay foorth: for those things which wee doe in ignorance and darknesse, wee haue not onely no comfort in them, neither learne any experience by them to be better directed afterward; but contrariwise we haue much to grieue our hearts and to accuse vs therby. And this I adde the rather, because wee see that *Gedeon* ouer-shot himselfe in this, who yet most worthily tempered wisedome and equitie with seueritie in the punishing of the men of Succoth and Penuel. Now because few of Gods children will beleeue this,therfore they see not,that the most offences that they commit,are abuses of good duties. They dare not sin grossely,and so long they think all is well: but when they are about good actions,they are soone
Note. ouer-shot: and why? They are there where they should be(being so occupied) they presume and suspect no danger: euen as the traueller riding in a most straight path or rode,hedged in on both sides, so that hee cannot goe amisse. But oh sillie man consider, thou bearest about thee a bodie of sinne, an euill heart,euen in a good heart: what wonder then if much euill cleaue to thy best actions, when no other thing is looked at, but the good? when the hypocrisie,ignorance,boldnes,pride, and other corruptions thereof lieth vnseene, vnpurged: nay when a corrupt humour sets a man on worke to doe a good dutie,that it may lurke vnder the vizor thereof: as anger and
Leuit.10.1. malice,vnder zeale and holy reuenge, which is as odious as *Nadab & Abihu* their offering Incense with strange or common fire. Is not hearing, prayer,
Luke 8.18. a good action? Yet our Sauiour saith: *Take heede how ye heare: Paul* saith,
Ephes.6.18. *Watch your selues in prayer*, Ephes.6. For if yee looke not narrowly to your selues in these,keeping your selues attentiue, reuerent, confident, humble, feruent,throughout them; the diuell will watch you so,that as good neuer a whit,as neuer the better when all is done. And if this be so,euen in things religious, how much more in those which are indifferent? For vnder this pretence,That to be angrie,merrie in companie, to eate,drinke,recreate the body,&c. are things neither good nor euill in nature; who forgets not this, That these all,change their nature when they come into action,and cannot be indifferently done? They are good or bad according to the manner of doing.

doing. Therefore though anger be not euill of it selfe, yet the Lord iustly challengeth *Ionah*, saying, *Doest thou well to be angrie?* meaning, so corruptly and carnally. Therefore, as easie a worke as men thinke it, to carrie themselues aright in all these: yet let them know, that if in any of them they transgresse the rule either of pietie, loue, or sobernes; the goodnesse, or indifferencie of the worke, shall not saue them harmelesse. For instance, if in their zeale, they neither aime at Gods glorie, nor the reformation of the partie, nor the moderation of the affection: their zeale is folly, rage, error, or any thing rather then holy zeale. But of this point I haue spoken in this booke often, and shall speake afterward, if God will. Let me adde this caueat to the Ministers, that in all their teaching, especially in the doctrine of these duties, they beware lest they teach men their libertie (which they learne too soone of themselues, and catch greedily from them) and be large therein: but slight and short in teaching the rules before named, to restraine the abuse thereof: rather be they short in the former, and warie and large in the latter, to cut off all lewd pretences. As wee see *Paul* doth, for hauing said, *Be angrie:* fearing he should haue disciples too many: he straight way addeth, [*but sinne not*] and this cuts the combe of the Libertine. So doth the wise Preacher, Ecclesi.11. *Reioyce young man, and take thy pleasure,* &c. *But know that for all this thou shalt come to iudgement.* Now if the best be subiect to these failings, what shall be said of the worst? Surely no wonder, if they regard not at all, whether it be good or bad they doe, but runne to their obiect, as the fish to the baite? Or if they doe enquire, then they doe it after the fact done, as *Salomon* saith of the sacrilegious, which bewraies a vile minde. For if they desire to heare it be well, what a prophanenes is this to desire that Gods rule were crooked, so their doings be streight? But if they thinke otherwise, they make the Minister of God a stale, and as for God himselfe, they make him a God of cloutes, who must take their frothie repentance and satisfaction in good part, be it what and when they please: but for themselues, they will be on the surest hand with him, first to satisfie their desire, and to inquire afterwards, whether they did well or no. Againe for good duties, they cannot doe them well, themselues being euill: as for indifferent: though they say, Let vs alone, if we know we may doe them, wee will take order good enough for the manner and end. For like fooles they runne into the contrarie extremitie, or else into monstrous excesse in the vse of the libertie. So that truly it is said of such, *They are set in slipperie places:* for they delight most of all to set their foote on the brinke of the ditch or riuer, who seeth not with what danger? but they loue not to walke vpon plaine ground, which they might doe safely: and so they slide suddenly, and in the end perish remedilesly.

Ionah.4.4. Eph.4.26. Ecclesi.11.9. Prou.20.25. Luke 6.46.

Gedeons mouing his sonne to fall vpon the two Princes, was to traine him to be acquainted with pursuing ill causes and persons assoone as he grew fit for it, and not to teach him from his youth to bee cruell. For that quickly pricks which will be a thorne, of it selfe, and needs no sharpning: either this or any other sinne. By this example (well approued by the best rule) Christians should frame their children betimes, and as their yeeres will permit, to discerne good from bad: and beware how they vse their tongues, or behaue themselues in the sight or hearing of their children, euen when they Doct. vers.20.

Note. are most tender: seeing they are apprehensiue enough of that which is lewd, and especially when their parents shall strengthen their inward pronenesse to euill by their authoritie: as (God willing) shall better appeare after in chap. 17. 2. As for this action of his, howsoeuer it may seeme crueltie to such as cannot iudge, yet it was pietie and obedience to Gods commandement. And youth in this age, had need in all wise manner to be moued, and (if it may be) perswaded, to the embracing and following of good instruction, and religious walking, they being so soone possessed by ill education and companie, of the sinnes of the time, as neuer more in any age or memorie then in this.

2 Although the act was good, that he was vrged to, yet feare and modestie in him being so young, was commendable: for there must be time to settle youth euen in that which is good, which takes not roote easily, much lesse growes to bring foorth fruite, especially when there is some shew and appearance of euill in it. As in *Gedeons* sonne vnexperienced in these kindes of manhood and courage, the falling vpon two valiant Princes by him a boy, it was to be commended that he feared to doe it. His father did well in vrging, but tendernes excused him, in not obeying. His example may worthily set to schoole too many youths too bold of their owne accord, without instigation, to attempt and set vpon not doubtfull but vile actions of theft, whoredome, drunkennes, swearing, ribaldrie and the like, odious both to God and man, as breaking all bounds of modestie, feare, and bashfulnes: the enioying of the which are comely ornaments in youth; and doe stand them in stead, while yet religion is to seeke with them, to keepe and holde them backe from great and shamefull euils, as bold fellowship with lewd huswiues and companions. And here iustly may we take vp a lamentation ouer our times, for the want of ciuill and godly education of youth: whereby sinne hath now so got the vpper hand, that the boldnes which wee haue seene in growne sinners, men of ripe yeeres, with astonishment, wee behold now with execration, euen in children and youth, new come out of the shell. And while parents (guiltie of the same, or at least irreligious) doe in particular neglect the care of such their children, by disswading, and discouraging them from the sinnes of the time, and by good education keep them from them, behold the disease groweth, ere they bee aware, common and desperate: and those parents are so few that shew their care this way, that it were well if religious parents often times did not nourish and winke at such euill qualities in their children.

Now when these two Princes see the youth fearefull, they (as men impatient of further delay) prouoke *Gedeon* himselfe to fall vpon and slay them, and so rid them out of the way. And they descant vpon the youths tendernes, as if *Gedeon* had not been well aduised what he did. The child (say they) doth according to his age: he is not fit for such a worke. The like discourse they make before, in their answer to *Gedeon*; *They were like thee* (say they) *like the children of a King*. Of both these together, because they bewray the same spirit and nature in them. First then in the 18. verse they denie not the fact, but describe the persons whom they slew, that they were Princes fellowes, as I haue said, and all to declare the greatnes of their courage and stomack: but they abase not themselues so low as to aske pardon, neither to craue any fauour.

fauour. And by this we may see,what are the props whereby wicked and desperate men stay vp and hearten themselues in their miseries and extremities: their props are prophane and diuelish magnanimitie, and a desperate loftie stomacke,which they call a braue minde,which will yeeld it selfe for no fault,neither blush,or seek any fauour,through a senselesnes of Gods wrath. And to ioyne therewith this second reply of theirs in this verse,they bewray the same here also,when they say,*Fall thou on vs*, or, *dispatch vs with thine owne hands*. And this I note of them not so much to their shame (who being Heathens,what wonder though they were no better reformed)as to the shame of such as come after them,who being in the Church, should be better, but yet are led by their spirit: who are so blinded and hardned by the diuell, that they thinke it an ornament to them, and a chiefe point of manhood,to shrinke for nothing, but to beare off all by the head and shoulders,as they say, and to seeme to men to set light by a violent death, as appeares in them who desperatly cast themselues off the ladder into hell, if God bee not mercifull: which contempt of death is yet contrary to their owne nature, and feeling within them. And this sinne resteth not in these only of the worst and most proiected sort,but reacheth to many professors: who if they haue done euill, yet set a good face, I meane,a bold,on it; but relent not in any wise,nor will be knowne to be such as they are, and know themselues to bee: of which sort wee finde *Gehezai* the seruant of *Elisha* the Prophet to haue been,who when his sinne was couertly bewrayed by his master, (saying, *From whence commest thou Gehezai*) answered boldly, and 2.King.5.25.
that with a lie,*Thy seruant hath been no where*, meaning but where he should be, to wit, about his businesse. This diuelish shamelesnes and hardning of heart is euer by the seruants of God to bee turned into relenting, melting, and meeknes of spirit, or else they may bee sure,with the wicked to meete with much sorrow. Of which point more hath bin said elsewhere, chap.2. and therefore I touch it here but by the way.

As touching *Gedeon*, he (as became him) dispatched them, wherein (setting aside the fault before mentioned) hee executed the vengeance of God vpon them being the ring-leaders, as before hee had done vpon the other multitude of the Midianites. And thus wee see a goodly end to the people of God of this sore affliction,if wee view the whole, both miserie and deliuerance out of it, and the ouerthrow of their enemies, as it hath been set downe from the beginning of the sixth chapter vnto this place. Let it teach vs thus to view and consider Gods great workes both in his visitation and chastizing his people, and also their behauiour vnder them, with his restoring them to their liberties againe, and his blessing of them. These are the treasures and riches that we should store not our bookes onely,but our memories also with,that out of them all we may learne the better to marke and obserue throughout our liues Gods dealing with vs,and how wee in faith, Note.
hope, and patience, may bee like the best of Gods seruants, and enioy the things promised,as they did,til we may with *Paul* learne by our experience, that hope shall not make vs ashamed: but beleeue for all times to come, that God who hath,and doth,he also will deliuer vs vnto the end.

Now lastly in this scripture it is added, that *Gedeon* took of the ornamẽts, which were in forme and shew goodly to looke vpon,and costly,as was fitting

ting for Princes, which were the furniture of their Camels: these ornaments (I say) with whatsoeuer else was of price, *Gedeon* tooke away: which could not be of small price and valew. Whereby, as we may see that God plucketh the prey out of the teeth of the wicked, (when he pleaseth) and giueth it to
Psal.3.6. the righteous, as *Dauid* speaketh in the Psalme, and as is to bee seene in the
2.King.7.16. 2.booke of Kings, chap.7. how he relieued his people in their famine and distresse, with the spoile and goods of his enemies the Aramites: so by this which God did here to *Gedeon*, that scripture is verified, which saith: *First*
Matth.6.33. *seeke the kingdome of God, and his righteousnes, and other things shall be added to you.* For while *Gedeon* in the simplicitie of heart, and desire of obeying God, did pursue the enemies of his people, intending that businesse wholly, and not minding earthly profit at all, behold, euen that also befell him, and was brought to his hands. And it is as easie to see and behold at this day, as it shall be alwaies found true, that while Gods seruants in all conditions and
Genes.28.21. degrees, seeke the Lord with all their heart, he prouideth other necessarie helpes for this present life, which they doe not so much seeke after. As *Iacob*,
Genes.32.10. when he had renued his couenant with the Lord in his iourney to Aram, confesseth at his returning home how liberally God had prouided for him. Oh how many may witnesse the same? For why? as the Lord is true of his
Hebr.11.6. promise, so he is a plentifull rewarder of them that seeke him. And as he regardeth such not meanely; so hee dealeth iustly with those that are vnfaithfull and worldly minded; that whereas they might seeme by their greedines and their vnwearied following their commodities (with the casting of care of things heauenly) to get all wealth into their hands, they oft times attaine not that which they pursue, and those that doe attaine it, haue got but
Prou.23.5. the winde in their fist, euen nothing, who see they cannot hold it, when they most desire it. And this is to teach vs contentment in a godly estate, yea
Prou.15.16.17. and 16.8. thankfulnes, and not to haue our teeth watering after the dainties of the other. A dish of greene hearbes is better in such a case, then a stalled oxe.

Vers.22. *Then the men of Israel said vnto Gedeon, Raigne thou ouer vs, both thou, and thy sonne, and thy sonnes sonne, for thou hast deliuered vs out of the hand of Midian.*

23. *And Gedeon said vnto them, I will not raigne ouer you, neither shal my child raigne ouer you, but the Lord shall raigne ouer you.*

The third part of the Chapter.

The sense and doct. of verse 22. IN this last part of the Chapter follow certaine particulars concerning *Gedeon*, and the first that is set downe, is the offering of the kingdome to *Gedeon* and his posteritie, by the men of Israel, and the reason which they render of their so doing: with his refusing it, in these two verses. The generall act of the people was good, in that they shewed themselues thankfull to him, for the great deliuerance which they had obtained by him (as Gods instrument) out of all the oppression of the Midianites, their enemies. And it bindeth all to the like dutie, when they haue receiued kindnesse. So both kindred, towne and countrey ought to shew kindnesse to him and his, by whom they haue receiued some great good and benefit. Thus did *Pharaoh* aduance

aduance *Ioseph*, and his brethren, and father, for that hee had preserued his Genes.47.6.
land in the famine, and it was complained of, that there arose another *Pha-* Exod.1.8.
raoh afterward, who did not know him. And *Dauid* remembred *Ionathans* 2.Sam.9.7.
kindnesse to him after he was dead, in doing good to his.

This caused *Salomon* to vtter this prouerb: *Thine owne friend, and thy fa-* Prou.27.10.
thers friend, forsake thou not. And so, (to descend to smaller kindnesse betwixt one neighbour and another) this thankfulnesse ought to bee shewed, that while both it and the fruit of it bee continued betwixt them, there may bee peace and good will, which otherwise (for the most part) is banished from men, vnlesse it be couered with dissimulation. For while the one scorneth to owe any thing to the other, professing that he can liue without him, and the other is backward in loue, whereby he might winne his neighbor: what is nourished betweene both, but strangenesse, suspition, vncharitablenesse, discord, and such cursed effects and fruits thereof? And now last of all in this matter, if thankfulnesse bee due for outward fauours and good turnes, how much more should it bee shewed for the greatest of all, as when one man hath by his industrie, labour, and loue, bin the instrument and meane, of the saluation of many? In which respect *Paul* wrote to *Philemon* thus: *I will* Philem.19.
not say (though he might) *that thou owest to me euen thine owne selfe.* And so other such may say, who haue receiued the like kindnesse by any of vs, as to be deliuered from the wrath to come by our teaching, though it little appeare by the requital of loue and kindnesse againe, I meane to procure their ioy who reclaimed them; by being shining lights afterward. But this hath been shewed at large vers. 1. before.

Now as I haue spoken of the generall act of the Israelites toward *Gedeon*, 2.Doct.ver.22.
which all may see to haue been commendable, in that they were thankfull, (though not without some weakenes) so yet their particular act in offering the kingdome to him, as farre of from allowance in them, that it was vtterly vnlawfull: for it was not in their power, and therefore they offered that which was not theirs, as shall better appeare by *Gedeons* answer in the next verse. We ought by this to beware, that we be not liberall of another mans right and good, in giuing that which belongs not to vs. As many loue for name and credit to be liberall, but it shall be of stolne, or (which is all one) of other mens goods. Euen so, (to shew it in another kind) neither may any man giue his soule to the diuell, as witches and coniurers, and many other though not so apparantly doe; for they are bought with a price: nor our bodies to be defiled, for they are redeemed, and made the Temples of the holy Ghost. This needs no long standing vpon: but by this we are taught, that as their sinne is great, as oppressors, gripers and gamesters, who inioy to their owne benefit ill gotten goods, and restore them not; so neither ought we to receiue of any man that which is not his owne, but ill come by, if wee certainly know it. Otherwise the receiuer is excused, who in his simplicitie doth presume charitably, that to be of the giuers proper goods, which hee knoweth not certainly to haue been badly gotten. Neither shall the simple affection of the receiuer, acquite the ill conscience of the giuer, whose sinne herein is double, both that he hath attained his wealth vnconscionably: and then plaid the part of *Achan*, in couering his stealth, what though it be vnder the faire pretence of religious and deuout liberalitie? Doubtlesse if *Ananias*

Actes 5.3. were guiltie of sacriledge,for detaining to himselfe a part of that which hee had alienated from himselfe,and consecrated to the Lords vse: how much more they who first rob others, and then feed the Lord with the spoile,as Lions doe their Whelps of that which they haue ill gotten? It is the cast of many caterpillars, when they haue sucked and drawne the blood of others all their life,like horsleaches ready to burst,they will satisfie for their villany, by paying the tithe or some shred of their vnrighteous Mammon to the vse of the Lord,or the Church: whereas this sanctifieth not the rest,that is behind,but maketh all their goods execrable to them and theirs,till restitution be made either in kind,or to the poore (the true heires of such goods) if it cannot otherwise be,to the pleasing of God,as a fruit of their vnfained repentance So no man ought to buy or hire that which is passed ouer to another before,nor couet wife, seruant, goods, of another mans (for that is nothing else but a taking of his right from him) nor to receiue stolne goods for

1.Pet.5.3. their aduantage. So neither should the Pope vsurpe dominion: S.*Peter* (whose successor he saith he is) forbidding dominion ouer the flocke,for he hath no such authoritie,as neither hath the best minister of Christ.

Vers 23. *Gedeon* answereth,God shal raigne ouer them,(an holy speech) for where shall they be found that will refuse a thing much lesse then a kingdome being offered? nay,how greedily would many haue fastened vpon a matter of small valew,being offered them,as the kingdome here was to him? But some will aske, Might not God raigne ouer them though hee had also? I say,Yes. Neither was he of the Anabaptists opinion, who thinke that such ciuill gouernment and subiection of people to Kings repugneth to Christian liberty. And God raigned ouer his people, when yet *Saul*,and after him *Dauid* raigned ouer them also: but his meaning was, that the order that God had set (of gouerning by such as had no continued gouernment,) should stand,and not be peruerted by or for him or his: but contrariwise,to his power he would hinder it. And God raigned indeed in the Commonwealth of the Israelites,which florished in *Gedeons* time, wherein the Elders were chosen by common consent,some ecclesiasticall to giue the meaning of the law,and others ciuill and temporall, as men call it, to rule the people thereby: in which office if they did not well carrie themselues, they were both punished and put from their places. And if any warre fell out, the Lord himselfe stirred vp Guides and Iudges, and they were not chosen by men,as appeares both by Chapter 1.1. and after neither did their children succeed them: and thus the Lord both in peace and warre ruled ouer them, and so *Gedeon* meant,that the office of the Iudge was no ordinary magistracy,such as the King is: but a temporary and occasionall, much like to the Dictatorship of the Romans,in respect of the vse wherto it serued: although otherwise of diuine election,immediatly,not by men. By this answere,the singular modestie, and the religious staiednesse and good gouernment of *Gedeon* appeareth: who hauing occasion so fairely offered of possessing and inioying the kingdome,refuseth it as resolutely, as they offered it earnestly. Hee is indeed the strong man, who standeth out stoutly,when the brunt commeth: now *Gedeons* sinceritie and courage is tryed: and now he plaieth the part of a truly heroicall captaine, in reiecting the tentation that was set before him. Which of how great force it was to batter and beate him down flat,

flat,although meane persons cannot easily conceiue, whose thoughts reach not so high,yet by the comparing of great things with small,may wel seeme to be forcible,seeing that a little preferment, fauour, commendation or reward doth so bleare the eie, and choake the conscience of many professors, as if it were a petty Paradise. In one instance consider of that which I say: *Gedeon* refused a whole kingdome, when it was offered him: and the most desire vnlawfully a small commodity of their neighbours in comparison of a kingdome,as his house and ground,wife and seruant, when they be denied them. And yet many a bold person would bee ready to say euen of *Gedeon*,He was a foole to refuse and neglect such an aduantage. Doubtlesse he did it not for any feare,or conscience of his owne insufficiency: hee had been a man fit for the place, if the office had been lawfull for him. But the respect he had to Gods commandement,was the meere cause that mooued him to denie and refuse. A worthy paterne indeed of a man truly fearing God,and making conscience of offending. And so it becommeth vs,both in sinnes of the grossest kind,as adultery,murther,oppression, (from which the feare of God doth best and most safely keepe vs,as *Ioseph* saith) and also in the matter of a mans priuate gaine,yea and that in the highest degree of a kingdome:it becommeth vs(I say)to keep our consciences pure and good. And yet for the smallest of these many a man,otherwise vertuous,would(as the cōmon speech is)straine a ioynt,and think,that for a kingdom he might venture to dispense with equity & conscience. And doubtles it is a great trial of a man what grace is in him,when a matter of commodity,promotion, honour,or the like,of the greatest valew,cannot surprise the conscience; so neere is euery man to himselfe;and indeed(when these temptations assaile) vtterly vnlike himself at other times.This example of *Gedeon* most properly taxeth ambitious and aspiring spirits,as wel Popish as other,such as *Absolons* was, not of immodesty onely,but of insolencie also,and intemperance,the cause of all confusion in euery state, especially being ioyned with discontentment and emulation. But it were to bee wished, that men of greater hope,had but a little measure of *Gedeons* grace, and were not rather led by the spirit of these whom I haue mentioned, to wit, that in meaner matters, and of lesse valew they did not hardly containe and keepe themselues within compasse from coueting and laying claime to other mens commodities, for the supplying of their owne wants, and to seeke increase of that which they haue,and not to looke after any thing which tends to the losse or hurt of other, but that they liued contentedly with that which is theirs, who ought in so liuely a glasse as this,to behold how honourable a grace this was in *Gedeon* to rest satisfied in his estate, as thinking that best befitting him, which hee might enioy with Gods good liking, and the quietnesse of his owne mind: and as for other endlesse wishing or coueting,to inhaunse himselfe, (which is most mens sinne) hee had got the victory ouer himselfe in that behalfe, which I thinke was a greater honour to him then all his conquest ouer the Midianites: it being an ouerruling of himselfe, and of his vaineglorious affection. But to the shame of many Protestants, I will adde one example,euen an Heathen might set vs to schoole in this dutie: who hauing subdued his enemies in battell,and returned home with triumph, was presented by some with a great masse of gold: but he repelled thē with this

Doct. vers.23.

Note.

Genes.39.9.

this answer; I had rather rule them that owe the gold, then be Lord and owner of the gold only, or rather to be a seruant, ruled and possessed by it. Oh well were it for vs, if the holy gouernment of our harts and affections were so pretious to vs Christians, as it was to many of them, who were Heathen: whereas they were drawne by a pride and ambition of praise, or at least bare loue of vertue, to contemne such offers, but we by religion, and hope of a farre greater matter, then the greatest earthly kingdome.

Doct.2. And this also more particularly teacheth, that all must endeuour in their callings and places, that God may raigne, as in all his heauenly ordinances, so especially in this of gouernment in Church, land, citie, towne, house; for

Psalm.2.1. that (I say) onely must stand, and all that is opposite must fall, Psalm.2. Religious gouernement is to be sought for, yeelded vnto, and imbraced, and not the contrary: but the limites and bounds of Gods holy word kept and preserued, which neuer repugneth to ciuill gouernment of the lawfull Magistrate, but confirmes it rather: so that God may bee obeyed, and equitie and iustice maintained, for the preseruation of outward peace and order in all things. And so I might say particularly of euery condition. But alas, what care is there had of this? but it is rather iustled aside at mens pleasure. For though wee pray daily, that God may bee glorified by the comming of

Note. his kingdome, and the guiding vs to the doing of his will: which if it might take place, what a blessed thing were it to see the superiors and inferiors, in all degrees and estates, liue together vnder the gouernment of one God, and mutually commanding and obeying each other in the Lord: yet wee see the quite contrary in mens practise. True it is, that the law of man stoppeth much disorder: and how could men inioy any safe and peaceable dwelling without it? but while the Lord is shut out of the conscience, the word and faithfull Minister of God despised, and in many places none at all to awake and prepare the people for the life to come, and the ordinance of God in Magistracie, which serueth to backe and authorise the Word, and to vphold other good order, little to bee regarded, and also little put in practise to restraine euill, but Atheisme, prophanenesse, and other great sinnes slightly punished, &c. behold, euery man runneth his owne course, and being wedded to his owne wilfull humour, without feare of punishment, walketh in his frowardnesse, atheisme, prophanenesse, scorne of religion, crueltie, oppression, contempt of the Sabbath, ignorance, &c. saying as they in

Psalme 12.4. the Psalme, *Our tongues are our owne*, wee will doe as we list, *who shall controll vs?* Surely none, but sinne and the diuell, rule and raigne at their pleasure, where the Lord by his word doth not, but is iustled aside: but let vs mourne for those things, till the Lord amend them: but in the meane season, let vs be sure that we be guided by him our selues in our whole course, or else hold our peace of and concerning others. But I passe now to the second thing concerning *Gedeon*.

THE

THE FIFTIE FOVRE SERMON ON THE EIGHTH CHAPTER OF THE BOOKE OF IVDGES.

Verſ.24. *And Gedeon ſaid vnto them, I would deſire a requeſt of you, that you would giue me euery man the earings of his pray; for they had golden earings becauſe they were Iſmaelites.*

25. *And they anſwered, We will giue them. And they ſpread a garment, and did caſt therein euery man the earings of his pray.*

26. *And the weight of the golden earings that he required, was a thouſand and ſeuen hundred ſhekels of gold, beſide collors and iewels and purple rayment that was on the Kings of Midian, and beſides the chaines that were on their cammels necks.*

27. *And Gedeon made an Ephod thereof, and put it in Ophrah his citie, all Iſrael went a whoring there after it, which became a ſnare vnto Gedeon, and to his houſe.*

NOw after this victory ouer the Midianites, *Gedeon* deſires to leaue a monument and memoriall of his thankes to God for the ſame, and for the great deliuerance of Iſrael. And thought it meet, that it ſhould be of ſome valew and price; and therefore he ſeeing the people ſo affected to him, that they could willingly haue agreed to make him their king, hee thought they would not ſticke at a ſmaller matter, but yeeld it to him: eſpecially, ſeeing it was not for his owne priuate, but for their common benefit: and the thing that he asked of them, was their earings, which were coſtly, which he obtaining of the people, made of them a Prieſts vpper garment, of great valew and richly ſet forth, called an Ephod, which was to be worne vpon their other apparrell: and this was the monument which he would haue remaine as a token of his thankfull heart. But it being ſet vp in a place of his citie Ophrah, becauſe of the forme, and coſtlineſſe of it, and for that it pertained to the Prieſts in the ſeruice of God, and to religious vſe, it grew to be worſhipped, which (through Gods iuſt iudgement iuſtly puniſhing Idolatrie in the poſteritie following, was the deſtruction of *Gedeon* and his houſe; ſo eaſily and ſoone did idolatrie and ſuperſtition ariſe vp among them againe. *The ſenſe.*

Here firſt his thankfull mind is to bee commended, and imitated of vs: thus ought our hearts in all benefits which we inioy, leade vs vnto God the fountaine of each good giuing, as Saint *Iames* ſaith. But this point hath been largely handled: reade notes vpon the 5. chapter, and elſewhere by occaſion of the like Scripture. Doct. verſ.24. Iames 1.17.

Againe, we may learne here, that when we are willing to pleaſure one another without taking any gratuitie againe, (which few will doe) wee may be Doct. verſ. 24.25.26.

be the bolder to ſue for ſomewhat to bee put to good vſes, as *Gedeon* intended here to doe, (though hee was deceiued) asking their earings to make a monument of thanks to God: eſpecially, I ſay, when wee haue refuſed to take to our owne priuate vſe, the commodity which hath been offered vs, (when it hath been thought we haue deſerued it) as *Gedeon* here did: in ſuch a caſe we may deſire ſomewhat to bee imploied to the ſeruice and glory of God by them that offer it vs: as to the relieuing of the poore, or other good ends. And in this alſo hee deſerued commendation, and was, and is to bee followed of vs. And as the people yeelded to him to a good vſe and end, ſo all good Chriſtians ought with all readineſſe to doe the like toward the relieuing and helping of the needy, by lending, giuing, or any other friendſhip yeelding, conſidering that Saint *Paul* ſaith, that free giuing and liberalitie hath great force to worke on men: for a bountifull perſon (ſaith he) *it*
Rom.5.7. *may be ſome man will die*; and ſo if one did much good by bodily helpe in comforting the needy and poore, he might be like to doe good by exhortation alſo: both which duties of loue it were to bee wiſhed might goe together, for thereby moſt good were like to be done. And ſo doing, we ſhould moue ſuch as thinke themſelues beholding to vs, to ſhew themſelues thankfull to God alſo, ſo bountifull to them that were in penury and want. And doubtleſſe if the honouring of our God were all in all with vs, and predominant in vs, this we ſhould mind and aime at in all our actions, to purchaſe this glory to him, to whom we are ſo infinitely beholding for all that we in-
Iudg.13.16. ioy. The Angell that appeared to *Manoah*, though he refuſed to eate, yet wil-
Eſter 7.2.3. led him to conuert the gift, into an holy preſent, or ſacrifice to God. *Aſſuerus*, to declare his loue to *Heſter*, promiſed to giue her what ſhe requeſted, euen to the halfe of the kingdome: but ſhe was content to reſigne her hope and aduantage that way, and turned the fauour ſhe found with the King, to the aduancing of Gods worſhip in and by the deliuerance of the Iewes
Nehem.2.5. from the miſchiefe of *Haman*. Good *Nehemia*, Butler to another King, finding him enclinable and fauourable to himſelfe, and pitying him in his heauineſſe: preſently offereth to him the cauſe of the Church of God, to conſider of, and deſires that he may by his meanes be comforted in the reliefe of
Dan.5.17.20. his countrimen the people of God. So *Daniel* hauing ſundry rewards offered him for his good ſeruice by *Nebuchadnezzar* and *Darius*, is content to to part with them all, ſo that the King wil acknowledge the Lord *Iehoua*, the
Exod.32. author of thoſe gifts which he ſo admired. And reaſon there is hereof: for
Rom.9.3. if *Paul* and *Moſes* engaged their ſaluation, for the procuring of honour to God in the ſaluation of the Church: how much more are wee bound to ſeeke it by the forgoing of ſuch a fauour as we may well be without, and need not accept of? Beſides, this wiſdome ſhould be in all Chriſtians, to vſe euery opportunity they may to the poore Church of God, eſpecially ſeeing ſuch occaſions befall not often, nor to all ſorts of men, in this kind. And further they had need of good diſcretion who ſhould perſwade men to conuert that ciuill kindneſſe which they offer them as friends, to a religious vſe, as Chriſtians: ſithence they may thinke it either vnſeaſonable, or meerely loſt which they are drawne to beſtow vpon ſuch matters, except themſelues
Pſal.16.2. be firſt perſwaded to the loue of religion, and delight in the Saints of God, as Pſalm.16. Therefore to knit the next verſe and the ſumme thereof, with this

this which belongeth to the same end,let both sorts learne their dutie. They who benefit others without hope of requitall, let them not doe it to make others obliged and bound to them, as seruants and vnderlings; but vse all the interest,credit,and loue they haue in and with them, (if they haue opportunitie to perswade them to loue and good workes, and to draw them to God, if they bee strangers; as the truth is, at the first, ignorant folke are more drawne by such inducements,then otherwise: or if they be alreadie Christians,let them labour to draw them neerer,as I haue said: saying thus euery man to the other: If I may preuaile with you any thing,or ye would gratifie me,preferre God and his fauour your selues,and exhort other to do so,and commend godlines also to them, and the poore members of Christ, to make much of them,and to be their delight,who excell in vertue, before all earthly commodities: as for your gratuitie, let the needie and distressed be partakers of it,and let them take my part, who shall blesse God for your pitie and bountie to them, and they shall yeeld you a tenne fold better requitall then I,being but one,can doe. And this bee said of them who pleasure other without looking for any requitall againe. The other who receiue benefit,and acknowledge that they haue been pleasured by them, and that they owe a duty againe: if their offer be not accepted by the partie,let them not then foolishly draw backe their hand altogether from euery good vse, saying; Seeing hee will not receiue this of me, I am discharged, and free from vnthankfulnes: as for others,I regard them not. For this sauours of a sinister meaning,not of a chearefull and heartie thanksgiuer,such an one as that good *Naaman* was,2.King.5.and these here mentioned, who readily 2.King.5.15.
answere to *Gedeon*,asking of them their earings to a good end, as hee intended it,wee are willing to giue that to thee,which thou askest to a good end and purpose: for it is like he told them,that he asked them not to his owne behoofe.

Vers.17. Gen.28.18.
Gedeon did well to set vp a remembrance of Gods kindnesse,as *Iacob* left a memoriall of Gods appearing to him, when hee went into Mesopotamia, changing the name of the place, and calling it the house of God: for there the Lord had promised him safe deliuerance from the wrath of his brother *Esau*,and to be with him whither he went, and to bring him safely backe againe: euen the like mind did *Gedeon* shew here,desiring to keepe a remembrance of Gods deliuerance there. But in making the Ephod,which was the signe thereof, *Gedeon* was very vnaduised, and dealt without due and good consideration. For in so weightie a case as that, and of so dangerous consequence,it had been meete that hee had first consulted with the Lord about it,and so (according to the resolution hee should haue receiued from him) to haue done: to wit, to haue abstained from such a worke: as vndoubtedly he must and would haue done,if God had bin consulted with,and might haue ouer-ruled. And this is the fruite of rashnes and carelesnes, whereas a small matter might haue preuented all. It was, I say, no better in *Gedeon* then inconsiderate,though his meaning were good. For God ordained not the Ephod to such an end,but onely for the Priests to weare in the Tabernacle when they offered sacrifice: and permitted it not to men to follow him therein,neither to make one for ciuil vses. It is charitably to be thought that *Gedeon* committed not Idolatrie himselfe, who had throwne downe

the Altar of *Baal* before with detestation, and cut downe his groue : but howsoeuer it was, as it is not certaine to vs; yet seeing hee did otherwise in setting vp the Ephod, then God had commanded, hee fell into a kinde of Idolatrie, or was at least a great occasion thereof, and so the Lord being offended, punished his issue and posteritie, rewarding them both with the vnthankfulnes of the people, and also with the crueltie of *Abimelech*.

Doct. vers. 27. So that though *Gedeons* meaning was otherwise, yet this displeased the Lord which he did, for that he consulted not with him in that strange work which he tooke in hand. Therefore we see that it is not enough to haue a good intent (as they call it) in that which we do to serue God in, but knowledge must goe before out of the word, to warrant and vphold vs in our attempts and doings. Rom. 14. 23. For *whatsoeuer is not of faith, is sinne :* and wee are happie when we do good things, but so, that we first know them to be such indeed, and not otherwise : Rom. 10. 2. for Israel had a zeale, but not according to knowledge. 2. Sam. 7. 5. *Dauid* would haue builded God an house, then the which who could haue gone about a better thing in all mens account and iudgement? But God reproued him by *Nathan*, and yet he himselfe consented to him at first, vpon the like good intent.

So, many haue since the daies of Queene *Mary*, and some still doe of a good intent, enter into the Ministerie, though many other intend nothing but to inrich themselues with liuing : whom the Lord alloweth not by his word, they being not able to feede his people with the foode of life. 1. Sam. 15. 22. So wee reade that *Saul* saued the fattest of the cattell (as he said) to sacrifice, contrary to the word of the Lord; which if it had been so, had been bad : but that was onely a false pretence to couer his couetousnes, and disobedience to the commandement.

Then *Samuel* reprouing him, was faine to answere him : *Hath the Lord as great pleasure in burnt offerings and sacrifice, as that his law should be obeyed?* Therfore good intentions (corruptly so called) cannot bee accepted of him, except they be directed by knowledge.

Of such intents arose most parts and points of Poperie : the orders of Monkes, the worshipping of the Sacrament, canonicall houres, free will, reliques, prayers to Saints, &c. Of all the which, and the like, the Lord saith, as Esay 1. 12. he did by the Prophet *Esay* in the like case, *Who required these things at your hands?* Esay 29. 13. And in another place, *In vaine doth this people worship me, teaching for doctrines, the precepts of men.* So that by all which hath been said, it is manifest how prone and readie wee are to Idolatrie and superstition. And what 1. Tim. 3. 16. other thing doth this teach vs, but that it is a mysterie to serue God aright and religiously : and that cannot stand with the common practise of men in the worshipping of God, who receiue not the word in the power thereof, to work vpon them effectually, and so as they may be cast into the mould thereof, but for fashion and orders sake.

2 Againe, *Gedeons* setting vp the Ephod, was the occasion of the peoples falling to commit spirituall fornication with it, through his letting it alone, and they worshipped it, as their fathers did the brasen Serpent : which therfore *Ezechia* commanded to be taken downe. *Gedeon* had done well therefore, if he had so serued the Ephod also, when he saw superstition to arise by occasion of it. And this is the best fruite and successe of blinde and ignorant

rant deuotion, that it draweth some mischiefe alway with it, as the grosse absurdities in Poperie, of which I spake, arose at the first vpon such beginnings. So that the thing which in these cases is to bee done, is, that all superstition and implements thereof be held out of the Church of Christ: but if any of them haue been suffered to remaine, the next is, that as soone as may be, they be remoued. And as for Gods ordinances, they ought not to bee turned from their kinde and right vse of seruing him in ciuill cases, (as the Ephod was appointed by *Gedeon*) as to make playes of them, or offer them any such abuse: as the Word and Sacraments. But I passe to another thing concerning the people.

Lastly, in that sundry of the people fell to Idolatry with the Ephod, who 3
had before worshipped God aright, with an vpright heart; and a plague of God fell vpon them for it, note we, that they who after they haue receiued the knowledge of the truth, doe fall to Idolatrie, doe neuer escape destruction, if they lie still therein, or some fearfull plague, although they rise out of it againe, and depart from it. *Salomon* was a witnesse hereof, both in himselfe, and in his posteritie, whose punishment is famous for harkning to his idolatrous wiues. And the Lord professeth himselfe in that case to be iealous, as a man that taketh his wife in spouse-breach, who (most certainly) will not spare the offender. Prou. 6.34.

Vers. 28. *Thus was Midian brought low before the children of Israel, so that they lift vp their heads no more: and the countrey was in quietnes fortie yeeres, in the daies of Gedeon.*

29. *Then Ierubbaal the sonne of Ioash went and dwelt in his owne house.*

30. *And Gedeon had seuentie sonnes, begotten of his body: for hee had many wiues.*

31. *And his Concubine that was in Shechem bare him a sonne also, whose name he called Abimelech.*

IN these foure verses another thing concerning *Gedeon* is set downe: and first it is shewed, how Midian for all the multitude and glorie thereof was brought low: whereby may be noted the sorrow of such of them as liued, and the shame and confusion both of the liuing and the dead, with the fruit thereof, to wit, a finall suppression of that enemie, and a long peace of fortie yeeres restored, all the life of *Gedeon*. Secondly, three more particulars concerning *Gedeon* are added: The first to his commendation: that hauing done the seruice for which the Lord extraordinarily called him, he willingly yeelded himselfe to a priuate life againe, as he professed against the contrarie, verse 22. The two latter were to his blame. First his polygamie in vers. 30. Secondly, his yeelding to the vnlawfull desire of his Concubine of Shechem, and making way thereby to the mischiefe that insued. *The sense of these foure verses.*

For the first of these, the text saith, *Midian* was subdued and brought low, &c. which being vnderstood of the multitude of them, teacheth, and proueth, that we ought to looke alwaies to the end of things, and not to the beginnings, and florishing estate of them, and this to doe, the Scripture calles sound wisedome. Thinke we of the godliest, and things of greatest account, pleasure, pompe, dignitie, wealth, buildings, purchases, solemne marriages, Doct. vers. 28.

or such like, I grant that the most men reioice and please themselues in them vainely and foolishly for the time, as if they had gotten a paradise; but when all may see them to fade daily with the enioyers thereof, and change to corruption, no wise man can or dare please himselfe or rest in them, as if they could make him happie; but as he seeth the end will be therof, so he will enioy thẽ from God, as things decaying and transitorie. What then? ye will (perhaps) say, shall he not be glad of, nor delight in them till he doe forgoe them, and till an end of them come? I answere, that I say not so. But hee

Note. shall know what the end of them all will be before it come, by the manner of vsing them. For he that seeketh by all these, to be more fruitfull in dutie doing to God, and in workes of loue to men, and not to take boldnes to sin the rather by occasion of them, this man may know that the end shall bee good, and in respect thereof, hee may vse them all comfortably, seeing hee vseth them warily and aright, as God directeth him, for in that he doth so, God also blesseth him exceedingly, which blessing few attaine thereto.

Deut. 32. 29. The Lord is brought in by *Moses* in Deuteronomy bemoning the want of practising this point of wisedome in men, saying, *Oh that my people were wise, and would consider their end.* And the Apostle asketh this question of the

Rom. 6. 21. Romanes, what fruite or pleasure they euer had in that, which in the end

Mat. 25. 3. 4. &c. brought shame to them? The wise & the foolish virgins giue cleere proofe vnto this: the foolish contenting themselues to bee without oyle in their lampes, that is, to walke securely, were therefore shut out: the wise waiting with oyle in their lampes, till the Bridegrome came, and therefore thus watching to the end, were taken in, and receiued readily. Looke vpon *Ab-*

2. Sam. 18. 17. *solon* for all the aduancing of himselfe, and on *Adonia*: looke vpon *Balta-*

1. King. 2. 25. *zar* for all his iunketting with his choice companie in the holy vessels of

Dan. 5. 6. the Temple; and vpon *Haman* though he onely was bidden to the banquet

Hester 5. 11. compared with 7. 9. with the King by Queene *Hester*, and for all his other honour that hee had, (which yet he himselfe did not a little boast of) was not the end of it greater shame, then the best of it was glorie?

Eccles. 11. 9. Looke vpon the young man to whom *Salomon* speaketh, who reioyced, as if he should neuer be old, nor meete with worse cheare, then iollitie and mirth: was it not told him, *he should come to iudgement?* And what better end

Luke 16. 25. of his delicious life found the rich man in the Gospell, then torments? And thus I might heape vp examples infinitly, both out of the Scripture, and out of our own experience, of them who had gotten much here, and they were many in number in al ages that did thus, as the Midianites (of whom I now speake) and were for their greatnes, and in their time, the talke of the world, yet hauing no sure hold of heauen, nor part in other happinesse then transitorie, came to naught, and were worse then nothing; so as one may say of them, as Christ said of *Iudas*, It had been good for them that they had neuer been borne. Therefore I conclude: blessed is the man that hath an eye to the end of his actions, and of all things which he beholdeth here vnder the sunne: and so dealeth, that hee may finde and enioy thereby a good end of his life: therfore when the holy Ghost to the Hebrewes commended the

Hebr. 13. 8. faith of some, he willeth the reader to *consider what hath bin the end of the conuersation of such.* And the Psalmist sendeth vs to the end of the godly; *Marke*

Psal. 37. 37. (saith he) *the end of the righteous, for the end of him is peace.* But for these that will

will be merrie otherwise, howsoeuer they goe to worke, their end will be in heauinesse, according to the words of our Sauiour, *Woe be to you that now laugh, for ye shall howle and weepe.* Note. Luke 6.25.

Now that it is said here, they had fortie yeeres peace after this subduing of the Midianites, it was a great benefit that God bestowed vpon them: and so all that enioy it, or a great part of it, shall see cause to say, if they reade and consider the bondage and woe that men are in to enemies and strangers. Therfore we should carefully looke what good may be done in such times of libertie and freedome from great disturbance, especially that when wee haue generally peace in the land, there be no priuate breaches with neighbours at home, nor in familie; but a quiet life with both; and the peace of a good conscience to Godward, chiefly and aboue all things procured. Looke of this at large in chap. 5. and elsewhere. Doct. 2. Deut. 28.48. Note.

Now that which followeth concerning *Gedeon*, in this verse is this: that it is said, after this victorie, *Gedeon* liued (after a sort) a priuate life, to proue and make it manifest that he desired not, as he had told them before, the empire, contrary to Gods ordinance. So it is with some offices among vs annuall, or temporarie. If hee had in this priuacie liued idlely, or wickedly, as one that had done enough before, and now waxt weary, it would haue been set downe as other faults be. That which wee haue to learne by this, is; that we so vse authoritie, countenance, preferment, or any such libertie which is more then common, that we remember it must be laid downe againe, and haue an end, and that also (perhaps) in this life: and therefore, that we swell not, neither be puffed vp thereby, neither forget what wee haue been: for that, and such like promotion or aduancement is but borrowed. And nothing is more common then to see age abased and in little regard: so that, The minde (as the saying is) is all in all: yea such as the minde is, such is the man. For else, what should be the priuiledge of a godly man in respect of other, both in life and at death? Some may better haue thousands (and vse them more soberly) then some can hundreds. He that makes his prosperitie his heauen, cannot but thinke the contrarie to bee his miserie and vndoing. But he that neuer ioyed too much in that he had, neuer laid it too neere his heart, when he lost or for-went it. It is the speech of a foole to say, It is most miserable to haue bin happie. A wise man is neither so lifted vp with inioying that which he knoweth is vanishing and mutable, as if it were happines: nor so deiected in the forgoing it, as if he had lost it, and as if his hope were past. The immoderate desire of the minde is like to him who hauing vsed his body to a plenteous and delicate fare, being afterward compelled to streighter allowance, pineth: and by the alteration of a full, fat, comely and strong body, into a thinne, meager, pale, and decaied; sheweth that the change of his diet hath made him vnlike himselfe. Whereas the sober minded resembleth him, who tieth himselfe to an ordinarie, as most agreeable to health and soundnes: and although hee come to an extraordinarie diet, yet he is a law to himselfe, he eateth no more of many, then he did before of a few dishes: So that as the one mendeth him not, so the other appaireth him not. Thus saith the Christian with the Apostle, *I haue learned to abound, I haue learned also to want:* in diuers estates to be the same, euen contented and thankfull. A rare portion aboue al earthly treasure: and such as he nee- Vers. 29. Doct. Philip. 4.12.

ded not be ashamed to confesse, he had learnd, for he was borne to no such priuiledge, as he was to be a free citizen of Rome, as he told *Lysias*, but was taught it by the Spirit of God only.

Wee haue great need to note this: for many by office, place, authoritie and superioritie in Ministery and Magistracy, haue, and doe daily forget themselues, and especially if great wealth accompany the same, yea sometime where there is no great matter in the persons to cause it. And therefore when God shall blow vpon their estate, and cast it downe, and they be constrained to come to abasement, and to their old condition againe, wherein they once liued, they scorne and cast it off, and shift by vnlawfull meanes to wind themselues out of it, by running into debt with other men, neuer meaning to pay, as both appeareth in many Seruingmen and Souldiers that haue been of any place, and other better borne then the common sort, and
Luke 16.3. many more, who say with the Steward; *Digge I cannot, and to begge I am ashamed*, and liue I must some way or other, but they will neuer fall to worke, or to the doing of any thing beseeming them for their maintenance, but hunt after pleasure, harlots, dice, cards, robbing, and cousening the simple, and beguiling sillie maides or matrons, to enrich themselues, &c.

And againe, this sheweth the follie of such great persons, as trusting to their greatnesse and wealth, as to a strong hold, prouide as little for their owne changes, as for the hardnesse which may befall their children: but bring them vp in all softnesse and delicacie, not so much as inuring them to any labour, or exercizing their bodies or wits to industrie and action: wherby it commeth to passe, that if their estate decline, they are left destitute and shiftlesse: and vrged by an vnhappy necessitie of their owne procuring to vse indirect meanes for maintenance.

verse 30.31. Another thing concerning *Gedeon* followeth, and that is, the setting downe of his many wiues, which was his great blemish. And it teacheth vs, that as well the faults and blemishes of Gods seruants are set before vs in the Scriptures, as their vertues: in which respect the Scriptures are vnlike to other stories or writings of men, carried partially through hatred or flattery to obscure the truth. So are *Dauids, Sampsons*, and *Peters*; and the faults and infirmities of sundry other approoued seruants of God: which (yet) is not done by the holy Ghost, that wee should seeke libertie to follow them, *for*
Psalme 32.10. *many sorrowes shall be to such*, but to teach, that wee, euen the best, should suspect our selues, being full of selfe-loue, to hide and winck at our corruptions and bad qualities, and therfore to keepe with all diligence our hearts, which we are hardly brought to doe, though they be out of measure deceitful, neither can we abide to be reprooued and shamed for the same.

Why the blemishes of Gods seruants are set downe in Scripture. And they are three. The first.

But seeing God hath for sundry causes, and in diuers respects left the infirmities and blemishes of his seruants in scripture to be knowne of vs, I will briefly note and set downe some of them, hauing so good and fit occasion offered, that so we may profit by them accordingly. He hath done it partly for our benefit, and partly to teach vs our dutie. Our benefit thereby is twofold. One, that if at any time we should fall into some grieuous sinne, and despaire of Gods mercy thereby, yet that wee may stay and vphold our selues by the examples of *Gedeon* and other such, who fearing God, did yet fall dangerously, and recouered themselues againe: that we, knowing that, may

may in the like case receiue hope of pardon likewise, if we call our selues home againe by repentance.

For in such cases when we are exhorted by Gods faithfull ministers not to cast away our confidence though we haue so offended, wee are ready to obiect thus: Oh there were neuer any of Gods children that fell so, and offended as we haue done, so that we may iustly feare, there is no remission nor pardon for vs to be hoped for. Therefore when wee shall heare of the infirmities of the godly, the cleere knowledge of this, much auaileth to stay vs from dispairing. This is not therefore to imbolden vs by their example to sinne, though we do yet stand by the grace of God, free from reprochfull euils, but to vphold vs, if we haue alreadie fallen dangerously, that wee faint not altogether. I say, it serueth for preuention of deadly feare after sinne, not to cause presumption in sinning. For if any will abuse this knowledge to licentiousnesse, hoping for pardon as they heare that others haue obtained it, when they had sinned in like manner as they themselues haue done, let them know that God will meet with them, as their boldnesse requireth, with terrors within, and shame without, till they shal wish that they had bin better aduised. And as they may iustly complaine that they sinned more wilfully and purposely, then the Saints of God did, (to speake of many of them) so they may feare that they shall not so easily find mercy and forgiuenesse, as they found. And this is one cause that concerneth vs much, why the Lord hath left the faults of the godly manifested in Scripture, as wel as their vertues. Another is, that wee hearing how some rare people in ages past haue falne, we should be more suspicious of our selues, and more wary that wee slip not into the common euils of the time wee liue in, seeing wee are much weaker in faith and grace then they were, and therefore are like more easily to forget our selues, and to fall grieuously, vnlesse we count it our happinesse (and oft tell it to our selues) to labour and endeuour by all meanes to perseuere in vprightnes vnto our end: and therefore wee are like to find it as hard to recouer our selues againe. And indeed the bitternesse which they tasted in their falles, were enough to deterre vs from following them, though we were sure to speed at length aswell as they. But few looke at the bitter, but at the sweet onely, and so are deceiued.

Note. *The second cause.* Note.

Another cause why God hath made knowne the blemishes of the faithfull that liued in former times, is, to teach vs our duty towards our brethren, that if we heare any of them to haue falne into any grieuous offence, and afterward when it commeth to their remembrance, that they take such a deep conceit for so displeasing God, and lay it so neere their heart, that they feare it cannot be forgiuen them, I say, when it thus falleth out, we are taught by this our dutie; and that is, to incourage and helpe to vphold them in meeknesse, and with our exhortings of them, and perswasions to rise vp and returne againe, to comfort them also when wee see them repent, and to beare with their infirmities, and not to condemne and forsake them, good things being found in them, remembring our selues who would be glad to be helped vp, when we haue falne, rather then to be shamed, forsaken, and left to our selues. To this end is that of the Apostle, *Brethren, if any be fallen by infirmity, you that are spirituall*, that is, indued with more grace, and seasoned with more fruites of Gods spirit, *restore such an one*, that is, doe your indeuour with

The third. Gal. 6. 1.

meekenesse

meekenesse to raise him, *considering your selues.*

The vse, in generall, of this whole discourse, is, to bee afraid to offend, seeing wee bee so vnwilling to heare of any rebuke for the same, and not to be bold to sinne by authoritie of the fathers, seeing we are not willing to take part with them in their punishments, but as shame and sorrow are vnwelcome to vs, so let the sinnes be also that bring them. For they quench faith, weaken grace, and loose our good name, beside the hindering of many duties. The Lord speaking of his faithfull ones, saith: *If they sinne, I will correct them, &c. but my louing kindnesse I will neuer take from them.* If then he meane not to forsake them, good cause why hee should punish and correct them, that so they may be stopped in their bad course, and driuen backe againe. As Saint *Paul* to *Timothy* saith, I am perswaded that the Lord had mercie vpon me, as well for other mens example and benefit as mine owne. And thus by such examples duly considered, and by the Scripture, wee haue consolation and hope. So that farre be it from vs to say: [Nay, if hee be fallen, let him shift for himselfe, I had better opinion of him then hee deserued, now I see, he is an hypocrite, a *Demas*, a reuolter.] But oh man, is this the way for thee to procure to thy selfe compassion from others, if thou shouldest fall so, and hadst the like need? If thou sayest, God forbid I should stand in such need. I answer thee: Thou shalt doe wisely in preuenting such an occasion: but that is not done by an high-minded conceit that such a thing shall not befall thee, but rather by feare of thy selfe, and thy frailtie. Neither by thy tendernesse to others shalt thou be made the more subiect to fall, but the more watchfull against falling. But lest thou shouldest say, I shall not fall, heare the Apostle saying, Lest thou thy selfe be preoccupated, and doe the like.

Note.

Psalme 89.31.

1.Tim.1.15.

That *Gedeon* had fallen wee haue heard: now it followeth, that wee see how. One of his particular blemishes was, that he had many wiues: as for the mentioning of his sonnes, it was of it selfe, neither with him, nor against him, but is spoken of, to make way to the next chapter. But poligamie, that is, the hauing of many wiues, was against the first institution. For though the Iewes did vse it, yet our Sauiour rebuketh it, and saith, it was not so from the beginning: and God forbad it the Kings themselues, (who might inioy the greatest liberties) and why did he so? euen because it turned their harts from God. For such hunt after pleasure, and forsake the Lord, which may be done also in single marriages, (I confesse,) but much more in poligamie being vnlawfull. For they who are giuen ouer to such licentiousnesse, or to any other like course, it besotteth them, and maketh them drunken therewith, in such sort as they become impotent to all that good is. Besides the inconueniences which haue accompanied Polygamy, disagreement, iealousie, hatred. So that God is displeased highly at the hauing of many wiues.

Doct.2.

Genes.2.24.
Matth.19.8.
Deut.17.17.

1.Cor.7.33.

1.Sam.1.6.

But some will obiect: What is this to vs, who abstaine from many wiues and are prohibited by law such licentiousnesse? I answere, yes very much: For this is not only true in Polygamie, that mens harts be stolne from God, but in single and lawfull marriage also, the same may bee, (as I haue said before) yea and most certainly will be, if men giue themselues the bridle, and consider not one end thereof to bee the restraining of them from strange lusts, and to liue holily, so as they be made more fit by their marriage to their seuerall feuerall duties,which the most doe not regard. For they who by their vnseemely speeches and offensiue behauiour towards other women,doe too apparantly testifie, that they liue vnchastly in marriage,and offend God grieuously thereby,much more would bewray their leaudnesse and badnes that way,vncleannesse of body also, but that either they are restrained by law and shame,or else their married estate is mixed with many fearefull and great troubles, which doe alay their lusts, in so much as many who would giue ouer themselues as farre as the worst; dare not, seeing they are so cooled and held downe by afflictions. They are wise that vse their marriage as an helpe,whereby they hold neerer to God,and become more dutifull,and they that doe otherwise,if they be the seruants of God, shall easily see their abusing of it by awknesse in Gods seruice, and vntowardnesse to all good duties : but if they be wicked and vnconscionable,they make that estate of marriage sutable to their other parts of life,that is to say,all naught.

In that it is said further of *Gedeon*, that hee had a concubine in Sechem, Vers.31.
that was another of his blemishes. Whereby as by other we may know,that they were vsed of men then, as well as wiues. They were inferiour to their wiues, and had no superioritie in the familie, but were as seruants. Which was euill also euen as Poligamy. In *Malachie* we reade, that they who after Mal.2.15.
the captiuitie had put away their wiues,and married strange ones, who also obiected,that a man of God did so,namely *Abraham*, wee reade (I say) that they were answered thus: that he *sought a godly seed*, and did it not of lightnesse,or wilfulnesse,so that although it was not according to the first institution that he did,yet in as much as it was not reuealed so clearely to be sinne in those former times in which he liued,as it was since,it was no iust defence for those,who comming after them, did it to satisfie their lusts when they had more light about the will of God, and knowledge of the sinne it selfe, and also what an euill end did follow it. And the same teacheth vs, who *Doct.*
haue a rule to guide our actions by, that wee may in no wise follow examples,no not of the good who haue done against those rules,but to try them by the rules,as *Paul* requireth it of the Thessalonians,*Trie all things,and hold* 1.Thes.5.
that which is good. And he willeth the Corinthians,that no man follow him, 1.Cor.11.1.
but as he followed Christ: as hath been noted largely before.

2 We are also here to consider one fruite of his taking of that concubine, euen by the name that she caused *Gedeon* to giue the sonne that hee had by her,to wit,*Abimelech*; which is as much as to say [My father is a king,] who kindled in him thereby the flame of bearing rule,to play the Tyrant,and to challenge the kingdome as due to his father, which yet hee refused both himselfe,and also that it should be giuen to his sonnes. But what better fruit might be looked for,when Gods ordinance was broken? (See the like in *Salomon*, 1.King.11.) And yet this she did who might worst haue done it, 1.King.11.3.4.
causing *Gedeon* to giue him the name of the Philistime Kings, who plaied the right part of a Philistime when he grew vp, and rose to place. For as it is cleare by the next chapter, that shee was a wicked woman, and of bad kindred,and had induced and trained *Gedeon* to her desire before, so there was none found like to that *Abimelek* her sonne, that we reade of in his time,neither could be much worse then he,either before or after him.

Let this be a watchword about names giuing: for they that are naught, will

will take euery occasion to increase their sinne, euen by occasion thereof, that if any of their name haue been noted aboue other for some bad qualitie, as stoutnesse and stomacke, bragging and boasting, pot-companionship, or such like, oh they must vphold the name, (though it be but a shaddow, as *Absoloms* pillar,) and so be sutable to their name, if it occasion them euill, and to keepe aliue the bad practizes and course of them that bare that name before them. Euen so names more aduisedly and wisely giuen to children (as I haue taught in another place) are good occasions to prouoke them to their duties.

3. Doct. vers. 31. Besides, we may see what men get, who are of any good note, by entring into so neere a league, and hauing so inward acquaintance with such dames and mates, which though it were in single and lawfull marriage, yet it threatens as farre as man may iudge, an extinguishing of the good sparkles of grace in them that are so matched. Which should cause the seruants of God to linke themselues in marriage with women, more like to themselues in religion and good behauiour. And for them for whom it is too late to giue this warning vnto, (who are too many) let them yet receiue and imbrace this instruction that is giuen them in the second place: that is to say, how they take counsell of such wiues or ill companions (in cases doubtfull and and dangerous,) as are malicious, high-minded, quarrellers, contentious, waspish, couetous and gripers, or in a word, voide of true religion. *Sampson* may be an example to all, both of hearkning too farre to such, and so *Gedeon* may be also, and likewise of opening and telling that secret which is not meet to be imparted vnto them, which *Sampson* did to his great reproch and abasement. But here an end of this seeing of both these last points I haue intreated purposely before, out of the former histories.

THE FIFTIE FIVE SERMON ON THE EIGHTH CHAPTER OF THE BOOKE OF IVDGES.

Verse 32. *So Gedeon the sonne of Ioash died in a good age, and was buried in the sepulcher of Ioash his father in Ophrah, of the father of the Ezrites.*

33. *But when Gedeon was dead, the children of Israel turned away, and went a whoring after Baalim, and made Baal-berith their God.*

34 *And the children of Israel remembred not the Lord their God, which deliuered them out of the hands of all their enemies on euery side.*

35. *Neither shewed they mercie on the house of Ierubbaal or Gedeon, according to all the goodnesse which he had shewed vnto Israel.*

The generall summe. NOw together with the Chapter, the holy story maketh an end of *Gedeons* acts: and maketh mention of his death and buriall, and sheweth what the people of Israel did afterwards. In this verse it is is said, he died in a good age. For seeing some of his faults haue been spoken of, to leaue them so, would haue bred some doubts, he hauing done many good things, therefore his end is here set downe, to shew, that both hee had the blessing of old age granted him, and also that it was blessed with many good things by God vnto him. The same that is said of him, is said of *Abraham:* that he should die in a good old age. Which speech here applied to *Gedeon*, and affirmed of him, though it be not to be drawne so farre as to prooue he died godly, but onely noteth fulnesse of daies, and prosperitie in this life, yet it is cleare that he died so, and obtained eternall life after, in that he is reckoned among the faithfull in the Epistle to the Hebrewes. Which is to good purpose to bee set downe, he being (though a godly man, yet) blemished, that thereby we may know he repented.

Genes. 15.15. Genel. 25.8. 1.Chro. 29.28 Heb. 11.32.

By this we are taught that we must stablish our faith, hope and other graces of God begun in vs at our first conuersion, that wee may bee rooted, grounded, and setled therein, as the Apostle willeth the Colossians, and that so the neerer we are the graue, the more glorious and fruitful our profession may be, and in our age we may more flourish then in our youth: which is a thing not easily found nor obtained. Therefore the Apostle Saint *Peter* also exhorteth saying: *Take heed, that ye be not led away from your stedfastnesse*; and sheweth how that may be like to be, euen *by the error of the wicked.* For by beholding how they walk, who haue no feare of God at all, and by harkning to their subtill counsell, and poisoned perswasions, we shall find to our cost, that there is no small force to draw vs after their cursed example, wheras we were in a good course before. If *Gedeon* so mightily and oft assisted and helped, did yet fal in such manner as we haue heard, what may we look for in so many and so variable cases throughout our whole liues? It is well seene in this age, what need they haue to profit by this doctrine, who ranne well sometime, as the Galathians did, but yet haue suffered themselues to be letted, so that they obey not the truth, which they began and professed commendably to doe.

Doct. vers. 32. Colos. 2.7. Note. 2.Pet. 3.17. Gal. 5.7.

Many faults both to the wounding of the conscience, and the offence of men, prouoke God daily in his owne children, and make faith to seeke, and hope to waxe faint, for that we doe not labour carefully to bring forth fruit plentifully thereof, and to hold out with all possible endeuour the profession of our hope with ioy. And if we haue trode awry, and begun with the wise virgins to slumber, yet through due and continuall attending vpon God, and daily and oft repairing and drawing neere to him, wee should not sleep therein, but make haste speedily to come home againe vnder the Lords wing and protection, where only true safety and good being is to be found: and that the rather, seeing the poore chicken and bird void of reason, after the least straying, longs by & by after the damme, and to be vnder her wing: and say wee therefore euery one with the Prophet to the Lord, *O forsake me not ouer long:* and euer and anone looke wee that all be well with our soule, that there be peace betwixt God and vs, and that our faith and repentance waxe not stale, nor loathsome to vs. And make wee no haste to rush into shamefull and reprochfull sinnes, for neither is the burthen and shame of them easily borne, nor the getting out of them; and the recouering of our

Matth. 25.5. Psalm. 119.8. Note.

ſelues againe from vnder ſuch bondage,eaſily obtained, when wee be once fallen into them; whereof,by many occaſions much hath been before ſpoken.

2 And hereafter the long mentioning of *Gedeons* acts followes his death: To teach vs,that to be the end of all fleſh,whether the life be ſhort or long, as *Dauid* alſo witneſſed in other words,ſaying; *I goe the way of all the world.* And great incouragement wee haue to prepare and haſte for death, if wee haue learned aright to dye,ſeeing with our being with Chriſt,which is beſt of all,there are with infinite other vnutterable prerogatiues, ſo many excellent and holy ſeruants of God gone before vs thither, to welcome vs. Of which point, ſee more by the like occaſion of *Ioſhua* and others, in the former proceſſe of this booke.

1.King. 2.2.

Verſ.33 34. Now the laſt of the things that followed after the death of *Gedeon*, is this, to wit, that the people of Iſrael (for all that wee haue heard God did for them) fell againe to Idolatrie,and that moſt ſhamefully. And by this we ſee what fearefull things follow the taking away of good gouernours which maintaine true religion. For they by their authoritie haue contained and held the people within compaſſe, who being dead, they fall away. Pray therefore earneſtly for them,and make we vſe of their liues, *that we may leade a godly and peaceable life vnder them.* For contrariwiſe when other that know not the Lord,riſe vp in their roomes,the people ſhall haue ſorrow their bellies full. The like may be ſaid of godly preachers and parents,what a loſſe it ſhall bee to the people of God, whom they ſhall leaue behinde,to forgoe them. But of this at large in the ſecond Chapter.

Doct.

1.Tim 2.2.

2 Their ſins were theſe two: One,that they tooke *Baal-berith*,as they called him,for their God: the other, that they forgot the Lord their God. This Idoll they called *the Lord of league*, whoſe Image they ſet vp. Herein conſiſted their worſhipping of him, that they acknowledged the good things that they receiued, to bee giuen them of him,and the remouing of their troubles to bee from him alſo. And to aſcribe theſe to a ſtocke,what was it but to goe a whoring after it, as here it is ſaid they did,from the true and liuing God? And hauing ioyned themſelues to him, they forſooke and forgot the Lord God, who had done all good things for them. And this and no better is the worſhip and ſeruice which our deuouteſt votaries in popery doe giue vnto the Lord at this day,as to him that will compare the religion of the one with the other will eaſily and ſoone appeare. See ſomewhat of this their ſinne in Chapter 2.11.13.

Furthermore, this example teacheth how inconſtant we are in all good beginnings and courſes,and how ready wee are to decline and turne away from thence, euery one to that whereto his falſe and deceitfull heart carrieth him: whether to Poperie or any other looſe and vnfaithfull ſeruing of God in hypocriſie: as to ſay, *Lord, Lord*; and to draw neere to him with the body,the heart being far from him: while no conſcience is made of dutie towards him. Whereas the only forgetting of the kindnes of the Lord our God, who onely hath fed, preſerued, deliuered and inlightned vs vnto the life to come, and who (in one word) hath been all in all vnto vs, I ſay, this onely forgetting him, and the ſuffering of his benefits to ſlip out of our mindes,

Math.7.21.
Matth.15.8.

mindes,is finne of it selfe most grieuous and great,without the other,as we haue seene chap.2.2,3. and in this chapter also I haue said the like of this point,vers.27. Note.

The vnthankfulnes of the people towards *Gedeons* posteritie is set downe in this verse, which is further expressed in the next chapter: as in this, that they suffered his sonnes to be slaine: their sinne is aggrauated hereby, that he had done so great things for them, as to deliuer them out of so fearefull bondage,as we haue heard they were in to the Midianites. But in this they did like themselues. For (not to repeate that which I haue said hereof twice in this chapter,vers.18.22.) we may be sure of this,(as we see here in these) that they who are vnfaithfull and vnthankfull to God,are not to be trusted that they will deale better with men. This both the heauenly order of the law of God teacheth,and many examples also. As *Abraham* said; *I saw that the feare of God was not in this place*, and therefore what trustinesse is to bee looked for to me of men? And likewise that example of the vnrighteous Iudge sheweth as much,that *neither feared God,nor reuerenced man.* This measure our Sauiour found among his owne countrey men, when he had done many great good workes among them, yet they would haue stoned him for them. And why? for they were not faithfull to God. Doe we our duties therefore of conscience to God,that so wee may not faile toward men. For otherwise from vs nothing is to bee looked for, but vnfaithfulnes to men,and euill example, vtterly vnbeseeming vs, when time shall serue to bewray and sift vs: which (as the prouerbe saith) is the mother of truth, and reuealeth that which was long hidden. Vers.35. Genes.20.11. Luke 18.2. Ioh.10.32.

Now to end the chapter with the answere of an obiection. It is marueiled at,that God suffered this Idolatrie and superstition so long vnpunished: For such as obiect thus,thinke that it fell out a little after the victorie,as it is sure *Gedeon* asked of the people the earings that made the Ephod,by and by after the victorie,whereas yet *Gedeon* continued fortie yeeres after this. But it is answered by S. *Austine*, who in such a case,being no article of our faith, may haue his iudgement approoued,and receiued,being likely; and not being answered by the Scripture. He saith, that though the gold was gathered soone after the victory,yet the Ephod was not made by and by,but long after,to wit,about the end of *Gedeons* life. Or if it were made sooner, yet it was not abused till toward his death. But of vncertainties we are not to ground any instruction,and therefore here an end. *Obiect.* *Answ.*

THE FIFTIE FIVE SERMON IS CONtinued on the ninth Chapter of Iudges.

Verse 1. *Then Abimelech, the sonne of Ierubbaal,went to Shechem to his mothers brethren,and communed with them, and with all the familie and house of his mothers father,saying,*

2. *Say,I pray you,in the audience of all the men of Shechem,Whether is better for you that all the sonnes of Ierubbaal,which are seuentie persons reigne ouer you,either that one raigne ouer you? Remember also that I am your bone and your flesh.*

3. *Then his mothers brethren spake of him in the audience of all the men of Shechem*

them all these words: and their hearts were moued to follow Abimelech: for said they, he is our brother.

4. *And they gaue him seuenty peeces of siluer out of the house of Baal-berith, wherewith Abimelech hired vaine and light fellowes which followed him.*

5. *And he went vnto his fathers house at Ophrah, and slew his brethren, the sons of Ierubbaal, about seuentie persons vpon one stone: yet Iotham the youngest sonne of Ierubbaal was left, for he hid himselfe.*

6. *And all the men of Shechem gathered together with all the house of Millo, and came, and made Abimelech King in the plain, where the stone was erected in Shechē.*

The summe and parts of this Chapter. THe summe of this Chapter I will first set downe, as vsually I doe, together with the parts of it, which are three. The first this: namely, how *Abimelech* seeking the kingdome, and hauing got the men of Shechem on his side, killed all his seuentie brethren, except one: and this to the seuenth verse. The second, the heauie prediction of his ouerthrow by that one brother *Iotham*, who escaped his bloodie hands, which denounced destruction to him, and to the men of Shechem. And this to the 22. verse. The 3. is, how that which was threatned & foretold by *Iotham*, the son of *Gedeon*, remaining aliue, came to passe, and was fulfilled, concerning the ruine and ouerthrow of *Abimelech*, and the men of Sechem, and that by the mutuall hatred and vexations that arose betwixt them. And this to the end of the Chapter.

Thus the Chapter being deuided, I will first speake of the former part of it, as it lieth in order, and handle the other two in due place.

The first part.

WE are to consider in this first part, how *Abimelech* after the death of his father, wounde in with the men of Shechem, to make him king, and for this purpose slew all his brethren saue one; and this to the 7. verse.

And for the effecting of this, it is said here that this *Abimelech* went to his mothers kindred: for he saw it was lost labour to attempt so horrible a fact by his fathers friends helpe, or any other: and by his subtiltie, and flatterie, he wonne their hearts to be willing to hearken vnto him; they nothing respecting the common benefit of the land, but their owne priuate commoditie: and so helped him forward by money, which much aduanced his purposes: and thus being fleshed (for the more secure enioying of his will) he was inboldened to kil 70. persons saue one, of his brethren, and then (as they thought) the coast being cleare, these Shechemites went about to make him King, and performed it accordingly. And thus the house of *Gedeon* was ouerthrowne, and most detestable vsurpation, and tyranny by *Abimelech*, came in.

Doct. in vers. 1 Here first we may note by *Abimelechs* going to his mothers kindred to further him, when he went about this mischieuous intent, in seeking to be king; we note (I say) the cast of wicked men in the compassing their desires; that is, when they intend any euill, they wil repaire to such places and companies, as they thinke are for their purpose, and (if they haue conuersed with better before) yet they then take no more pleasure in their company any longer. Not that they neuer goe to bad company, but when they goe about

about some especiall euill. For it is their meat and drink, and pastime to conuerse with such as they themselues are, (as neere as may be) continually; but if they be sorted by education, cohabitation, or other occasions with better then themselues. (as it comes to passe oft times) yet euen there, if they grow to affect, and set their hearts on some particular more mischieuous practises then they were wont in times past, they will (if it be possible) giue them ouer, as no companions meet for them, and breake out to other companie, and conuerse with those that bee of their owne disposition, and like themseldes. The reason is, they be not onely more wearie of the good company that they were in, then they were before; but they see, that they cannot follow their bad purposes so currantly while they bee among them, neither looke they for any aide thereto at their hands, as they doe by the other: but know, that they shall bee suspected, disswaded, hindred, and broken off by them from their ill purposes. And what maruell? for this changing of company, as the good for the bad, ariseth vpon smaller occasions, then vpon the minding and intending of such mischiefe, as this *Abimelech* here went about. For they in the sixth of *Iohn*, when they had taken a pritch against our Saui- **Iohn 6.66.**
our, it is said of them, that they walked no more with him, and much more and sooner men doe this, when they purpose wickednesse. *Absolon* there- **2.Sam.15.10.**
fore when he intended to rebell against his father, got him away, and gathered companie fit for such a purpose, his fathers house was a prison and wearisome vnto him. And *Iudas*, when he went about to betray his Master, forsooke and left the company of him, and the Apostles, and went to the Pharisies, the most deadly enemies of Christ, and lincked himselfe in with them. But most clearely we see this in the like fact of *Adoniah*, 1.Kin.1.reported by **1.King.1.25.**
Nathan to *Dauid* in this manner: *Me* (saith hee) *thy seruant, and Zadocke the Priest, and Salomon thy sonne, he hath not called*: (why? they were not for his tooth) *but Ioab the captaine, and Abiathar the Priest*, and some of his younger brethren, men fitter for his ambitious humour: them hath hee called; crie before him, and they say, *God saue King Adoniah*. And euen so it is still at this day, as I haue said. For there are many bad mixed with the good, and company with them in sinister respects, for some benefit they looke for, or credit thereby, or for their safety, who yet when they see their time, wind out from them, and ioyne to other companie, much like to *Simon Magus*, when he saw the Apostles were not for him. And it is an ill signe when they doe so, I meane, to forsake the societie and fellowship of good people, and company with the bad. For though there was no great hope of some of them, when they were at the best, and when they were by meanes of their calling and imployments sorted into the company of the godly, because they had no pleasure nor delight in them, but rather their hearts were farre from them, euen then, when in place they were most neere them: yet they were in the way all that while, to good, and to be wrought vpon, or drawne on, one time or other, while they abode in such places and companies, if God had been pleased to worke in them: but when they leaue, and forsake them, and so bewray themselues in their colours, though they should meane no worse; then their woe commeth vpon them, and they wrap themselues deepely into mischiefe and misery, with little hope of recouery, or getting out againe, yea, or being stopped in that their bad course.

And yet this I say,that such as keepe company with those that are religious,and take no good by them,they are deepely bewitched, couering their
Luke 13.26. hypocrisie,with the cloake of good companie: as Christ told them,who answered him,that they had eaten and drunke in his company : although for the most part,this prooueth true of them, that if a man once spie out their leaudnesse,and will not allow them in their euill course, but tell them of it, they will away from them, if they can,forthwith,and count them their enemies. But, as they are wearie of such without any iust cause, so they must know,that they from whom they depart,are wearie of them for good cause; and desire, (if they may doe it lawfully, and can haue no good hope to re-
Heb.11.24. claime them) to depart from them also,as *Moses* did, (when hee was able to iudge what hee did) from the house of *Pharaohs* daughter, and as *Salomon*
Prou.14.7. counselleth vs to doe in a case much like,saying: Seest thou a man in whom there are not the lippes of wisdome,depart from him.

The vse that the godly ought to make of this, is: to learne of such as are wiser in their kind then we are in ours; that is, alwaies to be carefull to vse, and delight in godly company, as they doe in the contrary; and by no meanes to depart from,or forsake it; whereby not onely we may shew and giue proofe,that we our selues not only warpe not,neither imagine,nor set our hearts on euill,while we company with,and cleaue fast to them that are good : but also that through their godly instructions,counsell,reproofe,and example, wee seeke to get all possible good by their company. And if we should at any time decline by some occasion, yet that we labour to bee brought backe againe into the right way, and so continue therein : and as
Psalm.15.4. for the fellowship of the leaud,let it be to vs more odious,then ours can bee to them,as I haue noted. The bad also may make their vse and profit of this doctrine,in this manner,let them that be not wholly past hope,but walking
Psalm.1.1. vp and downe,as the Psalmist speaketh,in the counsell of the vngodly,as yet vnresolued what to do, let such (I say) if they haue any care of themselues, draw and gather to good company. For want whereof,and by the contrary,they grow to be leaud persons,as drunkards,whoremasters, theeues, idle ones,and such like. For,as I haue noted, that a bad man, that hee may the better doe euill,departeth from the good : so it is true also, and much more that because a man draweth not neere the good at all,therefore he is the easilier carried to that which is naught. And as they are iustly to be suspected to be badlie disposed,who cast off good company,which they haue seemed to imbrace: so they are to be pitied,and exhorted to the frequenting of the good,who,for want of it altogether,haue fallen into bad company,and bin seduced thereby. Both are faultie,though the former more then the latter. For the latter would be glad (such as are of the simpler sort of them) to bee aduised,and profit much by wholesome counsell: the former who haue enioyed it already,are wearie of it,and seeke to shake it off: the latter,although they are flexible,and easily drawne away by ill example : yet they contriue not mischiefe of themselues for the most part: whereas the former,through a secret lingring after their lusts, doe not need others (alwaies) to call them on,but they themselues rather poyson other, and like *Abimelech*, draw others to them : no companions proouing so leaud,as they who breake from the good.

Thirdly,

Thirdly, let them that are among the good (ſo placed by Gods prouidence) acknowledge it to bee a great mercie: and beware of that ſubtiltie and falſehood of heart, whereby they depriue themſelues of the fruit of it. Let them ſay thus: If credit, gaine, commendation, or fauour (all which I may obtaine by the cleauing to the godly) ſeeme ſo much to be deſired: how much more deſirable is that, for which a good man himſelfe is to bee deſired, I meane, his grace? which as it may well goe with the other, ſo it will make his companie to be alway precious, and much eſteemed. Contrariwiſe, what is it that makes a man count good men odious? Surely a bad purpoſe of miſchiefe leſſe or more: this is that which makes him to be rather where his heart is, and whither his luſt carries him, then where his bodily preſence is. Conſider then what an odious thing is that, which cauſeth ſuch odious effects? It is a foule part to depart from the good. How much more to flee to the other aduerſe partie, I meane the tents of the vngodly? and moſt of all, that which cauſed both theſe, a luſt of the heart after their bad qualities. Indeed, *for the deſire of a man* (be it good, or euill) *a man will* Prou.18.1.
ſeparate himſelfe: meaning from all which might hinder it. *Gehazi*, for his couetous deſire, will withdraw himſelfe from his maſter: *Demas* from *Paul*, &c. Yea ſurely, for his ſins ſake a man will deuide himſelfe from father, mother, kindred, as Chriſt ſaith. Is not this odious? much more odious then is that for which a man wil do thus. Again, there is great cauſe of this meditation, becauſe ſome (not knowing thẽſelues to be ſo euil, as indeed they be) ſuſpect not the temptation to euill, ere it aſſaile them; and therefore are no ſooner tempted, but they are alſo foyled. *Hazael*, when he came to the Pro- 2.King.8.13.
phet *Eliſha* did reuerence and acknowledge him ſo farre, as hee ſaw well inough what good he might haue taken by him, and at that time he framed himſelfe to diſlike that euill which the Prophet told him he ſhould worke, yea, he deteſted it: but when afterward he plaied the cruell Tyrant againſt the Church of God, he ſhooke off all due remembrance of him, and of his owne words to him, which were good then, euen as many doe in the like caſe. No wonder, for he was falſe-hearted, and neuer loued him ſo, but hee might hate him as much, when time ſerued.

Laſtly, as for ſuch as will boaſt that they are for all companies, good and bad; and can apply themſelues (like that fiſh) to all colours, and keepe their bad purpoſes to themſelues, let ſuch impious fellowes (farre worſe then the former) feare leſt he that found out *Abimelech* for his ſinne, will not let them eſcape ſcotfree for theirs, which are not inferiour to his. Touching the infection of bad company, more elſewhere ſhall be ſpoken in a fit place.

This ſonne of the concubine, ye haue heard, went to, and among them Verſe 2.
with whom he was likeſt to preuaile, and to this end, that he might be made King: the which his father vtterly refuſed for himſelfe, and his; and yet this monſter, borne out of time, regarding neither God, nor father, moſt impudently ſought the kingdome againſt his will and liking, yea and againſt all right. Now it followeth, what his deuice and reaſon to them of Shechem, was to get it. One was this: that it was better he alone ſhould be King then ſeuenty of his brethren. But it might haue been anſwered, that it was neither needfull, nor lawfull, that hee, or they, ſhould reigne ouer the people. His ſecond deuice and ſhift was, not for the publike, for that hee was neere

them and their flesh. The third was, seeing he would (he told them) bee for their priuate benefit: for that he pretended to them, that he being of their kindred, hee would chiefly seeke their peace, profit and preferment. All which was but cousonage, subtiltie, and flattery.

Doct. 1. Here in that this wicked instrument, the sonne of a good man, rose vp to attempt, and worke the mischiefe which his father abhorred, wee may see, what wicked posteritie come oft times of a godly seed, and how vnlike the parents in goodnesse: whereas one would thinke, that they should rather labour to resemble, and to be like those their godly parents at the least. The generation after *Ioshuahs* time, degenerated from that which was before it. *Ely, Samuel*, and *Dauid*, most of the good Priests, Prophets, Kings, had wicked children, euen as is to be seene in all ages. The reason is; first, the want of good education, when they are vntaught, and ill gouerned. Secondly, as the best corne breedes chaffe, so the godly beget their children not as they are godly, but as they are men naturall and sinfull: neither is Gods grace tied absolutely to them, for their parents sake. Thirdly, pride, stubbornnesse, wilfulnesse, and seeking of libertie in youth; and among the rest, this is not the least, the multitude of bad examples, I meane which are fit enough to poyson the best natures, though they haue both instruction, and outward gouernment. So that many leaud youths are trained vp at the great cost of their parents, who yet lose all, and their hope also, their children not walking in their steps.

Oh what multitudes are there of such in our age? In which (yet there is more done for making them good, (especially in some places) then hath been in former times, though they are rare, who offend not herein euen in the sight of others. A thing much to be lamented, to see so many youths vnlike their good parents: but where none or weake meanes are vsed to make

Note. them better, it is not to be marueiled at. The woe to both, is not knowne cōmonly, til it be so felt, that it is past remedying. The beholding of the contrary, as it is rare, so it is goodly and beautifull. But it is a great cause, why the death of childrē before they come to proofe, should be borne patiently, seeing it is not to be doubted, but that most of them are taken away at the best, and who knoweth to what woe they might be brought, if they should liue? It is to be lamented that the examples of good parēts being so few, yet euen of these few, few (to speake of) preuaile with their children: from whence

1. Sam. 8. 5. the common complaint of all sorts is, as theirs to *Samuel*. A good father: but the child walkes not in his steps. For the infinite bad patternes of gouernours, are generally embraced: none fearing to follow where they haue led the dance, no, though it bee to destruction, as if all the beasts of the forrest should each follow the tract of his fellow, to the den of the Lion, because till they be within the den, and past recouery, there appeares in the footsteps no danger. It is said of *Iacobs* ewes, that beholding the pilled roddes laid in their water-troughes, they conceiued particoloured lambes forthwith: and so a man would thinke that so neere and domesticall examples, as good parents are to their children, (who are nourished by them, grow vp with

2. Sam. 12. 3. them, and are warmed by their heate, as *Nathan* speakes of the poore mans sheepe: yea haue the benefit of the familiar instruction, and conuersation, of such as are of their owne disposition, and nature:) a man would thinke, (I say)

ſay)that ſuch ſhould take after them in grace, as they doe reſemble them in their viſage,or naturall properties. A man would thinke,that they ſhould (as it were)through a mutuall feeling of the ioy which a good parent hath of a wiſe child,and of the ſorrow by the contrary: that they ſhould alſo reioyce in following their goodneſſe. Thus wee might thinke, and thus it ſhould be,if God in his ſecret iudgement had not prepared ſome (euen of them alſo)to the euill day. It is ſaid of *Elie* his children: they hearkned not to their father,becauſe God had determined to deſtroy them; to wit,for the inexpiable offence they had cauſed to the people by their polluting the holy things of God. And ſo alſo,it is pitifull to thinke that the other ſort,the poſteritie of bad parents,dare venture ſo confidently to goe where their anceſtours haue gone; as it were taking ſinne by tradition from them,yea filling vp the meaſure which they attained not to, as our Sauiour ſpeaketh. This,in a manner,is generally ſeene: and where it is in a few otherwiſe, there another father, euen the Father of Chriſt hath reuealed it from heauen,fleſh and blood hath not taught it. And this dregge of Poperie is naturall,without teaching: to make it a ſtrong piller of a mans religion to doe as the forefathers haue done. In the ſtory of the Church it is reported, that a certaine Heathen Prince hauing receiued ſo much light of true religion, that hee was content to bee baptized: yet when hee came to the water,ſtopped,and asked the Miniſter this queſtion: Whether haue more of my anceſtors (being vnbaptized) gone to heauen,or hell? To hell,ſaith the Miniſter. So will I then,ſaid he,and refuſed Chriſtianitie vtterly. Yea doubtleſſe,nature teacheth no better then this,euen rather to go to hell with the parents, then to heauen without them. Both theſe,I ſay, are lamentable: as for the vſe that both ſorts are to make thereof,I ſhall not need to inſiſt vpon it here, hauing oft vrged it in other places.

1.Sam.2.25. 1.Pet 1.18. Matth.23.32.

Now of his ſhifts,which I will put together for breuitie ſake, matter ariſing ſo plentifully. And marke by what fraud he goeth about it,inſinuating with them,that if he be not King ouer them,then his ſeuenty brethren muſt reigne together. But that he thought they would neuer allow, or conſent to. Secondly, where hee telles them,it were better be ſo,that he reigned; it was vntrue alſo, for that is beſt alwaies that God appoints,who did deteſt this. Thirdly,in that he ſetteth out himſelfe,as though hee ſhould ſay, who is fitter for your benefit then I? they ought to haue knowne, that in creating of Magiſtrates,the publike,and not the priuate commoditie is to be reſpected.

The vnfolding of the ſecond verſe.

That which we haue to learne hereby, is this: that all ſhifts and ſubtile practiſes are ready at hand with them that intend miſchiefe: and that which they goe about,is by lying, cogging, and falſhood. But as for the Lord in their dealings, he muſt ſtand by, and a farre off. The reaſon of both is,the heart of men is euill aboue meaſure,and is deepe, and hath many abominations in it. They deuiſe,and goe to worke without him,and we ſee likewiſe that thereafter they proſper. To theſe may bee added other,and ſome that profeſſe the Goſpell,who ſhould be aſhamed to be found ſo groſſely to degenerate,as to vſe like practiſes to the other, though they be couered with ſome fairer ſhewes,who caſt off God,and ſay in their hearts, depart from vs, we deſire not to haue acquaintance with thee. Theſe ſhal one day know and

Doct.2. Ierem.17.9. Iob 21.14.

that

that to their cost, that they should haue been examples vnto other in good life, as they did professe, without which they shall surely come to naught. Besides the subtiltie of the hart, there is another cause of this, euen the craft of Satan, (who rules in his children) teaching them how to contriue, and warpe all subtile shifts, and policies, both to atchiue their euill purposes, and to defend them being brought to passe: And some of his schollers finding this trade to follow their hand, as they desire, make it their chiefe worke, to inuent euill and mischiefe, and excuses to couer it withall: they
Genes. 3.12.13 are not where they would be, if they be otherwise occupied. Our mother *Eue* learned it from the beginning, of him the father of shifts and lies, (for they goe together) for her posteritie: though some seeme to haue it entailed vnto them, aboue others. As, who almost, can be so suddenly come vpon, but he hath a shift in readinesse? and though all bee not a like plausible, yet (as the prouerb is) a bad one is better then none at all. By this let none thinke that all policie is forbidden: for *Nathan* and *Bathsheba* had plotted a wise course, but that was to the great good of Church and Common-
1. King. 1.12. wealth, & that by honest meanes, against *Adoniah*, as appeares by 1. King. 1. and the substance of the deuice was true, holy, and to a religious end, for it tended to serue Gods prouidence. But their practise warranteth not *Absolon, Adoniah*, or any such as they, whose policie is wicked and cursed: much lesse the hellish plots of Iesuites, and Papists, for the bringing to passe their designes, the setting vp, or tolleration of their idolatrous religion, though holinesse, and the Catholike cause be still pretended, and authoritie of their supreame Vicar. The titles are goodly, but the boxes are full of cursed drugges and poyson, as lying, slander, calumnies, treason, murther, cōfusion:
Matth. 5. all badges of the prince of darkenesse, whose Vicar he is. *Salt is good: but if it hath lost his sauour, it is good for nothing:* Wit and spirit, present speech and policie are good, but if they bee poysoned with those ingredients, they lose their sauour, grace and beautie, and are good for nothing, but to be vsed as proppes of the diuels kingdome. Better were it for the cunningest craftes man in this trade, to be defeated in all his purposes, and to be conuicted and take shame of them, then by such meanes to compasse them, or being compassed, to bolster them. Neither is there any counsell against the Almightie: his hand shall find them out at length, and countermine them, as (blessed be his name) hitherto hee hath done, euen the deepest and furthest fet-
Reu. 2.24. ches of them. Let all sorts learne by this, and namely the simple hearted, to thank God that he is no more acquainted with the depth of Satan, I meane either the depth of sinne, or the depth of subtile practises and shifts thereof: and they who are more ready wittied, let them turne it from playing the aduocate to such a fruitlesse client, and submit it to the simplicitie of the word, to be guided thereby: which (when all is done) will prooue the safest, when the other shall be as *Adams* figge-leaues.

Verse 3. Now behold here in these men who were of his mothers kindred, how soone they hearkened vnto this corrupt motion of that *Abimelech*, and so approoued of his deuice and suite, that they durst propound it to the rest of their neighbours, which was too shamefull for themselues to open their
1. King. 1.9. eares vnto: Like vnto whom is that practise of those Courtiers of *Dauid* in the aduancing of *Adoniah*, among whom were also many of his brethren and

and kinsfolke. By this we may see how kindred are blindfolded to beare one with another; breaking through shame, modestie, yea and honestie also; regarding no other thing but this, that they are their flesh, and they take part with them, be the matter that moues them neuer so bad. For example, how are parents blinded in their children, and carried by them almost to any perswasion: and that without all Christian wisedom or regard: being sometime incensed by them against those that are good; and yet not reprouing, but winking at their childrens faults, and giuing them their will so farre till themselues blush, & smart for it, to see to what boldnes they grow thereby, nor taking it in any manner contentedly, if their children though neuer so iustly be called to their answere for their doing, and corrected: but reuenging it rather, and that with spitefulnes. Euen so, what disorders are faine to be suffered in townes, while euery one (forgetting the Apostles speech, that it is an higher degree to back a sinner, then to commit sinne) holds with his Rom.1.32.
owne kindred, so that none must stirre against them, but the towne is diuided into factions, and parts taking for their cause, (and so it is also betwixt carnall friends) where as kindred (being neerer to a man then other good acquaintance, or companie) ought to bee the first that should bridle, controle, and helpe to hold vnder their kinsfolke from ill rule and disorder: and as for friendship, men should reach it out, and shew it, but according to conscience, not daring to abuse the bond of nature, to brotherhood in euill. The which produceth dangerous effects both to the partie wronged, the parties defended, and also the parties themselues who countenance them: as here, both the whole common-wealth, *Abimelech*, and the Shechemites smarted all by this confederacie. And the greater, and the more authoritie such friends, kindred or parents be of, the more this doctrine toucheth them: For as a common townesman may doe in a towne, so a great person may doe in a shire, a Prince in a kingdome: euen set all in a combustion for a few malefactors sake, as the Beniamites, chap.20. did for the defence of those Sodo- Iudg.20.
mites of Gibeah. Let these therefore learne of the common speech, [*Vsque ad aras*] that is, as farre as in conscience I may, I will doe the part of a friend vnto you, and of a parent: but if ye draw me beyond that, I leaue you: neither will I (to pleasure you) make God my enemie. Depart from me: yee shall finde no aide at my hands, yee adulterers, riotous, ill companions and Psal.101.6.
workers of iniquitie. And let all sorts take their lesson, if not from the holy Ghost, yet from an heathen, who saw cause of prescribing this rule, That especially this must be lookt to, lest a man commit any thing iniurious, or vnlawfull for his friends sake: as he that professed he would burne downe the Tower of Rome, if his great patrone willed him so to doe. Such amitie fitteth Robbers and Traytors, better then Christians. Who should duly weigh, whether the matter bee such as will stand with their profession, credit, and equitie: otherwise to betray them is faithfulnes, and to punish thē, and (as the law was) to cast the first stone at them, is good seueritie, rather then to betray good order, the towne, or Common-wealth, by their ambition, or iniustice. Men will admit of this in generall, and say, God forbid else, but when it comes to the push, they shew they haue the same disease which the other haue; (as these Shechemites had the same sore which *Abimelech* had) and so are loth to smart for them, but rather smother their owne

owne sinnes, in other mens. But of this I say the lesse, because the two next points aime at the like end, and may serue as an inlargement hereof.

Vers.3.4 But (to passe from these) wee may see here as great a fault in the men of Shechem, as we haue seene in the kindred of *Abimelech*. They who should haue trembled at the hearing of such a matter propounded, being so monstrous, and horrible; and should haue carried it to them that were in authoritie: behold how they applaud and like of it; yea and procured money also to the furthering of it: which, all wise men see, was done of them in great lightnes, and rashnes at the least: yea, that was one of the smallest euils in their hearkening to them. And by this note the ficklenes of the multitude, how easily it is to bee carried euery way as with a blast, neuer weighing or considering what sound reason leadeth them to in their doings, much lesse aduising with the word of God.

Doct.

A cleere and notable example of this ficklenes and lightnes, wee haue in the Gospell, of them that one day honoured Christ, and set him vp, crying *Hosanna*, before him, and bowing to him as a King: but a few daies after, when the Iewes and Pharisies rose vp against him, they cried in another manner, *Crucifie him, crucifie him*. So that wee see how such are not to be rested in, who though they hold with religion, as other doe, and good order in words, yet except they be seasoned with sound and sauing knowledge, and grace to gouerne themselues in the course of their liues, it is nothing. But such as giue themselues to sobrietie & staiednes, are highly to be esteemed, & so vsed with all good discretion; considering how soone flesh may be puffed vp, and ill counselled, yea & they are to be incouraged to such staiednes and constancie, in a Christian and well ordered course: which they that are fickle, not regarding, but holding on in their inconstancie, they may reade their destinie, that as miserable as they are alreadie, they shall daily waxe worse and worse, till they dye as they haue liued. But this offereth it selfe often: therefore I spare any further discourse of it: Here I will stay for this time.

Luk.19.38. *compared with* 23.13.18.

So in the former chap. verse last, compared with the 22.

Compare (for another proofe hereof) 2.Sam. 19.43. *with the* 20.2.

2.Tim.3.13.

THE FIFTIE SIXE SERMON ON THE NINTH CHAPTER OF THE BOOKE OF IVDGES.

More of the third verse.

NOw to proceed, wee haue seene how these wofull men of Shechem, who bewraying by the forementioned act of leaning to a bad request, the exceeding wickednes that was in them, haue yet branded themselues with another note of infamie like the former, which doth much aggrauate their sinne; namely this: that liuing in the fellowship of honest citizens, who should haue punished euill doers, and haue chaced them away with their very countenance, yet behold,

behold,there were no worse to be found there then themselues. They who should haue made the worst afraid of their iniquitie, by their executing of law and iustice vpon the committers; euen they put the common citizens, and better men then they were, in danger of their liues by their wicked dealing; and did indeede cause them both to lose their liues, by bringing in an vsurper and tyrant, to spoile and make hauocke of them. We know next to the Prince in a land, are the Peeres and Nobles thereof: these it most concerneth to assist the supreme gouernour in the execution of iustice and gouernment. And yet we see, by comparing this with the Chronicles of diuers lands, that these often haue been the forwardest in defending the worst causes, in attempting against the State, yea and (in the vacancy of the throne and kingdome) to further and helpe forward vsurpers in their vnlawfull claime, against the vndoubted heires. Whereby we learne, that there are no worse then some of them who liue in ciuill societie with others; who also are trusted with the peace and safetie of towne and citie, and yet by the iust iudgement of God, pursuing them, break out and bewray themselues sometime to be notorious offenders, and are brought forth oft times by their due deserts, to shamefull execution with other euill doers; Euen as we reade of one who liued in the tents with other, when Israel abode in the desert, after they came out of Egypt, yet being a blasphemer, was take out of the hoast of Israel, and stoned to death, like the worst malefactors: and so some (to come to our time) with *Ananias* are found, though they bee citizens and headborowes, to be forgers, sacrilegious, &c. Others, of the same condition with *Achan*, prooue arrant theeues, and as he was, are put to open shame and reproch, as well as rogues and masterlesse hang-bies; and some are found with *Zimry* to be whoremongers, yea worse then the incestuous, and no better the Sodomites, and do publikely receiue their punishment due thereto. As also all the spies, being yet choice men among the Tribes, yea of the chiefer sort of them, yet perished for their collusion and dissimulation, except *Caleb* and *Iosbua*. These are not light and small matters that such as are substantiall, and of good reputation among their neighbours, should bee brought forth thus to be set on the stage to be gazed on with the worst, who might and ought with the best, to haue been pursuers and punishers of other euill doers: and their infamy shall neuer be put out with God (beside the shame that befalleth them here before men,) without vnfained repentance, which is no common thing, as the world (yet) accounteth it. And to passe from these, there are other some so vile, irreligious, and monstrous in another maner, yea and euen of them who yet beare it out among men, as if they were to be allowed and iustified, their sinnes being not punishable by the law of the land, nor to be taxed by the Magistrate, so that the Lord doth execution vpon them himselfe, causing their prophanenesse, atheisme, and miserlike worldlinesse to rise vp against them, and driue them to hang themselues with their owne halter, as did *Abitophel* the great counseller, and *Iudas* the Apostle, when he became a traitor. These whom I haue now mentioned, and many other of bad note, being found among the ciuiller sort in cities and townes euery where, who yet should helpe to suppresse vagarant and vnruly persons; Oh, what are good, faithfull, and friendly neighbours

Doct.2.in verse 3.

Leuit.24.14.

Iosh.7.25.

Numb.25.8.

Numb.14.37.

worth, and how highly to be accounted of? such I meane, as among whom one may dwell peaceable, and without feare, and in whose faithfulnesse a man may rest? And as such may much reioyce, though their infirmities hold them vnder, so yet they who flourish and lift vp their heads on high, and count themselues the onely happie people, because they are more righteous, as they call it) that is to say, counted honest, and ciuill dealers, and such as cannot be blemished with any open blot and staine of infamie for oppression, falshood, vncleannesse, and yet void of religion, euen these also (so many of them as will shew themselues wise indeed; let them (I say) know they are in little better case thẽ the other in Gods account, seeing they hate to be reformed. And for all their vaunting themselues, and the high conceit that they haue of their good estate toward God, as if they were the only religious persons, yet while they submit not their neck to the Lords yoke of obedience, but abhorre and scorne such as they thinke go beyond them in sincere piety, who make conscience of stricter matters, (as the world count them) as idle speech, pride of life, foolish iesting, filthy pleasures, railing, slandering, lying, deceiuing, &c. euen they, most certainely haue God their
Luke 13.3. aduersary, and because they repent not, they shall likewise perish. Doubtlesse it were (I deny not) to be wished, that there were no worse in townes, then these of the ciuiller sort, and it were greatly for the benefit of the commonwealth, that grosse villanies were rooted out among them, & common vertues practised, as the outward worshipping of God, and peace with men. But yet these, (as the Scripture testifieth) are farre from happinesse, as before hath been noted: the which I say, partly lest these men should deceiue themselues and others, with an erroneous conceit of that good which is not in them, (while they search not their hearts, and purge out the filth that is there, and yet glorie of repentance: and partly, that Gods people may see cause of endeuouring after a further measure of grace and true holinesse; rather then to faint therein, and breake off their good beginnings. And the
Note. Lord doth oft times therefore plucke out such whole and ciuell men, (as they loue to bee counted) by the eares from their fellowes, and for the example of many other, he suffereth them to disguise themselues grossely by falling into the sinnes for which they haue scorned and disclaimed others, as adultery, and boasted themselues to be free from them. This (I say) God is faine to doe to them: and then they crie out of their hollownesse, ignorance, vnbeliefe and euill heart, (being so conuicted,) which hath laid them in the dirt. These before were no sinnes with them, neither would they be brought once to thinke so; whereas yet now that they haue committed the grosser, they accuse themselues of smaller also. Therefore they are happy, who lay the foundation of their peace, credit, safety, and true welfare toward God, who lay it (I say) deeper, then that storme or tempest, wind or weather may cast it downe: neuer ceasing, till they haue by faith purged out the strength and poyson of those corrupt and bitter rootes of the euill heart, and by the same faith haue obtained and found mercy with God, that they may feare him, and for a good conscience sake, goe vnder (if it must needs bee so) discredit with bad men, rather then for credits sake to smother conscience, which building soone decaieth

decaieth with the sandie ground-worke thereof.

But now to returne to the Shechemites againe, I haue not yet noted nor Verse 4.
set downe the particular sinne, which they added to the rest, that is to say, that they help forward this cursed impe *Abimelech* to vsurpe the kingdome, by giuing him such a peece of money out of their common treasurie, which was the house of their Idol Baal-berith (of whom we spak before cha. 8. end) with the which he was able to hire a band and company of leaud fellowes to guard and runne before, and follow him, as *Absolon* did the like, when he tooke in hand such a like worke. Whereby we may see to what vses ma- Doct. v. 4.
ny put their goods, and how commendably they imploy them, which they are put in trust with. As for feeding the hungry with them, or cloathing the naked, or pitying the oppressed, it is too base a matter for them to looke Marke 4. 7.
after, though they shall know one day, and that to their cost, that they haue the poore among them, to this end, that they may doe good to them. But the thought of such things is as far from them as the East is from the West: yea it is death to them to part with the very shreds to good vses: but they Iames 4. 3.
empty their purse to the bottome to bestow vpon their lusts, in roytous life, in drinking, whoring, and other excesse, till they bee brought to a morsell of bread: or else they be of another disposition, namely, to gather and increase their substance endlesly, neither they themselues, nor any wise man can tell why: for if they haue posteritie to leaue it to, (which yet many want) they should leaue them but that which remaineth after they haue done, in their time and place, many good deeds to diuers ciuill and religious necessary vses: and otherwise accursed are they in that which they haue, which for the most part doth no other good then the pleasing of the eie of the owner, while they know many smart and are in penury, (that I say) nothing of their wicked increasing of great part of it by oppression, and defrauding of men; whereof we haue too many wofull examples among vs from time to time. The Lord, therefore, hath giuen them no heart to doe good with it, which if they had, they should consider also, that there is somewhat else to bestow cost vpon, as well as vpon themselues, but especially vpon their lusts: I meane, the worship of God, procuring a good Minister, relieuing the distressed, of all kinds, as their abilitie will reach. But they shew that God and his word are of meaner account with them then their lothsome lusts. Touching this abuse of mens wealth and outward blessings, sundry kinds of doctrine haue occasioned vs to speake before, neither shall it bee needfull to make any set discourse vpon it in this place. Onely I will adde a word or two touching this. *That they tooke these peeces out of the treasury of Baal-berith.* Whether they tooke it out of their treasure, appointed to idolatrous vses (for it is probable they had such a treasurie, in imitation of the treasurie of the house of God) or whether their common treasure, was in some place of that Temple, there laid vp as in a safe repositorie, and free from the violence or sacriledge of robbers, (of which vse of temples, especially in times of war and danger of pillage, we reade in Prophane and Ecclesiastical writers euery where) of this, I say, I will not affirme, neither can I. Only I encline to the former opinion: and do think that they robbed their Temple, to supply the want of *Abimelech* (and sacriledge may wel stand with treason and tyranny, which spare neither things holy nor prophane.) But vpon coniectures I

will collect nothing. Whether soeuer they did, sure it is, that they thought their Idoll a sufficient treasurer and keeper of this siluer, (or else they would not haue made his Temple the treasurie) and durst trust him with the preciousest things they had: who yet had neither eies to see it, or hands and power to defend it from robbers. This is no wonder (may some man say) that they durst trust him with their money, who durst venture their liues and
1.King.18.28. soules vpon his protection, as they in the daies of *Eliah*. 1. King. 18. did. I answer: It were the lesse wonder indeed, if wee saw not Christians, worshippers of God (who professe themselues to ieopard their saluation vpon his promise) to be yet farre behind these Idolaters in this thing. For they will not venture nor cast their goods vpon his safegard, nor thinke the Lord a meet and trustie keeper of their wealth; they will put no more in his hands then they are willing to lose. To such we may say: Is he not much beholding to you the whilest? He hath giuen you liuing Temples, not of stone temples, not of *Baal*, but of his owne making, euen the poore members of the Lord Iesus; Into these he commandeth you to cast, not your superfluities, but some of your substance: hee promiseth to be the ouerseer and steward of this treasurie, he will reckon and returne againe such beneuolence of yours, double and trebble vnto you, yea tenfold, (which is vse and gaine enough) nay, an hundreth fold, rewarding it with euerlasting habitations: For why? he hath vndertaken, and is become the Surety (as I haue said) to repay all such loane againe abundantly. But wee thinke these to bee but words: and keepe the principall fast, let the interest goe where it will for vs. As for these Temples, we count them Sepulchres, deuouring al, asking *giue, giue*, but neuer returning ought againe: and as they in Ecclesiastes, who
Eccles.11.1. thinke all lost and cast vpon the waters, that is well bestowed. But these Idolaters and their confederates in Baal-berith, shall stand foorth, and witnesse against such, to their shame.

Doct.2.in vers.4. Again, when they had thus helped him forward, we may see what maner of persons he hired & prouided to bring his wicked purpose to passe, to wit, such as were empty, light-headed, and naught worth, and which were lewd and loose, and were carried headlong to that which they did, and not by sound reason. Whereby we haue a description of such graceles and wicked hangbies, what they are, and wherefore they serue; which shall be to good purpose to note, as for other causes, so for this one; to wit, that we may see what iustice should be done and executed on such: who liuing idly for the most part, further then they needs must must worke, should be laid for as of late yeeres they were by that Honourable Counseller of worthie memorie, and kept from ranging about. But seeing they are seldome punished, the best vse we can make of them, is to beware of them. First they are, if we will know them, such as haue spent all, and liued idlelie, without practising any profitable trade or calling: and how haue they spent it? full leaudly and badly, in gaming, whoring, gusling, caualering, fray-making, &c. and yet hanging in mens debts. Secondly, they are male-contents both with their owne penury and the welfare of others, yea with the State it selfe (often) of the Common-wealth, wherein they liue. Thirdly, they are such as are not to be ruled by reason, much lesse by religion. But their disposition is, to run on head to bee set on gadding, rouing, &c. And wherefore stay or waite they?

they? but euen for such troublesome times as these here were? and for some tumult and insurrection, that they may fish in troubled waters, desiring a change of the present condition of these peaceable times, as a fit occasion to practise and set a work this their diuellish disposition, which in peace and gouernment, is, as it were emprisoned in them: some by ioyning themselues with vaine and loose persons like themselues, and wandring to and fro, if there be no imployment for them at home, into forren countries, not through a desire of getting knowledge or experience, much to trafficke for their maintenance, but to trie their fortunes (as they prophanely speake) being wearie of their owne countrey, wherein they are defamed for their leaudnesse, prodigalitie, and needlesse debts, or other dishonesty: others being readily hired, to sort themselues with such as will rifle mens houses, and companions in helping to make a head, and if none of these hit, (as they say) nor come to passe; then fall they to robbing by the high waies. And such dangerous and diseased members haue there alwaies been, and are in al Common-wealths. In the booke of the Acts, in two or three Chapters, the Acts 17.5,8.
Iewes got such hang-bies to make stirres and tumults in cities, and then & 19.29.34.
charged *Paul* to be the author of them; when he yet was in danger of his life by them; and all to make him seeme seditious, and a raiser of trouble where he came. Euen so such there are at this day, idle companions, who cannot choose, but like Vultures and Cormorants, pray vpon other mens goods: who might easily haue been staied from these courses while they were young, if they had not been suffered to haue their owne will so farre, til this trade (as miserable as it is, yet because it is ioyned with ease) waxed sweete vnto them. And againe, if they had not been saued and kept from prison and correction, when they had so iustly deserued it: which correction if the ciuill Magistrate, or the Head-borrowes of townes wherein they lurked, had neglected; yet their owne parents and kindred should haue seene exe- Deut. 22.19.
cuted.

And if such as worke not, ought not to eate, why are they suffered, whose 2.Thes.3.10.
life is idlenes? Let such therefore be purged out from among vs: and in all places let prouision be made, that they who are idle and vagrant, be restrained, and set on worke, (though they haue somewhat of their owne) that so, (will they nill they) as they will doe no good, they may bee compelled to stoope to good order, and be held in from doing mischiefe at least, that this euil may cease which threatneth so great danger to Church and Common-wealth: which (I must needs say) is hard to doe; considering how such persons flocke together to such places of the land as are populous and frequented, where they may be in harbour and the safer from search and punishment: but then, that which we cannot amend, let vs lament, and blesse God if we be free from such molestation in the places where we dwell.

When this *Abimelech* saw how his bold and shamelesse deuices and at- Vers.5.
tempts prospered, and how he thriued in them, he waxed much bolder, and
tooke heart to goe fall vpon his innocent brethren, and slew them. And *Compare*
herein is verified that of *Salomon*, Eccles. 7. *There is a wicked man* (saith he) Act.12.2.
who continueth in his malice: meaning, because he prospereth, and is not resi- Eccles.7.15.
sted. Thus *Adonibezek*, chap. 1. staied not till he had serued seuentie Prin- Iudg.1.7.
ces shamefully after his cruell humour, but was fleshed more and more by

his ſucceſſe. O horrible and vnnaturall blood-ſhedding crueltie! Here wee may ſee what monſters are in the world, worthily to be driuen frō amongſt men, and to be made ſpectacles and gazing ſtocks by open and moſt ſharpe puniſhment inflicted vpon them. Such were *Athaliah*, *Haman*, and *Abſolom*. Such were they who wrought that bloodie maſſacre in France, and they who were the chiefe doers in the perſecution here in England, which may be remembred by ſome that yet liue; and they of the Gunpowder-treaſon come nothing behinde, that I ſay no more. But how much more cruell are they who murther many ſoules for want of due foode? But touching the ſinne of crueltie I haue ſpoken in chap. 1. 7. and chap. 8. 20. and forward. There let the reader ſupply this place from thence.

Obiect. Many, not ill minded, deſire to know why God doth ſuffer ſuch abominations. *Anſw.* I anſwere, that God knoweth the cauſe, who ruleth iuſtly, and who (as a godly father ſpeakes) ordereth the euill appetites of the wicked, to fulfill his prouidence, though he infuſe not euill into them; as he wrought the ſaluation of his elect, by the fall of *Adam*, and the treacherie of *Iudas*: and yet wee are not, neither ought, to bee altogether ignorant why God doth this. Wee are not to appoint the Lord how to gouerne the world, nor by whom, nor how he will be glorified. And he who may marueile that God is patient toward the bad, how can he thinke himſelfe too good to ſuffer for his own deſerts, be the inſtruments neuer ſo euil, when our Sauiour ſuffered for vs without cauſe? But if any of vs bee without danger and hurt by ſuch wicked perſons, who are one of Gods ſcourges to correct vs, let vs reckon it among the great bleſſings of God, and vſe it accordingly.

Verſ. 5. doct. 2. But in this verſe let vs proceede further with *Abimelech*. He conſidered that his ſeuentie brethren might be like to hinder and reſiſt him: and therefore what did he? hee reſolued to diſpatch them all, and ſo hee did, except one. The hainouſnes of the fact, deterred him not from going through ſtitch with it: he would not leaue it by halues, nay he could not be quiet till euery obſtacle and hindrance was remoued, and each eye-ſore taken away. It bewraieth a moſt fearfull propertie in the workers of euill: that cannot deſiſt nor leaue of, till they haue brought their vngodly attempts to a full and perfect end: wherein the godly ſeldome match them in contrarie actions. A man would haue thought theſe ſeuentie men had been a great blocke in an vſurpers way, to keepe him from proceeding currantly in his bad courſe: and *Abimelech* ſaw that to, but yet it was not a barre ſtrong enough to keepe him from villanie, but he broke it (as it were) to peeces, rather then it ſhould ſtand vp in his way to hinder him from his purpoſe. For that, he was reſolued to goe forward with: and therefore whatſoeuer oppoſition ſhould come againſt it, hee would beare it downe, as floods and windes pull downe hils, bankes, bridges, gates, trees, and whatſoeuer comes in their way, and yeelds not to them. Woe be to him that meetes a Beare robbed of her whelpes; and yet better ſo, then croſſe an vſurper of his ambitious deſire: although theſe his brethren had not croſt him, but by ſilence and ſitting ſtill. Ambition is a raging monſter we ſee, and although it thirſt after honour, yet ſeldome is it aſſwaged without blood, if occaſion and opportunitie ſerue. Nothing is ſo holy, ſo pretious, ſo neere, which it prophaneth not, defloureth not, and deſtroyeth not. Euen his owne ſonne, if hee

had

had stood in his way, had tasted of the same sawce, which his brethren did, as it is reported *Herod* the great did, in the massacre of the infants. But it became him well enough to keepe that to himselfe by villanie, which hee had inuaded by wickednes before. Euen as his successors at this day, these Italionated diuels, and disciples of *Machiauel* both practise and defend, according to his rules, that a kingdome gotten by force, must be preserued also by violence. Againe, he that will rule, must not stand nicely vpon vertues, but (when occasion serues) play both the lyon and foxe, and worke out his enemies by fraud or crueltie, any way, so he can doe it. Againe, let them strike once, but (as *Abishai* said) strike home, and kill all at once that stand in his way and sit in his light. For to kill often is odious, but to make a riddance all at once, roote and branch, is with such, policie, and a necessitie pardonable. When I thinke of this fact of *Abimelech,* I could not but thus resemble it to these monsters, who lately offered to giue vs an experiment of the like enterprise in their powder-treason: which, as no age euer matched, so no age shall euer forget it, to their eternall shame, and the Lords endlesse praise. For as they were *Abimelechs* in ambition and crueltie, so the Lord made them *Abimelechs* in confusion. *Abimelechs* ioy lasted not: theirs was but hope, and yet made them ashamed. The Lord sent a spirit of diuision betweene him and Shechem: so hee did betweene these, one betrayed the other. *So let thine enemies perish O God, &c.* Therefore let all wise men (for all are not great ones) circumspectly take heede and beware what sinnes they resolue to commit: for surely whatsoeuer they giue ouer themselues vnto, they will make no bones of the necessarie attendants thereof, be they neuer so hideous and horrible. As it is hard to say, whether this parricide or his ambition were greater, saue onely that the former serued the latter. Men little dreame how deeply they plunge themselues, when they vndertake any sinne: themselues often are astonished at themselues, but that when they haue begun, they must play the men in going forward, and not shrink for it. *Herod* himselfe was not willing to behead *Iohn:* but when he had said the word, he must not goe backe, (he thought) for his credit sake, therefore hee went through. Hee might thanke his luxuriousnes, and iollitie, which caused the oath, and the oath the murther. So saith the Apostle; Because men set it downe, they will be rich, they meete with their match, and fall into many temptations and snares, &c. Tush, tell not them of trifles, of lyons in the way, they are busie in pursuing their game, and they will get it, whatsoeuer it cost them, for they haue so decreed and set it downe. Well, learne to resolue onely vpon that which is lawfull, and so be free from any great inconuenience, and goe through it with commendation: for all other resolution is diuelish. I would bee larger in this, but that there followeth in the sixth verse a doctrine not much differing from this argument.

Match. 2.

Iudg. 5. last verse.

1. Tim. 6. 9.

But in this bloodie act of *Abimelechs,* one of his brethren escaped his hands: and in that one of them was preserued from his crueltie, and kept out of his reach, it was done by Gods speciall prouidence, both to hold him in feare, seeing hee that was kept aliue, was the lawfull sonne of *Gedeon,* and borne of a lawfull wife; *Abimelech* himselfe comming but of a concubine: and further, it was also a good dashing of his ioy. And moreouer, wee see there was good vse of the Lords sauing aliue of that one of his brethren, *Iotham*

Doct. 3.

tham I meane, because of the prophecie that he vttered; therein foretelling the destruction of *Abimelech*. To teach vs, that although the committers of euill haue their humors satisfied, and their turne serued, and things to fall out euen as they would wish, yet there is, and shall be euer, somewhat reserued to vex and pay them home, euen here in this world, and to giue them a taste of further torment. For example, who had better successe then *Haman?* and yet by *Mordecay* (who was of no place to stand with, or to crosse him) how was his ioy quailed by him? rather then there should be none to resist him: yea, and that which was very vnlike to be, came vpon him, for by
Ester 7.10. & 9.10. *Mordecaies* counsell, and well handling the matter, *Haman* was ouerthrowne with his whole house.

So *Herod* and *Herodias* had nothing that troubled them, but *Iohn Baptist*;
Marke 6.20. and yet when they had taken *Iohn* out of the way, our Sauiour Christ rose vp, who (through this that *Herods* conscience put him in feare) kept him at
1.King.22.8. that stay, that he could not bee quiet. *Ahab* had been at hearts ease, but for *Eliah*, and yet afterward *Michaiah* vexed him as much. *Gehazi* sped well a
2.King.5.25. while; but at length his master dashed all. And all this is a sauour of their woe before it come, vnlesse they be feared & driuen from their bad courses thereby, and so humble themselues to seeke mercy; as that third Captaine
2.King.1.13. of *Ahaziah* did to *Eliah*, seeing the danger. And thus God feareth the whole rabble of the vngodly, and by other terrors also: when his word wil not doe it, his workes shall; and euen thereby, I meane by the casting them downe by the law liuely preached to them, and the feare of death, iudgement day, and hell; hee doth so torment many a man, that all his shiftes and deuices cannot deliuer him there-from; neither is al that hee hath able to comfort him, and cry downe this voice of the Ministery, although it worke no true feare of God in him to repentance, but onely awake and astonish him. True it is, that some, though they bee apparantly crossed by God, yet they feele it no more then the dead palsey, as we see in *Nabal*. But in that they be hardned, they are in worse case. So then God dealeth thus commonly, that the wicked shall haue somewhat to make them lesse eager of their pleasures; as either paine, sicknesse, or some such thing, or else inward feare, or the like. Although (alas) what although they should neuer be interrupted? they should yet be but caried to hell merrily, when others goe mourning. And when Gods seruants fall to the like sinne, as to nestle themselues in the deceiuable inticements of this world, hee giueth them the like medicine to cure them of their disease, that they
Note. shal euer haue one thing or other to hold them in vnquietnesse, and to feare them with: which is euer like to light vpon them, to vexe and sting them, if they shall dare delight themselues in any euill thing, or to rest in that which is transitory; and so goe from the Lord. As the feare of losing a good wife, their nearest companion to them, to partake their commodities and delights with them; or their crosses and decaies in the world, to make them easilier borne, which affliction disquieteth them much, and dampeth all their earthly repast. So also, he exerciseth them with weakenesse of body, meannes in estate, petty losses, &c. and al to weane thē from the breast (as it were sucklings) by laying such bitter and distasteful corrections vpon them.

Vse. The vse of this is, to rest and ioy our hearts in nothing here below; but to see,

see, that our delight bee in the fauour and feare of the Lord continually: which is the one thing (though we may make them two) that is necessarie. Prou 24.27. Luke 10.42.
And if nothing will rouse vs out of spirituall slumbering in earthly prosperitie and peace, (wherein to lie senselessely and sottishly, is more then to haue one foot in hell already) let this doe it, that wee know not how soone wee must leaue al, and goe to iudgement, and to the yeelding vp of our account. And yet if the Lord crosse vs in our enterprises that bee euill, we may know the worst that he meaneth toward vs, is, that he would stop vs in our race toward destruction and misery, that it may not come vpon vs.

When *Abimelech* had so vnnaturally slaine his brethren, which ought to Vers 6. *The sense.*
haue stricken such a terror into the men of Shechem that they should haue abhorred him, and pursued him openly, calling the rest of the Tribes to ioyne with them therein, till he had receiued his due punishment: he so subtillie woound in with them, and they were so credulous, that they beleeued, for all that hee would deale well with them, as hee had promised them; and therefore proceeded (O fearefull to be spoken) and vndertooke to make him King: and this they did in a place that pertained to them, none of the other Tribes being either called, or made acquainted with the matter (who yet had a farre greater stroke therein then they) which must needs raise great dissention and deuision betwixt them. But this they regarded not, seeing they had taken in hand the effecting of the other.

Here we see, when one sinne is intended of a man to be committed, it go- *Doct.* 1.
eth not alone, but draweth with it many other, as companions to it. For neither can it be brought to passe without the helpe of other, neither can a man take pleasure in it without the company of other sinnes. He seekes to be King, and how many sinnes doth he adioyne, to the effecting of it? As he here vsed fraud, flatterie, and cousonage, and rose vp, and drew after him a band of seditious hang-bies; he slew his brethren; and when he was made King, what contention did he cause among them?

It is too manifest, that sinne is no solitarie bird, nor is euer seene out of Rom. 13.13.
company. Euen as S. *Paul* teacheth to the Romans, how strife carrieth enuying with it; and gluttony draweth drunkennesse; and chambering, wantonnesse. And this is the more to be marked, because wicked persons alleage for themselues, when they are reprooued for their faults, that al men are sinners, yea some sinne grossely in many kinds, and for themselues, they say, they hope, if they haue done amisse, yet they may be borne with, seeing it is but one trespasse: and further they will say, euery one for himselfe, Such a man hath this blemish, and such a one that: all haue some one or other, and so may I haue, and what then? But to this it is to be answered, where one chiefe sinne is committed, there are many other as handmaides to accompany it. As in the sinne of *Achan*, *Dauid*, *Ananias* and *Saphira*, with many others, is to be seene. Therefore if we thinke it be a shame for vs, to be char- Note.
ged with many, then take we heed of any one, for it will not goe alone, and if we thinke it a small matter to bee rebuked for one, know we for certaintie, that one will bring and draw many to it: and he only is happy, that wisely taketh heed of all. But this doctrine I haue handled before: therefore the lesse shall serue. Looke backe into chap. 1. vers. 7.

Moreouer, let the foolishnesse of these men of Shechem, who beleeuing *Abimelechs*

Abimelechs faire words, went by and by and made him King, let it (I say) teach vs wisdome. For it is a singular good watch-word to all Christians, that we doe not regard so much the speeches of vaine and loose persons, as weigh and compare their actions one with another, that we may profit by them, and not be beguiled. As the prouerb saith; what should I hearken to, words, when I see deeds contrarie. His were vile and horrible, as they saw, therefore they ought not to haue regarded his words. For he that is faultie in a great matter, is not to bee trusted in a small. For example; if (as our text teacheth) a man be vnpitifull to his owne, as this *Abimelech* was, he will certainly be without pitie and compassion to other, howsoeuer for vaine glory he may shew pitie sometime, and in some case; but that will not hold, neither is it to be rested vpon: for one swallow maketh not summer. So if one will contend and fall out with, disclaime, and deceiue his neere friend, let not a stranger trust him. For though such an one bee now in fauour with him, yet they may twentie waies be easily estranged one from another, as we see it commeth daily to passe. So if a man liue not peaceablie and kindly with his wife, hee may say what hee will of his agre-ing with others, but longer then while his corrupt and inconstant humor bee pleased, he will liue kindly with none. This *Dauid* aimed at, and meant in his answer to them that brought tidings of their murthering of *Saul*, and of *Ishbosheth*: for what likelyhood gaue they of any more fidelitie to him, if the time should haue serued?

Note.

2. Sam. 1. 16. & 4. 12.

So to prosecute this point in more particulars, wherein the truth of it doth best appeare; let vs not be deceiued, but wise; if we see, that a man be not faithfull to God, let vs not thinke that he will bee to vs. So if one helpe not his poore neighbour in his need, there is small liberalitie or neighbourhood in him at any time. If a man bestow not the Sabbath in godly exercises and religious duties, it is sure he doth little that way on other daies. and if he doe; yet it is not of knowledge nor conscience, whatsoeuer he doth, without which it is nothing worth. So if a man cannot be appeased in a small matter, let him say what he will, it is sure, hee will much lesse bee in a great: and yet men commonly say, any thing but this I would doe for you, or could yeeld vnto, when yet a small matter is requested of them.

Note.

So, to enlarge the argument from the greater and more likely, to the lesser: if thou canst not trust them, whom thou hast long knowne faithfull, though thou gettest many new friends, thou shalt neuer be bold soundly to rest vpon them. Also if a man will seeme repentant, and leaue not an il outward qualitie, he hath not (certainly) yet begun to search and purge his euil heart. If the righteous find much adoe to be saued; he is farre from it, that taketh his libertie at his pleasure. And who is little troubled about seeking assurance of his saluation? If one day spent and taken vp in a godly life bee sweet, what were many, may the whole life, if it were passed therein? If we faint in afflictions, and yeeld readily to temptations, we may know by that; our strength was neuer great. Againe also, (as our Sauiour saith) *If ye be vnfaithfull in the smallest things, who shall trust you with the greatest treasure?* And so (to say somewhat of Gods dealing with vs) if God haue helped vs in the hardest, when we sought to him in feruentnes and truth, he will by the same meanes, helpe vs in smaller danger. If he spare not his owne, (as he did not

1. Pet. 4. 18.

Psalm. 84. 10.
Prou. 24. 10.

Luke 16. 11.

the Prophet,who disobeyed him at Bethel) much harder shall the state of the bad be,as *Ieroboams* was,who hard of the others punishment. And if we be sure,that he hath giuen vs his Christ,the greatest of all gifts; much more will he giue the smaller,being sought with the like mind. Thus we may take good by *Abimelechs* words,and bee bold to say,that hee set not more by the men of Shechem,then by his brethren,whatsoeuer he said. 1.Kin.13.25.35.

Now one thing I will adde, or repeate rather, hauing handled it in this Chapter more at large; I meane, touching these men of Shechem, who went and made *Abimelech* King, for all the abomination that they saw hee had wrought,who ought rather to haue pursued him to the fearefullest death,as I haue said. Out of whose practise wee may clearely see, that there are none so vile and odious persons, shewing openly their wickednesse to the world,but they are applauded and approoued of some in their odious and bad practises: and none are so godly, but shamelesse beasts there are, who openly wil defame them,and speake maliciously of them;yea,(if need be)to their faces. The reason is, that they who commend and maintaine these vngodly ones,are as vile and bad themselues as they, as I prooued before out of the Apostles words. And for further proofe of this which I say, let that be considered of *Iudas*, when hee had betraied his most kind and louing Master,yet how was hee incouraged to it before, and rewarded for it by thē that went then for masters in Israel, euen for the chiefe pillers of the visible Church,yea,teachers and lights to others?though the fact was afterward cried out of by the traitor himselfe,saying: *I haue sinned in betraying the innocent blood.* And all experience, aswell as Scripture, prooueth the truth of this point; which shewes how full of sinne and euill doings the times are. And yet they who applaud such, goe for honest citizens and townesmen,till they bee bewrayed by the Lord, and till their wickednesse breake foorth,euen as the others doth. Which rightly verifieth the prophecy of our Sauiour,who foretold, that in these latter daies,the abundance of iniquitie should bee such, that it should cause the loue of many to waxe cold. So that I conclude,that they are happy who are wise to turne away from, and to abhorre the sinnes of the times they liue in,but especially,if they abhorre sin in themselues secretly,that they may be farre from committing it openly,and feare to offend God,for the loue they beare him. But I leaue the rest to the next Sermon.

*Doct.*3. Rom.1.last. Luke 22.5. Matth.27.4. Matth.24.12.

THE

THE FIFTY SEVENTH SERMON ON THE NINTH CHAPTER OF THE BOOKE OF IVDGES.

Verse 7. *And when they told it to Iotham, he went and stood in the top of mount Gerazim, and lift vp his voice and cried, and said vnto them: Hearken vnto mee you men of Shechem, that God may hearken vnto you.*

8. *The trees went foorth to annoint a king ouer them, and said vnto the Oliue tree; Reigne thou ouer vs.*

9. *But the Oliue tree said vnto them; should I leaue my fatnesse wherewith by me they honour God and man, and goe to aduance me aboue the trees.*

10. *Then the trees said vnto the Fig tree, Come thou and be king ouer vs.*

11. *But the Figtree answered them, Should I forsake my sweetnesse and my good fruit, and goe to aduance me aboue the trees?*

12. *Then said the trees vnto the Vine, Come thou and be king ouer vs.*

13. *But the Vine said vnto them, Should I leaue my wine, whereby I cheare God and man, and goe to aduance me aboue the trees?*

14. *Then said all the trees vnto the Bramble, Come thou and raigne ouer vs.*

15. *And the Bramble said vnto the trees, If yee will indeed annoint me king ouer you, come, and put your trust vnder my shaddow: and if not, the fire shall come out of the Bramble, and consume the Cedars of Lebanon.*

16. *Now therefore, if ye doe truly and vncorruptly to make Abimelech King; and if yee haue dealt well with Ierubbaal and with his house, and haue done vnto him according to the deseruings of his hands.*

17. *(For my father fought for you, and aduentured his life, and deliuered you out of the hands of Midian.*

18. *And yee are risen vp against my fathers house this day, and haue slaine his children, about seuentie persons vpon one stone; and haue made Abimelech, the sonne of his maid-seruant King ouer the men of Shechem, because he is your brother,)*

19. *If yee then haue dealt truly and purely with Ierubbaal, and with his house, this day, then reioyce ye with Abimelech, and let him reioyce with you.*

20. *But if not, let a fire come out from Abimelech, and consume the men of Shechem, and the house of Millo: also let a fire come forth from the men of Shechem, and from the house of Millo, and consume Abimelech.*

21. *And Iotham ran away, and fled, and went to Beer, and dwelt there, for feare of Abimelech his brother.*

The second part of the Chapter.

The summe of this 2 part of this Chapter.

WE haue heard how *Abimelech* and the men of Shechem prospered, and pleased themselues in that which they had done. Now in the rest of the Chapter, and first in this second part to the 22. verse, is shewed that God would haue them blancked and damped in the midst of their

their doings, and first by *Iotham*, one that was reserued for that purpose. Therefore when it was knowne to *Iotham*, the youngest sonne of *Gedeon*, (who escaped the bloodie hands of *Abimelech*) that the men of Shechem were gathered together to make him king, hee waited his opportunitie, by Gods directing of him, when they should meete together, and came to a place where hee might be heard of them, and that was mount Gerazim, which was neere to Shechem, on the top whereof hee stood, to tell them of their doings, and how they should speed for them. That he came thither by Gods instinct, three reasons doe proue, as also *Iothams* words in the 7. verse. First, in that he went safe away after: which to reason was not likely. Secondly, for that it came to passe, as hee prophecied. Thirdly, the thing was good, and to good vse, and not found fault with. His reprouing and denouncing against them, for more plainnes he set down by a parable, giuing them to vnderstand a truth by a thing imagined, as by a maner of speech more plausible and perswasiue, then if he had made a direct inuectiue against them.

The opening of the parable. Herein first let vs see the meaning of some things in this scripture, which are hard to be vnderstood, before we proceed further. In parables, we know there must be no precise agreement with truth looked for in euery circumstance, nor sense wrung out of euery word, but the scope and substance must bee looked to and regarded. By the oliue therefore, vine, and figtree, briefly, hee meaneth such of *Gedeons* familie, as might haue been profitably employed. By the Trees seeking a king, hee meaneth the Shechemites. By the bramble *Abimelech*, good for nothing. And as the bramble, which is one of the worst shrubs in the field, ought not to be taken aboue any of the best trees, for any principall vse, but is most fit to bee burned: So neither ought *Abimelech* to haue been preferred before *Gedeons* sonnes, who yet would not raigne. Therefore both *Abimelech*, and they who chose him, should be, as they had deserued, euen worthily cut off. In this scripture are two things: the one a preface, desiring to hearken to him: with a reason, lest God hearken not to them: the other, to what they should hearken, to wit, to the laying out of their sinne, to verse 16. and to the punishment denounced against it, to vers. 22. *The parts two of the parable.*

Doct. out of all the verses generall. In that *Iotham*, when hee knew certainly the premisses, being stirred vp of God, went thereupon and told the men of Shechem of their doings, and denounced the iudgement of God against the same: it teacheth, that it pleaseth God, who set him aworke, and his will is, that iniquitie should be laid open to the committers thereof, and be resisted as speedily as may be; and that all, as their place and calling giue leaue, ought to be ready to goe against it, and pursue it. The Ministers by zealous teaching to deface it; the Magistrates by punishing; the gouernours of families in their places to do both. These are, as they are bound, to preuent and take order, as they can, lest such euill things should come to passe: and so to roote out, and reforme, when they are come. For thus both Church and Common-wealth is, and should be preserued.

Vse. The vse hereof, and in a manner of all which in the first three doctrines I noted, touching the contrarie fact of the kindred of *Abimelech*, and the men of Shechem, is, that they who doe euill, ought iustly to feare, for God hath set many to pursue them, yea euen their owne kindred; and though they escape one way, they shall be taken another. Wilt thou then liue without

Psal.112.1.& 8. feare euery way? feare God then, and doe well: for if ye doe the thing that
1.Pet.3.12.13. is good, who shall harme you? *For the eyes of the Lord* (as the Apostle saith) *are* (as the mothers vpon the child, that it may take no hurt) *ouer the righteous, and his eares open to their prayers: and the face of the Lord*, euen his anger, *is against them that doe euill.*

Vers.7. *Hearken*] By this speech of *Iotham* note, that as all instructions and warnings sent vs of God, ought to be hearkened to; so more particularly, they
Reuel 2.29. Doct. out of verse 7. who heare not the crie of the innocent being wronged, shall crie them-
Prou.17.15. selues, and not be heard. Note it against the monstrous oppressors and hard dealers of our time; who in letting and lending, regard neither equitie, the common benefit of both persons, nor the case of the poore, but wring from them what they can into their own hands, and vse other as they list. Iudge-
Iames 2.13. ment shall be without mercie to such as are so mercilesse. Consider what
Genes.37.28. a plunge *Iosephs* brethren were brought vnto two or three times, for the crueltie they had shewed to him most vnnaturally; when they sold him thither, from whence they hoped he should neuer returne to trouble them any more. God and man shall leaue such in their most miserable distresse, as in the destruction of Ierusalem, and in the death of *Saul* and *Iudas* we may see: but the mercifull shall finde mercie. This iudgement of God in measuring
Matth.7.2. out such measure to the mercilesse, as they haue met out to other, I haue oft obserued to be paid to them who haue been cruell, as to the bodies so to the
Note. soules of men; who for their own pleasure depriuing many, that were hungrie, of the food of life, haue (for all their bodily abundance) dyed miserably in darknes, without any comfort or instruction.

But alas, who beleeueth our report, till he see it verified? But men laugh and sport themselues in that they haue scraped together, wee haue it in our coffers, say they, and about vs: and as for God, tush, we hope, he will do neither good nor euil, we hope neuer to be put to any such plunge as you speak of: others indeed haue found the truth of this by wofull experience, but as for vs we hope to morrow shall be as to day, we feare it not. But oh wretch! what if the Lord in mercie cull out some one of many to be a wonder and example to the rest, sparing others the whilest; doest thou so abuse this his patience, to thy condemnation? What if thou be that odde person whom God will set vpon the stage? might not *Adonibezek* haue said as thou? But put case thou escape this plague from men, is there not a God who can bee cruell with the cruell, as well as froward with the froward? as the Psalmist speaketh: that is, match them to the full? Wilt thou vrge him to deale with thee as once he did with an engrosser and griper, arming mice and rats to
Note. oppresse him by sea and land, till they had eaten the flesh from the bones without pitie, as hee had done many mens before? If thou saiest this is rare, and not like to befall thee. Well, yet there is one way behinde, which shall surely meete with thee: and if thou canst shunne that, then say the Scrip-
Luke 16.24. tures are fables: and that is, when thou art in hell thou shalt crie out as *Diues* did, for woe and paine, desiring reliefe: But it shall be answered to thee, as to him: No; remember, the time was when thou feltest not the miserie of the oppressed: Now thou criest out in thine anguish, and none heareth thee. But by diuers occasions this is spoken of and handled in this booke.

To conclude therefore, (with a word or two touching another kinde of oppression) I haue obserued this, that some Protestants haue dealt hardly with,

with,and vncharitably defamed others; euen men of the same religion,and (which aggrauateth their sinne) such as they knew durst not giue them the measure backe againe,which they offered them. Now these men afterward falling into the hands of Papists, (men of another disposition, cruell like lyons, and stinging as scorpions) haue been so vnpleasingly and despitefully handled, by the slanderous railings of their Iesuites and Rabshakees, who haue vexed euery veine of their hearts: that they would haue bought off the blemishes and scarres with a price if they could, which the pennes and tongues of their enemies haue defiled thẽ with; sparing neither age,person, gifts,or place. And al to teach thẽ to deale gently with the innocent lambe, if they would auoide the tongues and teeth of woluish aduersaries & lyons.

Now to come to the parable: By the trees seeking a king,was meant, as I said, the Shechemites slipperines and inconstancie, who could not be content with Gods gouernment, gouerning them, as he had done, by many, and raising them vp a Iudge in their trouble by other nations, to deliuer them: but they would yeeld to be gouerned by one and haue king,(euen as sometime after the whole nation of the Iewes did follow them in: 1.Samuel 8.) contrary to that which God had appointed. Which practise of theirs teacheth vs,that we soone grow wearie of Gods yoke and of his ordinances, by obeying the which yet wee might doe well if wee could see,and loth wee are that God should raigne ouer vs. Indeed we say, and in words seeme to pray otherwise,as in the second and third petition; Thy kingdom come; Thy will be done: but who admitteth it? And no marueile. Vers.8. 1.Sam.8.5. Psalm.2.3. Luk.19.14.

For flesh is vnruly,and in the most there is no worke of the spirit,and the operation of it is weake in the best of vs, especially as we goe to worke. By meanes whereof,we see how ill it goeth with the most at this day. For they hauing no more then nature in them,seeke libertie to liue as they list,and to follow their owne way. From whence arise so many troubles and garboiles to them in their liues;when yet Gods yoke is the only easie yoke,and vnder the wing of his protection only is peace & safetie. Oh,one day in his house, to be nurtured by him,euen in this life,is better then a thousand in any estate of pleasure whatsoeuer: and yet wee haue libertie to enioy much euen that way also. Looke more hereof in chap.8.in *Gedeons* answere to the people offering him the kingdome. Note. Matth.11.last verse.

The other sonnes of *Gedeon* are compared with *Abimelech,* as the good trees are with the bramble. And yet they, who were more excellent then he,would not raigne: much lesse should *Abimelech,*who was farre lesse worthie,and yet he did. By the trees here,and *Gedeons* other sonnes,who would not raigne, though they mought, nor the trees, as the vine, oliue, and figge tree, that would not leaue their state for an higher, nor their sweetnes for any other; all of vs are taught to keepe compasse, and to frame our selues willingly to abide in the estate wherein God hath set vs (as indeed the only and best estate for vs) and not to breake out of our range and compasse, to affect that which is not for vs. And as gifts are required thereto,and calling; so we should attend thereupon,and imploy our time on that,for which we are fitted: yea and looke to find most sweetnesse therein. For as wee are taught to pray for our daily bread, euen that successe and measure of blessing that God seeth best; so that which he sendeth, wee should hold to bee best for vs. A worthy proofe we haue hereof in *Dauid,*who,though he were Vers.9.10.to the 16. *Doct.out of th former verses.*

designed to the kingdome, yet he professeth himself so modest & sober min-
Psalm. 131. 2. ded, that he looked not at any thing too high for him, but possessed his soule in silence and patience. Noting by the way, that to auoid this pragmaticall humor and ambition, a man must get an humble hart, much occupied about the wel ordering of his owne affections, & finding work enough at home.

But the most of vs reach at things beyond our compasse, or by our wit, policie and skill, thinke to get all into our net; and meddle with those which we are not trained vp vnto; and so we suffer our gifts to lie a rusting. Yea surely, this is the case of the most; either they will haue all or nothing, though they beg for their labour. Busie bodies many are, the priuat man prying into the Ministers calling, and finding fault with him; but blind and vntoward to seeke what is amisse in himselfe: not vnlike to *Absolon*, who being a subiect, who should rather haue prayed for grace fit for that estate, forgets himselfe grossely, and pleaseth himselfe to thinke how fit he was for an higher, and what he could doe in his fathers place farre better then hee,
2. Sam. 15. 4. and wisheth he were put to the triall, 2. Sam. 15. Whereas, if the foot be vnfit to doe it owne office, much lesse able will it be to bee the head of the bodie: and, indeed, such as these are euer censuring other in their places and callings, as insufficient, not looking to their owne duties. Let vs leaue (euerie one) this course, and haue euer in mind this answere of the Vine and the other trees; *Shall I leaue my sweetnesse, &c.* Lest we be as ridiculous as he, who bearing his head aloft in viewing the starres, fell into the ditch, for want of looking (in the meane while) to his owne standing. Rather let vs bee content, though we haue not as wee would, and rush wee not in hast, and without consideration to places and changes of dealings for aduantage: but let vs be sure, that we haue the Lord alwaies going before vs, or let vs looke for it, that he will most certainely ioynt vs. Yea let vs count it our chiefe praise, to be faithfull in our owne condition and calling: and no discredit to bee ignorant and vnfit for anothers, seeing the Lord requires no more of any, thē according to that he hath. And yet it is not vnlawful with such respects, in the decay of our trades or such like occupying, to enter vpon some other dealings for our necessary maintenance, (if need so require) and to shun and auoid idlenesse: but let them be such as are fittest for vs, and likest to helpe vs, but with this prouiso in any wise, that they be not too many, lest wee bee clogged with them, nor beyond our abilitie, that wee bee not cast behind hand by them. And so when we are driuen by necessitie, we cannot be charged as many may, I meane these banckrouts, and such as are weary of their callings, who being discontent with meanenes, aime at great dealings, neuer asking a questiō about their so vnaduized changes how God aloweth therof; and therfore with the trees they lose their sweetnes, (as we see by their answer, they must haue done, if they had left their places) yea, they must forgoe it whether will or no, when they make such changes, and cannot keepe it, although they would full faine. But of this point in part see chap. 8. 23.

Doct. 2. We may further learne here by the answer which is supposed to haue bin made by the trees, to wit, that they did so contentedly rest in that estate of theirs which God set them in, and which pleased him, and was profitable to men; we may learne (I say) by this, that God hath done much for vs, to whom he hath giuen a sweet contentment to rest and abide in our callings, and to vse them with faithfulnes and diligence. For why? (as I haue said) there

there are few that do so; and beside, we are bound in all things to be thankfull: and also that is one principall part of our welfare. But we must take it thus, that first we see, we be receiued into fauor with God, and then that we labor to be in deed, and to be counted faithful of him, that so we may be put 1.Tim.1.12.
in his seruice, for else neither can we walke in our callings aright, neither find this sweetnesse therein, that I speake of, but a carnall reioycing, so farre as we prosper, and not for that we serue the Lord in them. But this I enlarge not, being onely an vse of the former doctrine, and mentioned therein.

Now whereas it is said of the trees, that they ioyed God and men, wee *Doct.3.*
must know, that the oyle and wine were vsed in the seruice of God in the Tabernacle: the oyle many waies, as to annoint Kings, Prophets, and Priests, and to burne in the Tabernacle, and to be mixed with offerings: and the fruit of them al, were meat or medicine also, and comfort to men. Herein we must note the goodnesse of God in making euery creature to yeeld such vse and benefit to vs, insomuch as the vnlikest of other are not exempted from doing this seruice to vs, no not the Toade and the Spider, with the like of that kind, & yet by sin they are become noisome to vs, which before sin cōmitted, were not so. This (if we shuld go through the creatures) serues vs to meditate on, to the admiring of Gods kindnes, wisdom and power, seeing euery creature yeeldeth such variety of helpe to vs for our great refreshing and comfort. And yet our ignorãce of many excellent vertues and qualities which lie hid frō vs, in many of them, greatly hindereth vs in this dutie, though we see inough to set vs on work thus to occupy our selues about thē.

The naked and dead earth, as it appeareth in the Winter time, to yeeld to vs, and to all liuing creatures here below, food and nourishment, and to cast such a beauty into our eyes by the varietie of the furniture of it in the Summer season, Oh what an admirable thing is it? The sunne to giue heate and light daily to cherish the creatures, what a great fauour of God is it, as common a matter as we make of it? and so we may thinke of the rest. These are Rom.1.19.
the visible things of God, to make him knowne to vs, who is inuisible. The goodly varietie of meates, drinkes and medicines, which hee hath appointed for our refreshing, health, and comfort, which not only our owne soile, but also other countries afford to vs; also that he alloweth vs to eate of the Note.
fat, and drinke of the sweet, who can thinke of all these, but with wondring Nehem.8.10.
at the loue of the giuer of them in this his large and free bounty: and especially considering, that wee haue peace, health, and other publike and priuate blessings with them, as I haue noted chap.5. And yet who knoweth not, that these serue vs here only in this temporall life? things eternall are of another kind, and farre more excellent. Yea, and yet that which we see in the creatures, is nothing in comparison of that which should haue been, if the sinne of man had not blemished and defaced the first beauty of their creation. And howsoeuer (in great prouidence) the Lord haue released the curse due vnto them: yet they come short of that they were, when God saw all was good, and so blessed them. And all these his creatures for our need and Christian delight, may we enioy, boldly and without feare, who are his redeemed ones by Christ, and so restored to the right we had first in them: and this we may doe with Gods good liking, if we haue learned how to vse them to their kindly ends, euen to admire at (in our beholding them) the

 wis-

wisdome, power, and bounty of the Creator; gathering from that wee see, proofes of his mercy, prouidence, and loue to vs, in supplying vs with the good things we see not. For by these (in part) he would haue vs know him: as himselfe said, Doe yee see how the grasse of the field, the Lilies, and other plants are cloathed with beautie in their seasons, and beautifie the earth with their leaues, flowers, fruites, the colour, the sauour, the abundance of them? Then think (saith he) much more will he furnish you, if you can beleeue it. But further, this wee must take great heed of, lest these things, being neere and sensible to vs, cause such a through vewing, and deepe beholding of them, that our affections be snared by them, and held from ascending vp and mounting vp to the Creator: cursed be that view which causeth them to be loued with the loue of him that made them, and himselfe excluded from the heart of him that enioyeth them. Lastly, this also is to bee highly regarded, that we quicken vp our selues thereby, to chearefulnesse in his seruice, which is that good and ioyfull hart he speakes of in Deut. 28. breaking out into a sutable fruitfulnesse in duty toward him, who hath enlarged himselfe so greatly to vs. For else, when men swimme in blessings, hauing corne, wine and oile, or (as the Israelites had) the milke and hony of Canaan, in all plentie; and yet either know not God aright, or if they doe, abuse their liberties, and break out of their bounds; alas, they turne this varietie of Gods bounties and fauors, into accusations against themselues and punishments: they find no sweetnesse in them to purpose, while they enioy them, and they hasten also the remoueall of them vnseasonably, and when it shall bee full vnwelcome. Only the faithfull possesse them here, and are led by them to long after the fruition of him in fulnesse hereafter, who is much more glorious in himselfe, then in them: and in heauen where his honour dwelleth, then here vpon earth, which is but his footstoole.

Matth. 6. 28.

Deut. 28. 47.

4 By *Abimelech* and the Bramble, which sought that they were vtterly vnfit for, let vs marke, that where ambition is, it maketh the vnworthy to take vpon them that, which the more worthy will not, but vtterly refuse to doe. For this cause wee must search our selues better in this point. For want whereof, the most are deadly sicke of this disease, and feele it not. It is bred in all by nature to aspire, both in Minister and people. That which a graue and godly man dares not doe in the Ministery, that euery youth and bold fellow almost dares, for his commoditie, thrust himselfe into many preferments, and is not ashamed. So that which honest and ancient inhabitants abhorre, and flie from, as to contend and quarrell, to iudge others, and puffe vp themselues with a conceit of their gifts, and to thinke other fooles in respect of themselues, that (yet) dare other doe, who in the best things come short and farre behind them. The time hath been, when (through a reuerent and high conceit of the worke of the Ministerie (though erroneously and amisse, I must needs say) some men altogether with-drew themselues from it, as thinking themselues wholly vnworthy of it, and so buried many a talent in the earth. But that was the extremity of modestie: wee complaine in our age of the contrary ouerweening of our selues, and vnderprising of it, so that we can easily answer *Pauls* question [*To these things, who is sufficient?*] by another, who is not sufficient? Indeed, since mē looked to the benefit, and not to the burden (which so occupieth an honest man, that hee thinks

thinks lesse of the other) and enquired rather into the quantitie of it, rather then his owne qualitie and worthinesse: while nothing but flourishing in apparrell, iollitie, pleasures, good cheare and booncompanionship is thought to be the complement of the Ministery, the answer (I confesse) is easie, if the liuing be therafter, who is not sufficient for these? But, Oh Bramble! where is thy sweetnesse? do men gather Grapes of thornes, or figges of thistles? doest thou thus teach in season and out of season? is this thy feeding, thy watching, thy planting and watering? Is this to cheare (and not to grieue rather) the heart of God and good men? Oh who shall heale thy barrennes? other barren creatures haue been cured by a miracle or art: the wombe, the earth, the waters: and if thou wert an Oliue, a Vine, or Figge-tree, (though not so fruitfull) there were helpe for thee, by cutting, digging, compassing, remoouing; but being a Bramble, who shall make thee fruitfull? Is it because there is no Oliue in the forrest, that thou exaltest thy selfe? who neither hast oyle of vnderstanding, nor oyle of grace (much lesse thy vessell full thereof) that of thy abundance others may be refreshed? Yea, who if thou haddest thy due, and the Lords forresters, thou shouldest not (I say not) haue place aboue the other trees, but not be allowed to stand among them at all. But I conteine my selfe. Matth.7.16. 2.Tim.4.2. Note.

In this part following of the parable, *Iotham* denounceth against the men of Shechem and *Abimelech*, saying: If yee haue done well, in that yee haue done, reioyce: else your ioy shall God breake off: Let vs by this see, that all reioyce in their doings, according to that they are, whether they be good or bad: but let vs be perswaded, that to be the durable and sound ioy, which God alloweth, nay commandeth vs in all our doings, (as we see Deut.28. and elsewhere) to wit, that which commeth from well doing, and a good conscience. But all other ioy is either wicked, as *Hamans, Adonijas* and *Absolons*: or vaine, and to be repented of; as the young mans in Eccles. and is a compound of bitter and sweete: but the bitter is durable, the sweete soone vanisheth, when men are merrie, and in their mirth suffer any knowne sinne, or dishonour of God among them, their reioycing is not good; but Christs woe meeteth with them, when he saith, *Woe be to you that now laugh, for you shall waile and weepe*. And when in the common course of our life, we are led by the affection of ioy, which hath no good ground nor warrant, such ioy is euill, and shall be turned into sorrow and woe. And yet I deny not, but mirth, yea euen naturall mirth in things transitorie and indifferent is allowed, so that it be moderated; yea, and especially if it be vsed to nourish spirituall ioy; to which end it is ordained of God, and for the supporting of our greatest infirmities, euen as all other of Gods earthlie benefits are likewise. Ver.16.17.18.19 Deut.28.47. 2.Cor.1.12. Rom.15.13. Eccles.11.9. 2.Cor.5.6. Luke 6.25. Note.

And by this speech of *Iotham*, wee gather, that although good and bad meete together, and both seeme to be merrie in their seuerall companie; yet there is a greater oddes betwixt them, then a man would imagine. For the vngodly mans mirth is bred in the tongue and countenance, and therefore is controlled by an heauie sad heart, which tels him, that if he considered aright of the matter, hee hath small cause of being merrie, but to turne his meriments into heauinesse. The godly mans ioy is heartie, entire, sound, and therefore lasteth: and he cannot checke himselfe iustly, except it be for that *Doct.1 out of the former verses, 16 & 19.*

that he is not so merrie as he ought to be. And (as *Iotham* saith here) the wicked though they reioyce together, yet they adde not each to the other any sound, but onely frothie and deceitfull ioy by their fellowship: the reason is, because the ground of it is societie in euill. But the godly, as they ioy in secret, both in Gods fauour and their happie estate, and in the good duties which they doe, (as appeareth both in their going about them, perfor-
Note. ming them, and the fruite of both) so when they meete together, their ioy is encreased and multiplied, euen as mirth is doubled by musicke and pleasure. Whereas therefore the Christian complaines of much sorrow, within and without, his corrupt affections, his loosenes, his crosses, reproch in the world, bad example, abundance of iniquitie, temptations: let such a man know, that euen this sorrow of his, is a good ground of his reioycing, seeing that his sorrow is good. He sorroweth for euill to see it so to abound, but his sorrow is not euill. His conscience still is good, and so long his ioy is warrantable: onely the ill conscience marres this feast of a quiet minded and
2.Cor.1.12. merrie hearted Christian. My reioycing is my good conscience, saith the Apostle. But if a good man will doe as a bad man, his ioy is like his. As for affliction, if it come vpon him in his innocencie, though it may dampe his outward mirth, especially if he be not fitted for it, yet it takes not ioy from his soule, but it shall returne againe double and treble. For their names be-
Luke 10.20. ing written in heauen, and they knowing it to be so, no affliction, no nor the greatest malice of Satan can blot them out thence: and therefore affliction (to the godly) is compared to sowing: now we know sowing is the cause
Psal.126.5. of haruest, wherein is great ioy. Therefore let them beware, lest by their disguising themselues and wounding their consciēce, they cause not to themselues needlesse complainings, feares and sorrowes, or halfe ioy in stead of sound, and so doing, they shall not neede to feare that Gods fatherly corrections shall hurt them. And if they will see good daies, and liue chearefully,
1.Pet.3.11. let them looke that out of a good heart, they bring foorth no other but good
Luke 6.46. fruites, to bee reioyced in, and flee euill of all sorts, yea though the world count them but peazants and meacocks for their so doing. The time shall come when all such iollie fellowes shall ioy as *Abimelech* and the Shechemites, that is, shall sit downe and put their heads betweene their knees, for sorrow, shame and miserie, and yet a greater sorrow is behinde.

Vers.17.18. *Iotham* in mentioning his father, saith that he put his life in danger to deliuer the Shechemites: and so againe, he requireth of the men of Shechem that they deale accordingly with his posteritie, that is to say, in vprightnes and righteousnes. Wherein he speaketh as the Scripture doth euery where, that men who haue had good measure offered them, and stand vpon their knowledge, ciuilitie and honestie, and much more their profession, should not behaue themselues as others, who walke by example onely of the common sort, and their own sensualitie and will. Neither is that any better, that some alleage, that they do as much as law enioyneth them, when as yet they may be conuicted of palpable iniurie, and vnthankfulnes. For a good man, if there were no law, will be a law to himselfe: Oh! how much to be accounted is that faithfulnes, which requites loue with kinde dealing? but it is rare to be found, but yet on the contrarie, that is barbarous to yeeld euill for good, as many doe, and as these men of Shechem are heere charged by

Iotham

Iotham to haue done, when yet wee haue learned, that wee ought to render good for euill. But I referre the reader to the first and last verses of the 8. Chapter, wherein I haue more at large spoken of this point. Rom.12.21.

Here in that he foretelleth, that one of them shall destroy another, that is: *Abimelech* the men of Shechem, and they him, euen as it came to passe; it may teach vs, that all ill practises and doings shall haue an euill end. The kingdome, on his part was wickedly sought, and on their part as wickedly granted; and how could the end be good, the worke being euill, howsoeuer for a time it appeare not? Who were greater or faster knit in consent one with another, then *Iosephs* brethren, about sending and selling him away far from them, where he should neuer trouble them, as they counted it, and hoped, any more? But what came of it? were they not after strangled, or rather haltered with that they had done? When there arose but a little trouble against them, did they not then crie out and confesse, that their cruell handling of him, yea and that long after, was the chiefe cause of it? Vers 20. Doct. Gen.42.21.

So, who are neerer ioyned together then theeues? Yet there commeth a time of pealing one another, wherein they cry out, Oh we are vndone! woe to vs that euer wee were linked in a confederacie together. Who greater friends then the wicked that conspire together against goodnesse and good men? but when it is bewraied, and they by a greater, and an ouerruling power are called to a reckoning, what deadly hate is there betwixt them, as we reade of *Iudas* and the wicked Priests? And in shew, where is there greater loue then betwixt these caualering and drunken companions, who (forsooth) will be called the only good fellowes? Doe they not embrace each other as *Ioab* did *Abner*, in their armes, when they goe about their pot-companionship? And yet, ere they arise from their ale-bench, one of them stabbeth another, as *Ioab* thrust *Abner* thorow with his weapon, euen while he embraced him. Call yee this loue? It is diuelish loue then, which brings foorth such fruites. Therefore let our beginnings and attempts be alwaies good, yea and well followed also; or else, let vs neuer looke that the end of them shall bee any better: this one thing being excepted, that repentance come in the way, for then it may end well, in that it is repented of: but this is not the thing that the vngodly propounded to be the end of their wicked acts, neither if it were, could they be sure to obtaine it, for it rarely befalleth such. But reade of this point in the 22. verse following, which mentioneth the fulfilling of this prophecie. Matth.27.4. 2.Sam.3.27.

In this last verse, after the speech of *Iotham*, it is said that hee fled to hide himselfe for feare of *Abimelech*. And no marueile though he fled: for men haue been impatient in hearing rebukes in all ages; euen as there may bee no reproofe, either of mens estates or doings, admitted or borne, be they neuer so vnsound or wicked: especially by those who are great in the world, for the most part. That of *Hoseah* the Prophet doth sufficiently testifie it, saying: Though by swearing, lying, stealing, adulterie, &c. the land do mourne, yet let no man reprooue another: meaning, that it should bee in vaine. And our Sauiour foresaw this, in willing his Disciples to flee from citie to citie: noting that men would not beare reproofe, but through the loue of the darknesse they were in, they would hate the light, especially to be reprooued, and the messengers of God that were the bringers thereof. Verse 21. Hos.4.4. Matth.10.23.

Reade

2.Chro.16.10. Reade how *Asa*, a good man, handled the meſſenger of God, *Hanani* the Seer, when hee brought his meſſage from God: he was wroth with him, and put him in priſon. Many, who know their owne ſtrength what they are able to doe, becauſe they are of great wealth and authoritie, how iuſtly ſoeuer they are reproued, will not ſee that, but pretend that Preachers ſeeke to bring their necks vnder their girdle, and to dominere ouer them: and that they alleage to be the reaſon, why they refuſe to be reproued by them. But let their conſciences tell them, that they feare them not in that reſpect, they being men of ſmall account in the world: but yet they take occaſion to ſhake off their ſermons or priuate companies, vnder that pretence and colour. But they hope by this meanes, that they may attaine moſt eaſily that which they haue ſought, and doe deſire; to wit, that they may more boldly goe forward in their ſinnes, while there is no man that ſhall haue acceſſe or allowance to tell them thereof. But what followeth ſuch doing, but this; that they goe forward in them ſtill, till they ring in euery mans eare, and are in euery mans mouth to be talked of, and they alſo dye after the ſame manner, that is, without repentance, being bereaued of all their greatnes, and left helpleſſe and hopeleſſe in great baſenes and contempt. Farre are ſuch off from the eſtate of the wiſe, who pray, Let the righteous ſmite vs, that ſo we
Pſal.141.5. may not fall into the hands of the wicked, to be bought and ſold of the vn-
Ierem. godly at their pleaſure. All the world well nigh ſings this note with the
Hoſ.4.4 wicked people of Anathoth, *Preach to vs pleaſant things*, but let none reproue. For though there was neuer more neede, yet to that point they are
Heb.13.22. come, that euen baſe ones will not admit it, when yet wee ſhould all ſuffer the wholeſome words of exhortation.

The reaſon why reproofe is ſo vnwelcom, is, becauſe the worſe that men are, the more daintie & iealous they be to be handled roughly, or to be told plainly of their faults, and to be drawne out of them: as wee ſee the tendereſt faces can leaſt endure the nipping weather: and the galled fleſh can abide no rubbing. For the truth is tart and bitter to them, few can admit it, except it be tempered with ſome ſweetnes of flatterie: which though a man know it to be dangerous, and as the vipers ſting, killing by ticking: yet men had rather be tickled to death, then healed by corraſiues. We reade of one in hiſtorie, who was cured of an impoſtume by the ſword of his enemie, which opened an iſſue in his fleſh, and let out the corruption. And till the Lord giue wiſedome to ſuch to ſuffer their enemies (for ſo they call the
Gal.4.16. Miniſter, as the Galathians did *Paul*, for telling them the truth) to wound them: their owne ſelfe-loue will nouriſh ſuch impoſtumated matter within them, as will breake inwardly (for lack of vent) and deſtroy them. This is
Prou.10.9. an euill ſpirit in men, that neither they will be innocent, (for then they
Note. might walke boldly through the pikes) nor yet abide to bee called to queſtion. They will both deſerue blame with the formoſt, and yet (with the forwardeſt) be reuenged vpon him that ſhall controle them, though it bee by Gods commandement. So that, neither Scripture, Miniſter, no nor God himſelfe, may ſtand vp againſt them: they are lawleſſe and exempted perſons. But oh man conſider, if thine enemie ſhould wiſh thee a ſhrewd turne, he could not inuent a greater then this, that thou ſhouldeſt want an admoniſher to warne thee, by the refuſing of whom, thou more hurteſt thy ſelfe,

then

then thy greatest enemie can hurt thee. The Lord threatens it against the Iewes, when hee denounceth the most seuere punishments against them. Therefore in that thou maist be reproued, (especially in publike, where no man is priuie to the matter but thy selfe) think it a greater portion, then many (of farre higher place) enioy, and profit thou (if thou be wise) by it accordingly.

Some might think that *Iotham* ranne away, because he said more then he durst stand to: but we must know, he put his life in Gods hands, and hauing discharged his duty, auoided (as much as he could) the lions mouth & danger, being not bound to put his finger into the fire wilfully: and yet (as it is like) not afraid thereof, if God had giuen him into his enemies hands, and called him to seale the truth by his blood. And therfore, let none condemne such of rashnes or cowardise, who hauing rebuked sinne in such as are boisterous and malicious, shift for themselues, and prouide (as they may) for their owne escape and safetie. Rather this condemneth the cruell disposition of them whom they reproue, who when they cannot iustly conuince such of error or slander, rashnes, or the like; but haue their owne conscience condemning them for the same offences: yet will not suffer those to liue by them in peace, who haue done their duties, and discharged their conscience in iustly reprouing. How shall such be brought to be conuicted, that so they may relent and amend, who cannot endure to be accused? And it is the mercie of God (considering the spitefull nature of the wicked) that any godly *Iotham* or Minister of the word may bee suffered to keepe his standing, and to awake and admonish the vnruly that hee may be saued: and is not compelled to flee, and runne away, for feare of his opposites, when hee hath reproued them, although hee hath but told them truth for their good and benefit, and that in a kinde manner. If God did not muzzle them, doubtlesse it were as hard for them, as for *Iotham*, if euery lewd offender might haue his will, as in some places, such beare too much sway, and deterre the Minister (being weake and fearefull) from medling, in challenging the sinnes of the place, and laying hard against the offenders, when yet God hath charged them streightly to denounce against them. But why doe such hinder the course of their Ministerie? Verily because they themselues may sleepe secure in their sinnes, as *Herod* thought to doe, when *Iohns* mouth was stopped.

THE

THE FIFTIE EIGHT SERMON ON THE NINTH CHAPTER OF THE BOOKE OF IVDGES.

The third part of the Chapter.

Verſ.22. *So Abimelech raigned three yeeres ouer Iſrael.*
23 *And the Lord ſent an euill ſpirit betwixt Abimelech and the men of She-
chem, and the men of Shechem brake their promiſe to Abimelech.*
24. *That the crueltie toward the ſeuentie ſonnes of Ierubbaal, and their blood
might come and be laid vpon Abimelech their brother which had ſlaine them, and
vpon the men of Shechem who had aided him to kill his brethren.*
25. *So the men of Shechem ſet men to waite for him in the tops of the moun-
taines: who robbed all that paſſed that way by them, and it was told Abimelech.*

The ſenſe. NOw it followeth in this third part of the chapter, how both *Abimelech* and the men of Shechem were deſtroyed; with the occaſions and meanes thereof, which were two: firſt the diſcord betwixt them and diſſenſion: ſecondly open warre, both which made way thereunto. Theſe are to the 42. verſe: and the deſtroying one the other to the end of the chapter. For the firſt, it is ſaid that the Lord ſent an euill ſpirit betwixt them, euen the ſpirit of Satan, and therefore there muſt needs be diſcord betwixt them, as in theſe verſes appeares, to the 26. And being thus at diſſenſion, they were prouoked to fight, till each ſlew other, as I haue ſaid. But before I enter into, and lay open theſe things, this is to be conſidered, firſt, that is ſaid here, that *Abimelech* ruled ouer Iſrael three yeres. Which words are a preparatiue to that which followeth: for thus they are to be taken; that after theſe words of *Iotham*, thus vttered, *Abimelech* raigned three yeeres notwithſtanding, and the men of Shechem and he made a ſhift to hold together ſo long. All which while a man would haue thought *Iotham* his parable had been but a dreame and deluſion: But when three yeeres (a ſhort time to ſpeake of for a King to enioy his crowne) were come about, then the Lords threat began to take effect, (for how ſhould it be otherwiſe?) though a little while it were deferred? Now if the time had been long, men might eaſily haue forgotten *Iotham*, but being within three yeeres thus fulfilled, who might not remember the prophecie and note the accompliſhment thereof? Thus the Lord will haue his iudgements ceaſe vpon his enemies: ſo that they who ſee them, may ſay, This is no caſuall miſchance which hath befallen them, but the hand of God purſuing them manifeſtly, for ſuch or ſuch a tranſgreſſion.

It

It is not said, that hee was Iudge ouer Israel, for they were raised vp by God, but hee ruled and vsurped, as Tyrants vse to doe. And to begin first with his prosperity in that God gaue him this short time to inioy his desire, and to dominere as he did, it is to teach vs, that he doth for some little time, giue wicked men their longed for desires; and yet not for that he applaudeth them therein, but that they may haue time to repent, and to bethinke themselues what they haue done, and how they haue gone to worke, and how many waies they haue prouoked God; and that if they refuse so to do, they may see that they be iustly reiected, and that God had no pleasure in them, in their greatest florish. *Zimry* and *Cozby*, *Chorah* and *Haman*, with the Rich man in the Gospell, and others many, a short time they had to worke, and accomplish their desires, and take their pleasure, and enioy the lust of their hearts. And indeed so short a time had need bee well improoued, while it lasts, for when that time was ouer and past, what heare yee, euen this, that their folly, nay their shame and madnesse, was manifested and spoken of in all places. Neither should their reproch and downefall haue been so notable, if they had not proudly passed their bounds, and carried themselues too loftily before. Many waies, wee see, God hath to destroy such. Sometime he suffers them not to plant themselues at all, but crosses them in the enterprise, as *Absolon* and *Adonija*: sometimes hee suffers them to take deepe roote, and giues them a long time, but it is with much vexation and vnsetling; as *Pharao* and *Ahab*. And otherwhiles he lets them flourish but a short time, and puls them vp ere they bee halfe rooted, as this *Abimelech*. Whether he keepes them from attaining that which they seeke, or keepes them vnder, or plucks them vp againe, let them learne by them all, that he is wise, and knowes how to handle them, and to shelter his owne from the annoyance of them. *Dauid*, Psal. 37. speaking of this third sort of flourishers, whom he compares to the greene Bay tree, (which though it be barren, yet keepes the colour both Winter and Sommer) addeth this, that *they are suddenly and horribly consumed*: and it is the argument of many Psalmes, and the summe of that which *Iobs* friends so much insist vpon, (though they apply it preposterously) That the happinesse of the wicked is short. So that wee must not wonder if they plie their worke apace, and take the vttermost of their libertie: for the diuell teacheth them so to doe; who rageth the more violently, knowing he is tied by a short tether. Doubtlesse their short iolitie, is the vantage of the Church, which hath many a breathings betwixt whiles, by their discontinuance: euen as wee see Sushans perplexitie vnder *Hamans* malice, was turned into ioy, in his ruine. Naturall Philosophers obserue, that the creatures which are most noisome and hurtfull, are some way or other so restrained (either by paucity, short life, or the like) that they cannot doe the harme they would. But if God did not restraine men as wel as beasts, they would waxe more monstrous.

Doct. vers. 22.

Psal. 37. 35. 36.

And be we wise, though the world bee set on wilfulnesse, and mischiefe, let not our teeth water after their dainties: the best whereof is a short flourishing, to tickle fooles with a desire of the like; but they see not their day comming, which yet is at hand, like a whirle-wind and tempest to scatter their pleasures and glory; and like a fire to deuoure and consume all, most fearefully: which painted estate of theirs, all may see to be farre from the

grace which the Lord wisheth to his people, when he saith, Oh, that they
Deut.32.29. were wise to consider their end. And yet the worst end of the other is not seene. And Gods mercy is great in cutting them off so soone: who else should liue with them, besides the preuenting of much iniquitie, which would make their account heauier. For all this, one followes the steppes of another, and the child, when he comes into his fathers place, beginneth not at first, to weigh the shortnesse of his life, how soone he shall be, as his father is, that is, cut off from al, that so he might apply his heart to wisdome,
Psalm.90.12. but taketh possession of his place, as if he were riuited into it for perpetuity, and will not so much as thinke of any change or remouall from thence.

But to goe forward: this euill spirit that was sent betwixt them, being
Vers.23. the first occasion of their ouerthrow, was the diuell; by whose malice and subtiltie, ill will and hatred were kindled betwixt them, yea and inflamed:
Doct. and this, with the breaking their promise, doth shew vs clearely, that the league and friendship of the wicked is soone broken off: For why? it hath no good ground. And although there be some outward things which vphold it, as hope of profit, pleasure, preferment, and the seruing one of anothers turne; although (I say) these and such like, patch vp an agreement betwixt them for a while, yet their hearts are inconstant, and many things fall
Note. out to breed alienation of affection one from another, and a pritch is soone taken, many conceits arise, and reports are carried betwixt them, and who can reckon vp all: And yet if there were no other cause hereof, (as yet there is, for they daube vp their friendship with vntempered morter, which falleth away) this were inough that is spoken of here, that God can send an ill spirit betwixt them, euen then, when they are most strongly combined and knit together: and cause them to breake their promise one to another, and iarre and disagree. And although it bee a great reproch to them, that their contentions should break out and be knowne, (as if both consent together to smite the righteous) and therefore in wicked policie they doe what they can, to hide them; yet otherwise they are diuided, and strongly incensed one against the other, which also breaketh out sometime, and so confirmeth this truth, that though they seemed to be glued in friendship and familiaritie together, and make men beleeue, that their loue is firme, yet their league is rotten, and they grow to bee at defiance one with the other, and that oft times betwixt themselues secretly, before it breake foorth in the sight of
Vse. men. The vse whereof is, that we make no such wicked and cursed leagues. Secondly, that we account no otherwise of them where they be made, but as of the Spiders web, soone swept downe: and thirdly, praise God highlie when wee see them broken. For that turneth to the great benefit of the Church, and the diuers members of it: as we reade that the diuision of the
Act.23.10. Pharisies and Sadduces turned to *Pauls* deliuerance from their rage. But let the godly continue their league, that their loue may be strong, as a threefold
Eccles.4.12. cord, that is not easily broken. Neither let them neglect their mutuall examples to profit thereby; but rather be ashamed that heauen should not tie them together faster, then hell tieth the vngodly: yea, let them bee ashamed (I say) that euen the smallest trifle and a very conceit of one against another, is enough to estrange them, as it too often falleth out, and to set them at defiance betwixt themselues, till the wicked laugh them and their profession

to

to scorne: whereas these cursed leagues of the malignant hold sometime longer, though they be bound together with rotten threads, through wicked policie, which oft reneweth them, (except the Lord disioyne and separate them) especially if their concord and agreement be in opposing the innocent.

And seeing God curseth and scatters these combinations of the wicked, as fast as they vnite and strengthen themselues, as Psalm.2. saying of them Psalm.2.1.
as *Iacob* did of *Simeon* and *Leui, Cursed be their rage, cursed be their counsell:* let Genes.49.7.
not the godly so much feare their bandings, and fast knittings of themselues together, as looke patiently till this curse, as a moth, consume them. *Iehoshaphat*, 2.Chron.20. seeing Moab, Ammon and Seir confederate to destroy 2.Chron.20.3.
him, feared at the first: but when he saw the sword of each against other, till they had made a riddance of all, he was comforted; euen as that mysterie of the late matchlesse treason, with what deepe secrecie was it carried, how strongly complotted, how firmely were the agents thereof vnited? euen as firmely as oth, vow and the Sacrament (abused) might knit them: but the Lord (blessed for euer by his name) sent a spirit of diuision betweene them, they were detected and discouered by each other.

And in that it is said, that the Lord sent this euill spirit betwixt them, wee Doct.2.
may note, that though God be not the author of euill (as some would (perhaps) be too ready to gather) yet that sinne which is in the wicked, hidden in their hearts, and neuer so secret, he bringeth forth at his pleasure, and lets it breake out at his commandement, ruling, and ouer-ruling the same. And they that nourish it in themselues, and doe not giue it a vent by repentance, may euer iustly feare, and doe sometime too truly find, that as water pent in, breakes out violently in some place or other: euen so the sinne that is inter- Note.
tained in mens hearts, shall one time or other breake out, to their shame in their liues. But as the stinke of the dunghill riseth not from the Sunne, no more (assure we our selues) doth sinne proceed from God.

Also by this diuision betwixt them, we may note, that when God suffers Doct.3.
diuision among the wicked, or an euill spirit any way to leade them, it is to punish their leaud fellowship, and to reuenge the sinne of both parts, and to make each the others executioner. And yet, Oh what a sweet libertie it is thought to be, to inioy fellowship with such? We see that the thatcht hou- A Simile.
ses which stand close together, though they fence each other from the violence of weather for a time, yet if one be on fire, it serueth but to hasten the consumption of the other. And so there is no knot so wickedly knit betwixt men, but (while it lasteth) it bringeth (I grant) some benefit to the confederates: but when once the Lord hath dissolued the band, their greatest vnion turnes to the most deadly enmitie that can be, and is as the diuision of bre- Prou.18.19.
thren, stronger then the brasen barres of a palace or citie gates. And first, grudges secretly being conceiued, they are nourished by iealousies and suspitions exasperated by daily iniuries, till they breake out into hatred, and end in extremitie. These things are commonly seene: but who beholdeth Gods iustice therein? or is thereby flayted and feared from hauing any thing to doe with such? or made wise to lay a better foundation of their amity and friendship?

Vers.24. Furthermore, by this, that God would haue the blood of the innocent sonnes of *Gedeon* reuenged vpon *Abimelech* and the men of Shechem, hee teacheth vs, that hee will reuenge the innocents cause, and so he made the
Genes.12.3. blood of *Abel* cry out for vengeance. The Lord will blesse them that blesse his, and curse them that curse his. And the greater the persons are, and the wrong that is done to them, the more God will pay them home, who are guiltie of transgression and spite against them. As when the Lords annointed are stricken at, as lawfull Kings, and Gods faithfull ministers; for which
Psalm.105.15. cause he saith, *Touch not mine annointed, and doe my Prophets no harme.*

Therefore those runnagate Iesuites, that roote out and kil Christian Princes, and subuert kingdomes, so farre as in them lieth, hath the Lord branded with a mark of perpetual infamy, and of his iust displeasure, at the gallowes; though they being brazen faced, and hard-hearted, cannot by any meanes be brought to repentance. *Iudas* hath left behind him a sufficient testimony of the wofull estate of those that hurt the innocent, his words are these, out
Matth.27.3. of despaire, and a perplexed conscience; *I haue sinned in betraying the innocent blood.* Therefore he that seeth so many to studie to hurt such as would liue in peace by them, by murthering, by robbing, or oppressing, and vexing the being harmelesse, what doe they, but cause talke euery where to goe of the Lords threats of reuenging them, and bring them also most certainely vpon their owne heads, that I say no more. But of this point I haue elsewhere entreated.

Doct.2. Also, in that it is said, that the men of Shechem did strengthen *Abimelechs* hand, by giuing money to hire base fellowes to kill his brethren; in that, I say, that such as liued in the citie, and should haue helped to settle, and see good order kept, yet were such euill men, euen incouragers and furtherers vnto murther: we see, that there are in cities, and townes, oft-times, vile persons couered with the vizor of honest citizens and inhabitants. For in no worse account many goe, who bearing office to punish and beate downe disordered persons and disturbers, are yet themselues as bad and noisome as any other. Which admonisheth all such, as liue ciuilly in townes, to search themselues, that they may bee found faithfull also, and that they rest not in the opinion, that is conceiued of them for the place that they are in; who, as we see in these, may be farre worse then the base ofskourings, which fall into their hands to be punished: but if they keepe from open staines, yet another thing is to bee looked for in them, to wit, that their hearts be good also. But of this point I will not here repeate the same things which I handled before.

Vers.25. This dissention was so hot betwixt them, that it brake into ciuill warre, by meanes whereof, none could passe in safetie. And wee cannot be ignorant, how dangerous those times be. But by this we may see, what troubles and dangers (as robbing one another in the high way) one vile person, or a few, may raise vp: who may be fitly compared to a firebrand cast into a barne of corne: euen such mischiefe wrought this *Abimelech*. Such a one was *Absolom*, and those caitiffes who slew the two French Kings: and the same may be said of the Authors of the Gun-powder-treason. No torture can be too great for such. Such desperate persons and diuellish should bee cut off at first,

first, when they bee found out, and not suffered to liue to doe greater mischiefe. Touching the benefit of peace, and the like publike blessings, see chap.5.and else where in this history.

Vers.26. *Then Gaal, the sonne of Ebed came with his brethren, and they went to Shechem, and the men of Shechem put their confidence in him.*

27. *And therefore they went into the field, and gathered in their grapes, and trod them and made merry, and went into the house of their gods, and did eate and drinke, and cursed Abimelech.*

28. *Then Gaal, the sonne of Ebed said, Who is Abimelech? And who is Shechem, that we should serue him? is hee not the sonne of Ierubbaal, and Zebul is his officer? Serue rather the men of Hamor, the father of Shechem, for why should wee serue him?*

29. *Now would to God this people were vnder my hand, then would I put away Abimelech; and he said to Abimelech, encrease thine army and come out.*

OF the first occasion of *Abimelechs* and the Shechemites destroying one another: the next occasion of the mischiefes that followed, is here set downe, namely this; that they being thus incensed, one against the other, they fall to open warre, and to set it forward, there came in the way one *Gaal*, and the men of Shechem hired him for their Captaine to be for them against *Abimelech*. And by his helpe they went out, and gathered their grapes, which otherwise they durst not haue done, and made merry, and cursed *Abimelech*. And that boaster *Gaal* hardned them against him, affirming Thrasonically, that he would put him downe. If the men of Shechem knew him not, as the Scripture sets not downe from whence he came, but his behauiour bewraied him. If (I say) they knew him not, they did foolishly, to receiue and rest vpon him, being a stranger, though a boaster: and if they did know him, what madnesse was it, to take and trust in him, though a stranger, yet a boaster? But howsoeuer their sinne was great, in their intertaining of him, yet indeed, it was of and by God (who hereby hastned their destruction) that they should light vpon such a Captaine; themselues being such souldiers, they might well goe together; and no wonder, if boasters and the ambitious so easily accorded, although if they had not been giuen vp to themselues, they would not haue trusted to him. Thus the men of Shechem prouided for themselues, and how *Abimelech* did the like, it followes after. *The sense.*

And as the doing of the men of Shechem was foolish, dangerous, and (as it prooued) their ouerthrow; so it giueth warning to them that can receiue it, to beware of resting vpon all rotten holds, and broken staues. Of which sort there are many, with which, men are deceiued as grossely, as they of Shechem were by this their folly, to cast all their welfare vpon a boaster. The Psalmist mentioneth some of these, when he saith: *Some put their trust in chariots, and some in horses.* The Prophet *Ieremie* teaching men to shunne the same danger, saith, *Let not the wise man glory in his wisdome, nor the strong in his strength, nor the rich in his riches, but let him that glorieth, glory in this that hee knoweth me, saith the Lord.* If we may not rest on men, much lesse on weaker *Doct.* *Psalm.20 7.* *Ier.9.23.*

 staies

ſtaies, as ſome doe in their preſent eſtate of peace, wealth, habitation, wife,
friends, health, and the like.

Ier.17.5. The ſame Prophet ſaith: *Curſed is he that maketh fleſh his arme, and truſteth*
in man, and his heart departeth from God. So the Prophet *Dauid* crieth out,
Pſalm.146.3. ſaying: *Truſt not in earthly Princes,* who cannot ſaue others, nor themſelues.
2.Chron.16.7. And to King *Aſa* it was ſaid, *Becauſe thou truſtedſt in the King of Aram and not*
in the Lord, from hence foorth thou ſhalt haue warre. In God onely our truſt
Prou.3.5. muſt be repoſed, *Salomon* ſaith, otherwiſe we may vſe mans helpe and other
Pſalm.127.2. meanes, but all in vaine. And the vſe of this doctrine is, that we ſhould retaine in all dangers and troubles, our hope and confidence in Gods promiſes, and for other ſlippery helpes, our comfort is thereafter as wee reſt in them: and this appeareth more clearely, the greater the matters are, in which we doe ſo.

But this doctrine hath been diuerſly occaſioned before. One thing I will adde to anſwere ſuch as might ſay, Theſe Shechemites had no other ſhift now, but to ſhroud themſelues vnder this, or ſome ſuch like defence, who therefore can blame them if they ſought ſhelter againſt a tyrant where they could get it? I anſwer. To ſeeke ſuccour againſt an vſurper is lawfull, ſo the meanes be according: but this vſurper was ſet vp by themſelues, neither did he any greater violence to them, then they to him; and therefore for this, I ſay, they might thanke themſelues, for that they brought wilfull bondage vpon themſelues. Indeed, as the caſe ſtood with them, either they muſt fence their citie and people (whom they had brought into the ſnare being led by them) againſt *Abimelech*, or elſe yeeld and periſh. But what a curſed thing is this, for the men either to vſe vile perſons to be their patrons in their deſperate quarrels, or elſe to bring themſelues to that point, that they might be come vpon by one that ſought and waited to deſtroy them? Therefore let not men defend their ſins by this plea, that they are driuen to a ſtraight, and haue no remedy, but to fall vpon the ſmaller inconuenience, that they may auoid the greater: For who brought this wretched choice vpon them? God alloweth his children to walke at large vnder his gouernment, and keepes them from ſuch ſtreights as theſe. Who then cooped them into ſo narrow a roome? Surely their owne ſinne: when men haue liberty, they are wearie of it, till they be ſtreightned and driuen to their ſhifts. Therefore this defence is as bad as the crime it ſelfe: for if men haue fallen into extremitie by one ſinne, they muſt not redeeme and auoid it by another, nor doe euill that a ſuppoſed good may come of it. What then? Humble themſelues for the firſt ſinne, and caſt themſelues vpon Gods hand for the iſſue
2.Sam.24.17. and danger, & ſo auoid the ſecond, as *Dauids* example excellently ſheweth. For who are they, that hauing ſinned, they ſhould ſcorne to beare the ſhame of it? And eſpecially if the extremitie they auoid, bee but onely a puniſhment bodily: (as cōmonly that is the ſtreight which men ſeeke to ſhun) and they ſin doubly by prouoking God through indirect meanes, and al to ſaue themſelues frō momentany trouble & danger. Indeed of two euils temporall, the leſſer may be choſen to auoid the greater, but not of two euils morall and mortall which are ſinnes, much leſſe when the one is a temporall euill, the other morall. For by this meanes an adulterer may ſay, I haue no way

to

to shift but one, to buy off my shame, except I would bee shamed for euer. But O thou wofull man; if thou haue deserued it, beare it; if God haue laid it vpon thee, as the Church did in *Micha*, saying: *I will beare my punishment, because I haue sinned:* and thinke not by such a shift to escape shame being guiltie, vnlesse thou fall into a greater without recouerie. Mich.7.7.

The Shechemites were so afraid of *Abimelech*, that they durst not gather their grapes, which were as their haruest: therefore they hired this *Gaal* to helpe them, who was (we see) seditious, a boaster and a deceiuer. Now by his conduct they goe foorth into the field, and in great lasciuiousnes, reioyced, and in their Temple cursed *Abimelech*. Vers.27.

By this, among the manifold discomforts in warre, which in other places I obserue, let this one be numbred, ỳ men are thereby cut off from the fruits of the earth, & from their haruests, by which they liued all the yere: which being spoyled, how farre is their life from death? and yet worse then death, to lie in feare of it, pinched with penurie. They could not goe out of their doores, nor reape their fruites, till now they made this shift by *Gaal*: and yet neither were they safe in their houses: these besides many like effects of warre most frearefull, are at such times brought against them, who are by warre set vpon. So that a man would thinke, that knoweth this, that such as are preserued from it, and the like sore oppressions, would binde themselues while they liue, to submit themselues to God in all dutie, and that most willingly. *Doct.*

And no doubt so would they most readily couenant to doe, when they are vnder such oppressions, vpon condition, that they might then obtaine a promise of deliuerance from them: which sheweth that there is good cause why they should doe so: but can we say (who marke it) that men doe thus? In smaller troubles, we see (alas) the contrary. I remember what is said in the Psalme: when the Lord *smote the people, they sought him, yea, they sought him early:* but what was there found in them when it came to the triall, but false heartednes and vnfaithfulnes? which I vtter with griefe, as knowing how commonly this is offended in. And wee that doe but heare of such things, I meane of warre, throughout this booke and other stories, and see it not, through the long continuance of peace, wee (I say) doe not weigh the greatnes of the benefit, such is our vnthankfulnes ioyned with blockishnes, but abuse our peace to sensualitie, and thus we deale with God in many other things? Psal 78.34.

But hauing oft obserued and bewailed this follie in men in other places, and seeing it followeth here expressely, what they did when they were rescued by that *Gaal*, and gathered in their fruites, I will note it from hence. And what was their behauiour therein, thinke we? verily most brutish, and vtterly vnbeseeming such, as had euer serued the Lord. For, like mad men, they did eate & drink, and made merrie without measure, cursing their enemies, and praising their Idols. Which teacheth vs, that it is hard to say, whether the wicked are more to be pitied in their miseries and calamities, or in their deliuerances out of them. For by them they are held in some awe and feare: but when they are set free, they are most dissolute and vnruly, and more offensiue by excesse therein, then they are by impatience, and vnquietnes in their calamities. But in both they are greatly to be pitied. 1.Sam.30.16. Note.

And although their bodily estate be to be lamented greatly, yet is it farre worse with their soule, as is manifest in their breaking out so fearefully and damnably into all manner of sinne with greedinesse. Instances hereof in all
Note. conditions are too many. In such as haue some religion, (because they haue no more store of it) who seeth not, that they are euer most loose, secure, forgetfull, when they are most at hearts ease? And in the badder sort it is more manifest: who are quailed in their crosses, and held downe by them from much euill: but if they bee at hearts ease, oh the loosenes, sawcines, quarrelling, lashing out of needlesse and great expences; rioting, swearing, that may be seene in them, and scorning those that seeke to reclaime them, though they be such as they ought to heare, and whom they owe duty vnto, and therefore should readily heare them, whereas they regard nothing in their prosperitie, but curse and blesse with one mouth, I may say (almost) with one breath. But to leaue these, let the best looke well to themselues herein; I meane, that in both estates they may yeeld another manner fruite of their peace and prosperitie, and bee carefull to haue a good conscience. Of which argument, seeing much is spoke by occasion in the former processe of this storie, I cease to say any more.

To proceed: These two, *Gaal* and the Shechemites hauing each hearted the other, and helped forward their defiance of *Abimelech*, by feasting and iollitie, which are great meanes (yea as oyle to the flame) to prouoke the proud stomacke of a man, they now being well heat with meate and
Vers. 28. drinke, presumptuously aske, Who is *Abimelech?* We may say truly, where and when doe the wicked make an end? For they goe from one sinne to another, as one that runneth downe an hill, and staieth not. Now after all the rest, they boast against him, and defie and deface him, and that in his ab-
Doct. sence. Which teacheth the vnmeasurablenes and vnsaciablenes of the wicked in sinning, how they goe on from one to another, and neuer are willing to make an end: and in stead of repenting for the former, they adde greater sinnes vnto them: and by that course harden their hearts in all manner of euill doing, as they bee able, with greedinesse, and so grow past feeling vnto vtter impenitencie.

Many, after they haue done euill, haue some remorse, as the brother in
Matth. 21. 31. the Gospell, who when he had not obeyed his father, sending him to work in his vineyard, but refused; hee afterward bethought himselfe, and went.
Ierem. 8. 5. 6. And the Prophet *Ieremy* wondred that they who offended, relented not. But when men goe from one sinne to another, and cast not vp their gorge,
Gen. 25. 31. it is almost past hope to reclaime them. *Esau* when he had sold his birthright, the signe of eternall life, which one would haue thought had sinned fearefully enough in so doing; yet he could not stay there, but he must also iustifie the wicked fact that hee had done, saying: *Of what valew is this birthright vnto me?*

But if this sinne rested onely in such as I haue spoken of, wee that feare God might be sure, that it could not be committed by vs: but when we see how *Peter* was taken in this snare, to sinne againe, after he had once or twice denied his Master, and that with swearing, and cursing himselfe, if he knew him, and had been ready to haue done it an hundred times more, if occasion had been offered; how may not the best of vs feare the falling into it?

For

For in thus giuing place a little,and in ſome things taking libertie to goe againſt conſcience,it is the next way to goe further, as wee haue heard. The beſt remedie againſt it,is,while we may to preuent it,and to be ſo farre from ſuch a courſe, that we rather *in feare and trembling to make an end of our ſaluation*; but if we haue already fallen,then as ſoone as we can to riſe out of it. Philip.2 14.

Now this *Gaal* wiſheth that he were king(for we muſt know that all the men of Shechem were not of one minde) and this is the meaning of the phraſe of ſpeech that he vſeth,ſaying:*Who ſhall giue this people into mine hand?* Verſ.29. The like ye may reade in the Pſalme: *Who will giue me the wings of a Doue:* Pſal.55.6. that is,oh that I had them.Euen the ſame that *Abſolom* wiſhed in a caſe much like this of *Abimelechs: Oh that I were made Iudge in the land.* Thus did this 2.Sam.15.4. *Gaal:* which noteth the pride and ambition that was in this baſe fellow, his boaſting being not farre off. Which ſinnes in him, with the like in *Abimelech*,brought to paſſe his and the peoples deſtruction.

To teach vs to beware of all ſinne, and of theſe particularly, ambitious *Doct.* pride and boaſting, with the like, in the which is wrapped vp, when they come to their full growth, irrecouerable miſchiefe to the committers and intertainers of them,as all ſinnes doe threaten no better,if they be not ſpeedily broken off by repentance. Whereunto Gods deare ſeruants being ſubiect,euen as ſome of them haue tried and found it ſo alreadie,that great ſorrowes haue accompanied them long time,as the fruite of ſuch ſinnes: Pſal.32.10. *Dauid, Sampſon* and others: ſo we that remaine are taught,if we will be wiſe, to auoid carefully the beginnings and occaſions of euill: ſo ſhall we be ſure to be free from great woe. As for boaſting, it is but the ſuperfluitie of the corrupt and proud ſcornefull heart,ariſing not alway from ſome worthineſſe or eminencie,but a bare windie conceit of ſomewhat which is not. As we ſee in the body when the gall is too full,it ouerfloweth and coloureth the face *A ſimilitude.* with the excrement of that humour: and when the inward parts are tainted,the outward are full of breakings out and ſores: ſo when pride is at the full,it ſwelleth,and breaking out of the heart, vtters it ſelfe by the mouth and behauiour. But put the caſe there be ſome excellencie in him that boaſteth: doth boaſting beſeeme ſuch a man? nay, doth it not impeach his worthineſſe? Therefore he that will auoid boaſting,let him ſoberly thinke of,and vſe Gods gifts both inward & outward,knowing who he is,whence he receiued them,how naked hee were without them, and while hee hath them,they are but borowed, he himſelfe is naked and deſtitute. Neuer was an humble man a boaſter: except his boaſting were as *Pauls*, of his infirmities: or of his gifts,to honour the giuer, and diſgrace the enemies of Gods glorie. Touching the particular point of ambition and the preſeruatiue againſt it, let the reader ſee more in the former chapter in *Gedeons* refuſing the kingdome, and alſo in this chapter in *Iothams* bramble aſpiring to bee king ouer the trees. Here therefore I end.

THE

THE FIFTIE NINE SERMON ON THE NINTH CHAPTER OF THE BOOKE OF IVDGES.

Verse 30. *And when Zebul the Ruler of the citie heard the words of Gaal, the sonne of Ebed, his wrath was kindled.*

31. *Therefore he sent messengers to Abimelech priuily, saying: Behold Gaal the sonne of Ebed and his brethren be come to Shechem, and behold they fortifie the citie against thee.*

32. *Now therefore arise by night, thou and the people that is with thee, and lie in waite in the field.*

33. *And rise early in the morning as soone as the Sunne is vp, and assault the citie; and when he and the people that is with him shall come out against thee, doe to him what thou canst.*

34. *So Abimelech rose vp and all the people that were with him, by night, and they lay in waite against Shechem in foure bands.*

35. *Then Gaal, the sonne of Ebed, went out and stood in the entring of the gate of the citie. And Abimelech rose vp, and the folke that were with him from lying in waite.*

36. *And when Gaal saw the people, he said to Zebul; Behold, there come people from the toppes of the mountaines: And Zebul said to him, the shadow of the mountaines seeme men vnto thee.*

37. *And Gaal spake againe, and said: See, there come folke downe by the middle of the land, and another band commeth by the way of the plaine of Moonenim.*

38. *Then Zebul said vnto him; Where is now thy mouth that said, who is Abimelech that we should serue him? Is not this the people that thou hast despised? goe out now, I pray thee, and fight with them.*

39. *And Gaal went out before the men of Shechem, and fought with Abimelech.*

40. *But Abimelech pursued him, and he fled before him, and many were ouerthrowne and wounded euen vnto the entring of the gate.*

41. *And Abimelech dwelt at Aranna, and Zebul thrust out Gaal and his brethren that they should not dwell in Shechem.*

IN these 12. verses is shewed how the broile grew hotter betwixt *Abimelech* and the men of Shechem, & how they warred and fought one against the other, whereby their destruction drew neerer. And first, how *Zebul*, when he heard of the boasting of *Gaal*, sent word to *Abimelech* thereof: (for hee was his officer to gouerne the citie in his absence) and he gaue him aduice, what he thought best to be done, and that is set downe in the foure first verses. In the next foure it is shewed, how *Abimelech*, according to *Zebuls* counsell, came out with the men that were with

him

him neere to Shechem, and lay in wait for *Gaal* and his retinue. And thus the matter went forward of the destruction and ouerthrow of the men of Shechem, and of *Abimelech*, as I haue said, and as in this third part of the Chapter was foretold, and in the verses following doth clearely appeare. In the last foure verses is shewed how *Gaal* and *Abimelech* met together, not farre from the gate of the citie, and many of them that followed *Gaal* were ouerthrowne and wounded, and he himselfe cast out of the citie. But now let vs pursue these verses more particularly. First, this must be knowne, that as the men of Shechem had hired *Gaal* to bee their Captaine; so *Zebul* was for *Abimelech* as a Deputy and Lieutenant set there by him, to hold the people in subiection from rebellion and mutiny.

And it is said here first, that *Zebul* could not beare the insolency of *Gaal* against *Abimelech*, both for that he was vnder him, and also for that he saw the bragging of the other was very shamefull & insolent, but his wrath was kindled against him, and hearing the proud words and crackes of *Gaal*, he was sore troubled thereat, and sent word to *Abimelech* thereof. And from hence let some thing be noted: By the one, that is, this boasting of *Gaal*, which was meere froth and words without substance, and so grosse, that *Zebul* being seruant to *Abimelech*, could not beare it, wee may see the shamefulnesse of this sinne of bragging and cracking: which none can abide, nor heare willingly. For why? Boasters doe not consider how they can make good that which they say, but in the pride of their hearts speak so, to get praise of those who heare them, as when they are vrged to stand to their word, then to their shame they are driuen to run away, and to goe from their word also, as afterwards this *Gaal* did: or else the Lord himselfe disableth them to performe that which they boast they would doe, as hee did *Benhadad*, when hee braggingly challenged all *Ahabs* goods, and as he did *Saul*, vaunting that he had now *Dauid* safe enough in his hands, when hee was inclosed in a citie that had gates and barres. So that both God and man are enemies to boasting: man, I say, not onely religious, but euen ingeneous and ciuill abhorre it. To shame all such as delight in it, and to perswade all that are fit to learne better things, to practise lowlinesse and humilitie in stead of such disguisednesse. And this bee said of *Zebuls* wrath that it was kindled against *Gaals* boasting.

The summe of these foure verses more specially.

Doct. out of these foure verses.

1. King. 20. 3. 1. Sam. 23. 7.

Now followeth the other thing, that *Zebul* was incensed against *Gaal* for, and that was, because his bragges were against *Abimelech* his Master: and therefore he sent him word thereof, and yet there was no such consent and wel-grounded loue betwixt them, but for that he set this *Zebul* ouer the city in his absence, which was but an outward fauour, that soone changeth, especially betwixt such as they were, (and for that he was a man (as it seemes) discreeter and more politicke, then some other. And this act of *Zebul* in that he could not beare this defiance that *Gaal* gaue out against *Abimelech*, being hi master: this (I say) teacheth, that much lesse ought a Christian to heare God dishonoured, no nor his Prince railed on, or to bee rebelled against by Popish enemies, or leaud subiects, but his heart should rise against it, and he should in the speediest manner bewray, and seeke remedie thereof, and that not for feare of law (which holdeth the concealers thereof as accessaries) but much more for conscience sake.

Doct. 2.

Euen

Euen as a naturall child cannot beare it, if he heare his father reproched: and therfore the blasphemies against God giuen forth by Atheists and malicious enemies, (such as those were of cursed *Rabsachee*) against *Moses*, and Christ, the Scriptures, and worship of God. And such as that was of the
John 9.24. Pharisies, who said to the man that was restored to his sight, *We know that this man*, (meaning Iesus) *is a sinner*; and finally whatsoeuer such (as there are many of this kind, not fit to be spoken of before Christian eares) they are all intolerable, yea and meaner reproches giuen out against him, ought not to be suffered, as swearing, forswearing, filthie talking, or the like; but rather,
1. Cor. 6.20. we should honour God in our bodies and soules, for they are Gods. And because hee that loueth him who begat, loueth him who is begotten also; therfore let this naturall affection and kind for Gods honour, descend from him, to the meanest of his Saints, yea let it make our eares and cheekes to glow and burne, when we hit into such company as make it their game and pastime to deride and traduce them whom we know zealous and sincere Preachers and professors of Gods holy truth. Let the Lords example teach vs, who professeth, that he had as liefe men should touch the apple of his eie, as so touch his holy ones. And if wee find not such reproches to touch vs to the quicke and search vs, so that we step foorth, and stand out in the defence of such innocents when there is cause; but secretly and willingly giue way to such speeches, as if they displeased vs not, but we beare, yea and brooke them too, wee are no better then false-witnesse-bearers against our
Exod. 20.16. neighbour, Exod. 20. we shew our selues, I say, not weake and feeble; but (it may be feared) none at all, or rotten members of the body which feele not, neither are troubled any whit when they are hacked and lanced, wounded and torne by the tongues and teeth of dogges and swine, and therefore as *Dauid* called the Ziphims strangers, because of their falsehood, (though otherwise Israelites;) so these indeed are, forrenners, vnnaturall, men of another houshold and familie, although they otherwise may be (by outward profession and dwelling) neighbours and brethren.

Doct. 3. And moreouer this his faithfull aduertising his Master of the treason, and the wisest way to oppresse it, teacheth, that faithfulnesse betwixt religious friends had need to be well witnessed, lest this dutifull loyaltie of *Zebul* towards his Master *Abimelech* put it downe and condemne it. We know, that such trustinesse among Christians abideth not, or is very rare; and yet in some particular case, it falles out, that men who are strangers to religion, will goe farre one for another: which ought to prouoke vs, as we haue better reasons then they had to shew it to our brethren; so especially when occasi-
Prou. 3.29. on is offered, to let our innocency and faithfulnesse appeare, and bee seene;
Rom. 12.9. and alwaies to prouide, that our loue bee without dissimulation, that so it may bee safely rested on in time of need by them that depend vpon vs: touching which dutie of faithfulnesse both in loue and the fruits of it, let the Reader see more in the history of *Caleb* and elsewhere.

The clearing of vers. 34. to 42. In these other foure verses it is shewed, how *Abimelech* strengthened himselfe by the aduice of *Zebul* his officer, and by the message that he sent him, and how he prepared foure bands of men, and lay in waite al night for him, and the men of Shechem, not farre from their citie. And further how *Gaal* comming foorth of the same citie to goe to heare of, and seeke *Abimelech*,

pretending

pretending that he would set vpon, and inuade him, *Zebul* came out together with him,(as though there had been no subtiltie or conspiracie intended) to the end that *Gaal* might suspect nothing. And it being earely in the morning, when it was not yet cleare light, and *Gaal* hauing some shimering of *Abimelechs* bands and scouts,(as soone suspecting that which he feared) hee bewraied as much to *Zebul*, that hee saw men lie in waite, yet knowing nothing: but *Zebul* on the other side, bare him in hand, (to draw him on further) that he feared without cause, and tooke the shadow of the mountaines for men, for they are not vnlike them a farre off in the dawning morning. But vnto that *Gaal* replied, that it was otherwise, and he was afraid indeed: in the meane while, light more clearely comming on, and *Gaal* and *Abimelech* more neerely approching one toward the other with their armies, *Gaal* could not goe backe with any conuenience, as hee gladly would haue done: whereupon *Zebul* then cast his bragges in his teeth, for *Gaal* had challenged him before, and had contemptuously spoken of him, saying: who is *Abimelech?* and so he must needs goe forward, and comming neere *Abimelechs* bands, was sore chased by him.

Now in *Gaals* returning toward the citie for shelter, he was thence shut out by *Zebul*; by meanes whereof, *Abimelech* preuailed exceedingly, and slew many of the men of Shechem, and so *Iothams* prophecy began to bee verified, that he should destroy them.

Now to note somewhat from this part of the story, first in the readinesse Doct.vers.34.
of *Abimelech* to put in execution *Zebuls* counsell, we may see our selues taxed of a double fault. First, in that he shooke off al tediousnesse and toile, and that for a bare vncertaine hope of preuailing against *Gaal* his enemy, whereas we hauing a sure hope of blessing, and that plentifull in all that wee obey the Lord in,(for in obeying him there is great reward) yet we are slow and Psalm.19 11.
backward: whereby we verifie the prouerb, That a Lyon is in the way, and we are ready to faint. And this is our iust reproch, that bad men in an ill case Prou.22.13.
should be forwarder then we in a good, hauing yet so great and large incouragement by the reward that is promised vs in that behalfe. Whereof in the former historie, I haue largely spoken in the examples of *Iuda* and *Simeon* in the 1. Chapter, and since by diuers occasions.

The second thing to bee noted in *Abimelech* is, that *Zebul* being but his Officer, is not disdained of him, but he is aduised by him, to furnish himselfe against *Gaal*: and yet *Zebul* hauing familier talke with him, hee might haue been like enough to haue been vnfaithfull to *Abimelech* his Master: It set- Doct.2.
teth many of vs to schoole to learne, who refuse better aduice, and that in matters of greater waight: Nay wee scorne oftentimes to bee counselled, though it be for our good, in the best things: especially, by our inferiors; which folly while *Naaman* committed, he had done it to his owne vtter vn- 2.King.5.13.
doing both of body and soule, if he had not bethought himselfe, and taken better aduice after, then at the first, when he receiued the Prophets answere in so ill part. And what lost *Dauid* by hearkning to the counsel of a woman? Nay, he blessed God highly for it himselfe afterward. But such is the foo- 1.Sam.25.32.
lish pride of men, not onely in matters of the world, but euen in ghostly and heauenly, that we thinke it to bee our vtter discredit and shame to confesse our selues to be defectiue or vnable to mannage euery businesse that per-

taines to vs, well and sufficiently. Whereas who knoweth not, that euery foole can easily runne himselfe out of breath? but hee had need be a wise man that should stop his own bad course, and settle himselfe againe in good order and frame without the helpe and counsell of other. Nay, do not prodigall and licentious persons more imbezle and weaken their estate, credit, health, and the good of posteritie oftentimes, then ten wise men can turne their hand to restore or redresse againe? Such is the case of the soule indangered deeply to Satan and hell: But who (among hundreds of such) is willing to be aduised in time, till thrift and stocke, hope and helpe be quite past recouerie? Indeed when all is in the bottome, yea and worse; then men aske and enquire after Thrift, Sobrietie, Discretion. But oh, had it not been much better for such to haue admitted counsell before, against an irrecouerable mischiefe? Counsell after the euent is no counsell, but either lamentable pitie, or bitter rebuke. It were to be wished this folly were only bound in the hearts of youthfull *Rehoboams*, (although euen they shall finde it sharpe enough to be taught by Mistresse experience) and not as well in ancienter yeeres: whose commendation it ought to bee, to shew foorth the example of staiednes and wisedome to the younger sort: But if they be neither able to aduise themselues, nor willing to be aduised by other, what remaines but that euen the heathen Poet condemne them to be miserable? Therefore be glad of counsell for soule or body, and make much of it: the time may come when it will be precious and desired: when for want of it the body is turned into prison, beggerie, and rags; and the soule, after many grieuous plunges, to hell. If *Pauls* aduice (as ill a Pilot as he was) had been reiected to the end, what had become of them that should haue scorned to
Act.27.31,32. be beholding to him? Act.27. I meane of them ẏ sailed with him? Remem-
Prou.20.18. ber therefore what the wise man saith: Establish thoughts by counsell: and
and 15,22.27.9 know that without it, thoughts come to naught. And as ointment and per-
1.30. fume reioyce the heart, so doth the sweetnesse of a mans friend by heartie counsell. And further, they that refuse counsell, shall eate the fruit of their owne way, and be filled with their owne deuices.

Verse 35. to 41 *Gaal* also as well as *Abimelech* was earely vp to follow his matters, going out of the citie to see what was done, and whether hee could perceiue any danger to be at hand: to our shame it may be spoken, who are backward, where it were more meete for vs to be speedy and forward in all that concernes and belongs to our peace and happinesse, as I haue said before, in the example of *Gedeons* hastie pursuit of the Medianites.

Doct. out of these verses. But though he was earely vp, yet (as it appeareth in the storie) he was neuer the neere in the end: to teach vs, that it is not earely rising, and late going to bed, nor all the care that may be taken, is not sufficient to bring our attempts and businesse to passe, if God please to blow vpon our endeuours: but this is all in all, that the Lord alloweth of our doings being with an vpright heart taken in hand, and according to knowledge, and that we are vpon good ground perswaded (as wee ought to be) that he will vouchsafe to
Psal.127.1. blesse the same. So saith the Psalmist, Except the Lord build the house, that is, gouerne and dispose all things pertaining to the familie, they labour in vaine that build it: and except the Lord keep the citie, the keeper watcheth it in vaine. And yet I deny not but God doth suffer the wicked oft times to prosper,

prosper,but not long, as neither he did here this *Abimelech*: or if long,yet to a greater ouerthrow.

A pregnant example hereof is *Ieboram*, (and his father *Ahab* is another) who intending a voyage against their enemies of *Aram* and *Moab* (hauing rebelled) failed not in their outward preparation, and politike deuices to ouerthrow their enemies;for they prouided themselues of men,munition, and confederated themselues strongly against them: but neuer considering that thẽselues had rebelled against a greater Lord,euen the Lord of hoasts, they went on headily fearing no controlement,nay thinking they had God pinned,yea bound to them. But the one found to his cost that hee went to worke against the edge,and desperatly : The other,though he were spared for the time to a more notable ruine, (as it came to passe afterward) yet hee found himselfe plunged and driuen to an extremitie before that, by want of water; which threatned the losse of his beasts,and his owne,and his peoples destruction. Which was enough to proue that he played the foole in getting two Kings of his side,when God being shut out,and not sought to, laughed him to scorne and was his enemie. 1.King.22. 2.King.3.9.&c.

Oh then, where are the hearts of the people who regard not this, but looke that by their toyle and moyle (as they say) all should bee brought to passe, as they would haue it? And doe neither commit their affaires and dealings to God by prayer,neither goe to worke by his direction, nor consult how they may please him, but rashly and by their owne wit goe about all,and then look that it should fall out according to their desire. And therfore when they thriue not, neither prosper, as they would, they are as mad men impatient and outragious: and if they speede better, and haue good successe,then they praise their owne wisedome and their good hap and fortune in stead of God. Looke more largely for the handling of this point,in the example of *Sisera* his preparation against *Iabin*.

But before I come to the successe that *Gaal* had by meeting with *Abimelech*, I will note that which went before it. To the which end it is said here, and it is to be obserued,that *Gaal* was now in the triall timerous: who had boastingly said before,who is *Abimelech?* now he was afraid(I say)as soone as the least suspition and likelihood of danger arose and appeared vnto him: for he looking out as soone as he was able to discerne in the dawning, perceiued a band and companie of men a farre off: and as he did better discerne them,he was more afraid : so that he said as much to *Zebul* his enemie, and thereby bewraied his dastardlines vnto him, who had heard before of his great brags and boasting against *Abimelech*. Whereby wee may cleerely, as in a glasse,obserue the propertie and disposition of boasters: who prate and bragge of great matters, but effect small,or rather none at all. Like to *Benhadad*, who triumphed ouer *Ahab*,arrogating to himselfe all that was his: but was glad after to send a few of his men (that were left of two mightie armies) with ropes about their neckes to sue for his life,and their owne, vnto the same *Ahab*,to his exceeding great shame, when they had small hope to obtaine them. Vers.36.37. Doct.

So that this example laieth out a boaster in his colours; noting him to be one,who out of his vainglorious and frothie humour, vndertakes great matters,but performes nothing lesse, and therefore in stead of honour purchaseth himselfe shame by his folly. Commonly the boaster is no bodie in the triall: like vnto a torrent or standing water, which in winter swelleth and runneth amaine, when there is no vse of it; but in sommer and droughts, when it should coole and refresh, that is, when it should stand any man in stead, it faileth and is drie. The impotent nature of man boasteth of all the gifts of God, inward and outward, interuerting and holding backe thankes from God, by presumptuous bragging of it selfe: but for the most part, these gifts are rather supposed to be, then be indeed in the boaster: and therefore when the triall comes, the Thraso or bragger is ridiculous to the beholders. *Amaziah* boasted of his valour greatly, and prouoked *Iehoash* without cause, when he needed not: but hee sped thereafter, and was sore foiled. So the late miscreants, I meane the powder-traytors, how boasted they of their deuice, when it was almost at the vpshot? God and man (say they in that letter of theirs) haue decreed the ouerthrow of these English heretikes, &c. But God had decreed the contrary, and turned their boasting into shame, euen when they looked for a perpetuall destruction, vpon the vpholders and embracers of the Gospell, and the ouerthrow of the Gospell it selfe. So did *Goliah* challenge *Dauid*, by words to this effect; I will chop thee as small as hearbes to the pot, (as the common phrase of the swaggerer is) but hee was chopt himselfe head from body, with his owne sword. The Pharisee boasted of his righteousnes, liberalitie, deuotion, thus: I thanke thee Lord, I am not as this Publicane, &c. but the Publicane went away more iustified. The worldling in *James*, boasteth of to morrow: To morrow (saith he) we will goe to such a place, and make such a gaine, &c. But the Lord was forgotten, and therefore they thriued as *Iehoshaphats* ships that went to Ophir for gold, for they were broken. So *Hezekiah* gloried of his treasures, *Nebuchadnezzar* boasted of his buildings, *Achitophel* of his policie & counsell, (see his words) *Herod* of his wit and eloquence: and now adaies, who is so naked but hee hath somewhat to vaunt of? And if of nothing else, yet of this to his neighbour, that he was in the towne before him, whom he contendeth with, and ouer-croweth; and will be there when he is gone: So another boasteth of his skill in his profession or trade; another of his selling deare, or buying cheape; of crossing his aduersarie and matching him, &c. for boasting hath not so small acquaintance as men thinke: yea, for a need, if a man be prouoked but a little, he will bragge of his pride, and not blush to say to him that is his better, Though I haue not so good a purse as thou, yet I haue as proud a stomacke as thou, for thine heart: euen thus may ye heare the poore man contending with the rich. But O earth, earth, earth, consider what thou braggest of, for euen thy glory is thy shame: of thine owne mouth shall he condemne thee, who professeth to resist the proud. As for them that boast of worse matters, who say, They will quench the zeale of these precise ones, (as they terme honest men) and will wearie and pursue them, till they haue made them eate their word, and to renounce their precisenes: as Psal. 2. These (I say) are as neere to the Lords despight, and to disappointment as the rest: and therefore he scoffeth at the boasts of such enemies, casting their brags in their teeth, and saying; Tell the towers and gates, see the walles of Sion, &c. As if he should say, What? haue they cast downe all these, looke well, and consider, yee shall finde that not a stone thereof is remoued. So bad

A similitude.

1. Sam. 17. 51.

Luke 18. 11.

James 4. 13.

1. King. 22. 48.

2. Sam. 17. 12.

Ierem. 22. 29.

1. Pet. 5. 5.

Psal. 2. 3.

bad a member wee see the tongue is, and boasteth of great things, to small purpose. Therefore, to make vse hereof, let not the wise, strong, rich, boast of their wisedome, strength, and wealth: but hee that will boast, let him boast that he knoweth me, saith the Lord. And he that can boast of this, shall not feare arrogancie, seeing this knowledge of God is euer seasoned with humilitie and loue. Let vs consider this, that the sinne of boasting seldome goeth without vsurping Gods honour to a mans selfe, and lying: Both most capitall crimes against the first and second tables. It is grosse for a rich man to boast of his worth and wealth: but for a man to borow of this man and that great summes, and to boast how well monied he is, how absurd is it? Be able to say (if need be) vtter it, of thy well vsing thy gifts, that thou regardest it as much as them: or else thy craking of the gifts themselues shall be a witnesse against thee, in the giuing vp of thy account; yea rather let the best say: To vs O Lord belongeth shame, and confusion of face, we haue small cause of boasting, if we saw our selues in any sort, as we are, and our vilenes.

Ierem.9.23. Note. Iob 31.25.

Nay, let none boast so much as of to morrow, they know not what one day may bring foorth. Man is a worme, meane and base, if he were laid out in his colours: But being as he is, he should rather breake into admiration, and say with the Prophet, O Lord, it is thy mercie that we be not all consumed, rather then to boast of things aboue his reach. It is absurd and ill beseeming euery way, but especially it is odious, and as dangerous, when it is vsed against the people of God, as *Iezabel* did against *Elias*, and *Rabsakee* that railing heathen against the good King *Ezechias* and his men, boasting and threatning them, and all to discourage them from the true seruice of God, as I haue said. And this of *Gaals* boasting: now of *Zebuls* answere.

Prou.27.1. Lam 3.22. 1.King.19.2. 2.King.18.27.

When *Zebul*, who being for *Abimelech*, saw the boastings of this *Gaal* against *Abimelech*, as he sent him word thereof, when he heard of them by other, that hee might prepare himselfe to come forward and fight with him; so now he heard him himselfe, he fleshed him on, and matched him in another kinde, to wit, in subtiltie and dissimulation, while yet he spake faire, and seemed to be friendly to him, as here wee see. For hee went out of the citie with him, to the end he might suspect nothing, when he had yet giuen warning to *Abimelech*, to lie in waite for him, against the time hee should come foorth, and to be readie to set vpon him: and in the middest of the feare and danger that this *Gaal* was in, *Zebul* subtilly deceiued him, as if there had bin no cause of feare at all: egging and drawing him on subtilly, so that he could not for shame, when yet full faine he would haue broken away from him. Where, besides that wee may note the dissimulations, lyings and slie subtilties that be in the world, euen among such as pretend great loue and friendship, as is to be seene in this *Zebul*. Which point I haue spoken of alreadie in this booke: so wee may see how men of euill qualities are matched and meete together, as he was with *Gaal*. For if we marke wee may see, that one is a boaster, another a dissembler, and a subtill vnderminder, a third a quarreller, and contentious liuer. Other tainted with sundrie other dangerous and bad qualities, of which the Apostle speaketh; these I say all, liue and deale together. Is it not therfore the great goodnesse of God, that one deuoureth not another? Yea if the Lord should not bridle him for the vpholding of the peace of the Church and Common-wealth, they could not possiblie

Vers 36.38. Doct.vers.38. 2.Tim.3.2.

dwell together, nor liue and conuerse the one with the other, nor stand in any sort, no, not as they doe, but being of so contrary and bad qualities, they must needs as fire and water destroy one another. And whereas the good Magistrate and faithfull Minister with other assistant Christians, doe labour to throw downe the workes of darknesse, and of the diuell, and so to bridle the rage of the turbulent and vnruly sort of people; herein it may be spoken with griefe, the opposition against pietie and goodnesse is so great, that although (the Lord working not by miracle, but by meanes) somewhat bee done for the incouragement of his; and the restraining of the other; yet but little in respect of that which might be, and that were to be desired and looked: because such good instruments, the most of them are too faint to fight the Lords battels against his so fierce, subtile, and many enemies. The like prouidence of God I noted before touching *Abimelechs* hiring vaine fellowes vpon the fourth verse of this Chapter. And to that, I may adde, that the Lord doth vse one wicked person to deuoure and oppresse the other, that so his owne people may enioy the more peace and safetie. As we see here, that this politicke dissembler *Zebul* (a right picture of our subtile Machiauilians now adaies) smoothes and flatters this *Gaal*, and serues his humour, (as one that would make his fellow drunke, drawes him on leaudly to drinke pot after pot, till he be quite turned ouer) by a pretended shew of friendship, that so his intent and plot to betray him to *Abimelech*, might in the meane season take the more sure effect.

Doct. 2. Secondly, from hence let vs note, how one sinner (being opposite to anothers drifts and purposes) goeth to worke, in the defeating of his enemy. Euen thus that (as the prouerb saith) one naile driues out another: they haue no way to go beyond each other, but this, who shall vse his weapon skilfullest, and most mischieuously. They all fetch their wiles out of one budget, and their arrowes out of one quiuer: either subtiltie or force is their weapon: the sligh and treacherous *Achitophel* runnes to the budget, the cruell and malicious *Esau* to the quiuer: here lies the point, who shall draw out the subtillest and cunningest fetch, or who shall take thence the sharpest or deadliest arrow. Both shoot in the same, I meane the diuels bow, but the skill is, who shall ouer-reach, and ouer-shoote each other therein. And he that prouides them this artillery, will be sure to be the gainer which part soeuer loseth: hee will prouide, that his kingdome shall increase, euen in the opposition of his subiects: they fight as fast for him as they doe against each other: *Zebul* and *Gaal* serue two Masters here (in one sense) the one *Abimelech*, the other Shechem, and the one by his boasting seekes to out-face the other. The other by his conniuence and dissembling seekes to root out him. But loe in the meane while both serue one Master the Diuell, hee reioyces as much in the spectacle, as *Ioab* and *Abner* did, in the beholding their young men to play, (as they cruelly called it) but in good earnest to cut each others throat. If men in their cursed doings and tradings thus in sinne, would consider that themselues are sure to goe by the walles, and forfeit their soules to him with whose engins and tooles they appugne each other, yea if they considered, that their quarrels serue to no other end, but to make a pageant for the diuell to laugh at: If they could see into the issue, that hee who winneth, winneth hell, and hee that loseth, loseth heauen: the gaines are

(Margin, beside "ioyces as much in the spectacle": 2. Sam. 2. 14. — beside "yea if they considered": Note.)

are onely Satans: oh how would this quaile them and dampe them in their leaudnesse? Put case that in the same ship vpon the sea, two men walke contrary steppes to each other, the one crossing the other in their motions: doth not the ship carrie them both one way? Can they (will they, nill they) resist the motion of the ship wherein both saile? Euen so all sinne hath one motion, though sinners mooue diuersly; let them striue each against other neuer so eagerly both must yeeld to one motion, their sinne wil bring them both to hell. The prodigall man walkes with quite aduerse steppes to the couetous, but both steps tend to hell. One great man seekes to ouerthrow another: hee that is subtill takes the vantage of him that is ambicious, and laies such a traine for him, as by following his ambicious plot, he incurreth the danger of the law, and so supplants him; but both the wisdome of the one, and the folly of the other is hellish. So that the closer and deeper the one is aboue the other, the sooner he may subuert him: but a subtiller then both, goeth beyond them, and will (at length) ouerreach them both. One man vnderhand worketh mischiefe against another: and he againe vnsheaths his tongue against him: the former is like to put downe the latter, but his owne sinne will as fast vndoe him. So the buyer would match the seller by his dissembling: the seller would cosen the buyer by his boasting and praising of the wares: but indeed both deceiue themselues aswell as each other. The vse is, to teach men not to thinke themselues safe and warrantable, because they resist euill, except they dislike and hate it also; for they may sinne as fast in resisting it, as in allowing it. Againe, let it teach men to abhorre this estate which admitteth no peace, no sound consent and vnitie: but is a fountaine of confusion: and to embrace that profession and practise, which commeth from the God of order, and is as vniforme in the meanes as the end, and vniteth them that embrace it, in the league of loue and peace. As for those that are better minded, let them beware of this errour of the wicked: let them not thinke their libertie hereby restrained, because they may not match the vngodly in their kind to play the Cretians with Cretians, the Foxes with Foxes: this is not their profession, they are bought with a price to serue the Lord in their bodies and spirits. The other indeed being disswaded from this practise, answere for themselues: That if they did not sweare, cosen, lie and temporise with the world, they could not liue, euery one would ouer-reach them, they should greatly disaduantage themselues in forgoing that liberty. But let the godly oppose their innocencie, with the wisdome of the spirit, to the subtiltie, and all other leaud qualities of the wicked: and if they cannot match them thereby, let them willingly take the foile, and submit themselues to God, rather then returne euill for euill. *A Simile.*

This vrging of *Gaal* by *Zebul* alleaging his owne words, that he had said, Verse 39.
[*Who is Abimelech*] made him goe forth against him, but ful soone he turned his face away from him, and fled: where we may see how God shamed him for his bragges, and that euen among the men of Shechem, where hee had made his boasting: that they, as well as he, might take shame for their rash and most vnwise aduenturing to set him vp for their head and guide, in whom they saw nothing but bragges. Thus doth God daily put to shame both boasters and such as aduance and cleaue vnto them: as what

boaster is there, if he can make a flourish, but some base and vnsetled persons or other will admire and applaud him, which God doth most iustly suffer them to doe, the one to deceiue, the other to bee deceiued, accordingly as they haue prouoked him, and yet in great mercy he doth it, to humble, and bring them to repentance, when they cannot but with shame see what they haue done: although we see (the more is the pitie) that few are the better thereby, or make any vse thereof, but runne into some other bad course, if they be made openly ashamed of that. Which I speake as well to giue a watchword to both, to bethinke themselues betimes of taking a better course, as also to the great comfort of them that are wary and aduised to shun and auoide such deceiuers and base flourishers, and doe take like heed and

Doct. verse 39.40. care to keepe themselues from euery euill way. But to returne: in that this *Gaal* was driuen so cowardly to flie, who had made so great bragges of courage and manhood, we see what many doe shew themselues to bee in triall: for without grace there is little difference. And I doe not onely meane hereby grosse and great braggers, of whom I haue spoken already, but others also in that kind, though as it is counted in a lower degree. For example: how many may we see, who shew great liking of good things, and who professe their forwardnesse in religion, and to dislike others that doe not so, as if they were before-hand themselues in comparison of many? and yet it is cleere that either they haue small or no vse of religion, (when they be at the best) no, not as many of them haue, whom they disgrace and condemne, or else they reuolt in time for all their faire shewes, and thereby doe openly bewray that there is nothing but froth to be found in them. Which is no small cause of griefe to the best, that there being but few that do make any great profession, yet that many of them should deceiue themselues and

Prou. 28.14. others. In stead whereof, let Gods true seruants feare alwaies, as the blessed doe, their infirmities and vntowardnesse, which they feele to be in them, and giue no occasions to any to thinke of them better then they are, but

2. Cor. 10.6. walke in vprightnesse of hart toward God, and not neglect to honour him, as they shall haue opportunitie in giuing good example to others.

Verse 41. And while *Gaal* the Captaine of the men of *Shechem* fled, many of them fell and were slaine, according to the Lords foretelling, and for that their sin against *Gedeons* house: and their boasting defender himselfe (as he tooke vpon him to be) was cast out of the citie with his brethren, that they did not so much as remaine in it. And by this let all learne a further lesson, then to

Doct. shunne and auoide boasters; to wit, that they neither put themselues vnder the shadow of flesh: for euen so they shall be serued, (as these men of Shechem were) who repose their confidence in man, or in any earthly thing. And this doth cleerely shew the beginning of the destruction of the men of Shechem. But of the argument now handled, I need not repeate that

Prou. 12.2. which hath been spoke vpon sundry occasions heretofore: as for *Gaal*, we see he rosted not that which he got in hunting. *Gaal* thought by crakes and

Verse 41. boasting to winde in himselfe and his brethren with the men of Shechem: as for *Abimelech*, hee knew hee got into the kingdome by tyrannie, and hee thought it liker for many to preuaile then one. And although commonlie it commeth to passe that men stablish themselues and theirs, by flattery and cosoning, yet here it was otherwise. For hee was frustrate of his hope, and

as

as we see here,cast out by *Abimelech*. And so God dealeth oft-times,that *Doct.2.*
though many vnworthy persons lift vp their heads, and build their nest on
high against the darts of missfortune, (as they call it) by pride, extortion,
crueltie,boasting, &c. yet God many times hindreth the course of such,
and throweth them downe: as he soone broke off the ill course that *Iudas* Matth.27.4.
tooke to be rich: *Ioab, Abner*,and *Achitophel*,who were neere to the King in 1 King.2.32.
whose daies they liued,yet in time they were cast downe from their great- 2 Sam.3.27. 2.Sam.17.23.
nes and glory which they had.Oh how hath he done the like in latter times
since,that if such wil needs darken and obscure Gods glory and the Gospell
for their owne pleasure,or the setting vp of themselues; they may see with
their owne eyes, as also all that applauded them, that they haue receiued
their due reward,when God hath cast them downe with shame,and yet the
worst is behind; which abideth such,whatsoeuer changes they meet with
here in the meane season.And this being the best state that sin bringeth (in
this life) which I haue now mentioned, let it feare the godly to taste of the
dainties of such,(as they count them) lest they with *Eue* reaching out their Genes.3.
hands after them, doe taste also of their punishments in such wise, as they
wish with many stripes,that they had neuer done so.

Verse 42. *And on the morrow the people went out into the field,which was told Abimelech.*

43. *And he tooke the people and diuided them into three bands, and laid waite in the fields and looked,and behold,the people were come out of the citie,and hee rose vp against them and smote them.*

44. *And Abimelech and the bands that were with him rushed forward, and stood in the entring of the gates of the citie, and the two other bands ran vpon all the people that were in the field and slew them.*

45. *And when Abimelech had fought against the citie all that day,hee tooke the citie, and slew the people that was therein, and destroyed the citie, and sowed Salt in it.*

45. *And when all the men of the Tower of Shechem heard it,they entred into an hold of the house of the god Berith.*

47. *And it was told Abimelech that all the men of Shechem were gathered together.*

48 *And Abimelech gate him vp to Mount Zalmon, he and all the people that were with him,and Abimelech tooke axes with him, and cut downe boughs of trees, and tooke them,and bare them on his shoulder, and said vnto the folke that were with him,What yee haue seene me to doe,make hast and doe like me.*

49. *Then all the people also cut downe euery man his bough,and followed Abimelech,and put them to the hold,and set the hold on fire with them.*

50. *So all the men of the tower of Shechem died also, about a thousand men and women.*

AFter the forementioned slaughter, and holding *Gaal* out of the citie, *The summe to*
the Israelites in Shechem thought among themselues,that they would *verse 46.*
be auenged of *Abimelech*, as it seemeth; and they went out of the citie to
pursue him. They neuer considered what a punishment they had sustai-
ned already, by their rash putting themselues vnder that vaine-glorious
boaster

boaster *Gaal*, but vnaduisedly followed their quarrell. But he vnderstanding it, tooke the aduantage of that their attempt, and so disposed his bands of souldiers, that hee set two of them to take those that came forth of the citie, and slew them, and hee and another band rushed to the entrance into the citie, and hauing fought against it the whole day, took it, and slew the people in it, and destroyed the citie, and sowed salt in it.

The clearing of verse 42.

If the men of Shechem had gone out of the citie, but to walke, or to doe some businesse, as some (perhaps) would thinke they did, *Abimelech* should not haue needed to prepare two or three bands of armed men to set vpon a few, scatteringly here and there, and those vnarmed, comming forth to their worke; or if they had gone out vpon pleasure, what had he gained, to haue gone forth with bands against a few persons? But it is cleare therefore (as I said) and most certaine, that they went out in warlike manner to fight with *Abimelech*, (though they went without *Gaal* their Captaine) being much prouoked and incensed for the losse of their neighbours, whom *Abimelech* had slaine the day before. For they were many, and for that they were now heated very much: and more in spite, rashnesse, and desire of reuenge, rather then good aduisednesse they went to worke: being driuen and put to their shifts, as they thought, and that somewhat they must doe to him, either that they must ouerthrow him, or else they saw that hee would surelie root out them: for to this it was now come, that the word of God by *Iotham*, might be fulfilled. And by this we see to what desperate shifts men are driuen by their falsehood, crueltie, rashnesse, vaine, confidence in man, and by the like sinnes: and what wise man would looke for any better end of such doings?

Doct. gathered generally to verse 46.

If God had brought vpon them that trouble in their innocencie, hee would haue taught them how to beare it, whatsoeuer had been like to haue followed: but now they runne vpon the swords point, and therefore both they that sought to fight with him abroad, and they that waited for to set vpon him and his men in the citie, are both of them destroyed. This is the best end that sinne bringeth vpon the committers. And thus wilfulnesse, stomacke, and stubbornesse bring many to destruction, while they who are contrary minded are in peace. So contention, whoring, drunkennesse and riot, doe the like in their kind: and they that seeme to bee safest, and freest from danger being of that sort, may looke for no better fruit nor end of their euill doings, but shame, sorrow, and a miserable death, though not by enemies, as these men of Shechem found it, whether it bee in their beds, or wrought by their owne hands, all is one, if repentance breake not off their euill course.

Note.

The which while Gods seruants behold, and see to what a wofull end their euill doings bring many, who yet in their iolitie thought themselues the only wise men of others, and all fooles who walked in their innocencie and vprightnesse. I say while Gods seruants see this, they shall praise him highly, for that they followed a better course by Gods direction; and euen now (I say) when they see Gods threats executed vpon euill doers, as they were told that it should be so in the middest of their prosperitie and iolitie. And all that come after them, shall see good cause, and haue incouragement to hold on a Christian course, and to turne neither on the right hand, nor on the left, although they shall see pietie and good conscience to be iustled to the walles, and scorned, yet shal the worst day of these that practise them, be farre better then the best of the other, for all their setting out of the matter for a while; and when their time commeth in which they shall smart, then shall Gods seruants reioyce in their owne sinceritie and innocencie. Let the reader looke backe to the former chapter, and inlarge this point by adding thereto, that which hath been noted touching the sinne and iudgement of Succoth and Penuel. Note.

Now followeth the further proceeding in, and laying foorth of the ouerthrow of the men of Shechem. *Abimelech* might for all the force of them goe and dwell safely in his house, as he did, at Arnmah, not farre from Shechem, their power being weakned, and *Gaal* thrust out by *Zebul*. But yet they rose vp against him, as we haue heard, of stomack, if possibly they might any way be reuenged: But their so doing being told to *Abimelech*, turned to the destruction of them that did so, and to them that were in the citie, with it also; as appeareth in these foure next verses. Reade them in the text. The Lord hauing purposed their ouerthrow, did thus goe forward with it: for he hath many waies to execute his iudgments threatned vpon his enemies. It was a iust cause to astonish the rest, when he began with the formost: but alas, where there is no counsell from God to direct them, what can they do, but waite their time to follow their fellowes in the like iudgement? Euen so, God sometimes sweepes away all the companie of bad men and euill workers in some one place at once, as hee did whole kingdomes in *Ioshuas* time, and made his people possesse and inhabit them. Sometime he keepeth them vnder and wasteth his enemies by degrees, and one after another, as here: as before I noted out of the space of *Abimelechs* raigne, where the same point hath been handled. *Verse 42 to 48. still continued.* *Doct 2. out of these verses.*

So they that marke it, shall finde, that though hee giue them their scope and libertie for a time, which hee doth, that they may repent; they in the meane while looking after no such thing, (I say) they that mark it, shall see, how God either beginneth to blow vpon their prosperitie, as the East wind in the Spring beginneth to nip and hold in the leaues that were comming foorth, or else as a great frost doth all at once kill them; so doth he suddenly send desolation vpon them, one way or other, when their time is come. And therefore let no seruant of God feare, or be dismaied for the greatnes and pride of such, for in a small time their glorie and iollitie shall vanish, it shall be no more seene; there is a greater then they, who will surely cut off their hope, and lay their glorie in the dust. Oh that the righteous could then praise God, for that hee hath kept them in all those times of danger within their bounds, not suffering them grossely to reach out their hands to iniquitie; and when they haue seene such workes of God to be shewed on his enemies, then euer after to bee more firme in their couenant keeping with God. Note. *A Similitude.* Ecclef. 5. 8.

These things being thus brought about to the killing of so many of the men of Shechem, a thing so vnlikely in their first making of *Abimelech* king; it shall not be amisse to consider a little of it, the spoile of the men being so great, and yet so small likelihood thereof, till the Lord sent an euill spirit betwixt *Abimelech* and them. Who would haue said in the time of their *Doct. 3. out of the former verses.*

their agreement and loue, that was betwixt them, that they ſhould haue growne to this point, to become vtter enemies? and while they were ſo neerely ioyned and knit together in amitie and friendſhip, that they could be thus alienated, and at the vttermoſt defiance one with the other? They who were promiſed by *Abimelech* to be aboue all other reſpected and preferred; who would haue ſaid, that they of all other ſhould be hardlieſt handled, yea deſtroyed? But wee muſt vnderſtand, that there were two cauſes hereof, and the one riſing from the other. The one was this, their loue was wicked and curſed, and bound together with rotten bands. The other was this; that the wrath of God burning like fire, brake and conſumed theſe bands: whereby hee raiſed an euill ſpirit betwixt them, to the deſtroying each of other. And let all that are wiſe, bee inſtructed hereby, that where men are, as theſe were, companions and friends in euill, and that they are not linked together by the feare of God, and the loue of goodneſſe, that their fellowſhip will not hold long, what likelihoods and ſhewes ſoeuer there be of the continuance thereof: And the more euils that it is compact and framed of, the deadlier and more violent ſhall the breach of it be. If it be not accompanied with wicked practiſes, as theirs here was, yet euen the ſecret moths of ſelfe-loue, priuy pride, and the ſeeking of commoditie therby, being the grounds of this agreement and fellowſhip; euen they wil conſume it as the moth doth the garment. It is a worke of great difficultie for the beſt intended loue euen betwixt good Chriſtians to be held firme, and kept vnbroken: and there muſt be renuings of couenants oft times betwixt them; and all little enough, the diuell ſo ſets in to raiſe and make diuiſion among brethren. For why? It is a good note of their welfare and happineſſe to be knit together in brotherly loue. So ſaith our Sauiour: Hereby
Ioh.13.35. ſhall men know that ye are my Diſciples, in that yee loue one another. But if men be brethren in euill, as if they be more neerely knit together, becauſe they both ioyne in a bad cauſe, ye haue heard Gods ſentence of ſuch agreement alreadie, it ſhall ſurely come to naught, as this betwixt *Abimelech* and the men of Shechem did, how vnlikely ſoeuer it ſhall ſeeme to be ſo in the time of their peace and loue: And the ſame I ſay of their fellowſhip, who are both of them vnreformed, although it bee not for ill ends and purpoſes entred into by them. And let this which I haue ſaid, make vs wiſe in ſeeking loue and friendſhip one with another. But here, the occaſion being fitly offered, I end.

THE

THE SIXTIETH SERMON ON THE NINTH CHAPTER OF THE BOOKE OF IVDGES.

NOw followeth the further destruction of these men of Shechem. For when their citie was destroyed, they fled to a double fort, which was their castle for the strength of it: euen the house of their god *Baal-berith*, as they called him, with whom they had made a couenant, and therefore hoping that there they should haue been safe. And these were the chiefe and wise men of the citie. And *Abimelech* hearing of it, came and destroyed both them and their Temple. Vers.46.

In that these hoped there to finde ease and defence by the holinesse, as well as the strength of the place, wee may see, that when men haue no religion nor acquaintance with God, how wise and great soeuer they be, what poore shifts they haue to prouide for their safetie: euen to thinke, that the holinesse of the place, their gods of wood or stone, or the reliques of Saints, or some such rotten props shall free them from their troubles and feares: No, although they should seek to the true God, in their haste, which is much liker to worke their good, yet their hearts being farre from him, and they without confidence in him that he would helpe them: euen that seeking of theirs should not be able to deliuer them. Doct vers.46.

But all these are bruised reedes, and spiders webs: much like the helpe that *Baals* Priests obtained by calling on him; whom for their deceiuing of 1.King.18.40.
the people in such a manner, *Elias* caused to be slaine. Euen such helpe doth the wilful generation of Papists and Seminaries at their death in their greatest need, obtaine themselues, and their superstitious votaries whom they haue deluded, and brought into the snare with them. Of whom one (a principall ring-leader) at his death, was constrained to renounce the opinion of merit, and humane satisfactions for sinne, although he was loth to haue that gap opened to the people, for shame, whom they had so grossely seduced. Another (yet liuing and of greater reckoning in the Popish Church) Better I meane, is forced to confesse, that for the auoiding the perill of vainglorie and carnall presumption, it is the safest of all to repose a mans whole confidence in the onely mercie of God in Christ Iesus. And by this we see that howsoeuer (for sinister ends) they suppresse the truth, and abuse their sillie Proselites: yet when they are cōpelled by the force of their conscience, or the terror of death, to put away lying, and equiuocating, which few of them attaine to, but dye in hardnes of hart, wherein they liued: but whē it falleth out otherwise, thē they confesse & renounce their cōceits, as bruised reeds, to be vnable to support thē: which as it is commonly vnprofitable to themselues, so yet it should serue to deterre others from venturing and resting so

boldly vpon their vngrounded assertions. To omit other there was a third, of long and great account and reckoning among people of that religion, whom I visiting vpon the death-bed, was an eare witnesse with sixe or seuen other of that place, then present also; that the partie, then shortly after deceasing, renounced the dunghill stuffe of that religion, and reckoned all Poperie as a deceitfull trade, and particularly the chiefe points thereof, who yet had long been a stiffe and stout defender and maintainer thereof. Oh therefore blessed are the people whose God is the Lord *Iehouah*, and who
Ioh.17.3. know him the onely true God, and whom he hath sent Iesus Christ, for this is eternall life. But as these men of Shechem here were slaine in the Idolatrous Temple of their Idoll *Berith*, for their blindnes and putting their confidence therein, so shall all be serued that rest on such proppes, that is to say,
Matth.27.3. they shal be left in the briars, as *Iudas* was of the Priests, whom he trusted in. Let the reader looke backe to the fifth chapter, and the 30. verse, where the answere of *Sisera* his mother to her selfe, and her wise Ladies to her, is recorded: and there he shall finde this point further inlarged.

Vers. 47.40.49. As I said they were slaine in the Temple of their Idoll, which they put their trust in, so it was done by *Abimelech*, who followed the matter to the purpose, when he heard whither they fled. This was his kindnes to the men of Shechem, that made him king. He promised other matters to thē, vers. 2. that he being their bone, and their flesh, he would regard them aboue all other. And now we see here that all was but flatterie: for to what end came all but to this, that they had no greater enemie then him? True it is indeed, this fell out according to that which *Iotham* before had denounced against them: to wit, that fire should come out of the bramble and destroy the Cedars of Lebanon. But this excuseth the fact of *Abimelech*, no more then the counsell and purpose of God touching the deliuerance of Christ to death,
Act.2.23. (A good watch-word) excused *Iudas* the traytor, and the Priests and other who put him to death. This is good therefore, and an vse to be made of this doctrine, (if euer) now needfull, and therefore to bee heard and regarded; namely, that wee take heed whom we trust and giue credit vnto; that is to say, not such as wee haue not proued to be faithfull, as the men of Shechem may teach vs, who too rashly and readily trusted this deceiuer, and false hearted *Abimelech*.

Ioh.2.last. Our Sauiour would not commit himselfe to them that were said to beleeue in him, for he knew what was in man. Much lesse ought we to doe so, who know there is much falsehood and doubling in them whom we trust, and that they are ignorant, prophane, and hypocrites. Therefore *Salomon*
Prou.27.10. going as neere the marke as he could, gaue this counsell about trusting of men: Thine owne friend and thy fathers forsake thou not, &c. So that if it may be, some proofe should be made of their faithfulnes and vprightnes first, before we rest vpon them, especially if it lie in vs to doe it. And it being so necessary a gift, this faithfulnes I meane, the Apostle requires it in seruants, the meaner sort of persons, as one of the two necessary duties that should be in them, (the other being diligence) without which they cannot doe their duties well, that we may see thereby how needfull it is in all other about greater matters.

And as this sinceritie is rare to finde, according to that which *Salomon* com-

complainteth of, saying, Where shall one finde a faithfull man? And *Paul*: Prou.20.7.
All haue not faith, that is the fruite of faith, which is faithfulnes and true 2.Thes.3.2.
heartednes: so it should cause vs to begin with our selues, and vrge our own hearts for vprightnes first, and not to marueile that we finde it not in others, if it be not in our selues: as that we may be trusted vpon our word, and approue our selues such as we would be taken to be. And then by our obseruation and experience of the good dealing that wee can finde in any more then in other; thereafter let vs giue credit vnto them: and yet I meane such good dealing, as hath been learned by the preaching of the Gospell, such as is according to knowledge. And by the same vprightnes and good dealings men should bee led in chusing their companions in mariage, and not to hearken to euery glosing tongue that can make faire and large promises, which haue deceiued thousands: and also in seeking of seruants, or to haue them (if it may be) the children of the faithfull well and religiously brought vp: and the same care should be had in chusing executors comeprimitters, and such as we would put in trust. To the which if it be demanded, where such shall be found, that they may be trusted in matters of importance: I answere: beside that I haue said already, that euery one which will aske this question, must first begin himselfe to practise sinceritie, that so hee may the better complaine of the want thereof in other; this I adde, that some who call for it and finde it not, are worthie to goe without it, although I doe not hereby excuse them that are void of it, and offer the contrary euill measure. And they, who I say are worthy to goe without it, when they would full gladly finde it in those whom they deale with, are such as are carping, biting, Note.
scoffing, and accusing of them for their precisenes, who labour and endeuor to keepe their consciences pure and good. Too many there are in this age, who cannot so soone perceiue a man or woman to withdraw themselues from the sinnes of the time, and to bee afraid to offend, as the common sort doe, but by and by they cry out of them, that they are Precisians. Now they who can allow none to be vpright and conscionable in their waies and life, it is no matter though they meete with such in their dealings, as shew small conscience and vprightnes toward them, God being iust to make others to measure out to them as they haue measured to others, as *Salomon* saith in an other kinde, Eccles.7. to teach them to know what an vpright hearted man Eccles.7.23.
is worth, and to make much of such, rather then to discourage them. One example shall serue for all; A cruell Landlord cries out of his vnfaithfull Tenant, that he hath broken his day, and (it may be) is runne away with his rent. But who is in fault? The poore Tenant that dares not appeare before his Lord to craue indifferencie, or the cruell Lord who hath borne him in hand, that he hath let him a good peniworth; whereas indeede hee hath so racked and fleeced him, that he is fitter to begge reliefe, then to pay his debt out of the farme, hauing had nothing neere sufficient (out of his owne labour) to vphold himselfe. As for such, let them crie out of vnfaithfulnes till they be weary, who will pitie them? Let the dead bury the dead, as our Sauiour saith, they are serued as they haue deserued, and let them reape as they haue sowne. Further I answere, let vs lament and pray against such vnfaithfulnes, for that it is so common. At least let vs pray, that we may be free from hauing to doe with such: for vnfaithfull men commonly are also vnreaso-

nable: at least that we be not beguiled by them, ere we be aware, as *Abner* and *Amasa* were by *Ioab*: which (except the Lord giue a man wisedome to discerne) cannot alwaies bee auoided. Besides where least trust hath been found by experience, let men be wise to repose least trust in them. For who will put precious liquors in a broken vessell, hauing proued it to be vnfit for vse? or through folly venter to dash our foot against the stone, which we remember hath hurt vs? Therfore I say, let men trust no such, of whose fidelity and truth they haue no proofe, but rather the cōtrary, or no further at least, then they may without any great detriment to themselues: and where they must needs trust some such, let them bind them the more strongly. And so let those that vndertake suretiship, beware that they lose not their liberty and bring themselues into bondage, and their estate and posteritie to wilfull penurie. Most of all, let Christians beware of them, that vnder a colour of loue, seeke to vndermine them, to betray them, to get somewhat from them, which might tend to the danger of their brethren, or to the wounding of their owne conscience; which I speake because many silly Christians thinke themselues happy if they can get countenance or benefit by such as are their superiors, not knowing that the benefits of the vngodly are forked, and bring more backe then they bestow. *Boner* did more mischiefe by his flattering poore men, till they abiured the truth, then by all his crueltie: for which cause, *Salomon* admonisheth well of such, saying: Be not desirous of their daintie meates, for it is deceiuable meate. But where without inquirie and obseruing in the best manner we can by our selues and others, we rashly beleeue euery one who can speake vs faire, (as indeed, Faire words make fooles faine, according to the prouerb) I say, they who are so light of credit, I send them no further then to this present example: let them looke what became of all the smooth words and faire shewes that this *Abimelech* made to these men of Shechem his kinsman and mothers brethren, in whom they reposed such confidence: for as they had no greater enemie then him, euen so neither let these looke to find any better measure.

2. Sam. 3. 27. & 20. 10.

Prou. 23. 3.

Now though this may bee laid forth in all kinds of fellowship among men, yet it is most commonly seene in their earthly dealings, wherin scarcely any promise is kept, and most liuely it is to be seene in marriages. What solemne, kind, and ioyful beginnings haue many of them had? so as it might worthily haue prouoked the beholders thereof to praise God, and reioyce for such a goodly ordinance of his, so like to bring foorth such answerable fruit to those beginnings. And betwixt the couples themselues, so marrying and comming together, what liking betwixt them, and delightings one in another, as if they could neuer be enough, neither might one be well out of anothers sight; but in continuance, longer or shorter, how haue all these been turned into the contrary?

Note.

What dislike and wearines hath there been one of another? what alienating of affection, crossing one the other, chiding, railing and reuiling, separating from bed and board, (while yet they must needs liue together) and afterward an vtter casting off the one the other? I speake not this of the heauinesse which the Lords chastisements meeting and taking hold of them, doe raise in them, to the which, all, euen the best are subiect, wherein they both should and haue promised to be companions, and one to helpe the other

ther to beare the burden: which kind of behauiour would preserue their loue, as it doth betwixt some others: I speake not (I say) of these corrections of the Lord, but of the mischiefe that their euill and corrupt hearts, false, raging, proud, wilfull and inconstant, haue wrought betwixt them, they being disguised, and nothing like the persons they seemed to bee at their first meeting. Oh therefore if towards men wee bewray this disease, then how much more is it to be feared in professing our repentance to God, it being secret and a thing hid from men? and in comming to the word and sacraments, what need haue we of this vprightnesse?

In these two verses it is shewed, by what meanes he slew them: and that was, by cutting downe boughes from trees, and bidding his men doe as he did, and putting them to the hold, and setting them on fire, till all the men of Shechem that were therein, died. And there we may see, what force is in example, especially if it be bad. Touching which, though I haue spoken at large before, especially in chap. 1. the end where the sinne of the most Tribes in neglecting the Lords charge is recorded: which I desire the Reader to turne vnto, yet vnto so apt an occasion as this is, somewhat I will say here of it also. *Gedeons* men followed him in carrying their pitchers and lampes after him in great danger to feare the Midianites: but that was as commendable as this was wicked and cruell, and most commonly followed: yet it is not to be denied, but if there were some to giue good example, there would be some followers of them also: as in meeknesse, humblenesse, innocencie, faithfulnesse, mercy, pietie, patience and the like. And namely, if rich men would for their parts begin to the rest, and go before others in deeds of charitie, and sell for lower prices to the poore, (when things are deare) then the common prices be, and would be examples in mercy, in harmelesnesse, in gentlenesse, and such like. Vers. 48. 49.

It is hard to say, what good might be done thus? and by hauing religion and holy instruction in high account, and louing heartily, and well esteeming of Gods people. But to this it is come, that men, and the wealthier sort especially, whereas they might bring on many to Christian practise by well doing; they haue (alas) cold loue to good causes, but are slow and backward, and therefore deadnesse and vnprofitablenesse is to bee seene thicke and threefold in other that should learne of thē, the diuell labouring, when he cannot make all sorts alike in wickednesse, to leaue as few to giue countenance to good things, as may bee. And men bee so vnapt to learne to performe duties aright, that except they see good examples before them, they cannot tell how to set vpon, or goe about them. But as for euill courses, they need none to goe before them therein, they can find the way thereto without guides, though they are much more fleshed and drawne on when they haue other to breake the ice to them. But where the best examples are giuen, let this bee our rule, that wee follow them no otherwise then as they follow Christ: and they that doe so, let them perswade vs to al zeale and forwardnesse in duties of the first Table, (as to the reuerent receiuing of the word preached, and the right manner of preparing our selues to the Lords Supper, and such like exercise) so in no wise follow we the common sort in their behauiour and practise about duties to men in the second Table. Note. 1. Cor. 11. 1.

But let vs goe forward: The vnweariednes also of this cursed *Abimelech*, in

in his businesse is to be marked, how from one thing to another he toyleth himselfe: yea and that not without perill of his life. A base worke, one would thinke to goe vp to the mountaine, cut downe boughes from the trees, and bring them on his necke, and set them to the hold to burne it. But good enough for him, and thus will men toile and indanger themselues for their pleasure and profit in most base manner, though it come to nothing, but that they soone lose all, as hee did. So doe all sorts of men for a poore liuing, which yet they oft faile of notwithstanding. Whereas in the
1.Tim.6. meane while, godlinesse, which is the great riches, lieth dead by them, and by no perswasions can they be brought to seeke after that with the least delighting therein, whilest yet God alloweth them time and trauell enough for things meet and necessary. For example, how duly come they to Sermons and to the Lords Supper? though they might reape no small benefit thereby: and so doe they accordingly sit wearie and sleepie at the preaching of the word, when they be there. And yet the most part of men (these two actions with prayer being excepted) shew not so much resemblance of religion in their whole life beside. But oh, that euen Gods faithfull seruants did not grow (many of them) to the like point, shewing much vntowardnesse at the Word and Sacrament, when yet they haue approched to both, with great reuerence and chearefulnesse in former times. If men be asked, how they can endure such toile and paines as they take for the world, while they be so cold in duties to heauen-ward, their answere is: Man is borne to labour; and the world is hard. If we labour not, we shall neither haue food nor rayment. This makes them (as the Psalmist saith) to rise earely, sit vp late, fare full hardly, and all for a poore liuing. Ah poore soules, and what when they haue got it, (not to speake of this, how many waies they offend God in getting it, and yet they are oft times disappointed of that which they seeke: either by their leaud spending it, or Gods curse vpon it:) but I say, What when they haue it? Doe ye not see, that at the solemne day of death, when they count all their great gains, and fruit of their labor, that their soule is yet vnprouided for? Was all their life little enough to feed and clothe their bodie, and thinke they (vpon so short a warning) to prouide for their soule? Is not a soule of much more value then a body is; nay then a world? And yet in getting saluation for the soule which the bodie shall fare the better for also; yea, euen here it shall bee the better able to doe earthly labour, with chearefulnesse, and without vexation; who will put his finger in the cold water for it? Who thinks not euery little time bestowed that way, toylesome and tedious? More particularly, to giue all diligence to obtaine faith and repentance, as we are commanded, how vnwelcome is the charge thereof vnto vs, which yet is easilier obtained, and with more assured successe, if wee so seeke it as if wee would find, and is a more durable possession, and of more necessary and daily vse, and farre more pretious gaine, and that which exceeds the riches of Princes without it. Vpon the death-bed al this is confessed, and yet not once in a whole quarter thought of, while men haue life and strength, because they want heart and will thereto.

Doct. from verse 1. to this 50 And generally let all learne this by the men of Shechem, how they ioyne themselues to the acquaintance of wicked men for hope of gaine, pleasure or preferment: for God will meet with, and recompence such, as they deserue,

ſerue,at one time or other. As here may be ſeene, where *Abimelech* for his great promiſes,was repaired and cleaued vnto:but what got they in the end who did ſo? Nay,while they ſought much, what did they not loſe of that which they had,euen to their very liues themſelues?

So they that intend that,and ſeeke commoditie at the hands of ſuch,doe as I ſaid in the laſt point ſaue one, euen bring themſelues into bondage to them,if they haue any conſcience to accuſe them. For beſide this,that they are taken vp with ſuch thoughts, to wit, what gaine they ſhall get by them, after which manner the diuell occupieth them, to draw their minds from being better imployed : beſide this,I ſay, it muſt needs goe ill with them, if they profeſſe the Goſpell,and ſeeke to keepe a good conſcience,when they ſhall conſider,that by ſuch as Papiſts, Libertines, prophane and bad liuers, they be held in hope,and flattered,where the more they get,the more they loſe, and they are then in beſt caſe,when they haue leaſt to doe with them. But alas,the moſt ſuſpect not the ſeruitude that ſuch labour to bring them into,(for) the borrower is a ſeruant to the lender,and much more the receiuer to the giuer: while they hunt for the precious ſoule of him whoſe benefactors they would ſeeme to bee, aiming at this marke,(eſpecially ſome of them) euen to make them the children of hel as fully as themſelues be. And yet (which is farre worſe) they being ſo neere lincked in fellowſhip with them, they are ſo bewitched by their enchaunting and intiſing words,that they cannot tell how to bring themſelues backe againe out of the Maze wherein they are. I grant ſuch make ſhift to digeſt thoſe things till the day of their viſitation come,but then they be at their wits end. Prou.22.7.

Verſe 50. *Then Abimelech went to Theber,and beſieged Tebez and tooke it.*

51. *But there was a ſtrong Tower within the Citie, and thither fled all the men and women,and all the chiefe of the Citie, and ſhut it to them and went vp to the top of the Tower.*

52. *And Abimelech came vp vnto the Tower, and fought againſt it, and went hard vnto the doore of the Tower to ſet it on fire.*

53. *But a certaine woman caſt a peece of a milſtone vpon Abimelech his head, and brake his braine pan.*

54. *Then Abimelech called haſtily his Page that bare his harneſſe,and ſaid vnto him,draw thy ſword and ſlay me,that men ſay not of me a woman ſlew him, and his Page thruſt him through,and he died.*

55. *And when the men of Iſrael ſaw that Abimelech was dead, they departed euery man vnto his owne place.*

56. *Thus God rendered the wickedneſſe of Abimelech which he did vnto his father in ſlaying his ſeuentie brethren.*

57. *Alſo all the wickedneſſe of the men of Shechem did God bring vpon their heads,ſo vpon them came the curſe of Iotham,the ſonne of Ierubbaal.*

THus we haue heard how God puniſhed the men of Shechem for their ſinne againſt *Gedeons* ſonnes: Now how *Abimelech* was alſo plagued for the ſame: that the prophecy of *Iotham* might bee verified vpon them both; is laid foorth in theſe words,and followeth vnto the end.

To the former two miſchiefes that *Abimelech* wrought againſt the men of Shechem,in that he deſtroyed their Citie, and the people that were in it, *The ſenſe of verſ 50.51.*

 and

and their strong place and hold that the rest resorted to for safetie, and burnt it: to these I say, the holy story addeth how hee went about another. As thereby shewing, that he was not yet satisfied with the blood of the former: and therefore that he went further, to wit, to a Citie neere adioyning, called Thebez: which also as it is probable, though vncertaine, either ioyned with the Shechemites, or at least refused to be subiect to *Abimelech*, and going against that, tooke it also. Thus we see how this cruell base-borne Tyrant proceeded in his bloody attempts, and thereby also is shewed what extremitie these people of Thebez, were brought vnto. For they were all driuen to shift for themselues in a Tower that they had in their citie. Wherein though they might shelter themselues for a day, yet they could not long liue, but must needs bee famished at least, by any thing that they could see. These and such like dangers men lie open to in this changeable world, whereof they see no likelihood a little before. Which may teach vs the vncertainty of al things here below, in which yet men repose their confidence, and that no man can vpon good ground say, that to morrow shall bee like to day. As by that speech of the Lord, in the 12. of Luke, to him that bad his soule take the ease, eate, drinke and bee merry, seeing hee had laid vp much good in store, I say, by that speech may bee seene, when the Lord said vnto him, Thou foole, this night thy soule shall bee required of thee, then whose shall those things be, which thou hast prouided? euen the day before he died. And lest it should bee thought to bee his case alone, this he added: So shall it bee with him that laieth vp treasure for himselfe, and is not rich toward God. Therefore how many may we see and heare of, who are fearefully taken away from all? and many other are wasted, and haue their estate changed, as if they had neuer inioyed it? And such as regard not these things, are like to haue much to doe, when they shall see their owne prosperitie so to fade in like manner: Oh it shall be vtterly vnwelcome. And who can say any lesse, then that in smaller changes by losse, sicknesse, pouertie, diseases; it is hard stooping to them when they come, yea although they be thought of before, and in some sort prouided for? All this is said to teach the wise to liue here as strangers, and to make heauen their home, though they walke vpon the earth; and to warne the foolish to seeke wisdome, that while they cling fast to earthly staies and delights, they bee not with the foole before spoken of, cast out hence from all, and then vtterly to seeke of the true happinesse also.

Vers. 50. 51. Doct.

Luke 12. 20.

The opening of the 52. verse to 56.

But now it followeth, that after all this done to them of Thebez, the Lord brought on the time of his confusion, I meane *Abimelechs* also, as well as of the men of Shechem. And for the effecting of Gods iudgement vpon him, it is said, that when he had sped so well, as we haue heard, he attempted the Tower that was in Thebez, to take that also, and being drunke with his former successe, and therefore looking for the like there, hee receiued his deadly wound as his due reward, and that by a woman, to his great disgrace; who cast downe a peece of a milstone from the top of the Tower, he going close to the doore of it, to set it on fire, and broke his braine pan: whereupon he being not strooke quite dead, and yet past possibilitie of recouery, called presently for his page to thrust him thorow, to preuent the shame (as he thought it) that it might else haue been said, to wit, that a woman

man had slaine him, and so hee came to his end also.

By this last attempt of his, he hauing sped so well in the former, wee may see, how the wicked are fleshed by the successe that they haue in their bad courses, and that they bee so blinded therewith, that they make no stay, till they be cut off in the middest of them. For they make account, that they shall doe as they haue done: and dreame of no resisting of them. They say to themselues like them in the Psalme: Tush, the Lord will doe neither good nor euill. Is it not time then that God should make them feele that power of his in displeasure, which they will not acknowledge by teaching? and by this their going forward, til God stay their course, we see they cannot breake off, and this makes their sinne the greater. The like we shall obserue (God willing) in the Beniamites, chap. 20. of this booke. So *Herod* when hee had slaine *Iames* with the sword, and saw that it pleased the Iewes, he went about to take *Peter* also, till in his attempt the Lord cut him off. And what maruell though God vsually deale thus? the wicked will not know him, but they do measure their future successe by the former, which he will make them see to be a wrong ground. Doct. 3. verse 51. 52. Acts 12. 2.

For they thereby being imboldned, goe further from God, and by their successe, through the corruption that is in them, they are made more vnfit to returne to him againe. But all must know, that the word of God followed and obeyed carefully of vs, bringeth the good successe indeed, in which wee may rest, yea and in that only. For what blessing soeuer it pleaseth the Lord to send vs in outward things (as hee promiseth many) saying to those that doe so, that other things shall be cast vpon them; we haue also inward comfort thereby, which neither can be bought with money, neither can be taken from vs: which maketh vs glad to vse and imbrace all good meanes for the strengthening and stablishing of vs: which the other being drunken with earthly peace, make no account of. And both these being considered, the godly haue small cause to repine at the successe and ioyfull proceedings of the vngodly: the Lord giues them their scope, that he might bring the more sudden desolation vpon them, while they looke to morrow should be like to day, and much better. Neither should it grieue the godly, that themselues are often crossed, and denied the successe they dreamt of, and desired: seeing either their enterprises were euill, and therein to bee crossed is a blessing: or lawfull, but vnlawfully followed, and therfore Gods promises were stretcht further by them, then indeed they reached: or although their doings were religious, yet it may be, they were vndertaken with too much confidence in the goodnesse thereof, and in the meane season themselues who are the doers, not looked into, nor well purged from other sinnes which may easily set behind the successe of their best actions. But doubtlesse, where a Christian offends none of these waies, he shall neuer want successe: and the fruite thereof shall be farre other, when it is least, then the wicked mans who ventureth onely the more boldly vpon the next onset, because of his former good speed, (as *Abimelech* here:) but he shall with *Paul*, beleeue that God, who hath well begun in him, will giue good successe, both in mercies and deliuerances. But I haue handled this point at large in this historie before. Note. Matth 6. 33. Note.

In this Scripture is set downe, that this wofull instrument had his deadlie

wound;

Vers.53. wound; and by what meanes: euen in a base manner, by a woman breaking his skull, by throwing downe vpon him a peece of a mil-stone: where wee may further note by Gods cutting off this cursed instrument *Abimelech*, in the middest of his iolitie, and before hee had done any more mischiefe, that the prosperitie of the wicked is both short and vncertaine, when and how it shall come to an euil end. Which although I noted in general before out of the short time of his reigne: yet a little I wil adde thereto by this present occasion here offered. Now this their speedy taking downe is wrought by the Lord, not only by the many waies that he hath to meet with, and to punish

Note. them, but also because they are euer putting the Lord, as it were, in fresh remembrance by their renewed and continued prouokings of him, what hee oweth them. And in the meane while, he is not idle, when he is still and patient toward them, for hee knoweth and appointeth the time, and the

Psalm. 37.36. meanes to subuert them. So the Psalmist saith: Though the wicked flourish like a greene Bay tree, yet a little while, and his place shall haue no resemblance of such a one to haue been there, and hee shall bee no more found.

Behold this verified in *Zimry* with his *Cosby*, in *Chorah*, the Rich man men-

Luke 12.20. and 16.27. tioned in the Scriptures, and in many other in our owne experience, who while they prosper, are decaying: but they that abide, and remaine in the power of faith, hope and patience, as of Gods seruants is required, and are thorowly set a worke in them, they shall see good daies, and be well liking; and yet euen they also, if they withdraw themselues from their confidence, and will giue themselues to liue by eye-sight, as other doe, they shall see the Lord can soone change his course, and their sorrowes will bee exceedinglie multiplied like other mens. *Dauids* feet had well nigh slipt, when hee beheld the present flourishes of the vngodly, til God drew him out of his own

Psalme 73.17. fancie into the Lords Sanctuarie, and taught him this wisdome, to compare them with himselfe, as well in one part of their estate as another, and the bitternesse of their end and reward, with the plausiblenesse of their iollity, when they are in their flower, and their slipperinesse, when they are at the

A similitude. best. Therefore as in a picture such as will throughly view it, take not some note of the knee, or foote, or any one part of it, but the whole; for otherwise

Note. they should see nothing to any purpose: so view wee the whole course of Gods dealing with the wicked, as well the ending, as the beginning, and his proceeding with them, and thereby our hastinesse in desiring their dainties, will be abated full soone, and our opinion changed; as *Dauids* also was in iudging the bad to be happie, after that he had better considered their end. Lay we also sure hold on this, that as the time and terme of the wicked is stinted and appointed: so say we of the Lords dealing with our selues, *Yet*

Heb. 10.37. *a little while, and he that commeth, will come and not tarrie*, to bring our full redemption.

Doct. 2. Furthermore, we see here, in that *Abimelech* had his deaths wound, and after was slaine; that he had not his will on the people of Thebez, as he had on the other: but as he suffered him to destroy the men of Shechem, which fled to the Hold of their God Baal-Berith, so yet he saued the men of Thebez and their wiues, who betooke themselues to the Tower that was therein for shelter. Wherein we may note, that God doth oft times plague them whose

whose iniquity is manifest, as the sinne of these men of Shechem was, when other who haue not sinned in the like manner, though they be not (yet) religious, are spared and borne with, as these men of Thebez were. The reason is: the sinne of the one sort is manifest and grieuous, and cannot be hid and crieth for vengeance: the other, either through ignorance, or for that they haue not so wittingly or grossely offended, are borne with, that they may come to repentance. And yet this is no excuse to them, who liue in the light of the Gospell, and haue knowledge, if they liue and abide vnrepentant, though they be not grosse offenders. Neither on the other side haue they any cause to flatter themselues, whose sinnes are notorious, though they be not by and by cut off. The vse of this doctrine is in this respect to incourage them, who doe but walke in the way of the vngodly, but stand not stiffely to maintaine their euill doings, that seeing God giueth them time to repent, and beareth with them, they should not harden their hearts, but take all occasions to turne vnto him. And for such as are not fit to heare this doctrine, but goe forward in euill, they may euer feare, that Gods vengeance is comming. Now he being brought to bee past all hope of life by the blow the woman gaue him, we see, that hee who sought such glory as to be made King, yea and obtained it also, though most vniustly; euen he did yet come Doct. vers. 54. to such shame and reproch, (as hee counted it) as to be slaine by a woman, and not so much as by the meanest man of warre. Neither did it serue *Abimelechs* turne any whit at all, that the last stroke was giuen him by a Page, hauing had his deadly wound by the woman before: onely it bewraied his pride, which encreased the shamefulnesse of his foile. And yet for him to be slaine by a Page, was it such an honour to a great King so valiant and victorious, as *Abimelech* now thought himselfe, being in the top of his hopes, and hauing brought vnder his enemies? Therefore where God will set his brand of shame vpon a man, it is but folly for him to striue against him, or to elude him. It was as confidently giuen out that *Abimelech* was slaine by the hand of a woman, as that *Sisera* was dispatcht by *Iael*: as for the Page, hee slew (as we may say) a dead man in a mockery. If this verifie not the saying, [*God resisteth the proud*,] what doth? When men that haue carried thẽselues 1. Pet. 5. 5. aloft, and borne their heads on high, as the tall Cedars, being terrors to their inferiors, especially of the more religious sort, are thus brought to shame, as he was, is it not notable to see them as much abased in their death below the meanest, as they aduanced themselues aboue the greatest before? It is re- Note. ported of a Pope that he entred in like a Fox, ruled like a Lion, and died like a Dogge: if he had also been buried as that proud *Iehoiakim* or *Iezabel* like an Ier. 22. 19. Asse, what could haue been added to his shame? and yet a liuing Lion, to 2. King. 9. 37. be made a dead dogge is basenesse enough. Therefore we may clearely see by this that the seeking of glory, as *Salomon* saith, is no glory, but the glory of Prou. 25. 27. such is their shame. For although for a time it may hold and last, yet in a short time it shall vanish and end with reproch, whatsoeuer else goe with it. And so it is generally in all pride and vaineglory, as I noted out of *Gaals* example before, it shall end with shame; and contrarily, the humble and lowly in mind shall be exalted. For there can not one tittle of Gods word fall to 1. Pet. 5. the ground, but it must be verified, to the comfort of the one, and the iust rewarding of the other.

Doct.2.in vers.54. In this verse let vs further see (for the Lord would not giue him the honor to be slaine in warre) what he did, when he had his deaths wound: doth he crie for mercy? was that (as it ought to haue been) thought vpon? And yet the most past grace will lightly desire, that he may haue three words before he die, for then (though it be to small purpose) he thinks to aske mercy: but the glory that this monster had hunted after in his life-time, that was all that hee regarded, euen now at his wofull end, as his words testifie, to wit, That it might not be said, that a woman slew him, declaring thereby, that he more feared infamy then damnation. The multitude of desperate wretches that die in all ages with as little hope of saluation, as hee did, maketh it lesse to be considered and bewailed: but what is more fearefull then to thinke, a man should go to hell so apparantly, and (as it were) visibly?

Where wee are to obserue, that such as mens thoughts and affections are in their life time, such they bee commonly at their death. They loued not Psalm.109.17. Note. blessing, saith the Prophet, and therefore it is farre from them in their need: Psalm.109.17. so it is said elsewhere, they sought not after God, neither desired acquaintance with his waies, while they liued, and therfore God ordinarily suffereth Prou.1.24. them not to begin to doe it at their end. They remembred not their maker in the daies of their youth, neither shall they haue grace to doe it at their Eccles.11.1. death: but as they are mercilesse, so God iustly recompenceth them with iudgement without mercy, in their latter yeeres. And the like we reade of *Saul*. But yet for all this is one of a thousand (thinke we) of such as he was perswaded to repentance in the time of his iolitie? nay doth not one follow anothers course to condemnation daily, and from age to age?

And such as haue their libertie to aske three words before they die, how vse they it? what come they to? but euen to worse then nothing? Euen as *Abimelechs* few words did, [*Let it not be said, that a woman slew me.*] And so 1.Sam.31.4. their three words are vsed, as *Saul* vsed his at his death: [*Draw out thy sword, and thrust me through.*] And as that wicked man mentioned in the booke of Monuments, who when he was haled violently on a bridge by his Horse into the riuer, being put in minde of his three words, he said thus: Horse and man to the diuell. A notorious adulterer there was a few yeeres agone, who also had poysoned many youthes by his vncleane conuersation, and lewd example, and tongue: he liued till he was threescore yeere old, to resemble him to the sinner whom *Salomon* speakes of, Eccles.7. neuer could hee bee brought to sauour or taste either preaching or praying, which yet hee saw many zealously did round about him: he might haue spend fiftie pound land by the yeere by his marriage; but being visited by God, in a strange manner, and losing his maintenance by the death of his wife, his bodie sore plagued with paine, and diseases, when he lay like a lazer in a barne, (for thither he was thrust, through pouertie, and there he died) now to come to the point, for the which I alleaged this example, hee being moued by such as came to him, when they saw in what miserie hee lay, to call vpon God; hee answered with fearefull oathes: Is this a time to pray? The which seeing he was neuer acquainted with in all his life, (wee see) hee was farre off from it, shunned and lothed it at his death, by Gods righteous iudgement.

And as wee haue heard that it is commonly so with the vilest persons at their death, as it hath been in their life; so it were good wisedome for

vs to seeke the Lord while he may be found, in the daies of our youth, lest if Eccles.12.1.
we should not goe about it till death, it should not bee a sound turning to God, but in mood and passion, by violence and in feare onely gone about: and who knoweth not that late repentance is dangerous? And so let them reioyce and blesse God, who haue made the Lord chiefe with them in their young yeeres, and haue counted his seruice perfit freedome, such shall not neede to feare that God will frowne vpon them, and forsake them in their age, or at their death, but (as many haue done) shall reioyce most for this, that they made the Gospell their solace in their life time, and Gods fauour their portion and ioy, and would not for all the riches of the vngodly, haue done otherwise: for so they should haue been then vtterly to seeke how to be saued. Oh one sweete fruite of a godly life (beside many other enioyed before) is a most Christian and comfortable death: so saith the Psalmist; Marke the end of the righteous, and ye shall see that the end of such a man Psal.37.37.
is peace. As for *Abimelechs* Page, he was as he had been trained by him, one fit to serue him onely in euill. Like master, like man; such an one, as hath many followers, of which sort of hangbies few vnder such masters, as themselues be, few of them are (I say) found to come to good. But both of them, desperate, rash, murtherous, and fraught with such sinnes as commonly accompanie these. Yea, and yet such hold vp their heads in the world, for whom, who seeth not but that the prison is fitter, where they may be kept from doing mischiefe, rather then to commit many lewd parts at libertie abroad. But seeing such are past admonition taking, let thẽ that are teachable, learne to take such seruants to be neere at hand to them, who may in danger giue aduice to them, if need be, as *Naamans* seruants did, to the preseruing of 2.King 5.13.
his health, rather then to be as too many are, that is to say, furtherers of their vtter vndoing or death. And such as deserue well (as *Ioshuas*, and the seruants of *Cornelius* were) let them (I say) be well incouraged and rewarded, which are to be reioyced in, of their masters, when the other being intertained but to their owne, and their masters vndoing, or great detriment, shall load both themselues and them with their bellies full of shame and sorrow. Of this argument I spare to speake more heere, being as much (and a great deale more) as is like to be regarded, of such as I speake of.

Thus we haue seene the wofull end of this cursed *Abimelech*, and of the Verse 55.
wicked men of Shechem, who had been the furtherers of him to the mischiefe that he wrought. And after these troublers of the land were taken away, there was peace, and euery man left off from the worke that *Abimelech* had drawne him to, and went home to his owne place: where first it may be seene, what stirre, disquiet, and trouble one vile person may make in the Church or Common-wealth, the Lord so punishing the peoples sinne, as partly I noted before in this chapter. *Absolon* was but one man, but how did he disquiet his father and the whole land? Likewise *Sheba* the sonne of *Bicry* that raised a new commotion against *Dauid:* and so the Prophet *Elias* told *Ahab* that he troubled all Israel. And so I may say of *Achan*, and of *Kora*, and of many other: euery of these was but one in his attempts: but each of these, what plagues and mischiefe wrought they by their seuerall sinnes, though most of thẽ priuate persons, to the whole state of the Church and Common-wealth of Israel? If wee compare the sinnes of the whole

body with the ſinnes of a few, wee ſhall finde that the ſorrow which few brought vpon the whole companie, came little ſhort of the plagues which God inflicted vpon the whole, when all prouoked him. Although alas, what ſpeake I of particular actions? *Adam* his ſinne firſt brought a feareful confuſion into the whole creation? What wonder then if this contagion and peſtilence hath euer ſince, and ſtill doth cauſe the like diſorder in the places where it rangeth? whoſe deformitie (yet) and the miſchiefe that it workes, though we ſee as it were with our eyes, who (almoſt) is not bewitched with the painted beautie thereof?

But to returne: when *Achan, Sheba, Abſolon* were taken away, behold all was whiſt againe, and a great calme there was after ſo horrible tempeſts. The whole Church is as a ſhip; in which if there be one *Ionah*, what tumult makes he? but caſt him out, and the danger is ouer. And as this is true of great ſinners and publike offenders: ſo it is true of more inferiour and priuate perſons: as of Magiſtrates in their precincts, Headborowes in townes, Maſters and parents in families ſeeing (but for the badnes of ſuch) the reſt ſhould be in peace.

Doct. 2. And further, by the rooting out of *Abimelech*, let vs confeſſe it to bee a great benefit, when ſuch authors of miſchiefe, and workers of iniquitie bee taken away: and therefore giue all our endeuour for the maintenance of peace, and to make holy and right vſe of it, while we enioy it. For as wee may ſee by theſe, that ſought peace after the death of *Abimelech*, euen ſo the moſt that are vſed to trouble other, in time waxe wearie of it.

Verſ. 56. 57. In theſe two verſes is the ſhutting vp the whole chapter: *Iothams* prophecie is verified, and Gods iudgement thereby declared, how hee rewardeth iniquitie. Of which this I ſay briefly, ſeeing in ſome ſort it hath been tou-
Doct. ched already, that they who take ill matters and bad in hand, ſhall haue ſmal cauſe to reioyce thereof in the end. For their ſinne will finde them out, when they thinke leaſt of it. And it is moſt like alſo, that looke what way they haue ſinned, euen the ſame way their ſinne may be puniſhed, as here it was, Stone for ſtone. *Abimelech* killed his brethren vpon a ſtone: and he is killed by a weake woman moſt vnlikely with a ſtone. The like wee haue heard of *Adonibezek*, and of *Oreb* and *Zeeb*, who tooke their death where they wrought miſchiefe.

Matth. 7. 2. Oh how doth God recompence into their boſome in full meaſure heaped vp and running ouer, vnto ſuch? The which they will not foreſee and ſo preuent, vntill they ſmart, and be paſt recouerie. If this cannot moue any of the like ſort, to take warning by ſuch watch-words, in time to hate their bad courſe, and that with deteſtation at leaſt, let thoſe that haue ſhunned and declined from ſuch euill waies, reioyce with thankſgiuing, and that vnfained, for that they haue been preſerued from them, and that they haue choſen the good way to walke in it, howſoeuer they haue had many prouocations vnto the contrary.

2 And laſt of al, we may ſee here that as God reuenged the innocent blood of *Gedeons* ſonnes, ſo God will take part with ſuch innocents. Hurt them not therefore, for the time will come when thou ſhalt pay deare for thy ſo doing: of which point looke more in the former part of the hiſtorie.

The end of the ninth Chapter.

THE

THE SIXTIE ONE SERMON ON THE TENTH CHAPTER OF THE BOOKE OF IVDGES.

Verſ.1. *After Abimelech, there aroſe to deliuer Iſrael, Tola the ſonne of Puah,*
the ſonne of Dodo, a man of Iſſachar, and he dwelt in Shamir in mount Ephraim.
2. *And he iudged Iſrael three and twentie yeeres, and died, and was buried in*
Shamir.
3. *And after him aroſe Iair a Gileadite, and iudged Iſrael twentie and two*
yeeres.
4. *And he had thirtie ſonnes that rode on thirtie aſſe colts, and they had thirtie*
cities, which are called Hauoth-Iair vnto this day, which are in the land of Gilead.
5. *And Iair died, and was buried in Kamon.*

THE ſumme of this Chapter is briefly this; that the children of Iſrael hauing enioyed peace and libertie for a time vnder *Tola* and *Iair*; fell againe afterward to Idolatrie. Whereupon the Lord alſo did againe deliuer them into the hands of their enemies: wherfore they calling vpon God, were at the firſt ſharply reproued: but afterward truly repenting, they obtained fauour with God, and were releaſed of their ſinnes, as before time. By occaſion whereof, entrance is made into the ſtorie of their deliuerance in the chapter following. The parts of it are three: The firſt containeth the time of their peace, to verſe the ſixth: The ſecond, a new defection and reuolt of the people from God, to verſe the 17. The third mentioneth the preparation that the Ammorites made againſt the children of Iſrael, and the peoples and Princes meeting and comming together to conſult and agree how to goe againſt them; and this is to the end of the Chapter. *The ſumme of the Chapter.* *The parts 3.*

The firſt part of the Chapter.

GOd raiſed vp theſe two Iudges, to wit, *Tola* and *Iair*, after the former, to keepe the people in the true worſhip of God, and in outward peace. Here to ſpeake ſomewhat in this firſt part, of both theſe two Iudges of Iſrael ioyntly together, and afterward, ſomewhat ſeuerally; this is to be noted of the former, that after the ouerthrow of that curſed *Abimelech*, the people of Iſrael had a long time of peace in both their daies, that is, 45. yeers. Where note, that though God iuſtly puniſheth the ſins of mẽ, as he did theirs here, yet he doth ſtill remember his people, and regard them, ſending them peace againe afterwards, euen as after a ſtorme and tempeſt commeth faire weather: and he hath ſaid, that the rod of the wicked he will not ſuffer to lie al- *Doct. out of verſ.1.2.3.*

Psal.125.3. Exod.34.7. waies on the lot of the righteous; God will not keepe his anger for euer toward them. It is his great fauour to his, that they who are exceeding bad, liue not very long, and that he vpholdeth his owne people many waies. In deed when God is prouoked, ſome muſt & ſhall ſuffer, as here by the plague many thouſands in citie and countrey haue been ſwept away of late, who if they haue been readie for their departure, and haue repented, it is well; they haue gone vnder Gods hand in their ſufferings the better. And ſo let ſuch as are preſerued aliue, when others are taken away, turne to the Lord with al feruencie and ſpeed, that ſo they may teſtifie that they may make their profit of Gods ſparing their liues, and that they may ſo procure the continuance of peace and the Goſpell to their poſteritie. Let Gods people (I ſay) do this, though other haue no eares to heare good inſtruction: and be well aſſured, that though carnall reaſon ſee no ſuch thing, God will doe much at the earneſt ſuite of his; yea though they be but few. As we ſee he would not haue deſtroyed Sodome, if there had been but tenne righteous perſons found Matth.24.12. there. But (alas) through the abundance of iniquitie the loue of many decaieth, and few are wiſe to vſe their outward peace, or health, or other benefits of God to their good. And as for the moſt, (which is not to be wondred at) they vtterly reiect the things which concerne their peace for euer. As in the daies of *Noe*, the people (liuing in darkneſſe) ate and drunke, married and gaue in marriage, euen as they doe in theſe latter daies of the ſonne of man, before he come in his glorie; of whom ſome ſhall in their aduerſitie, when he ſhall awake them, deſire but to ſee one good day, and it ſhall be denied them. They neither labour to keepe outward peace each with other (which were no hard matter, while the common enemie is held vnder, and that there be peace in the land) nor yet betwixt God and themſelues, but nouriſh vile luſts (the fruite of Sodome) in themſelues, through fulnes of bread Note. and abundance of wealth, the daughters of peace. But the worſt is, that theſe fierie darts of mens luſts are throwne at God himſelfe (who hath gran- Act.9.31. ted vs theſe daies of peace to a farre other end, as Act.9.) and at his ſeruants who are the beſt pledges of our peace. Is this the recompence (ſaith *Moſes* in Deut.32.6. Deut.32) which ye make the Lord, for your outward peace and ſpirituall libertie? And iuſtly may it be demanded of vs: Is this the thanke God hath at your hands for your peace and freedome from Egypt and Canaan? Conſider therefore that in our thus warring againſt, we fight againſt our ſoules, 1.Pet.2.10. as the Apoſtle *Peter* ſaith: and againe, by this, that we ſerue not God purely in this our proſperitie, the diuell himſelfe (a great word to ſpeake) is deceiued in vs, who tooke it for granted long agoe, as hee ſaw reaſon for it, that Iob 1.10. when a man is hedged in with bleſſings, (and eſpecially this ſtrong hedge of a publique peace) he would ſerue God without queſtion. Indeede hee requireth a further matter of vs, euen that wee ſerue him in time of affliction alſo: but is this likely, when wee doe it not in peace? But of this matter I ſpare to adde any more heere, hauing vttered my minde of it before in the fifth chapter and elſewhere.

Of the firſt three verſes ſtill. Theſe two, *Tola*, and *Iair*, are not ſaid here to haue riſen vp to iudge Iſrael as intruding themſelues, but as following Gods appointment, who raiſed them vp as good gouernours to ſaue and deliuer his people out of their enemies hands, ſo was not that vſurper *Abimelech*, but a waſter and a ſpoiler.

So

So are they whom God sendeth in mercie to rule, nurcing fathers, and such as teach, be full of loue and compassion to the people; for he graceth them whom hee counteth faithfull, and putteth in his seruice euen to that purpose. 1.Tim.1.12.

Somewhat I haue said before touching Gods calling and the manner of it, yet by this occasion I will adde somewhat. God in a generall prouidence *Doct.2.* of permission may be said to raise al that rise vp in place of gouernment and authoritie. By premission, when he resisteth not them who raise vp themselues vnlawfully, as *Abimelech.* In which respect the Lord tolerateth many (in his secret will) to doe many things against his reuealed will; he permitteth, I say, not causeth them, for then one will should be contrarie to another. Secondly, he actually blesseth many, and raiseth them outwardly himselfe, (though their rising be to no purpose) as *Ieroboam.* Thirdly, he raiseth vp and blesseth other; (their attempts being lawfull, and not indirectly vndertaken, but according to his will) whereas he doth onely trie the other, by raising them, whether they will raise and aduance him or no, and set him vp as chiefe, and procure the like from others: so, if they forget him, as *Ieroboboam* and *Saul*, that then hee may honour himselfe vpon them, when hee Exod.14.17. could get no honour by them.

This the holy Ghost expresseth liuely in *Pharaoh*, Rom.9. But the last and most speciall kinde of raising is, when beside common gifts, the Lord raiseth a man, as well vp to the life of grace and holinesse, as inhaunseth him in the world, adorning him with more rare gifts, as meekenesse, wisedome, faith, holy courage, zeale, and the fruites of true loue to his Church and Gods glorie. And these onely may be said most properly to haue been raised by God, and neither by men, nor themselues, and therefore to be Gods fauourites indeede. There are many that rise in the world, who grow further from goodnesse: I speake of such as are apparantly raised, and some of them from the dunghill to honour, learning, wealth; but they were in more hope to Godward when they were lowest in the world: since, they waxed proud, idle, scornefull, their hearts rising against God and his seruants; and to euill ends abusing the steps and degrees of honour and estate, by which God hath raised them, thereby prouoking the Lord to pull them downe to their former ebbe, euen the lowest staier of shame. According to that of *Samuel* to *Eli* vttered from God; Those that despise me, I will set nought 1.Sam.2.30. by, but honour them that honour me. This rule will not be vnmeete to try our rising by, for euen Heathens saw somewhat, when they could say; No good man waxeth suddenly rich. And as torrents, and standing waters bewray some sudden and great tempests and raine more then vsuall: so mens sudden risings bewray the immoderatnes of their affections, exceeding the measure of iustice and religion. And let this serue to quiet them whom God lifteth not vp to great place, if hee haue raised them vp with his Christ from death to the life of grace, and quickned them by faith to the liuely hope of glorie.

But I proceede to note something of these two Iudges seuerally out of the verses following.

To begin with *Iair*, hee was of the halfe Tribe of *Manasseh* a Giliadite, *The summe of the third, fourth and fifth verses.* hauing many sonnes, seeing they had many wiues in those daies: his sonnes rode, in token of their greatnesse; and euery one of them was a Ruler ouer a Citie, and therefore their father must needs be a man of great Nobilitie. Now to giue some light into this, it is said in the booke of Numbers, that

Numb. 32.40. & Deut. 3.14. one *Iair* tooke many Cities of the Canaanites, and they were called the Cities of *Iair*: not that I say, that the man who is here mentioned of that name was he, seeing there were 300. yeeres betwixt them both, but being both of one place, there is little doubt, but that the heere mentioned, came of the family of the other, and so those Cities (it is most like) fell and came vnto him.

Doct. 3. out of the 3. first verses. Now from hence we learne, that God choosing out of one Tribe, as well as another, as by those that haue been mentioned before in this story, and these here, may appeare, to wit, *Tola* of *Issachar*, a poore Tribe, and *Iair* of *Manasseh* very rich: by this, I say, we may see that he would giue to none of them any cause to complaine, no not the meanest, (as they might otherwise (it is like enough) haue taken occasion to doe) that he had not chosen out of one Tribe as well as out of another, the deliuerer and Captaine ouer the people. Teaching vs by his example to be without partialitie in our dealings, and iniurious to none; which is a singular vertue, and shewed by *Salomon*, as a companion of his wisdome, in deciding the cause betwixt the

1. King. 3.27. two harlots, he leaned to neither, but dealt indifferently with both.

And such indifferency we should shew in our actions through our whole course, that wee might not be iustly challenged for the contrary, but to practise equality in comparisons and censures, and in one or other our dealings, we shewing good reason if we at any time do otherwise, not doing as some, whose office being to professe the punishing of wicked persons, will yet for fauour on the one side, or spite and malice on the other, not only be partiall, but also extenuate the fault of the guiltie partie, and charge the innocent and honest to be in greater offence, then the guiltie, which is the peruerting

Prou. 17.14. of iustice, and the direct way to nourish and multiplie iniquity, and this some will doe the rather, if the innocent partie be zealous of the Gospell.

When the Lord sent Manna from heauen to feed his people, he made a law against mens greedy snatching it vp one from another, prouiding that he that gathered more then his fellow, should part with the ouer-plus, to make the portion of the other equall, so that none could complaine that he was neglected in that heauenly dole. Men of meane estate murmur that this abundance of the earth is so vnequally diuided by God, that some haue al, some neuer a whit. But so to doe in that case is more equalitie, then if all had alike, for a difference there must euer bee in estates, some rich, some

Iames 2.5. poore. But who seeth not (euen in this) Gods indifferencie? *Know ye not brethren* (saith *Iames*) *that God hath called the poore of this world to be rich in faith and good works?* Meaning that not many rich are vouchsafed this honour: and therefore in that the poore are betrusted with the Gospel, which

Matth. 11.5. is the Treasure and Manna of heauen, and receiue it willingly, Matth. 11. whereas the rich haue other matters to busie themselues about, are they neglected through partialitie thinke we? But if any of low degree, want his part in the best things also, he may thanke himselfe for his abasement: who will pity him who shortens himselfe of his allowance? there would (doubtlesse) be lesse complaining among the better sort of people; (as for the vnruly

ruly and idle,they ſeeke their owne ſorrow) if men wee ſo prouided for, as God allotteth to them : for neither ſhould many men become poore through their leaudneſſe, and they that otherwiſe muſt of neceſſitie be ſo, ſhould both comfort themſelues in God, and be the better regarded by others through a larger contribution of his beſtowed vpon them.

Therefore againe I ſay, let this ſeemely vertue find fauour with them, whom the entertainement of it might much aduantage. Such as haue the rating of inferiors for publike duties, giue great cauſe of complaining, by their partialitie, through friendſhip or diſlike : yea and ſcape themſelues (proportion being obſerued) more eaſily then the meane ſort of people. Which is groſſe,that men will ſeeke for the higheſt place of countenance and honor aboue others, but in matter of burden and charge,put the baſeſt vnderling before themſelues.

More particularly,in that the Lord chooſeth out of the poore and baſe Tribe of *Iſhaker*,this *Tola*,to Iudge Iſrael,it was to teach vs the truth of that prouerb,that a mans gift makes him to ſit among the mighty,and aduanceth the baſe and the meane,who ought not to be deſpiſed for want of wealth,if God hath giuen them gifts. How little this truth hath been regarded alwaies, *Salomon* declareth,who ſaith what he had obſerued,that a poore and wiſe man deliuered a citie ſore aſſaulted by the mightie, and that he did by his wiſdome ; but none remembred this poore man. And in another place he ſaith,There is an euill that I haue ſeene vnder the Sun, that folly is ſet in great excellency,and the rich in wiſdome and vertue ſet in the low place, I haue ſeene ſeruants on horſes,& princes walking as ſeruants on the ground.

Doct.particularly out of verſe 1.

Eccleſ.9.15.

Eccleſ.10.6.7.

This, ſeeing hee calleth an euill, hee well inſtructeth the children of wiſedome,to iuſtifie her whereſoeuer ſhee bee found, howſoeuer ſhee bee iuſtled and oppoſed by the carnall. And as the Queene of the South ſaid to *Salomon*, Happy are thy ſeruants that attend on thee, and who may heare thy wiſedome : ſo becauſe a greater then *Salomon* is heere, wee ſhould count it our felicitie to heare him,and count their feet beautiful that bring glad tidings. And to receiue ſuch,as men of God,and as his Prophets, what meane ſhew ſoeuer they make in our eies,and to commune with them when they are dead,while we reade their holy works,when we cannot conuerſe with their perſons,being taken away from vs out of this life. Thus *Dauid* out of a mean family,and *Saul* alſo (though deſtitute of grace) were excellently gifted with courage for warre, and gouernment in peace, ſo that few of the nobleſt (doubtleſſe) might compare with them. So that the meanelier they were deſcended, the more admirable they were in themſelues, not being beholding to any predeceſſors for the ſpirit and good parts that were in them : but laid the foundation of Nobilitie to their poſteritie. Therefore ſo long as the baſe by birth, maintaine worthily the places of high office and honour whereunto their excellent gifts haue lawfully aduanced them : not degenerating by pride, crueltie, and couetouſneſſe, (the common companions of men bred meanely, when they are got aloft) I ſay,when ſuch are not regarded ; it is a great contempt not of them onely, but of God in them, (for hee that deſpiſeth the poore,deſpiſeth his Maker, and much more, hee that reprocheth them in authoritie) to call them vpſtarts,or to defame them by their baſe blood,that ſo their more eminent ver-

1.King.10.8.

Rom.10.15.

Prou.17.5.

ties may be blemished. A common disease among the factious, and flattering followers of great and vicious persons, to staine the honour of such as are more truly noble then they, in vertue and wisdome, by this; that they are but men of yesterday, and cannot shew the Armes, which their patrons can. But whether is it better (as hee in the history answered) to raise vp a new, or to bury the old Gentrie and Nobilitie? Of this the lesse, because I haue said somewhat in the two points before not impertinent hereto.

Verse 3.4. Now as we haue heard that God chose out of *Isshaker* a poore Tribe, *Tola* to Iudge Israel; so also, we see here that he chooseth the Noble to bee Gouernours, as he did this *Iair* here, who for his wealth, was able to giue a City to euery of his thirtie sonnes. To teach vs that Nobilitie is no let to the gouerning of the common-wealth, but the honourable and mightie hauing examples of their ancestors to prouoke them to vertue, and many other helpes and complements to the well discharging thereof, they may be seene in many respects to be the fittest: this being added, if they bee not lifted vp with insolency and high conceit of themselues, which they haue no cause to do, if they consider that they came of nothing, and are but wormes meat, and also, if they would weigh their mutable state, and how full of lamentables changes their liues be. And to say the truth, it is an vtter shame for vs, that when God hath done much for vs, we should be found vnfaithfull. Neither is high place any greater impediment to priuate godlinesse, then publike gouernment. Although if euery man might tell his owne tale, there is none so poore, nor any so rich, but will alleage somewhat, why they should not be tied to dutie precise, but liue as they thinke good, and bee released from this burden, as they count it: whereby, what doe they but lay stumbling blocks in their owne way. Therefore wee may boldly giue it foorth, as a rule in Christian practise, it is a miserable and vnlawfull estate of life, which cannot stand with the daily and carefull practise of Christianity. Somewhat (I deny not) must be yeelded to the occasions and vnseparable businesse, which attend vpon greatnesse: but yet so farre foorth onely, as men defalke and detract nothing from the substance of that high and great due, which the greatest owe to a greater then themselues. But yet if men dare goe thus farre, they shall find, that God wil not giue his honour to another; but rather his iealousie wil breake out against them like fire, that maintaine their honour by treading his vnderfoot, Psalme 2.

Doct. oue of verse 3. and 4.

Psalme 2.9.

Vers. 2.5. This be said of those things which were seuerall in these two Kings, and which they did in their life; now of that which was common to them both, I meane their death. For so it is said of both, that they died, and that was, when their dutie, each for his time, was discharged in procuring and maintaining Gods true worship, and outward peace to their countrie a long season: the they gaue place, and were gathered to their fathers, & their bodies were laid in the earth, in hope of the resurrection. To teach vs, that all of vs, are here to doe our duties in our callings, to serue God therein: who hath giuen and committed to our trust talents, with a charge to occupie them till he come, and allowes none of vs to bury them in the earth, but straightly forbids it, to wit, to bee idle, and to suffer our gifts to rust in vs, and to this end, we inioy euery man his proper gifts. The Lord hath set vs our habitations, and stinted our time of dwelling in them, with commandement, that

Doct. out of vers. 2. and 5. Luke 19.

we

we ſhould not be idle nor vnprofitable in the knowledge of our Lord Ieſus, Act.17.26.
nor in our particular calling, but to attend thereunto, for profitable vſes to
our ſelues and others : and hath for that purpoſe, appointed that we ſhould 2.Pet.1.8.
haue comfortable fruite thereof in all neceſſarie things of this life, to incourage vs to our duties, that ſo we might be none of the refuſe, and idle hang-byes in the world : and in both our generall and particular calling to ſerue God for conſcience ſake and with comfort. To this end I ſay, God hath ſet vs here, alwaies to haue our eye vpon our departure, and with good father *Barzillai* to prouide for our graue. 2.Sam.19.37.

2
And when wee haue thus diſcharged our ſelues, and the Lord ſhall giue vs warning by ſickneſſe, paine, diſeaſe of our end to bee at hand, or call vs home with ſmall warning, wee ſhould be readie for his comming, to yeeld Note.
our ſoules into his hands, and our bodies to the graue for a ſeaſon, in hope of receiuing them againe : which ſhall be no hard matter for vs to doe, who haue, as ſtrangers here, prepared for it before, as wee haue learned to doe. Neither ſhould we looke or deſire to haue any more abode or continuance here, but giue ouer our ſelues in peace, and willingly commend our ſelues vnto the Lords ſafe keeping, as I haue ſaid. And therfore in the meane time we ſhould ſoberly vſe all the tranſitorie helps of this life ; as wealth, friends, wife, and our life it ſelfe, ſo that they may not be clogs with their deceiuable ſhew, to hold vs from farre better things. And in the meane while take the Note.
beſt vſe of them to profitable ends, and doe the good that wee may doe by the helpe of them, ſeeing in the graue there is no ſuch thing to bee looked for. And ſo the remembrance of the time well paſſed, ſhall be moſt comfortable : but as for thoſe that are calling in for their cheare and merry making in this world, otherwiſe then they are ſure they ſhall be able well to giue their reckoning for it hereafter, ſuch can neither poſſibly dye well, nor willingly, vnleſſe they bee deſperate. To the which purpoſe I haue ſpoken elſewhere, as the diligent reader ſhall finde. Eccleſ.9.10.

The ſecond part of the Chapter.

Verſ.6. *And the children of Iſrael wrought wickedneſſe againe in the ſight of the Lord, and ſerued Baalim and Aſhtoroth, and the gods of Aram, and the gods of Zidon, and the gods of Moab, and the gods of the children of Ammon, and the gods of the Philiſtims, and forſooke the Lord, and ſerued not him.*

7. *Therefore the wrath of the Lord was kindled againſt Iſrael, and he ſold them into the hands of the Philiſtims, and into the hands of the children of Ammon :*

8. *Who from that yeere vexed and oppreſſed the children of Iſrael eighteene yeeres, euen all the children of Iſrael that were beyond Iorden in the land of the Ammorites which is in Gilead.*

9. *Moreouer, the children of Ammon went ouer Iorden to fight againſt Iudah, and againſt Beniamin, and againſt the houſe of Ephraim : ſo that Iſrael was ſore tormented.*

10. *Then the children of Iſrael cried vnto the Lord, ſaying, Wee haue ſinned againſt thee, euen becauſe wee haue forſaken our owne God, and haue ſerued Baalim.*

Now

The scase of these verses.

NOw followeth a new reuolt of the people of Israel, and this is handled to the 17. verse, wherein the things to bee considered are these: to wit, a double repairing and returning by them to God, when hee afflicted them by their enemies for their sin in forsaking him. In their first seeking to him, they had the repulse, for their repentance was not found. In the second, God deliuered them, they seeking to him in repentance. In the former note these foure things: First their sinne, which was a ioyning to the nations among whom they dwelt, and this in the sixth verse. The second is Gods punishing them euen by those, whom they ioyned with in Idolatrie: which is shewed in the next three verses. The third point is their crying to God: and lastly, the fruite thereof, in the tenth verse, and so forward. The fruite was diuers: for first God denied to deliuer them, to the fifteenth verse. But at the second crying of the people to God, hee deliuered them: which is set downe in the next two verses vnto the seuenteenth. Now let these things be looked into more particularly. To returne therefore to the sixth verse, and to begin with the peoples sinne, it is said, after the death of these two Iudges, in whose daies they had enioyed peace fiue and fortie yeeres, that the people fell againe to prouoke God, as wee haue heard their fathers did. And how? by committing Idolatrie after the manner of the seuen nations, that are here mentioned. For both that was liking to the flesh, and besides, they thought those nations that did so, liued in more abundance, and in more pleasure, then themselues did; for many delights to tickle the flesh forward they adioyned to their false worship, to draw away their hearts from seruing the true God aright, whom, it is said here, that they forsooke. Thus much for the summe of this verse, and therein of their sinne. And here are diuers things to be considered.

The opening of verse 6. more particularly.

Doct vers. 6.

First it teacheth, that we should not greatly marueile, that so many in this our age giue themselues to Popish religion, seeing Idolatrie hath in most ages been so common: by reason that it hath so many player-like toyes and bables of sights to bleare the eye, and sonets to deceiue the eare, that it maketh them thinke they be in a peece of paradise, while they embrace and are made drunke with such fond conceits, when indeed they be thereby caried (as it were) fast asleepe to hell. There is nothing that moueth or delighteth them in all the word of God, rightly vnderstood, but only blind deuotion in their false religion, wherein they haue been nuzled vp, and then a fond and fantasticall conceit, that they shall goe to heauen thereby. As for the authoritie and warrant of their Masse, and other trumperie; in the beginning of the world, nay in our Sauiour Christs time, and many hundred yeeres after, there was no shred nor ragge of it vsed or knowne, especially to any such end, whereas the true seruing of God was alwaies (as now it is) euen from the beginning.

Heb. 11. the whole.

And how prone people are to worship God with ease, (for so farre they like, whether it be sound and true, or counterfeit) it may be seene not onely in Poperie, which is coyned for the purpose to deceiue the simple, with strong delusions, but also in our religion, which for the outward manner of it is holy, pure and good, and consisteth in hearing, prayer, and the vse of the Sacraments for the substance thereof. And yet many of them who allow it,

as

as the true manner of worſhipping God, what doe they (for the moſt part) but draw neere to God with their bodies, but their hearts are farre from him? As if they would ſay, they would gladly goe to heauen, but they would haue an eaſie way thither; but to ſerue God in ſpirit and truth, which is the direct way thither, they cannot bend themſelues thereto: whereas there is as great delight in the worſhipping of God aright, and that by the Lords allowance and promiſe, (which in the two former kindes; of popiſh, and the other, of only outward worſhip are wanting) as great delight, (I ſay) and as ſound in true performing it, ſo farre as fraile fleſh may attaine to, as there is reward promiſed thereto, which is vnutterable. Ioh 4.24. Pſal.84.1. Pſal 19.11.

In this verſe alſo may bee ſeene, what fruite this people yeelded to the Lord of their long enioyed peace, euen as wee haue ſeene their fathers did, and that was, how they fell to laſciuiouſnes, and forgetting of God: a ſufficient watch-word whereof they had giuen them before by *Moſes*. Now for the laying out of this ſinne both in them and our ſelues, how fearefull and great it is, let vs onely conſider of it thus; Seeing this point hath been largely handled already, if the diſeaſed perſon pained with the ſtone or ſtrangury, or the famiſhed, and hee that is in penury, or the man that is in exile and baniſhment; if theſe (I ſay) might be ſet free from that which oppreſſeth them, what would they not readily offer, and couenant to doe, in the ſeruice of God? yea and that much more feruently then other men? Therefore how grieuous is their ſin, (let all men iudge) who may in health, in wealth, at eaſe, and in outward peace doe this, I meane, ſerue the Lord, which is the thing that he requireth of them, and yet they can by no means be brought to it? But this I leaue to be further conſidered, as euery one ſhal ſee cauſe. *Doct.*2. Deut.6.12. Note.

But more particularly, in that it is ſaid, they forſooke the Lord, it may be marueiled at, that they ſhould forſake him, whom they had loued and ſerued before. But by this we may ſee, what force there is in ſinne to beſot and make drunken, them who giue ouer themſelues thereto; be it whoredome, the loue of the world, or any other: For it is able to bereaue them of ſound reaſon, to turne away their delight from prayer, and all good practiſe, and to forget the ioy that they had in both, ſometimes; and yet to blindfold them ſo, that they ſhall not ſuſpect any danger to be toward them for al this, while they may merrily ſerue their humour therein. *Sampſon* and other went farre this way. And let the beſt of vs feare, leſt we be carried away of our luſts to loue and like where wee ought not, and tempt we not God, but let vs reſiſt the beginnings of euill: wee know little what may befall vs in time, if wee dare deale looſely and vnfaithfully with the Lord, and ſuffer our ſelues to be led away from our ſtedfaſtnes. This boldnes and careleſneſſe, if it thus be ſuffered to beare ſway in vs, may cauſe this ſcripture in time to be ſaid of and verified in vs, that we haue forſaken the Lord our ſtrength. And yet becauſe men are cunning to deceiue themſelues, hoping that as long as they embrace not another religion, they ſhall not become ſuch, nor iudged ſo hardly of, though they take vp their delight in ſins that pleaſe thē; I thought it not therefore amiſſe, to giue this caueat, that in vaine doe ſuch men worſhip God, though they draw neere to him with their bodies, while they ſuffer their hearts to goe another way: and it is a kinde of forſaking of God, *Doct.*3. Note.

though

though not in so high a degree as the other, and as in time they themselues are like to come vnto, and their labour is lost that they bestow in seruing God, while it is accompanied with such anoiance and vnsauourines, he vtterly abhorreth it. This phrase of forsaking God, is taken from wedlocke, when either partie renounceth interest and fellowship in the other, and departeth away: euen as the phrase of [selling them away] vsed in the next verse on Gods part, importeth the like action in the Lord, as iustly giuing ouer his part in them. As they had resigned their right in him, their husband, (who had married himselfe vnto them) vnto strange Idols: so the Lord put ouer his interest in them, vnto strange Idolaters, alienating himselfe from them, as the commoditie which is sold changeth the owner, and becomes the right of another man. Now then let not men thinke they may at their pleasure breake their couenant (as the knot of marriage) with God; thinking they may returne to him as they list, and when they list, (as *Sampson* to his companion, and the Leuite to his concubine) for neither will it be so easie for them to doe it, neither shall they finde God so ready in their hastie seekings after him, vpon each occasion to admit them.

And this is said of the peoples sinne, and by occasion thereof. Now we
Vers.7.8.9. haue heard of that, being the first point of the foure: in these three next verses is set down Gods displeasure conceiued against them for it. For when they had thus prouoked him by their sore transgressions, he prouoked them also, by that which did little like them: for hee stirred vp the Philistims and Ammonites against them, who vexed them sore for many yeeres. And this they did, not onely in the land of the Ammorites, beyond Iorden to the children of Israel that dwelt there, but they waxed more bold, and passed ouer Iorden & made warre with the tribe of Iuda, Beniamin, and Ephraim: so as they were not able to resist them. And what should wee say to all this? It must needs be granted, that this was an heauy bondage that they were vnder. But what remedie? If it had been any lesse, it would not haue moued nor wrought vpon them. They would not complaine, nor crie to God for a little. For if they had, they should haue been heard, and kept from so great extremities, that they should not haue vexed them.

Doct.vers.7.8. So that, to say no more of this, we may all see here, that when wee come vnder sore afflictions, which in a manner take heart from vs, and make our liues wearisome, we may thanke our selues for it: God vseth not to cast his punishments vpon men all at once, but by peece meale, and by degrees, and giueth warning of them for the most part, at least by his word alwaies: that
Prou.22.3. so (as wise men seeing the plague comming) they may preuent them; or else he laieth his hand more lightly vpon them, that they may at the first repaire to him, and intreate him to stay it. If it be otherwise, that he suddenly, and at once take away the righteous with the wicked, they shall haue no cause to complaine of that, for they shall rest in peace. If God remoue not his punishments, yet if they be reconciled to him, and liue obediently, hee will giue them greater grace of faith, hope, and patience, to beare the burthen more easily, and with farre greater contentment. All the danger is, if they harden their hearts, and bow not meekely to God vnder their burthens, that is more against them, then all their outward calamitie and bondage.

We

Wee haue heard how God punished the people for their committing 2
idolatrie,and suffered their enemies to oppresse them sore and a long time. But this was not al which is here expressed,though that was very grieuous, as all may well see. But with this,it is to be noted,how they also by their sin, turned the Sun shine of Gods fauour into most darke and vncomfortable displeasure. This men purchase to themselues by their wilfulnesse and rebellion,when they might otherwise go out and in before him, to their good liking,and dwell most safely vnder the wing of his protection all the day long. What madnesse is it to cast themselues into deadly feares and vnquietnesse and anguish of soule for the Lords displeasure, as sharpe arrowes sticking fast in them,with reproch,discountenance of Gods seruants, and many other crossings and discontentments? But of Gods anger and wrath,reade more in Chap.2.14. Here I end. Deut.33.12.

THE SIXTIETH TWO SERMON ON THE TENTH CHAPTER OF THE BOOKE OF IVDGES.

WE heard in the former verses how God afflicted this people for their sinne: in this verse,the holy story setteth down how this oppression by the enemies reached to the people beyond Iorden, as well as them that were on this side onely. Wherein that thereat was verified (whereof before hath been spoken) that they and their idols,should be as snares vnto them,euen to their destruction. But besides this we see,that this miserie did spred further in time, then to those that were on this side Iorden, for it reached euen to the Israelites also, which dwelt beyond Iorden. So that although the enemies began with them first, who dwelt in the land of the Amorites,yet seeing the people on both sides of Iorden had communicated with the nations in their sinne,they were therfore both plagued alike by the enemies. And so it fareth with vs: for if many ioyne together in prouoking God,they shall smart together, by bearing his corrections. And though the Lord begin, as I said before of Shechem and *Abimelech*,with some at the first apart, yet he will,as the fire burneth one house after another,he wil,I say,deuour the rest with the former at length, as by the plague we haue heard he hath done. Vers.9.

Now in that it is said in this verse,that they cried to the Lord,saying: we haue sinned,I haue spoken of this before,as also of this,that they were long in miserie ere they complained,therfore I wil not repeate those two points, onely this here is to be noted,that they did not crie vnfainedly at the first, but for the smart they felt,but hauing the repulse of God, and they seeing Vers.10.

that they preuailed not thereby, they did after, set themselues to seeke the Lord, and to repent in the truth of their hearts, as is shewed afterwards: and that they did not at their first seeking to him, come in true repentance, it appeareth by the Lords reiecting of their cries, and his bidding them goe to their gods, whom they had serued, for helpe; which hee would not haue done, if they had turned to him in truth: for hee is
Exod.34.7. full of compassion, and readie to receiue those that are of an vpright heart.

Doct. And by this wee may see, that many men, when they are in extremities, confesse their sinnes to God, as *Saul*, when hee feared the losse of his kingdome, and crie to him, when yet it is otherwise hardly wrung from them, neither doe it they sincerely; and yet I will not say, that they here, or that all
Note. other such, of whom I speake, doe it in hypocrisie: but this I say, that in their need and hast they crie, onely they consider not that God looketh for truth at their hands, neither resolue afterwards to looke aboue all things to keepe their couenant with God, neither therefore indeed doe so: but like *Ahab*, bow for the time as a bulrush, and afterward forgetting, through carelesnes and negligence, what they said or promised; whereas they who in truth and vnfainedly repent, and turne to God, looke duly and constantly to their
Psal.119.106. promise that they made to him, as *Dauid* did, who said, I haue sworne, and will performe it, to keepe thy righteous iudgements. And there had need to be no lesse in them, that couenant with God, a man would thinke, vnlesse they will boldly and grossely shew, that they despise him, and helpe to fill
Psalm.78.34. the Church with reuolters, as they were, that we reade of in the Psalme. The vse of which I repeate not, but referre the Reader to the places before mentioned.

Verse 11. *And the Lord said vnto the children of Israel, Did not I deliuer you from the Egyptians, and from the Amorites, and from the children of Ammon, and from the Philistims.*

12. *The Zidonians also, and the Amalekites, and the Maonites did oppresse you, and ye cried vnto me, and I saued you out of their hands.*

13. *Yet ye haue forsaken me, and serued other gods: wherefore I will deliuer you no more.*

14. *Goe and crie vnto the gods which yee haue chosen, let them saue you in your tribulation.*

The sense. IN these verses it followeth what God said to them in these their cryings to him: When the people had called vpon God, and began, as it seemed, to repent, God answered them indeed, but sharpely and roughly, as appeareth in the text, whether by the high Priest, or by some Prophet. But why he so hardly reproued them, the reason was, to awake them further, and to bring them to sound and constant repentance, to the which they were not yet come vnto. As if he should haue said to them, Yee seeke to be deliuered, but ye doe it, to the end that ye being set at libertie, may returne to your old byas againe, and follow your lusts, and serue strange gods. But who could haue thought, that you would hereafter, saith the Lord to them, haue reuolted from me? Did you not call vpon me at other times, and were heard? Is this

this the first,and when I deliuered you, yet he haue forsaken me,as is to bee seene this day,for the marke ye stil beare of it,and haue cast me behind your backs. I deliuered you from the Egyptians,Ammorites, Ammonites, and other,and in stead of the thanks, ye by and by forsooke me,and fell to serue strange gods. O horrible! Thus therfore the Lord (as we haue heard) now casteth them in the teeth with their doings. And namely with their Idols, as if he should haue said,yee see now what your gods (as you call them) are able to doe for you. For if they could haue helped you, I see, that you would neuer haue sought to me: I will not therefore deliuer you,and if you seeke to them,ye see they cannot. Briefly to end this; their state being thus *Doct.* laid open by the Lord before them,I note (or rather repeate) out of the whole answere which the Lord makes them heere: that it is not so easie a matter for men to deceiue him, who knoweth their hearts, and the guile, falsehood and flattery,that is in them,as to beguile men, who in charitie do (as they ought) iudge the best of them by that which they heare and see. To heare some men in their good pangs, either when some great blessing befalles them, or when they are held vnder by some great affliction, (as by the feare of death) and kept vpon the racke, or when they haue heard some powerfull Sermon which hath searched them to the quicke; or when they behold the great workes of Gods power, as thunder, lightning, winds and tempest by sea or land, or when they see Gods hand vpon other men,or to be heauy vpon themselues any other way: vpon such occasions (I say) to heare the speeches,and see the behauiours of some men, Note. what words of thanksgiuing,of trembling,of admiration,nay, what confessions and prayers breake from them, with earnest couenants and vowes of repentance; I say to heare these things at such times, would make a simple-hearted Christian crie out as amazed, and not feare, boldly to affirme,God be glorified; doubtlesse these persons are throughly changed, and truly penitent, and God is in them of a truth, surely *Saul* is become a Prophet of God: and thus in their simplicitie doe many iudge of such, by occasion of that which they see in them: and who, except they bee well experienced, should not say the like in that case, and cursed are they that deceiue such: yet thus they speake of them,till they are afterward as much astonished to see the contrary in them. Thus wee see, they deceiue men, whereas the Lord, as wee may see in this example,will not, nor cannot bee so easily deluded by them, neither wil so soone be satisfied with these their speeches: but still waiteth for the truth and vprightnesse of such as vtter them,and giues no credulous eare vnto them,but doth more then suspect them,for he calles them to further proofe of their soundnes and affection towards him, and expostulateth with them,for that he finds it not so with them. *Saul* (as 1.Sam.15.24. and 30. I said, fearing his kingdome) confessed the sin which was laid to his charge, 1.Sam.15. But the Lord professed (for all that) he had reiected him,chap.16. 1.Sam.16.1. So the people in Deuteronomy being in feare,and strongly possessed there- Deut.5 29. of,in all hast,protested they would obey the Lord in all things which *Moses* should tell them from the mouth of God: But the Lord smelt them and found them out presently: for thus he saith to *Moses*, This people saith wel, all that they haue said: but I will not take their word,and why? Oh there is no such heart in them,saith he, as their tongue would seeme to import. For euen as a leaud houswife, who is runne away from her husband, or any ill debter, who is fled for debt, if they be taken and terrified with the law, they will not sticke to say and sweare to any conditions which are offered them, so that the present danger and shame may be remitted: whereas yet they are as treacherous and loose afterward, as euer before; as the issue prooues (in theeues and other malefactors) euen so, when vile persons are vnder Gods punishments; (from whom they see, there is no breaking away by strong hand) what will they not say, in accusing and condemning themselues? Nay, who can shame them as they will themselues for their sinnes? or who can so denounce and pleade against them as themselues? What will they not promise, vpon condition of release from the present woe they are in? And yet when these men come to the triall, they flie touch, and recoile againe, as if there were no witnesse to conuince them, and as if all they said, had been spoken in a trance. Oh therefore, those forced exclamations and complaints, which either for horror and feare a grieued soule maketh, or which a body pinched, and in distresse, compell a man vnto: how may they be taken for approoued testimonies of repentance, either by themselues, or by other? Yea such as know they haue often abused the Lord thus, (as if they had him at command to order him as they list, vpon each flattering promise, whereas it is his wonderfull mercy that hee will forbare them, and offer them meanes of searching themselues better: let them repent therefore of this playing wily beguily with God: Oh how should this terrifie them, and scare them, that the Lord still counts them but hollow persons, rotten at the heart, and false in their couenant, and therefore that hee will at one time or other, reckon with them for all their villany and hypocrisie, which they durst couer vnder the vizard speeches of humblenes and truth.

1.King 5.22. As for vs, who haue learned and practised better, let vs beware that, as *Paul* bids *Timothy*, not to lay hands suddenly vpon any; so that we doe not lightly iudge well or commend the estate of any man vpon so slender euidence, let his constancie speake for him: time (the mother of truth) shall prooue him: in the meane season, lift not thou such an one vp to the third heauen in one moode, when in another thou shalt bee vrged to condemne to the nethermost hell: but be sober, and leaue him to God, to whom (as to his master, who knowes him) he standeth or falleth.

Vers.11.12. More particularly in these two verses, he telles them what deliuerances he had wrought for them, bringing his benefits to their remembrance, to prick

Doct of verse 11.12. their consciences. And therefore to speake the truth, what incouragement could they haue in comming to God in their need for helpe, whom they had dealt so treacherously with before? especially, they hauing no testimonie, that they came in remorse and shame for their former reuolts, and with firme and resolute perswasion, both that God would pardon them, and that themselues would no more fal from him. So, how can any of vs in our need, doe as they did, but we must looke for the like answer from him? And so we haue, though not by voice from heauen, yet by the fearefull accusation of our consciences, and by his word in canonicall Scripture. And as for men that haue bin so dealt with by any neighbours, yea though it be but once, if they haue been beneficiall to them, they wil soone shew them their minds, that is, how greatly they detest such vnthankfulnesse and falsehood. But how

we

we should be moued by the hearing of Gods benefits brought to our remembrance, and of such like matter I haue spoken largely in the second Chapter,vers.1.2.3.

This speech of the Lord,namely,[*I will deliuer you no more*] because afterwards he did deliuer them,giuing occasion of some doubt and difficulty, is to be considered of vs accordingly, I meane with more regard. His meaning is this: Yee (O people vnworthy to be beloued) haue abused my facilitie and gentlenesse,and you seeing me easily entreated heretofore to helpe you,plied mee with your cries and complaints, till yee had gotten that yee would haue,euen deliuerance from your enemies,naming many sorts vnto them. But when yee got once elbow-roome,saith the Lord,(whereas I looked to haue been the God of your worship and seruice,aswell as of your saluation) ye turned your backs vpon me,and rebelled against me: If this bee the fruit of my loue and tendernesse, that I must haue the worke to deliuer you,but euery stocke and stone,euery Idoll of Ammon,Moab,&c. go away with the thanks and reuerence,and get all the obedience and worship from me,I will helpe you no more,except I see better fruit come of it: and otherwise I haue done with you, goe seeke to them whom yee serue for succour and reliefe. So then we see this refusall is conditionall: and is applied to them for their former idolatry,and their present vnsound dealing,and reacheth onely to the present time, though they cried vnto him: as if he had said: At this time,in the case you are in, I will not deliuer you,I will not helpe you,as fast as you complaine,but when I shall see it meete, that is, when I shall see your repentance sound, then I will giue you another answer. So that it is manifest I say,that he speaketh but conditionally,and thus we must vnderstand it; for otherwise (they not hauing committed the vnpardonable sin) this speech should haue been contrarily to other Scripture. Where the thing which is to be noted is this: that God after the manner of men, sheweth his fearefull speeches, as hee did heere,that he is offended with vs, (and for the same cause doth oft afflict vs) to the end he may make vs search out,see,and feele some special sinnes,they are sore and grieuous in his sight, and yet of vs nothing or little regarded. By this meanes therefore, he bringeth vs to such a sense of them,that we are not able to looke vp,but our hart (to the iudgement of flesh) doth faint within vs, as may bee seene in these heere.

Vers.13. | Doct. | Note.

This *Dauid* felt,when he said,Innumerable troubles haue compassed me, my sinnes haue taken such hold of me, that I am not able to looke vp: they are more in number then the haires of mine head, therefore mine heart faileth me. So in another Psalme, we may see the like. This doe mens sinnes bring them to, when God citeth them, and seeth it expedient to awake them,though he doe not this often,especially to the reprobate,and yet with slender,or rather no vse nor benefit to them,when he doth it; they haue so many shifts to wash it away, and so harden their hearts, that they cannot profit thereby,but with great vse and comfort to his owne children,in the end especially,how terrible and feareful soeuer the beginnings and proceedings also sometime are,or seeme to be vnto them.

Psalm.40.12. | Psalm.32.4.

And so he terrifies many at their first conuersion with the feeling of his wrath and heauy displeasure iustly kindled against them,for the odiousnesse

and detestation of their liues past, so that they fall into a kind of despaire, as
Actes 2.37. the people in the Acts did at *Peters* sermon, saying: Men and brethren what shall we doe? And yet a little before, they made light of their sinnes, which then so pricked their consciences, and had no sense of them. By all this that
Note. hath been said of this matter, we may gather, what manner of thing sinne is, if it appeare in the proper colours of it, and as it is indeed; to wit, the most fearefull of all things. Many thinke this true that I say, of murther, adulterie, idolatrie, and such like. But the truth that I haue vttered, is verified of other sins also, which yet seeme lesse odious: as of anger, impatience, worldlinesse, distrust, tetchinesse, pride of heart, sloth and idlenesse, the leaudnes of the eie, self-loue, deceiuing, reuenge, and the rest whatsoeuer they be, if they come clearely to the conscience to be felt and duly considered.

And because we make them such common matters, and are so little grieued for them, the Lord is therefore driuen to awake vs, as heere hee did this people, to make vs astonished, and stung at the heart for those sinnes which wee thought were small, or none at all, while wee lay nuzled and drowned in them.

For if God open our eyes once, to see them as they are to be seene, and
Note. as they may be felt, with the shame, foulenesse, basenesse, sottishnesse in the committing of them, and the danger that they bring; wee iudge euen so of them, as well as of the rest.. For what horror doth adultery breed, when it is thought of after the committing? it is as an arrow shot through the liuer? But of that, ye will say, there is no doubt: so what is anger, when it is past, to him that offended by it but shame, and so I may say of all other. A view hereof, may bee taken in *Saul*, when God pursued him for his sinne, and
1.Sam.28.15. made him crie out, saying: What shall I doe? for God hath forsaken me, and speaketh no more to me. And what torment (thinke wee) felt *Iudas*, when of himselfe he said, I haue sinned in betraying the innocent blood? And when his sinne so wounded his conscience, that the halter made an end of his life? And *Adams* transgression also, which was diuers from both the other, what wrought it vpon him? was he not so terrified for it, that he
Genes.3.8. fled from Gods presence as farre as he could, to hide himselfe in the thicket among the trees? And if I should reckon vp an hundred more, who all sinned in a diuers manner, one from the other; which of them hath not abhorred his owne, as if no other had been so vile, when God makes him see it.
Note. Therefore the Martyrs, rather then they would commit sinne against their conscience, and feele the terrour of it, chose to lose their liues rather, as wee may reade plentifully in the booke of Monuments. True it is, men doe not alwaies see, nor feele this, neither can they be brought to be moued and astonished for their sinne, except they be by the Lords strong hand thus forced and vrged. But by this (to end the matter in hand, we may iudge what shall be the horror of the Iudgement day it selfe, when all such things shall fully be made manifest. And for vse of all this, let vs learne, seriously to haue all sinne in horror and detestation, yea euen then, when it puts on an harlots face, and hath most force to deceiue vs; lest that which we heare, strike and wound vs at the heart, when wee looke for no such thing, but shall find it most deadly vnwelcome vnto vs.

*Doct.*2. Another thing herein to be marked, is, that although they had dealt deceitfully

ceitfully with the Lord, both in their former abuses of theit deliuerances, and now also in their complaint which they make for new helpe: yet the Lord leaues them not in this case, which had been enough to haue hardned them, and made them quite desperate. But euen by these words of defiance, whereby hee seemeth wholly to abandon them from protection, yet secretly he drawes them to a deeper searching into themselues, and to a far more serious meditation on their estate, that so hee might grant them their desire, and receiue them to fauour againe. Oh vnspeakable and admirable kindnesse of the Lord, thus to draw water out of the rocke, and to fetch light (as it were) out of darknesse. If God be so gracious to his children when he seemeth to frowne; then how sweete and pleasant is his amiable countenance? and how delightfull are his promises and his incouragements? If he cannot forget himselfe so farre to his children (though degenerate) as to put off the habit of affection towards them, euen when he would play the Iudge: then how pleasant is his louing kindnesse? Therefore, although it is not easie for him that is fallen, and departed from God, to see this intent of God toward him, in the time of his threats and terrors, yet they knowing it to bee so, they must grow to beleeue it, in the time of their neede, for it magnifieth Gods deepe rooted and tender loue to his children, when they haue offended, and it makes matter of vnfained thankes and praise, when the worst end of his anger and displeasure shall appeare to haue been this, that remorse and repentance might be wrought in those who had offended him, that so they may be receiued of him againe. The vngodly see not, neither finde any such fruite of Gods renouncing their complaints and confessions, or his terrors of word and workes against them for their sinne: his voyce is as the voyce which sounds in a deafe mans eare: or if they heare it, they either rebell the more, or else runne away from him through feare? But did this present terror so worke in these? No, the Lord meant better to them, though he spake roughly, (because indeed faire speech was no fit medicine for their disease) and they were drawne to him by the secret condition, more then driuen from him by the open threat. So strangely doth the same speech and word of God instruct or teach wisedome, yea put hope into the beleeuer: and vtterly disanimate and turne off the wicked, or at least no whit profit them. For as God intendeth a thing, so shall it worke: all shall worke for the best to them to loue God: Sweetnes shall come out of bitternes to them: whereas the other hauing no such promise, finde no such effect. Christ (saith the text) looked vpon *Iudas* comming to betray him: and so did he (as Matth.chap.26.reports) looke vpon *Peter*, hauing denied him: These lookes were frowning lookes both of them: but the worke of them was diuers: *Peter* by that looke was touched with compunction, and went out a repentant person: the other an harned and wretched person, not mollified by the same aspect, because there was no bountie in it.

Note. Rom.7.8. Gen.3.10. Rom.8.28. Luk.22.47. Matth.26.61.

3 Lastly by this point, let Gods children learne a double dutie, as well as take occasion of thanksgiuing: I say such of them as haue declined and gone out of compasse, let them wisely obserue what Gods meaning is toward them in his word or workes of affliction. Let them first take heed, lest they giue eare to his subtiltie who would prompt them with this suggestion, Thou art alreadie gone from God: and behold now he seekes to be rid of thee Note.

thee altogether, and to feare thee quite from him. Auoid Satan (let them say) this were to renounce my right in God by faith, and his right in me, which is his free loue : this were to put no difference betweene the beleeuers priuilege, and the vnbeleeuer. No, no, this dealing of God, I see is, as it was to his people of Israel, and the Niniuites : it hath a condition annexed to it, which argueth, God is more desirous to forgiue me, restore me, heale and settle me in good estate againe, then to forsake me. If hee had meant so, what needed he to haue redeemed me at all? or now to haue spoken conditionally? Therfore I will euer hereafter highlier esteeme of that life which hath the promise of Gods fauour annexed thereto : and whereas I see my selfe now frowned vpon by the Lord for my boldnes & wilfulnes in stolne liberties taking, and the pleasures of sinne, my peace wasted, my spirit abated, my faith weakned, my ioy, willingnes to pray, &c. appalled : I will therfore now giue my selfe no peace, till I haue searched out my sinnes, repented of my houerly confessing them, and my drowsie sottish lying in them : I wil not cease powring out my soule to the Lord, that his terrors may astonish me, and driue me to lay my sinne to heart, and to bee so ashamed of them, that God may accept my humiliation and sorrow, and giue me faith to rest in his promise of pardoning and restoring me againe. Secondly, let this also teach Gods people to indent seriously with the Lord, to vse his former blessing and old deliuerances past thankfully, if they desire to obtaine new: remembring how God here vpbraides these Israelites, saying : How dare ye come to demaund deliuerance at my hand, hauing so shamefully abused the former?

Note.

Vers. 14. *The opening it.*

In these words [*goe crie to your gods*, &c.] Doth God (thinke we) bid them goe and sinne? No, in no wise : but he speaketh, as he doth oft times in the Scriptures, in another manner then the words seeme to meane, which if we marke not, wee shall easily fall into great errors and absurditie. It is a most grieuous casting them in the teeth, by an ironicall mocking of them with their Idolatrie : as if he should say, Now yee proue and see what your gods
1. King. 18. 27. can doe. As *Elias* did the like to the prophets of *Baal*, when he had them cry aloud to their god *Baal* : perhaps he is asleepe (saith he, &c.) he did not (all may so meane) that they should crie to him, but to vrge to marke well what a god they worshipped.

Doct.

Therefore by thus speaking, and bidding them goe seeke helpe at their Idols hands, they hauing shaken off the Lord, he teacheth vs (as it standeth with good reason) that they whom wee haue serued, and committed our selues to, must pay vs our wages : and to them the Lord iustly doth, and will send vs to their patronage in our greatest need, euen to our conuiction and horror, yea destruction, if he take vs not, as he did these here, to his mercie. Contrariwise, but yet according to the same equitie our Sauiour answered
Math. 19. 29. *Peter*, when he said, that he and his fellowes had forsaken all, and followed him, and therfore asked him, what they should haue, he said an hundred fold here, and after eternall life.

They therfore that haue trusted, and still doe in man, and haue made flesh their arme, shall know by experience one day, that they haue trusted to a bruised reede. So God will answere the workers of iniquitie, that serue Satan, Depart from me, I know you not. So let them know whose portion is
Luke 13. 27.

in

in stolne pleasures of sinne, that there will come a time when they shall be infinitly more bitter, then euer they were sweete, and that thereafter they shall feele smart and sorrow in full measure, when there shall be no remedie nor redresse. So Papists shall be sent for helpe to their Pope, Saints, Pardons, Pilgrimages. For God doth threaten all such impenitent ones, who haue cast him off by their dead workes, that as he neuer did, so hee neuer will acknowledge them for his. Note. Reuel. 18.7.

And such patrons they shall then finde to bee cold comforters in those torments, which they shall feele, as for their other sinnes, so by the remembring how they sought shelter by and from them, vnto whose seruice in their life time they addicted themselues. Thus a wise parent, guide, or superiour is taught to answere a scape-thrift and lewd wretch, that hath brought himselfe into need, prison, and miserie; by idlenesse, gaming, prophanenes, bad companionship, and such like doings, when hee seekes to them for helpe; thus (I say) hee is to answere him: Get you to them, to whom, and whose counsell ye haue hearkened and followed: who (it may be) are in the same miserie, or worse then themselues are in, and therefore vnfit enough to succour or helpe them. And if God manifest his nature here, that this shall be his answere to such as liue after this manner, then let vs learne and conclude, that no man shall end well an euill life: this being added, vnlessed it be changed before by repentance: and therefore that it had been good for such that they had neuer been borne.

Briefly to conclude this doctrine with some other vses thereof: wee see secondly by this, that God doth import no lesse, then that (by the law of like equitie, and by vertue of a farre stronger couenant) if this people had persisted faithfull in his seruice, he could not haue denied their suite for help and defence against their enemies. Otherwise, by what reason doth he now shake them off, and send them to their Idols, whom they had serued? except he had meant, that himselfe would haue besteadded them, if they had cleaued to him for succour by faith, & attended him by bringing forth the fruit of their confidence, I meane obedience. And what a sweet prerogatiue is this for which wee haue the expresse grant of the King of heauen, that so long as we keep a couenant with God, so oft we may also claime from him (in reuerence be it spoken) the libertie of sonnes and seruants, to bee defended and guarded against all inward or outward aduersarie power of our saluation?

This is that approching with confidence to the throne of grace, this is that freedom of spirit which calls God father, whether ẏ resistance be made by some lust, or some diuels instruments, or the diuel himselfe: what libertie is this, that a Christian may (with hope which will not make him ashamed) Rom. 5.5. pray against it, with assurance of being heard, euen as Christ himselfe was in that which he besought his father for? And why? Because he is within the couenant, and therefore warreth against all euill, therefore hee may boldly pray for grace against it, that he be not foiled: for he is about Gods worke, and the Lord is a louing Master, he will not see his seruant frustrated of his hope in his seruice.

Thirdly, these words note out this, That it is wisedome for a man to bestow his chiefe cost there, whence hee lookes for best recompence, and acknowknowledgement in the time of most need. The steward in his kinde, is commended for this policie: who would shew curtesie to such as he knew in a day of hardnesse and want, would be readiest to remember it with thankes and requitall. The contrary folly the Apostle to the Romanes taxeth; what fruite had ye of those things whereof yee are now ashamed? A man is not ashamed of that labour which hath brought him in plentifull gaine; but of that which answers not his cost and hope. Men that haue runne themselues out of breath all their life, groping after a blind happinesse, in their vnprofitable, superstitious, prophane course; at length seeing themselues deceiued, wish they had serued a Master who might haue saued them and receiued them into euerlasting habitations: But he answers them, bidding them go, see, if their money will saue them (their god) or their lusts (their masters): as for me, I had none of their seruice, neither shal they haue any wages frō me. Thus the Lord is faine to vpbraid men (though not by word, saying: Go to your Idols, yet in effect, in that he leaueth them shiftlesse) or else who should perswade one of an hundred, that he soweth among thornes, or loseth his labour and cost, when he casteth it, and himselfe away vpon one Idoll (a broken staffe) or other? And the truth is, such a bewitching nature these Idols are of, (not Popish onely, but spirituall also, set vp in the loue of the heart) that they possesse their seruants with an opinion of fruite, which is to be obtained, (if they could hit vpon it) till at length with other like themselues, when time and strength, thrift and cost is all spent and wasted, they crye out miserably, (like theeues at gallowes) they were deceiued: leauing an example for others (if they bee wise) to profit by; as for themselues, neither rule nor example could doe them good, as wofull experience witnesseth in too many other.

Luk. 16. 4.

Rom. 6. 21.

Vers. 15. *And the children of Israel said vnto the Lord, Wee haue sinned, doe thou vnto vs whatsoeuer please thee: onely we pray thee to deliuer vs this day.*

16. *Then they put away the strange gods from among them, and serued the Lord: and his soule was grieued for the miserie of Israel.*

The sense of verse 15. 16.

THe people hauing receiued an hard and sharpe answere of the Lord to them, to wit, that hee would not heare them, laid it neere to heart, and cried againe to the Lord (how soone after, it is not here expressed) confessing their sinnes, casting away their Idols, (which at their first suing to God they did not): now in stead thereof, they serued the Lord, whom they had forsaken, and beside all this, they submitted themselues to him, to doe what he would to them, resting confidently perswaded of his mercie, and so obtained deliuerance, which they had earnestly sued for and sought, out of that present calamitie: for the Lord was intreated of them, and granted their desire.

Doct. ver. 15. 16.

Now if it seeme strange to any, that in their first crying to God, their sute was reiected, wee must know, that they sought not to him for it in the vprightnesse of their hearts, as is said before; and therfore God meant to hold them on the racke, as it were, and not onely to keepe them in suspence, but also to hold them in a deepe feare, by denying helpe to them. Secondly, to bring them to a through repentance, as indeed now they did shew signes of it,

it,and those also effectuall,which they did not before: and for this purpose he draue them more throughly to examination of them themselues, then they had done before. So that we see at first, they gladly would haue been deliuered,but in the meane while they would not cast away their Idols and other sinnes,but would still walke in the waies of their owne hearts. Which setteth before vs a common disease, that is too oft euen in Gods deare children: that in our afflictions we crie to God for mercy and helpe, and faine would haue the punishment taken away, but so, that we would haue libertie to liue as we did before,and hold fast our sinnes still, and abide in them, Note.
for they are dearer to vs then our owne flesh. Euen after this manner many of vs too oft and boldly deale with the Lord: so that repentance is hardly attained vnto,no,not euen then,when we are to sue to the Lord for ease in our trouble. As may bee seene in *Dauid* himselfe in the 32. Psalme, that it Psalm.32.5.
was painefull to him to confesse against himselfe: we need not the speech of the people of Anothoth to *Ieremie*,to preach vnto vs pleasant things: and againe,that we will not heare the law of this thy Lord: neither to follow *Demetrius* the siluer Smith in the booke of the Actes; for these were wicked Actes.11.25.
both of them. And how did they foile themselues; they of Anathoth, to retaine their pleasures; the other to vphold his wicked gaine? But that it should be so with vs in any manner,who are of the better sort,how can it be borne! And yet it may iustly be complained of, Oh euen the better sort of men will not be reformed. Insomuch,that when affliction is vpon them,of which they would most willinglie bee eased,yet they cannot be brought to see or amend any thing that is amisse, because they flatter themselues,& are great in their owne eies,while their iniquitie is found worthy to be hated. And yet there are worse then these,who murmur vnder their affliction,and doe what they can,to hide their sinnes.

And here more particularly,as it is cleare,that this people saw they did euil 2
in worshipping strange Gods,but would not acknowledge it,til God draue them to it by his sore iudgements: So when we see,and will not see,how we prouoke him by any of our speciall sinnes,let vs feare,that he will,if wee will not abhorre,and be weary of them by his instructions,and warnings which he giueth vs,that he will (I say) bring vs thereto by sharpe correction. So that the best is to iudge our selues,that we be not iudged of the Lord.

But by this,that the Lord so hardly vrging this people,they fell to a more serious searching into themselues,and so came to better state, wee may see, that as hardly as Gods people are brought to confesse and renounce their sinnes,hauing fallen,as at sometimes they haue done; yet when they see and feele the hand of God against them, and no release nor issue of their trouble is seene by them; many are drawne thereby to sorrow and repentance. But when they haue not felt Gods anger kindled against them for their sinnes first,they can hardly for the most part,abide to be told of them, nor to heare of his iudgements for them,but shake them off, if they can possibly. But if God doe purpose to bring such home; he wil so worke in them, that he will make them feele both his threats and his displeasure so fierce and smarty,that rather then they will still liue vnder the feare thereof, they will run through fire and water to escape both, though no other bodily affliction be vpon them.

Thus

Thus many haue been brought home, when the Lord hath tamed and subdued them by afflictions, especially inward: for if they rebel not through pride, but stoope vnder their burden, there is good hope of them; euen as
Note. the high minded, who doe kicke against the pricke, and are refractarie and wilfull, doe surely come to euill. Now therefore, seeing we may find that mercy from God by our afflictions, which we neuer felt before in our prosperitie, why should wee storme at the comming of them, but rather looke
Iames 1.2. for some good by them, as the Apostle *Iames* wisheth vs to doe, when he telleth vs, that it is matter of greatest ioy, when we fall into many of them?

4 And lastly in this matter, in that they returned to serue the Lord, know we that this is the end of all our repentance to serue God, with chearefulnes throughout our life, euen as it is a chiefe end of our liuing here, for that to doe is indeed to bring foorth fruit of amendment of life; and when that
Luke 1.74. worke faileth in vs, I meane, that the waies of godlinesse are not pleasant vnto vs, let vs know, it is not wel with vs, but that the diuell hath much preuailed against vs.

Now in the next place in these two verses, let vs lay together the signes of the peoples repentance, which are these fiue. The first, their confession; the second, the submitting of themselues to the will of God; the third, the putting away of their Idols; the fourth, their returne to a godly life; the fifth, their confidence in God, taking no nay, neither making any doubt of his helpe. And for our instruction, these things are here mentioned in this maner, that though they be not all vsually in Scripture expressely set downe in
Ier. 31.33. the repentance of men together, yet other are in sundry places, as in *Ieremie*, *Hosea*, &c. and these also may be found in such as were penitents, if wee will
Hose 14 2 3.4. examine the stories of such, and search them out. In *Hosea* they may bee all
Psal. 1.1.2.3. found, though not all named: in *Dauid* also, in *Zacheus* likewise. And so by
Luke 19.8. them all ioyntly laid together, let vs, whensoeuer we list, looke to approoue our repentance to be sound and good: but seuer wee them not in any wise one from the other. For to confesse alone without the rest, may bee an vn-
2.Sam.12.13. certaine testimony, as is to be seene in *Sauls* confession, and yet in some it is sufficient, yea, sure and good, as in *Dauids*, when he vttered this bare confession to *Nathan*, I haue sinned. But to leaue euill, and doe good, with a resting on Gods promise, and a submitting of our selues to his holy will, I say all these together with confessions are signes of repentance infallable: euen as on the contrarie a failing in some of these may easily breed question about the sufficiencie of true repentance, where the Scripture doth not otherwise commend it.

And in that the holy story thus setteth it forth, that when the people thus repented, the soule of the Lord was grieued for their misery, euen as he was angrie with them before for their reuolting, it doth admirably commend
Ioel 2.18.&c. Gods mercy, as it is oft set downe in the Scripture: which is not spoken, as
Ionas 4.2. though God were mooued with affections, but those things which are noted to be in men, are ascribed to God, and so it is spoken after the manner of men, euen as they are first grieued for the misery of those whom they pitie, so God is said to be grieued for them, receiuing them to mercy.

So that we may truly say, that God exceedeth in mercy towards poore sinners, that haue sore prouoked him, when they vnfainedly turne to him.

And

And as this is true of his affection to them, so is it also of the fruites of his fauour, as elsewhere I haue noted at large. And to this end is that oft repeated saying in Exodus: I the Lord am gratious, slow to wrath, ready to forgiue, Exod.34.7.
and repenting for the euill that I brought vpon them. And as the Lord was wholly theirs, now they repented, notwithstanding all their former abominations, which blotted out and darkned in them all sound comfort, and so is to all other in their case; euen so doth he change the estate of wofull people by that reconciling them to himselfe, no otherwise then as the foullest and most tempestuous day is vnto the most comfortable weather, and constant Sun-shine. And they need not know what these changes meane, but walke in Gods fauour continually, as they doe who continually delight in his law, Prou.23.17.
and in his feare. But of these points from the fifteenth verse hitherto, I speak briefely, because I haue handled them vpon the like occasions before, in the second and fourth Chapters of this booke.

THE SIXTIE THREE SERMON ON THE TENTH AND ELEVENTH CHAPTERS OF THE BOOKE OF IUDGES.

The third part of the Chapter.

Verse 17. *Then the children of Ammon were gathered together, and incamped in Gilead: and the children of Israel assembled themselues together, and incamped in Mizpeh.*

18. *And the people and Princes of Gilead said one to the other, What man is hee that will begin to fight against the children of Ammon? he shall be head ouer all the inhabitants of Gilead.*

In these two verses, being the last of this Chapter, (to Vers.17.18.
passe from the repentance of the people of Israel, which I haue spoke of) it followeth now, as we may see, the Ammonites were not satisfied with vexing the people of God, as they had long done, but now they went about to put them to the sword, and to take their cities and lands from them for their owne. But marke we this: the Lord so dealt with his people, and prouided so well for them, that they their enemies could neuer goe about it in better time in respect of the Israelites. For now they had turned to God by repentance, and he had receiued them into his fauor and protection: this caused the Lord now to stand with him, who before was against them, so that they did know they had his direction and help to go about to deliuer thēselues out of their bondage and miserie. The Ammonites, seeing

Gilead was a goodly citie, and richly furnished, they laboured and determined first of all to destroy that: Israel was assembled in Mizpeh (while the other camped in Gilead) but that was too farre off from aiding the Giliadites their brethren, (who were then besieged by those Amonites.) Therefore as they were directed by God, they propounded betwixt themselues, namely, the Princes to the people, that he who would begin the battell against the Ammonites, he should be guide to them, and Iudge ouer them. And that they were led hereto by God, it may appeare by this, that the Lord raised vp those that were Iudges ouer them, and after confirmed *Iphtah* in going against them.

Doct. vers. 17. The story being thus laid foorth, I wil here stay a little, and say some thing of them, both the Ammonites and Israelites. And first this: if the children of Ammon had gone about to take the cities and ground of the people of Israel into their hands and possession, and oppressed them by warre, before Israels repentance, and turning to God, they might easily haue done it, for none of them durst, or had any heart to resist them, as appeareth in the story: for they suffered them to oppresse them, till now in the last yeere especially, they were sore distressed and tormented by them. And besides; they then had God also against them. But now after they sought the Lord in the truth of their hearts; he was now with them, and they were heartned and imboldned to resist, and stand against them, by the hope they had in him, as wee see they did manifestly declare. By the which wee may see how God keepeth many euils and troubles from his deare seruants, till hee hath made them fit for them, and them able to goe vnder them: whereas if they had come vpon them before, they had been vtterly ouerwhelmed by them. For as he turneth many afflictions away from them altogether, which they saw not how they could auoide, euen so hee deferreth many, so that they shall not touch them, till he hath strengthened their shoulders, and put courage into their hearts, and so made them able to beare them. And yet he leaueth them not vnexercised with one or other more small and easie, as he seeth it profitable for them, and that they are fit to beare them.

Doct. out of vers. 17. 18. Note.

But if any of vs well consider it, we shall find that his goodnes hath herein exceeded toward vs, and who can choose but see it, that at his first inlightning of vs by faith, when wee were weake, and might easily haue been dismaide, hee hath kept many of our sinnes from our sight, when by those which we saw we were hardly kept from despaire, and sundry troubles also; which if they had appeared to vs, when as yet wee were nothing able to heare of them, much lesse to beare them, they would haue swallowed vs vp, and haue driuen vs to vtter desperation. And as this is true, we vnderstand it of our first conuersion, or after; euen so is it also with vs throughout our whole life. He spareth vs, to the end we may be better incouraged to serue him faithfully in that which we know, that so afterward we may be fit to see more, both of our sinnes, and also to take part of the afflictions which abide vs. Euen as wee vse our children tenderly, while they bee young, but after they be growne vp, we set them to worke, and shew them that they must labour, and suffer some hardnesse, they being now better able to goe vnder it.

Note.

1. Sam. 23. 27. Thus did the Lord cal backe *Saul* from the pursuit of *Dauid*, when it was likely

likely that he could not haue escaped his hands if he had been let alone. So when *Nashash* the King of Ammon might easily haue destroyed the Giliadites at the first onset, while they were vnarmed: the Lord stopt him, and caused him to hearken to a needlesse condition, whereby the time being 1.Sam.10.
protracted, they had helpe sent them in the meane season, and ouerthrew them. In this kind of dealing the Lord resembles a friendly person, who spying a furious enemy comming fiercely with weapon against his neighbour, vnarmed and vnprouided to meet him, stayeth the rage of the one, till the other haue got himselfe armor fit to encounter him, or may escape his hands, or when hee hath done so, he commits them together, knowing that the innocent partie hauing the better cause, will easily foile the doer of wrong. Thus the Lord often doth, although when he seeth his time, he can also either quite diuert the enemy, as he did the King of Ashur from comming against weake Ierusalem: or else take his peoples part (as *Moses* did the Is- Exod.2.12.
raelites against the Egyptian) and fight for them while they stand still and looke on. So he did to *Pharao* and *Zenacherib*. Now when the Lord reserues his people till such a time of strength and courage, not suffering (as I may so say) the Canaanites to come vpon his people, (being weake through their late circumcision) it is a greater fauour, then if he remoued their triall wholly from them: for in this, they haue onely proofe of Gods goodnesse: but in the other, they haue (beside that) a triall of their faith and grace more precious then gold; which triumpheth, hauing got the victory ouer the enemy, whether spirituall or earthly. *Thomas Bilney* a godly man, during his imprisonment, had a strong assault giuen him by his owne flesh against the paine of the fire, which he feared he should not be able to endure. And who knoweth what he would haue done, if the triall had been hottest, when hee was weakest? But the Lord so suited the time, that when fire was put to him, he that feared the foile, of weake became strong (Heb.11.) and ouercame Heb.11.34.
the fire, by yeelding his whole body to wast it, whereas his finger could not before abide the candle. It is a great grace therefore to beleeue, that (as the Apostle implieth) God wil keepe from vs such afflictions as we are not fit to 1.Cor.10.13
honour him in, but liker to be ouercome of our corruption, and betray our Note.
cause. If any obiect the foiles of diuers seruants of God, preuented and taken vnawares by strong trials, as *Cranmer* in the first assault of his enemies forced to yeeld to that which he ought not, &c. Let such know, God hath a diuers end of a diuers method: and teacheth men humblenesse, and knowledge of themselues by such assaults as they cannot answer, to the end that they may be abler for those trials afterward, hauing renounced themselues, and got firmer hold vpon the alsufficiencie of God, without whose protecti- Note.
on they are weake, as other men. Now then let men beware how they abuse this dealing of God to their owne hurt. For seeing God by this bolding off, and forbearing of trials which wee could not beare, doth require both exceeding thanks, vpon serious recording of this manner of his dealing with vs from time to time: as also a growing daily in strength to suffer greater troubles hereafter, (a grace not common:) how grossely do they inuert Note.
and abuse this purpose of God, who make no other vse of his sparing and dandling them in the lap and armes, but to weare out the feare or expectation of affliction altogether? whereby the longer they are free, the weaker

they are to suffer? What difference in this point, will ye make betwixt these and such, as to whom affliction is euer vnwelcome and intolerable? I meane the vngodly? Let all Christians beware (therefore) of this softnesse and tendernesse.

Doct.2. Vers.17.18. Furthermore, we haue heard in the seuenth & eighth verse, that the Philistims and the Ammonites sore vexed Israel eighteene yeeres: and in all that time they neuer durst take vp weapon against them, vntill they repented; but then they began with good courage to resist them, and assembled themselues against them. By the which, it may be noted, what liberty and courage true repentance bringeth with it. The reason is this: when men in their conscience see, that they haue dealt trecherously with God, and haue nourished and followed the desires of their owne hearts, contrary to that they knew they should haue done, they haue no hope in him at such times, neither feele any heart or strength in themselues to deale against their enemies either ghostly or bodily.

Leuit.26.17. This is that plague that God threatneth in Leuiticus, that his people should not be able to stand before their enemies, if they sinned against him: Iudges 5.8. and in the fifth Chapter of this booke, it is said, when Israel had prouoked the Lord, there was no heart in them to stand against those that held them in bondage. So that wee see, how sinne disguiseth men, and how preposterously it causeth things to goe with them, when they are inchanted and carried away with the allurements and pleasures of it. Which prooueth the contrary to be true, to wit, that the seruice of God is perfit freedome: and that it is faith and godlinesse which onely giue courage and boldnesse as to a Lyon by well doing. And seeing it cannot be denied, that no bondage is like this to be bondmen to our lusts, let all looke to receiue from God both reward and punishment in this life, and hereafter accordingly as in their liues they haue sought either of both. See Iudges 5.8. and the notes vpon it.

Doct.3. verse 17.18. This order that the people tooke for the choosing of their Gouernour, was by the Lords direction, as we may after see by his confirming it, in sending his spirit vpon *Iphtah*. He did it as by an outward incouragement, to stirre them vp to fight against their enemies. Euen as he did the like by *Caleb*: who incouraged the people by the like meanes in such a like case, saying, Iudges 1.12. in a difficultie of winning a Citie, Hee that taketh it, to him will I giue *Achsah* my daughter to wife: which though the people ought to haue done, I meane, to fight against Gods enemies for his commandements sake onely, yet they had neede of spurres, and were the better drawne on by such incouragements. Euen as Magistrates and Ministers owe duty of conscience to God in their place to beate downe sinne, and aduance the Gospell: but yet they are the better heartned thereto, when both sorts are incouraged by the high Magistrate, and the Minister beside, by the readinesse of the people to their dutie. And so euery other in his place shall be better set forward in well doing, by temporary incouragements, though Gods commandement be the strongest motiue. So husbands and wiues should liue kindly together by bond and promise each to other for conscience sake; but yet they doe this much better, when each respecteth the other, by yeelding mutually that which they owe each to other.

THE ELEVENTH CHAPTER OF THE Booke of Iudges.

Verſ. 1. *Then Gilead begat Iphtah: and Iphtah the Gileadite was a valiant man, but the ſonne of an harlot.*

2. *And Gileads wife bare him ſonnes, and when the womans children were come to age, they thruſt out Iphtah, and ſaid to him, Thou ſhalt not inherit in our fathers houſe: for thou art the ſonne of a ſtrange woman.*

3. *Then Iphtah fled from his brethren, and dwelt in the land of Tob; and there gathered to Iphtah idle fellowes, and went out with him.*

IN this Chapter the perſon is mentioned, who ſhould goe before the people of Iſrael in the warre againſt *Ammon.* And the ſumme of this Chapter with the parts (which are foure) is here further ſet downe to be this. Firſt, the calling of *Iphtah* is mentioned vnto the 12. verſe. The ſecond part is, how he ſeekes to appeaſe the Ammonits by meſſengers, moouing them by reaſons to deſiſt from warre, but all in vaine, to verſ. 29. The third part containeth the ouerthrow of the Ammonites by *Iphtah,* to verſ. 36. The fourth ſheweth what fell out after; and particularly how hee performed his vow which he had made to God (if he might get the victory) in verſ. 32. and this is to the end of the Chapter. *The ſumme and parts 4.*

Now to come to the firſt part, before *Iphtah* became their Guide and Captaine, it is ſhewed how vnlikely it was that he ſhould be ſo: therefore he is deſcribed in the firſt verſe, to haue been the ſonne of an harlot, who (ordinarily) might be admitted to no ſuch place. In the ſecond and third verſe it is ſhewed how his brethren did therefore (whether through pride and ſcorne or emulation or both) expell him out of their fathers houſe, ſo that he was faine to flie into another land, and ſomuch the more hee was vnlike to be gouernour. And yet God ſo brought it to paſſe by his prouidence, that the Princes of Gilead, euen ſuch as had driuen him away, were conſtrained to ſend for him againe, euen him among all other, (whom they had baniſhed from their fellowſhip,) to bee their guide, according to their decree made in the former Chapter, to wit, ſeeing he had of all other begun warre with the Ammonites: and ſo vpon agreement betwixt him and them, hee yeelded to them, and the Lord ouer-ruling the action he was elected Iudge ouer them, and this to the 12. verſe. *The firſt part.*

Now of theſe more particularly, as they lie in order. And firſt how he is deſcribed, namely, in theſe two points. One, that hee was the ſon of an harlot, being the ſonne of *Gilead:* the other, that he was yet a valiant man, and of great courage, and fit for warre. So that by the firſt he was baſely accounted of, as he was baſe borne; by the laſt, he came to good eſtimation and credit among men, as he well deſerued. *The firſt verſe.*

For the firſt, whereas *Gilead,* the father of *Iphtah* tooke to him an harlot beſide his lawfull wife, we ſee, he did not obey the commandement of the Lord in Deuteronomy, to wit, that there ſhould be no whore in Iſrael. And *Deut. 23. 2.* if it be demanded, why God forbad ſuch as were borne in baſtardie to enter into the congregation of the Lord, that is, to beare any office in the Church, it was not forbidden, for that the man ſo borne was worſe then others, but that the people might know, how greatly God abhorred whoredome, and this was but a iudiciall constitution appertaining to the Iewes. And in that *Iphtah* so borne, was yet set in authoritie ouer the people, (which thing God forbad) we must know, that hee made not that law to himselfe, but for the Iewes, that it should not be lawfull for them to preferre any such, but as for himselfe, who hath authoritie to call him into question for that which hee doth.

Doct. vers. 1. Now for instruction, we see here by this that *Iphtah* was begotten of an harlot, that the law of God (forbidding that there should bee any whore in Israel) was not obeyed, euen as before wee haue heard of *Gedeon* his concubine: whereby we see, how little Gods law is, and hath been regarded in all ages of many, whether this one law, or what other of his soeuer wee vnderstand it of. As for this, of and against whoredome, that it was neuer more common then in this age, woful experience proues it to be too true, so that there want now no such offenders more then in former times: I may truly say, in number they farre exceed them, as if the antiquitie of corrupt example in this kinde, were enough to license men to continue it still. And so it is in all other kindes of sinne, verifying to the full the Apostles prophecie to

2. Tim. 3. 1. *Timothy*, that in the latter daies shall come perilous times: for men shall be louers of themselues, couetous, proud, boasters, and infected with diuers other sinnes. And for this cause commeth the wrath of God vpon the children of disobedience: and no marueile that wee haue many plagues, seeing God is not obeyed almost in any thing. And so may euery one particularly say to himselfe, as he is most obedient, so shall his blessing be. And as this sin in any man had been bad enough, so in *Gilead* a great man, and who should haue punisht it in others rather, (being the father of a familie) what a reproch was it? Euen as in *Dauid*, in *Sampson*, in *Iuda*, and in *Reuben*. For alas, when a meane person sees the commandement of God to be of no greater force, then that euery great man is bold to dispense with it, he growes to thinke it but a scare-crow, and saith boldly (as the strumpet in the Prouerbs) Tush, tis but a trick of truth. But for such tricks of youth the Lord in wrath

Numb. 24. 9. destroyed 24. thousand of Israel. Yea when the great enemie of the Church *Balaam* being frustrate of his cursed attempt against Israel, (for they are cursed who can finde in their heart to curse Gods people) sought how to bring an equiualent plague vpon the Congregation, he could inuent no more fit and mischieuous a plot, then to intice them to vncleannesse with the Moabitish women, and to Idolatrie with their heathenish gods. Therefore how great a iudgement of God hangs ouer this land for the lust of the eye, (a maine branch whereof is filthines) and the vnlimitted lust of all sorts, (especially in places of darknesse) wee can more easily coniecture, then perswade

Note. them that are guiltie, to redresse it. Oh it is lamentable that such spots of our assemblies are suffered boldly to spit in the face of modestie, and to hold vp their heads aloft, as hauing the better end of the staffe, I meane greater aduantage against their accusers (commonly) then they against them. How should this moue vs to sue to the Lord, that such should be noted and shamed for inordinate persons, that the rest may blanke and feare by their example, and so the anger of the Lord be staied, as once it was by the zeale of

Numb. 25. 8. *Phinees*, for the Lords cause, thrusting thorow *Zimri* and *Cozbi* for their shamefull

shamefull abomination. So should the word preached be more forcible, when the transgressors should see the price of their boldnes; and so should the law of the Magistrate take better effect, and not become ridiculous. And so should not we feare that plague which *Iehu* denounceth vpon *Iehoram* (saying, What peace?) seeing the abominations and whoredomes of thy mother *Iezabel* are still in great number. Of which I say the lesse, because I haue noted it as the fruite of all sinne as well as this, in the former parts of this booke. Onely I say, if the vngodly sort will not take the Lords bridle to restraine their flesh from this lewd course, (for adulteries, as our Sauiour notes, are the breakings out of the filthie heart, euen as the sores and scabs of the body are the fruites of a corrupted blood) then let the people of God learne this dutie, euen to possesse their vessels in holinesse, to keepe themselues vnspotted and pure, and to preserue their bodies and spirits in chastnes, except they wil make of the temple of the holy Ghost, a stie of vncleane and loathsome lust, fit to driue the spirit of God away. And otherwise the Lord shall set a marke vpon them, worse then the brand of a theefe, euen a marke of infamie, which I dare not promise that repentance it selfe shall quite wash off, while they liue, but that the staine shall still continue. For this sinne is of a scarlet dye, as *David* speakes, Psal. 51.

2.King.9.22.

Note.

Psal.51.2.

Now to end this verse, by that it is said that *Iphtah* was a valiant man, we must know that in those times of warre, courage and valiantnes was a gift much set by and of good vse. So that though he had a blemish vpon him in that he was the sonne of an harlot, (which was not his sinne) yet the Lord couered it (as I may say) with this excellent gift of fortitude, that made him much desired. It was a crosse to him (all may see) that hee was thus abased, and yet if he had not been vnder that, or some other such chastizement, it had been like he should haue been a worse man, and in greater danger. For such blemishes in the body, are occasions through Gods worke, to turne the minde to better matters, and to bring it in loue with them, and to hold from the partie greater troubles thereby.

The remnant of verse 1.

Doct. 2.

As we reade of *Mephibosheth, Ionathans* young sonne, that he being lame on his feete, could not resist *David*, as *Ishbosheth* his vncle did, (to his great toyle and little preuailing) but liued peaceably in the Kings fauour and fed at his table: and how could he haue been in better state? whereas if he had enioyed his limmes at libertie, it is hard to say whether hee would not haue been stirring, and taking part with *Ishbosheth* to his owne ouerthrow: which had bin very like to haue befalne him, whẽ *Abner* forsook him, if he had not bin preuented by violent death. Thus doth the Lord (as *Paul* speaks) clothe the more vnseemly parts with most honour. And in our experience many worthie men for their excellent parts (both in Church and Commonwealth) haue yet had their deformities. One among the rest of late and godly memory, Master *Perkins* that worthy instrument, being lame of his hand, testified often, that his defect was the occasion of his training vp to learning: as being vnfit thereby for other employment. Wherein Gods admirable prouidence appeared, in making him lame, that his blemish might be an occasion of doing good to the Church. Indeed the common speech is, that Nature noteth some men, for their sinister and notorious qualities: (by how much the rather all such had need pray much and vse good meanes to

2.Sam.9.3.
2.Sam.2.9.

1.Cor.12.23.

rectifie

rectifie and perfect their inner man, and purge out their corruption, lest this imputation be iustly cast vpon them) but wee must know that God hath a further stroke then Nature, and laieth his hand vpon many, that hee might be glorified by them, and shew his workes on them, as (in a sense somewhat
Ioh.9.3. diuers) our Sauiour speakes of the blind man, Ioh.9 So that such as are notable for their grace and gifts, as the other are notorious. Naturally we pitie such as are deafe, lame, blinde, and we doe well, (for it is the part of a cursed *Cham* to deride such) but the Lord oft turnes pitie into admiration, yea and condemnes by such, the shamefull vnthankfulnes of them who haue no bodily blemishes, but inwardly are tainted with all that naught is. God had done his part (to vse the phrase) one way to *Absolon*, who had not a wemme from top to toe, but who had a more disguised soule then that faire bodie carried within it? Euen as we see, the compleatnes of many a mans person, drawes by degrees to the halter: many a womans beautie makes her a strumpet. Whether then of the two is more to be desired, a copper ring with a precious Iewell set in it, or a golden with a common peble?

While many children haue their parents liuing with them, (who are their glorie) how bold, sawcie, and lewdly disposed are they, so that they were better vnborne. And other in the meane while, being depriued of their parents, which chastizement is nothing vnferiour to a blemish or scarre; how haue they been driuen to liue vnder good gouernment, and in good order?

For vse hereof, let vs not wonder, though the Lord mixe troubles with blessings, and (as I may say) blemishes with beauties, wants with perfections.
2.Cor.12.7. *Paul* lifted vp to the third heauen, was not so safe as being buffeted. A little abasement may preuent the greatest of all, yea I say, that some chastizement
1.Cor.11.32. laid vpon vs by the Lord, doth keepe vs oft times from perishing in the world, and so sicknesse and pouertie doe take heart from sinning, whereas health and wealth imbolden thereto. Therefore if thine affliction come from the Lord, (I meane when no apparent cause of thy drawing it on thy selfe can be seene, and so as thou sufferest not for euill dealing) waite for some speciall good to come thereby vnto thee, and to that end, labour to make vse of it.

Note. And if it bee an hindering of thy bodily commoditie by losse, disease, paine, and such like, looke that it be to the benefit of thy soule, and that thou haue a rich and large supplie that way, for so the Lord is wont to deale with his: and that to the end they may see cause to say as *Dauid* did, it is good
Psal.119.71. for vs that we haue been afflicted. It was sometime the speech of a vertuous and religious gentlewoman, well exercised in Gods nurture, that if there had falne to her any hard trouble, and heauy crosse, (as there did many) she did confidently looke for some great blessing more then ordinarie, which was for the most part some addition of new grace, or a quickning of the old.
Rom.8.28. And Saint *Paul* saith the same in other words, that as God sendeth our afflictions
Note. for our good, euen so we should looke for them to be to vs; which if we did, they should not be so vnwelcome to vs as now they be, nor so discontentedly borne and gone vnder, as commonly and for the most part they are.

Vers.2. For the blemish of his bastardie, wee heard how his brethren thrust him out, which was an vniust and cruell dealing with him. For what had hee done?

done? and as for their fathers shame which they raised therby, they ought to haue couered it,as they had bin able,rather then to haue reuiued it. And who seeth not that the sonne for his part had sorrow enough in that he was so branded with disgrace for it,so that there was smal cause that his brethren should adde more affliction vnto it.

By the shamefull fact of them,here we are taught to beware that wee doe not despise any in their affliction, being base, meane and contemptible for the same commonly in the world,and especially if there bee any good parts and gifts of God in them, whereby they may bee like to bee profitable to Church or Common-wealth. Yea and without respect of this also, for because Christ died for them and they are our brethren. For we are taught of God how to carrie our selues toward thē,though the wicked will be taught by nothing. We learne in the Psalme,that he is happie that iudgeth wisely of the afflicted,and that wee should pitie them, and mourne with them that mourne. And in such cases it were our wisedome to put the case, and suppose; what if such affliction and abasement were cast vpon our selues,would we not desire to be pitied and regarded? And besides this,we haue learned, that iudgement shall be to the hard hearted and mercilesse, and that without mercie. And therefore to adde sorrow to their bands, who are alreadie wrapped deeply therein, as it is a great sinne, so it threatens to the committers,that they shall not goe vnpunished,but receiue the like measure themselues at Gods hands for their so doing. And sometime they suffer the like disgrace and harme at their hands to whom they offered the iniurie. For when God lifteth vp their heads out of aduersitie, whom they haue abused and done the wrong vnto, (though they thought that they being once downe,should no more get vp againe and recouer) they take stomacke and reuenge the iniury that was done them much more eagerly. As *Ioseph* might haue done to his brethren, (their owne consciences being witnesses,when he was aduanced) for their vnnaturall dealing with him in his meane estate, and would most certainly haue done so indeed,if the feare of God had not staied him.

Doct.

Psal.41.1.

Iames 2.13.

Gen 50.17.

But although there were no feare of any such reuenge to come by pitilesse dealing with others; yet this were enough to disswade a true Christian from it,yea and from any hard measure offering to any brother liuing by him, how meane soeuer; that (beside other inconueniences) by so doing, hee should bring himselfe into an hard conceit with him,and so hee should neuer after bee able to doe him good by counsell and good instruction, exhortation,or comfort,as the other should stand in need of it. And that hope no seruant of God should lose, (especially the Minister,it being so precious a thing to helpe saue a soule) to wit, to harden the heart of the meanest against him by vnchristian handling of him, that he should therefore refuse to take any good by him afterward. And yet I do not for all this, say,that we must tolerate and winke at any in their sinnes and euils.

Note.

In great persons sometimes crueltie and wrong is shrouded vnder the name of policy. For when as (according to the rule of their master *Machiauel*) they seeke to bring vnder and discredit their corriuals and men of equall worthinesse, or it may be (better then themselues) they practise this principle, *When he is going, downe with him*; if he rise vp after he be sunke, if he be

comming vp the hill againe whence he is fallen,sinke him againe,thrust him backward,tread vpon him, that hee get vp no more. Thus dealt *Daniels* aduersaries in the Court of *Darius:* Thus dealt the enemies of *Dauid* in *Sauls* Court. And there be many petie and lower kinds of this iniurie among inferiours : as when the heire of the deceased or intestate partie (hauing the stroke in his hand) defraudeth both mother and brethren of their inheritance and portion, domineering ouer them, and driuing them to vnequall conditions,or else to endlesse and bootlesse suites. So the like may be said, when men mocke others euen for their affliction, (which secretly vpbraideth them of it selfe) as crookednes,blindnes,&c.of which more (God willing) shall bee said hereafter in his due place. In the meane time,let these consider the reward of mocking such, in the example of those Bethelites,
2.King.2.23. 2.King.2. (being but children) and of those Philistims how they smarted, that made *Sampson* their may-game (and yet but Heathens) what shall be the portion of Christians,and men of discretion then thinke we ?

The law had dealt seuerely against *Iphtah,* thrusting him out of the publique place of worship : But these thought that not enough, except they draue him also out of the number of the people of God amõg Meshec and Kedar,I meane Infidels.Let *Dauid* speake what a bitter punishment this is :
1.Sam.26.29. who saith to *Saul,* Cursed be they who haue cast me out from the inheritãce of the Lord.To returne therfore,woe be to him that curseth the innocent: but double woe to him that addeth affliction to the Lords affliction. If
Gen.21.9.10. *Ishmael* were cursed for mocking *Izhak:* doubly accursed were those Baby-
Psal.137.7. lonians, who seeing Ierusalems ruine, cried, Downe with it,downe with it, race it to the ground. As hailestones vpon the ripe eares of corne are vnseasonable : and as the putting out of that mans eye who hath but one,that so he may be vtterly blinde,is cruell : so is the adding of sorrow to the heauie hearted. This caused the Lord to make this law to the Iewes : Grieue
Exod.22.21. not the stranger: it is enough for him that he is from his place,and euen that alone makes him sad in heart. Let the rule of the Apostle conclude this:Reioyce with them that reioyce, and weepe with them that weepe : remembring thy selfe,and doing as thou wouldest haue others do to thee. For who
Rom.12.15. seeing his neighbours house on fire in one place,wil take some of the brands and set it on fire in other places that it may be quite destroyed ?

Verse 3. Now followeth the third verse, wherein wee see, that by his brethrens hard dealing with him,he was faine to flie whither he could for shelter,euen thither among strangers,where he might haue miscaried altogether, if God had not greatly regarded him. Whereby wee may see,that the iniurie and oppression of some causeth the innocent to vndergoe much hardnesse. A thing that may long enough be complained of, before any one of many so offending,will amend it. Great cries and complaints are heard euery where of the inferiours and vnderlings, what wrong and hard measure is offered them by the mightie, or such as haue power ouer them, as pitilesse Landlords,and such as haue men at aduantage, who when they are put to their shifts for money,make them take it vp on conditions that vndoe them,with such exactions as they were as good flea the skinne from their bodies. So vngodly parents,who labouring to raise some one of their children, and casting off the rest,compell them to seeke their fortune s (as they prophanely speake)

ſpeake)and driue them to extremities. Alſo ſtepfathers and mothers, and cruell maſters and dames,may be reckoned here among many doers of iniury,for I can giue but two or three inſtances among many, leſt I ſhould bee tedious; let the reſt in other kinds be conſidered by theſe.Theſe with cruell dealing,as depriuing them of neceſſaries, and laying heauy burthens vpon them,cauſe the poore orphans and vnderlings to runne away, as *Eſau* did *Iacob*,and being ſhiftleſſe,to ſtarue or miſcarrie. And euen ſuch is the dealing of the reſt,who are cruell and void of mercie. Let them take warning: for if the poore and oppreſſed crie in the eares of the Lord, they ſhall bee heard,and ſhall pay to the full, for the iniury which they haue offered. I would be loth to do the leaſt wrong; for God will make it come againſt him that ſhal be bold thus to prouoke him,and grieue his neighbour,when it ſhall ſting as a Serpent,and be deadly vnwelcome.

It were a wiſe part for a man to iudge of his ſinne,as he iudgeth of the many dangerous effects that follow vpon it. But who ſeeth it an abſurd vnſeemely thing in the wealthy,to play the Lords and controllers ouer the baſer and poorer ſort? Not being content to make them their drudges and ſlaues to doe their meaneſt workes: but both in word and deed taking liberty to vſurpe ouer them,as if they had been only made for them to crow ouer? Sometimes rating them with reproches, nick-names, vpbraiding them by their pouerty,(which is to deſpiſe their maker)otherwhiles making a pray of them, and racking them for the poore commodities they buy, whereas yet for their worke,they will driue them to the loweſt wages that may be,as hard as times are,and all things deare and chargeable,which the poore ſtandeth in need. But now when the worme troden vpon,turneth againe,and draweth out the onely weapon it hath, the tongue I meane,to reuile and raile moſt diſdainefully vpon the rich, for their miſfortunes and oppreſſion,then I ſay euery wealthy perſon can ſay,this is odious.And ſo it is indeed: but was not their dealing as bad which prouoked them? They doe badly,but by them God will teach the wealthy how to conſider wiſelie of the eſtate of the poore. Therefore when men being exaſperate,turne to ſhifting,euery man can ſpeake againſt them: but who conſiders the greatneſſe of their ſinne who vrge them? The law of neceſſitie(we know)is hard to vndergoe. And when theſe ſhifters turne vpon their oppreſſors, not only with tongue, but with hand alſo, reioycing in ſtealing and purloyning from them,doe not then all crie out and complaine of the dammage they ſuſtained? And yet their ſtealing was cauſed by the others robbery: onely the one being a rich theefe ſtole openly,the other for feare in ſecret:and defends himſelfe by this,*That he hath but robbed him,that firſt ſtole from himſelfe.* Indeed it is Gods mercy,that (oppreſſion of the poore being ſo rife, as who ſeeth not that all the gripings wherewith one rich perſon oppreſſeth another,are in the vpſhot wrecked vpon the pooreſt, who can worſt make his part good?) that there is ſo little harme done in this kind: and in great part the cauſe is in the good gouernment ciuill which reſtraineth ſuch. But if we ſhould reade or heare of the diſorders of other places(wanting ſetled order and execution of law) it would amaze vs,and teach vs to practiſe that equitie and moderation of mind towards our inferiors, which might preuent ſuch ill meaſure at their hands,or rather Gods hand who will reuenge it.

For all this hardnesse that *Iphtah* sustained at their hands, yet this is worth the noting, that God prouided for him in a strange countrie, where he was able to maintaine diuers that resorted to him, and to frame them to fight against the enemies of God. And thus the Scripture is verified, that when father and mother forsake, the Lord taketh vp. As he dealt with *Ioseph, Hester, Mordecay*, and many others. And this protection of his, if it reached onely to the maintaining of such needy and distressed persons in their bodily necessities, and temporary sorrowes, it were much: but to bring them also into fauour with himselfe, that in so wicked a world they may bee weaned from the defilements of it, and that in better sort then many thousands, who haue father and mother to bring them vp, this is no lesse then admirable. Oh therefore what madnesse is there in them, and how are they to be pitied, who in the multiplicitie of dangers and miseries that swarme euery where, cling not nor cleaue neere vnder Gods wing, where only safetie is to be found and enioyed? And yet where they seeke it any other way, they haue got that which will not stand by them, if they get any thing, and yet their account is to come.

Doct. 2. vers. 3.

Note.

Now although this be a priueledge of the faithfull, onely to haue God their prouider for, and vpholder, yet euery hang-by catcheth the speech by the end, and saith, I hope God will prouide for me aswell as he hath done, &c. Wheras yet, neither haue they any faith to beleeue it, nor grace to beare their crosse, when they fall into any vnlooked for extremitie: no, nor yet applie themselues vnto any such meanes (as through Gods blessing) may giue hope of sufficiencie. How can a man shift and vse bad courses to maintaine himselfe, and yet (in truth) say, he beleeues God will prouide? For first he beleeues no further then he sees how he can bring his desire to passe, (which is not faith) and (which is worse) he vses vnlawfull meanes, whereas God makes no promise, but to the obeyer of his commandement, but curseth wicked practizes. *Iphtah* here was prouided for: But how? First, God gaue him a gift of valour aboue others, and then taught him how to set his gift on worke to good purpose, and so (beleeuing that God would not be wanting) he obtained the fruit of his labour. Now this is not the course which all such take, as yet with great confidence will professe. They doubt not, but God will feede them, hauing giuen them a mouth, and clothe them, hauing giuen them a body, yea and saue them too, seeing hee hath made them. These hopes are blind hopes, neither is faith the parent of them, nor contentation and thanks the fruite of them, when they enioy their desires, much lesse patience and depending vpon God, when they are frustrate, as often they are.

More in vers. 3. In this verse a further thing then wee haue yet heard, is laid out. For by Gods prouidence, *Iphtah* had set these men that resorted to him, who were needie, hee had, I say, set them against the Ammonites, and they carried away from them what they could get. And in the meane while, they warring against Israel, and namely Gilead, a great and wealthie citie, the Princes of Gilead had agreed among themselues with the people, that hee who first began warre with the Ammonites, should be their Captaine and guide to rule ouer them. And thus it came to passe, that they sent for him, I meane *Iphtah*, to intertaine him for their Captaine, whom before they had cast

out

out from among them as hath been said.

Now here in the end of the third verse, where it is said, that hee vsed the seruice of certaine wandering fellowes, who (it appeares) had no dwelling place constant, and set them on worke against Gods enemies, (for how could they haue been better employed?) as *Dauid* also did: we learne that such as are idle, needy and without imployment, should be brought by the wisdome and godly care of men, as the Magistrate and other, and ranged within compasse, vnto some worke profitable, and to the maintaining of themselues, and putting them out of their idle course. For such vagrant persons waite but to doe mischiefe. Doct. 2. vers. 3. 1. Sam. 25. 7.

So then, these are neither to be cast off altogether for their bad qualities, (but pitied and relieued in their misery) nor yet too much nourished and harboured in houses or townes, but (by them that are religious, and make conscience themselues of spending their time) whether Gentlemen (who entertaine many into their houses that are shiftlesse when they are out of office) or others, and their gift that is in any of them, as of wit, courage, or skill, &c. is to be wisely directed to the fittest and most profitable obiect, lest it breake out to outrage, being not gouerned. And this being done betimes, labour and exercise (by habit and vse) will be more welcome then idlenes, besides the cutting off of much sinne, both against God and man. Whereas for the want of this prouident care, wee see that many growing vp to mans estate, in the practise of leaudnesse and licentiousnesse, waxe impudent and incorrigible, filling the Church with noysome example and offence, and the Common-wealth with theft and beggery. But I will not repeate that which I haue said of this before, chap. 9. 3.

Much good hath been done of late yeeres to diminish the number of such, and to cut them off from a rogueish life, by enioyning them to labor: and if it were not crossed, I meane this good order, by the foolish pity of some, who incourage them to continue this begging and idle life, by giuing reliefe to them, rather then to the needy that dwell by them; much more good might yet be enioyed thereby. And further, they who take such into their seruice, or being able, ought so to doe, when there is cause, if they would instruct them, and rule and looke to them carefully, as *Iphtah* and *Dauid* did, wee should not haue such disorders, and outrage in Church and Common-wealth as we haue: neither should it be such reproch as it is, to keepe such bad ones in mens houses: for though they are rude and bad themselues; yet by good care had ouer them, they might be brought to better order. This being added, that if they will not be ruled and kept in compasse, that they be deliuered to the Magistrate, and committed to the house of correction.

THE SIXTIETH FOVRE SERMON ON THE ELEVENTH CHAPTER OF THE BOOKE OF IVDGES.

Verse 4. *And in processe of time the children of Ammon made warre with Israel.*

5. *And when the children of Ammon fought with Israel, the Elders of Gilead went to fetch Iphtah out of the land of Tob.*

6. *And they said vnto Iphtah, Come and be our Captaine, that we may fight with the children of Ammon.*

7 *Iphtah then answered vnto the Elders of Gilead, Did not yee hate me, and expell me out of my fathers house? How then come yee vnto me now in the time of your tribulation?*

8. *Then the Elders of Gilead said vnto Iphtah, Therfore we turne againe to thee now, that thou maiest goe with vs, and fight against the children of Ammon, and be our Head ouer all the inhabitants of Gilead.*

9. *And Iphtah said vnto the Elders of Gilead, If yee bring mee home againe to fight against the children of Ammon, if the Lord giue them before me, shall I bee your head?*

10. *And the Elders of Gilead said vnto Iphtah, The Lord be witnesse betweene vs, if we doe not according to thy words.*

11. *Then Iphtah went with the Elders of Gilead, and the people made him Head and Captaine ouer them: And Iphtah rehearsed all his words before the Lord in Mizpeh.*

The summe of these verses.

IN these eight verses, we see how God brought to passe by his prouidence, that the Princes of Gilead, who with *Iphtahs* brethren, had vniustly expelled him out of the citie, were driuen by their owne law to desire him home againe, and to fight against the Ammonites for them; which that they might the better effect, they goe themselues in a solemne manner to the place of his banishment, euen to the land of Tob, and with entreaty in all humblenesse, offer him the gouernment, and chiefe command in the battell against Ammon. *Iphtah* at the first casting them in the teeth with their vnkindnesse beforetime, (as it was meet that such discourtesie and disgrace as they had offered him in time past should not be altogether buried in silence and be vnmentioned) requireth of them good assurance of their fidelitie, because it might be doubted, that their present necessity draue them to make this offer, rather then any loue towards him. Which being tendered and granted to him accordingly; he yeeldeth to their request, and went home with them, and (the Lord ordering the businesse) there he found the whole congregation ready readie to confirme the election of the Elders of Gilead, as also, afterward, the Lord himselfe did: and so *Iphtah* was made their Captaine, and proceeded to the worke whereto God had appointed him.

Generally this teacheth how strangely God turneth the times and state Doct.ver.4.5.6
of things by his wisdome, whereby he ruleth and disposeth them: and this he doth for the triall and comfort of his, and contrary to and against the expectation and desire of their enemies, as here he did to *Iphtahs* comfort, and to the crossing of them of Gilead, raise this warre. To teach vs all that are fit to learne, to depend vpon him alone, and to haue his word for our direction, that so we need not be ashamed whatsoeuer come to passe.

Whereas if we haue followed our owne humor, either in crossing, and wronging any, as they here did *Iphtah*, we may be driuen to stand in need of them, and to seeke helpe at their hands, as they did at his, which will not a little crosse vs; or if we haue reproched our selues, by bragging and boasting, we may receiue the foile at their hands, whom we haue so abused, and so we may with shame bee made to eate our word; or if we haue proudly set vp our saile, or doe depend vpon vncertaine hope of future commodities, and momentany preferment, wee may bee disapointed to our iust reproch, and that easily; the Lord so altering and changing things as he doth. And herein his daily frustrating of many mens hope, who depend vpon blind fortune, promising to themselues, that all shall be, as they wish, vtterly shutting God out from their attempt, might make vs wise.

An example hereof in the King of Aram, as in many other, is to be seene:
who oft appointed his armies secretly against the King of Israel; but he was 2.King.6.10.11
disapointed by God of his expectation, till he raged and fretted at it. Here-
vpon S. *Iames* reprooueth his resolution of man, that hee will himselfe, and Iames 4.13.14.
of himselfe say of these changeable things; to morrow we will goe to such
a citie and gaine, &c. when yet *Salomon* telleth vs, we cannot tell what one Prou.27.1.
day may bring foorth. And yet men cease not to determine what they will doe, and how they will thriue, reuenge, take their pleasure and passe the time: and so we reckon of, and deale about seasons, that although all know
the weather altereth the price of things, yet wee will sell and buy our com- Note.
modities before hand, when wee know not how to make good, and performe couenants to other, or how other will to vs, no, neither are willing, if prices alter, to stand to our word: which yet God doth bring to passe ofttimes, to the ioynting not of such common doings onely in smaller matters, but also of the richest in their greatest affaires, and that a thousand waies according to his good pleasure. And therfore it were our wisdome to submit our selues to his prouidence in all things, and not to stand stiffely vpon our owne will, seeing he will breake our stomackes in spight of our hearts, by disappointing of vs, and except we doe so, we shall neuer be quiet.

But to returne againe, we see that God brought this about principally for the good of his seruant *Iphtah*, and to worke his enlargement, though to the shame and conuiction of his aduersaries. *Iphtah* neither himselfe made any meanes, by messengers, writing, or suite of friends, for his returne out of banishment: neither would the Lord permit him to doe so, but prouided better for him, that he should haue a calling to it: for if he had returned blindly home, as a priuate exile, what great matter had it been, or how could Gods worke haue been seene in it, as now it was? But behold, the Lord will rather haue *Iphtah* abide sometime in distresse and basenesse, that hee may bee fetcht home with publike consent of his nation, as *Ioseph* was out of prison; and that they did not so much to the gratifying of him, as themselues: the greatest persons of Gilead requesting it at his hand, and professing themselues highly beholding vnto him, if hee would grace them by returning, who had disgraced him before, by casting him off. Nay, and he must not to his be sent for, but come for, not by friends, but by his ranckest enemies, not to former estate of a subiect, but to be a Lord and Gouernour. A carnal man hearing of this, Oh how his teeth water and his fingers itch at the successe of *Iphtah*, and how doth he wish he might haue his desire vpon his enemies, and triumph ouer them as he did? But oh foole! this is no prerogatiue for thee to claime, it is the glorie of innocencie, the fruite of faith, of patient waiting vpon God, and committing a mans waies to him in wel-doing. Such another example (lest wee should say this is alone) is *Mordecai*. The Lord might haue put it into the Kings mind to peruse the Chronicles and recognize *Mordecaies* well deseruing long before he did: but alas, that had been an obscure fauour in comparison. God meant his worthy seruant farre better then so: he would haue this breake out when it was most seasonable: and the season was, when his prouidence might be most manifested therby. Therefore when great *Haman* was working his ouerthrow, and al the Churches; then is the opportunitie to bring forth the record: that so (all vnder one) the aduersary may be defeated with shame, the Church notably deliuered from danger, and *Mordecai* not rescued onely, but brought forth out of trouble, with the highest honor that his rankest enemie could be forced to giue him. Come forth (ye disciples of *Machiauel*) and set your braines on worke in the politiquest manner ye can, and see if ye can teach your nouices such a way as this, so famously to supplant your opposites, and set vp themselues in their roome! ye cannot doubtlesse, or if ye could, yet ye teach them but diuelish policie to contriue it, whereby you and they haue more cause of shame and repentance, then boasting and insulting. Therefore (not to digresse) now *Iphtah* is busie about Gods matters (neuer thinking of a reuenge of his owne priuate wrongs) and loe, the Lord is as busie about *Iphtahs* affaires, and contriuing how he may bring him foorth out of his trouble. Is not this enough to perswade vs to make God our Factor and Aduocate to pleade for vs, and bring about our matters? yea to tie our owne hands behind vs, from putting them forth vnlawfully in our owne defence? May we not say now, there is a truth in those words, Roll thy waies, or cast thy care vpon Iehouah, and he will giue thee thy hearts desire? Did he not so to *Iphtah?* Euen that issue which he would haue desired and sought by reuenge, or euill meanes (if he had been a bad person) I meane to haue his enemies to be his pages to conduct him home as their Commander; that I say obtained *Iphtah*, not by vsing euill meanes, but without vsing any at all. Was not this as a man would haue it? What needed here any shifting, any stirring, any plotting? Did not God effect it without these? So when *Ioseph* in prison was forgotten by *Pharaohs* Butler to be set free, how did the Lord remember him, to bring him foorth with farre greater honour. Thus hee dealt with his, where they relye on him. And if hee did this for *Iphtah*, a poore

Note. *Doct.* 2. *Psalm.* 37. 5.

poore souldier, a bastard, and banished, and for *Mordecai* a despised stranger, and for *Ioseph* a poore prisoner, as wee haue heard; will he not doe the like to vs, if we would cleaue vnto him as our allsufficient God, and honour him by putting ouer all to him, to deale wholly for vs, while wee sit still, and goe about his seruice? And what lesse can we doe then trust him with our matters, and wholly giue vp our selues to be doers of his work, when as our Master professeth himselfe to be wholly ours, and to bring our matters to passe, which our selues (with much labour and more sinne) should neuer be able to compasse?

We haue heard how *Iphtah* was repaired vnto by the chiefe of Gilead, and what a free and large offer they made to him if hee would goe with them: thus had the Lord prouided for his seruant. Now followeth his answere: *Iphtah* therfore (as he might well) told the Princes of Gilead of their fault, by so good occasion and opportunitie as was offered; and how iniuriously they had dealt with him, in driuing him out from among them against all right and law: and hereupon hee demanded of them how they could now in their streight seeke to him among all other? and indeed they could with no sound reason request fauour of him whom they had hated; and as for him, hauing receiued such measure from them, how could hee trust them? And they could not denie it, which was a shame to them to remember: but now they would preferre him (they said) to make him recompence, and the rather to perswade him thereof, they confessed the whole matter vnto him. But if he had been as wilfull now they stood in neede of him, (which he saw very well) as they had been cruell and spightfull against him before; hee would neuer haue condescended vnto them, but would haue held them on the racke. *The summe of verse 6.7.8.*

We learne here, that God doth oft make vs stand in need of their helpe whom we hate and despise. First to the end wee may see our fault in hating them, and take shame for it, as there is cause. Secondly, to ouercome enuie, which if we had not need one of another, would grow very strong. For this cause did the Lord so dispose, that the Tribes euer needed one another, (as we see through the stories of this booke and the bookes of *Samuel*) that they might hold one with another against Idolaters, and might not hate each the other; and in a spirituall respect, so God made the people stand in need of the Apostles, whom before they had railed vpon in the second of the Acts. And so we, if we weighed it would neuer hate each the other, nor fall out as we doe too easily, one with another, considering the plunges we may be put to thereby, as when we are driuen to stand in need euen of them among all other, and it is in their hand to doe vs some great hurt. *Doct. vers. 6.* *Acts 2.37.*

And yet some doe so rest in their owne sufficiencie, through the want of wise foresight of the casualties which after may befall them, and through the pride of heart in their present estate, that they would stand in neede of none, neither be beholding vnto any, which is but a nourishing of the hardnes of their hearts, and high mindednes, that so they may further glorie in themselues: and therfore such will rather offer violence to themselues, then they will vse the helpe of any such as they like not: As *Ahab* spake of *Michaiah*, when he both stood in great need of his help, and was wished to vse it by godly *Iehosaphat*; No, saith he, for I hate him, and he doth not prophe- *Note.* *1. King. 22.8.*

 cie

cie good for me: but it had been better for him to haue been beholding to him.

So that in respect of such passions, it is some restraint of nature and bridling of the corrupt heart, in him that can seeke to his enemie. And seeing God doth make vs all to stand in need one of another, why should wee not make our hearts to bow and bend, especially when it shall be also for our owne good and benefit? Although I must say, that this is not so commendable in vs, nor profitable for vs thus farre to seeke to other, when we may feare the better thereby; (for a naturall man will straine himselfe for aduantage) but when we doe it to crosse our selues, and our euill hearts (which rebell in vs, and would carrie vs to the contrarie) and so stoope to the ouercomming of the poyson and corruption that is in them, and that also for conscience sake, that we may please God therein; this is a grace and worthie thing indeed.

This being done, we should doe well to help one another, and perswade each other to turne away to alienate rancour and stomacke from their enemies, as *Iacob* hath commendably gone before vs herein to *Esau*, and *Dauid* toward *Saul*, and the Prophet *Elisha* did perswade the King of Israel to handle his enemies kindly which fell into his hands. But yet on the other side we must take heed as well of flattering men in their euill, as hating thē: for wee may not sinne to obtaine and get mens fauour, but beare our crosse contentedly, if euer wee be driuen to seeke helpe of them whose sinne wee haue set our selues against; for why wee haue done our duties, though wee receiue ill measure for our good will, and God will make a way for vs, that al shall be well, and he will (if it be expedient) turne their hearts towards vs, for all that: but (as was said before) let vs make none our enemies by needlesse prouoking of them, but hold peace with all, (if it be possible) yea euen with them that are our enemies.

Gen. 32. 18.
2. King. 6. 22.

For how would these here haue done, if *Iphtah* had vsed them as they did him? Or what had become of *Iehoram*, 2. King. 3. if *Elisha* had persisted in his reiecting the motion which he made, because he and his father had scorned him and his predecessor *Elija* before? Therefore be wee wise, for God may so order it, that (to resist proud men) euen they whom we haue prouoked in our rashnes, may be in place to doe vs much hurt, and that none saue the very persons whom we haue scorned, can helpe vs in our neede. When *Saul* was newly created King, there were some iust of this humour (and therefore they are called sonnes of Belial) who defied him: Tush, say they, what new vpstart is this? how shall such a base fellow saue vs? so that they would not acknowledge nor take him for their King. But shortly after, how should they haue done (when *Nahash* came vpon them) if that despised fellow (as they accounted of him) had not holpen them? Then there was seeking to *Saul*: and after the victorie it was demaunded by the people, who were these that spake against *Saul* so despightfully, saying, Shall he raigne ouer vs? bring them foorth, and let them be slaine. Therefore (that we may auoid this shame and imputation of folly to be in our extreames, now to abandon a man as nothing worth, and after to seeke to him, acknowledging him to be our onely helper) let vs learne this moderation towards all, as neither to be burdensome to the greatest, nor yet beare a scornefull minde toward

2. King. 3. 13.
1. Sam. 10. 27.

ward the meaneſt. If the Samaritan, and the man that fell among theeues had knowne each other before,and the one ſcorned to be the better for the other,is it like the one would haue looſed and relieued the other in that extremitie? Yet we may well thinke (in ſuch a caſe) hee muſt haue been of a rare proud ſtomack, that would haue lien ſtill wounded and in paine,rather then be beholding to him that was there to helpe him. And let me giue the poore a caueat, concerning this humour (for they that muſt depend vpon all, yet hauing a proud heart, wiſh that all depended vpon them, and ſometimes will vtter words to that effect) and I ſay this vnto them,It ill becommeth the richeſt: and euen they may bee ſure at one time or other to ſmart for their proud ſtomacks: but much worſe it beſeemeth the pooreſt, who rather (as *Salomon* ſaith) ſhould vſe all entreatie. Let ſuch breake their hearts,and make holy vſe of Gods affliction vpon them, and ſubmit themſelues to the bearing of their burthen, that ſo the hearts of the wealthier be not iuſtly hardned againſt them.

Alſo we ſee here in their deſiring the helpe of *Iphtah*, whom they had before expelled, that oft times the things which men reiect, God chuſeth to doe great enterprizes by. Which as it was moſt cleerely verified in our Sauour,who being the ſtone which the builders refuſed,was made the chiefe corner ſtone; ſo was it alſo liuely verified in the Apoſtles after, *Paul* himſelfe ſaying of himſelf: For all the good he had done,and the reſt, we are al made a gazing ſtocke to the world,to the Angels,and to men. And ſo at this day, by whom doth the Lord gather his Church together,but by them that are counted the abiects of the world? or whom doth he make members of his Church,but them and thoſe to be deareſt vnto him, who are not counted meete to liue on the earth? Therefore let no faithfull ſeruant of God be diſmaied for the diſcourteſies and diſcouragements which he ſhall meete with by the vnthankfull world; the Lord ſeeth their workes, and hath them in neuer the leſſe account,but will plentifully reward them: of which point I need not ſay much,hauing ſo often handled it in this booke alreadie.

Doct.2.verſ.6.

Acts 4.11.

1.Cor.4.9.

THE SIXTIE FIVE SERMON ON THE ELEVENTH CHAPTER OF THE BOOKE OF IVDGES.

NOw let vs proceed with *Iphtah* his anſwere made to the Elders of Gilead: Firſt therefore in this hee repeateth and rippeth vp their fault,which in times paſt they had committed againſt him: telling them, that they now comming to him in their diſtreſſe, he (as he might well) marueiled at it, they neuer hauing made agreement with him. And it is eaſie to be ſeene, that in all this,hee anſwered, as he might lawfully doe,putting away all gall and bitternes; for it was

Verſ.7.

meete they should secure him. And euen so it is lawfull for vs, by so good an occasion as was offered to him by them, to doe as hee did, in a like case: to wit, to rehearse mens great iniurying of vs, when they would make nothing of them. And yet all is not necessarie to be followed and practised of vs alwaies, which Iphtah said to them here, and namely his repeating of their fault, but as the partie is able and fit to beare it, and as the weightines of the matter requireth. But without due regard had, the ripping vp of matters and faults betwixt such as haue been at variance, is oft times a reuiuing or an increasing of strife betwixt the parties. But these men of Gilead seeing they were many, and their offence had bin great and apparant in excluding him, therefore hee maketh mention of the iniurie which they had offered him, he hauing so good opportunitie, and doing it so meekly and kindly; and yet *Gedeon* did wel before in not ripping vp, but burying an iniury done to him by the men of Ephraim, and passing it ouer in silence, when yet they had sore prouoked him.

Doct. in vers. 7. Note.

Note. Therefore herein we must craue of God the spirit of wisedome to direct vs how to deale in the like cases, and whether to repeate wrongs done vnto vs, and how farre, and when: as if they be but words, and in heate and passion vttered, then to passe by them. But if it shall be found expedient to rehearse our wrongs, yet this must be resolued of by vs, to doe it without bitternes and prouoking of them who haue hurt vs: and if we can make them see their fault, it is well: but to this end, in the affection of our loue let vs goe about it, and seeke it at their hands, but not to cast them in teeth with it, to ease and satisfie our stomackes thereby, and so stinging them, but earnestly desiring their good in any thing that wee say to them, neither denying to them (for all that mentioning of their offence) any helpe wee can yeeld to them for their benefit. And when we shall see cause to speake, let vs also take heed of harshnes and tartnes in speaking, whereby our hearts will otherwise easily be incensed, and set on fire against them before we be aware.

Doct. vers. 8. Now in their answere to his exprobration made against them, in vers. 7. let vs in this verse note, that they doe not deny, but confesse that they had iniured him, but indeed they shew that they (conueying it cleanly another way) are vtterly vnwilling to heare of it: telling him why they came to him, namely to make him their Captaine for their deliuerance, by which kindnesse offered to him, they hoped (they said) to make him amends. Where we may learne, that it was commendable in them, and to be followed, in that they doe grant that they had faulted and iniured him. So is it euer to bee done of vs: and contrarily, that the washing away of mens faults, (whereof they may iustly bee conuicted) by facing, lying, or otherwise hiding, or cloaking, or extenuating them, must be carefully auoided. By which meanes wee doe but lay them more open before God, and as it were, put them in remembrance of them: the onely way to couer them, is by confessing and renouncing them, for to such belongs the promise of forgiuenes, which is called the true couering of them by God himselfe, Psalm. 32. For if wee haue sinned, wee ought to acknowledge it, according to the nature, qualitie and kinde thereof: whether to God or man, publikely or priuatly, yea if it be to one: according to S. *Iames* direction, in these words: Acknowledge your faults one to another. And if we cannot be brought to do

Prou. 28. 13. Psal. 32. 1. Iames 5. 16.

so,

ſo,and that willingly; much more hardly,or not at all, will we offer further reſiſtance of,and violence to our corrupt nature,which ſome ſinnes doe and will require. And yet if we come to yeeld ſo farre,yet if we doe it houerly and for faſhion,or to get that which we ſeeke,by our ſo confeſſing,howſoeuer it may bee commendable before men, yet before God it is nothing worth.

But in that they haſted from hearing much of that matter,it being harſh in their hearing,and ſore againſt them, it bewraieth a corruption to be noted in vs which is ouer common,to wit, how vnwilling we are to haue our faults brought to light; we care not how little and ſeldome we heare of any thing that is againſt our corrupt nature, or euill practiſe, againſt which yet we ſhould be ready to heare the hardeſt, knowing that wee are not debters to the fleſh, but enemies to it, and that profeſſed. A token (no doubt) of a filthie and hard heart,much putrified: for ſhould we not be ready to purge out the poyſon and putrifaction which will burſt and kill vs? *Doct.2.* Note. Ioh.3.19. Rom.8.12.

In particular,the practiſe of moſt men is like theſe Gileadites; for if they haue ſlandered their brother by whiſpering reports in corners (where they thinke they are ſafe enough from comming to light againſt them) and afterwards are charged to make them good, or take the ſhame thereof by eating their word, they can cunningly winde themſelues out of that argument,by turning their ſpeech to ſome other matter, which they thinke will better pleaſe their accuſer, at leaſt which may couer their owne lewdneſſe. And if they be preſſed with it, oh then (ſay they) let vs heare no more of that,ye ſpeake out of ſeaſon,&c. Is this honeſt dealing? to lay on loade of reproch vpon the innocent, and to aggrauate conceits or falſe rumours againſt them, and when the truth ſhould bee brought foorth to the ſauing and preſeruing of our brothers good name,then to leaue him in the briars vnconſcionably? Let *Ioſephs* brethren condemne theſe, who confeſſed their ſinne againſt their brother and concealed it not. Note.

If it be the propertie of a ſeruant of God,to hunt and purſue himſelfe for his inward ſinne, yea though it be but one,as wee reade *Dauid* oft to haue done; what ought we to doe for many,and thoſe alſo manifeſt before men? But if men doe accuſe and iudge themſelues no ſorer for their ſinnes in priuate,aggrauating and bewailing them to God, with taking ſhame to themſelues for the committing them,then they giue teſtimonie thereof to men: alſo,if they doe not more reſiſt them aloue,then they loue to heare of them by others, it is no marueile that they be ſo bad as they are. And as it is too common to take a priuate reproofe vnkindly, nay rebellioußly, and with hating him that offers it,which yet he is commanded of God to doe: euen ſo in publique hearing it fareth; inſomuch as if ſome mens conſciences be touched in any liuely manner, (which is an wholeſome warning) yet wee ſee how vnwelcome it is to the moſt,and excepted againſt, though without the leaſt cauſe of ſo doing, but of the contrary rather, to wit, of yeelding thankes for it. The vſe is,that if we cannot be willing to heare of faults, we ſhould in no wiſe giue libertie to our ſelues, nay nor by any violence bee brought to commit them. But of theſe points,ſee chap.9.in *Iothams* fleeing from his brother,&c. Pſal.51.3. Pſal.73.3. Note. Leuit.19.17.

Now out of the offer of the Elders, compared with *Iphtahs* ſpeech in Verſ.9.

the

the ninth verse, demanding assurance thereof, (for he did indeed vrge them about it, as he had cause) a question may arise, how they could offer this to *Iphtah* to be their Iudge, and how he could take it with a good conscience? Deut. 23. 2. First, seeing they had no authoritie to offer it. Secondly, seeing he and they both had this blocke in their way, that a Bastard might not enter into the Congregation of the Lord to beare any office. The answer is to both questions one: that the Lord directed them thus to doe, who is bound to no law: and that he guided them herein, the whole story through the Chapter testifieth. The Lord excludeth such in Deuteronomy from bearing publike office: and that to terrifie men from begetting Bastards, who are in this world reprochfull, and lie open to much miserie. And yet how this forbidding that sinne preuaileth with men, this the commonnesse of the sinne, and this prophane practise of adulterers too too much bewraieth, who thinke that by this meanes, of bringing Bastards into the world, (that is the pitie they take of them) they shall shunne the wearisome company of the wife, and tediousnesse of children, with the vnwelcome annoiances that they count to accompany both. But oh monsters! doe they thinke by auoiding the burden of the lawfull wife and children, to escape the blot of vnlawfull libertie, euen reprochfull whoredomes? Doth not God set a brand both vpon them and their cursed fruit? For it is prooued by experience, that besides the discouragement which bastards are oppressed with, as of scorne, and opprobrie in the world, (which of it selfe is enough to hold them vnder) the Lord denieth them (commonly) good education: so that they prooue vagabonds, curseth them with a more then common indisposition and aukenesse of nature, to retaine instruction and gouernment. Note. And lastly, there are few of them who are not tainted with vile and odious qualities, such as they deriue from their vitious and vncleane parents. And therefore the greater is their sinne, who for all this his prohibition, most wickedly fil the world with them, & cause them to be brought into so great calamitie. Yet as the innocents cannot doe with it, so (God bee thanked) they are not shouldred out from the hope of saluation, for there is no respect Actes 10. 34. of persons with God, if they feare him. But if they were cast off by the Lord, yet such is the vnconscionable beastlinesse of those gracelesse persons, that for their owne filthy lust they would thus endanger them, as the loathsome practise of those vncleane Locustes, the Popish Monkes and Friers, both in this land and elsewhere hath abundantly witnessed to the world in former ages. See more in the first verse of this Chapter.

Vers. 10. 11. *Iphtah* hauing found ill dealing at their hands before, as we haue heard, for that they were not lead by conscience and the feare of God, when they cast him out, but by partialitie, vsed crueltie against him; he did not therfore trust them vpon their word, but requireth an oath of God at their mouthes, as may be gathered by their making God a witnesse of the promise which they made vnto him, and so tieth them to a sure couenanting with him: For it had not otherwise been wisely prouided for by him: and therefore when he went with the messengers to Mizpeh, he rehearsed these things there before the Lord, that so the promise which they made, might stand sure, God being desired to be the beholder and witnesse.

Doct. vers. 10. And here let vs learne, that when men haue dealt vnfaithfully, and dishonestly,

nestly, they haue no wrong offered them, if they bee not credited as before, no, although they bee bound by bond, (whereas their bare word was taken while they went for honest men) for they haue giuen iust cause to other to suspect their credit. And by this, which I say, may be noted, that one cause why men are in lesse credit now adaies, is their vnfaithfull dealing. And whereas some cannot be trusted, nor borrow vpon their word or bond, but for want of credit doe goe without that which would stand them in exceeding great stead, for their vpholding and maintenance; it is the fruit of their owne doings, and that which they haue sought by their owne vntrustinesse, and breaking of their promise, whereby they haue lost their credit together with their honesty. Note.

For in these daies many care not to deceiue, yea, and vndoe others, and therefore come to nought themselues also for the most part, whereas some other being faithful and conscionable; vpon their bare credit, liue and maintaine their charge by borrowing, and by other mens forbearing them. And whereas it is obiected on the behalfe of these vnthrifts and deceiuers, that they must be borne withall, though they cannot pay that which they haue borrowed: I answer; Some of them see no likelihood that they can repay so much as they will seeke to borrow, and take into their hands, of other mens goods; which argueth little honesty, and therefore are well content to wind it from them cunningly and craftily, whereby also they impouerish some; others will not diminish their occupying in the least manner, though they goe aboue their reach, nor detract from their belly and pastime to pay the owner, therby shewing that they care not how he come by his due and right, or whether he euer haue it againe or no.

Now while these things are thus, we may note that the beautie of religion is such, if it be planted in men soundly and indeed, as that it winnes credit to him that hath it for contrary dealing, and maketh him to be approoued for his faithfulnesse, conscionablenesse and honesty: whereas he that is void of them, liueth in vtter discredit and iust reproch. And whereas ye will say, some of them that make shew of religion, doe yet deceiue and deale vntrustily with their creditors. I answer, it is not the shew of religion, but the practise of it that carrieth the beauty with it that I speake of: and if any that be taken to be religious, offend this way, know wee that it is not their religion that imboldneth them to such dealing, but that they haue so little of it. And so it is true also, that some that haue credit deseruedly, doe, for the sweetnesse of the gaine, if they take not heed, hold their due from the owners sometimes, though they may little reioyce in it. And let them know, that their sinne is the greater: but yet all this notwithstanding, there are some who dare not, neither will by any meanes be brought to doe so. And if ye aske me, Why then doe men take bonds of such as are of approoued honesty, and haue not broken nor lost their credit; as if they were no better trusted then other common men? I answer: Not because they be distrusted, but first, seeing all are mortal, and so men might lose their goods, if they had no securitie for them by those in whose hands they are: and secondlie, that contention may not arise betwixt the posteritie of both parties that shal come after. And againe, seeing there are such deceiuers in the world, as would

would prouoke euen the honest to contention, if they can see any hole open, or espie any aduantage.

And this rule holdeth also firme and good in religious actions before God. For as it is the honour of a Christian to continue constant in his loue to the truth, and the Church of God, the fruit whereof is a sound and good report: so if a man begin to warpe and bewray his hollownesse or treachery in either; his staine is not easily washt out, neither can he looke for that currant estimation or reuerēce which before he had, nor scarce obtain so much afterward as to be credited, for all his profession. Although men will betrust their vessels with oyle or wine, while they be sound & whole, yet if they begin to leake and run, they will not commit any thing vnto them, which is in
Mat. 16.16.17. danger of losing. Our Sauiour asked *Peter* but once, Whom sayest thou that I am? and tooke his word, when he deserued no other: whereas afterward
Iohn 21.15. hee was not satisfied with one nor two professions of his affection, *Simon* louest thou me? good reason, he had made a great cracke in his credit, and
Note. therefore he that had forsworne Christ, deserued not vpon his owne bare word and answere, to be beleeued. And those who haue deceiued the opinion of the Church touching their religion, by falling into error and schisme, or their pietie and honesty, by grosse offences; may thanke themselues, if euer afterward the people of God haue them in a iealousie. As we reade in the Ecclesiasticall historie, that when once the baptized partie reuolted either from his religion or good conscience, (as *Miriam* by her arrogancie) the Church admitted him not without serious repentance and confession of his fault. But if he slipt the second time, they practised greater seueritie towards them, enioyning them not repentance only, but (for a space of time) to remaine out of the Church as infamous. Yea, some euen of the reuerendest Fathers of those times, as *Cyprian* and others, grew to this erronious opinion, that such were not to be admitted without rebaptization, as if their former seale had been quite puld off by their sin, I meane the seale of forgiuenesse. Therefore let all Christians looke to their standing: the di-
Note. diuell (if it be possible) will quite ouerthrow them; but if he cannot, hee will foile them, and take away the crowne of their reioycing, which is their faithfulnesse and constancie. And he is an impudent person, who hauing foully dishonored God and his profession, wil hold vp his head boldly, and claime his old priuiledge. Doe we not see that among men, one periured, or a forger, is disabled from euer bearing any witnesse, against or for any, in publike court? And haue not all men such a one in suspition? Doth not treason taint euen the blood of the traitor, so that (euen when he is loyall) he goeth for no better? and hee who hath got a patent of restitution, or pardon for his fellonie, doth he not forfeit it by a second offence in the like kind? But of this enough.

Vers. 11. Another thing worth the marking is this, that in as much as *Iphtah* went so easily from his iust quarrell that hee had against them of Gilead, and had so soone done, when he had wisely told them that which concerned them to heare, and when they had assured him of that which he demanded; by
Prou. 16. this I say, we are taught, not to hold in our harts an iniurie against vs by any, but soone to remit an offence, for it is an honour to passe by it. He mentioneth

neth the matter but once to them, and once requireth security, but goeth no further. And who seeth it not to be a great grace in any man to doe so? for therein he doth after the example of the Lord himselfe, who doth not follow things against vs hotly, but sheweth great lenitie and kindnesse. And as we should not be rigorous and cruell in our dealings, to prouoke men with our bitternes to wrath, so should we make an end of controuersies, as soone and in as few words as may be, as for other causes; so, not in the least respect for this, seeing in many words commonly there is much sinne. Of this somewhat was said before in vers. 4. but especially looke backe into Chap. 8. verse 2. Exod. 34.7. Note.

And further learne what hath been the religiousnesse of an oath in times past: to wit, such that if it were once offered and taken, there was no more question, but the controuersie was ended. As we see *Rahab*, hauing it granted her by oath of the spies, that she and her fathers house should bee saued aliue, at the destruction of Ierrico, rested satisfied. Therefore men must looke to what they sweare: seeing an oath is not to bee violated, vnlesse it were made for the accomplishment of euill: in which case the keeping of it were double sinne; (as *Herods* was) and the least euill therein is great. And as heed must be taken, how men sweare, so must they who offer the oath to other, that it be so done, that they to whom it is ministred, may be free from snare, so that they may doe it (as the Prophet speaketh) in truth, righteousnesse and iudgement. *Doct.2.* Ioshua 2.21. Marke 6.20.

Therefore such as draw men by oath to fulfill their desire, and to doe things against conscience, haue the more to answer for. Men then must not be drawne and forced thereto, to which they cannot yeeld, nor of themselues rashly sweare to doe that which they approoue not, but abhorre. *Iphtah* doubted no more after the oath, but goeth after the army. But an oath is not strong enough now adaies to hold a man fast, neither can wee safely rest in it, for the deciding of controuersies, although the Lord hath taught vs otherwise. Now for the further ratifying of the couenant betwixt them, it is rehearsed before the Lord in Mizpeh by them: for thus the men of Gilead say, We couenant with thee before the Lord, to doe, as we say, and that he may punish vs, if we breake it. Therefore such as are common swearers are not to be admitted to this solemne oath, either in accusation or decission of controuersies. For (as I said) they haue lost their credit: they haue often falsified their oathes, (for how should a common swearer auoid common periury?) and therefore that which another man vseth reuerently, and with conscience, such rush vpon commonly and carelesly, through a prophane habit: being herein worse then Heathens, who counted not such worthie of societie, but *intestabiles*, as they called them, that is, such as were not to be admitted as witnesse. And commonly such they are, who prostitute themselues for gaine to sweare falsely before the Magistrate: of whom there are many, and some the Lord shoaleth out from among their fellowes, as notorious monsters, branding some with infamie and misery, and terrifying the consciences of other with hellish feares, if not with despaire. And a step to this sinne, is the abusing of the tongue by false asseuerations, or contestations: as to say, Verily it is thus, or so: As sure as I am in this place it is true: God knoweth I speake no more then truth: I take God to witnesse, &c. Heb 6.16.

Whereunto commonly men ioyne deprecations with *Peter*, if they bee not beleeued. And yet all false. This I say, neuer goeth alone: the common lyer, the false asseuerer, will not stick, if need be, to be a false swearer also. Therfore (to shut vp) let men account of oathes as diuine bands and pledges: cautions of our fidelitie and truth deposed, and left in the hands of God himselfe: which he that dare forfeit or breake, let him be sure, that God (to whose censure he yeeldeth himselfe) will find him out, if not in this world, (as many are) yet hereafter, when hee shall giue him his portion in the lake that burneth with fire and brimstone for euer. As indeed what punishment can equall that sinne, which ouerthroweth all ciuill societie and (the sinewes thereof) religion it selfe?

THE SIXTIE SIXE SERMON ON THE ELEVENTH CHAPTER OF THE BOOKE OF IVDGES.

The second part of the Chapter.

Vers. 12. *Then Iphtah sent messengers vnto the King of the children of Ammon, saying, What hast thou to doe with me, that thou art come against me, to fight in my land?*

13. *And the King of the children of Ammon answered vnto the messengers of Iphtah, Because Israel tooke my land when they came vp from Egypt, from Arnon vnto Iabbok, and vnto Iorden: now therefore restore those lands quietly.*

14. *Yet Iphtah sent messengers againe vnto the children of Ammon,*

15. *And said vnto him, Thus saith Iphtah, Israel tooke not the land of Moab, nor the land of the children of Ammon.*

16. *But when Israel came vp from Egypt, and walked through the wildernesse vnto the red Sea, then they came to Kadesh.*

18. *Then they went through the wildernesse, and compassed the land of Edom, and the land of Moab, and came by the East side of the land of Moab, and pitched on the other side of Arnon, and came not within the coast of Moab; for Arnon was the border of Moab.*

19. *Also Israel sent messengers vnto Sihō King of the Amorites, the King of Heshbon, and Israel said vnto him, Let vs passe we pray thee, by thy land, vnto our place.*

20. *But Sihon consented not to Israel, that hee should goe through his coast: but Sihon gathered all his people together, and pitched in Iahaz, and fought with Israel.*

21. *And the Lord God of Israel gaue Sihon and all his folke into the hands of Israel, and they smote them: so Israel possessed all the land of the Ammorites, the inhabitants of that countrie.*

22. *And they possessed all the coasts of the Amorites, from Arnon vnto Iabbok, and from the wildernesse euen vnto Iorden.*

23. *Now therefore the Lord God of Israel hath cast out the Amorites before his people*

people Iſrael,and ſhouldeſt thou poſſeſſe it?

24. *Wouldeſt not thou poſſeſſe that which Chemoſh thy god giueth thee to poſſeſſe?*
ſo whomſoeuer the Lord our God driueth out before vs,them will we poſſeſſe.

25. *And art thou now farre better then Balak the ſonne of Zippor, King of Mo-*
ab? did he not ſtriue with Iſrael,and fight againſt them?

26. *When Iſrael dwelt in Heſhbon,and in her townes,and in Aroer, and in her*
townes,and in all the Cities that are by the coaſts of Arnon three hundred yeere? Why
did ye not then recouer them in that ſpace?

27. *Wherefore I haue not offended thee; but thou doeſt me wrong, to warre a-*
gainſt me. The Lord the Iudge,be Iudge this day,betweene the children of Iſrael and
the children of Ammon.

28. *Howbeit the King of the children of Ammon, hearkned not vnto the words*
of Iphtah,which he had ſent him.

I*Phtah* being now ſtabliſhed their Captaine and Guide, as wee haue heard, it is ſhewed in the verſes now read, how hee went to worke againſt the Ammonites,and that was in this manner. Firſt,hee ſendeth meſſengers to the King of Ammon,with reaſons to appeaſe him,if it may be,and hold him from warre,but he hearkens to none. His quarrell was for land,which Iſrael had now enioyed full 400. yeeres, and yet the King of Ammon claimeth it, and being denied it,now maketh warre with them for it. Now more particularly let vs heare their reaſoning about the matter: the which to auoid tedious neſſe, I will not at large ſet downe firſt,but lay it out in the verſes,as they be in order. *The ſenſe of theſe verſes in generall.*

In theſe two verſes, *Iphtah* demands of the King of Ammon by his meſſengers,why he made warre againſt him, and what iniurie hee had offered him,why he ſhould doe ſo. The King of Ammon anſwered him, that Iſrael had taken away part of his land,when they came out of Egypt,and this he required to bee ſafely deliuered, and reſtored peaceably to him,and hee would depart from moleſting his countrie,but otherwiſe he would not. Of theſe in their order. *Verſe 12.13. particularly.*

Firſt here let vs conſider *Iphtahs* dealing, who before hee goes to warre, debateth and enquireth about the matter,to ſee if by this meanes the enemy might be appeaſed: in a word he vſeth the beſt meanes he could deuiſe to keepe peace: which ought to be obſerued as a rule,that ſo we ſhould do before the attempting of warre with nation, or ſuite with any perſon. According to the generall rules: As much as in you lieth haue peace with all,and againe, Enſew peace and follow it,though it flee from you,(for it is a precious treaſure.) So in this particular eſpecially: We know how carefully we labour,to preſerue a member of our body before we will cut it off. So much more we ſhould deale in this caſe,to preſerue many bodies of men and perſons rather then commit them to the hazzard of warre,(as making no more account of the liues of Chriſtian men,then of dogges,oxen,or ſheepe,or to ſuffer ciuill and priuat enuy, contention and ſtrife, to the loſing of many ſoules. And ſo did the ten Tribes deale with their brethren on the other ſide Iorden, that is, they did preuent and ſtay much that might haue riſen,and Doct.ver.12. Rom 12.18. Heb.12.14.

blood-ſhedding. For when after their departure from them, they heard
Ioſu.22.33. they had committed a grieuous treſpaſſe againſt the Lord, for the which they thought they had iuſt cauſe to make warre with them: yet did they not follow their owne mindes, nor giue full credit to the report, but did firſt wiſely ſend vnto them to know the certaintie, and thereby they were ſatiſfied. But I doubt not of the eaſie conſenting to this part of iuſtice, as being a point diſputed and agreed vpon by Heathens and their practiſe in their warres, as alſo your Moraliſts, whoſe poſition it is: That an honeſt warre, is to be preferred to an vnequall or hurtfull peace, and no otherwiſe. To leaue this therefore and to come neerer to our ſelues, the ſame rule is to be kept in priuate controuerſies betwixt men, that law be not attempted, till all other meanes be firſt vſed: and a great ſinne it is among Chriſtians, to runne by and by to law, and to the ſuing one of another, as too many vſe to doe, hotly, raſhly, and wilfully, though themſelues ſuſtaine moſt hurt by it, who doe ſo, as being authors of the contention, and ſuite. Likewiſe the ſame may be ſaid of offenders in other kindes, who if they haue been lead away by leaud counſell or companie, and yet relent for it afterward, and take admonition againſt it willingly, they are to be vſed more fauourably (ſo farre as by the law they may be forborne:) euen as the ſtiffenecked and ſaweie, and bold defenders of their ſinne are ſharply to be dealt with, leſt they grow paſt recouerie, and doe as the waters, euen ouerflow all places where they come.

Some controuerſies ſhall (no doubt) alwaies ariſe betweene man and man, touching things, the equitie whereof is vnknowne, and vncertaine it ſhall be whoſe the right is. But if contentions proceeding from manifeſt wrong, or from vngrounded ſurmiſes, were at the firſt taken vp, and cut off, (in which commonly moſt raſhnes, heate and diſtemper is bewrayed) yea if trifling quarrels were troden vnder foote; then neither ſhould men haue
Note. ſo many needleſſe ianglings, and thoſe which are ſerious and could not bee auoided, ſhould more indifferently be handled and decided, either priuatly or (with peaceable conſent of both parties) by trauerſe of law. Yea I ſay, if themſelues could not hit vpon agreement, they would yeeld to the diſcretion and loue of ſuch as might compound their differences: rather then multiplie one ſinne vpon another, as fiercenes of words to the gall of their ſtomacks, and other actuall purſuite each of other to both the former; ſhewing themſelues vnappeaſeable and inexorable. It is the pride, bitternes and enuie of the heart, rather then the weightineſſe of the cauſe, which oft prouokes men to the heate and ſtomacke which they vtter and bewray (all may ſee) in their iarrings each againſt other. And therefore they are ſo farre from *Iphtah* his practiſe, that they reioyce they haue any pretence of debate and ſuite againſt their neighbour: and follow it in ſuch eager and odious manner, that all may ſee they ſue not becauſe they haue cauſe, but are glad they haue any occaſion (ſuch a delight they haue therein) that they might fall to ſuite. The claime of a whole Tribes inheritance, did not ſo ſtirre *Iphtah* to wrath againſt this vſurper, as many of vs would bee ſtirred againſt him that would challenge a few acres of our poſſeſſion: what doe I ſay? nay, againſt him that contendeth about a twelue penny matter with vs; and yet wee ſhould exceed them, that goe many degrees before *Iphtah* in the meanes of knowledge and acquaintance with Gods will in particuler duties, if we did well

well consider it. Let such doings be heard of among Heathens: as for Christians, if one partie will not heare of his dutie, let the other giue him ouer, and let him contend (if he will needs) with his owne shadow. Doubtlesse in many contentions, if either party were wise, the others folly should soone appeare, and the contention which growes past recouerie should cease, and be at an end.

2 And further *Iphtah*, by asking what wrong he had done him, that he came to warre against him, giueth all to vnderstand, how absurd and odious a thing it is, to doe wrong and deale hardly with them who haue done no iniurie to vs: and therefore hee saith, If I haue done wrong, good reason it is that I should satisfie the challenge, &c. For if that be foolishnes when wee doe but meddle with a matter that belongeth not vnto vs, and with the which we haue nothing to doe; yea though wee meane no euill thereby, if that (I say) be folly; and as *Salomon* saith, all one as if a man plucked a curst dogge by the eare: then to hurt any willingly, and to bee cruell and iniurious to him, that would liue in peace by vs, is an high degree of iniquitie. And if we ought to sustaine a double iniurie, rather then to offer to reuenge one, how great a sinne is it to doe wrong, or hurt any man, wee not being prouoked by him? It is abomination; euen as it is to let the guiltie goe free, and yet many make no conscience hereof. But I haue spoken of this point in chap. 8. in *Gedeons* protestation to *Zeba* and *Zalmunna* and in other places.

Prou.26.17. Matth.5.39. Prou.17.15.

The King of the Ammonites sends him word, that Israel had taken away part of his land, when they went out of Egypt toward the land of Canaan, and therefore he made warre with them. But how true this was, ye may see in Deuteronomy, where the Lord speaketh thus to the children of Israel, when they should passe by them: Thou shalt not lay siege against the children of Ammon, neither make warre against them, for I will not giue the land of the children of Ammon into thy hands. And in the 37. verse, *Moses* tels them, they obeyed the Lord therein, saying: Vnto the land of the children of Ammon thou camest not: nor vnto any place of the riuer Iabbok vpon which it bounded. So we see, that whereas it is manifest, that the Lord suffered not Israel to meddle with Ammon; yet the King answers boldly, they did.

Vers.13. Deut.2.19. Deut.2.37.

This teacheth that such are to be found, who neither meane well & simply, neither care what they say: but as their hearts are full of falsehood and deceit, so their mouthes are full of lying. The Lord himselfe had said, the people of Israel should not, neither did they meddle with the Ammonites, as the forementioned scripture testifieth; yet their King boldly and vntruly auoucheth, that they tooke his land and enioyed it as their owne. The which, who should not be ready to beleeue, being so boldly auouched, and that by a King? Euen so, many care not what lyes they coyne, nor how shamelesly they lay claime to other mens goods, and how boldly and impudently they set against the truth in many other dealings. And this they doe either for their commoditie, as this King did; or for their credit, and to set a colour on their doings, as the old Prophet of Bethel did, by lying, and *Gehazi* also when hee had gotten the tallents of *Naaman*: or for both respects together, as *Ananias* and *Saphira*; and *Saul* also: See his answere

Doct.vers.13. 1.King.13.18. Acts 5.5.

 1.Sam.

1.Sam.15 20. 1.Sam.15. Let the credit of ſuch be with vs thereafter. In ſtead of this dealing wee ſee the beautie of truth and faithfulnes, without which,how can

Epheſ 5.25. men liue one with another? Put away lying therefore, as the Apoſtle willeth,and ſpeake the truth euery man to his neighbour.

*Doct.*2. In this vnreaſonable and abſurd anſwere of this King, compared with *Iphtah* his wiſe and equall proceeding, we ſee the contrarietie of mens diſpoſitions: there are ſome that ſtriue by all poſſible meanes againſt contention and vnpeaceablenes: there are others againe, whoſe delight it is to be euer at debate and oddes with ſuch as full gladly would liue at peace,as *Eſau* with *Iacob:* and all becauſe they would make a gaine and bootie of them that are honeſtly minded,or haue their will of them ſome other way. They know a godly man will buy his peace deare, rather then want it: and they wil lay loade enough vpon ſuch therefore,to ſee what they can wring from them,although without all colour of equitie. Beſides, peace is vile and of no price with an vnrighteous perſon, there is nothing to be got by it,hee ſaith: but when the water is troubled,then is his ſeaſon to caſt in,and therefore all is fiſh that comes to net. Who ſeeth not that this King was miſchieuouſly minded,in that he ſhapeth ſuch an anſwere as either (being yeelded vnto) tended to the vndoing of a Tribe; or if not,threatned implacable diſ-

1.King.20.3. ſention? So *Benhadad* ſends this meſſage to *Ahab,* Thou and all thou haſt are mine,deny it if thou dareſt. It is plaine he was ſet vpon warre, who ſent ſo proud a challenge, as excluded all poſſibilitie of agreement and peace. And ſuch there are in all places, who (if they might haue their mindes) would chuſe warre,rather then to liue in peace, that they might boldly rifle their houſes whom they grudge at, and whom they could not ſuffer to liue by them,except they might poſſeſſe them,and all they haue,as *Hamor* ſpake

Gen.34.23. of *Iacob* and his ſonnes to the men of his citie: Therefore ſeeſt thou an vnrighteous perſon? wonder not then if thou heare of vnreaſonablenes to come from him: for theſe two goe yoked together,(though feare and danger of law doe oft reſtraine the inward corruption from breaking out) ſo hideous a monſter is iniuſtice,if it might be ſeene in the colours! As for this practiſe of lying, forging, ſubborning, concealing truth,and impudent facing out an ill cauſe (as an ill title, to goe no further) for aduantage ſake, though to the treading downe of the poore innocent,nay, to his vtter vndoing,when was it more common then now adaies? And this euill (as well as other ſcurfe and iniquitie) will cleaue to the better ſort too, (if the diuell

Epheſ.6.14. can) and he will alſo, except they walke armed with their breaſt-plate continually.

Verſ.14.to 19. In theſe fiue verſes, *Iphtah* ſends word againe to the King of the Ammonites,that it was not ſo as he affirmed: they tooke no part of his ground to them: and then proceeds further by reaſons to perſwade him to deſiſt from his attempt. As firſt thus: Iſrael ſent meſſengers when they came out of Egypt,to the King of Edom to goe through his land, and he not yeelding to them, they were faine to goe a great way about, by a long and tedious iourney in the wilderneſſe: ſo they deſired to paſſe by *Moab* alſo, and could not be ſuffered. But did they make warre with either of both? No, they choſe rather to abide long in the deſert, and to goe farre about (as I haue ſaid:) ſo farre is it off, that they did them any wrong, that they choſe rather to offer violence to themselues So that they did no iniurie to any. And was it like then, that they would offer violence to any? and consequently, not to thy predecessors, the children of Ammon.

As *Iphtah* heere giues not place to vntruth, though hee preuailed not: wherein he honoured the Lord, in bearing witnesse to a good cause; so let vs know, it is our dutie to doe: namely to bring the truth to light, as much as in vs lieth; if it be but to bring them to shame who resist it, for they worke much mischiefe and iniquitie thereby: and to hold sinne from multiplying, as it doth greatly by lying. And haue we it in greater detestation, then some of them who would be taken for honest men, for as much as we know that the Lord hath linked such as loue to make lies among dogges, Inchanters, and whoremongers. And let vs remember that which *Salomon* saith: Hee who iustifieth the wicked, (lier or other) is as abominable to the Lord, as he that condemneth the innocent. And the Apostle puts the consenter to euill (whether to lying, swearing, &c.) in an higher degree of sinners, then the committers. As who seeth not, that the Pharisees and Iewes which hired and fleshed the false witnesses against our Sauiour, were worse then the false witnesses themselues? Thus *Samuel* conuicted *Saul* of his lye, 1. Sam. 15. *Elisha* argued *Gehazi*. Nay *Paul*, Galath. 2. did openly checke and detect dissimulation in *Peter*, and resisted him to his face. The truth is, men in generall hate lying, both the coyner of it, and the teller of it: but in particular, there are so many occasions fall out, (as sometimes when a man in fauour of his kinsman will not sticke to sweare against conscience to purge him of adulterie) to lay men open who doe so, that their generall hatred thereof, is turned into a speciall liking of it, or a tolerating it, and conniuence at it. Neither is it strange, that they who are not iust and armed with the breast-plate of righteousnesse, should want the girdle of veritie. Some for bribes, fauour, flatterie, friendship, commoditie, and such like partiall and sinister respects, will (to vse the prouerbe) not sticke to say, The crow is white, if their great patrons, or such as they depend vpon, wil say it before them: and others for feare, are driuen to conceale the truth, and to heare a falsehood iustified, who are as bad as lyers, and coupled with them, Reuel. the last. And yet we must know, that euery vntruth is not a lie, except we know that which we report as an vntruth, to be so. Yet must we beware that we offend not therein, neither by vttering rashly whatsoeuer we heare spoken of other (but as it may doe good:) neither in telling the truth are wee bound to vtter all the truth, further then we shall see it expedient to doe so.

Doct. ver. 14. 15

Reuel. 22. 15.

Prou. 17. 15.

Matth. 27. 20.

1. Sam. 15. 14.
2. King. 5. 26.
Gal. 2. 14.

Iphtah not onely withstands an vntruth, but also sheweth reason: so wee must withstand vntruth by reason, approoued of all and of the Scripture it selfe; so that they who will not yeeld to it, may shew themselues vnreasonable, and so they are to bee accounted, and no better, who wash away all sound reason, which they are not able to resist, breeding quarrelling and contention hereby: wherein the Pharisies and Priests went before other, neuer resting in the most sound reasons, wherewith our Sauiour in commoning with them, did conuince them, but withstood them shamelesly. So when other alleage reasons to vs, it is our dutie to yeeld to them: as *Laban* himselfe though an Idolater, answered *Abrahams* seruant, in that matter hee dealt with him for; seeing the report which he made of things vnto him, to be

Vers. 15. 16. 17.

Gen.24.50. be so currant and reasonable, I can say neither lesse nor more, saith hee, for this thing is of the Lord. But more of this in the 28. verse by way of vse hereof.

2 Now what his reason was we haue heard: to wit, that the children of Israel did offer violence to themselues, rather then they would in the least manner wrong other: therefore they would much lesse take away so great a portion of ground from him with whom they had nothing to do, neither were prouoked by him. Where we learne this, that we should neuer finde sweetnesse in comming by any profit amisse, and namely with the hurting and wronging of other. First, seeing wee thereby prouoke God against vs, Gen.12.3. for God is the auenger of such things: and what is our life, if God be against Matth.7.2. vs? Besides, as we deale to other, so shall we be dealt with againe: and lastly, besides an ill name, wee shall haue an ill conscience also, as wee may see in *Iudas*.

And as we should offer hard measure to none, so least of all to the poore, and to such as cannot beare the losse, and are not able to stand with vs in suite. For wee being by the commandement of God to relieue them, what Rom.12.13. pleasure should wee take in plucking from them? and God threatens to heare their crie against their oppressors. And yet how are the poore griped and pilled? But he that obserueth it, shall find, that either God maketh themselues who so wrong them, to crie out of it, for feare of his reuenging hand, one time or other: or else it shall be to them, I meane their sweete morsels (as they count them) which they take in by wronging other, as the Israelites Numb.11.33. Quailes were, who died with them, while they were in their mouthes. Euen so shall they haue small liking of their iniurie they doe, that I say no more. But let them rather make restitution, and that speedily, while they may, in token of their repentance, which is the onely good end that can be made of such doings. This point hath oft come to hand and largely been insisted vpon. See verse twelfth. Only let vs marke the example of *Iacob* for the proofe Gen.31.39. of the doctrine, who rather then he would giue *Laban* (a quarrellous and vnreasonable man) the least occasion to challenge him for pillage and robberie, did more then he needed, euen make good euery sheepe, which was casually destroyed or perished, with his owne. Now if all this our good dealing, doe not preuaile with our euill aduersarie, nor stop his mouth, yet (as *Iacob* answers *Laban*) the Lord who seeth vs in secret, will take our cause into his owne hand, and plead for vs; whereas otherwise, although all men should stand out for vs, yet our conscience and God being against vs, wee should not be able to stand vnder our burthen.

Vers.19. to the 25. Another reason *Iphtah* setteth downe in these verses, thus: *Sihon*, king of the Ammonites, would needs come out against vs, as wee were going toward Canaan, and God gaue him into our hands, so that by him wee enioy this land which ye contend for, and which he enioyed; and therfore what haue ye to doe to claime it? or what right haue yee vnto it? For yee neuer possessed it, but *Sihon* of whom we wonne it by the law of warre. So that if the Lord our God hath cast him out, and giuen his land to vs, commest thou in who hast nothing to doe with it, against vs to possesse it? Hee further in the 24. verse sheweth that which he said cleerely by a similitude, thus: Yee Ammonites worship the Idoll *Chemosh* for your god, and you thinke that the

the land which yee possesse, yee inioy it by his benefit, and so by good right: so we haue this by the benefit of the true God, and therefore we possesse it by very good right. And as for *Chemosh*, hee called not that idoll a God, for that hee tooke it to bee so, but for that the Ammonites so iudged it to be.

We may see here, how farre we may lawfully enioy such things as are taken in warre: and that is, when the warre is lawfully taken in hand, as by Israel it was. That which we thereby obtaine by good successe, that may we enioy, as giuen into our hands by the Lord. And to speake of things more priuat, the same may be said of all that God giueth vs by the good will of our friends, or by our lawfull dealing, and by Gods blessing in our calling. But yet with this watchword, that wee honour him therewith in Christian life, and glad the hearts of Gods people thereby: which we ought as well to do, as to be able to prooue and shew, that the commodities we enioy, are no fruites of our owne rapine, oppression, couetousnesse, and euill conscience, but indeed the bequests of our father, which, as *Iacob* said, the Lord our God hath bestowed, as a blessing vpon vs his seruants, seeking first the things that concerne our happinesse and God his kingdome, and receiuing from him these smaller things againe, in token of his allowing and approouing of vs. But this is an vsuall argument in this booke, therefore I passe by it.

Doct. vers. 19. to the 29. Genes. 32.10. Genes. 33.5.

More particularly, let vs note out of this verse, in that Israel would not (and was guided by God therein) when he had great need, so much as goe through the land of *Sihon* without his leaue, learne we hence I say, that no man may vsurpe or challenge to himselfe another mans right, but euery man is to be content with his owne portion and allowance; yea in this the Lord will haue the meanest free from the tyrannie of the greatest, and taketh the cause of the poore into his owne hand, against their potent enemies, though there be none vpon earth that can iudge them, as in the case of *Ahab* and *Iezabels* extorting *Naboths* vineyard, doth appeare. And the reason is good: for next to the good of the Church, the Lord hath a special care of vpholding of societie among men, by order and good gouernment, which are ouerthrowne when proprietie in goods and commodities is taken away, by the vnequall vsurpation of the greater ouer the smaller. And in truth, as there is small oddes betwixt beasts and men, when the common bands of equitie are broken: so much lesse is it like, that a Church can bee setled and established in such confusion: and the greater is their sinne, who euen in the Church exercise this mischieuous practise, whereof not God (who is the God of order) but Satan is the author, euen as he is of all other disorders. Therefore let none be troublesome or iniurious to other, more then he would be content, that another should wrong or hurt him in that which is his. None should be oppressed in bargaining, or otherwise, as the Lord by the Apostle hath giuen in charge; which if it were well regarded, much complaining of iniurie and hard dealing would cease. But this is a branch of the other.

Doct. vers. 19. 1. Thess. 4.6.

It came of the Lord, that *Sihon* did not only deny passage to Israel through his land, but also that he should prouoke them to warre, that he might giue him and his land into their hands, and withall giue them passage through his country. Euen so it is, that many doe wilfully and stiffely oppose themselues

Doct. vers. 20. to the 23.

selues against the innocent,as by suites of law,vntill their wealth bee consumed, as the fat of lambes against the Sunne. Others meddle needlesly, where they haue no cause oft times, neither can by any reason bee disswaded,yea and some with their betters,through a proud stomack(contrary to the counsell of *Salomon*)because the Lords meaning is, to let them fall into euill,and to suffer them to meet with their match, that they may pay for their griping of their vnderlings,and smart for their owne sinne. For otherwise he would,as he is able,hold them back some way. And thus adulterers, drunkards, cauillers,and such wilfull persons,go forward,but to their confusion. And so *Elies* sonnes were hardned, that they might be destroyed. And *Pharao* in not suffering Israel to depart. So *Ahab* would not heare *Micaiah*,that so he might fall at Ramoth. And had *Iudas* proceeded on to betray his Master,(thinke we)hauing had so faire a warning by him a little before(enough to haue cooled his courage, and to haue holden him backe from such an attempt)but that he was a cursed vessell of wrath appointed to misery? And happie is he who relenteth and meekely submitteth himselfe to God by resisting his wicked attempts, and stopping his bad course: lest by kicking against the pricks,he goe forward to his sorrow and destruction. And this is much more verified in such as will take no counsell by the reproofe of the law of God,but turne away their eares from it,yea liue a long time vnder it vnprofitably,till they waxe obdurate: surely thus they do,because they of al others are the vnhappy people,whō the Lord hath not purposed,by his promise and the ministery of the Gospell, to conuert and saue. Else why should it not be the case of all,aswell as of some? Now if any will cauill against this and say,either that God is bound to deale with them as he did with *Paul*,whom hee saued by violence as it were: or that God in so hardning men,is the author of their perdition: I answere to the first, that God is a free agent,& bound to none of his creatures,he need not at al stop them in their euill course,much lesse to striue with them, when they breake through his opposing of them, as *Balaam* did in his iourney to the King of *Moab*. For the latter I say,that the Lord need not cause any mans destruction,for if he stay him not,he runneth on to it of his owne accord: and as for the Lord,he finds matter of sinne in him(he neede not infuse any)and therfore if he doe not mollifie the heart, it waxeth hard of it selfe without his hardning of it.

1.Sam.2.25. Exod.14.8. 1.King.22.28. Numb.22.18.19.

Doct.vers.21.22. 1.Pet.5.5. And here further we see,that the wilfulnesse and stiffeneckednesse of euill and rebellious persons redoundeth to the benefit of Gods seruants many times,who haue to doe with them. The reason is,that God resisteth the proud,and giueth grace to the lowly. Whereby it commeth to passe, that such wilfull persons meete with much hardnesse, they prouoke other against them, and although they want not power, yet by crueltie,violence, and rashnesse,they runne themselues against a rocke,and contrarily al goeth much the better with the other, (for the most part, though sometime they be borne downe) and in suites and comprimises their innocency and good dealing is seene and rewarded. Thus the Lord gaue sentence on *Dauids* side against *Saul*,and chose him,rather, then his house, and rewarded the innocencie of the one,and gaue vp the other to a reprobate sense.

Doct. vers.23.24. And by these two verses we see,that Gods seruants may with good security, titie, and boldnes, vſe and inioy the poſſeſſions and goods which God hath giuen to them, and by much better reaſon then other, who think that to be their owne which they haue, howſoeuer they haue come by it: whereas theſe haue no ſanctified vſe of any thing they enioy, hauing no right nor title to it from God by Chriſt who is heire of al, although the meanes be lawfull which they vſe: but beſides that, they come vnlawfully (many of them) by much of it: they I meane. The other not only haue right to it by Chriſt, but alſo haue ſought it by a good conſcience, and the vſe is accordingly bleſſed vnto them. This I ſay we may learne by that *Iphtah* anſwered the King of Ammon thus: Thou thinkeſt it to be thine which *Chemoſh* (as thou imagineſt) hath giuen thee much more we may enioy this land of the Amorites which the Lord hath giuen vs. But this I toucht in the 18. verſe.

In the frame of this argument wee may obſerue the arguers diſcretion. He conuinceth his aduerſarie, by a ground confeſſed by himſelfe, handling it comparatiuely after this manner: Thou (ſaith he) thinkeſt thou haſt good right to that which is giuen thee, and that by *Chemoſh*: ſo doe I account my ſelfe to hold that firmely, which *Iehouah* my God hath granted me. Wee know he might haue ſaid, much more may I lay claime to *Iehouah* his gift, then thou to thy Idoll, who indeed hath no more authoritie, then deitie. He might haue diſcourſed much (and that truly) touching the difference betweene God and an Idoll, Heathens and Iewes, the true Church of God: But to what purpoſe? he might haue been ridiculous, but he could not (by ſuch diſpute) haue conuicted him. To teach vs, that all men muſt not bee alike handled in confutatation of their errors, hereſies, prophane cuſtomes: but by grounds acknowledged by themſelues, they muſt bee vrged to confeſſe the truth of concluſions which they would not acknowledge. No man putteth new wind into old veſſels: No man puniſheth a Frenchman by Engliſh law: for why? he takes not himſelfe to ſtand bound to a law which he neuer conſented vnto: the law Ciuil is not like the Common law. Sometime we may take the true confeſſion of our aduerſarie, as an argument againſt him: and this is the more forcible of the two; both becauſe it is a truth, (and therefore of it ſelfe confuteth the contrary neceſſarily) and alſo becauſe we conſent with him therein (wherby we ſhew that wee would not diſſent from him at all, if it were poſſible to auoid it.) And ſometimes wee may vſe his owne confeſſion againſt him, though it be falſe, ſo it bee to conuince him, and doe him good, (for otherwiſe we muſt not abuſe his errour to hurt him:) and this manner of arguing, though it conclude not directly, yet it is ſtrong againſt him that holdeth it. The Apoſtle *Paul* being to conuict the Athenians of their falſe worſhip, firſt argues from an abſurd confeſſion of their own, abſurd in reaſon, Ye worſhip (ſaith he) an vnknowne God, as the title of your Altar importeth, and therfore ye know not how ye worſhip: whereupon doubtleſſe your worſhip is a prepoſterous, and falſe worſhip. And we know *Paul* vſeth one kind of Apologie to Heathen *Feſtus* and *Felix*, another to *Agrippa* a Iew borne. This teacheth vs in dealing with any aduerſary of the truth, to ſmite him with his owne weapon, not with Gods weapons, drawne from the Armorie of the Scriptures, which are truths by reuelation only, not by nature; and therefore to ſuch as they are vnreuealed vnto, they are as *Pauls* doctrine of Reſurrection was to the profane Stoicks.

The

The Church smiteth not the Infidell by spirituall Censures: because he is not capable of spirituall direction and doctrine. There are none so erronious, but they hold some truths: and the truths which they hold, may serue to infringe the errors they maintaine. And so when they are brought to suspect or renounce falsehood, they may the sooner be perswaded to admit the truth, which before their strong preiudice will not suffer them to doe. The Heathen by confessing a Deitie, may by graduall consequences, be forced to acknowledge an vnitie: and so by the workes of this deity, vrged to confesse a worship due thereto, and that inward aswell as outward, as also to see the folly of his manner of worshipping. And thus being prepared, hee may the better be instructed in the truth. The reason of the former point is, because all truth is vniforme, and repugneth to all falsehood, though it be not discerned so to be but by demonstration. So the Popish Transubstantiation, the Lutheran Vbiquitie, are best confuted by their owne positions and confessions (as also other their errors and heresies) and not by our own. Neither will it be hard to doe so, since that it is impossible, but that he who writes many truths should contradict himselfe in his errors ere he be aware. And let this course be vsed against the ignorant and vngrounded: neither let vs presently raile vpon such or abandon them, because they are not perswaded by the things which are forcible with vs, but let them be kindly drawne on, by little and little, and not driuen further of. Thus much bee said of that which hitherto hath passed betwixt *Iphtah* and the King of Ammon.

THE SIXTIE SEVEN SERMON ON THE ELEVNTH CHAPTER OF THE BOOKE OF IVDGES.

Verse 25. NOw to proceede: In communication betwixt the King of Ammon and *Iphtah*, it followeth, that he vsed another reason to the King of Ammon by his messengers: and that is prescription, & long continuance of time, euen 300. yeeres well nigh: all which time this ground was neuer claimed. No, nor *Balac* the King of Moab, when Israel was newly come into the cities belonging to it, and dwelt in them, neuer challenged it, nor contended for it, when yet hee stroue with them, that they should not enter into his owne borders. Now this reason of *Iphtah* must be vnderstood to follow vpon the former more pertinent reasons, after this manner. He had prooued directly, that this land was no part of the Ammonites land: now he proues further, that Ammon could lay no iust claime to it in any second respect: as because it was a part of the Amorites land, bordering

ring vpon them. For (saith he) then might Moab aswell (nay better) challenge it then the Ammonites: which yet neither they did, nor had done in 300. yeeres space before. If the reason be not thus considered, it concludeth nothing: for it doth not directly follow, that Ammon had no title to it, because Moab had none. Thus *Iphtah* answered him, and then committed the successe to God. But the King of the Ammonites did not hearken to him.

Although *Iphtah* sheweth that for 300. yeeres, Israel enioyed the country of the Amorites quietly, yet hee brought other reasons also, drawne from right and reason aswell as fact and possession: which made that more strong as we haue heard. All which laid together, did sufficiently prooue that the land was theirs, and that the King of Ammon did trouble them vniustly, and without cause. This I say, for that we may know, that prescription of time, as it may fall out, (though seldome it doe so) is no sufficient reason, to hold our commodities by: but that there may be right on the other side, and good proofe for the same: and yet our law, supposing a great likelihood of right to be on our sides, when we haue long enioyed our lands, hath well determined the controuersie, by giuing it to vs, when it hath been long enioyed of vs and our predecessors, seeing (otherwise many endlesse contentions might arise) because it is not like that any aliue can alleage any good reason against so long a cōtinuance of time, neither can bring any thing certaine from former times to ouerthrow it. And the equitie of the law aimeth at that which most vsually, though not generally or infallibly, holdeth for the most part ordinarily. Doct. verse 25.26.

2 And where *Iphtah* saith, that *Balak* King of Moab stood against Israel stiffely to hold him from going through his land, yet hee stroue not with them for the recouering this land of the Amorites, which he might as iustly haue done, as he the King of Ammon did, hee prooueth thereby, that he had nothing to doe with it, nor any right vnto it. Teaching this thereby, that when men are deadly set against their aduersaries for any matter, seeking thereby to vexe them in the sorest manner they can, they would shew their rancor, in bringing foorth greater crimes and accusations against them then they doe, (whereby they might much more easily bring them downe) if they were prouided with any. And whereas they seeke to blemish their names, or to impouerish their estate, or to afflict their persons by restraint of libertie, imprisonment or banishment: they doe as the old Serpent, bite at their heele, because they cannot breake their head, but they would be gladdest of all to shed their blood. God indeed plucks them back, and so they vomit not their poison out, to so great mischiefe as they conceiue it, but fall short: but their poison is nothing lesse deadly for all that, they want but matter to worke vpon. And this is manifest by these two signes: the one, that they are content to take the slightest occasions, and rather choose to be ridiculous in their malice, then not malicious: the other, that both they aggrauate their slender accusations, with slanderous additions of their owne inuenting, and combe both the warpe and the woof, both the crime and the amplification thereof in the diuels forge, their lying hearts and braines, because the innocency of their aduersarie yeelds them no iust exception. Thus those enemies of our Sauiour (for want of matter) suborned false-wit-

nesses: which periurie argued, they would not haue spared to produce true
Dan.6.5. and greater crimes if they could haue found them. It is noted of *Daniels* aduersaries, chap.6. that wanting matter of treason, they were faine to bring out his religion against him: which (as they contriued the matter, by the law they made for the purpose) toucht his life also: but if they had found ought to lay to his charge in the other, they would rather haue vsed it.

This doctrine serueth to answere them who pretend for the couering of their malice, that whereas they vexe their aduersarie one way, they could doe it many waies, and say, that they haue greater and more causes to pursue them, then that one which they alleage. But all such speech is bragging and boasting without iust cause: for if they had greater, doth any man doubt but they would take their aduantage by vsing them, when as they prosecute the smaller so hotly against them?

Doct. vers.27. Vpon the forementioned reasons, he concludeth, that hee gaue him no cause to make warre with him, as he had done, but hee had been stirred vp vniustly against him. And as *Iphtah* was bold to accuse him, and auouch his owne innocencie, hauing so good proofe for both, so euery one that can proue the goodnesse of his cause, shall bee able boldly to defend his owne innocencie, against his aduersaries and accusers, to their shame and iust reproch, and their owne peace and comfort. Whereas other must be driuen to vse shifts, as lying, dissembling, boldnes, heate, multiplying of words, and false witnesses, as may be seene in the cause of the Priests and Pharisies accusing our Sauiour before *Pilat*. The truth seeketh no corners. See notes vpon verses 14. and 15.

2 And so hee appealing to the most highest for his simplicitie in the matter, to be iudge therein, he endeth his message. Thus must wee be able to doe, I meane not to be afraid, to make the Lord iudge in the cause, that so, though we be iustled to the walles by our vnequall Iudges vpon earth, yet we may rest in Gods testimonie of and vnto vs and our cause, and therefore,
Prou.28.1. not fearing man, may be confident; verifying the prouerbe, *The righteous*
Iob 31.35. *is bold as a lion*. In the same kinde *Iob* speaketh, saying: *Though mine aduersary should write a booke against me, would not I take it vpon my shoulder and binde it as a crowne to me?* Meaning it should be to his commendation. But seeing the men of the world see boldnes so much to preuaile in the defence of their bad causes, therfore they face out matters themselues thereby. Wherby this watch-word is needfull to bee giuen them, that men looke not so much how boldly they stand in the defence of themselues and their doings, as how truly: for that which in a good cause is courage, in an euill is impudence.

Vers.28. But though *Iphtah* had said enough, and that also to good purpose, yet we see that it moued the King of Ammon nothing at all, but as he had taken a bad cause in hand, so he meant to defend it vnto the death; euen as men too commonly doe, who hauing begun an ill matter, doe purpose to goe forward. So that we see wise and sound reasons, and perswasions, howsoeuer they be vsed, both to purpose and in season, so that they (who can iudge) would thinke they might be like to preuaile and moue (especially not knowing the corruption of the heart, which couers it selfe with shew of honestie) yet with the wilfull they doe no good, nor with any such as bewray themselues

selues (being put to it) to be resolute to do wrong, and of a preiudicate mind, or possessed of strong passions. Therfore it is that *Salomon* saith, *A word more entreth into the wise, then an hundred stripes will auaile with the froward.* This humour possesseth many, whom it would not easily be thought to be in, and therefore (being discouered) so much the worse beseemeth them, euen ciuill courteous persons, still, and sometimes religious: because, either they suspect not themselues, and so are ouertaken by any occasion suddenly falling out: or else they nourish this serpent in their bosome wilfully. *Naaman* was taken with that tech, (and no marueile he being an Heathen (when he heard the Prophets answere, by what meanes he told him he should be healed. But highly to be commended was *Dauid*, who receiued the counsell of *Abigail* (a woman) so readily, to turne him from a cruell and wicked resolution. And euen so, they who are obstinate, (as thinking it a discredit to them to desist) shall meete with more shame by proceeding: but happie are the meeke and tractable, who receiue the wholesome words of exhortation, and stop not their eares from good counsell, but submit themselues without respect thereto: such shall deliuer themselues from great euill. And (a man would thinke) such behauiour doth better become professors of the Gospell, then wilfulnes and obstinacie. Concerning the vse, whereof I haue spoke somewhat by the like occasion in the 21. and 22. verses: let the reader ioyne them both together. Prou.17.10.

Vers.29. *Then the spirit of the Lord came vpon Iphtah, and hee passed ouer to Gilead, and to Manasseh, and came to Mizpeh in Gilead, and from Mizpeh in Gilead, he went vnto the children of Ammon.*

30. *And Iphtah vowed a vow vnto Lord, and said, If thou shalt deliuer the children of Ammon into mine hands,*

31. *Then that thing that commeth out of the doores of mine house to meete me, when I come home in peace from the children of Ammon, shall be the Lords, and I will offer it for a burnt offering.*

32. *And so Iphtah went vnto the children of Ammon to fight against them, and the Lord deliuered them into his hands.*

33. *And he smote them from Aroer vntill thou come to Minneth, twentie Cities, and so foorth to Abel of the vineyards, with an exceeding great slaughter. Thus the children of Ammon were humbled before the children of Israel.*

The third part of the Chapter.

IN this third part it is shewed generally, that *Iphtah* ouercame and subdued the Ammonites. And in particular, first how God gaue him the spirit of courage and fortitude to this end. Secondly, that before hee entred the battell hee made a vow to the Lord, that if hee should get the victorie, hee would offer that to him, which should first come out of doores to meete him. Thirdly, how after this he went forward to Gilead and Manasseh, and came to the place where the Ammonites were: and so lastly, how (fighting with them) the Lord deliuered them into his hands. *The sense of these fiue verses.*

In this verse it is shewed how *Iphtah* came to the Ammonites: from Mizpeh in Gilead (for it is distinguished from that Mizpeh, that is in the Tribe

 of

of Iuda.) Before that, the Lord had furnished him with gifts of his spirit fit for warre,both valiantnes of mind and strength of body,as was said before.

Doct vers.29. And by this it may appeare, that the Lord had appointed before, that hee should be their Iudge and deliuerer, though it was vnknowne to the people when they sent to him to haue him to be their Captaine.

Now for our instruction and benefit, heere wee may see, that when the Lord appointeth any man to any speciall calling,hee giues him gifts for the discharge of it. When *Moses* was to be sent to *Pharao*,hee alleaged his vnfitnes and vnsufficiencie to speak to a King,the Lord prouided for that,before he began to discharge it. The Apostles likewise whom Christ left weake and vnfurnished for such a worke as they were to take in hand after his ascension, to wit, to preach the Gospell to the most nations of the world,yet before they tooke it in hand, he made them meete for the worke they went about.

So *Iphtah*, when hee was to fight against the Ammonites, for the deliuering of Israel, hee was by the spirit of God indued with gifts for that purpose,euen farre greater then he had before,now when hee was set about a greater worke. So the Ministers much more, as the calling is farre more excellent,when hee sendeth them to any people to conuert them,and make them of his militant Church,hee stirres them vp by loue, zeale and labour, to set their gifts of knowledge a worke, and maketh a great change among

Note. the people by their ministerie. They who are vnfit to doe the Lords message to them to whom they are sent, are not sent by him, but seeke themselues and their owne profit,and not the peoples. It is worthie our view to behold the difference of men called by God, and such as climbe in by another way of their owne framing. Both doe one and the same worke,but the one sets himselfe aworke,the other is set aworke by God. The one (after his fashion) goes about it: but how? awkly and vntowardly, by setting a bold face vpon the matter, by carrying a great shew, and bearing sway,by preaching what and when he pleaseth,and in the manner he liketh best: but errand he hath none to doe to the people, (no more then *Cushi* had to *Dauid*) and thereafter is his welcome. For as hee faileth of the end of his office,so loseth he the honour of it; except with a few flatterers and hang-byes. Alas they haue enterprized a long race and iourney,without prouision to enable them to runne it through: It is not the habit that makes the Minister,nor the learning (though that comes neerer) degree, dignitie, or applause of man, which onely will carrie this worke through stitch: It is this, that God hath said to him as to *Paul* and *Moses*; *Goe, I will be with thee:* that is, fit thee, embolden thee,(for a Minister hath enough to discourage him,euen from within himselfe,as I haue noted elsewhere) yea beare thee out against opposition,and encourage thee by blessing thy labour: otherwise all thy prouision is to little purpose,thou maist stand like a foole,errandlesse & speechlesse. Now being called and separated by God, (and therefore also qualified) though thy selfe a weake earthen vessell, yet what precious treasure doest thou carrie? How admirably doth the Lord make way for him, making high hils to stoope, and lie leuell before him,procuring honour from the consciences (not the countenances onely) of such as they haue wonne to God from the power of Satan and darknesse, by conuerting and sauing them.

them. And by stopping the mouthes of such as might despise and discourage them, saying: Who is this new-found babler? what, will hee beare downe all, and thinke to haue vs tyed to his girdle? No, no, he deales for his Master who sent him, and therefore seekes to bring yee vnder the yoke and girdle of Christ: and therefore let the discouragements be neuer so great, this worke shall prosper: and euen out of the mouthes of blockish, brutish, sauage and ignorant, yea prophane ones, the Lord shall procure credit to his Ministerie, (when he hath changed them thereby) and these shall iustifie wisedome against all cauillers, scorners and enemies thereof. Let them be of neuer so many kindes, as in this age there are many, who (contrary to the manifest fruite they see) impeach either the sufficiencie of their calling, or the worthinesse of their message. Oh therefore how lamentable is it, that all congregations are not thus furnished, and made partakers of so blessed an ordinance of God! Therefore the Lord Iesus, to shew how pitifull a case it is, to see the people dispersed, as sheepe hauing no shepheard, he not onely had compassion on them himselfe, but also willed the Disciples to pray to the Lord of the haruest to thrust labourers into the haruest, seeing none are forward to that worke, except the Lord stirre them vp thereto. This point hath been spoken of before, I therefore will not be tedious therein to the reader. Note. Matth.9.38.

The vow, that I said before *Iphtah* made, is heere shewed what it was: Vers.30.31
namely, that he would in token of his thankfull heart, offer and dedicate to the Lord that thing that should first come out of his house to meete him, if he returned with the victorie. This vow, though hee meant well, was ill made and in great ignorance, in that he did not make it more distinctly and aduisedly. For what if a dogge had first met him? which is a fauning creature, and had been like enough to haue first come foorth to meete him? hee could not haue offered it to the Lord, it being vncleane, and so forbidden to be made a sacrifice. His words haue this meaning when he saith (It shall be the Lords, and I will offer it for a burnt offering) that is, I will offer it in sacrifice, and it shall be a burnt offering to the Lord, for hee meant simply, that he would offer the first thing that should meete him; if he had thought of his daughter, would he haue made that vow? And will any say, that in so vowing, he meant, that if that which should first meete him, should not bee fit for sacrifice, he would offer it to virginitie, and yet perhaps it should not be fit for that neither? as if it had been a dogge: and if he had meant to offer it to virginitie, as some hold he did; did hee not see that his daughter had been most like to haue bin the partie vpon whom his vow should haue bin performed? For who had bin liker to haue first come foorth to meete him then she? And would he (thinke wee) haue vowed that which might haue turned to his owne, and his daughters so great sorrow? Therefore I say, hee meant no offering of that which should meete him, to perpetuall virginitie. Neither are those words of his to be taken disiunctiuely, as some think they may, thus: That which first commeth forth to meete me, shall be the Lords, or I will offer it. For though the Hebrew letter ו be so taken sometime, yet very rarely: and so little reason is it, that it should be so taken heere, being most commonly taken coniunctiuely, as they well know that haue any vnderstanding in the Hebrew tongue, yea and oft in some one chapter, as may

 easily

easily be shewed. As for example in Genes. 32.1.2.3.4. foure or fiue times it is so taken in 3. or 4. verses. So in Genes. 33.1.2. as oft in two verses, and Genel. 45.1.2.3. As many times it is found to be, and in most Chapters (if not all) throughout the old Testament this word (ו) signifieth (and) coniunctiuely, not (or) disiunctiuely, as I haue said before. Therefore heere to take it otherwise, there is small reason for it, especially the sense of the place not being amended thereby. For to vnderstand it disiunctiuely thus, [*It shall be the Lords, or I will offer it*] what sense can it haue thus? If it be be not fit for sacrifice, it shal be the Lords: How should it be the Lords? they say by offering it to perpetuall virginitie, if it be fit thereto, for so some vnderstand it, as I haue said before? But where did God require virginitie to be inioyned to any children by their parents? or what example haue we thereof in Scripture? And yet if he had meant so in vowing, we know it had been most like to bee his daughter, I say againe, that should first haue come foorth to meet him. Therefore what sense can there bee in it to take it so, that hee would offer it to perpetuall virginitie, if it were not fit for sacrifice? For this cause I conclude, that the words are to bee vnderstood coniunctiuely, and the latter clause to be the exposition of the former, thus: It shal be the Lords, and I will offer it in sacrifice.

And if it be asked, whether *Iphtah* offended in making such a vow, which some think he did not, because it is said here, that the spirit of the Lord came vpon him: and againe, seeing he is reckoned in the Epistle to the Hebrewes among the faithfull. I answere, first to the question, and after to the reasons: to the question, that if hee had vowed simply to be thankfull, he had done well: but in such a vowing as this was, hee sinned greatly, as shall appeare better, when we come to his performing of the vow afterward, vers. 39. And to the first reason I answer, that the spirit which is said in this verse, to come vpon him, was the spirit of courage and fortitude for war: although it is not denied that he was a beleeuer, and had the spirit of sanctification also. But what hindred, but that hee might in some particular actions, through ignorance or weaknes, offend, as *Gedeon* & *Barak* did, and yet they were the true seruants of God, and obtained the victory also, for all that? So many sound Christians among vs there are, who yet tread awry sometimes, and so did *Iphtah*: and this one answere may serue both the reasons: And this of and concerning his vow, till the 39. verse before mentioned.

Hebr. 11.32.

Doct.

Now as he offended not in vowing (for that tended to the praising of God, though as he made it here, he faulted greatly) so wee may bee perswaded, that it is a lawfull thing to make a vow to God. Whereby I meane neither the generall vow of faith and obedience required and performed, both in the old and new testament, neither that speciall vow that was ceremonial onely, practised in the old Testament, and some where in the new (to wit, in the first age of the Church) but I meane that speciall vow, which is a promise made to God, touching some duties to be performed to him, and to a good end: and this vow (if it be made accordingly) is lawfull, and belongs to the Church both of the old and new testament. Such a vow was *Iphtahs* (in respect of the godly intent thereof) but that it was not lawfully made, nor in a right manner, as hath been said. And such are ours, when we pro-

Gen. 28.20.

mise as *Iacob* did, that if God deliuer vs from such a danger, wee will more carefully

carefully and constantly walke with him afterward.

And so when to helpe our dulnesse and infirmitie, wee set our selues by firme couenant, to prayer and reading, more then ordinary, for measure or for frequency and feruency, and to giue set almes, for special causes knowne to our selues, or to keepe set times of fasting for a season, as there shall bee cause; or if we perceiue and find our selues prone to drunkennesse, and in danger to fall thereto by drinking wine or strong drinke, wee may vow to abstaine for so long a time, as may bee fit to keepe our selues from sinning. And although wee bee bound already hereunto by the word, yet may wee more solemnly, and for the better bridling of our rebellious nature, renew the same bond in a vow, to this end, to helpe our dulnesse, for want of zeale, and to make our selues more forward in duty to God, and loue to men; as *Dauid* did: *I haue sworne* (saith he) *and I will performe it, to keepe thy righteous iudgements.* Psal.119.116.

These kinds of vowes are lawfull, so as they be agreeable to Gods word, and stand with Christian liberty, and bee agreeable to our calling, both generall and particular; and be in our power, and made deliberately, not rashly and the end of it be good: whereas not Popish vowes only, are failing in these, but euen *Iphtahs* also in many of these points. And although vowes made in this manner, are no part of Gods standing and constant worship by themselues, yet neither are they wilworships, nor yet simply left to our arbitriment alwaies, but to be vsed as helpes and furtherances to godlinesse, wel approoued by the experience of the Saints, as to preserue the gifts of faith, prayer, repentance, and other vertues of the mind, so also to testifie our thankfulnesse to God, for blessings which wee haue receiued of him. And with this minde, *Iacob* vowed in the way as hee went to Aram, as I said Gen.28.20. before.

Now this vow of his, as it was a more then vsuall token of his thankfull heart, which he indented before hand to expresse, if God should giue him the victorie: so wee must know that it proceeded from a rare feeling of the spirit of God, exciting and quickning him vp to such feruencie. Gods people find not themselues alway in one tenor and tune, either for inward ioy and comfort in God, or for outward forwardnesse to dutie. *Paul* had his 2.Cor.12.9. lifting vp into the third heauen, and hee had also his buffeting to abase him lower then the earth. *Peter* was rauished in spirit, when he was in his heauenly Act.10.11.&c. trance before his going to *Cornelius*, but we know hee had as rare ebbings at other times. *Elias*, a man of men, for grace and familiaritie with God, and that appeared by his reall assumption into heauen bodily: but he was in a poore case, when he was faine to flee from *Iezabel*, and goe 40 daies fasting and mourning for the misery which lay vpon him and the Church: besides his weaknesses which be bewraied, and therefore is called by S. *Iames* a passionate man, one that was clothed with the like infirmities that others had. It were to be desired, (& we heare men make great moane for the contrary) that there were alway in vs that abundance of grace, faith, feruencie, chearefulnesse, which is at some odde time. But the contrary befalleth most men, partly the Lord so disposing of it, because hee knowes wee were not able to beare it, but would turne it into a distemper, (euen as too much good blood in the bodie makes a pleurisie, and when there is more water in the channel then it can containe: it must needs ouerflow the bankes, and doe harme) and partly our selues procuring it, who nourish not in our selues such motions, nor make wise vse of them, by setting them a work, and applying them to some fit obiect, (as *Iphtah* here did) but delight only in the sweetnesse and pleasure which we feele, and so suffer the heauenly flame to vanish, for want of laying on fewell to preserue it.

And although the Lord causeth his children, euen here, sometimes in health, sometime at death to enioy such vnspeakable feelings and operations of the spirit, (which hee doth to giue them such a taste of heauen, as may cause in them a restlesse longing, til they come thither) yet he knoweth, they
Math.17.4. would say with *Peter, Master, it is good for vs to be here,* and would thinke of no departure, if this should be an ordinarie diet. Therefore he rather considers, what they can digest, then what he can afford, and saith, *My grace shall neither be giuen in superfluitie, nor yet in penury, but it shall be sufficient.* And let vs learne to account so of it, as the best for vs. Onely let vs beware, lest by our giuing way to our flesh (the counterpoise of the spirit) that is to the earth to our sensualitie and lusts; we bury and quench the spirit, and smother it from appearing in the beauty thereof; and also lest wee cause it to be heauy and sad in vs, and so our selues to bee blockish and sottish, rather then heauenly and ioyfull: which is to choose to feede with swine, when we might eate Angels foode.

Vers.32.33. In these two verses is not only set downe the victory, which God gaue to *Iphtah* ouer the Ammonites, but it is also particularly amplified and in larger manner described. As that many fell in the battell; and that hee ouerthrew twentie of their cities; and that hee brought the Ammonites in subiection to him. Where wee may clearely see, what it is that encourageth vs, and setteth vs forward in our duties doing. Euen the Lords appointing and calling vs thereto, as of the publike calling of the Minister I spake before: it is true of the priuate duties also. Husband and wife from thence haue their hartning on to liue mutuall helpers one of another to their Christian and peaceable conuersing together, and passing their daies sweetly, and bearing their crosses contentedly; euen from hence, I say, that they beleeue God hath ioyned them together to that end. So the Magistrate, and all other in
Note. the seuerall duties of this life. And want of this faith, is enough to make mens liues ouercast, as the weather is with clouds and tempests, and to fill men with sinne and sorrow. Other things which might bee noted from hence, haue been mentioned before, but besides them of these two a little.

Vers.33. In that the King of Ammon went by the worst in the battell had with *Iphtah*, it shewes what wilfulnesse brings a man, or the contempt or reiecting of good and sound perswasions, such as *Iphtah* vsed to disswade him from warre. For though he were an Heathen, yet he knew by the law of Nature, that he ought not to offer iniury to the innocent. And we know that when
Rom.1.19. the Gentiles knew God onely by the light of nature, and did not honour him accordingly, he gaue them vp to their hearts desires to fulfill them against nature. Much more, they who haue light in the word of God, hauing no regard of good instruction and admonition, shall come to naught, especially the despisers thereof, vnlesse they take shame and abashment to themselues for it, and so come to better state: according to that which is written,

He that knoweth his Masters will,and doth it not, shall bee beaten with many stripes. Luke 12.47.
But more of this punishment vpon wilfulnesse, see before set downe by the like occasions,and by name in Chap.8.14.

2 And in that hee lost twentie cities which hee had of his owne,and lost those also which he fought for,which were none of his, it liuely setteth before our eies,that many not contented with that which is their owne,while they claime to,and seeke that which belongs to other men,either by colour of law, or otherwise; they lose that which they sued for, and spend and consume that which they had before. The Lord doth oft times requite their vnconscionablenesse that way: and yet in great mercy he dealeth with them in so doing, to keepe a heauier iudgement from them, who would (most certainely) be worse,if they should by their corrupt and bad dealing speed better,and be suffered to haue successe. Note.

I will cleare this point by example and instance. *Pharaoh* not contented to haue oppressed the Israelites (for many generatiōs) with bondage; would needs pursue them, when they were gotten out of his clawes,though hee had smarted many waies for not letting them goe. But what came of it? seeing he sought vniustly to encroach vpon Gods possession, he not onely failed of that hee desired, but lost also that which he ventured, euen his owne life,and all that hee had, and his people also,in the middest of the sea. The same is verified in other parts of vnrighteousnesse: *Sampson* not content to liue with credit and honour in his owne land, and within his compasse, would needs breake out among the Philistims,& there hit into *Delilas* company,which his soule entirely loued,(though vnlawfully) and was made a vassall to a base mistresse. But behold a short time this pleasure of sinne lasted: for loe, his louer rewards him with treason, and then *Sampson* (poore man) is faine to forgoe his mistresse by force, (who could not be plucked from her by conscience,) and that which he abhorred,that he was made to vndergoe,(and that by them whom he most hated) to wit,a painefull bondage while hee liued, beside shame and sorrow, and after all, an vntimely death. I will instance first in the sinnes of the second Table. The murtherer and thiefe can by no perswasion bee brought to labour with his hands, and to doe the thing which is good: tush,it goeth vtterly against him to bee put to labour,and to worke hard all the yeere long for a poore liuing: hee can bring in all at once,and get great booties,to liue at ease, and plentifully for a long time,as he imagineth,and is not that a merry world? yes while it lasteth; in his kind,but how long is that? He gets two or three purses,and in the fourth enterprise he is taken in the manner. Doth hee not then (thinke you) wish from his heart, that hee had obeyed Gods ordinance, and been hard at work,(as much as he loathed it before) rather then to haue put forth his hand to violence? For he seeth,that neither he hath obtained that which he sought for: and that ouerthrow which he little looked for, that hee hath brought vpon himselfe. He lay in waite for the life and goods of another: therein he was defeated,but this will not satisfie for his sinne, he must giue life and goods to boote,and all to make amends by mans law. What needed he haue feared the law (which is not made for the iust, but the transgressor) if he had holden himselfe content with his owne? But men say they must venture: nothing venture nothing haue: till by venturing all,they lose all: not

Exod.14.28. Iudges 16.20. 1.Tim.1.9. Note.

not money and body, but soule also, if God be not more mercifull. These things notably lay foorth the folly and fruit of sinne, euen in outward respects: and yet it is as manifest in spirituall. For to adde another instance in the first Table: Many there are that say, they hope that God is not so hard a master, neither wil punish sinners so seuerely as the Ministers would beare them in hand: others goe further, and will enter vpon Gods prerogatiue, saying euery one for himselfe, I cannot beleeue that God hath reiected so many thousands, and will saue so few: (meaning, that if God doe so, hee is cruell.) But oh foole, as *Paul* saith, what gettest thou by disputing against God, nay by bereauing and spoiling him of his iustice, (oh sacrilege and vnrighteousnes in the highest degree?) Surely, as *Austin* saith (speaking hereof, *That which they would haue, they lose, but that which they would not, they haue* (euen woe) *for euer.* They would get heauen by disanulling the decree of God: that shall they neuer get, (for the Moone keepes her course, though dogges barke at her:) and they would scape hell too, but that (will they, nill they) must be their portion for euer. But what fruit see we in the liues of most men, of this and the like doctrine, driuing and scaring them (a man would thinke) forcibly from all kind of vnrighteousnesse. But I passe from this to that which followeth.

THE SIXTIE EIGHT SERMON ON THE ELEVENTH CHAPTER OF THE BOOKE OF IVDGES.

Vers. 34. *Now when Iphtah came to Mizpeh vnto his house, behold his daughter came out to meet him, with timbrels and dances, which was his only child: he had no other sonne nor daughter.*

35. *And when he saw her, hee rent his clothes, and said, Alas my daughter, thou hast brought me low, and art of them that trouble me: for I haue opened my mouth vnto the Lord, and cannot goe backe.*

36. *And she said vnto him, My father, if thou hast opened thy mouth vnto the Lord, doe with me as thou hast promised, seeing that the Lord hath auenged thee of thine enemies the children of Ammon.*

37. *Also she said vnto her father, Doe thus much for me: suffer me two moneths, that I may goe to the mountaines, and bewaile my virginitie, I and my fellowes.*

38. *And he said, Goe: and he sent her away two moneths: so she went with her companions, and lamented her virginitie vpon the mountaines.*

39. *And after the end of two moneths, she turned againe vnto her father, who did with her according to his vow, which he had vowed, and she had known no man. And it was a custome in Israel:*

40. *The daughters of Israel went yeere by yeere, to lament the daughter of Iphtah the Gileadite, foure daies in a yeere.*

THE FOVRTH PART OF THE CHAPTER; Of the executing of his vow.

WHen *Iphtah* had gotten the victorie,he returned home to *Mizpeh*,for there he dwelt:and therfore we heard before,that he made a league with the Gileadites,before the Lord in *Mizpeh*. And behold(for now I returne to his vow) to the bewraying of his deepe folly in making his forementioned vow) the first that came foorth to meete him was his daughter, which so troubled him, that his ioy for his triumph, was turned into most deep and bitter sorrow : but she,when she vnderstood her fathers vow,submitted her selfe,onely desiring a time to bewaile her virginitie. And hee after her returne,performed his vow on her. And it was a custome that the daughters of Israel went foure times in the yeere to bewaile her. *The summe of these verses.*

Now to peruse the verses particularly,it is said here,that when he had bin made ioyfull by the victorie; at his returne, his daughter was the first that came forth to meete him with trimbrels and dances: for so they were wont to celebrate the worthy acts of Princes and great men: As they did (I meane the maides) to *Saul*: thus they vsed to expresse their publike thanksgiuings to God. Now to the aggrauating the griefe of *Iphtah*, it is said she was his onely childe,and he had no other. Vers.34. Exod.15.20. 1.Sam.18.6.

And in that his daughter came the first to meete him,who must be done to (he thought) as he had vowed : all may see what effect comes of rashnes, and how vnbeseeming a companion it is to a wise man, who should ponder his doings, and weigh his words with reason,yea religion, euen in the ballances of the sanctuarie,that is,by the word of God, before they be vttered. The best fruite of it is sorrow and repentance. It is a true saying; Rashnesse doth nothing well,as in *Herods* rash promise and oath is to be seene.The like had *Dauid* done, if he had not bin staied by *Abigail* against the house of *Nabal*. Doct. Mark.6.23. 1.Sam.25.34.

Much like was the wilfull and rash act of the Prodigal,who would needs goe see the merrie world abroad,(as he thought it) yea and he might in no wise be staied from his purpose, as though hee had gone about some great and weightie worke, when he had gotten his portion into his hands to that end; but to what extremitie of miserie brought he himselfe? The same may be said of the rashnes of choller, whereby men smite out teeth and eyes out of the heads, yea and breath out of the bodies (sometime) of wiues, children,seruants,or any of them,whom they light vpon,in their fume : also of the rash bargaines and suertiships which are made and vndertaken in the world,and a thousand mischiefes besides. Likewise of the protestations commonly made in this manner : I pray God I sinke where I stand,if it bee not true that I say;or,Gods curse be vpon me.Which *Peter* himselfe through rashnesse and forgetting himselfe,did fall into. Therefore it behoueth all to be wise and well aduised in their vowes to God,and promises made to men, that they snare not themselues,neither bring needlesse sorrow and woe vpon their owne heads. And euen so,when they be aduisedly and circumspectly made, according to the rules before set downe, vers.30. then in no wise Luke 15.13.

Eccle.5.3. Psal.15.4. Psal.119.106. to goe from them, but to performe them as *Dauid* did, Psal. 119. Of this look more in the historie of *Gaal*, chap. 9. and elsewhere.

2 Furthermore in this verse wee are taught, that God is to bee praised publikely for the publike benefits which wee receiue in common, as both here wee see in *Iphtahs* daughter, and in many other places I haue shewed, although not in the same manner, and *Moses* also, *Miriam*, and *Debora*, with sundrie others did: and that as for other reasons heretofore set downe, so to teach posteritie by our example to doe the like. But of this after. God would haue the first fruites consecrated to him, that wee might vse the rest with thanksgiuing.

And in that she was his only childe, it must needs increase his heauinesse, that by his vow he had brought vpon himselfe, when he saw he must be depriued of her: and to this his sinne brought him, in his rash vow making, or whatsoeuer other sinnes they were, that others may beware thereby. And by this we learne, that God for mens sinne will not spare to depriue them of that which is most deare vnto them. One reason hereof is, that the Lord meaneth to humble them deeply, and to cause them to descend into themselues more seriously, and to purge out the sinne that waiteth them a mischiefe, and so to preuent it. And therefore this vse wee should make of it, that whensoeuer the Lord dealeth so with vs, wee should know it is for the hardnes of our harts, which otherwise and without such breaking of them, will not be softned. And let vs the lesse marueile at it, when we finde it to be so; for though he haue often gone about it by gentler meanes, yet we know they haue not preuailed: so that wee haue driuen him to deale more hardly with vs, as wee count it, and to handle vs more roughly, as to wound vs so deeply, by taking the things from vs, which are most deare vnto vs. And if we are not to be accused for that our hearts are hardned by the deceitfulnes of sinne, but that wee relent, yet let vs know, that God hath sufficient cause to afflict vs; as to exercise and prepare vs for greater, and to hold vs here as strangers. But of this in another place; although I haue often obserued it, before in the seuerall stories, of the punishments which fell vpon the idolatrous Israelites.

Note.

Vers. 35. *The sense.* By this verse it may appeare, how sore *Iphtahs* daughters meeting of him did trouble him, as both by his words hee testified, saying; Oh thou that shouldest haue been my chiefe earthly comfort, thou (I say) art one that hast chiefly cast me downe. Also by signes thereof hee shewed it, in that hee cut his garments for sorrow, after the manner of the Hebrewes, when they saw that some great calamitie was suddenly befalne them, as in *Ioel* and other places it appeareth. And he shewes the reason, that hee hauing vowed to offer her to the Lord, he might not (he said) goe backe: such was his ignorance, that he knew not there was libertie giuen by the Lord, in that case to redeeme that which a man had vowed amisse.

Ioel 2.13.

Doct. This verse affoordeth vs many good lessons, and first by this, that she was such a trouble to him, after hee had gotten the victorie, and that the Lord pulled him downe so sore thereby; by this (I say) we are taught, that God seeth it expedient thus to deale with his seruants oft times, that when hee hath exalted them by some great fauour bestowed vpon them, lest they ſhould take too much delight therein, and ſo become ſurfeited therewith; hee addeth ſome affliction to it, or taketh away ſome part of the benefit, which point I haue at large handled in chap.8.verſ.1. of this booke, yet I will here adde ſomewhat. This appeareth therefore in ſundrie particulars; as in our goodly ſhew and likelihood of fruitfull harueſts, and hope of other commodities, commonly wet or drie, cold or heate immoderate, and other changes and caſualties cut off a great part of our hope.

So in marriage, wealth, credit, and ſuch like, the Lord addeth ſickneſſe, Note.
ſome loſſes, or other affliction, or holdeth the feare of them ouer our heads, (as the parent doth the rodde ouer the childe) to weane vs from too great pleaſure taking in them. Euen as we reade in all ages he hath done the like: So *Iſaak* and *Rebecca*, in their kind and comfortable marriage, had *Eſau* their ſonne to bee a vexation to them, in his moſt wicked marriage, and before Gen.26.35. and verſ.7.20.
that, ſometime a famine, and ſometime the ill dealing of ſtrangers with them. So *Iob* for all his wealth, had his croſſes and namely his wiſe, yea hee Iob 1. and 7.1.
was ſo acquainted with this truth, and Gods dealing with his deare children, that hee ſaid in the middeſt of his proſperitie, that he looked for his change.

And who doth not ſee it neceſſarie, that the Lord ſhould deale thus with vs? For elſe it ſhould bee found ſo to be with vs, as it was in the daies of Matth.24.37.
Noah, when they did eate and drinke, marrie and were married, and made that the chiefe end of their liuing here: whereas godlineſſe being the great riches, and a day paſſed therein, being better then a thouſand in any eſtate beſide, the Lord would haue vs claſpe about that, and be ready to learne by Note.
little and little, that wee haue no hold of any tranſitory thing here below though lawfull, but we ſhould count one thing neceſſary, though we be occupied about many. Luke 10.42.
And to make good the doctrine that I haue gathered out of this verſe, to wit, of Gods keeping vs vnder, ſome way in the middeſt of our proſperitie, I conclude, that if *Paul* had neede to be buffeted, leſt hee 2.Cor.12.7.
ſhould be lifted vp aboue meaſure, we may lay our hand vpon our mouth and ſay, God hath moſt iuſt reaſon to deale thus with vs, as I haue ſaid. Now if hee ſeeth it meete thus to exerciſe vs, leſt wee ſhould bee lifted vp, then much more if we haue already been ſo, and paſſed our bounds in any ſuch manner.

Now to goe forward: by theſe words of *Iphtah*, (Oh my daughter thou Doct.2.ver.35.
art of them that trouble me) and by the deepe and ſudden ſorrow which they teſtifie to haue then poſſeſſed him, by them I ſay wee may ſee and obſerue another thing, that the beſt delights and greateſt pleaſures of this life, in which wee haue had exceeding comfort, as hee had in his daughter, may poſſibly and doe often turne to our great ſorrow and diſcontentment. We ſee the ſame in *Iacob*, when his ſonnes hating their brother *Ioſeph*, had dip- Gen.37.33.
ped his coate in blood, to hide their owne ſinne, and brought it to their father, to make him thinke that he had been ſlaine by ſome wilde beaſt; when he ſaw it, hee brake out in a great paſſion, and ſaid, This is my ſonnes coate, an euill beaſt hath deuoured him. Oh what heauineſſe tooke hold of him, euen from and by him who was his ioy and moſt deare vnto him? And thus it is with vs, as it was with them. So conſider how deare *Abſolom* was 2.Sam.18.33.
to his father *Dauid*: and when word was brought him of his death, how

heauily did he take it? how did he wish and desire that hee might haue lost his owne life, to haue saued his, as his words vttered in most patheticall and lamentable manner, doe testifie, where he thus crieth out: Oh *Absolom*, my sonne, my sonne: would God I had died for thee, oh *Absolom* my sonne, my sonne. Euen so what sore disquiets and corsiues, are many children to their parents, wiues to their husbands, and these againe to them, and one deare friend to another? And what vexations haue many mens goods been to them, as their house and land, when they haue brought them to naught, and when they haue seene they must forgoe them? And how haue other mens pleasures stung them at the heart, when they hauing been the ioy thereof, they haue forsaken them? Oh if men durst or could be perswaded to bewray it, when they haue seene they must dye, and leaue all, how haue they been wrapped in deadly sorrow and thraldome thereby, so neere were their hearts knit to their earthly delights, that they haue been able to thinke of no good thing to helpe them to saluation, and to make their account well to God, no nor to entertaine any good aduice and instruction, if it had been offered them. And what may bee the reason of all this? Truly this, seeing they haue so greatly abused them, by setting them in the Lords place, and their harts vpon them so impotently and fondly, directly contrary to Gods commandement, giuing this charge: If riches encrease, set not your hearts vpon them. And to make this their sinne the greater, they must know, that they who are not brought as yet to faith in Christ, and true repentance, so that they bee by him intitled to them (who is Lord and heire of all) they haue no right to any of their lawfullest pleasures and profits, no not their children by Gods allowance, hauing lost the same right by *Adams* sinne, which indeede once was giuen in *Adams* innocencie. And yet euen the godliest must vse them soberly, and learne to enioy them with Gods allowance (as they may, when they resolue with contentment to leaue them, and when they are put to necessarie, profitable, & godly vses) for that is (indeed) to learne to want them, (as we are commanded, and haue example thereof) when God will so haue it: And otherwise they who haue had most, shall wish they had had least. And if yee will aske, if there be nothing that men may safely and boldly reioyce in: I answere, Yes, let them reioyce in beleeuing, in hope, patience and a good conscience: that ioy shall not be taken from them.

Note. 1.Tim.6.17. Psalme. 2.Tim 3 4. Phil.4.12. Rom.5.3.

Doct.3. Besides in this verse, in that *Iphtah* said, his daughter troubled him, and yet it was by no ill behauiour, let it be an instruction for children, that they had not need to be crosses to their parents, by loosenes and disobedience: for their parents are many waies grieued by them in other respects; as to see them crossed and brought behinde hand in the world, by pouertie, or for that they thriue not in their outward estate, so for their other sundrie troubles that befall them: and with these, when they looke to haue them the staffe of their old age, then if they see them taken away by death, or crossed by their awke and bad matches; if then they also with the like to these shall vexe them in their life, how can they chuse but bring their gray haires with sorrow to their graue? Monsters therefore and vnnaturall children are they, who knowing that from their very conception & birth, they are occasions of griefe and heauinesse of heart, to their parents many waies, who take thought

thought for them also afterward in euery part of their life, how to bring them vp and prouide for them, monsters (I say) they are who doe yet adde more heart smart, and greater griefe to them by their vnrulinesse, stoutnesse, loftines of minde, riot, ill spending their time, and goods with lewd companions, and many other euill waies, euen so many as who can reckon them vp? But this point hath been diuersly occasioned already, and more directly concernes the 36. verse following.

And because he saith he could not goe backe, but must execute his vow, 4
many marueile he should be so ignorant, that he knew not the law in Leuiticus concerning the redeeming of a sonne or a daughter in such a case, for so might hee haue done. But hee being driuen out of his fathers house, because he was base borne, and banished, & fell to a souldiers life, it might the rather be therefore, that he was lesse acquainted with the law of God. But it is more marueilous, that being so famous a thing, that the high Priest should not be consulted with, by the motion of some of his friends especially, there remaining two moneths before the vow was put in execution. But his ignorance it was, that held him in that grieuous error. Leuit. 27. 2. 3.

And it is a watch-word to all Gods people, to labour against it, seeing he being ignorant of this one point, brought such sorrow and woe vpon his owne head: for who findes not likewise, that want of knowledge in some one point, or want of care to remember that which he knowes (which in effect is all one) hath been a sore blemish to him among his betters, who can espie his ignorance? or else through the want of it, hee hath runne vpon rocks, I meane indangered himselfe, to doe that to his shame and griefe; which, knowledge thereof would haue guided him, to haue done to his owne great comfort. Oh seeke we therefore sauing knowledge, and all that is necessarie while we may, and as wee may, it is a crowne to an humble and sanctified person: and in a doubtfull case, doe we not, as *Iphtah* here did, to neglect the seeking of resolution, when and where we may haue it. And let them who liue vnder an ordinary Ministerie vnprofitably, repent betimes, and redeeme the time: for it is a great plague of God, to bee euer learning, and neuer comming to the knowledge of the truth. And such as want meanes, let them quicken their appetite the more, and labour to set the best price vpon knowledge and wisedome, which is the holy vse of it. For hee that matcheth these with the most precious iewels, and searcheth after thē as gold, hee is like to finde them soonest. The other passeth by them vnknowne at vnawares, as he that walketh ouer mines and treasure hidden in the earth, neuer the wiser. 2. Tim. 3. 7. Note. Prou. 2. 5.

But the text giuing occasion rather to vrge this care vpon the better sort, we may iustly bewaile it, how long it is ere euen many a good Christian attaine to that measure of competent and necessarie knowledge, which might guide his course. I speake not now of exact knowledge in all points, much lesse of curious knowledge of things lesse pertinent, which yet many seeke after more greedily, then they doe the other; like distempered stomackes, which feede vpon trash rather then good nourishment. Now what makes it so difficult a thing as it is? Sometime an inuincible defect in nature: in which case I confesse, a tractable and modest minde may pleade an excuse from God: in others a conceit that if Christ be knowne in any sort, it skils not whether other matters bee knowne or no; (which is a fooliſh opinion and collection.) Others and the moſt heare badly, or adde no priuate helpe of their owne reading, or vſe of the memory by conference. Therefore as contraries be cured by contraries, ſo let euery mã ſeeing his diſeaſe, addreſſe himſelfe to the cure. We ſee that ignorance in the law of the land, ſometimes breedes a man ſuch trouble and loſſe, as makes him rue it all his life long: much more then, a man would thinke, in the law of God. For example, many a man through ignorance (though otherwiſe wel-minded) is drawne into bad company, and by ſuch, entiſed to leaudneſſe, or made drunke, or ſnared by raſh promiſes, bargaines, ſuretiſhips. Others ioyne with their religion, abuſe of their lawful liberties, and are ouertaken therein groſſely, in vnlawfull gamings, and ill ſpending of the time, laſciuiouſneſſe, fooliſh mirth, and many other blemiſhes. Some doubting of the lawfulnes of a thing which they earneſtly deſire to doe, entangle themſelues, which (if they had knowledge) they durſt not doe. So it is rare, but a goodly ſight, to ſee a man order his ſteppes by knowledge, and to haue fellowſhip with the light, and the contrary (beſides the other named inconueniences) much diſhonoureth the profeſſion it ſelfe of the Goſpell.

5 Further, to omit that he might haue redeemed her, as I ſaid, and to ſpeake no more of his ignorance in that point, note we this, that his care was great in keeping a good conſcience: a good conſcience I ſay, according to the knowledge he had, though I confeſſe it cannot bee in it ſelfe a good conſcience, which is not a ſound conſcience. But an euill conſcience it may bee, euen to doe a thing lawfull, if it be contrary to that which a man is perſwaded, though erroniouſly. And it appeares *Iphtah* ſought to keepe a good conſcience, in aſmuch as he ſpareth not his onely child, to the end that hee might pleaſe God, as he thought, by performing his vow. For there was nothing elſe could cauſe him to bring ſuch ſorrow vpon himſelfe by offering his only daughter in ſacrifice, but the ſhunning and auoiding of a greater ſorrow, namely, the bringing of God to bee againſt him, as hee feared hee ſhould haue done, if he had not offered her according to his vow.

His care to keep a good conſcience in that he thought he knew, teacheth all Gods people, in that which they know to be faithfull. Better is he by many degrees, who in that which hee knowes is carefull to doe the ſame; then another who ſwelleth with pride, and is puffed vp with great knowledge in the letter, when he ſeeth not the end of it, much leſſe attaineth to it; which is by loue to edifie, and doe good to himſelfe and others by it. But in them who be vpright hearted toward God, as the good women were, that accompanied our Sauiour on earth, that is, verified which hee ſpake. If ye know

John 13.17. Matth.5.19. theſe things, happie are yee if yee doe them. &c. And contrarily, he that offendeth in the leaſt (teaching others ſo to do) ſhall be leaſt in the kingdome of God. Now to this we muſt adde that which (in part) was toucht before that men muſt beware of that corrupt conceit of Popery, that conſcience (for ſuch is all true deuotion) may bee in a thing where knowledge is not. Nay, they go further, for they are ſo bold as to ſay, that deuotion is the fruit of ignorance. It proceeded not from *Iphtah* his ignorance, but from his grace, that he was ſo deuout. That which ignorance propetly brings forth, is error and wilworſhip: deuotion is neither cauſed by ignorance, no, nor yet

yet by knowledge without faith and grace, though knowledge must guide and perfect it afterward.

Now to this lamentable complaint of the father, to wit, *Iphtah*, let vs heare the kind and dutifull answere of the daughter. My father, saith she, if thou hast vowed any thing to the Lord concerning me (as she perceiued by him he had, for euery word is not recorded in a briefe history) I yeeld obediently to thee, and am willing to confirme and helpe to make good thy vow. Her obedience, or rather desire of obedience to her father, was highly commendable, euen as his was to God, but yet in the respect before named, to wit, because she thought her fathers vow was lawfull, as himselfe thought; it must bee performed and kept: for shee ought and might haue denied to haue yeelded, where her father had so vainely and needlesly vowed, if she had knowne that her father had had libertie by the law of God to redeeme her. But she to please God, as shee supposed, and that her father might not offend him neither, by breaking his vow, did submit her selfe, and makes no exclamation at the heare-say of it, nay doth not so much as question about, and discusse it with a scrupulous mind. And marke further that she saith, it was not grieuous for her to die, seeing the enemies of God were ouerthrowne. Vers.36.

This her readie and obedient affection (setting aside the error thereof) is a cleare glasse for youth to looke in, to shew their readinesse in obeying their parents, it being agreeable to the law of God, which is required of them, and so in obeying their gouernours set ouer them. And as shee said in her owne case for her selfe, so should they say, euery one for himself vnto them, farre bee it from mee, that I should procure, or bee a meane of your sorrow. Children that are teachable may heare her, and learne when they may or must speake, and how to doe it. And that is thus: that whereas reuerence, obedience and thankfulnesse is required of them, so they bee readie accordingly in the performing of them all vnto them to doe their duties. Doct.1.

Their humble and kind words should comfort and glad their parents hearts, and yet they should looke carefully to be found sutable also in their deeds. And these were as double armour to them, when the wicked children wound and lay open their parents to reproch among the bad sort, and are corruption to their bones. These should make them not to be ashamed of them, as their children. And blessed is the man that hath his quiuer full of such arrowes, they shall defend him from the ill tongues of his enemies. Euen so the common ill behauiour of the most children, and namely, their words and answers, which they giue to their parents, chattingly, stoutly, saucily, (yea and with gybes and taunts, some of them,) they are to their parents, as I haue said, reproch and poyson to their owne soules. But to make this point more full and cleare, here let all good children learne this duty from God, that with their ready and willing mind, submitting themselues to their parents, they ioyne also wisdome and sound knowledge, to direct them wherein to obey, that so they may not commend their affection onely, but the whole duty to their father in heauen, aswell as to their father in earth. I speake not this, as if I would teach them to contest with their parents, or descant with them about their lawfull demands; but to beware lest by obeying man in a good intent, they offend God in the maine. Neither Prou.12.4.

doe all parents make conſcience what they vrge, but require a ſtrict obedience without controle. And they that doe make conſcience, yet require their due often ignorantly: and would be full loth to doe it, if they knew it vnlawfull, as *Iphtah* doubtleſſe would. Indeed I confeſſe this duty lieth ſtreightlieſt vpon the parent, to know what to demand, but the child (if hee neglect) is bound to performe the ſame, which might of the other be lawfully demanded. And let none thinke that by this rule, the inferiour is euer a whit priuiledged: no doubtleſſe, hee obeyeth the parent and gouernour beſt and moſt, who obeyeth in the Lord vpon knowledge.

Doct. 2. And in that ſhe ſaith, Seeing thou art reuenged of thine enemies, I am well content to dye, it was a ſpeech that might well haue become the experiencedſt ſeruants of God, though vttered by a young damſell. Oh let ſuch examples be our inſtruction! for as *Paul* ſaid the ſame words in a like caſe; ſo the Lord inſtructeth vs to doe the ſame. So that wee haue cauſe to ſay and thinke it, that our liues ſhould not bee deare to vs, in reſpect of the welfare and peace of Gods Church and people: for her proſperitie ſhould bee our deſire and ioy. As wee are taught by the example of that rare noble man *Nehemiah*, more famous for grace and godlineſſe, then for his greatnes and aduancement: who being asked of the King, why his countenance was caſt downe, and ſad; he anſwered, Oh my Lord the King, why ſhould I not bee ſad, when the houſe and citie of the ſepulchers of my fathers lieth waſte, and the gates thereof are deuoured with fire?

Actes. 1. Iohn.

Nehem. 2. 3.

Commendable alſo was the anſwere of *Mephiboſheth* to *Dauid*, when hee was ſafely deliuered from the rebellion of *Abſalom*, and reſtored againe to be the vpholder and welfare of the Church: thus he ſaid, What are all my goods and ſubſtance to mee, ſeeing my Lord the King is come home in peace? And *Paul* ſhewed by his words to the Romans, Chap. 9. and 10. that ſo earneſt was his deſire and prayer to God for Iſrael, that they might be ſaued, that he would pledge his owne ſaluation to purchaſe theirs. And hee telleth King *Agrippa*, that ſo as he and all that heard him that day, were added as true members to increaſe the Church, hee was content to beare the bands and hardneſſe himſelfe alone, hee (I ſay) could haue wiſhed that hee might haue borne all the brunt, to free them from it. Such loue ſhould wee beare (and not pretend) to the Church of God, that a great part of our ioy ſhould bee diminiſhed, vnleſſe ſhe might ioy with vs. But we may complaine with the prouerb, Euery man for himſelfe: but they are happieſt that weepe and reioyce with her. For wherein ſtandeth our happineſſe, and whence haue we our chiefe cauſe of reioycing? Haue we it not from hence, that we are members of that holy Catholike Church of Chriſt, which (being his body) is knit and compacted by ioynts and ſinewes together, and draweth from him (as her head) life and grace? And partake wee not euen here ſingular fruit from this communion of Saints, not only by the ſweet conuerſing with them, whom wee are next vnto, and dwell among, but by the prayers of ſuch as wee are onely preſent with in ſpirit, though in place farre diſtant? Therfore next to our communion with our Lord Ieſus himſelfe, what ſweeter meditation haue we then of our fellowſhip with his bodie? whereunto he hath granted ſuch ſingular priuiledges, and which hee hath beautified with ſo many admirable gifts and graces? in all which wee

2. Sam. 19. 30. Rom. 9. 1. & 10. 1. Actes 26. 28. Note.

haue

haue our parts,if we haue any part in her. What thinke we? Is Christ diuided: Is his body subiect to dismembring? Can any of vs draw from the head,any influence of grace,if wee will be singular by our selues,or separate our selues from our brethren? Doth not a great part of our felicitie hereafter,consist in this,that we shall haue fellowship with the Saints in light,euen the light of Gods and the Lambs immediate presence? For these reasons,let vs bee perswaded to enlarge our selues, and not to bee streightned within our selues,as if we neither had any part in the sorrowes or prosperitie of others. For as there is a duty required of vs toward the whole body, to pray for the peace of it,and mourne for the grieuances thereof: so especially for that part thereof,whose estate is best knowne to vs: and with *Dauid* we must say,If I forget thee(O Ierusalem)let my tongue cleaue to the roote Psalm.137.5. of my mouth,and my fingers forget to play. And againe,For Zions sake,I will not hold my peace,&c. till her beautie breake forth as the light,and till Ierusalem be set vp,the glory of the earth. And this affection should bee so strong,that it should ouerflow the bankes of the Church,and extend it selfe to the borders and confines thereof: and be earnest with God,for them that are yet strangers and aliants,that they may be made members of this bodie, and citizens of this Citie: that the Kingdome of Christ may bee stretcht out from sea to sea,and he may rule farre and wide throughout the world. And it will become vs aswell to entreate the Lord, to pitie the many thousands of them that sit in darknesse, who cannot discerne betwixt the right Ionas 4.10.11. hand and the left,as the contrary ill beseemed *Ionah*,who was checkt for his labour. And further,seeing the varietie of the necessities and estates,both of diuers particular Churches,& members of each,(some of them knowne to vs)is manifold: we must thinke this duty not easily discharged, without a great measure of loue,and an heart dilated therewith,and well purged of selfeloue. There are many that pretend this office to the Church(being indeed Schismatikes and Heretikes) out of a preposterous loue of a communion,out of vnion.But let them know the Church acknowledgeth no such bastards,neither hearkneth after those that would, vnder the pretence of a new deuised communaltie of their owne, draw her to either a separation from her head,as Papists doe, or from fellowship with the body of Christ, as they who terme themselues of the separation doe.

When *Iphtahs* daughter had answered her father,as he had giuen her occasion,she made a request to him for her selfe, as in this verse is shewed,saying: Giue me leaue to goe to the mountaines, to bewaile my virginitie, I and my fellowes. For it was counted a reproch in those daies, to die childlesse. And a solitarie place as she asked,was fit for that purpose. Now that she would not without leaue doe euen that which was good,she sheweth clearely,and we may see,that much lesse would she haue done as *Dinah, Iacobs* daughter did,to range and roue,idlely,needlessely and dangerously. Vers.37.38.

Which may teach our youth,and particularly the maidens of our age, to learne this point of obedience of her;namely not to bee their owne caruers, to cut out their liberty to themselues, while they be vnder the gouernment and authoritie of their parents or other; to go where they list, and to thinke themselues too good to craue leaue,especially,for their lawfull going forth: which to doe agreeth not with sto t and loftie stomackes,and therefore the Doct.

most of them, going commonly to such places, & to such ends, as they wish afterward that they had staied at home, doe with shame and sorrow, reape the iust fruit of their disobedience: whereas by crauing leaue they might haue been answered by them with whom they should haue consulted, that such goings foorth had not been for their good, and so might haue been staied at home with safety. And if shee asked leaue for her going abroad, how much more would she haue asked it in more weightie cases? But this is a branch of the generall duty of obedience, whereof much hath been said in Chap. 1. and elsewhere. Onely this wee may wonder at, that the daughter of *Iphtah*, a man ignorant (no doubt) and vnaquainted with many things, concerning the will of God; and therefore none of the fittest to season his children with religion, (especially considering his banishment, and maner of liuing) that she (I say) should yet attaine to this excellent courage, and shew so rare a patterne of obedience, as that few mens example in the Scripture may compare with her in the one: but assuredly, the greatest part of the children of the most carefull and religious parents (for al their knowledge) come farre short of her in the other. But where grace is, there nature and sexe is not to bee respected: that which the Author to the Hebrewes saith, That by faith many waxed strong, is truly verified in this worthy damsell, among the rest.

Note.

Heb. 11. 34.

The 2. point in this verse.

The leaue she asked, was to this end, that for two moneths she might go and bewaile her virginitie, and comfort her selfe with her companions, (which were virgins also) on the mountaines in solitarie places: for it was among women a reproch in those daies, and lamented, to be barren, and so it was by her, that she should die a virgine without issue. For it was a kind of curse of it selfe to die so. For God had commanded men from the beginning, to replenish the earth. And the Hebrewes desired to encrease a holy seede and Common-wealth: and they hoped, seeing the Messiah should come of the seede of *Abraham*, that he might possibly come of theirs.

Now in that some thinke, that seeing she asked to goe bewaile her virginitie, that therefore she was not offered in sacrifice, but only kept from marriage, and was vowed by her father to perpetuall virginitie while she liued. I answere: That cannot bee, seeing neither God did euer command, or require of any, to vow the virginitie of their children, and so tie them to it, neither could *Iphtah* mind or meane that, when hee made his vow, as I haue said before, for hee saw that it had been most like that his daughter should haue been shee, that should haue met him, as it was so indeed. Beside his daughter was not consenting thereto, which of necessity she must haue been, if his vow had been made of that. And besides when he returned, and met his daughter, how was he stricken with great griefe, shee not knowing why: and what sense had there been in this, when hee made his vow, that he should meane thus? [The first that meeteth me, I will offer her to perpetuall virginitie.] But his lamenting it, and common sense sheweth the contrary: and if any other but his daughter (as what knew hee) had met him, what authoritie had he to vow her to virginitie? And if yee will say, nay; he meant his daughter, I haue answered that, and besides, how can his vow of a burnt offering be expounded of virginitie.

Likewise the absurditie of the fact, and his vnnaturalnesse to his owne child

child,and hauing no more,and the Lord not requiring it of him, what had it been lesse then madnesse in him,(though it had been in his power to doe it) to haue either vowed, or intended any such thing, and much more to execute it? Therefore although he did as ill (I grant) through ignorance,in offering her,yet it cannot be that hee vowed her to virginitie,but hee meant when hee vowed, to offer that as a sacrifice that should first meete him,and he thought he might. But if ye aske,why she said,she would go and bewaile her virginitie, if her father meant not that, I say virginitie is here expressed because she more grieued that she should dye a virgin,then simply that she should dye: for in as much as losing her life she died childlesse, it was all one as if she had liued all her life long in virginitie. The meaning then is, she lamented that she must dye a virgin.

That which we are to learne here, is this, that the afflictions which God laieth vpon his seruants, ought both to be grieuous to them for the present time, and also according to the measure and continuance of his afflicting hand: so ought the measure and continuance of their sorrowes be. The whole booke of the Lamentations of *Ieremy*, is a plentifull witnesse of this truth,for it containeth a bitter continued complaint, made in the behalfe of the Church,for the desolation which was vpon her, euery part and circumstance whereof is laid in the ballance, to prouoke her to a due correspondent heauinesse and humiliation vnder Gods hand. And so ought it to be with vs also. First,because we haue none laid vpon vs, but we deserue them by our sinne,and wee must be led to repentance by them, or else wee abuse them. And besides,the greatnes and continuance of aflictions argue,for the most part,that we are not sufficiently humbled,nor repent as we might doe, for our sinnes; nor call vpon the Lord effectually as wee should. But most men turne away their eye from that which is vnpleasing,and carnally solace themselues with their outward blessings,that so they may auoid all heauinesse,or choke it. Doct.2. Heb.12.11. Lam 3.39. Note.

The vse hereof is,to reproue the stoicall blockishnes of those that be not moued with afflictions, and to reproue them againe on the other side, that by continuance vnder the crosse, doe grow hard hearted and rebellious; which condition is a fearefull signe of Gods reiecting of them. Also to teach vs the heauier and longer that troubles are vpon vs,the more earnestly to labour with our selues,to grow in repentance,zeale and feruencie of prayer. But oh how soone doe euen the better sort of Gods people faint or waxe blockish vnder them,if they doe no worse,especially being grieuous and long vpon them? Yea and how doe they exceed in the other extreame oftentimes, in laying their crosses too neere their hearts,and aggrauating them beyond measure? which sinne *Iob* himselfe,when his troubles exceeded,was not free from. Iam.1.5.

Now to performe this solemne worke,she chose both a solitarie place fit for the purpose, and also farre from her fathers house, to weane her selfe from thence,or for to auoid recourse of her friends vnto her. To teach vs, that there fall out times and occasions to bee solitarie, euen as it is it selfe commanded vs of God,and that both extraordinary, as here, and in priuat fasting,and ordinary also for meditation; and these both the one and the other we should vse to our good when we haue cause,either longer or shorter Vers.38.

ter time to goe apart by our selues, knowing that this is a speciall action of religious worship, and therefore requireth seperation from hindrances. So did our Sauiour Christ for a time, after much preaching and being in companie, goe into some solitarie place, with his Disciples, as it were returning to himselfe, that hee might haue more freedome for heauenly contemplation and prayer. So in the time of great lamentation, as the people did
Zach.12.12. mourne for the death of *Iosias*, and in the time of *Zachary* the Prophet, whē the familie did it apart, one member of it from another, the husband apart, and the wife apart. But fondly doth Popery abuse such examples, to maintaine Monasticall life, and such like fancies, when they were vsed in the best manner, (if euer well vsed) but now much more, when they haue brought them to such abomination as they are come vnto, that it is but a couer for much and great wickednesse.

And this point deserueth our obseruation: that she being now in heauines, wisely chose the fittest exercise to set it in on worke, and did not yeeld to her passion, which then would haue made her loggish and vnprofitable, but vsed it to a singular good end, euen to fit her selfe for her death and departure. In mirth and ioy how hard a thing is it to recall home our wandring senses and straying affections, and retire our thoughts and mindes from rouing in euery corner of the world, our wofull experience can tell vs. Sorrow hath likewise many and those grieuous annoiances attending it, but that of the two (the comparison being equall) is the fittest trumpet to sound this retreit. And as naturally it contracteth the body and the spirits, so if it be taken heed vnto, it bringeth the superfluous and noisome cares, delights and desires of the soule into a narrower compasse. And when a man is wholly at home, is he not fitter for any good dutie, then when hee is absent in great part from himselfe? Therefore as the day of griefe is a season and opportunitie for some good dutie, which at other times is to vs vnseasonable, so let vs vse it accordingly, that is, redeeme it. Solitarinesse (I confesse) is not fit for euery sorrower: and yet it is necessarie for the better doing of this dutie. I therfore distinguish of persons: Such therfore as are ignorant, and yet oppressed with heauinesse, for that they doubt, and are vncertaine of Gods fauour, for their sinne, and especially if they bee pressed with melancholy. To these I giue this counsell, that they auoide solitarinesse in their pangs of griefe, and melancholike passions, and giue not vantage to their enemie the diuell to finde them alone, (as neere as they can) lest they finde his delusions and temptations the more forcible, as *Iudas* in his perplexitie did, when hee went aside from all companie. But let their sorrow driue them to aske counsell, and make their cases knowne to such, as can ad-
Luke 4.2. uise or comfort them. The diuell was bold to assault our Sauiour himselfe in his solitarinesse. But to returne and to speake of the point. If a suruey were taken, I doubt wee should finde few houres (I speake not of weekes or moneths) dedicated by the most part of Christians, to this heauenly worke of vsing solitarines for meditation, especially for preparation to dye, to make vp their accounts against they should be called for. Oh they look to liue long, they are not in the case of this maide, who was within two moneths of her dying day, and applied them wholly to fit her for death; but they are made drunke with an vnsatiable desire of liuing still, and therefore tell

tell not them of such sad vnwelcome matters. But oh fooles! are they not suddenly taken (and as vnprouided) within few daies and houres of their death, as they were many yeeres before? Therefore to leaue them: when the Lord at any time iustly occasioneth vs to be sorrowfull and pensiue, let vs beware of blockishnesse (which commonly accompanieth them, who in in their mirth thinke of nothing but iollitie) and say wee euery one thus to our selues: Now the Lord calles me home to the practise of a dutie, (which indeed ought to be oft in vse) to meditate of my estate, to vnburden my mind and soule of those manifold, needlesse and noysome thoughts and affections, which I haue ouerloaden my selfe a long time withall: now the Lord will haue me bent to search out my errors, corruptions, and disorders of hart and life, and going aside to ease my stomack of them, confesse, loath, renounce and aske pardon of them. Now the Lord will haue me to pray, that his spirit may be restored to me in greater measure, that I may returne with more libertie to his seruice, and beware that I be not againe surfeited, with that which now I haue vomited vp, as the world, pleasures, vaine desires, vile and loathsome lusts. This is a good vse indeed of heauinesse: the Eccles.7.2. house of such mourning, is better thē the house of feasting. And to this end, oh it were to be wished, that damsels as well as other, liuing in these daies, would set forth themselues to the world, not in pride, boldnesse, nicenesse and curiositie of fashions, but in modestie, grace and wisdome (as this maiden here did) which were another manner of spectacle, then to see many golden rings in a swines snout.

Now whereas it is said here, (to fill vp the measure of her due commendation) that she returned at the time set, vnto her father, to doe to her as hee had vowed; the faithfulnesse, constancie and obedience of the maid is not onely to bee commended, but admired. For why did shee so, but to serue God therein, as she was perswaded? Such keeping of couenant and promise made by her, when it was to the forgoing of her life, doth vrge all in smaller matters, much more to keepe promise, and to make conscience of their word, and that not only towards God, but euen to men also. The like we see in *Paul*, who hauing his liberty giuen him, both in his iourney towards Rome, and at Rome also (where hee was *Nero* his prisoner) whereby hee might haue made many an escape and shifted for himself: yet neuer attempted any such course, but faithfully returned to his Captaine, and to his Keeper, (though to the perill of his life) rather then he would procure safety by breaking away, by distrusting God, or by vnfaithfulnesse. A good cause will seeke no such shifts: and our great Iesuits, if there were in them that zeale, which they pretend, they neede not by breaking oath, nay prison, prouide for themselues, as sundrie of them haue done, to testifie what a good cause they haue to maintaine, who betray it so grossely. And this further condemneth that common vnfaithfulnesse and falsehood (which also I haue noted before, but cannot too much complaine of) at this day practised, to the vtter vndoing of many thousands, by breaking both promise and bond, and running away with mens goods, or playing the banckroupts, and all to defeate them.

Vers.39. Doct.

Now in that it is said, he did to her according to his vow, it is a sufficient Vers.40. proofe, that he vowed her not to virginitie. I haue in ẏ verses before shewed

how

how these words are to be vnderstood: to wit, that he sacrificed her, as his vow was to doe, to that which should first meet him, and did not tie her to liue a virgine: and therefore I say no more of it, lest I should make a needles repetition: and if I dissent herein from any, they are those who confessed, it was but their opinion, in that they thought otherwise then I doe: and I haue shewed my reasons of this my assertion. Now though hee did so performe his vow vpon his daughter of meere conscience, (for he thought that he ought to keepe and performe that vow which hee had solemnely made, though it fell out vpon his owne daughter) yet this that he did consult with none in all that time about it, (which is admirable that he did not) doth admonish all in doubtfull and dangerous cases to aske counsell, and seeke resolution. But withall let them take this: to seeke where they ought, namely, in the Scriptures, or at the mouth of the godly and learned, to be resolued by the Scriptures. See before verse 30.

Vers. 39. 40. It is said further, that it was kept as a custome of the daughters of Israel, that they went to bewaile the daughter of *Iphtah* foure times in the yeere. Some translate the Hebrew word to talke with, and to comfort; other to bewaile: the word yeeldeth both significations. But whether of the two is to be vnderstood in this place is easie to see: for the vow of *Iphtah* being taken in this meaning, that he ment thereby to offer her in sacrifice, it followeth of necessitie, that these maides bewailed her when they met, and did not talke with her, shee being dead. For although the Hebrew word indeed signifieth, both to common with, and to bewaile, yet I haue shewed that the latter sense here is to be imbraced. Now in that they held this as a custome to lament her that she was sacrificed, it appeares they sought this thereby, that it should not bee forgotten, and besides that, it is like enough they did it, that all parents might be warned to make no such vowes.

Doct. This custome while it was not abused, nor brought to any superstitious vse, was the lesse to be misliked, whereas otherwise, it had been fit to breake it off. accordingly should customes be thought of, and dealt with. For as they agree with Gods law, and with charitie, they are to be obserued and kept, but otherwise, as they be superstitious and prophane, to hinder, or put by Gods worship, or when there is danger that they will grow to such abuse, they are to be broken. Also when they tend to the maintaining, of needlesse charge and expences, the hurt and hindring of any, or bee otherwise vnlawfull, (as there are many such at this day maintained and keept) they are to be abolished. And therefore the blind and wicked practise, of spending the twelue daies at the Natiuitie in play, reuell and disorder, also the leaud customes still retained in some parts of this land, to keepe their prophane customary feasts and drinkings on the Sabbath, with al other misrule of like sort, are vtterly to bee rooted out, and better plants set in their roomes, if it may be: of which I say no more, hauing before more fully discoursed thereof.

THE

THE SIXTIETH NINE SERMON ON THE TWELFTH CHAPTER OF THE BOOKE OF IUDGES.

Verse 1. *And the men of Ephraim gathered themselues together, and went*
Northward, and said vnto Iphtah, Wherefore wentest thou to fight against the chil-
dren of Ammon, and didst not call vs to goe with thee? we will therefore burne thine
house vpon thee with fire.
2. *And Iphtah said vnto them, I and my people were at great strife with the*
children of Ammon, and when I called you, ye deliuered me not out of their hands.
3. *So when I saw that yee deliuered me not, I put my life in mine hands, and went*
vpon the children of Ammon: so the Lord deliuered them into mine hands. Where-
fore then are yee come vpon me now to fight against me?
4. *Then Iphtah gathered all the men of Gilead, and fought with Ephraim: and*
the men of Gilead smote Ephraim, because they said, Ye Gileadites are runnagates of
Ephraim, among the Ephramites and among the Manassites.
5. *Also the Gileadites tooke the passages of Iorden before the Ephramites, and*
when the Ephramites that were escaped, said, Let me passe, Then the men of Gilead
said vnto him, Art thou an Ephramite? If he answered, Nay,
6. *Then they said vnto him, Say now Shibboleth: and he said Sibboleth: for he*
could not so pronounce: then they tooke him and slew him, at the passages of Iorden:
and there fell at that time of the Ephramites, two and fortie thousand.

THe summe of this Chapter consisting of two parts, is this, first, the sedition of the Ephramites, but to their owne cost. For they quarreling with *Iphtah* for a light or rather no cause, and comming to make warre with him, many of them were slaine by him, and others of them in flying, were in the like manner put to the sword, and this to verse 7. this is the summe of the first part. The second declareth and setteth downe the time of the gouernment of *Iphtah*, and of the three other Iudges, who succeeded one another, and of their death and buriall, to wit, *Iphtahs*, and the other, who were these, *Ibzan*, *Elon* and *Abdon*, and this to the end of the Chapter. *The summe and parts 2.*

The first part of the Chapter.

IN this former part, these two things are contained: First, the bitter contending of the Ephramites with *Iphtah*, threatning to burne him and his house with fire: and *Iphtahs* answere and defence to verse 4. The second thing is, how *Iphtah* killeth diuers of them in the skirmish and fight, and others of them in their flying away, to verse 7. *The first point.*

The

Verse 1. The sinnes of these Ephramites, which they shew here in one action, are many: of the which it shall not be amisse to take a view, as the text offereth occasion, in the most whereof I will bee the briefer, because I haue handled them already, vpon the like fact, Chap. 8. 1. The first is sedition, in rising against their lawfull gouernour *Iphtah*; and this came of pride, whereby they attributed so much vnto themselues aboue other. Then their vnthankfulnesse to him, who had farre indangered himselfe to the Ammonites before he got the victorie, for theirs, and the safetie of their brethren. Thirdly, their false accusing of him, that he had not called them to helpe him in the conflict, boldly making a lie in so charging him, whereas hee had called them, and they refused to come, which shewed their disobedience to him, who by his authority might command them: and lastly, their threatning to burne him and his house, a fruit of their sedition; and to void this their stomake of the baggage in it, it is said they went Northward to Gilead against *Iphtah*, that is, to contend and fight with them.

The sense of the 3. first verses.

Doct. To make some vse hereof, first we see, that such as beare the face of honest men, and liue in countenance among their neighbours, as these Ephramites did, may yet possibly become and proue seditious. Pride of it selfe is able to set men forward to it, as it did *Absolon*, and these here. Much more, ease and idlenesse, ill counsell and enuy, with such like. And though the sprigges of it bud forth full fast, and are readie too easily to yeeld fruit in all, yet we must haue an especiall care, that they grow not: but let them be pruned off, yea and a digging at the roote betimes had need to be, that the branches may wither. See what I haue noted of this point out of the face of the Shechemites, chap. 9. 2. 3.

Now for the remedie hereof, seeing pride and discontentment are the causes hereof, let the heart bee kept with all diligence, from nourishing of such affections and thoughts, and to cracke pride, and pull it downe, thinke we of our selus as we are: euen such as if we could see our faces in the cleare glasse of Gods law, should appeare more loathsome, then the most deformed Lazer: such is the filthinesse of our inborne corruption, and foule litter of most monstrous sinnes that proceed from thence, so farre off should we be from swelling and thinking our selues to be great, yea, petty Angels as we are readie to doe, whereby we imagine we be too good to be in subiection to our betters in the Lord, yea, or to the Lord himselfe, in obeying his word. There are many who accuse the sincere preachers and professors of the Gospell, as seditious and tumultuous, yea, enemies of good order, &c. A man would not thinke, that the accuser were like to bee stained with the crime, which he chargeth vpon another. But when for want of the feare of God, some of the ciuillest, and such as stand for law and gouernment in townes shal be puld out for notorious malefactors, either in this crime of sedition, as *Demetrius* and his fellowes, or in any other riot and disorder; while they whom they chargde shall be found innocent, then they wish they had been a little preciser in that kind, and confesse that onely conscience can resist these temptations to sinne. They make a shift for a while to conceale their leaudnesse, but if forcible occasions and prouocations assault them, they haue no power to withstand them. Thus much of this. Looke vpon the quarrelling of the Ephramites with *Gedeon*, Chap. 8.

Note.

Secondly,

Secondly, their bitter and causelesse contentions, threatning to burne him and his house, where they had cause rather to haue been highly thankfull to him, doth teach of what mettall and disposition some be, that they cannot liue in their place innocent and harmelesse with other, but take vpon them to dominere ouer them, holding them in feare of them, when yet the Lord hath commanded, that wee should not be many masters, neither suffer any to liue in feare by vs. Such were the Iewes against *Paul*: for this sin of contending with others, though it be odious wheresoeuer it be found, yet when it is raised for religion, it is monstrous: and they that hate their neighbours for their weldoing, and for that they cannot ioyne with them in their vnfruitfull and shamelesse workes of darknesse, but reprooue them rather, such I say hate them with a deadly hatred, and cannot in their disliking and malicious conceits against them, be pacified or reconciled to them, their wrath is vnapeazable, as we reade that *Cains* for that very cause was towards his brother *Abel*, that his brothers deeds were good, and his euill. 2 James 3 1. 1.Ioh.3.12.

This ought to teach vs, not onely to liue peaceably with those that are quietly disposed, though they be not framed to liue Christianly; but also to doe our best to winne and perswade them to looke after the life to come, and to feare God; and that first by our innocent liuing among them, and good example giuing vnto them, and then by little and little drawing them forward, by good instruction, admonition, or otherwise, as there shall bee cause. But especially it should vrge vs to be more neerely knit in brotherly loue, one Christian with another, and to beare the infirmities which we see each in other, and helpe one another out of them: rather then to take a pritch and conceit one against another, and so to cause strangenes and breaking of fellowship, wherein many offend greatly, till they be forced by the hard vsage, that they finde among the bad sort, to make more account of their brethren afterward, then they did before. But of this often.

To the former doctrine, this may be added as a limme or branch of it, that ciuill men not Heathenish onely, as the King of Ammon, chap.11. but Professors also sometimes (as we see these Ephramites did) to adde strength to their contentions and braules, and to giue them more libertie therein, will, I say not, sticke to set out their dislikes, and accusing of other with lyes and false chargings of them, that so they may seeme to haue iust cause to hate and contend, as that wicked *Ziba* did bring into disfauour & disgrace, that innocent man *Mephibosheth* with *Dauid*, as much as in him lay, with lyes and false accusations. Let the odiousnes of such dealing, make the speaking of the truth to be more set by of vs, and yet for loues sake to our brethren not to vrge the vtmost that we may doe, though we might doe it iustly, which is the right and kinde shewing of our loue to them. Let the reader see chap.11.13. 3 2.Sam.16.3.

And by the vnthankfulnes of these Ephramites, which it is no marueile to see in them towards *Iphtah*, they being branded with such grosse euils, as we haue heard to bee in them, let vs learne what Gods seruants may looke for in this world, for all their loue and labour in procuring the peace and welfare of other, and in bringing them to good: truly, vnthankfulnes they may looke for, if not ill will and the fruite thereof: and that recompence is rendred them for all their good will, to go about to bring the wicked world 4 to a better point, I meane in labouring to acquaint them with God. They owe them more then all that they haue is worth: as wee may see by *Pauls* words to *Philemon*: yea and it is cleere also by the word of God, that they are beholding to them in great part for their liues; as we reade, that for ten righteous mens sake Sodome should not haue bin destroyed: euen for this they are (I say) beholding to the same good seruants of God, as well as for the welfare of their soules, who by their holy prayers and other good endeuours would be helpers to them, if they might be regarded of them: yea to say much in few words, if it were not for them, the world could not stand, so that they haue all that they enioy for their sakes, and more might haue at Gods hands, but that they willingly withhold it from themselues.

Phile. 19.

Gen. 18, 32.

And what doth the whole rabble of them yeeld againe to Gods people (thinke we) but vnthankfulnes, (vnlesse it be a few whom God inlightneth to beleeue the truth) euen as *Iphtah* did receiue at the hands of the Ephramites, whom he set at libertie, yea and that with all indignitie, discourtesie, and bad vsage. But to omit them, with whom there is little hope of good to be done, this I say to them who desire to glorifie God by bringing foorth much fruite, let them not be discouraged, but beare it contentedly at their hands, it is the onely recompence that the vnthankfull world can yeeld to such; as Christ himselfe found and foretold it vs, saying, *I haue done many good workes among you, for which of them doe yee stone me?* And againe, *If they haue not knowne me*, saith he, *neither will they know you*. For the fuller vse hereof, looke in chap. 8. verses 22. and 35. also chap. 8. 1.

John 15. 9.

John 10. 32.
Iohn 16.

5 Lastly in this verse, whereas this sinne of contending and dissembling in these Ephramites, is found to be not in one, but many generations of them, as partly we haue heard already in the 8. chapter of this book, where we see the Ephramites did the same to *Gedeon* then, that these their posteritie did here to *Iphtah*, and afterward the like pride is read to be in their posteritie; it teacheth how a sinne keepeth in a kindred, for many generations after, as treason, whoredome, flatterie, dissembling, and such like, and such taints and staines are not worne out, till speciall grace of God doe worke and effect the same. But of this before, chap. 8. 1. for in these points I shunne tediousnes of purpose.

Vers. 2. 3 In these two next verses is set downe the answere of *Iphtah* to these Ephramites, by which answere it is cleere, that he vsed all meanes, like a wise and well gouerned man, before hee would take vp weapon against his brethren the Ephramites, notwithstanding their bold prouoking of him, and he Iudge and gouernour ouer them, and might therefore by his authoritie haue beaten them downe. And the summe of his answere was this; that they laid a false accusation to his charge, for contrariwise, at such time as he was sore prouoked by the Ammonites, and driuen to make warre with thē, he sought helpe of them, and they would not goe foorth with him, but put him to his shifts: and when he fought with them, to the perill and danger of his life, the Lord deliuered them into his hands: Therefore he demands of them, what cause they the Ephramites had, to assault and set vpon him in that manner they did. Thus much of *Iphtahs* answer.

Now let vs a while consider of this more particularly, as wee haue done before of the Ephramites quarrelling with him. Where this commeth first

to

to be noted by their disordered contending with him, not in course of law, *Doct.*
but seditiously and with tumult, how one affliction arose to this good man after another: as the trouble ẏ he had by his daughter was accompanied in some sort with this, that came to him by his neighbours the Ephramites. Whereby we may see the condition of Gods people as in a glasse, that they are euer wrapped into new combats and troubles daily, so as the end of one is the beginning of another. As wee see in the booke of *Iob*, it is said of his troubles, how one complaint came to him in the necke of another: and yet (which is more to bee marueiled at) God of his goodnesse so worketh by them, that they who will be ruled by him, may see them turne to their profit and benefit, according to the saying of the Apostle, to wit, that all things turne to the best to them that loue God. The like saith S. *Iames*; Count it (my brethren) matter of the greatest reioycing, whē ye fall into diuers tribulations. And it is a double mercie of God that it is so: For we are so corrupt and defiled, that if things succeed with vs after our desire, we are exceedingly lifted vp, and forget our selues, in such wise that our pride is intollerable, and we shamefully disguise our selues, so that such as feare God, and behold vs, knowing we are but wormes meate; are greatly grieued to see our insolencie. Therefore to keepe vs from such disguisednes, and the danger that commeth thereby, what a fauour of God is this, that he after some prosperitie, doth vse to exercise vs with new combats and afflictions, and all to hold vs vnder, yea, and much to benefit vs. For as it is better to goe to heauen with one foote, then to hell with both; so he will rather saue vs with putting vs to some paine and griefe here, rather then to lose and forgoe vs vtterly, by suffering vs to enioy vncertaine and momentany prosperitie and the pleasures of sinne for a while. Of this hauing spoken what I thought fit in chap. 11. vers. 34. and 8. 1. I adde no more here.

Iob 1.16. *Rom.* 8.28. *Iam.* 1.2. *Mark.* 9.45.

Onely this watchword is necessarie to be taken of vs, that although wee be now and then (as *Iphtah* was before, chap. 11.35.) humbled with some afflictions, so that for the time we be brought to obedience, and subdued as it is meete for vs to be; yet because wee doe so soone wash them off, therefore we haue need of many, and those also strong afflictions, (as *Iphtah* had) as mallets to beate vs downe one after another, and bruse vs that so we may be meekned vnder the mightie hand of God; and we must be importunate with him in our prayers, that we may be more and more accustomed daily, to beare the crosse patiently and contentedly, till hee haue perfected and brought to his appointed measure, the good worke that he hath begun in vs. And whereas the succession of heauie afflictions much dismaieth vs for the most part, (though alas they are not worth the naming in respect of Christs, whose afflictions wee should be conformable vnto; nor yet to the glorie (which through him) they worke vs, as the Apostle saith, I say it should be otherwise, and we should cast one eye eft vpon the righteous and equall dealing of God, and eft vpon the cause within our selues, as well as vpon the greatnes of the affliction, or the multiplicitie of them, as hath often been noted before in handling this argument.

Note. *Luke* 9.23. *Rom.* 8.18.

Secondly here we see, that answer is to be made to false accusations, when *Doct.* 2.
they bee proudly giuen out against vs, and are to our reproch and hurt, as

these of the Ephramites were against *Iphtah*: such (I say) are not to be suffered to passe, lest the authors of them bee imboldned thereby, to doe so still,
Prou.26.5. yea and goe further. So *Salomon* teacheth, saying: Answere a foole according to his folly, lest he be wise in his owne conceit, and so he waxe bold to make a practise of it.

For though wee walking in our innocencie and vprightnes in all good
Eccles.7.21. conscience, should not regard the taunts and vniust reproches of euill tongues, which they commonly send after vs, much lesse hearken what they
Note. say of vs, for then wee should neuer be quiet; yet in weightie matters that touch our profession, and the credit thereof, we ought (if we can obtaine it) to vse the helpe of the Magistrate, both to restraine the slanderer, (in which respect *Mephibosheth* complained to *Dauid* of *Ziba*) and to procure vnto him his due, vnlesse he repent. But especially take wee heed that we giue them
1.Pet.3.17. no iust cause to speake euill of vs, while wee suffer as euill doers, for so wee bring a double punishment vpon our selues.

And because much seed of contention is sowne in the world by bad persons, this I say further of it, that it is our part and dutie to roote it vp, as fast and as much as in vs lieth. And if ye aske how that is done: I answere, besides that which before I said, we should carefully looke that we take all in good part, if it may be; but if it cannot be, yet in defending our innocencie,
Note. let vs shew all meeknes, and striue against all bitternesse: if the offender see his fault, we haue good blessing of our labour; if not, it is lawfull to goe further, and according to the greatnes of the fault, so let satisfaction be vrged at his hands: but in any wise, let vs see that wee keepe the vnitie of the spirit in the bond of peace. This I thought good to adde to that I haue said before in the eleuenth chapter in *Iphtah* his answere to the Elders of Gilead, and in his replie to the King of Ammons lying answere.

To come more particularly to the matter, we see, that whereas they make this the chiefe cause of their quarrell against him, that he called them not to helpe against the Ammonites, hee telleth them hee did call them, but they
*Doct.*3. would not come. So that he conuinceth them of a lye. But who would thinke, that so many should consent together so boldly to maintaine a false matter? And men of the visible Church and of the tribe of Ephraim, one of the famous tribes among the rest. Therefore they who at this day doe carrie their heads aloft, both for their profession and outward estate in the world, haue great cause to suspect and feare themselues both in and about this sinne and the like. But to terrifie and withhold men from standing stiffe
2.King.5.27. in a lye, let that fearefull example of *Gehazi* preuaile with them, with such like in Scripture.

The heart of man is false and naught, and will easily carrie men to that which is odious and vile, especially if the matter sauour of profit or pleasure, and selfeloue shall so blindfold them, that they shall not see the euill they haue done, till they smart for it, vnlesse they be such as keepe a narrow watch ouer their hearts, and a searching into them faithfully, to finde out that which is amisse. And this that it may be done, God hath giuen vs two
Iohn 3.19. especiall good helpes: the first is our comming to the light, that our euill deedes may that way be made knowne to vs. The other, our owne examinings

nings priuatly of our waies,and arraigning of our selues before God,that so Psal.4.4.
we may cast out such filthinesse, of lying, dissembling and the like sins. See Lam.3.40.
branch 3.of verse 1.

These Ephramites dealt with *Iphtah*, as the men of Succoth and Penuel Doct 4.ver.2.3
dealt with *Gedeon*, when hee followed the Princes of Midian, to wit, *Zeba* and *Zalmunna*: for they dealt roughly and vnkindly with him. So these when *Iphtah* their gouernour sent to them for helpe, they most vndutifully denied it,and yet (which was much worse) they came and quarrelled with him, now when hee had got the victorie, for that (as they shamelesly affirmed) he had not called them to the battell,and so they would bee thought to haue deserued as much fame and commendation in that victorie, as *Iphtah*, seeing they boasted that they were as ready to haue gone against the Ammonites as he,when indeed they meant it not.

Therein they bewrayed two foule faults, very odious and to bee taken heed of: the one, hard-heartednes and barbarous vnkindnes, not to helpe their brethren in their need,the case being their owne as well as theirs; and this was ioined with disobedience,in that *Iphtah* was their gouernour. The other fault was their subtiltie, in that they did (which way, and on which side soeuer the victorie should goe) prouide for themselues. By the first we are taught to beware of this vnkindnes and incompassionate hard heartednes, to bee senselesse of the miseries and necessities of our brēthren; but to be moued with pitie toward them in their distresses: and this wee should doe,as for the commandement of God and other causes, so for this that we our selues are subiect to fall into the like troubles, and doe also at one time or other. In which case our consciences beare vs witnesse, that we are iustly forsaken of other,and left to sinke in our sorrowes,and smart by our calamities,and that none should offer themselues to pitie vs,seeing wee shewed so little mercie and kindnes to other before in the like troubles, but were rather hard hearted towards them. And it is (doubtlesse) one cause (as wee Note.
may see by the euill seruant, who had no pitie on his fellow,and therefore his master was wroth with him,and deliuered him to the tormentors) it is Matth.18.34.
one cause(I say) why God afflicteth vs, for as much as we should otherwise neuer pitie our brethren in their troubles,but thereby we learne commiseration towards them. Looke chap.5. in *Deboras* complaint of the Tribes: and chap.8.vers.6.and 8.

The other fault was their subtiltie and double dealing; for they hauing Doct 5.in vers.2.3.
an ill conscience propounded this to themselues,that if the Ammonites had the victorie ouer *Iphtah*,then they should be free from hurt and danger,seeing they had not stirred against them to aide him; and if *Iphtah* should preuaile against them (as he did) then they would come forth,florishing boldly with a lye,affirming that they had cause to take it hardly,for that hee got the victorie proudly with a few,(and would not call them to bee partakers with him) and so they did indeede. And thus they had, as men say, two strings to their bow. This falsehood is so common in the world,to deale subtilly, as it is hard to know whom to trust, as *Salomon* complaining asketh, where a faithfull man shall be found? Touching this vngodly policie and Prou.20.7.
subtiltie,enough hath been spoken vpon the like occasion before. Now of

their hollow heartednes and falsehood (the ground of it) I will adde somewhat more particularly.

Subtiltie and bad policie appeares in three things chiefly: the remedies. This sinne, as it is committed many waies, so in three things especially I obserue it. First in the professing of religion: secondly, in friendship betwixt and among men: and thirdly, in mens bargainings and worldly dealings. For remedying of the which (for it were very long to discourse at large of thē) this should be done: For the first, because many professing, are brought to like religion for credit, profit, and vainglorie, and so fall from it againe, by small occasions: therefore take this for instruction, let the power and beautie of the Gospell perswade thee to become a professor of it, rather then Note. hope of profit, or the seeking of credit thereby, &c. and when thou hast felt it to haue wrought in thee (by the powerfull preaching thereof) faith, and a new life; and when thou seest how safe and well liking that hath made thine estate to be vnto thee, in comparison of all that was before; this (by Gods blessing) shall worke faithfulnes in thee, to honour and beautifie thy profession, so as thou shalt not start aside from it, as too many other doe; and otherwise thou shalt neuer hold out in thy profession, what faire shewes so euer thou makest; or if thou doest, yet thou shalt reape no fruite in peace, nor haruest of such profession, because when it was at the best, it was not sound.

The second remedie. To passe to the second: for the remedying of doublenes and dissimulation in friendship, let this be one chiefe rule: Chuse thy friend for his goodnesse, and his excelling others in pietie and vertue, especially hee being ap- Note. proued to be a continuer therin, and one that is free from strong affections, as choller, anger, tetchines. And loue him still for that, (seeing the thing that Prou 19.19. is to be desired of a man, is his goodnesse) whether there be other kindnesses enioyed therewith or no; which if there be any and faile, yet hold the principle still, and nourish it, by thinking true friendship to be both rare and Prou. 27.10. precious: and let not that counsell of *Salomon* be forgotten; Thine owne friend and thy fathers forsake thou not. And beware thy selfe of tetchinesse Prou. 17.9. and conceits against him; yea though thou thinkest he hath giuen thee cause; or of the tale-bearer, which would set diuision betwixt him and thee; neither repeate any matter which ought to haue been buried and forgotten, which may easily alienate him from thee; and in no wise let hope of earthly commoditie tickle thee, or the want thereof coole or diminish affection in thee towards him: So faithfulnes in friendship will be preserued, and hollownes and dissembling auoided: otherwise, like the league of fooles, it will be soone broken off.

The third remedie. Note. And to remoue falsehood and vntrustinesse in bargaining and worldly dealings, thinke not that good for thee, that thou seest is euill and hurtfull to another, especially to a meaner man in wealth then thy selfe, but most of all to a poore body. And when the worth or value of the ware or commoditie shall be agreed vpon, plainly and without subtiltie, be willing to giue a Gen. 23.16. penny for a penniworth: and as *Abraham* weighed the siluer, according to the manner and custome of the time to *Ephron* the Hittite, for the peece of ground that he bought of him, to bury his dead in; so do thou pay currant money and coyne for it, according to couenant, that as neere as may be, there

there may be equalitie to both. If a day be set for paiment, keepe it, at least let there be no fault in thee, but let it be seene that thou art disappointed and hindred from paying, against thy will: and so if the Common wealth be regarded of thee, not thine owne priuate onely, thou shalt come neere the rule that our Sauiour giueth for earthly dealings: that is, looke what ye would that men should doe to you, euen the same doe yee vnto them: So shalt thou not be guiltie of double dealing and falsehood. And if thou thus shunne in these three, hollownesse and subtiltie, thou shalt haue great cause to reioyce in and for thine vprightnes and sinceritie, and not easily brought to halting or dissembling in other matters. Matth.7.12. Note.

Now let vs proceed: *Iphtah* answers further to the Ephramites, When I saw you would not helpe me (saith he) I put my life in mine hands, meaning I aduentured without you, and rested on God, going foorth with smaller helpe, when I could not haue greater. And by this paterne wee are taught, that we hang not, neither depend on other men in the good things we take in hand. For example, that neither in those things that concerne our owne happines directly, (I meane the seeking of faith and conuersion, nor which pertaine to sanctification of life & godlines, as mercie and loue, righteousnes and innocencie) we must neglect any good dutie, because we see other backward in it; but rather look we to the examples of the forwardest and most faithfull both in their generall and speciall calling, and in no wise let vs regard to follow them that come behinde in good things. As all will acknowledge that we should doe so, in the preuenting a mischief neere at hand, as *Iphtah* did here in following hard the Ammonites, when the Ephramites refused to helpe him. *Abigails* wisedome and care is to be commended and imitated by many degrees before *Nabals* folly and senselesse blockishnes. Euen so let vs say with *Ioshua*, If other will not goe and ioyne with vs, yet we and ours will serue the Lord. When our Sauiour saw many offended at his doctrine, and departing away, he asked *Peter* in the name of the rest, Will ye also goe away? *Peter* answers; Whither shall we goe (Lord) if we forsake thee, who hast the words of eternall life? Be we sure therefore we prouide ill for our selues, if we pinne our zeale and forwardnes vpon others, and gather not strength enough from our owne assurance of Gods peculiar goodnesse towards our owne soules, to keepe vs close and firme in our purpose of cleauing to him and that daily. Who doth so, is wise and builds vpon the rocke, and no assault shall batter his building: as for the declining or starting backe of others, he leaueth that, saying thus to himself: They stand or fall to their owne master: and whether they haue euer been truly perswaded of Gods fauour towards them or no, I cannot tell: But I know in whom I haue beleeued. Therefore if other men will be blind, shall I put out my owne eyes? If I see the world generally disposed to coldnes, loosenes, and luke-warmnes; shall I presently repent me of my zeale and forwardnes? Haue I resolued vpon no better grounds, then may be shaken with euery blast of winde, the frowning of my betters, the want of encouragement from men, or because I see these things are not in price and account among such as cannot iudge? If I onely serue God faithfully, of many that liue in the same towne carelesse and prophane: will God be ashamed of me before so many, or rather will hee not acknowledge me and reiect Doct.6. 1.Sam.25.33. Ioshua 24.15. Ioh.6.68. Matth.7.24. Note.

them

them for all their multitude? Oh then what a wretched part were it for me to be ashamed of him before men! or to feare base and sinfull man (whose
Math. 10.28. breath is in his nostrils) more then God, who can cast body and soule into hell? But of this point see chap. 8. verse 11. compared with former.

Doct. 7. In saying, God deliuered the Ammonites into his hands without their helpe, as it is manifest he did, wee see first how gratiously God prouided for this his seruant: that whereas hee could by no meanes procure aide from these Ephramites, the Lord dealt so for him that hee needed them not, but went through as prosperously, as if he had obtained their best assistance. For why? God will not forsake his, that trust in him, hee is their helpe and defence in time of neede, in so much that if father and mother forsake them, hee taketh them vp. This is a thing which greatly flesheth the vngodlie, (who alas little know what refuge the righteous haue in time of neede) to wit, that if they haue friends, might, and wealth, they thinke they can ouermatch their aduersarie: and then they thinke hee hath no shift, (as for the Lord, they exclude him) but he must either fall into reproch, or make shipwracke of his conscience: although if God see it expedient, hee disappointeth and frustrateth their hope. Thus the enemies of *Dauid, Daniel* and our Sauiour, insulted, when they had contriued their purposes so mischieuously to manward, that they saw no way for them, whom they pursued, to escape: Now (say the Iewes) let vs see if God will helpe him at this pinch. But oh fooles! if God were farre off also from his, when you are hottest in your furie against them, ye said somewhat indeed: but loe, he is then neerest them, to carrie them through and laugh their enemies to skorne. *Iphtah* was desirous here of the Ephramites helpe; but being denied, the Lord so wrought that they were the first that complained, and not hee: There needed no Ephramites helpe, the Lord of hoasts being on his side to make a supply. And let this be added as an encouragement to them whom I spake of in the last doctrine; that their nakednes and solitarines, I meane want of mens countenance and furtherance, ought rather to driue them to cling more closely
Prou. 16.7. vnder the Lords wing, who is able to make the enemies of his people their friends, if their waies doe please him: if not, hee can vse meanes to vphold
Note. them without their helpe. For either he can so muzzle them, that they shall not hurt them, as they would: or hee can enable them with such courage and boldnes, that they shall contemne their contempt, and little regard their opposition: or if they be such as may doe them any hurt, yet the Lord can so grace them, that they shall goe vnder that crosse willingly and bee rather confirmed, then vnsetled in their good course thereby. And let all such as would willingly bee religious, saue onely for the reproch with others, yea euen their owne flesh would cast vpon them: let such (I say) labour to beleeue this, and that temptation shall little trouble them. Againe, obserue from hence what blessing God giueth by weake meanes, when men goe to worke in their simplicitie and in a good conscience: which in all good attempts ought to encourage them that offer themselues willingly to the
Iudg. 4.6. worke, as the tenne thousand of the men of *Zebulon* and *Napthali* did in the Lords battailes against some hundred thousands in *Siseras* armie that came against them. In such a case where God hath set vs on worke and heartned vs, let vs not be discouraged by our meanenesse, which in shew of reason is indeed

indeed able to doe little: which hereby I may perswade, that they haue not been the greatest men of account, that haue brought greatest light in the Gospel vnto men, but such as are very meane in the iudgemēt of the world; euen so, in many other of his dealings, he effecteth great matters by weake meanes. See that which is noted vpon *Iphtah* his victorie in the eleuenth chap. and 32. verse, being the same words.

Vpon these premisses *Iphtah* concludeth with an interrogation, asking them wherefore they were come to fight against him? As if he should haue said, I saued your liues, you sitting at home with ease, what reason haue yee therefore thus to come against me? By this we may learne, that when wee should do good to all by Gods commandement, it proues vs to be of a most bad disposition, when we shall be found iniurious and hurtfull to the innocent, as these men of Ephraim were against *Iphtah*; and so I may say of those that doe vs hurt, and no good, though we liue innocent by them: whereas the Heathens doe good to such as doe good to them, &c. The vse of this doctrine is, that we so liue among men, that wee may not be charged iustly, nor conuicted of wronging any: and yet not to rest there, but to be ready to doe them good, as it may stand with our calling, and as we shall be able, so shall wee be sure neuer to feare accusations of vnkinde and vnbrotherly dealing; but if any be brought, we may answere them as *Iob* did, If mine aduersarie write a booke against me, I will take it on my shoulder, reade it who listeth. *Doct.8.* *Math.5.46.* *Iob 31.36.*

9. As touching their reiecting this Apologie of *Iphtah*, the point hath been handled before in the eleuenth chapter (although this wilfulnes farre worse became them, then the Heathen king of Ammon) yet somwhat I will adde by so fit occasion. It is like their wilfulnes troubled *Iphtah* not a little, especially being their gouernour, who was loth to haue turned the edge of the sword vpon his owne people (if it could haue been auoided) and besides yet could not suffer it to haue his graue and iust defence so slightly reiected. But what other fruite was to be expected at their hands, who came ready armed to trie the matter by force? Was it like they would stand debating and reasoning long with him, who came with a preiudicate and resolute minde to the contrary? It is not said indeed, that they gaue not eare to him, but their reall refusall to hearken, appeares in their proceeding to warre. But yee will say in the eighth of this booke, their predecessors bewraied the contrary, for their wrath was appeased by the answere of *Gedeon*. I answere: Indeed being vsed like froward children and condiscended vnto, that is, their proud and angrie humour being pleased, they gaue ouer with much adoe: they had bin beasts if they had not: nay doubtlesse, they could not although they would (for an angrie man cannot continue in his anger so long as he would, the fewell being remoued:) But is this the praise of a man, that being humoured (as I may say) he giues oner? No, though it be the honour of the appeaser, yet it is his shame, because he should haue ouercome himselfe before; his shame I say in that respect, although indeed he that desisteth by any meanes, is better then the implacable. But to returne: If there had been but a dramme of good nature and indifferencie in them, (for religion they had none) would they not as well haue abated their spirit towards him by their hearkning to his sound reason, as their fathers

thers did before to *Gedeons* mildneſſe? Yes doubtleſſe: but it is as impoſſible
to order an vnreaſonable paſſion by reaſon, as to be mad with reaſon. Let
this then ſet before our eyes (who are Gods Miniſters) the diſpoſition of
the moſt of our ordinary hearers, that ſo wee may learne how to be armed
againſt that diſcouragement. We are yoked with ſuch ſtiffenecked and op-
poſite natures, as winde about their fingers, the moſt ſerious charges we lay
Hoſ.6.4.&c. vpon their conſcience, and (as they in *Hoſee*) we declare vnto them the large
and weightie things of the law, and they account them as a ſtrange thing,
that is, after long information, fare as if they had neuer heard, and make
them as words of courſe, or as if wee ſpoke in an vnknowne tongue vnto
them. We looke that they ſhould receiue them as from God, (and ſo ſome
few doe) and yeeld, ſubſcribe, and hearken: but it is not ſo: we may ſay to
Matth.11.17. them, We haue piped vnto you, but ye haue not danced, &c. And why doe
they not conceiue our meaning, and of the tune of our ſong? Yes, but they
are otherwiſe reſolued, they haue another courſe to runne, (as thoſe Ephra-
Hoſ.6.4. mites had, of whom God complaineth that hee knew not how to entreate
them) and therefore they hearing vnderſtand not, ſeeing will not ſee, but
winke and harden their hearts againſt vs. Muſt not this needs grieue vs? Yes:
and ſo it ought to make vs mourne: but how? moderatly, as the Phyſition
ouer the patient, whoſe diſeaſe was paſt his skill, ere he medled with him.
And indeed ſo it ought to be: let vs feede them, and if they caſt away their
meate, or thriue not with it, they diſcredit not vs that diet them with a good
ordinary. We could wiſh, that we could find them appetites as well as food:
but this is paſt our skill: they died not of a famine, but of a ſurfeit: the
meanes were vſed, and therein we reſt, and ſay; we are a ſweete ſauour to the
Lord in them that periſh. It is manifeſt by the ſigne, that Gods will was to
reiect them: that God would not perſwade them by vs, and then (alas) how
ſhould we perſwade them? we haue ſaued our owne ſoules, their blood be
vpon their owne heads, they died not for want of phyſicke. Now of this
their wilfulnes (I meane the Ephramites) againſt *Iphtah* came ciuill warre
betweene them. Of which in the next Sermon.

10 And laſtly, in that ſo many could agree together in ſo wicked an action,
(no leſſe then two and fortie thouſand men, for ſo many loſt their liues
thereby:) we may ſee how eaſily men agree together in euill: as traytors,
rebels, and other confederates in euill, doe. Whereas it is hard for a few,
yea dwelling together in one towne and of the better ſort, to agree toge-
ther about a good matter, or againſt the euill committed therein, though it
be to their owne great eaſe and good to doe ſo. For why? the moſt of them
that ſhould ſeeke the puniſhing of ſinne, as are farre gone themſelues, and as
deepe therein, (in one kinde or other) ſo that they muſt hold backe for
ſhame, and that, leſt their owne puniſhment ſhould be procured, in vrging it
buſily vpon others. Beſides this, men are commonly of their owne corrupt
nature, ſlow and backward in doing good.

The vſe of this is, to purge and clenſe our ſelues with all care from that
2.Cor.7.1. which is euill both of ſoule and bodie, and to keepe our hearts with all dili-
gence, that good life may come from thence. So ſhall wee neuer neede to
Prou.4.23. feare that wee ſhall be vpholders of ſinne in other, or agree with them who
are ſuch. To the which purpoſe it is good to note, by what degrees wee
grow,

grow, either to that or any other height of sinne, which euen heere may bee learned by the example of these Ephramites. In whom as in other of like sort it may bee seene, that first anger was kindled against *Iphtah*, and bred in their hearts: then wrath followed, which is continued anger; next to both, hot contention; and then consent to ioyne in warre, and to band themselues against him, who was both innocent and helpfull yea euen to them. But this point I haue handled heretofore. Thus much of the Ephramites quarrelling with *Iphtah*, and his answere.

THE SEVENTIETH SERMON ON THE TWELFTH CHAPTER OF THE BOOKE OF IVDGES.

NOw followeth the fight and cruel warre that was between the Ephramites and *Iphtah*. For they, as wee haue heard, would in no wise relent, at the sound and good reason that *Iphtah* brought to disswade them from battell, but were resolute to proceed therein. Wherefore he fought with them, and ouercame them; and that they might not escape, hee preuented them, and tooke the passages ouer the waters at Iorden before them, that they could not passe ouer, and returne home, but there also many of them were taken and slaine. Vers. 4. 5. 6. *The summe of these 3 verses.*

But to come to the verses seuerally: In this fourth verse, whereas it will be marueiled at, that *Iphtah* made ciuill warre with these Ephramites; such are to know, that as they could not be staied nor disswaded from making assault vpon him, and therefore it had been free for him, in that respect, he being in such a streight to defend himselfe, although he had been but a priuate man: so, much more, he being, as he was, to wit, head and chiefe ouer them, had the sword and authoritie put into his hands, whereby he was not onely to goe against forreine enemies, but also to suppresse and punish the rebellious and seditious of the land, when they should offend in that manner. And the Lord gaue him the victory ouer them, who had despised him, and sought against all right of law to take from him the gouernment ouer the Gileadites, and to cast him out by strong hand, hee being rightly possessed of it. *The summe of verse 4.*

All which being duly considered, and the punishment and destruction which befell them thereby, euen the losse of two and fortie thousand mens liues, who by no perswations would yeeld to peace: it laieth out the heauy and iust iudgement of God against those who are vnthankfull, wilfull and seditious; and it is worth the noting, to see what such proud spirits bring vpon themselues, and how they trouble themselues, who seeke to trouble others. For either God taketh vengeance of such by men, as vpon *Achan* he did Doct. vers. 4.

Iosh.7.25. did by *Ioshua*, who said vnto him, Seeing thou hast troubled vs, God shall trouble thee this day, when they stoned him to death: or else the Lord doth
2.Thes.1.6. it himselfe without meanes, as when it is said, He will recompence tribulation to them that trouble his. To teach vs to follow peace with all men and
Heb.12.14. holinesse, without which no man shall see the Lords face.

Of this fruit of mens wilfulnes and the deare price it costeth them, I haue noted somewhat elsewhere. To knit vp the point therefore, marke how iustly God met with these Ephramites, and what a shame it was vnto them, to be the first disturbers of peace, and good order, and to be so foully foiled and beaten, by them whom they prouoked iniuriously. When it falleth out so, (for it falleth not out alwaies so) what a cutting of their combe is it, and a pulling downe of their proud stomacke? And if they should carrie away the field, and preuaile alway, who should liue with such? But for the defence of the innocẽt, and the preuenting of that confusion which would otherwise ensue, (for what is more intollerable then a boaster, when hee hath his will) the Lord resists such, and pares their nailes: so that their hornes are but short, though their hearts be full curst. And seeing all will say, that when a makebate and contentious person is put to the worse, he is well serued, to teach him to liue within his bounds, and meddle not with them that giue him no cause: let vs prouide in our dealings with others, that both our cause be honest and well grounded, and that our affections be
Note. sutable, not carried with passion, heate, and rage against him, who hath wronged vs: for if it fall out that wee be defeated, and put to the foile, (as we may looke for no other in such a case) and God himselfe take against vs in our bad courses, how shall wee be able to hold vp our heads for shame, when men reioyce at our ouerthrow? Surely hee had need be impudent, who should beare God and men and his owne conscience downe altogether, and not blank for all the shame which his owne boldnes hath brought vpon him. But as for such as measure all by the successe they haue in their leaudnes; thinking it becommeth them well enough, while they prosper, more shall be said of such in the 5. and 6. verses following.

2 In this verse a reason is added, why the Gileadites slew them of Ephraim, to wit, because they railed on them, for these Ephramites which branded themselues with so many foule sinnes together, as we haue heard, (which was too bad) yet added this to the rest, that they railed on them also. These railing words were vsed before in their contention with *Iphtah*, vpon which the Gileadites were doubly incensed. For seeing they quarrelled with *Iphtah*, and threatned him so, what wonder if they grew to disgrace the whole familie of which he was? The meaning then is, Gilead smote Ephraim, because Ephraim, besides their sedition, added disdainfull and reprochfull termes, and (because they dwelt betweene two tribes) they tooke occasion to call them, Mungrels, hang-byes, and men of no set tribe, but Neuters.

So that by all that hath been said, though the tribe of Ephraim was a famous tribe among the rest, and none of the meanest, yet we see how the best for birth and descent, may possibly degenerate and grow companions with the base and shamelesse, as these here who had worthily such measure offered them by their brethren, for their leaudnes, quarrelling, tumult and railing. Now if those may thus disguise themselues, then how easily, nay how

how vsually (thinke we) may it be seene, that very vile abiects and ofscourings may dwell among worthy and right honest seruants of God and good christians, and be of their kindred also? For as many vagrant and idle persons doe hang about Princes courts, who are neither hired, nor belonging to the house, but shifters for their bellies and backes, offering themselues to runne of meane persons errands: so are there in townes and cities, vnruly and disordered fellowes, either shrouded vnder the wing of their godly kindred, or nestling themselues among other of good note for religion and honest behauiour, some without callings, brought vp to no labour, some without liuing, but all voide of grace, ready to be set a worke in doing mischiefe if opportunitie serue. Note.

Such in diuers cities we reade of in the booke of the Acts of the Apostles, who waited to bee hired to make tumults and vprores therein. And yet I would haue none to take me thus, as though I meant, by such as I speake of, the poore folke in townes, who are in meane estate to liue: of whom I say this, that many of them follow their calling diligently, and labour painefully for their liuing, and where the Gospell is truly preached, some of them are religious and approoued good christians, I speak of that which I know: although I deny not, that there are of them also, many idle hangbies which may be reckoned worthily among the other that I spake of. The vse of this is to helpe to weede out such (as men haue abilitie and authoritie) and chiefe men in townes, and all other to bee furtherances hereunto, and to preuent idlenesse, irreligiousnesse and liuing without callings, from whence such annoyances doe arise. Looke more about this before in chapter 9. 4. and 11. 4.

We haue heard of the subduing and killing of many of the Ephramites in the battaile before mentioned: now it followeth how the rest were slaine. And that was, by taking the passages at Iorden before them, and there as many as they found to bee Ephramites they slew; all that were put to the sword, and that lost their liues at one time and other, were two and fortie thousand. Now because many passed ouer Iorden of the Reubinites and Manassites, as well as of them who were Ephramites, therefore they tried them by their language and speech, whether they were Ephramites or no, and that was by their tongue in pronouncing. For when they bad them pronounce *Shibboleth* in a more full manner, they could not, but said *Sibboleth*, being not able to pronounce so, and by that meanes they were discerned, and so taken and slaine. Vers. 5. 6.

The first thing to be noted here, is the occasion which moued the Gileadites to vse this policie, to bid the other say [*Shibboleth*] and that was, because these Ephramites being asked who they were, made a lye to saue their liues, and denied their tribe. It is true which Satan said, *Iob* 2. Skin for skin, and all that a man hath, he will giue for his life; euen truth, honestie, and all. And few will marueile at (it may be) or blame these for lying in so weighty a case, as life it selfe is, because they thinke that if they should be put to it as these were, it were no more then they might and should doe to saue their life. Indeede I confesse life is sweete, and if lying be lawfull in any case, it is in the case of the perill of life. But it is one thing for a man to omit some dutie of the law for mercies sake to our owne life, another, to commit an Doct. Iob 2. 4.

expresse sinne against the negatiue of the law. Therefore although it bee lawfull for a man to preferre his life before the doing of some dutie commanded (put case it be the Sabbath daies duties) yet a man may not before a Magistrate answere falsely, or equiuocating-lye, vnder colour of mercy in sauing his life. For it is not onely the omitting of some dutie, but the doing of a grosse fault: herein therefore the rule is true, Euill must not be done, that good may come thereof. And the negatiue rules of the law admit no exception, except God dispense (as he did with the Israelites in robbing the Ægyptians) who is aboue the law. And hence it followeth, if lying bee a sinne, that it is as well a sinne to lye, in the defence of a mans life, as it is to lye needlesly, or to please. All three, the officious, the vaine, and the shamelesse lye, are of the same cloth, though not the same colour, nor equall and of so deepe a dye. And to vs Christians it should seeme no hard condition neither, to cast our selues vpon God, rather then be beholding to a lye for our life, if the case should so stand. Better it is not to liue, then to liue with that (which is worse then any death) an accusing conscience. As the abiured Protestants in the time of persecution can witnesse. It is not the fond and foolish pretence, or colour warped by the subtile braine of man which can diminish one iot of the commandement of God, much lesse disanull it. He that will saue his life, by euill and indirect meanes, shall lose it when all is done: as we see these Ephramites gained not by their lye, but were conuicted of it, by the same tongue that made it, as it were with one breath. The truth is, as the case stood with them (they fleeing before their enemies in so bad a quarrell as this was) little better was to be looked for at their hands, then to lye and shift for themselues, hauing brought themselues into the briars by their contention, rebellion and railing before. But let vs beware, we bring not our selues into such streights by our sinne: for we shall finde it a matter hard enough to helpe our selues in extremitie of danger and trouble: which God brings vpon vs, if we be not the better fenced with faith and a good conscience. But the danger of the former is desperate and remedilesse, as elsewhere I haue more fully declared in the Shechemites and their Captaine *Gaal*, chap. 9.

Exod. 11. 2. and 12. 35.

Note.

Matth. 16, 25.

Doct. 2. Secondly, whereas the text saith of these Ephramites, that they failed of the full pronouncing of the word, we see that although all the Tribes spake in one language, yet euen therein such a difference was, that one spake not as the other (for we see that these Ephramites could not pronounce, as the Reubinites and the Manassites did) euen as also the Greekes haue great difference, and we Englishmen, namely southerne and northward, differ much one from another in our dialect or manner of pronouncing, though we all speake one language. This should teach vs, that as oft as wee heare or thinke of any hurt or detriment comming thereby, we should call to mind, and bee humbled in our selues, for the sinne of them that caused the confounding of language first, the fruite whereof remaineth among vs at this day, and ought iustly to humble vs, for that much toyle and time is now spent in learning to vnderstand languages, which might else haue been otherwise bestowed. And also by strange tongues wee see how the wicked keepe many from vnderstanding the pure word of God, as the Romish Prelates long haue done, which could not haue been, if there had been but one

one language and speech ouer the earth, as once it was. Besides with what difficultie, in respect of this which I speake of, doe many trauell into forraine lands, to exchange their wares and commodities, or to other ends and purposes? For except they haue learned their languages, they cannot speake to each other, but by an interpreter? What labour is there bestowed in the translating of the Scriptures and other writings, which else might haue bin spared? which when all is done, commeth short of the naturall tongue and language. Not to insist in the inconueniences which arise by Translations, euen controuersies in religion, about faith, which had been (in some part) cut off, if one and the same language bee generally embraced: and they which translate best, attaine not vnto that significancie of words and proprietie of meaning, which the naturall language would affoord them, and that without difficultie. These and other like discommodities arise from this diuision of tongues: although they that liue at home in their owne countrey, and conuerse with such as are of the same speech with themselues, doe not so much obserue them: let such consider, that it is Gods mercie, that this confusion reacheth no further then it doth, but is confined though within so large bounds as it is. And againe let vs know, that mens dishonouring God by their tongues, by periury, yea or swearing, by blasphemie or cursed speaking, and specially by imprecations, might bring a deeper iudgement vpon them in person (though the generall little trouble them) euen the taking away of their speech altogether; which kinde of examples, neither experience of former ages, nor our owne haue been wanting in: although if God should smite as oft as he is prouoked, there should bee no end. I conclude this therefore, let it bee a watchword against abusing our language, lest wee prouoke (as many daily doe) some curse and punishment from God, and bee made examples to feare others, seeing other mens would not admonish vs.

Lastly from hence, that they slew such as could not pronounce the word, we learne, that as these lost their liues in returning homeward, though they escaped in the battaile, so when wicked men passe by one danger, yet they shall fall into another. For the Lord being against them, they are neuer safe nor free from feare or perill of some euill to light vpon them, although not by and by. For which cause the Prophet *Amos* saith, If a man flie from a Lyon, a Beare shall meete him. And euen so we see it to be by experience, if such escape by lying, friendship, money and such like, by the hands of men, God himselfe will certainely meete with them, by the pestilence, or arrest them by some strange disease, debt, imprisonment, shame, or some other visitation: or els the worme of conscience as a serpent shall bite them; and if they haue their conscience seared as it were with an hot yron, yet this plague shal take hold of them, euen an hardned heart which cannot repent, and so they dying (for few of them seeke to get out of that plunge) they doe most certainely perish vtterly without any recouery, being throwne into that gulfe that is bottomlesse, where is weeping and gnashing of teeth.

Doct. 3.

Amos 5.19.

Note.

And although such ill disposed persons dye not alwaies by companies and multitudes, as they did heere, and at the flood in *Noahs* time, and as it commeth often to passe, according to the occasions that are offered, (and therefore it is the lesse marked) yet he that obserueth it, shall finde that they who bewray that they are not vpright harted, but dissemblers and hollow, and that they haue no sauour in the Gospell and good things, and by their behauiour, speech and companie, doe testifie their bad liues; I say such as obserue it, shall find that now one, and then another, and some by one iudgment, and some by another, shall verifie that which I say, namely, how such pine and wanse away secretly in ignorance or impenitencie, or bee arested apparently with such visitations of God, as in which they testifie the same. See my notes vpon the ninth chapter in the death of *Abimelech* and the men of Shechem.

The second part of the Chapter.

Vers. 7. *And Iphtah iudged Israel sixe yeeres: then died Iphtah the Gileadite,*
and was buried in one of the cities of Gilead.
8. *And after him Ibzan of Bethlehem iudged Israel,*
9. *Who had thirtie sonnes, and thirtie daughters, which he sent out and tooke in*
thirtie daughters from abroad for his sonnes. And he iudged Israel seuen yeere.
10. *Then Ibzan died, and was buried at Bethlehem.*
11. *And after him iudged Israel, Elon a Zebulonite, and he iudged Israel tenne*
yeeres.
12. *Then Elon the Zebulonite died, and was buried in Aijalon, in the countrey*
of Zebulon.
13. *And after him Abdon the sonne of Hillel the Pirathonite iudged Israel.*
14. *And hee had fortie sonnes, and thirtie nephewes, that rode on seuentie asse*
colts, and he iudged Israel eight yeeres.
15. *Then died Abdon the sonne of Hillel the Pirathonite, and was buried in Pi-*
rathon in the land of Ephraim, in the mount of the Amalekites.

Vers. 7. to the end. *The summe.*

IN these verses following, is contained the time of the reigne of *Iphtah* and diuers other, that were Iudges in Israel, together with their death and buriall in their owne cities, where they dwelt and aboad in their life time. Wherein that which is said in common of them both, I wil speake of ioyntly, as of the time how long they gouerned, and of their death and buriall: for they are all set downe alike. Other things herein contained, I will seuerally note as occasion shall be offered in the text. And first of the time of their being Iudges ouer the people.

Doctrine in generall out of all.

It is said *Iphtah* had that place sixe yeere: *Ibzan* seuen yeeres: *Elon* tenne, and *Abdon* eight. All which being but one and thirtie, were a small number for foure to enioy the place one after another. Whose office, as it was to deliuer the people out of the hands of their enemies, so (doubtlesse) they did, if there were cause, by their being in bondage, or else they kept them in peace, that they were not oppressed nor brought vnder of their enemies at al. And that was a great fauour of God to Israel, that they changing their Gouernours so oft, yet they are not said betwixt the time of the one and the other to haue been in their enemies hands; which when it was so, is expresly set downe in the former examples and stories. Thus the Lord hath blessings of all sorts for his Church, & is not willing to change them into punishments, till our abuse of them turne them to our owne bane. And as these 31. yeeres of of peace, vnder foure gouernours were granted to Israel, so it was their owne sinne and reuolt from God, which brought vpon them so long or a longer time of warre and disquiet: the Lord could haue allowed them their peace without interruption, if they could haue serued him in it without vnsetling and wearinesse. And as he dealt with them, so would he with vs also: who as he hath vndeseruedly continued our peaceable daies euen in the times of our late change, (a worke of his most worthy to be had in remembrance) so he would haue freed vs from plagues and dearth also; but in that he hath allaied our peace with such domestical punishments, as these late yeeres haue witnessed, wee may thanke our selues, and marueile that they haue been no sorer, for (doubtlesse) hee hath therein remembred mercie in iudgement. Our peace is from him, our troubles wherewith it is accompanied are caused by our selues, and farre more bitter should the cup be, if we were made to drink it, as we haue tempered it: but the Lord in mercie holds back from vs, confusion, and bondage, to our enemies, which hee inflicted often vpon these Israelites. But more particularly, this teacheth that it is a great mercy of God, when in the change of Princes and Gouernours, there falleth not out some great detriment and hurt to the people, especially when the changes are often. For that is counted a punishment, as *Salomon* saith. For the transgression of the land, there are many Princes: and the state of the Common wealth, if it bee in peace and prosperous, is then like to change to the contrary. It caused *Dauid* when he heard of the death of *Saul*, who was not very commendable in his time, yea although hee knew that hee himselfe should succeed him, it caused him (I say) to mourne with a great lamentation, saying: *Ye daughters of Israel, mourne for Saul*, how much more would he haue done so, if he had been religious and godly? The same I say of inferiour Magistrates who helpe to vphold and countenance the Gospell, and doe maintaine peace in their precincts and corners where they dwell. The losing of them is with great danger, besides feare of worse to follow: and of faithfull Preachers the like may be said also: though there be many instructers, yet there are not many fathers: the taking away of them therefore will not be without much cause of griefe also, for who knoweth what shall follow?

Lam.3.39. Prou.28.2. 2.Sam.1.24. 1.Cor.4.15.

The vse is to stirre vs vp to thankfulnes for Gods goodnesse to vs and our land, in respect of the late peaceable succession and present prosperitie and health of our Soueraigne: which indeed all are willing to take part in, but few take the paines to consider how much they owe to God for such a benefit as this; which as a knot containes in it all the particular blessings which we enioy as infolded in it. Much lesse doe they weigh that ouer-ruling power of God, which swept downe, as a cobweb, the long contriued plots of the Popish practisers for a forreine gouernment, and defeated in a moment and derided their hopes, by setting the crowne vpon the head of the true apparent Heire, our gratious Soueraigne, without the least contradiction of so many enemies. The sensuall abuse of this blessing, hath now caused the Lord to abate somewhat of this his fauour, by abridging vs of a part of our hoped welfare, in the death of our late enioyed noble Prince. The which (among other vses) ought to teach vs first to bee earnest suters to God for the long life and prosperitie of the young Prince: secondly, to teach vs so-

brietie, that seeing there fall out such changings in our liues, so that no man knowes what shall come to passe, & what troubles may fall out in our daies,
Col.3.1. therefore to set our affections on things not subiect to change, euen to furnish our selues with knowledge and grace, whereby wee may bee fitted for the best estate while wee liue, and after death to enioy durable honour.

Doct. vers. 7. Of *Iphtah* to say a little particularly, when hee had so many and great troubles, for the short time of his abiding in his place, as three are set downe at large: his dangerous battaile with the Ammonites, the vnlooked for forgoing of his only daughter, and this bitter prouoking of him by the Ephramites, this teacheth (besides that which hath bin said hereof before, vers. 2.) what great afflictions they haue, who are of calling and high place in the world, who in comparison of many thousands are thought by their wealth to haue a little paradise in this life, (and doe indeed enioy many outward priuileges aboue other) and what then may the life of meaner persons be accounted but a vale of miserie?

And especially the liues of such I may say, who are in penurie and want with many other calamities which accompanie it, and yet haue no hope of saluation neither; which were able not a little to asswage the force and anguish of such tribulations. All which I speake to shew how great the madnes of men is, and that of all sorts and conditions, who for all their daily and manifold afflictions which cannot be expressed, are yet so wedded & glued to this world: as that they are not fit to heare of a departure from hence, no nor to bee brought to a sober and moderate vse of it, nor by the strongest perswasions to looke after and waite for immortalitie, so as they may enioy it. Now let all iudge how little cause they haue to doe so.

It might bee thought a benefit, that the long life of man is so shortned from nine hundred yeeres to scarse halfe nine score, if men duly weighed
Gen. 47.9. how euill they are, as old *Iacob* told *Pharao*; *Few and euill haue the daies of thy seruant been.* But oh, at what a rate would most men buy the lengthening of their miserie? a madnesse so much the more extreame, because they want that which might much allay the vanitie and vexation that falleth out in their life, I meane faith and grace. Others, on the other side, meeting with much, yea and that stinging trouble in their liues oft times, waxe discontented, desperate, and wearie of liuing, and yet without all willingnes to dye, saue through a necessitie of their owne making, thinking thereby to auoide that, which they encrease thereby. A third sort lay all their miseries vpon their pouertie: whereas (alas) if they had the best estate and happinesse vpon earth, *Iphtah* might teach them, that they should be neuer the neerer their desire, for they may haue sorrow and vexation enough for all their wealth.

Doct. of vers. 7. 8.9.10.11.12. 13.14.15. Now of the death and buriall of them I say this: as they all died, with all other vnto this day, so it liuely admonisheth that it is the way by which all that yet remaine must goe, and who knoweth how soone? that wee may mind and prouide for it. And as they were buried in the places where they dwelt, (as *Iphtah* in one of the cities of Gilead, &c.) so we should submit our selues thereto, with such other abasements as accompany it, (though flesh rebell against them) and this wee should willingly doe for the hope of the glorious

glorious resurrection. But of death and buriall before. Thus much therfore be said of the Iudges ioyntly.

Now this is seuerally said of *Ibzan*, that he had thirtie sonnes whom hee liued to marrie, and thirtie daughters whom he also bestowed in marriage, for so long hee liued together with them. And this is set downe to shew, that the great number of children is reckoned, as then it was, for one of the great blessings of God. Therefore the Lord promised to *Abraham* his friend, that his seed should be multiplied as the starres of heauen, and as the sand of the sea. And so sung the Prophet in the Psalme: *Thy wife shall be as the fruitfull vine on the sides of thine house, and thy children like the oliue plants round about thy table:* and then he addeth this, *Loe thus shall the man be blessed, that feareth the Lord:* calling it not onely a blessing, but more then common. Doct. vers. 8. 9. Gen. 15. 5. Psal. 128. 3.

And it doth the more condemne the vnthankfulnesse of them who doe what they can to auoid that blessing, and doe of purpose shunne the occasion of hauing their part in it, by marrying with full purpose and resolution, where they may be sure they can haue no children. Whose fault may be the lesse, if it be of simple ignorance, but else it may be reckoned as a companion with theirs who grudge and murmur, for that they haue so many children: which ariseth partly of distrust in Gods prouidence, partly fearing that they shall not haue wherewith to nourish them; partly of pride, who see they must pull downe their countenance, for because of the number of them, and cannot set foorth themselues with the wealthiest of their condition, to braue it iollily in the world, for that they be plucked downe with such a companie of brats, as they terme them. And yet as bad as these sorts are, farre more grosse and barbarous are they, high or low, Minister or people, who rather then their countenance should in the least manner be abated by mariage and multitude of children, do not only liue in continuall whordome, zodomie, and such like vnnaturall and filthie vncleannesse, but are glad (though most vniustly and in dissimulation they doe it) to be counted and numbred amongst them that liue chast, which sinne shal bring the swifter damnation to them: They are loth to abase themselues (as they count it) by stooping to Gods ordinance: but God hath many waies to pull them down, and make them stoop (as I haue noted in the former chapter) though they escape it one way and time, yet hee meeteth with them another: for *fornicators and adulterers God wil iudge*, as the Author to the Hebrewes saith, and the experiments thereof are infinit in all kinds of iudgements, by scripture and experience, both of old and daily: Although what neede wee goe farre? That which they shunne by their auoiding marriage, the most pull vpon themselues, by the contrary course, as I haue said. Now what remaineth, but that they who haue and count children a blessing, endeuour carefully to make them the children of God also, that so they may be to them a double blessing? Which is done of few, especially as the case requireth, that is, with carefull and constant looking to the religious bringing vp of them, and the marking of their disposition, and the sinnes which they are most prone and inclined vnto, that they may in due time and good manner helpe to remedie it accordingly. Heb. 13. 4.

Another thing that is seuerall in these verses, is this, that this *Abdon*, the Vers. 13. 14.

the last that is reckoned, had fortie sonnes, and thirtie sonnes sonnes, and these were of place, and some countenance, riding stately, and not as meaner persons going on foote. Whereby it appeareth (to say no more of the number of children) that they had peace then, and were free from oppression by the other nations that dwelt about them. For they must not else haue had such elbow roome, nor their libertie so to shew themselues boldly and openly, but to hide their heads as well as meaner persons, and to lay their iollitie aside.

For our instruction this wee may learne, that in the time of peace, when there is freedome from warre and persecution in a land, there is great prosperitie in euery kinde, as multitude of people, building, purchasing, and growing in wealth and promotion. For though the plague and famine sometime sweep away & diminish the number of people, yet they through Gods goodnesse not continuing long, nor sore, are the sooner outgrowne: but the other, I meane warre and persecution, make strippe and waste, as we say, euen as the violent fire burneth all where it commeth, and the raging waters drowne. But when they cease, there is plentie for the most part going with peace, and there is with both great outward prosperitie.

Which is to bee acknowledged a singular great fauour of God, and to such as are able to vse it aright, it giueth much libertie and encouragement, to liue well and happily. And otherwise what is all iollitie and abundance, if we haue not learned, and be not fitted for the right vse of it? The which how few regard or looke after, but onely seeke to passe their precious time, in ease, vanitie, play, idlenesse, whoring, drinking and such like: and the ciuiller sort to minde little else, then to encrease and gather wealth, the most of them not knowing why, but to content & please themselues thereby: to see (I say) how fondly, nay madly so many doe vse this peace and liberty of quiet liuing; it is much more to be bewailed, then the benefit it selfe is to be reioyced for: And to thinke, how in this time of peace, good preaching should be in vse throughout all parts of the land, to hold downe Poperie, Atheisme, prophanenes and other sinne, and that which should be all in all with vs, to bring many people to God, and yet how little is done this way, it cannot without much bewailing bee thought on. Now if in this earthly mansion of ours (wherein wee are absent from the Lord, and liue as strangers for a time) he can allow his people so liberall and comfortable a supply of earthly refreshings meete for them, vntill they shall no longer stand in need of them; then what is like to be their entertainment at home in heauen (thinke wee) and what prouision will the Lord make for them there? where all sound reioycing is without end or measure? A great meanes (doubtlesse) to prouoke them to serue out their time with cheerefulnesse and faithfulnes, when they consider that all things are theirs, both here and hereafter: all good things serue to make vp the happinesse of them who are Christs, who is Lord of all. And this be said of that which is to be considered of in these Iudges seuerally and apart, and so of the whole chapter.

Note.

THE SEVENTIE ONE SERMON ON THE XIII. CHAPTER OF THE BOOKE OF IVDGES.

Verſ. 1. *But the children of Iſrael continued to commit wickedneſſe in the ſight of the Lord, and the Lord deliuered them into the hands of the Philiſtims fortie yeeres.*

2. *Then there was a man in Zorah of the familie of the Danites named Manoah, whoſe wife was barren, and bare not.*

3. *And the Angell of the Lord appeared vnto the woman, and ſaid vnto her, Behold now thou art barren, and beareſt not: but thou ſhalt conceiue and beare a ſonne.*

4. *And now therefore beware that thou drinke no wine, or ſtrong drinke, neither eate any vncleane thing.*

5. *For loe thou ſhalt conceiue and beare a ſonne, and no razor ſhall come on his head: for the child ſhall be a Nazarite vnto God from his birth, and he ſhall begin to ſaue Iſrael out of the hands of the Philiſtims.*

HEre before I giue the ſumme of this Chapter, as I vſe to do in the entrance of euery Chapter, I will firſt lay downe the ſhort ſumme of the foure Chapters next following; containing the ſtorie of *Samſon*. And it giueth good light to the matters therein contained. This Chapter ſetteth downe his birth: the next his *The ſumme.* mariage, the 15. ſome of his acts, the 16 his death. For the firſt of theſe it is ſaid that the Iſraelites being for their ſins brought into the hands of the Philiſtims, and oppreſſed by them, *Samſon* is promiſed of the Lord to his parents, to be borne as a reuenger of them: and the Angell of the Lord inſtructing them what to doe about the child, confirmed the promiſe by a ſigne, and at the time it was performed that *Samſon* was borne.

Agreeable hereto are the parts of the Chapter, which are three: firſt, The *The parts 3.* 1 appearing of the Angell to *Manoahs* wife, with a meſſage to her of a ſonne, 2 that ſhe ſhould beare, to helpe Iſrael againſt the Philiſtims, to verſe 6. Then his ſecond appearing to them both together, *Manoah* and his wife I meane, 3 to the fifteenth verſe. Laſtly, the ſigne that the Angell gaue, that the thing he promiſed ſhould come to paſſe, as it did indeed of the childs birth, and this to the end of the Chapter.

The firſt part of the Chapter.

THe holy ſtorie ſheweth in this firſt part of the Chapter, that God ſent *Verſ. 1.* tidings and hope of help againſt the Philiſtims, and that is done in this, and

and these foure next verses following: and that was because the people hauing fallen againe to prouoke the Lord, hee deliuered them into the hands of the Philistims, and that for fortie yeeres. But here it is said, hee thought vpon their bondage, and went about their deliuerance. This their bondage when it began and ended, is hardly gathered for certaintie: but most likely it began after the death of *Abdon*, and continued almost to the time of *Heli*.

Doct. vers. 1. Of the sin of Israel, that they added to worke euill in ẏ sight of the Lord, for so are the words: meaning, as they had done before in times past, and as their fathers had done before their late peaceable gouernment, so they did now againe. For this must be vnderstood of the body of them, not of particular persons: who (there is no doubt) committed sinnes against the Lord, but not so boldly, grossely and openly with consent. But now they fell to that, and most like to idolatrie among the rest. And now the Lord had omitted to punish them, and had giuen them peace, they fell againe to their old byas. This teacheth how naturall it is, for all flesh to decline, and to fall to those sinnes which once they abhorred.

Our latter works should be better then our former: but how rare is this to Note. be seene, no not in the better sort? no, vnlesse it be in them, who do obserue their own frailtie, & how many waies they are ready to fall, and lay daily for especiall grace of faith and good gouernment, & knowledge without fainting and wearines, as at any time they haue done, since they first began, else I say it is hardly to be found. And no lesse had need to be done of them, because both old and new prouocations to euill are so many and strong, and euer in the way, that they will otherwise preuaile one time or other. And therefore men should know and consider, that they waite for a reward of great price, and no man is crowned except hee striue for it lawfully, and to the end: therefore they should not be weary of weldoing, neither faint in their good beginnings. But (oh to bee lamented) many of the forwarder sort in times past, are now growne to tempt God boldly, and take vpon them to stint him in their prayers and other seruice, and detract from it, and coldly goe about it, much like them who are driuen to worke dead worke with their creditors, and are constrained rather to pay them therby the debt that they owe them, then that they haue any wages to receiue for the same: which kinde of worke, all know how vnwillingly and wearisomly for the most part it is taken in hand. And to speake a word of those who are not ingrafted into Christ at all by faith, and to shew how awkly they come forward, in the sincere receiuing the doctrine of the Gospell, (though wee Rom. 2. 4. know, and so may they, that the Lord beareth long with them, to the end he may bring them to repentance) yet how many of them may we obserue, who though they liue vnder good teaching, doe not verifie the Apostles 2. Tim. 3. 7. words to *Timothy*, of the wicked & vngodly, *viz.* that both for knowledge, 2. Tim. 3. 13. they are euer learning, but neuer obtaining it, and as for their practise, they waxe worse and worse, rather then that they haue so much as any purpose to set their hearts to seeke after true repentance. For the fuller handling hereof, let the reader looke backe into the former Chapters, wherein the other reuolts of this people are mentioned.

In that it is said, God gaue them (when they had thus prouoked him) into the hands of the Philistims, as he vsed (when they fell to the like sinnes) to sell them to other nations about them; and they and their fathers had so often found it so, that they might haue knowne (if they would) that they should finde some such like thing againe as oft as they reuolted from him. The Lords thus dealing with them, I say, not onely laieth foorth their boldnes in sinning (which I haue spoken of) but it certainly testifieth also what God will doe to them, and to all others in such a case, to wit, that hee will surely be auenged of such his enemies, who dare so boldly tempt him; yea one time or other he will most certainly doe it. And so let vs and especially such as take aduantage, by deferring of Gods executing his iudgement, to settle themselues the more to doe euill, let vs tell to our owne hearts, and that not doubtingly, as the woman answered of the punishment to the Serpent, which God had certainly annexed to the eating the forbidden fruite, but assuredly. And this let euery one that is wise apply to himselfe, as a most vndoubted truth vpon the committing of those sinnes, to the which hee is most in danger, or else hee must looke to smart afterward. But of this point and the next in this verse, namely that he did so long continue the people in bondage to the Philistims because of their sinnes, I haue spoken in another place. Doct.2. Gen.3.3.

The Lord purposing to raise vp one that should helpe his people, doth first appoint his parents, and them he mentioneth and describeth in this second verse: and sheweth in the third, how he sent word to the woman by his Angell, that she should beare such a childe, as should helpe to auenge their enemies: in the fourth hee directeth her how to vse her selfe who should beare that childe, and that she should not eate or drinke any forbidden or vncleane thing: in the fifth he shewes a reason hereof, to wit, because the childe should bee no common person but a professed Nazarite. And therewith he declareth what he should doe, that is, begin to saue Israel out of the hands of the Philistims. Vers.2.3.4.5.

Touching the first of these points, of describing the parents of *Samson*, I would say the more, but that I see the holy Ghost omitteth and passeth by the commendation of their godlinesse here, which yet by that which followeth appeareth to haue bin great. But yet I will borrow somewhat from other places in this chapter to this purpose. We may obserue in Scripture, that vpon the like occasion sometimes a very liberall roome and commendation is allowed to the parents of worthie instruments. One for all may serue, of the parents of *Iohn Baptist*, Luk.1.6. not so much described by circumstance of place and outward condition, as by their grace and godlines. This is here omitted, and yet so as by the sequell of the historie in this chapter, it may appeare they were a worthie couple: and the holy Ghost (as it were) leauing it to the discretion of the reader, to make vp their description by the good fruites and effects which are after recorded of them both, as (God willing) shall be noted out of the text, I doe here make mention of it, as being to good purpose, in the first mentioning of them. Briefly then, let vs note from this practise of the spirit of God, how much it auaileth to the due setting out of a good posteritie, to see from what manner of parents they are descended, (the godly progenitors, being the crowne of a good progenie) especially if the vnworthinesse, and vnsutablenes of the yonger, depriue them not of that honour which their elders haue purchased for them. The godly parents are the roote whence the children (euen by promise and couenant, Exod.20.) are to deriue blessing vpon themselues, if they bee faithfull. Hence is it, that all beleeuers are honoured with the spirituall priuiledge of being the sonnes of faithfull *Abraham:* a greater by farre then to bee his degenerate children by carnall propagation, Iohn 4. Secondly, this insinuateth to Parents the dutie of care and gouernement: seeing when the children are named (as in the booke of Kings commonly) there the parents are set in the forefront, to beare the blame, or to carrie away the honour: if their children deserue well, they may claime the praise of it iustly, as a blessing and rewarde of their education: to the shame I speake it of such loose persons, as whose childrens religion shameth the ignorance and vngodlinesse of their parents. Thirdly, this redoundeth to the honour of God, and his faithfulnesse, when one posteritie after another, for some generations shall bee found to know the God of their fathers: in whose steps to walke it is to them a worthy commendation before men, but much more in the sight of God, as *Timothy* a godly childe and grandchild, is commended.

Exod.20.

2.Tim.2.5.

Doct. verse 2. and the rest.

Secondly here, in that the Lord doth raise a deliuerer out of the tribe of *Dan*, in which this place Zorah was, neere to Eshtaol, and verse 25. sheweth; this tribe being one of the meanest: It teacheth that God will serue himselfe by the meaner sort as well as by the mightier and greater, when it pleaseth him. For if he furnish them with gifts fitting, for that he setteth them about (whereof they are as capeable as the other) thereby he enables them for the worke, which not their birth or wealth alone can doe, as we haue seene before. Therefore it is not for vs to scorne and reproach such, whom the Lord by their gift will exalt, though this be to be added, that neither meane nor mighty shall haue any cause in the end to reioyce in their preferment, otherwise then they haue well and rightly vsed their place, and themselues in it with their gifts. And as I haue said of outward place and aduancement in the world; so I say of inward grace and gifts of the spirit. That euen out of the meane or middle sort of people, the Lord chuseth many, yea most to be heires of saluation: and to vse our Sauiours words, Matth.11. to be seasoned with the Gospell by beleeuing (for so I expound the words.) And doubtlesse in comparison of these, few great ones are called: nay many who haue striuen against mediocritie of estate (which yet *Agur* preferreth as the best to serue God in) they haue forsaken their owne mercy. See more in the tenth chapter, 1.2.3. verses thereof.

Matth.11.5.

1.Cor.1.26.

Doct. vers. 3.

The Angell speaketh to her of her barrennesse, that she might receiue the message of bearing a childe more thankefully and ioyfully, for barrennesse in those daies was generally holden a kinde of curse, as I noted in chap.12. the end, and fruitefulnesse a blessing: but wee see that God turneth this curse to a blessing, and it was counted no doubt by this woman, a great worke of his mercy, that hee gaue a childe to her being barren, as well as of his power, as *Dauid* reckons it. Thus doth the Lord make way for the thankfull entertaining of his mercies, by laying before vs our want and insufficiencie: and yet all is little enough to procure that affection, (except it be a little at first) for in a very short time our mindes are changed with the time, and

Psal.113.end.
Luk.1.37.

and we rather looke vpon that we enioy, then looke backe vpon our former penurie, or the author of our change. So that the Lord is faine to vpbraide vs, by his vndeserued kindenesse (as hee did *Dauid* by his taking from the sheepefold) in stead of reaping the fruite thereof in praise and dutie: which is verified well in many of them that haue mourned and complained long of the heauie burden that oppressed their conscience (which they feared, as *Hezekiah* once did, that they should neuer bee eased of) and at length met with such comfort, as they long wished for: for although at the first obtai- Esay 38.10.
ning thereof, they indented with God, that hee should bee all in all with them, yet in time they haue worne out the remembrance of such kindenes, as *Pharaohs* butler did *Iosephs*. Let such and all others whose conscience Gen.40.23.
beares them witnesse, that the Lord hath made them fruitfull of barren, Note.
(in what kinde soeuer) but that they haue brought forth sower grapes, and wilde oliues, and made themselues barren againe of fruitfull: let them (I say) looke backe and view the matter yet better, and pay their rearedges which they are run into with God, lest at length they wish they had bin beholding to God for lesse, except their fruit might haue made the Lord (as I may say) beholding to them for more then they haue yeelded. To him that Luk.8.18.
hath shall be giuen: hee shall receiue fauour vpon fauour, that keepes the old in precious remembrance and regard, occupying for him whose the talents are which are occupied: whereas he who hath not, shall forgoe still, till he haue lost all: that is, he that hath forgotten him of whom he receiued that which hee hath, shall both lose that for which he hopeth, yea and the principall to which he hath. This for one point.

Besides, by this example, the Lord sheweth vs, how hee turneth his cha- Doct.2. in
stisements to benefits vnto his people, as the issue of *Iobs* afflictions witnes- verse.3.
seth. For if they from whom he taketh away any good things, and correcteth, receiue not greater outward benefits then they forgoe; yet if they waite on God, they shall haue proofe of the graces that are in them, as faith, patience, and obedience (as oft I haue already noted in this booke) which are farre more sweete to them then any outward libertie which they lose and forgoe. So then let the people of God prouide to walke before him with vprightnesse, and they shall see whether their life bee not replenished with comforts, and they followed with many a token from God of his loue to them, and pleasure in them, by all which they shall finde their daies vpon earth to be sweetely passed, and they exceedingly well prouided for, till they be taken to glorie.

The Angell in prescribing to the woman, that shee should drinke no Doct.vers.4.5.
wine, nor eate no vncleane thing said so, because the childe that she should beare, should be a Nazarite to the Lord: who (by the law of the Nazarite) was himselfe to bee tied to certaine ceremonies, for that time of his so being: the one was that he should (also) abstaine from wine; secondly, that no rasor should come on his head; thirdly, that hee should not touch or come neere any dead body: of this reade further in the booke of Numbers. Now a Nazarite was one that was separated from others, and more parti- Numb.6.2.&c.
cularly such a one as serued the Lord in a more strict manner then other did: as for *Samson*, who was to continue this estate throughout his life, he was a peculiar person and therefore a type of Christ, not onely in death, and that

most victorious, but euen in life, wherein our Sauiour fulfilled all righteousnesse.

The signification of the Nazarite was this, that the Lord would haue all that come neere vnto him, and will be in his seruice, to be separated from the common sort, which doe not examine their waies after the rules of Gods word, but walke after their owne hearts desire. And hereby, and vnder a ceremony, hee requireth that of his, which in plaine words he doth elsewhere; saying, ye shall therefore be perfect as your father in heauen is
1.Pet.1.16. perfect: also purifie your selues euen as I am pure: Be mercifull euen as your heauenly father; And be ye holy, for I am holy. Insomuch that in another
Heb.12.4. place he saith, without holinesse, no man shall see the Lord. And the signification of the Nazarite, doth exclude all that are vncleane and vnsanctified, from the Lords presence, fauour and seruice. True it is, the ceremoniall rule is abolished: for in the Church of the new testament, it is not permitted to any man to vowe any regular seruing of God according to outward obseruances and orders, with placing any religion therein; no not so much as to retaine the obseruation of the Nazarite, much lesse to inuent new rites and orders, and yet such are holden the onely religious men and women at this day in the church of Rome, as haue solemnely entred into some order or other (as they haue many confused orders of their owne forging) and therein ayme at perfection. But to let these and their disorders goe: the equitie of this institution still remaineth firme, and bindeth vs. For the Lord will haue all his to know, that they are not set here to liue, no nor to serue him as they list, or bee as seruants that be at their owne hands, but hee tieth them to a rule and an order, according whereto he will haue them to walke.
Rom.12.1. But this rule is spirituall first, then vniforme, and bindeth all without excep-
2.Cor.7.1. tion. The summe whereof is (as I haue said) to giue vp themselues in bodie and soule to the Lord in all inward subiection of heart and outward obedience of life strictly: with clensing themselues of all superfluitie and filthinesse of either body or minde.

2 The ceremonies also here required to be vsed of the Nazarite, had their signification: those which are mentioned in the text are these two: the one, the suffering of the haire of his head to growe and not to be cut off, for the time that their vow of being Nazarites remained, for they vowed it either for a certaine number of daies, moneths or yeares. But when their vow was at an end, and the time of keeping it expired; at the offering of sacrifice and burning the flesh in the fire, they cut off their haire and burnt it in the same fire. And after that they were free, and returned to their former course of life. Although it was otherwise with *Samson*: for he was by the Lord appointed a Nazarite for his whole life: though that was not according to the common manner of being made Nazarites. The signification of it was, that much time should not be taken vp in too nicely trimming and looking to our bodies, seeing we know they must be consumed to the earth, and become wormes meate; and therefore a ridiculous folly to forget that, and to please our selues in such deceiueable fancies. And also when the minde is set curiously on that worke, as it is a dangerous token of pride, so it bewrayeth that it slenderly regardeth the inward apparrelling of it. But as this nicenes and curiositie in the weaker sexe (who spend too many good houres,

houres, vainely and vnfruitefully in this kind) argueth pride & folly: so there is a foule abuse in men about this matter, and that is their disguised wearing of long haire. I thinke there are few of them who will defend themselues by the practise of Nazarites: if they did, yet the world would conuince them, as being (for the most part) furthest off from the strict worship of God, and sincere walking after his will, as the Nazarites did: if they doe not also mocke and skorne those that embrace it. Me thinkes it is strange, and argueth somewhat more then common for the badnesse thereof, that among many changes of corrupt English fashions, worne out and expired, yet this vnnaturall fashion (as *Paul* calles it) for a man to weare long haire, 1.Cor.11.14.
hath suruiued them all. I know some nourish it for amarous lightnesse of minde: others as a supposed ornament to their person, or marke of gentrie, or at least imitation of gentlemen. These, as I thinke, might more wisely forbeare it now, (seeing it is become the fashion and habite of the basest swaggerers and ruffians, and the diuels marke which he hath set vpon many that wil not be reformed) then at the first, when they vsed it, either as ensigne or ornament. It was the speech of a worthie and reuerend Iudge of the land, That the vse of the long locke was first taken vp by branded fellowes, for a couer of their shame. And that honourable personage in his circuit, sitting in the place of iustice, vpon malefactors, practised according to the former obseruation: commanding all whom he saw beset with such deformed haire, to be immediatly cut or shorne, whether to discouer their earemarke, or to shame their vnseemely guise, I know not. And yet many of them (farre enough from Nazarites all may thinke) set as much by their haire, as if they had put religion therein, and were as loth to haue sheares or rasor to come vpon it.

The signification of the abstaining from wine or strong drinke, was not 3
simply to forbid the vsing of it to all (for wee see in *Nehemiah* the Lord gi- Nehe.8.10.
ueth his people libertie to eate of the fatte, and drinke of the sweete) but it was commanded them that were Nazarites, for the time that they continued so, to abstaine therefrom: the signification (I say) thereof was, to teach Gods people, that they should auoide all excesse that way, lest thereby they should dull and blunt the powers of their mindes, and so they must of necessitie vse them to shamefull ends, which were giuen them to farre more excellent purposes: which I say to the iust condemning of all beastly drunkards, and such as are their pot companions, though they can better beare drinke without open disguising of themselues, then the other: who yet spending their time wickedly, and in needelesse and brutish deuouring of it, are nothing inferior to them in sinning: but in sundry respects are much worse then many of them. But of this sinne by other occasion I haue spoken. This particularly be said of the rule of Nazarites, and the caueats thereof: more generally this I adde to the former, that by these prohibitions and such like, the Lord would teach vs, in how high account hee hath an heart well mortified and purged from the drosse and superfluitie of lusts and concupiscence which it is stuffed withall. Wee see how he enioyneth his Nazarites not so much actuall worship, as a straight restraint of the flesh from all vnlawfull excesse, which he shadoweth out by these two, of diet, and decking the body, & abstinence in both. Doubtlesse if it were possible

for a man, to equall the Angels in obedience, and cheerefulnesse, readinesse and integritie of seruice, yet if it were possible againe, that the olde man with his desires and passions, might still remaine aliue with them, as wrath, malice, couetousnesse, vncleanenesse, hollownesse, loosenesse, pride, vncharitablenesse, an vnruly tongue, &c. the religion of this man were altogether
Prou.23.26. vaine. There are reasons of this: 1. The Lord saith, Sonne giue mee thy heart, he meaneth not a rotten heart and corrupt (he needs it not) but an heart well searched, and well drained from sinfull affections and lusts: such
Note. an heart he calleth for, and chuseth. For he knowes, that where a mortified heart is, there also is an heart quickned to the life of God, and the more fit for dutie, both within and without. 2. The chiefe seruice of God is inward; and this inward stands especially in repentance, which first consisteth in the change of the euill habites and qualities of the soule, ere new be put in. For no man grafteth vpon a rotten stocke; nor puts new wine into old vessels. 3. A christian man fetch surer euidence from hence of his reformation, then from any particular dutie to the affirmatiue commandements of the morall law: and more soundly distinguisheth himselfe from an hypocrite. I seperate not the parts of repentance, but diuide the false from the sound by this rule: many a good Christian is behinde hand in this worke (and euer shall be, for no man is pure) and hardly forgoes some one or few old relikes of *Adam*: and therefore looke how much a man profiteth in this peece of religion, so much hee groweth more truely religious.
Note. The vse is, that they who haue chosen the easier course of seruice, I meane to doe good duties, doe better tend that other part of christianitie, which hath been lesse regarded by them; and that they trauaile in denying themselues, ouercomming their passions, abstaining from, and crucifying their corrupt nature, where it is strongest in them, and so shall their religion prosper, and better beseeme them. For though it be the harder part of the two, yet time bestowed therein, will counteruaile the labour most plentifullie.
Rom.8.12. And for a good man to be a debter to any lust, is most vnseemely, but to be a seruer, fulfiller, and obeyer thereof, and to haue the weapons of sinne still vnmortified, and fighting in him against righteousnesse (as *Paul* speakes) is monstrous: Thus much of the Nazarite.

Doct. vers. 5. In this verse, the Angell telleth the office of the childe that should bee borne, to wit that when he should come to age fit for it, he should begin to deliuer his people from the bondage of the Philistims. Wherein the Lord declareth his tender loue and care of his people: who when they are oppressed and in tribulation, doth pitie them, and thinketh euen before, of easing and redressing their sorrowes; whereby he would draw them to relenting for their sinne, and to be ashamed of their prouoking of him to punish them, and of the hardning of their hearts, by lying still in their offences, without humbling themselues and crying to the Lord for mercy and deli-
Obiect. uerance. And if yee aske why hee doth not as well take them out of their troubles, as well as he pitieth them therein, and why he suffered this people to lye in bondage so long to their enemies, till *Samson* grew vp and was able
Answ. to deliuer them. I answere: he were willing and ready to doe it, and much more, if it might be good for them; but that cannot be, while they still harbour and nourish their sinnes, but they would procure vpon themselues greater

greater vexation by continuing their wicked course, if the Lord should deliuer them, before they repent for the same, as hath bin often proued by the example of these Israelites, crying for ease, but neuer heard, till by repentance the Lord was grieued for their miserie. So that Gods suffering their oppressions to hold them vnder a long time, as this his people was by theirs, namely from the birth of *Samson*, till hee came to mans estate, and after; it was not for that he taketh pleasure in afflicting his, (hee professeth the contrary) but it is for that they relent not, neither cast themselues down before him, to draw compassion from him, by their lamenting after him. And therfore their long abiding vnder their tribulations, doe argue exceeding hardnes of heart in them, whereby they procure the same. Iudg.10.16. Lam 3.33. 1.Sam.7.2.

Obiect. And whereas men cauill with God, and say they cannot bow their own hearts, nor force them to relent, God must soften them and breake them, or else he is the author of their miserie. *Answ.* I answere, they can binde heauie burthens vpon his shoulders, which themselues will not take vp with the least of their fingers. And that appeareth by the slight account they make hereof, and their dealing so carelesly in so weightie a matter. For although the Lord can pull out the stone of the heart (as the Prophet speakes) and make it an heart of flesh: yet if this were the thing they desired, they would first apply themselues to that grace of his, which is able to worke this effect in them, and then put ouer and commend the blessing of their labor to God: which while they neglect to doe, they haue that within them which shall witnesse against them, to be the wilfull causes of their own desolation. The Lord is not bound to them, in the least respect, to minister the meanes of the word, in afflictions, benefits, examples, help by others, much lesse grace to be humbled and repent. Therefore in that they vse none of these ordinances of his, to the wholesome ends to which they are appointed, the sin is theirs: he is guiltlesse, in that he hath offered them more faire, then themselues were willing to accept of. Neuer did the Lord leaue any to himselfe, hardned and impenitent, who desired to profit vnder his doctrine and discipline. Therefore let men beware they ouerreach not themselues in their subtiltie: for as bold as they are in speech here, yet when they come to answer the Lord face to face, they shall be dumbe: and of their own mouthes shall the Lord condemne them. To the which end more might be added, if the point came not so often to hand throughout this booke, as oft as the relapses of the people are mentioned. See also the first branch of the doctrine vpon the 7.8.9. verses of the former chapter. Thus much of the first part. Ezek.36.26.

The second part of the Chapter.

Vers.6. *Then the wife came and told her husband, saying, A man of God came vnto me, and the fashion of him was like the fashion of the Angell of God exceeding fearefull: but I asked him not whence he was, neither told he me his name.*

7. *But he said vnto me, Behold thou shalt conceiue, and beare a sonne, and now thou shalt drinke no wine, nor strong drinke, neither eate any vncleane thing: for the childe shall be a Nazarite to God, from his birth to the day of his death.*

8. *Then Manoah prayed to the Lord and said, I pray thee my Lord, let the man*

of God whom thou sentest, come againe now vnto vs, and teach vs what wee shall doe vnto the childe when he is borne.

9. And God heard the voyce of Manoah, and the Angell of God came againe to the wife, as she sate in the field, but Manoah her husband was not with her.

10. And the wife made haste, and ranne and shewed her husband, and said vnto him, Behold the man hath appeared vnto me that came vnto me to day.

11. And Manoah arose and went after his wife, and came to the man and said vnto him, Art thou the man that spakest vnto the woman? and he said, Yea.

12. Then Manoah said, Now let thy saying come to passe: but how shall we order the childe and doe vnto him?

13. And the Angell of the Lord said vnto Manoah, The woman must beware of all that I said vnto her.

14. She may eate of nothing that commeth of the vine tree: she shall not drinke wine, nor strong drinke, nor eate any vncleane thing: let her obserue all that I haue commanded her.

Vers. 6. to 15. *The summe.* NOw it followeth how the Angell appeared the second time, and that to them both, to wit, *Manoah* and his wife: and that was thus. She like a good wife went and told her husband, that such an one, some Prophet or man of God appeared to her, and told her of such a thing, and what she should doe, but she said, she answered nothing to him againe. Then *Manoah* besought the Lord, that he might come againe, and hee appeared againe to the woman, who immediatly went and called her husband, who finding the man of God in the field, asked of him, both of the former message, which he had brought to his wife, and also what they should do to the child, when it should be borne, and he answered him, euen as he had before said to his wife.

Here the woman in her telling her husband of the messenger, describeth him thus: The fauour of the man of God (saith she) that appeared to me, was (as an Angell of God) fearefull; for so the Hebrew word is translated, which signifieth also wonderful: and so it is like she said and meant, though it be translated fearefull. And to preuent all doubts and suspitions, further she telleth him, that neither she knew him, nor from whence hee was, neither did he tell her his name. But this onely hee said to her, that she should beare a sonne, and she must abstaine from wine, and eate no vncleane thing, for the childe should be a Nazarite from his birth vnto his death.

Doct. vers. 6. But let vs now peruse these verses throughout more fully. Touching that which she vttereth of the reuerend presence of the Angell, I will not insist in it, hauing elsewhere noted the substance thereof. I begin with this sixth verse, where first know we this, that the woman by and by going to her husband simply, to signifie the matter to him, as soone as she receiued the message, which equally concerned them both, did as became a good wife. For so it behoueth that married couples should communicate their mindes one
Ephe. 5. 31. to another, matrimony being a societie betwixt two, as if they were but one. For they ought to haue their fellowship together in imparting heauenly things one with another, and earthly also, euen as there were both, in this matter: heauenly, seeing the message came in the name of God and from heauen; earthly, seeing it was of and about a temporall comfort or blessing pertaining

pertaining to this life, to wit, of the bearing of a ſonne. This example betwixt two godly couples, doth commend to vs the ſociable and kind agreement and liuing together in mariage, that both be of one minde in good things, and ſhew foorth their inward conſent in affection, by the tokens of communion in outward things concerning them both, as *Abraham* and *Sarah*, *Iſaac* and *Rebecca*, with many other did. And as God hath commanded that it ſhould be thus: ſo in like manner it ſtandeth with all ſound reaſon, that they who are ſo neerely linked together in cohabitation and fellowſhip, ſhould be neerely affected, and agree together moſt kindly. Therefore *Salomon* wiſheth the husband to reioyce in his wife, and that ſhe ſhould be as the louing Hinde and pleaſant Roe before him. And ſo we ſhould ſee cauſe why mariage ſhould bee counted a ſingular benefit, as the Scripture calleth it. Concerning the which, though ſome couples voide of religion, haue ſome ſhadow hereof, ſeeing they agree in vpholding the familie, and in gathering wealth one with the other: yet they are out and in, their loue is not conſtant, but full of vnſoundnes, diſlikes, diſſimulation, inconſtancie, and vnquietnes; for they want the principall, which is ſome true meaſure of the feare of God, for that is the chiefe ſtaier of debate, and the nouriſher of true loue betwixt them: which ſhould therefore be laid for at their firſt comming together, or elſe will hardly be wrought in them after. But this kinde agreement betwixt couples, is ſo farre from the moſt, that ſtrangenes and wearines one of the other, doth ſoone meete with them, with other blemiſhes manifold, which deface the beautie of mariage exceedingly. And yet leſt while I vrge this conſent, ſome couples ſhould catch more libertie then I or the Lord allow them, let me adde that their agreement muſt be in things warrantable, or elſe they rather band themſelues together againſt the Lord, and abuſe his ordinance. For they are not yoked together, that they may ioyne their wits & wils to do miſchief, as *Ahab* and *Iezabel*, *Ananias* and *Saphira*, which is not to be helpers of each other, (as they come together to that end) except it be to euill and to hell. This I ſay, becauſe many couples are neuer at one, but when they conſent in euill: then they are as cloſe as barke and tree, where they ſhould differ and diſſwade each other: but in good duties their mutuall affections are ſo farre from ioyning, that they are repugnant and diuided each from other as farre as may bee. By vertue of this holy concord, great is the bleſſing, and ſweete is the fruite of this ordinance. In all duties of the familie, as education of children, in all actions of Gods worſhip, in the workes of loue to the Saints, in the vſe of their lawfull liberties, &c. with freedome of minde, what ioy and contentment ariſeth in this vnanimitie and amitie betweene them? which otherwiſe is much impeached. And the fruite of this accompanieth them in their inward troubles of mind, and outward croſſes of body and eſtate: the one being ſtrengthened, comforted, reſolued, and holpen by the wiſedome, knowledge and aſſiſtance of the other. Yea ſurely the precious memorie of this agreement remaineth as a pledge in the boſome of the ſuruiuor, when death hath made a breach betweene them. But woe to him that is alone: double woe to couples that are diuided: where the one ſcorneth to communicate with the other: and the wife chuſeth any to breake her minde to, rather then her husband.

Prou. 5. 19.

Note.

But

But (to returne) as the woman is to bee commended for telling her husband; so the more she deserueth it, seeing that the partie that appeared to her, was taken of her to be a man, and his message to her, being barren, was, that she should beare a childe. This might haue raised strange thoughts in her, as doubting & wondring how this should be; and some woman would haue concealed such a matter, lest her husband should haue had her in iealousie and suspition about it: and againe, seeing that if he should haue heard of such a matter by some other and not by her, it might haue been hardlier taken of him against her. Betweene these contrary motions and conceits, some woman (I say) would haue been held in suspense, or would haue chosen silence as the safest: but she dealt simply, and did the best in opening it to him. And this teacheth that in faithfulnes about the mariage bed, there should be such holy loialtie and agreement betwixt couples, that there may not be the least doubting one of anothers faithfulnes, neither any occasion offered of the contrary, neither any suspition about it. Which by their religious and oft confirming one another, in their faithfull keeping of couenant, and concerning all things else betwixt them, and the free opening of their mindes each to other, and their agreeing together in holy duties and exercises of religion, might easily be. But where are these to bee found almost among the better sort? but to be sure they be reiected of the common sort, and thereby it may easily be iudged what manner of life they leade. Of this I say the lesse, because all will graunt, that if this amitie ought to be betwixt them in all actions mutually concerning each other, then especially in that office which is most essentiall and naturall to mariage. And the Greeke word, which *Paul* vseth in the former text, I meane *beneuolence*, although it doe admit a composition of two words, which signifie to be well minded, yet more properly it is deriued from the word that signifieth a bed, as noting that this containeth the other smaller beneuolences vnder it.

3 In saying to her husband, that she did not once aske the man of God, from whence he came, nor hee told not her his name, for it was needlesse: let vs bee taught by both, not to stay in company needlesly, and especially men with women, and most of all alone without other company, & where they may be in danger of doing or taking euill, or giuing occasion of suspecting any such thing to other. Oh the infinite mischiefe that hath been wrought hereby, I meane by the idle and needlesse meeting and tarrying together of men first, whereby one draweth another to some euill or other; and much more of men and women, whereby much whoredome hath bin committed, (yea and much that was neuer thought of before:) as by *Elies* sonnes meeting women in the Tabernacle, which although it was lawfull, yet they abused it monstrously. Particularly, let women learne of the Shunamite, 2. King. 4. that comely modestie and shamefastnes which is fitter for their sexe, then that boldnes and lightnes, which the most of them bewray, when they are in the companies, wherein they dare shew themselues. This woman therefore being called to *Elisha* his chamber (and yet not alone neither, but his seruant standing by) came before him, and stood in the doore, that is, she went not to him, but stood aloofe, as became a sober Matrone. But those daies are past: modestie is a burthen to many women, and further then feare or shame restraines them, grace and wisedome there is little in

Note.

2. King. 4. 15.

in ſome of them to doe it, as may teſtifie when the other bands are ſhaken off.

The laſt thing in this verſe is, her ſparines of ſpeech to the Angell; She asked him not any queſtion, but reſted in the meſſage. The little time ſhe ſtaied in his companie ſhe ſpent in hearing and marking, pondring (as *Mary* did) not inquiring and deſcanting about it. Admirable is it that a weake woman, hearing a report of a thing ſo ſtrange, ſo vnlikely, and yet ſo pleaſing, and that from a man that ſhe knew not, ſhould not once moue a queſtion. A leſſe occaſion by many degrees, had been enough to haue ſet ſome womans tongue on endleſſe running, and her eye and minde on rouing and caſting: but then we muſt thinke (if ſhe had bin of this humour) an Angell of glorie had not bin ſent to her. Oh rare woman, which maiſt ſet both men and women to ſchoole, to learne ſobrietie. If *Eue* had been as wiſe, ſhe had preuented a great deale of woe, from her ſelfe and vs. Curioſitie is a foule blemiſh in a man, but a far greater in a woman: and as this woman was chaſt, ſo ſhe was of few words, and both goe well together: For ſhe in the Prouerbs who is deſcribed to be light-footed and fugitiue, oftner and more in the houſes of others then her owne, is taxed alſo to be light-tongued, and talkatiue. This iangling and prating of women (a vice ſo deteſted in them by *Paul*) was neuer more rife in any age then ours. And (which is to be lamented) it is a diſeaſe incident to ſuch as (otherwiſe) are not of the worſt ſort neither: and all becauſe it is an impotencie and intemperancie, which iſſueth from the weakneſſe of their ſexe (in great part) which they thinke no diſcredit to themſelues, becauſe it is another nature vnto them. It is a nature vnto them indeed, but a corrupt one, which muſt be ſpied in time by thoſe that are wiſe, and corrected. I will not ſay, that ſuch are not fit for Angels company, they beſeeme not the company of a diſcreete or graue man: for a wiſe perſon would ſoone be wearie of them, though themſelues haue no ſtay of their vnruly member, till their breath faile them, or they be put to ſilence: no more then the wheeles of a Iacke, till the plummets be vpon the ground. I need not amplifie this: I wiſh that all praters and tatlers were but galled and gagged with this example here, and in the middeſt of their worke, made but to ſee their face in this glaſſe, which I think would trouble them more, then the glaſſe which the old Curtizan once looked in, and beholding her wrinkles and ſpots therein, crackt it aſunder becauſe it was ſo true a mirrour.

4 Luke 1.29. Prou.7.11.12.

Verſ.7. In this verſe is ſhewed, how ſhe told her husband what the man of God ſaid to her of the birth of the childe, and what ſhe ſhould doe her ſelfe, as we heard before verſe 4. and 5. of the which I haue ſpoken there: for this is a repeating of the ſame things. Onely this wee may learne by *Manoahs* wife, to report and relate things truly and aright as they were done, or as wee heard them related vnto vs. For through forgetfulneſſe, careleſneſſe, or of a worſe meaning, things are carried in ſuch ſort oft times, that by vntruths and lyes told out, much ſtrife and contention ariſeth, which bring and cauſe great trouble and annoyance. An example of many, may that be of *Ziba*, his falſe report to *Dauid* of *Mephiboſheth*, that he refuſed to goe with *Dauid* againſt *Abſolom*, when hee himſelfe withheld his beaſt from him, at ſuch

2.Sam.16.3. such time as he would full gladly haue gone,and whereon he should ride, because he was lame. Another is that of the Iewes slandering our Sauiour, that he said, Destroy the Temple, and in three dayes I will reare it againe. Matth.26.61. compared with Iohn 2.19.23. Whereas hee said destroy this Temple, meaning his body: so they that hearing Christ say of his beloued disciple *Iohn*, If I will that hee abide Iohn 21.23. till I come, what is that to thee, &c? gaue it forth erroniously, that hee said, I will that hee abide till I come, and so gathered that *Iohn* should not dye.

Concerning this soundnesse and fidelitie in reports hearing,bearing and telling,this I say,that he must bee a man well ballanced with grace, and girded with veritie,as a peece of his christian furniture,who lesse or more lieth not open to the diuell in this kinde, who will doe much to make them that goe for professors,to lose the credite of their godlinesse. Was it not a good- 1.Kings 13.18. ly ornament for the old Prophet (whose honour is to be true of his word) to be taken in a lye,both warpe and woofe,making and telling? Was it not a sweete nosegay to the Church, thinke wee, that two great and forward Acts 5.9. professors, should be drawne forth and censured for lyars, I meane *Ananias* and his wife? Euen christians rake vp the common scumme and scurfe of the age they liue in: and hauing heard reports, doe out of a corrupt vanitie, or a leaud and sinister intent, altogether corrupt the truth and text thereof with glosses and comments, additions and detractions of their owne ma- Psalm.15.2. king,Psalm.15. this is no good signe of a man that shall dwell with God, if we may collect by contraries. If the Lord require that wee bee wise, and beware of beleeuing euery thing, lest we become reporters of an vntruth vnwillingly: how shall they escape that cast each tale in their owne mould, and hammer it in their owne forge,ere they giue it out? and when it is broched, it is no more like that which they heard from another, then an apple is to an oyster, as the speech is. Whereas the breast of each honest man should be an harbour for truth to lodge in: and should be as precisely carefull to see it safely deliuered and vttered forth,as of a pledge or secret pawne left him by his friend. And let this worke a detestation of this Popish practise of lying and giuing foorth reports (yea and coyning them oft times) which they thinke will make for their vantage, not onely falsely, but so incredibly, and shamelessely, that the very hearers blush for shame thereof. It hath been, is, and euer will bee, one of the rotten pillars wherewith they stay vp their kingdome and maintaine their diuelish doctrine. But here I ende.

THE SEVENTIE TVVO SERMON ON THE XIII. CHAPTER OF THE BOOKE OF IVDGES.

IT appeareth that *Manoah* beleeued his wife, and therefore hee prayed to the Lord, that the man might appeare againe to them, who had brought the message to his wife, that they might not be left in doubt what they should doe to the childe, euen as they beleeued him that it should be borne. And the Lord heard his prayer and sent him againe vnto them: and hereby it was that the man of God appeared the second time, as in this second part of the chapter may be seene. Vers 8.9.10.

In that *Manoah* gaue credite to his wife, as appeareth by his prayer, to send him to them againe, we see that there was faithfulnesse and trustinesse betwixt them, in that as shee reported the message by and by that was brought vnto her, so hee beleeued it at her mouth accordingly. A liuely glasse for couples to looke in, to direct them in this poynt, how they should be true and trustie one to the other: according to that which *Salomon* speaks of a faithfull wife, Prou. 31. That her husbands heart resteth in her: and a man would thinke, that there had need to bee no lesse betwixt them, who must liue for their whole life time together. And much wearinesse and discontentment must there of necessitie bee betwixt them otherwise; as they finde, who respect not grace chiefly in their matches, but either to satisfie their eye, saying with *Samson*, giue me her for she pleaseth me: or else make them vp for wealth, or begin their marriage in a worse manner then by both the former. Such finde litle trustinesse one at anothers hand, as appeareth within a small time after: who yet haue that which they sought, and reape the fruite of their owne labours; when they meete with many curses in their matches, euen as God hath foretold them. But of this I will adde no more here, hauing so oft spoken of it. Doct. vers. 8. Note. Prou. 31. 10. Note.

And it is well to be marked, that in this doubtfull case of the childes bringing vp, about which they were carefull, but yet knowing not what to doe; in this doubt, I say, he therefore prayeth to the Lord, for direction by the appearing againe of the Angell, for he knew that God would not leaue them in suspence, about such a thing as he would haue them doe. Which should teach vs, that in all difficulties and doubts, as well as in other troubles, wee should seeke to God to guide and assist vs: they being matters in doing whereof, we must giue proofe of a good conscience, both as *Iehosophat* did, and as the Lord commandeth in the Psalme: saying, Call on mee in the time of trouble, &c. We can skill to complaine and make our moane, to euery one that wee meete with, what heauy affliction haue befalne vs, who Doct. 2. 2. Chron. 20. 3. Psalm. 50. 15.

yet cannot helpe vs, but rather increase our sorrowes; but with God, to whom they should chiefely complaine, and make their moane, men haue no acquaintance. But as it is with them in this, that they bee strangers to him, euen so they haue helpe, and thriue accordingly. Let the reader see chap. 1. 2. and often in this booke, touching this argument, as also the next poynt, which is answerable thereto.

Doct. vers. 9. As he sought to the Lord, so hee obtained that which he asked, to teach that it is not in vaine to pray, and as he seeing that God hauing sent to them a strange and vnusuall message, which *Manoah* did not well vnderstand, knew hee would not leaue him in suspence and feare, but would make his minde knowne to them more perfectly, and therefore prayed in faith: in like manner we are to doe; to beleeue that we shall obtaine that which we
Iam. 1. 6. pray for. He must pray in faith, and wauer not, saith Saint *James*, and in an
Iam. 5. 15. other place, It is the prayer of faith that must saue. And Saint *Paul* saith, that
Rom. 10. 14. we cannot call vpon him, in whom we beleeue not. Which I say, both because that is no prayer but babling, that is voyde of faith, and also for that such prayer of faith, euen by one, much more by many, being feruent, obtaineth most vnlikely things at Gods hands. And in all difficulties, this is the speediest remedy, (both because for the time present, it easeth the heart
Note. well, and for the time to come, giueth hope of redresse one way or other) and vnburdeneth the minde of that vnprofitable heauinesse which cloggeth it, and deteineth it from being well occupied. Although more particularly, the occasion that mooued *Manoah* hereto, was a trouble which concerned the married estate; which howsoeuer it neuer falleth out (in this kinde) now adaies to couples: yet in stead thereof, many other doe, as care of bringing vp the children, employing them in the fittest trade of life, bestowing them in marriage; defraying the charge of housekeeping, with many more such. In all which are there not many difficulties, feares, and doubtings, which arise in the minds of carefull and tender Parents and gouernours? Yes doubtlesse, and such I meane, so daily and successiue, that they will breede no small distemper, inwardly by fretting, carking and contriuing: nor disturbance in the family by impatience and discord, if a wise course be not taken to stay and preuent the one and the other. Now what course can bee like this of *Manoah*, who being troubled about a message, which God had sent him, doth repaire to the same God, and desireth him to free him from the feare and doubt which hee had caused: so should the husband and wife do together, that seeing the Lord is the ordainer of marriage, the blessing of posteritie is from him, and he hath vndertaken to prouide for them and theirs to many generations that feare him: therefore it would please the Lord to guide them in their gouernement, to frame their mindes to patience and contentednesse in their crosses, to giue a blessing to their education and care of their children, to blesse their labours and callings, that there may bee sufficiencie, and in a word to shew them the best way or issue out of those troubles of houshold and familie, which vnsettle and disquiet them. A man would thinke it were a iollie ease (in such cases) to haue God a mans friend, ouer it is with them, that neither haue God nor friend to counsell them, but vncomfortably to beare their burdens by their owne strength, which none at all is able to doe.

The

The Angell at the prayer of *Manoah*, appearing againe to the woman in the field without her husband, ſhe made haſt to tell her husband that he appeared againe to her, as hee had done that day already; which newes ſhee knew would not a little ioy his heart, and eaſe him of much doubting that troubled him. And this teacheth the wife another dutie to her husband, to fulfill his ioy, and to doe the things that may make him cheerefull and a glad man, as farre as ſhe is able: as on the other ſide, the husband ſhould, yea and that much more, doe the like to her againe. And ſuch countenance, geſture and ſpeech, with their whole carriage ſhould be betweene them, as might free them from feare or doubt of heartie loue and kindeneſſe, but rather by all good occaſions, might make one another ioyfull. As for brawling, chiding, prouoking each other, or ſecret diſlikings, tetches, or conceits, which might cauſe the ſame, though there will neuer want occaſions; nay if they ſhould, yet the euill heart miniſtreth too many, they (I ſay) ſhould be farre from them, eſpecially from neſtling, and being ſeated in them. Therefore *Salomon* ſpeaking of ſuch a woman, ſaith of her thus: Who ſhall finde a vertuous woman? For her price is farre aboue the pearles. The heart of her husband truſteth in her, euen as hers alſo ſhould reſt in him: for they haue many other troubles, and ſuch alſo as accompanie marriage, ſo that they haue little neede to trouble one another alſo, but ought euery way to allay and ſtoppe occaſions, or to remooue them by their ſweete and chriſtian ſocietie and liuing together. And therefore it is moſt abſurd, that one of them ſhould doe that, which may grieue the other; but monſtrous that one ſhould ſeeke to vexe the other.

Verſ.10.

Note.

Prou.31.10.

Note.

And indeed, where both are of one minde, and will, in good things, this is no difficult matter, thus to ioyne and worke together that naturall loue and content in each other, and ſo (which is the fruite thereof) ioy and peace in the good ſucceſſe they haue in their endeauours and affaires, may be procured and augmented, I ſay among ſuch as be of one ſound minde, it is more eaſilie obtained (though the beſt had need to watch for ſuch grace, that fickleneſſe, eſtrangement and wearineſſe, doe not breake in) but how ſhall this bee found among other couples, wholely corrupt, and voide of goodneſſe, ſuch as the greateſt number is? Surely not eaſilie, eſpecially if trials come (for alas the worſt make a ſhift to pleaſe each other while they proſper) as we ſee in that fooliſh woman, *Iobs* wife, who while things went well with them, is not ſaid to haue broken out ſo groſſely, but ſeeing her husband plunged into miſerie, added to his ſorrow by her vnſeaſonable ſpeech, whereas ſhee ſhould then (aboue all other times) haue ſpake ſomewhat in ſeaſon, to haue comforted him, when all other outward helps failed. No man (ſaith the Apoſtle) euer hated his owne fleſh, but nouriſhed and cheriſhed it: ſo that ſelfeloue might ſomewhat perſwade this dutie, that couples ſhould ſeeke the peace and welfare of each other. And if the example of our Lord Ieſus may preuaile (as we know married perſons are ſent to that rule to learne of him) then let them conſider, how tenderly hee careth for his Church and ſpouſe, by all meanes procuring delight to her, and auoiding moleſtation from her, ſaying: *I charge you wake not my ſpouſe till ſhe pleaſe*. This charineſſe and care of remoouing all ſuch things out of the way, as might cauſe each others heauineſſe and griefe, and bearing the

Cant.3.5.

burthen of each other, that the afflicted partie might bee eased, is the best way to witnesse in them this sympathie of affection, and like mindednesse.

Verse 11. Now when *Manoah* commeth to the Angell to be satisfied in his doubt, marke the manner of his speech: he vseth no long circumstance, but directly goeth to the matter. Art thou the man (saith hee) that appeared to the woman? Such was the simplicitie of that age, that one might aske of another that which concerned them, and be answered. How farre was that from the practise of our time? for now there is much courtesie, glosing and coloured hypocrisie and subtiltie, but little good meaning and honest simplicitie: neither shall a man be sure of the minde of his neighbour, when

Rom. 12. 9. he hath faire words enough tending that way. A shew of loue but with dissimulation.

Touching vnfaithfulnesse in dealings and conuersation among men, I haue elsewhere spoken chap. 12. 2. 3. to the which this as a limme thereof may bee added, which I am to speake of, to wit, vnfaithfulnesse in speech. Both are birds hatcht in the same neast of a false & deceitful heart, I meane

2. Sam. 3. 27. 2. Sam. 16. 3. as well *Ioabs* curtesie to *Abner*, as *Zibas* fidelitie to *Mephibosheth*. It is an equall ornament to a christian (say they what they can, that mislike the olde fashion) to be a plaine dealing and a plaine spoken man; for both argue he

Note. 1. Chron. 12. 33 is a plaine hearted man. He that carieth with him an heart and an heart, carieth about him, a tongue and a tongue, an hand and an hand, all double and dissembling, all abominable to the Lord, as *Salomon* saith. For though the clouen footed beast was cleaner then the whole-houed, yet the clouen hearted and clouen tongued man is more vncleane to him, then the single heart, and the vniforme tongue. In which respect the Iewes were brought vp to hate doublenesse and falsehood by the forbidden types of Plowing

Leuit. 19. 19. with two kindes of beasts, wearing two kindes of stuffe, and sowing two kindes of graine, to wit, at the same plough, in the same garment, and in the same field. But wee at this day haue both abrogated ceremony and substance too for the most part: and though (as in other points, so in this) we hold, that generally the equitie of morall commandements is eternall, yet in particular, this plaine hearted and faithfull communicating and dealing of men together, is abolished, as if it had been a meere ceremony. True it is, men haue not quite forgotten ceremonies in this dutie, but their new found ceremonies haue eaten vp the old substance sheere, euen as the leane

Gen. 41. 4. kine deuoured the fatte in *Pharoahs* dreame, I meane this, the affected apish or complementall speeches of the most men, haue quite consumed the trueth, simplicitie and honestie of the heart, that should bee found among them. I mislike not seemely and courteous speech, if it carrie with it the co-

Psalm. 55. 22. lour and temper of the heart, but I meane that which *Salomon* speakes of in the Prouerbs, when the words are soft as butter and oyle, sweete as honey, but the heart is sharpe as a sword, and bitter as wormewood, and hath seuen abominations in it. Indeed I confesse all haue not in them this cursed habit (it commonly being the cloake of the malicious and politique, whom a man may for the most part vnderstand to meane contrarily to that they speake) but it is also a vanitie and affectation of many others, to bee more full of shewes and courteousnesse, then to intend friendship or goodwill. Be it of malice or of vanitie, it is naught: if of the former, diuelish: if of the latter,

latter, frothie and superfluous. Sinnes stay not alway in the Court: they come downe also into the countrey, wherein many men are so hollow, that their consciences tell them, they deserue to be hollowly dealt with: they haue vsed vndermining questions to others, and so they haue answers, as sinister, indirect, and forked. So that now adaies, if a man would haue a plaine answere from another, he is faine to vse some slight or wile to get it out: for if he speake plainly, the other hath so many casts and conceits in his mind, that he feares aduantage will be taken some way against him, which can be no lesse then a token of a bad conscience. If it be a matter that wee would communicate, for redresse of any euill, in towne, familie, or person, we know not how to breake one with another about it, (the meaner to his better especially) but if wee doe, a slender regard shall be had of it. Euen so in friendly meetings at table, when we haue apparant cause offered of thankes by Gods benefits, yet euen there it is harsh to heare any words sauouring of Ephes.5.4. religion, or tending to edification, (although giuing of thanks is the speech with which our table should by the Apostles commandement be seasoned) but if there be not some to crosse them, that offer occasion of such speech, yet shall ye haue the most part winding away from (seconding or giuing liking of it) into other needlesse, worldly, or frothie speech, euery one as he delighteth to talke. And as our speech to men is many waies to be charged, so is our commoning with God seldome, and when wee haue any, full of coldnes, loosenes and wandring.

Manoah, vnderstanding the man of God, in that hee had said to his wife, Vers.12. and seeing that she had rightly related the matter to him (for the message which this man of God had done to his wife before, and she had reported to him, agreed with his second rehearsall thereof in all points) hee resteth in that they say: for so he answereth, Be it as thou hast said: or thus, I beleeue it shall so come to passe, although to manward it seemeth not likely. So whē wee haue receiued any message from God, and by examining and comparing one scripture with another, for the confirming of vs therein; we haue Acts 10.17. proofe what the will of God is, which we were in some doubt of before; we ought to cease discoursing, and though wee were held in suspence, as *Peter* was at the vision, till we were resolued, yet now wee should without contradiction or difficultie receiue it from God, yeeld to it, and rest in it. Euen as before we know it we were, according to the occasion offered vs, to doe as *Manoah* did, being vnresolued; that is, trie the spirit, whether it be of God or no, and to pray God to reueale it to vs: and therefore as our Sauiour speaketh, to search the Scriptures for further knowledge therein: according to Iohn 5.39. the example of the Beræans, who tried all things, holding themselues to the Acts 17.11. truth; as the Apostle counselleth the Thessalonians to doe. We see that all 1.Thes.5.21. naturall motions tend to a rest and quietnes: wherein the perfection and end of the thing so moued, consisteth. And he that runneth a race, attaineth not his purpose, till he haue reached to the end of his course, and then he resteth. And because I am come by occasion of *Manoahs* resting in that particular which he sought, and haue shewed that we also ought to doe the like: I will say something of that which we ought to rest in, after a more generall manner. My meaning is this: A Christians perfection and end which shall hereafter be full in the blessed rest of glorie, (the Sabbath of the Saints) is

begun euen in this life, and that is, when the minde, soule, and whole man is at rest, that is, enioyeth, feeleth, and possesseth that, for which they much
Note. trauailed and tooke paines. The rest of the minde is actuall resolution and certaintie of the truth against errour and doubting: and this is the fruite of seeking knowledge. The rest of the soule is, perswasion and assurance of Gods fauour and his alsufficiencie, being reconciled vnto vs, and this is the fruite of seeking faith. The rest of the whole man is his inward setlednesse, being the fruites of faith, repentance, and sanctification: and this is the end of seeking encrease and growth in grace. Now because all these are but imperfect in vs here, (for we know, beleeue, and grow, but in measure) therefore we must seeke still to know, beleeue, and be setled, more and better, daily. Howbeit herein stands not our happinesse, in that we are learning, laboring, endeuouring after, but rather in that which we hold, and haue learned and gotten. This laieth much to the charge of such as hauing long been vnder teaching, fare as if they neuer had heard: after tenne, twentie, and more yeeres asking, Oh that I were resolued of the truth! Oh that I might heare the way to saluation plainly described! Oh that this or that doubt, feare, temptation, lust and corruption were remoued! Why, O thou sluggard, what hath bin a doing all this while? Hast thou not bin iogged, pulled, and punched out of thy snorting and dead sleepe by the Ministerie, and doest thou now open thine eyes, and aske why no bodie would awake thee? It
Note. was thy sottishnes and lethargie, not want of rousing, which drowned thee in sleepe so long. Therefore if thou haue care of thy soule, beseech the Lord to bedew and moisten those drie clods of thy minde and soule, wherein the seede of the word hath lien so long vnprofitable, that at length it may take roote and fructifie. And cease not till by this meanes thou be resolued and setled about, and in the truth, that so thou maist rest safely, and not (as before) dangerously: rest, I say, not from worke and exercise of thy knowledge and faith (for the vse of both is to be occupied, when thou hast them) but from vncertaintie, error, doubting, and distrust. This point I desire the reader to compare with that I haue spoken touching *Gedeon*, chap. 6.

Vers. 13. 14. When *Manoah* was resolued that hee should haue a childe by his wife, though she had been barren, he asked what they should doe to the childe, of which thing they no lesse doubted: whereby hee still sheweth his desire of resolution in the doubts that remained: and teacheth vs to be wise in making our benefit of the company and familiarity of such as are able and willing to resolue vs, and pretend we not foolish bashfulnes, (when indeed it is but slothfulnes) or lothnes to be troublesome, lest by that meanes wee procure to our selues more trouble (then wee can easily auoide afterward) by such bashfulnes, ignorance, and sloth. But I will not repeate any thing. Now to this second demaund, the Angell answereth the same that hee did to the woman. But to the woman his prescription was; what she should do her selfe, and not what they should doe to the childe. So that it seemed he answered not *Manoahs* doubt: for when he asked what they should do to the childe, the Angell answered, what she should doe that was to beare the childe. But it was all one in effect, as if hee had spoken thus: That which I said that she should obserue, was that she should doe it, because of the child, and therefore much more he must obserue the same.

Againe,

Againe, whereas ſhe was bidden to abſtaine from that which was vncleane, and that might ſeeme a needleſſe charge, ſeeing the law forbad all people the vſe of vncleane things before that time: to that it may be anſwered, that after the Philiſtims had got dominion ouer the people, as confuſion in the Common-wealth and tyrannie grew; ſo religion among the Iewes began not a little to decay. No wonder then, if among other things of greater weight, this one point of the ceremoniall law was broken, that they fell to eate things vncleane, as well as that which was cleane. For it was common with the Iewes, vpon diuers occaſions to breake the ceremonie, as appeares by that 1. Sam. 14. See the place. And by this wee may learne that it ought not to ſeeme ſtrange when wee ſee in the places of ignorance and darkneſſe, ſundrie euill cuſtomes, errours, and prophane practiſes receiued and vſed: and no print nor ſtep of Gods commandements and ordinances remaining, but all worne out and forgotten. Alas, they are to be pitied and lamented, not wondred at and ſcorned. There are more waies to deface and race out religion, then warre and forreine tyranny. Bleſſed be God, we ſigh not vnder that burthen: no, nor yet vnder the bondage of Antichriſt: wee haue peace, and gouernment, free from a profeſſion of Poperie. Let vs pray the Lord to adde hereunto this mercie, that by the free paſſage of the Goſpell, we may be alſo cured of that blindneſſe which now poſſeſſeth many places, and keepeth the people in errour, ſuperſtition and all kinds of vngodlineſſe. Secondly, in that the Angell ſpake the ſame thing to *Manoah*, that he did to his wife before, about the ſame matter; we obſerue by his example, that it becommeth, and is meete for Gods ſeruants alwaies to ſpeake the ſame truth, in or about any matter, at one time and in one companie, that they doe at and in another: according to the Apoſtles words to the Epheſians, that they ſhould caſt off lying, and euery man ſpeake the truth to his neighbour; which is to the iuſt reproch and conuiction of them, who carrie two tongues in their head (as they ſay) and are ſuch as haue loſt their credit by reporting vntruth where they come, and doe hurt to other, as well as bring an ill name on themſelues. But this I noted out of the womans report to her husband, and in diuers other places.

[Margin: 1. Sam. 14. 32.] [Margin: Doct. ver. 13. 14] [Margin: Epheſ. 4. 25.]

2 By the other part of the Angels words, in preſcribing that the woman ſhould abſtaine from things forbidden and vncleane, ſeeing the childe that was to be a Nazarite muſt be borne of her; when yet the preſcription was chiefly for the child, we ſhould learne this: That when things which ſeeme leſſe likely are commanded or forbidden, much more thoſe which are more apparantly ſo. As if the ſeruant and childe muſt keepe holy the Sabbath, much more the parents and maſter ſhould doe ſo: and moſt of all the Miniſter. And if the appearance of euill be forbidden; much more the euill it ſelfe. And ſo if a ſmaller thing be commanded or forbidden, much more a greater. And this is to the iuſter condemning of them that both heare this taught them, and ſee many well gouerned chriſtians to giue them example herein, yet not onely follow them not, neither the doctrine which they heare, but offend in the ſhamefulleſt and foulleſt manner. And let vs know that if the Lord in his Commandements will haue all his ſeruants to vnderſtand by the great ſinne or dutie expreſſed, that his will is the ſame in all the

[Margin: *Command* 4.]

rest of that kinde, be they neuer so small and special: how much more then if hee manifest his liking or disling of a lesser euill (that is more secret and more doubted of) or of a lesser dutie (seruing to be of lesse necessitie) ought we to collect that he will not hold vs guiltlesse in those euils committed, or duties neglected, which are more manifest, as being either by the light of nature, or by apparant Scripture allowed or forbidden? If he will not hold him excused, who is not wise to gather the lesse by the greater: woe be to the carelesse, who being commanded to streine out a gnat, swalloweth a cammell. Thus much of this, I proceed in the text.

The third part of the Chapter.

Vers. 15. *Manoah then said to the Angell of the Lord, I pray thee let vs retaine thee, vntill we haue made readie a Kid for thee.*

16. *And the Angell of the Lord said to Manoah, Though thou make me abide, I will not eate of thy bread, and if thou wilt make a burnt offering, offer it vnto the Lord: for Manoah knew not that it was an Angell of the Lord.*

17. *Againe Manoah said vnto the Angell of the Lord, What is thy name, that when thy saying is come to passe, we may honour thee?*

18. *And the Angel of the Lord said to him, Why askest thou thus after my name, which is secret?*

19. *Then Manoah tooke a Kid with a meate offering, and offered it vpon a stone, vnto the Lord: and the Angell did wonderously, whiles Manoah and his wife looked on.*

20. *For when the flame came vp toward heauen from the altar, the Angell of the Lord ascended vp in the flame of the altar, and Manoah and his wife beheld it, and fell on their faces to the ground.*

21. *(So the Angell of the Lord did no more appeare vnto Manaoh and his wife) Then Manoah knew that it was an Angell of the Lord.*

22. *And Manoah said vnto his wife, We shall surely dye, because we haue seene God.*

23. *But his wife said to him, If the Lord would kill vs, he would not haue receiued a burnt offering and a meate offering of our hands, neither would he haue shewed vs all these things, nor would haue now told vs any such.*

24. *And the wife bare a sonne and called his name Samson: and the child grew, and the Lord blessed him.*

Ver. 15. 16 17. 18 *The summe.* IN this third part, followeth the signe by which they should be certified, that the thing told them by the man of God, should come to passe. But first *Manoah* doth two things: one, he desireth the Angel to eate: the other, hee asketh him his name, to both whereof the Angell makes answere. Of these first in order.

Vers. 15. Concerning the first, the Angel of God hath now done his message, and answered *Manoahs* doubt. But he kindly accepting him for the good tidings he brought vnto him, desired to retaine him, that he might refresh himselfe after his trauaile, and (as hee thought) his hunger, and therefore hee said to him, let vs stay thee while we make ready a Kid for thee. But the Angel hauing

uing no need to eate,drew *Manoah* from his purpose, telling him he would not eate,and led him to more heauenly matter, that is,to honour God, by offering a burnt offering vnto him.

In these two verses we may consider diuers things: first in *Manoah*, then in the Angels answere. In *Manoah* these two following: First his curtesie and thankfulnes in offering him to eate, (thinking hee had been a man) hauing brought such a message from God to him and his wife. And this confirmeth vs in that wee haue heard before,that where wee receiue kindnesse, wee should render and shew the like againe,as we can. And the godly vsed both,then,before,and after,to offer such curtesie to the seruants of God being strangers,though they brought no message to them from God, and it is called hospitalitie, as wee reade of the Shunamite, who requested *Elisha* to turne in as he came by, and built him a conuenient chamber for that purpose. They knowing that he who receiued a Prophet in the name of a Prophet,and a righteous man because he was so,should receiue the reward that such should. *Doct.1.* Matth.10.41.

It is not a thing so commendable in Christians to be kind towards them that deserue it,as the contrary is odious and brutish in them. Those that are commanded to doe well to their enemies, and loue them that hate them, what great thing is it if they loue and be kinde to the well deseruing? (Heathens and Publicans doe likewise) But to be vnkind towards them that haue been louing and well affected toward them, is not only worse then heathenish,but also then any beast will yeeld to another. Nay histories report that a lion hauing bin eased and holpen by a passenger that came by,of a wound which by some meanes had befallen him: long after acknowledged the benefit. For the Romanes vsing to behold the spectacle of men fighting with beasts: condemned malefactors to this death. Now among the rest this man being one,came armed into the place,to fight for his life: and(as it fell out)this Lion was the beast,which was committed with him. The Lion no sooner saw the man, but came and fell downe at his feete,holding vp his foote in the sight of al the people,and making no semblance of furie against his preseruer. The matter being enquired into, it was found that this man had taken a thorne out of the foote of the Lion and so eased his paine. This (being but a discourse of a thing of inferiour nature) I may be thought not so wisely to insert in so graue an argument: neither had I done it for the strangenes of it,but that I would thereby shame such boisterous,rough and barbarous natures, as being prouoked to this dutie of kindnesse, by the strongest meanes,yet out of a bitter stomacke, doe rather thereby take occasion of hatred and mischiefe,like *Saul*, who by *Dauids* innocencie and pitie to his life, was the more enraged against him. But these meete with their match, for God giues them ouer to be touzed and hampered by such as spare them not,and want conscience,when they are fallen into their hands, to teach them for euer after to abhorre such inhumanitie, I had said lionlike crueltie,but that I should wrong that creature, if I should ascribe mans euill qualitie vnto it.

Thus much of the first thing to be noted in *Manoah*,as I said before. The other thing here to bee learned out of the example of *Manoah* is this, with what reuerence we ought to receiue Gods message by them whom he sendeth Doct.2.vers.15.

deth to doe it, and to bee entirely knit vnto the messenger himselfe, for his message sake. *Eglon* a heathen king shewed this reuerence to the message of *Ehud* from the Lord, and *Gedeon* much more, with others. Beautifull should
Rom. 13.15. the feete of them be, who bring glad tidings (and yet the feete of such as went barefoote in those countries, were not very beautifull of themselues, but vnseemely) And so much the more precious and heauenlier that the message is which they bring, they doing the same in such manner as becommeth it. And therefore (blessed be God) we haue experience of no lesse in some, that they who apprehend and embrace the ioyfull tidings of saluation brought vnto them by Gods messengers, soundly, sweetly, and sauourly, euen to the assurance of pardon and happinesse, are knit to the messengers most dearely and vnfainedly for their worke sake, (though they be but the instruments, and sometime meane persons in the eye of the world) by whom God worketh and reuealeth his will and minde vnto, that they may beleeue.

Philem. 19. Which thing *Paul* knowing very well, told *Philemon* that hee owed himselfe vnto him, for the good he had receiued by his ministerie, whereby hee was truly turned vnto God; and what marueile? Therefore such messengers of God deserue not checks and taunts (as the wicked and vnthankfull world can doe no other then giue them) for their so testifying their affection to them. And they are iustly to be pitied, who hauing heard the message of God at the mouthes of such, yet haue their hearts no way inlarged to them, whereby they giue testimonie that they haue taken no good by their preaching.

Will an earthly King endure his Ambassadour to be lowred vpon, or a-
2. Sam. 12.31. bused thinke we? Look vpon *Dauid*, how he reuenged the indignitie which *Hanun* offered his seruants? And what did the husbandman to those that
Matth. 21.41. farmed his vineyards, and beate, wounded and slew his messengers? Hee
Iohn 15.1. Luke 10.16. that despiseth you (saith Christ this husbandman, Ioh. 15.) despiseth me, and him that sent me. Next to the contempt of the message, this despight of the messenger is most damnable. For by Pastors and Teachers, the Lord manifests his will, touching our liuing peaceably heere, and enioying life hereafter for euer: (which are treasures precious, farre aboue those of Princes) and therefore they are sauage people that lightly weigh them: But
Iob 33.23. they that haue found comfort by them, yea their reconciliation, as Iob. 33. speaketh: they that haue tasted of the good gift of God by them, and haue their soules bathed in this dew of heauenly knowledge, esteeme them worthie of more honour then they can yeeld them, and count them as a few men of a thousand, and are neerlier knit to them, then nature can knit them
1. Thes. 2.20. to their owne flesh. And so is the Minister againe to them, being as the crowne of his ministerie. And yet to preuent a cauill, I say not that they worship them as God neither, for all that: but indeed they make more of them, then common men: which little liketh them who would haue them thought of as men, not worthie to haue place in the Church, no, nor on earth at all. Therefore let all good hearers learne, first to bee riuetted into their doctrine, to get acquaintance with that first, and then, if their hearts can go against the messenger let them; but that cannot be, they must needs aduance themselues in ioy and affection to the instrument, if once God and his

his ordinance haue got any honour and loue in their hearts. As for ſenſeleſſe blockes, or cauilling controulers, either of meſſage or inſtrument, who take vpon them to carpe at their doctrine, or the manner of vttering, or the perſons that bring it, (as the trueth is, the wofull people make no other vſe of theſe things, but to iangle and cenſure them) they bewray themſelues to be no children of wiſdome as yet: what they may be, I ſay not, but yet they be not bred nor begot by her, for doubtleſſe they would then pleade for, and iuſtifie her. I haue often thought it Gods mercy to keepe the knowledge of ſuch diſcouragements from them that are to enter into this office (leſt they ſhould bee deterred wholly from it) till by experience they might be armed againſt it. To conclude then, if *Manoah* for a temporall benefit foretold him by the Angell, and but once appearing to him, yet becauſe hee was the meſſenger of God, ſhewed himſelfe ſo kinde as hee did to him, and as hee tooke him to bee a man, ſo hee was carefull to entertaine him, as it was meete ſuch an one ſhould be; oh how much more ought the teacher and meſſenger of God, and the people ouer whom he is ſet, and to whom he is ſent of God to guide them ſafely to his kingdome, yea and to whom he declareth the whole ſecrets of God, and that daily both in ſeaſon and out of ſeaſon, as *Paul* ſpeakes: how much more ought they (I ſay) to be knit in true loue the one to the other? Whereas there is ſcarcely outward peace and agreement betwixt the moſt of them, vnleſſe it bee in euill, as in vaine iangling and prating, drinking and gaming, and ſuch like ſpending their time together: and this of *Manoah*.

The words of the Angell follow: wherein firſt, that he denieth not, that he may be moued to ſtay with him if there were cauſe, but not to eate, if he ſhould make prouiſion for him: therein (I ſay) hee teacheth vs theſe two things; the one, that we may lawfully and willingly be perſwaded (vnleſſe there be neceſſitie to the contrarie) to ſtay together, one neighbour with another in company, after we haue done our earthly buſineſſe, if there be ſeene cauſe, and namely, if thereby we may doe good or take good one by the other, as to conferre, and vſe good communication together, for knowledge, edification, and their mutuall comfort and increaſe of loue betwixt our ſelues, or for the good of each other. In theſe reſpects (I ſay) neighbours may keepe company one with the other, after their other affaires and buſineſſe ended, which though it be not in vſe among neighbours, where no religion is, yet let not other loſe that benefit. But otherwiſe if they doe not ſo in tarrying together, I meane, inſtruct, edifie and comfort one another, and prouoke mutually to loue, and good works, it is much meeter for them to depart aſunder, each to his owne home and calling; rather then to fall to idle, needleſſe, or hurtfull iangling and ſpending the time in no good ſort together. This is ſomewhat like that which I haue been before occaſioned to ſpeake of in the womans wiſdome, ſhewed in departure from the Angell, as ſoone as ſhe had receiued his meſſage. There is a danger as well in mens too long ſtaying together with men as with women: and it is apparant, that many haue held out company longer then was meete, after their neceſſarie affaires were diſpatched, or their lawfull refreſhings by the creatures enioyed: becauſe they fall from eating and drinking, to drunkenneſſe, to vngodly gamings, to buy and ſell their neighbours, to plot miſchiefe, to wrangle,

Verſ.16.

Doct.1. verſ.16

wrangle, quarrell and bee at daggers drawing each with other: had it not bin well these had not met at all, or at lest, to haue bin parted in season? But on the other side, if time, place, and good occasion offered doe serue, it is the dutie of a Christian to redeeme any seasons in company to doe good therein, if it were but for this cause, that they meete not commonly nor oft together. And where there is willingnes, and as it may be thought, simplicitie and vprightnesse in them that desire it, there ought to bee readinesse and forwardnesse in him that can yeelde it (except other predominant reasons doe vrge the contrarie) without any strangenes and austeritie, and the rather, because the most part of the world looke after no such matter in their meeting together. And this wisdome we may learne by the Angels words.

2 The other part of his answere is this, that he would not eate, if he should prouide for him, because he was no man (as *Manoah* tooke him to be) and therefore had no need to eate. For though sometime the Angels of God did eate, as with *Abraham* and *Lot*, and did put on the shape of men when they had some message of God to doe, and so tarried the longer, yet here the Angell hauing done that he came for, and so hastning to depart, refused to eate, seeing it was needlesse.

Doct. 2. In this speech the Angell teacheth this, that the creatures of God ought not to be spent needlesly, but receiued for necessary vse: euen as our Saui-

Iohn 6.12. our taught long since, that the broken meate aud fragments should not bee cast away, which were left after the people had been satisfied. And this commendeth frugalitie and honest sparing, as it condemneth the prodigall lauishing and wasting that many stroy goods doe vse, who fatte their dogges, and famish the poore, for whom broken meate should be reserued. But of this I shall say more afterward God willing.

3 Neither is it vnworthy the noting for vs, to see how carefull the holy ghost is here, to cleare the good meaning of *Manoah* from any blame. Hee knew not (saith the text) that it was an Angell of the Lord, *q.d.* If hee had known it, ye may well thinke, he would not haue spoken so: but being ignorant, he is to be excused: I blame him not for it, no reason therefore that his simplicitie should make him subiect to hard censure. It is not simply indeed excusable in *Manoah*, onely because he was ignorant (for *Peter* was faultie for saying hee knew not what, being with Christ vpon the mount) but because he was neither bound to know, nor able of himselfe to know any such matter. See then how tender the Lord is of the credit of his good seruants, that whiles they in their innocency walke according to their knowledge, he auoideth all the blame that might grow to them by their vnauoidable ignorance: the Lord will iudge the worke of his seruants, according to that they haue; but as for the defect which is inuincible, it shall doe

Doct. 4. them no harme: this by the way. The thing I purpose to insist most in, is, that knowing afterward this messenger to be an Angell (otherwise then he supposed) was ashamed euen of his blamelesse error: how much more ought we to blush for our faultie errors, nay grosse ignorance, or (which is

Rom. 6.21. worst) wilfull sinnes? That which *Paul* Rom. 6. saith, implieth no lesse, That we being regenerate should be ashamed to looke backe into our olde profane course of blindnesse and badnesse: as if a deuout Papist (like *Ephraim* in the Prophet) being conuerted, should be abashed to consider the vnfruitfulnes

fruitfulnes of his deuotion, and kneeling to the Crucifix, and the image of the Virgin Mary, and a peece of bread, saying to these Idols, Fie vpon you, get you hence, they were blinde that made them, they themselues are like the makers of them, and I as blind that worship them. So should the proud boaster, that hath scornefully disdained his neighbour (in his heate and madnesse) being come to himselfe, and seeing he is no better then earth and a fire-brand of hell, be ashamed of himselfe, and say; Who am I, that haue thus basely forgot my selfe? So he that hath come iollily to the Sacrament, and yet profanely, because hee could discerne no more at the Lords boord, then his owne: when he seeth his boldnesse, and how farre hee hath ventured; how should it astonish him? The truth is, knowledge and grace haue no greater enemies then the ignorant, who (if they could see themselues as they cannot) how highly would they magnifie God for knowledge? if for no other cause, yet for this, that thereby they are made to see their estate far other, then they could euer beleeue it to be: and so resting thankfull, walke in the light thereof, and abhorre their former blindnes.

The Angel seeing *Manoah* deceiued taking him to be a man, led him further to more fit matters for him, bidding him make a burnt offering of the meate that he desired to refresh him with. For to no end was *Manoahs* speaking of meate to him, offering him to eate the kid of the goates. This speech of his sheweth that it is true wisedome to take occasion to draw one another forward to holy duties, and to communication of heauenly things. The most being earthly, and fast locked vp therein, *Manoah* was busie about prouiding for him, which through his errour, was to no end, therefore the Angell drew him to that which was profitable indeed. And so it well becommeth Christians to be ready to leade one another from vnprofitable expence of the time, to talke of things more diuine and fit to the edifying one of another: neither ought the wise christian to stumble at it when he meeteth in companie with such as are vnsauourie, whose tongues are their owne to set themselues on worke as they please. Alas what other is to bee looked for at the hands of such, as neuer learned how to gouerne themselues either alone, or in their priuate houses, or in the publike actions of Gods worship? How should their tongues be well seasoned in companie, or bring foorth sauourie and gracious matter, out of an vncleane heart abounding with the contrary? But rather let him pitie such, (for all bad men are not bad of malice) and by his milde and modest silence at least, and much more by speaking that which is likest to preuaile and doe good, turne off, and put by their superfluous and frothie talke: not fearing but that it will giue place, and cause the vtterers thereof to say, Indeed this speech of yours is farre meeter for the companie, and deserueth to be accounted of, and pitie it were that loose and vaine talke should haue put it by: pardon vs, for if we had knowne better, wee would haue vsed better. Is not this a good effect of Christian boldnesse (though no more then needs) thus to take occasion to breake off bad communication, and to bee farre preferred before an offensiue giuing place to ill speech till it haue gotten the vpper hand, so that it is too late to represse it? But to come neerer to the occasion of this text. A Christians dutie towards them that come behinde him in experience and the right vse of conference with such, is, not to make himselfe sport at their weaknes, or Doct. 5.

to ſcorne their ignorance, but to goe before them, and teach them how to ſpend the time more profitably. A man may diſcerne teachablenes, and an humble ſpirit in many, who out of a ſimple meaning, vtter that little good ſpeech that they can, or which comes next to minde, though they can little conſider to what purpoſe or edifying. Here is a fit occaſion offered to the other, with lenitie & ſoftnes to diuert rather then breake off ſuch ſpeech, to looſen the bands of it rather, then violently to cut them aſunder, that ſo the hearers may ſee themſelues wound into better communication ere they are aware, and ſecretly bluſh at their owne ignorance.

Doct.6. The particular that the Angell mentioned, was to counſell him to offer a burnt offering to the Lord. The ſignification thereof was, that thereby hee ſhould conſecrate himſelfe, body and ſoule, with the powers and parts of both vnto the Lord: and ſo he ſhould honour the Lord, as became him, and ſhew, that hee did thereby acknowledge himſelfe willing and readie to obey him in all things. Rom.12.1. And this is our true ſeruing of God to offer vp our ſelues wholly vnder his gouernment, as the Apoſtle ſpeaketh to the Romans. And ſo on the contrary, they doe nothing leſſe, who giue themſelues to follow their owne luſts, and the deuices and deſires of their wicked hearts, or who in ſome things wil yeeld him dutie, and by halues, as we reade that *Saul* did, for which cauſe the Lord rejected him. Let the reader looke more of this point in chap.2. and in chap.10. and elſewhere.

And further as *Manoah* for the kindneſſe hee receiued of the Angell, was bidden to offer to God that which he offered to him; ſo we ſhould not offend, who are Gods Miniſters, if in the like caſe we doe the like. As for example, if for our trauaile by aduice and counſell to any brother, either troubled in conſcience, or otherwiſe with ſome great and dangerous doubt; he being ſatisfied and quieted to his good contentment by our counſell, if (I ſay) he, the partie ſo counſelled by vs, out of a thankfull minde ſhould offer gratuitie to vs, (as many thinke it their dutie) I ſay, wee ſhould not offend, if we ſhould deſire him to giue it either wholly, or a part thereof, as freely to ſome very good vſe, if he be well able, as to ſome godly poore, as hee would haue done to vs, ſeeing we thinke it vnmeete for vs to receiue it, becauſe we would in no wiſe bring a reproch to our miniſterie, or giue occaſion to any, to thinke, that we doe baſely ſell the gifts of God for money. For if hee bee both able and willing (as *Naaman* the Sirian in the like caſe was) to ſhew thankfulnes, which we thinke it vnmeete to receiue, we ſhall doe a good dutie to helpe to benefit ſome other, where there is need of it, and ſo fit an occaſion is offered by Gods prouidence, to relieue him. Too few ſuch occaſions are offered of doing good in that maner, & if they be, yet they are not taken; and yet it is well knowne how many there are to doe good vnto, and how wee are commanded by God to take all occaſions thereof, as he offereth them. And if ye aske, why *Eliſha* did not worke vpon *Naaman* in that manner: I ſay, hee was an heathen, and a ſtranger, newly conuerted; and if he had requeſted any ſuch kindneſſe of him, it muſt haue been put into his hands to diſpoſe; in all which reſpects hee refrained. But of this I haue ſaid ſomewhat before, chap.8. in *Gedeon* his refuſing the kingdome and demanding the earings: the leſſe therefore ſhall ſerue.

Another thing I thinke good to ſtay about a little in this verſe, and that is, is,by occasion of a word the Angell spake. And that is this: that hee called that, bread, which *Manoah* called flesh: For when hee desired the Angell that hee might prepare for him a kid of the goates, the other answered hee would not eate of his bread: whereby who doubteth (will some say) but that both meant one particular thing? *Manoah*, that he would prepare some refreshing for him; and the Angell, that hee would not eate with him.

Here by the Hebrew word לחם which signifieth not bread onely, but all food, and so flesh particularly; by this word (I say) the Papists (who are faine to catch hold of euery thing that they thinke may serue for their purpose) take occasion to maintaine their transubstantiation; and they crie aloud, that the bread in the Sacrament may signifie flesh, as it doth in other places of the Scriptures. Where it appeares, that they are so hastie to alleage a proofe from hence for their purpose, that in the meane while they take one thing for another. For though the Hebrew word may signifie flesh, as it doth bread, yet they should remember that *Paul* wrote in the Greeke tongue, where the Greeke word ἄρτος signifieth bread, is neuer taken for flesh. And what gaine they by thus playing the Sophisters among the ignorant? For they who are able to iudge, do see ỹ they abuse the reader grossely in saying, bread may be taken for flesh, because the Hebrew word sometime signifieth so, when the Greeke word neuer signifieth so; in which tongue yet all that concerneth the Lords Supper, is written. And so while they goe about (with the dogge) to get the flesh that shineth in the water, they lose that which they seemed to haue in their mouth, and so both. And yet if the Greeke word ἄρτος did signifie flesh, as it doth bread, how doth it follow that it should signifie so in the Sacrament against sense, reason, scripture and truth? So wee see what substantiall proofes they bring to vphold and iustifie their absurd opinions and religion. This I say vpon this supposition granted, that the Angell and *Manoah* spake of the same indiciduall thing, which yet no man will grant to bee a necessarie consequence. For though *Manoah* meant flesh, yet the Angell might meane bread, both by a *Synecdoche*, meaning a refreshing by bread and meate: *Manoah* might offer him a kid, and he might answere (I will not eate of thy bread) in this sense; Prepare nothing for me, I will not eate so much as any bread, much lesse of thy flesh. Who is so simple as to thinke otherwise, except any should imagine that the meate was like to be set before the Angell, without bread? If bread were needfull also, what necessitie is it that both their meanings must needs be about the same particular? But I spare. Thus much of *Manoahs* desiring him to eate: the second thing followeth, of asking him his name: but of this in the next Sermon. *Doct.7.*

THE SEVENTY THREE SERMON ON THE XIII. CHAPTER OF THE BOOKE OF IVDGES.

Verſ 17.18. *The ſenſe.*

THus he ſtill ſeeing the man of God (as he tooke him to be) to ſhew ſuch grace in his ſpeech, was the more knit to him, and ſo deſired to know his name: and hee ſhewes him the reaſon, to wit, that when it ſhould come to paſſe, which he promiſed, *Manoah* might honour him with ſome reward: The Angell ſeeing it a needleſſe thing that he asked, did not anſwere to him in word: but thought it fitter to make himſelfe knowne to him in deedes then in words, and thereby to confirme the former promiſe made to them. And this to be the meaning of the verſe, the next words doe proue, namely, that hee did wonderfully; for ſo are the words in the originall: hee was marueilous, or he did wonderfully.

The Angel that reſolued there ſhould be no yeelding of gratuitie to him, for which cauſe *Manoah* asked his name, hee did not tell him: and yet who can deny but *Manoah* asked it vpon good conſideration, namely that hee might ſhew himſelfe thankfull to him, as he thought himſelfe bound to be? Wherein he gaue cleere teſtimonie of his honeſt and ſingle heart, in deſiring to take the opportunitie thereof vnto him afterwards for the kindneſſe that was offered him. Which is a neceſſarie duty, though it be not regarded nor looked for of them to whom it is due. But of this before.

Doct. verſ. 18. Now that the Angell did ſhew (as we ſee in this verſe) what hee was, by deeds rather then by words, he hath not onely left vs his example, but alſo confirmed vs in that the Scripture teacheth both Miniſter and people concerning that matter. And firſt of the former (who being a publike meſſenger of God, is called an Angel) my meaning is not that the Miniſter is liable to euery ianglers cenſure, for his allowance of him, or for his ſufficiencie. But let him get this Seale of his Miniſterie, which here the Angell bringeth out, to wit, the efficacie of working, I meane, both a powerfull teaching, and a powerfull example; and theſe ſhall be his iudges. By theſe they muſt iudge of him, who are able to iudge, and they who iudge by any other rule, are ignorant or malicious, and therefore diſabled to iudge. And the beſt Miniſters that euer were, neuer refuſed this Canon of doctrine and life to be examined by. Neither our Sauiour nor the Apoſtle *Paul* euer arrogated to themſelues ſuch libertie as to be receiued, the one for true Meſſiah, the other, for a true Apoſtle, vpon their bare word. It might haue opened a gap to euery ſeducing ſpirit, to haue ſtood vpon his owne worth, and (like Antichriſt at this day) to compell mens conſciences to acknowledge him a ſucceſſor of the Apoſtle, becauſe he (out of the abundance of his owne ſenſe) boaſted

boasted himselfe so. So that base testimonies are inartificiall arguments (all meere men being lyars) but to trie the spirits whether they be of God, is a needfull dutie: they that are so tried, haue no wrong done them; neither can complaine, if their charter bee demanded, I meane the power of teaching, and the power of godlinesse. These workes admit no appeale, though they be no miraculous works, (as the Angels here) yet they are demonstrations. In the 11. of Matthew, *Iohn Baptist* sends his disciples to Christ in policie to resolue them of the truth of his mediatorship: our Sauiour (when they had done their errand) doth not scorne them, or disdaine to giue account of his calling. But what manner of euidence giueth hee? *Goe* (saith he) *tell Iohn, what yee haue heard and seene, The blinde see, the lame goe, the poore receiue the Gospell. q. d.* If these workes will not euince what I am, take mee not for him that I goe for. So he tels the Pharisies, If I gaue witnesse onely to my selfe, I could not claime credit thereto: but the workes I doe, they beare witnesse of me, and further I desire not to be embraced. So *Paul* tels the Corinths, ye are my Epistle written in your hearts, &c. *q.d.* The spirit of God coworking with my Ministerie, to the begetting of faith, a new heart and life in you, hath sealed also this truth vnto you, That I am a true Apostle of Christ, against all gainesayers. And it is the dutie of all Gods Ministers to adde this commendation and allowance vnto the outward calling of the Church, their letters commendatorie I meane and licenses. And if hereupon wee may bee receiued, let vs not complaine: as for them who vpon this testimony from God, will not admit vs, either our persons, as factious Separatists; or the power of our Ministerie, as all vnbeleeuers and vngodly ones, woe be vnto them, for in not receiuing vs, they despise him that sent vs. As for their censures, we may appeale from them with our Sauiour; saying, I receiue not praise or dispraise of men, I haue another Iudge: And with *Paul*, It is a slight thing with me to be iudged of such, I passe not for your iudgement. And secondly let all priuat persons, that receiue the message of God by the Minister, know their dutie also, which is to declare what they bee by the good actions of their liues, rather then by their talke, and to bee examples to other in their conuersation, and not in their communication onely. So our Sauiour taught when he came to giue his life for vs here on earth: If ye abide in me, and my word in you, then are ye my very disciples indeed.

1.Iohn 4.1. Matth.11.2. 2.Cor.3.2. Note. 1.Cor.4.3. 1.Tim.4.12. Iohn 8.31.

Agreeable hereunto are his words in another place, Not euery one that saith Lord, Lord, shall enter into the kingdome of heauen, but he that doth the will of my father which is in heauen. Neither let any man desire to bee taken for better then he is, but submit himselfe to this touchstone which will bewray what mettall he is made of: and for as much as the inward duties of faith and pietie are vnknowne to others, let the workes of each mans calling say for him what he is, let a good magistrate be content to lose the credit of his profession, if he cannot maintaine it by vprightnes, courage in punishing offenders, & defending the innocent, being free from couetousnes, parcialitie, or iniustice. Let the husbandman approue his religion, by walking as a man of vnderstanding before his wife, and she hers, by submission in the Lord, and reuerence towards him: and so the other parts of the familie in their seuerall places. And otherwise, let them hold their peace as

Matth.7.21.

guiltie persons. Thirdly, this doctrine is to settle the best Christians to bee so still, notwithstanding the taunts and mockes of the vngodly, who bayte them with the names of hypocrites, and men of singularitie, seeing they declare that out by their good liues, which they imbrace with their hearts: and generally let all such take warning by this, as onely haue a name they liue, but are dead, and who speake well, but haue not hearts to doe thereafter, and as for such as reproach and scorne them who honour their profession with a life answerable, their iudgement sleepeth not.

It appeareth by that which is said here, that as the Angell willed *Manoah* to doe, euen so he did: I meane, offer a burnt offering vnto the Lord. Now where it is obiected that it was not lawfull for him to offer in any place, but at Ierusalem, and therefore that it was not lawfull for him to offer where the Angell met him; I answere, that it was lawfull to offer in other places while the Arke was carried about, and was stayed in no certaine place: but after the building of the temple at Ierusalem, then indeed that law tooke effect, and it was not lawfull to sacrifice elsewhere, but all high places were then to be taken away. And this I say, supposing the action to be ordinarie; but indeed this of *Manoah* had bin warrantable at any time, as being grounded vpon diuine warrant, commanding him so to doe.

Obiect.

Answ.

And whereas it is againe obiected, that *Manoah* not being of the tribe of *Leui*, but of *Dan*, ought not to offer sacrifice, neither was that according to the law that hee did: it is answered, that hee gaue the flesh and the other things to the Angell, whom he tooke to bee a Prophet, that hee might offer them, for the Prophets had an extraordinary calling, that though they were not of the house of *Aaron*, yet it was lawfull for them to sacrifice, as *Elia* and *Elisha* did: for when the Priests corrupted the pure worship of God, the Lord stirred vp the Prophets to restore it againe. But this was no Prophet, ye will say; I answere, no hee was not, but more then a Prophet: and therefore the flesh and the other offering being laide on the rocke, the Angell did wonderfully; hee raised fire out of the rocke, and consumed the sacrifice.

And the same we haue heard to haue been done in *Gedeons* sacrifice before: for although it bee not expressely said here, that fire was brought out of the rocke as there; yet seeing there is no mention of any fire brought by *Manoah*, and yet that the Angell is said to haue departed in the flame, it is most likely that fire was stricken out of the stone: the Angell ascended into heauen, as though he would vse the flame in steade of a chariot, and he dissolued the body which he tooke on him, and went away in the fire, which was a great wonder to them, for *Monoah* and his wife were stricken with a great feare, when they saw that he was an Angell of God: and after that, he appeared no more to them.

Doct. vers. 19. In that *Manoah* did as the Angell willed him, turning that which hee would haue set before the man of God for meate, into a sacrifice; it teacheth how fit and ready we should be, to be moued and ledde by good instruction to any duty that wee know not, neither thought of before: meekely receiuing the words of exhortation without resistance or vnwillingnesse.

2. Thess. 3. 4. This minde was in the Thessalonians, to whom *Paul* writeth thus: We are perswaded of you in the Lord, that both yee doe already, and will doe still

the things that wee commande you, meaning, that they resolued with themselues, to make the doctrine of the Apostles the rule of their life.

Thus should all Christians bee affected, like the paterne that *Paul* giues the widowes, that they should diligently be giuen not onely to the particular duties of compassion, Rom. 12. but to euery good worke. This commendeth the grace of God highly in all such as are thus prepared to serue God in euery part of their life, that as they shall see what the good and acceptable will of God is toward them, so they are ready still to new duties. And so it doth much checke and accuse them, who are slow and backward to any good thing that shall be required of them, and readily yeelded to by their brethren: they would be counted with the forwardest, but yet in duties that like them not, they will be reasoning against them, though in some other they shew themselues commendable. And yet for all that which I say, let it be clearely seene, that there is enough to binde their consciences, to that whereto they should yeeld, lest they be lead by company, will, or fancy: and there is cause of this readinesse and alacritie in receiuing the word by the people, if they consider that the Minister himselfe is tied to the like dutie in vttering it, according to that charge of *Peter*, feede the flocke of God with a ready minde, not of constraint: and the Apostle *Paul* confirmes it, There is necessitie imposed vpon me, and wo be to me if I preach not, &c. If then I doe this necessarie worke willingly, it is thankworthie: otherwise it is necessarie, and I must doe it without thanks. How shall this bee, if the people hold off and pleade libertie to take and refuse what they please? Therefore *Cornelius*, Acts 10. professeth himselfe and his, ready to heare whatsoeuer *Peter* should say from God to him. And when he saith [*whatsoeuer*] he meaneth, whether reproofe, or commandement, as well as comfort and instruction. This sheweth, that not all that doe some duties, doe them readily; but either for sinister respects or by halues: as he in the Gospell: who was bidden goe into the vineyard, answered, hee would, but went not: so, many heare zealously, but neuer weighing the worke of God, nor forecasting the difficulties, repent them of their forwardnesse. Others readily yeeld to the truth in their minds as sound and good, but their hearts come slowly forward, they delight not therein, nor approue it, as liking that it should gouerne them. Againe, some things which the word requires we yeeld to, (for the outward action especially) yea and stand stiffely in the defence of it, as *Iudas* did for the relieuing the poore, because (in a diuers respect) our desire concurreth with Gods commandement, euen corruptly peruerting the end and vse of a good duty to our own benefit, which ought onely tend to Gods glorie. But here we doe not obey readily, because the manner of obeying, which is for conscience sake, displeaseth vs: as the artificer liketh it well, that God calleth for diligence in his calling, for his coueteous minds sake; but to be occupied therein for the seruing of Gods prouidence, the auoyding of noysome lusts and temptations, the practise of his faith and patience, thankfulnes & contentment, he hath no readines thereto: yea this awkenesse is in the best, that they like any dutie should bee vrged which others are tardie in, and themselues prone vnto; but to be drawn any further, and to suffer exhortation and reproofe for their blemishes and errors, that is vnwelcome. So that readines and teachablenes humbly to

[Margin notes: 1. Tim. 5. 10. — Rom. 12. 2. — 1. Pet. 5. 2. — Acts 10. 33. — Matth. 21. 31. — Note. — Note.]

giue place, and curbe our contradicting and rebellious nature, where God hath manifested his will vpon good ground, is a rare gift of the spirit, and
Psalm.119.6. attendeth onely vpon them, who with *Dauid* haue a respect to all Gods commandements. Excellent is that speech of *Dauid*, O Lord thou saidst, Seeke my face; and I answered, Lord I will seeke thy face. Euen as the waxe applied to the seale, receiues the impression, and the holy instruments of musicke in the Temple sounded according to the skilfull blowing or fingering of *Asaph* and his brethren, so pliant and tunable should our hearts
Note. be to the voice of God, and make such harmony in his eares, as he himselfe hath made inwardly in them: as the seruant mentioned in the Gospell, whose obedience in going, comming, and dooing, seemed to be so prompt, as if it were the eccho of his Masters voyce. And such as haue attained any measure herein, let them looke to this one thing, that they be constant in so doing, lest (beside the expectation) the diuell in time by inward or outward discouragings or allurings, quite alter their temper, and make them first to heare without delight, remissely and coldly, and in time with dislike and resistance, as wofull experience witnesseth. Touching the particular kinde of *Manoahs* readinesse to turne the meate into sacrifice, see more in the peoples giuing to *Gedeon* the earings of their pray, which poynt is diuers from the former.

2 Further this consuming of the sacrifice with fire by the Angell procured in such a wonderfull manner, as it could bee no other then the worke of God, this, I say, was done for the confirming of *Manoah* and his wife: the
Iudg.6.17. which also was granted to *Gedeon* in the like case, and at the prayers of *Elia*, he did giue the like signe for the confirming of the people, that *Iehoua* the
1.King.18.24. God of *Elia*, was the true God, and *Baal* an idoll, and his priests deceiuers of them. By all which and many more such, the Lord testifieth, how willing he is, that his poore seruants should be free from doubtings and feare, which doe much distract and disquiet them.

For though he allow them not to looke for, or depend vpon signes now, as in times past, yet a most sure rule he hath giuen vs in his word to goe by,
Iohn 5.39. to the which he sendeth vs, saying; Search the Scriptures, for they beare record of me, and shew, what my will is toward you. And whereas it will be obiected to me that all cannot vnderstand the scriptures, and therefore that may be farre enough off from resolution in doubtfull cases: I answere, the Lord hath taken order, (if hee were obeyed therein) that throughout his Church there should bee preachers to reueale his minde to the hearers, and to haue their abode, and liue with the people, to the end they may
Note. helpe to resolue their doubts, as they shall arise daily in them, and so helpe to stablish their faith, and set them forward to the kingdome of glorie, all which the poore people haue neede of.

And if Gods matters were regarded of men but as their owne be, there would be such care to furnish all places, by them whom it concerneth, with fit and meete teachers (choyce being made alwaies of the best first, and they sought after) that both the rest of them who are students in Diuinitie might be well incouraged to follow their studie, and best examples, and the people well prouided for thereby, and so might grow to resolue themselues in many of their doubts, and be helped by their teachers in the rest, so as they might

might liue comfortably, which a few attaine to of many, and then it may be ſeene alſo, what other people goe without of their due, by wanting ſuch teachers, and they who are cauſes of it, may repent, which would bring great ioy into our ſtreetes. Note.

It is ſaid further here, that after this was done, the Angell did yet wonderfully in another thing: to wit, that when the flame aſcended from the altar toward heauen, he aſcended in it, *Manoah* and his wife beholding the ſame, that ſo they might know what he was who appeared to them, euen the Angell of God, whom they tooke to be ſome man of God, or prophet. Thus they were better confirmed about that which was ſaid to them concerning the childe. This, as the former verſe, confirmeth vs in that we learned there, namely, what a care the Lord hath to eaſe our infirmities, and to relieue vs therein: which being beleeued of vs, is no ſmall refreſhing and incouragement to vs. But of this poynt hath been already ſpoken much in the hiſtorie of *Gedeon*. Verſ. 20. *Doct.* 1.

Alſo it is ſaid here, that *Manoah* and his wife, when they beheld this, and knew, as it followeth in the next verſe, that he was an Angell of God, they (I ſay) fell on their faces to the earth for feare, as appeareth by his words to his wife afterward. For we may not be ignorant of this, that in thoſe times 2
the people were afraid at the ſight of an Angell, or in beholding any ſignes of Gods preſence, as in Exod. 19. we reade, and Iudg. 6. ſo I ſay, it was with them, and ſo it would be with vs, if we ſhould haue the like occaſions offred vs: the reaſon is, firſt our inherent ſinne, and the inborne corruption that is in vs: ſecondly, the accuſation of our conſciences, which tell vs what wee are in, and of our ſelues: to wit, moſt vile, rebellious, and diſobedient; the which ought to humble vs, when God by ſuch or other meanes, doth as it were, ſhew vs our face in a glaſſe, that through our ſin we be afraid, whereas we ſhould reioyce. Exod. 19 16. Iudg. 6. 22.

In that they did ſhew reuerence in ſuch caſes, it was their duty ſo to doe: and we owe the ſame, in reſpect of Gods ſpeciall preſence in the congregation. But as we ſee it was with them, that in doing a good thing they paſſed meaſure in their feare, and it was exceſſiue in them: ſo wee may beholde thereby, how hard a thing it is to auoyde corruption in our beſt actions. But as they went too farre in one extremitie, that they were too much afraid, ſo wee goe further in the contrary, for that wee come ſhort, and doe not feare the preſence of God at all, when we come before him in ſpeciall manner, or very little. So that the reuerend behauiour of the Fathers toward God, will be an accuſation of vs for the contrary, when yet we ought to carry our ſelues reuerently in all places. Let the reader looke backe into the 6. chapter and 22. verſe, where this argument is largely handled.

In that it is ſaid in this verſe, that the Angell hauing done that which he came for to them, departed, and was no more ſeene of them, it teacheth vs the ſame; to wit, that when we haue met together before the Lord to ſerue him, as for example, in the publike vſe of prayer, word, and Sacraments, and haue religiouſly ended theſe duties; then wee ſhould depart, euery one to his place, conſidering how many and great inconueniencies doe follow idle and needleſſe tarrying behinde, and loyterings: whereby we doe not onely forget ſuch good inſtructions as we haue heard (whereas while they Verſe 21. See Hebr. 2. 1.

be

be fresh in our remembrance, we might in our returning, either meditate on them, or reuiue the memory of them by good company, but also fall to drinking, playing, prating, and such like behauiour, as whereby wee doe much more hurt to our selues and others, then we got good by our hearing. The diuell hath more strings to his bow then one: and therefore if he cannot draw men to neglect the meanes altogether, hee will busie their heads with wandring, or oppresse their bodies with sleepe: but where neither of these preuaile, yet sometimes he windeth in with thẽ so by other deludings of them, that hee depriueth them of all fruite which they seemed to haue got, and that as easilie as they may be brought asleepe: and not least of all, by occasioning forgetfulnesse of that they heare, by needlesse company afterward, or some other improuidence. And while men are yet hot and glowing through the power of the word, hee doth cast cold water vpon their affections, and quencheth the spirit, which had kindled good desires in them before. And yet few are so wise as to suspect the danger, but thinke themselues safe enough, and well fenced from the diuell, they hauing so lately been taken vp in holy duties, as in hearing and prayer, and so are easily beguiled by him, that doggeth them, though inuisibly, from the Church, as well as to the Chruch, and in it. And this I speake not onely of the common abuse of the Sabbath, (which of Christians ought to be abhorred) but euen of other meetings occasioned besides, and not auoided. But let this be well considered after their publike hearing, besides the shunning of vnseasonable companies, that although I forbid not men to returne to their lawfull callings and affaires after hearing, whereunto the word fitteth them much better (and they are no enemies to the fruite which they haue gained in publique) yet I say thus much: first, that there ought to bee some respite betweene the one and other (if it may bee) so much as may serue to draw the minde and affections together, and settle some reuerence vpon them, that they rush not forward loosely to matters of another nature, as if with the foole in *Iames* they had forgot the hew whereof they saw themselues to be in the glasse of the word. Secondly, that if it cannot be that they
Prou. 18. 1. separate themselues to the reuiewing of the things they haue heard, Prou. 18. but it must needs bee that they haue to doe with others, as in markets and faires (where yet Sermons are vsuall heard by all sorts) or the like occasions: then let men watch more specially to their hearts and tongues, that neither they breake measure, nor forget the right manner and end of their companying together, but rather take occasion to season others with such things as they lateliest heard, then to driue out one nayle with another (to vse the phrase of Ecclesiastes) and lose all abroad which they should haue carried home for the prouision of their familie. But alas, as for the common sort whereunto shall I liken them? They are like to foolish market men, who hauing stored their purses with money, and their sacks with necessaries, steppe into some lewde house or other, where they finde such companions, as either by gaming, or drunkennesse, or iugling, picke that money out of their purses, and their commodities which they had bought, so that they send them home farre more bare and empty then they came forth. This dealing is bad enough at a market, but worse at a Sermon, or vpon the occasion of religious actions: worse, I say, because the former commonly falls

falls out against a mans will: but the latter wrong, men offer to themselues voluntarily. It is not to be wondered at that there are many such; for as they whom our Sauiour whipt out of the Temple, because they made *the house of prayer a den of theeues,* came not thither to serue God, but themselues: so now many come to the congregation, onely to meete their copesmates, with whom they are to deale, contract, buy and sell, and the like: the Temple is their place to them where they appoint to concurre: their market begins not for the most part, while Gods is done. This point is needfull to be enforced daily, where such meetings are.

How much more then, are the loose and vnaduised gaddings from our owne houses wantonly and wailily without any good end, how much more I say, are they full of danger? For of wilfull goings forth to euill ends and purposes (as in youth and masterlesse persons is to bee seene) I neede not speake, all doe know how odious they are, and what mischiefe they bring with them: the most are easilie deceiued about the other. *Dinah Iacobs* daughter, who went to see the maydes of the countrey, may bee an example to all such. It were meeter for Christians, to learne of *Dauid* in this behalfe, what to answere: when he was of his enuious brother *Eliab* asked what hee made there, (his father hauing sent him thither, namely into the campe) he answered him, is there not a cause? As if he should haue saide, haue I not cause to be here? then I might indeed be iustly found fault with. So let all aduised persons see cause of their being abroad, and that they are where they may defend their being, to the peace of their conscience. The most mischiefes that are now, or haue been, haue come by mens leauing of their calling, and going into company without cause, or hauing cause, by not returning in due time. But of this by the way, more shall be said of it in his proper place.

Gen.34.1.

1.Sam.17.29.

And this be said of the signe, and that which went before it: now is added to the former in these three verses an other thing, and that is a new trouble which befell *Manoah* and his wife, which was this; that because they had seene an Angell of God, therefore he concludeth, they should certainely dye. To whom his wife answered (as more strong in faith, and confident then he) wee shall not dye, and sheweth her reasons, as followeth to bee considered. Thus, as I noted in the story of *Gedeon,* wee see how a new trouble arose to the good man, and so doth daily to Gods seruants, maruelled at by them no doubt, but in great fauour brought vpon them by the Lord, and seene of them also that will trie it out, and receiue it meekely. But of this in the storie now cited.

Vers.22.23.24.

Doct.vers.22.

Psalm.119.71.

The trouble that oppressed *Manoah,* and that caused him to breake out into these words (we shall surely dye) was, for that they had seene the Lord. And by this we see what Angell it was, that was so called in the 21. verse? Euen the eternall word, whom here he calleth God, and in the next verse is of his wife called *Iehoua,* who sometime put on the shape of a man, and appeared to men, as also Angels did. And it is cleare in the stories of the scripture, that after good men had seene God thus, or an Angell, they were exceedingly terrified, and out of heart, and looked for no other then present death: for they knew what God had said to *Moses,* that a man should not see him, and liue: but they misunderstoode the words when they tooke them

See chap.6.14.

them to be meant of his appearing in a bodily ſhape, for many had often ſeene him ſo, and yet liued after: as both *Gedeon* did, and this *Manoah* and his wife, with others. The reaſon of this their feare, reade before in verſe 20.

Doct. 2. verſ. 22. The thing I note here, is this: what great weakneſſes oppreſſe Gods ſeruants oft times, as wee ſee heere they did *Manoah*, of which kinde is deadly feare, doubting, and diſtraction. And who can ſay, euen of the ſeruants of God, that they haue not been wound and wrapped in with ſuch ſore diſquietnes either in ſome ſore affliction, while they haue thought of the vttermoſt that might come to them by it, or when in ſome ſudden and deep paſſion, they haue feared ſome grieuous calamitie to bee comming toward

Note. them? In ſo much, as they haue made this reſolution with themſelues, that they were vndone.

And yet they haue ſeene that God hath giuen an iſſue out of them, and that they haue paſſed ouer their heads as a clowd: and they haue ſafely eſcaped and waded out of them. So that they haue not riſen from deliberate conſideration and grounded knowledge of Gods will, but from feare oppreſſing them, and too vnaduiſed and raſh iudging, and vnbeliefe, and oft times haſted on by melancholy: vnto the which as the beſt are ſubiect, ſo yet they muſt know, that grace and goodneſſe are ſmoothered and ouerwhelmed in them, when they fall deeply into theſe diſguiſing of themſelues, and therefore that they muſt bee carefull daily to watch and pray in faith, that no ſuch oppreſſing and turbulent thoughts and vexations take

Iohn 14. 1. hold of them, euen as our Sauiour hath giuen charge, ſaying: Let not your hearts be troubled.

Doct. 3. And to conclude, ſeeing it falleth out (as in this ſtorie is manifeſt) that good people may oft times be at this point, and are alſo (as *Manoah* was here being plunged into feare) to doubt ſo dreadfully of Gods fauour toward them, all may learne by this, how needfull it is, for them to gather and get all arguments and teſtimonies thereof before trials come, and in the daies of

2. Pet. 1. 10. peace to giue all diligence to make their calling and election ſure, that in

Acts 21. 1. their greateſt need they may be quiet and confident, and not doubt in time of triall. One way is to endeuour to haue a good conſcience alwaies both toward God and men: alſo to be the ſame in ſecret, that wee would ſeeme (when we walke moſt innocently before men) openly to be; with many

Rom. 2. 28. other ſuch fruites of faith: wherein the folly and ſenſeleſſe blockiſhneſſe euen of many of the better ſort may bee marueiled at, that they can in this ſo weightie a matter, and of ſo great vſe vnto them, be ſo careleſſe. Let the reader looke into the ſixth chapter, as I haue already referred him.

Verſ. 23. We heard in the laſt verſe, of the great feare that oppreſſed *Manoah* for that hee had ſeene the Lord. Now it followeth in this verſe what his wife did, when he vttered his feare to her, and in the next and laſt verſe is ſhewed that *Samſon* was borne. When the wife of *Manoah* ſaw her husband ſo troubled, ſhe was better ſtaied: and therefore counſelled, and by reaſons

Doct. verſ. 23. did perſwade him ſo to be alſo. Thus the Lord oft times ſpareth one of his children, and that alſo in the ſame houſe, when hee afflicteth another, and vpholdeth one when another is caſt downe, which is to bee marked of vs. And this he doth, as we ſee here in ſpiritual trials, as well as in bodily health,

and

and visitations: to the end that one may bee an helper and comfort to another. And if he visit all together, which is rarely seene, yet he supplieth their wants some other way, in giuing that grace to the parties asunder, that they were wont to enioy one by the other together. And although this mercie be little obserued, while it is enioyed, (men being readie to aggrauate their crosses, and amplifie them to the highest degree, but blinde in seeing Gods goodnesse in his afflicting them) yet such it is, as might full ill be spared, and when it is, it causeth men to accuse themselues of vnthankfulnes, which hath procured the increase and multiplying of their crosses. We know addition of miserie made him who thought it a small benefit to liue as a sonne vnder his fathers wing, to wish he might be entertained but in the place of a hireling. Luke 15.17.18

To returne to the point againe, this mercifull forbearance of the Lord is euen seene oftentimes in one and the same persons visitation: that although he lay his hand vpon the bodie, yet oft times the minde is free, and the spirit is able to sustaine the bodies infirmitie. Yet I spake not this, as if this were a token of Gods forsaking a man, when he seemeth to afflict on euery side: for then the Lord driues his people to cling to himselfe, when all props and crutches are remoued, lest they should sinke altogether. *Iobs* wife and himselfe were downe together, (as we may say) children slaine, cattell and substance destroyed, friends and kindred alienated. And this wrought (no doubt) strongly vpon his weakest part: but if the Lord had not been on his side, yea in stead of all comfort by wife, or others; he could neither haue resisted desperate impatience, euen at the hearing of the first heauie message that was brought vnto him, nor (much lesse) haue said afterward, Although he kill me, I will trust in him. Therefore although the Lord doe ordinarily thus measure out to his children, that all sorrow comes not at once: yet let none indent with the Lord, that thus hee shall deale alway with him. The Lord is tied to no certaintie, or necessitie in temporall crosses to his best seruants, saue onely to be their God alsufficient, and to minister vnto them the grace which shall be sufficient. Many haue fallen into such streights through infectious diseases, pouertie, trauaile, &c. that they wanted succour and comfort, from the neerest vnto them. Onely the Lord forsakes not his, being neerer to them in miserie, then nature can make the neerest friends to each other. Iob 1. Iob 13.15.

But seeing the woman here, though in regard of her sexe the weaker vessell, was yet the stronger in faith, to incourage her husband when hee fainted, let vs learne, that the husband may not despise his wiues counsell, when God shall grace her equally or aboue him. It is many mens cases to be honoured with such wiues, who by their faith, experience, knowledge, humilitie, innocencie, and such other good gifts of God, might hardly bee wanted, and are much to bee regarded. But they that haue these gifts, let them be farre from thinking on the other side meanely and basely of their husbands, remembring who commandeth them the carriage of reuerence towards them: Husbands againe must reioyce for them, and not scorne to take good by them, vpon a vaine conceit that their wiues will deny them supremacie, or (as many will say) crow ouer them. And yet those that want grace, and be otherwise ill qualitied, let them not leane much to their coun- Doct. 2.

 sell,

ſell, remembring *Ahab* and *Salomon*, in this ſinne, little differing. See verſ. 9. and 10. of this chapter.

3 Her firſt reaſon was this, and it was ſound and good: If God (ſaid ſhe) would haue killed vs, he would not haue receiued our ſacrifice. But he hath receiued it. And how knew ſhe that it was accepted of God? I ſay, ſeeing he it was that bad her offer it, therefore it was acceptable to him. And againe,

Doct. the manner was allowable, for that God had conſumed the ſacrifice with the flame. And we may ſay the like. That if God heare our prayers, and ap-

Acts 10.4. proue of our weake and poore courſe of life, wee may aſſure our ſelues that he loueth vs, and therefore will not in any aduerſitie forſake or caſt vs off.

Ioh. 9.31. But God heareth not ſuch as lie ſtill in their ſinnes. This reaſon of the woman (pithie and concludent) may bee further extended to this ſenſe: that ſeeing God had then allowed and accepted them and their offering, when they had leſſe ground to looke for it, nay were more vnlike to ſpeed of their deſires: then much more would hee now and in time to come teſtifie his loue towards them, hauing paſſed his word to them, and in token thereof, deuoured their ſacrifice. It was his meere goodneſſe (ſaith ſhe) to giue vs any acceſſe at all to his Maieſtie, to offer vp our requeſts and thankſgiuing to him, and to vouchſafe to ſmell a ſweete ſauour from our offering. He needed haue done no ſuch matter, it came from himſelfe, it was his free loue to vs, to reueile himſelfe to vs more ſpecially then to others. Doubtleſſe if hee had meant to ſlay vs, he would haue done it before, and ſpared all this labour: therefore these are arguments rather, that he will reueile himſelfe yet further to vs, and loue vs more dearely, and giue vs more cauſe hereafter to truſt him, and giue thankes to him. So that when ſhe ſaith, He meanes not to kill vs: ſhe implieth more, *viz.* But rather bleſſe vs more abundantly then before, ſo farre will he be from killing vs. And this argumentation of hers, is not vnlike to that of *Pauls*, Rom. 5. 8. If Chriſt dyed for vs being ſinners, much more being iuſtified in his blood, ſhall we be ſaued from wrath. And it ſerues as a preſident for Gods people, in their doubts and temptations, to rouſe vp themſelues from deadly feare, and to gather ſtrength againe to themſelues, by reaſon framed according to this of hers. And thus ſhould euery afflicted ſoule and conſcience reaſon in time of his trouble, and ſay to himſelfe: There was a time when I was out of couenant with God, had no promiſe to ground my faith vpon, and wanted hope: yet then the Lord viſited me in mercie, opened my eyes to ſee, and my heart to mourne vnder the burthen of my ſinne, to come to him for eaſe, and to finde forgiueneſſe. Since that time I haue had much doubting, and been troubled about beleeuing, and repentance, which haue driuen me to proue them, and thereupon I haue reſted, and found peace. Now therefore though I am tempted againe ſtrongly to thinke my eſtate to be vnſound and naught, yet I remember Gods mercies of old, and therein am and will be comforted. If God had meant to forſake and caſt me off quite, hee would not haue proceeded ſo farre with me as he hath done, he would haue let me lien ſtill in darkneſſe, vnbeliefe, hypocriſie, &c. and taken leſſe paines to call me, change me, reforme and gouerne me. Theſe betoken not hatred, but loue, no more then the deuouring of the ſacrifice argued that God would kill *Manoah* and his wife. Doubtleſſe the Lord who did owe me no ſuch fauour at all, ſhewed me me mercy freely, to the end he might shew me more in time to come, and finish his gracious worke in me. And thus I construe all his dealings with me hitherto, his enabling me to pray, and to beleeue, to hate sin, to grow in knowledge, and to inioy his blessing vpon all these to much encrease. Let others say as they will: I will not be so vnthankfull as to think he hath done all this in vaine, that were to mock and deceiue me: but I verily beleeue all was and is for good, and therefore that I shall see more promises fulfilled, till I see the Lord himselfe in the land of the liuing, &c. But here I end.

THE SEVENTIE FOVRE SERMON ON THE XIII. AND XIIII. CHAPTERS OF THE BOOK OF IVDGES.

OF the first reason of *Manoahs* wife, we heard in the last sermon. The second followeth, which was this: he appeared again & again to vs (saith she) & instructed vs what we should do, wherto also she said to her husband, we attended readily (as you know) and beleeued his words: (for thus we must vnderstand her, for as much as the word profiteth not, if it bee not mixed Heb.4.1.
with faith) therefore she concludeth, that they should not dye. And this, which was in her so commendable, is no lesse in so many of vs, as the like is found, but an especiall gift of God, to vphold our selues in *Doct.*
tryals, and then to beleeue God, and giue credit to him, when we haue nothing else to depend vpon. But if we be faint in trouble, then, as *Salomon* Prou.24.10.
saith, our strength was neuer great. And as it was no small trouble to *Manoah* so to doubt, in like maner shall we find it. Further, out of this second reason of hers rightly vnderstood, we learne, that although this is no good consequent, God hath sent his word among vs againe and againe, therefore he will not destroy vs, but loueth vs: yet let vs take it, as it was both meant of her, and practised of both her and her husband, to wit, that they receiued *Doct.*
the message at the mouth of the Angell, and beleeued his word, being confirmed by a signe, and then the reason is good, in this manner: God instructed vs, and we receiued it, therefore he will not destroy vs. And thereafter is our instruction. For if we imbrace and beleeue the doctrine of the scripture, that it is for our vse and benefite, and receiue it, not as the word of Iohn 1.12.
man, but as it is indeed, the word of God, and it be sweet to vs, as the honey 1.Thes.2.13.
to the tast, as the Prophet spake, then may we be sure that we shall not pe- Psal.119.103.
rish. But more particularly, the words of this second reason hauing relation to the Angels message, giue vs occasion to looke backe into the nature and quality thereof. The Lord (sayth she) hath told me, that whereas

 I was

I was barren, I should conceiue a sonne, and that he should be an instrument to saue Israel out of the hands of the Philistims. The time also he hath appointed, the manner of my dyet and abstinence he hath prescribed, adding the reason, because the childe must be a Nazarite. And this he hath not once to me, but the second time to vs both testified, and we haue rested therein, beleeued the report, and receiued a signe. What? shall we now thinke God will kill vs? How then haue we beleeued the message, seeing that if he kill vs, it is not possible that a child should be borne and begotten by vs, and therefore all the other particularities are absurd and friuolous. Or, if we still beleeue the word of God, how can we say, *God will slay vs?* Thus doth this woman bestirre her selfe to settle and restore her husband, by a strong reason drawne from their faith in the promise of God, which could admit no contrarietie, except God himselfe could be charged to be opposite in his performance to his promise. And this shewes how rarely God hath graced this woman, that she (a weake creature) should be able thus to rest her selfe, and vnder-lay her husband, by an argument of the greatest force, which might not be gainsayd, except grosse absurdities were granted, yea impossibilities, to wit, that God might falsifie his word. And in such cases as *Manoah* was, no lesse euidence of truth and proofe would haue serued the turne. It commendeth this duty vnto vs when we shall be tryed in the like manner, to wit, that we suffer not our selues with *Manoah* to forget who it is that hath made vs a promise of forgiuenes, and who
Iohn 10.28. hath assured vs that we shall not perish, but be kept to the resurrection day.
Note. It may be, that in some great and sudden feare, or trouble, the Diuell may quite spoyle vs of the remembrance of the grounds whereupon we haue built our faith, and strip vs naked of the experience of our faith, which in time past we haue had the fruit and benefite of, yea and the particular circumstances also, which haue added great force and likelyhood to the truth of the promiser: as we see in poore *Manoahs* example. But then should we step forth with this woman, and accuse our selues for this our forgetfulnes, as Christ did the two disciples, saying, *O ye dull and slow of heart to beleeue, &c.* and giue no place to our vnbeliefe, struggling against our weakenesse, as a
Note. strong man (whose hands and feet are bound by theeues) to breake the bands and get the vse of our ioynts and limmes, to help our selues withall. Then should we striue to call back the word of God to our minds, whereupon in times past wee built our faith and confidence: and so shame our selues, that wee did not still ascribe to God the honour of beleeuing him, which in times past we haue done. Nay more, we should embolden our selues thus, that we cannot be disappointed of our hope, (whether it be of any deliuerance present, or glorie it selfe hereafter) except God himselfe can be conuinced of falshood, which is impossible, and to say so were blasphemy; for he hath passed his word to vs, we haue been perswaded of it, and had cleare testimonie thereof at sundry times: so that it is as sure our state is good, as that Gods word (so much as in one iot or title) can not be frustrate. In things meerly temporall there may seeme a repugnance betweene the Lord his secret will, and his reuealed: I say, seeme, because men enlarge temporall promises further then they reach. But in spirituall pro-

mises there is neuer any repugnancie at all, where faith is ready at hand to argue with this woman thus: If this should be, God should be contrary to himselfe, which is impossible.

Now in this last verse, (for I referre the next to the Chapter following) Verse 24. the birth of the child *Sampson* is mentioned, as the signe thereof was giuen before by the Angell, and how the Lord prepared him for such a purpose, as to helpe his people against their enemies, by giuing him strength of body, and courage of minde. About his birth, after his parents had receiued a promise from God of hauing such a childe, yet there were many doubts in them, which now we see were all answered.

Euen so we are to know, that though there be many thoughts of heart, *Doct.* and much heauinesse in Gods people about the inioying of the sundry good things that God hath promised them before they be accomplished, yet wee see God in his appoynted time effecteth and bringeth them to passe. It is true, that by reason of the much vnbeliefe that is in vs, yea, though sometime it be well purged out of vs, we are euery while doubting Note. till we obtaine the things which are promised, and yet some of them we liue to see performed; and as certainely shall the rest be also, euen as wee see the promise that a barren woman should beare, came to passe to the parents that beleeued it, that Gods deed and his word may be one. And this is true in the promises of remouing any iudgements or crosses, as by the malice of the wicked, by paine, penury, or other oppressions, or of any blessings temporary, as well as of grace to beare afflictions, or to vse prosperity rightly, or of a good end of our dayes. How many and great promises had *Dauid* of the kingdome? yet through not only the long deferring thereof, but also the admirable and manifold oppositions that he met with, what likelyhood was there that he should euer haue inioyed it? in so much as vpon the sight of them, he brake out himselfe, and sayd, I shall surely dye by the hand of *Saul* one time or other, but yet came it not to passe that he inioyed it, and was stablished in it. Therefore let all those who haue a part in the promises of God, count it their singular priuiledge and honour to haue the Lord of heauen and earth thus bound to them, (as indeed to be out of this compasse is the greatest misery, though a man had all abundance) let such, I say, reioyce dayly that they are reckoned among them whom God hath assured to grace, enlighten, purge, gouerne, vphold, and hereafter glorifie. And let them watch and wait for the performance of Note. these promises, seeing that hee who hath made them, and in whom they are made is no man, that hee should change yesterday and to day, and the same for euer: renewing his mercy dayly. To hold this by faith is the beleeuers crowne: let him beware that none take away his crowne from him.

As the childe grew vp, so it is said, the Lord blessed him with common gifts of the spirit, as it is manifest that this is to bee vnderstood: but it is not so clearely seene that it should be vnderstood of the more speciall gifts also that are peculier to the godly. But yet forasmuch as the word [*blessed him*] is generall to both kindes, and not restrained to one kind only by the holy Ghost, we haue no reason to restraine it, but to take it generally, and the rather, for that the worthy actes he did were fruites of his faith, as we see *Hebrewes* 11. and it followeth after, that *Sampson* was indued with speciall gifts of grace, as well as with courage of minde fit for a valiant man, and bodily strength sutable to pursue his enemies. And this is said of *Samson*, as being a type of Christ, of whom it is said, that hee grew in fauour, &c. (Luke 1. last verse) as in yeeres and stature.

Doct. 1. Iam. 1. 5. Whereby we see, that all good gifts which wee enioy are of Gods free bountie communicated to vs: as the Apostle speaketh. And the graciousest, wisest, or hee that excelleth among men any other way, is beautified with the gifts which he hath, by God who giueth them. No man hath any thing of his owne, but sinne. The heart of man is onely, and alway euill: and as Luke 6. 46. the heart is, so is the man himselfe, that God may be all in all. Therefore it is a sinne to be bewailed in the most not meanely, that they make no haste to sue to him, for all good that they would haue, as wee repaire to the fountaine and spring for water, neither (hauing obtained them) doe praise him for the same, nor vse such blessings to honour the giuer. So that if any should desire or long for any gifts of God that wee haue, wee should not make them fall into an admiration at vs, but they should be sent to the author and giuer of them: and lest wee might take any part of Gods due and Gen. 41. 16. Dan. 2. 30. honour from him, we should answere them as *Ioseph* did King *Pharaoh*, and *Daniel Nabuchadnezzer*, The Lord hath reuealed the secret hereof to vs, but we haue no such wisedome in vs, more then other men. This bee added to that which heretofore hath been said by occasion of the like words before, as chap. 11. 21. 32. and many other places. And so much of *Samsons* birth, the chiefe thing in this chapter, and of the things pertaining thereto: now in this next Chapter I proceed to his mariage.

THE SEVENTIE FOVRE SERMON, CONTINVED IN THIS XIIII. CHAPTER.

Vers. 1. *And the spirit of the Lord began to strengthen him in the host of Dan, betweene Zocah, and Eshtoal.*

2. *Now Samson went downe to Timnah, and saw a woman in Timnah of the daughters of the Philistims, and he came vp and told his father and his mother, and said, I haue seene a woman in Timnah of the daughters of the Philistims, now therefore giue me her to wife.*

3. *Then his father and his mother said vnto him, Is there neuer a wife among the daughters of thy brethren, and among all my people, that thou must goe to take a wife of the vncircumcised Philistims? and Samson said vnto his father, Giue her me, for she pleaseth me well.*

4. *But his father and his mother knew not that it came of the Lord, that hee should*

should seeke an occasion against the Philistims: for at that time the Philistims reigned ouer Israel.

THis first verse is in some translations the last of the former Chapter, but I make it the first of this, as some other also doe. In this storie of *Samson* contained in foure Chapters, we haue spoken hitherto, concerning his birth, and that he was ordained to be an helper to Gods people against the Philistims: now in this next Chapter it followeth (to the further effecting hereof) that wee see how the Lord did strengthen him with further measure of the gifts, wherwith he had blessed him before, and more especially after his mariage. This is generally set downe in the first verse, and particularly laid foorth and declared throughout the whole Chapter, and in the next two following, to wit, the fifteenth and sixteenth. And in this Chapter his mariage is spoken of, seeing one particular occasion was offeted there to him, by which hee was mooued first to set himselfe against the Philistims, namely an iniurie wrought him at his mariage by them. Hereby (I say) he began to be stirred and prouoked against them, and to that purpose the whole Chapter discourseth at large concerning his mariage. *The summe of the Chapter.*

The parts of it are two. One is, how he was strengthened by the spirit of God; in the first verse. The second is, the shewing foorth of Gods gifts, wrought in him by the same spirit, both at the going about his mariage, and at it: and this is throughout the rest of the Chapter. *The parts 2.*

The first part of the Chapter.

HEre it is shewed, that as *Samson* grew in yeeres, the Lord strengthened him, & ofttimes the spirit of ŷ Lord came vpon him, that is, endued him with a burning loue of honouring God, and seeking the good of his people: and this he did, when he abode in his fathers house, who was of the tribe of *Dan*, and dwelt among them in their habitations, in that place which was betwixt Zorah and Eshtaol, which was neere the citie Ioarim. *Vers. 1.*

By this we may see, that the Lord openeth the hearts of those whom he will be serued by, as he did the heart of *Lydia*, and counteth them faithfull, and putteth them in his seruice, as he did *Paul*, and leadeth them by his spirit, as hee did *Samson*, to loue, desire, and endeuour to doe those things that please him, without the which, they should neuer goe about them to any purpose, much lesse be well carried through them. Of what place, state, or degree soeuer men are, thus they must be graced and fitted to their duties, although indeed God doe not now, as in times past, I meane, he dealeth not the same way that he did with *Samson* and many other then. For in those daies he spake to our fathers, and inlightened them after sundrie manners, but in these latter times, the outward meane that he vseth, is chiefly his word truly preached. But the spirit of God hath alwaies wrought grace in their hearts, what other meanes soeuer he hath vsed. But wee looke not for reuelations, nor Angels ministerie now, but while we giue heed to the doctrine of the Lord Iesus, which is plainly, soundly, and powerfully taught vs, the *Doct. Acts 16.14. 1.Tim.1.12. Heb.1.1.*

Lord inlighteneth vs with grace and power of the holy Ghost, and giueth
Ezek.36.26. vs another heart to serue him, (as hee saith in Ezek.36.) then wee had before.

This doctrine is a double linck of that golden chaine, mentioned by the
Rom.8.30. Apostle in these words, Rom.8. [*whom he predestinated, them he called, iustified, and glorified.*] There is no other way to seeke out the certaintie of our election, but by the meanes which serue to our calling: and our calling neuer goeth without the gift of faith, and the spirit of God sanctifying, which is the beginning of our glorifying in heauen. So that as predestination it selfe is manifested in time, by the inlightening and opening the heart to receiue the glad tidings of the Gospell: so when Christ is embraced by faith, the holy Ghost is giuen to the beleeuer, who quickens the heart with spirituall grace, and fitteth such a partie to the worke of God; both inwardly more renuing and changing his nature, and outwardly framing the life to his will. And thus he worketh in all his: though hee giue greater measure to some, (who are deputed and appointed by him, to greater imployment and seruice) I meane hee giueth them more zeale, courage, loue, diligence, constancie, experience, iudgement, and the like. And yet (lest any should erre about this point) know wee, that hee workes none of these without meanes: those therefore whom he will thus sanctifie, hee will also prepare, by stirring vp in them an earnest coueting of these graces, a speciall hunger and thirst after them, an high opinion and account of them, and a singlar affection of loue to them, with a feruent desire of honouring the giuer of them, and a studious endeuour by all meanes both of prayer and labour, to attaine them: yea looke what affections he worketh in such as he will bring to the certaintie and assurance of saluation: the like he preserueth and nourisheth in the beleeuer, for the encreasing of grace, and the inabling him to his seruice in better manner. He suffereth them not to sit still, or take their ease, till these gifts drop into their mouthes: nor to be indifferent, whether they attaine and come by them or no: but he causeth them to giue themselues no rest, till they bee satisfied from time to time with the good things that they desire. And in this sense and respect it is verified which is heere said, All whom God will be serued by, hee will furnish them with gifts for that purpose, as he did here *Samson*.

The second part of the Chapter.

Vers.2.3 WE haue heard in the former verse, how *Samson* was led and strengthned by the spirit of God: now it followeth to see how that grace was set aworke in him: and first in going about his mariage, to the which he was led by God, to make it with a Philistim woman, for it had otherwise been vnlawfull: which being spoken of throughout this whole Chapter following, I will lay foorth in this manner, referring all things about it, to these foure points. First, how he sought his wife, in these 4. next verses. Secondly, how he went to agree with her and receiue her, and what fell out by the way, to the tenth verse. Thirdly, what was done in their meeting at the mariage, which is set down in the eleuenth verse; and this to the twentieth. And lastly, what followed the mariage feast, and namely, that hee paied the

Philistims the apparell and linnen, and how hee tooke occasion by somewhat done there, to begin to vexe the Philistims, and this to the end of the Chapter.

Concerning the first, his seeking of a wife was thus: Hee going to Timnah a towne of the Philistims, he saw a woman there, whom he liked: and he desired his father and mother, that she might be giuen him: but they (as it is no marueile, seeing they feared God) disliked that he should deale with one that was an Idolater. Neuerthelesse hee was earnest for her, they not knowing then that God had moued him to take a wife there, to the end that hee might seeke an occasion thereby against the Philistims, who at that time were Lords ouer Israel. *The more particular summe of these verses to the sixth.*

Now in that *Samson* was growne vp to yeeres fit for mariage, and yet the people of Israel were still in subiection to the Philistims, and lay vnder oppression by them, (as they were before he was borne) wee may see cleerely that they were long held vnder of that calamitie. And so it commeth to passe oft times, that as it is long before God punisheth, so it is long before he cease punishing of his children. And that we may not much marueile at it, we may know that he doth so; first, that his correction may in some measure recompence the abuse of his patience: And secondly that hee may frame vs aright to his minde and liking, which is hard to doe at his first afflicting of vs, and long ere it be wrought in vs, because of our vntowardnes. For a little affliction and short, doth not commonly search vs deeply, nor bring vs very readily vpon our knees, and therefore such great sores must haue deepe tents, by longer continuance of the paine and smart. Some wee reade of to haue been afflicted twelue yeeres, some eighteene in the Gospell: as this peoples forefathers were long vnder the Moabites, and the Canaanites, and sore vexed by them: so famines haue bin continued, three, seuen, and more yeeres: which how vncomfortable, grieuous, and stinging they haue been, we may easily gather, by that which we sustained some few yeeres since, who saw the third yeere of famine to hold and continue, much more pinching and oppressing, then the former two: neither was it seene of the wise, how a fourth yeere could haue been borne, (if it should haue been cast vpon vs) without staruing and famishing to death of a great number of the people; so sore was the want of bread. To speake of particular mens calamities, in which also they haue lien long, it were endlesse and infinite. Let the vse of this doctrine to all of vs both persons and companies, be, not to make full account of present or speedie riddance from any crosse, by the which we are held vnder; and yet not to despaire, though we haue suffered long, not being relieued and eased, but abide patiently, and pray the more feruently: for God, before we shall fall into extremitie, will certainly come with helpe, though we know not how, and not tarrie. More of this the reader may finde in the former Chapters, as 13.1. and others. Doct. vers. 2. 1.King. 17.1. Ruth. 1.4. Acts 7.6.

Now to proceed: It is said in this second verse that *Samson* going downe to Timnah, saw there a woman of the daughters of the Philistims, whom in the next verse it is said, he desired might be his wife. But before I proceede further, a doubt ariseth about this attempt of his whether he did well or no: for this action of his, being in it self against the law of God, on the one side, namely to take a stranger and an Idolater to wife, his parents also being godly *The answering of a doubt in this verse 2. & 3* *Obiect.*

godly and disliking it; and on the other side he himselfe being led by the spirit of God, and renowned in the Epistle to the Hebrewes, among the faithfull of worthie memorie: these (I say) thus considered, breeds a question, how he could not onely like such a thing, but go forward with it, and bring it to passe, and in all the time not once calling himselfe backe. For though it be not to be denied, but a godly person may possibly slippe into a sinne wittingly, yet either he shall see his fault by and by, and dislike it, before he proceed to other duties, saying in repentance; What haue I done? as some did (by the lamentable example of *Ananias* and his wife) feare, or at least repent, when it shall be brought to his remembrance some good time after, as *Dauid* did. But neither of these we reade to haue been done of *Samson*, as though he had been either void of conscience, (which hee was not) or as if God had priuiledged him in that action, yea and (which maketh the question and doubt the greater) his parents themselues, who first withstood him, and disliked his attempt therein, did afterward consent, and his father went with him to the woman, and was at his mariage feast: what shall we say then hereunto? I answere: This thing came of the Lord, that *Samson* might thereby haue occasion to vexe the Philistims. And though the marrying with an vncircumcised woman was generally forbidden, yet the Lord giuing him a personal charge so to doe, (who is aboue his law, and not tyed to it) he offended not therein. As both the whole story following doth proue; where we may see, that God not onely brought it not against him afterward as a sinne, as he did *Dauids* and *Peters* sinnes; and there was as great cause, if *Samson* had been iustly to be charged in this, why hee should haue done the like to him: but God blessed him still afterward, and supported him in great difficulties and troubles raised against him by the Philistims, (except where he ranged and ranne after stolne liberties without his allowance) that all might see apparantly, God to haue been with him herein. And as for his parents, they knew not Gods minde in that matter at the first, and therfore, as they saw themselues bound by dutie, they were against him in his mariage. And in that they did afterward agree to it, who doubteth but that they had it reuealed to them by God, or that *Samson* himselfe told them, that God would so haue it? And all this was necessarie for me to say, for the answering of the doubt, and the cleering of this verse.

Acts 5, 11.

Answ. Iudg. 13 5.

Doct. in vers. 2. and 3.

By that which hath bin said of this point, as we see ŷ Lord may dispense with his owne law, as he did here, and with *Abraham*, where he hath giuen a personall commandement contrary to it: So where he hath done no such thing, know we, that neither wee may looke to be dispensed withall by any other meanes; nor contrary to his commandements, attempt the thing that *Samson* did heere, in seeking a woman, and taking her to wife from among Idolaters, or any other such like. A fact vtterly vnlawfull for vs to doe, and which shall be reckoned against the committer, as a capitall and great sinne. I put both the actions together, of his seeking and liking such a woman, for they are both of one kinde, though in degree one worse then the other (to wit, if he that seeketh such a wife, desist and leaue off, before hee liketh, and before he giueth ouer himselfe thereto:) but else, small difference there is betwixt them.

And great reason there is, that they should bee both odious to vs, for as much

much as there can be no true seruing of God in such matches; but it is to be looked for, that the great sinnes, namely Idolatrie and prophanenes in the one partie, shall deuoure, and as a canker, eate out the goodnesse of the other partie, rather then be auoided thereby: neither is it possible, that they who are so vnequally yoked together, can enioy the chiefe benefits of their marriage, without which the rest are little worth: for whereas they should consent and agree together in all good things, as in conferring, praying, and reading together, and to be of one minde in all other things of like sort and qualitie; they are contrary minded one to another, and draw an vnequall yoke; and what faithfulnes or loue (except it be in dissimulation) can there be betwixt such (especially on the behalfe of the worser partie) through the course of their liues? As they finde it, who will not be held from marrying in Popish kindred, and with persons well knowne to bee vncircumcised? which they finde, to the iust accusation and vexation of them long after. And no marueile, for we being straightly commanded to marry in the Lord, 1.Cor.7.39.
we are thereby iustly challenged for matching with Canaanites in a strange religion, or with such as are impious, and very scandalous in their liues, though of our owne religion, as in the second point of the next verse shall appeare. Let this be added to that which I spake of more briefly, vpon ver. 2. chap. 2. and other places.

Samson hauing broken the matter of his mariage to his parents, they giue Vers 4.
him answere in this verse, and a reason of that answere is rendred by the holy Ghost in the next. In their answere they obiect, the kindred and religion of the woman, that she was a Philistim, and vncircumcised, and doe further tell him, that he ought to take a wife among his owne people. Here his practise, that hee attempteth not the matter, without acquainting his parents with it, when hee liked the woman, doth condemne the common attempts Doct. in vers. 4.
of the most of our age about this matter, who haue so degenerated and turned away from this dutifulnesse of seeking their parents consent in their Note.
match, as *Samson* did, that they haue made an end, and done what they desired, with their wiues, yea many of them are vndone and readie to leaue them, before they begin to breake with their parents about it.

So that, whereas the Lord hath by commanding them to seeke their parents consent, prouided, that they should not rashly and vnwisely cast themselues into danger, and be led (as vnexperienced youth easily is) into depth of euils and sorrow, but well aduised and directed, as well as dutifull, therein to them; they not onely despise the counsell of God, but casting it and their parents helpe and furtherance behinde their backs, they doe therefore right soone both smart and sorrow for their hastinesse and wilfull proceedings. But herein they follow *Esaus* most cursed example, who against the will and liking of his parents, tooke Canaanitish women to be his wiues, Gen. 26.35.
whose sight and conuersation they could not beare nor abide.

A great part of the crossings and vexations in Marriage, doe arise and spring from this fountaine: for as they haue begun amisse, who thus goe to worke in their matches, so they proceed (for the most part) worse, because they neuer feared that God would sit in their light, till after many wearisome and oft complainings, and (sometime also, of their hasty and rash making vp of their marriage, though out of season, and too late) but most of all,

all, of the miseries which they sustaine: after all these, I say, they doe with paine and pensiuenesse end their dayes therein. But of the annoyances in marriage, which come of other causes, I haue no time here to speake. Therefore with one caution and watchword giuing both to parents and children, I end this point: And to them this I giue, that they doe not exercise a tyrannicall power ouer their children (as many doe) to draw them to such marriages, as they cannot yeeld vnto: to these, this I say, that they doe not lightly and hastily cast their affection where it cannot be fastned without great danger, when iust causes may be seene of breaking off their match, and that they proceed in them as God hath commanded, to wit, with their Parents liking and good will, vnlesse they will apparently resist God.

Doct.2. Now out of the answere of *Sampsons* Parents, we learne another thing, that the marriages of Gods seruants ought to be made with such as are like minded to them, not with the vncircumcised, and with those that be of an other and contrary religion, for so they say to him in this verse, *Is there neuer a wife of the daughters of my people, but thou must goe to the Philistims for one?* This to bee necessarily required of them, as commanded by the Lord, Deut.7.3. the seuenth of *Deutronomy*, with other scripture, doth clearely teach, namely, Exod.13.33. that the true worshippers of God may not ioyne themselues with Idolaters, and those that be of another religion. The reason is at hand alleaged by the Lord himselfe, to wit, for that they will be infected and corrupted by them. And besides, how can one hope that such shall be faithfull together, when the Papist, who is an Idolater, is vnfaithfull to God? Looke not in then at the dores of such persons for a wife, though much wealth be there. But forasmuch as many of the professors of our own religion are found to be bad, lewd, and of vild qualities, and those also arising from euil & distempered spirits; here lest any should stumble, and take liberty amisse, let them know, that it is likewise forbidden them of God, to cast themselues away vpon such vngodly ones: and to marry with any that be of their owne religion, if they be such: but they ought especially to looke vnto it, as they will answere it to God, that they be as well marryed in the Lord, as in their owne religion: for that did *Sampsons* parents include and vnderstand, when they vrged him to marry with the daughters of his people, that were not of the vncircumcised, but liued after the law of *Moses*, which was then the knowne truth among them; and this duty of marrying aright was afterward more clearely expressed and set downe by Saint *Paul*, when he giuing liberty to the widow to marry with whom she will, addeth this; that it be in 1.Cor.7.39. the Lord, that is, religiously, and in the feare of God.

For many otherwise professing true religion, are exceedingly disguised in their liues, so as whosoeuer be yoked with them, and meerely lincked to them in this fellowship of marriage or otherwise, must of necessitie either liue in deadly vncomfortablenes, if there be any better things in them then *Note.* in their companions, or else (which is worse) they shall fall to their manners and fashions, or match them some other euill way. So that concerning marriage, (for of that I speake here) it shall behoue them to be wise in so waighty a matter, both themselues, and their faithfull friends, and namely to enquire of, and learne both the disposition, and behauiour of those whom they seeke to make their companyons, that if they be tainted with any

any grosse and notorious vice, or in a high degree giuen to anger, wrath, impatience, currishnesse, stoutnesse, wilfulnesse, or be scoffing spirited, oppressed with melancholy; women particularly, of a stinging tongue, and Parret-like, or exceeding other in any such bad qualities: and so the man in some like manner disguised, I say, if these be, let there be great wisdome and care vsed to auoyd matches of such qualitie and condition.

For although in this act of *Samsons*, God did put in himselfe to leade him, yet otherwise, these speeches of him; that he saw a woman in *Timnah*, (whom he desired to marry, and that she pleased him well) were no way to be allowed in him as sufficient causes to rest in, neither therefore in vs of proceeding therein. The pleasing of the eye, and fancy, are both very dangerous to aduise vs in this case, yea vtterly insufficient, if they goe alone; though where better things accompany them they are allowable, yea and ought to haue place in both the parties, I meane, that both the eye and the heart be pleased, contented, and satisfied. For seeing marriage is for a mans life time, it is meet there should be good liking the one of the other, to the well bearing of all molestations, crosses, and aduersities that may befall couples: yet with this liking, the one of the person of the other, there must also be good graces and qualities, as I said before, to goe therewith. For who knoweth not that the eye is blind, and the heart deceitfull: by the one, sinne is let into the other, as light into the house by the window; and whatsoeuer is done by them alone, without better aduisers, doth surely come to an euill end: as that one example may testifie long agone giuen, that the sonnes of God saw the daughters of men that they were faire, and they tooke them to be their wiues, and so iniquitie multiplied.

Note.

Gen. 6.2.

Now that we haue heard how the parents of *Samson* consented not to him, that he should take a Philistim woman in marriage, the reason is rendred in this verse, that they knew not that it came of the Lord; to the end that the Philistims might first giue occasion to *Samson* by iniury offred him, to be afterward auenged of them the more iustly. So that they followed their knowledge that they had in the law of God, in denying their consent to such a match. And therefore when they knew not that this marriage was of God, they disliked it, as their knowledge in Gods word directed them to doe. And in that they yeelded to it afterwards, they did so when they were made acquainted with the will of God by their sonne, or otherwise, to wit, that God would haue it so, for they would not else haue yeelded, and gone from their professed obedience to that law which forbad it.

Vers. 5.

And their example ought to be our instruction, that as they haue done, so we should know we ought to doe, that is to say, that we follow the light and knowledge which we haue of the will of God. Of the which if we be perswaded that it is the truth we should sinne if we did contrary to it, for we should goe against our consciences in so doing. Thus did *Peter* while he did not yet vnderstand the vision, he followed the knowledge that he had in the law, but after, when he was clearely and fully instructed in the contrary by the vision, and saw that God allowed him so to doe, he then changed his minde, and still did after his better knowledge.

Doct. vers. 5.

Acts 10.28.

It was commendable in *Abimelech* toward *Sarah*, that he would not haue taken her to him, if he had knowne she had been an other mans wife: and

Gen. 20.

alſo that being admoniſhed afterward by God that ſhe was ſo, yet though he were an Heathen, yet he followed the light he had in not touching her, which was the wife of an other man. And *Pilate* alſo did well, while he de-
Luke 23.4. fended Ieſus againſt the Prieſts bitter and falſe accuſations according to the knowledge he had of his innocencie. And this much more well becommeth vs who are Chriſtians, that according to the light we haue of Gods will, ſo we ſhould doe, euery one according to the meaſure that he hath, yet euer ſeeking to be inlightned more and more, and confirmed in our knowledge, leſt wee ſhould be deceiued; and to bee well grounded, leſt our conſcience be erroneous. But to doe againſt it, I meane that which we are perſwaded to be the truth, (which yet is the moſt mens caſe) it threatneth ſore ſuch perſons, that they will make ſo many wounds at length in their conſcience, that they will neuer be kindly healed: See more of this in Chapter 11.35. and the caueat there propounded.

2 Now whereas it is ſaid, the Lord (or *Samſon* by him) ſought occaſion from the Philiſtims to fight againſt them, (and therefore was this marriage ſought by him) though he could many wayes haue plagued them, and defended his people from them; yet ſeeing he would not doe it by open warre, but by one man, he muſt haue a fit occaſion thereto, which by this marriage was offred, that by priuate iniuries done againſt *Samſon* by the Philiſtims, he might more fitly take occaſion openly to vexe and annoy them. And it appeareth that while they were thus vnder the dominion of the Philiſtims, there were certaine couenants made betwixt them, which might not without great danger raſhly be broken by the Iſraelites. And further, *Samſon* was but a priuate man, as farre as any could know, and therefore God would haue a ſufficient occaſion of fighting againſt them to be offred, that if in ſuſtaining any iniury by them, he ſhould againe make any requitall, it might be thought of them that he rather reuenged his owne priuate wrongs, then the publike againſt their nation; although it cannot be denyed but that the Lord might, if it had pleaſed him, haue armed *Samſon* as well as he did *Othniel*, *Ehud*, and other in the like caſe, to haue chaſed and ſubdued them by profeſſing it openly.

Doct. But now, for that which concerneth our inſtruction out of this place, though God would haue *Samſon* doe thus, yet (as by the like occaſion I noted before out of the ſecond and third verſe) wee haue neither warrant nor authoritie to doe the like, ſeeing wee haue a plaine commandement from God of the contrary: to wit, that wee ſhould auoide all occaſions either of doing, or of reuenging wrongs: and that we ſhould ſuſtaine ſome hurt and damage rather, then offer the leaſt, without the which there is no liuing in any peaceable manner among moſt men in this world. He that is fit to beare
Note. iniurie, and ſo to buy and redeeme quietnes thereby, may more eaſily enioy it, then ſome other: but if he be noted for offering wrong, he ſhall haue his loade of trouble in that one reſpect, as he well deſerueth, beſide many other waies: and therefore wee are commanded to follow, and inſue after
Heb. 12.14. peace, (yea although it ſhould flie from vs) and holineſſe, without which no man ſhall ſee the Lord. Whereof ſeeing enough hath bin ſpoken elſewhere, I need not here inſiſt longer therein. And thus much of the firſt of theſe 4. points in this ſecond part of the chapter, that is, of *Samſons* ſeeking a wife.

THE

THE SEVENTIE FIVE SERMON ON THE XIIII. CHAPTER OF THE BOOKE OF IVDGES.

Verſ.6. *Then went Samſon and his father and his mother downe to Timnah, and came to the vineyards at Timnah, and behold a young lion rored vpon him.*

7. *And the ſpirit of the Lord came vpon him, and hee tare him, as one ſhould haue rent a kid, and had nothing in his hand, neither told his father and his mother what he had done.*

NOw followeth the ſecond generall point in this ſecond part of the Chapter, to wit, firſt, the double iourney of *Samſon* to this woman, which was to bee his wife: (in both the which, hee was accompanied with his father and mother:) whereby it appeareth that they knew Gods will then, about his marriage, better then they did before: and ſecondly, what fell out in both iournies by the way; and this to verſ.11. His firſt going to her at Timnah, with that which fell out therein, is laid foorth in theſe two verſes, and that is this: That as he went with his father and mother, (he going aſide from them out of the way) a young lion met him, roring on him, and the ſpirit of the Lord came vpon him, and though he had nothing in his hand, yet he rent him in peeces: but hee told not his father and mother what he had done.

And by this that fell out by the way, God would giue to *Samſon* a proofe of the ſtrength that he meant to endue him with afterward, that hee might be bold to looke for power to doe greater things. And now, this being ſaid, it remaineth that wee obſerue more particularly that which concerneth vs, out of this ſtorie. And firſt this: that when his father and mother vnderſtood that his mariage pleaſed God, they went downe with him to the woman whom he ſhould marrie, to finiſh the agreement betwixt them, and to countenance and further him euery way in it. So parents, when they ſee *Doct.* that their childrens attempts, either that, or any other way, bee pleaſing to God, they ſhould be ready to helpe and free them by all meanes from delay, and trouble and griefe thereby, as much as in them lieth; euen as in the contrary they are bound to croſſe and hinder them, leſt if they ſhould allow them in their euill courſe, their childrens ſinne, beſide their owne bad example, ſhould be chiefly laid to their charge. And this aſſiſtance of theirs vnto *Samſon*, is further mentioned in the 8. verſe of this Chapter: therefore let this onely bee here noted, that parents be very warie leſt they turne that authoritie and power of theirs, which God hath giuen them for the good and benefit of their children, that they turne it not (I ſay) vnto the deſtruction or damage of them, by laying the bridle in their necke, and so embolden them to euill, by their allowance, counsell, or example.

2 Now in that a young Lion is said to haue met him, (not a whelp) which had been like to haue fawned on him, and played with him, but one that was full growne, (for the word signifieth one of full growth) and therefore neither pleasant, nor kinde, as sometime they be, being as yet not growne: in that (I say) such an one being cruell and fierce, did set vpon *Samson*, as the nature of them is to doe; which thing so falling out, suppose we in that case, that he had gone about any vnlawfull businesse, behold what ill successe had followed it? Euen as we reade for example, how it fell out to the man

1. King. 13. 24. of God, who came from Iuda to reproue the Idolatrie of *Ieroboam* at Bethel, who, seeing he transgressed the commandement of God afterward, in going into the old Prophets house to eate bread, (which God had forbad him to doe) loe, a lion met him, when hee was gone out of the towne, and slew him.

And it was an apparent correction of God vpon him for that; for though in other things he had obeied God to his high commendation, yet because in that one thing he had done contrary to the charge giuen him, (he being told by the old Prophet of Bethel that he might do it) we see what an heauie iudgement befell him. It teacheth, that we ought to see in all the manifold actions of this life, that we looke wee haue good warrant for the taking in hand of them, and the going about them, lest we meete (I say not) with a

1. King. 21. 20. lion, but with the Lord crossing of vs, worse then a lion could hurt vs, some way to our little liking in the middest of the hot pursuite of our desires, and that either with outward resistance of vs, as he did *Ahab* by *Elias*, when he was going to take possession of *Naboths* vineyard; or with inward wound of conscience, as most commonly hee vseth to doe, to such as haue know-

Rom. 2. 4. ledge; or with hardnesse of heart, which alwaies hindreth and keepeth away repentance. And by occasion of *Samsons* iourneying out of Iuda to Timnah of the Philistims, I say more particularly, let such as trauaile, (whether within the land, or beyond seas into forreine countries) see, that their errands are lawfull and warrantable, not expresly crossing the Lords charge,

1. King 2. 43. (as that of *Shemei* did *Salomons*) lest although they scape *Shemei* his punishment, yet a worse befall them. Remember *Dina*, and *Gehazi*. Nay, see they not onely that their businesse be good, but look they also that their affection be well and orderly carried thereto: otherwise their seeking after noueltie, curiositie, vanitie, (I speake of them that doe so) or their sinister intent any other way, will marre their action of trauailing, be it neuer so lawfull. And as that is nourishment to one creature, which is anothers bane; euen so is trauaile to sundrie sorts of men, though to some other it be good and profitable. It is apparant that many trauellers who went out with no euill purpose, yet being vnarmed against euill, and not strongly resolued to depart from it, haue rushed vpon the pikes, tempted God, cast themselues vpon streights, and indangered their bodies, liues & consciences manifold waies. I speake to such as professe to haue God the directer of their waies: as for others, let the dead bury the dead. That is a iourney well vndertaken, which a man can take in faith, and sanctifie it by prayer, and so commit himselfe therein to Gods protection and blessing. And surely if we goe otherwise to

worke,

worke, wee are as able to beare meekely and patiently; either disappointment, ill successe, or any hard accident that shall befall vs, as wee are to encounter a Lion, if he should meete vs. But beside these vntimely and vnseasonable trauailings abroad, there are other no lesse dangerous at home, or neere at hand: and among the rest for example sake, when the Sabbath is abused to wanton and waily gaddings, to stage-playes, gaming houses, drinkings, on which yet by Gods commandement the most lawfull common actions and ordinary businesse ought not to bee done, which may bee done on other daies. This is one instance of many other wicked iourneyings and trauailings on that day, which are as vsuall with the ill disposed, as it is ordinary among the better sort to heare the word preached, or to vse any other religious exercises. But although such persons haue no stoppe in their way to turne them backe, neither doe meete with the opposition that *Balaam* did, to hinder and crosse their desires; yet they shall reape the wages of their iniquitie, as hee did, and wish they had kept at home, and been free from such company, with many stripes.

The meeting of a Lion by *Samson*, which was (as wee haue heard) with the perill of his life, yet was to him, as God did vse it, an occasion to trie, declare and shew foorth Gods power and strength in him, which should else haue been hidden. For the spirit of the Lord stirred vp in him an extraordinary gift of might and manhood, more then is to bee found in the strongest person, whereby he hauing nothing in his hands, did yet teare the Lion in peeces, one part and member from another, as if it had been a young kid or lambe. *Vers. 7.*

By this example wee may learne, that though the crosse be to vs as fearefull, when we see it comming toward vs, as a Beare or a Lion is to meet with, yet the Lord who loueth vs, as hee did *Samson*, doth vse by his quickning grace, to hearten vs against it, so that wee finde it to turne to our great good and benefit. But let this be marked which I say: that God doth by his speciall grace bring it thus to passe, not that we should looke for it by extraordinary meanes, though he dealt so with *Samson*, but wee are to beleeue and waite certainly for it, because he hath promised it, and by the helpe thereof, we shall not need to doubt, but that such strength shall be granted vs, as shal put away feare, or at least abate and restraine it: but without that help from God, we shall feare and be troubled, when wee doe but heare of the crosse or danger, as at the sight of a lion, yea and be disquieted and ouercome with the heauinesse that we haue for it, as if we should meete a Beare. *Doct.* *Note.*

We haue too many examples of this weaknesse and feare in Gods deare people, as in the seruant of *Elisha*, who when hee saw an armie of Aramites compassing the house, cried out, and said, Alas (master) what shall wee doe? So in the Disciples the like is to bee seene, who through their vnbeliefe, thought they had seene a spirit, and were sore afraid, when yet that which they feared was Iesus their Master, comming toward them, to comfort thẽ: So that we of our selues indeed, are most timerous euen when we haue little cause, much more otherwise: but yet when great afflictions oppresse vs, God being with vs, as I haue said, we are able through his might, to do great things, as the Apostle saith, I am able to doe all things through the helpe of Christ, who strengtheneth me. Yea so great oddes is there betweene one *2. King. 6. 15.* *Matth. 14. 26.* *Phil. 4. 13.*

and the ſame man oppreſſed with feare, though for a ſmall trouble, when he
Note. is taken on the ſudden, and with a great one, when hee is prouided for it, as betweene the heate of the leaſt candle, and a greateſt fire. He that fainted at the one, when he was weake in faith, eſcaped and ouercame the force of the other, being aſſiſted therewith, as hath at large been ſhewed in *Gedeon*, at one time afraid to goe and behold that campe, which after hee blanckt not both to encounter, and to conquer.

2 And this whole ſtorie of the Lion, all that conſider, may vnderſtand, that it tendeth directly to this end, to prepare and make *Samſon* able to beare the diſpleaſure and enmitie of the Philiſtims, which was afterward raiſed vp againſt him, the Lord giuing him ſtrength for that purpoſe: and that it might miniſter matter for the riddle which he did after propound to them, whereby they did ſore prouoke him. By the firſt, learne, that when God indueth men with excellent gifts betimes, (as he doth many) he thereby declareth, that hee will both double and multiply them in thoſe perſons, and alſo vſe them to ſerue him to ſingular purpoſes, if their proceeding be not hindred
Note. by ſome ſiniſter practiſes of theirs, to ſtand in their way, or by the diuell and his inſtruments ſubtilitie, diuerting his good gifts to bad purpoſes. This is apparent by that which God did worke in *Samſon* in his firſt yeeres of diſcretion, and when hee was yet but young, compared with that which followed afterwards when he made ſtrip and waſte of the Philiſtims. Euen ſo when he will worke (I ſay) in more ſpeciall manner by ſome in future age, he will giue ſignes thereof in younger yeeres; which is notably to be ſeene in *Dauid*, who in the great danger he was in by *Goliah*, (when *Saul* told him that he was but a boy, but hee whom he vndertooke to fight with, to wit *Go-*
1. Sam. 17. 36. *liah*, was a man of warre from his youth) anſwered vnto *Saul*, Thy ſeruant kept his fathers ſheepe, and there came a Lion, and likewiſe a Beare, and tooke a ſheepe out of the flocke; and I went out after him and ſmote him, and tooke it out of his mouth, and when hee roſe againſt me, I caught him by the beard, and ſmote him and ſlew him. Therefore this vncircumciſed Philiſtim (ſaid hee) ſhall be as one of them; ſeeing hee hath railed on the hoaſt of the liuing God. And the like is manifeſt in *Samuel*, whom becauſe the Lord meant to make a more then ordinary inſtrument of his glorie, in the function of both Iudge and Prophet: therefore he reuealed himſelfe familiarly by viſions vnto him, in his tender age, yea before he ſeemed to be of diſcretion, and ripenes of yeeres and iudgement, the Lord began that work in him early, which in time to come, he meant to accompliſh in great meaſure. So that we ſee that the religious and prudent training vp of young ones in the knowledge of God, and of themſelues, and good literature, (being the ordinarie meanes now adaies to promote this worke of God in time to come) is not to be deſpiſed: much leſſe the towardlineſſe of ſuch as whom God in their youth ſhall begin to grace aboue others, is to bee ſnibbed and checked, as the practiſe is of ſome brutiſh perſons to ſcorne and reiect ſuch, ſaying: Tuſh, what reckoning make yee of ſuch? A young Saint, an old Diuell.

This truth is exemplified in many young perſons at this day, who by good education doe ſhew very great towardnes: as ſchollers in the Vniuerſitie in their learning, and other in the countrey, both young men and

damzels

damzels in such things,as wherein they are trained vp,and both sorts in the practise of Christianitie farre differing from the common sort of youth, who are saucie,disobedient,and prophane,and giue fearefull signes of mischiefe working,and sustaining miserie afterward. And out of them hee raiseth excellent instruments, some fit for Magistracie, and some in other places to doe much good in the Ministerie,not to be teachers onely, but also fathers begetting many children to God,and others to bring foorth much fruite to his glorie. And herein that prophecie is verified,that in those daies the Lord would powre out his spirit vpon all flesh; not old men onely, but euen the tenderest, young men and maidens. A fruite (no doubt) of that vnction of Christ Iesus the arch-Prophet of his Church, who began at the age of twelue yeeres to giue demonstration of strange forwardnes, for wisdome and grace, because in his riper yeeres hee was more fully to declare that he was annointed with the spirit without measure. *Acts 2.17.* Luke 2.52.

These therefore whom I spake of before,if they vse well the gifts of God, as *Dauid* and *Samuel* did,which they receiued in their youth,shal (after they haue gotten experience) see how God prospereth and inlargeth them to their sound and great reioycing,and the good of many other, and helpe to to cast downe, and destroy the workes of darknesse,and of the diuell,in places where they bee not too strongly resisted and set against,by such as loue darknesse more then light, because their deeds are euill. But if after they haue begun well, and in their younger yeeres giuen great hope,if (I say) they comming further into the world, shall be dazled with the deceitfull beautie of it,as though they had found a btter portion then grace, and shall be blindfolded with profit, pleasure, and promotion, so that thereby they cannot do their former workes,they shall complaine too late (when all these must forsake them) that they were once in the way to do well,if they could haue seene it. And all may see, that howsoeuer they woond out of the diuels hands in the first maine temptation,wherein they were in danger to be brought to despaire, and in the next also, which tended to bring them to presumption; yet that he hath preuailed against them in the third,about the glorie of this present world,and thereby hath deceiued them. Note. Matth.4.8.

And thus much be said of the first thing which I mentioned now last in this verse,to wit,of the gifts of God appearing in *Samson*, in the first yeeres of his discretion: of the second, namely, that this storie doth minister matter of the riddle afterwards,I will speake in place, where I shall haue a fitter occasion offered,namely in the fifteenth Chapter.

Lastly,in this verse in that it is said, hee told not his father nor mother of 4
this that hee did to the Lion, it shewed both that neither hee himselfe was vainglorious, (for then not onely they, but other should soone haue heard thereof) but also it appeareth,that he saw no cause nor end of vttering it to them at that time. So let vs learne when to speake, and when to hold our peace,and to be silent, euen when our speaking can doe no good; or more hurt then good, or when it cannot but doe hurt. And by this rule, which guideth vs how to be silent,and when; let vs also learne how to speake, and when,namely, when wee see it may doe good,and no hurt,or more good then hurt. The same is repeated of him in verse 9. and agreeth with that which I haue often vrged in the generall, to wit, that wee should shew all

godly wisdome as well as vprightnes in our doings: as our Sauiour Mat. 11.
Math. 11. 7. would not commend *Iohn Baptist* before his Disciples were gone, lest it should haue as much hindred them, as profited the people.

Vers. 8. *And he went downe and talked with the woman those things that were pleasing in the eyes of Samson.*

9. *And within a few daies when he returned to receiue her, he went aside to see the carkeis of the lion: and behold, there was a swarming of Bees, and hony in the body of the lion.*

10. *And he tooke thereof in his hands, and went eating, and came to his father and his mother and gaue vnto them, and they did eate: but he told not them that he had taken the hony out of the body of the lion.*

11. *So his father went downe vnto the woman, and Samson made there a feast: for so vsed the young men to doe.*

12. *And when they saw him, they brought thirtie companions to be with him. Then Samson said to them, I will now put foorth a riddle vnto you: and if you can declare it me within seuen daies of the feast, and finde it out, I will giue you thirtie sheetes, and thirtie change of garments.*

The sense of verse 9. NOw it followeth according to the diuision made in the second verse of this second part of this Chapter, how *Samson* went to agree with the woman, and his father and mother with him, as we heard they did in the seuenth verse: and that his father, when they came thither, did that which pleased him in concluding the match with her. For that is the sense of this first of these verses: to wit, that where it is said, he did speake the things that pleased *Samson*, we should vnderstand that to be meant of his father, that he talked with the woman to the good contentment and liking of his sonne: also heere is shewed, what fell out at this their next going vp in the way when he went to receiue her, and this to the 11. verse.

Verse 8. But here I must a little stay the reader, by occasion of a doubt arising out of the 8. verse, to wit, in that it is said, *Samson went aside to the carkeis of the lion, and tooke hony out of it.* For seeing he was a Nazarite, as appeareth by cap. 13. 5 and chap. 16. 17. it may bee thought that *Samson* either sinned against the rule of the Nazarite, or else had a speciall dispensation to breake it. Touching the rule, wee reade Numb. 6. and particularly vers. 6. that it forbad *comming at a carkeis*. And yet we should be vncharitable in casting the blame of wilfull sinne vpon *Samson*, and as rash in iustifying any dispensation, seeing neither of both are mentioned or intimated in the text. The answere is, *Samson* neither sinned against the rule, nor was dispensed with by God: and the reason is, He was tied to no such rule. And seeing it will be demanded still, How then could he be a Nazarite? I answer againe, that we must make a difference betweene Nazarites: Some were borne Nazarites, and by an immediate ordaining of God, separated to this profession. Others voluntarily vndertook the vow according to the Ceremonie. Both sorts had something common, both the profession of a more strict and pure worship of God, and some ceremonies annexed thereto. But they differed herein, that as the former sort were necessarilie tied to that estate, and that for their whole life, so they had priuiledge allowed them to be exempt from some

ceremoniall

ceremoniall obseruances which the vowed Nazarites were tied to. For as the vowed Nazarite was voluntarie, and for a certaine space of time onely, so for that time he was bound indifferently to all the Articles mentioned in Numbers. *Samson* then (I say) was no voluntarie or vowed, but a borne and ordained Nazarite extraordinarily. And therefore though it be probable that hee was tied to more then his long haire, as namely to abstaine from strong drinke, (as his mother was) yet it is cleere that he was free from this ceremonie of touching the dead and sundrie other. Of the like ordination was *Iohn Babtist*, as by the text appeareth, Luk.1.15. This answere is applied by them who hold our Sauiour to haue been a Nazarite (not by the place of his education onely, Matth.2.23. but by profession also) to salue the obiections of his drinking wine, comming to the dead, &c. but how soundly I will not here enquire: onely this I say, if that could be proued that our Sauiour was a professed Nazarite, then those obiections hinder nothing, because they onely oppugne the vowed, not the ordained Nazarites. But of this, thus much. Now I proceed to the doctrine.

First, here by *Samsons* father and mother going with him to conclude the mariage, it teacheth, that when parents see that the match which their children vpon iust occasion propound to them, and desire their consent in, is of the Lord, and pleasing to him, they ought (as I said before) to be ready to further and accomplish it in the best manner, and with the best conditions that they can: so their children may in reuerence desire them, that seeing God doth allow and blesse them herein, that they would not hinder them. But if they make their matches so that their parents and guardians may not, neither dare be seene in them, as it is a great blemish to themselues, so it is iust that they bee both held backe by them, and their attempt staied therein; let them therefore submit themselues to the Lord, and giue their parents the honour that is due to them, lest they make them most strangers in this work, who should be chiefe doers in the same, and by that they may know, that their prospering therein shall be small. But for this point, let the reader see that which I haue noted of *Caleb*, chap.1. *Doct.*

After *Samson* and the woman had agreed about their mariage, hee went againe afterward and tooke her to bee his wife: and what fell out in the way as he went is shewed. By the first of these two, in that he married her afterward and tooke her for his wife, when he had now first consented with her to liue together as man and wife, and that with his parents agreeing thereto; all these doe proue that the vniting of one man and one woman together in mariage, is a solemne ordinance of God, and appointed by him, and so it is likewise blessed by him, where hee is obeyed in it: and that the loose and brutish liuing together otherwise, (as one man with many women, &c.) is most vnfitting a Christian, and contrary to Gods ordinance, and bringeth foorth most noisome euils: euen as the parting and separation of one of the married persons from the other, saue for adulterie, is odious. And this of the first of the two points be said briefly, seeing occasion is offered to speake more particularly of it elsewhere. *Verse 9.10.* *Doct.*

The second thing in these two verses, to wit, what fell out in the way as he went, was this that *Samson* went aside, as he trauailed to his marriage, to see the carkeis of the lion which he had rent in peeces, and what was become

come of it. And hee found in the body of it, a swarme of Bees, and hony: a strange thing to behold, for those creatures loue the sweetest places, and not those which are vnsauourie. But the Lord had so brought it to passe, and that his father and mother should eate thereof, and yet not know from whence it came, to the end that it might minister matter for the riddle that he propounded at his mariage, whereby occasion arose to him of pursuing the Philistims. Thus God prepared the hony in the body of the lion, and directed him to finde, eate, and giue it to be eaten.

Doct.2. in verse 10.11. By this that I haue now set downe in these two verses, wee may see, that when God pleaseth either to punish or blesse, as here hee did both, (for hee intended a blessing to Israel, and a punishment to the Philistims) he will vse meanes for the effecting of the same, though wee see not alwaies how, and extraordinarily, rather then they shall faile, and not come to passe. And so Exod.14.22. when he purposed to deliuer his people out of *Pharaos* bondage, and none saw how it could bee, they being hedged in (as it were) on euery side, hee made a way (we see) for them thorow the red sea, as it had been by the high way, and drie ground.

Euen so be we perswaded, that he hauing appointed and purposed to do vs good in this life, who feare him, and to bring vs well through all difficulties, as he hath promised, and to finish our course with ioy; he will most certainly doe it, though wee see not how, but it may seeme oft times to vs impossible, for he hath many waies to bring his will to passe. Euen as hee did, 2.King.6.17. when he deliuered *Elisha* the Prophet from the armie of the Aramites, by an armie of heauenly souldiers, and when hee promised great plentie of corne by his Prophet on the next day, when yet at that present they were almost famished, he did (I say) performe it, and that by the meanes of foure leprous 2.King.7.16 persons, in so much that a great man neere to the King affirming, that although God should raine downe corne out of heauen, it could not bee so; yet he liued and saw it so, though he liued not to eate of it, euen as the Prophet had told him. And so be we perswaded that whatsoeuer he seeth expedient for vs, he will bring it to passe, though we see not how, hee hath waies enough; and that which he doth not for vs, wee must willingly submit our selues to want and forgoe, as knowing that it were not good for vs to haue it Note. granted. Whereas wee in our troubles and feares either about grace to bee granted vs, or deliuerances to bee wrought for vs, doe either smoother our faith, by feare and despaire of helpe, or breake foorth into open murmuring and discontentednes, which in time causeth vs to shift and make way for our selues by vsing vnlawfull remedies. And by this meanes we double our affliction, both for measure and continuance oftentimes: or else shake it off, as the asse doth his burthen, not staying Gods leisure, till hee ease vs: so that when the next commeth, we are vnfitter for it, then for the former. Now if Note. we (being in our selues most shiftlesse) could behold that alsufficiencie of power which is in God, and the varietie of meanes which his wisedome can worke by, for our deliuerance, this confused and distrustfull behauiour of ours should in great part be cured. Especially, seeing whatsoeuer power he hath in him to succour vs, his distressed seruants, his loue setteth him on worke to shew and exercise it, and all for our exceeding benefit and good. 1.Sam.23.27. *Dauid* saw not before *Sauls* comming against him, by what meanes God

would

would rescue him, neither was it needfull seeing he had promised so to doe: howbeit he waiting by faith the issue, he was deliuered, and so saw how the Lord wrought it for him: and thereby gathered, that so hee was able and ready to do often in the like danger, rather then his promise should faile and be falsified. Thus wee should hearten on our selues to waite with pacience through all difficulties, till we haue finished our course with ioy. Note.

2. And in that he tolde not this either to his father or mother, which was very like he should haue done, (it being a strange thing to finde honey in the carkeis of a Lyon) and we are all giuen to tell such things to our friends, as are seldome heard of, and are like to be wondred at, as newes very welcome to them, yet I say, in that he signified it not vnto them, it was wisely done of him to conceale it, whether he then thought to make a riddle of it, or no, it is vncertaine, as after he did: for then, if he had told it to them, it might easily haue been knowne to many, and so it had been like to haue by some meanes been disclosed to and among the Philistims, as wee see it was afterward, when he tolde it to his wife onely. It confirmeth vs in the former doctrine out of the seuenth verse: namely, that we be very wary to conceale things that need not bee vttered, especially secrets, when wee see no good can come thereby, but by concealing them there may. And because it is not easie for a man to foresee euery inconuenience which may come of vnseasonable speech; therefore it is the wisest way for vs to cut off al talke, whereof wee see not some good reason to moue and warrant vs to vtter it. Now if there grow any inconuenience thereby, notwithstanding our care and respectiuenes, wee shall haue the lesse to accuse vs, as we see in *Dauids* fact, 1. Sam. 21. I meane in his requiring the shew bread and armour of *Golia* from *Abimilech* in the presence of *Doeg*, necessitie draue him to aske it, and Christ defended the fact, and therefore hee had lesse cause to bee troubled, though much hurt arose by it. To them that obiect, that *Samson* tolde the riddle to his wife, which was more dangerous then to haue opened it to his parents: be this taken for an answere, that he offended greatly in so doing. And we may learne by it, that we may possibly shew wisdome in some part of our life, whereof yet wee may faile, without great heed taking, afterward. 1. Sam. 21. 6, 9.

We haue heard how *Samson* went to take his wife, and what fell out by the way. Now followeth the third point (in this second part of the Chapter) to wit, their meeting to accomplish his mariage, and what things were done thereat, and they were especially foure. The first, he made the Philistims a feast, in this verse. Secondly, what the Philistims did to him: verse 12. That is, they prouided thirtie companions to be with him; Thirdly, *Samson* propounded a riddle to them, with condition what they should haue, if they could tell him the meaning of it, within seauen dayes, and contrariwise: and this to the middest of the 15. verse. Lastly, how they laboured to know the meaning of it, but could not, till the seauenth day, and then they tolde it to him, hauing gotten it of his wife before: and this to the twentieth verse. Vers. 11. to 20. *The summe generally to ver. 20*

The first of these 4. things mentioned in this verse, was, that he made them a feast: his father going downe with him againe, (no doubt) to be a comfort to him in that strange place, and to countenance him, as I haue noted *The sense of vers. 11. particular.*

ted twice before in verse *6.* &c. And it is added, that *Samson* did that according to the custome of the place, for so the yong men were wont to doe at their mariage. Here by this custome (not vnlawfull in it selfe) we see it hath been an vsuall thing to call friends together at such times of marrying their kindred, to feast and reioyce one with another. It hath been the practise of the good, as well as of the bad: neither is it our commendation, simply to shunne the ciuill or indifferent actions of common men, and the multitude; but this indeed is to bee looked to, that wee conforme not our
Rom.12.2. selues to the euill manner of vsing them in the age we liue in, Rom. 12. And
Ioh.2.1. as for this one custome and fashion of feasting, as *Samson* vsed it, so Christ was present at a marriage feast in Canan a towne of Galile, where many were met together, and he approued their feasting.

Gen.29.22. And as for the bad, *Laban* made a feast, and called together the men of the place, when he gaue his daughter to *Iacob* to wife. So also did the young men of the Philistims vse to doe at such times. The action therefore hauing been the practise as well of the godly as of bad people, in it selfe is indifferent to be vsed, and as it may be done lawfully, so it may also be omitted, because wicked men haue vsed it, who doe nothing well: and therefore as it falleth out for the most part, that the greatest number that meete at feasts are none of the best, it may be seene oft times more conuenient to omit the meetings of such, lest much wickednesse should be committed by them, and lewdnes in tongue and behauiour, to the dishonour of God, which is the more easily done, when they haue well filled themselues.

Or if it cannot be altogether let passe, yet a smaller company would bee gathered, especially of such of our friends as are of the best sort of people; and for the other, if they must needes be there, they should so bee placed at the table, that as few of them be set together as may be, and that it bee obserued, that they may bee soone interrupted and broken off, (by such as sit neere and are better minded and wise withall) if they should fall in any offensiue behauiour. As for our Sauiour Christ, hee gaue good example at the marriage where he was present, and took occasion, by the miracle which he wrought there, to hold them occupied in good talke, and to turne the people away from the contrary; and we as farre as we may see our companie to be to good ends, as that we may be like to doe good, or take good, so and thereafter to vse it. And this be said of this point here, hauing before touched it, and hauing occasion to speake fullier of it afterwards.

2 Further, by this that is said here, that the young men vsed to make a feast at their marriage, and therefore *Samson* did so, we see the force and strength of custome how it preuaileth, and is as the Medes and Persians law was, that is, not easily broken. Such a custome that was, that the people at their desire had a prisoner deliuered & set free to them at the Passeouer: by meanes
Matth.27.15. whereof they asked *Barrabas* a murtherer, rather then Iesus. Such customes as are bad are continued still, whereby disorder and reuell is maintained, euen fruits of darknesse, into the which the people is so reuited, that though the preaching of the Gospel hath bewraied and brought to light the shame and odiousnes of them, yet they can hardly bee broken almost in any places. As the prophane spending the greatest part of the Lords Sabbath in carding, drinking, feasting, and such like abomination, and other such, in

euery countrey after the manner thereof, making it a day rather held to *Bacchus*, or *Saturne*, then the Lord. And the same may be said of the riotous and intemperate mispending of the twelue daies, and certaine other daies in the yeere, farre worse passed, then (I say not Papists) but euen Heathens oft times vse to doe. And except the putting downe of Faires, that were wont to be kept on the Sabbath (which with much ado were some yeeres agone abolished) I remember not many more ill customes ouerthrowne and put out of vse. As for the ouerthrowing of many blind, dangerous, and disordered Alehouses, (for there is vse of the honest, for the necessitie of trauellers) it hath indeed very commendably been gone about by some honourable and worshipfull persons; but yet through the vpholding of them by some gentlemen and others, to their small credit, they remaine still, to the working of much euill and mischiefe thereby in most places. As for those that are good customes (to say no more of the bad) they ought; and other that be not hurtfull, may be suffered and continued. And in that respect (I take it) did *Samson* here, after the manner of the young men, make a feast to the Philistims.

But to proceed, they being on both sides met at the marriage, I meane Vers.11.
Samson and his friends on the one part, and the Philistims on the other, the holy storie sheweth what the Philistims did: to wit, they tooke thirtie yong men (for they had choice enough) but the friends of *Samson* being strangers there, could not command such a number, neither is it like that the Philistims would haue liked it: so that it cannot be meant of *Samsons* friends, that they took thirtie men to countenance and honour him, but of the Philistims, who when they saw what manhood and stomacke was in him, and that they had neede to beware of him, they gaue him thirtie men (pretending they did it to honour him) to attend vpon him, which indeed they did for feare of him.

In these Philistims we may obserue two things: the one is, their policie: the other, the care that they had of, and ouer thẽselues, when they thought there was danger towards them, and cause of feare. Policie (I say) was in them, for that when they feared, they would not seeme so to doe, but couered it with a faire cloake, namely in appointing thirtie companions to him, as if they meant to set him foorth and countenance him. This the light of nature did teach them, to keepe themselues from danger and harme. Neither were the meanes euill that they vsed for that purpose, though it must be granted, that it was all one to them whether they were or no.

So much more we being more cleerely and fully inlightned by the writ- Doct.1.
ten word of God, may in great perill not seeme to feare, when it can doe vs no good (but it may put vs to reproch:) but vse such lawfull helpe, as wee haue at hand, to repell the same, though we let it not appeare. Euen as *Paul* did, who when hee was in great ieoberdie of his life by the Pharisies and Sadduces, and like to bee rent in peeces betwixt them, hee bewraied not to them what hee feared, but vsed that helpe that God shewed him, that was
this policie, that he said with a loud voyce among them that he was a Pha- Act.23.6.
risie: whereat there was a sudden diuision of his aduersaries, the one sect being against the other; and the Pharisies holding with *Paul* against the Sadduces. Onely let no man (by this that I haue said) iustifie his shifting and

vnlawfull policie in bringing himſelfe out of trouble: among which ſort of ſhifters at this day, the moſt bold and dangerous and diueliſh is this treacherous crue of Ieſuites, who when they haue brought themſelues into the briars by their villanous doings, ſeeke to relieue themſelues by lyings, equiuocations, and periurie, or flying (if they can) from comming to their anſwere.

2. The other thing to bee noted in theſe Philiſtims, was their wiſe care to keepe themſelues from hurt by *Samſon*, when they ſaw him to be a man to be feared, and this they ſhewed herein, that they ſet thirtie men of their own countrey, as if they would haue honoured him, (much like *Herod*, who pre-
Matth.2.8. tended that he would honour Chriſt, when he ſought to kill him) whereas they intended no ſuch thing, but to ſet them as watchmen to take heede that no hurt might be wrought by him againſt them. And as they did by the light of nature thus prouide for their owne ſafetie, ſo wee ought wiſely and warily to preuent danger, where it is comming towards vs: and to bee
Matth.10.16. wiſe as ſerpents and beware of men, as well as to be innocent like doues.

We haue great cauſe in theſe daies to beware whom wee truſt, and to whom we commit our ſelues by giuing credit to them. Our Sauiour hath
Ioh.2.24. left vs a good example behinde him, whereby wee may take heed how farre we commit our ſelues to men. For when he was at Ieruſalem at the Paſſeouer, many beleeued in him (it is ſaid) when they ſaw his miracles that hee did. But Ieſus did not commit himſelfe to them, ſeeing he knew what was
Note. in them. Teaching vs to be circumſpect, how farre wee truſt them, whom we doe not ſufficiently know. Many ſmart for that they are too light of credit: namely, for that when they heare faire words, and conditions, they are ready thereupon to put themſelues into their hands. Whereas they ſhould know this, that they who are not faithfull to God, will not bee faithfull to men, as Papiſts and looſe profeſſors. It hath been many mens vtter vndoing, who haue too raſhly put their eſtate and goods into the hands of them who haue made faire ſhewes of truſtines or friendſhip toward them. Other haue ſuſtained the like by their owne children, hauing a better opinion of them through blind ſelfeloue, then there was cauſe; and truſting them with almoſt all that they had, haue loſt all through their owne folly. The ſame I may ſay of vnwiſe and vndiſcreet lenders, and ſuch as haue vnaduiſedly brought themſelues into danger by ſuertiſhip, till with their loade of griefe they haue ended their miſerable daies in priſon or penurie.

But none are either more commonly deceiued, or more to be pitied, then ſillie and ſhiftleſſe damſels and maides, who care not into whoſe hands they put themſelues, till they complaine and crie out, that they haue not found truth and faithfulnes at their hands, who promiſed them great matters of quietnes, and liuing at eaſe: who haue in a ſhort time groſſely broke their couenant with them, by moſt contentious and vnquiet liuing, or left them with their charge to ſhift for themſelues: of which woful perſons England is full. For I muſt ſay the truth, that in moſt places there are few faithful people to be found. Let vs make the more account of them that are ſuch, and for the reſt, I ſay with our Sauiour, let the dead bury the dead: and let them match together, ſeeing they will needes doe ſo, who are both of them vnfaithfull. And ſeeing (in this ſubtile vizard age) we can hardly diſcerne oft

times

times betweene one and other, I meane betwixt the trustie, and the deceiuer; let vs with *Paul* pray God to deliuer vs from hauing to doe with such as haue neither faith, nor fidelitie in them. And so farre as by our narrow obseruation we can finde any hollownesse or falsehood in such as pretend the contrary, (as for others, they are more easily auoided) let it be a watchword for caution in time to come. All is not gold that glistereth: faire words are fit to beguile euen good people, whose innocencie makes them thinke that other are as themselues. But with the brest-plate of righteousnesse, (which serueth to keepe them from being offensiue) let them vse their head-peece, I meane wisedome and preuention of danger, that they may be defended from hurt by others. All know that none lesse deserue wrong then the harmelesse: yet none we see daily are more vsually beguiled, and made a pray to the spoiler for want of circumspection. 2.Thes.3.2.

THE SEVENTIE SIXE SERMON ON THE XIIII. CHAPTER OF THE BOOKE OF IVDGES.

Vers.13. *And Samson said vnto them, I will now put foorth a riddle vnto you: if you can certainly declare it me within the seuen daies of the feast, and finde it out, then I will giue you thirtie sheetes, and thirtie change of garments:*

14. *But if you cannot declare it me, then shall ye giue me thirtie sheetes, and thirtie change of raiments. And they answered him, Put foorth thy riddle, that wee may heare it.*

15. *And he said vnto them, Out of the eater came meate, and out of the strong came sweetnes: and they could not in three daies expound the riddle.*

16. *And when the seuenth day was come, they said vnto Samsons wife, Entice thine husband, that he may declare vs the riddle, lest wee burne thee and thy fathers house with fire: Haue ye called vs to possesse vs? Is it not so?*

17. *And Samsons wife wept before him, and said, Surely thou hatest me, and louest me not: for thou hast put foorth a riddle vnto the children of my people, and hast not told it me. And he said vnto her, Behold I haue not told it my father, nor my mother, and shall I tell it thee.*

18. *Then Samsons wife wept before him seuen daies while their feast lasted: and when the seuenth day was come, he told her, because she was importunate vpon him: so she told the riddle to the children of her people.*

19. *And the men of the citie said vnto him the seuenth day before the Sunne went downe, What is sweeter then hony? and what is stronger then a lion? Then said he vnto them, If yee had not plowed with my heiffer, you had not found out my riddle.*

20. *And the spirit of the Lord came vpon him, and he went downe to Askelon and slew thirtie men of them, and spoiled them, and change of garments vnto them,* which

which expounded the riddle: and his wrath was kindled, and he went vp to his fathers house.

21. *Then Samsons wife was giuen to his companion, whom he had vsed as his friend.*

Verſ. 13.14. NOw followeth the third thing that was done at the marriage, and that was the riddle that *Samson* put foorth to the Philiſtims there met together: the which courſe was in great wiſedome taken by *Samſon*, if it bee well conſidered. For if the cauſe bee ſought, why *Samſon* propounded this riddle, I anſwere: It was a pleaſant whetting of their wits, and miniſtred occaſion of mirth to ſet them about the inuenting and ſearching out the meaning of it, which was hard and difficult, that ſo in the meane while they might bee kept from manifolde offendings. And it was without ſuſpition to the Philiſtims of any euill intended by *Samſon*. And hee ſeeing that the ſeuen daies continue while the feaſt laſted (for ſo their manner there was to doe) was a long time for him and his friends to be in company and conuerſant among Idolaters, without much ſinne and offending God, hee could not haue taken a ſafer nor better courſe, then ſo to ſet them a worke and occupie their heads.

As for religious talke there was no place for it: to haue fallen into that, had been the next way to haue ſet them altogether by the eares at the firſt. And yet by the propounding of the riddle, they were held greatly within compaſſe from lewd and wicked talke, and ill behauiour, which could hardly haue been borne by *Samſon* and his friends: the which yet had otherwiſe ſo abounded with much other diſorder, ſuch as falleth out at thoſe kinds of meetings, (where yet one would thinke there ſhould be leſſe feare of it) as would haue bred moſt bitter contentions among them; the which by this wiſedome that hee ſhewed in putting out the riddle, hee ſhunned and auoided.

Doct. And by this practiſe of his wee may learne, when we be pent in companie, where no good things haue intertainment, but euill many waies is to be feared, (which companies are too common) how to bethinke our ſelues what is beſt to be done of vs. If it may bee, let ſuch companies be turned from altogether, eſpecially if they be our betters, who will take more libertie to offend, and yet beare it more hardly to bee reſiſted, or ſpoken againſt: whereby our griefe will be the greater, when we ſee no meanes to keep our conſciences quiet and peaceable, but that we muſt haue part in the ſin. But if it fall out ſometimes (as it may doe, that wee bee brought by Gods prouidence into ſuch companies by neceſſitie, when we cannot preuent them, if they be ſuch as we may be bold to ſpeake to them, they being of no wealthier ſort then we, or not much aboue vs, there is the leſſe cauſe of feare, or of any ſuch great danger to fall out: but yet euen there we muſt take heed that wee iumpe not, neither fall in with them, to iuſtifie and conſent to their offenſiue talke and behauiour: but if religious communication will not bee borne nor brooked of them, ſome other things indifferent (and yet not impertinent nor vnprofitable) would be thought vpon of vs, and miniſtred by

vs,

vs, to ſtay and preuent worſe, as fit occaſion may be taken thereof. And if ye aske what, I ſay, for example; the mentioning of the death of any among vs, and namely ſuch as are of note: and of any iudgements and plagues of God either preſent or lately fallen out about vs, as burnings, ſtrange death, and namely vpon drunkards; alſo the execution of malefactors, and ſuch like: which matters will be better borne to be talked of, then things meerly diuine: and yet by occaſion of ſpeaking of them, not onely ill communication may be kept away and auoided, but better alſo, and that which is to edification, may the eaſilier come in place. For to an honeſt Christian man it is a great griefe to loſe and bee cut off from his ſweete words, which flow from the abundance of the heart. But ſeeing this muſt bee borne oft Pro 23.8.
times, and worſe alſo at the hands of ſuch as are of wealth and power in the companie being ill minded, there; if we cannot reſtraine them, neither may haue place or liberty to ſpeake, when God is diſhonoured by them, in cauilling againſt the truth, railing vpon Gods people, or ſlandering the innocent, or by ſwearing, filthie talke, or any ſuch like; the beſt way will be to depart out of the company, or to giue no eare to them, if we may turne to other who are neere vs, or to ſhew diſlike in our countenance; or if they will needs aske our opinion, at the leaſt to ſhew our diſſent from them, but yet in meekneſſe and in a peaceable manner. But if the caſe be ſo, that wee may rebuke ſuch vnfruitfull workes of darkneſſe, God giuing vs occaſion iuſtly, let vs not carrie our zeale in our boſomes, as a ſword in a ruſtie ſcabberd, but vnſheath it to the defence of Gods truth, and his religion, leſt if we hold our peace in ſuch a caſe, the ſtones of the ſtreete will crie: which point hath elſewhere been opened.

Samſon, as it appeareth, tels them, he would propound his riddle to them ſo, that if they could tell it, they ſhould haue thirtie changes of apparell, and peeces of linnen, whether ſheetes or ſhirts, &c. and if they could not tell it within ſeuen dayes, then they ſhould giue as much to him: which was a kinde of wager laying, and their ſport was for loſſe on the one ſide, & gaine on the other. Which kinde of dealing, I meane after this manner of wagering for gaine, (ſeeing he had his direction from God therein, and warrant in ſpeciall to practiſe it) cannot be counted vnto him for ſin, neither ought any to ſtumble at it.

I might here take occaſion to ſpeake largely of the like actions and exerciſes among mē to that which was in this place vſed of *Samſon*, but I ſhould be too long. This is all that I will ſay, that as the moſt handle the matter, they doe grieuouſly ſinne againſt God: as when men play or wager either in a couetous deſire to winne, or when they are angry and paſſionate in playing or wagering; or when they ſweare and blaſpheme the name of God in their play; or when they fall a quarelling, or goe together by the eares amidſt their paſtimes and wager-laying; or when they are immoderate in their playing, ſpending whole nights and dayes therein, neglecting in the meane time the neceſſary duties of their vocation, and the moſt neceſſary duty of all others the ſeruice of Almighty God: of which ſort alas there are too many who ſpend moſt of their time in bowling allyes, and at trucks-bettings, and ſwearing vpon euery caſt; prophane men, that make ſo little account of their time as to paſſe it away ſo idly; let them take heed that they be not driuen as many haue been in time to desire one houre to repent, and yet goe without it: or last of all when they thus play or wager away all their maintenance. And for such kind of gamesters who haue not money competentlie to maintaine their familie, much lesse for the reliefe of others, though *Paul* biddeth them that stole to steale no more, but labour with their hands, that they may haue wherewith to helpe the poore (for which two ends it chiefely serueth) and yet haue enough to play away, let them with the rest of their companions take heed, that among many other punishments of God, which they draw vpon themselues, this be not also one and not the least, that because they loue pastime they become poore men.

Prou.21.17. And we may wel thinke that if God denie to clothe the bodies of such with apparrell (for rags are their liuerie) much lesse will hee clothe their soules with grace here, or their persons with glory hereafter, except they repent; which is not at commandement, nor easily found of such.

Doct. vers.14. We haue heard of *Samsons* wagering with the Philistims in the former verse, and part of this: now it followes in the latter end of it how they gaue allowance thereto, and shewed their liking thereof, saying vnto him, Put forth thy riddle that we may heare it. And this sheweth, how readily wicked men turne to heare euen the godly (whom otherwise they dislike and scorne) when they speake pleasing things to them. Euen as *Ieroboam* King of Israel did greatly like *Elisha*, and spake kindlie to him when hee did that

2. King.6.21. which pleased him wel, in bringing the army of the king of Syria his enemie as prisoners into his chiefe Citie Samaria, hoping that thereby hee might haue his will of them in putting them to the sword. Oh when they fit their humour by words or deeds, they will change themselues on sudden toward them, and applaud them as if they were friends with them. And euen so is it with them in the construing of those actions that please them, such I meane as whereby they receiue benefit and fauour or aduantage: for these, they shall be aduanced aboue the skyes: but let them therewith ioyne admonition and good counsell, or so much as the mildest repoofe, especially if they take themselues crossed by them in their purposes of profit, pleasure, or will, (although neuer so iustly,) then they are the worst that goe vpon the earth, their goodnesse is remembred no more. Yea and this which I say may be extended to the best Ministers, who so long as the plausiblenes of their gift doth hold the bad in any admiration or affection, will shew the greatest signes of taking pleasure and delight in their company. But let the Minister leaue tickling of their corrupt flesh, and begin to search them a little, or bewray their corruptions which were hidden from them before, oh then hee

Gal.4.16. is bitter and irkesome to their taste, and becomes their enemie for telling them the truth, yea, then all his former desert is vanished with commendation and all: all which doe testifie too clearely, that they allow not of those who are godlie, either Ministers, or other for their goodnesse, which ought chiefely to be regarded, but for other causes. This must further teach the best sort to obserue themselues with the best circumspection how far they goe in humoring the wicked, to wit, so far only as they keepe bounds, that is, speake that which they may, for the turning them from euill, or drawing them to the liking of the best things by degrees, alwaies preseruing entire their liberty in reprouing, without any iust cause of blushing. As for them

that

that will not admit of ſuch kind of dealing, but like onely to be flattered, let them know their ſtomacks are diſtempered, and they in a dangerous caſe, (when they can take no liking of any thing but fleſhly and ſenſuall) euen as they are who will ſerue their turnes by flattering them.

Thus now of the firſt two things that were done at the feaſt, we haue heard, and of part of the third, to wit, that *Samſon* told them, he would put foorth a riddle to them, and how they readily apprehended it, and were willing to heare it. Now therefore in the former part of this verſe it is ſaid, he propounded it, which was the third thing done at the marriage, [*Out of the eater came meate, and out of the ſtrong came ſweetneſſe.*] Verſ. 15.

The meaning is, that hony which is ſweet, and meate to eate, came out of the body of the Lyon who is ſtrong, which I open and vtter, ſeeing the ignorant not comparing this with the 19. verſe, would not elſe vnderſtand it. In this latter part of the verſe it is ſhewed, that when the Philiſtims had heard the riddle, they toyled themſelues, and went about by their owne labour and wit to finde out the meaning of it, but could not by their owne helpe. And this is the fourth thing done at the Marriage, namely, how they ſought to find it out, & how they preuailed. But of this more in due place.

But I will firſt returne a little to *Samſon*, and ſhew how he made vſe of the works of God, which he conſidered and obſerued. For to his great benefit he gathereth a riddle, and raiſed thereby a queſtion out of the worke of God in the Lyon, which was a meane to hold much euill from among them. So it behoueth vs to marke things that come to paſſe daily, (which all fall out by Gods prouidence) and his dealing in and by them, that wee may learne wiſedome thereby, and take good by them. For as Preachers gather ſimilies by the things they ſee, reade, and heare, to illuſtrate that which they vtter in their Sermons to the people; ſo ſhould we by Gods iudgements vpon the wicked, and his bleſſings on them that feare him, we (I ſay) ſhould learne to profit by them, and to ſhun the one, and to get our part in the other, ſo as all may ſay, we haue made right vſe of them in deed, whereas the moſt part take no good by either of both, nor by any other of his great works: my meaning is not, that the generall adminiſtration of God onely in the gouerning the creatures (which he hath admirably made) ought to be noted, but ſpecially the ends of the iuſt and vniuſt: that to the one there is alwaies peace, the other cannot, no not at death giue teſtimonie of a good eſtate, nor depart with hope, nor encourage his companions to be like him, but dieth either with a wounding, yet deſperate conſcience, or is ſtricken like *Nabal*, with a dead Palſie of inſenſibleneſſe. Doct. verſ. 15.

But to proceede with this act of *Samſon*, in the latter part of this verſe, we ſee how by occaſion of this riddle much euill was ſtaied in that companie: for the time which would haue been otherwiſe very lewdly and ill beſtowed by the Philiſtims, was now buſilie taken vp about ſtudying and ſearching out of the meaning of the riddle: for ſo it is ſaid in the text, they could not in three dayes expound it. And hereby we may learne, that much ſinne may be ſtaied in meetings of friends & neighbours at feaſts and merrie makings, if there bee any perſons there, to intend and endeuour to preuent and ſtop it. And that is done by good and religious talke brought in, (if it will be admitted) or of things indifferent, yet tending to good ends: Doct. 2. ver. 15.

(as I haue sayd before) the which once occupying and possessing them, may put them out of their bad byas, which I haue oft seene done in my time: namely, much euill to haue been hindred, and put by, while by some in the company better minded then the rest, it hath thus been preuented carefully and wisely by christian & sauoury communication, and also kind vsage of them, and such like good meanes.

And to inlarge and vrge this matter a little further, of and about these Philistims, that as they were least hurtfull when they were most busie in seeking out the meaning of the riddle, so I may truly say this of the most of bad sort, that the greatest good they doe either in Church or commonwealth, or at least, the fewest euils that they commit, are when they be at their labour, and tyed to the works of their calling, euen as the theefe is fast from doing of euill when his hands are tyed behind him. For though euill persons are ill minded euen at their worke, and as ill occupied, if they haue opportunitie, seeing they are framed thereto, yet this can be nothing so much, as when oyle is put to the flame: for then they are at elbow roome, and much more when they be lincked in company with such as be like themselues, which is as far from that which ought to be, as may be, seeing euery part of a christian mans life should bring forth fruit. And it ought to be a great humbling of such when God shall open their eyes, (vntill which time they dreame of no danger) that whereas they are commanded in all that they doe, or goe about, to honour the Lord, they yet shall be by manifold witnesses brought against them, conuinced of the contrary. For whether they fast or feast, labour or be idle, whether they be alone, or in company, or whatsoeuer they doe, yea euen when they worship God in the congregation, their hearts are lusting after some euill, and far from goodnes. Therefore happy are those seruants, who when the Lord commeth may be found occupying their talent, so as they may be able to say, they haue been neither idle nor vnprofitable in the knowledge of the Lord Iesus willingly and with good aduisednes, but since they were taken into his seruice haue shewed themselues faithful & diligent: (alway except infirmitie) and yet euen then they are also occupied, namely in resisting the same.

Vers. 16. Thus we see that for three dayes they did beat their brains about finding out the meaning of the riddle, and we read no other but that they do so the other three dayes, till the seuenth came. But very probable it is, that they deuised among themselues (if need should be) that they would vse *Samsons* wife in the matter, to help them to come by the meaning of it, because it is said in this verse, that they came to her, and vrged her sore to get it of him on the seauenth day, when their hope otherwise was altogether past, although it is like they had sore vrged her to doe so before, then (I say) they threatned that they would otherwise burne her fathers house. And further they made a great matter of that they should lose thereby if they could not shew the meaning of it, as if they had been vndone by it, (and all this they ascribed to her bringing of him thither) if she did not learne the meaning of the riddle, and tell it to them.

Doct. And here by their seeking to get it by shifts and guile, when they could not finde it out by coniecturall wit, and deliberation, wee may see how like to these Philistims the most part of people are: who for a while keepe compasse

passe in their matters they deale in, and in their behauiour, as though they were well ordered persons; this (I say) many do for a time, while they haue no great prouocation nor temptation to breake out, but if they doe like stormes and tempests arise to stirre and disquiet them; loe, then they appeare in their colour, and make themselues knowne what they are, and what little gouernment they haue of themselues. *Saul* when *Dauid* being pursued of him, shewed him plainly, that hee had such aduantage against him, that hee could haue killed him, spake mildly and kindly to him: but 1.Sam.24.18. when he had thoughts put into his head, that *Dauid* sought his life, then he was most spitefully exasperated and incensed against him.

So in another kinde, while *Ananias* and *Saphira* his wife kept their possessions in their hands, there was no complaint made of or against them, neither were they accused to haue liued offensiuely: but when the Church was in need, and they for praise of men would doe as other did, according Acts 5.2.&c. to the Apostles perswasion, that is to say, relieue the poore, and so proceeded to sell some part of their lands, then they began to distrust that they should haue enough, and of a couetous minde kept away part of the price that they sold it for, and yet would make a shew to giue it all, swearing falsely thereunto. So many among vs liue peaceably, innocently, and vnoffensiuely, as honest neighbours, and well liking religion for a time, who yet in trials, and yet these not great, & particularly in matters of money or money worth, bewray that they are to be commended for none of all these shewes of goodnesse, but lay foorth themselues in contrary colours. Much like to that which Satan spake of *Iob*, (though amisse, and in another case) *Touch* Iob 2.5. *him, and he will curse thee to thy face.* And we may almost binde it for true, that if a man being laid to the touchstone of gaine, especially when no man knoweth what he doth, doe approue himselfe conscionable, he is an honest Note. man indeed. And as the Philistims did here fall to shifts, vnlawfull meanes, crueltie, and many other euill waies, who first did not so. In like manner we see among our selues, that some will shew themselues as faire chapmen as may be, like the bargaine very well, and boast they will not take good gaine tenne pound, &c. for it againe: also they will agree vpon couenants, seale the writings, take witnesses, appoint the day of payment or deliuerie; and what should I say more? yet let the ware or merchandise in the meane season waxe cheaper then was supposed, then begins the franke buyer to shrinke, palter, and shift dishonestly for himselfe: And so doth the seller commonly, if the price rise any thing: whereas they bought and sold before hand, pretending they were resolued vpon whatsoeuer euent to rest satisfied; if there were losse, to depend vpon God for restitution, and not to shrinke backe: Psal.15.4. if gaine, yet to confesse it equall and iust, to yeeld, and forgoe it without grudging, seeing God hath cast it vpon the partie. And the same humour is bewraied in such sellers, as comming short of the Note. price they would haue, yet being compelled to deliuer the commoditie, do change and impaire the qualitie, and goodnesse of it, or cut it short in measure, or vse other men gripingly, to make themselues amends: shewing plainly, that they regard not any thing in their contracts, saue onely to make a pray of their brother, and serue their turne by him, without conscience, or ciuill respect of the Common-wealth. So also when men cannot enioy

their

Note. their commodities, and thriue as they would, but decay, or feare that they shall; or if things grow deare, or by an hundred like occasions, they who for a time were of good carriage and behauiour, haue fallen to bad practises, and very offensiue courses to liue and bee maintained by, and thereby disguise themselues, as if they had neuer been well reported of, nor had been honest of behauiour. Yea, (and which is more) this taketh hold of many of the better sort euen of Christians, if they bee hardly laid at by trials, and prouocations, they too readily yeeld to do things euill and vnbeseeming them. All which, if they will not see and so amend and reforme such dishonestie, when it appeares to men, or secret falsehood, though God onely see it, they sufficiently bewray that God hath no pleasure in them. But if any break out in their liues offensiuely, and in such a wicked sort, whē they be not strongly laid at and prouoked to doe so, they doe worse then these Philistims, who were sore prouoked and neerely driuen (as we haue heard) (the time drawing neere in which they must giue the meaning of the riddle, or else suffer inconuenience) before they fell to subtiltie and violence, and yet euen therin we see they disguised themselues grossely.

2 And heere it shall not bee amisse to marke the wrangling and dishonest contendings of these Philistims, when they saw they must lose; and what commeth of playing for money, or wagering. Euen in this our age, where the vsers of them are of the same mould and nature with these Philistims, the same may be seene: Among many other euils, which I will not here set downe, these that are mentioned in this place, to haue been practised of them, are for the most part, companions with play and wagering. That is to say, discontentment, quarrelling, contentions, denying, and breaking the couenants, and seeking to doe this by force and by threatnings. As these here are not ashamed to require that *Samson* should tell his wife the meaning of the riddle, that she might declare it to them, which was as much as to goe from their couenant, and so with dishonestie to deny it. But of these mischieuous fruites sutable to the causes, I said somewhat before.

But in the meane season this further marke (for the aggrauating of the fact) how small a matter it was, that they could haue lost thereby: which I doe not so much speake, as though I would cause marueiling, that the vncircumcised and irreligious people should contend for so small a matter, who did the like throughout their life; but to the end I may fitly take occasion hereby, iustly to charge numbers at this day, what a great and grieuous sinne they commit, who fall out one with another for a lesse matter then for a change or suite of apparell, when yet they professe to bee guided by knowledge in the things which they doe. But it is lesse marueile that they so breake out at their playing to winne one anothers goods, when as they will doe as much in their lawfull bargaines, that is, quarrell and striue (that I say no worse) for a groate or a shilling valew, as I said in the former point in a more generall sort.

Oh the mischiefe that many doe, yea and vpon a small occasion, and for a very trifle. For these were ready to burne downe the house and her, and all that was in the house, rather then they would lose the valew of a suite of apparell: So, how much is spent by men in their rage and heate at the law for a twelue penny matter, though not so much for the thing, as the satisfying of of the will and spitefull stomacke of the man. Yea what vndoings withall of one another are seen, and that in one age after another, lest they who come after, should seeme to learne wisedome by them that went before them; both wofull and long experience doe too lamentably teach. Beholde how great a fire a small sparkle kindleth: that is, when it falles vpon matter fit for it. This be said for amplification of the former point, and of the whole for this time. Iam.3.5.

THE SEVENTIE SEVEN SERMON ON THE XIIII. CHAPTER OF THE BOOKE OF IVDGES.

HOw earnestly the Philistims vrged *Samsons* wife to get the meaning of the riddle of him, wee heard in the former Sermon: now the holy storie setteth downe, what followed their threatnings of *Samsons* wife, that she might get the meaning of the riddle at his hand. First she sued to him in most earnest maner to know it, and and required of him, that as hee loued her, hee would declare the meaning of it vnto her: who answered her by sound reason, and gaue her a deniall. But she not satisfied therewith, desisted not, but was importunate with him, and weeping to him the rest of the seuen daies after the first three were past: for so are the words to be vnderstood in the 18. verse [*she wept before him the seuen daies, while the feast lasted*:] then, I say, hee told her the meaning of the riddle on the seuenth day, and she declared it to them, and they to *Samson*, and so the controuersie was ended. Vers.17.18.19. The summe.

And first let vs marke the womans dealing with him: thou louest me not, saith she, but hatest me. That had been hard indeed at the first entring into their marriage, though a thing which falles out often in the marriages of many vnaduised couples. But her words were not true, neither therefore by and by so to be beleeued, as she vttered them, to wit, that hee loued her not: yet if it had been so, wee all see had been guiltie of a foule and great crime: whereby before we proceede further, let vs note this: that in the iudgement of an heathenish woman, there should bee no hatred but neere and vnfained loue betwixt couples in marriage: much more among Christians should it be verified, Neuer any man hated his owne flesh, &c. Such an absurditie (I say) is not to be admitted, but to be abhorred, which causeth (that I say no more) wearinesse one of another. The falling out among those is much more to their great shame: yea, and so is the diminishing of loue also which maketh ready way to hatred, seeing loue ought to be strong as fire, which cannot be quenched with many waters. But they prouide ill Verse 17. Cant.8.7.

for

for this, who make their marriage (when yet it is void of grace, and the feare of God) the onely ground of louely and delightfull qualities: whereas the best things that are in it, beside these, are flitting, and momentanie, and so is the loue ẏ is grounded on them: but the true and christian loue is constant, and bringeth foorth much fruite. And this is a point of such importance, that the Apostle includes all the husbands dutie therein, that hee loue his wife: as if he should say, Where that is, other good things are not wanting. For hee being the head of relation and vnion, from whom must flow and descend to the wife all comfort and welfare; he must know, that he is thorough this loue, to communicate himselfe to his wife, in all free, bountifull, and plentifull affection, and dutie: whereupon it followeth, that she is to him againe in all reuerend submisse, and yet cheerefull manner, fitted and framed. Yea so weightie a point is this of loue, (I speake not of frothie, hot, and foolish loue, which is vanitie of vanities) that except the heart of the man bee knit to the woman in the Lord, as to one not onely religious and well qualified, but also as the onely person, whom he can delight in, and liue within this speciall kinde of fellowship: except this (I say) it is not the generall chusing of a good woman, which will serue the turne, neither shall the seuerall and mutuall offices which concerne each party be euer currantly or constantly performed, much lesse the whole life, and the estate of marriage blessed or comfortable.

Doct.2. Further, by her weeping, when she had no iust cause, wee may note the subtiltie of a bad woman, to complaine bitterly of that, which her husband gaue her no occasion of. For what though hee told her not that which hee ought not to doe, must he therefore hate her? and although the Philistims threatned her, did that proue that he hated her? I say therfore (to leaue her to her selfe, and such as she was) let no iust cause of vnkindnesse be offered by a Christian husband, and let it be well testified that he doth so, and if she will then (as many women doe) dissemble, and charge her husband vniustly, and knowes that she doth so, and that onely to bring him to the bent of her bow, or to make her owne cause seeme tolerable and good, and so seeke (as she did here) to draw him to inconuenience; if (I say) she doe thus, let it make all Christians wise and warie of such fetches, and teach them that they in the meane while, giuing them all due that belongs to them, take heed that they be not ouercome of them that way, or in any such case. As for example, if a spitefull woman will call her husbands loue into question, because hee will not reuenge the falsely supposed wrongs which another hath offered her, as she out of her impotent humour pretendeth: Or if a proud woman will thus vpbraid her husband, for not satisfying her demaunds touching costly attire, or allowance of more money, then his estate will admit. So also if a iealous woman, to iustifie her base and vncomely conceits and behauiours to her husband, shall make her case good, by alleaging that he is cheerefull in other womens companies, though he do it with sobrietie and warinesse: In all these cases let the husband see that he be innocent, and then beware how he prostitute or imbondage himselfe to such of his wiues passions, lest by yeelding a little, he lose his libertie: but yet let it be done kindly and peaceably anger and bitternes.

Doct.3. Now further, in that she chargeth him that he loued her not, because he

tolde

tolde her not of that secret that in no equitie it concerned her to know; what reason had shee so to doe? But shee drew her reason from a wrong ground: that is, that women must know their husbands minde in al things, or else they thinke they loue them not. If this had been her error alone, I would haue said no more of it. But behold, it is a fondnes and follie that possesseth many women. I confesse that in things common to them, and that concerne both, either pertaining to soule or bodie, or this present life, there be a free and readie communicating of all such things betwixt them, for the woman hath a right therein, as well as the man: but seeing there are many things of secresie besides them, which lie waightily vpon the husband, but doe nothing concerne the wife, yea and dangerous to bee tolde foorth, and many women weake to conceale them, the husband in no wisedome may impart them vnto her: and yet for all that, he shall not be iustly charged with want of loue. But more of this in the next Chapter (God willing) saue one.

Samson withstood his wife at first by good reason, namely, this, that he 4
had not told it to his father, nor mother, whom yet he loued dearely, and long; she was but new marryed to him, neither had he proofe of her faithfulnes, wisedome, and silence; but otherwise his reason had not been good, seeing a man may impart some things to his wife rather then to them, and in denying her request he did well. So we should with reasonable answers withstand vnreasonable sutes, and then we shall shew our selues well fortified by the word and sound resolution out of a good conscience, when we can giue a sufficient reason of our refusall: and otherwise we are as like to be drawne to sinne, although we be not greatly sollicited by the importunitie of others, our selues being vngrounded or vnarmed against the subtiltie and loose disposition of our owne hearts, though we thinke neuer so well of our owne strength. But it must be granted, that the greatest danger is when beside our owne readinesse and pronesse to euill, we haue prouocations also, and those strong by inward temptations and outward occasions. In auoyding and resisting both, *Ioseph* hath giuen vs an example worthie our following, who was neither snared nor inticed inwardly, when he saw he might easily haue had such desire satisfied, neither being allured with words and flattery, did so much as hearken to his whorish mistresse. Now as I haue spoken to men, so a word I will adde to women, and that is this, that if they were wise, they would learne to shake off the bold and shamelesse sutes of such as should dare demaund that of them, which were their dishonestie, reproch, and vndoing, namely, to prostitute their chastity to any of them at their pleasures, who hauing once spoyled them, doe leaue them so. But of the fruit of dalliance more afterward.

It is said here that she would not be answered so by him, but was impor- Verse 18.
tunate with him all the rest of the seauen dayes of the feast, after the first three, in which they could not finde out the meaning of the riddle, and so she woon and obtained at his hands at last that which she sought: and so shee told it to her people and countrey men the Philistims. These three things may be seene in this verse distinctly, her importunate vrging of him, his impotencie in being ouercome of her, and her telling the exposition of the riddle to the Philistims her people. And they minister seuerall instructi-

ons to vs. First by her importunate vrging of him, when no reason would answer her, wee may see, how vnreasonable shamelesse, and bold, and yea vnwearyed wicked persons are in the following of their bad suites, so that they will neuer giue ouer, but thinke they shall preuaile by one meanes or other, at the least, by their importunity: wee can not doe the like, nor come neere them either in seeking to further goodnes by men, or in suing to God for it; but a small denyall, and a weake withstanding of vs by men, makes vs soone weary of our honest attempts, and so we may faint by and by, and in like manner giue ouer in making our requests to God, yea, and that for great matters if we preuaile not at once. How vnlike are we to the woman
Luk.18.8. of Canaan, who would take no repulse, nor be discouraged by the hardest answer that was giuen her. And our Sauiour hath taught vs, that if we were importunate with him, we could not faile, nor goe without that which we aske, our requests being made according to his will. And this is one speciall point of wisedome, wherein the children of light are to learne of the children of this world.

Doct.2. Now further to passe to the second thing of the three, we see that by this following him thus with continuall vrging of him, he yeelded to her suite, and told her the meaning of the riddle. So that he who withstood her at the first, was afterwards ouercome. It teacheth, that when we haue ouercome a temptation at the first assaulting vs, (which one would thinke were hardest to doe in respect of times following) yet we may possibly be ouercome of it afterwards, and be giuen ouer to it: as for example, whether it be to such vnlawfull demaunds as this was, or to incontinencie, filthy gaine, seeking, or any such like. The reason is, because we are fickle and flexible, and doe not strengthen our selues to be constant at one time as an other in a good thing, neither be oft instant with God by feruent praying, watching, neither couenanting against sin, or not looking carefully to the keeping of them, neither disgrace sin: by meanes whereof, Satan taketh his aduantage against vs one time or other.

Euen so the same *Samson* here spoken of, did afterwards the very like, who withstanding the inticements of a subtile woman as now he did at the first, and that with full purpose (for a time) to doe so still, yet yeelded by long perswasion vnto her vniust and vnreasonable request at the last. It is no marueile to see it thus in some particular sinne and temptation that one is brought to yeeld at last, who resisted at the first: for we see it to be so in the generall liking and imbracing of the whole doctrine of the Gospell. That some, who receiued it with ioy for a time, yet fall away from the loue of it afterward, as if they had neuer imbraced it. Therefore, much more they who haue resisted a sinne for a time, may possibly afterward fall into it notwithstanding. And it ought to make the best of vs constant in watching against all euill as well as at the first, remembring that our Sauiour his charge is peremptory and indefinite reaching at all times [*Watch.*] As for them who neuer haue had any sound proofe of the forgiuenes and death of sinne wrought in them by the power of the Word, no marueile if this inconstancie bee seene in them, that they please themselues ouer-much in their good actions, and soone are discouraged either from within or without themselues by the least occasion. The best people must plie God with their

their prayers to hold out, and to build vp daily vpon a good foundation. Can a rush grow without mire? or can a man be watchfull to persist in the good course which he hath seemed to like, or in hating the sinne which hee seemed to haue disliked, when there is nothing to set him forward in a matter of such difficultie? Flesh and blood cannot inherit the kingdome of God: neither is Satan diuided in himself. Reioyce not men in their shewes therefore, but get the assurance of Gods fauour, and not patch vp an euill heart with a fewe colours of goodnesse which are not ioyned with substance.

Also this weaknes and follie of *Samsons*, before I passe to the third point, 3
teacheth another thing: that when we haue ouercome an hard difficultie, and greater temptation, yet we may be afterwards ouercome of a small one. For he had concealed the opening of the riddle to his father and mother, to whom he had farre greater reason to tell it, as hauing so long proofe of their pietie, loue, and faithfulnesse; rather then to her a stranger, and whom hee knew to bee void of the most of them, if not all. And it is like hee tolde not them, lest they should by some occasion haue opened it to the Philistims, as his wife did now vnto them.

His follie in bewraying it to his wife, was like the sin of the man of God, who came to reproue *Ieroboams* idolatrie at Bethel. For he hauing a charge giuen him of God that he should goe into no house in that wicked place, to 1. King. 13. 8. 9.
eate or refresh himselfe, did well and carefully obserue it in the place where it was hardest to doe it, that is the Kings house, and yet behold hee was ouercome, and went from his charge, through foolish credulitie, where he might much more easily haue kept it, that is, to his fellow. For hee being inuited home by the King, he withstood it, not fearing his displeasure: but when afterwards he was moued by the old Prophet of Bethel, to goe to his house and eate, he went with him contrary to the commandement of the Lord, and was therefore after his departure slaine of a Lion in the high way.

The reason hereof both in him, and as many as offend that way, that they are ouercome of a smaller sinne, when they haue ouercome a greater, is this; that men are more afraid of committing that, and distrusting themselues, seeke the more feruently to God for helpe, and obtaine it: but when it is a Note.
smaller sinne, we doe not so much suspect and feare our selues, and so being vnarmed and ill prouided, we doe the easilier fall into it. And thus it commeth to passe, that when we haue slaine a Lion, a Beare foiles vs, and hauing deuoured a camell, a gnat chokes vs, that is, wee auoid the harder inconuenience, and yet bewray and shew our weakenesse in a smaller, which wee might more easily haue ouercome. And so it fareth with vs in repenting, that for a great trespasse we are easilier brought to relent, seeing wee know that wee were more hardned in and by the committing of it, and yet in a lesse offence wee shall hardlier bewaile and confesse it, seeing the heart in committing of that doth not see so much euill. Therefore it is well with Gods seruants, while they liue by their former experience, and renue their care of pleasing God. and feare of the contrary: for then they shall bee so farre from this distemper, that they shall be able (with the same Prophet at

another time) to beleeue that hee who deliuered them from the Lion and Beare,(the more dangerous) will not suffer the Philistim to preuaile.

4 Now to come to the third point: whereas it is said, that when *Samson* had opened it to his wife,she did by and by tell it to her countrey men, the Philistims; it appeareth, that all her weeping to her husband was but dissimulation and falsehood, treacherie and vnfaithfulnes, euen a packe of mischiefe she did bewray to lie hidden in her heart, vnder that faire shew of kindnesse and loue. To teach vs, that we should not giue credit to the outward shewes of goodnesse and simplicitie,so as we rest in them as sufficient proofes thereof,and when we haue no better testimonie in them that will seeme such. For the heart of man is a deepe gulfe full of abomination: and such as are subtile can waite their opportunitie to get and obtaine that which they seeke. And yet iudge we none before the time,and till God shall lay them open,but waite and trie them. Many pray to God, but it is onely as S. *Iames* saith, to bestow amisse that which they aske, euen vpon their lusts. And so doe many pretend faire to men, when there is no such thing in them,but dissimulation and hypocrisie.

Ierem. 17. 9.

Iam 4 3.

Verse 19.

Now they had got the knowledge of the riddle by the woman, they bring it forth to *Samson* before the Sunne went downe on the seuenth day. A most grosse part played by them, to seeke it out that way, as *Ahabs* act was in killing *Naboth*, when *Elias* met him,and said to him, Hast thou killed and taken possession? But it may giue warning to vs,to haue no more to doe with such,then we must needs. For this is so common,that falsehood, violence,and vnconscionablenes is crept in euen among men of better profession,so that they who deale with such, cannot tell when they haue made their couenants and bargaines sure enough. For not onely they flie from their word, but also from witnesse and writing too, if there be the least hole to be found. Which is to make men more faithfull themselues, and more wise in taking heed of others.

Note.

2 Besides,note the vnweariednes of these men,that after they begun,they neuer gaue ouer labouring, and perswading the woman by flatterie and threats,sweating at it,till they had that which they sought,and yet had little hope of comming by it by her meanes, who was wife to their aduersarie *Samson*, with whom the wager was laid: who if she had been faithfull to him,might as well haue fetched the water of the well of Bethelem, (by going through an hoast of armed men for it) as they should haue got it of her.

Oh the toyle that lewd fellowes will take for their pleasure and profit, and to bring their wicked purposes to passe. If they haue no successe at one time,yet they take no discouragement at it, but set vpon it another. They that take such paines for trash, a man would thinke should take some for grace. But oh that they who professe to loue goodnesse, could be brought to doe but halfe so much to bring good things to passe, and to seeke happinesse for euer,as they doe in hunting after the pleasures of sinne, and filthie gaine,which are but for a moment. I haue said somwhat of this in the womans importunitie, though indeed she was woed to this by these, and these were the first that swaied her motion. But she (of the two) was the

Note.

more

more like to preuaile with him, then they to draw her to bee a partie with them. Therefore strange was their confidence and presumption in attempting to goe thus betweene barke and tree, and obtaining their purposes by so desperate a meanes, as were no lesse then the setting husband and wife together by the eares. But what will not such aduenture, as are set vpon mischiefe? A right Embleme of the cursed brood of Iesuites, negotiators for the whore of Babylon, whose furie no attempt, no sedition is impossible vnto vs.

And to shut vp this matter about seeking out the meaning of the riddle; 3
now let vs heare *Samsons* answere, when they brought in the meaning of it, after this manner: [What is sweeter then hony, or stronger then a Lion] he said in effect to them againe; And what is more vnfaithfull or vntrustie then a woman? Hee answered little lesse, when hee vttered these words to them; If yee had not ploughed with my heifer, ye had not found out my riddle: which was as much as if he had accused them of falsehood, and vniust dealing, and her of vnfaithfulnes to her husband.

By this learne one property of a wicked woman, that she is more true and trustie to strangers, then to her owne husband. And yet to speake as the truth is, she is neither constant nor sure to either of them, if a third come in Note.
the way betwixt both. But she that will deale so with her friend, namely her husband, what, thinke we, would such an one doe to her enemie? And if shee would doe it without iust cause, what, if she should be prouoked? Whereby let other be admonished. But oh faithfulnes, how precious and much to be desired art thou? And of *Samsons* wife and the Philistims thus much: of *Samson* himselfe I will say more in the next Sermon.

THE SEVENTIE EIGHT SERMON ON THE XIIII. CHAPTER OF THE BOOKE OF IVDGES.

NOw I will end the Chapter with *Samson*, and shew what Verse 20.
was done by him then, after the feast was ended: which is the fourth and last branch of the second part of the Chapter. We haue heard how ill hee was dealt with by the Philistims, yet (as the storie relateth) he did performe that, which they challenged as their due, which yet in deed they had iustly depriued themselues of by their bad dealing, if *Samson* would haue stood with them. But the Lord strengthened him, so that he paid them with the apparell of their owne countrimen. And hauing slaine thirtie men of them, and answered the demaund of the other that wagered with him, he was greatly offended with his wife, and went away from her to his fathers house, not telling her whither hee went, and in the

the meane while, she was giuen away from him by her father to one of his companions. And these things fell out after the marriage feast.

It is said heere, that the spirit of the Lord came vpon *Samson* againe, that we may know that he was guided thereby, in that which hee went about, when he slew the thirtie Philistims at Ascalon, and was thereby strengthened also to doe it. This example of his is not to bee followed of vs, I confesse, but we must do things in our vocation which God haue commanded generally in his word.

2 The apparell of these thirtie men of the Philistims whom hee slew, hee gaue to them that told the meaning of the riddle. So that although he fell into their hands by subtiltie, yet doth he not shift them off, and serue them according to their dealings with him, but satisfie them: for though no mention be here made of the linnen that hee gaue them with the garments, yet we must vnderstand it thus, that hee gaue them all, though the chiefe onely be named, it being the manner of the spirit of God to expresse the whole oftentimes by a part: and besides, wee know, they would not otherwise haue been contented and satisfied. So we are to know that it doth not become vs who are Christians, to yeeld ill measure to them that offer it to vs, as we see that neither *Samson* did, but to ouercome euill with good: which (it must be granted) will hardly be yeelded to, and the flesh affordeth much Rom. 8. ill counsell against it: but we are not debtors to it, to fulfill the desires of it, but to practise innocencie, through many prouocations to the contrarie. Nay further, although wee should pretend that wee vse our aduantage against him that hath wronged vs, to this end that we may play stopgame (as we say) with him, and saue our selues harmelesse, although we doe not depriue him simply of his owne, euen this (I say) is not permitted vs: except the aduantage be such as wee may lawfully take, and would haue taken against him in equitie, whether he had giuen vs occasion of reuenge or no. As for example, if hee haue wronged vs in our bargaine through our ouersight, we may not prouide for our selues by some ouersight of his: but if he stands not to couenant, or deny vs our due, we may lawfully seek our owne, after all other meanes to come by it haue been vsed, so we haue no respect of reuenge. And this is the streight rule: but where is the practise of it, euen among them that know it, and professe it should be so, to let others goe? But we thinke our condition vnequall, if we may not deceiue the deceiuer, and preuent his subtiltie with the like, and play the Cretians with the Cretian, that is, dissemble, cogge, and lye with him that makes no conscience, as if Christianitie might not meddle in this businesse; which yet is as apparant a relike of the old man, and the lust of our flesh, from which we should be purged, as any other, if *Paul* may be beleeued. Oh what occasion doth the common sort take to recompence euill for euill? They then shew themselues in their kinde and colours, when they can hit them home, who haue stood in their light neuer so little, and they loue to talke and glorie of it, when they haue done. But to say a word more of them, though it was not expressed in the agreement betwixt *Samson* and the Philistims, that the meaning of the riddle should be declared by their owne finding out, and not by falsehood, or indirect meanes: yet who doubteth, but that they meant so? In like manner, this departing from innocencie

nocencie in bargaines and contracts, and going to ſhifting, and againſt that which is honeſt and iuſt, vnder a pretence that euery particular cannot be mentioned and ſet downe, it is a great fault among men, and proues them that deale ſo, to bee farre from vprightnes: but thoſe that yeeld of their due rather then ſtriue endleſly, to be odde people.

But to paſſe from this, and to come to another point, namely of *Samſons* 3
wrath kindled againſt his wife for telling the riddle to the Philiſtims, and therefore going away without her to his fathers houſe, or at leaſt, not telling her of it, that act of his is not to bee iuſtified. For hee ought not in ſuch a moodie manner to haue departed from his wife, and leaue her in a wondering at his ſo ſudden going from her, and giuing her cauſe to feare at his returne home, a renuing of his diſpleaſure toward her againe: he ſhould not (I ſay) haue left her (a young woman new married) in doubts and feares, what might befall her: but he ſhould haue told her fault vnto her, as ſhee had been fit to heare it, betwixt them two, and ſo after a kinde reproofe, and a counſelling of her to be better gouerned, to haue ended the controuerſie, and either to haue taken her with him, or at leaſt not to haue gone away frow her ſullenly in diſpleaſure.

This ſheweth what a fault ſullennes is, when we bee angrie with any bodie, and yet wee will not bee knowne of any ſuch thing, neither ſhew the cauſe peaceably and plainly, why we are grieued, that ſo we might make an end of the matter, and be ſatisfied (if it may be) with the anſwere giuen vs, or at leaſt beare it patiently by little and little, and ſo cut off anger; but either to goe out of the companie diſcontented and vnquiet, or ſaying nothing, but broyling in our ſtomackes to the great griefe and offence of the partie againſt whom our anger is kindled and conceiued, thus to doe (I ſay) is a thing vtterly vnbeſeeming a Chriſtian. But if queſtion bee made which of the two is worſt, either open or ſecret anger; I ſay, the bewraying of it, and the letting of it appeare, if we be ſo impotent that we cannot bridle and ſuppreſſe it, is of both euils farre more tolerable, then this ſmoothering and keeping in of it, though both be vile and odious.

For as if an houſe be ſet on fire, it is farre more dangerous, and threatneth greater miſchiefe to the ſpeedie conſuming of all that is in the houſe, when the flame is pent in, then when it hath vent to breake foorth: Euen ſo, the anger that is hidden and concealed, is farre worſe then that which ſheweth it ſelfe; as may be ſeene in *Abſoloms* hidden wrath (breaking into murther) which except it bee in a high degree inflamed, (and that bewraieth much follie) will ſoone vaniſh and come to an end: whereas the other imagineth euill, and bringeth it foorth, when hee thinketh and ſeeth beſt. Yet I grant there are degrees in this ſullennes, but it is too vnbeſeeming a Chriſtian, when it is in the loweſt degree that is; yea though it goe away in time, when the ſtrength of it is ouer, without any further hurt doing.

The remedie here, is to weigh the follie and ſhame of ſuch diſguiſing of our ſelues. Alſo to conſider what and who wee bee, that take the matter ſo hotly, which is done againſt vs, who haue prouoked God as many times as we haue haires on our head. And how much greater cauſe we giue to God to be diſpleaſed with vs we ſhould conſider, and whether we could like that the Lord ſhould ſo hide his diſpleaſure againſt vs, and execute it vpon vs, when we would not,neither are aware of it. Thus,and by such like meanes, we should goe about to resist and asswage it. And if it bee hardly done at the first,yet afterwards it will be done more easily, if wee labour for it, and so in times chace it away altogether, further then that some reliques of it will remaine in vs,as after some sore ague. Causes (I confesse) there are of separation betweene married persons,but euery man must not be his owne iudge,but either the Ciuill Magistrate, or else those that are appointed by God in the Church to bee iudges in these and such like cases,must determine. For what manner of society were there like to be among men,if each husband vpon euery tetch might for a shorter or longer time,leaue the fellowship of his wife? To be sure,this practise is one meanes (besides many more)of much vncleanenes,confusion of blood and posteritie,beggery of the parties and families so forsaken,and of what other riots and disorder God knoweth. For where the sacred ordinances of God(which are the religious bands and securing pledges of peace, vnion and order) are once leapt ouer,and troden downe, who can limit within any bounds the mischiefe like to ensue? Therefore let none of such as are guiltie in this kinde, plead *Samsons* example,who had as little libertie giuen him herein as they.

Now whereas some obiect,that *Samson* herein gaue place to wrath, and rather withdrew himselfe, then abode with her, lest hee might possibly haue broken out further: I answere,*Samson* in not dealing outragiously in words or deeds,is to be commended: howbeit his going away in passion, is not thereby excused, seeing this did not amend the matter, but made it worse. And although the partie offended may sometimes auoid (as *Ionathan* did) to alleniate such as are displeased in the companie, yet this followeth not, that the partie offended of the married couples) may depart from the offender,and goe away for adoe: for thereby he nourisheth his own humour,& prouoketh the other further,rather thē slaketh it in either.

Vers.21. But to goe forward,and so to draw to an end,here we may see what men get by such dealing. For while they be sullen,and take displeasure,and will not bewray it,the other against whom they conceiue it, are impatient, and cannot beare it,as we see here *Samsons* wife and her father not enduring this manner of his departure from her in dislike and discontentment, they (no marueile) breake off their loue,and turne and shew it to another. This was the good he got by his inconsiderate dealing. And if we marke, wee shall finde,that such rash follie and vnaduised dealing (as this of *Samsons* was) is commonly recompensed with some such vnwelcome crosse and trouble, and all through their owne fault who cause and prouoke it: so that they would after buy it off with labour and cost,when it is too late; which by a little wisedome and patience they might altogether haue remoued, & kept away. As may appeare by that fact of *Absolom*, who being secretly incensed against *Ammon* for abusing his sister(whereas he ought to haue accused him to his father, and committed the righting of his cause to him vnder God,without nourishing of a reuengefull humour;) what brought hee to passe thereby,and what ensued of it? but *Ammons* murther,*Dauids* sorrow, a breach in the familie,and to *Absolom* himselfe an vnpleasing exile from his fathers Court and presence. But farre different was *Dauids* behauiour, being prouoked by *Shemei*: he leaues the man, and looks into himselfe: *It may* *be be I haue deserued* (saith he) *that God should suffer him to curse me;let him alone.* A most worthie president. Therefore,let the angry and sullen person come foorth and shew what he hath gained by his folly,saue the name of a foole, and the brand of reproch,and we will recant and call backe that wee speake. No wonder if the mad man, casting fire,darts,arrowes,and deadly things, haue some of them light vpon his owne pate. It is iust also with God to bee displeased with such,and resist them,while they are vniustly displeased with others,and meditate how to reuenge. Many euen vpon the sudden in their vnaduised rage haue killed their dearest friends, (as *Alexander* is reported to haue done in his drunken fume) and after being sober, they haue been readie to reuenge themselues for their madnes. Others leaue prints of their anger in the faces or bodies of such as they light vpon, and some they kill forth right: which they then repent of when either they haue smarted well in the purse,or be drawne forth to punishment which is appointed for such furie and outrage. Let it teach vs, to shake off wilfulnes, impatience, and heate passions, and in stead of a little pleasing of our selues through follie, not neglect wise and kinde dealing, which shall not be repented of. And to this end we must vse to meditate,both of our own corruptions of pride, selfeloue,anger,loosenes,tetchines,frowardnes,and the like; how many and foule they are; and also of our selues,who are but wormes, dust and ashes; and therefore no such as may not be crossed: and last of all,we should consider of those whom wee are wont to bee offended with: that they are but men and mortall, and therefore subiect to humane infirmities; and what maruaile then,if they doe things sometime that we like not,and which doe crosse vs,seeing they doe to vs, but as we haue done oft to other. And wee being sicke of the same disease, and being infected with the same originall contagion and poyson,should rather pitie them,then bee angrie and out of patience with them. But it were infinite to set downe that which yet might be said to good purpose of anger,and remedies against it. This for this time by occasion of *Samsons* sullen mood at his departing from his wife then.

As for the fact of *Samsons* wife and her father, so soone to be aleniated from him, and she to be giuen to another, it is not to bee marueiled at, neither any reason to be asked of it,they being not led thereby,much lesse by a better guide in their doings,but by will,and strength of flesh,whereby they were readie to take very slight colour and pretence of reason for their doings, as hath been noted before, and as shall further appeare in the next chap.vers.2. And so we must looke for no better measure at the hands of wicked and vnreasonable men, if we giue them the least occasions, who are commonly carried to outrage without any occasions: to teach vs to haue as little to doe with them,as wee may: and when wee must needs,take wee heed that we make all sure on our sides,(as possibly we may) to auoid euill and perill by them. But if it fall out afterwards, that wee bee in danger to them,and that they haue aduantage against vs,(as who is not subiect to that and to the like?) wee must beare it patiently, committing the successe to God,with well doing. And here an end of this Chapter.

THE

THE SEVENTIE NINE SERMON ON THE XV. CHAPTER OF THE BOOKE OF IVDGES.

Verſ.1. *But within a while after in the time of wheate harueſt, Samſon viſited his wife with a Kid, ſaying, I will goe in to my wife into the chamber: but her father would not ſuffer him to goe in.*

2. *And her father ſaid, I thought that thou hadſt hated her: therefore gaue I her to thy companion. Is not her younger ſiſter fairer then ſhe? take her, I pray thee, in ſtead of the other.*

3. *Then Samſon ſaid vnto them, Now am I more blameleſſe then the Philiſtims: therefore will I doe them diſpleaſure.*

The ſumme of the Chapter.

I Will proceed, keeping the order that I obſerue in the reſt. And firſt to begin with ỳ ſumme, it is thus much: *Samſon*, when his wife was denied him, vpon his returne to her, tooke occaſion to ſet on fire the corne fields of the Philiſtims, and to kill them, being armed againſt them: whereupon they came into Iudea, to fight with the men thereof, vnleſſe they would deliuer *Samſon* into their hands bound: who therefore did ſo. But his bands being broken by the Lord, he ſlew a thouſand of them with the iaw bone of an aſſe: and being thirſtie after his labour, he obtained water from God by prayer: and ſo he was refreſhed againe.

The parts 4.

The parts of it are foure. The firſt, how *Samſon* tooke occaſion to hurt and to bee reuenged vpon the Philiſtims, to verſe 9. The ſecond, how the Philiſtims got him to bee deliuered bound into their hands by his owne countrimen: to the midſt of verſe 14. The third is, how he was ſtrengthened by God, ſo that he brake the cords, and ſlew a great many of them: to verſe 18. The laſt, how he thirſting after his labour, and obtaining water of God, was refreſhed. Of which in order, as the text giues occaſion.

The firſt part of the Chapter.

The ſumme of the firſt part.

COncerning the firſt part, and the woe that hee wrought them, the occaſion was, that his wife was denied to him, when he returned to take her, and was giuen to another, as appeareth in the firſt two verſes: hereby hee was prouoked, as we ſee in the third verſe, and ſo he ſet vpon and hurt them in their commodities, being ſo prouoked, as is ſhewed vnto the 9. verſe.

Verſe 1. And firſt it is ſaid, that after a while he came to his wife againe, & brought a Kid with him to make merrie with her, and to ſhew thereby that he was reconciled to her, and was purpoſed to liue with her againe. For he hauing in in absence considered his fault,in going from her in such a manner as he did, resolued and thought good now to cut off all occasions of griefe from her, and of separation,and to renew and recouer his decayed loue againe. If all that will condemne *Samson* for his choler would shame themselues as hee did here (in returning, which was a condemning of his departing) when they haue bin ouertaken as he was,it were well : or if men could be brought out of loue with such their wilfull doings, by considering that for the time they banish God out of their thoughts, and make a man slaue to his rankest enemy. But by this we see, that though good and bad haue passions,carrying and ruling them, yet where grace dwelleth, they shall be found out in time,and that shall be done to the vanquishing of them which the strength of corruption in those that want grace, will not suffer a man to marke and resist them. Sinne nourisheth it selfe (especially anger) by selfe-loue : smoothing it selfe vp with *Ionah* his conceit, [*I doe well to be angrie*] and so *Samson* would (perhaps) haue answered, if hee had been demaunded a while after he departed from her. But now at leisure he recanteth, and by returning, condemnes his departure,as I said ; much like the sonne,that being sent into the vineyard,bid his father doe his worke himselfe for him ; but after, comming to himselfe againe,did as he was bidden and went. Whereas a lewde person hauing sinned, pleaseth himselfe in it, and doubleth it with *Esau* in his taking strange wiues ; or if hee relent, it is for shame and terror onely as *Iudas* ; as I haue noted in *Abimelech* before, chapter 9. *Samson* in his cholericke pang, went away with resolution (likely) of neuer returning, but to let her goe as she deserued. But now in cooler blood he appeaseth himselfe (as the Musitian did *Elisha*) and demurring of his doings, confesseth, that though his wife deserued ill measure,yet it became not him who in so great heate sought to marry her : to deale so despitefully against her, and that presently vpon his marrying of her.

Doct. Ionah 4.9. Mat.21.29. Gen.28.9. Mat.27.3. 2.King.3.15.

And more particularly, as *Samson* here vpon better consideration returded to his wife againe, so it must be granted of all that there should not be any long displeasure conceiued betwixt couples, (if it cannot be auoided but that some will be,) and specially that it is too much that there should be any separation betwixt man and wife,vnlesse it be with consent,and in loue, and that also but for a while, and as the Apostle willeth that they may giue themselues to prayer and fasting, and so to come together againe, lest the diuell tempt them to euill. This I say were to bee wished : but if there fall out worse matter betwixt them, it ought to cease betimes, as wee see here *Samson* returned to his wife within a while after hee went from her. For if the prayers of married persons ought not to be broken off through dissention any day, as S. *Peter* chargeth ; much lesse ought there to bee a separation for a longer time.

1.Cor.7.5. 1.Pet.3.7.

Therefore seeing many occasions fall out hereof betwixt couples in marriage, by reason of much conceitednes one against the other, waywardnes, inconstancie in loue, falseheartednesse,and such like ; let such as abhor and would shunne this and the like wearisomenesse of their companions, neuer cease till they renounce and disclaime those corruptions, and pray oft and earnestly against the same, and arme themselues with many renued couenants, that no such thing may bee betwixt them. So shall they the better

Note.

keepe

keepe other in order who are vnder them, when they shall see no breaches nor brawles betwixt them: yea and they shall be fit to set other couples together who are at variance; but they shall ill doe that abroad, if they maintaine not peace at home.

Obiect. But by occasion that I said, that married couples should not be absent any long time one from the other; it is obiected that many are, who through necessitie of following their calling, cannot chuse but be a long time one from another, as many Lawyers, Merchants, Sea men and other: and therefore how can that charge that is giuen by the Apostle to the Corinths stand? to wit, that there should be no long absence betwixt couples. I answere: because that charge is no better kept, therefore is much euill committed, I meane through long absence one from the other, and many complaine how they smart by meanes thereof, and yet redresse it not, nay say plainely, they see not how they can.

1 Cor. 7. 5.

Answ.

And I say further, that men suffer much sorrow, and sustaine great troubles through their owne fault, who seeing what their callings are, and that absence must fall out betwixt them, doe neither labour for more grace themselues to beare it the better, neither seeke such yoke-fellowes as excell other therein, neither faithfully take order betweene themselues carefully to looke about them euery way to auoide danger. For God is not contrarie to himselfe, neither commandeth he contraries: as that there be no long absence one from another: and yet that they shall follow such callings as of necessitie require it. But if the last must needes be; then certainely they may bee helped and relieue themselues in the first. And if they both feare God (as otherwise what promise haue they that God will blesse them in any thing, or what speaking to them is there about any such matter? If (I say) they feare God, then by good order taking, betwixt themselues, and by oft and earnest praying on both parts, for quiet and chaste mindes and bodies, vsing therewith all good meanes for the same as neede shall require, then they shall attaine redresse against it, and God hath promised to such, that with consent they may be absent each from other, without the many vnquietnesses and other inconueniences, the which yet doe most certainely meete with such as be not so qualified: who if they fall into adulterie, and the like euils, it is the fruit of their sinne which God punisheth, I meane of their irreligiousnesse, vnfaithfulnesse, and such like, as they fall out to bee; who is able to say what or how many?

2 It followeth in this verse, when *Samson* would haue gone into the chamber to his wife, to do the dutie of an husband to her, the father the Philistim, would not suffer him, for he had giuen her to another! Oh wofull act, but especially before he had spoken with him. But we neede not wonder at that; for what reason doe such professe to yeelde of their doings? By this dealing of the Philistims, wee may see, what a sore punishment it is to haue to doe with such vnconscionable men, that will boldly hold our right from vs, and so deale with vs, that wee cannot make any reckoning, no not of that which is our owne, if it must come through their hands, neither can be sure of our owne, if it be owing and due vnto vs by them.

And what bondage is this, that another should haue power and authority ouer our goods? Nature it selfe being the foundation of propriety in each mans goods,and abhorring community, as the cut-throte of ciuill society and common-wealth. As if the labourer when he had done his work, must nor looke to receiue his wages; or the man who hath lent wares for money, should be denied it: as though hee that listeth, should claime or detaine another bodies goods. And to that point things are come in many places, that for the heathenish vnconscionablenesse that is grown vp in this world, a man cannot say that any thing hee hath is his owne, there are so many waies to defeate the owners of their due. And so are men pursued with other open wrongs,that they may well say,as *Samson* had cause to complaine; you deale with vs as Philistims. The vse of this is, to account of honest and faithfull men much the better,and in dealing with other bee wary and circumspect; also be ready to offer all good measure to those with whom we haue to doe. But this point offereth it selfe often. Note.

And as for *Samson*, who was denied his wife when hee returned to her fathers house to take and enioy her, all may see what a punishment it is. But when men bring it vpon themselues by their owne sinne,as he did, they are the lesse pitied. And this is true of the finall disappointment of the vngodly, as the example of the foolish Virgins sheweth, excluding themselues from that place, which yet they desired. Let euery man therefore auoide occasions of troubling himselfe as well this way as otherwise, by giuing liberty to his corrupt affections and lusts; wherein *Samson* failing, by going from his wife in a sullen and discontented manner,rather then wisely saluing vp her offence, now brought it to passe that hee was denied her when hee would gladly haue enioyed her. Thus doth a mans sin crop off the blossome which should after in season yeeld fruit. And this and such like are the fruites of our sinnes, which neuer yet, no not the pleasantest, did vs any good. This hurt among many other commeth; that therby we are depriued of our best liberties,when we would enioy them,and all because wee did,in our sinfull mood set light by them. But of this enough in the last verse of the former chapter.

Her father to excuse his cursed act, in giuing his daughter to another man,tels *Samson*,he thought he had hated her, therfore (he saith) I gaue her to thy companion, and then hee offered him her sister, as being fairer then she. Wee may learne by this his first speech, that wicked and vnconscionable men, when they haue offered great wrong to their neighbour, make a light matter of it: they thought (they say) they might haue done as great a matter as that, without offence taken thereat, and that they had cause to doe so; and they thought it would not haue been so hardly taken; yea and many bid them goe seeke their remedy,where they can get it. So in the History of the Church, *Iulian* the reuolter being solicited to deale more indifferently with the Christians, vsed to answere: Tush, they haue no wrong done to them, for their Master commands them being smitten on the one cheeke,to turne the other. So did the cruell *Pharaoh* vpbraid the poore Israelites groning vnder their burthens; saying to them, *Yee are idle,* and want worke: and the Babylonians so taunted the poore Iewes mourning vnder captiuity; *Sing vs some of the songs of Sion. Rehoboam* also being willed to mitigate the heauie hand which his father held ouer his subiects, answereth; Tush,yee had too good measure shewed yee by my father; my little finger Verse 2. Mat.5.39. Exod.5.17. Psal.137.3. 1.King.12.14.

ſhall be heauier then his loines. And as ſlightly bad men deale with the Lord in his ſeruice: they thinke their drawing neere to him with their bodies is ſufficient ſeruice, though their hearts be farre off, when yet he himſelfe pro-
Math.15.9. feſſeth, that in vaine doe ſuch worſhip him.

1.Sam.13.9.13 So *Saul* thought he might offer a burnt offering and a peace offering to the Lord, (though it was contrary to his commandement) and would needs imagine it to bee well pleaſing to him ſo to doe, taking it harſhly that *Samuel* preſſeth him ſo with his diſobedience. But hee ſhould haue obeyed God, and not haue followed his owne fancie.

But to returne to their dealings with men, whom when they haue ſore hurt and wronged, they make a light matter of it, and ſay, they meant no harme; they are like the man in the Prouerbs, that fained himſelfe mad, and
Prou.26.19. caſt firebrands and arrowes, and ſaith, he was in ſport: ſo they deale deceitfully and wickedly with their friend and neighbour, and ſay, they are in ſport, that is, they meane no harme. But if the leaſt iniurie bee offered them (as was heere to this Philiſtim by *Samſon*, going from his daughter but a while) they will make of a little matter a great, rather then be ſatisfied with ſuch an anſwere, that the party thought it would not be ſo hardly taken. To
Eccleſ.11.9. conclude, as *Salomon* ſaith to the young men; *Reioce in thy youth, &c: but bee ſure God will bring thee to iudgement:* ſo I may ſay to theſe men while health and iollity laſteth, and none to controll you, tread your vnderlings vnder your feet, and winde God himſelfe about your fingers: make a ſlight matter of ſinne, and ſay, it was but a tricke of youth, it was but a ſmall matter, I did it but once; as many at this day make a But of *Adams* ſin, he did but eate an apple (a matter of nothing) and loe both he and all his poſterity muſt die
Gen.25.32. for it. And doe ye as *Eſau* did, Tuſh, what great matter is it to ſell my birthright, let it goe? Sooth vp your ſelues (I ſay) with the conceit of him that thinkes God is (as the Papiſts paint him) but a good old man and ſits idle, hee will neither doe good nor euill, wee may vſe and deale with him as wee liſt. But when God ſhall take the wild Aſſe in her moneths (who being
Ier.2.24. light, cared for none of her purſuers) I meane, when he ſhall viſit theſe men, and ſet before their face their vnconſcionablenes and hard meaſure, which they haue offered and made nothing of, (as if other men were made to bee their teniſ balles, and the obiects of their wrong and ſcorne) then their ſin ſhall not ſeeme a ſmall But, but a great hill and mountaine vnto them, and they ſhall cry out, ſaying, We neuer felt the weight of our ſinne till now; it was light in committing, but the puniſhment is greater then wee can beare.
Heb.13.4. And as the holy Ghoſt threatens adulterers, *God ſhall iudge them*; ſo let theſe know, that ſeeing they are too ſtout and ſtately for common men to meddle
Iam.5.4. with, God will take them in hand, and (as *Iames* ſaith) bee an aduocate for the innocent againſt their oppreſſors. This bee added to the former point,
2.Theſ.1.6. to this end, that as there I counſell others to haue little to doe with ſuch Cormorants: ſo by this marke and cognizance, and the like (as the next point noteth) we may know and auoide them the better. Thus much bee ſaid of the firſt ſpeech of *Samſons* father in law: the next followeth.

2 And that was, that he offered him his wiues ſiſter to be his wife. For hee reſpected not how neere ſhe was in blood, but feared him, becauſe hee ſaw that hee was a man of a great ſtomacke, and did fret ſore againſt the Philiſtims,

ſtims, therfore he offered him her to appeaſe his wrath, and yet many of the Heathens did know that ſuch marriages were vnlawfull,and made lawes againſt them. Thus he thought to put him off. Euen ſo wicked men, when their bad dealings are found out, and they in ſome danger and feare by meanes therof, marke what recompence they offer: and that is worſe then if they offered none at all, (as hee did heere) and ſuch as they cannot take, nor be the better for, being (for the moſt part) againſt conſcience: for either they promiſe them faire and goe from it: or if they pay their debts,and ſatisfie for their wrongs which they haue done, it ſhall bee done moſt vnwillingly,or with other mens loſſes and harmes.

By this act of his father in law, *Samſon* tooke occaſion to vex the Philiſtims, the Lords enemies: for hee ſaw that his father in law did but mocke him,and ſo he took not the condition that was offered him, but ſaid,I haue receiued wrong of you Philiſtims,and my dealings ſhall be ſeene to be better then yours, if it come into queſtion. Ye haue giuen me iuſt cauſe to ſeek reuenge. But yet we muſt know,that this hee did as one appointed by God thereto, and not as a man to eaſe his ſtomacke vpon them for his own pleaſure. So we may in no wiſe reuenge our enemies in the heate of our hearts, (howſoeuer wee hardly heare that ſaying)but leaue vengeance to God,and bridle our vnruly affections,that they may not carrie vs to euill againſt men; but ouercome their euill with doing them good. Although I denie not,but where we are commanded of God to purſue euill,we muſt goe about it readily, as *Samſon* heere did. But heere I end theſe verſes. Verſ.3. Rom.12.21.

Verſ.4. *And Samſon went and caught three hundred foxes, and tooke firebrands, and turned taile to taile, and put a firebrand in the middeſt betweene two tailes.*

5 *And when hee had ſet the brands on fire, hee let them goe into the ſtanding corne of the Philiſtims, and burnt vp both the ſhockes, and alſo the ſtanding corne, with the vineyards and oliues.*

6 *Then the Philiſtims ſaid,Who hath done this? and they anſwered,Samſon the ſonne in law of the Timnite, becauſe he had taken his wife and giuen her to his companion. And the Philiſtims came vp, and burnt her and her father with fire.*

7 *And Samſon ſaid vnto them, Though ye haue done this, yet will I be auenged of you,and after that I will ceaſe.*

8 *And he ſmote them hip and thigh,with a great ſlaughter, and hee went downe, and dwelt in the top of the rocke Etam.*

Samſon hauing gotten occaſion to ſet vpon the Philiſtims, the holy ſtory in theſe fiue verſes ſheweth how hee vſed it, that is to ſay, theſe two waies: firſt in ſpoiling their commodities,their vines and oliue trees, and burning vp their corne; and then in taking away the liues of many of them alſo. The firſt of theſe two vexings of them is ſet downe in theſe two firſt verſes, and he did it in this manner. He got three hundred foxes (which abounded in thoſe places) and the tailes of them hee bound together,and put firebrands in the middeſt of them, and ſent them into the corne of the Philiſtims, which then was ripe, and burned vp heapes or rickes of corne gathered in,and that which was ſtanding alſo. *The ſumme of theſe verſes.*

Verse.4.5. It is but a folly for vs to aske why hee plagued the Philistims that way among all other. It is sufficient that the holy Ghost hath set it downe that he punished them very sore euen that way, as we may conceiue. For a fire being kndled in many places, and spreading further and further in euery place where it was kindled, much hurt might soone bee done thereby; as appea-
2.Sam.14.30. red by *Absaloms* dealing with *Ioab* in setting his corne field on fire. But much more these wild creatures (being terrified with the fire) running too and fro, and carrying it through the fields might doe greater mischiefe. A thing (doubtlesse) vnlikely to haue come to passe so; but the more vnlikely it was, the more it admonisheth vs, not onely that our commodities and riches are subiect to losse sundry waies which we may conceiue, but euen that way also that we cannot thinke. For who would haue thought (though by windes, wet, and drought they might haue lost their fruites) yet that they should haue been spoiled this way? But the reason is, for that there are so many casualties and changes in this transitorie life, and we are liuely put in mind of it hereby. Possesse we therefore these earthly benefits, as if wee did not, and so we shall be lesse addicted to them. For no man can shew to how many vnlikely dangers mens goods lie open, beside those which are common and ordinary. We haue heard of late, that many mens commodities being brought in (and so in likelihood past danger) haue been in great part destroyed by vermine, as mice and rats.

Luk.12.20. Therefore they are called vncertaine riches, seeing no man hath any hold
1.Tim.6.17. of them, but one mans they are to day, and another mans to morrow. Besides, we ought not to set our hearts on them, which we cannot keepe, neither thereby giue occasion to our selues to be disquieted when God by any meanes shall depriue vs of them. But minde we better things, and those not
Mat.6.20. seene with mortall eye, which shall also be witnesses that wee haue treasure laid vp for vs in heauen. And when wee walke in the discharge of our callings, whereby, through Gods blessing we encrease our substance, yet euen then regard we more the commandement enioyning vs labour, then the profit: and comfort we our selues in our good conscience in comming by and vsing them, with Gods promise of good successe, rather then by reckoning our commodities before we enioy them. But of this point I haue said more elsewhere.

2 The next thing in these two verses is this, which we are to make our profit by; that when the Lord giueth vs opportunity, and offereth vs occasion to do him seruice, we should be wise to see it, & ready to vse it, that we may so testifie our obedience both to God and men. For so did *Samson* here. The Lord would haue him set vpon the Philistims, but so, that he should first be prouoked by them; lest if he had done it without iust occasion offered him, they might not haue pursued him alone, but all the land; as they made much adoe for the hurt he heere did them, till they knew that some of their brethren, the Philistims, had prouoked him, and that thereupon hee sought to be reuenged on them; as in vers 6. Looke more in *Gedeons* story.

Vers.6. Before *Samson* proceed any further against the Philistims, to pursue them in their liues, it is shewed in this verse, that there was hot enquirie among them who it was that had so spoiled their commodities. And they learned that it was *Samson* that had done it: and further the reason was rendred why he he did so, and that was, because the Timnite had taken his wife from him, and giuen her to another. Which when they vnderstood, they went by and by and burnt her and her father with fire: for they considered that they had done him great wrong, and thought that he auenged himselfe on other of them for that which they had done to him.

In this verse, by the earnest inquirie after him that had done them so great displeasure, we may see, that by the light of nature they did this, (euen as it is lawfull for vs to doe in our owne cases by the help of the Magistrate) to seeke to finde out such as haue done much euill in the Common-wealth, and that were troublesome. But yet herein we must differ from them, that as these heere did eagerly pursue the doer of wrong to themselues, (more then the disorder) so much more wee that are further inlightened by the word of God, ought to hearken after such offenders, and to procure their iust punishment as we may; rather for their sinne, then to auenge our selues thereby. As *Salomon* dealt with *Ioab*, who had ioyned himselfe with *Adonijah* against the Lords annointed: for hee commanded him to bee slaine, that the blood which he had shed causelesse, might be vpon his owne head. And great is the sin of them, that rather then they would incurre the least danger and displeasure at the hands of bad persons, worthie to be cut off, or sore punished; doe suffer them to goe on in their wickednesse, rather then to withstand and bring them foorth before authoritie to receiue their due; yea rather, if they can, they will bee readie to excuse their fault and defend them: but if a trespasse be committed against themselues, there is no measure in pursuing their enemies. But a fitter occasion to handle this, will be offered in the 21. Chapter. *Doct.* 1.King 2.34.

2 When the Philistims vnderstood that *Samson* had thus spoyled them, because the Timnite had giuen his wife to his companion, they went (it is said here) and burnt both him and his daughter, and the house ouer their heads. But why did they so? For the Timnite was not he that hurt them. No, but seeing they could not come by *Samson*, to take reuenge on him, therefore they punished them who were the occasions of *Samsons* spoyling them, though they were in no wise consenting to it, nor knowing what hee did. A most vnreasonable act, to fall vpon them who were no way guiltie of the hurt done to them. The Lord (indeed) did most iustly hereby reuenge that villany, which they had all of them offered to *Samson*, but this they looked not at: God onely ouer-ruled their appetites, that in one and the same act (most iniurious in it selfe) yet the Lord executed his most righteous iustice against these malefactors, arming one wicked person against another, and preparing a way thereby to reuenge these Philistims themselues, as shal appeare afterward.

But here we may see the madnes and outrage that is in men. For though these were Heathens, and therefore might bee thought to haue none to match them in grosse wickednes, among such as are baptized: yet behold, they who are destitute of grace among vs, (further then the feare of man restraineth some) are let loose to as great sinnes. For proofe whereof, behold the dealing of those furious Iewes, Acts 18. who when they could not come by *Paul*, fell vpon *Sosthenes* his companion, and beate him: and at this day the Papists when they cannot come by the heretike himselfe (as they terme him) Acts 18.17.

him) vſe to draw his picture, as exactly as they can, and with great deſpite burne it in the fire, ſhewing what they would doe to the perſon. Not vnlike to the practiſe of ſeditious ſouldiers, in chopping them as ſmall as herbs to pot, who oppoſe them in their mutinie. And we ſee it commeth to paſſe ſometimes, that when vile men are giuen ouer to furie, paſſion and moode, he ſhall beare the blowes that commeth next in their way, though hee was in no fault, and whatſoeuer is next them, be it knife, dagger, cudgel, or whatſoeuer elſe, whether it beate out the eye or tooth, or breake arme or legge, all is one with them, when they be moodie: euen as ſhe-Beares that are robbed of their whelpes. Nay, ſo little are they led by ſound reaſon, that when, through their owne raſhnes, they haue hurt themſelues at a doore, or fall, by ſtumbling at a ſtone, they curſe the one, and beate the other. But if they ſuſtaine damage or loſſe by any neighbour, they are not ſatisfied, till with the Philiſtims they haue their blood, at leaſt till they ſeeke it, though the hurt done to them was againſt their will, who are thus doggiſhly purſued of them.

Touching ſuch rage and madnes I haue ſaid ſomewhat heretofore, to diſcredit it, and diſſwade men from it: both by ſhewing the hideous face thereof, and the curſed fruites iſſuing therefrom. As who beholding *Lamech* in
Gen. 4. 23. his furie and outrage, and hearing the terrour of his words, would not abhorre him and his qualities? And yet there remaine among vs men of no better diſpoſition, (though they will not ſpeake ſo plainly as *Lamech* did) who could in their rancour eate the very heart of their enemie with garlicke, as the ſaying is: and yet nouriſh this ſerpent in their boſomes ſtill, and fight not againſt it with the ſword of the Spirit, nor confeſſe themſelues to bee beaſts for their yeelding ſo farre, whereby their whole Chriſtianitie is called into queſtion.

Doct. 3. But another thing in this verſe is not to be omitted, that whereas *Samſons* wife being threatned by her neighbours before, that they would burne her, except ſhe told them the meaning of the riddle; ſhe (as wee haue heard) to auoid the danger, did tell it them, to the griefe and great hurt of her huſband; and yet now behold, ſhe could not auoide it, but by the Philiſtims was burned for all that. For by and for her telling the riddle to her people, ſhe was ſaued from burning, but *Samſon* went from her, and for that her father gaue her to another to wife: for that, *Samſon* ſpoyled the Philiſtims corne and commodities; and for that cauſe they burned her and her father; and ſo the riddle, the declaring whereof ſaued her life, the ſame was the occaſion of loſing it. Euen ſo, that which ſhee ſought before by vnlawfull meanes and ſhifts to ſhunne, I meane burning; by the ſame vnlawfull ſhifts
Gen. 37. 27. ſhe procured it. And ſo it was with *Ioſephs* brethren, when they ſought to be rid of him, becauſe of his dreames of ſuch honor that he ſhould haue aboue them, which he told them of, and they in no wiſe could abide it, and therefore they ſold him into a farre countrey: euen thereby they brought him
Gen. 39. 1. and 20. compared with 41. 40. &c to that honour, cleane contrary to their mindes and liking, as is cleere in the ſtorie.

And what is more manifeſtly and manifoldly proued by experience among vs then this, that whereas many ſeeing great troubles comming toward them, doe ſeeke by euill practiſes, as lying, ſwearing, forſwearing and

ſuch

ſuch like,to winde out of them; what may bee commonlier ſeene (I ſay) Note.
then this, that thereby they bring farre greater and ſorer, if not the ſame troubles vpon themſelues? For while they ſeeke to auoid worldly ſorrow for a while,which had come by their trouble,but much leſſe,they are plunged into a farre greater, euen to torment their conſciences with deadly ſtings of ſorrow by their ſinne,which of a long time will not bee plucked out. So the Iewes ſought libertie by putting Chriſt to death; yet when Matth 28.11
thereby he roſe roſe againe from death,it cut their hearts deeplier,and imbondaged them much more, (I ſpeake of ſuch as were not ſeared with an hot yron) and ſo much the rather for that they haue thereby brought his blood vpon them,and their children vnto this day.

I ſtand the rather vpon this, becauſe it is thought a fooliſh part for a man to beare a diſcommodity patiently, rather then to ſhift it off by vnlawfull meanes,and is counted a point of wiſdome to fall rather into the hands of bad men,though by yeeding to ſinne, then to commit his caſe to God, with confidence in him: for what account is made of that,though it bee againſt a mans conſcience? As many Politikes cenſure *Daniel* for his vpright Dan.6.10.
perſiſting in the ſeruice of God,after the decree was made againſt him by the Princes. What? (ſay men) had he no ſhift nor euaſion to deliuer himſelfe,and elude his aduerſaries,but he muſt wilfully fall into the ſnare? Oh foole! learne by this example the truth of that denunciation; *He that will* Matth.16.25.
ſaue his life,(that is, giue skinne for skinne, conſcience and all to ſaue it) *he* Iob.2.4.
ſhall loſe it: that is,either be diſappointed for his ſhifts,God not giuing him fauour in the eyes of his enemies,who count him but an hypocrite for all his ſhifting) or if he ſeeme to gaine ſomewhat thereby in one kinde,yet he ſhall neuer enioy his penniworth with comfort, but rather with a checking and vpbraiding conſcience,if he doe not at length with wearines renounce it,and caſt it away, as *Iudas* did his wages of iniquitie. But *hee that loſeth his* Matth.27.3.
*life,*that is,truſteth God with his moſt precious liberties,rather then he will runne vpon the pikes to haue his will,*he ſhall finde it,*as *Heſter* did, by ſauing Note.
it; or as the good Martyrs did,by changing it for eternall life,after the ſhort enduring of trouble,which their good and quiet ſpirit,and the hope of reward ſhall make tolerable. Oh that men would once learne to meaſure gaine, not by the preſentnes, but by the cleerenes, and worthineſſe of it! they ſhould by this meanes auoid many a ſinne,with the ſhifts that attend vpon it, beſides preuenting of many after-reckonings of ſorrow and puniſhment, which an euill conſcience makes vnſufferable: eſpecially if the ſame miſchiefe light vpon them,which with ſo deare a price they ſought to auoid. Very Heathens could ſay,that vengeance would not ſuffer the guil- Acts 2 .4.
tie to eſcape,though they might ſhift for the preſent. But the word of God teacheth vs the cauſe: becauſe the God of vengeance is the Lord of hoaſts, and hath a hundred ſouldiers armed to meete with his enemie, though he Amos 5.19.
haue eſcaped one. It is as if a man hauing ſhunned a Beare, ſhould meete with a Lion: he hath eſcaped the former,but he is ſtill in chace,neuer at reſt till he be deſtroyed,and hee had been better to haue yeelded to the firſt. The ſtory of al Churches verifie this truth in the examples of abiuring hypocrites,who met with worſe meaſure when God took them in hand,then

1.Cor.1.20. they shunned at the hand of men. *For the wisedome of man is foolishnes with God.*

Vers.7.8. Now in these two verses the other way is set downe whereby *Samson* hurt the Philistims, and that was in their bodies, which hee so lamed and pained with kicking them with his feete, that he did beate life out of them. And so wee are to vnderstand those words in the 8. verse [*hippe and thigh*] that is, with a necessary supply added for making the sense runne the roundlier, thus; his foote put foorth to their thigh with a strong blow, and had no other weapon to fight against them, but his foote; spurning them as sluggish persons, not able to resist him. This as the best exposition (in my opinion, leauing others to their own iudgement) of these words [*he smote them hippe and thigh with a mightie plague*] I set downe, not troubling the reader with other opinions about it.

Doct. Now by this extraordinarie strength that hee had, thus to spurne and tread them downe euen to death; and the slauish dastardlines of the Philistims, on the other side as much to bee admired, that they seemed not to striue or fight for themselues a whit: wee may see how mightily God assisteth his seruants, whom he setteth about his worke, when he will haue all to see that it is he that bringeth it to passe, and not they. As in *Gedeons* vanquishing the Midianites that couered as grashoppers the face of the earth

Iudg.7 7. for multitude; for he did it with a very few, euen three hundred men. And

2.Chro.20.17. so he dealt with *Iehosaphat*. For when the children of Ammon, and Moab, and mount Seir, came to cast him and the people of Iudah out of Gods inheritance, with a fearefull and an exceeding armie, the Lord sent a messenger to them, saying: *Feare not for all this great multitude, for the battell is not yours but Gods. Stand still, moue not, and behold the saluation of God towards you, To morrow goe out against them, and the Lord will be with you.* And (to make vse of this doctrine) I say, that if wee haue eyes wee may see, that God assisteth and helpeth his, in their trouble, feare and neede, beyond all that mans reason can reach vnto, when they depend on, and trust in him: yea hee brings them into danger oftentimes and straits, and all to this end that his power in deliuering them, may be seene in their weakenes, and fighteth for them as sensibly as he did for *Iehosaphat*, or for *Dauid* against *Goliah*. Of the which truth *Ionah* is a liuely proofe, who was receiued into the fish, (when he was cast into the sea) preserued in the belly of it, and cast vp to land by the extraordinarie prouidence of God, rather then hee should be lost and forsaken.

Samson hauing thus slaine them, hee went and abode in a place called Etham, an high rocke, which belonged to the tribe of *Simeon*, in the borders of Iudah. And therefore it is said in the next verse, that the Philistims came and pitched in Iudah to seeke for him. But before hee thus slew them, as is said in the 8. verse, that is to be marked which he said, and is set downe in the seuenth verse; that when he saw that they had burned the Timnite and his daughter, seeing they were onely an occasion of their losse, he said thus to those Philistims; If yee haue done thus to them your neighbours, and of your owne countrey, who did not hurt you, what would you doe to me, if I should fall into your hands? I will therefore be auenged of you, before I

cease.

ceaſe. Thus much for the cleering of theſe two verſes.

Out of this verſe wee may note, that if men be cruell and outragious a- Doct.verſ.7.
gainſt them that were onely the occaſions of their hurt, though they neuer ſought nor intended it; how much more will they ſhew their fury and madnes againſt them, who haue done the hurt and wrong vnto them? This may fitly be gathered from the reaſoning of *Samſon*. And ſo wee may well conclude and ſay; that if wee will bee exaſperated againſt ſuch as doe but come in our way, or were onely preſent where wee ſuſtained ſome reproch or iniurie; how much more, if we light vpon him that hath done the wrong to vs, will wee ſhew our ſelues vnreaſonable? For hee that cannot beare a little, much leſſe will beare a great deale. Fall not we (as neere as we can) into the hands of ſuch. So hee that will beate the ground at which he ſtumbled, will much more fiercely riſe againſt him, who hath caſt him wilfully on the ground.

Further, in that *Samſon* ſaid, hee would be auenged of the Philiſtims before he ceaſed, hee ſpake as it became him, ſeeing God had appointed him
to doe ſo. So are all in authoritie ſet in place by God to be a terrour to the Rom.13.4.
wicked, euen as they are for the comfort of thoſe that are good. For it is a
grace, and no eaſie matter to puniſh ſinne aright, and to ſeeke to winne the Prou.17.15.
offender. And it is as great an offence for them to doe that worke of the Lord negligently, as it is to fall vpon the innocent haſtily and cruelly. So all priuate perſons, and Preachers of the word eſpecially, ſhould doe likewiſe: to wit, make that ſinne odious to themſelues and others (as farre as lieth in them) which the Magiſtrate is to puniſh, and they to reproue: euen as they ought to be like affected to all ſin, becauſe God abhorreth it. Here-
in ſaying with good *Leui*; *Who is my father? I know not euen my father*, if hee Deut 33.9.
goe about to hinder the worke of God: and herein follow wee our bleſſed
Sauiour, who came to deſtroy the workes of the diuell. But I haue oft no- 1.Ioh.3.8.
ted this before, therefore I preſſe it no further.

That which in the former verſe he was ſaid to threaten, the ſame in this Verſ.8.
verſe he is ſaid to doe and accompliſh. That is, to ſmite them with a great plague and in reprochfull maner: ſetting (as it were) his feete vpon them, or ſpurning them vnto death. This, if it had not been commanded by God,
had bin cruelty. So that here we may learne to know, that except we haue 1
our charge from God to execute vpon men ſeuere and ſharp puniſhment, it is meere crueltie to ſet vpon it, which wee ſhould in no wiſe like, much leſſe delight to attempt: no more then wee would be willing to haue the like offered to our ſelues. But haue wee compaſſion and commiſeration ouer ſuch as are in miſerie any way, as we our ſelues would in like caſe deſire the ſame. This is a branch of the former, often touched before.

That which is ſaid of the rocke Etham here in in Iudah, is to ſhew that 2
he abode there, till hee was after taken from thence by the men of Iudah, and carried to the Philiſtims: which was ſoone after. Of which I know no more to be ſaid, ſaue onely that we may ſee that he did not goe to hide himſelfe in a corner, as though hee durſt not ſtand to that which hee had done, but being like to be apprehended he went, God directing him to take that patiently which they ſhould doe to him, and to depend on him for iſſue, though to a defenced and high place, yet to an open, where he was knowne

to be, and was easily remoued from thence, when the men of Iudah came vp thither to carrie him bound to the Philistims, he committing himselfe to Gods prouidence, whose worke he had done. For though he went thither from the Philistims, yet he was euen there in a place where they gouerned.

So let all bee wise, to doe that for which they may not bee driuen to flie for it: but so answere to it, and bee armed to beare that which comes vpon them for the same. As it falleth out oft times, that euen for that which they haue well done, some instruments of the diuell or other will bee ready alwaies to molest and bring trouble vpon them for it. Notwithstanding the Mat.5.12. which, yet they may reioyce as our Sauiour willeth them, and bee glad if 1.Pet.3.17. Prou.28.1. they be persecuted and reuiled for his sake, that is, for well doing. But let no man suffer for euill doing, for hee shall bee forced to hide himselfe, and runne away; the wicked flying, when no man pursueth him. And yet (all that I haue said notwithstanding) it is not denyed any man, to rescue himselfe from the open wrong of the vnconscionable, by any lawfull meanes, neither ought it to preiudice the equity of our cause.

THE EIGHTIETH SERMON ON THE XV. CHAPTER OF THE BOOKE OF IVDGES.

The second part of the Chapter.

Vers. 9. *Then the Philistims went vp, and pitched in Iudah, and spread themselues in Lehi.*

10 *And the men of Iudah said, Why are ye come vp against vs? and they answered, To bind Samson are we come vp, and to doe to him, as he hath done to vs.*

11 *Then three thousand men of Iudah went to the top of the rocke Etam, and said to Samson; Knowest thou not that the Philistims are rulers ouer vs? what is this that thou hast done to vs? And he said vnto them, As they did vnto me, so haue I done vnto them.*

12 *And they said vnto him, We are come downe to bind thee, that we may deliuer thee into the hand of the Philistims. And Samson said vnto them; Sweare vnto mee that ye will not fall vpon me your selues.*

13 *And they spake vnto him, saying; No; but wee will bind thee fast, and deliuer thee into their hand: but surely we will not kill thee. And they bound him with two new cords, and brought him from the rocke.*

14 *And when he came to Lehi, the Philistims shouted at the meeting of him.*

The summe of these verses. HOw *Samson* vexed the Philistims, we haue heard in the first part of this Chapter: In this second is shewed, how they pursuing him, got him to bee brought bound vnto them. And that was after this manner. First they came vp against Iudah where *Samson* was, threatning to fight against them, vnlesse they brought *Samson* bound

bound vnto them. And this is in vers.9.10. Secondly, they of Iudah fetched him from the rocke Etam, where hee was, and brought him bound vnto them: vers.11.12.13. And thirdly, when he came to them at Lehi, the place heere mentioned, the Philistims shouted for ioy that hee was come, thinking to haue some great hand ouer him: and this is in a part of the 14. verse.

But to come more particularly to these three points, it is said first, that the Philistims came with an armie against Iudah in that part of it which was neere adioyning & conterminate to their owne countrey, here called Lehi, which signifieth a cheeke or iaw-bone, and tooke the name from an act that *Samson* did in that place afterwards, in slaying many there with the iaw bone of an Asse. Into Iudah, I say, they came, putting the men thereof into great feare, for that *Samson*, who had done them so great hurt, had his abode among them, and was (as they tooke it) harboured and maintained in that euill which he had wrought against them, by them of Iudah. And when they demanded of the Philistims, why they did so come against them, seeing they had not broken their league with them; they answered: that they did it for the great hurt that they had sustained by *Samson*, and him they would haue to be deliuered vnto them, or else they would make warre with them. Vers.9.10.

The Philistims did in this, but as any like them, nay many farre better, would doe in the like case. Nay, there are few to bee found, either nation against nation, or man by man prouoked, who are not ready enough to seek reuenge, yea to passe their bounds therein exceedingly, rather then to come behind in such cases: who though they doe euill, as the Philistims also did, yet if any man would aske whether a Christian must put vp all wrongs and iniuries? I answere; he may defend himselfe in his innocent case, and stop the course of his aduersarie, so as it bee without malice and a reuenging mind, of which more is said in another place. Neither doe I affirme, that sin is to goe vnpunished, by this debarring of euery man in his priuate quarrell from reuenge: for (as that officer of Ephesus told the seditious Citizens) If ye haue ought against these men, there are aduocates; so I say, in cases of weight, there are Magistrates, who are to looke to this, that neither by the impudency of the wrong doer, nor the impotency of the reuenger the common-wealth be disturbed: And so much more in the sinnes committed against the Maiesty of God, ought the Magistrate to bestirre himselfe, if hee doe as behoues him: wherein he is no reuenger, but rather one that stands in the gap to stay Gods hand from being reuenged vpon the whole body for the disorder of a few bad members, as in *Phinees* his story is manifest. But that which I complaine of is this: that whereas men are so hot one against another for bodily trespasses, and temporary harmes done vnto them; yet their owne speciall sinnes, which doe themselues infinite harme, they haue no heart to goe against them; no neither are wise enough to beleeue what deadly enemies they bee vnto them. And thus wee may find it in all kinds of offenders. A thing worthy to be bewailed, if it were duly considered; especially in those who hauing found them by wofull experience to haue wrought them more sorrow and iust cause of complaint, then their rankest enemy could possibly haue procured them. Doct.vers.9. Act.19.38. Numb.25.8. Note.

As for reuenging of others; that should alway be ready to feare and hold

Rom.12.19. vs from it, which is written, Rom. 12. *Vengeance is mine, saith the Lord, and I will repay it.* For whiles men are ouer busie in quitting themselues of their enemy, they both exasperate him, and make God a party against them, and so they find the harder match of it. *Dauid* durst not reuenge when he could
1.Sam 26.10. haue done it, but answered; *As the Lord liueth, either the Lord shall smite him, or his day shall come to die, or he shall fall by the sword, or otherwise: as for me, I will*
1.Sam 24.13. *not smite him; wickednesse be with the wicked, but my hand bee not vpon him.* But
1.King 19.2. we (though wee can doe nothing) yet please our selues in *Iezabels* humour, and her sonnes, saying, *God doe so to me, and more also, if I make not Eliahs head*
2.King.6.1. *as the head of one of these to morrow.* So said *Iehoram* of *Elisha*. Whereas before we can bring our purpose to passe, we are our selues preuented by God, and our nailes pared, and we laid full low oftentimes, more fit to be pitied, then to reuenge. Doubtlesse, if we could moderate our selues, and take the Apo-
Rom.12.19.20 stles counsell to the Romans [If thine enemy hunger, feed him] Rom. 12. wee should sooner make our aduersary submit himselfe vnto vs, and acknowledge his offence with shame and griefe, then wee shall euer doe it by opposition: which were a double victory both ouer him and our selues. See that example, 2. King. 6. 22. compared with the end of the 23. verse.

Doct.vers.10. Now by this their seeking of *Samson*, and requiring of the men of Iudah with threats, and in armour, to bring him bound to them, as in this verse it appeared they did) we see a new trouble arose against him, for the faithfull
1.Sam.17.8. and diligent performance of his dutie: euen as *Dauid* receiued many discouragements for his well doing, and namely by *Saul*, and those many and great, and before that, of *Eliab* his brother, in offering himselfe to fight against *Goliah*. But so God hath prouided in his wise disposing of things, that wee cannot bee forward in any good cause, but commonly for the humbling of vs it shal cost vs trouble: as either by our owne corrupt nature crossing and hindering vs, seeing we are renued but in part, & the flesh resisteth against the spirit, when we striue to doe well, and to renounce euill: or else by outward affliction befalling vs for the same. As oftentimes ill will of men is ready to meet vs, for labouring to keepe a good conscience, and that many waies shewed and testified: as by railing vpon vs, and speaking euill of vs, persecuting, and other vnreasonable measure offering vnto vs, because wee cannot brooke, and digest the sinnes of the times that wee liue in, nor
1.Pet.4.4. walke after the bad examples of other, as Saint *Peter* speaketh. But oh, little know wee or consider, that by such opposition the Lord trieth what courage is in vs, and whether wee were like to honour him by suffering greater things for him, when we can so easily beare smaller reproches for his names sake, and make them our crowne, counting our selues happie that wee may suffer for well doing. Moreouer this manner of our liuing, and such carriage of our selues, bringeth another way great reioycing. For what ioy or comfort is like to that which ariseth from a good conscience? which *Salo-*
Prou.15.15. 2.Cor.1.12. *mon* therefore compareth to the continuall feasting of the vngodly. But this hath been often vrged.

Vers.10.11.12. This bee said of the first of these three things in this second part of the Chapter, to wit, of the Philistims comming armed against the men of Iudah to require *Samson* of them. Now the next point followeth thereof; that

is

is to say, how the men of Iudah, being sore afraid of them, went and bound *Samson*, to deliuer him vnto them. And this they did after they had asked of them why they came against them, and they had answered; to haue *Samson* brought bound vnto them. The which they went about immediately, as shall further be laid out in the 11. 12. and 13. verses.

But the men of Iudah demaund of them in this 10. verse, why they took vp armour against them, seeing they (according to agreement with them) submitted themselues to them, and paid their tribute, and had not prouoked them by rising against them: vpon which condition, they had promise of the Philistims that they should enioy peace, and liue without feare. But they answered for themselues, by pleading how *Samson* had spoiled them, who was one of them, and if they would (they said) defend his doing, then they would fight and make warre with them: but if they would deliuer him bound vnto them, they would depart: for they would (they said) do vnto him, as he had done vnto them. Vers.10.

They of Iudah thought they had great wrong offered them by the Philistims, whiles they themselues did none to them: for they did not defend *Samsons* fact. And the Philistims thought much that they should be opposed by any of Iudah, they hauing made peace with them vpon conditions, and would hurt none but him (they said) that had hurt them. By both wee learne, that it is more then heathenish, and a thing that reasonable men doe marueile at, that peaceable and innocent people, who giue themselues to leade an harmelesse life, should be hurt by any, and that they should not bee quiet and in safety by them with whom they liue, and to whom they do no harme. So saith *Salomon*; *Intend no euill against thy neighbour, seeing hee doth dwell without feare by thee.* And they who enioy such peace by them, haue that earthly benefit that God alloweth them; which how great it is, who doth not know? Doct. vers.10. Pro.3.29.

But on the contrary, the vnpeaceable (for the most part) doe reape the fruit of their vnquiet liuing, answerably. For it must be granted, that vnrighteous people, and such as shiftingly hurt & wrong others, procure to themselues much hatred, trouble and sorrow; and the breaking out of men that way, doth cause the exclamations, disquiets and complaints that are in all places. But God doth pay such home, and requite the leaud and bad dealings of vnconscionable men oft times in this life, causing them to find such measure as they offer to other. From which dealing yet how farre they should be, euen this teacheth; that both the Philistims, and they againe, the men of Iudah, do claime couenant keeping of the heathen Philistims, and challenge them for the breach of it, as being against the light of nature. And how much more should Christians keepe couenants which they haue made for peace one with another, howsoeuer things fall out, and not breake and goe from them dishonestly, when by Gods prouidence they sustaine some hurt thereby. Euen as wee reade in the Psalme: If thou hast sworne to thy neighbour, disappoint him not, though thou shouldest lose thereby. Sundry are the bands which tye men (otherwise lawlesse) to dutie and peace. The generallest is the common band of humanity. Then our Baptisme, profession, the Communion (for so we call that Sacrament) and among some, Matrimony, consanguinity, affinity, friendship, partnership, neighbourhood; Psal.15.4.

yea the law or comprimize hath bound some from offering violence. Here are lincks enough, a man would thinke, to make a cord not easie to be broken: but where a boysterous and vnreasonable spirit, nay brutish, beareth sway, what is there, either holy thing or ciuill sufficient to containe men? Euen as *Samson* did with those new ropes, so doe these with such bands of loue and amitie, shamelesly and at once, breake all in two, like flax. But here an end of this.

Vers. 11. Now to goe forward, wee haue heard that the men of Iudah answered the Philistims, that they had not risen vp against them, and therefore marueiled why they came to make warre with them. Whereupon ariseth a

Quest. 1. question, whether they did well in yeelding so to the Philistims, and in answering them so, to wit, that they had been subiect to them according to agreement. Also, whether they did well herein, in offering to yeeld *Samson* to them? And now (as is said in this verse) in forsaking him their countrey man and auenger, nay in apprehending and binding him, and so to deliuer him into their hands? For God had raised him vp an helper vnto them, his people, against their enemies: and should they be so vnthankfull as to offer him, their Iudge and helper, into their enemies hands?

Againe, (to make the doubt the greater) it was said in verse 4, chapt. 14. that it came of the Lord, that *Samson* should take occasion against the Philistims, that he might sore vexe them; and should they of Iudah then helpe them to cut him off, who was giuen of God to be such an helper to them? And whereas he was not so openly and professedly suffered to shew himselfe such a one, as the other Iudges did; *Othniel, Ehud* and the rest: but only in priuate manner to vexe them, as they gaue him occasion,

To this the answere is; that so God had appointed, who would thereby haue the enemies curbed, and their force weakned, for the ease and quiet of his people, and yet he would not giue them a ful deliuerance, whom he had so often proued to be vnfaithfull and vnthankfull toward him.

I say therefore that hereupon it may seeme that the whole course of the words and deedes of the men of Iudah toward *Samson*, was faultie and euill, for ought that hath yet been said to the contrary, and their yeelding him vp to the Philistims, as they did afterward, was no better then that which they are said in this verse to haue spoke and done to him: to wit, that they went so speedily about the apprehending and binding of him, and so sharply rebuked him for the hurt he did to the Philistims, whereas they fared the better for it, and saw it was to the easing of them.

Answ. To all this I answere, that it is not certaine that the men of Iudah knew any such thing that *Samson* was giuen them to auenge them of the Philistims, (though it was told to his mother by the Angell in the 13. Chapter, verse 5.) and that may bee gathered by the words of the men of Iudah to *Samson*, when they spake to him so sharply and said, that they must bind him, and so deliuer him to the Philistims: which had been absurd for them to speake, if they had knowne that he was set by the Lord to deliuer them. Besides, God gaue them no commandement to breake their league with the Philistims, which they had made with them, being brought vnder of them, neither had hee giuen them any meanes to defend them by violence and armes against them, therefore they were to commit the successe to God:

and

and it cannot be laid to the charge of the men of Iudah as their fault, that they did so to *Samson* in deliuering him vp into the Philistims hands, notwithstanding that God in his prouidence had called *Samson* to be their auenger. And wee must obserue that by this deliuerie of *Samson*, the Lord still gaue further heart as also opportunitie to him to afflict these Philistims more then before, as shall appeare in the fifteenth verse. So that the Lord thus carrying the businesse, wee must not (without apparant cause) condemne the fact of the people. Yet hereby I doe not altogether cleere them from blame. For there is no doubt of this, but that the men of Iudah were too much afraid of the Philistims, and too ready to keepe themselues from danger by them, and to stay them from making warre against them. And though it had been commanded them of God to haue kept *Samson* from them, yet seeing it had been with the perill of their liues, it is like enough they would not for all that haue done so, but would haue deliuered him vp vnto them: onely indeed they are the lesse to be charged, because (as I said) they had no commandement of God to doe so, which excuseth the fact, but not them, because they looked not at these grounds, neither were guided by knowledge. So then thus I conclude (and let the reader marke): The fact of the people of Iudah had been bad and grosse, if they had left *Samson* to shift for himselfe, against an expresse commandement from God, and if he had bidden them to take *Samson* for their helper, and to assist him: for then they ought to beleeue, that hee would both haue directed them what to doe, and would also haue assisted them. But this not appearing by any necessarie proofe, they are onely to be charged for this, that they proceeded herein vpon sinister causes, and not by the warrant of knowledge; as appeares by their fleshly fearing the Philistims, because they were strong: and they did not cleaue to *Samson* in this respect, seeing they saw not that they were like to be eased greatly by him against them, and thereupon were so ready to goe about to apprehend him, and to aske him what hee meant to prouoke the Philistims against them, they being yet vnder their dominion.

So that this wee may learne hereby; That howsoeuer God promised to be with vs in all our waies appointed to vs by him to walke in, as hee did to these men of Iudah, yet if we cannot doe so without opposition, displeasure and resistance by men, wee commonly looke, as they did, to the strongest side, with fleshly and carnal eyes, I meane, to the power of man, and not of God, and so we soone goe out of the way: which is not like to be without our great hurt. And yet maruellous it is to see, what slauish mindes are in vs, that how plainly soeuer God reueile his will to vs, in and about any particular dutie, we will haue an hundred shifts and excuses why we cannot (as we say) but indeed dare not walke in the approued beaten way, which God hath laid out for vs. Doct. vers. 11. Note.

No tongue is able to expresse the innumerable breaches of Gods commandements, and fearfull sinnes which are committed thus and by this occasion: and all to shunne an outward and temporary danger and discommoditie; but the inward violence and smarting words which wee make in our consciences thereby, we doe not at all, or very little regard them: which therefore arise after, and sometime many yeeres after to trouble, yea and torment

Gen.42.21. torment vs. As the fact of *Iosephs* brethren did vex them more then twenty
Psal.25.7. yeeres after; and *Dauid* was sore troubled, when he remembred the sinnes of his youth.

And this to bee true both Scripture and experience teach vs, that while men runne into sinne, to auoid outward trouble and danger, and yet make nothing of it when they haue done, lest they should too much disquiet themselues; yet that God doth afterwards make their doings as prickes in their eyes, and thornes in their flesh; that thereby we may know, that they who hold vp their heads most iollily after their sinne committed, as though nothing were amisse with them, shall not so easily goe away with it; but their sinne which they haue made their dearling, shall sting them in their bosomes, and rise vp and strangle them, as it oft doth, and make their liues
Numb.25.8. wearisome, if it put not also an end to them; as the sinne of *Zimry* and *Cosby*
Numb.16.32. did; *Corah* also and his company. But where might one make an end of this discourse? Looke more of this in the storie of *Gedeons* demaund of the men of Succoth and Penuel, and in this Chapter, verse *6*.

Vers.11.12 To the question of the men of Iudah, demaunding of *Samson* what hee meant so to prouoke the Philistims against thē, by hurting them (he knowing that they, euen all their land, were vnder them, and subiect to them) he answereth them; As they haue done to me, so haue I done to them; meaning, according to my charge. *Samson* might haue been like, if hee had followed carnall reason, to haue fallen vpon them, for that they knowing him to haue so greatly hurt their enemies, and he knowing himselfe to be their Iudge and helper, saw yet that he was so roughly dealt with by them: for
Exod.5.21. they might seeme to deale with him as the Hebrewes dealt with *Moses*; who being oppressed by *Pharao*, told *Moses* that he made them stinke in the sight of *Pharao*. *Samson* (I say) knowing that which he did, might haue bin like to haue slaine these men of Iudah for their slauish fearing of the Philistims, and for their sloth and dasterdlines in yeelding to them, and setting themselues against him.

But he kindly answered them, and told them gently what he had done to them, and why. And when they shewed him that they must binde him, and carrie him to the Philistims, hee rageth not against them, neither hurteth them, he only requires an oath of them (and vpon that condition he would yeeld himselfe to them) to wit, that they would not kill him themselues: the which he did, because hee loued his countrey, and would in no wise shed the blood of any of his citizens; which (yet) hee saw hee must doe, if hee should fight with them by hand-blowes. Such was his loue to them, that he would rather be deliuered to his enemies, then that his countrey for his cause should come into danger: and his faith in God was as firme and constant. In whose mercie he trusting, doubted not to commit himselfe to his enemies, and to defend his nation from them with the perill of his life. And this teacheth, that we should haue regard of other, as well as of our selues, in so much that though we haue power in our hands to hurt them, yea and though some cause be offered vs to deale hardly with them, yet wee should forbeare, and rather in godly wisedome passe by an offence, except greater euill and inconuenience doe come thereby.

For (alas) what pleasure should we take in seeing euill fall vpon our brethren,

thren, when we might haue held it from them? which *Iob* in no wise would be brought to doe. And as we should euery way haue regard of this toward our neighbour, so in our families we should shew this wisedome, care, and loue toward them that are vnder our gouernment. For the Lord sparing vs, where we haue deserued hard measure at his hands, nay we receiuing many and continuall blessings from God, why should wee not also deale well with other? So *Iob* gaue his seruants leaue to plead their cause, and hearkened to them, if they were wronged. And of his neighbours hee said; I was not moued with ioy when euill came vpon them that hate me, neither suffered I my mouth to sinne, by wishing a curse to their soule. All these commendable graces in *Iob* are condemnations of the spitefull and malicious, who glory in cruelty against other, and seek to hurt and wrong them, whom they should kindly regard.

Iob 31.29. Note. Iob 31.13. 29.30. See Hester 10. last verse.

Nature hath engrauen a loue in vs to our countrey, but grace must season, ripen, and direct it. And a shame it were for Christians to come short of Heathens in this point. And yet there are memorable examples among them of such as for the procurement of their countreys good, doubted not to deuote themselues to execrable deaths, and offer themselues of their own accord to assured slaughter. But what shall I say of this nation of ours? Those *Decij* and *Marcus Regulus* shall rise vp in iudgement against many cursed vipers, degenerate miscreants of this our nation, who (hauing some of them more bonds to obliege them to loue and loyaltie then this alone, I meane, fauours from Prince, dignities and rewards more then for their desert) yet haue attempted and taken vp armes against their owne parent, and sought to shed her bowels vpon the ground: some out of pretensed conscience, but most out of hellish rancour, discontent, pride, and vnthankfulnes, haue raced out the image of all loue, dutie, or allegiance to God, King, Religion and Nation: sorting themselues into two treacherous rankes of runnagates, the one shrouding themselues as souldiers vnder forreine Popish Princes, and waiting their opportunitie to doe mischiefe: the other creeping into Cloysters, and there taking vpon them the mark of Antichrist the Pope, the deadly enemie of our Religion and State, and renouncing their owne countrey and seruice thereto, to the end that they may returne againe and worke the ruine thereof by their cursed policie.

But to leaue these and shut vp the poynt, let *Samson* teach vs, both Gouernours, Ministers, and people, to vnite our loue to our nation and the Church of God therein, by al meanes wishing her peace, and procuring her welfare: and pray God that they may more and more doe it, whom it concerneth to roote out all aduersarie power which might threaten it. As wee see, *Paul* cannot thinke of his nation, but he bursteth foorth into prayers for the saluation of it, not doubting (as a loyall souldier) to pledge not his life onely, but his soule for it. And *Dauid* when hee beheld his people standing amazed at *Goliah*, breaketh out thus; What is this vncircumcised Philistim, that he thus brayeth against God, and the hoste of Israel? Thus let it be with vs, and not onely content our selues with that common loue that standeth in the communion of peace, wealth, ease, pleasure, and liberties: for then the least discontent for the want thereof may preuaile so farre, as to cause vs to forsweare all religious or ciuil interest in her that begat and nourished vs.

Rom. 9.3. 1. Sam. 17.26.

 The

Verse 12. The oath that he required of them, was for the ſecuring of him; for hee thought himſelfe ſafe if he had an oath from them, that they would not kill him: becauſe then hee doubted not, but that hee ſhould breake his bands, and eſcape the hands of the Philiſtims, and vex them againe. This his example teacheth vs to take heed how wee commit our ſelues into the hands of men, and whom we cannot ſafely truſt; and ſuch as are not faithfull to God, except wee haue good ſecuritie for our ſo doing, (yea though they make ſhewes of friendſhip and loue) but much more when they bewray themſelues to be ſuch. Neither hang we the peace of our conſcience vpon men; for they that haue none themſelues, will not tender and regard vs, but put vs to our ſhifts. Looke in the former chapter more at large hereof.

And here wee ſee, that men venture their liues vpon the ſecuritie of an oath. He putteth his life into their hands, when they had ſworne they would
Ioſh.9.15. not kill him. So the Gibeonites thought themſelues ſafe, when the Princes of Iſrael had ſworne to grant them their liues: and *Rabab* was ſatisfied, when
Ioſh.2.12. the Spies had promiſed her by an oath, that they would ſaue her and her fathers houſe, when they came to take Iericho the citie wherein ſhe dwelt. Such an account hath been made of an oath, euen among the Heathens; as hath been noted in the ſtorie of *Iphtah* and the men of Gilead, chapter 11, verſe 11.) by the like occaſion. Therfore moſt fearefull it is, that ſuch as goe for Chriſtians breake and goe from their oath which they haue made to witnes their faithfulnes to their brethren, putting their truſt in them; wheras their bare word ought to haue tyed them: much more this condemnes ſuch as lay vnconſcionable oathes on people, and vrge them to ſweare to that, which is in no wiſe to be vrged vpon them.

Verſ.13. Now they did as they had ſaid to him, I meane, they bound him with two new cords, and brought him downe from the rock: loe, thus they dealt with him, and deliuered him into their enemies hands. Now in that they were conſtrained thus to bring him bound to them, euen as a ſheepe to the ſhambles, (and as if men ſhould deliuer their dogges to the wolues) and ſo muſt bee depriued of ſuch a great benefit as hee had been to them almoſt twentie yeeres, in deliuering them from the oppreſſion of the Philiſtims, (God giuing them no commandement to aſſiſt him:) note wee, that it falleth out many times, that wee muſt (and cannot auoide it) be depriued (the caſe ſo requiring) of our beſt helpes and meanes of our health, peace, libertie, and other commodities. And God will haue vs feele the ſmart thereof, to make vs know our ſelues the better. And how ought this to bring vs out of loue with our ſpeciall ſinnes, which are the cauſes hereof, or of like vnquietnes and diſtraction in our liues? And if we deſire to keepe the beſt things wee haue, to our comfort, then let vs offer violence to ſuch our ſins, as looſnes, inconſtancie, hollow-heartednes, wilfulnes, ſtoutnes, worldlines, or to any other as they ſhall ſit more neere vs. Touching this fruite of ſinne, wee haue had occaſion to ſpeake often, and through this booke.

Verſ.14. The men of Iudah to ſhew their diligence, and to purge themſelues from blame with the Philiſtims, brought *Samſon* from the rock bound vnto them in that place Lehi before mentioned, nigh the borders of the Philiſtims, and yeelding him vp ſo into their hands, at leaſt going about ſo to do: (for elſe, if he had eſcaped before they ſaw him bound, and before they had receiued him

him into their custody,they might haue been thought to deale fraudulently with the Philistims,and not to haue bound him,) I say when they brought him to them, in that manner,I meane fast bound,they shouted with a great noise for ioy : so glad they were,when they had him their enemie, so neere them,euen in their hands,and (as they thought) past escaping.

Behold heere the ioy of the wicked, wherein it consisteth, and how it is caused. In a word, when their desire is accomplished ; howsoeuer it bee : as in the apprehending of a great enemy of theirs, (as heere it was with the Philistims, when they had got *Samson* bound) so in their aduancement, in feasting, in play, vaine pleasures,and such like. But as for good things,as the certainty of the fauour of God, the assurance of eternall life, other heauenly tidings of the Gospell,the setting vp of the kingdome of Christ,or the ouerthrow of idolatry or some great sinne, finally in holding and keeping a good conscience (which yet is continuall feasting) they know they cannot reioyce in these. Whereby a man may iudge more certainely of their estate to Godward, then the Physitian may of the state of his patients disease, by feeling his pulse. *Doct.* Prou.15.15. Note.

And to speake as the truth is, what resting is in such ioy,how lawfull soeuer the things are in which they reioyce ? but a sudden sorrow may follow as greatly stinging and tormenting them, or such as will at least a while after vndoubtedly take hold of them, in this changeable world (if no other way) by losing and forgetting that which caused such reioycing. And these moods and passions) which are as meere extremities, as the noonetide is to midnight) are nothing beseeming the faithfull seruants of God,but doe vtterly disguise them, who haue learned to take vp their delight in the other things holy and heauenly, which I haue last mentioned,and such like : and in their reioycings in and about these outward to bee carried alwaies in a meane,and with measure. Note.

And because I know, that vpon that which I haue now saide, it will answere these demands and questions, whether it be vnlawfull to reioyce in such lawfull things as God giueth men to enioy in this life, as victory ouer enemies, promotion, wealth, and such like : I answere,no,as I said before : so as withall we desire and resolue to make right vse of them, so farre as wee know how, or may learne : but to rest in them is vnlawfull, for that were to trust in them, which is idolatry. Also to exceed in reioycing for hauing them, is to take away our ioy from better things, if we haue any, or to hinder it,that there may be none ; of which fault to be conuinced, *Iob* in no wise could abide it. I thinke it not vnfit heere, (though I might bring hither his owne words, which doe cleerely shew that hee was a paterne of rightly enioying riches (to set downe the obseruation of the right learned Father Master *Beza* concerning this point. Hee well weighing the story of *Iob* and his practise this way, speaketh thus of him about this thing. *Iob* (saith he) lost his goods without any great griefe, therfore he enioyed them when he had them, without any great loue. Thus wee haue heard in this second part, how the Philistims preuailed thus far to the satisfying of themselues in seeking reuenge vpō *Samson*, that they caused the mē of Iudah to bring him bound vnto them, to their great reioycing. Now followeth the third part of this Chapter, wherein we shall see how flitting and short this their ioy was. 1.Tim.6.17. Iob 31.25.

THE EIGHTIE ONE SERMON ON THE XV. CHAPTER OF THE BOOKE OF IVDGES.

The third part of the Chapter.

Verſ. 14. *And the ſpirit of the Lord came mightily vpon him, and the cords that were vpon his armes became as flax that was burnt with fire, and his bands looſed from off his hands.*

15. *And hee found a new iaw-bone of an Aſſe, and put forth his hand, and tooke it, and ſlew a thouſand men therewith.*

16. *And Samſon ſaid, With the iaw-bone of an Aſſe, heapes vpon heapes, with the iaw-bone of an Aſſe haue I ſlaine a thouſand men.*

17. *And it came to paſſe when he had made an end of ſpeaking, that he caſt away the iaw-bone out of his hand, and called that place Ramath-Lehi.*

The ſumme. THe ſumme of the words which I haue now ſet downe is briefly this, that firſt *Samſon* broke his bands: after that, hee ſlew a thouſand of them: and laſtly, gaue a name to the place accordingly. To proceed firſt with this other part of the 14. verſe, for the former part was ſpoken of in the former Sermon, it is ſaid concerning the firſt of theſe three points, that while the Philiſtims were ſhouting for ioy at the deliuering of *Samſon* bound vnto them: the ſpirit of the Lord ſtrengthened him in ſuch wiſe, that he did as eaſily breake the cords, as if the fire had burned flax. Wherein ſtill let vs marke, that the Lord is ſaid to giue ſtrength to *Samſon*, that we may ſee that he was with him, and aſſiſted him in all the great acts that he did againſt the Philiſtims.

Which many in reading the ſtory not marking, do not vnderſtand it, but take it amiſſe, as though *Samſon* had done all that he did againſt them, cruelly and ſpitefully; when (yet) all may eaſily ſee, that ſtrength and rare courage and labour, which hee had not of himſelfe, were requiſite for the doing of

Doct. 1. the things that hee did, if hee had been neuer ſo malicious. And ſo in all the duties that we performe, to the magnifying of the Goſpel, and our holy profeſſion of it, more then other doe attaine vnto, let vs looke that the Lord ſet vs about them, and goe before vs in them by his word, and be the perſwader of vs thereto by his ſpirit, (whereby onely wee are inabled.) that ſo neither fancy, nor moode, and paſſion may be ſaid to leade vs therein: which may eaſily come to paſſe in the doing of good things; as by the like occaſions I haue often obſerued.

2 And heere it is very profitable to note, how ſhort and momentanie the great

great ioy of the Philistims was at the beholding of *Samson* bound: for loe, the Lord vnbound him immediately, and so turned al their ioy into as great sorrow. This may be learned here, how flitting the reioycings of such are, as be not guided by the spirit of God, but follow their fleshly humour therein; the best of them are fickle and momentany, yea euen the pleasantest of them as the cracking of thornes vnder a pot. Onely this caueat I would haue the reader to obserue, that what I speake of these vncircumcised Philistims in this & the next point, I applie not vnto their particular condition (being not enlightened, but destitute of all feeling of their misery, or sinne,) but I take occasion by the iust iudgement of God vpon them for other sinnes against their knowledge, to put all bad persons in mind of the woe which hangeth ouer them for their vnbeleefe, wilfull louing of darkenesse more then light, and the seuerall sinnes issuing thence, and by name the abuse of earthly blessings. And this I say of all such; The wicked flourisheth (as *Dauid* saith) like the greene bay tree, that doth not as other trees cast or change her leafe, no not in winter: so doth their iollity appeare aboue other mens: nay it seemeth in the eyes of fooles, to be such, that they liue (as they suppose) in a little paradise: and yet within a while there is no remainder or token of any such thing left behinde, but desolation onely and confusion to be seene, but of their estate to Godward, as a secret I ceale to speake of.

Eccles.7.6.
Ioh.3.19.
Psal.37.35.36.

Nabal swimming in wealth, did make a feast as the feast of a King, and his heart was merrie with wine, but about ten daies after, he was taken from all, and died; and his heart died the next morning, after he heard he should die, and hee was like a stone, when his wife told him what had been intended against him. And how was *Hamans* heart lifted vp by his aduancement and great fauour with the King? So that he could not containe himselfe, but he must needs tell forth to his friends, what prosperitie he had; and yet he had as good hold of it, as can be enioyed in this world, being backed and vpholden by the mightiest that was in the land vnder God. But how soone was all his honour laid in the dust, and his ioy ended with most bitter anguish and torment?

1.Sam.25.37.
Ester 5.11.

The Scriptures and experience are full of such examples. Hee that hath liued and obserued the courses of those, who in diuers ages haue seemed most happie of other of their condition, and haue most giuen themselues, as their state and place would giue them leaue, to take the vtmost of their liberty in the merriments of the world, (and yet what haue they been, but play and other vaine pleasure taking in pampering the body with eating and drinking, company keeping with such as themselues bee, or in gathering wealth, and such like) they (I say) who haue marked such things, what haue they seene but this, how soone they haue been taken from them all, neuer looking for it, nor thinking of it, and yet others oft fearing it, and many of them in such manner plucked from all, as if a man would say, God would haue all to marke and speake of it. For if *Salomon* could finde nothing in all his royalties, dignities, and pleasures, but vanitie and vexation, doe other comming after him, looke to find better then he euer could? no, this world affordeth no better.

Note.
Eccles.2.11.

So that it may iustly grieue him, that knoweth that all such shall come to fearefull iudgement, who haue made these fading and deceiueable pleasures their

Eccles.11.9.

their greatest ioy, to thinke they haue been no wiser, but to trifle out their pretious time, in which they might haue taken so much good; I meane,
Note. they might haue sucked out of the Gospell true comfort here, and saluation afterward for euer. And this is the right vse that should bee made of this doctrine, to wit, of the momentanie ioy of the godlesse and irreligious in this world, that wee should seeke durable ioy, and that which is also most sound and sauorie, namely, the assurance of Gods fauour heere on earth, (till wee enioy it most perfectly in heauen;) and a Christian and godly life, which is the only sweet companion and guide, that leadeth vs thither.

Vers.15.16. *The sense.* The first of the three things in this third part, wee haue now heard, and that was, how he brake the double cord wherewith he was tied. The second is set downe in these two verses, namely, that when hee had escaped out of their hands, yet it was so farre off, that all they who were there present could apprehend him againe, that he slew a thousand of those Philistims, there gathered together to see him, & reioyce at the bringing of him thither bound. But ye will aske how he could doe so, being but one alone, and yet naked also and vnfurnished of weapons; I say, the Lord, as we haue heard, strengthened him: and for weapon, though he had none, a new and moist iawbone of an Asse by Gods prouidence lay by, which he tooke vp, and made that serue for the purpose, as if it it had been sword, staffe, or other weapon. And when hee had slaine them, hee shewed what heapes hee had made with so slight a helpe or instrument.

Doct.vers.15. Heere we see that these Philistims lately so exceedingly ioyfull, did not onely lose their ioy, but their liues also. And this may tell vs yet a heauier thing then the former. For it teacheth, that for the most part, looke what fearefull and blind estate the blind and bad people liue in, and chuse to repose themselues in, in the same they continue for the most part, and end their daies. For is there almost any place left for amendment? Therfore the
2.Tim.3.13. Apostle saith; The wicked and the deceiuer wax worse and worse, and *when*
1.Thes.5.3. *they crie peace, peace,* and all things are safe, then commeth destruction suddenly vpon them, before they be aware, as the trauell vpon a woman with child, and they shall not be able to auoide it.

Luk.12.20. When the rich man in the Gospell reioyced most in that he had, he was
Dan.5.27. nearest a wofull end. So *Baltazzar* when he was drinking wine merrily with his Princes and Concubines, in the vessels of the Temple, then the fearfull hand-writing appeared on the wall, hauing this meaning, God hath finished
1.Sam.15.33. thy kingdome. So *Agag*. And as such liue, so they die. Although I denie not, but God, where it pleaseth him, can giue a new hart, where it is sought, and cause such vanity to bee distasted, as wherein men haue delighted, and worke sound reioycing in stead thereof. Therefore chuse wee the best delights, and so the longer we hold them, the soundlier wee shall enioy them, vntill we keepe them vnto our end.

Vers.16.17. Another thing that he did, was, that when he had slaine an heape, he correcteth himselfe, when hee smote them on both sides with the iaw-bone, they preasing about to take him; and he saith, two heapes, or many: as if he should haue said; heapes vpon heapes had been slaine by him. And seeing
Iudg.15.18. hee knew that God gaue him the strength thereto, hee being a godly man, why doth he vtter these words, but that al might see and acknowledge what

a great

a great worke God had wrought by him, and that by a weake meane, euen with the iaw-bone of an Asse? To teach vs, that where the Lord will haue vs execute iustice without pitie vpon euill doers, we must not faint, nor be negligent to doe his commandement vpon them, as *Samson* did here, *Ioshua* before on *Achan*, *Ehud* vpon the King of Moab, and *Shamgar* on the Philistims. God will haue the wicked smart for their trespasses openly committed; to smart (I say) by men according to the weight and hainousnesse of them, and vtterly forbiddeth foolish pity to be shewed in such a case; according to the saying of *Salomon*: It is an abomination to iustifie the wicked. The like may be said against that foolish pity which ariseth in vs, when wee behold Gods immediate hand vpon them, and yet wee ought not then for all this to insult ouer them: but we must ascribe honour to God, with those 24. Elders in the Reuelation, and *Dauid* vpon the death of *Nabal*. Iosh 7.25. Iudg.3.21. & 31. Prou.17.15. Reuel.5.14. 1.Sam.25.39.

Now followeth the third point, that as *Samson* honoured God in shewing what hee had done by him, in slaying heapes of men, euen a thousand, so he added this thereto; that he gaue a name to the place where hee did it, as a memoriall thereof, that all posterity comming after, might know vnto the end of the world, what great things God did for his people against their enemies. The name of it he called *Ramath-Lehi*; as if he should haue said, the lifting vp of a iaw bone, which remaineth as a monument of Gods mighty worke by him euen to this day. Thus, and by this meanes Gods seruants haue praised him in times past, as in the booke of Numbers, *Ioshua* and other, is to bee seene, as well as other times by songs and dances, that wee all may marke and remember his benefits and great workes, and praise him among the generations following, to the quickening and comforting of his people, and the feare of his enemies; although not in the same manner that some haue done in ages past. But of this before, once or twice. Vers.17.

The fourth part of the Chapter.

Vers.18. ***And he was sore athirst, and called on the Lord, and said, Thou hast giuen this great deliuerance into the hand of thy seruant: and now shall I die for thirst, and fall into the hand of the vncircumcised?***

19. ***But God claue an hollow place that was in the iaw, and there came water thereout, and when he had drunke, his spirit came againe, and he reuiued: wherefore he called the name thereof En-hakkoreh, which is in Lehi vnto this day.***

20. ***And he iudged Israel in the daies of the Philistims twentie yeeres.***

NOw followeth the fourth and last part of this Chapter: wherein is shewed, what an exceeding great thirst *Samson* had after the slaughter of these Philistims, and that he prayed to God, and he gaue him water, so that he reuiued: and so he praised God there. And the time that hee iudged Israel, is in the last place adioyned and set downe, which was twentie yeres. *The summe.*

By this thirst of his, the Lord would haue him to know himselfe, and to be held vnder, lest by that which hee had done to the Philistims, hee might haue been lifted vp aboue that which was meet. Thus he dealeth with his; intermixing his chastisements with blessings, that both they may be held in humility by the one, and yet may haue sufficient encouragement to abide Note.

constantly

constantly in a good course,and not forget the Lord and become high minded,as they are easily brought to bee by the other, to wit, his benefits. And
2.Cor.12.7. thus the Lord saw good to deale euen with *Paul* himselfe,who was buffeted by Satan, when hee had been lifted vp to the third heauen by the rauishing of Gods spirit: yet hee had that humour remaining in him,which needed setling and cooling,that his ioy might be kept within holy lists and bounds.
Iudg.11.35. And the same I haue noted in that famous accident of *Iphtah* his daughter: whom God set on to abase him, that hee might proceed on to the triumph more soberly. Wee must thinke Gods seruants are deare to him,when hee sticketh not to bereaue them of their preciousest delights, to the end they may hold their delight in him,and not turne their sweetnesse into bitternes,
Note. I meane,their holy reioycing, into fleshly presumption. The reason hereof is, because else God cannot trust vs in the businesse he sets vs about, except hee giues vs coolings and abasements to consume the superfluity of our hypocrisie,conceitednesse of our selues,pride and security: which are as vnfit
Leuit.10.1. dealers in heauenly matters,as *Nadab* and *Abihu* their strange fire was to kindle incense or offer sacrifice withall. And secondly, the Lord honoreth many of his deare seruants (whose faith and setlednesse in grace,and freedome from such grosse staines hee is priuie vnto) by giuing them the proofe of their patience, vprightnesse and humility, presently after the exercise of their thankfulnesse and reioycing: that so the crosse suddenly comming vpon great blessings, or deliuerances, they may approue themselues soundly religious, in that they are fit to goe vnder the one without murmuring,as well as they vsed the other without foolish lightnesse and vaine glory. And it is a rare gift for a man by his wise carriage vnder such kind of afflictions, to shew, that hee waited for his abasement, euen in the greatest welfare, as *Iob*, in the height of his prosperity looked for his change. Whereas the common sort of professors, if God endow and furnish them with any priuiledge aboue others; as good successe and thriuing in the world,victory ouer their aduersary in sute of Law, credit and good account, either for labour in the the Ministery, or for profession of the Gospell, liberty to heare the Word, and to enioy the Sabbaths, fellowship of the faithfull, or the like; they presently are sicke of a spirituall Plurasie, and rankenesse of corrupt blood, which if God (by some sudden change) abate not, would soone oppresse
Note. them. And this nurture wee should all learne,that wee may keepe compasse in our liues,and neither turne to the right hand, nor to the left, which is a great portion,and sauoureth of much grace and godly wisedome. For if we swell, know wee for certainty, that God will pull vs downe, and lest wee should faint and be loden with trouble to our discouragement, hee will put vnder his hand in due time to lift vs vp againe. And if wee regard to bee guided by his word, his handie worke and corrections shall bee fewer, or more fauourable, and fruitfull in vs. As for hypocrites and time-seruers, God vseth no such discipline toward them, but lets them fall from one extremity into another. See that I haue said of this in the eleuenth Chapter.

2 In that this extreme thirstines did not breed in him murmuring against God,for that he who had done him such seruice,should now be suffered to miscarrie,as it were,and to fall into the hands of Gods enemies,as they fell into

into his; it is to admonish vs, that we should beware of that sinne of impatience, and breaking out against God when we are crossed, (as wee are too prone and ready to doe) as though he must helpe and deliuer vs when wee would, or else he doth vs great wrong: euen as *Mary* in the want of wine at the marriage, looked vnwisely that Christ should prouide it by miracle by and by. Nay rather, let vs know that we are euer vnprofitable, and that God seeth we haue need oft times to be spurred forward, and therfore with *Samson, Dauid*, and other his people it behoueth vs to sue humbly to him, that so his helpe may be the more sweete vnto vs when it commeth: and that we thinke not our selues too good to waite vpon him patiently, but rather with importunitie call vpon him in the meane season. We make a good shift while the Lord spares vs; but if once he lay his hand vpon vs, then we verifie that which Satan spake falsely of *Iob*, that is, we curse him to his face. Not vnlike in this to him, that seeing himselfe and his hoste in perill by thirst, murmured, saying; What? hath the Lord brought three Kings together and their armies to destroy them? And the like was his behauiour after in the famine, of which we reade, 2. King. 6. So the Israelites in their returne from Egypt, of whom the Prophet complaineth, Psal. 95. And these (the more is the pitie) are our presidents which we follow (yea euen in pettie trials) rather then *Iob*, who in the middest of his miseries, was so far from charging God foolishly, that he blessed him, and reioyced in suffering tentation, as S. *Iames* saith, are blessed: and therefore as wee heare of his patience, so we see what end the Lord gaue him. Farre are wee from considering that our owne sinne being the cause why we suffer, we may well bow our shoulders to beare our affliction. Or, that he who sent one, might haue sent tenne, and set them on tenne times deeplier, and might haue begun sooner. But this I haue oft vrged by occasion of shewing what the power of faith is in the well bearing the crosse; without which patience is a stranger.

Iohn 2.3. Iob 2.5. 2. King. 3.10. 2. King. 6. 30. 31. Iob 1.22. Iam. 1.12. Iam. 5.11. Note.

3 He vpholdeth and strengtheneth his prayer by two maine and strong pillars, that hee might be confident that God would heare him. One was the acknowledging of his power and mercie in the late victorie: for thus he saith; Thou (O Lord) grantedst by thy seruant this great preseruation to thy people. The second, this: I am thy seruant, and in this businesse against the Philistims I haue done thy worke, which thou settest me about, therefore leaue me not now to this reproch. And this, with that in the last verse, that he is said to haue iudged Israel, doe still proue that God in all this resisting the Philistims, did appoint him to it, and that hee is not to be blamed as a priuate man, that did rashly and furiously take it in hand, as some more ignorant and hastie then wise, will be bold to iudge.

Our instruction is from hence twofold: first, that the remembring of Gods former benefits and fauour doe adde great force to, and cause much feruencie in our prayers, (this being added, that wee quench not the same by any sinne committed against conscience) for then we may be sure God will heare vs, as he hath done oft before. And here that of the Apostle hath place, Experience bringeth hope, which maketh not ashamed: because God is not changed, and therefore wee suing to him feruently as in times past, may rest the better perswaded: but the forgetfulnes of Gods former kind-

Rom. 5.4.

nesse, and our vnthankfulnes, doth on the contrary as much weaken and coole our prayers. For we can nothing so confidently looke for help from God, whom by nature wee are afraid of, as when wee daily remember his
Ioh.15.9. former kindnesse, and that it abides for euer towards vs: and yet (which is much to bee pitied) few awake out of this drowsie forgetfulnes and vnthankfulnes wherein they lie.

By this wee see, that it standeth euery Christian very much vpon, to hold his confidence and comfort in the promises of God, whereby hee may stay himselfe and be vpholden in his trials, till God giue a good issue. For why? The benefit hereof doth not onely reach to the present time, but prepareth him also for all crosses in time to come, to entertaine and beare them the better. Because his experience formerly, being ioyned with this, *That the*
Isai.59.1. *arme of the Lord is not shortned*, makes euery new triall seeme more tollerable. Whereas hee that vpon occasion of each sudden and vnwelcome trouble, fetcheth help rather from his head, then his heart, and falleth rather to contriue fleshly shifts, how to auoid or ease him of his distresse, (like *Saul* in get-
1.Sam.16.17. ting him a Musitian to heale him of a troubled conscience) then to meditate of God his former mercies; doth make euery new crosse more heauie to himselfe then other. I confesse, such haue an experience, but it is like their hope, neither shall helpe them. For thus they argue: Such a sicknesse I recouered of, therefore I looke to breake this too. Loe, their experience breedeth a rotten confidence in them, and makes them presume of that which often they faile of; and when they faile, they are either like *Iehoram*, very lions; or as *Nabal*, meere blockes. The case is plaine; They digge to
Ierem.2.13. themselues pits which will hold no water, but forsake the Lord and their
Iona.2.8. owne peace, for a vaine conceit; and as *Ionah* saith, While they embrace lying vanities, they forsake their owne mercie, whereof they haue no promise. And so at length that is verified of them which is written by the Prophet,
Amos 3.19. Though they escape a Beare, yet a Lion shall deuoure them: yea and often that which they least feare shall be their vndoing. Now this caueat let me
Note. adde to the doctrine, lest I be mistaken. I say not that a Christians experience breedes hope of the selfesame outward issue and manner of deliuerance out of his trouble, which hee hath before time found. Neither durst the three children in the third of *Daniel*, expresly auouch that God would
Dan.3.17. worke a miracle for their deliuerie; and yet they had faith neuerthelesse to beleeue that he would bring them well thorow: which I speake to controle the phantasticall spirits of some, who affirme that ỳ not recouerie of a disease (as it might be the plague) is the fruit alway of vnbelief. If we could beleeue the promise (say they) in Psalme, we should not feare that sicknesse, nor dye thereof. Contrariwise let vs know, that the act of faith is euer carried according to the qualitie of the promise. *Pauls* faith was not expresly carried to
2.Cor.12.7. beleeue, That the pricke in his flesh should be remoued, and yet he had experience of many deliuerances) but that Gods grace should bee sufficient. And he beleeuing this had the fruite of his former experience, because hee obtained an equiualent supplie.

4 This be said by occasion of the first prop of *Samsons* prayer, to wit, the rehearsing of Gods former goodnesse: the second followeth, that he was his seruant, and had done his worke in that his great labour against the Philistims.

stims. And by this we must know, that it is a thing very materiall to be able to proue our selues Gods seruants. For by what right can we else claime any place in his house, otherwise then as strangers? But if we be so, then we doe him faithfull seruice (as the Apostle saith, his seruants yee are to whom ye obey) yea and that wee performe ioyfully and without feare all our daies, (for it is not a seruice in name, but perfect freedome indeed) and so doing wee may claime the benefit of seruants, that is, protection. Rom.6.16.

The Angels had this title to be called the seruants of God. And as he said he was his seruant: so particularly he shewed that he was so in this: for he said, I haue not pleased my selfe, nor serued mine owne humour in killing these Philistims; but I did thy worke, and fought thy battailes: Euen so in our particular actions, wee are to looke to be guided by God, to proue that we are in the state of seruants, and not hangbyes: and then we may be able with boldnes to say, we haue a good conscience in all things, and where we are accused, yet to be at peace, else God might also discharge himselfe of his promise vnto vs. It is no small priuiledge (as I haue noted elsewhere) that whiles we are well occupied, wee may boldly sue to God for blessing. And so did *Samson* here. For if earthly masters tye themselues to prouide sustenance for their seruants, not looking that they should be troubled with the care of any thing, saue their labour; then with what boldnes might *Samson* here call vpon the Lord, that he might not perish for thirst, being in the heat of his worke? For it might else haue turned to the dishonour of the Lord, to suffer him to miscarrie for want. Oh that men would trie the Lord in this, and commit their waies to him in well doing, to see if he would not effect their good desires, and else let them not wonder that he seeme an hard master to them. Heb 1.14.

Now followeth the substance of his prayer, and that was, that he hauing 5
imployed himselfe to glorifie Gods name, might not be deliuered into the hands of the vncircumcised: and hee saith further; I being set by thee (O Lord) to iudge ouer thy people, suffer me not to come into their hands and power, contrary to that which thou promisedst to me, till I had fulfilled thy worke. So wee should be earnest with the Lord that wee may not liue nor dye to the dishonour of his name: but to bee kept (if it may bee) from iust reproch. Such requests can none make, that set themselues on worke without God: though they counterfeit, or make great florishes, as *Ioab* did. See 2.Sam.10.12
2.Sam.10. And whereas ye will obiect, that he did yet fall into reprochfull euils afterward, for all this his prayer: the answere thereto is, that he neglected the nourishing of the grace that hee did now pray in; and further answere will by more fit occasion be made hereto, in the next chapter: therefore I will deferre it to that place.

When *Samson* had made his prayer thus, in his extreame thirst, the Lord, Vers.19. *The summe.*
as it is manifest in this verse, caused water to come foorth of the hollow place of the iaw, breaking out of the tooth, which stood therein, and so hee drunke and was reuiued. And therefore he gaue a name to the thing done accordingly, calling it, the Fountaine of him that prayed.

By this that the Lord heard *Samsons* prayer, and rather gaue him water extraordinarily, then he should perish; it teacheth the same to vs, that rather then we shall miscarrie, he will prouide for vs, though we know not, neither

1.King.17.6. 2.King.4.7. ſee how. As he fed *Eliah* by the rauens, and the good widow with the increaſe of her little oyle, till it paid her debt, and maintained her and hers, and preſerued *Ionah* in the fiſhes belly, and againſt all likelihood brought him ſafe to land. So God hath many waies to comfort his, and vphold their eſtate, and he is as willing as he is able to doe it, and that by his extraordinarie prouidence, rather then they ſhould faile. And if he ſee it not expedient alwaies to doe ſo; yet he doth more for them a great deale, then if he gaue them their deſire; for hee worketh in them contentation and other grace: and ſooner ſhall the ſtones of the ſtreete bee turned into loaues of bread, and the water of their wels into drinke, before they ſhall periſh euen here, vnleſſe he doe better things for them. Cleaue wee therefore to him inſeparably, and be we not remoued from our ſtedfaſt confidence in him, for he that hath ſaid it, will alſo doe the ſame. But this point commeth often to hand.

2 Of this water *Samſon* drunk, and was reuiued againe, being neere to death before, as in this verſe appeareth. Whereby wee may ſee theſe two things: One, that thirſt is a moſt deadly and intollerable paine, as wee may well ſee by the thirſt that our Sauiour complained of on the croſſe, for it is reckoned as one part of his paine. And as thirſt is, ſo is hunger: by either of which to dye, is, as a lingering, ſo a moſt weariſome and grieuous death. Like vnto the which ſeeing there are many other kindes of death, wee may ſee from how many deaths, and thoſe moſt painfull, God keepeth vs. For we might eaſily miſcarrie both this way, as *Samſon* was like to doe, and by infinite other waies, if God did but hold backe his helping hand. Which is the more to condemne our blockiſh vnthankfulnes, who neuer or ſeldome reckon vp, as daily we ſhould, ſuch benefits and deliuerances among other, neither are thankfull for them. And ſeeing hunger and thirſt are ſo biting and painfull, and nakedneſſe like both, we muſt be pitifull to ſuch diſtreſſed people, and moued with bowels and compaſſion toward them: remembring Chriſts words, *I was hungrie, and ye gaue me meate*, &c.

Ioh.19.28. Math.25.35.

The other thing heere, is, what a ſmall refreſhing did preſerue *Samſons* life, euen a little water in ſo homely a manner prouided for him, as wee ſee here mentioned, did comfort and reuiue him. What ſhould this teach vs, but that wee ſhould marke how many comfortable refreſhings wee enioy from God, (in compariſon of the which, this was meane and ſmall) without the which we ſhould haue been much diſtempered in our bodies, and thereby vnquiet and vnſetled in our mindes alſo? as meate in our hunger, drinke in our thirſt, reſt after wearineſſe, eaſe and aſſwagement of paine and diſeaſes. All which, while we be pinched with them, doe better teach vs, how much the freedome from them is to be accounted of. Oh a little intermiſſion from the paine of the ſtone, the anguiſh and extremitie of the gowte, or the like diſeaſes, how doe wee price it? euen farre aboue much treaſure that cannot be valued.

Pſal.68.19. O then, when we bee free from all kinds thereof for a ſeaſon, yea and loden with benefits alſo, on the other ſide, to make our liues comfortable, (both grace and other good things) which makes them all ſauory; what (thinke we) ſhould wee yeeld vnto the Lord for them? Therefore *Samſon* gaue a name to that place alſo, as he did before to the other, according to the occaſion

occasion offered; to testifie his thankes to God for hearing his prayer, by sending him water in his exceeding thirst, in which he was neer vnto death. The doctrine out of this place hath been taught before sundry times; and last of all, out of the 17. verse. Onely this I wish might bee annexed to the doctrine of thankesgiuing that it bee continued, and specially for that great deliuerance from the feare of euerlasting torment, that it bee continued all our life long. As in the song of *Zacharias* wee are taught that God will giue Luk.1.74.
grace thereto. And great reason there is that wee should doe so, seeing wee reape and enioy the fruit thereof all our life long.

But this other thing out of this place I will not omit, and that from the 4
name of the place, which hee gaue. For hee calling it the fountaine of him that prayed, meaning, which God extraordinarily prouided for him, when he prayed to him in his thirst; it teacheth vs, not onely what rare effects and fruites spring of feruent prayer, as S. *Iames* saith (that feruent prayer auaileth Iam.5.16.
much) and as we finde, that thereby wee obtaine grace against daily sinne and corruption: but also, when such fruit is obtained of God by vs, it should well appeare, as it did by *Samsons* leauing a memoriall of his thankfulnesse in the place. So much more should we, who doe not once, but oft, yea and that in one day, receiue many blessings (as effects of our prayers) from God; wee should (I say) let those places bee witnesses of our remembring Gods kindnesse, there so plentifully shead vpon vs. That if such places could speak, they should be well able to testifie, that we had not been barren nor silent in yeelding praises vnto him there. And this not our houses onely, and cham- Note.
bers should witnes, but our gardens, & the fields, yea and the high waies, by which we haue so often passed safely & without danger, should do the like.

Now for the shutting vp of the Chapter, the holy story addeth this, that Vers.20.
for the space of twentie yeeres, while the people were vnder the dominion of the Philistims, *Samson* did continue in his place iudging Israel, that is, helping them, and vexing the other; whereby wee may gather, that although the Israelites were not freed out of their hands altogether, yet they had many great calamities kept from them, by meanes that *Samson* was euer in the way, and at hand, to crosse and disquiet them. And therein we are to marke, that the Lord hauing oft deliuered his people, and yet seeing them to reuolt from him after, and not to bee better for it; hee holds them vnder now the longer, and yet he lessened their bondage, and made it the more tolerable by the helpe they had by *Samson*.

We may hereby learne, that seeing we, when we haue liberty, peace, and other blessings, and also inlargements from affliction, doe not yeeld to the Lord the fruit that is answerable to so great kindnesse of his, and that also looked for at our hands, but wee forget it, and wax vnprofitable, yea and Luk.17.17.
grieue the Lord with our returning to our old euill course againe; therfore he doth the longer and the straitlier hold vs vnder with one crosse and trouble after another, and wee either haue not so good meanes to come out of Note.
them, as he would else giue vs; or we profit not by them, as some of his worthie seruants doe; neither enioy sweet and comfortable daies as wee might doe, and that with his good liking; for all the which wee may thanke our selues. And it is his great mercy that it is no worse with vs.

But take we heed that we tempt not God still in such manner, that while

Esa.5.2. hee looketh for grapes, wee bring forth wild grapes; that wee lie not in our sinnes, which we cannot be ignorant, that they doe much displease him, for God will not be mocked. As he left heere vpon this people a long continued bondage, so will hee deale with vs, as hee hath done heretofore; namely, that although he haue taken the heauie yoke of bondage from the necke of Note. his people in this land, I meane subiection to Idolatry and Poperie, yet hee will leaue matter of sorrow enough by scattering the most part in ignorance, and without good and diligent teachers and guides, & cast the spirit of bondage vpon the rest. Euen as he dealt heere with this people who were vnder the Philistims a long time, that is, before *Samson* was borne, and all the time till he grew to be able to set vpon them, and all the twentie yeres while Leuit 26.21. he iudged Israel, and so continued after that. Yea and hee will punish vs yet seuen times more, if we continue in our euill course.

And let vs obserue a farre different manner of God his visiting the godly, and his punishing the wicked. The people heere by their breaches of couenant and daily reuolts from God were faine to bee inured to affliction, and particularly to bee in seruitude to such as hated them: and yet because the Lord had chosen them from among all nations, to be a peculier people vnto himselfe; therefore his eye could not see their misery, but hee must needs pitie them, and euen then when hee could not but bridle them, hee must needs prouide that their bondage may be tolerable. Wee may thanke our selues for any straitnesse and trouble that befals vs: but in that wee see any light of comfort through a creuis, or haue any breathings and relaxation, it is Gods indulgence: who thereby sheweth that he could bee content the rod were burnt, and might not be vsed at all, forasmuch as he is content to shake it ouer vs only, when as he might beate vs with many stripes. And to say the truth, he holdeth vs vnder rather to preuent greater offences, and sorer punishments for time to come, then deale with vs after and according to our former and past transgressions. Let this teach vs to bewaile and bee humbled for our hollow and false-hearted dealing with God in our promises of amendment, and for our formall thankesgiuing for the blessings wee enioy, and for that wee retaine no more fruit thereof, but become as bad or worse afterward, as euer we were before. And let vs chuse rather by a sound and well ordered course to enioy the constant feeling of Gods loue, and the Ioh.15.10. fruition of his blessing, then by our breaking out, to cloud and blemish our owne happinesse by the mixture of many vnwelcome afflictions. And againe, let it serue to alleniate and qualifie our rebellious nature, which commonly deemeth that God hath quite hidden his face from vs, if all goe not currant and smooth with vs, as in time past. For why? The fauour of God is not like to his displeasure, because sinne is not like obedience: but is it not much, that in the middest of displeasure, and when he hath been so oft prouoked by vs, he forgetteth not to shew mercy to vs? whereas if we looke to the wicked, we shall finde that it is nothing so with them: for neither doth 1.Sam.2.25. the Lord exercise them with afflictions alway, to restraine them; but suffereth them to goe on to perdition: or if he doe punish them, yet he sweetens Mat.27.3. not the crosse to them, but smites them in wrath, and giues them euen here a taste of that eternall displeasure of his, which they shall feele endlesly and easelesly hereafter.

THE

THE EIGHTIE TVVO SERMON ON THE XVI. CHAPTER OF THE BOOKE OF IVDGES.

Vers. 1. *Then went Samson to Azzah, and saw there an harlot and went in vnto her.*

2. *And it was told to the Azzahites, Samson is come hither, and they went about, and laid wait for him all night, in the gate of the City, and were quiet all the night, saying, Abide till the morning early, and we shall kill him.*

3. *And Samson slept till midnight, and arose at midnight, and tooke the doores of the gates of the City and the two posts, and lift them away with the barres, and put them vpon his shoulders, and carried them vp to the top of the mountaine that is before Hebron.*

THE summe of this Chapter is thus much. The Philistims hauing been oft plagued by *Samson*, as in part wee haue heard, they laid for him to kill him. And they hearing that he was at *Azza* or *Gazza* as it is called, (one of their chiefe Cities) they set watch for him in the night to take him, but were disappointed. After that they vsed meanes in another place, and there they apprehended him, and cruelly handled him, and made themselues pastime in bringing him before them to be scorned and laughed at, till at the last, he pulled down the house vpon the chiefe Princes of the Philistims, and many of the people, being met together to sport themselues, and laugh at him, in beholding him their great enemy so disguised and abased, and so there he lost his life with them. *The summe of the Chapter.*

The first part of the Chapter sheweth how *Samson* escaped the hands of the Philistims lying in watch for him at *Azza*, and this to the 4. verse. The second declareth how at another time they laying waite for him, tooke him at the house of *Delilah* in the valley of Sorek, to the 21. verse. The third part sheweth their entreatie, euen their cruell handling of *Samson*, after they had apprehended him, and what came thereof, to the end of the Chapter. *The parts*

The first part of the Chapter.

IN this part is shewed how *Samson* came to this City *Azza*, and there went into the house of an harlot: which being heard of by the Citizens, they laid wait for him, but tooke him not: (for to the great disappointing of them) hee at midnight tooke the posts of the gates vpon his shoulders, and carried them to the top of a mountaine, in the land of Israel, betwixt Hebron and the Azzahites. *The summe of the first 3. verses*

Vers.1. Heere more particularly it being said that he seeing in the City a woman which was an harlot,) for so the Hebrew word is to bee translated heere, though it signifie also a victualler) he went in to her: which phrase is as much as that hee being not her husband, had vnlawfull companie with her; as in chapter 15.1. that phrase of speech is taken for the companying of husband and wife together, as also in many other places it doth appeare; so that it is cleare, that *Samson* in this first verse is said to haue vnlawfull companie with an harlot, neither is there any shew of reason to take it otherwise, against the significatiō of the phrase, as that he saw a victualler, & went in to her, that is, into her house: for their houses were knowne to bee for the receiuing of passengers by some signes, or report, & not by meeting the victuallers in the streets, and so accompanying them home. Sure it is, that this was an harlot, whose house he went into, and he went in thither to an ill end, euen to haue company with her (as I haue said) in an vnlawfull manner: therefore to

Doct.vers 1. seeke any other exposition to salue the matter, is needlesse.

It hath been well seene in this storie, that *Samson* (notwithstanding some faults) was one of the deere seruants of God, as also, it is confirmed that hee

Heb.11 32. was so in the Epistle to the Hebrewes. And yet now behold, hee is snared with an harlot, nay made drunke with that which was pretious to him, and deceiueable in her. This is wondred at, and raiseth doubtfull thoughts of heart in many of Gods weake people, to see a man so beloued of God as hee was, to be left to himselfe to fal so shamefully. They desire therfore to know how this should come to passe, that *Samson*, otherwise so good a man, should be thus bereaued of his former good mind at this time, yea so disguised, and become so vnlike himselfe, and that in so short a time after hee had serued God so commendably in the former Chapter, vers. 16. &c. and that he who could ouercome, and by his strength slew a thousand at one time, and that without weapon, should become so impotent, thus to bee ouercome of a poore sillie woman, yea of an harlot. But it teacheth, that such a thing may possibly befall the deere seruants of God. Such frailty they are subiect to, and such corruption remaineth still in them, that they may possibly forget God for the time, (a fearefull thing to thinke of,) and the holy estate they are in, and bee soone carried by occasion from their stedfastnesse in faith, knowledge, and other grace to such fearfull sinnes, and thereby it was that *Samson* fell into this sinne of whoredome, his heart not being armed against vncleannesse, nor he vpholden in his former chastnesse and grace.

2.Sam.11.4. And therefore let vs know, that the people of God (as *Dauid, Salomon, Io-*
1.King.11.4. *nah*, and others did giue too good proofe of) haue not God his grace
Ionah 1.3. so pinned to their sleeues, but that they may possibly fall either into this, or other reprochfull and foule sinnes, partly by the forementioned meanes, and partly by the inward suggestion of the heart, giuing liberty thereto; besides this, that there are many other outward occasions and

Note. prouocations among which they walke, with bad examples, whereto they are in danger of being fashioned and made like to them, which may first teach vs all to see that there is great cause why the best of vs should not trust our corrupt nature, nor content our selues to deale slightly in looking to our vow and couenant made with God against al sinne and wickednesse; but bee fast knit and vnited to him by faith vnfained, and true loue for

for his infinite kindnesse to vs, so that wee might not bee let loose so farre, as to prostitute our selues to any such villanie and reproch: but rather for the same his goodnesse to vs to be so farre off from it, as that we should rather be daily drawne to endeuour to please him in all things, and that with readinesse: yea and to watch thereunto constantly for all power from God to arme and inable vs thereto: well considering with our selues, that they are not our great words and boasts of our chastnes, honesty, and grace, which will stand vs in stead, in the time of tentation and triall, neither are cold prayers and endeuours able to weaken strong tentations in vs, but we must looke for strength, and hearten on our selues by diligent and reuerent vsing of al good meanes appointed of God for this purpose, and yet to know that we are great gainers thereby. And to speake more particularly of this sin of *Samsons*, we must (as we shall see cause) arme our selues against dallying with the least tickling of vs thereto, and with the forementioned meanes vsing, as hath been said) to attend our particular callings, and auoide idle and vnnecessary goings abroad; (which *Dinah* did not, and therefore smarted) whereby wee shall obtaine no small liberty and freedome from the same. These things being duly regarded of vs, and feruent prayers offered vp oft and constantly to God for assistance and blessing; there is no feare, (God hauing so spoken) that wee shall bee strongly possessed of smaller sinnes, as anger, impatience, &c. much lesse tainted either with this vncleannesse, or with any other reprochfull euils: but rather, by daily and renued care and watchfulnesse, wee shall gather experience, and hope of being vpholden from the same vnto our end. But if good things grow in meane account with vs, yea if wee hold them not in an high price and reckoning, then begins our woe, and then we lie open to infinite dangers. The vse of this is to make the best of vs to feare and suspect our selues, lest we should fall, seeing we haue not grace at commandement, but as we make much of it.

Note.

Gen.34.1.2.

Note.

And further heere, as in fittest place, I thinke good to adde this; that seeing *Samson* did afterward recouer and rise againe; therefore this should secondly serue to hold any that haue been deere to the Lord, (and yet haue fallen as *Samson* did) from dispairing of Gods mercy toward them, and rather encourage them to cling againe in all true submission to him for mercy. And much more ought our knowledge hereof to stay vs from condemning such for Apostates, who haue so offended, though it cannot bee denied but that they haue stained their credit which they had for godlinesse, with such blemishes. Sundry among vs not considering themselues, are too readie to fall to such rash and vncharitable iudging of other: and it is (as they thinke) a good piece of religion (to their small commendation bee it spoken) that they can censure others, vntill their vncharitablenesse, high mindednesse, and rash iudging with the diuels malice & subtilty together, haue brought themselues into the like or worse case, and iustly exposed them to that reproch which they in their distempered mood did most spitefully draw vpon others. But of this point the seuerall relapses whereof the former story is full, hath ministred occasion to entreate: let the reader compare the seuerall places for his owne benefit.

Note.

Another thing in this verse is, that it is said, he was carried to this sinne by his eye. For hee saw a woman that was an harlot, and he went in to her. So that

Doct.2.

that the occasion of his sinne was his vngouerned eye, the euill heart being soone inflamed and prouoked thereby. And so it is oft times with many o-
2.Sam.11.2. ther. Thus was *Dauid* deceiued, and (though that is lesse to bee wondered
Gen.39.7. at) *Iosephs* Mistresse. So all experience teacheth, that the eye is a glasse window to let sinne into the heart, though it haue little neede of helpe, for it is it selfe a fountaine of filthinesse, out of the which as smoake out of a fornace, all wickednesse doth proceed and come. Our wisedome shall be here, and it is the vse wee should make of this doctrine, to keepe our eyes continent, while we walke in the middest of the allurements of this world, and there-
Iob 31.1. fore to make a couenant with *Iob*, not to looke vpon a woman, lest wee be caught and snared with that which is precious in her, but rather, where our
Matth.5.29. eye offendeth, to plucke it out, and turne it away from such alluring obiects.

Oh it giueth great ease and rest to vs with safetie, ouer that they finde, who will giue libertie to themselues that way, I speake euen of those that repent for it afterward: as for other, they haue no eare to heare, till their eyes bring both soule and body so set on fire, to destruction. And the like I may say of the eare, the tongue, and companie, which all of them, euen as idlenesse and venturing to meddle and deale, where we haue no calling nor warrant, threaten infinite mischiefe to vs, as not onely that example of the
Prou.7.5. foole in the Prouerbs doth testifie, (whose rouing about the streetes made
Gen.34.2. him a bootie to the harlot) but *Dinahs* also, and many other doe witnesse, who, when they were catcht in the snare, though not the same, (for the neg-
Note. lect of this rule carrieth all sorts into deepe danger) haue cried out bitterly, when it was too late. But who could perswade them to doe otherwise before? or who by such examples can teach others wisedome, till they haue bought it and paid for it dearely themselues? For as in this sinne of dalliance, so is it in the rst: men thinke they are wise enough to guide their own
Ierem.10.23. way, though God be shut out, (whereas the Prophet *Ieremy* denieth that it is in man to direct his own way) and they that are not so bad, yet they think they may be bold to goe vpon the brinke, though they fall not into the water, but when they are fallen in, (for what other thing may they looke for) then they wish they had abridged themselues a little of their libertie, rather then to haue taken a whit too much: then no precisenes, (which hath sometime been scoffed at in others) nor any setting watch ouer heart and eyes is too much. And to say the truth, God (who is onely wise) knoweth what hee doth, when he lets such bold persons (seeing they will needes) fall dangerously: not onely that others might learne to beleeue those admonitions concerning such offences, when they see examples, but euen for the offendors themselues, that their pride may bee crackt, their loosenes corrected, themselues made more priuie to their owne corruption, and glad to liue euer after more thankfully vnder Gods gouernment.

And yet this I say further about this point, that some who glorie to bee counted virgins, and therefore refuse mariage, and the rather to shun other discommodities accompanying it, they shall haue small reward for their so doing of God; but their sinne breaking out another way, as by Sodomie, and the nourishing of vncleane lusts, and so being doubled, they shall haue their punishment accordingly.

But

But seeing this sin of *Samsons* was committed immediatly after the great Doct.3.
seruice that hee did to God against the Philistims, mentioned in the latter end of the former chapter, (from the which worke he came to this citie *Azza*, where hee saw the woman) by this (I say) wee may see, that when wee haue praised God (as he did at the victorie he had gotten) and after we haue serued him in any good sort and manner, yet euen then are wee subiect to offend, and breake out against him some way, as occasion may be offered, Note.
and euen then are we not free from danger of falling, no, not after so firme standing: whereas it might be thought that we be then out of perill for many daies after.

Indeed it were meete it should be so, I meane, that wee should be better fenced and strengthened against euill of all sorts, when we haue been well occupied and taken vp in dutie to God before, and I confesse, (as all will grant) that if wee consider it well, that wee should after and by such seruice Note.
done to God, as *Samson* did against the Philistims, we should (I say) be fenced against all the sweete baites of sinne for a long time afterward; and it were meete, that by such good spirituall refreshing of our soules, we might be the fitter to proceed cheerefully and readily from one dutie to another, at least to be farre from such disguisings, as this of *Samsons* was. But as the diuell handleth the matter, who slightly and couertly worketh thereby in vs securitie, and a pleasing of our selues in the good that we haue done, we are sometimes easily led to dreame, and imagine, that wee hauing now been well occupied, we may more boldly take our libertie, and by good right remit and slake our care that we had before: to the which wee are all prone by the rebellion of our wicked nature. To be forward any way to sinne after we haue been fleshed on by ill companie, and such like inticements, it is a thing not to be marueiled at: but after we haue been well occupied, and haue done faithfull seruice to God, then to break out amisse, and to go (like *Cain* and *Iudas*) out of Gods presence, as it were into the diuels shop forthwith, about his worke and busines, this (I say) would not easily be thought, that wee might be brought vnto. But yet through wilfull ignorance, that wee will know no better, neither will see, when yet wee doe, or through sloth, pride, loosenes and securitie bearing sway in vs, wee may possibly bee misled, yea and that easily and full soone, after this manner, as I haue said. The vse of this is, to reproue them who will say: What? must wee euer be in seruing of God? The which speech how vnsauourie it is, and vnbeseeming professors of the Gospell, all may see, who know, that the seruice of God is perfect freedome: and they shall see also, when for the neglecting of it, they haue well smarted.

And if that will not stop their mouthes and answere them, let that saying of our Sauiour bee added to it: to wit, that when wee haue done the Luke 17.10.
most, we are but vnprofitable seruants, and that we come farre short of that which we ought to doe: yea and that all meanes vsing will not fray away Satan and noysome temptations, except we watch and pray to resist him Matth.26.41.
alway, as frailtie will permit. These things and the like, if they be duly considered, we shall see small cause to flatter our selues, as though wee might take some libertie by authoritie to sinne.

What these men of Azza did, when they heard that *Samson* was there, is Verse 2.
shewed

shewed in this second verse: to wit, that they went about presently to take him, and compassed the house, and lay in waite for him in the night, purposing (though they were disappointed) to kill him in the morning. This diligence in them without delay, being heathens, to preuent a mischiefe, putteth vs to blame and iust reproch, who are Christians, if wee bee not much more carefull to doe the like. For thereby wee preuent, or cut off at least, much inconuenience, when it is alreadie begun, if wee doe not also hinder and marre the growth thereof, that it goe no further. As for example more particularly, if disorder, lewd meetings, to drinkings, gaming, whoring, and such like, bee sprung vp in our countrey townes, or houses among vs, all should be hinderers of them (that are such workers of euill) as they may, and oppose themselues against them, both Magistrates, Headborowes of townes, and Masters of families: so for the apprehending a Iesuite or Seminarie, and such as are knowne to carrie traytors hearts against their Prince and land, or any that come to sow their heretical and Idolatrous cockle and darnell among the Lords wheate, also if any should goe about to aleniate the people from the true worship of God, from publike hearing the Gospel preached; we should be as forward as these Philistims, in hunting them out of their holes, and bringing them foorth, rather then to haue our sloth, and backwardnes in such good attempts to be condemned, and that iustly, and especially by the diligence of such as these Philistims were.

Against all which abominations wee should so ioyne together for the rooting out of them, that they who can lend no other helpe hereto, should yet enquire after them where there is cause, and to tell and bewray their haunt, as they did here tell the citizens of Azza, that *Samson* was there. And so all of vs with the poore people at the building of the Temple, (who brought morter to set forward the same, when they could doe no greater thing) all of vs (I say) are to doe our best endeuour, at least to shew our forward and readie mindes to doe the good we can therein. But lamentable is the sloth and backwardnes that is shewed in setting Gods matters and businesse forward, when yet no time nor labour, no, nor cost, is enough in following our owne: much like them who are mentioned by the Prophet, Habac.1.4. who dwelt in sieled houses themselues, but suffered Gods house to lie wast. But more of this before oftentimes, and lately in the former Chapter by the like occasion.

Vers.3. But it is said in this verse that *Samson* escaped their hands, for all their labour and diligence to take him, and not onely so, but also did them further hurt: whereby we may see, that God did not by and by punish him for all his great sinne committed, but gaue him time to thinke of it; whereas if he had forthwith chastised him, hee had dealt with him but iustly. But seeing God oft times dealeth so with vs, I meane, not to pursue vs by and by after some wilful and knowne sinne committed, here lest we should misconceiue of his so doing, learne we the end of his forbearing any of vs, when we haue prouoked him: for we know that he should doe vs no wrong, if he should forthwith lay his hand vpon vs, yea and that in some sharpe manner. The 2.Pet.3.9. reason of Gods deferring, the Apostle *Peter* setteth downe: who telleth vs, that the Lord is patient to vs in such cases to this end, euen to bring vs to repentance: loe, this good he meaneth vs by forbearing vs. And though it be be no wise mans part to tempt him at all, in hope of being spared, as *Samson* heere was, (because sinnes can neuer be without feare, though they may be without outward danger for a time) yet if wee haue done so in times past, for the time to come, doe we so no more.

For so our Sauiour speaketh to the man in the Gospel who had been hea- Ioh.5.14.
led of his disease, (and the caueat & watchword is as fit for vs) Goe thy way and sinne no more, lest a worse thing befall thee. So the best that we can do in such a case, is, to iudge our selues speedily, for the euill we haue done, that we bee not iudged of the Lord, which will bee sharpe and smartie. Euen as
Samson found it afterward, and as other doe in the like case find it daily. And 1.Cor.11.31.
yet without due regard had, our corrupt hearts will driue vs vpon the common rocke; to wit, that wee shall hurt our selues that way which many doe, euen to cry peace, peace; if God deferre to punish, and to thinke (for so wee loue to flatter our selues) that he fauoureth vs, when he doth not by and by
strike vs: euen as the wicked said in the Psalme, (because the Lord did (as it Psal.50.21.
were) hold his tongue, and did not by and by smite him for his sin) that he was like vnto him, that is, of his mind, and allowed him therein; but God answered him, I will reproue thee, and set thy bad doings before thee, that thou shalt acknowledge them whether thou wilt or no, and so I will shew how I fauoured thee.

The second part of the Chapter.

Vers. 4. *And after this hee loued a woman by the plaine of Sorek, whose name was Delilah.*

5. *Vnto whom came the Princes of the Philistims, and said vnto her, Entice him, and see wherein his great strength lieth, and by what meanes we may ouercome him, that we may bind him and punish him; and euery one of vs shall giue thee eleuen hundred shekles of siluer.*

6. *And Delilah said to Samson, Tell mee, I pray thee, wherein thy great strength lieth, and wherewith thou mightest be bound to doe thee hurt?*

7. *Samson then answered vnto her, If they bind me with seuen greene cords, that were neuer dried, then shall I be weake, and be as another man.*

8. *And the Princes of the Philistims brought her seuen greene cords, that were not dry, and she bound him therewith.*

9. *(And shee had men lying in waite with her in the chamber,) Then shee said vnto him, The Philistims be vpon thee Samson: And he brake the cords as a threed of tow is broken when it feeleth fire: so his strength was not knowne.*

10. *After, Delilah said vnto Samson, See thou hast mocked me, and told me lies, I pray thee now tell me wherewith thou mightest be bound.*

11. *Then he answered her, If they bind me with new ropes that were neuer occupied, then shall I be weake, and be as another man.*

12. *Delilah therefore tooke new ropes, and bound him therewith, and said vnto him, The Philistims be vpon thee Samson (and men lay in waite in the chamber) and he brake them from his armes as a threed.*

13. *Afterward Delilah said vnto Samson, Hitherto hast thou beguiled mee and told me lies, tell me how thou mightest be bound. And he said vnto her, If thou plattest seuen lockes of mine head with the threeds of the woofe.*

14. *And she fastened it with a pinne, and said vnto him, The Philistims be vpon thee Samson, and he awoke out of his sleepe, and went away with the pin of the web and the woofe.*

15. *Againe she said vnto him, How canst thou say, I loue thee, when thine heart is not with me? thou hast mocked me these three times, and hast not told me wherein thy great strength lyeth.*

16. *And because she was importunate vpon him with her words continually, and vexed him, his soule was pained to the death.*

17. *Therefore hee told her all his heart, and said to her, There neuer came rasor vpon mine head: for I am a Nazarite vnto God from my mothers wombe: therfore if I be shauen, my strength will go from me, and I shall bee weake, and be like to other men.*

18. *And when Delilah saw that he had told her all his heart, shee sent and called for the Princes of the Philistims, saying, Come vp once againe; for hee hath shewed mee all his heart. And they came vp to her, and brought the money in their hands.*

19. *And shee made him sleepe vpon her knees, and she called a man, and made him to shaue off the seuen locks of his head, and she began to vex him, and his strength was gone from him.*

20. *Then she said, the Philistims be vpon thee Samson. And he awoke out of his sleepe, and thought, I will goe out now as at other times, and shake my selfe, but hee knew not that the Lord was departed from him.*

The summe of these verses. IN these verses is set downe the second part of the Chapter, wherein *Samson* sinned againe, in like manner as before, but he had not the like issue as he had out of the former wicked fact. For God did not arrest him vpon that trespasse, nor pursue him; but seeing hee made no benefit of that his conniuence, when hee went away without punishment, but proceeded to the like sinne againe; behold he now paid dearly for both, accordingly as he tempted God farre by this sinne of whoredome. For here it is said, that he loued another woman of the Philistims, and when they vnderstood it, they considered by what meanes he vexed them, and that was by the great strength of body which he had, whereby hee wrought them great mischiefe: and they by and by enticed and flattered the woman, and easily wonne her, by promising her a great summe of money, and so agreed all of them together therein, to perswade her to get of him by subtilty, where his great strength lay, that so they might when they knew it, vse some meanes to weaken him, and then handle him afterward at their pleasure. The which practise she being so hired, readily went about; and he being made drunke with the sottish and inordinate loue of her, suffered her to moue such questions to him about it, that although hee held her off a while, yet at last hee told her all his heart, euen that which she asked of him, how he might bee made weake, till hee saw too late with *Adam*, that God was gone from him, and that hee had lost all the great strength which God had giuen him. *Gen.3.7.*

In these verses (containing the second part of the Chapter) seeing they are many, and the matter of them much; therefore for auoiding confusion and tediousnesse in the handling of them, I will draw them to these two points. The first, how by a new occasion the Philistims laid wait for *Samson* againe

againe. And this is to the end of the fifth verſe, and that was in this manner: to wit, by moſt earneſt ſuing to *Delilah*, to learne where his great ſtrength lay: The ſecond, how ſhe neuer ceaſed til ſhe had found it out, and brought them word of it, to verſ.21.

And firſt touching *Samſon*, the holy ſtory relateth what the occaſion was of purſuing him; in verſe 4. and then how the Philiſtims thereby were moued to lay for him, in verſ.5. The occaſion was, that he caſt his affection vpon another woman, not an Iſraelite, (but of the nation of the Philiſtims) and the holy ſtory expreſſeth the place where ſhee dwelt, which was the plaine of Sorek, and the womans name whom he loued was *Delilah*. By this that is ſaid of *Samſon*, that hee went to another woman as before; note that filthy luſt is not ſatisfied, by yeelding to it (no more then anger and wrath is) that is, onely for the time, but breaketh out, and rangeth ſtill yet further. For as the fire, when it is broken out into a flame, ſtandeth not ſtill, but taketh hold of one houſe when it hath burned another: Euen ſo it is with wicked luſt: It is not one woman, two, or twenty, that can ſatisfie the vnbridledneſſe, and outragiouſneſſe thereof, but it would, if it might be ſerued and yeelded vnto, goe as farre as *Salomon* did, euen to defile a thouſand. As *Iehu* in his anſwere to *Iehorams* demand of peace, 2.King.9. tels him that his mother *Iezabels* witchcrafts were without number. The reaſon hereof is, becauſe the vnlawfull pleaſure of ſin doth (as the bait doth the fiſh) egge on the ſinner to goe forward, and blinds him from ſeeing the manifold vnfruitfulneſſe thereof. Like gameſters, who will neuer leaue off their trade, while there is a pennie left them. Which ſheweth, that the wickedneſſe of the heart is in that one kind, as in many other, out of meaſure ſinfull. For what though there bee no cleare proofe of this alwaies that I ſpeake of, I meane the vnſatiableneſſe of mens filthie appetite. It is ſo, partly ſeeing the ſinne is ſecretly committed, for the moſt part, and therefore can hardly be knowne to many how far it proceedeth: and partly, for that ſuch as ſinne in that kind, can hardly haue ordinary opportunity to effect that which they deſire. But the truth of that which I ſay, appeareth by this, that it hath been found out, as by other waies, ſo by the confeſſion of ſome, who haue gone farre in that wicked courſe of life, and howſoeuer they may haue come ſhort in the number of ſo many as a thouſand with *Salomon*, yet they haue made it vp to the full, in the long lying in the ſin with them who were their leaud companions, when they haue not been intercepted, but haue had their full ſwinge. So true is it which is affirmed of the guilt of ſinne, that it is infinite, both in reſpect of the tranſgreſſion againſt an infinite Maieſtie, and alſo becauſe the ſinners appetite (though actually finite) yet extendeth it ſelfe to a deſire of multiplying ſinne infinitely, if it could. And it is death to bad men to thinke that their euill courſe ſhould bee ſtopped, or that they may not do as in times paſt they haue done: yea becauſe that age and death, if no other thing, muſt needs end all their iollity.

Doct. verſ.4.

A ſimil.

2.King.9.22.

And not to inſiſt in this inſtance alone, it may bee ſeene in ſundry other kindes of ſinne, (as theft, prodigality, drunkenneſſe and the reſt) how the heart is out of meaſure ſinfull, and giueth not ouer euill doing, till it want opportunity, or till it muſt ceaſe by neceſſity, and that violence bee put vnto it. It delighteth the old ribald to ſee and heare, and report the pageants, ſtories, and practises of vncleannesse, which he remembreth he hath wrought, and though his old bones cannot bestirre them so liuely as in times past, yet old *Adam* within is aliue, and as lasciuious as euer. The angry man, when hath he done? till he haue none to be angry with, or till hee be cut off, so as he cannot shew it. But I might bee endlesse, if I should follow particulars. How oft (thinke wee) had *Peter* been like to haue denied his Master, who did so three times, and vehementliest at the last, when yet hee did it onely through feare, of meere infirmity, and not professedly, which had been much worse? neither yet were the occasions very strong or great by which he was brought thereto, but euen the words of a silly damsell.

Prou. 4. 18. The vse of that which I haue said is this; that both in tentation to the sinne of vncleannesse, (and the obiect thereof) and to any other sinne, wee keepe our hearts and eyes with all possible obseruation and diligence from allowing or liking the offer of it, in any sort, but that we curbe them vp and tie them short. For though carnall reason would perswade vs, that the giuing of a little liberty to our fleshly affections, and couetous desires, would
Note. content and satisfie them, so as they would not desire to reach any further, (as some man will say, If I were worth but thus many hundred pounds, &c. I would rest content) yet this were a grosse bewitching of vs to thinke so, seeing without Gods speciall grace, as money encreaseth, so doth the loue thereof also; yea it were the next way to bring vs into vtter and extreame bondage, and to prouoke vs further to endlesse ingaging of our selues there-
Mat. 26. 41. unto. Nay, rather ioyne we prayer with watching, and that we fall not from our vprightnesse, so shall we be sure not to fall into any such tentation. I say the lesse of this, because I haue handled it in the speech of *Adonibezek*, in cap. 1. vers. 4.

THE EIGHTIE THREE SERMON ON THE XVI. CHAPTER OF THE BOOKE OF IVDGES.

2 TO goe forward where I left, heere note wee another thing; to wit, what vse and benefit wee commonly make of Gods long sufferance and patience, and that is this: euen to goe forward by spirituall delusion, in our sinnes, without making any question, that God will call vs to any account for them; but flatteringly to tell our selues, and to be perswaded that all is well, as long as God lets vs go vnpunished. Whereas, who should bee ignorant of this, that the patience of God toward vs is to the end we should acknowledge it with vnfained thankes: (for he might iustly haue punished vs, as he hath done others, when he spared vs) and that to the end

end wee ſhould turne againe to the Lord by true repentance, rather won- Rom.2.4.
dring at his lenity in ſo doing,then with much adoe enduring the penalty. and when we be enlightened,and come to our ſelues,and ſee that wee haue tempted God,we ſhould in no wiſe flatter our ſelues,leſt the Lord be forced thereby to tie vs ſhorter, and vſe more ſharpeneſſe then we ſhal like well of. The like I ſpake of *Samſons* eſcaping in the former verſe. Onely this I adde, that it is a fearefull thing,when the loue and conniuence of God, which is a Note.
chiefe bridle to containe his faithfull people in obedience, is become an occaſion of the greateſt licentiouſneſſe in them. It argueth that their tender nature and filiall affection is waxen hardened,and degenerated into ſlauiſh and deſperate boldneſſe.Like to him who preſuming himſelfe ſure enough of his maſter, fell to waxe wearie of worke, and to take vpon him iollity, as they doe who reckon without their Hoſte. But there ſhall no one thing ſo much ſting them at the heart when God is come to take correction on them,as this; that they were neuer well,till they had turned the loue of a father, into the iealouſie of a foe: whoſe ſwift wings in taking reuenge ſhall be ſure to recompence the delay of his leaden feet,ſlow to puniſh,as *Samſon* himſelfe in the ſequell found to his coſt.

Thus much of *Samſons* ſinne: now it is ſhewed how the Philiſtims tooke Verſ.5.
occaſion thereby to get him into their hands,and that was, by dealing with the woman whom he loued,to intice him to tel her where his great ſtrength lay,that ſo they might doe to him as they deſired; but withall, to the end they might draw and perſwade her thereto, they offer her (the chiefe Princes of them, I meane) a large ſumme of money. By this we may ſee the wiſdome and readineſſe of the men of this world in going about to remedie any bodily miſchiefe that is comming toward them. As ſoone as they heard where *Samſons* haunt was,the chiefe of them went thither, and tooke order for the ſuppreſſing of him,and that not without their great coſt and charge. Oh this were commendable indeed, if it might bee ſeene in vs, yea and ſo much the more, where greater miſchiefe hangeth ouer vs, I meane, if wee could offer like violence to our ſinne, and giue it no reſt, till wee had rooted it out,as they heere effected that which they went about. The which (yet) all may ſee,that we haue greater cauſe to doe, then they that are in the moſt emminent danger of any temporall or bodily euill. But here to ſee both our ſloth and our follie,it is both admirable and lamentable. But of their prouidence, together with their coſt, conſent, and diligence I haue noted more by the like occaſion in the former verſe.

It is no maruell that they counſell her to deceiue him by inticements and 2
allurements, ſuch as harlots haue good skill in,and fooles that are woond in with them, are eaſily deluded by. For *Samſon* by the ſtrongeſt reaſon and perſwaſion of the wiſeſt carnall friend, would neuer haue been drawne to this ſlauerie and ſhame,which a baſe companion brought him to, by delu- Note.
ſion and deceiuing of him. Whereby we may learne, that when we are carried away to ſinne, and are giuen ouer to our luſts,we depart not only from religion, but alſo from ſound wiſdome and reaſon, and are not in our right mindes,(as they ſay) but are deluded, mocked, diſguiſed, euen made very fooles,as *Samſon* was heere, if not mad and beſide our ſelues; as it was ſaid of Luk.15 17.
the prodigall ſonne when hee had ſpent his goods with harlots,hee came to himſelfe

himselfe at length, whereby it is cleere that he was before beside himselfe: and as we reade of the foole in the Prouerbs, that hee followed as an oxe to the slaughter.

Prou 7.22.

And if we be such, then it is our due to bee shoaled among such, and to be driuen from the companie of sober and wise men. Yet thus was *Samson* deceiued and deluded, when he was drawne and inticed by that wicked woman, to vtter this secret, namely where his great strength lay. The vse that we should make of this, is to abhorre that sinne, and all fellowship with such persons, and labour to retaine godly wisedome, to guide vs in holie feare of offending, rather then to take part in the pleasures of sinne for a season, so shall we not be deceiued and deluded, as otherwise wee cannot chuse but be, yea and that in most sottish manner, as *Samson* here was by her inchantment brought to bee. Let this bee sufficient to shew, that there is enough in the corrupt heart of man to humble him in the sight of God and the world, if he were not in the depth of darknesse, yea though there were no more but this, that there is such a rebellion and deformitie in the inferior appetite of the soule, through originall sinne, that whereas it was created most obedient and subiect to the pure light of the vnderstanding in all things, now it is so infeebled and infatuated, that it resisteth the iudgement of the minde, and led away by the strength of any allurement, euen contrary to that knowledge, which still remaineth to guide it. So that it is degegenerate and become most brutish and sottish, and so bewraieth it selfe euen in them that otherwise goe for none, of the simplest, or vnciuill sort.

Doct. 3.

This offering of her money by these Princes of the Philistims, and that also in such liberall maner, which was as much as an hundred pound a piece of our money well nigh, by the estimation of the shekell, which they reckoned by, [for a common shekell was as much as twentie pence with vs, and therefore eleuen hundred want little of an hundred pound at that rate.] This offering (I say) of so many hundreds to her, according to the number of the Princes that came to her, might easily draw on to their purpose such an one as was but light, inconstant, and false-hearted to *Samson*, (as harlots are) without respect of the money.

Doct.

Which teacheth vs, that this hireing of people for money, hath bin, and is as readie a way to draw them to any lewd practise, as it is commonly offered, & hath bin in all ages, but neuer more then in this, and especially by the Popish crue in the attempting of desperate murthers, &c. The like hath bin noted in the fact of *Abimelech*, chap. 9. who hired lewd fellowes with the money of the Shechemites: and that wofull example of the Priests preuailing thereby with *Iudas* one of the twelue Apostles, to betray his Master, and in hireing the watchmen, Matth. 28. to defame the Resurrection, may be notable presidents hereof. And I mention this point to this end, that seeing it is as common as odious, that it may not reach also to Gods faithfull seruants, to doe either the one or the other, either to set a worke others, or to sell their helpe either to corrupt, or to be corrupted by money, (for they go together, and are mutuall causes and effects of each other) to bring wicked purposes to passe; which in so euill an age as this is, (farre more subtile and skilfuller then the former to doe mischiefe) may too soone preuaile by custome

Iudg. 9. 4.

Mat. 28. 12. 13.

ſtone euen among them. Touching the coſt they were at, ſee more in chap.17.2.

Thus wee haue heard how this wicked woman was hired by the Phili- Verſ.6.7.8.9.
ſtim Princes to this wofull worke of deceiuing *Samſon*, which was the firſt point of the two, (as appeareth in the fourth verſe) in the ſecond part of this chapter. Now it followeth, how ſhe went to worke, and preuailed, and this is the ſecond. This is declared and laid foorth in the verſes following, to the 21. But ſhe not obtaining at one time that which ſhe ſought, ſhe ſet vpon him ſundrie times. Foure ſeuerall attempts are expreſſed here to haue been made by her to this end; and the firſt of them is to bee ſeene in theſe foure next verſes. Of theſe therefore as they follow in order.

In her firſt attempt, we muſt not thinke that ſhe went about it ſimply by Doct. verſ.6.
asking him the queſtion, where his ſtrength lay; but as they had taught her to deceiue him, ſo there is no doubt but ſhe flattered him, pretending that ſhe marueiled at his ſo great ſtrength, and that ſhe reioyced not a little, for that ſhe had a louer indued with ſuch an excellent gift and qualitie; and therfore that ſhe, as one louing him againe, and truſtie to him, for his kindneſſe towards her, deſired of him to know where that great ſtrength of his did lie. By this we ſee, what boldneſſe, men (though furniſhed with excellent gifts) doe cauſe and cheriſh in harlots, by hauing fellowſhip, and keeping companie with them. *Samſon* was a man ſo ſpoken of for his manhood, that ſuch as were of good courage, durſt not be bold to looke him in the face, yet ſhe a baſe houſewife, dares boldly demaund of him weightie matters, and the greateſt ſecrets. So the whoriſh daughter of an whoriſh
mother, *Herodias* I meane, being ſo farre admitted as to dance before *Herod* Matth.14.6.
the King, & being permitted to demand what recompence ſhe liſted, euen to the halfe of his kingdome, ſhamed not to aske the head of *Iohn Baptiſt:*
whom not onely all the people, but euen *Herod* himſelfe reuerenced and Mark.6.20.
ſtood in feare of. And theſe are the wares which the ſtrumpets fardall is ſtuft withall, euen ſubtiltie, crueltie, falſehood (all ſo tempered together in this demaund of *Delilah*, that a man knowes not which qualitie of them all is predominant) and among the reſt, this (whereof we now ſpeake) inſolent impudencie and ſhameleſneſſe. It is the practiſe of this curſed kinde euen at this day with their Paramours, to demaund of them vnreaſonable pledges of vncleane loue, as appeares by the embezeling of their patrimonie for their maintenance, and ſometimes cauſing them to ſpend euen their blood in their quarrell, or by their occaſion.

It is a true ſaying, that too much familiaritie breedeth contempt. But much more if it be in euill, and in no euill ſooner then in this kind, I meane
in whoredome. A thing notoriouſly exemplified in that harlot *Iezabel*, Note.
who ſo much abuſed the remiſſenes of *Ahab*, as to inſult ouer him, as her 1 King.21.7.
vnderling. It is the common phraſe of them that are the companions of harlots, to call themſelues their ſeruants, and them their miſtreſſes. But in deed they are their vaſſals and ſlaues, and yet their bondage, as great as it is, and ioyned with miſerie, is ſweete to them, although (indeed) but a ſweete poyſon: but it is a reward good enough for ſuch employment. And yet many chuſe this kinde of life, as a libertie, rather then honeſt mariage. But to returne to that which I ſaid of familiaritie, it is not meete for the beſt to

swell (I confesse) and to bee high minded, but humble and meeke toward all; yet with grauitie, whereby the bad may be afraid of them, and not think them fit companions for them, except they change their qualities, and the good may cling and ioyne to their companie and acquaintance, without feare. But to haue familiaritie with the bad in euill, is vtterly vnlawfull, and serues onely to confirme and make them bold in wickednesse. Thus is many a man, otherwise worthie, as *Samson* was, brought into meane account by indiscreete and vnseasonable laying open his minde, where hee should not: euen so did he imbolden this woman thereby to aske him how he may bee bound and hurt; the which how absurd a thing it was either for him to incourage her, or for her to propound to him, who seeth not?

Note. Tit. 2. 7.

Vers. 7. *Samson* in answering her, who should not haue admitted her to speake to him of any such matter, and telling her how hee might be bound, did make way to all the euill that followed. For if she had been repulsed and beaten back from such boldnes at the first, she should haue had no incouragement, or much lesse (no doubt) to haue proceeded further, as she did afterward. It was as great wisedome in *Samson* to answer her in this, as it was in *Balaam*, when he answered the words of his Asse. It was time (he should haue said with himselfe) for him to thinke that hee had gone farre enough in prouoking God, when hee opened the mouth of the dumme beast to reprooue him.

Numb. 22. 29.

So should *Samson* haue thought, that when he had imboldned a wicked woman to tamper and meddle with him about that which touched his life, and concerned his soule, to bereaue it of the furniture of the graces of God, he should haue thought (I say) that it was time to cease speaking to her, or to admit her to speake of any such matter to him: yea to turne vtterly away from her rather, and vtterly to giue her ouer. *Ioseph*, when his whorish Mistresse lay at him day by day to yeeld to her wicked request, the Scripture testifieth, that yet he hearkened not vnto her, neither would be in her companie.

Gen. 39. 10.

So if any of vs haue made vagaries and outstrayings, yea though not so grossely as *Samson* did, neither in fellowship with lewd women, (which were horrible) but if it be but in fond and filthie lingering after them, and their whorish companie, when our consciences shall accuse vs for so doing, and warne vs to desist and breake off betimes, from such longing and lingering after them, as they who haue nothing to doe with them, and when withall we set before our eyes the shame and sorrow that will fall on vs by that which we long for, and hast after: then (I say) let vs thinke, it is high time for vs (if wee haue vnhappily gone so farre) to breake the brood, and scatter the mists of such idle and filthie thoughts and wicked lusts, and with astonishment aske of our selues, what haue wee done? and by the helpe of our faithfull and feruent prayers to throw them all in the dust, and not with *Samson* to dally with them, as he did with his *Delilah*, but marke and thinke seriously vpon the end thereof. And so doing, wee shall to some purpose make our benefit of this example of *Samson*: otherwise wee may with the common sort wonder at, and condemne his follie, and our selues play the fooles in the like or a worse kinde. It is not strange, that he who purposely had prostituted himselfe to the will of an harlot, and was now in the pur-

Note.

suit

ſuit of his luſt, could not then breake the bands of his ſinfull deſire, when it had ſnared him: for the time of preuenting this miſchiefe was, when hee was firſt enticed: now the matter was gone ſo farre that being vnder feete, he had ſmall liſt or ſtrength to riſe vp, and call himſelfe to a ſerious remembrance of his offence. And *Delilahs* lap and armes was no fit nor likely place or occaſion of ſuch thoughts or meditations: wiſedome was driuen out of his breaſt by corrupt affection: the blow was ſmartie enough, but hee had loſt his feeling. So that there is no more miſerable a ſight, then to behold a man when he is intangled with the ſnare of his owne luſt, or any ſin that waſteth the conſcience, for then is hee ſhiftleſſe, and cannot helpe himſelfe, but is readie to beare any burthen which ſhall be laid vpon his ſhoulders, rather then to riſe vp from vnder it. Therefore great is the loue of God to that man, who not hauing at firſt preuented the beginnings of ſinne, but been ouertaken with the deceitfulnes of it at the firſt view, yet vpon more aduiſed conſideration of the danger which it leadeth vnto, ſhall awake and rouſe vp himſelfe, and flie from it as from a ſerpent. Note.

And for his ſhifting her off with a lye, as though he would both ſatisfie her, and yet keepe himſelfe in ſafetie, by not bewraying the ſecret; his wiſedome and commendation was alike in both. For as he dealt fooliſhly in anſwering her at all, ſo did hee as ill in looking to ſtop her mouth with a lye. Which forewarneth vs, not to ſhift for our ſelues, nor looke to make our part good by lying, though the way lie open thereto, and is then too readie at hand, when we ſee no other way; which ſinne in all kinds thereof is condemned, howſoeuer little account be made of it. And the rather it is to bee taken heed of, ſeeing we oft times runne headlong into it, (as I haue ſaid) when wee ſee no readier way to ſhift for our ſelues, and (as wee thinke) to ſaue our credit, and auoid greater danger. And ſeeing there was no other to bee looked for, then that *Samſon* (being in the caſe hee was at this preſent) ſhould prouide for his owne ſafetie by a lye, (a poore ſhield for him, whoſe innocencie and watchfulnes ſhould haue been his defence) let vs beware of entring acquaintance with any ſin, for it will bee coſtly in the maintaining, and draw a man by a wretched neceſſitie to adde thereto many other ſins: euen as *Samſon* muſt ſeeke couert and ſafegard to himſelfe by a lye (for want of better) except at firſt daſh he would haue gone through ſtitch, and haue told her the matter. Touching his dallying humour, and his playing wilie beguily with her, as if he had had wiſdome and skill enough to ſhift her off with trifling anſwers, if the hardeſt ſhould come; although it ſauoured ſomewhat of confidence and conceitednes of his ſuppoſed ſtrength, (much like *Peters* raſhnes, when hee was told by his Maſter that he ſhould denie him) yet in the ſequell it bewraied his more then common folly, as hee that had had but one eye, might eaſily haue ſeene that no leſſe euill could follow: which alſo ſhall appeare in due place hereafter. 2

Luke 22.34. Mat.26.34.35.

She, as if hee had told her the truth, as ſhe verily thought hee had, went about forthwith to make proofe of his words: for whereas hee told her hee ſhould be weakened, if he were bound with ſeuen greene withes or cords, ſhe cauſed them to be brought to her foorthwith, and ſhe bound him with them, though indeed hee brake them: (oh wonderfull ſottiſhnes in him to ſuffer it!) and ſhe had certaine of the Philiſtims lying in waite in a cham- Verſ.8.9.

ber

her thereby; who should be ready to take him, if he had been weakened indeed, as she supposed he was, and looked for it. Thus wee see whereto her flattering words tended, euen to seeke his life. And this is as good as they may looke for, who haue neere fellowship and secret company with such companions.

For though as *Salomon* saith, her lips drop as the honey combe, euen as
Prou.5.3. if she were pleasure it selfe to a man, yet her paths leade to destruction, and an whore will hunt after the pretious life of a man. We haue read of many, who partly haue been most wofully handled of the strumpets themselues, whom they haue trusted with life and goods, and partly haue bin deliuered by them into their enemies hands to be slaine. And what maruell? For she that hath sold her selfe, will much easilier sell her Paramour. And therefore
Prou.7.27. well did the same *Salomon* giue warning, that shee is to bee shunned as hell mouth. But though bodily danger be so much to be feared by her, yet that is the least; spirituall hurt is farre greater. But by the occasion of this which I say, I adde; that the sin of them is farre more grieuous, who abhorre common harlots, who might easily bewray them, yet will not refraine from making those (or going about it at least) who were honest before, to stoope to their lure, and so become whores and dishonest; which thing of the better sort is more to be feared. Of this falshood and trecherie I haue said somwhat in the former Chapter.

Vers.10. Thus much of the first attempt of *Delilah*, by the which though she preuailed not in that which shee sought, yet this shee gained, that shee was the more imboldned to set vpō him again, as hauing receiued no check nor discouragement by him, for that which she had done already. Therefore shee is not discouraged, but attempteth the matter the second time, as in these next three verses is to be seene. And she boldly said to him, that hee had deceiued her, and told her lies, which might iustly cause her, she said, to doubt of his loue to her, and therfore now she required better dealing at his hands, or else she should be much grieued.

1 This shamelesse behauiour of hers should teach vs, that all boldnesse in euill is an high degree of sinne, and we should keepe our selues farre from it: as not euen to dare open our mouthes to a woman to hearken and consent to a filthy and vncleane demand or motion, wherby also she may know and be priuie to the wickednesse that is in vs. The same I say of boldnesse in any other sin, as boasting, threatning, slandering, lying, swearing, challenging of any to fight, or any other like vnto these, & it is fearfull to heare any of these, or to see them committed with such boldnesse as they are. Oh modesty and bashfulnes, what seemly & comely ornaments are they, euen where conscience is as yet wrought by the word, but wanting? for they doe keepe and preserue many from shamefull euils oftentimes, who haue no religion to
Note. guide and defend them. But boldnes is and ought to be vsed in the defence, commendation, and sute making for good things, and therein to be shewed, and when it is so employed, it is then in kinde. This point I will not heere enlarge, seeing it often commeth to hand.

Vers.11. Now followeth *Samsons* answere to her sute in the second attempt. And that was much like the former. If, saith he now, I be bound with new ropes that neuer were occupied, I shall bee weake, as another man. Wherein wee see

ſee he dallies with her ſtill,and ſuffers her to demand that of him which was not meet in any ſort for him to haue ſuffered, yea and anſweres her alſo about it. For what though he held her off with a lie? yet ſeeing hee did not refuſe to anſwere her about it,and charge her to ſpeake no more of it, (being a ſecret not to bee vttered) and alſo in that hee doth ſo the ſecond time, when he had tried already,that ſhe ſought to know it onely to the end ſhee might deliuer him into the Philiſtims hands; in theſe reſpects,I ſay,as it was palpable dotage in him to doe ſo, euen ſo it was the next way to ſet her forward in ſoliciting and importuning him,till ſhee got it at his hands. It was therefore a further degree both of his ſinne, and alſo of the bringing on of his miſery. He might haue been made wiſe enough to haue refuſed to heare her any more about that, hauing ſeene before, that the Philiſtims lay in the chamber iuſt by,(if opportunity had ſerued) to binde and take him.

And this may teach vs,that it is no better then ſottiſhneſſe to bee ſo impotently giuen ouer to a mans appetite,and either this way in lingring after,or clinging to a wicked woman,or in purſuing hotly any other ſinne, ſeeking the fulfilling of a mans deſire, ſo that he can no way bee remoued from it; and that eſpecially when neither proofe of former danger thereby,nor feare of preſent euill,nor the foreſeeing of any to come, (and yet all certaine and apparent) can hold him from it. And though in this groſſe manner Gods ſeruants bee not commonly enchanted and bewitched (which were monſtrous) yet let vs not reſt in that, nor in any like impotency, as in hunting greedily after the wealth of this world, and ioying in the pride of life, &c. but ſo bridle wee and keepe vnder our wicked hearts, eſpecially when wee haue had faire warnings before, as he had, that they bring vs to no ſuch like ſlauery and bondage, but that we abhorre them more then at the firſt, (if we did then entertaine them, eſpecially we hauing had proofe, as he had, what woe will follow. *Doct.*

The more I conſider this fact of *Samſon*, the more I thinke of that phraſe which the holy Ghoſt vſeth to deſcribe ſinne by; I meane that of drunkenneſſe. And as by other occaſions I note other properties of a drunkard, wilfully ruſhing into it; ſo I obſerue this one of venterouſneſſe and boldneſſe. Well ſaid he that deſcribed drunkennes (among many other properties of the diſeaſe) that it puts into man a maruelous confident hopes, ſo that it dareth fight with any man without weapon, whom ſobriety durſt not encounter with,though well armed. And no wonder, for when the braine is ouercharged,and nature oppreſſed, in ſtead of the purelight and vnderſtanding of mind; there is ingendred a frothie conceit and appearance of that which is not,and in ſtead of the ſpirit and vigour of the affection,ſucceedeth a degenerate boldneſſe and foole-hardie ventrouſneſſe: as all men can iudge that the boldneſſe of a drunkard comes rather for want of wit, then preſence of courage. Euen thus fareth it with *Samſon* in this diſtemper and ſpirituall drunkenneſſe of his. Still he makes his companion anſweres, faire and farre off, flouriſhing and caſting about, as if he had skill, and ſtrength enough to match and goe beyond her; whereas alas it fareth with him as with the man I ſpake of, who thinking himſelfe ſtrong enough to goe alone and vpright, tottereth and falleth at euery turne. For although the ſecret was not yet vttered, yet theſe preambles of dalliance and trifling, what were they but

but as the nibling of the fish, or the hopping of the bird about the bait and snare which she hasteneth, and yet would not seeme to hasten vnto? Doubtlesse, if *Samson* his grace had not been in great part imbezeled and feebled, ere his locks were cut off, he had carried a truer measure of himselfe, and better iudgement of his owne case, then to thinke himselfe his owne man, and able to resist, when his mistrisse, or rather his lust, had him bound in chaines, and laid vnder feet, as foiled and vanquished. Ah poore *Samson*, (it may be said) thou wert strong enough to match Lions, and thousands of men: but grace stands not in the bignesse of bone, and strength of armes, or greatnes of stomacke: thy lust and thy harlot are stronger then the Lion, or mightie men. Therefore let this be enough to conuict all such of folly, as are of *Samsons* humour. Tush, ye must not tell them of bad company, nor stealing of liberty which God denieth them; they would not haue you think they haue shaken hands with the feare of God, they would bee as loth to part with a good conscience as others: yea, (it may bee answered) so thought *Samson*; he would haunt the harlots house, and yet secretly keepe his goodnesse too, for all that. But how, and where lay the strength to effect this? Poore soule, onely in his foolish conceit and boldnesse, and indeed onely there lay the foundation of his woe. For if he had felt his declining and weakenesse, then had he with astonishment shaken off his louer, and departed. But now hee feareth nothing till all be too late, and this makes him to sport and play in a matter of the greatest importance and danger. Therfore to all such bold persons as say, Turne me loose to any company, and the strongest enemie; If I be foiled, laugh at me: To such I say; yea, we shal be sure you shal be laughed at, though the wise will pitie you rather: but who shall giue you counsell to escape it before? truly he that can perswade you to walke humbly, and with feare of your owne frailty, and to watch against, and suspect your owne frailty and falshood of heart: hee (I say) may keepe a mischiefe from you, and hold you from venturing and dealing with such an aduersary, as you know will master you. But if you looke to escape danger, and yet reiect this grace, then know for certainty, that these kinds of Merchant-venturers alwaies make shipwracke, and bring in no better gaine. All the grace that a man hath, is little enough to quench the dart of tentation suggested; which yet is but the beginning of the sinne: and shalt thou, adding fewell to the fire, and helping the diuell forward by inward prouoking thy selfe to sinne, thinke to quit thy selfe well of it in the hottest assault? If God try thee, his
2.Cor.12.9. grace shall bee sufficient for thee: if thou wilt tempt him, and trouble thy selfe, know thou hast no promise of safety, or to be kept harmeles, but maiest looke certainely for thy downefall: as for thy owne wisedome, grace is not propped vp by such pillers, but shall totter and reele as an house which hath lost her foundation: yea they that goe to worke thus on their owne head, most assuredly with *Samson* shall fall, and bewray their folly at last, to teach them by the experience of fooles, that wisdome, which the word and other vnhappy men could not doe. Then shall they see there was oddes betwixt keeping innocent, and wilfull offending; they shall finde, that the strength of the one is not like the other, though they were little aware of any such matter.

Vers.12. The issue of this second attempt was altogether as it was in the former: for

for she bound him with ropes againe, and had company lying ready for the purpose at hand,(if there had bin any worke for them to do,) though as yet he fell not into their hands. And let this teach vs, not onely to feare and suspect trechery and vnfaithfulnesse in leaud women which we know;(as this was such an one;) but generally also wherein soeuer wee haue to doe, beware we that we defile not our hearts and hands in any wicked actions and practises, whatsoeuer shewes and promises are giuen and offered vs. Remembring the words of our Sauiour, Bee wise as Serpents, and innocent as Doues,and beware of men. Mat.10,16.

Which I doe not say, as though I would teach men vncharitablenesse, (charity being not suspitious) but to giue warning to Gods seruants to beware how wee put our selues into mens hands, and trust their faithfulnesse vpon a faire word or countenance, which our Sauiour willeth vs to take heed of,and giues vs example also, in that he would not commit himselfe to men,though they speake him faire,and giueth his reason thereof, *For he knew what was in man*. But while we doe thus, we do not iudge of men what they are,(but are warie,as we be counselled) or what religion is in them, further then we haue proofe thereof by their words and deeds, and yet that we do not so, finally neither,but for the time onely,while they lie in knowne euill, or not knowne to be reformed. So that neither are wee on the one side, to iudge men without ground and warrant, neither yet are wee on the other side,to commit our selues into their hands,(hauing that knowledge and experience that wee haue of mens vnfaithfulnesse how common it is) vpon a bare shew. But heere an end for this time. 1.Cor.13.5. Ioh.2,24.

THE EIGHTIE FOVRE SERMON ON THE XVI. CHAPTER OF THE BOOKE OF IVDGES.

THe third attempting of *Samson* by *Delilah* followeth in these next two verses: For shee seeing hee dealt so slightly in the matter,and that he did not in good earnest forbid her to meddle any more about it, but still dallied with her,she tooke his deniall but in sport,and therfore sets vpon him againe,not despairing,but that by importuning him, shee might in time preuaile and ouercome him.By this we may learne,that if we resist sinne houerly,(and in that so waighty a matter as this was,as striking at our happinesse) and deale slightly and loosely about it, when all that wee can doe against it is little enough to withstand it,wee can giue no further token that wee will fall into, and commit the sinne it selfe,and that shortly. Vers.13.14. *Doct.*

For the diuell and his wicked instruments that lie in the way to deceiue vs, and to draw vs into the snare; they are wise in discerning, and artificiall in marking how we goe to worke, and how farre we hold backe from yeelding to tentations: If we doe it earnestly with strength of reason resolutely to disswade our selues from the same, and be feruent and constant therein, we put them to their shifts to inuent arguments of greater force, whereby they may be in better hope to preuaile with vs. As the diuell dealt with our Sauiour according to his resolute and strong deniall, in most slie and subtill manner. But if we refuse the bait but faintly, as *Balaam* did (for al the shewes he made) the wages of iniquity that was offered him; or if we shew that we feare not the danger greatly which is like to ensue, but stand strongly in our owne conceit, that wee can easily withstand the sin in the vpshot, and that we haue no need to be counselled about or against it, as the most at this day do so deceiue themselues; the diuell hath what he would at our hands, and doubts not but to draw vs into the snare to commit the sinne shortly, euen as these that I speake of do finde and feele to their cost, for all the confidence that they seeme to haue.

Mat.4.4,5. Numb.22.38. 2.Pet.2.15. Iud.11.

Doct.2. *Samson* in this third attempt, was so far off from giuing her ouer, hauing twice tryed that she sought his life and vtter vndoing, that yet hee answeres her the third time; such was his effeminate sottishnesse: so that howsoeuer hee thought still to conceale the secret from her, and to keepe himselfe free from vttering it, euen as before thitherto he had done; yet hee began now in this third attempt, to slide and slip in further, and to stagger as a drunken man, little considering what he did. For hee was tampering about his lockes now before he told her the very thing that she asked, and so came neerer to the bewraying and vttering that which shee sought of him: as if hee could hardly conceale it from her; saying to her, that if his lockes were fastened to the threeds of the woofe with a pin, hee should be weakened, and be as another man. And she, thinking indeed that hee came now more neere the very point, seeing he spake of his lockes; she by and by made triall of his words, and hauing done so, she called the Philistims againe to set vpon him; but as yet hee held backe from yeelding to her, and once more withstood and deceiued her, although hee had much adoe (as we see) to keepe it from her.

Doct. Whereby wee may see, that when men giue themselues liberty and full scope to talke too and fro of things dangerous and hurtfull, and take liking therein, and will auoid no occasions, nor resist no tentations drawing and leading thereto, they shall not chuse but bee snared and caught therewith, though they intend no such thing, (as it came to passe to him) and so they shall hardly forbeare and containe themselues from running headlong, and being giuen ouer thereto. For when they are led away of their owne concupiscence, as Saint *Iames* saith, they are inticed also, and snared, so that they cannot well go off nor on, but more ready to consent, as wee see *Samson* did afterward, telling his whole heart vnto her. Euen so I say, men shall by oft and long tampering with the sinne whereto they are too neerely affected, come more readily and speedily to the consenting to it, and the committing of it, who should rather turne away, and weane themselues, and that betimes, from the least liking or longing after it, much lesse should they hasten it on by liberall talking of it. For if we will suffer our selues to be impor-

Note.

Iam.1.14.

tuned

tuned in all cases,medling with them when we need not,who doubteth but that we shall much easilier yeeld thereto. Those whom commonly wee call men of good natures, being once tainted by leaud company, grow first dissolute,and by degrees desperate : but they wax rotten by degrees,as wee see fruit by long lying doth. And as wee see in the running out of the houre-glasse, that euery part of the sands course is the hastening of the houre to an end, though the last passage of it be the actuall ending thereof : so may we say of *Samson* his dallying,and houering replies, that euen the first, second, and third were the preparations to the final bewraying of the secret,though the fourth onely confessed it actually. If the fourth had been away,the matter had been whole,but the fourth was in the first,in the second, and in the third(though more obscurely)enfolded. Alas,at his first shifting he thought hee might haue proceeded still. But as the secret at the first dash was too waighty to vtter : so after two or three dalliances, the tentation preuailed, and was too strong for him any longer to shift off, withhold, or resist. And the like let vs know,euen as this also is, to be spokon vnto vs.

The fourth attempt followeth, in the which shee gaue him the deadly blow. For when no warning will serue, how can a man chuse but fall into the danger,(how great soeuer it be) which he would by no meanes auoide while he might ? But let vs heare the dealing of them both. She is growne now more subtill then before. For wee are not to thinke that these things were done betwixt them on one day,or on foure daies together, (as the acts are heere set downe to be in number foure) immediately following one another ; but with some space betwixt them, that she might take fit occasion in a more subtill manner to renue her suite and request againe. Shee beginneth therefore with him in this manner ; that whereas hee had told her hee loued her, shee subtilly answered, shee saw hee loued her not,because his heart was not with her, but hee had mocked her now three times, and had not told her that which she asked of him. And through her subtill and secret winding into him, and her impudent importunity, and earnest vrging of him,for all his wisedome (as he thought) in holding her off with lies and delaies,in iesting manner ; yet he thinking by her following of the matter,that she was in good earnest with him,in saying hee grieued her because she saw he loued her not, he was brought thereby to pitie her, and to be so wounded with her subtil flattering of him,and dissembling with him, that he was sore vexed to see her so grieued: and therefore as great woe as it was like to bring to himselfe,he neuer duly considered it,but was ouercome and told her according to her desire, all his heart, euen how hee might bee brought to lose his strength. This for the summe of these three verses. Vers. 15.16.17.

But now let vs weigh these things more particularly. In the 15. verse, by the subtilty the woman had learned now at the last(who told him he loued her not, when yet she knew he doted on her)we see how artificiall the wicked do easily grow, (for herein we need not doubt but that ỷ like offenders now, are like her) and how soone the deceiuers in their attempts doe waxe worse and worse, and more ripe in subtilty and deceiuing, then they were before. So saith *Paul* to *Timothy*. So that if there were any to obserue it,how (for the most part) men are fitted to this trade; to wit, that how meanely and bungerly soeuer they go to worke in comparison, when they begin the Doct. vers. 15. 2. Tim. 3. 12.

world, I meane for subtilty, ouer they doe afterward: but how soone they grow ripe in this faculty, and that in euery kinde of euill dealing, as experience sheweth too cleerely; I say if men obserued it, they would confesse no lesse then I say.

Whether we speake of them that begin in vnlawfull trades and courses, as in whoredome, oppression, flattery, beguiling, or in any such; or in those which are lawfull; as buying, selling, letting house and land, or other earth-
Luk. 16. 3. ly dealings, (as may bee seene in the vniust Steward, what euill practises are vsed in all these,) and what cunning and craft are found out and inuented, to goe one beyond another, otherwise then in times past, for the most part they haue done; it is admirable to consider it. In all which they shew plainly, that they do not to any purpose, mind nor set their hearts vpon any better things, howsoeuer some of them will beare vs in hand that they doe, and that they will serue God as well as the best. And not only so, but (that which would lesse be thought) how long is it, before they that imbrace the Gospell grow to be experienced, and well seasoned with such true and sauing knowledge of holy doctrine, as whereby they abhorre such dregges and doings, and attaine to the finding of the Christian life to be meate and drinke to them. And how few are there that doe so? So that it may worthily bee complained of, yea lamented with teares, if there were euery where such as could doe it, to see both the fewnesse of this latter sort, and how many there be euery where swarming of the former. But of this ripenesse of sinne elsewhere. Yet this I adde, (that which I vtter with griefe) euen these ripe headed and nimble fellowes, who grow so soone masters of their trade before they haue serued halfe a Prentiship, shall rise vp and condemne many of the better sort for their block-headed backwardnesse in matter of religion and Christianity, after so long training vp in Gods schoole. This age should bee ripest in grace and skill how to passe the time most fruitfully and ioyfully: and neuer age had such dullards and dunces in searching into themselues, and trying whether they be in the state of saluation or no, and in seeking acquaintance with God, considering that it hath the helpes of all former examples, and present meanes to this purpose, greater then euer age had since the Apostles time. If it be, who shall domineere ouer others, and set vp himselfe, who shall cogge and cosen, or goe beyond his neighbour to deceiue him, and who hath more strings to his bow to shift, scrape, and rake pelfe together howsoeuer; then our age may commence the highest degree in this profession. Skill and ripenesse in mischiefe is not bounded only within them of *Delilahs* trade (though doubtlesse the strumpets of old ages were punies to them of ours for all subtilty and villany) but extends as farre as the Prince of this world hath any subiects. But if ye go to enquire who hath made the Christian life easie, by constancy in obedience, who liueth a sweet life and void of sorrow by resolute purpose and endeuour of abstaining from all euill, and by watching ouer his heart and life alwaies, also who enioyeth that
Note. liberty which God alloweth, to rest assured of his loue, and so to goe in and out before him, from one duty to another, without vnsetlednesse, wearines, and disquietnesse. In a word, if ye enquire who is the man that hath so im-
Mat. 19. 29. proued the doctrine of the Gospell, as that hee hath found that hundredfold measure of contentment for reiecting lying vanities, so that hee is become

come a light and example to others, like those Thessalonians whom *Paul* 1.Thes.1.7.
calles paternes, and those Saints whom *Dauid* calleth excellent: If (I say) Psal 16.3.
inquirie be made after these (which yet are the best of all other) yee shall finde or meete with few, that see into them, affect them, or can answere any great matter about them: Oh, euery little is enough in godlinesse, men are content with mediocritie heere, which in godlinesse is a vice, and no vertue. So that there is a perfection and mastership in Gods trade also, and without comparison the greatest gaine: but the worke is tedious, or men vnhappie that cannot hit vpon it.

Samson being so blindfolded with her beautie, that hee was now become sicke for seeing her grieued, so that now he must rest no more with her, but in good earnest he must vtter his secret to her, or else he loued her not, as she charged him; and how could she beare that vnkindnesse at his hands, that she louing him so dearely, (as she made him thinke she did by her subtiltie) he on the other side should not care for her, he being (I say) thus blindfolded, this oft and importunate vrging him by her, so wounded him, that rather then hee would haue a thought that hee was cut off from her loue, (which was death to him to thinke) hee could hold her off no longer, but told her that which she asked of him, till hee felt too late that hee was vndone, to make all others afraid by his example, to make a sport of sinne, and to trifle in matters of such consequence.

Here this may be learned by *Samson*, that they who will be companions Vers.16.
in sinne iestingly, and in dalliance (thinking yet with themselues, that they will goe no further) they shall fall to it in good earnest, and shall not bee able to auoid it. This might bee exemplified in many particulars. I pray giue vs leaue to be merrie, saith the wanton, we meane no harme: No, but harme waiteth you by your dalliance. An angrie and moody person (who yet knowes how dangerous a sinne anger is) giuing reine to himselfe; and resisting no occasions, in time strikes and wounds, and at length kils in his rage; yet ye must let him alone, he cannot but be angry, he saith, being prouoked, but when he hath spoken he hath done. Nay, many a man hath vndone himselfe ere he hath done, and all by dallying with his sinne. It is ill playing with Beares, and Lions, or fierce creatures, for there is no amiable Note.
qualitie in them: but sinne of all other is the most hideous monster, and no man is more in danger to be deuoured of it, then hee that playeth with it. This, not onely the prophane of the world doe proue to bee true, to the shame of many of them which would be better thought of, but euen the godly doe finde it so, when for yeelding to their lusts and bad desires too farre, they haue no power ouer themselues, but are brought to that point, that either their consciences disquiet and sore torment them, or they bring foorth in the sight of all men the sinne, which they too much gaue ouer themselues vnto, and delighted in; as we haue heard of *Dauid*. Let it bee a warning to all how they dally with sinne, and iest about it, he is neerer them then they are aware, Satan I meane, who drawing them to goe on the brim and banck of the riuer, will plunge them headlong into the bottome and depth of it; but let men rather be farre off from treading in the steps that leade thereto: as I haue before obserued out of his three-fold dallying answere, and therefore in this will be briefer.

2 Another thing heere of *Samson* let vs learne, that it is euen death to men to bee put from their vnlawfull delights and pleasures, when they haue once giuen ouer themselues brutishly and sottishly vnto them, as hee was vexed almost to the death to heare her to tell him, she must forsake him, and could not loue him, if his hart was no more toward her, then she saw; which yet she spake but in grosse dissembling. All bondage is grieuous; but what is greater then bondage to an whore? when a man cannot but cling to her, and be at her lure, whose heart is false toward him, and seeketh his destruction. We must take heed that we rest not in the best things that are subiect to change, but much more that wee hang not our securitie vpon deceitfull pleasures, & especially of all other, vpon a wicked & alluring woman, who rather then *Samson* would once thinke of forgoing, behold, he shameth not
Note. to abandon God, conscience and all, not to speake of the outward mischief that ensued. And surely if this be true of *Samson*, who sinned against conscience all this while, what shall we say of them who commit secret filthines with greedines, and yet without remorse? What a death is it to them (think we) to be pluckt by violence from their old acquaintance, which by custom
2.Sam.12.3. is become as the poore mans lambe, whom *Nathan* describes to *Dauid*, euen as his sonne? Therefore when men haue liued a long time in a lewd course without let, how welcome is death to them that makes an vtter separation betweene them and their lusts, which liued before in as streight league and
Note. vnion as the soule and body together? Oh bondage vnspeakable! to bee inwardly linked to the loue of that which can neither be enioied but with extreame miserie, nor forgone but with intollerable vexation. Let this be one motiue among others to humble the sinner before God, and to shew him how out of measure sinfull his corrupt nature is: as also to teach him not so eagerly to pursue his lusts, except he will bring a world of sorrow vpon himselfe, when the time of forsaking them is come. For what though at the last cast many a man renounces the old courses of vngodlines, and repents him, yea and is ashamed of his doings? this is when the conscience is terrified by some violent feare or griefe: not while hee hath his will, and prospereth in his euil. And yet, alas, who seeth not that these terrors when they seaze vpon any, (for we must not think they seaze vpō al, many dying sots as they liued without feeling) for the most part vanish away and come to nothing; so that those great penitents, if they get vp and recouer their maladie, how far doe they put from them the remembrance of the former trouble, and shew,
Note. that it was distastfull vnto them, and forced them in the bitternes thereof to say any thing; but now they are at libertie they returne againe as naturally to their byas, as the stone falleth downward. Oh therefore pray and labour that it may bee good, which ye set your hearts on and delight in, being accounted of you as most precious: for the end else will be more bitter in the parting, then euer the loue was in enioying. Loue the best things and feare not to exceed measure; for besides the vnspeakable and sound ioy they affoord, this they also yeeld, euen a perpetuitie, they shall neuer bee pulled a-
Iohn 16.22. way, as our Sauiour saith, this ioy shall no man take from you.

Vers.17. Now he was so wrought on by her, that as wise as hee thought himselfe, in purposing that shee should neuer know that which shee sought at his hands; yet because he gaue place to his wicked affections, he was not onely snared

ſnared and in danger as before, but now told all vnto her: to wit, that there neuer came raſor on his head: but if his lockes were cut off, he ſhould loſe his ſtrength; which was as much as if he had told her, how they might take his life from him, and bring all ſhame and ſorrow vpon him, as they did in deed: and yet more then this, hee might (though to ſmall effect) haue ſaid to her, to wit, beſide all this euill which I ſhall ſuſtaine hereby, I doe alſo ſet the Lord againſt me, to depriue me of his grace, and all this for thy ſake: for thus much (doubtleſſe) he ſuffered for her.

By which, ſo many good obſeruations ariſe, as a wiſe man may be to ſeek with which to begin firſt. But briefly of two or three. One is this: that we ſhall not need to complaine of the hurt and wrong that other doe vnto vs, which how common it is, all places doe witneſſe; for none are greater enemies to vs, then our ſelues. Were hee not a monſter of men that ſhould offer but the one halfe of this vnto vs, that *Samſon* did to himſelfe, as here may be ſeene? But behold, all this, and no leſſe, doe ſome, nay very many, offer to themſelues. We ſtorme, rage, and crie out of other, if they hold but a little of our due from vs: and much more, if wee ſuſtaine greater hurt by them; whereas we by our ſinnes, worke our owne woe, and yet through blind ſelf-loue we are neuer angrie with our ſelues, when yet wee could finde in our hearts to purſue others vnto death. Oh rend we our hearts for our ſins, and be deeply diſpleaſed with our ſelues for them. All theſe Philiſtims could not haue done *Samſon* the miſchiefe which he did himſelfe by his owne folly, or rather madneſſe. But if they had attempted any ſuch matter againſt him, as to make him infamous, as hee made himſelfe, would he not ſtreight haue reuenged it? Nay, did hee not reuenge it in the ſequell? But, to leaue him (who ſinned not in reuenging) and come to our ſelues; who is he that dare but iuſtly reproue vs for a fault, (be it neuer ſo groſſe) but he ſhall haue our badge and liuerie preſently, and we thinke him our enemie, and watch our ſeaſon to be euen with him, as *Eſau* dealt with his brother *Iacob*. And yet ſo farre is a louing reproofe from hurting vs, that if wee were the men wee ſhould be, it might keepe the hurt we ſpeake of, from lighting vpon vs, and be as a precious balme vnto our heads. Well then (will a wiſe man ſay) I ſee theſe men are iealous of themſelues, and their owne hurt, if they can endure no other to touch them but they will flee in his face, they will be long enough (it is to be hoped) ere they wrong themſelues willingly. Indeede the reaſon is ſenſible, but the proofe is moſt prepoſterous. For that man that will not take the loſſe of a penny at anothers hand without ſtorming, will ſpend many a pound to haue his wicked deſire ſatisfied; nay he will vndoe himſelfe and ſtrip himſelfe of all he hath; and yet thinke neuer the worſe of himſelfe when hee hath done; nay, no man may tell him of it neither. Therefore if we will preuent outcries and late repentance for time to come, (for there is a time when ſuch fooles crie out; I am loſt, I haue vndone my ſelfe) let vs learne that the way to become our owne beſt friends, is to be greateſt enemies to the ſinne which moſt preuaileth in vs, as that which threatneth our greateſt deſolation. God will take that mans part againſt himſelfe, who moſt ſtriueth to hate himſelfe, I meane the corruption within him, which is as deare to him as himſelfe. And till wee be come to this point, that we can haue as heartie indignation at our ſin that we haue moſt

Doct. 1.

Note.

Gen. 27. 41.

Pſal. 141. 5.

Note.

Note. delighted in, as wee haue against others for no cause, or sometime against our selues for being circumuented and ouershot in a bargaine by a cunning cosener; we are farre from repentance, or from that estate that a wise man should rest in, though the worke bee difficult (I confesse) which I speake of. But about this businesse though a man haue many, and those great enemies to hinder him; yet his sinfull heart is more dangerous then all, and by the trecherie whereof onely, all other enemies doe him mischiefe. And doubtlesse the diuell and the strongest allurements rebound backe, and hurt not, neither enter, where the heart lieth not open to euill, and vnfenced against it. The euill that remaineth in the best, occasioneth all externall euill enemies to stirre it vp and encrease it. The pure Angels haue the diuels their enuious enemies. Nay, sinne makes God our enemie, (not for euer, if euer we were reconciled to him) while it lieth harboured and vnremoued: but otherwise, though hee correct vs, yet hee loueth vs, as a father his children. The cause is much more the enemie, I meane sinne, then the effect, which is Gods enmitie. And therefore when hee afflicteth for sinne, count not him our enemie, no nor the crosse which hee inflicteth: but patiently beare it, and say, I will goe vnder my triall willingly, seeing I haue sinned, and turne my griefe against my chiefe enemie, knowing that except that, which is my sinne, vndoe me, no other thing shall, but turne to my good rather.

2 Also by this that *Samson* was brought to that which hee neuer meant to bee, to wit, to vtter his secret to a base housewife, by the following him on with her importunitie; note what force is in it. The widow by importunitie ouercame the wicked Iudge, to grant her iustice, though he had no mind so to doe. But let vs see that it be for good, when men be importunate with vs for any thing; or else turne wee away from hearing them, as *Ioseph* did from his alluring Mistresse. And let vs specially vse this importunitie and earnest suite, as our Sauiour hath willed vs, that is, to God in our prayers: for if the wicked Iudge would be moued (saith our Sauiour) to heare the poore widow, lest she should make him wearie, shall not God auenge his elect that crie to him day and night? Of this more largely in the 14. Chapter by the like occasion.

Luke 18.5.
Gen. 39.10.
Luke 18.7.

3 Againe, me thinkes this answere of *Samson* to such a strumpet, [*I am a Nazarite*, &c. *if my locks be cut off, I shall be as another man*] sauoureth of incredible sottishnes, and argueth plainly, that a wretched sinner, who breaketh not off his course, till he be in the heate and power of his sinne, can no other doe then yeeld to the tyrannie thereof; as hee that is bound hand and foote is carried whither his creditor or aduersarie, not whither himselfe listeth. It cannot be enough to excuse *Samson*, that if he might haue had his will, hee would rather haue chosen to haue kept his secret: So it is like, but who brought him into the stockes, and set him by the heeles, who brought him to this streight, that hee would not but doe that which hee desired to shunne? Himselfe, his headstrong lust, which hauing once got the hand ouer him, vsed him impotently, and made him a stark beast and slauish foole. He knew the sorrow which must ineuitably ensue vpon his betraying himselfe, yet hath he (I say not the grace, that was now vnder boord) but not the strength to containe himselfe. I said my minde touching this vpon the 4. verse, [*Entice him*, &c.] but now the execution of the plot doth more liue-

Note.

ly

ly present to our eyes the nature of sinne, that it takes wisedome from a man first, and then imposeth what conditions it pleaseth: knowing that a man would neuer be such a vassall, so long as he is in his right minde, and not out of his wits. As *Samson* could say, I am a Nazarite, &c. so he could haue said, By this sin, I shall make my selfe of the purest worshipper of God, the most prophane creature and execrable. But *Samson* would not say so, at least not weigh it, but desperatly runnes vpon the pikes. Doubtlesse he had not had the power, though his saluation had lien vpon it, at this time to preuent it: (but blessed bee God who holdeth his election, when men haue lost their grace in their feeling) *Samson* had lost his eyes, ere the Philistims put them out. This let me a little more enforce vpon so iust an occasion, then I did in the fourth verse. Who will not boldly auerre and affirme this, and say; Tell me what sinne is, and proue to me by good euidence, that it will bring such sorrow as *Samsons, Peters, Dauids, Salomons,* did to them; and then if I commit it, count me a foole indeed? Put in one thing more, and I will beleeue thee; If, when the occasion is offered, Gods grace bee stirring and effectuall in thee by watchfulnes and iealousie ouer thy selfe, then thou wilt abstaine vpon that meditation. But (alas) who finds that grace in the strength of tentatiō, who sought it not before? without which, yet thou maist haue matter enough in thy minde to disswade and flaite thee, (I will not denie) but thou shalt haue small list or power to weigh and ponder it, nay thy intangled and drunken heart will make a sot of thy minde, and a most disguised beast of thee. An heart infatuate with lust, stoppeth and freeseth vp the passage of the knowledge, that it cannot succour the poore distressed and embondaged soule, but leaue it to shift. We conclude then, *Samsons* sin was not presumptuous, but impotencie, yet vnauoidable, the case standing as it did. Oh then still learne; men haue not quit themselues well, as soone as they haue spoken a bold word against sinne in generall. For when it comes to particulars, what doe men? I will haue his blood (saith a cursed *Cain*) though I be hanged presently, yet hee knoweth the shame and woe thereof. Of some Iewes (not all, for some knew well enough) the Scripture saith; *If they had knowne, they would not haue crucified the Lord of life.* And sometimes, I denie not, ciuill men are kept from crimes by this meane, and good men from offending, though strongly tempted to goe through stifly. But this is no rule. And I still say to thee, (that shall reade this) beware of dalliance, and venturing farre: for thou shalt haue no power to withdraw, when thou wouldest, who wouldest not when thou mightest. Trust not thy selfe, thy strength in this case will be a brused reede. The best lawes leaue as little to the Iudge as may be, because man is subiect to corruption: and except Gods grace be a law within thee, suspect that in a strong pursuite of lust, thou who art as Iudge to aduise thy selfe, wilt hardly be a law to thy selfe to gouerne thee. But if thou be fearfull to giue a little libertie to thine heart in euill, a great Note.
shall not master thee: if thou feare anger, thou shalt be no murtherer: if thou flee from the baite, the snare shall not catch thee. Euer beare this in minde; Sinne as it groweth, it will be predominant and get the masterie. And a man may as well be mad with reason, as sinne with reason, and think to moderate himself when he will yeeld once, and be euer a slaue: for sinne will

will force thee to yeeld after, euen as a strong fit of an ague maketh him to doe, whom it strongly shaketh. Thus much for this time.

THE EIGHTIE FIVE SERMON ON THE XVI. CHAPTER OF THE BOOKE OF IUDGES.

Doct. 3. in vers. 17. NOw to proceed in the story, because we see how *Samson*, though otherwise indued of God with singular graces, yet was most impotently giuen ouer to the loue of women, when wee doe not reade, that hee was else tainted with other sins; let it admonish vs, that we may possibly be more weake in resisting, and more prone to the committing of some one sinne, then of another, and it shall not bee amisse for vs to think, seeing we haue so many examples of it in Scripture, that this sin of his is more common among the most then other. The which I say to this end, that euery one of vs should obserue our selues, where we see our selues weakest, and there to vse most meanes to strengthen our selues against the same, as watching, prayer, reading, and this not houerly but heartily, if we seeke to be the better thereby, and in no wise to dare be bold to commit it, seeing we cannot but bee as sure of ill successe, as *Samson* was before hee did it. When the husband-man suruaies his ground, he vseth not to fence where the quick set is strong and thicke, but where the hedge is thin or troden downe; wee loue to lay on load where there is no need; but if there be a blemish in our liues which makes all the rest disgracefull, and therefore requireth more labour to blot it out, wee cannot abide to set our selues to amend it, nor so much as to take knowledge of it. And yet one dead flie corrupts a whole pot of the sweetest oyntment, and the sweeter, the sooner. How did *Salomons* excessiuenesse in this kinde, defame all his other excellency and gifts? And doe we not see by experience the truth hereof? He is an honest man (saith one) but a couetous, an hasty, an vncharitable, a breaker of promise, and one or other interposition there is to eclipse his light & credit. Yea and (as *Paul* in the like kinde spake of the house of *Cloe*) there is cause. Now in this so weighty a case what do we? euen tush off the matter, and say, One infirmity is none: and wee hope that our many good qualities (in our conceit at least) must priuiledge vs, and license vs for a few scapes? Alas we erre foully, one secret lurking companion is enough to betray the house: and when we are espied, what say men of vs but this, Nay, hee that will doe thus, or thus, will do worse, I dare not trust him in any kind, if occasion serue. Oh, cast out that diuell by watching, fasting, prayer, and oft renued couenant, which lurketh

Eccles. 10. 1.

1. Cor 1. 11.

keth behind to doe mischiefe, when many others seeme to be cast out. And till then, beare not thy head on high, for doubtlesse God will not suffer such a one to prosper: and what doe we professing, if we take this liberty, except we wil haue our good deeds shame our euil, and become execrable because of their company, as Israel was for *Achans* sinne. Wee will not keepe a seruant in our house (otherwise none of the worst, but painfull) for some leaud qualities sake, though he would giue vs his seruice, and shall God endure vs? A man may feele what the sin is, which hee cherisheth, as well as the meate he loueth: and he that doth know it, let him know God is not mocked: let him not suffer that sinne to rankle and fester in him, but labour to purge out euery superfluity of flesh and spirit, and to sanctifie the whole lumpe, that it may bee seasoned in euery part, and the conscience may bee good in all things. Iosh. 7. 12.

Now we haue heard that she had brought him to tell her where his great strength lay, let vs shut vp this second part of the Chapter, and see what followed vpon this, which is set downe in these next three verses. First, shee caused the Philistims to come yet againe to her, in better hope then they did before. And then causing *Samson* to sleepe vpon her knee, his locks she caused to be cut off, & the Philistims were there ready to take him, and he thinking to doe as hee had in times past done, and to free himselfe out of their hands, he found too late, as *Adam* after eating the fruit, that the Lord was departed from him. Vers. 18. 19. 20. *The summe.*

Heere in that shee and the Philistims hauing been disappointed and deceiued so oft, euen three times at the least, yet for all that are not discouraged nor wearied, but goe on still, yea and preuaile at length, we may see how euill persons are not withheld nor discouraged from their bad attempts, but take hart, and go forward after many repulses. The reason is, they haue hope to preuaile, and doe not commonly misse of their purpose, following it so earnestly, and going so substantially to worke as they doe; God suffering them to goe forward, seeing hee is purposed to destroy them. This is most cleerely to bee seene in the spitefull and shamelesse attempts of the Priests against our Sauiour in seeking his life. Doct. vers. 18.

Though *Pilate* had three times alleaged his innocency to them, and giuen them their answere to desist, yet could they not bee made to leaue off, but procured by themselues their false witnesses, and other confederates, in such wise that they had that which they sought before they made an end. But if this diligence and vnweariednesse in good causes bee sought for in them, who yet are such as would gladly effect them, where shall they bee found? Nay, they are soone answered and put off, as faint suters. *Ester* indeed, and some other did ieopard their liues, in and for a good cause, to preserue the Church of God in their time: but how many followers of them may be seene? Indeed many logs are in the way to hinder goodnesse, and much discouragement is giuen to such as would bee forward, but yet mens backwardnesse for all that, may in no wise be excused: For what know we whether the Lord may one time or other, giue successe, and are wee too good to tarrie his leisure? But of this often before. Luk. 23. 22. 23. Ester 4. 16.

The Philistims hauing better hope to preuaile then in former times, as shee had giuen them to vnderstand, they came with their money in their hands, 2 hands, ready to be paid according to their promise. Where besides that we may see, that the wicked spare no cost to bring their bad matters to passe, while we who follow better causes, looke vpon our penny and draw backe, who shall begin: I say, beside that, ye may see, that they will not breake promise, but bee liberall to such as further their businesse, when they like well the successe which they haue therein. But I would I might not truly say, that in better attempts there is oft times a drawing backe euen of that which was promised; so farre off are men from furthering goodnes: but they deale heerein, as the most doe in other promises, though aduisedly made by them, for therein the like is done. Which elsewhere I haue also bewailed.

Vers. 19. When this impudent and shamelesse woman had brought the Princes of the Philistims together, as we haue heard in the former verse, it is shewed in this, how she made him sleepe vpon her knees, and caused the seuen locks of his head to be shauen off, and that shee began to vex him by calling the Philistims when that his strength was gone from him.

Doct. This was a most base thing and vtterly vnbeseeming him, that hauing excellent gifts of God, he should become a slaue to such an whorish mistrisse, as to bee made to sleepe vpon her knees. Hee that would not turne his face from a thousand men, now to lie downe at the feet of a leaud woman. Oh sottish follie almost incredible! Thus they who for their gifts might bee reuerenced, (that I say no more) and for such good graces as are in them, might go before many; are brought to shame for their abusing of them, and the sins which are come in the place of them, and no way more commonly,
Note. then by a base housewife. For as a mans gift bringeth him to honour, euen
A simil. so the same person, if he deface his gifts, is despised, as a faire and comely garment, when it is soiled in the filthie and lothsome channell of mire and dung. For hee that cannot keepe credit and honour when God hath giuen it him, is worthie to be without both, and be had in derision.

This is memorable which the Lord spake of *Hophni* and *Phinees*, for this
1. Sam 2. 30. sinne among others: Them that despise me, I will set light by. Mens good parts neuer set them vp so much, as their leaudnesse defaceth them. How
2. Tim. 4. 10. vile did sinne make that traitor *Iudas*? What contempt was cast vpon *Demas*, when he had forsaken *Paul*? How base, and what a by-word doth many a mans vncleannesse make him? nay many a professour of good hope, though he haue repented, yet what a brand of contempt and disdaine doth
Gen. 49. 4. hee carrie about him to his dying day? As *Ruben*, in Genes. 49. his dignity being gone? But we are not yet come to *Samsons* punishment, the basenesse we speak of, is a companion rather then a fruit of sin. But doubtles, it would neuer appeare to many a man (who thinks his sin his ornamēt) how vile his
Note. occupation is, if sometimes hee saw it not in the base seruice it puts him to. Very heathens saw no lesse, who describe it by the shadow of a mighty Giant, enamored with a strumpet, who made him lay aside his harnesse, and sit spinning with the distaffe betweene his knees. And yet many a ciuill man, out of his discretion, would shun many a sinne for shame. As for example: Seeing a man of good quality and sort, giuen to drinking and gaming, and so farre giuen ouer to them, that hee will rather make the basest fellow in a towne his companion then sit out, which hee thinketh he may doe, yet hee will loathe the basenesse of that sinne and such like in other, and count it as

repugning

repugning to common honesty. But to returne to them, who being men of good parts otherwaies, doe shame themselues with grosse sinnes, they are well enough serued, who will needs venture so farre, and for their owne lusts, will forsake the seruices of Gods house, the meanest whereof is honorable.

The next thing that followed was this, that shee caused one to cut off his locks, that is, the haire that couered his head. And this is the deadly wound that she gaue him. For therewith his strength failed him, and grace likewise forsooke him.

Heere we may see, that by degrees a man shall bee brought to the lowest ebbe and depth of sinne, as *Samson* now was, he broke the law of the Nazarite, which was solemne, as the law of wedlocke betwixt couples; and therby made himselfe profane and loose, who had liued in the most holy estate of other. Yea this sinne, if comparison should bee made, was farre greater then the breach of the law of wedlocke, seeing that is but one particular, but this is a general setting open the doore to many sins. Oh, how little thought he, or thinke we, that we shall euer commit them, before wee begin to tamper with odious and fearefull sinnes? (as *Hazael*, when the Prophet told him the euill that he should doe, answered, Am I a dogge, that I should doe this great thing? Yea and after we haue begun also to dallie with the means that leade to them, we yet thinke to keepe farre enough from them. But yet we see heere what followeth in the end. But wherein this abasement stood shall appeare in the particulars that follow, the losse of strength, and Gods presence, when his locks were cut off. For the former of these, it is said, after this, that his strength failed, and was gone. And heereupon some may obiect and say, Did his strength lie in his haire? I answere no: but he lost that, because it was the commandement of God to the Nazarite, (such an one as *Samson* was,) that no razor for the time, should come vpon his head. Which commandement *Samson* now brake, by telling her so much, as caused the cutting off of it: and by that he going from Gods ordinance, the Lord departed from him, and left him to himselfe, which hee found to bee weakenesse, and therewith woe enough. The obiection being thus answered, this teacheth what followeth such outrage, and cōtempt of Gods ordinance, to wit, the losing of such good things as we enioyed before. So that such actions doe not onely hold many good things from vs, but also they depriue vs of those which we had. Some sinnes depriue vs of one benefit of God, and some of another. As riot, ill company, spend our goods: drunkennesse and whoredome waste our bodies: cares of this world, and voluptuous delighting in riches, doe as a moth eate vp our religion; and our Sabbaths are lost by ill vsing them: euen as *Samson* lost his strength, whereby hee had slaine a thousand at one time, without either helpe of any man, or vse of warlike instrument. All haue not *Samsons* strength to lose, but all wilful sinne wasteth a Christians strength, alacrity I meane, and cheerefulnesse of spirit to the duties of Gods worship. I said enough of this point vpon cap. 5. in the complaint of *Debora*, that there was not a speare found nor courage to vse it among the fortie thousands of Israel. Let the reader looke backe to that place. Heere this I will say; The faithfull vse and imployment of God his heauenly graces and gifts is the onely way to keepe and augment them: vse

[Margin notes: *Doct.* 2. — 2. King. 8. 13. — Ier. 5. 25. — Iudg. 5. 8. — Note.]

a gift and haue a gift: employ it not, and lose it. If this bee the fruit of bare sloth and neglect, how much now of contempt and wilfull sinning against knowledge? So that we shall not need greatly to care how we may lose our grace, for not only the quencher, but euen he that nourisheth it not (as fire) shall soone enough lose it. *Adam* and *Eue* had strength giuen them to stand in their good estate; and seeing they wilfully spoiled themselues of it, they brought vpon themselues a weakenesse, so that they could not but sin. So they that haue had better things in them, and are now become luke-warme professors, or secure, sottish and sleepie conscienced, and couetous; how decline they in their zeale, and lose their gifts, and sauour not at all religious exercises, but wax barren of grace, and at length fall to leaud company, follow the common fashion of the world, nay become disgracers of the truth, and of the louers thereof, as most repugnant to their practise? Neuer was a poore vnarmed traueller falling among theeues so bereft of money, of apparell and of all comfort: or a gamester shrigged of all, being ouer-reacht by a false handed cosoner: or a tree so stript of her beautiful leaues and fruit, by the violence of a tempest; as poore *Samson* heere was of the gratious furniture of the spirit, by the vnkindly assault of his sinfull lust. Oh what a difference was there betweene *Samson* when he was himselfe; and betwixt his disguised nakednesse which his sinne caused? The vse heereof is, to teach vs, that seeing hee grew to this low ebbe by the degrees forementioned; therefore we promise our selues no priuiledge beyond him, otherwise then by preuenting the meanes leading thereto. And let vs not thinke that the grace we haue, seeing it cost vs much paines to obtaine, much hearing, long practise, vse of many good meanes, with watchfulnesse and prayer, let vs not thinke (I say) that therefore wee need feare no such sudden losse of it. Ah foole, it comes in a day that came not in seuen yeeres: and as the houses of *Iobs* children were blowne downe all at once, so may a mans goodnesse and strength bee all wasted suddenly by a dangerous fall, yea the fruit of many yeeres growth and gaine may perish in a day; though I denie not, but vsually it paireth by degrees rather through sinnes committed daily, and duties neglected. The strength of a Christian lies in his faith, as truly as *Samsons* did in his lockes: and if faith be quailed by wilfull sinning, (as how can a man feele God louing him, when he giues leaue to himselfe to offend him,) then how much more if the fruites also decay, as feruency, care, feare, diligence in good duties, &c. As the one growes to vnbeleefe, so the other degenerates to deadnesse, carelesnesse, and loosenesse, &c. Now whereas some cauiller lying in the wind for aduantage, might say, I see *Samson* is condemned for shauing of his lockes, therefore long haire is no such blameworthy habite, as some would seeme to make of it: I answere him two waies. First, that this guise of *Samson* was not common, or generall; for then it had been only permitted as indifferent to all, but personall and belonging to the vow of the Nazarite, which now is abolished. As that other of abstaining from strong drinke was; which I suppose the greater part of them that plead for long haire will not so easily yeeld to abstaine from. Secondly I say, though this liberty were to be further extended, yet in all equitie, those might challenge it of most due, who are most proportionable to the Nazarite in the pure worshipping of God. Now these in the former respect see small cause

Note.

to

to vse any such habite, but condemne it as most vnseemly. The wearers thereof are most of them prophane, no worshippers; and the best of them (I suppose) are none of the most pure worshippers of God. Therefore let this abuse returne to the heires of them that first inuented it for a couer of the shame, which their lewdnes first brought vpon them. But enough to a wise man was said of this vpon the thirteenth Chapter: as for the foole, though hee were braied in a morter, yet would not his follie depart from him. Prou.27.22.

It is said further in these two verses, that when his strength was gone, she began to vexe him, by calling the Philistims, who were at hand, to fall vpon him, and handle him at their pleasure; and so they did. Oh, wee see it is an easie matter to bring miserie vpon one, when he shall not onely be destitute of earthly helpe, but haue God against him also. Euen so it was with *Iudas*, when the time of his visitation came, that hee was vtterly forsaken of God: but beside, hee had cast off his Master, and the Disciples who had been his fellowes; and the Priests, his pretended friends had cast off him. So *Samson* was forsaken of his louer, hated of the Philistims, and the Lord had left him; and therefore how neerely was the prouerb verified in him, *Woe to him that is alone*. Not vnlike to that thriftlesse debtor, who by his folly is come vpon by his creditor, haled to prison, forsaken of his friends, and destitute of all comfort; who might haue liued in a comfortable manner, and haue been a comfort to others, if he had been wise and carefull in managing his businesse. The vse of this is thus much, that if we should fall into this danger, as to haue men, yea and friends against vs, (as sometimes it may befall vs for a good cause) yet to lay this foundation strongly; that the Lord forsake vs not, which (doubtlesse) he will not doe, if we forsake not him. Touching her cruell trecherie in betraying him thus, when he had reueiled himselfe to her, it detecteth the like vnfaithfulnes (wheresoeuer it be found) in Christians to be more then monstrous, and such false-hearted ones to be farre worse then Philistims. Vers.19.20. 2.Chron.15.2.

Samson being awaked by her, did not by and by see what was done to him, but thought hee would doe as hee had before done, namely by his strength to shift for himselfe, but he could not: for the Lord was departed from him, leauing him (as hath alreadie been said) both without strength of body, (which he had before) aud the vse of all grace to guide himselfe, or comfort his minde. By this we see, that when God hath deliuered men oft times out of danger, they looke still that he should doe so, neuer thinking how iustly he might haue plunged them deeply into the same long before, neither weighing their owne securitie, who little regarded to profit by their deliuerances past. Vers.20. *Doct.*

This is the exceeding blockishnes and senselesnes of men, who (as the Prophet saith) are wise onely to doe euill, but not any good. They looke they should doe as they haue done in all things that like them, and they will do as they haue done in all that please them. But in all this, what allowance haue they from God, or libertie to do so? Nay rather, why do they not consider that God is against them in that their bad course, and therefore hast out of it, and they seeing the plague to hang ouer their heads, why do they Iere.4.22. Note. Prou.22.3.

 not

not hast out of it, and with the good Captaine, humble themselues to God,
2.King.1.13. as he did to *Elias*, and craue pardon?

Oh! let the best of vs know, that wee may not nestle our selues in any ill course, though wee haue been bold with the Lord in times past that way, when wee were as yet lesse experienced, to tempt him farre, and deceiue our selues, (as we haue done) imagining that we shall doe as well as in former daies. For in this changeable world, such changes come oftest to them that change not from their euill courses, and besides, God will not be mocked. As for the bad who crie peace; their case is much worse. Thus *Corah* perished and his companie, when yet he thought that all should haue been
1.King.19.2. with him still, as it had been in times past. And by this was *Iezabel* deceiued, that threatned *Elias* should lose his head on the morrow, little weigh-
2.King.9.33. ing what one day doth bring foorth: but she a little after lost her life, and
Isai.57.21. that in a fearfull manner. For why? There is no peace to the vngodly, saith God. And thus *Samson*, though no reprobate, yet now a miserable reuolter, fared; who knew not that God was gone from him, and looked to escape as he before had done, but was disappointed and deceiued.

And this palpable deceiuablenes is bred in vs, to dreame of God as hee did in the Psalme, who said, that seeing God did as it were winke at him and
Psal.50.21. held his peace, when he did euill, therefore he was as hee himselfe, and approued his bad course, and would doe neither good nor euill, so that there was no change of his prosperitie, as he thought, to bee feared. And (I confesse) God suffereth long, and in this his administration here below doth oft times let such as he meaneth to destroy, goe on without stop, and prosper, as the oxe fatted to the slaughter: whereas hee meeteth with his owne children in mercie, (though with smart and bitternes) rather then that they should perish. Howbeit, neither is this course generall, (as appeares in the many examples of them in Scripture and experience, whose sinnes haue gone before hand) and where it doth hold for this life, yet it faileth at death.
Isai.65.20. Then to be sure their course is altred. The wicked man, as the Prophet saith, (though an hundred yeere old) is accursed: and a day commeth, whereof it shall be said, It is not as yesterday. Let this terrifie all vngodly ones, lest God come vpon them at vnawares, and alter their condition to their most intollerable vexation. Let thē rather as men amazed by the terrors of God, shake hands with, and renounce their stale course, wherein they are setled, and as it were frozen. And let them trie whether by vnfained humbling their soules, and obtaining mercie with God, they finde not that it was happie for them that euer they changed their estate. For I doe them to vnderstand, that there are persons who make a farre other vse of Gods sparing them, then *Samson* did here, and doe not occasion themselues to sinne more boldly still, and yet to promise themselues peace as in former times. And further, I say, that there are men to bee found, I say not, who may, but who ought to looke for, and build vpon it for certaine, That it shall be well with them as at other times, and so faith teacheth them to speake; and they are such as haue obtained fauour with God, that they might beleeue in him, and in token thereof walke in his waies: euen they to wom God hath giuen such an heart as to feare him, and endeuour to obey him in all his Commande-

mandements, they (I say) may assure themselues, and shall finde it to goe well with them alway. Marke that I say alway; to day as yesterday, and now, as in times past. And so had *Samson* found, if hee had walked according to this rule. For, be it knowne to all such as haue fully purposed to cleaue vnto God without warping or falling off, (which he did not) that it is their sinne if they doe not fully account of it and beleeue it, that their soules shall be alway liking, and they to be in fauour with him, and blessed of him. So that if men desire to haue to morrow to be like to day without change, (I meane any substantiall change, though otherwise their faith and comfort is intended or remitted through their weaknesse) let them be reuited by faith and care of obedience, vnto him, who is the vnchangeable alsufficient God of his elect. But let them not thinke this promise entailed to them by the bare bond of their election, or adoption, but by their constant care to keepe both, by holding fast a good conscience: but if they waxe dissolute, let them look that their good daies shall be changed into sorrowfull. God giueth no man any certaintie of his outward estate, peace, health, wealth, friends or prosperitie; much lesse granteth any man securitie in an impenitent course. Note.

And lastly, whereas it is said, that the Lord was gone from him, the meaning is this, that hee had taken his strength from him, and the graces which he had enioyed, were so feebled, darkned, and drowned in him, as if hee had lost them altogether; and so (doubtlesse) he had, if it could haue been. A fearfull spectacle to behold; such an one as he had been, to wit, before the most in gifts and grace, to be brought to this point, by his sinne, as to cause the Lord, who had loued and done so much for him, so to leaue him in the hands of his enemies, to vse him at their pleasure. But what he was brought vnto, I meane, to what depth of miserie, sorrow, and shame, it shall better appeare in that which followeth. 2 Note.

But yet God forsook him not finally, but after, he returned to him again, and brought him to repentance, as shall be further shewed in the end of the Chapter. Now to finish this second part of it: let vs consider of *Samsons* estate by *Sauls* dolefull complaint, when he used the same words, which the holy Ghost doth here of *Samson*: namely, that the Lord was departed from him. By both which, though the difference (I confesse) in the persons was not small, nor in the issue of their troubles like: behold, to what wofull estate mens sinne brings them; and that Gods owne children are not free; but if they will follow the sinnes of other men, they shall be punished here like other men. Oh! how doe many verifie this, who haue in their time shined as lights, and been the supporters of many weake ones, who haue blessed God for their counsell and example: whose flower was neuer so glorious, as their fade & decay was ignominous. They haue wished themselues in the state of the meanest of those, who haue admired them in their welfare: their conscience hath plaied the hangman within them, they haue to the astonishment of their beholders, called themselues outcasts from God, who hath hidden his face from them, withdrawne all confidence from them in their prayers, all sauour in hearing, and sense of his goodnesse which in times past they enioyed plentifully. And why this? Themselues haue bewraied, some by pride and conceit of a perfection obtained, separated themselues from the fellowship of their brethren, as hearing the word, and 1.Sam.28.15. Psal.89.31. Note.

and vſe of other meanes,and ſo by degrees waxt looſe and hardned. Others beguiled with the ſnares of the world : others with pompe, not a few with voluptuouſnes, or other ſinfull luſts, haue cried out of their eſtate, not for their loſſe of ſome outward bleſſings,as *Naomi* did,but euen the chiefeſt, I meane inward peace toward God, and hope of pardon. And yet ſuch of them as were not hypocrites, God hath made that very affliction vnder which they haue groaned,to break their hearts & to reclaime them, though their former grace and honour they neuer recouered. And the like danger lye all open vnto,who dare tempt God as they did, and waxe wanton, as if grace ſhould abound by the abundance of their ſinne. Such as are in this caſe I ſhall ſay more to, in the handling of *Samſons* ſorrow and afflictions that followed his fall : but happie they,that by preuenting this diſeaſe,need no ſuch phyſick. The meanes I obſerued and ſet downe at large in the firſt verſe.

Now it muſt not be omitted that is added,to wit,that he knew not that the Lord was departed from him. No wonder, he felt not the ſmartie effect of it as yet : he fared as he who is robbed in the night of all his treaſure, or wares of his ſtorehouſe ; but till the light of the day he miſſeth nothing. But then, oh what an inuentorie makes hee of his ſeuerall loſſes ? And ſo did this poore ſelfe-robber in this place. When the Philiſtims came vpon him,there was no power to reſiſt, then it appeared indeed that he was robbed to purpoſe : and he might with ſorrow his belly full recount his damages at leiſure. I feare me,it is the caſe of many, (who lie as *Samſon* did without his locks on *Delilahs* lap) to conſider little what their owne ſinne hath brought vpon them. It was thus with *Dauid* and *Ionah* in their ſlumber,as with *Samſon*,that they were robbed : but it was night with them,they could for the time ſee no harme done. Mens relapſes from God are dangerous and frequent, and their repentances rare and few : how ſcape they then ? Can they keepe the Lord cloſe vnto them,retaine their zeale,ioy,and comfort in his promiſes,more then poore *Samſon*, committing either the ſame or as great offences ? No, no, they haue euill conſciences, cold comfort, few (and thoſe faint) prayers, and leſſe fellowſhip with God: yea in their ſenſe they feele no election, no aſſurance of ſaluation. In their ſenſe,did I ſay ? They haue none : they goe on and on,and miſſe none of all theſe, during this obſtupefaction and benummednes of conſcience ; but beare off all without remorſe or complaining. Oh wofull people ! And yet in times paſt, while they had life and a working conſcience in them, a leſſe blow then this would haue guſtered and flaited them,and they could ſoone haue grieued for the decay of the leaſt grace, the want whereof now little troubles them. It is wofull to loſe grace,but more to feele no ſuch loſſe. And yet yet this and ſuch like,mens wilfull ſin cauſeth to thē. The vſe is,to teach vs not onely to abhorre the cauſe hereof; but to eſteeme it a mercie of mercies,to haue a tender conſcience,a watchfull heart, an effectuall and operatiue : which may make our liues both plentifull in good duties, and in ſound comfort ariſing therefrom. And a further vſe is to cauſe vs to feele and abhorre the leaſt temptation to that ſinne which moſt certainly will procure a ſenſeleſnes herein, and an vnprofitable lying vnder that burthen. And this of the ſecond part of *Samſons* apprehenſion,and the ſeuerall worthie

A ſimilitude.

Note.

Note.

thy instructions arising therefrom, bee spoken. Now of the consequents thereof in the next Sermon God willing.

THE EIGHTIE SIX SERMON, ON THE XVI. CHAPTER OF THE BOOKE OF IUDGES.

The third part of the Chapter.

Vers. 21. *Therefore the Philistims tooke him, and put out his eyes, and brought him downe to Azzah, and bound him with fetters, and hee did grinde in the prison house.*

22. *And the haire of his head began to grow againe, after he was shauen.*

23. *Then the Princes of the Philistims gathered them together, for to offer a great sacrifice to Dagon their God, and to reioyce: for they said, Our God hath deliuered Samson our enemy into our hand.*

24. *Also when the people saw him, they praised their God, for they said, Our God hath deliuered into our hand our enemy and destroyer of our countrey, which hath slaine many of vs.*

25. *And when their hearts were merrie, they said; Call Samson, that hee may make vs pastime. So they called Samson out of the prison house, and hee was a laughing stocke vnto them, and they set him betweene the pillers.*

IN these fiue verses of this third part of the Chapter, it is shewed what manifold outward vexations were brought vpon *Samson* through his many sinnes, (though the Philistims, who were the instruments thereof, intended no such thing) but yet it is shewed, that in these tribulations he did repent, as we reade *Manasses* to haue done in his afflictions. Heere is shewed also what great ioy the Philistims had, (both Princes and people,) for that they had got him into their hands, (though that their ioy lasted but a while,) and how they praised their Idoll Dagon for it: and gathered themselues together a great number of them, to make themselues pastime, by bringing forth *Samson* at their pleasure to that end, euen to be laughed at. These things are set forth in these verses: and in the last of them is shewed, that they set him betwixt the pillers, whereby *Samson* made preparation to the mischiefe that hee brought vpon the Philistims by and by after, in casting downe the house vpon them. *The summe.* *2.Chron.33.12*

And first, in that God thus gaue *Samson* vp into the hands of his enemies, and punished him as we see, it was iust that the Lord did to him, (he so prouoking him as hee did) by the vncircumcised Philistims; by this (I say) wee learne, that if need bee, and if they breake out boldly against him, hee must *Doct. vers. 21.*

 make

make his owne deare children to smart, as well as he loueth them, as the A-
1.Pet.1.6. postle *Peter* speaketh. For as he brought them into the hands of his enemies, as is heere to be seene, euen so he vseth to doe to other of his; when there is cause, and he seeth it meet. The reason is, to the end they may rise vp againe out of their falles, and repent: for the working of the which, affliction (through Gods blessing) fitteth them rather then prosperity (which they are so ready to abuse,) as presently shall appeare in this story; and in the meane while the wicked, going on in their sinnes, are the readier for iudgement, which one time or other meeteth with them, and taketh hold of them. And if he should not thus take downe the pride and boldnesse of his in tempting him, they could not be brought to good. This being knowne to be so, there is no cause why wee should discontentedly beare our afflictions, especially we our selues hauing giuen iust cause thereof. And as for them that reioyce in our troubles, or (which is more) do themselues trouble vs: I say no more but this, that except they repent, and so become true worshippers of God with vs, the Lord shall trouble and vex euery vaine in their hearts, so farre their troubles shall exceed and goe beyond ours: as God threatneth in the
2.Thes.1.6. second Epistle to the Thessalonians, and we may see in the calamities of *Diues*, and especially if they be compared with *Lazarus* his comforts. But before I come to lay out his troubles in particular, let vs see this one thing which is not to be omitted, which is this: In *Samsons* punishment wee may discerne a more euident proofe of Gods iust and equall proceeding to reuenge, then in euery relapse mentioned in Scripture, (which I note that we may be the more afraid to tempt him:) For as wee see *Samsons* disease was very grosse and grieuous, and his sinne began to bee seated and habited in him: hee had scaped once before, when the Philistims laid wait for him at Azza, verse 2. and 3. and then God spared him, and gaue him a safe conduct, putting him to further proofe. So now behold his sin not being subdued and abhorred, as an vnkinde itch that is not killed by a milde medicine: he prouoketh God a fresh by the same sinne that hee did before; and the fire (being but raked vp as it were in hot ashes) catching hold of new and fit matter to worke vpon, flameth out amaine the second time. Therfore much water wil not now quench it, much lesse the letting it alone was like to heale it. What then? doth God deale with him as before? no: now he taketh him in hand, and paies him home, and makes him see hee dallieth not with the dallier, and so he is faine to beare the penalty of this, and the former too. So he dealt with *Dauid*. It was no very extreme dealing for two so great and so rebellious sinnes, as Adultery and Murther, to take away the child borne in adultery, especially after so patient a respit all the while betweene. But *Dauid* had forgot that gentle correction, for so hainous offences; and therefore waxed hee bold once againe with the Lord who had shewed him such lenity: and so prouoked him againe in grieuous manner, by his ambitious numbring his subiects. But did he escape as cleerely then, as before? No; God remembreth both; and as the story well witnesseth, sets himselfe to a resolute course of reuenge, and so hee did, till hee made *Dauids* heart ake, so that he saw his boldnesse in tempting God, how little it gained him. For hee stayed not till the Angell had well slaked the matter of his ambition, by slaying seuentie thousand of his people. Let it be a watchword to vs, that if God

haue

haue once mercifully passed by some wilfull offence of ours, by sparing vs, that (I say) we count it for a great aduantage and fauour; for if we will dare to be bold to prouoke him againe, we may iustly feare that his scourges wil bee smartie, as *Samson* and many other found them to bee. That I say no more.

Wee haue heard of the many sinnes that *Samson* committed, and of the inward vexation of his mind, in that God was departed from him, though he saw it not by and by: Now I will (as I purposed a little before) lay out more particularly his outward miseries, as they are set downe in this verse, and that is done by heapes one after another. First it is said, they tooke and apprehended him, who was before at liberty, and yet they did not then forthwith put him to death, they would not bee satisfied with so short a reuenge, nor so bee rid of him, that hee should suffer no longer paine then so; but they meant to keepe him aliue, and so hold him as vpon the racke, in much torment and vexation, which might bee worse then any death vnto him; therefore they then plucked out his eyes, and thereby they prouided, that he should not see any more to doe them mischiefe: then they lead him to one of their chiefe Cities, and put him among their rascall prisoners, and made him grinde there as an horse. All these with their apurtenances duely considered, it may easily be seene what a depth of miseries he was plunged into. And yet all this they did to him, beside their mocking and laughing at him, when they were disposed to make themselues pastime thereby, and to bring him forth to that purpose. Doct. 2.

By this we see, that where many sins are committed, there it is certaine, that many iudgements of God are to be looked for, to bee heaped vpon the persons that doe commit them, euen heapes vpon heapes, if wee haue eyes to behold it, as the Psalmist saith, Many sorrowes compasse such about, on euery side; and what cause their many sorrowes and troubles, but their many sinnes? *Saul* though a King, yet found it so, and seeing his life was full of iniquity, he could not be free from many plagues, till the last of all made an vtter riddance of him. The Scriptures are full of examples, both of the godly, who haue turned aside, and of other who transgressed many waies, and how both sorts were punished accordingly. And although many escape long, and other flourish and prosper in the world for a while, yet are they not altogether void of them; for those which are inward doe sting them for the most part, and the other are in a readinesse, and shall bee thought to come too soone, how farre off soeuer they seeme to be; and the greatest iudgement of all is, (to whom soeuer it shall so fall out,) that they are suffered to go on without any. But when destruction commeth vpon them, happy shall they be, who haue kept their hearts pure and good. Psal. 32.10.

But further heere let vs note, that our sinnes doe not onely keepe many benefits from vs, but also bring many iudgements, as shame, pouerty, sorrow, bondage, prison, and any other misery vpon vs, and beside them all, they do quench the graces of God in vs: as faith, hope, a good conscience, the feare of God, and the rest; which men make little matter of, because they see they are in little account and price in the world. But to be short, he that hasteth after his wicked hearts desire, and will giue himselfe liberty any way which he knowes God doth not allow him; though it bee not altogether Doct. 3.

ther so grosse and shamefull as *Samsons* sinne was, he hasteth his owne misery,) as in time appeareth to himselfe, and is alwaies to be seene of him, that will obserue and consider it. *Samson* was deepely drunken, and therefore his vomit was the stronger. One or two ierkes makes a sturdy boy but to dance: but when hee is stung to the quicke, his stout stomacke comes downe, because he sees no remedie. The hardened heart cannot repent, neither without this violence will it be meekned. A subtil traitor, Iesuite, or other, at first examination is as farre off as the Moone, and will bee knowne of nothing: but being held well to the racke, hee will confesse all. If there bee so much good to be done by seuerity, God will vse it rather then faile of his purpose. Let it teach men to try God no further then they thinke themselues well able to stand out in it, and to beare his angry countenance, and if by venturing too far, they finde their opinion of Gods lenity confuted, and themselues loden with sorrow; let them rather vse the same to meeken their hearts, then to cry out of their misery. For great trouble commonly argueth strong rebellion, and long trouble an hard heart. It is a singular mercy of God, to haue it tamed by the continuance of the punishment, but small cause of reioycing, to haue it remoued, and the heart left in obstinacie. The more we hasten this cure, the shorter shall be our sorrow: for God delights not to punish long and much together. But to returne to *Samson*, be it granted that *Samson* needed whipping. Must it therefore needs bee with a whip of so many strings, and were there none meete to see execution done, but they that had no measure? who (as the Prophet complained of the Edomites) aimed at nothing lesse then the punishing of his sinne, but wholly at the satisfying of their reuenge. Did God bring vpon *Samson* the personall hatred of the Philistims, for the publike good and his honour, in doing his owne worke vpon the enemies of the Church; and now is hee made a prey to their teeth, and an obiect of their furie? Oh! consider thou that obiectest, while *Samson* simply went about God his worke, God bound himselfe to shelter him from his enemies, to the which end hee furnished him with extraordinary strength, so it was literally verified in him, *One shall chase a thousand*. God stood to the making good of all harmes that could befall him in his owne quarrell, and else *Samson* might iustly haue complained. But hee would haue his owne worke goe forward, and Gods too: he had other businesse that required hotter pursuit then his masters: euen wicked and leaud businesse, which crossed the other, and therein hee was his owne man, and not Gods seruant, looke what charges or damages befel him in that imployment, he was himselfe to defray and stand to. And so we see, that as he vsed not his gift, but abused it to his owne lust; so God bereaued him of it, and sent him among other masters to pay him his wages for his owne worke. For this, God tooke himselfe highly wronged, and therefore hee takes *Samson* in hand to purpose, making his worst foes the arbiters. I denie not, but euen herein he shewed him fauour; but I speake of his physicke, which procured his recouerie. And if wee thinke that God is fittest to minister that which is fittest for quality, let vs ascribe this to him also, that can do it as wel in the quantity as he listeth. In bodily diseases this is in the second place one chiefe thing: for the same measure workes not vpon all. The tenth of this would haue killed *Peter*, yet lesse then this would not haue stirred *Samson*.

Rom. 2. 5.

Note.

Psal. 137.

Deut. 32. 30.

Note.

He

He had returned to his filthinesse without doubt, if the restraint had not been so forcible. God is mercifull, and delights not in extremitie; but he is iust, and cannot be faced out with boldnes. Lam. 3.33. Exod 34.7.

Now in that *Samson* was thus led away in paine to such base worke, in so reprochfull a manner; we see that withall this, he was constrained to leaue and goe from his louer also, to whom he was so neerely knit, and for whose sake hee suffered all this woe, and much more; which how sore and hard it was to beare, who doth not see? All which hee might haue been free from, and haue continued in the happie estate wherein he was before, if he could but haue shaken her off, and alienated his mind from her, and yet now must leaue her whether he would or no; and who seeth not what cause hee had, and what faire warnings so to doe before? Doct 4. in vers. 21.

Euen so, obserue wee, that if no perswasions will serue to draw vs from some speciall sin, (whether this which *Samson* was deluded with, or any other) yet that God knoweth waies enough to scare vs from it; and this one among the rest, that as he was, wee shall be plucked from it by violence, though we would not, and that also as he was, with shame and sorrow our bellies full, and shall wish too late that we had been wiser in time. So saith *Salomon*, There was a young man among the fooles, destitute of vnderstanding, going toward the house of an harlot in the euening, when the night began to be darke, who with her subtiltie inticed him, and he followed her straight waies, as an oxe that goeth to the slaughter, and as a foole to the stocks for correction, till a dart strooke thorow his liuer, as a bird hasteth to the snare, not knowing that she is in danger. And this is the best end that commeth of following our wicked hearts desire, to the committing of sin, whē by no meanes we can be reclaimed frō it. And it is a great matter worth the marking which I say, that when the Lord puls not the vngodly from their filthie pleasure wherein they liued, and doth not restraine them, it is the immediate forerunner of their finall woe. But when he plucks the godly from those baites, by which they are allured and indangered, he dealeth kindly with them, recalling them from woe to repentance, and the enioying of many good things. For he is wont to deny that in fauour to his children, which he granteth to the wicked in wrath. One point hereof we see in those two (who died one death both bodily and spirituall) *Haman* and *Iudas* I meane: the other in the eleuen Apostles, as wee shall see by and by. Concerning the two former, when the one was taken from his pompe, the other from his peeces of siluer (which he rid himselfe of, as hastily as euer he coueted them greedily:) the next newes we heare of them, after they had giuen ouer themselues to the sinne intended, is, that they both were hanged, and ended their cursed life in a cursed death. To whom we may adde that foole in the Gospell, with *Achitophel* and infinite others. When they were in the top of their wickednesse, and were not held backe by God, then was their end neerest at hand. But the other, to wit, the good Apostles were graciously weaned from the pursuite of that which would haue bin their bane. For when ambitiously they sought and that with striuing, who should be the greatest and chiefe among the rest, our Sauiour held them from it, so as he made them ashamed to thinke that they had gone about it. And what lost they by it? Nay what gained they not rather? for they learning humilitie, Prou. 7.6. Ester 7.10. Mat. 27.5. Luk. 12.20. 2. Sam. 17.23. Iohn 13.14.

litie, found that sauour and sweetnes in his seruice afterward, and in his loue, (as appeareth by their great lamentation that they made for his departing from them) that it made way to their enioying of most worthy and precious benefits after their Masters ascension. Euen so, as hee wrought in
Note. the Apostles, he doth the same in his other elect people: who when they see they cannot enioy their desired vnlawfull liberties without their vtter vndoing, then they begin to thinke it is high time to looke about them, and doe see that it were depth of folly to refuse and forsake their owne mercie,
Ionah 2.8. (as *Ionah* speaketh) for looking after lying vanities, and so they resolue to renue their old acquaintance with their God, and to returne to him their first husband, and to fall to their old diet againe. But oh mercie of God inualuable, that they may do so. And though it be with some bitternes to thẽ, because the flesh sauoureth no goodnesse; yet it is fauour on Gods behalfe toward them vnutterable, and that which could ill haue been spared, euen themselues being iudges. Therefore, to returne, let all such as must be thus roughly vsed, as *Samson* was, I meane, to be bereaued and plucked from their sinne so deare to them, and that with violence ere they will giue it ouer, let all such (I say) beware, lest when God shall thus crosse them, they like blind idiots and wilfull rebels fight not against God, and increase their owne miserie by renuing their old sinnes, and seeking forbidden pleasures or gaine,
2.Pet.2.22. which is little better then with swine to returne to their mire. And such as neither forbearance, nor violence will doe good vpon, they may feare their case to be bad, (or others for them may) seeing God vseth commonly no other remedie that will cure their maladie.

And by this we see, that the end of sinne is not as the beginning and entrance into it. For then the diuell most slighly and cunningly sheweth a foole all the pleasure and profit that it bringeth, (as he iudgeth it to be) yea and offereth more to their conceit then they shal euer finde, as it may be fittest to allure and blindfold them; but in no wise suffereth them to thinke of
Note. Prou.24.7. that which will follow in the end, that is, their vndoing; for such wisedome is too high for a foole. And so the diuell, to winde vs into the sinne, commeth as a tempter; but when he hath brought vs to commit it, and we then begin to see what we haue done, and in what wofull case we be left, then he commeth as an accuser, leauing vs in the briars, as he did *Iudas*, when we are meerely destitute of all helpe, to shift for our selues. Of which all the former stories of these Israelites are a plentifull witnes.

And here, because I am shewing the miserable ends of sinne, when men will needs follow their wicked lusts, it were (and so I haue thought good to admonish the reader) it were good (I say) for him that is inticed strongly
Note. with the baites of any sinne, whereby he seeth himselfe in danger, to set before his owne eyes, as particularly as he can, the wofull effects of his former yeelding to, or dallying with the deceitfull allurements thereof, the holie Ghost here doth set downe foure or fiue which followed *Samsons* sinne. As if a professor should forcibly be haled to vncleannes with any woman, and that he seeth not likelihood to turne away from her; let him answere himselfe thus: This my sinne it is abhorred of God, who is my delight, and it will set him against me, and make him mine enemie: it will be a most grieuous reproch to my profession, if I yeeld to it, it will be a burthen of conscience

science importable : the losse of grace by it will be vnspeakable : the griefe of the godly vnutterable, the fleshing and ioying of the wicked vnsatiable ; and besides all, vtter vndoing to me it will be for euer : and the iniurie to the partie, to whom I should offer such discurtesie, neuer to bee recompensed. And let him oft, as he shall see cause, twit and crosse his carnall humour, and answere himselfe, what got *Eue*, when she had tasted that which being forbidden her, was yet in her deceitfull fancie, for many causes to bee desired? And let him say further : Doe I thinke long, till I crie out with her, that the thing I so impotently hast after, hath been my great sorrow and vndoing? All meanes shall be found little enough to obtaine deliuerance from such bondage. And seeing it is no speaking to vs at the very instant of going about the committing the sinne, let this and such like meditations be vsually and seriously thought on by vs before, if we be wise.

Lastly, in this verse, one thing more I thinke good to note : and that is, *Doct.* 5.
the care that these Philistims had to set their prisoners to worke, as they set *Samson* to grinde at the mill among the rest, as they did the other : which were worthie the following them in by vs Christians, (though I would they shamed vs not herein) that knowing how ill occupied the malefactors be in the prison, they might by good imploying of them in some honest labour, not only get somewhat toward their keeping, (many of them being starued for want thereof) but also be staied and held from much idlenesse and mischiefe, which they otherwise will doe, as at this day is to be lamented and seene in most prisons. Wee see the commoditie of setting them to worke in prison, by appointing worke to the poore who liue among vs at libertie :) who being diligently set to worke, doe both maintaine themselues, and many of them a great charge, and also are kept thereby from many offences and sorrowes. Nay further, if heathens haue gone so farre in ciuil policy (though not for hatred of the sin, themselues being as bad in other kindes) as to prouide for order in so confused a companie of prisoners ; then might it well become Christians not onely to doe the same, but to goe a little beyond them, and regard the welfare of their soules also, both during their imprisonment, and before the time of their execution. As that godly Captaine *Iosbua* did to *Achan*, chap. 7. My sonne (saith he) giue glorie to Iosh 7.19.
God, confesse thy sinne, and disburden thy conscience, that though thy bodie be punished and destroyed for a season, yet thy soule may bee saued in the day of the Lord. A pitifull thing to consider, that such should be left to themselues, to fulfill the measure of their sinne, till death approcheth, and not to be laboured nor dealt with about the most weightie matter of their saluation. Which thing would moue vs more then it doth, but that we see so little care had by many Ministers, to teach painfully their people who walke at libertie, and are well paid for their labour.

In this verse it is shewed, though not so cleerely, (that all doe see and Vers. 22.
vnderstand it at the first view) how *Samson* sitting in the irksome prison in paine of body, but greater of mind, did think of his euil course, and frõ what estate he was falne, and what miserie he was in, and repented for it, after due consideration of it, as the prodigall sonne did. But ye will aske how that appeareth, that we may rest perswaded of it, seeing it may bee doubted of as well as of any other part of the storie? I answere : seeing it is not so cleere

in this verſe, I will ſay the more about it, fetching light heereto from other Scripture. And firſt in this verſe, thus much may be gathered, that the holy Ghoſt ſetting downe this growing of his haire againe, giueth vs this to learne by it, that it was a manifeſt token that hee returned to the eſtate of a Nazarite againe alſo: (for it being a common thing for the haire to grow againe, there was no other end of mentioning it) which was the moſt perfect ſeruing of God, and that we may know hee could neuer haue done, except he had repented.

Secondly, it appeareth to be ſo, by his prayer to God afterward, verſ. 28.
Iona 2.2. whereby we vnderſtand, that he beleeued in him, (euen as *Ionah* did the like
Rom 10.14 in the Whales bellie.) For as the Apoſtle ſaith; How can we call vpon him, in whom we beleeue not? And if he beleeued, then hee alſo repented: for faith and repentance cannot bee ſeparated. The third proofe of his repentance, is, that he was a Nazarite of Gods owne ordinance, and therefore the elect of God, and one that muſt of neceſſity returne againe after his fall, or elſe he could not haue been one of the Lords, as it is certaine he was, being a Nazarite. The fourth is, the teſtimony that is giuen of him in the Epiſtle to
Heb. 11.32. the Hebrewes, where hee is reckoned among them who liued, and died in faith. And now that it is proued that he repented, let vs make our benefit of that his example.

Doct. In him therfore, as in a glaſſe, we may ſee the vnſpeakable mercy of God, to great ſinners: for who in all likelihood would haue ſaid that hee ſhould haue come to repentance, whom wee haue heard to haue ſo odiouſly, ſo
Note. long, and ſo many waies gone from God, and to haue followed his owne wicked luſts? But hee being one of Gods elect, it was impoſſible that hee ſhould periſh, though hee muſt needs ſuſtaine much woe in this preſent world, euen as we haue heard he did. Which alſo is to be ſaid of *Dauid, Salomon* and *Ionah*, with other. And as ſuch an one is to be pitied much, whom God hath called and reclaimed from his old bad courſe to faith and amendment of life, when we ſee him afterward to wallow in the filthie mire of his former euill life againe; for wee know his puniſhment is like to bee moſt fearefull and heauie; ſo the offending party muſt know, that ſuch an one ſhould, as *Manaſſes* did by the tribulations that hee fell into, bee broken hearted and repent, and beleeue, and ſhould haue no peace, vntill he can do
Note. ſo. And therefore iuſtly are all ſuch to bee complained of, who hauing ſo faire warnings from God when they haue fallen, are not for all that brought home againe, and humbled. So then, the conſideration of this point ought little to nouriſh the conceit of preſuming to offend God vpon hope of impunity. They that plead this, and the like example of *Samſon, Dauid, Salomon*, and others ſuch, do ſhew that they ſinne with boldneſſe, and preſumptuouſly beare themſelues vp in hope of forgiueneſſe, becauſe thoſe forementioned ſeruants of God obtained it, who ſinned not of preſumption as theſe doe, who reaſon thus, neither do they know therefore that they ſhall finde the like mercy in their need. For how monſtrous and irregular a concluſion is it, for him whom the loue of God ſhould keepe from ſinning, to preſume to ſin, becauſe God loueth him, and will neuer dampe him? Thou that makeſt ſuch concluſions, feare that mercy belongs not vnto thee. But know it for certaine, though thou haſt thought thy ſelfe ſure of ſaluation, hauing

uing sought after it, and hast begun to reforme thy selfe, yet if thou degenerate and offend wilfully, (for thy vnauoidable errours and weakenesses I speak not of) the Lord shall fill thy life, thy soule, and conscience, with such perplexity and distresse, that thou shalt neuer enioy good day after thy satisfying of thy rebellious will: and if thou die so (whosoeuer thus sinnest) thou neuer wert a sonne, and beloued of God, but a bastard and counterfeit. Doe we not see what death hath befallen such impudent cosoners, as (being vile and base borne) claime to themselues the names and inheritances of great persons dead long since, as if they were yet liuing? The like penalty and far greater shall lie vpon thee, (oh foule imposter and deceiuer) that pleadest the name of a regenerate one, being an arrant deceiuer and hypocrite. But to returne, as for the better sort, let them often coole and quench the dart of such a tentation with this, that as sweet as liberty seemes, God will finde a way to make it bitter enough ere he leaue them, though hee meane not to cast them off: witnesse heereof be this famous example of *Samson*. And on the other side, if they haue thus fallen, let them follow the example of this man in his repentance, and so doing, let them apprehend him, and comfort by his recouery, (for to that end the Scriptures were written) in their owne particular case. And beware they, lest the diuell (who is euer an accuser in the end, though a tempter in the beginning,) draw them to runne further and deeper in, because they haue already aduentured so farre. And so hauing escaped both rockes of bold, or secure, or of desperate proceeding in sinne, they shal be encouraged to seeke till they finde mercy: the which (lamentable it is to see) few doe, though the number of reuolters be many, the greater signe that they neuer were of the number of them whom they seemed to goe out from, and therefore returne not, as Saint *Iohn* saith. For of the other it is verified, They goe farre that neuer returne.

Note. 1.Tim.1.16. 1.Ioh.2.19.

But to leaue this point concerning reuolters, this doubt is as hardly answered, whether they who neuer were conuerted vnto God as yet, may bee in hope to obtaine mercy of him, in such depth of sinning. For as such goe farre, and lie long in their sinne before they thinke of any such matter; so when they goe about it, they are cast by a deadly feare almost into desperation. Therefore what shall such doe? I answere as they in the Acts did, who came, being pricked in their hearts for crucifying the Lord Iesus, to the men and brethren, euen the Apostles, and asked counsell of them what they should doe, and so obtained remedie. For there being great likelihood and hope that they are of Gods elect, when they grow wearie of their wicked liues, they haue great cause to be incouraged, (if they know their liberty) in broken and melting hearts to seeke mercy at Gods hands, and not to giue ouer their hope, neither despaire.

Acts 2.37. Iam.4.9.10.

In which case, *Mary Magdalene*, out of whom were cast seuen diuels, did stay her selfe, and the penitent theefe did obtaine mercy, and *Paul* himselfe, as farre gone in a Pharisaicall conceit of his owne righteousnesse, as the rest of the Pharisies, who neuer repented, and was euen madde in persecuting Gods saints, and therefore in no meane danger: yet he (I say) who had bin a persecutor, an oppressor, and a blasphemer, was receiued to mercy, and obtained pardon. And why was this? Surely not onely for his owne comfort, but also to magnifie Gods goodnesse, for the encouragement of other great

1.Tim.1.13.

sinners, that should come after him, such as (of whom I now speake) that they (I say) might be heartned and encouraged to looke for the same vpon the like humiliation. The rest I referre to the next sermon.

THE EIGHTIE SEVEN SERMON ON THE XVI. CHAPTER OF THE BOOKE OF IVDGES.

NOw to goe forward with *Samson*: it is to bee considered in this verse (it hauing been proued that hee repented) in what place and estate hee was in, when God brought him backe to repentance. And that was, in the irkesome prison; when he was blind, and loden with paine, and sorrow enough. But oh will some say, what encouragement could hee haue to minde repentance, in that loathsome place, and irkesome condition, where rather all was against him, that might haue been an helpe therto? Indeed I confesse that his so comming home to God in humbling himselfe, and looking for mercy in that vncomfortable estate that hee was in, is a thing almost as admirable euen as his fall was, and the depth of misery that he fell into.

Note.

Doct. But by this and other such examples, we see how God doth oft worke, as before we heard he went about to doe in him, that hee worketh (I say) that grace in a man, while he is in misery, which in prosperity is rarely seene and found to be in him: as I haue occasion to say oft: And it is the more worthie our noting, seeing hee dealeth not so with all in their trouble, nay it is rare to behold, and the case but of few. For the most are carried to impatience and cursing, when they feele Gods heauie hand vpon them, and to bitternesse, against God himselfe, for his so handling them; neuer looking to their owne deserts, for so there were hope that they might be easily brought to confesse that God did all iustly, yea and shewed mercy also in iustly punishing them. And thus he dealeth with men that are brought to good by trouble, I meane hee bringeth them to a due and through consideration of their vilenesse and prouoking of him, that they are glad to seeke reconciliation with him: euen thus, I say, hee draweth and perswadeth them to take vp their thoughts, for their exceeding benefit, when hee meaneth that they shall take good by their affliction.

And he it is (being onely able) that pulleth downe their proud and loftie lookes, by the remembring and considering what they haue done, (his holy spirit directing them) & makes them ashamed therof, and breaketh their stomackes, and maketh them thirst for mercy, after that they can thinke that there is mercy for such, and loathe their leaud liues, vnto the which gratious

worke

worke they were before most opposite. Thus in sicknesse some are brought home, that in health could not abide to heare of such a returne. Thus *Iosephs* brethren, *Manasses*, and others bewailed their sinnes in trouble, who when they were void of it before, could by no meanes be brought to the least consideration of any such matter. Let none therefore maruell, though God pursue them hardly, after wilfull transgression, and turning from him, and bring many troubles vpon them, for hee intendeth their good thereby, which is a great matter; and seeth that they will not be brought to repentance otherwise. And what a mercy of God is it, that when wee are in the way to vtter vndoing, and we thinke little that the end of such afflictions will be any better, but rather the hastening of our misery? yet that hee intends to draw vs thereby to greatest happinesse, as in the former examples may be seene. And though this fell not out at the first, yet let vs humble our selues vnder Gods hand, and not harden our hearts in the least manner against him, and in time we shall most certainly finde it so, euen as *Samson* found the prison, hunger, and shame, farre better companions for him then his so much desired *Delilah*, as great oddes as there may seeme betweene them. Enough hath been said heereof in the like stories, and particularly vpon chapter 10. vers. 10. Gen 42.21. 2. Chron. 33.12

Now to returne to the Philistims a while, and to leaue *Samson* in his sorrowes, we see how they giue thankes to their god for victory ouer him. I say the lesse of these Philistims, because the light they had reached not so farre as to condemne them heerein: their enemy they got, and him they paid home to the full: no wonder: they tooke *Samsons* vexing of them, a great piece of wrong done to them, if they should not now they had vantage ouer him, haue done their vttermost to destroy him that sought their ruine, they should haue dealt foolishly. And therfore they little regarded by what meanes they came by him, or how cruelly they dealt with him. But to let their cruelty passe, not to be maruelled at; what shall we say of many professors, who shew little better practise in the like cases: who hauing by most vngodly meanes and deuices obtained their desires and purposes against such as they spitefully pursue and hate, are so farre from repentance for it, that they exult and triumph as conquerers, with praising God for that they haue bin auenged of their enemies; herein declaring that they giue thankes for those things, for which they should haue been much grieued. And as these Philistims got *Samson* into their hands, but by an harlots meanes, and by fraud and subtilty most shamefull: Euen so, wherein glory many of the other, but in that which is their shame? as in reuenge had of their enemies, in oppressing and peeling the innocent, in humbling and abasing most vilely chast Matrones and Virgins, in getting their will vpon the deere seruants of God, (as the Priests did against our Sauiour) and other such villany. Thus men ioy in things which they should be ashamed of, as the Apostle saith of worldly minded men, that their glory is their shame: but to reioyce & glory in the Lord, who should be our onely glory, they haue no desire that way. Vers. 23. Phil. 3.19.

Another thing in the Philistims note, that they praise Dagon their god, offring a great sacrifice to him, and making a solemne reioycing together, for deliuering *Samson* into their hands. Thus they were blindfolded, as Idolaters that knew no better: This they learned of the Israelites, who did praise the Lord *Iehouah*. Heereof, (not to bee tedious in saying that which Doct. 2.

 hath

hath oft times been taught) let this be sufficient to say, by their example to our shame, that if we should not be feruent in setting out the Lords mercies and deliuerances with praises and thankes, and that ioyfully, wee shall haue the Philistims, who were Idolaters, to rise in iudgement to condemne vs.

Vers. 24. This verse sheweth, that as the Princes did, so did the people, in all things they followed them. Where we see, that the examples of our superiors and betters are of great force to draw vs after them. It is a truth whether in good or euill, but specially in euill, whereto wee are prone enough of our selues, without any to draw vs: and therefore much more when we haue them also, as patternes to goe before vs. When the people had taken them strange
Ezra. 9. 2. wiues of the Idolatrous nations in the daies of *Ezra*, it was told to *Ezra*, but with this addition, that the hands of the Princes and rulers was chiefe in that matter. Good cause there was therefore that the Apostle required, that
1. Tim. 2. 2. there should be supplications and prayers made for such to God, who being set in these places by him, to the end wee may liue an honest and peaceable life vnder them, they shall the better performe it, and giue vs also the better example, when the people doe feruently craue it of God. The same is to be said of the Minister, gouernours of families, and of other superiours. See more chapter 9. 48, 49. and other places of this worke.

But while I am speaking of the Philistims, I will here, as in the fittest place note another of *Samsons* punishments; for as it was his great sinne, so it was also a punishment of sinne, that he opened the mouthes of the vncircumcised, to praise Dagon their Idoll, as though hee had been able to haue taken him out of the hands of the God of Israel, and to deliuer him to them to vse him at their pleasure. And so did hee likewise highly dishonour his owne God, as though he had not been able to saue him from Dagon. And this (no doubt) troubled *Samson* when hee came to himselfe, as much as the other punishments pained him. So it is certaine, that *Dauid* was sore troubled, as
Psal. 51. 1. 2. appeareth in the Psalme, when hee remembred and thought vpon his sins, when among other things, after he came to repentance, among the which, this was none of the least, that hee had caused the enemies of God to blas-
2. Sam. 12. 14. pheme. For he being threatned of God by the Prophet, for that offence very sharply, doth yet acknowledge, that God should deale iustly in punishing him for it; thereby declaring that it much grieued him. And that euill seruant, which hauing buried his talent in a napkin, was arraigned for it, and answered for himselfe, that, He knew his master was an hard man, reaping where he sowed not, and gathering where he strewed not; hereby de-
Luk. 19. 22. 24. faming his masters worke, and discouraging his seruants: what reward had he? For as a starued and ill thriuing and ragged seruant makes all men think that his master is a bare man and miserable, and therefore they shunne his house: so doe these. And the dishonour heere is the fouller, because the diet and wages of his attendances is infinitely greater then any other. And let
1. Pet. 2. 12. both these warne vs, that we haue our conuersation honest before men, that they may not iustly speake euill of vs, as of euill doers: for if they do, it will goe to our hearts when we shall come to repentance, to thinke that we haue caused our holy profession, and the Gospell it selfe to bee ill spoken of. For we are not set heere by God to lay stumbling blocks in mens way, and so to cause them to fall, (woe be vnto such) but to conuert sinners from their wic-

ked courſe, (as *Dauid* promiſed to doe) and ſo by our good workes which they ſhall ſee, to cauſe them to glorifie God for vs, when hee ſhall viſit and haue mercy on them. Pſal.51.13.

This verſe ſheweth, that al the indignities and iniuries that the Philiſtims had offered *Samſon*, with the griefe that God brought vpon him, were not thought to be enough of them to make them ſatisfaction, but when their hearts were merrie with feaſting, they muſt needs haue him brought into a ſolemne place before them, to laugh at him, being ſo diſguiſed, and loden with miſeries as he was, and to be ſcorned by them, that ſo they might ſatiſfie themſelues with ſport and paſtime thereby, euen as they deſired. And they were aboue three thouſand of them (according to the receit of the roome) and they of the chiefeſt that did thus meete there. And to this end it is ſaid here, that *Samſon* was fetcht out of the priſon houſe, and ſet before them. Verſ.25.

Here we ſee the vnnaturall crueltie of the Philiſtims, who could not bee ſatisfied with all wrongs offred to *Samſon*, but they muſt make him a laughing ſtocke, and loade him with taunts and reproches alſo. Which though it be a vice ſo foule, as by the light of nature ſome Heathens abhorred it, I meane to ſhew immanitie to the miſerable; yet it is of that ſort of vices as might eaſily preuaile with ſuch as put out this light by brutiſh paſſion, and impietie. As appeares by the monſtrous crueltie of the Romans, who vſed to behold with great pleaſure, the ſingle combats of malefactors condemned, and their Sword-players ſhedding each others blood. Therefore it is the leſſe to bee maruelled at in the Heathens: but by occaſion of it, let vs know who are Chriſtians, that it is to be reckoned among vs as a moſt cruell thing to adde affliction to the afflicted: And when puniſhment is inflicted, that is it ſelfe anſwerable fully to the treſpaſſe, yet for all that, to be inſatiable in the deſire of reuenge. A fearefull example is that of the Prieſts againſt our Sauiour, whom when they ſhould haue highly honoured for the great workes that he did among them, not only preferred a murtherer before him, and vniuſtly got liberty of *Pilate* to crucifie him, being Lord of glory, but alſo railed and ſpitted on him, and moſt ſhamefully reuiled and mocked him in the middeſt of his agonies: and indeed herein they reſemble their father the diuell, who then moſt inſulteth when hee hath a man vnder: but the Lord is alway neareſt to his, as he was to *Ionah*, in their extremities. Doct. Mat.27.17.1. Ionah 2.9.10.

Now although God for his euill doing doe iuſtly puniſh ſuch an one; yet we ſhould be moued with ſome pitie toward him, and not to adde vexation to ſuch as God ſmiteth. And therefore wee reade, that the Lord afflicting Iſrael for their iuſt deſerts, by ſending them through the long and vaſt wilderneſſe; yet when the King of Edom would needes vexe them alſo, by forbidding them paſſage through his coaſts, was diſpleaſed with him: And therefore the Prophet *Amos* writeth thus; *For three tranſgreſſions of Edom, and for foure, I will not be intreated, neither turne to him*, and addeth that, as the reaſon, becauſe he did purſue his brother with the ſword, and did caſt off all pitie toward him. And for that cauſe ſaith, hee will not leaue him vnpuniſhed. Amos 1.11.

The vſe is to vs, to beware of all crueltie, and eſpecially if it be mixed with enuie: for which cauſe *Salomon* ſaith, *Anger is cruell, and wrath is raging, but who can ſtand before enuie?* Thus *Dauid* prayes againſt him, who purſued the Prou 27.4.

Psal.109.15,16 man whom God afflicted, saying; *Let his daies be few, and his prayer be turned into sinne: because he remembred not to shew mercie, but he persecuted the poore man, and him that was contrite in his heart,&c.* But these things wee reade and despise, as if God would be mocked. See more of this in other places of this booke, and by name vpon the fourth verse of the first chapter.

2 And here consider againe, notwithstanding such disguising of *Samson*, as wee haue now heard, and that he was thus brought into an high degree of shame, contempt, and miserie, whereby it might be thought that he was no better then an abiect and castaway; yet consider we (I say) that he was euen now reclaimed from his forementioned sinnes, and reconciled to God againe, as I said before, and say it againe; that none may mistake me in so saying; and by that which I haue set downe of his repentance, God sheweth how deare he was to him, for all that hath been said of his fall: not that he had merited, by his patience in the prison, forgiuenes of his sinnes: but he acknowledged them there, beleeued the pardon of them, and, as it became a godly man, he repented, as before hath been proued; else these had turned him quite off from God. This did greatly extenuate and asswage his miserie, ouer it was with him before he thus turned to God. So that the Ionah 4.6. Lord who prouided for *Ionahs* body the shelter of a gourd, lest the extremitie of the heate of the Sunne might haue added affliction to his disquieted minde: euen hee (I say) did much more gratiously preuent this poore prisoner his seruant, with mercie and fauour, against the time that his enemies grew to the height of their malice; lest it might otherwise haue been intollerable. Yea and hereby the Lord animated him to beare the indignitie the more quietly, because his strength was now also renewed, and thereby he knew God had called this despitefull rabble together, to be auenged of them.

Heereby let vs learne, that whatsoeuer men haue been in their euill liues heretofore, and howsoeuer they haue brought vpon their own heads much misery thereby, yet there is much comfort to bee taken in them, both by themselues and by others, when they haue truly renounced and cast from them the workes of darkenesse, to haue no more fellowship in them, but do shelter themselues vnder Christs wing, as the poore chicken vnder the hen, that he may couer and remit them. And this only is able to make them hold vp their heads, when so many sorrowes and troubles doe othewise oppresse them. But oh then, how happie and sweet is this vniting of vs to John 15.11. Christ by faith, when we are so resolued that we may abide in his loue, that wee carefully seeke to enioy and preserne it, and doe wisely decline other things which doe make that benefit seeme farre lesse gainfull and beautifull Prou.18.14. vnto vs then it is. It is truly said by *Salomon*, that it is the wounded spirit which makes the trouble waighty; and the spirit of a man, free and cheerefull through a good conscience, and supported by God, which beares him vp in his affliction. And howsoeuer the proofe hereof is sweetest in affliction sent vpon vs in our innocency; yet it hath place also euen in crosses which are drawne vpon vs for some sinne, when wee haue humbled our selues truly for them, and haue not delayed to seeke reconciliation with his Maiesty for them. For then a man recouereth his particular confidence in God, and seeth that his affliction hauing done that for which it came, shall

ſhall ſpeedily bee remoued, and a ſupply of patience giuen the whileſt, to vndergoe the triall. Therefore oh fooles, that cauſe God thus to puniſh them : but double fooles, who abuſe their correction, and lie vnder it impenitent ; for theſe ſhall need no Philiſtims to adde ſorrow vpon ſorrow, ſeeing they make their burthen double and treble by their ſin aggrauated, and by a conſcience hardened againſt God. Note.

Verſ. 26. *Then Samſon ſaid to the ſeruant that led him by the hand ; Leade me that I may touch the pillers that the houſe ſtandeth vpon, and that I may leane to them.*

27. *Now the houſe was full of men and women, and there were all the Princes of the Philiſtims : alſo about the roofe were three thouſand men, and women that beheld while Samſon played.*

28. *Then Samſon called vnto the Lord, and ſaid ; O Lord God, I pray thee think vpon me : O God, I beſeech thee ſtrengthen mee at this time onely, that I may bee at once auenged of the Philiſtims for my two eyes.*

29. *And Samſon laid hold on the two middle pillers whereupon the houſe ſtood, and on which it was borne vp : on the one with his right, and on the other with his left.*

30. *Then ſaid Samſon, Let mee loſe my life with the Philiſtims : and hee bowed him with all his might, and the houſe fell vpon the Princes, and vpon all the people that were therein. So the dead which he ſlew at his death, were moe then they which he had ſlaine in his life.*

31. *Then his brethren, and all the houſe of his father came downe and tooke him, and brought him vp, and buried him betweene Zorah and Eſhtaol, in the ſepulchre of Manoah his father : now he had iudged Iſrael twentie yeeres.*

NOw it followeth in the end of this third part of the Chapter, to conſider the iſſue of this their dealing with *Samſon*, and that is, the deſtruction of many of the Philiſtims, brought vpon them by his meanes : hee himſelfe loſing his life with them. But before he did it, he tooke his beſt opportunity to bring it to paſſe. For he being ſet betwixt the pillers, as was ſaid in the former verſe, hee asketh of the ſeruant that led him, to ſet him ſo, as hee might feele them with his ſhoulders ; which he ſpake, as though hee would haue eaſed and reſted himſelfe, being wearied with grinding in the priſon, and by bearing his chaines and bolts: but intending indeed to ſeeke the beſt opportunity to caſt downe the houſe vpon the Philiſtims. The ſumme. Verſ.26.

Here firſt marke this, that he notwithſtanding he had loſt his eyes, which ſhould haue guided his body, yet hee was not vnmindfull of the worke of his calling, namely, to plague the Philiſtims, Gods enemies, and therefore he vſed the help of the ſeruant to further him there to. We ſhould all learne to remember and conſider (for all our troubles and diſcouragements) thoſe weightie charges and duties which are in our power to performe, that wee leaue them not by occaſion thereof, neither lay them aſide, as wee are eaſily brought to doe thereby. So that although wee haue not all incouragement and abilitie thereto, as were to be deſired ; yet we ſhould vſe that which we haue, and may come by. Rare is the example of *Ionah* in this behalfe, that being in the Whales belly, where for ſtreightnes of roome, noiſomenes and ſtinch Doct. Note.

ſtinch hee could (a man would thinke) doe nothing; yet euen there made his faithfull prayer to God, and vpheld himſelfe by faith.

For notwithſtanding we are diſabled altogether to performe ſome duties by neceſſitie; yet thoſe which wee may, wee ſhould with *Samſon* labour to performe, and haue a care to diſcharge them. I ſpeak this, for that many profeſſors of the Goſpell hauing receiued a checke from ſome of their betters, for being more forward in religious duties then other, or then is well liked, and for making more conſcience of their waies, then the moſt; I ſay, they ſuſtaining a rebuke for the ſame, are diſcouraged, and are ready to leaue off their Chriſtian courſe altogether, at leaſt their feruencie and forwardneſſe: which is vtterly vnmeete for them to doe; for ſo they ſhew that they feare man more then God, and ſo they cut him ſhort of his due, as they thinke good, which is in no wiſe tollerable. Whereas if they were ſeruants, tenants, or otherwiſe inferiours to ſuch ſuperiours as ſhould abridge and depriue them of ſome helpes and liberties, which might further them to the diſcharge thereof; yet ought they not through feare to giue ouer the duties which they may performe, but the rather conſtantly to hold out therein, and practiſe the ſame in al points as they may. For what ſhall all help of man
Exod.16.26. be to them, if God be againſt them? *Moſes* would not leaue the leaſt dutie vndone, to pleaſe *Pharao*. I remember what I haue read of a valiant Roman Captaine in a fight by ſea, that firſt hee aduenturing to put foorth his hands to catch at the gable of the enemies ſhip, with eagernes to ſurpriſe her, and draw her to his owne Nauie as priſoner, loſt his right hand by the ſword of the enemie: which being cut off, he haled againe with the left hand, thinking to pull her away, but in the attempt loſt his left hand alſo; when he ſaw himſelfe diſarmed of his hands, he (being neere) fell downe, and with his teeth drew the ſhip with ſuch violence, that hee wonne her in the deſpite of the defenders thereof. I bring in this as an alluſion, to ſhew the exceeding reſolution of carnall men in the aduancing of their purpoſes for honour, wealth, or fleſhly proiects: but in this matter of our holy profeſſion, wherein God is highly honoured, if wee bring forth much fruit, who takes not a repulſe by the ſmalleſt diſcouragement, either from being zealous therein, and an ordinary worſhipper of God, or for being carefull ouer his family, or a liberal relieuer of the diſtreſſed Saints, or from walking in his particular calling with a good conſcience, or to be ſhort, from ſeruing God inwardly and outwardly, with labour, and attendance as the cauſe requires? Alſo who being ſhut out one way, ſeekes paſſage another, trying all meanes rather: yea and though diſappointed in part, yet to do ſomewhat, rather then nothing? *Paul* indeed being reſtrained from publike preaching ſat not ſtill, but did what he could in priſon, ſo that his bands were as famous as his li-
1.King.19.4. berty: not ſaying with *Elija* (therein weake,) Take my life now (Lord) for *Iezabel* giues no permiſſion to thy Prophets to teach openly, but makes a racket of them. If we may honour God in publike, let vs: if not, then a-
Note. mong a few: if not ſo, yet in our family: if we be ſequeſtred from al theſe, yet in our ſpirit, and that ſhall be our diſcharge before God. But if any ſhall ſay, I haue offered God my ſeruice in his Church, and hee refuſeth it, therefore he muſt pardon me if I haue the ſmaller liſt to be otherwiſe occupied: this is madneſſe and follie, or elſe ſloth and hypocriſie. Oh, ſaith many a ſon,

wife,

wife, seruant, ye little know what a father, husband, or master, or landlord I haue, to discourage me; otherwise I can tell what I could doe in seruing God, as well as other: Well, marke what *Paul* saith; If thou be a seruant, (though streitned) doe as thou maist: (the worst master cannot make thee cold without thine own consent) although if thou be free, vse it rather. And therefore it was a great sinne in *Dauid* when hee was driuen to his shifts by *Saul*, to offer his helpe to *Achish* against the Church; make the best of it that we can. For, want of incouragement must not coole our affection (though it may hinder action) much lesse may it excuse discontentment, or that which is worse. And seeing such sullennes argueth that there is no resolute purpose indeed, to dutie; therefore many such grow loose and conscienles in their trouble: (for affliction will search a man) and others being in time inlarged and set free; are as barren hypocrites after, as euer before they were plentifull in their complaints of their miserie. We must thinke *Zachary* and *Elizabeth* had as many dismaiments as we, vnder *Herod*, and in so corrupt a time: let vs be as they, and wee shall be borne with for being no forwarder. But here an end for this time.

1. Cor. 7. 21.

1. Sam. 27. 2.

THE EIGHTIE EIGHT SERMON ON THE XVI. CHAPTER OF THE BOOKE OF IVDGES.

Vers. 27.

HEre to goe forward, as *Samson* was preparing to bring to passe that great slaughter of the Philistims, so the Lord had prepared the persons for him to execute it vpon them. Therefore it is said here, that the house was full of men and women, and all the Princes of the Philistims were vpon the house, prouision being made where they might best see: aboue three thousand men, to behold *Samson*, and please themselues therein. Which cleerely laieth out the folly, yea the vaine and deceitfull folly of the ignorant and irreligious, who haue been, and still are so readie to flocke together by hundreds and thousands to satisfie their eye, and to behold that which may prouoke foolish laughter, with what danger soeuer.

And yet if this be so to be disliked (as who of sound iudgement will not affirme it so to be) what may be said of them who now long after, as also in yeeres past and yet still in the light of the Gospell, haue inuented other maner of spectacles to delude the simple withall: euen shamelesse shewes, and most dangerous stage-plaies, omitting none to play a part in them, that may increase sinne; as some to play the vice and foole, so disguising themselues, as if they were void of reason: some to resemble the diuell, by which counterfeiting Doct. 1.

terfeiting they make the mentioning of diuels in the Scripture, to be onely a ridiculous iest, and matter to laugh at, that so they may be the bolder to sinne, and the lesse feare diuell or damnation: and some are brought on the
Deut.22.5. stage in womens apparell, God hauing commanded the contrary, and said, It shall not be so. In the which meetings they doe not onely with the Philistims please their eye, but also strongly are incensed and prouoked to lewdnes and lust, which some of them were nothing so much acquainted with before. Whom if God should shew some such strange iudgement vpon, as vpon these here, (as we haue heard that some of them haue had lately faire warnings in that kinde, while they haue been in the middest of their pastimes) I denie not but it were lamentable; but doubtlesse not lesse (what doe I say? nay by farre more) deserued then this. But these must be left to the Magistrate, who should not in vaine beare the sword, but to the terror of offenders.

Of like sort to the Philistims meetings to laugh and please themselues in beholding *Samson* brought foorth to be a gasing stocke among them; of like sort, I say, are the brutish flockings together of some parts of our countrey, who on the most Sabbaths through the summer haue vsed, and that very lately (I am sure) and still they may, for ought I know, to feast, drinke and dance, with much misrule accompanying them: misrule, ye may well gesse what, by that which I haue mentioned; as if God had neuer commanded better things, saying yet aloud in their eares, Remember that ye keepe holy the Sabbath. All which prophane customes with the like, let them perish and come to naught, and holy assemblies to heare sermons and to pray, rise vp, and bee duly and reuerently frequented and vsed on the contrary. Of these lewd customes I haue elsewhere spoken.

Doct. out of vers. 26.27. I noted before the slauishnes which *Samsons* sinne brought him to, while he committed it, in the 17. verse, reseruing the other, to wit, the basenes and shame which followed after it, to this place, as more proper for it. That which God threatned to the whole body of his people for renouncing his seruice, that they should lose their headship ouer the nations, and become the taile, that befell this one man *Samson* for his wilfulnes. Not vnlike to that which *Noah* (by implication) prophecieth of the Church in the two heads therof, *Shem*, and *Iaphet*, that *Cham* should be vnder, and a seruant vnto them, while they dwelt in the tents of God, but otherwise *Cham* should hold his dominion ouer them. *Samson* was made a Lord in some sort ouer these Heathens, to rule them, and so he did while he held his honour in the seruice of God: but being wearie of it, loe hee is made the most vile vnder-
Note. ling to them, and loden with all despite that malice could lay vpon him. We will neither beleeue that there is honour in seruing God, (whereas yet the
Heb.1.14. Angels haue no greater, and the greatest Kings vpon earth hold their Maiestie, in seruing the Lord and maintaining his truth inuiolable) nor shame and miserie in the contrary. But *Samson* (doubtlesse) saw the former, the more cleerly, when he was so oppressed with the latter: and that in so foule a manner, as that he who weigheth the storie, shall neede no further proofe of the deformed and vile nature of sinne. Euen thus was it with *Adam* when he had sinned: whereas before he was the soueraigne Lord ouer the creatures, hee became the vilest and worst of all, if God had not restored him.

Thus

Thus the euill Angels not content with the highest honour,became diuels, abased to the lowest and cursedest ebbe of shame. And this particular I thought good not to omit,(though I haue said meetly enough of the other parts of miserie which this sinne of his caused) to the end that such as like *Samsons* diet so well,may know by that time God hath tamed them so, and fetcht them about as he did this poore offender,he will make them buckle and stoope to his lure,and be glad of the meanest roome in his house,as the prodigall that wished himselfe an hireling of his fathers,in his wretched pe- Luk.15.19.
nurie,whom the place of a sonne before liked not. As for them who thinke it their reproch to weare Gods liuerie at all, they are rather to be hissed at, then confuted by this text,let them goe like vagabonds and *Cains* vpon the face of the earth; but as their true shame is herein, that God vouchsafes them no roome in his Church,so the time shall be,when their shame shall breake foorth to their confusion,then when there shall neither be place for them to hide their heads in, nor cloakes left them to couer their shame, much lesse to haue entrance into his kingdome. Let rather such as goe for Christians,who enioy the honour of good report among the best for their religion,and haue been hitherto kept from reprochfull crimes,and the fruit thereof,that is shame among the godly, and from being a byword to the wicked: let such,I say, look about them by this example,and beseech God to shew them yet more cleerely the priuiledges of their sinceritie,and godly care of obedience,(which euen here are glorious,ere glory it selfe be obtained) that so they may cleaue fast vnto him still,and beware,lest catching at some other shadow of glory,by forsaking their zeale, and following the common sins of the time,they become most ridiculous pageants of scorne to them,whom before they held in awe and reuerence,by the admiration of their vertues. Sure it is, that if they will venture with *Samson* to breake out to doe euill for the hauing of their owne pleasure, or to auoid a little trouble,they shall as he did,reape a great deale for it.

Before *Samson* set vpon this worke,he besought the Lord to inable and Vers.28.
assist him,and we must know,that his prayer was feruent and effectuall, offered vp in faith,and obtained that he sought. And whereas he may seeme to seeke reuenge in his prayer,wee must consider,he was the Lords instrument to bring to passe his worke; and for good successe in that, he intreateth God to assist him: Euen as the Apostles did in the Acts; when the Act.4.29.
Priests had forbidden them to preach in the name of Iesus, which he had commanded them, they besought God to stop and hinder their threats from hauing effect,and prayed, that with all boldnes they might vtter and preach his word. The same did *Samson* against these enemies of God, and God heard both alike; both him,and the Apostles. Though God had promised them both all necessarie assistance,yet his grace was not so pinned to their sleeue,as that they might alway make account of it, without seeking of it by the prayer of faith, as in *Elia* and *Elisha* appeareth, and wee haue toucht it in the prayer which he made for supply in his deadly thirst, when he was about Gods worke in chapter fifteenth, where I also obserued the ground of that libertie which Gods faithfull seruants haue in their accesse to God by prayer.

And in effect *Samson* prayeth thus: O Lord, seeing I am brought now into so great a company of these Philistims, whom, I being blind, shall neuer be able to pursue, as thou haddest commanded me, they being enemies to thee and thy people; and seeing thou hast restored my strength to me in this so good an opportunity; seeing it is thus, saith he, in token that I beleeue no lesse, I beseech thee to grant, that I may now bee auenged of them, and that they may be payed home for the iniurie they haue done me, by plucking out mine eyes, and other woe which they haue wrought mee thy seruant, whereby I haue been hindred from doing thy worke among them. Thus we see how it fareth with Gods people, and what their behauiour is in their affliction: to wit, that they testifie their beleeuing in him, by feruent supplication to him in such time of their need; shewing thereby, that they make him their onely refuge and stay.

Doct. And by this we are taught, how earnestly and diligently we should go about the Lords businesse, when we may, and haue opportunity, and chiefly in our tribulation; namely, with feruent prayers suing to him for helpe in the one, and successe in the other; which seeking to him, the Lord doth much regard and commend: and (as hee here did) to oppose our selues against his enemies, wherein we finde and can proue that they bee so. For as
2.Cor.9.7. the Lord loueth a cheerefull giuer, so hee loueth a cheerefull doer of his businesse. And so should wee bee also, and the rather seeing there are but few that are forward and readily minded in Gods matters, howsoeuer in other attempts they runne when they should draw backe. But of this latter point, euery where almost through the booke.

Vers.29.30. In these two verses is shewed, how *Samson* setting his shoulders strongly to the pillers of the house, he said; My life perish with theirs. And the house fell on the Princes and the people, so that many more were slaine by him at his death, then he slew in his life, and he died with them.

Doct. of both. Here we see for one point, the momentanie and flitting estate of the ioy of the wicked. And this is their bane, their vexation, and chiefe heart smart, that when they haue feathered their nest, as they say, and prouided great wealth, pleasure, and honour, whereby they giue shew to fooles that they haue gotten a pettie paradise here on earth, yet when they haue done, they
Note. want one chiefe thing to helpe them to hold and keepe still their deceitfull and pictured felicity, and that is, length of time and daies: that they may containe the enioying of it to themselues. This they cannot buy nor compasse, as they can all other things to their liking, and for want of this, all the other leaue them, fade, and giue ouer their vse, as if they had neuer been theirs, and yet withall, send them also to a farre worse conditon. What prouision haue many made in sumptuous and goodly buildings, with fat pastures, and commodious grounds laid thereto, and all commodities more neerly adioyning, as fish-ponds, burrowes for coneyes, doue-houses, parkes, orchards, gardens, and what not, that may bee deuised for their pleasure: as
Eccles.2. *Salomon* speaketh of himselfe.

Note. And heerein one followeth another, as farre as by their wealth they can reach, and when they looke now to enioy them, and so to shew their happinesse thereby to other, then, or after a very little while, Time denies her seruice

seruice to them, and will performe it no longer, without which all the rest are to them as nothing, nay vexation of spirit also. Thus death the Lords messenger comes oft on the sudden, as the sergeant or bailiefe arresting, and taking them away from all their pleasant delights, as *Samson* was violently from his *Delilah*, vntill they cry out againe, when they see how they are plucked from them, but all in vaine, seeing there is none to rescue them. The same may be said of those, who haue prouided yeerely reuenewes, to auoid dangers, and maintaine fleshly reioycings. All which though they be Gods good benefits, and may be lawfully enioyed, yet when they are set in Gods place, and made the delights of men, in stead of his fauor and gouernment, they are cursed with the vsers of them.

And thus when they must be taken from them against their will, and they can enioy them no longer, they say in themselues, O death, how vnwelcome art thou to vs, who haue taken vp our pleasure heere? And haue they nothing else to say? where is now their wisdome, (who went for the wisest of other in their prosperity,) that hath bewrayed them to bee meere fooles, and left themselues then nothing? Why did they not rather obey God therefore, who charged them that they should not lay vp their felicity here below? Why did they not giue credit to him, who told them, as he told the rich man in the Gospell, There is no certainty of any earthly thing till to morrow? Therefore must such become by-words for their follie and wilfulnesse, in euery common mans mouth, (as I know not wherfore their doings serue, but for matter to talke of,) who looked to haue been famous here for euer by their vnsatiable gatherings, and great prouision making of earthly abiding and prospering.

Note. Luk.12.20.21. Note.

For he that hath said to him, who was as well setled in momentany rest as these, when he thus comforted himselfe, [*Soule, eate, and drinke, and take thine ease, thou hast much good laid vp for thee for many yeeres,*] Hee I say that spake thus to him; *Thou foole, this night will they fetch away thy soule from thee, and whose then shall be the things which thou possessest?* He saith as much daily to these; and who can then pitie them, if they will not be warned? Much like a great man that died a few yeeres agone, who when sicknesse grew fast on him, and would not bee shaken off, as hee hoped it would haue been, at the first comming of it, when he could get no helpe against it, but that death approched and drew neere, hee vttered these words now at last; whereby it is cleere that he had little thinking of any such thing before; Why? now I see that all is vanity. Another hauing builded a goodly house, when hee had shewed the commodities and pleasantnesse of it to a plaine countrey man, asking him how he liked it; he answered: I like it well, if a man might keepe it alwaies. Thereby marring the ioy of it, who could not commend it, but together with the deadly and vnwelcome remembring the momentanie and flitting estate thereof, and the vncertaintie of enioying it.

Luk.12.19.

And all the ioy of the wicked is no better then I haue said; and yet that none may thinke the Lord to deale partially, bee it knowne that if his owne people degenerate, and partake with the other in their sinne, and play the fooles with them by reioycing in euill, and things transitorie, as their paradise, they shall smart with them likewise, and for the time enioy no better priuiledge then they doe. Therefore let vs bee wiser, and imbrace and proſeſſe that ioy which cannot be taken from vs, neither ſhall euer be repented of, that we haue ſought it, and that is our reioycing in the Lord, in his word, in his ſeruice, and in his Saints; and to be ſhort, in his all-ſufficiencie. And this bee ſaid more fully of this point which yet I handled by the like occaſion in chap. 15.

2 Againe heere let vs marke at what time and when the ioy of the Philiſtims was damped and taken from them. And that was, when they were met together to ſport themſelues, and bee merrie, and when they were furtheſt off from any thought of trouble or death, or of loſing and diſappointment of their paſtime, euen then was the houſe throwne downe by *Samſon*
1. Theſ. 5. 3. vpon them. Like to that which the Apoſtle ſpeaketh; When men cry peace, peace, and al things are ſafe, then ſhal ſudden deſtruction come vpon them, as trauell vpon a woman with child, and they ſhall not be able to eſcape: e-
Dan. 6. 25. uen as *Baltazar* alſo was moſt fearefully threatned the loſſe of his kingdome in the middeſt of his banqueting.

This doctrine doth mauellouſly croſſe our vile nature, who giue our ſelues leaue, when health and welfare meet together and abide with vs any time; to make our ſelues drunke with them, and to take our fill of them. And therefore we cannot away with this, to heare of any change, nor to be awaked out of our carnall drowſineſſe: and for this cauſe, ſeeing men will
Luk. 21. 34. not hearken to the Lord, bidding vs watch, and beware of ſuch ſurfetting and ſpirituall drunkenneſſe; therfore he leaues many in the ſnare oft times,
Prou. 22 3. wherein like fooles they be taken. And by this we may ſee, when God hath begun iudgement before with his owne, ſo that they eſcape not, that it ſhal much more grieuouſly meet afterward with his enemies; and therefore
1. Pet. 4. 18. that their iudgement ſleepeth not. This I enlarge not, hauing ſpoken of it in the place before mentioned, chap. 15.

3 The caſting downe of ſuch an houſe, (we know all) it paſſed the ſtrength of a common man. And as he had his ſtrength reſtored to him againe, as we ſee, ſo had hee alſo his inward grace, as appeareth by that which hath been ſaid of his repentance, and his prayer of faith. Now therefore ſince that, the caſe being thus altered with him, we muſt behold him as another man, then when he was beſotted and made drunke with the wicked woman. And here let vs marke what a difference there is betwixt the time of grace in a man while God guideth him, and the time of bondage when God letteth him follow the deuices and deſires of his wicked heart, as may bee here ſeene in *Samſon*. Oh, grace if it could be ſeene with eyes, as we can ſee but a darke reſemblance of it by ſome outward ſhewes thereof, it would in an admirable manner draw vs to loue it, as the meekeneſſe of *Moſes*, the loue of *Ionathan*, the zeale of *Dauid*, and the like: and ſo would the fouleneſſe, loathſomnes and terribleneſſe of ſinne, cauſe vs to abhorre it, as the diuell: as in *Iezabels* cruelty, *Ioabs* malice, *Hamans* murtherous mind is to be ſeene.

Oh what a ſhame it is for a man that hath been reuerenced and highly regarded for his approued innocency, faithfulneſſe, and conſtancy in good carriage, to become a foole in Iſrael, a baſe, ridiculous, and contemptible
Note. perſon! And againe I ſay, oh how glorious and worthy a thing it is, to ſee ſuch an one to be reformed, and caſt into the mould of the Goſpell! Looke vpon thy ſelfe, if euer thou diddeſt ſerue God vprightly, theſe vertues here

ſet

set downe,had place in thee,yea prayer was sweet to thee;and hearing,with such like fruites of amendment were pleasant: but when thou hast suffered thine heart to carrie thee after the corrupt inclination thereof, thou art then become vtterly disguised,as if thou haddest neuer been the same person.

I will here onely adde this,how sinne maketh men impotent, and taketh heart from the committers of it,as I haue shewed other waies, how loathsome and odious it is. Reade that one example to this end, in this booke. When the Lord brought warre vpon his people for their Idolatry, by the Canaanites, it is said that the people were so put out of hart with the thinking of their sinne, and so appalled in their consciences, remembring how they had transgressed, that among fortie thousands of them, there was not one that durst take vp speare or shield against the enemie. But of this point plentifully before,and particularly vpon those words,[That he thought hee would doe as at other times.] But here an end. Iudg.5.8.

THE EIGHTIE NINE SERMON, ON THE XVI. AND XVII. CHAPTERS OF THE BOOKE OF IVDGES.

NOw to proceed with *Samson* vpon this, that hee casting downe the house vpon the Philistims, died also with them: it is demanded,if he did not kill himselfe, which if we finde that he did, then all the commendations of his renued repentance falles to the ground, and is washed away by this his last so wofull a fact, and that also aduisedly done. Hereto I answere,that it cannot bee said hee killed himselfe: indeed he died with them, but the end that he propounded, was not that he might die,neither did he desire it; but he sought reuenge vpon Gods enemies,which was the worke of his calling, and that which was like to bring and procure it: but what was that but a faithfull seruing of God, though with the losse of his life? euen as the Apostles did.If they preached Christ,they saw it would cost them their life, and that they should be slaine if they would needs preach him: now when it fell out so indeed by their preaching,shall we say therefore that they killed themselues,and that they sought their owne death? No, no more then a zealous and diligent Preacher,who by his paines in study and his ministery,empaireth and spendeth his strength and health,can be said to be the procurer of his owne vntimely death,for he hath spent his strength in his calling, to which end God gaue it him. *Obiect.* Vers.30. *Answ.* Note.

And as *Paul* said,he was ready to be bound,and to die for the Lord Iesus, so *Samson* said, let me lose my life with the Philistims. He runneth not rashly to death,but followeth his vocation, and if death come therewith vnto him, Act.21.13.

him, he yeelds to it willingly, and the rather because he had brought this necessity vpon himselfe by his owne sinne; and hee could no otherwise pursue Gods enemies then with hazard of his owne life. Euen as valiant
The vse of it. souldiers who seeke not death, but yet looke for no other. The vse of this to vs is this, that as wee should abhorre the least sinne this way, yea the very speech or thought intending and seeking our owne death, so yet it is our duty to walke in the estate in the which God hath set vs, in such wise, that we be not onely ready, fit, and willing to die; but also if God will in our faithfull discharge of our duties, meet with vs by death, as hee did with the
Mat.16.25. Apostles, then to bee readie to yeeld to it, and to remember, That hee who loseth his life for Gods sake shall finde it. And therefore let neither our life, nor any thing we haue, be thought too good for him who requires it. And though all lose not their liues, yet many doe forgoe other commodities, which were not commendable in them, if it were not for Gods cause. Very Heathens (when they spake according to their light) saw it to be vnnaturall for men to deuoure themselues. And as the souldier may not disranke himselfe or forsake his station, without his Emperours permission who hath set him in his place; so neither ought any to destroy his owne life and soule by wilfull death, but waite the time that God hath appointed. Indeed the Heathen saw not thus much, that a man might not auoide apparant perill of
Plinius. violent death, whether by an incurable disease, (as one of them starued himselfe to death to free himselfe from the stone) or by the pursuit of their enemies. This they made themselues erroneously beleeue to be magnanimity, and the waiting for death (in that case) cowardise. And like to them are many brutish people among vs, who in some great distresse of mind or shame which their owne sinne hath brought vpon them, bereaue themselues of their liues, like *Iudas*, and *Abimelech*. And others being crossed but in a small matter, are ready to wish themselues as deepe in the ground as they are high too. And euen Christians often forget themselues, and haue this pang vpon them to curse the day of their birth, and to desire death. I doubt not, but many doe it in rashnesse, (for if death came and offered it selfe, they would recant,) but howsoeuer it bee, both this rashnesse, and the other madnesse is vtterly vnbeseeming Christians, and a token of an vnsauorie heart, little seasoned with the doctrine of confidence, and patience. And if a wise man weigh it, there is more cowardlinesse in preuenting trouble or crosses by violence, then enduring them patiently. And let such as the diuell hath woond in withall so farre, as to worke vpon their melancholy, and terrours of conscience, or weakenesse of nature, by such dangerous tentations as these; to drowne, hang, stab themselues, abusing the Scripture, and such examples as this of *Samson*, to that end; let such (I say) bee fenced well against his malice by this instruction, answering with our Sauiour in
Mat.4.7. the like case; Auoide Satan, I dare not tempt the Lord my God.

2 But to returne a little to *Samson*: It is so farre off from equitie to condemne that last act of his, in losing his life with the Philistims, that it was far to be preferred before his other annoying of them, and euen his greatest auengings of them. For he slew many more of them now at his death, then he did in his life. And was therein a liuely figure of our Sauiour Christ: who though he destroyed the workes of the diuell in his life, (euen as hee

came

came to the same end) and foiled him shrewdly many waies; yet at his death he triumphed ouer him, & led him captiue. Both their acts, I meane *Samsons* and Christs, doe shew, as in a glasse, what we all should doe: namely, endeuour to doe the best good at our death: which shall the better bee done, if we lay for it in our life. For, liue well, and dye better: because wee ratifie and confirme all the good we did while we liued, when we iustifie it at our death. And this is one fruite and peece of honour, that a good life receiueth, that a good death followeth it. Oh therefore begin wee betimes to feare God, and as we are commanded, remember we our maker in the daies of our youth, and let it not bee tedious to vs to nourish those good beginnings, that our last end may be like both; or else an hundred to one, that we shall haue small cause to reioyce in our end, that I say no more. 1.Ioh.3.8. Note. Eccles.12.1.

And the like (in this particular) may bee said of the death of the righteous, which is said of *Samson*, yea and much more. And it affoordeth no small encouragement to al such as are faithfull in the work of the Lord; I meane, in rooting out and destroying the enemies of their owne soules, especially the corruption of their nature, and the fleshly lusts which issue frō thence. Their watchfulnes and diligence in suppressing them ought to be daily, their prayers constant, their faith in Gods almightie power, (to which nothing is impossible) as armour, ought continually to be exercised in the assaulting of their concupiscence and the fruites thereof. And though they yeeld not at the first, because they are strong and mightie; yet hauing receiued their deadly blow at first, by the death of Christ, they shal decay sensibly, and at death be quite abolished, as the walles of Iericho fell downe the seuenth day of the compassing thereof.

Thus *Samson* dieth with the Philistims, but in a most contrary and vnlike manner. For they dyed in riot, idolatrie, crueltie and impenitencie; but he in faith, and (as *Stephen* did) in calling vpon the name of the Lord. So let it be well laid for, and looked to, that though wee must dye with the bad, yet we may in no wise dye as they doe. And so the outward manner of death, though in paine, disease, and kinde of death, it bee one, and the same, to vs and them, (as the Wise man saith, to wit, As the foole dyeth, so dyeth the wise) yet all that can iudge will say, that wee must not measure the godlines and happy estate of men by outward things, though they fall out alike to both. And by this let vs beware, that we feare not death with the wicked, who say in token thereof, we must dye; but waite wee for it, saying: Come Lord Iesus, come quickly, reioycing to thinke we shall dye. Act.7.59. Eccles.3.19.

This is a priuiledge bestowed vpon the faithfull, who prouide to dye in faith, (as the Author of the Epistle to the Hebrewes saith of the Patriarkes, and among the rest of *Samson*) to wit, that God putteth a difference betwixt their death, and the death of other; though the world cannot discerne it in the generall and common abasement of the body and flesh; yet I deny not, but sometimes this difference appeareth also euen in the manner of dying. For though some are so bereft of sense and reason by the force of their disease, and others by Gods disposing so of them, that euen the best are either much disguised in their sicknesse, or at least giue no great testimonie of that excellent grace which is in thē; yet in the grace they liued, therein they die: and vsually, and for the most part, it may be obserued, that a well passed life Heb.11.34. Note.

Psal.37.37. bringeth a good death, and oft times sheweth plentifull and apparant signification of confidence, comfort, and spirituall triumph in death, which it is impossible to finde in the other. Witnesse hereof is the death of the Martyrs, (a thing at this day much sticking in the stomacke of the Papists, if they would speake the truth) compared with the desperate or diffident death of their Iesuites, and Seminaries. I instance in these, because they arrogate most to themselues in their sufferings for the Catholike cause, as they call it. But as for other bad persons, (except deeply deluded) wee shall behold in them manifest signes of distrust, feare, impatience: and the best is, crying out of their dangerous estate. Therefore let this be a comfort to all such as hold their purpose entire of cleauing to the Lord in beleeuing his promises, and obeying his will; that as their dying may differ from the vngodly, so they (in Gods account) shall differ, though their death differ not. A great stay to them against temptation to the contrary, and against the base and common condition of their bodies, and the dishonour thereof, lying on their deathbed, laid by the walles, or in the graue. He that hath put first a difference between them and others, by faith purifying their hearts, and then by his precious account that hee maketh of them; shall eminently testifie that difference after he hath raised them out of their vilenes and ignominie, and clothed them with incorruption and glorie.

Psal.116.15.

2 And lastly, to make an end with *Samson*, we haue seene in this story, how grieuously he fell, and withall, that he turned againe to the Lord, and called vpon him, and was heard. To gather the story therfore into a short summe, according to my vsuall maner of dealing in cõtinued histories, let vs learne, that if at any time we haue sinned against the Lord more willingly and wittingly, then by meere infirmity in our ordinary course of life we vse to doe; (for Gods seruants, though they attaine not to that measure of grace in the seruice of God that they desire, yet neither doe they oft or commonly goe against their knowledge, and smother it, but yet the diuell that layeth a snare for them, and lyeth in wait continually to catch them therein, may easily, and is like sometime to finde them worse prouided.) Here therefore if it fall out, that they be taken in such a trippe, and outstraying, and met withall by God in pursuing them; let them not lie still, as the horse in the mire, as making light of their sinne, and putting the due consideration of it farre from them; but as soone as they can, labour they to come to themselues againe; and consider seriously from whence they are fallen, & how it is with them in that estate, and how they are estranged from God, and giue no rest to themselues, till with the prodigall sonne they resolue with broken hearts to goe againe to their father who is their refuge, and say: We haue sinned, receiue vs graciously: and so God, who offereth to raise vp such as are fallen, will, with the father of the prodigall, receiue and welcome them ioyfully. And so with *Samson*, and others, who haue slidden as he did, let them renue their couenant more strongly with the Lord, that it may hold firme for the time to come, euen to death, as his did, against all sinne, and especially that which hath foiled them most, lest it returne back more strongly vpon them, as waters which were ill stopped. And lastly, let them returne againe humbly and penitently for mercie, and it shall be, according to their faith, granted them. But I trow, they are most happie, who feeling and finding how sweete

ſweete the Lord is, and how gainfull his ſeruice is, will prouide, as they are
taught,to abide conſtantly in his loue, as hee willeth them to doe,not put- Ioh.15.11.
ting the matter vpon a venture,nor vrging the Lord to ſuch a ſharp manner
of diſcipline,through their boldneſſe, as this of *Samſon* was; all this (I ſay)
they will doe and that gladly alſo,except they long for woe,and ſtand vpon
thornes till they haue brought ſorrow vpon themſelues, and doubled at
leaſt their owne labour,and trouble in recouering their welfare againe.

By this verſe it appeareth, that at this ſtrange ſpectacle of the caſting Verſ.31.
downe the houſe vpon the Philiſtims and their Princes, the reſt of them
were ſo amazed, that they ſuffered the kinſmen of *Samſon* to come thither
and carrie him backe againe vnto their land and inheritance,and to burie
him there. Which if they had conſidered aduiſedly,they would haue taken
them and the reſt,being vnder their power, and haue put them to the moſt
cruell death; as the Gibeonites deſired of *Dauid* certaine of the kindred of 2.Sam.21.5,6.
Saul to be hanged vp to reuenge themſelues on him,(on *Saul* I meane) who
ſlew ſundrie of them, contrary to the league that *Ioſhua* made with them, Ioſh 9.23.
which was,that they ſhould not dye,but cut wood and draw water for the
ſeruice of the Tabernacle.

Thus wee ſee God ſometimes appalles the wicked,ſo as his people may
fare the better by it; as by caſting them to the ground who ſought Chriſt Ioh.18.6.
to take him,wee ſee hee might eaſily haue eſcaped their hands,if he would,
and that he had ſeene it expedient. And euen ſo, by their feares, or multi-
tude of buſineſſe,as alſo many other waies, the Lord putteth his hooke in
the noſtrils of the wicked,ſo that they deſiſt and leaue off from moleſting
and vexing his faithfull ſeruants, though it be ſore againſt their will: euen
as *Saul* was called away from purſuing *Dauid*, when he was in great danger. 1.Sam.23.2.
But if the Lord ſhould reuenge their wrongs vpon their aduerſaries,as hee
ſeeth it not alwaies expedient to do,he ſhould make a riddance of the wic-
ked from the earth, and ſo the innocent and righteous ſhould not haue
their faith and patience tried by them, as hee hath appointed them to be.
But ſeeing he is patient toward them,therefore they ſhould be much afraid
to goe on in their cruell courſe againſt them, as wee ſee the Prieſts by the
counſell of *Gamaliel*, thought good,and ſaw cauſe to be ruled by him in let- Acts 5.35.40.
ting the Apoſtles goe,who had before intended moſt cruelly againſt them;
what was it,that hindred them from their purpoſe,but this,that they feared
that the Lord would haue reſiſted them,who(indeed)ſo terrified them,that
hee conſtrained them to let them alone. Thus as well as by the death of
ſome that are maliciouſly minded againſt the faithfull; other of their com-
panie are ſo aſtoniſhed and appalled,that they deſiſt from their wicked at-
tempts,and are in ſuch feare, that for the time they cannot tell what they
may doe. Thus (to conclude) God eaſeth the ſhoulders of his ſeruants ma-
ny waies,as wee ſee,of the burthens that oppreſſed them, and many other
waies,that cannot be expreſſed, and not in the leaſt manner by taking their
oppreſſors away in the middeſt of their floriſhing and crueltie, that wee
may ſee he knoweth how to deliuer his, and ſheweth accordingly in due
ſeaſon,that he doth not forget them; and all to this end,that they may not
faint from their good beginnings, nor be diſcouraged in any good courſe,
but hold it alwaies beſt to depend vpō him,as Iſrael by *Pharaos* drowning, Exod.14.28.
and

Eſter 8.17. and *Shuſhan* and the Prouinces by *Hamans* abaſement, with the like, found it. And though in ſome hot and fierie trials this be hard for the faithfull to go vnder, yet after they haue borne the brunt, they would not for any good haue done otherwiſe. (Note.) But of the ſundrie waies whereby God vſeth to ſuccour his, and ioynt their enemies, I haue in another place diſcourſed at large. Therefore thus much be ſaid of this point, and of the whole hiſtory of *Samſon*.

THE SEVENTEENTH CHAPTER.

Verſ. 1. *And there was a man of mount Ephraim, whoſe name was Micah.*
2. *And he ſaid vnto his mother, The eleuen hundred ſhekels of ſiluer that were taken from thee, about which thou curſedſt, and ſpakeſt of alſo in mine eares, Behold, the ſiluer is with me, I tooke it. And his mother ſaid, Bleſſed bee thou of the Lord, my ſonne.*
3. *And when he had reſtored the eleuen hundred ſhekels of ſiluer to his mother, his mother ſaid, I haue wholly dedicated the ſiluer vnto the Lord, from my hand, for my ſonne, to make a grauen Image, and a molten Image: now therefore I will reſtore it vnto thee.*
4. *Yet he reſtored the money vnto his mother, and his mother tooke two hundred ſhekels of ſiluer, and gaue it to the founder, who made thereof a grauen Image, and a molten Image, and they were in the houſe of Micah.*
5. *And the man Micah had an houſe of gods, and made an Ephod and Teraphim, and conſecrated one of his ſonnes: who became his Prieſt.*
6. *In thoſe daies there was no King in Iſrael, but euery man did that which was right in his owne eyes.*

IN this Chapter, before I enter into the handling of it, as I vſe to do in the other, I muſt ſtay a while, and ſay ſomthing for the ſatisfying of the reader; and that not onely about this Chapter, but alſo all the other that follow to the end of the booke. That which I meane, is this: Whereas it may be, by the ignorant, thought, that the things mentioned in theſe fiue Chapters following were done in order of time, after thoſe things which goe before; I finde by conference of Scriptures that they were not, neither can it be that they ſhould. But it appeareth that the acts ſet downe in them, were done long before. And becauſe it may ſeeme ſtrange which I ſay, I neither will nor dare affirme it barely becauſe any other man ſaith ſo, but I will ſhew my reaſons out of the Scripture.

The acts mentioned in theſe fiue next Chapters, follow not the former in order of time.

I affirme therfore, that the things that are ſaid to haue been done in theſe Chapters following, were done before the times of any of the Iudges, or at the leaſt at the end, and after the death of *Othniel*, mentioned in the firſt Chapter, or in that vacation of thoſe eighteene yeeres vnder *Eglon*, while there was no Iudge in Iſrael. And they may not inconueniently bee reckoned to the ſecond Chapter, and the eleuenth verſe, and thoſe that follow it, which doe mention the horrible wickedneſſe of the people of Iſrael after *Ioſhua* was dead, and the chiefe rulers who ouerliued him. My reaſons that theſe things were done before the times of the Iudges, or thereabout, are theſe.

The

The first is,that it is said in the next Chapter,that the Tribe of *Dan*,being *Reason* 1.
a populous tribe, did inlarge their borders at that time, which (if it should
be vnderstood to follow the storie of *Samson* in the former Chapter,a recko-
ning being duly made, must be full three hundred yeeres from the diuision
of the land. Against the which therefore(as nothing like to be so)that in the
19. of *Ioshua* is opposed, where it is said, as here it is, that the border of the Iosh.19 47.
children of *Dan* was at that time lesse then sufficed : therefore the children
of *Dan* went vp and fought against Laish,euen then ; and taking it,smote it
with the edge of the sword,and enioyed it for their inheritance, and dwelt
in it. So that if they of *Dan* then tooke it, it followeth that the story in the
next Chapter,where they are said then to haue taken it, is to bee referred
to that time mentioned in *Ioshua* 19. which was three hundred yeeres be-
fore,and not to the time following immediatly after *Samson*, according to
the order of the Chapter as it is set. And this is my first reason why these
fiue Chapters follow not the order of time,as they be placed.

Another reason why these Chapters cannot bee vnderstood to bee set 2
downe according to the order wherein they stand, and the time in which
they are thought to haue been done, to wit, immediately after *Samson*, but
are to bee referred to the former times, that were three hundred yeeres be-
fore : another reason for it,I say,is this ; that *Ionathan* the Leuite,mentioned
in these two Chapters, is said to haue been the nephew of *Manasseh* the son Iudg.18.30.
of *Moses*, and the sonne of *Gershom* nephew to *Moses*, who were dead well
nigh three hundred yeeres before the death of *Samson*,and therefore vnlike,
or rather impossible that he should liue after *Samson*.

Thirdly, whereas the acts of these fiue Chapters followed one another 3
at the same time,it is manifest that at the war of the Beniamites, chapter 20. Iudg.20.28.
Phineas the sonne of *Eliazar* the sonne of *Aaron* ministred before the Lord
at that time,and asked counsell of him,if they should go against *Beniamin* to
warre. And the same *Phineas* aboue three hundred yeeres before the death
of *Samson*, appeased the wrath of God by thrusting through *Zimri* and *Cos-* Numb.25.8.
by in their tent,while the people of Israel were on the other side Iordan,and
were not as yet come into the land of Canaan. Therefore the acts mentio-
ned to haue been done in these fiue Chapters, could not bee done after the
death of *Samson*, as they by their placing may be thought to haue been ; but
long before : vnlesse we grant that *Phineas* and the rest, as *Ionathan*, and the
Danites that went to Laish, liued three hundred and more yeeres, which
none then did : for three or foure generations before that,in *Moses* time, the Psal.90.10.
daies of a man were reckoned but threescore yeeres and ten, or fourescore
at the most,to speake of,and those also with paine and wearinesse.

To these may this be added, that the Citie Ierusalem, then called Iebus, 4
part whereof fell to the Beniamites, at the peoples first comming into the
land of promise, and part of it was in the hands of Iudah : this Iebus was
now said to be possessed of the Iebusites, in the 19. Chapter. Now that Iudg.19.10.
which was giuen to *Beniamin* three hundred yeeres before, and enioyed of
them.Iosh.18.being taken from the Iebusites,could it be in the possession of Iosh.18.28.
the Iebusites so long after, being driuen out so long before? And though Iosh.15.63.
they were not wholly expelled,(as Iosh. 15.) yet part of them was, Iudg.1.
And the men of Iudah who tooke it,slew the inhabitants with the edge of Iudg.1.8.
the

the ſword, and burnt the City with fire. The other part of it was, as I ſaid, pertaining to *Beniamin*; and though ſome remained to the time of *Dauid*, yet they enioyed not the City, though they could not bee wholly caſt out; but were onely in holds, as may be ſeene, 2. Sam. 5. Therefore that which is ſaid of Iebus in the next Chapter, that it was called the City of the Iebuſites, is not to bee vnderſtood to haue been ſo called now after the death of *Samſon*, but three hundred yeeres before, when it was not yet giuen to *Beniamin*, nor taken by *Iudah*.

2. Sam. 5. 6.

I ſay therfore, that in this and the other 4. Chapters following, is ſhewed that the Common-wealth of the Iſraelites was moſt corrupt both in religion and manners, after the death of *Ioſhua*, and the other good rulers that ouerliued him: for in a ſhort time after, by little and little, another generation aroſe, which knew not the Lord, and the whole tribes fell to Idolatry, and horrible wickedneſſe, of both which an example is ſet downe here; one of their Idolatry in the 17. and 18. Chapters; and another of the monſtrous life that was then in vſe among them, which is ſet downe in the other three Chapters following.

Iudg. 2. 10.

The ſumme of the Chapter.

This being ſaid of the time when the acts of this and the Chapters following were done: I proceed now after the manner that I vſe in the former Chapters, to ſet downe the ſumme and parts of this. The ſumme of it is this: That a woman, mother to one *Micah* in this Chapter mentioned, loſt a good ſumme of money, (as it might be, about an hundred poudd after our reckoning) which her ſonne *Micah* had ſtollen from her. This money when he (hearing how ſhee curſed for the loſſe of it) had reſtored to her againe, ſhe beſtowed it vpon idolatrous vſes. For ſhe procured a molten and grauen Image to be made with part of it; and her ſonne made other Images and ornaments for them both, of the reſt of it, and hired a Leuite for the better furniſhing and ſetting out of the matter, to be in his houſe, as his Prieſt with him. The parts of the Chapter are two: the one, concerning the Idolatry of the woman and her ſonne, vnto the 17. verſe: the ſecond, how *Micah* hired himſelfe a Prieſt for the purpoſe, to the end of the Chapter. And by this example we ſee how Idolatrie in thoſe bad times was firſt brought into a priuate familie, which after ſpread into a whole tribe.

The parts, two.

The firſt part of the Chapter.

The ſumme of the 4. firſt verſes.

IN the firſt part, we are to conſider of the woman, in the ſixe former verſes. And here firſt of the things which are ſpoken of her before her Idolatry, as they are laid out in the text. Where (after that ſhe is ſaid to bee the mother of this *Micah*, a man of mount Ephraim) it is added, that certaine money which ſhe had vowed to the Lord, was ſtollen from her by her ſon: whereat ſhee curſed the theefe, not knowing who hee was that had taken it away. And when he confeſſed his fault, and that he had it, ſhee bleſſed him: who reſtoring it to her againe, ſhee anſwered him, that ſhee had vowed it to the Lord for his vſe, and therefore bad him take it againe. So ſhee tooke two hundred ſhekels therof, to make a molten Image of it, and put it in the houſe of *Micah*: and (as it may be gathered by her owne words) added the reſt to other like apurtenances thereunto.

Many things offer themselues to vs heere worthie the noting. And first this: that this *Micahs* mother had of her superfluitie and great wealth, wel nigh an hundred pound to vow to superstition and idolatrie, (for so it appeareth) and that they were both very wealthie, in as much as hee was able to make, maintaine, and furnish an house or chappell of Images, (not of the meanest mettall) and to adorne them, and she to increase them. This sheweth, that howseuer many want and are in great need, (whose penurie should be relieued with the superfluitie of others) yet in the meane while there are, who haue more then they can tell well how to bestow or imploy. But alas, they haue no heart to doe good with it, especially to others, neither wil be taught to lay aside, as God blesseth them, to good vses and ends: nor to themselues to doe the best good, namely, that they may bring foorth much fruite, that so their soules may fare well. Yet this was not the fault of these two, that they had no heart to lay it out, for that they were ready enough to doe, but they did it amisse, and to idolatrous vses. For though they thought they did well imploy it, yet they were superstitiously and blindly led to that which they did. And as it was the sinne of these, that their zeale was carried amisse, through want of knowledge, (which yet excuseth them not, seeing they were the posteritie of the visible Church, and in likelihood themselues lately of it) so others, whose knowledge is greater, offend in their kind as grossely. For, either they cannot depart from it at all and forgoe it, I meane, any portion of their superfluitie, (which is one extremitie) or they lash it out vnlawfully vpon their lusts, either in voluptuousnes, as adulterie, drunkennesse, and such like, which is another and more dangerous extremitie: and to one of these, though not all in a like measure, tend the most mens vsing of their goods. Few aime at the best manner of disposing them. If they did, God hath giuen enough; that as it was in gathering the Manna, he that gathered lesse then a homer, wanted not, and that hee who gathered more, had nothing ouer: So for the condition of euery man, God hath giuen sufficient: yea, and for the sin of men, causeth the sea to drowne much wealth, and much to be lost on the land; as if he would haue vs thereby take knowledge, that he had rather it should be lost, where only it doth no good, then to be in the hands of wicked men, where it should doe much euill and hurt. Therefore let vs bee ready to imploy our goods to the comforting of other euer way, and so, as we also may haue all possible good, by the well vsing of them. But a fitter place for the pursuit of this point, will be that which is said after in the third verse.

Doct. ver. 1. & 2

1. Cor. 16. 2

Ioh. 15. 9.

Exod. 16. 18.

Note.

Now it is said, that all this money, while she had it in her possession, was stollen from her. Nothing is said of the manner of this fact, but barely and simply it is set downe that it was so. To teach vs, among other things, how fickle and vncertaine the hauing and enioying of worldly goods is, and how soone they be lost, and how many waies, (for who suspecteth his owne children) they being one mans to day, and another mans to morrow. As *Benhadad* said to *Ahab* by his seruant, Thy siluer and gold is mine: and a very little while after, all that *Benhadad* had, and he himself was at *Ahabs* pleasure, and he was driuen to begge his life of him. Thus it hath bin with good and bad in all ages. Which yet I say not, as though wee should set all at sixe and seuen, and not labour for commodities, (for God hath commanded vs so to

1. King 20. 31 32

 doe)

doe) and make ſmall account of Gods goodneſſe in giuing theſe earthly benefits vnto vs, (for they are his great bleſſings for ſingular vſes) and wee are
Epheſ.4.28. commanded to be occupied in our callings for the obtaining neceſſaries for our life thereby.

But to ſuch changes hath God made the condition of earthly ſubſtance
1.Tim.6.17. ſubiect, that we may learne not to truſt in vncertaine riches, (as we are moſt prone and ready to doe) but in the liuing God, that we may liue with him; and that we indanger not our ſelues by wronging or offering violence to any for comming by them, which are ſo ſoone loſt; but doe good with them rather, and be rich in good workes, and not follow the example of the wicked world, who commit all miſchiefe to get them, and in vſing them. Ther-
Matth.6.19. fore our Sauiour chargeth vs, ſaying: *Lay not vp treaſure for your ſelues vpon earth, where the ruſt and moth doth corrupt, and where theeues breake through and ſteale: but lay vp your treaſure in heauen.* We haue ſaid enough of the ficklenes of outward things, by one occaſion or other, in the moſt of the former chapters.

3 Her money was ſtollen by her owne ſonne. For many children make a light matter of ſtealing and plucking from their parents, as though it were their own, euen while their parents liue. But ſuch make no conſcience, who dare ſo doe, to defraud their parents. This aggrauated *Micha* his ſin in that he robbed his owne mother, who yet of himſelfe was rich, and needed not to fall to ſuch practiſes, and ſhe was in houſe with him, and (as it is moſt like) they vſed all things in common together, and at leaſt the money was like to fall to him for his ſhare: and yet all this notwithſtanding, behold his ſin, that he could not forbeare, but that he muſt needs put his hand to it before the time. This ſheweth ſin to be out of meaſure ſinfull, in that they who commit it (ſetting aſide a lewd & wanton humour, and an heart ſo full of naughtineſſe, that it muſt haue vent ſome way) oft times haue no more need to do it, then to put their hand in the beares mouth. Of this ſort are the waily, idle, and needleſſe oathes and ſpeeches of ſome, the medlings of buſie bodies in other mens matters, and (that which is more dangerous) in things that are
Note. too high for them; alſo the ſtealings of rich men, as this *Micha* was: with the whoredomes of married perſons, and thoſe lyes which we call ieſting lyes for pleaſure ſake, and the drunkenneſſe of ſuch with their lewd companions abroad, who yet may be well and with ſufficiencie ſatisfied at home, with an hundred more of like ſort.

Though al ſin be vile & odious, (for no ſin is neceſſary becauſe ſome are needleſſe) yet to be ſure, he that ſinneth, when he hath no need, and therefore wanteth excuſe euen to God and man, as he that committeth adultery, or the like, to be ſure (I ſay) he troubleth and deſtroyeth his owne ſoule. Re-
2.Sam.12.8. member how *Nathan* inlargeth the ſin of *Dauid* by this circumſtance, that he hauing many wiues, robbed his poore neighbour of his onely wife, and killed her husband alſo, for the better concealement of his adulterie. And this was ſo inexcuſable euen in the cenſure of the offender himſelfe, that he abhorred it, and condemned it moſt deeply: and therefore thinke not that God will take ſuch by the hand. Beſides, this teacheth parents to traine vp their children religiouſly, and to diſgrace and make odious all ſin to them, as well as to follow them with other inſtruction, and good example; that

lying,

lying, swearing, stealing, and the like, may, through Gods blessing, bee farre from them; which, with such other like sinnes, will easily and soone fasten vpon them, vnlesse by good education they be weaned from them: as shall appeare in the next point saue one more cleerely.

Now in that he being an Idolater, was also a great theefe, we may note, 4
that they who dare fall to Idolatrie and false worshipping of God, are not to be trusted in duties doing to men. So *Abraham* said to the King of Gerar, of all, as well as Idolaters, that where the feare of God is not, there is smal likelihod that the feare of man will preuaile: and so hee will say, that doth rightly consider it. For howsoeuer a deceiuer may for a time, and while he is not greatly prouoked, neither hath any occasion offered him, or is held in by strong outward bridles or inducements from outrage, may (I say) shew good example among men, and walke without offence toward them; yet when he shall see his time, he will shew what he is, as wee see in seruants, in children, in friends betrusted with great matters, bewraying at length an vnfaithfull heart: and the reason is great: they are false to God, and what man then shall looke for any better at their hands? euen as the holy Ghost saith of the Iudge, that hee neither feared God, nor reuerenced man. And much the rather is this true in Idolaters; seeing that euen he who is of sound religion, as I haue said, yet if his heart be not vpright, may possibly bee a deceiuer. Gen.20.11. Luke 18.2.

Among other vses of this point, this is one, and not the least that we pray for such as are in authoritie, that they may religiously prouide, that their people may feare God, (at least want no ordinary meanes that may draw them thereunto) and therefrom be conscionably carried to obedience outwardly towards men. Seeing the most forcible meane to containe men within compasse, is the feare of him, who can cast body and soule into hell, rather then him who can but destroy the body. Besides, that nothing is secret to God, before whom all things are naked and manifest. Whereas the seuerest Magistrate can proceed no further then by witnesses, himselfe not being priuie to the conscience or fact of the offender. But of this elsewhere. Concerning Idolaters in particular, euen the deuout and especially Papists, this president of *Micah* is sufficient to stop the mouthes both of them, and of their abettors, who iustifie their innocencie and good behauiour towards men. Whereof there were more cause and colour, if the rotten hollownesse of their hearts brake not foorth into hideous and horrible vnrighteousnes, as vncleannes, crueltie, murthers, treasons, lyings vnder the maske of ambigious speeches, and most slanderous defamations not of meane persons, but of Princes, and their gouernment, besides periuries, breaches of league and promise with many more, and some of them maintained by them in Schooles, as well as practised. The deuoutest of them are the least euill persons, but the rest are little better in their iudgements then in their practise, euen Atheisticall and damnable in both. For who seeth not, but that the late monsters of opinions and positions which they haue broched, flow from no other fountaine, but a resolute and malicious purpose to serue their owne turnes, and hold vp their tottering kingdome, though with the ruine and ouerthrow of all their opposites? So destitute they are of all ground of Scripture or sound reason. Matth.10.28.

Doct. 5. These eleuen hundred shekels, when hee heard his mother curse for the losse of them, he confesseth he had them: but lest ye should think, that confession went with any sound repentance, yee may see him bewray the contrary. For as though he had been ashamed to be taken for a theefe, (whereas Luke 23. 40. 41 the penitent theefe, like him, in the Gospell, did freely acknowledge it, and to the full testifie, that he was out of loue with the sinne) hee here extenuateth his sinne, saying: The shekels which were taken from thee, it was I that tooke them: but ye must marke that he saith, he did but take them, but not steale them; which extenuating of the fact, was farre from one that repented: let it be a warning to vs, that we make not light of sinne, for then wee will fall to commit it; neither confesse wee it slightly, for then wee will returne to it againe. He that meanes to turne vtterly from it, will with *Daniel* Dan. 9. 5. in the ninth Chapter, aggrauate and deface it, and with the people in *Samuels* time, make his speciall sinne which hee is guiltie of, and confesseth; hee will, I say, make it more odious, then all his other sinnes: so did they say to 1. Sam. 12. 19. the Lord, Forgiue vs our sinnes, especially this that we asked for our selues a King. But of this, to wit, the danger of extenuating sinne, and the nature of true repentance, I haue distinctly spoken in other places.

THE NINETIETH SERMON ON THE XVII. CHAPTER OF THE BOOKE OF IVDGES.

Doct. 6. NOw to proceede with *Micah* and his mother, this is further to be marked in him her sonne, that when he saw his mother so troubled for the losse of the money, and heard her curse for it, hee did not suffer her to lye still in that estate, but made haste to quiet her, by telling her that he had it. Which I note of him, though a bad man, to the iust condemning of those, who seeke to vexe their parents, and to doe that which they know will grieue them at the heart, when yet they can doe otherwise. If ye aske how: I answere, besides many wilfull parts played by them otherwaies, they doe it by their irreligious, prophane, and vnthriftie course, in spending their goods wastfully and riotously: whereas not onely children should not grieue their parents, but neither one neighbour or stranger should vexe or disquiet another. But all should procure the Note. peace and welfare of other, and not seeke to vex them, which a man would thinke were a goodly sight to behold, and that because God is bountifull and rich in mercie toward vs, who haue ten thousand times more prouoked him to reuenge, then the worst enemie we haue hath proked vs. And therefore cruell and rigorous are they, who are so hard hearted that they can reioyce in other mens harmes, & laugh at the shrewd turnes that befall them, (pro-

(prouoking thereby the like to be done to themselues) so farre is it off, that they either pitie or seeke to rescue them in their oppressions.

Further he saith, that when his mother missed the money, she cursed. By cursing so, she might meane as well her hard happe, (as such count it) as well as him that had stollen it. Both she might doe: but whether of both soeuer it was, vnsauourie and vngodly it was. And yet hearing newes of it againe by her sonnes confession, she is in another extremitie, and blesseth him, as fast as she cursed before. These distinct points let vs a little consider of, ere we goe from this verse. And for the first of these, wee see in this woman, as in a glasse, the cursed nature that is in most people, (except corrected by grace) that when any thing crosseth them, or befalles them otherwise then they would, it driues God out of remembrance and the consideration of his prouidence, or of their owne iust desert which hath brought it vpon them, and so they let passe their dutie, which in such accidents God calles them to practise. That which is presentest with vs, is wrath and reuenge; which seeing we cannot haue to the full vpon the supposed wronger of vs, therefore that toole which is readiest we draw; euen a venomed arrow out of the quiuer of a poysoned heart, cursing, banning, and swearing and such like. Not that men content themselues with this, (saue onely to vent the fome of their wicked hearts presently, which else they thinke would burst) for when they come neerer the partie, they will requite him ten for one, & hit him home to purpose, as the Philistims did *Samson*. But till this come, they will bee doing with the other. And the greatest impotencie men bewray in this kinde, when the casualtie is such as they see not how they can redresse it, but it must bee stood too howsoeuer. Thus did the Iaylor, when his prisoners were fled. Thus men doe when their goods are impaired by ill debtors, suertiship, cosonage, ill bargaines, robberie, nay euen when Gods more immediate hand crosseth them, as in trauell by sea or land, in their haruests and commodities, by vnseasonable weather, bad successe or the like. And then they let the arrow flye, light where it will, sometimes vpon God himselfe, (for he that curseth his lot, curseth God, and if he were within his reach, he would surely challenge him) and sometimes vpon men, nay sometimes vpon the senselesse creature it selfe wherein they are crossed, or which crosseth them, by the side wherof, they wound God himselfe. Wheras *Iob* spake not foolishly, neither charged God in al the euil that befell him. And *David* looked vp to God, when all Ziglag was destroyed by enemies, and in *Shemies* grosse abusing and wronging him. Let such behauiour therefore be farre from vs, being fitter for Heathens or Idolaters.

Doct. 7.

Note.

Act. 16. 27.

Note.

Iob 1. 22.

2. Sam. 16. 10.

But besides this, we see, that it is a very bad thing for parents and gouernours to shew ill example any way by cursing, swearing, or any like in the presence of children or other. For that greatly aggrauateth the sinne that was too odious of it selfe, though done of them in secret. As all open sinnes are more dangerous then couert faults, because of the extension, and offensiue example; so no examples so noysome as the sin of parents before their children. No example is so forcible to draw, both because nature helpeth the conueiance, and besides, causeth the childe to thinke it becommeth him to resemble his parents, and besides it giueth hope of impunitie. And yet this is the trade and way which most teach their children in their youth, to the end they may be ripe and masters thereof in their age. For though sinne oft doe runne in a wicked blood, (as I haue said before, chap. 12. 1.) yet by daily practise and obseruation children are more rooted in their parents vices by imitation. The like (if not worse) is the breaking out of husbands before their wiues, Masters before their seruants, Magistrates or Ministers before their subiects and people: these examples descend and soke into the inferiours farre more deeply and infecteously, (I say not then good examples doe profitably) but more then from equals or meaner persons. Hereof

Gen. 4. 23. 24. a shew was that of *Lameg*, raging and playing the mad man before his two wiues. How shamefull also was it for *Saul* to shew such wrath and reuenge

1. Sam. 19. 1. 11. & 1. Sam. 20. 30. 33. in the presence of *Ionathan?* For a parent to lye, raile, sweare in the hearing of his children? Nay to patronage such sinnes in their presence, as some will tell their young ones, if they thought they would proue precise seruers of God, they would neuer giue them penny: what is this, but to spurre them to that which the strongest bridle can hardly keep them from?

Gen. 9. 21. It is as goodly a sight, as *Noahs* vncouering himselfe before his children. Oh men thinke, their children can spie nothing amisse in them, they may sin by authoritie, and shall they stand in awe of their children? No, stand in awe of God, and then your children shall see that in your godly speech and behauiour, mixed with sobrietie, that shall make them stand in such awe of you, that they dare not disguise themselues before you, or behind your backes; which else no terror will driue them from, though seueritie may make them simper and dissemble in presence. And this I adde, because men thinke to binde beares, and will say, Though I doe so, or so, I will make my childe doe thus and otherwise.

But to end these verses with the other point, wee see by this what is the goodnesse of those who would bee taken for good people, but yet are not guided by God: Euen that which we see in this woman; and that is, cursing going with blessing: and so it is with the most, in taking their troubles, or vpon the newes and hearesay of any crosse befalne them, they are readie to curse; and when their humour is serued, and they pleased, then on the other side they blesse; so from one mouth commeth cursing and blessing, as

Iam. 3. 9. the Apostle speaketh, in such the case being altered. If an affliction meete with them, they could finde in their heart to charge God for it; and if the contrary thing befall them, they can change themselues into new colours, and as if they had not abused their lippes so foully, they fall to blessing of God: but they please him as much in so doing, as in the other; so that, as such blessing with the tongue bringeth no blessing from God, so such cursing falleth oft vpon themselues and theirs, who sticke not in their rage to wish and call for it vpon others, who shall bee free from the curse that is causelesse, neither shall it come neere them. It is not to be wondred at, that men vnsetled and vnsauourie should runne into such extreames; for if their doings were laid before them, they would answere for themselues without blushing, that they doe well herein. When we see sweete seasons (say they) and good haruests, and all to our liking, what should we do but blesse God, and be thankfull? Indeed when we cannot plough the ground, because it is so steely with droughts, nor sow by reason of immoderate wet, or when we see the corne and grasse come to his perfection, then to be in hazard by weather,

weather, who can beare it or behold the losse and destruction of the creatures without griefe? No, it is true, if there be no more then corrupt nature in thee, thou wilt finde some excuse or other to salue thy cursed and vngodly doings withall. But if grace had once seasoned thy heart, or purged old *Adam* in any measure out of thee, thou shouldest finde no such distemper of affections, nor inconstancie in thee, but presently thou shouldest take thy selfe in the manner, and say; Oh what fountaine is this which sendeth forth bitter and sweete out of me? shall I receiue good things from Gods hand Note.
and not euill? shall I serue him for aduantage? but if hee touch me, shall I then curse him to his face? That which were grosse to offer to a base man shall I offer to God, to count him my friend onely then when hee pleaseth me, but if hee crosse me neuer so little, then to count none so great an enemie? I abhorre such dealing: If I did well in blessing him, I doe shamefully in the contrary, and my thanksgiuing is a stinking offering in Gods nostrils, in stead of a sweete sauour: for God hateth a man of a double tongue, as well as a double heart, out of the which the tongue speaketh. And if men would by such qualities as these, learne to search out the rest, (for these goe not alone) and by all laid together, would giue iust iudgement vpon themselues and trie their estate; they should make good vse of such instructions. And to be sure the lewd and prophane neuer heare any particular sinne reproued, to purpose, till it driue them quite out of conceit with themselues Act.2.37.
for the superfluitie of euill that lurketh in them, and the world of woe and desolation which (without mercie obtained from God) it will at length bring vpon them.

Now to proceede to the third verse: The woman, when her sonne had Vers.3,4,5,6.
restored the siluer, answereth him, that she had dedicated it to the Lord, euen for her sonne to make a molten and graued Image. And she took part of it, and gaue it to the founder, and hee made such an Image as she desired, and she put it in the house of *Micah*. And he had a house of gods, and made with the rest of the money all garments and ornaments fit for a Priest, signified by the Ephod, the vpper garment of the Priest, which was ẏ chiefe; and when all other things fit for Idolatrie were prouided, then he brought the Images, which are here called Teraphim, into the house of his gods, (as he called them) and made his sonne his Priest. And whereas it might be said, Was all this abomination done in Israel? how could that be? It is answered in the sixth verse, as the reason of all; there was then no ordinary Magistrate in the land to see good order, and put downe the contrary, and that was the cause.

Whereas she had dedicated the money to the Lord, all that heare what Doct. vers.3.4.
she said, would thinke her meaning was, that she had vowed it to the vse of the Tabernacle, and seruice of God, which had been commendable in her; but she did so dedicate it, to the making of an Image, not to the intent to worship false gods, but the true God, euen *Iehouah*, though in an vnlawfull manner. Whereby wee see two kindes of Idolatrie haue been, and are practised in the world: one, when a strange god is worshipped, or made for that end: another, when the true God is worshipped therein, but not in such manner as hee hath commanded, but by and in Images, or some other way that men haue inuented: and of this second kinde was this womans sinne.

So when an Image is made by any & set vp, to bring God to remembrance, we must vnderstand, that although they doe it of deuotion, intending no other thing then to worshippe him thereby, yet all such doing of theirs is but meere ignorance, and superstition, and that which God doth vtterly abhorre.

Exod 32.4. Such as that was of the children of Israels deuising, in making a Calfe to worshippe, mentioned in Exodus; and such as now is practised in Poperie, who professe when an Image is set vp before them, they pray not to it, but to God, whether it bee the Crucifix, or the picture of the Virgin *Mary*, (as they call it) or any other, neither worship they it, (if ye will beleeue them) they say, but they doe so, to put them in minde of their Sauiour, which is little better. But whatsoeuer they meane or intend in such their doings, their worke is accepted of God, euen as this womans was; and that is, that he taketh and counteth it for Idolatrie. But let vs all, as well as Idolaters, beware that we offer not to God any seruice or sacrifice, whereby we should but mocke him, as *Micahs* mother did. Whether it bee will-worship which he neuer allowed, or done in hypocrisie, which he detesteth, as well as Idolatrie most of all condemned: but let vs alwaies be guided by his word in the worship which we offer him.

2 As she had dedicated the whole summe of the money to the Lord, which she tooke againe of her sonne, so accordingly she put to the founder a part of it, to make a molten Image, and the rest of the eleuen hundred shekels she gaue backe to her sonne for the like vse, to wit, for the maintenance of his Idolatrie. The which doing of hers (seeing she was so franke in bestowing, and yet reaped no fruite of all her cost) doth giue iust cause of wondring, and lamenting, that such Idolaters as they were, and as they of our time be, can so readily lash out their money vpon that for which they shall neuer be
Esay 55.2. the better, (for in vaine doe all such worship God) and yet many of vs are so slow and backward to lay out our money (that may bee well spared) to comfort the hearts of Gods people, and to other good vses, when wee yet may reape and enioy most certaine yea and that vnspeakable fruite thereof. I meane when we beleeuing that we are beloued of God, do shew this fruit of our loue and thankfull heart to him againe, that wee maintaine his true worship with our goods, and also pitie and incourage the true worshippers of him, I meane his poore members, as he requireth, of which poore sort he might haue made our selues to be. But oh, it grieueth me to speake it, that for such good vses, to wit, for the refreshing of Gods poore Saints, and the
Iere 48.10. furthering of the true preaching of the Gospel, men haue so small deuotion, that they thinke all too much that is bestowed that way. But they shall receiue their reward accordingly: though they hold the truth in the letter, as long as they serue God negligently and pinchingly: whereas we haue lear-
Ioh.15.9. ned of our Sauiour, that his heauenly father is not honoured of vs, (neither then shall we of him be) except we bring foorth much fruite. And because in the entrance vpon this chapter I referred the reader to this place, as a fit occasion of vrging so important a dutie: therfore I will here adde somwhat to the former. This I say therefore: there is not that lauish expence and needlesse lashing out of mens money in some kinds through the land (God be thanked) which hath been, I meane in bestowing much meate & drinke

vpon idle ones,and gamesters,and rogues; but wherfore is it spared,which was wont to bee ill spent? To clothe the poore naked members of Christ, thinke we? or to feed their hungrie bellies? to relieue either poore students in the Vniuersitie, or Christian poore and distressed ones in the countrey, or any other good way? This were a good change indeed,and a wise frugalitie, to spare from the wicked and vile vses, to the making of friends that may receiue men into eternall habitations. No,no,but the Popish rout spareth for the maintenance of fugitiue Iesuites and Seminaries,and the vpholding of the Popes kingdome: the other, that they may the better defray the great charge which the seruice of their lusts puts them to,I meane pride of life,the lust of the couetous heart, and vncleane eye, all which neuer so swarmed in this land as at this day,and yet neuer so great and generall complaints,and penurie,nor so many and daily vses of reliefe as now, in so great increase of pouertie,as the people is increased. Well, gorgeous apparell, royall feastings,costly pleasures, great summes laid vp,and purchases made for the vse of posteritie, may presently giue contentment to the flesh; but Note. when the Lord shall call for a reckoning,these expences wil not be allowed, nor this account taken for currant, but a wofull backe reckoning shall bee exacted at the hands of these euill stewards, for such wasting of their Masters goods. And that pinching and niggardly contribution to Christs vse, being laid with the huge summes that men bestow vpon their lusts, shall be an inditement sufficient against them, to their condemnation. Few there Matth.25.26. are alas,able to doe any thing to purpose towards the easing of the generall burthen: and therefore that among those few, the most should want an heart (as a wofull miser confessed vpon his death-bed) oh how lamentable is it? Till better prouision be made by the Church,I grant tis no easie thing to be brought to passe(most men being so wedded to the penny) but in the meane time let vs know the law of God bindeth all his people,that as they are freed from Ceremoniall cost in sacrifices, Temple and the like, so the Lord Iesus himselfe hath substituted in their roome his poore members,vndertaking the payment of all which they take vpon his score, to the infinite aduantage of their creditors.And this should be enough to perswade them that be not desperatly couetous, to inlarge themselues in mercie and loue to Christ, by comforting the bowels of the religious poore, except they will proclaime that if Christ himselfe were present, they would suffer him to pine and starue for any helpe he were like to haue from them, when yet they are well able to helpe. They that are rich in good workes,I wish them the true fruite of their practise, as I nothing doubt but they shall enioy it, euen mercie with God in time of need: And for other, seeing euery penny to good vse commeth so hardly off with the most of them,I aduise them to take a better course with themselues against their owne vncheerefulnes, by a solemne setting a part of somewhat,as the Apostle willeth,(according to 1.Cor.16 2. their abilitie, or yeerely receits) when it commeth to hand,for the seuerall vses,which by their owne obseruation, or the information of others, they shall see to be most needfull to bestow vpon.

To conclude,let many of vs Protestants beware,that the bountie of many carnall or Idolatrous persons,rise not vp in iudgement against our niggardlines. They hauing nothing to set them on work, saue ciuilitie or blind

deuotion,

deuotion, are bountifull to others, and yet themselues not a whit the betrer for it. But we (though we pretend that wee haue obtained mercie at Gods hand, which should set vs forward to shew mercie to others) are so shut vp in our selues, that if we may fare wel, little care we what becomes of others. Let vs amend, by being wise for our owne good, in shewing mercie, and that with cheerefulnes.

Vers. 4. 5. But I proceed in this first part of the Chapter. When *Micahs* mother had caused the Image to be grauen, and then couered it with siluer, she put it in her sonne his chappell or house of gods, (for he had such a place, as we haue heard, where hee did his deuotion) and furnished it with such manner of stuffe, as with Priests garments, the Ephod, and other ornaments; and there he put Teraphim, that is, Images which he made with the rest of the money of his mothers. And that hee might want nothing for the purpose within his owne doores, he made his owne sonne, who was neither of the order of *Aaron*, nor yet of the tribe of *Leui*, (who onely might minister before the Lord) yet he made him his Priest rather then he would want one. And in deed the Priest was good enough for the seruice he was put to, both being abominable. In this mirror we may behold what confusion was growne after the good gouernours *Ioshua* and the rest were dead. It may well bee said in the second chapter of this booke, verse 10. that then another generation arose after them, who knew not the Lord, but serued Idols; in which times these cursed doings of *Micah* and his mother had place in all likelihood, as in the entrance of the chapter I haue declared.

So that we see how it was there and then, when the people declined and turned away from the religion of their forefathers, and when the times grew to be corrupted, we see what shamefull examples there arose of such things, as a little before could not haue been abidden; among whom this *Micah* is to be reckoned, who was alreadie come to be one that had brought strange and false worshippe into his house, and was fallen farre from *Ioshuas* practise, who said in his time, whatsoeuer other did, he and his house would serue the Lord. And let it teach vs (if we be wise) that if some good meanes faile among vs, disorder will soone winde in, to our great discomfort. Wherby let vs be warned, we I say, who desire to please God in the vprightnes of our hearts, that while we haue the light, we walke in it: and that not onely we do so, while the light is among vs, and good examples remaine to incourage vs, but let vs then, euen before the times of danger come, strengthen and vnder lay our selues in such wise with resolutions and purposes daily renued so to continue; that if declinings from good courses arise among vs in our daies either in religion or manners, yet we may abide stedfast in both, and turne not aside with the vnstable and inconstant multitude, and those that degenerate, that so our old age, by a constant walking with God, may be crowned with honour, as (no question) it shall by so doing. Wee little know what may fall out to be done, yea euen of vs who intend against all euill, if the times grow corrupter, and wax worse and worse, except we make faire worke before hand by clinging close vnder Gods fauour and gouernment.

Note.

Note.

And although by Gods mercie wee are freed from the greatest yoke of bondage, I meane Idolatrie; yet as they that touch pitch, cannot chuse but

be

be defiled, so they who haue to doe, and conuerse with the prophane and filthie ones of the world, where they may doe what they list, how can they keepe their garments vndefiled? I meane their liues vnstained, and their consciences pure and good? Wee haue too much proofe of that which I speake, in our owne parts of the countrey, how many of good hope and forwardnes, haue by bad examples, yea and by their owne declinings in the middest of so many prouocations, been brought to be disguised in their liues most shamefully: and yet I am certified, and I easily beleeue it, that there are farre worse people in countries further off.

But to goe forward, in that it is said, that he being but a priuate man, had 2
yet an house of gods, and all furniture for the same, (of which point I spake
in part before in the second verse) we may see in what base things men take
their delight, to wit, in such as doe not profit them, (as the Prophet *Esay* Esay 55.2.
complaineth) yea and in such as bring great hurt and annoiance vnto them. He complaineth in his time thus of the people: Wherefore do you lay out your siluer, and not for bread? and your labour without being satisfied? And what better may bee said of the most in these times? but if they bee such as professe any religion, (the rest are (I confesse) further off from God then they) how is their care and cost bestowed, with their labour and trauaile, but vpon the false worship of God? whether we regard the substance, it is with a great many Poperie, superstition, or such like: or the manner of it, it is lip-labour, and hypocrisie. But such seruing of God though hee abhorre it, agreeth well with their prophane humour, and crosseth not their carnall corruptions. But for the varietie of good bookes, whereby they may doe themselues much good in deede, how many rich men be at cost, or take vp their delight that way, to furnish their houses with such precious ornamēts,
as *Micah* filled a chappell with Idols and all furniture for them? Is there not Note.
(thinke we) good incouragement giuen to students and Preachers, to set foorth their godly labours, to be buried in the dust, and couered with cobwebs, and to lie vnoccupied? But to leaue them, and to come to men of meaner estate, who cannot doe much that way, in being at cost with good books; yet what pleasure take they in keeping some constant course in seruing of God, by praier, recording such good instructions as they haue heard in publike, or in reading good bookes of smaller price, which they may easily come by? No, no: these are wearisome and vnwelcome: and why so? euen to the end that they may trifle out their precious time, & so lose their part in the happinesse which is both promised by God, and preached.

Furthermore by this that *Micah* and his mother, being both Idolaters, 3
had trained vp his sonne after the same manner, and more then so, had committed another great sinne, to wit, to make him Priest to serue in his house of Idols, contrary to Gods commandement in a double respect, wee may see the heauie estate of the children of Idolaters, and of such as haue no acquaintance with God, whose lot is for the most part, to be trained vp (poore innocents) vnder such as they are, which is a very deuoting them to the diuell. Whereas mens posteritie should bee through their many gene-
rations, consecrated to God and his seruice, as *Samuel* was by his mother; 1.Sam.1.27.
and *Timothie* was not only brought vp by his vertuous mother to know the 2.Tim.1.5.
Scriptures from a childe, but he had also his grandmother commended by

Paul

Paul for her religion. Whereas they who are Idolaters, or wicked in their life,depriue their children of their due,I meane godly education, and as much as in them lieth,corrupt and ſpoyle them betimes. To teach the children of religious parents,to count their portion great, when they ſee that by ſubmitting themſelues to the godly education of their parents, they in ſo doing ſubmit themſelues to God alſo,and pleaſe him in the ſame,wherein they pleaſe them. And for the other,they receiue their deadly wound by their bad bringing vp for the moſt part, obſeruing the ſuperſtitious precepts of their parents,as of *Omry*,or beholding their bad examples and abiding in their religion and ſteps,(for ſo they muſt doe,they ſay, yea and wil doe,as their fathers did) euen to the day of their death. Now touching this inormitie of making a common man a Prieſt, it was as monſtrous vnder the Law, as if in our time a man of occupation without gifts ſhould boldly take vpon him to diſcharge the Miniſters office. And the like cor-
2.Chro.13.9. ruption crept in when *Ieroboam* ſuffered euery baſe perſon to thruſt himſelfe into office to ſerue at Dan and Bethel. Of which more God willing in the next verſes. In the meane while, note we that a baſe and ragged ſhift will ſerue mens turnes,for fault of a better,if they be ſet to commit any ſin which is for their profit or pleaſure, or the ſatisfying of their corrupt affection. As in moſt ſinnes we ſee it verified,and ſuch patcherie well becommeth ſuch tradeſmen. If a man of worſhip be addicted to his pleaſure,riot, gaming,vncleannes,or the like, tis a baſe and vnſeemly companion that wil not ſerue the turne with him for a need,rather then the buſineſſe ſhould be hindred. And whereas this *Micah* hauing broken the maine Commandement which concerned the ſubſtance of Gods worſhip, made no bones of breaking the ſecondary law of Ceremonie, touching the qualitie of the perſon who was to miniſter: let it teach vs to beware how we pull out any maine ſtone of Gods building,leſt therewith wee pull it downe vpon our heads,and many ſmaller with it out of the building.

Verſ.6. The reaſon is added in this verſe, why ſuch ſtrange and groſſe abuſes grew vp ſo ſoone after good order in the daies of the good gouernours *Ioſhua* and the reſt: namely, for that now there were no ſuch in the daies of
Gen.36.31. *Micah*,that is,no ordinary Magiſtrate,for ſo the word is taken,Gen.36. and therefore euery one did what ſeemed good in his owne eyes. And this ſheweth (beſide that which I haue ſaid thereof) that it was an horrible part which that *Micah* and his mother wrought. Now this is that which this place doth doth cleerely ſhew vs, and giueth occaſion to be noted among other things,to wit,what confuſion groweth when good gouernours faile and are wanting: of which I haue ſpoke at large in the beginning of the peoples declining after the death of *Ioſhua*, in the ſecond and the Chapters following.

But that which I will now ſay, is this, that although there bee Chriſtian Magiſtrates,yet except they execute the lawes carefully and conſcionably,
Rom 13.4. defending the good,for which end they are ſet in place,and purſue the vngodly, without partialitie, it will be by the many foule inormities which may lie vnpuniſhed,that much iniquitie will ſwarme, though it cannot be compared to the hauing of none. And what the people will then doe, we may ſee here: that euery one doth that which liketh him, following his owne

owne minde and will. And what is more dangerous then ſo to do? Ther-
fore howſoeuer it bee with others, our Sauiour hath taught vs to deny our Math.7.21.
ſelues, to haue no fellowſhip with the vnfruitfull workes of darkneſſe, and Ephes.5.11.
to renounce our owne will and to be ſubiect to his; the obeying whereof
is the direct way to happineſſe: for ſo hee teacheth, He that doth the will Luke 9.23.
of my father which is in heauen, he ſhall enter into the kingdom of heauen. Math.5.22.

THE NINETIE ONE SERMON ON THE XVII. CHAPTER OF THE BOOKE OF IVDGES.

The ſecond part of the Chapter.

Verſ.7. *And there was a young man out of Bethlehem Iuda, of the family of Iuda*
who was a Leuite, and he ſoiourned there.
8. *And the man departed out of the citie from Bethlehem Iuda, to ſoiourne*
where he could finde a place: and he came to mount Ephraim to the houſe of Micah,
as he iourneyed.
9. *And Micah ſaid vnto him, Whence commeſt thou? And he ſaid vnto him,*
I am a Leuite of Bethlehem Iuda, and I goe to ſoiourne where I may finde a place.
10. *And Micah ſaid vnto him, Dwell with me, and be vnto me a father and*
a Prieſt, and I will giue thee ten ſhekels of ſiluer by the yeere, and a ſute of apparell, and
thy victuals. So the Leuite went in.
11. *And the Leuite was content to dwell with the man, and the young man was*
vnto him as one of his ſonnes.
12. *And Micah conſecrated the Leuite, and the young man became his Prieſt,*
and was in the houſe of Micah.
13. *Then ſaid Micah, Now know I that the Lord will doe me good, ſeeing I haue*
a Leuite to my Prieſt.

THis ſecond part of the Chapter ſheweth that this *Micah* hauing brought that new and ſtrange worſhippe, *The ſumme of theſe verſes.* namely Idolatrie into his houſe, ſo pleaſed himſelfe therein, that now wanting nothing to the ſetting of his new trade on worke but a worke man, I meane a Prieſt; now (I ſay) he tooke the opportunitie offered by a Leuite, who ſought a ſeruice, and takes and entertaines him. Before he was content (as we heard) with his ſon to ſerue for a Prieſt, though none might be by the law, but ſuch as came of *Aaron:* wherby we ſee, that the law of God is little regarded where men are ſet to haue their owne will. But now behold, accordingly as hee wiſhed, there is offered him a Leuite, as little to his commendation, which hee much better liking, (as the taking of his ſonne before for that buſineſſe) and him he took, and therefore receiued him into his houſe, neuer examining him, nor prouing him by inquiring about him further, that he might well & throughly know his behauiour, but makes him his Prieſt forthwith, applauding himſelfe in his ſucceſſe, and reioycing not a little in his ſuppoſed well doing.

Verſ. 7. 8. But firſt in theſe two verſes it is further ſhewed, how *Micah* got him a Leuite to be his Prieſt in his ſonnes roome, and that was thus: This young man *Ionathan*, who is here deſcribed by the place where hee dwelt, and the familie he was of, and by his tribe, (for the Leuites were ſcattered, through all their tribes, in their dwellings) went about to ſeeke a place where hee might ſtay himſelfe, hee wanting maintenance, and (as it fell out) came in his trauell to this *Micahs* houſe, and by that meanes hee ſtaied and abode there. Where firſt wee may ſee another note of the badneſſe of the times which then were; in that the Leuites, which were appointed by God to ſerue in the Tabernacle, and were alſo prouided for by him of maintenance (of whom this man was one) they, I ſay, (many of them at leaſt) were now (as appeareth by him) left deſtitute of both. So this man had neither imployment, dwelling, nor maintenance, but went about to ſeeke them all.

Doct. verſ 7. By this we ſee, when it goes ill with the Magiſtracie, that it goes not hard with the Common-wealth onely, as wee haue ſeene in part, but with the Miniſtery alſo. For when there are either none, or when they be not carefull in their places to do the good they are ſet for, the Miniſterie which ſhould bring foorth many children to God, maketh his houſe but a barren family: for ſome are driuen to ſeeke a place, as this Leuite did, which is a very baſe and vnmeete thing, and vnfit for thoſe that are to ſerue God in ſo holy a calling: ſome come into their places by money, which cauſeth them to be leſſe regarded of the people, neither do the moſt of them any good among them: although they haue ſome gifts: and many of them are not able for want of fitneſſe, to direct the people aright, I meane ſoundly and plainly, vnto true happineſſe, and many are offenſiue by their ſcandalous life. In ſtead of all theſe, and many other abuſes, good gouernours will ſeeke for, and incourage thoſe that bee worthie onely or of good hope, and prouide that they may preach and attend on their charge with cheerefulnes; to the which end they are appointed by God, and ſee that they may not go about to ſeeke a place, as wandring perſons; whereas they who are beſt backed and incouraged, doe good little enough. And as the Church and Common-wealth are knit together as the ſoule and body into one, ſo that they (like enemies) laugh and weepe, fare ill and well together, as two in one ſhip either enioy ſafetie or miſcarrie alike; ſo ought they to conſent and accord ſweetly together, for the preſeruation of each other. The ſoule we ſee followes the temper of the body: and the body is as much affected with the diſtemper of the ſoule, neither of both well; if either be out of frame. And it is as true, that ſeldome that Common-wealth is happy, wherein the Church and Miniſterie hangeth downe the head. And that is, partly by the prouidence of God, iuſtly puniſhing the neglect of his ſeruice, and partly by a naturall reaſon: namely, becauſe the light of knowledge not reſtraining, and the rule of conſcience not gouerning; the corrupt nature of man can not but breake ſquare, to commit all vnrighteouſneſſe with greedineſſe, although

though there be law and penaltie to keepe men in awe; much more where Anarchie and confusion is. Therefore let the Magistrate backe the Minister with authoritie, and by the sword of iustice, sharpen the edge of the sword of the word, that it be not despised and made vnprofitable; and let the Minister requite him againe, in forcible perswading the conscience, and working vpon the soule, till hee haue brought mens thoughts into subiection to God, so that they neither presume to despise authoritie, nor forbeare to transgresse for terror so much, as for Gods sake, and conscience, which is no small vantage to the Magistrate, as some will themselues confesse. But some will aske perhaps, Why? what confusion was there in this, that the Leuite thus trauailed to seeke liuing and worke? Indeed I thinke well, there be some that thinke no otherwise of the Minister then of another tradesman, who goes about the countrey to enquire for worke: and they are such as thinke that a Minister should doe like *Paul*, that is, worke with his owne hands, that they might be the lesse troubled to maintaine him. But to leaue such Gargarites, I answere to the point, first this disorder there was in it, that as I haue said, the Leuite was not employed (if he had been worthie) in the priuate instructing of the people, and the publike at the Alter, or the like. The like disorder it were that the Minister should, as this Leuite, goe seeke himselfe a place; it is sufficient that he is willing to giue the Church an account of the gifts which God hath giuen him for her vse, (being demanded lawfully) but a place must seeke vp him, (and not he it) and approue, welcome and entertaine him in the best manner fit for the well discharging and executing of his dutie. Such as call themselues, let them shift as they can: Gods ordinance they haue violated, if discredit, discouragement, or Note. ill successe befall them, the mends is in their owne hands. If God had sent them, he would haue seene to them. But secondly there was confusion in this, that the Leuite was compelled to runne about to seek reliefe, although he had been setled. For what a shame is it for the people, (if their neglect be the cause) or for a Minister (if prouided for) that he forsakes his studie, publike teaching, and watching ouer the people, and roues about the countrey, tendring his seruice to preach here and there among strangers for money, as some base straglers doe? Whereas the Lord hath wisely prouided an exemption not onely from roning, but euen from ordinary domesticall employments, buying, selling commonly, marketting also and traffique in the world, and all to the end that he may be wholly taken vp in the worke of God; whereto who is sufficient? as the Apostle saith. But 2.Cor.2.16. wee haue them that are sufficient for all things now adaies, which makes them sufficient for little or nothing (God helpe) that they should be.

This young man is here described by the place of which hee was, to wit, Doct 2. vers.7. of Bethlem Iuda, as being borne, and brought vp in a familie there: as also by his stock, tribe, and profession, that he was a Leuite: As if the holy Ghost would tell vs, it was no strange thing, for in likelihood there were in other places that went wandring vp and down without calling, and maintenance (Leuites I meane) as well as he. For it was at this time as in the daies of *Nehemiah*; that is, when the Leuites had not that sufficiencie (which by the Nehem 13.10. law I haue before shewed they ought) to maintaine them, they went (by an vnwelcome necessitie) from their seruice, seeking where they could be better prouided for. So here, for that men were giuen to Idolatrie, and there were no Magistrates, to see the people pay their tithes; the Leuites, as this young man, went wandring vp and downe a begging.

This sheweth, that it is a great crosse vnto a man to be without a calling: because it is an occasion of great vnsetling, and inconuenience thereby, yea and to take one that is vnlawfull, and with bad conditions, as this man did, to become an Idolater. And so, a good mercie of God it is on the contrarie, for a Christian to be setled in a lawfull calling. Wherein although many trials and difficulties doe arise, yet they are by Gods prouidence mixed and accompanied with many blessings, to keepe men safe and free from many annoyances by both. For as if a mans life were loden with troubles, there could be no libertie nor incouragement to good duties: so if these benefits of God should not oft goe with burthen, seruice, and difficultie, all would be out of order on the other side. As for shewing the fruite of idlenesse or want of employment, I will forbeare heere to speake; hauing often vrged the inconueniences thereof before in this booke. Onely let this vse bee made hereof, that if it fall out, that the good seruants of God bee either through the decay of their trade, or by their owne pouertie, or by any other occasion, forced to leaue it; let them consider, and take aduice in the best manner that they can, to supply that by taking paine in some other, or in a Christian sort, settle themselues in some good doing for their maintenance, and so be free from idlenesse, and as little as may be, burthensome to other. And let all faithfully discharge dutie therein with diligence, and make no haste to trie how miserable it is to liue without a calling. But as for them, who are trained vp to none, neither will change their idle course to learne or practise any, or vnder the colour of seruice to men of place, neglect Christian employment, which might stand by them in age: for these, I say, beside this, that they are vnprofitable, and increase beggerie in the Common-wealth, sinne in the Church, and waite the mischief of both, being fit tooles for the diuels hand and workmanship: besides this (I say) themselues hasten their owne sorrow, for they are oft times cut off as caterpillars of the Common-wealth, by vntimely death, which they haue themselues long before sought and procured. There are euery where, idle headed, shifting, discontented, and schismaticall persons, that haue callings, but are wearie of them, and picke any quarrell against them, to giue them ouer. Nay, many Christians hasting to be rich, and finding but small and leisurely gaines to come in by their callings, will all vpon the sudden be ouer head and eares in great dealings, (wherein their skill is small, and their successe lesse, and their weake estate maketh them as vnfit as both) till at length they become scarce worth the tooles of their shop, in which they had been wiser to haue kept themselues. For they lose that one way, which they get another, by that time they haue counted all. Oh, infinite is the gaine of a calling holily and constantly walked in, wherein is exercise of faith, equity, mercie, thanks and patience; freedome from noisome temptations, from iangling, swaggering, pot-companionship, beggery, rapine, stealth, besides an vnquiet conscience; whereas in seruing of Gods prouidence by labour, the minde of the diligent is alway quiet, yea the very sleepe of such a man is sweete.

Note. Note.

Vers. 8. 9 How this young man went about to seeke a place to dwell in, wee haue heard:

heard: now in these verses following, it is shewed, how hee found a place wherein he was staied, and that was with this *Micah.* Where we are to consider, first of their communing about it, and then of their agreement in it; after diuers questions and answers had passed betwixt them. Therefore it is said, after the young man by trauailing came to the house of *Micah* in mount Ephraim, *Micah* demanded of him, from whence hee came. And when he vnderstood he wanted a seruice, and was a Leuite, (a fit morsell for him) few other questions needed, (which yet had been requisite, they being strangers one to the other) but *Micah* by & by agreed with him to take him into his seruice, and the Leuite likewise to serue him, and be his Priest; and consecrated him thereto, and then reioyced greatly in that which hee had done.

Now in this *Micah* wee may see how rashly and vnwisely hee goeth to worke in hiring this stranger. For as soone as hee vnderstood that hee was neerer the Priests office then his sonne, he agrees with him by and by, and neuer examines him further, neither staies till he better knew what his conuersation was: which if he had bin but a common seruant, he ought to haue done, and much more inquirie ought to haue been made into such a one. And yet (lamentable it is to thinke) his practise is followed to this day of the most: who inquire not of the fitnesse and conuersation of the Minister, but if he be of either the Vniuersities, and haue some sight into the Latine tongue, and can make friends, or haue abilitie to giue more then another, he is the man that the people must content themselues with, howsoeuer the better sort seeke a worthie one. And some congregations of an honest minde, but indiscreetly, wanting a man who might supply the defect of their ordinary Incumbent, take vp euery stray that can deceiue them with a counterfeit shew of zeale or other gifts: and some runne away with their money which they borrowed: others leaue ill sauour behinde them some other way; to the shame not of themselues only, but also of such as brought them in, and admitted them. Which slight manner being vsed in so weightie a matter, we see what great inconueniences it bringeth into townes and parishes; whereas great care ought to be had (we know) in prouiding a meet Minister. And as in this, so triall ought to bee made in other conditions and estates of men, of the faithfulnes of such as wee trust with our goods, and education of our children, or in other weightie and doubtfull cases. But of this poynt in the next chapter, verse 20. by the occasion of the euent hereof, more, God willing.

Doct. vers. 8. 9.

Note.

As *Micah* vsed no examination, where he ought, so the chiefe cause was, that he was meerely led by his foolish appetite. Wherein he is a liuely and cleere paterne of the most people in their doings. For if they like a thing, they will haue it, and if they haue a minde to doe any act, they are carried after it violently, as with a whirlewinde. And in this very matter whereof the text intreateth, what makes many Patrones so resolute in their choice of Ministers, but a fleshly appetite, a foolish minde to some one person in a sinister respect, as of kindred, friendship, gaine, or suite of others. Whereas it is cleere, that a man endued with good gifts should be sought; euen as such also ought to be ordained, as both by the aduisednes of the Apostles in the choice of *Matthias*, Act. 1. and the aduertisement of *Paul*, not to *lay hands suddenly*

Doct. 2.

Act. 1. 21. 22.
1. Tim. 5. 22.

denly vpon any man,&c. as also the practise of such as presented any to the Church, and of the Church in accepting and admitting any to the Eldership or Ministerie, (in the purer and primitiue Church) what deliberation, maturitie, triall of gifts, prayer and solemne courses were vsed, at the separation and ordaining of any to this holy function, as the ancient stories of the Church doe abundantly testifie. But to leaue this instance, euen thus it fareth in other matters, as it did in this of *Micah:* if there be liking betwixt two persons, especially wealth, it is enough, without other considerations, to make a marriage. The same I may say of a seruant, or any other such like thing. Nay there shall scarce a question be asked by many, whether there be any fault or vice in him or no. It is enough that he is liked and desired. Yea though it be sacriledge which a man would commit, there must be no inquirie nor question, whether it bee lawfull and expedient, or no, till it bee

Note. done: *Samsons* answere is as much as needeth, with the most, giue her me, for she pleaseth me. It was sometime thought very meete which was said in the prouerbe, to wit, Two words to a bargaine; that is, that men should vse aduisednes and consideration in their doings: but now, one will serue; that is to say, rashnes, where a mans will is as good as the greatest wisdome.

Prou.20.18. But *Salomon* bewraieth the shame of such, whē he saith: *Stablish thy thoughts by counsell, and by counsell make warre*; requiring aduisednes in all things. But they of whom I speake, who are as wise as *Micah*, may fitly be compared to a childe, who esteemeth more of a red apple then of pearle; and are like to *Eue*, who desired and chose the forbidden fruite, rather then heauen or paradise. But a word is enough to those who are wise.

Vers.10. As he was blame-worthie for his slightnes, so yet this must bee granted, that he gaue him (as the times then were) indifferent good consideration, he being so destitute as he was: as, meate, drinke and apparell, with some money (of a shekell yee haue heard before) meete enough for the priuate seruice he should do: so that yet he would not take the vantage of his want, and hire him for nothing. Therein he went before many of better religion, who are to prouide a Minister for the people, who could be content to haue one to doe the things required by the law, but themselues that hire them, (whether they be Ministers, or haue Impropriations, and must prouide one for the place) they (I say) little regard whom they put in, either his age, gifts, or gouernment, so he may be gotten cheape: but can be content to goe away with the profits themselues, and neuer blanke for it. A most wofull corruption, and to be much bewailed, being so generall, yea and the fault of them (as much as any) whom it least becommeth to defraud the Church. I am credibly informed, that some Colledges in the Vniuersities, as their leases come out, haue by decree among themselues, appoynted both better maintenance to their Curates, and also reserued to themselues (at euery vacancie) the election of their Ministers themselues, and haue accordingly furnished some of late with men of better desert, then before had the place. Which act as I mention to their commendation, so I desire both the continuance of it where it is begun, & that their example may be as seed cast into the earth, bringing foorth an hundred for one, by the imitation of all such as whom this care lieth vpon. But to leaue this, and to come to other abuses of like kinde, euen so it is in base seruices. Few are willing to giue the workman his due, and that which is answerable to his labour and trauaile, but can be content to haue it for little or nothing. Thus euen those seruants and poore artificers and labourers, that are willing to vphold their estate, and not become burthens to townes where they dwell, are impouerished, and the number of such increaseth who pay dearest for almost all commodities, and the rest are inriched. And to make an end of this matter, plaine, indifferent, and good couenants are in most dealings neglected, (though fewer euen of them are well kept and performed) whereby arise so many disagreements, suites and controuersies, (as we heare daily) to the disquieting and grieuing of almost infinite persons.

This superstitious man *Micah* said well (as hee thought) that hee would haue this Leuite for a father in his house to him and his: who yet hired him for idolatrous seruice, to the which the other was content to yeeld. Euen as many rash persons at this day, will giue the like termes of reuerence to godly Preachers, when they please them, like *Saul* to *Samuel*, chap. 15. and 1.Sam.15.13.
Ieboram to *Elisha*, [*My father, my father, &c.*] but neuer tooke a dramme of 2.King.6.21.
good by them, much lesse were euer, or euer sought to be gotten to God by them. And yet we know, there is a relation betweene the father and the childe. But these counterfeits are as soone weary of their great reuerencing of such, and the wise Minister lookes for no lesse, euen that their *Hosanna* should turne to a *Crucifie him:* for no violent thing is continuall. Againe, this agreement of these both herein sheweth this one thing; to wit, that there are numbers of men, who as long as they do any such seruice to God as others doe, they neither regard nor enquire how he requireth men to worship him, nor in what religion. An easie religion and soone learned, but a thing most lamentable: for seeing it is the solemnest and weightiest matter of all other, we should foreknow and be sure, that we please God therein, and not follow our blind fancie and corrupt minde in the worship that we offer him: as I haue sundrie times admonished in this booke. For thereby it commeth to passe, that it is with many in common, as it was with *Micah* in his house, that we count them for fathers to vs, who do but deceiue vs, as neither hauing in them skill nor will, or not both, to do vs any good. We should not rest altogether, no not vpon them who are meetest to be called fathers; for our Sauiour commandeth, *Call no man father on earth, one is your* Math.23.9.
father, &c. much lesse take them for such who are not. For it is a degree which euery Minister attaineth not vnto, to bee a father of the people, as the Apostle saith, that is, to beget them to God, and so to nourish & bring 1 Cor.4 15.
them vp to his seruice. And it is not common to see such as can wisely goe in and out before the people in example, ouersee them in the Lord, and protect them from danger, or by their experience, aduise, comfort, and resolue them in their doubts and particular cases, and compound their differences. But by this poynt (not to stand longer vpon it) let men learne the weight and necessitie of *trying all things, especially spirits,* whether they be of God or no: and not ascribe to euery idiote the honour of the chiefe workmen in Gods house: as many will ridiculously compare a most base fellow in the Ministerie (because he is in the place) with the best deseruing, though the vices in him be more eminent, then any good gift discernable. And hereby they puffe vp such (being spunges and bladders of themselues easi-

ly blowne vp) in a conceit of that which is not, as this Leuite also by the fondnes of *Micah* was: whereof more shall be said in the next Chapter, verse 4. in his boasting.

Vers. 11. 12. This hireling committed two great sinnes in this action of his agreeing to be with *Micah:* For (to say a little of him also, as I haue done of *Micah*) though hee were not so prouided for, yet hee must not change his religion for the feeding of himselfe, and the filling of his belly. And his sinne herein aggrauated highly, for that hee was a Leuite, whose office being to serue God about the Tabernacle, it was the more horrible for him to turne to a contrary worshipping of God, which in the people was most odious: whereas he should haue abhorred it rather, and cried out against it. The other sinne of his was, that being a Leuite he would vsurpe the Priests office also, as *Corah* did. Which how grieuous it was, may be gathered by the
Numb. 16. 9. words of *Moses* to him and his company. Thus he saith to them: Seemeth it a small matter vnto you, that the God of Israel hath separated you from the multitude of Israel, to take you neere to himselfe, to doe the seruice of the Tabernacle of the Lord, and to stand before the congregation, and to minister vnto them, but ye must take the office of the Priest also?

Doct. The example of this man setteth before our eyes the wofull condition of such as making profession to serue God, doe yet both vsurpe that which belongeth not to them, that is the Ministerie, for the which God hath not fitted them, or be content to fall to plaine Poperie for their bellies sake, so as they may get wealth and commoditie. Whereas all should magnifie and honour their profession, and be ashamed to bee found discreditors thereof by their conuersation. Much more we of the Ministerie. But it is apparant that for earthly benefit both the one and the other doe easily turne aside from a good conscience, as this hireling did. Oh necessitie is a strong cord, to draw men on to great offences, as shall bee further cleered in the next Chapter, verse 20.

Vers. 12. Againe, it is said, that *Micah* consecrated him to be a Priest, that is, filled his hand, as the Priests of the Lord, when they were ordained, offered something to the Lord, which was called a filling of their hands. And so *Moses*, when he consecrated *Aaron* and his sonnes, put in their hands the breast or shoulder of the beast, or some other thing that was to be offered. But what authoritie had this Idolater to doe so to him, but onely that he did apishly imitate *Moses* in this; as in many other points, both hee and other Idolaters did? And the other was proud of his preferment, little considering that he vsurped, as *Corah* did, (who was swallowed vp of the earth for it) but glorying thereof.

Doct. This act of *Micah* doth condemne the doings of al those to be like odious, the which are done by apish imitation of God, or his good seruants, when they haue not onely no commandement to follow them, but rather the things they doe are contrary to Gods word. Of the first sort are the obseruing of the Iewish ceremonies at this day, because they were vsed before Christ, for a season, and that by Gods commandement. But their date being expired, the Papists which do thus retaine them in vse, shew themselues not onely ridiculous, but also blasphemously to challenge the place of God, by taking to themselues authoritie to make lawes to binde the conscience.

To

To these may be added such as make allegories of the Scriptures,because God doth so: and to imitate Christ in his fortie daies fast, by abstaining so long from the eating of flesh,whereas they are not to follow him in his miraculous workes,any more then in the workes of our redemption,but onely in his morall duties. Of the second sort are the doings of such, as follow the examples of Gods seruants,in things which they did by a personall and peculiar commandement, which they in obeying did serue God, but other following them therein without a commandement, doe sinne. Therefore wel said the Apostle,Be ye followers of me,as I follow Christ,that is,where 1.Cor.11.1.
ye haue a commandement,as I haue. To these may bee added such as say, Why should we not haue reuelations,and visions,and do miracles,because the Apostles had and did so? But of the abuse of examples in Scripture, how diuersly men corrupt them, I haue distinctly spoken before,in his due place.

Now in that it is said,that the hireling dwelt with him, and was glad of 2
the promotion,it is no marueile. For who is not so, that being vnworthie of preferment,is yet aduanced to it? For such being vnmeete for it,and hauing as little minde to vse it well, they must needs be ioyfull when any such thing befalleth them. Whereas they who haue a dutie laid vpon them,with a commoditie,and make conscience to discharge it,they fearing much their owne vnfitnes to doe the duty,and their vnworthines to be made partakers of the benefit that goeth with it; their light and carnall ioy for the commoditie is much abated; and they reioyce most in the desire they haue to doe their dutie. But they that look for nothing but the satisfying of themselues, and to liue pleasantly, or most chiefly that they, with this Leuite,are lifted vp,when liuing and commoditie come in, for that is all they looke for, and their very felicitie. More of this poynt let the reader see in the next Chapter,verse 20.by the like occasion.

Now in the shutting vp,the holy story tels vs, how well this *Micah* the Vers.13.
Idolater pleased himselfe,when hee had thus brought his matters to passe. He saith,that now he knoweth that God will doe him good, and prosper him,for that he had got a Leuite to be his Priest. A speech at the least of an ignorant and superstitious person. For a wise man knoweth,that prosperitie is no token of happinesse,and that he blessed himselfe for that which he had cause to bewaile. But now hee thought he should haue many come to his idolatrous seruice,and he should haue benefit by their oblations and sacrifices,besides the credit he expected, and contentment he presently tooke in this his deuice. Out of this,let vs(for conclusion of the Chapter)obserue a double instruction, neere bordering each vpon the other. The one from the matter of his exultation,the other his blessing himselfe thereupon. For the former of these,the matter was, now he had a Leuite to his Priest: that is,he had his wish, the world went well on his side. True it was indeed, he was hit pat in the hand now in that it fell out that a Leuite wanted a seruice, and his seruice wanted a Leuite,and both met together to make a bargaine. A man would say,If hee had made a deuout prayer to God for some good thing,hee could not haue been so fitted,not better at least. So wee noted of *Abimelech* his successe against *Schechem*: and againe,the Philistims against *Samson*,and like to both was the hap of *Iudah* in his meeting of an harlot,

Gehazi

Gehazi his treasuring vp his bootie, *Hamans* speede against his enemies. These all shew, that God giues bad men their hearts desire in many euil purposes they enterprise. Not al I confesse, for then who should liue with them: but some, to the end he may the speedilier bring them to shame and punishment. For as the Quailes were the destruction of them that murmured for them till they had them: so commonly the wicked mans fall is neerest, when he hath his will most: for like a brute beast hee then is readiest to surfeit to death: when he is fullest, he is neerest bursting. Witnesse the examples forementioned. The godly are stopt and ioynted as often: which for the present is harsh to them, if they might carue for themselues, but in time they see there was more wisedome in him that crossed them, then in the eager pursuit of their desires, either bad, or badly followed. But of this elsewhere distinctly.

To returne and conclude this first point, (for I haue toucht it often) let it be no fleshing to bad men when their euill causes, no nor when their lawfull businesse take good effect, themselues being out of Gods fauour. For God who denieth many things to his in mercie, laugheth and bestoweth vpon his foes in reuenge. His gifts to them are snares, which cause them to fall into vtter ruine. And whereas the foolish world is so set vpon wishes and foolish desires: as the angry man, that he had his lust vpon his enemie: the couetous, that he had the wealth of such and such a great person: the ambitious and voluptuous, that their sensualitie might bee satisfied, &c. let them from hence learne, if God serue their turne, there is cause they should tremble (if they had feeling) to consider how speedie their decay and desolation is: seeing now their turne being serued, they doubt not but their case is good, and therfore they resolue to abide still in their stale course wherein they are setled. But if God turne their iollitie and triumph into sorrow, by making them to find no sweetnes in their great successe, (as they
1.Sam.8.14. who would needs haue a King, and had him, but vpon hard conditions) or if he crosse them altogether, so that they prosper not, as *Ahab* in his going to take possession, if either the Lord stop their course by terrors of his word, or by countermining them in their bad designes, as *Paul* at Damascus gates, let them not rage and raile that they are preuented, but say, It is a faire warning for them, let them desist while they are well, and not kicke against the prickes, lest God giue them ouer on plaine ground, and striue no more with them, but giue them ouer to their will, and to their woe all at once. And let the people of God, when they see the bad carrie the world thus in a string,
Psal.73.2. bewray that they stumble not with *Dauid*: or if they doe yet recouer themselues with him, and say; Oh, how are they (in the middest of all) suddenly and horribly consumed! Psalme 73. whereas their priuiledge is great, who may aske and haue whatsoeuer they desire at the hands of God in the name of Christ, without any such feare of an ill farewell, or token of displeasure.

2 But I haste to an end: now come wee to the second point, the fruite of this his good hap. *Now I know the Lord loueth me*, saith *Micah*, *seeing hee hath giuen me a Leuite to be my Priest*. Thus wee see how men blesse themselues in that which God curseth, and for which they ought iustly to bee humbled: as if a deuout Papist should say thus, for that he hath got a Popish Priest to

shriue

ſhriue him. The reaſon is, they cannot ſee cleerely into things: but when they can ſerue God in that eaſie and fleſhly manner that they deſire, and then may alſo thriue in the world,oh they count that they attaine to a peece of paradiſe: and yet the Lord denieth them not farre greater bleſſing, if they would ſerue him better. Thus the ſuperſtitious pleaſe themſelues in their blindnes,and in their muttering of certaine words,(which they count prayers) as the *Creede,* their *Aue Marie,* and their Commandements,with the Lords Prayer in an vnknowne tongue; and in croſſing themſelues. In this error liue the Papiſts like the Phariſies,and many ignorant ones among vs: yea their beſt learned,who approue the truth of their hereſies, becauſe God hath giuen them earthly proſperitie. The which cannot be remedied without a ſound Miniſterie, with a ſpeciall bleſſing of God vpon the ſame vnto the effecting thereof: which is the right way to redreſſe all other diſeaſes. But they onely may reioyce aright,who can ſay,they reioyce in him, and hee who can truly ſay, The Lord loueth me, for hee hath changed my heart,he vpholdeth me in my integritie: and they who in ſtead of all ſuperſtition and other deluſions, know themſelues to bee truly reconciled to God,and that their names are written in heauen; and count his ſeruice daily,to be perfit freedome,labouring for a good conſcience in all things. But enough of theſe points, ſeeing they are mutually infolded each in other. Thus wee haue heard of theſe two,to wit, *Micah* and his Prieſt, like maſter, like ſeruant, a hard thing to ſay whether of the two was the better man. And thus much of the bringing of Idolatrie into a priuate houſe,till wee heare more in the next Chapter what came thereof.

Philip.4.4.

Pſal.41.12. Luk.10.20. 2.Cor.1.12.

The end of the 17. Chapter.

THE

THE NINETIE TWO SERMON, ON THE XVIII. CHAPTER OF THE BOOKE OF IVDGES.

Verſ. 1. *In thoſe daies there was no King in Iſrael, and at the ſame time the tribe of Dan ſought them an inheritance to dwell in: for vnto that time, all their inheritance had not fallen vnto them among the tribes of Iſrael.*

2. *Therfore the children of Dan ſent of their family, fiue men out of their coaſts, euen men expert in warre, out of Zorah and Eſhtaol, to view the land, and ſearch it out, and ſaid vnto them, Goe and ſearch out the land: Then they came to mount Ephraim, to the houſe of Micah, and lodged there.*

3. *When they were in the houſe of Micah, they knew the voyce of the young man the Leuite; and being turned in thither, they ſaid vnto him, Who brought thee hither, or what makeſt thou in this place? and what haſt thou to doe here.*

4. *And he anſwered them, Thus and thus dealeth Micah with me, and hath hired me, and I am his Prieſt.*

5. *Againe they ſaid vnto him, Aske counſell now of God, that we may know whether the way which we goe, ſhall be proſperous.*

6. *And the Prieſt ſaid vnto them, Goe in peace: for the Lord guideth your way which you goe.*

7. *Then the fiue men departed and came to Laiſh, and ſaw the people that were therein, which dwelt careleſſe, after the manner of the Zidonians, quiet and ſure, becauſe no man made any trouble in the land, or vſurped any dominion: alſo they were farre from the Zidonians, and had no buſineſſe with other men.*

The ſumme of the Chapter.

THE holy Ghoſt hath ſhewed in the former Chapter, as we haue heard, how Idolatrie was brought into a priuate houſe. In this he ſheweth how it came into a whole citie and tribe. For it was ſet vp by the tribe of *Dan*, in the place that they went to dwell in, (to wit) Laiſh. And more particularly in this Chapter is ſhewed how the children of *Dan* hauing their inheritance too ſmall for them, ſought to inlarge it, and ſent to Laiſh to view it, and vnderſtanding by thoſe whom they ſent, the ſtate of the place, thither came ſixe hundred of them with their children, cattell, and ſubſtance, and tooke and poſſeſſed the place, and then brought in Idolatrie, and ſet it vp there. And firſt the holy Ghoſt ſhewes the cauſe of this great wickedneſſe, as hee had done in the former Chapter, ſpeaking of the like matter. And the cauſe is alleaged to be this in both places, namely, that there was then no ordinary Magiſtrate in the land of Iſrael, to hold downe ſuch wickedueſſe. But yet the holy ſtorie begins not this Chapter with their euill facts in particular, and their ſetting vp of Idolatrie; theſe (I ſay)

ſay) are not ſpoken of here in the beginning of this chapter, but firſt of all, the occaſion thereof is largely ſet down, (to wit) this: that the Danites ſent certaine men to goe ſee and view the place that they ſhould dwell in: (for vntill that time they were vnprouided of a conuenient dwelling) and theſe lodging at mount Ephraim as they went on in their way, carried with them *Michas* Prieſt, with his Idolatrous furniture, which they tooke by violence out of *Michas* houſe, and went on their way; and being once ſetled in the place they went to, they erected Idolatrie there. This for the ſumme of the Chapter.

The parts of it are foure. The firſt, the children of *Dan* ſend men to ſearch the land: to verſe 11. The ſecond, the ſixe hundred who were ſent, robbed *Micha*: to the 27. verſe. The third, they deſtroy Laiſh, and build it againe; to verſe 30. And laſtly, they ſet vp Idolatrie there: and this to the end of the Chapter. *The parts of the Chapter foure.*

Of the great benefit of ſetled gouernment and Magiſtracie, and of the diſcommoditie by the want thereof, (which the firſt verſe giueth occaſion to ſpeake of) I haue ſaid that which I thought meete, more then once vpon the like words. I will therefore paſſe from this, to that which followes in this firſt part of the Chapter, and begin with this firſt verſe. It is ſaid heere therefore that the tribe of *Dan* not hauing roome enough to dwell in, (for we heard in the firſt Chapter of this booke, that they were pent in on the mountaines, and could haue no place in the valleys) a little after the death of *Ioſhua*; they now (I ſay) ſought to inlarge their bounds, where they had been aſſigned them, but were withholden from them till now; partly by their owne ſinne, in that they did not goe about to expell the Ammorites, but ſuffered them to waxe ſtrong; and partly by the negligence and ſloth of their brethren, who would not helpe them. And this ſeeking of a place by theſe men of *Dan*, a little after *Ioſhuas* death, doth proue that the acts of theſe fiue chapters are to be referred to thoſe times, as I haue ſaid in the former chapter. They therefore wanting dwelling roome, ſent certaine to the place firſt, to ſee how they might in the beſt manner come by and enioy it, who in their trauaile, as it lay in their way, came to mount Ephraim where the houſe of *Micha* was, and lodged there. *Verſ. 1.* *The ſumme of verſe 1. & 2.*

Though the Danites had been long without ſufficient roome to abide in, yet they did well now in ſeeking out the reſt of their inheritance to dwell in, (for ſince the diuiſion of the land to that day, which was another generation after well nigh) they enioyed it not wholly, they did now therefore as became them, to wit, ſeeke to recouer that which belonged to them by Gods appointment. Their practiſe is our inſtruction. For we ought not to be ignorant of this, that the Lord doth allow, that men ſhould ſeeke for neceſſary things to this preſent life, and haue a care to prouide for their owne, by the lawfull meanes that he hath appointed, & following of their calling. It is no matter of ill report to doe ſo, but rather the part of an Infidell to do otherwiſe. And one way to do this, is to ſeeke, and deſire by lawfull meanes to enioy their owne, euen that which falleth to their portion and lot howſoeuer, as occaſion ſhall be offered, as theſe Danites did. And in like manner it is as lawfull for them by diligent labour, wiſe prouidence, and honeſt frugalitie to labour to encreaſe the ſame, and liue of it. And this I vtter the *Doct. verſ. 1.* *1. Tim. 5. 8.*

plainlier and more fully, that men may know their liberty which God hath giuen them in this behalfe, and that they may not thinke it to be worldlines when they walke in their callings, seeing it is a duty rather inioyned them of God to doe so, onely let them see, that they be well gouerned in the executing of the same. And therefore it argueth great ignorance in some, or a worse thing, that if any trouble befall them, they impute it to their calling, and thereupon begin to thinke it vnlawful, and seeke to leaue and goe from it. But while this is allowed and iustified, which I haue spoken of, to wit, that men may and should liue of their owne, and follow their vocation, I must not forget, nor omit to shew how this liberty is abused of many, for which cause I gaue that watch-word of well vsing it in the last sentence but one. I say not of the common sort, who vse nothing well, but euen of those who professe to doe well: for through greedines of commodity they so easily fall to offend God, and that many wayes, in vsing the world, that they
Note. are hardly good husbands, but they waxe worldly minded, and too apparently shew themselues such, to the offence of others, as well as to their owne hinderance, so that they rarely prooue good Christians also.

Of this there is great cause why we should be put in minde while we are occupied here below; howsoeuer we couer our doings with this pretence, that the things which we be occupied about, be lawfull. For commodity hath such force to worke vpon our corrupt nature, that when there is any hope of comming by it, we runne headlong after it: and so forget our selues, that if we neglect not, or lay aside prayer and other good exercise all together, yet we shall be in danger to choake them so, that they shall not
Note. bring forth fruite in vs, to any purpose; as innocency, humility, sincerity, loue, patience, and the like; and thereby, great question may bee made whether we haue any faith and sound heartednes in vs or no.

Few are found who so wisely behaue themselues, that while they be oc-
Luk. 10. 42. cupied about many things, yet one thing is counted necessary of them, yea
Note. very few that goe about their worldly affaires with holy & pure mindes, neither wronging and hurting other, nor impairing their owne grace; but shewing by their dealings that their conuersation is in heauen, though
Phil. 3. 20. they be on the earth. And yet this which I say, iustifieth not the idle, ill husbands, and runneawayes from their wiues, with rogues, and the sluggards that *Salomon* speaketh of, for they, I say, offend and sinne in another extre-
2. Thes. 3. 10. mity; and therefore according to the Apostles rule, they not labouring, should not eate nor be maintained. But to leaue these, and returne to the other, if such men cannot keepe their conuersation honest and good, betwixt worldlines and idlenes, while they be free from sicknes and great affliction, how shall they be able patiently to beare and goe vnder that, when it commeth? That which I haue spoke of diligence in our callings, and of an honest desire of enlarging our estate and ability thereby, especially where charge encreaseth, and the prices of commodities are so enhaunsed, that the ordinary and former expences of family and other matters will not serue the turne: Of both these I say, I will something more fully speake. I say therefore, that it is a more elegible course of life, for a man to be so busied; then either to auoide the world vnder colour of deuotion (as the olde Monkes, more deuout then discreet, were wont to pretend or doe,) or to

incurre

incurre the contrary idlenes and vnprofitablenes, (the companions whereof commonly are vncleannes, riot, lewd companionship) to the shunning whereof, the walking in our vocation was, among other endes, first ordained. This indeede I confesse, that the malice and cunning of the Diuell is such, as that he can as well make our imployment and diligence in action become a snare vnto vs, as vacancy and sluggishnes. For if a man be busie in his minde how to serue Gods prouidence in the increasing his estate, (though both his intention bee religious and his action limited within boundes of iustice towards others, without shifting, rapine, fraude and oppression) it is tenne to one if the diuell winde not so within that man, that he shall offend against the rule of sobriety. So that either the sweetnes of the world following his hand shall breede an hearty loue of it, in him: or the ill successe in attaining, or in spending, and keeping shall be a vexation vnto him. And whether of these two snares (thinke we) are more perilous? For the former, it commonly causeth immoderatenes in the minde, and lesse priceing of things farre more excellent, and (ere it be espied) through a defect in meanes vsing with feruency) a sensible death and decay of some graces, and a cooling and declining of such as remaine. And a tying of God to his one and the same strict course of dealing, in the measuring and dealing out of his blessing, euen as the party appoints and sets him downe how, and an expectation of the same successe at one time as another. The latter, vsually is ioyned with a resisting of God; as sometimes a rash change of the calling, borrowing other mens goods vpon promise of large recompence, which is not in their power to performe, and an endlesse pursuit of that which flieth away as fast, be it pleasure, or profit; beside affliction of minde; and at length defrauding of others, and vtter ruine to themselues that caused it. Therefore let that golden meteyard of mediocrity be here imbraced in the sober vse of our liberty: which standeth in this, that as we shunne not action, I meane labour, through any colour; so yet we neuer approue our selues in such kinde of action, as depriueth the spirit of religious action, or the person from outward fruitfulnes of duty in both Tables. Againe, that at our entrance into this busines we couenant with the Lord, that neither gaine nor losse shall empeach our sobriety in the one, or contentation in the other.

Now to passe to the second verse, their sending certaine strong men, to Vers.2.
see how they might in best manner, and with least danger (for a few might goe without suspition) take and possesse the place that they sought, rather then rashly goe about it, especially they hauing so many enemies on euery side of them; this dealing of theirs, I say, doth commend to vs their wisedome in that they did so: yea though it was a portion allotted them by God, yet it behoued them to serue his prouidence, for the comming by and Doct.vers 2.
inioying it, in the wisest manner that they could goe about it. And from hence we should take instruction against not onely indiscreet dealing in enterprising religious actions, but also rash and vnaduised going about our owne matters. As if we haue right to any thing, and yet it requires care and prouidence to compasse it, or if we haue likeliehood thereof onely, or whatsoeuer honest thing we attempt; herein I say, we are not to runne forward with open crie as it were: (It is mine, I will haue it, whatsoeuer it cost

me:) but consideration is to be had, and aduice to be taken, (as need shall be) how we goe about the busines. And the like is to be said in our aduising of other; as *Salomon* gaue example betwixt the two harlots, and *Ioseph* to *Pharao* about sauing and reseruing of corne: for besides that rashnes doth nothing well, wee know, that we bring many troubles vpon our selues thereby, which by circumspect and wise dealing might haue beene preuented and auoyded. And yet if troubles come, notwithstanding all our care and diligence vsing; yet we may rest quiet, seeing we know that wee haue not been vnaduised, but haue laboured to doe our duties with a good conscience. When *Samuel* told the people that they should not aske themselues a King, if they had hearkened to him, it had gone well with them; but they were so set to desire one, nothing well considering what they did, that they answered nay; but we will haue a King to raigne ouer vs, as other nations haue: behold therefore how they thriued in their so doing, for God sent a sore tempest, and cast great feare vpon them thereby: as is to be seene in the 12. Chapter.

1.King.3.27. Gen.41.33. 1.Sam.8.19. 1.Sam.12.18.

And if in one thing, rashnes and wilfulnes may hurt so grieuously, (as in many examples and daily experience is seene and may bee shewed) what may be looked for in many such actions through our liues which are accompanied with them? For thereby manifold vexations doe needlessely and without cause continually oppresse and disquiet men. And is it any marueile? for when they will none of Gods counsell and direction, (as he willeth, saying: Establish thy thoughts by counsell, &c.) but will follow their owne mindes, and rashly runne on in their bad courses, (God foretelling them the danger) is it not good reason that they should smart? But of this often, in the example of *Iuda* and *Simeon*, in the practise of *Iael, Gedeon* and his seruant, *Iephte* in his embassage to the King of Ammon, and through the history of this booke.

Prou.20.18.

It is said further, that the fiue men that were sent forth, came to mount Ephraim, where *Micahs* house was, and lodged there, most likely with him, or at least, the place being well neighbored, as appeares by the story, their way lying by that place; A great fauour of God it is (as it was to them) so now to vs (though little considered) that whē men must trauaile from their owne houses (which of necessity doth oft fall out to the most) that they may rest safely and without danger in their trauaile by the way. For who doth not know (as it fell out to the Leuit and his concubine in the next Chapter, by the wicked men of *Gibea*) what fearefull robberies and murthers haue bin committed, both by lewd and dangerous persons in the open high wayes, and also by such as haue receiued men into their houses to lodge, who comming thither in their innocency, and hoping to finde safetie and protection from euill there; haue bin sore endangered and disquieted, if not spoyled also of their goods, and murthered? For there is much falsehood in many strangers, it being so common, (with great griefe I vtter it) euen among those who are familiar with vs. Great cause there is therefore, seeing choice may be made of their lodgings and resting places, why especiall care ought to be had by trauailers, where they lodge, and rest, and by Magistrates, whom they giue authority vnto of receiuing strangers into their houses, as their guests; not onely for the auoyding of the fore-

Doct.2.vers.2. Iudg.19.25.

forenamed spoiles and murders, but also of other disorders, as moderate drinkings, drunkennes, gamings, riot, whoring, and the like.

But to returne to the fiue men of *Dan*, which are here mentioned, and Vers.3.
are said to haue lodged there, because the other sixe hundred men of *Dan* by their meanes, committed a shamefull and great trespasse; of the which a fitter occasion shall be offered to speake afterwards. In the meane while, (I say) to returne to them, I will shew what fell out in that place, when the men were come thither, which is set downe in the foure next verses following. And that was in effect this, they knowing the yong man, (like enough by this language) that he was a stranger there, for though the Hebrewes spake all one tongue, yet they had diuers idiomes or manners of pronouncing their words, as we heard by the Ephramites: they questioned with him Chap.12.6.
about the cause of his comming thither, and when they knew by his relation that he was a priest, they asked of him, if their iourney should bee prosperous, and he tooke vpon him to answere them, that it should.

Out of this story let vs obserue as followeth: and first by these dainties Doct. vers.3.
seeking acquaintance with this Idolatrous Leuit, either by lying at the house of *Micha*, or being there in his company, we see what euill came of it, both now in mouing him to aske counsell for them, and in their returne thither afterward. This should teach vs a good point of wisedome and warines, how farre and to what end we seeke acquaintance with strangers, or ouer neere familiarity with neighbours; as we may here see good cause of this watch-word, for though many grow soone familiar together; (and oft times, as soone repent it,) yet *Salomon*, well experienced, hath taught vs, if Prou.14.7.
we see that there bee not in a man so much as any sauour in good things to like and allow them, but much more if swinish reiecting or doggish contempt of them, as partly by his words wee may perceiue, if wee obserue them, and partly by his doings, we should then seeke no further fellowship with such a man.

It is, I confesse, our duty to auoid morosity and austerity of behauiour, which argueth either vnnaturalnes in vs, or that we thinke fewe worthy of our acquaintance, through too high imagination and conceit of our selfe sufficiency. It becommeth vs rather to be harmelesse and vnoffensiue to all, euen in that respect, and to yeeld and giue them their due in curtesie, or reuerence, as their state requireth, and as occasion is offered, though they bee bad. And this is enough for vs towards all in generall: but if we haue dealings with them afterwards in any ciuil case, then it behoueth vs to proceed with them according to equity, without neerer familiarity, except they be such as we may doe good to, or take good by. For what commeth of that fellowship betwixt men where one of these two be wanting? they being euer in extreamities; or ready by the least occasion to offend, and that ma- Note.
ny wayes in their conuersing together with vs. For sometimes they are too merry, vaine, and light, and so commit much sinne that way; or at other times in contention & strife one with the other, or exasperated against each other; and what mischiefe and euill is wrought betwixt, and among such, the whole world well nigh is a witnes. Beside this, in many other respects also, as of the idle and needles expence of time, (if not hurtfull and dangerous) and of their substance and goods, another fruite of needles and hasty

acquaintance. All of these in respect (I say) being duely considered, who doth not see, that it had been much better their familiarity had neuer been begun, but that they had in stead thereof, attended and followed their calling? But if the acquaintantance of men may bee to good end and vse, as *Dauids* and *Ionathans* was, so that they may both be like minded in good things, or well inclining thereto, one sharpening the others edge, then let them as they may conueniently, haue acquaintance together: but so, as they intend and purpose with consent, that their fellowship may be to this end, euen to helpe and further one another in know-
Hebr. 10.24. ledge, and the practise thereof, prouoking one another to loue and to good workes, and so that their loue tend to this end, that they may thereby become better Christians: and with this, let them aduise one another, as they bee able, about their outward estate, to follow their particular calling with diligence and prouidence: and if they haue any earthly dealings together, (for who are fitter then such to contract and haue dea-
Note. lings together?) let them in all plainnesse without dissembling, and voide of selfeloue, as they can, shew their innocencie and good dealing: and take heede that the desire of priuate profit, or conceitednes and secret grudges make not a breach of loue, and so worke a decay of their grieuous fellowship betwixt them. But oh, it is to be lamented, how few there be, who are meet couples to associate and linke themselues together in such fellowship. One of the Heathens speaking of this, complained that few were fit for a vertuous person to be inward withall, and therefore concludeth that of the common sort of people; Few are enough, one is enough, none is enough. And though it were a shame that it should be so among vs who are Christians, enlightened with knowledge of the word: yet a wise man marking on the one side the frothie, vaine, iangling and prophane acquaintances of the baser sort, whom a pot of beere in an Alehouse, or a booth in a Faire,
A simil. makes acquainted, (who like the ditch in a sudden raine soone filled and soone empty, are as easily diuided asunder) and obseruing on the other side,
Note. how short, slight, and vntempered the acquaintances of the better sort are, (who yet haue so excellent meanes of entring and maintaining the same) I say a wise man noting both these, might wonder not a little, and resolue, either to liue more retired and priuate to himselfe, or else determine to ground and maintaine the fellowship which he must haue, vpon other maner of termes and with more carefulnes, then the most familiarities euen among them that goe for Christians, are vpholden by. Wee haue heard of the Danites seeking acquaintance ouer hastily with the new made Priest: now see we how it was accepted.

Vers. 4. This hireling in *Micahs* house, as desirous to haue them to heare of his promotion (as he counted it) as they were rash and hastie to enquire of him, was as ready to take acquaintance of them: and shewing himselfe as wise as they, and tels the men readily, what he was, and how *Micha* dealt and agreed with him, and that he had hired him to bee his Priest. And thus speaking to them, he shewes how glad he was to tell out his prosperity, such as it was, (to be sure, it was great in his owne eyes, he remembring how lately he came from beggers state, and very nothing:) hee thought it therefore great credit to tell them of his promotion, whereas (if he had bin wise) he would haue

haue been ashamed,being a Leuite,to be knowne to be an Idolater, & therfore would rather haue said nothing. For if a foole (as *Salomon* saith) while he holdeth his peace,is wise (noting it to be a point of wisedome to keepe silence,when there is no cause to speake) then on the contrary, he sheweth his follie, who vttereth that which should bee concealed and is his owne shame. Prou 17.28.

But by his vanting and foolish words we may see,how vainglorious wee are,and desirous to be taken and accounted of in the world for such as bee of worth, and that it should be knowne to the vttermost what wee are, and wee sticke not to say, wee would men should know that wee are not of the meanest: whereas it falleth out oft times,that we repent such folly,and wish such words in againe when it is too late. The like we see S. *Iude* to obserue in those false teachers, that they speake swelling words and proud things. And S. *Luke* describing *Simon Magus*, Acts 8. saith of him that hee deluded them of Samaria by his inchantments,saying of himselfe,that he was some great man. But if we desire to haue our vertues knowne,let our practise shew our godly conuersation in meeknes of wisedome, as S. *Iames* speaketh: and let our patient mindes,and our profiting in other fruits of the spirit,be knowne to all men: howsoeuer let vs not seeke a name by talke and vaine florishes to be better thought of then we giue cause, which of all things the Apostle *Paul* abhorred, saying: that hee would haue none thinke of him aboue that which he seeth me to be,or that he heareth of me: but be we indeed good, rather then seeke to be so accounted, seeing that which is to bee desired of a man is his goodnes. *Doct.* Iude 16. Acts 8.9. Iam.3.13. 1.Tim.4.15. 2.Chron.12.6. Prou.19.22.

My meaning is not,by condemning this vanitie in the light headed and vndeseruing, (for commonly the vessell is emptiest where the sound is greatest) to iustifie that inward and seated pride,that is in others more close and secret, though they haue somewhat to commend them aboue their fellowes. That vice (somewhat distinct from this, for euery proud person is not by and by a vaine boaster) other occasions shall be offered to vnmaske and disgrace. But for the other, what is it but the rawnes and frothie superfluitie of an indigested and vnsetled minde? Of the which I will say more, God willing, in the next Sermon.

THE NINETIE THREE SERMON, ON THE XVIII. CHAPTER OF THE BOOKE OF IVDGES.

Verſ.4. TO goe forward where I left, in verſe 4, with them that loue to ſet out their folly in ſhewing their greatneſſe (as this fooliſh Prieſt before mentioned, did) by their birth, wealth, learning, and friends that they haue, they ſhew themſelues little wiſer then children; who through want of wit, doe breake out and talke of euery trifle, and tell their fellowes how farre they come ſhort of them. And who laugheth not in his ſleeue at ſo palpable a folly and weaknes in them? yea (and as men vſe to doe with Naturals, (though I commend it not) to bring them into a fooles paradiſe, that they may make themſelues ſport in making them ridiculous: ſo doe many, when they light vpon ſuch vnwiſe perſons, make a paſtime of ſoothing thẽ vp in their humour, that when they haue made thẽ drunken with their owne imagined praiſe, they may laugh at their nakedneſſe and folly.
Iudg.9.38. So that ſubtile *Zebul* did with that vainglorious boaſter, and fetherie *Gaal*, Iudg.9, when he had him in his vaine: whereas rather ſuch fooles ſhould be checkt and taken downe; there being no way to keepe the wilde figge tree from mounting ouer the wall, and ſhewing it ſelfe, but cutting and holding ſhort. In deed if there could be place for wiſedome, where folly hath taken vp the roome, thoſe that commend thẽmſelues for ſuch completnes, ſhould be aſhamed to be ſo blind as not to ſee others make them laughing ſtockes for their folly: and ſo take vp themſelues for halting, when the creeple begins to deride them.

If we ſeeke to be commended for our wealth, promotion, perſon, and ſuch like, what is more vaine? They are changeable commodities, and vaniſh in a ſhort time. And as in ſetting foorth our ſelues in and for thoſe
Note. things which are not ours, we robbe God of his honour, whoſe ſuch gifts are: ſo therein, to thoſe that are wiſe, we bewray our owne folly. And as by
Prou.25 27. ſeeking glorie that way, we goe without it: (for the ſeeking of glorie is no glorie) ſo the gaine we ſhall haue thereby is this, the more we ſet by it, the greater our vexation ſhall be, when we forgoe it. Of this boaſting humour enough hath been ſaid of *Gaal*, chap.9. in the ſtorie of *Abimelech*.

Verſ.5. But I proceed in the ſtorie. Theſe men of *Dan* vnderſtanding that he was a Prieſt, by and by aske counſell of him. Here we may ſee in them one fruite of fooliſh and needleſſe acquaintance, that one oft draweth another thereby to great ſinne and wickednes. The men who were ſent were valiant and ſtrong, and fit for that they were ſent about: but in this they ſhewed themſelues to be without all ſauour of godly wiſedome, who being not the

the meaneſt of a tribe in Iſrael, were ſo ſoone moued to aske counſell of a vainglorious hireling, yea, an Idolater: before they knew him better, or to haue any thing in him worthie ſuch a calling, and by attributing ſo much vnto him, they cauſed him to thinke highly of himſelfe, and that hee had that which he had not. For he tooke vpon him by and by to anſwere them, as though he had conſulted with God, and had bin one indeed whom God had ſet in the place and reuealed his will vnto him: And ſo one of them drew the other to great ſinne. But what infinite euill commeth of haſty and raſh acquaintance ſeeking and taking, rather then any good, for the moſt part, I haue ſaid already in the third verſe: ſutable whereto is that which hath been at large ſaid of ſomewhat neerer acquaintance between the men of *Sechem* and *Abimilech*, chap. 9.

But this further laieth out the wickedneſſe of thoſe times, that theſe fiue men choſen out of the whole ſixe hundred of the men of *Dan*, for their wiſdome and fitneſſe to be ſent about ſuch buſineſſe, and therefore ſuch as had been like (ſome of them at the leaſt) to haue found out and diſcerned this Leuit hired to be an Idolatrous Prieſt in a priuate familie; yet none of them could ſee any thing blame worthie in him, to admoniſh and tell him of, but rather approued him in his euill courſe, and therefore were as bad as hee. This is lamentable (I ſay) and ſhewes that the corruption of thoſe times did not reſt in a narrow roome, but ſpred farre into diuers tribes, and that in few yeeres after the good gouernours, who liued awhile before, ſo that few were to be found, not infected with the common diſeaſe. And by this we may obſerue when diuers perſons dwelling farre off, ſhall meete, as theſe did, and communicate the euill and vnſauourines that is in them, one to an other, corrupting one another with their profane tongues, as with ſtinking breath, the one no way fit, nor able to vtter a good word to the other, but ſhew themſelues vaine, looſe, profane, (as little other is to be ſeene among the moſt) oh how doth it bewray the times to be euill and wretched? Such grow ſoone acquainted being of like qualities and conditions. And little better is to be found in moſt countries: whereby it may (and that not hardly) be gathered, into what a narrow roome religion and goodnes is driuen. The Prophet *Eſay* ſeeking to bring many vnto eternall life, found them almoſt all vnfit to be ſpoke to, and deuoted another way. And our Sauiour preaching to many, in ſorting them out, concluded that three ſorts of foure, were euill. See chapter the firſt in the deſcription of the generall negligence of the tribes, where the vſe of this is propounded. 2

Note. Eſay 55.1. Mat. 13.19, 20.

But further we may learne here, in this that theſe men did require of the Leuite to aske counſell for them of God, that they knew it was the manner in Iſrael to doe ſo. And they better knowing that it was a cuſtome there to goe in their doubtfull caſes vnto the Prieſt, then how to vſe that libertie, yea commandement aright, and as they ought to haue done; giue vs to learne theſe two things. One, that it is a point of great ignorance and irreligiouſnes, when we be at a ſet, in doubts and difficulties (about matters of conſcience I meane) not knowing what to doe, and yet wee haue not learned to ſeeke to God for reſolution thereof: for though we haue not now any high Prieſt to aske counſel for vs in that manner, as the people of Iſrael then had, yet wee haue the Scriptures to ſhew vs the minde and will of God in all 3

Iohn 5.39.

things

things that concerne vs, and are willed by our Lord Iesus to search them; and if we say, we cannot finde out the resolution of our doubts, and direction fit for vs, why doe we not goe to the men and brethren and aske them? Touching which point at large hath been spoken both in the first chapter, verse the first, and in the storie of *Iphtas* daughter. But as there are some who
Act. 2. 37. make no question in any thing, but through neglect, or through boldnesse, either smother and conceale their doubts, till they vanish, to their greater hurt, or rush through boldly till their consciences cause them to blush, (at least till their shame breake forth openly) so there are other as wise as these
Note. Danites, who will enquire indeed, but without regard whom they aske counsell of, and therefore are neuer the neere, who looke at no other thing but that it may be to them as they desire, and would haue it. Whereas wee know there is great oddes in Counsellers, according to that of *Iob*; that he
Iob 33. 23. who can declare to a man his reconciliation, is no common man, but one of a thousand. And it is as if he had said, In the terrors of conscience or the agonie of temptation, there had need be great choice of men, whom a man would open his minde vnto. For not one of many hath knowledge, experience or tendernes, loue, discretion, and discretion enough in such a case to relieue the distressed. God hath taken order in deed, that in euery Congregation there should be a man in stead of the high Priest, able to teach and resolue doubts from the words of the Law and the Gospell: but the sinne of men hauing violated this prouision and ordinance, many a one who wants aduice, runnes by and by to him, who by his place ought, but by gifts is most vnfit to giue satisfaction: euen as poore *Samuel* ranne to *Eli*, when God called him. And what gaines such a one by the bargaine? Euen as much as those poore people who ranne to *Rehoboam* to seeke reliefe of his Fathers impositions, and were burdened twice as much as before. Yea, whereas their wound was great when they went, these rude Chirurgians make it worse. For whether they salue all with sweete words (there being a corrupt sore which needes launcing) they cause the wound to rankle: or whether they prescribe remedies, yet they are so improper and indirect, that
Note. they make the disease lesse curable. But the most of them cure such by crying out against the best Physitians, and being not able themselues, neither will suffer others to meddle with them. As for those who (being in deede profane) yet will seeme in their doubts of some particular, to aske counsell; they chuse such as are like themselues, and who will speake to their humor, I meane, smoothly, and iustifie them in their worst doings, reiecting others as *Ahab* did *Micaiah*. And what gaineth hee (thinke wee) that will needes write by rule, and yet of purpose make his ruler crooked? I haue said enough of this by another occasion.

Doct. 4. The other thing that I said is to be learned out of this verse, is; that as these men followed the example of the people of Israel rather then they knew how to doe it aright, (for else they would haue been more wise, and better aduised in their asking, I meane they would haue knowne him, his religion, and authority from God to giue counsell:) so there are many, which doe things that are good, but they doe them not aright, nor in good
Esay 1. 12. sort as we reade in Esay that when the people offred sacrifices to the Lord, yet he asked who required them? so that God is not pleased with such doings.

ings. For either they doe them not vpon good ground, as not hauing authority from the word of God for the same, but onely follow example, and doe as they see other doe; or else doe them not with mindes that desire to serue God therein, and so they lose all their labour: and yet such is the common seruing of God among vs. For the former of these two, I meane prescription of example, they incurre a double error: for either they mistake the ground it selfe in generall, or they faile in the particular applying of the same to their owne practise. They mistake the ground either when they plead an extraordinary fact for the defence of an ordinary, as when *Samsons* reuenging the Philistims, or vse of long haire is brought to iustifie the like: or when they falsely presume that example to bee warrantable which is wicked, as *Iosephs* swearing, *Abrahams* equiuocating, *Samsons* dalliance. They offered againe in application of examples, through want of obseruing circumstance, and especially the manner of doing, which is most vsuall in the abuse of things indifferent. And so it falleth out that they doe that very action badly, which another did commendably. Touching the latter, which I noted to be a corrupt minde in doing good things, it extendeth further then the particular abusing of examples: and taxeth such as are willing to be led by rule and precept, so ye vrge no more then the letter, as (among other) the second commandement is a sufficient proofe. The Lord commands the vse of word, Sacrament, prayer, and externall worship: but if ye presse the manner vpon them, I meane spirit, that is vprightnes of heart, and truth, that is sound knowledge, they bid ye farewell. So that both their seruice is onely to giue God their parings and out-side (Pharisaically) without any substance: and so as ye leaue them a worship, it skils not greatly what it be, a twined thread would leade them from our Church seruice to a Masse. The truth is (and the Lord knowes) this onely distinction would pare away the most of our worshippers at this day. And when they are challenged for it, then they runne to their last refuge, we doe as others, they say if we doe not well, God haue mercy vpon thousands, &c. Indeed such haue need of mercy, but who shall pitty them who pitty not themselues? if ye know these things happy are ye if ye doe them: but ne- Iohn 13.17.
uer looke to doe them well, till ye know your ground, which is no example of others, but Gods charge, whereto solemne promise and penalty is annexed.

Now followes the answere of the hireling: who seeing in what account Verse 6.
the men of *Dan* had him, though he was neither true Priest, nor had any gifts fit for the place, yet he answered as boldly, as if he had receiued an answere from God by inspiration or reuelation. Euen as *Zidchia* the chiefe Baalite, and his fellowes answered *Ahab, Goe and prosper*. So saith this poore 1.King.22.11.
counterfeit Priest; God goeth before you, and will direct your iourney, and 12.
he being with you, will prosper you.

Here besides the apishnes and affection in this counterfeit, who imita- *Doct.*
teth the Prophets, as if he had been one of them, besides this (I say) we see the boldnesse that is in the blinde and vngodly: they will beare as great a shew as the best, of that good which is farre from them, as though it were in them. Many in the Ministerie that are farre enough behinde those that they should learne of, and labour to bee like vnto in gifts for the discharge

of

of their dutie, and grace meete for christians, yet make that good by deprauing and detracting from the gifts of such as farre excell them, by ostentation of frothie and vnseasonable quotations, and speaking beyond the capacitie of the meane, and in a word by vaine flourishes and boasting, which they want in substance of learning and goodnesse: which ought not to moue the better sort to carnall indignation at the sight of it, the iniquitie of the times being such, as wherein among fooles the boldest are more applauded then the wisest: but with patience to possesse our soules, and learne to content our selues with Gods approbation of vs. I marueile that such are not afraide, that God will finde them out, and lay them open; which it were
Luk.19.44. better for them that he did, then to recompence them in the ende for all, with woe, when they shall not bee able to beare nor auoide it. This I am sure of, that many of them dare vndertake and put forth themselues further both in speaking, writing, and action, then the most learned graue experienced dare doe.

And so it fareth with many of the people in their place and condition. They haue a name they liue, many that would seeme forwarder then other, while they may professe without danger and trouble, but they delight
Psal.119.105. not in the word, neither will they make it the light to their steps, and lan-
Matth.23.3. terne to their feete: they say, and doe not; nay, as they hate to be reformed indeed, so they are ashamed, especially in some companies, to bee taken for vpright hearted Christians, and yet in other companies rash and bold to
Note. speake that which is good, but that many knowe it to be but froth and hypocrisie in them. And others, though they are most ignorant and farre from any sauour of goodnes, yet puffe vp themselues with a conceit of their
1.Thes.5.3. good estate, crying peace to themselues when there is nothing but danger, and dreaming that because they can delude men with a shewe of ciuility and freedome from grosse enormities, therefore they shall escape also the Lords censure, who yet hath assured them, that without faith it shall goe wide with them when the Sonne of man commeth to iudge the earth. And yet there is no kinde of people which are more hardly driuen from their holdes, or conuerted, then these Pharisies.

And to ende this point, seeing that which occasioned this boldnes and presidence in this vpstart, was the fleshing and flattery of these Danites: beside this, that commonly we see that vaine glorious fooles shall not want flatterers, (though to their owne destruction) a fit couer for such a cup: we also must learne both to beware of this basenes, and prostituting of our selues to such as seeke for countenance from vs vndeseruedly, but deale plainely with them, lest we become accessaries to that pride, mischiefe and insolency which we cause in them: and euen so likewise, when others applaud vs for any gifts of God in vs, (except our conscience doe it first) let
Acts 12.23. vs be affraid to rest therein, and to swell as *Herod*, considering how God re-
1.Pet.5.5. sisteth such.

2 Behold therefore how quickly their base dealing in approuing him, whom they ought to haue controuled, workes in him the like study to please and humour them, for he by and by shapes them an answere to their liking, but not from God, (Goe and prosper.) Thus the wicked through the iust iudgement of God are made the mutuall coadiutors and causes

causes both of ingendring and nourishing of sinne in each others, as the Apostle saith, They waxe worse and worse by this trafficke and tradition of sinne from one to other, one deceiuing, the other being deceiued, till both receiue the reward of their vnrighteousnes. And this is all the good they doe each to other, in the profession of such kindnes each to other; euen to encrease delight in sinne, hardnes of heart, contempt of the word, and better examples; as *Pharaohs* sorcerers did to him, and the false Prophets of *Ahab*, with others. A point worthy to be insisted in: but I will not degresse. I say therefore (to returne againe to the point) that this Priest and hireling saw he should hit them pat in the hand, and please them exceedingly, if he answered that which they desired: (although he had nothing to answere from God indeede, neither knewe he what would follow) therefore he thus spake to them, (*ye shall prosper.*) Herein he hath bewrayed another sinne which raigneth commonly in the world, and is not suspected to be so, because among those that haue no iudgement, it is taken for a vertue of facility and courteousnes. And that is, a soothing and flattering one of another, and a yeelding to them in that which they desire; It is as great a sinne to speake or consent to mens liking, when yet they deserue to bee reproued, as it is againe in the other, to desire to be so dealt with and flattered. 2.Tim.3.13.

It was the sinne of the false Prophets: and what bred it in *Ahab*, but this, euen to hate the true Prophets of God for that they durst not, neither would flatter him also, but speake the truth, as God commanded them? Of this sin the Lord complaineth in *Ieremy*, saying; They haue healed the hurt of the daughter of my people with sweet words, saying; Peace, peace, when there is no peace. Euen so it is still, if men tell the truth, and deale plainly, (how kindly soeuer) and cannot skill to sooth them, they cannot be brooked: and this makes such as are conscionles, to engage their soules in the damnation of others. Some are in the contrary extremity, in censuring others most sharpely and bitterly and without iust cause as it pleaseth them, being themselues vnfit to take the least rebuke, howsoeuer they doe more then deserue it. 1.King.22.8. Ierem.6.14.

To leaue both sorts, I will end with the third, as bad as the two other, who sooth vp themselues, as they whom I haue spoken of, doe other, flattering, and deceiuing themselues, as though all were well with them, when destruction at hand hangeth ouer their heads. But as he that telleth the truth to other, shall in the end finde more fauour, then he that flattereth; so he that telleth the truth to himselfe, and iudgeth himselfe because of his transgressions, he shall be safe, and not be iudged of the Lord, which will be more vnwelcome. Note. Prou.9.7. 1.Cor.11.31.

Thus we haue heard how these spies that were sent foorth by the tribe of *Dan*, came as farre as mount Ephraim toward Laish the place they were sent vnto: now in this verse it is shewed how they came thither, and what they found when they came there; namely, that the inhabitants liued quiet and void of care, as the Zidonians did, for they of Zidon being none of the seuen nations, were not disquieted by Israels comming into the land of Canaan, and therefore liued safe, euen so did they of that place. *The summe of verse 7. to the 11.*

The reason is added, there were none that troubled them in the land, or made them ashamed for any euill they did, neither had they gouernment among them by inheritance, and the freer they were from feare. Also it is further added, in what respect they might easilier subdue and ouercome that people, to wit, first, because they were farre from the Zidonians, with whom (it is like) they were in league: and next, because they had no dealings with other: whom if they had confederated or communicated with, in contracts and bargaines, they might for that cause haue had helpe by them. These things the spyes that were sent, did take view of, and oberue diligently, (whereby it appeareth that they were wise) and thus they carried word backe againe, as the verses next following, to the eleuenth doe declare.

Doct. vers. 7. 9. 10. First, in that it is said, that the people there was secure and voide of care, liuing in great plentie, and no scarcitie of good things, and much libertie; it confirmeth vs in that which is oft noted, euen in this booke, namely, that for the most part, abundance breedeth carelesnes and securitie, though it is to be granted, that there were in these other causes thereof also, as the ignorance of God. But seeing bare knowledge remedieth it not in many that haue it, we need make no doubt, but they who wanted it, were secure much more; so that they turned all good things to an euill end. God can inable vs (we doubt not) to bee better thereby, I meane by our abundance, and to bring foorth the fruite thereof, but sure it is that few attaine it: and therfore God giues vs many checks and warnings by dearth and famine, and other punishments, (if we haue eyes to see them) lest beside his displeasure, we be driuen to serue him by sorrow and penurie, who might haue done it with ioy and plentie. Now if they who haue knowledge, are yet farre from doing thereafter, and namely in vsing his benefits aright, what is to be looked for in other, as I said before? But of this often.

And further, in that it is said, that there was no gouernour by succession, (for so it is best translated) and therefore the people being their owne gouernours were in lesse awe, we may note, that where there is one to rule in a land constantly, and so by succession, it is a greater meanes to hold the people within compasse, and much more, when other helpes are there with it, as ẏ Gospel: (which nothing hindreth but that it may be so likewise vnder an inferiour Magistrate, though chosen but for one yeere.) Snch a benefit

2. Sam. 1. 17. 24 it was to liue vnder one chiefe ruler, that *Dauid* feared danger, when hee heard that *Saul* was dead (seeing such changes are seldome without) though he himselfe was then to succeed: much more then in greater likelihood. The vse of it is, that all such as enioy that benefit, be more thankfull, yea and euen they that are particularly ruled by inferiour gouernours, seeing they rule with more ease and peace, being backed and authorised by the chiefe. The exemplifying and inlarging of this point, I leaue to the Politician, or Philosopher, whose principle it is, that of all other states and gouernments, the Monarchie or rule of one gouernour, constant and hereditarie is the best. That which my scope especially aimeth at, is, to presse vpon vs of this English nation, the vse of this point, which if any people vpon the earth haue cause to make, then haue we aboue all the rest. That which I say, briefly is this: That howsoeuer we commonly looke at the personall and domesticall benefits which wee enioy apart and seuerally from others, and giue thankes

thankes for them more then for publike and generall, which wee hold in common with all our brethren: yet we must learne in our praisings of God, to lift vp our eyes higher to behold the great fauour of God toward our land, in bestowing the blessing of blessings vpon it, (outward I meane) which is the roote and foundation of the inferiour and particular, I meane constant gouernment, and that of one, whereto not election, or will of others, but nature and blood hath title of succession. If we knew or had read of the confusions of all estates in all times past, and the miserie of those subiects, whom priuate contentions for gouernment haue tossed and turmoyled by occasion of euery vacancie, wee should see cause enough of thankes for this mercie. And it would make vs to thinke those burthens and seruices which lie vpon vs, toward the vpholding of regal state and soueraignty, the more equall and indifferent. I haue in the fifth Chapter spoken to this purpose, but vpon so good occasion I will adde to it somewhat here. Therfore of that I say a plentifull witnesse are those bloody warres euen in this land, in the daies of our forefathers, arising vpon question & claime of title, which now (God be thanked) being wel setled & compounded, and strengthened by the happie entrance of our late Soueraigne, & the apparent succession of his royal issue, and that, when we iustly feared great distraction by the false pretenders of other titles, I think it is no smal addition to ẏ weight and cause of our thankfulnes. But doe wee yeeld this fruite of such a priuiledge? Doe we (in this setled peace and freedome at home, or from forrein warres) edifie our selues in knowledge, faith and the feare of the Lord? In deed those Churches in the booke of Acts, which had but an interim and Act.9.31.
breathing time in this peace betweene whiles, did so improue it: but are we so happie to imploy ours, hauing bin constantly continued a long time, to imploy it (I say) in such manner? No, no, and yet wee haue the Gospell also giuen vs and maintained among vs without any mixture of other religion, (blessed bee God) as a companion, yea the seasoner of the other blessing. Oh, if wee had been vnder those short and contrary gouernments of *Edward* the sixth, and Queene *Mary*, and had seene by comparison, what benefit this is which wee speake of, wee should acknowledge and yeeld our thankfulnes by great feruencie and fruitfulnes, for without these, thankfulnes is hypocrisie. But now this setled blessing (for aboue fiftie yeeres continuance without breath) hath made vs drunken, and riueted vs into carnall ease, and extended our thoughts and desires to a long abiding here below, and besotted vs so, that heauenly things are in small account with vs. Thus we (to vse *Moses* his words) deale with the Lord, like a most vnthankfull nation. And yet we had been like to haue been much worse, if hee had not held vs vnder with many crosses.

Againe, in that there were none to make other ashamed for their ill doings, but the wickedest citizens were suffered to goe on without reproch by 3
meanes that the Magistrate was set slothfull, wee may see where there are some that rule, yet if there bee nothing regarded but outward peace, there may, yea and will certainly be enormities and many vile sinnes committed. For when there shall bee none that will put them to shame and sorrow for them, what marueile though wickednes swarme in such places? But it goeth much better with them, among whom the lewd and wicked are rebuked,

and iuſtly cenſured for their euill doings, eſpecially by thoſe that are in authoritie: and the ſame may be ſaid of townes and families. Of the which neglect of duty in the Magiſtrates, though I haue ſpoken by ſundrie occaſions, yet this I will now adde, that it ought to bee the wiſedome of all gouernours, and eſpecially the chiefe, vpon due conſideration of this point, to wit, that ciuill lawes and penalties cannot containe their ſubiects in awe, except they fetch aſſiſtance from thoſe lawes that binde the conſcience, therefore to prouide for godlineſſe firſt, by diligent and ſound preaching throughout their dominion, and then for peace and honeſtie. Doubtleſſe, where the former is wanting, the latter (though forced with neuer ſo great ſeueritie) preuailes little. And correction without inſtruction may for a time compell, but (as the heathen ſpake of feare) it is a bad watchman for continuance, or in ſecret. God, who workes oftentimes great effects by ſmall meanes, they being mightily bleſſed to thoſe ends, is able to reſtraine the bad, and containe the good within bounds much more forcibly by the ſweete bands of his word, binding the ſoule to obedience, then by the ſtrongeſt ciuill terrors: but much more both together ſhall ſweetly conſpire to that purpoſe.

4 Laſtly in this verſe, where it is ſaid, they were farre from neighbours, as the Zidonians, with whom they were neereſt in league, it may teach vs, that it is a great benefit to liue by neighbours, that there may be at hand alwaies ſome to helpe in time of need. This was alwaies, and is true among the heathen. But much more it may be truly ſaid of vs, who liue where the Goſpel is ſoundly preached, who, beſide the other helpe that we haue in common with them, and may enioy one by another as they doe, may haue alſo farre greater vſe each of other by edifying our ſelues in exhortation, and inſtructing one another, then they can. To the great ſhame I ſpeake it, of ſuch neighbours as are vnciuill, miſchieuous, and better affected to ſtrangers, without reſpect of any benefit they haue by them, then to ſuch as dwell neere them, to whom they are noyſome and ſiniſter: veriſying that ſpeech, The further off men be one from another, the better friends they be: whereas neighbours ſerue both to be comforts each to other by reioycing together in peace, and alſo to be helpers, and ſuccourers in time of danger and diſtreſſe. Others dwelling neere together as in cities and townes, liue in ſmall loue together, but in diſſenſion, ſeeing among them that be of the ſame trade, one eateth vp anothers gaine, and ſo haue ſmall helpe one of another, but rather a burthen, by contentions and ſtrife; or if they liue in any fellowſhip together, they be the worſe one for the other, for the moſt part, as by gaming, drinking, and other miſrule. And their commendation is little greater, who hauing but few neighbours by them in the countrey, yet wiſh them further off from them, (ſo little they regard their helpe or neighbourhood) and all to this end, that they may haue the more roome, and occupying: who ſo as they may haue that, it appeares can be well content to liue alone, till their mouthes are filled with earth. Of this ſort are they that pull downe houſes, townes, in ſome part of the land, yea Churches and all, to inlarge their owne borders and deſtroy the Common-wealth. But concerning the right vſe of this bleſſing, I haue elſewhere ſpoken.

THE

THE NINETIE FOVRE SERMON, ON THE XVIII. CHAPTER OF THE BOOKE OF IVDGES.

THE REMAINDER OF THE FIRST part of the Chapter.

Verſ.8. *So they came againe vnto their brethren to Zorah, and Eſhtaol: and*
their brethren ſaid vnto them, What haue you done?
9. *And they anſwered, Ariſe, that we may goe vp againſt them: for wee haue*
ſeene their land, and ſurely it is very good, and doe you ſit ſtill? be not ſlothfull to goe
and enter to poſſeſſe the land.
10. *(If ye will go, ye ſhall come vnto a careleſſe people, and the countrey is large)*
for God hath giuen it into your hand; it is a place which doth lacke nothing that is
in the world.

WHen theſe ſpyes had viewed all things well, they brought word to their brethren, according to that which they found, (as hath bin ſhewed in the former verſe) when their brethren demanded of them what they had done. They told them how commodious, large, and copious the land was in all good things, and eaſie to bee enioyed of them, the people there being careleſſe, and for incouragement they added this, that God had giuen it into their hands, and therefore they were to make ſpeede, and not delay the time. Verſ.8.9.10.

Here (not to repeate the ſame things againe that I noted in the former verſe) occaſion being offered ſo to doe by the repeating of the ſame words, we ſee howſoeuer there was little religion in them, yet they were ſpeedie, wiſe, and truſtie in the buſineſſe that they were ſent about, which indeede concerned their owne benefit, as well as their brethrens. So wee may finde it oft times, that men who haue no true feare of God, yet in their earthly dealings, and namely ſuch as bee for their owne profit, they ſhall be found carefull and forward enough, vnleſſe they be ſome ſlothfull perſons, that are not meet to liue in a Common wealth. For why? ſelfloue leadeth them to be forward, and to goe readily about their owne profit: in ſo much, as they runne too headlong after it. Doct.

And this is the cauſe why we ſee it ſo common a thing among our ſelues, that when there is no heart nor affection in men to godly duties, yet to the world they are ſo eagerly and impotently carried, that they neede no ſpurs to pricke them forward, being too ready of themſelues, there being hope of profit. But let the ſeruants of God giue their greateſt diligence to the ne-

cessariest duties, and the holiest seruices of God, that so they may doe the meaner workes, as it becommeth them, that is, aduisedly, vprightly and soberly, remembring alwaies that one thing is needfull, that so they may mo-
Luke 10.42. derate themselues in and about the seeking of the commodities of this life, which grace is rare, and enioyed of few, and yet without which, the men are surfited with cares, and voluptuousnes, as Christ hath plainly shewed in the third sort of hearers. And yet my meaning is not, that they should bee
Matth.13.22. negligent, nor vnfaithfull in and about their earthly dealings, but diligent, wise, and prouident: but for such as haue no more to witnesse the fauour of God to them, then their diligence about earthly businesse, (which was apparantly to be seene in these men of *Dan*) they may know, that they are vtterly to seeke of it, euen as they were. See more of this vpon vers.10. and elsewhere in this booke, the dutie of prising the best things in the best manner.

*Doct.*2. Also their commending of the land for the commodities, and plenty that was therein, doth not only shew vs the abundant riches of God, who hath replenished sea and land with all good things in their kinde, to the end that we may seeke such things at his hands; but more especially it teacheth this; that when we our selues liue where we see and inioy such plenty of the good things of the earth, as it is said, this countrey did inioy, (whe-
Note. ther these spies were sent,) which wanted no good thing, we may not only admire and magnifie God, who so beautifieth his footestoole, and prouideth so for vs, that we may eate of the fatte, and drinke of the sweet; but we ought to be led also hereby to consider the glory of his habitation, and to set our hearts vpon those things which are aboue, yea and to beleeue,
Colos.3.1. that he which hath such store in his hands, and that also here on the earth where we be but strangers, will not let his deare children want any thing needfull for the vpholding of their poore life, nor forsake them in their necessities: which should bee a strong encouragement to vs to honour him with the best things that we haue, and count his seruice perfect freedome,
Iohn 4.10. and to be prouoked to seeke better things at his hands: so our Sauiour told the woman of Samaria, that he would haue giuen her (if she had but asked it of him) the water of life; euen the refreshing grace of the holy Ghost, which preserueth vnto eternall life. If poore parents out of their small prouision, doe yet bestow vpon their children necessaries, how much more shall the Lord prouide farre better things for his? And hee, a man would thinke, who is so rich, should be attended, and sought vnto, for all good
Iam.1.5. things, (and especially, also seeing he giueth plentifully, and casteth none in the teeth,) if we would bee rich in deede, and haue no sorrowes therewith.

*Doct.*3. In that they incourage their bretheren to goe speedily to the land, because God had giuen it into their hands, we see that commonly as men are effected, so they indeuour to effect others. The spies that were sent first to
Numb.13.28. search out Canaan, being smitten (the most of them) with feare, discouraged the brethren from setting vpon it. Earthly minded and politike men wil be alwayes talking of worldly affaires, prouidence, thrift and good husbandry, so that they who heare them, are not a little whetted on by them thereunto. And as sweete odors strawed among linnen or apparell, leaueth their

their sauor behinde; so doe men where they become, leaue such impressions and sauors among others, as their owne mindes, affections and tongues bewray and expresse. The word preached layeth open to the eye of the soule, most apparently the treasures of wisdome and knowledge, and setteth forth the riches of the loue of God in Christ to all that will take their part therein, with the plentifull graces wherewith he beautifieth the beleeuers, with their priuiledges in this life, and the glory hereafter; the meanest of all which farre excelleth the plenty and variety of Laish: as S. *Paul* speaketh of godlines, 1. Timoth. 6. and many more easily, and with lesse cost and trauaile be come by, then Laish was. But where shall wee finde a man (a spie in a spirituall sense of Canaan) who hauing heard these things of the City of God, commeth away with such affection, zeale, and fulnes of matter as these from Laish? who stirres vp his fellow as the woman (that good spie) Iohn 4. did her neighbours by her narration of that she had seene in Christ, and heard from him, and this among the rest, that hee would haue giuen her water of life for the bare asking? ye will say, men see not that in the word, which these saw here, and I confesse in deede there is the cause. But why? because there are not these sights, or that they want eyes? Therefore be we ashamed of this stupidity and sottishnes: and let both the Minister first striue to be well affected himselfe with these matters, that as Gods seer, he may not only shew these wonders to the people, but breath into them affection, sense, admiration at them, and moue them forcibly to embrace and make after them. And then let the people readily yeeld to their report, and quicken each the other toward grace and heauen, as doubtles these Danites did each stirre vp the other here by the very words whereby the spies had excited them, as appeares by their practise and consent in the verse following.

A simil. 1. Tim. 6. 6. Iohn 4. 29.

Besides this, they vrge vpon them this point of wisdome, (not the smallest euen in earthly affaires) to shake off delay and dalliance, and to take hold of the opportunity now offered them. As if they had said, though Laish be quiet, secure, plentifull, and in likelihood easie to be taken, yet it will not offer it selfe, it will not be got by sitting still, the booty will not fall into our mouthes. Nay if this vantage be ouerslipt, who knoweth what may fall out betweene the cup and lip as it were, to defeate vs of Laish? as this, that possibly they smelling out our enterprise may fortifie themselues, &c. Behold how these spies play the heraldes, not informing onely, but preuenting error and sloth, and encouraging their brethren. And the truth is their words were pleasant, and so might haue bred in the people a dreame of ease, as if Laish had been taken in conceit already: therefore they call instantly, take the season, arise vp, delay not, delay in dangers is gainefull: in benefits commonly dangerous. Learne we that are Christians wisdome from hence for our vse: who though we haue no newes of a countrey to be possessed without great danger, (for if we did, we needed rather a bridle then a spur, as appeares by our practise in this land for the compassing of a farre dispermeanor thing offred vs. And when wee finde our hearts by the hearing of God his terrors, or promises, to stoope, encline and bee drawne towards God and goodnes, let vs say: this is my season, now God offreth grace, now the coast is cleare, and now the onset is easiest in all probability, and

Doct. 4.

hope of ſucceſſe. Farre bee it from me to dally with theſe glad tidings (as a man rockt a ſleepe with muſicke) or to thinke I haue my part in them, by delighting in the report. So in the encreaſe of grace, or the ouercomming of a corrupt affection, when the deſire is greateſt, or the worke is begun well, then are our ſeaſons of eager purſuit, and our opportunity of fighting: if we ſtay till our deſire be quencht; or our heart hardened, we may ariſe and take vp armor but out of ſeaſon: let vs ariſe and worke in ſeaſon, with

Note. theſe Danites. For I tremble to ſpeake it, the opportunity of many a man to be a Chriſtian, or to be a better Chriſtian, was once, but is not now with him ſo, at leaſt it is much leſſe, by his vnſeaſonable dalliance, (for I ſpeake of one who may ſo be charged) and ouerſlipping his ſeaſon.

Doct. 5. But to returne againe to theſe ſpies, and their confident wordes, it may be asked how they knew that that the Lord had ſo ſurely giuen Laiſh into their hands, they being faithles Idolaters, wanting communion with God: for if they meant, that he had giuen it them in the diuiſion of the land, there were among them, that knewe that as well as they, and rather better long before; I anſwere, they ſpake ſo vpon the words of the hireling the Leuit, whom when they moued to aske counſell of the Lord for them whether they ſhould proſper in their iourney, hee anſwered as if hee had bin Gods mouth to them, yea, Goe and proſper; from this anſwere (I ſay) of his, (which they as readily beleeued, as the other did boldly vtter it) they brought word to their brethren, that God had deliuered them into their hands.

Whereby we may ſee that confirmed which we heard before, that they who are wiſe enough to deale in matters of this life, as theſe men of *Dan* were, both the ſpies, and they which ſent them, yet in heauenly things they are oft times moſt childiſh and void of true wiſdome. For who would in ſo waightie a caſe, if they had bin wiſe, haue giuen credite to an vſurper of the Prieſts office, and an Idolater? if you will ſay, they tooke him for a Prieſt, I anſwere their blindnes was the greater, as theirs is, who among vs cannot diſcerne a good Miniſter from a vaine, and counterfeit deceiuer.

1. Cor. 1. 20. It is no marueile, though S. *Paul* ſay the wiſdome of this world, is fooliſhnes with God. It grieueth the good Miniſters at this day, to ſee the labour and vnweariednes of ſuch as goe for wiſe men, to be ſo forward about matters of profit, vaine pleaſure, and preferment, of which they haue no certaintie till to morrow, and the pleaſures that are on the Lords right hand for euermore, they doe not once looke after them, or very ſlightly, yea rather a great many doe make a mocke of them. But to end; their ſo light giuing credit to the counterfeit hireling, ſo farre as they report thereupon his anſwere to their brethren, euen as if they had receiued it from God, this (I ſay) teacheth further what deadly danger ariſeth of haſty harkening to vngrounded reports, and the greater, the waightier they bee corrupt, and yea though wee receiue them from our acquaintance, being not approued for their vprightnes and honeſty. But how men are confirmed in error, and otherwiſe hurt by ſuch acquaintance, I haue ſpoken vpon the 6. verſe in the entrance thereupon. But it followeth.

The ſecond part of the Chapter.

Verſ.11. *And there went from thence of the family of the Danites out of Zo-*
rah, and out of Eſhtaol, ſixe hundred men, appointed with weapons of warre.
12. *And they went vp, and pitched in Kiriath-iearim in Iuda: wherefore they*
called that place Manaheh-Dan, vnto this day: behold, it is behind Keriath-iea-
rim.
13. *And they paſſed thence vnto mount Ephraim, and came vnto the houſe of*
Micha.
14. *Then anſwered the fiue men that went to ſpie out the countrey of Laiſh, and*
ſaid vnto their brethren, Doe ye know that there is in theſe houſes an Ephod, and
Teraphim, and a grauen Image, and a molten Image? Now therefore conſider what
ye haue to doe.
15. *And they turned thitherward, and came to the houſe of the yong man the*
Leuite, euen vnto the houſe of Micha, and ſaluted him.
16. *And the ſixe hundred men appointed with their weapons of warre, which*
were of the children of Dan, ſtood by the entring of the gate.
17. *And the fiue men that went to ſpie out the land, went vp and came in thi-*
ther, and tooke the grauen Image, and the Ephod, and the Teraphim, and the mol-
ten image: and the Prieſt ſtood in the entring of the gate, with the ſixe hundred
men, that were appointed with weapons of warre.
18. *And theſe went into Micahs houſe, and fetched the carued Image, the E-*
phod, and the Teraphim, and the molten Image: then ſaid the Prieſt vnto them,
What doe ye?
19. *And they ſaid vnto him, Hold thy peace: lay thine hand vpon thy mouth*
and goe with vs, and be to vs a father and a Prieſt: is it better for thee to be a Prieſt
vnto the houſe of one man, or that thou be a Prieſt vnto a tribe and a family in Iſ-
rael.
20. *And the Prieſts heart was glad, and he tooke the Ephod, and the Teraphim,*
and the grauen Image, and went in the middeſt of the people.
21. *So they turned and departed, and put the little ones, and the cattell, and the*
carriage before them.

WE haue heard of the ſending out of the ſpies, of their returne, and the newes they brought to their brethren: Now in this ſecond part of the Chapter it followeth to ſee, what ſpeed the men of *Dan* made, when they had receiued ſuch good newes and incouragements by the ſpies, to goe to the place, and where they reſted, and what they did by the way, and when they came there. For the firſt, how they haſted to take their iourney, it is ſaid in this verſe, that vpon the returne of the meſſengers with ſo good tidings, they by and by tooke their iourney, and made no delay, well furniſhed, if they ſhould poſſibly haue bin ſet vpon, or reſiſted by the way, or when they came there. *Verſ.11. The ſumme of the verſes.*

In that they went ſo readily and chearefully toward the place when they ſawe ſo good reaſon to moue them, ſeeing they were encouraged by the word brought them by the fiue meſſengers, it is no marueile, but yet they wanted the chiefeſt inducement, which was to haue God tell them ſo. For what *Doct verſ.11.*

what though the hireling tolde the spies as from God, that they should prosper, yet sixe hundred men of Israel Gods people should not haue bin all so void of sound iudgement, godly care, and vprightnes, as to haue taken the bold word of an Idolatrous Priest, for Gods word. Euen so wee haue proofe that the soundest reason of all to leade vs in our matters, is the word of God, against the which there is no exception, and yet that doth little moue or preuaile with vs, in the duties imposed vpon vs, to yeeld vnto it, especially with any forwardnes. Wherein we may see another point of our corrupt and vile nature: For if we be moued and sollicited to any thing which is liking and pleasing vnto it, be it earthly and transitory: nay vnlawfull also, we are easily inticed by it, and carried away with it, notwithstanding the absurditie of such dealing: but let vs be aduised by the word of God only, to any thing that shall be good and profitable for vs, and see reason from them to draw vs thereto, (and yet that promiseth another manner of benefite then all carnall reason or perswasion can doe) yet how hardly we are carried the best way, it is lamentable to consider.

Note.

I am weary of making this complaint, which I haue done so oft, I will rather helpe to remedy it, as I am able, which I endeuour to doe by these two reasons. The one this: we are not debtors to the flesh, and therefore should not be slaues to our wicked lusts, the yeelding to them, being our vtter vndoing. On the contrary, if we be led by the spirit of God, and obedient to the will of God, and not our owne; this shall fill our liues with blessings, which, who is it that desireth not to inioy, and be free from the contrary? The second reason is this: if men of the world be readily carried by earthly perswasions to seeke after that which liketh them, is it not a shame for vs who haue giuen our selues to the Lord, to limpe and come behinde them in seeking farre better things being prouoked and incouraged thereto by him? This backwardnes in vs to good duties, sheweth what commendable grace of God it is, which is said to haue bin in the Thessalonians, that they were ready to any thing taught from God before they heard it. For is the Gospell more barren of sweet inducements and motiues, or the Ministers thereof lesse alluring and perswasiue, then earthly men and matters are? Take but this example here, how preuailed these spies so soone with their brethren to goe forward to Laish? By the maine argument of welfare and commodious dwelling, and the ease of obteining it? And yet this welfare came farre short of happines. For neither was it continuall, nor certaine: a time came when it forsooke the possessors of it, and as they tooke it from others, so others might also bereaue them thereof. And as easie as it was to get, yet it was casuall. But that which God by his Ministers induceth vs to, namely that we will be reconciled, beleeue, lay hold of eternall life, &c. is such a portion as (to vse our Sauiours words to *Martha*) shall neuer be taken away from them that choose and preferre it before other things; and such, as neither is bought with siluer, but freely giuen, nor casuall in obteining, but assured to such as will but truely desire it. And though the blessings of Laish were his also, whose these heauenly gifts are, which I spake of, yet the oddes is as great as Laish and heauen. The very name of a gift commonly is gracious, and preuailes wheresoeuer it goeth: but doe these so? If a man in a deepe ditch or dungeon, had one hand reacht him

Rom.8.12.

2.Thessal. 3.4.

Luke 10.42.

him (as *Ieremy* had ropes) to draw him out, need he to be perswaded ? yet when Gods Ministers haue said all they can, and done their best to prouoke men to accept this offer of God, reaching them the hande of mercy and saluation, they cannot preua le with them, but they had rather lie still and die in their misery, then bee beholding to him for rescue and deliuerance. And as the Prophet *Esay* complaines, so may these Orators, and say, Who hath beleeued our report ? And with our Sauiour, Matth. 11. *We haue piped vnto you, but ye haue not danced.* Oh blockish people, oh deafe adders : (for what is more deafe then that which stoppeth it owne eares) that will not be charmed by the wisest inchanters, I say not these men of Laish, but euen your selues shall be your owne iudges and condemners in that the smallest commodity could doe more with them, then heauen could doe with you, which if ye would take but the tenth part of the paines to get, which ye do to get the other, ye might as easily gaine as the other : But ye are more fit (like sensuall beasts) to bee giuen ouer to a fleshly religion, and to Popish perswaders, and carnall counsellers, who may draw you by deceitfull reasons, for these matters are too high for such as sauour not the things of God, but like beetles are blockish, and drowned in the earth.

Esay 53.1.

Matth. 11.17.

In their iourney they must needs rest by the way, and the place where they pitched their tents at the first resting place in their iourney, was this *Kiriath-Iearim*, or as the word *Kiriath* signifieth, the citie of Iearimites, neere vnto that, I say, they made their stay, which was a citie in Iuda. At the which place seeing no mention is made of any thing they did there, saue onely of the name that they gaue to the place, (for so I vnderstand the words [*They called*] that is, the Danites themselues) called it *Mahaneh-Dan*, that is, the tents of *Dan*, as if they had said, in this place the people of *Dan* pitched their tents, when they passed thereby, seeing, I say, there is no mention of any other thing done there, I will proceed, hauing no occasion offered from the text to say any thing of it. Onely of their giuing of that name to the place, let this be noted, that it was no leauing of a remembrance of thanksgiuing for their rest in the place (that suted not with their other behauiour) though that was an vsuall thing with the Fathers to doe in those times, and many did intend it, by giuing names to places where they abode : as *Iacob* did ; to whom the Lord appearing in the way, he called the name of the place Bethel, that is, the house of God. And in this booke *Samson* did twice the same in one chapter. But wee finde no such good in these, who yet had cause as well as other, offered them to doe so, by their resting in the place, if they had been well disposed, but their fact was matter of iust, yea great reproofe and reproch rather, and sutable to the two notorious acts of theirs, which they committed at Mount Ephraim at the house of *Micha*, as in this chapter doth appeare. Euen thereafter, and in the like iollitie, we may well think this giuing that name to the place to haue been. Namely, that it was done of a vaine folly by them, and with a braue minde, as they now call it, who seeing they could shew it no other way, and had no heart to doe it the best way by thanksgiuing, would doe it thus, being lifted vp by their hope they had of well speeding in the place to the which they were going. And it doth liuely set foorth in their colours the rude and almost mad behauiour of loose, disordered, and light headed fellowes, in all ages, who cannot passe by

Vers. 12.

Gen 28.19.

Iudg. 15.17 19.

by the high waies and townes, but they must shew what they bee, and of what disposition, and that such iolly fellowes passed by, and that they doe shew as well by their lewd and vndecent hallowing and iangling with their voyces, and also by doing other shrewd turnes where they come. As in their vnrulines, and drunken mood, such as those were, cast downe mens gates, barres, and stiles, as they goe in the way, steale their fowles, and disquiet the innocent whom they passe by.

Vers. 13. to 22. the summe. And this be said of their first resting at *Kiriath-Iearim:* In these verses following is shewed, how they came next to pitch at Mount Ephraim, where *Micha* dwelt. And here wee are to consider what they did there. For there they spoyled and robbed him of his gods, and carried away his hireling the priest with them, who when he saw that it was like that his going with them should bee for his preferment, hee willingly departed without leaue, and changed his old master for new; and so they went their way, putting their young ones, their cattell, and their precious substance to be carried before them, lest they should haue been troubled with them, if any (as it came to passe) should pursue them.

Doct. ver. 13. 14 The next place that is mentioned of their stay (as I said) was where *Michas* house was: for nothing is said of any thing they did betwixt their two resting places, seeing it is like they did nothing worth the setting downe. But when they came there, the fiue messengers told the rest of their brethren this: That there were in that place, Gods, (as they termed them) and that many, and an Ephod the Priests garment, and there was the Priest, whom they had moued to aske counsell for them, when they passed by in their former iourney; (it is like enough) they did the same now in this their iourney, as they had cause, euen as they before had done, to wit, consult with him. They had sped well, they said, by asking counsell of the Priest before, and therfore measuring things by the euent and successe, as commonly the most doe; for more certaintie, as they thought, they did take him with them.

And it is an vsuall thing with men still at this day, that where they haue sped well, as they count it, there they hope to doe so still, and therefore follow the same course, how vnlawfull soeuer it hath been, euen as these Danites sought neerer fellowship with this deceiuer, imagining that hee had greatly pleasured them before. The gamester, when hee seeth that he is a winner, he is set on thornes to be at it againe, (for hee doth not see that the Prou. 21. 17. diuell hath made it a snare to take him in) and so goeth forward, till either he lose all, and then verifieth the prouerbe, that he who loueth pastime, shall be a poore man; or till hee make a trade of that his gaming, to his vtter destruction. And so the whoremonger when he hath escaped sundrie times, Prou. 23. 35. waxeth bold, like him in the Prouerbs, They haue smitten me, saith he, but I was not sicke: therefore I will follow it yet still.

Thus *Samson* escaping the Philistims hands twice or thrice, he dallied so long with his *Delilah*, that the Philistims came vpon him in deed at length, and bound & brought him to great bondage and miserie. And what makes men bold to sinne against God, but this, that they hope to escape punishment, as they haue before done? but in the end they pay for all. And as these measured all by successe, so they haue done in Popery, charging our religion as false, seeing they can alleage that great prices haue risen since it was set vp among vs. But to leaue all these erroneous and deceiuable courses of these and such like, wee should and ought of all other to practise this point, which I haue now handled, that seeing we haue sped well, nay so exceedingly well in the true seruing of God, we should still hold out resolutely in continuing therein, and that without fainting and wearines.

The next thing here mentioned, was this: that these fiue men came into the house of *Micha*, where the Leuite was, and kindly saluted him there, as if there had been very sound friendship betwixt them since they had asked counsell of the Lord by him before: and they brought him forth vnto the six hundred that stood without the doore, and while they staied him there, the other fiue went into the house, and fetched out thence the Idols, and the Ephod. And when they came out with them, the Priest amazed to behold it, asked them what they meant by their doing so: but they soone stilled him, and stopped his mouth, and bad him bee content, and goe with them also, and bee their Priest: which they told him, was better for him to doe, then to be in a priuate house: who forthwith was well pleased with their offer, and readily accepted of it, and went with them, who then was well pleased that they should take all his implements with him. Vers. 15. 16. 17.

It appeareth that they thus saluted him, that they might the easilier draw him to consent to go with them, and to be the lesse set against their doings, when they should bring out his Priests garment, and implements of Idolatrie to carrie them away. By the which wee may obserue another practise of profane and dissembling people, that their shewes of friendship & kindnes are but to an euill end, and to couer some mischiefe which they intend. Thus *Ioab* saluted *Abner* and *Amasa* in a most friendly manner, but it was to couer his bloody and murtherous heart; for forthwith hee thrust his weapon into them and slew them. Doct vers. 15. 16. 17. 2. Sam. 3. 27. 2. Sam. 20. 9. 10

So *Absolom* kindly inuited his brother *Ammon* to a feast, but it was to get opportunitie to kill him, as he had taken order with his seruants, and commanded them before. So though all such intend not one and the same wicked end, yet for the most part, they meane ill euen when they pretend loue and good will each to other. Therefore *Dauid* complained that hee who sought his great hurt, was he that seemed his familiar friend. We haue the same in daily practise among vs: what euill is wrought vnder friendly and kinde pretences? Many vnder faire shewes doe secretly plucke their neighbours commoditie from them, yea and when they haue broken their mindes to them and asked their aduice, about some bargaine, and purchase, and as counting them their speciall and trustie friends, haue looked for their helpe and furtherance; they haue bin preuented euen by them, while they haue sought the same commoditie themselues out of their hands, about which they consulted with them: And about seeking of wiues the same may be said: for while some haue consulted with a friend about a fit companion in mariage, the supposed friend (what a fearfull thing doe I report?) hath depriued the other of that hee sought, and broke his minde of vnto him. 2. Sam. 13. 26, 28, 29.

And no better are the faire and flattering words of many chapmen, who doe the more deceiue men thereby, either with bad wares, or making them

pay deare for them, that are nothing so much worth. Oh how long might I stand in laying out the many sinnes of this kinde daily committed? But to leaue them, although all such do not alwaies intend euill, when they make faire shewes, yet this at least they doe, most commonly, to wit, that they meane not as they speake or pretend, but dissemble or flatter: neither may credit be safely giuen vnto them in that which they say: but that which is not much vnlike, this (with griefe I vtter it) is not only among the bad sort,
Note. but also a blemish euen among those who are otherwise good people, that they hardly speake well one of another behinde their backes, that I say no more, though they agree well when they meete together. I deny not, but there may cause be giuen: but what though it be so, they should through loue couer their infirmities, and be sorrie for them, rather then tell them out to their reproch, especially while they make shew of the contrary. Let the vse hereof bee this, to discouer and bring out of loue with vs that corrupt disposition of nature, (one of the cursed fruites of originall infection) I meane to hollownesse and falsehood of heart, and to make sinceritie and truth more esteemed with vs. For doubtlesse as slight a matter as the most make of trecherie and dissimulation, (who thinke it rather a gift in themselues and deseruing high commendation, then a foule blemish) yet let them know, their hearts are as false and deceitfull to Godward in the matter of faith and obedience, as their actions to manward and in duties of loue, are hollow and vnsound. And though I doubt not, but many that vse this occupation care as little for Gods account of them, as for good report among their brethren, (of whom I say, Let the dead burie the dead, and so leaue them forlorne monsters as they are) yet some others I know are not so deeply dyed with this tincture, whose hearts neuerthelesse are like their doings, loose, and dissembling, and yet would be loth to be therefore condemned and cast out as refuse, aud damnable hypocrites. To these I speake now, and tell them that they dawbe with vntempered morter, and declare that they little search or examine themselues by the fruits that come from them, and therefore they nourish in themselues a rotten and hypocriticall heart in stead of a sound and vpright. And as for their nice distinguishing betweene false dealing with God, and dissembling with their brother, they go but betweene barke and tree: for let them know, God abhorreth to be serued with that heart, hand, or tongue, which dishonoureth him by hurting and deceiuing their neighbour. For hee who playeth the false traytor with him whom he seeth, how shall hee be found to deale plainly and sincerely with him whom hee seeth not? Therefore you who cannot be pulled nor disswaded from this trade of yours, and yet would seeme to professe the Gospell, take your selues in hand seriously and timely, and suffer your selues
1. Sam. 15. 30. to be conuicted of ranke hypocrisie before God, (though with *Saul* yee would also retaine your credit among men if it might be) bewaile this sin vnfainedly, and cease not till God haue giuen you the grace to purge it out from your heart and practise; lest by your dallying ouer-long, the diuell who was your greatest setter forward and abettor in your peace and iollitie, become in the day of sicknesse and trouble, your deadly aduersarie to condemne you: and lest your conscience being opened by Gods terrors play the hangman within you, in such wise, as the best friends ye haue shall

not be able to comfort you against your owne despaire and finall impenitencie. I haue spoken of this poynt purposely before vpon chapter 9. verse 36. where *Zebul* vseth all cunning to draw forth *Gaal* out of the citie to the hoste of *Abimelech*: therefore I will proceede no further in it, but end.

THE NINETIE FIVE SERMON, ON THE XVIII. CHAPTER OF THE BOOKE OF IVDGES.

NOw therefore to leaue this, as I said before I would, here note another foule part that these men of *Dan* plaied by the way, as they were in their iourney. For beholde, they enter into a mans house by violence, and take thence what they list: whereas strangers should be harmelesse toward all, & themselues feare rather to take hurt by other: for what though the things they tooke, were idolatrous implements, they counted of them we see, as *Micah* also did that lost them, for precious commodities. If they had taken them away, for the detestation of idolatrie, yet had they not been to be iustified therein (much lesse in this) no more then *Rachel* in stealing her fathers idols, whatsoeuer her purpose was. Thus wee see how common a thing robbing and spoyling is: a lamentable case, that of these sixe hundred wee reade not of any among them that were against that odious and violent fact: and were it not for mans law, that is somewhat strict against such doings, yee should haue many open and grosse theeues, whereas now they be but secret, and coloured. Doct. in vers. 16.17.

It is too true, one mans teeth water after another mans commodities, though if the least part of his owne be withholden and taken from him, hee cannot beare it in any sort, neither is there any reason he should. But why should hee not learne thereby to forbeare, and hold backe both his heart from desiring, and his hand from laying holde on his neighbours goods, measuring him by himselfe, who would be glad safely and peaceably to enioy his owne. To recken vp the particular sinnes of this kinde against the eighth commandement, it would bee too long, and they may be found in many Catechismes: so that it is a poynt of Christian practise, and dutie, to containe our selues within those bounds, that wee may bee free from hurting any, and from giuing iust cause of complaining thereof. And yet wee are bound to more, I meane to be contented with, yea, and highly thankefull for our daily bread, which God of his goodnesse bestoweth vpon vs, as the Apostle teacheth, saying: If we haue meate and drinke with apparrell, 1.Tim.6.8.
let vs be content therewith: and besides this, to yeelde willingly of that which we haue, to the necessitie and reliefe of other: according to the same

Ephes.4.28. Apostles rule, let him that stole, steale no more, but labour with his hands, that he may haue to giue to others.

The generall dutie of righteousnesse euery man will allow, as commendable and necessary: and in deed nature teacheth heathens no lesse, especially toward them that deserue no bad measure at their hands. By how much the more was this part of theirs vile and odious, thus to deale with him (*Micha* I meane) who had deserued no such measure at their hands, but kindnesse: who if hee receiued not those fiue spyes as guests into his house, in their former voyage, yet it is manifest, that he hurt them not being strangers. Of the which particular I haue said my minde in another place. But to returne to the point; though rapine, and oppression haue an vgly hiew in the generall, yet the diuell (the cunningest painter of bad faces) can make the speciall acts of wrong and vnrighteousnesse seeme beautifull: for men in this age leaue the plaine song, and effect the descant; and so much will they seeme to detest iniurie in the generall, as they loue the conueyances and policies whereby they nourish it in the particular. One man iustifies himselfe by this, that hee relieues such as are in distresse for money, by lending them, but hee ties the borrowers, to such conditions, forfeitures, and incumbrances, as make them oft times to yeeld vp their right and estate into his hands at an vnder valew, rather then to be beholding to him for any kindnesse, further then it standeth with his owne profit. It is a foule fact for Note. a man to hurt his neighbour; but to doe it so closely, as that the poore innocent must thanke his malefactor for doing him a shrewde turne vnder colour of kindenes, how abominable is it? And yet many such prankes are daily plaied in the world, by oppressors, extortioners, and bad executors, subtile comprimitters, protectors of Orphanes, and in a word, by smooth but vnconscionable men, where they can espy their pray, and sease vpon it securely. If *Dauid* hearing of this trespasse but in a parable, abhorred it so farre, as to reade sentence against it, (himselfe being a party and guiltie) saying: the man that hath done this shall dye the death (and yet to steale or take away a Lambe is nothing so much as to swallow vp an whole inheritance, or great summes) then with what securitie shall the vnparciall Iudge of the earth, punish this sinne where he findes it? Especially it being commonly committed by such Cormorants, as *Nathan* there describeth, not stealers for neede, but for lust, hauing themselues wealth at will, yea, and some of them whole flocks of sheepe, when they oppresse the poore of his onely Lambe.

Vers.18 Though the sixe hundred men of the Danites stoode at the dore of *Micah* well armed, yet when the Priest saw them bring out of the house the Ephod, Teraphim, and molten image, he was much moued at it, as thin-
Act.19.27. king with *Demetrius* the siluer Smith, that his trade and so his maintenance would downe and faile him, and therefore he spake to it, asking them what they meant thereby. Hee could doe no lesse, seeing his liuing lay vpon it: but when he saw that he should sustaine no losse, but be a gainer by it, he was well content to let it goe, and all the idolatrous stuffe to be taken away, and that was all that he regarded, and not either his religion toward God, (whose Priest he thought himselfe to bee) or his faithfulnesse and dutie to his master, to whom yet he promised it.

And

And by this motiue of theirs to draw this Prieſt (for of his acceptance we will ſpeake after in verſe 20.) wee ſee, that a number doe meaſure their religion to God and ſeruice to men by their belly: and all that they doe, is ſo long done, as that their commoditie may remaine; but if that faile, neither the one dutie nor the other is regarded of them. And whereas it will be demaunded of mee, if God doe not allow men to liue, in and by doing both, I anſwere, yes: but ſo as men are not to goe from thoſe duties, if maintenance fayle to their ſight and iudgement: for if we be vpright hearted to God in his worſhip, and truſtie to men, God hath promiſed, and hee will make good his word, that we ſhall be prouided for. The hope whereof ought to incourage vs to doe our dutie without fainting. But bee this knowne, that if we depart from both, or either of them, when the liuing is taken away from vs, that we enioyed by them, we neuer faithfully diſcharged our dutie when we did it beſt, while we had our liuing thereby: and if it ſhould be ſo, that in doing dutie to God and men, we could not be maintained as we haue been before, yet I affirme, that we muſt follow the Lord in a meaner eſtate euen as through good report, and bad report: yea, and that a man were better by many degrees not to liue at all, rather then to liue without them. But more conueniently of this in the anſwere which the Leuite makes them. *Doct.* *Matth.6.33.*

Theſe fiue men, when the Prieſt ſpake to them (as we haue heard) at their bringing forth of his idols, they (I ſay) ſoone ſtopped his mouth, telling him, that he ſhould haue no cauſe to complaine, nor his eſtate be any thing the worſe, neither he loſe any thing by that which they did, for he ſhould (they tolde him) goe with them, and be their Prieſt, which (they ſaid) was much better for him then to remaine in a priuate houſe. Thus wee ſee how men thinke with commoditie and preferment to ſtoppe the mouthes of all ſuch as ſtand in their way to hinder their wicked doings, and to ſpeake againſt their ſinnes: and ſo they preuaile to maintaine them. And to this poynt the world is come, that if any bee priuie to their euill doings, which are otherwiſe ſecret, they bee hired with money to conceale it, or if their lewdneſſe be open and manifeſt, then they bribe ſuch as ſhould helpe to puniſh them, as the Prieſts did the watchmen, who kept the Lords ſepulchre: and as for anſwering ſuch as aske how ſuch foule faults can goe vnpuniſhed; it is the eaſieſt way of twentie to giue it forth, that it is a falſe report and a ſlander. Much like to this, is their practiſe in Poperie: for if there be any ſuch among them, yea, or among others, (if they will play the fugitiues) as excell the common ſort in wit, dexteritie, learning or any other gift, which might either make for them or againſt them, they are ſure to bee choaked and corrupted with gifts, as offices, benificies and dignities, for the better aſſuring them to the Catholike cauſe (as they call it) and the conuerting of all their labours, ſtudies, and enterpriſes to the aduancement thereof, and the oppoſing of the contrarie part. And it is admirable what an exceeding zeale and emulation they breede in the mindes of their young nouices, by the rewards which they ſet before them, as they know, who haue ſeene their practiſe euen from the loweſt of the degrees which are taken in their Vniuerſities, to the higheſt preferments which they beſtowe vpon their Champions. *Verſe 19.* *Note.* *Matth.28.13.*

Iudg.16.18. Thus the Philistims with money did winne her that was *Samsons* companion, to yeeld and deliuer him into their hands. Thus *Simon Magus* (Act.8.18.) thought for mony to buy the gifts of the holy Ghost: declaring thereby, that he sawe that to be the way to obtaine the thing he sought, that is, to get fame and great wealth, though he failed and was disappointed in that particular. And how came that to passe? Surely, because hee dealt with them who would not be corrupted with money: thus whoremongers, when their wickednes is like to come forth, doe with money, easily and cleanely winde out of shame and punishment; or if they meet with honester Iudges in Courts, who will not be corrupted, they will by money intice the harlot, to lay the euill fact vpon another, though it be by lying, and false accusing of the innocent, they care not, so as they themselues who are the euill doers may escape. And thus for money open sinne is couered, or coloured, so as it holdeth vp the head oft times, and is not punished. A watchword to all that desire to keepe a good conscience, to arme themselues against this sinne that they be not corrupted with money to conceale, consent to, or to commit any sinne, forasmuch as there is such force in it to draw euen those who haue good things in them, to great iniquity and euill. And so it pleaseth some to iudge of vs, who preach and haue maintenance of the people, that we dare not tell them of their sinne, but flatter them: which indeed were like enough to be true, if they whom we receiue maintenance of, were grosser offenders then other: but if it be otherwise, we shall be easily freed from flattery, and they that are wise will iudge, that we sought rather them, then theirs, and that we labour to make them good Christians by our preaching to them, rather then to inrich our selues by their contribution; which all may see can be but small. But this I handled by occasion, in the story of *Samson* and *Delilah*.

Doct.2. in vers. 19. To returne therefore to these men: whereas they aske him, if it were not better for him to be Priest to many families in a tribe, then to one man: or if the like question were moued now, whether a great commodity be not to be preferred before a lesse; to both the answere is alike; that it is better, if it be with good conditions; as that God be pleased thereby. But otherwise as a dish of greene hearbes is better with peace, then a stalled oxe, with an ill conscience; so I say to both questions. But when little and great are both euill, as his seruing in a priuate house, and to a part of a tribe was: there the least euill was his priuate, being among a fewe, though neither of both were good: and therefore in accepting their offer, hee sinned of the two more grossely.

Prou15.17.

Note.

But in this case there is no necessity to doe either of both, when both, I say, the greater and lesser are euill; for then God hath laid no such burden vpon men that they must doe the one or the other, much lesse auoide one and choose the other, and as men most commonly doe the worser of the two. Therefore neither let vs bring any such bondage vpon our selues, as to allow and beare with our selues herein: as for instance sake to doe a small iniury to our neighbour, so as we shunne a greater. So ye shall heare many light and vaine persons alleage for themselues, that rather then they would be idle, they will spend an afternoone or a whole day, (they speake of the least) in gaming, and good fellowship, with such as themselues be. As if they should

should say, rather then they will be idle, they will be ill occupied. Some ignorant idiots hold this olde relike of superstition still, that when they are reproued for praying for the dead, they answere, Better pray God bee with them then the diuell: whereas of these are both of them forbidden by the Lord: and the best of all is in that case, and the onely good, to say neither. For in all our prayers our Sauiour teacheth vs to be ready in faith, which for the dead we cannot doe. This I say, of such vnlawfull choices as may be auoided easily: wherein yet fooles alway needlessely incurre one extreame to auoid another. And the same may bee said of all other instances in this kinde, euen when there is ineuitable danger insuing on both sides: that the lesse sinne is neuer to be admitted to auoide a greater, seeing none at all is allowed by God, or tollerable: whereof see Chapter 12. verse *6*.

When the Leuite heard this, it is said, his heart was glad; so that although Vers. 20.
before, when the fiue men brought the Idolatrous trash out of *Micahs* house, he then spake to them in great dislike of their doings, and asked them what they meant by so doing; yet now he was well satisfied, when he heard that his departure, and the carrying away thereof, should bee to his preferment. This was the part of an hireling indeed: let his master be depriued both of Doct. him, his seruant, and of his costly furniture which he had prouided; yea let him lose both together, he careth not. A notable description of an hireling, who hath no regard of any thing but of his belly: and so as he himselfe may fare well; he leaues others in the bryars, whom hee is bound yet by couenant and duty to regard as himselfe. Such are all they, who against conscience, doe wrong and wring them with whom they deale, respecting no equity nor honesty, but their owne aduantage and benefit. For it is with the most, as with the vniust steward, that if they can inioy their former commodity no longer, they be ready for any other, how bad soeuer the conditions be. It is not to be denied, that a good turne, or a commodity, which commeth into a man, especially when hee was in distresse for the want of it before, maketh glad the heart, and warmeth the spirit of him that receiueth it, both for the seasonablenes, and also for the benefit and vse thereof. Howbeit there must be a good consideration had, whether the manner of getting and comming by it be lawfull or not: for when the desire of obtaining, or the delight in any earthly good already possessed, letteth passe this wisedome and drowneth it, it is no hard matter to gesse at such a mans disease, and the temper of his corrupt heart, as it were, by the pulse handled and felt, which I speake, to the ende that men may learne how to iudge of themselues aright, (without partiality or selfeloue) by that they feele within: for if their couetous, vncleane, profane, loose, voluptuous affections which doe commonly stirre in them, doe also rule and carry them, though there be neuer so faire wether abroad, so that no man can openly conuict them, yet it will bee ill with them at home in secret, yea all such doings will surely come to naught. And if men will not marke such secret passages of their hearts, as in this kinde, if they swell sometimes, though they can bite in reuenge, and if they will linger after stollen liberty, though shame keepe them from open filthines, leaping for ioy when they haue their pleasure of their enemy, or haue got commodity into their hands vnlawfully; these (I say) though they breake not out to laughter in

the sight of men, yet if they will smother and nourish these corruptions, without checke and controlement, when they breake forth (as in whom doth they not more or lesse) in time these men will either breake out openly and shamefully, or be so full of their sinnes, as that they shall not containe themselues, but in euery of these betray and accuse themselues as grossely as either *Lamech* or *Iudas* did in the one, or as this vnconscionable hireling did in the other: who (it is like enough suspected himselfe of theeuish or couetous desires, as little as his master did, till the occasion in the money that he had stolne from his mother, offered in time, bewrayed him.

2 But while this hireling dealeth thus with his master, it is to bee considered, how iust a thing it was with God to punish this *Micha* his master thus, who had dealt so slightly in the receiuing him into his seruice, neither knowing what he was, nor what was in him, and yet would hire him, thin-
2. Chron. 13.9. king as *Ieroboam* did; that who would, might bee a Priest, that could offer seuen rams: but herein *Michas* sinne appeared to be the greater, in that he knew that this Leuit belonged to the visible Church, yet he would turne and perswade him to become an Idolater: and euen so this hireling, though not without great sinne, serueth him accordingly. It should teach men in generall, not to be bold in prouoking and sinning against God, for he will be one time or other auenged: and particularly it should teach them to see whom they receiue into their house to doe them seruice. For according to
Psal. 101.7. their care, so may be their hope of blessing. If *Dauid* was commended for saying, That no deceitfull person, nor such an one as telleth lyes, should dwell in his house, then much lesse ought such to be entertained into our seruice as are scorning Ishmaelites, or taunting Edomites; nor swearers, drunkards, whoremongers, fauourers of Popery, or cauillers against the preaching of the Gospel, except they would renounce all such bad courses, and promise willingly to be subiect to good gouernment, and that they desire to be reclaimed.

For when we care not whom we take into our house, wee must looke to be serued thereafter: we looke for diligence, truth, and trustines in our ser-
Note. uants, but we take not the way thereto, when we be not first faithful to God our selues, nor make no better choice, nor traine them no better when wee haue them. If we will aske, where we shall finde such seruants? I answere, if ye seeeke for them among your good friends, though a farre off, as ye will doe for good breed of cattle, and teach them kindly, and giue them good
Note. example, and procure the preaching of the Gospell in your townes, or carry them with you, where it may be inioyed of them, if you haue it not at home: and if ye say, ye cannot doe these things, then I say, you care not for good seruants that may serue God, but for such as may serue your selues, and then you are very like to want both. And whereas you will say, there are not good ones enough for all; I answere, all will neuer seeke them; but doe you that professe, labour for them that are religious, and for the rest, let the dead bury the dead. This I haue added according to that which I promised in the 17. Chapter for a more full explication of the sinne of *Micha*.

Vers. 21. In this verse it is said, that these men of *Dan* did not dally in bringing out the Idols, but they carryed them away with them, Priest and all, and none are

are said to haue found fault, either with the theft, or the Idolatry intended, among them, and the carrying of those Idolatrous implements away by those fiue, out of *Michas* house, but they all agreed therein together. Onely in their iourney we may see, that through an euill conscience, they put their children, cattell, and stuffe before them, lest any euill should befall them by those that they thought would surely pursue them.

So that we may see, that there is in wicked men a checke and sting of conscience for the much euill they doe, but fewe of them take warning thereby, to accuse themselues, and to goe forward with that worke of penitently turning to the Lord from the euill they goe about, though they haue a faire warning thereby, and a good furtherance thereto. And this point hath his truth in all degrees of euill persons, from the Heathen, to the worst hypocrite. In so much that the Apostle chargeth the former sort with it thus, That they had their thoughts accusing or excusing them. And of the other, that of our Sauiour may serue, Iohn 3. That men hate the light, because their deedes are euill, although they knowe full well that they are so, and yet fight against their owne light and knowledge that God hath giuen them; yea and heathens as well as Christians, haue had enough to doe to resist the terror of their guilty consciences, as the histories and fictions of *Medea, Theseus*, and the like haue witnessed. And for the striuing against such their light of nature, the same Apostle doubteth not to say, That God gaue them ouer to a reprobate sense, to commit things as much against nature, as many among vs doe against the light of the word. Oh therefore that is a grace of God peculiar to his beloued ones, when the word, or when the conscience warneth them, not to slubber vp their sinne, and wash it away slightly in time, but to count it as Gods voice to turne them backe, seeing such checks would otherwise be a further witnes against them. For they being warned of Gods displeasure thereby, and not seeking to returne to him againe, they haue the more against them, and they are another time the more hardned, so that they shall not bee able to seeke the Lord in their necessity, as they shall haue great cause to doe, but still to be further off; and euen so shall their iudgement be, for if their conscience accuse them, God is greater, as the Apostle saith.

Doct. *Rom.2.15.* *Iohn 3.19.* *1.Ioh.3.20.*

THE REST OF THE SECOND PART OF THE Chapter, to verse 27. and the third part to verse 30.

Verse 22. *And when they were a good way from the house of Micha, the men that were in the houses neere to Michas house, were gathered together, and ouertooke the children of Dan.*

23. *And they cryed vnto the children of Dan, and they turned their faces, and said vnto Micha, What aileth thee, that thou commest with such a company.*

24. *And he said, Ye haue taken away my gods which I made, and the Priest, and ye are gone away; and what haue I more? and what is this that ye say vnto me, What aileth thee?*

25. *And the children of Dan said vnto him, Let not thy voyce be heard among vs, lest angry fellowes runne vpon thee, and thou lose thy life, with the liues of thy houshold.*

26 *And*

26. *And the children of Dan went their way: and when Micha saw that they were too strong for him, he turned and went backe vnto his house.*

27. *And they tooke the things which Micah had made, and the Priest which he had, and came vnto Laish, vnto a people that were at quiet, and secure, and they smote them with the edge of the sword, and burnt the City with fire.*

28. *And there was no deliuerer, because it was farre from Zidon, and they had no busines with any man: and it was in the valley that lieth by Beth-rehob, and they built a City, and dwelt therein.*

29. *And they called the name of the City, Dan, after the name of Dan their father, who was borne vnto Israel: howbeit the name of the City was Laish at the first.*

The summe to verse 27. WE haue heard of the wicked part that these men of *Dan* plaid at mount Ephraim, and what they did to *Micah*. Now it is shewed in these verses, that when they were departed thence, *Micah* with the helpe of his neighbours, followed after them, to see if they could recouer the things that they had taken away: but all in vaine, for they could not. But they were threatned euen the losse of their liues also, if they returned not, but would needs goe forward to follow after them: and so hee with his helpe, were faine to returne home againe, as they came.

Doct. vers. 22. It appeareth that there was a streete of houses, and many neighbours neere to *Micah*, who being made priuy by him, what was done by the men of *Dan*, they gathered themselues together, and went after them, and made an outcry when they came neere them. This teacheth, that the mightier haue need of the meane, and one of the helpe of another: as *Micah* here had of his neighbours, and *Iuda* of *Simeon*; and wee should know, (Iudg. 1. 3.) that it is the condition of vs all, to stand in neede of the aide one of another, and that we cannot liue of our selues. Which vexeth the hearts of many scornefull persons, who would be beholding to none, neither would be seruiceable to any. The vse to be made of it, is to cast off statelines and disdaine, and that we should not despise, no not the meane, but vse them kindly, and liue innocently among them, but yet so, as we communicate not with them in their sinne, howsoeuer that should alienate them further from vs: we must commit the successe to God, who can draw their hearts to vs if need be, for all that, as hee did the Egyptians to the Israelites, and make (Exod. 11. 3.) them see, wee haue giuen them no cause of their so being incensed against vs.

But set we not light by them, for so, in our greatest need, we may be put to our shifts, when of all other, they onely are able to doe vs good; as it falleth out sometimes. And to this end we may remember, that when the Israelites had cast out *Iphta* from among them, both vniustly and cruelly; (Iudg. 11. 2.) afterward, when they stood in need of him, so as without him they had been spoiled by the Ammonites, they were driuen with shame to craue his helpe, (Iudg. 11. 7.) and if he had not bin a man of a peaceable spirit, and void of desire to reuenge, their scornefull and vnkinde dealing with him, had been their ouerthrow and vndoing, and might haue taught all other by their example to liue peaceably with meaner then themselues. Therefore well saith the Apostle to this purpose, *The eye cannot say to the hand, I haue no need of thee, &c.* (1. Cor. 12. 21.)

And

And as *Micha* had need of his neighbours,ſo they were ready to helpe him ſo farre as they were able: which likewiſe teacheth, that it is the dutie of men againe,to lend their helpe to their neighbours in their neede, and not to withhold it from them: which while ſome froward, ſpitefull, and vnkinde perſons haue done,onely of a bad minde,they haue been left as miſerable ſpectacles to be looked vpon for their waiwardnes,and tetchy mood.

Let the men of Succoth and Penuel bee examples to all men of this that I ſay: who ſcornefully denying to ſuccour *Gedeon* in his great need, as hee paſſed by them to purſue the Midianites,receiued this for their reward,that they of Succoth euen the chiefe of them (Aldermen,as we call them) were Iudg.8.16. torne in pieces with briars and thornes of the wilderneſſe: and the men of Penuel had their tower throwne downe, in which they ſo greatly truſted and gloried. Like to theſe are ſuch as vpon a tetch and a pritch taken againſt their honeſt neighbours,wil remoue their dwelling,and depart from them, only to ſatisfie their owne peeuiſh minde, and to ſpite and hurt their neighbours,till either they be conſtrained with ſhame to returne to them againe, or to wiſh they had neuer ſo yeelded to their owne froward mindes,when Note. they ſee how God hath croſſed them: which to ſuch ſtomacks,is no meane puniſhment: as I haue not once or twice before obſerued in this booke.

Theſe men of *Dan* ſhew themſelues to haue been moſt vile and lawleſſe Verſ.23. perſons,that when they had robbed the man, and hee ſought his owne by crying after them,they aske him what he aileth: thereby declaring they did not onely not pitie him,who was much grieued,but alſo ſcorne and mocke him. This ſheweth the ſenſeleſſe vnreaſonablenes of thoſe men, who when they haue wronged and hurt their neighbour,make nothing of it,but threaten they will doe them more hurt. Shewing themſelues to be ſubiect to no law nor equitie, who doe not weigh what meaſure they offer to other, but truſting to their might and ſtomacke,doe what they liſt; much like them, who when they haue taken away a mans cloake, will haue his coate alſo. Such are not fit to be liued withall, for they will not themſelues put vp the leaſt iniurie: and they who hold their neighbours at the like point, though they doe not boldly ſay ſo,are in the next degree of ſin. But wee who confeſſe wee haue been otherwiſe taught of God, ought to abhorre vnto the death,all ſuch dealings,and meaſure other by our ſelues,and offer not that to them which we would in no wiſe our ſelues goe vnder. For be wee well aſſured, that though they bee not able to make their part good againſt vs, God will be auenged of vs.

It is a thing harſh and vnpleaſing to caſt a man in teeth with a benefit: but it cuts the heart-ſtrings in two,to doe a man a ſhrewd turne, and to bid him put it vp,leſt he ſuſtaine a greater at their hands alſo. It was wont to be odious,to breake a mans head,and afterward to apply a plaiſter: but a thouſand times worſe to heale a wound in the fleſh with a wound at the heart. Not vnlike to that of *Iehu* to *Iehoram*, (though warranted by God) who meeting him wounded at Izreel, ſtrooke him with an arrow to the heart. It had been crueltie in the higheſt degree,if God had not borne him out. And ſuch is the cutting and curſed ſpirit of thoſe,who after the fleaing of the skin off,and eating the fleſh of their poore aduerſaries; doe threaten Note. them to make dice of their bones alſo.If *Reuben* could ſay, his brethren were

Gen.42.22. iustly followed with Gods reuenging hand, in that they had not pitie vpon their brother *Ioseph* crying in the bitternes of his spirit vnto them; what (thinke ye) do such deserue, as ioy in making the burthens of them heauier,
2.Chro.10.10. who sunke vnder them before already as *Rehoboam* did? For as it is the perfection of bountie to reioyce in their well doing, whom we haue releeued: so it is the height of crueltie to insult ouer the oppressed. And seeing both the open stealth, and this outragious dealing of these Danites, was one wofull fruit of wanting gouernment: let it teach vs to count it a blessing worth somewhat, that by the good lawes (which are as hedge and ditch to keepe out such incrochers) wee enioy our owne commodities free from such monstrous cormorants, and open spoylers of vs, yea and from vsurping ty-
2.Thes.3.2. Gal.5.10. rants who might make our liues irksome to vs, as *Iezabel* made *Elias* his life to him. Pray we that we may long (and with fruite) enioy this blessing, to be deliuered frō such vnreasonable men, as would leaue vs stript of all, with the mends in our owne hands. And seeing they are most like to fall to this who (being conscienslesse) haue others at aduantage, and feare no superiors to controle them; let such also learne to know they haue a Master in hea-
Coloss.4.1. uen, who can pay them home to the full, for their vsurping ouer them whō they oppresse, whether Landlords, Guardians, or the like, and that hee will also doe it accordingly. *Pharaoh, Edom* and the heathen nations, with the crucifiers of our Lord Iesus, were met with at length, for their adding sorrow to sorrow vniustly and cruelly vpon them who mourned vnder their burthen, and cried out in the agony and anguish of spirit, and could not be heard.

Vers.24. He answereth them they had taken away his Gods, and his Priest, in the which he ioyed, and had nothing left wherein he so much delighted: and had he not cause then (said he) to complaine? As if hee had said, hee could haue been content to haue lost all that he had, rather then his Gods. Marke wee here the vehemencie of his affection to this trash, and no more vehement, then brutish: oh how neerely his heart was knit thereunto. And yet we know hee was grossely bewitched and deceiued: for (to speake as the
1.Cor.8.4. truth was) his Idols were nothing, and his Priest could doe him no good, no not that way that hee most imagined and looked for: but for the euill they wrought him, who doth not know that hee did set the Lord against him, I meane those his cursed doings? The Prophet *Esay* complaines of the
Esay 44.19. sottishnes of those Idolaters of his time, who said to a third part of the tree, whereof they both made a fire to warme them, and heated their ouen to bake their bread, yet said to it, thou art our God, and were so bewitched as to fall downe and worship it. The like we see here in *Micha* calling them his gods, whom yet we see he was faine to rescue by force, but they could not deliuer themselues, nor their owner from this wrong and indignitie.

But how admirable is this, that error, fancie, and imagination should so feruently and neerely draw mens heart and loue to a stocke and an Idoll; and yet that the cleere knowledge of the true God in Christ alsufficient to helpe his beloued ones, and neuer leauing them thus in despaire, can so hardly winne affection to him, for the infinite goodnesse which hee hath done, and is still ready to doe for them? and further he hath prom sed to do
Ephe.3.20. that which passeth all that we can thinke of, and yet all this cannot knit our hearts

hearts to him,and cause vs to make him our song,and our delight. Oh while Papists dote vpon their Crucifixes and Images, which can doe them no good, but deceiue them, that professed Christian's cannot account it the greatest portion, and their felicitie to know that the Lord *Iehoua* is their God alsufficient, who will suffer them to want nothing that is good for them.

Oh with how much adoe can they, I say, reioyce by their beleeuing, (which is the greatest ioy in this life) while the other are rauished with a meere and deluding fancie, to wit, that the sillie creature framed by a man, is the Creator almightie, who hath made heauen and earth. This Idolater *Micha*, with such other, may teach vs how to set vp the Lord in our hearts, and esteeme of his Maiestie. For how much more ought wee to set our hearts on the Lord, and our affections on heauenly things, and to make him our ioy and felicitie? But withall consider the blindnesse of them who count them their gods which men may steale away: such was *Laban* and the Idolaters of our daies. Rom.15.13.

When *Micah* had plainly laid open his griefe and the wrong which they had done him, they were so little moued at it, that they threatned to proceed further against him if he returned not. And thus to their former wrong that they did them, and the scorning of them, they adde sharp threats to him also, who yet sought but his owne. But it verifieth the prouerbe, Whom a man hath hurt, him hee hateth, because hee knoweth hee seekes reuenge, and that on him who did him the wrong. But I will adde nothing to that I haue alreadie said of it. Onely this I note, how the wicked goe from euill to worse: in so much, as when they should be ashamed and wearie of their euill past, they are readie to runne to further mischiefe. And as it is with these and was with those Danites, so are many at this day at the same point: who make no vse of their precious time, though they had more need to seeke to be reconciled to the Lord, and that speedily for their sinnes past; rather then to runne further in debt with him, who must bee left to the iudgement seate of God, who shall giue them their desert in his due time; and let all that loue the Lord Iesus and their owne soules, depart from iniquitie; yea abstaine from all shew of euill, that so they may bee sure they shall neuer fall to the depth of wickednesse, that these men of *Dan* were come to: and such like to them are growne vnto. Of the proceeding of sinne, I haue oft spoken. A most cursed relike of corrupt nature, to hate him whom we had more need to make amends vnto. Vers.25. 2.Tim.2.19. 1.Thess.5.22.

THE NINETIE SIXE SERMON, ON THE XVIII. CHAPTER OF THE BOOKE OF IVDGES.

Vers.26. NOw to proceed, *Micha* is constrained to returne as hee came: but as farre off from obtaining any reconsideration and repentance for his sinne, (though God had giuen him occasion enough) as he was from obtaining any redresse of his wrong. But he that so foolishly boasted of his good hap, as he counted it, to wit, that he knew God loued him, for that hee had giuen him a Leuite to be his Priest; might he not more iustly haue said, I hope this is some likelihood to me, that the Lord will loue and be mercifull to me, in that hee hath taken both Priest and Idols from me? as *Ephraim* did, who hauing bin most blind-
Hose.14.8. ly deuoted to Idols; yet repenting, cried out, saying: What haue I to doe with Idols? But to let him passe, learne we not onely how vaine a thing it is to glorie of that which is a shame to vs, as wee see here *Micha* did: but also how hard it is for such kinde of persons to be brought to true repentance.
Heb.3.13. And so it is for all such as are hardned by the deceitfulnes of sinne: which should cause all to be the more afraid to yeeld hastily or at all to their owne lusts, vnlesse they could as easily come to themselues againe, and cast them off when they would. It is an easier matter to robbe a couetous man of his money, then of his couetousnesse: for though the fewell being remoued, the flame is allaied, yet if the fire bee not quenched, it will lie long vnder the ashes, and in time breake foorth againe. Euen so, *Micha* returned without his Idols, but not without an idolatrous heart within him, which was enough to set him on worke againe, and vndoe him. Much like to the bankrupt, who being wedded to his occupation of borrowing and liuing vpon it, which hath before wasted him, though he breake often, yet he will set vp againe, and fall to his trade, be it neuer so little stocke which hee hath to begin againe withall. It was but a womans weake conceit which supposed,
Gen.31.34. that if her fathers Idols were stollen, he would renounce his false worship. As for *Micha*, his error had so ensnared him, that he rather imagined God to be further of, and his condition more woful through this losse, then before: whereas he should rather haue imagined God to be highly offended with him, and his trade, the Leuite and his implements being thus stollen away, whereby before he assured himselfe foolishly, that God loued him. What shall we then conclude from hence? That his bad successe should haue of it selfe alone driuen him from his profession? No, in no wise, for the best persons and their causes may outwardly be crossed. How then? Let it teach vs the miserie of all such people, as whom their sinne hath so blindfolded, that they can neither see any thing to disswade them from entring vpon it, nor from

from obstinate continuance in it. Whether they thriue outwardly or not, God accurseth them, and plagueth them for their resisting the cleare light, and not receiuing the truth in loue, and with simplicitie of heart. Now seeing the prince of this world hath blinded them, that like bats and moles they should not see the beautie and glorie of the Gospell: therefore they are giuen ouer to beleeue lies, and the Lord suffreth them to be strongly deluded by the spirit of error or profanenesse. So that if they prosper, they doe (as the Philistims) sacrifice to their Dagon: if not, yet they will admit no preiudice of their corrupt Religion or practise. But all this while they see not their sinne which brought them into this maze: that is, an hatred of the light, and loue of darknesse, lest they should be reformed. Let vs therefore count it a great mercie of God, that we haue escaped this mischiefe: and as we are enlightned by the truth, so see we that we walke therein, and know our selues approued by God, by that inward testimonie and comfort of his spirit.

The third part of the Chapter.

OF *Micahs* pursuing the men of *Dan*, but all in vaine, we haue heard in the fiue former verses: Now in these three following, wee see these men of *Dan* went away with the Priest of *Micah*, and his idolatrous implements, and came vpon the men of Laish, and burnt their citie, and slew them, there being none to helpe, and that afterward they builded it againe, and dwelt in it, and gaue it a name after *Dan* their father. Vers. 27.28.29.

As the men of *Dan* did with *Micahs* Idolatrous trash, so haue the Papists taken to themselues strange ceremonies both from the Iewes & Heathens, almost infinite in their Masses, and Seruice. From the Iewes, oile, water, incense, salt, lights, and many other; which in the time of the Law were not idolatrous, when they stood in force by Gods word. And those which they receiued of the Heathens, as the worshipping the bread, the praiers to Saints, the falling downe before Images and Relicks, praiers for the dead, and such like, these (I say) were superstitious and idolatrous before, and still are with them, and no better then they were while they were vsed of the Heathens. But serue we God in spirit and truth. Doct. vers. 27. John 4.24.

As for these men of *Dan*, though they tooke the citie as they might lawfully doe, yet was there nothing commendable in them in that which they did: but many euils were committed by them, which caused their habitation, which might haue been a sweet blessing to them, and a pledge of eternall habitation in glorie after the dissolution of this temporall life, to be nothing else but a temporarie abiding place to them. And their wicked liues depriued them of their sweet communion with God, and of all reioycing soundly and aright in him: and all because they went thither (as I said) defiled with foule sinnes against both Tables, especially theft and Idolatrie, with other shamefull blots and staines in their liues, which draue God from among them. So let vs know, that they prouide no better for themselues, who enter into their dwellings, marriages, inheritances, or vpon any other temporarie prerogatiues with vncleane hearts, bodies, or liues. The reason hereof is manifold; First the title which any man hath to his outward portion, standeth in his spirituall interest and right to eternall life: Euen as Canaan in that respect was giuen to be the possession of the Church, and taken from the Heathens as intruders and vsurpers; So that he who hath not Christ, and yet hath all other things, holdeth a possession without title, which no custome (be it of neuer such continuance) can warrant against reentrie or forfeiture. Secondly, as his title is crackt and naught, so his vse

Tit.1.15. is impure and profane. To the vncleane (saith the Apostle) all things are vncleane. As they hold them not in God, so they vse them not for him, nor to his honour or seruice, but the seruice of their lusts, sensualitie, or pride of life. As the Leper by his touching so lewd persons, polluted the best ordi-

Psal.50.16. nances of God, the most spirituall, I may say it, much more the temporall benefits of God which stand in things indifferent. Thirdly, their hearts are so profane, that it is a most vnsauorie thing vnto them to sanctifie any blessing, dwelling, marriage, recreation, either at the entrance vpon them, or in the vsing thereof, by praier, thanksgiuing, mercie, or the like (which we haue expresse charge of) and therefore they must needs defile them by wantonnesse, riot, ease, idlenesse, securitie, voluptuousnesse, and a thousand such lusts, which fret into them, as the disease of leprosie that I spake of, did into the bodie, or wals of the person and dwelling tainted therewith. And therefore God his curse is in their buildings, marriages, fruit of their bodies, and the rest of their pleasures and commodities, seeing they are founded in crueltie, rapine, vncleannesse, couetuousnesse, and other sinnes. And though it appeare not at the first, yet the secret curse of God, which maketh all these execrable, will in his time breake out, either to the worlds eye, as in beggerie, shame, vtter extirpation and ruine, or assuredly to the destruction of their soules eternally, who haue so corrupted them. And this may all be verified of these Danites here: who though they seemed to account the habitations of these Heathens impure (as appeareth by their ruinating and new building of them) yet themselues being no whit better in their worshipping of God, nor manners, then the inhabitants whom they destroyed, they defiled their new buildings by the wickednesse they brought with them, as much as the other had done by the taint which they left behinde them. The vse is, that wee sanctifie the Lord in our hearts, and make him chiefe, and also dedicate our selues and all we haue, to the glorie of his name,

1.Cor.6.20.15. yea, euen our bodies to be Temples for his spirit to abide in. And that we remooue from his presence whatsoeuer might make him to loath this mansion of his in vs, by sweeping out such draffe, and clensing our selues from

2.Cor.7.1. all that is filthy of the body and minde. So shall we haue the Lord, with his perfuming grace, which is farre more fragrant and sweete then *Aarons* oyntment, to sweeten our hearts, and dwell with vs: whilest the vngodly labour to driue him furthest off from their consciences, companies, and dwellings.

2 It is said, that the men of *Dan* came vpon the people of Laish being improuident and secure, so as they destroyed them with ease: where we haue somewhat to note out of their condition wherein the men of *Dan* found them, and somewhat of the effect that followed. They found them quiet, that is, safe and sure (in their owne opinion) and therefore without mistrust. The summe is, that through long peace and continuance of outward

prospe

prosperitie, they were both within themselues at ease, and as they would be, and feared no danger by other forrein enemies. It is no wonder (being Heathens) that a rich and plentifull citie waxed secure and sensuall: for without especiall grace, wealth and welfare, hearts ease and abundance, will make euen Protestants turne profane, like Atheists. I meane it will make them thinke they are the onely happie men, and especiall when the thought of death is absent, (as what is so forcible to put away the remembrance of the euill day, or to put into the heart a foolish conceit of an eternitie here, and an earthly paradise) they will be ready to thinke themselues pettie gods vpon earth. Wee see what it is then which men so mightilie striue and scuffle for in the world, euen that which (without Gods feare, a thing little thought of with such) is able to make a man like a diuell in the flesh. For whereas the diuell beleeueth God and trembleth, behold the Iam 2.19.
heart of such a man, as I speake of, is so lockt vp, and he so entrenched within his safe holde and strong castle of wealth and greatnesse, that he thinkes himselfe out of Gods reach, and gunshot. Preach to him of dutie, of the promises, of terror, all enter alike: he is too good to obey any superior, and therefore command him nothing: he is as well as his heart can wish, therefore offer him no promises: and he hath made a league with hell and death, and therefore terrors are but as a noyse of many waters, which may well sound in his eares, I will not denie but they reach not to his conscience. And this we haue seene, and see daily in men, whose hope is only in this world, that so they may haue their fill of pleasure, wealth, and honour, their feare of God, or Diuell, care for Heauen or Hell is all alike. I remember what one of the Popes (a belly-god) spake of his peacoke, (a diet forbidden him by his Physitians) Giue it me saith he in the spite of God: So saith euery other monster in his kind, giue me my desire here, and take Gods faire promises for hereafter who will, I will looke to my bodie, I will eate and drinke, and say to the wedge of gold, Thou art my right hand (which, Iob.31.28.
but so much as to haue said, *Iob* counted it all one, as to denie the Almightie) yet they say to him, depart from vs, we desire no acquaintance with thy wayes? what profit shall we haue if we pray to thee? Nay, not onely Iob.21.14.15.
such as haue these things in possession, but euen poore people in their desires, shew themselues as brutish: Here is much preaching, and professing (say they) but it was a merry world when we might go to Church to heare a Masse, and haue our bellies full: this new learning hath eaten vp all hospitalitie. Is there such force then in pelfe and trash, to make a man denie God, renounce his truth, giue ouer Religion, and conscience? yea doubtlesse, there is in our nature abundance of *Esaus* prophanesse: but to be of Gen.25.33.
Dauids minde, Psal. 4. Lord shew vs the light of thy countenance, and thou Hebr.12.16. Psal.4.7.
shalt make vs more ioyfull then they who inioy much in the world: Or to chuse with *Salomon*, 1. King. 3. That we may please God rather then our 1.King.3.5.9.
selues, that must come from grace. Let it teach both such as hast to be rich, and such as are alreadie; to be sober minded, to checke themselues for the contrarie, and lay before their eyes, the examples of such vile men in Scripture, as haue degenerated in this kind, abhorring not them onely, but themselues in them, that they may not become like to them by degrees. And let feruent prayer be ioyned therewith, that the Lord would guide

their hearts to the loue of his Maiestie, and keepe them from the putting their confidence in any thing below, which might alienate them from trusting in the liuing God. The deceitfulnesse of riches, and carnall ease, shall else assuredly carrie them to this fearefull extremitie.

Doct. 2. in verſ. 27. Now secondly, the little mistrust of this people of Laish, was another cause of their ruine. A great follie it was for so sufficient a citie to be vnprouided and fenced against whatsoeuer might befall them from forreine violence: and commonly men binde surer in these cases. But in matters spirituall, these secure men of Laish are the right mirror of most professors: who hauing to deale with an enemie of so inuincible strength, diligence,
1. Pet. 5. 8. subtiltie and crueltie, as the diuell is, (so described by *Peter*) themselues being so weak, carelesse, and simple as they are: yet as if they had a priui-
Note. ledge, walke at libertie, so that the diuell need not watch them a mischiefe, for they lie open euery way for want of watchfulnesse and armour: as in *Samsons* storie hath appeared. This is that which one time or other will light vpon such, and now much more in the light of the Gospell where men haue knowledge, and regard not. So in the daies of *Lot*, the people did eate and drinke, marrie, and were married, till fire came downe from
Matth. 24. 37. Heauen, and destroyed their cities, Zodome and Gomorra. So were the Amalekites come vpon that burnt Ziglag, and when they had done, they
1. Sam. 39. 16. lay scattered on the earth like beasts, eating, drinking, and dauncing, for the great pray that they had taken, and *Dauid* came vpon them, and smote them from the twylight, euen to the euening of the next morning. And while men so crie, peace, peace, at this day, as too many doe, they may looke
1. Thess. 5. 3. for the like successe. The sound and safe securitie, is the quiet and holie resting vpon God in all stormes & tempests, and this commeth from faith, which is to be sought of all, whereby onely quiet rest to our hearts can be obtained. See more in the 15. Chapter and 16. in *Samsons* destroying the Philistims.

Verſ. 27. 28. These people of Laish had no fellowship with other, neither cared for them, and therefore now in their need there was none to helpe them, being farre off from neighbours. And it was now verified in them, that is a common prouerbe, He that careth for no bodie, no bodie shall care for him: And he that stoppeth his eares at the crying of other, shall crie him-
Prou. 21. 13. selfe, and not be heard; and iudgement shall be without mercie to them
Iam. 2. 13. that shew none. Euen so, despise we none, neither set we light by any though meane: for in so doing, it may come to passe, we may stand in need of their helpe, and then we may be sure it shall be farre off from vs.

I knew a woman of great wealth, and chiefe among the neighbours that dwelt by her, who scornefully esteemed of them, and regarded not the poore. And it being obserued by the Preacher a right godly man, he tolde it to her, that so should it be vnto her, namely, that she should be so requited. And after a fewe yeares, (when yet her wealth was increased, and she preferred to higher estate by marriage) God a while after visited her with the plague in the middest of her iollity, and so she was carried from compa-
Note, nie into an obscure place, where she could haue no resort, no, not of the meane, vnto her, but dyed desolate, and destitute of the helpe, which had bin like enough for one farre inferiour to her, to haue inioyed, but that the Lord

Lord was minded to leaue an example of that which he hath threatned, and executed vpon many other, to wit, that iudgement shall be without mercy to the mercilesse, an heauy and hard estate to the hard hearted, as to *Iezabel* a cruell persecutor, a cruell death was appointed. Iam.2.13.

When these men of *Dan* had burned downe the City, because (it seemeth) it was not to their liking, they bestowed labour and cost to builde it vp againe: and they did nothing therein to be misliked. But was there any answerable care in them to pray for Gods blessing in their habitation? and to set vp his worship that there might haue bin a spirituall building among them also? Nay, but contrarily, they fell to flat and grosse Idolatry. By which we may see, that men can labour euen till they toile againe to purchase and obtaine an earthly dwelling, which can be but for a while, but as for an heauenly, they will take no paine for it, whereas wee are taught that we should account most chiefly of that in comparison of this: we haue here saith the Author to the Hebrewes, No dwelling or continuing City, but we seeke one to come. Vers.28. *Doct.*2. Hebr 13.14.

The same may be said of foode and wealth, that we should not labour so much for the food that perisheth, but for that which abideth vnto eternall life, and godlines is the great wealth and riches: as if it should be said, that gold and earthly treasure is but the smaller in comparison of that. And yet who hungreth after the bread of life, though he thinketh himselfe to haue neuer enough of that which procureth worldly pleasure, and goeth into the belly? or who careth for the treasure and riches of wisedome and knowledge, when yet in desiring of the earthly pelfe, hee shall be found vnsatiable. Ioh.6.27. 1.Tim.6.8.

When they of *Dan* had finished their worke in building the City, they gaue it also a name, which thing was vsuall in those dayes in many other matters, then at the birth of their children. And the name which they gaue to it was *Dan*, after the name of their father: which they did not to keepe a memoriall of his vertues, they themselues being loaden with vice; but that there might be a vaineglorious remembrance of the name continued, like *Absaloms* piller. Euen so it is a common thing with men to seeke their owne glory, when they can be well content to lay the glory of God in the dust, and (which is all one) to haue it buried: whereas yet, who knoweth not, that the wise man should not glory in his wisdome, nor the strong in his strength, nor the rich in his riches; but let him that glorieth, glory in this, that he knoweth me, saith the Lord. So vaine is the glorying in all that is momentany and earthly. The contrary duty hath been often forced, and insisted vpon by the practise of *Gedeon*, *Iephte*, and *Samson*. Touching the vaineglory of these *Danites*, see verse the 12. of this Ghapter. Vers.29. Ier.9.23.

The fourth part of the Chapter.

Verse 30. *Then the children of Dan set them vp the grauen Image, and Ionathan the sonne of Gershom the sonne of Manasseth and his sonnes, were the Priests in the tribe of the Danites, vntill the day of the captiuity of the land.*

31. *So they set them vp the grauen Image, which Micah had made, all the while the house of God was in Shilo.*

The summe. IN these last two verses of the Chapter, the holy story sheweth, that when these men of *Dan* sawe how all came to passe to them as they desired, and as the Leuite had tolde them; and that they were now setled in their dwelling, they were so possessed with this error, that their Priest had brought them all the good successe that they had, that now they setled him and his posterity in the Priesthood, and set vp that Idolatry and false worship that the Priest vsed: who fell himselfe from the true seruing of God, that had been lately before vsed in Israel in the dayes of *Ioshua* and the good rulers after him; and had patched vp such a seruice (as *Micha* had done) and what could that be better then Idolatry and superstition?

Doct. vers. 30. This was the thanks that they gaue to God: and they continued in that Idolatrous course till the death of *Eli* at the least, when the Arke of God was brought from Shilo, and taken by the Philistims, and when Israel was in captiuity to them, and this was forty yeares at the least, for so long *Eli*
1.Sam.4.18. had iudged Israel. Of the efficacy of error in these men of *Dan* so grossely deceiued in ascribing so much to the pretended Priest, and all because his words fell out to be true that he spake of their good successe: Of this (I say) and by this we may obserue, how strongly the spirit of error bewitcheth many, that they shall be perswaded most resolutely, that thing to bee true which yet all that list, may see to be cleane contrary. The reason is: men are most prone and ready by their corrupt nature, to beleeue error and lyes: and therefore much more, when there be many of their minde, and most of all if there come profit or pleasure thereby.

And this is in great part, when men refuse and reiect the truth which they see, or may see, (as these might haue done) then the Lord suffers them to fall to their owne desires and deserts, and giues them strong delusions to beleeue lyes: that all they may be damned that beleeue not the truth, but
2.Thess.2.12. haue pleasure in vnrighteousnes. This is most liuely seene in Antichrists kingdome at this day, who could not so grossely maintaine a religion patched vp with so many vntruths, fancies, and inuentions of men, if the Lord did not giue them vp to their owne delusions: as to worship the creature, in stead of the Creator; to trust to their workes to be saued by them, when the best of them are like a filthy and defiled cloath, and to boast of their righteousnes, yea and workes of supererogation, when yet it may easily be proued that their sinnes are as the haires of their head innumerable, and when
Luk.17. the best haue done the most good they can doe, they are but vnprofitable seruants. After the same manner are they deluded in the profession of the Gospell, who draw neere to God in their bodies, their hearts being farre
Matth.15.9. from him, and professe that they knowe him, but with their deedes they de-
2.Tim.3.5. ny him. To whom may be added, they who measure the truth by the successe they haue, who if they thriue and prosper by the direction and counsell that they take, as these men of *Dan* did, (after the hirelings answere) they seeke no other proofe, that it is the truth which they follow and imbrace. See verse the 26. of this Chapter.

Doct.2. But let this be added to the former: namely, that we may see and obserue by this setting vp this Leuit by the men of *Dan*; how from supposed causes of desert, some are raised vp, and their posterity after them, as this counterfeit Priest, and his children were; who yet deserued no such matter

ter as to be preferred or his posterity prouided for. If they please to fauour them whom they wil set vp, and thinke they haue cause, as these Danites did, it is enough: infinit such things the Lord suffereth to be done, not that we should applaud them who are vnworthily helped and set vp, as *Baals* Priests were by *Iezabel*, but in Gods purpose, to be instruments to doe and execute, his will to speciall purposes. And they in due time, shall giue their account, who haue not vsed that their prosperity for good, but abuse it any way, as this Leuit did to Idolatry.

Also we may see here, what thankes men giue to God for his manifold 3
mercies. These hauing gotten habitation in very commodious manner, they ascribe it to their Idols, and their supposed Priest. Whereas they being the posteritie of the visible Church of God, should haue bin ashamed so to turne away from the true and liuing God, and to giue his honour to stockes and Idols framed by a sinnefull man. Herein being no better then heathens: for so did the Philistims praise *Dagon* for deliuering *Samson* into their hands. The Papists praise their seuerall patrons, Saints, as they call them for their seuerall cures and deliuerances: and therefore although they ioyne God with them, yet they are an abomination to him, who will not haue his honour giuen and diuided betwixt him and cursed Idols, or creatures, and to leaue them, euen wee who professe the Gospell, though wee giue thankes to God, (and yet many of vs ascribe too much to our owne wisedome, and so detract from God) for all that, we honour not God with, and for the good things which he giueth vs, but sin against him the more, because we inioy them to flesh, and hearten our selues in seeking our will. But enough of this in Chapter 16. vpon that acclamation of the Philistims.

For, the Priest (as they called him) the text importeth, that he being taken in by these Danites to be a worshipper of false gods, woond in his posteritie also into his place after him, (though no doubt with the consent of those Danites being so addicted to him) whereby it may appeare, that when darknesse couereth all things, and so the vile and the vnworthy creep into the Ministerie thereby, as they long haue done in this land; that the hurt which commeth thereby, is not only the deceiuing and leauing of many in blindnesse and ignorance, for one generation, and for their time, but successiuely and for many ages after them. And in this land so they haue done, blind Idols I meane, as long as they could be suffred, brought vp their children to follow them in their occupation and trade, to get their liuing easily and idely, as they themselues haue done; some of them couering their dishonest doings with an honest shew of sending them to the Vniuersity two or three yeares, to stop mens mouthes withall: whereby they haue runne into the sinne that *Paul* findeth fault with; namely, that being yong schollers, they are puffed vp, being no better stored of learning for the discharge of their duty, then of grace, to guide their liues aright therein. Now if there be admitted to the Ministery fitter persons, (as it is not to be denied but some are.) and there is more knowledge in many of them, and those also of the posterity of Ministers, then there hath been in former times; it is to be wished also, that they approue themselues to bee fit Ministers of God indeed, by seeking ability to diuide the Scriptures aright, and by their faithfulnes, loue, and diligence in their Ministery, and painefulnes,

1.Tim.3.6.
Note.

at their study and constancy in their good conuersation, to bee lights to other. And as the sonnes of this Priest continued their Idolatry, and their Priest, and his sonnes after him in his place a long time, so would such as I haue spoken of, doe likewise, if the light did not hunt them out of their corners by such as are in authority. For the continuall sounding of this speech in the eares of the Bishops of former yeares, that they had let into the Ministery men of occupations and trades, as seruing men also, and other like, who were good for nothing; this (I say) with the distast that it bred in the eares of some in authority and in high place, did at last giue a deadly blow to that practise, and broke off that custome of making such base persons (I meane Artificers and their like) Ministers in the Church. Euen so now another abuse is brought to light also, to wit, that many who haue bin in the Vniuersity three or foure yeares, are vsually taken into the Ministery, who are as vnfit by their skil and gifts in Diuinity to instruct the people, (the most of them hauing not learned the principles in catechising themselues) as they be vnable and vnmeet to gouerne them, who (for the most part) are vnable to guide themselues? Oh I say, that this euill crept into the Ministery, might be remoued also with the other, and that the chiefe inquiry by them in authority ouer the Ministers, that it were (I say) of the sufficiency of them, their diligence in preaching, and good life, and that the offenders might be amended or remoued. And because I haue now mentioned a great abuse in the Church, as I haue done many other, (especially the scandelous life of many Ministers;) it may perhaps be asked of me if I can as wel set downe any remedy of it: I thinke it not amisse to adde a sentence or two about it; not taking vpon me the office of determining the case, but leauing it to them whom it concerneth.

Therefore this is all that I say: that for the time to come I doe heartily desire, this euill may be carefully auoyded, and no more such vnworthy ones admitted to the Ministery; and not only so, but that there may be better inquiry made for their sufficiency and fitnes to teach by the learned to Acts 1.21. whom it belongeth, and for their innocent life by the testimony of those who haue best knowne their conuersation. And for those, who are in already, I know not better what to say, then to wish and desire that or the like order to be taken for the enabling of them to doe their duties, which my selfe in my time haue seene practised and put in vse by a right reuerend father, an Archbishop in this land, and that was this. That within fiue or sixe miles compasse of some great towne, all the Ministers of that Deanry did euery fortnight assemble together there in the publique place, and three or foure were appointed by moderaters designed for that purpose, to interpret and speake out of a peece of Scripture before the rest of the Ministers, and such of the people as would come to the publike assembly to heare them. Now there were three or foure of the ancient and best approued Ministers appointed to ouersee and be present there also, and euery day of their meeting one of them to speake with the other, three out of the same text; and after the breaking vp, al the Ministers went apart among themselues from the people, and the foure ancients and moderaters, spake in allowing, or finding fault, and incouraging them as they sawe cause. And the reason of this order taking, the right reuerend father alleaged to be this: seeing many were admitted

admitted into the Ministery young and raw, hee saw no way (hee said) to draw them from idlenes and other manifold wayes of mispending their time, to diligence at their study, sober behauiour, and the fitting of them in their places, to doe the people good, no way so likely to be effectuall as this. And who can say any lesse? and so God blessed it exceedingly while it continued: for this I say, and doe well remember, that the Ministers which resorted fortnightly to that place that I did, (being about forty) so applied their study, and liued within compasse in that precinct, (I was yong then, and could take no viewe in other places what was done) but of that meeting that I was of, this I dare affirme as true, that as it was also commonly reported, the Ministery in that place was greatly changed and bettered in their behauiour, sober, vnoffensiue, and well beseeming their places, and they so gaue attendance to reading priuately, that they exercised their Ministery at home with good liking and hope of the profiting of the hearers, who before that had not done so, and they that had made good beginnings were much amended. And I see at this day now full forty yeares since that time, and that with much griefe of heart, that the Ministery in great part is behinde them whom I speake of, in sober carriage of themselues, diligent teaching and study, that I say no more. And this by occasion of this hireling the Leuite, I thought not vnfit nor vnseasonable to set downe; and so an ende of the whole Chapter.

The end of the 18. Chapter.

THE NINETIE SEVEN SERMON ON THE XIX. CHAPTER OF THE BOOKE OF IVDGES.

Verse 1. *Also in those dayes, when there was no king in Israel, a certaine Leuite, dwelt on the side of mount Ephraim, and tooke to wife a Concubine out of Beth-lehem Iudah.*

2. *And his Concubine plaied the whore there, and went away from him vnto her Fathers house, to Beth-lehem Iudah, and there continued the space of foure moneths.*

3. *And her husband arose, and went after her to speake friendly vnto her, and to bring her againe: he had also his seruant with him, and a couple of Asses: and she brought him vnto her Fathers house, and when the young womans Father saw him, he reioyced of his comming.*

4. *And his Father in law, the young womans father restrained him, and he abode with him three dayes: so they did eate and drinke, and lodged there.*

5. *And when the fourth day came, they arose early in the morning, and he prepared to depart: then the young womans Father said vnto his Sonne in lawe, Comfort thine heart with a morsell of bread, and then goe your way.*

6. So

6. *So they sate downe, and did eate and drinke, both of them together: and the young womans Father said vnto the man, Be content, I pray thee, and tarrie all night, and let thine heart be merrie.*

7. *And when the man rose vp to depart, his Father in lawe was earnest: therefore he returned and lodged there.*

8. *And he arose vp early the fifth day to depart: and the young womans Father said, Comfort thine heart, I pray thee, and they tarried vntill after midday, and they both did eate.*

9. *Afterward when the man arose to depart with his Concubine and his seruant, his Father in law, the young womans Father, said vnto him. Beholde now the day draweth toward euen: I pray you tarrie all night: Beholde the sonne goeth to rest; lodge here, that thine heart may be merrie, and to morrow get you early vpon your way, and goe to thy tent.*

10. *But the man would not tarrie, but arose and departed, and came ouer against Iebus (which is Ierusalem) and his two Asses laden, and his Concubine was with him.*

The summe of the Chapter.

IN generall, these three chapters following, set downe another grieuous sinne with the punishment, and some redresse. Particularly, this chapter laieth out an horrible fact committed in those dayes (when there was no ordinarie Magistrate in Israel) of a Leuites Concubine, who after she had plaid the whore, departed and ranne from him to her Father. And how her husband went to take her againe, and as he returned with her at Gibea (where he lodged) she was abused villanously all night by the men of the place: and being found dead in the morning, her husband carried her home, and cut her bodie in twelue peeces, and sent them to the twelue tribes through the land, to the end hee might moue them to see the trespasse punished.

The parts three.

The parts of the Chapter are three. The first containeth the things that are mentioned to haue gone before the foule fact, and they are foure: to vers. 22. The second containes the horrible fact it selfe, to wit, that a Leuits wife was abused all night by the men of Gibea till she died: to verse 28. The third part, how her husband carrying her home with him in the morning, diuided her, and sent her into all quarters of the land, that they might auenge him of the wrong doers.

The first part of the Chapter.

The summe of these ten verses.

IN the first part, as I haue said, wee are to consider of the things that went before the foule fact, which were said to be foure: to verse 22. The first was the womans whoredome, and her hiding it by going to her fathers house, and this to verse 3. The second, her husbands going after her to take her againe: to verse 4. The third, his entertainment at her fathers house: to the 10. The fourth, his departure, trauaile homeward, and lodging at Gibea: to verse 22.

Before I enter into the matter of this first part; because it is said that a certaine Leuite tooke a concubine from Bethlem Iuda, I thinke good to cleere a doubt a doubt that might ariſe from hence : for it may ſeeme that he tooke a concubine,that is,one that had liued before in the faſhion of a concubine,to be now his lawfull wife, as though ſhe had been a concubine before. But as I ſee no reaſon thereof; ſo (queſtionleſſe) wee are to vnderſtand it, that hee tooke her to be his concubine onely. And therefore in Hebrew it is thus read : he tooke a woman a concubine,that is,a woman to be his concubine: and hee tooke not one that had been a concubine to bee his lawfull wife. And the name that is giuen her throughout the Chapter,is concubine,not wife, which were diſtinct names of two diuers perſons; as wee may ſee by *Ketura*, who was *Abrahams* wife, and *Hagar*,who was but his concubine : the one, lawfully ioyned to a man, and partaker of all things with him : the other onely a bed companion.

Now I come to the firſt part of this Chapter,I meane the womans euill fact,which cauſed the Leuite that had taken her to be his concubine,to goe to Bethlem Iuda,was this : to wit,that hee hauing taken her from Bethlem Iuda,where her father dwelt,ſhe had plaied the harlot;and then ranne from him to her fathers houſe, where ſhe continuing a long time, euen foure moneths,and not returning home, hee went thither to take her againe, and to carrie her home,and this is in the firſt three verſes. *The ſumme of the firſt three.*

In the firſt two verſes wee will ſtay a little,as occaſion ſhall bee offered, about her fact,and her hiding it at her fathers houſe. Firſt it is ſaid, that this Leuite dwelt as a ſtranger on the ſide of Mount Ephraim ; which is to bee marked,becauſe the Leuites had cities appointed them to dwell in with the ſuburbs,but yet they went and dwelt in other places,I meane in the townes and villages of other tribes, to teach and inſtruct the people there. Thus God prouided to haue the people taught. The like care he hath had alwaies, Doct. verſ. 1. although not by the ſame meanes, or in the like manner. As as Sauiour a little before his departure teſtified,charging *Peter* if he loued him,he ſhould Ioh. 21.16. feede his lambes and his ſheepe. And this order hath he taken by himſelfe and his Apoſtles,commanding that it ſhould ſtand faſt for euer. But the diuell hath found out many waies to hinder and break off this holy ordinance of God, and they are principally foure. Firſt the irreligiouſnes and couetous mindes of Patrons, who for the moſt part will beſtow the liuing vpon none, but they will bee paid for it one way or other, and ſo they cauſe him that buyeth it,to be faint in the dutie of preaching, and to breake both the law of God many waies,(and namely in forſwearing himſelfe) and the law of man in comming in by money. Secondly,the little conſcience and care of thoſe who haue vpon too ſlight triall of the partie preſented for the liuing,or no triall ſometime of his ſufficiencie in life & gifts of knowledge in the Scriptures, & of preaching,haue admitted him vnto it. Thirdly,the vnconſcionablenes of the Miniſters and Incumbents,that take little pain in ſo weightie a charge to labor after the ſaluation of their people,by doctrine & good example,neither for a gift of handling the Scriptures moſt profitably. Fourthly,the ſin of the people,that care not who be ſet ouer thē,either ſuch an one as is well qualified and approued for his fitneſſe to doe them good, or one that is inſufficient, all is one with them. The vſe hereof is this : that as all ſhould pray the Lord of the harueſt, to thruſt labourers into the harueſt; ſo for all the forementioned foure kindes of perſons particularly, as Math 9. laſt.

they desire the prosperitie of the Church, so to further a good Ministerie.

This Leuites concubine, as the holy storie recordeth, plaied the whore while she kept with her husband and remained with him. And thus wee are to vnderstand the words in this verse, where it is said, that she plaied the whore, against him, or there; for so the words are to be taken and vnderstood, and not that she committed the whoredome with the Leuite: which yet some hold, but without any reason: because though she was concubine to him, yet (say they) she had not her fathers consent, therefore (they say) she liued in whoredome with him: but how proue they that? seeing when he came after to her father for her, he receiued and entertained him kindly, heartily and with great ioy, and so sent her away with him. Therefore it is cleere that he had his consent, and by consequent, that she liued with him as his concubine, and that she committed that wickednesse euen while she was with him, against him, as it is in the text, but not with him, as some fancie and imagine that he did.

This sinne of the woman is aggrauated many waies: as in that she was a woman, and therefore the more shame to her: then in that she was ioyned to an husband and not single: thirdly, in that she was the wife of a Leuite who was a publike person, in which place she ought to haue been a light to other. And from this wee may learne first that many women (which sexe should be more modest and bashfull) are as readily carried, at least allured to the sinne of vncleannesse, as men. I speake it not to extenuate it in men, whom the Lord will most certainly iudge and plague for it, because they are the stronger of the two to auoid it: but yet in a woman it is monstrous, as is to be seene in the harlot which *Salomon* describeth in the booke of the Prouerbs from the 8. to the 24. verse. And therefore as many women haue di-
Prou.7.8. uers blemishes, yea staines in them, which will hardly bee blotted out, so I cannot tell whether any be more shamefull in them then this: especially seeing some of them doe not necessarily goe with other, but this hath many companions or handmaides attending it, of the like sort that it selfe is. The vse of this is, that we count it a singular grace of God, (and therefore labour for it) when both men and women doe content themselues one with the other; without nourishing or admitting strange lusts to carry them to outward vncleannes, euen as it is a grace of like valew in the vnmarried to bring chast bodies and mindes to marriage, or their graues.

2 Secondly, that this sinne in the Leuites concubine was committed by a married person, it sheweth this sinne of adulterie to be out of measure sinfull. And whereas in single fornication necessitie is alleaged, (which cannot iustly be, seeing God hath prouided a remedie against it) yet married couples haue no such occasion) no, not the least) to plead for their so offending: but that it is their foule and filthy yeelding to their outragious lust,
Note. and satisfying of their lewde eyes, and yet more horrible it is, when it shall not bee once done only by importunate impotencie ouertaking them, (which yet were wicked, as it was in *Dauid*) but when it shall come to be made a trade and become an vsuall practise with them.

But here I must giue a watch-word to them that are in danger to fall into this sinne, and yet by some speciall fauour of God haue been kept from it; and that is this: That as the other who haue falne to it, haue their consci-

ences

ences branded with horror,and their persons oft times,namely when they are knowen to be such with reproach: and these who are in danger therof, be in the next degree vnto them, because they are much looking that way, and their thoughts oft times too fast fixed thereon: I say this watch-word I giue to such. First, That they take no liking of any woman,for that which seemeth pretious to them in her, but disgrace and condemne all such dis- coursing thoughts, as the path-way to the action it selfe: for though her lips drop as an hony combe, & her mouth be more soft then oile,yet she is as corruption to his bones that hunteth after her,and her paths (most certainly) leade vnto destruction, and the end more sharp then a two edged sword. Secondly, That they neither allow this libertie to themselues, to suffer their eies to be satisfied in looking vpon such parties, for that is as a glas-window to let sin into the soule,which *Iob* abhorred to doe. Then let them hold those liberties with prayer, not for fashion, but feruent,making like vse of their reading,as the matter they reade shall giue occasion. And with all these,let them oft tell themselues,that this is an vnthankfulnesse to God not to be suffered, for their lawfull marriage and other his benefits to looke after their neighbours wife, or seruant, from whom by strait charge and threats, as by hedge and ditch, he hath separated them. Lastly,if for all these meanes vsing,they shall yet sometime finde, not onely vnstaiednesse, but also impotencie to resist,they must by fasting and prayer set themselues to cast out that limme of the diuell.

Caueats about Whoredome. The first. Prou. 5. 3. The second. Iob. 31. 1. The third. The fourth. Note. The fifth.

3 Againe, in that she was the wife of a Leuite, who had charge in the Tabernacle about the seruice of God, she ought the rather to haue kept her selfe,farre from whoredome, and from smaller offences,which because she did not, her sinne was much the greater. And so we are to take it: for so is the shamefull breaking out in a Ministers wife, (and therefore much more in him) a farre greater dishonour to God,then when it is done by a priuate person, as we may read of *Hophny* and *Phineas* the sonnes of *Eli*: and so in an other kinde, of *Iudas* an Apostle. In like manner it may be said of the Magistrate, if he liue loosely,and be offensiue that way, I meane, in the life in vncleannesse, who is by his place to punish offenders zealously, and by his faithfulnesse and iustice, as by an angrie countenance, to driue away iniquitie. And the same I say of professors, in respect of those which are none; and alwaies such as I speake of,should haue this in remembrance and due consideration,that as all persons are in place more noted for worth and greatnesse: so should they be furthest from sinne of note rather then such as be of smaller reckoning.

Prou 29. 4.

4 When this woman had wrought wickednesse,as we haue heard, she feared her husband, and durst not come in his sight, and sought shelter at her fathers hand, and therefore fled to him to Bethlehem Iudath. She should haue been astonished, as if an arrow had pierced through her liuer: but it appeares that to haue been farre from her. By which we may see,how hard a thing it is to vse the best remedy to heale and plucke out the sting of sinne, (if it haue once been deeply setled in vs, and hath got strength in vs) so that we may recouer our selues, and be whole againe, as before we committed it. Many with shifts hide and extenuate their sinne,but such shall not prosper: other run to their friends, as she did,and thinke they should help them,

Prou. 7. 23. Note. Prou. 28. 13.

 but

but that doth only flesh them, and hold them from repentance: Other though it be said in the Psalme, That no man can make satisfaction for his owne sinne. Many run (as they haue been taught by their blind and superstitious Priests) to popish penance, and to almes giuing, to relieue mens bodies, for the sauing of their owne soules; and flie to patrons as to Saints departed, but all these increase their sinne and their debt thereby, yea, and men haue twenty waies to shift of repentance for a sinne, as from one root spring many branches: But in a melting and broken heart to flie to Christs satisfaction, and then to lay hold on his merits by a true Faith (as they did sometimes on the hornes of the Altar) which Faith is able to quench the

Ephe. 6. 16. fierie darts of the diuell; this (I say) which is the onely remedie, as a great number doe not soundly and cleerely know it, so many of them that doe, yet when they haue most need of it, as this woman had here, cannot vse it and take benefit by it, that so they may also be reformed: but either they feare their sinnes are too great (they say) and therefore God will not forgiue them, or else they doe houerly and not hartily confesse their sinne and aske pardon without vnfeined repentance, and therefore they also goe without it.

5 It is further said, that this woman the Leuites concubine abode foure moneths at her fathers house, and sought not to reconcile her selfe to her husband, which made her fault the greater, and the rather for that we see that he was like to haue receiued her againe, in as much as he came afterward to her fathers house for her. And though she also could haue desired the same, seeing at his comming for, she departed willingly with him from her fathers house, yet she could not (we see) of her selfe offer and seeke it. As it was with her, so it is with many, if they haue trespassed against their neighbour, they could wish hartily, that other men would take vpon them to end the matter betwixt them and the other, but through the badnesse of their hearts, they themselues cannot goe about it, but they shun him, and keep from him: not one of fortie, shall be found to consider of his fault, and so relent, and seeke agreement, and to make peace with him, though who doth not see great cause why he should doe so? Euen as the Apostle

Iam. 5. 16. *James* also wisheth, saying: Acknowledge your faults one to an other; and pray one for another. But they harden their hearts (which were hard enough before) who haue done the trespasse, and so they aggrauate their sinne, and come not out of it, till either they be brought to agreement by other, or till time weare it out, or they themselues meeting by occasion, af-

Note. ter brawling and chiding wash it away, and make an vntoward and broken end of it. And as one man dealeth with another; so the most deale with God, that is, when they haue offended him, they aske not of themselues,

2. Tit. 3. 13. saying; what haue we done? but being hardned, go foreward and doe worse, and so liue more estranged from him: and in the same estate they should die, if God should not visit and quicken them by instruction, admo-

Iona. 1. 7. nition, and checke of conscience, as he did *Ionah, Peter*, and other, before

Math. 26. 74. 75 they of themselues returne to him againe.

Vers. 3. This be said of the woman: now of the Leuites going to his concubines father to take her againe: which is the second point in the first part. He seeing her not to returne to him in so long time, went with an Asse to bring her,

her,and an other to carrie neceſſaries to her fathers houſe,and ſo to take her againe: whether he were wearied with ſolitarineſſe, or moued with compaſſion towards her, or both, it is not expreſſed: but he giuing her aduice, (as it is verie like he did) and perſwading her to repentance, promiſed her to receiue her kindly againe. She ought to haue been put to death by the Law: but ſeeing that was not looked vnto for want of gouernment in the land, he thought it the beſt to take her againe, and it appeared that ſhe was not alienated from him, though ſhe had done wickedly: for when ſhe ſaw him, ſhe brought him into her fathers houſe, (who could haue hidden her ſelfe, if ſhe had hated him, and would not haue come in his ſight:) and her father alſo was glad of his comming. Deut.22.22.

The trouble that fell on this man doth put vs in minde, how many are croſſed and diſquieted with griefes in this world, among which, this is none of the leaſt, to be puniſhed with a bad wife, and namely this way among many other, I meane by vnfaithfulneſſe, and breach of the marriage couenant. There is no doubt, but it doth ſore afflict and grieue them, on whom it lighteth. And to omit other troubles, which it were infinite to ſpeake of, theſe that fall out in marriage betwixt couples, are not without the fault of one of them, or both: either by drawing them vpon themſelues needleſly by their ſinne, which may eaſily be done many waies, (and the more and greater ſinne cauſeth more of them and greater alſo) or by bearing them amiſſe, I meane impatiently and vnquietly when they come. So that if ſuch doe not bend themſelues to all duties doing, and lay for it alſo aboue other things, and to preuent needleſſe troubles, and auoid conceits one againſt an other, they may make their reckoning to find ſmall comfort in their married eſtate, but their vnquietneſſe will drowne and aſſwage their greateſt delights therein. And more particularly, for the vnfaithfulneſſe, that is found in one of the parties, or both, concerning the marriage bed, ſeeing it is oft times Gods iuſt puniſhment: for their irreligious, vnaduiſed, and wilfull matchings of themſelues, ſuch, if they breake not off their bad behauiour, and make haſt to take a better courſe, may looke for little better, to fall out in their liues then vexation and ſorrow their bellies full: God will ſurely meet with them one way or other. But they ſhall haue moſt peace, who giue the feweſt and ſmalleſt occaſions. Doct. Note.

His concubine bringing her husband into her fathers houſe when ſhe ſaw him, and ſhewing thereby that ſhe was glad of his comming, as not hauing turned her heart from him, though ſhe did but her dutie therein, yet it might poſſibly haue been much worſe with her, hauing ſo offended, as ſhe had done. And her ſo doing, doth condemne their practiſe, who falling into the ſame, or the like ſinne that ſhe did, doe vtterly alienate themſelues, and turne away their loue from their companion, continuing in their filthy trade of whoredome ſtill, and cannot bee reclaimed. In compariſon of whom, this woman and the like, are not in the higheſt degree of ſinners: but ſeeing the offence of ſuch is paſt when they haue ſinned, and cannot be vndone againe, they muſt be pitied and laboured with, to be brought to repentance, as ſhe was here, and as the inceſtuous perſon was, who is mentioned in the Epiſtle to the Corinths. And herein, the Leuites ſeeking to 2 1.Cor.5.5. 2.Cor.2.7.

reclaime her was commendable, as theirs also is, that doe the like, whomsoeuer it doth concerne.

Doct. 3. It is further said, that the concubines father reioiced, when he vnderstood that her husband was come to take her againe: therfore we may well know that she had caused heauinesse to him, by her comming from her husband to seeke shelter by him. Thus do many lewde and bad children cause much griefe to their parents, by their loosenesse and vnrulinesse, and as otherwise and before they take that in hand, by stoutnesse and disobedience; so this way in making their matches against their parents minds, and for the most part reap the fruit of it, euen long after: some of them repent their so doing, but the most of them continue as they began, that is, carelesse, and wilfull, and so marrie themselues to sorrow and bondage, as long as they liue.

4 But his reioycing to see a making vp of the breach, that was betwixt them, doth teach vs, that we should count it a good fauour of God, when we are freed from many common troubles, and namely this way, I meane by children, and to see loue and agreement among them: and that also when they are so matched, that there be no iarring nor vnquietnesse betwixt them, nor with their companions, and when there hath been any, to see it speedily broken off and ended. But especially, when they being both heires of the
Psal. 133. 1. promise of life (do as the Prophet speaketh) dwell together in godly vnitie, Then it is beautifull to behold, euen as to see the fields in Summer season fruitfull by the refresing dewes and sun-shine.

Vers. 4. We haue heard now, the first two things of the 4, in the 3. first verses before, to wit, of the womans fact, and how the Leuite came to the house of the father of his concubine, and that he was glad of it; now to the 11. vers. of his interteinment, and abiding there: and afterward of his departing homeward with her from thence. For his interteinment: her father embraced and made much of him: and they did eate and drinke, & lodge there three daies, both the Leuite and his concubine. Whereby it appeareth that her father set them together againe, and made them friends. This their practise commendeth to vs the meeting of friends, their reioycing, and taking their repast (as they are able) together.

Doct. The thing it selfe, as we may reade of *Iobs* children by his commande-
Iob. 1. 6. ment, is not only allowable but commendable. And *Iobs* children did vse it by course, sometime in one brothers house, sometime in anothers, for the increase of loue among themselues, and to such ends, the meeting of friends (as I haue said) is well to be liked. But as wee see in *Iehosaphats* familiarity with *Ahab* being an Idolater, that it brought him to offend God, till he was reproued for it by the Prophet of God, so in such respects it is to be taken heed of and auoyded. And yet they were as brethren, the one King of Iudah, the other of Israel. And that should warne vs to beware of offending of God, euery way in such our meetings, and if we see that some of the kindred for their corrupt religion, or profane behauiour cannot be companied with, but that the rest shall be tainted and hurt by them, they shall doe best to forbeare the fellowship of such, howsoeuer with and among others it be allowed and commendable.

But (seeing it is manifest here in the text, what good vse was here made by them of their meeting) I will further shew what the end of such feasting of of friends and reioycing together should bee, by that which was done by them whom I now speake of. Whereby also we shall see, what is to bee taken heede of therein. They in their meeting together were reconciled; the Leuite I meane and his concubine: which could not bee done, but much good speech must of necessity passe betwixt them, and bee vsed of them to and fro. And as the very Poets say, that all things aduisedly taken in hand, are done to some ende: so we that are Diuines, and Saints by profession, and taught of God, we (I say) much more should hold this for truth, and teach, that all should be done to a good ende: as *Salomon* saith, Ponder the path of thy feete, and let all thy wayes be ordered aright. Prou. 4. 26.

Therefore it is not to be intended of vs, that we should vse our fellowship to offend God thereby, as many of them doe, who vse all other things to that ende; no, neither when we meete, to fall to euill by occasion offred in the company, though we neuer intended it before; as to iest, laugh, prattle, sweare, talke ill of other, and filthily, to contend, to winne one anothers money at play, and to be drunke. Much better it were not to meete, then that we should leaue such ill sauour behinde vs, and to make the very place a witnesse thereof against vs. But we should in stead hereof intend to vse our company and fellowship to good ends. As to edifie one another with good and sauory communication, to make peace if there bee cause, and to confirme our loue one with another (after debating of our earthly busines, or refreshing our selues together) if there be occasion to doe so. And to such and the like end should the meetings and feastings of friends and kindred be. Oh therefore the many meetings to euill ends how hurtfull and wofull are they, and therefore how shall they be able to answere for them who vse and frequent them. Note.

When they had made merry together, the Leuite and his concubine with her father three dayes, on the fourth day the Leuit arose early to depart, but the olde man perswaded him to dine and lodge there that night also, and he did so. For their father was desirous to knit them firmely together: which was the liker to be, the longer and oftner that good counsell and perswasions were beaten into them. Verse 5. 6. 7.

And we may learne hereby, that ancient and experienced men doe wisely, when they cast and feare the hardest (as this man did here) that may befall the yonger sort vnder their authority and gouernment as children and other: they had neede to haue an eye vpon them and to obserue them, how they carry and behaue themselues, not once but oft, yea though they bee not the most vnruly; both when they are married, and also before, and namely they are to take order for their innocent, religious, and peaceable liuing together in the family and with the rest of the seruants: as it may be; because we know that youthes especially in one house are either commonly stomacking one another, or els knit in a bad league together against their gouernors, and ready to keepe one anothers counsell, to the disaduantage of them; and so likewise those that are married and liue by themselues, are oft vnpeaceable & vnquiet. And the little care that they haue of their either agreeing together, or of their other behauior, doth cause so many disquiets and troubles in families, and so oft breakings out againe, when they haue been set at one together. To this end did this old man labour to stay the Doct. Note.

Leuite and his daughter,to knit their good will each to other more firmely.

Verse 8.9. On the fifth day, when the Leuite rose againe to be gone, he was earnest againe to stay them, such was his care ouer them, and his feare, lest after their departing from him,they should some way be diuided and alienated

Gen.45.24. one from the other, (euen as we see how *Ioseph* was faine to strengthen his brethren against falling out,as seeing cause,when they went from him) and for this cause this father of the concubine could haue wished, if it had been expedient, to haue stayed them both still with him for a longer time. And surely it is to be lamented, that the natures and disposition of people are so crosse, peruerse and crooked,that married couples can so hardly agree together,or with other of their kindred,otherwise then from the teeth outward: or that they do so discontentedly remaine in the house of their parents,how great soeuer their need be to doe so: or that other vnmarried, bee so ill gouerned, their stout, stomackfull,profane,disobedient, as complaint is made of it euery where; though it be (as it is not to bee denied) otherwise with many, as it is meete.

But to returne to the point in hand, let vs marke how great the care of parents is, for the good of their children, and their feare lest they should

1.Sam.2.29. not doe well. Looke vpon *Eli* and *Dauid*, how tender and deare their chil-

1.King.1.6. dren were to them, so as they grew into extremity that way, and offended through blinde affection toward them: it is the case of many thousands. And all that they respect and looke to,is the welfare of them,though themselues haue no benefit thereby, but rather be at great cost,as well as in great care for their well doing. And yet all this should not be repented of, if it were regarded of them, and kindly accepted of their children: but that is commonly farre from them. For whatsoeuer they receiue, they holde it as their due, and that which they would haue, they looke for it, howsoeuer it be with inconuenience to parents and other of the kindred,which is grosse pride and vnthankfulnes.

Vers.10. In this verse it is said, that the Leuite refused to stay all night, and yet hee tarried the most part of the day with him:for it is said,when he would needs depart, the sunne grew towards going downe, and the day declined a pace. Now whether the Leuite hasted home about needfull busines, which was not like, (seeing he would not then haue tarried so long, neither haue lyen by the way with great inconuenience) or whether he was weary of tarrying,he chose no fit time to depart in, as shall appeare in the next verses. By this their departing together so willingly, we see they had bin agreed and reconciled. So let our fruite shew, that our meetings are to good ends, as I haue said before.

Doct.2. But it teacheth, that it is no wisdome for men to sit together howsoeuer, or to continue their meeting so long,as that thereby they come out of season to their lodgings, and to be preuented by the darknes of the night of comming to the place they purpose: for many are the inconueniences, which may fall out, both by the way,and when they come to their resting place. What men are driuen to doe by necessitie, I speake not of, but when they may choose. And though regard of their owne safety and thrift,ought to teach them so much, yet so ought religion to teach them the same also. For as it tendeth to the good of their bodies and the welfare thereof, and

who

who knoweth not, that the regarding of them aright and in good manner, is to the tendring of the soules good and welfare also? And thus much bee said of the Leuites going vnto and abiding at the house of the olde man, his concubines father, being the second point in the first part of the Chapter, and of his departing thence: Now of his trauailing forward and his lodging by the way, the next verses testifie, and the place where he lodged being Gibeah, what fell out both by the way and there.

THE NINETIE EIGHTH SERMON ON THE XIX. CHAPTER OF THE BOOKE OF IUDGES.

THE REMAINDER OF THE FIRST part of the Chapter.

Verse 11. *When they were neere to Iebus, the day was sore spent, and the seruant said vnto his master, Come I pray thee and let vs turne into this city of the Iebusites, and lodge all night there.*

12. *And his master answered him, We will not turne into the city of strangers that are not of the children of Israel, but we will goe forth to Gibeah.*

13. *And he said vnto his seruant, Come and let vs draw neere to one of these places, that we may lodge in Gibeah, or in Ramah.*

14. *So they went forward vpon their way, and the sun went downe vpon them, neere to Gibeah which is in Beniamin.*

15. *Then they turned thither to goe in and lodge in Gibeah: and when he came he sate him downe in a streete of the city; for there was no man that tooke them into his house to lodging.*

16. *And behold there came an old man from his worke out of the field at euen, and the man was of mount Ephraim, but dwelt at Gibeah: and the men of the place were the children of Iemini.*

17. *And when he had lift vp his eyes, he sawe a wayfering man in the streets of the city: then this olde man said, Whither goest thou? and whence camest thou?*

18. *And he answered him, We came from Bethlehem Iudah, vnto the side of mount Ephraim: from thence came I; and I went to Bethlehem Iudah, and goe now to the house of the Lord, and no man receiueth me to house.*

19. *Although we haue strawe and prouender for our asses, and also bread and wine for me and thine handmaide, and for the boy that is with thy seruant: we lacke nothing.*

20. *And the olde man said, Peace be with thee: as for all that thou lackest shalt thou finde with me: only abide not in the streete all night.*

21. So

21. *So he brought him into his house, and gaue fodder vnto the asses, and they washed their feete, and did eate and drinke.*

Vers. 11. *The summe.* NOw in this third point of the first part, his trauailing forward is mentioned, and his lodging place, and what fell out by the way there. In the trauailing of this Leuite and his concubine homeward, they came to Gibeah, and there were at last receiued into house of an old man, no other offering to receiue them. But more particularly, it is said in these first foure verses, that the Leuites seruant seeing the day was spent, aduiseth his master to turne into the citie of the Iebusites, and lodge there. That citie was called Iebus, and at that time, in the possession of strangers, afterward called Ierusalem, the citie of the most high God, and inhabited of his people. His master would not turne in thither, because it was against the law to haue familiaritie with strangers: but hee bad him goe forward to Gibeah or Ramah, cities of the children of Israel, and they came to Gibeah in Beniamin, when the Sunne was neere downe.

More particularly of verse 11. 12. 13. 14.

Doct. ver. 11. 12 Here the seruants aduice was good in respect of the time, the Sunne being neere downe, to aduise to take vp their lodging before the darknesse should grow vpon them: but that citie Iebus being inhabited by strangers, Idolaters, for such these Iebusites were, his master did wiselier to turne from them. And by this we may see that we must not alwaies measure things indifferent by the outward likelihood, but we must goe further, that is to say, to see that it be not hurtfull to our spirituall welfare, which is for our bodily benefit. As for example, it were a commoditie for vs to be befriended of Papists, and to haue kindnesse shewed vs by them: but when they seeke to yoake vs thereby, and to bring vs into bondage of conscience, we must not once looke vpon, nor hast after such friendship and fellowship, but vtterly refuse it. Fellowship also and neighbourhood is seemely and commendable; but to vse it to drinking, playing, or any other disorder, to the quenching of grace in vs, and the nourishing of sinne in other, and to deuise euill any way, it is in no sort tollerable. So it cannot be denied, but that it was better for them to haue taken vp their lodging at Iebus, in respect of the time that night drew on, and therefore inconuenient for them to seek their lodging further. But seeing that place was inhabited of the enemies of God, and Idolaters, they knew not what euill might haue befalne them there, therefore they did well to take away the occasion thereof: and yet as it might haue come to passe, as if they had bin driuen by necessitie to lodge there, they should not haue offended if they had done so. Euen so that which is not meerely euill and vnlawfull, though it bee inconuenient, yet vpon necessitie may be done, so as there be good aduisednes and due regard had therein, and a greater inconuenience auoided thereby.

Doct. vers. 12. 13. 14. The Leuite did well and commendably in refusing to go in to Idolaters: for though it fell out ill with him by going to Gibeah, yet that was vnknowne to him. And there was more likelihood to haue taken greater hurt at Iebus. More fully I adde this to the former point: that wee may learne to shunne fellowship with Idolaters such as are in our time, such as scorne

and

and turne from the true worſhip of God. If hee would not take a nights lodging among them: much leſſe ſhould we oft eate and drinke with them vſually, and without iuſt cauſe, not at all, neither to vſe their fellowſhip in other things. And though many profeſſing the Goſpell, haue diuers blemiſhes, which we haue great cauſe to be ſorrie for, yet there is hope they may be reclaimed, one time or other, whiles they will heare the Goſpell preached. But the other refuſing vtterly to heare, are without hope to be reclaimed: and we ſeeing they will not come together with vs into Gods houſe, we (I ſay) ſhould not conuerſe with them in their owne houſes.

The Leuite in thus ſpeaking that hee would not goe in among ſtrangers to lodge with them, and to teſtifie the ſame he went forward to the next citie: he did therein as became him in another reſpect, to wit, in that he gaue good example thereby of his religious mind to his concubine and ſeruant, euen as he did in other things. Wherein they that follow him, ſhall ſhew themſelues commendable, by ſuffering their light to ſhine among men to the glorifying of God. And that not onely in the world to ſtrangers, where for ſhame or commendation they will oft times abſtaine from offences and keepe within bounds; but in their owne familie, and towards thoſe with whom they liue and conuerſe, though too many will ſay (very vnwiſely) that they will not be ſubiect to their children and ſeruants, to forbeare for their ſakes that which they thinke good to doe. Therfore S. *Paul* ſaith, This is my reioycing, that in ſimplicitie and godly pureneſſe, I haue had my conuerſation in the world, but moſt of all toward you, O Corinthians; among whom I haue liued and had mine abode. And this is to the iuſt condemnation of thoſe, who profeſſing to ſerue God, doe yet walke very offenſiuely and looſely among their neighbours, and doe wrong, contend, deceiue, ſlander and what not? And in their families likewiſe they brawle, talke idely and vainly, and haue no regard how they behaue themſelues, ſeeing they are commonly and daily in their companie, neither are afraid of any, who may call them to an account for the ſame. *Doct. 2.* 2. Cor. 1. 12.

Whereas it is ſaid that the Leuite when hee was come to Gibeah, ſat downe in a ſtreete of the citie, ſeeing there was no man that tooke him into his houſe to lodge him, it appeareth that there was not ſuch vſe of Innes among them as is now. For if there had, hee might haue gone to ſome one, and not haue ſitten in the ſtreete, looking to be bidden and taken to lodging by one or other of the citie. But they vſed to carrie their prouiſion with them, for themſelues and their beaſts, their iourney not being long, nor far, and wanted nothing but roome and lodging. So much the more vncourteous was the dealing of theſe men of Gibeah, that it being a cuſtome among them none would bid him to lodging. Verſ. 15.

The euill dealing of theſe men of Gibeah, doth lay out the vnciuill and vnkinde dealing of many among vs, who performe not common duties to their neighbours, as ſaluting one another, neither communicate in mutuall borrowing and lending of neceſſarie things, yet of no value; nay the fetching of fire and water one from the other to the benefit of both, and the hurt of neither, when their ſtomackes are vp againſt each other, are withheld and denied betwixt them; and but as for the lending of helpe and hand mutually each to other in weightier matters, how farre off is that betwixt them? *Doct.*

Theſe

These are small things, but yet such as if they may not be communicated together betwixt neighbours, it argueth a kinde of rude and barbarous behauiour, and that they know not themselues; or a worse thing, as spite and cankred malice to be among them, which breakes off all neighbourly duties vtterly, and so maketh their liues deadly, vncomfortable and wearisome.

It may well be said, that those things are scarcely neglected among the most barbarous people. But it will bee obiected, that there is no cause to complaine of these things among vs; I say, yes, in some places, through meere vnciuilnes: in other, not so much through that, as through spite and malice, which hindreth this communion and fellowship betwixt them. The kinde vse of this point of neighbourhood, is with them that feare God, and are religious, who being like minded in the hope of the glory to come, and making conscience of other greater duties, doe make the same of these, which are not to be omitted, though they be small, and yet to be vsed without burthening one another. Which if they bee not in vse among them, better it were to liue in a poore cottage by a woods side, desolate and without companie, then to dwell with such neighbours. They therefore that en-
Note. ioy such habitation, as where they may haue both the benefit of peace, helpfulnes, and also Christian communion in partaking of the Gospell by publique sound preaching and priuate exhorting, and mutuall comforting one of another, they haue a great libertie giuen them of God in this part of life in respect of many other.

Vers.16,17,18,19,20,21. While no man receiued the Leuite into house, there commeth in the streete by him an old man out of the fields from his worke, who was but a stranger there in Gibeah, though he was come thither to dwell, but was of Mount Ephraim, but they that were of the place, were of the tribe of *Beniamin*. He questioned with the Leuite, whence he came, and whither he was going, who answering him, he tooke him into his house.

Doct. ver. 16.17 This old man seeing them standing there as strangers, and not receiued into house by any man, he passed not by them, as the Priest and Leuite (spo-
Luke 10,31,32. ken of in the tenth of *Luke*) without pitie passed by the man that fell among theeues and was wounded of them; but asksd him of his iourney, from whence he came, and whither he would, that hee might the better minister helpe to him, as hee did afterward. Commending to vs by his practise our dutie in such like case. That where God shall offer to our sight or knowledge the distressed and lamentable estate of any of his poore seruants, (alwaies excepting sturdie rogues, and idle and stout beggers) we should not stop our eares, nor turne our backes vpon them, as though we owed no dutie to hearken after them.

But when we see, we may be some helpe to them, regard we them, if wee our selues would desire such compassion to be had of vs in the like case, and be not hard hearted toward them nor senselesse of their griefe. So wee are
Phil. 2.4. commanded by the Apostle to doe. Brethren (saith S. *Paul*) looke not euery one on his owne matters, but euery man on the things of other men. Againe, Beare ye one anothers burthen. And this is so to be done at one time, as that we do the like many times, euen while we shall be able, for occasions shall neuer bee wanting. As gathering for poore Preachers, decaied Christians, young couples comming together in neede, or to any other like good vse.

vse. It falleth out that such taking knowledge of mens calamitie and distressed estate, is both a great comfort to the afflicted, and is not vnrewarded to him that sheweth compassion, and that from God directly, or else from some other, whom he stirreth vp thereto. For the first, what a comfort compassion ministreth to them that are afflicted, let the example of *Boaz* to *Ruth* in her meane estate testifie, who being a godly young woman, and comming out of her owne countrey, Moab (an idolatrous land) for the worship and feare of the God of Israel, with *Naomi*, into the land of Iudah, *Boaz* a rich and religious man told her what good report hee had heard of her rare pietie and vertue. This his taking knowledge of her, and his incouragement that hee gaue her being a stranger, how it affected and comforted her heauie heart, her owne words declare: for thus she spake and answered him: Oh my Lord, thou hast spoke to the heart of thine handmaid. For in effect she saith, Thou hast comforted me much, in that thou hast taken knowledge of any thing done by me, and so shewest that thou hast respect of my poore and meane condition. And why? for a word in season is like apples of gold and pictures of siluer. And by this we may well thinke what good it might doe, if men of wealth would thus looke after, and incourage the poore godly; and generally if they who are free from affliction would pitie them, as this old man did here the Leuite.

Ruth 2.8. Ruth 2.13. Prou. 25.11.

Thus I haue shewed how it would comfort the afflicted, if they who are free themselues from trouble, would pitie them: And how true it is that they who doe so, shall not lose their reward, that saying of our Sauiour doth well proue: Whosoeuer shall giue to one of these little ones, which in the sight of the world are vile and abiect, but a cup of cold water onely in the the name of a Disciple, verely I say vnto you hee shall not lose his reward. And againe: Come ye blessed of my father, and enioy the inheritance prepared for you: for I was hungrie and ye gaue me meate, &c. This made *Nehemiah* pray thus (and he beleeued it should be so to him as he prayed) Remember me O my God, and wipe not out my kindnesse shewed to thy people, &c.

Math. 10.42. Matth. 25.34. Nehem. 13.14.

2 This old man dwelling in Gibeah, yet because he was of Mount Ephraim, and was but lately come to Gibeah as a stranger, therefore the holy storie doth not omit to set it downe, neither can I see any other reason of his so doing, but this, that he should not be shoaled among those wicked men that dwelt at Gibeah, neither counted as one of them, as if he had long had his abode among them, his behauiour being vnlike vnto theirs. Therefore if the Lord would seuer him from so bad a people, and would not haue him taken to be one of them, but a stranger of another place, it should be a strōg motiue to vs, to shoale our selues as farre as wee can, from the children of Belial, and the workers of iniquitie, that as wee abhorre their doings, so wee may shoale our selues from their company, and that so men may see that we are not of them.

3 And when it is said that he dwelt at Gibeah, being of Mount Ephraim, seeing the cause is not set downe why he came to dwell there, wee can neither commend nor discommend him for it, he might haue cause to remoue to the place, and yet ignorant of the wickednesse of the people. But by occasion of his so doing, I thinke good to giue a caution or caueat to the reader,

der, and that is this: That we make not choice (if it lie in vs) of our dwelling in a place where Idolaters and prophane persons inhabite (especially where they rule) in hope of getting commodity there. If wee doe we shall pay deere for it, and wish our selues away with much losse.

If this man did it for his priuate commodity, and would come among such wicked people for his benefit, (which is not likely,) then he sought his
Gen. 13.10.11. owne sorrow; as *Lot*, who made choice of Sodom for the fertilty of the ground, but his soule was vexed with the vncleanly conuersation of the wicked Sodomites: if he went to dwell at Gibeah vpon necessity, he did best to liue innocently among them, as it seemeth he did, and so let vs doe: but if we rush in among the vile, when we neede not, and that willingly, wee haue heard what is the best that shall come of it.

Vers. 18.19. The Leuite answered the olde man, whither he went, and from whence he came, and saith, no man receiued him to lodge: which seemed hard to him, seeing he left Iebus of the Idolaters, because hee would come thither, he went to Gibeah a city of the Israelites, where he looked for so much curtesie, especially he said so, seeing he did not meane to put him to charge that should entertaine him into his house, saue onely for roome and lodging: and by this his speech it appeareth (as hath bin said before) that such curtesies were vsuall amongst them one toward another.

By this that he left Iebus for the Idolatry of the place, and chose Gibeah because it belonged to the people of God, and yet he found not common curtesie, but as we shall heare in the verses following, most odious dealing; we must know that sometimes it shall be so, that places and persons are not so religious and good, as they are reported and imagined to be: as by that
Reuel. 3.1. which is said by S. *Iohn* of the Church of Sardi, that it had a name it liued, but was dead. To teach all, not to please themselues in the name that goeth of them, or the place where they dwell. Not euery one that saith Lord, Lord, shall enter into the kingdome of heauen, but few are chosen, though many be called: and woe is pronounced by our Sauiour against such as had
Mat. 11.20. much preaching: Woe be to thee Corazin, saith he, woe be to thee Bethsaida, for if the workes which haue bin done in you, had bin done in Tyre and Zidon, (most prophane & wicked cities, neere adioyning and well knowne vnto them) they had repented long agoe in sackcloth and ashes. And yet for all this, men must be professors, or els Christ will be ashamed of them.
2. Cor. 12.6. So then betwixt both, let vs know and looke to it, that we be indeed as wee
1. Pet. 3.4. be accounted of for our profession; and that we in no wise seeme to men to
1. Tim. 1.5. be forwarder in good duties then we be in deed: and to this end be we sure that the hidden man of the heart be pure and cleane, as a witnes of our faith, which is before God a thing much set by.

2 Further in that the Leuite said, he had all prouision meete for him and for his beasts, and sought not to bee a burthen to his countrymen, which of them soeuer should receiue him into his house: his speech doth well teach vs, that no man ought to thrust himselfe into other mens houses to put them to charge, or otherwise to be burdensome to them, as they would be vnwilling that other should offer the same to them, which doing and offering of discourtesie, is oft times an occasion of hard thoughts betwixt neighbours: It is that vnequall measure that none should offer. But if there be

be necessity to those whom it most concerneth; and if the kindred bee not able nor willing to supply the necessity of such, it should be made knowne vpon the sight thereof, consideration should be had by one or many, not onely of hospitall intertaining of such, but of further helpe, as there shall be cause for their reliefe: and where need is, there if any will offer such courtesie of themselues, as they see cause so to doe, it is to be counted friendly kindnes, and a good fruite of Christian neighbourhood.

The olde man when he had heard the Leuites complaint, bad him take no thought, for all that thou wantest (saith he) thou shalt haue of me, come into mine house therefore, and remaine not in the streete all night. So hee brought him into his house, and gaue the asses fodder, and he and his concubine did eate and refresh themselues. This olde mans practise commends to vs a double duty: the one that we should be ready to remoue griefe from our brethren, and to quiet their troubled mindes as we may, and not suffer them to remaine vpon the racke, I meane in paine and griefe, when we may conueniently, and without any great detriment to our selues, ease and helpe them. For griefe and heauines doe much hinder the minde from doing any duty: especially they being deeply seated in the heart, and turbulent passions of themselues, and therefore the easing it of them, is a setting of it at liberty. *Vers.20.21.* *Doct.1.*

2 The second duty we learne is, more particularly the duty of hospitality: which as farre as neede required, he did vnto this Leuite. The like kindnes is to be shewed by vs to strangers sad in heart, being knowne to be brethren, that they be vsed of vs kindly and in all courtesie, and if we be not able our selues, yet to commend them to such, as are of ability among vs, to be receiued and lodged: but in no wise to grieue them, being already heauy hearted. To the iust reproch of such, this may be noted, as mocke and iest at them, and in the deriding of their simplicity are ready to set them in a wrong way, asking of them to know the right, or to abuse them any other way, whereas they are sad enough, in that they be strangers. Thus did not this old man, but they washed their feete there, the countrey being hot, and did eate, they and their asses, and rested there to the good refreshing of them.

The second part of the Chapter.

Verse 22. *And as they were making their hearts merry, behold, the men of the city, wicked men beset the house round about, and smote at the doore, and spake to this olde man the master of the house, saying, Bring forth the man that came into thine house, that we may know him.*

23. *And this man, the master of the house went out vnto them, and said vnto them, Nay my brethren, doe not so wickedly, I pray you, seeing that this man is come into my house doe not this villany.*

24. *Behold, here is my daughter a virgine, and his concubine: them will I bring out now, and humble them, and doe with them what seemeth you good: but to this man doe not this villany.*

25. *But the men would not hearken to him, therefore the man tooke his concubine and brought her out vnto them, and they knew her, and abused her all the night vn-*

 to

to the morning: and when the day began to spring they let her goe.

26. So the woman came in the dawning of the day, and fell downe at the doore of the mans house, where her Lord was till the light day.

27. And her Lord arose in the morning, and opened the doore of the house, and went out to goe his way, and behold, the woman his concubine was dead at the doore of the house, and her hands lay vpon the threshold.

Verse 22. to 28. IN this second part followeth the horrible fact of the men of Gibeah: In the which consider first, their foule attempt and demand: Secondly, how they were disswaded by the olde man: Thirdly, how they refused to be perswaded, but went forward: Lastly, the fearefull effect that followed the fact, for they killed the woman the Leuites concubine among them.

The summe. These men wrought a great villany in Israel: For they did first beate at the dores of the house of the olde man, to breake them open (when he and his guests were quiet within) that they might draw out the Leuite a stranger in the house, and that to deale vnnaturally with him, as the men of Sodom did offer the like villany to the two Angels, whom they tooke to be men, who had entred with *Lot* into his house. (Gen. 19. 5.) But howsoeuer the Leuite escaped from the hands of these wicked men of Gibeah, yet they did abuse and that most shamefully, the Leuites concubine all night till she died thereupon: and though the olde man came out to disswade them, yet he could not preuaile. Oh horrible villany! and yet as vile and odious as their attempt was the more odious, for that they in the house were at their meate not prouoking them. But to bring this Scripture more neere vs, in this that the Leuite and the olde man, made their hearts merry by eating and drinking together, we may learne that it pleaseth God well, that we should after wearines, trauaile and labour, refresh our selues according to our condition; and it is lawfull and free for all the children of God to doe so by Gods owne allowance, for he hath giuen his people double cause so to doe, namely, first, in that he prouideth such refreshing for their bodies, and so they may bee merry in considering that both he ministreth the same to them; and secondly for that they haue a right to the creatures by Christ, who is heere and Lord of all: and though profane and vnsanctified people bee merry at their meate also, as they would be through out their whole liues in their kinde, but that they are yoked and curbed with crosses, yet it is in a farre different manner from the other. Sure it is we are in danger to breake out into excesse, euen while we doe that which we may lawfully doe, as *Iob* did feare the same by his children, when they feasted together. (Iob 1. 5.) And therefore also it is said to be better, to goe into the house of mourning, then of feasting: (Eccles. 7. 2.) which I say, to the end that it may make vs weary of offending in the vse of such liberties, and to be carefull to haue the Lord present with vs, that so we may bee merry in the best manner. And yet this eating our meate together ioyfully, and in gladnes of heart, giueth no place to profane merry-making, which is caused by answerable behauiour, neither doth God allow that, but abhorre it: and yet againe, I meane not that men should with lowring countenance eate their meate together and in vnquietnes; which wee are as we may, to auoid, but yet vsing such cheerefulnes as may be accompanied with thanksgiuing, which is easily hindred when we eate with the profane and bad, euen

euen as also it is by crosses and afflictions, if great heede be not taken.

But while the old man and his guests were refreshing themselues toge- 2
ther, thinking no hurt to any, it is said, that wicked men of that place beset
the house, intending villanie against the Leuite. By the which we see, that Note.
while the innocent walke in their simplicitie, neither suspect any euill from
other, nor minde any towards other, yet it is attempted and practised
against them by such as are badly minded: Oh the world is full of such,
who are so farre from procuring the peace and quiet of other, that it is
meate and drinke to them, to crosse, vexe, and disquiet some, yea, though
they be not prouoked by them: Which is spoken to the iust reproofe and
condemning of them that doe so, seeing the Heathen haue light enough in
them by the law of nature, to conuict them, that such dealing is odious
and vnnaturall. But *Salomon* giueth admonition about this more plainly;
saying, Intend no hurt against thy neighbour, seeing he dwelleth without Prou 3.29.
feare by thee. And why? for God will take part with him against thee, and
looke thou for the like measure againe. Nay, though thou hast been pro-
uoked by him, and that he hath done thee wrong, yet let it be doubled Matth 5.39.
vpon thee, rather then once reuenged againe, as our Sauiour comman-
deth. And howsoeuer the disobedient and vnruly doe giue and set them-
selues to commit such works of darknesse, yet thou, who fearest God, ab-
staine from them, and flie such things, and striue, and thinke it worth thy Rom.12.1.
trauaile, to ouercome their euill with good.

In that these wicked men of Gibeah aske to come into the house, that 3
they might know the man that was gone in, that is the Leuite, they doe
meane a most filthy thing and horrible wickednesse, by those words, and
in so speaking, to wit, that they might commit the sinne of Sodomie.
Whereby we may see what monstrous and vnnaturall sinnes are commit-
ted in the world, euen such as a man would not thinke, who is himselfe of
a better minde. But it is no marueile to them that haue vnderstanding, for
the heart of man is exceedingly corrupt, and out of measure euill. Like the
sea, that fometh vp myre and dirt. Lust is raging, and as flaming fire, hard- Note.
ly quenched, and as the angrie man in his wrath, so concupiscence is vn-
bridled, and blinde, and not willing to take knowledge what it doth.

And as all sinne of this kind, is filthy and odious to God; as first forni-
cation, then adulterie, thirdly incest; so this Sodomie and the fruit of vnna-
turall lust goeth beyond the rest, which is as the Apostle termeth it, Man Rom.1.24.
with man to commit filthinesse. This sinne the Lord hath branded and set
his marke vpon it in the booke of Genesis, laying out the vilenesse of it by
the punishment: which he in times past inflicted vpon the committers
of it. As for the iudgement that fell on these men of Gibeah, I shall set it Gen.19.11.24.
downe in the next Chapter, where there shall be a fitter occasion offred:
but I speake now of the men of Sodom, who were like them. For they Note.
were burnt with fire and brimstone from Heauen, as they burned in filthy
lust, one against an other, the loathsome smell whereof, their shamefull
fact resembled. Yea, and the verie place bare the marke of their wicked-
nesse, in that it was made barraine. For though it had been a most fertile
and fruitfull soile, for which cause *Lot* chose it, yet the Lord made it vtterly
barraine, euen as those wicked Sodomites sought barrainnesse, by their

lewde doings. Now whereas it is demanded, why God punisheth not this sinne still in the like manner, seeing it is certaine that it is in practise still; it is to be answered, that this sinne (as we are to hope) is not common through whole places, as cities and townes, though it be too common with some persons, and they sometime liue among the good, for whose cause they are spared. Againe, he oft defers punishment: euen as he doth not alwaies inflict & send the same: and such sinnes breake out oftentimes with the like which accompanieth them, so that they fall thereby into the hands of the Magistrate, and are that way reuenged. Oh therefore how many and great iudgements doe they auoide, who studie to liue well and religiously free from this and other euils?

4 But an other thing followeth in this verse, of these wicked men of Gibeah, that they goe not onely about the sinne of Sodomie before mentioned. but also they tell what they will doe, and without shame professe it, which doth greatly aggrauate their sin. And this teacheth, that as the committing of any vnknowne wickednesse is odious, and especially such as this is; so to professe and to loue to speake of it, and affirme that they will doe it, or boast that they haue done it, is meerely shamelesse. For while men though otherwise badly disposed, blush & are touched with some bashfulnesse and shamefacednesse, though they cannot conteine themselues, yet there is hope of them: but when they iustifie their bad doings, and boldly speak what they haue done, or what they will do in that behalfe, they are almost desperate, & giue small hope of amendement: without speciall grace.

Vers. 23.24. Now followeth the second point of the 4. The good man seeing the horrible attempt of these wicked men, went out to them, and in kind manner besought them, that they would doe no such thing, alleaging reasons to disswade them: yea, and considering the vilenesse of the thing which they went about, in the detestation thereof, as not weighing throughly what he said (for in good aduisednesse, he would not so haue said) he offred his owne daughter, and the Leuites concubine, to vse at their pleasure, hauing respect therein of his faithfulnesse in safe-keeping his guest the Leuite from their outrage. But farre better (I confesse) he should haue done, to regard the safetie of them all three, as well as of one of them, because he owed the like dutie to them all in that behalfe.

Doct. vers. 23. But to obserue somewhat out of this; First this commeth to be considered, that God declared his goodnesse to these wicked men, in that he stirred vp this old man, to admonish, reproue, and labour to bring them from that filthinesse, who were vtterly vnworthy of such a benefite. And yet such is his goodnesse, how vile and bad soeuer men are, he doth some way seeke to reclaime them, if they could doe but so much as to see and obserue it. And we (I say) are to account it a great fauour when he doth so, because when men are hardned and giuen vp to their lusts, for want of holding them backe from the fulfilling of them, as he did *Paul* by the vision, *Ionah* by the tempest, and other by like meanes, they haue no power to call backe themselues from their intemperancie, nor to restraine themselues from their outrage, as we may see by *Hophni* and *Phineas*, and why were they let loose and suffred to runne on without admonition? verily because God meant to destroy them.

(Act. 9. 3.4. Ionah 1.12. 1. Sam. 2.25.)

In

In sicknesse, and other visitations of God, many a one being spoyled and made naked of all grace and goodnesse by his sinne, is in no wise able to stir vp himselfe to repentance: but yet if God offer him instruction, and exhortation by other, which are able wisely to minister it, we see oft times, that it returneth not againe in vaine, but much auaileth. And so Saint *Paul* willeth vs to admonish the vnruly. But woe to him that is alone, and hath none to aduise and perswade him. The vse of that which I haue said is this, that till hope of doing good to such be past, we should not giue them ouer, but pity them, and by all good opportunities seeke to performe this dutie, where wee shall see it to bee laid vpon vs, and giue not ouer for euery discouragement. 1.Thes.5.14.

He vsed reasons to perswade them, first by kindnesse, calling them brethren, though they were wicked, and he lied not in so calling them, for they were of *Beniamin*, and he of the tribe of *Ephraim*, both sonnes to *Iacob*. And when such are dealt withall, they must be handled gently, for they shake off and scorne all sharpe speeches, especially if they be their betters, and are not opposed by such as are in authoritie. Secondly, they are disswaded by the shamefulnes of the fact. And thirdly by this reason, that hee had taken protection of him, as his guest, and therefore hee must see him to bee safe vnder his roofe. So we should by sound reason goe about to perswade as the case requireth, either to that which is good, or to disswade thereby from the contrary: and to vse these or any of them, when the like need requireth.

In that this old man did offer his daughter vnto them, and the Leuites concubine, wee must consider hee was in a streight, looking chiefly to one thing (to keepe the Leuite from hurt) loth to doe the one, to wit, to put foorth to them the concubine and his daughter, but abhorring the other deadly, namely to offer to them the Leuite himselfe to their shamelesse lust. And being thus astonished, and on the sudden to seeke what to doe, he fell to that inconuenience: for it was not easie for him to see what he ought to doe in such amazement and vnlooked for distraction. Therefore we are to pray God to keepe vs from such streights, for euen so did *Lot* himselfe in the like case, euen as this old man: but seeing sometime it cannot otherwise be, but that we shall fall into such streights, so that either wee must come into some great trouble in this life, or doe against the knowne truth of the word of God, we must learne it throughly, and resolue vpon it oft times to commit our selues to Gods gouernment and prouidence thereby, whatsoeuer it shall please him shall come to passe, seeing it cannot bee but good that hee doth: but alwaies wisely and carefully auoiding occasions of such streights, seeing they commonly put vs to our shifts, and plunge vs into depth of danger: and so doing, if it be to our bodily hurt, yet it shall bee for our soules good; and that hurt hee can and will turne away also, if it shall bee expedient. Doct. vers. 24. Note.

And whereas some demaund, if the old man did not well in offering the woman rather then the Leuite himselfe, to their outragious lust, because it was the lesser euill of the two, and of two euils we must yeeld to the smaller, (they say) before the greater. I answere, wee must vnderstand that generall rule of outward troubles and discommodities of this life (and not of sinne) for in that case it is in deed better for vs, if we must needes goe vnder one, to Obiection. Answ.

Note. Matth.5.19. chuſe the leſſer, but we cannot ſay ſo of ſinne, nay, yeeld to any, how ſmall ſoeuer it ſeeme to vs, to the end we may ſhun a greater, for our Sauiour hath taught vs that no ſinne is little: For we haue an other as generall and true a rule as that, to wit, That we may not doe euill, that good may come of it; as if we might benefite our neighbour by the making of a lye; or if a lewde perſon would threaten to kill himſelfe, if an honeſt matron ſhould not conſent to ſerue his wicked luſt.

Verſ.25. It appeareth, that the old man added ſome ſuch thing, as that he wiſhed they would deſiſt altogether from deſiring either the Leuite or the women, becauſe they had refuſed to hearken to him before, therefore (it is ſaid in this verſe) that they tooke but the Leuites concubine only, leauing the mans daughter and the Leuite himſelfe, without further attempting to draw him out, as they at firſt threatned to doe. But in that they would not leaue off till the woman was brought forth to them, it ſheweth what an high degree of ſinne it is to be ſo hardned, as not to regard and hearken to
Heb.13.22. admonition and exhortation. For as we haue heard, that they muſt be mi-
Luk.23.43. niſtred, ſo muſt we know, that they ought to be receiued. Good incouragement we haue hereto. The penitent Theefe tooke much good by Chriſts words; ſo, who can tell what good exhortation and perſwaſions
Prouerbs. may doe now, if they be regarded? But he that hardneth his heart againſt them, ſhall ſurely come to euill. As our Sauiour hath taught vs, ſaying, Oh Ieruſalem, how oft would I haue gathered thee together, as the hen
Matth.23.37. doth her chickens, but thou wouldeſt not: therefore behold, thine habitation ſhall be left vnto thee deſolate.

Verſ.25.26. The third thing of the 4, (as in the 22. verſe is to be ſeene) now followeth, which is, that the Leuites concubine was put forth to them, when the wicked men of Gibeah could not be diſſwaded from their villanous attempt: ſo the Leuite put her forth to them, to keep himſelfe out of their hands. But by that which was ſaid of the old mans act, in offring her and his owne daughter; it may be gathered without any repetition, that this his ſo doing is to be iudged of as the old mans was, to wit, euill and naught, though he did good thereby to ſaue himſelfe. To omit that therefore and ſay no more of it, that euill may not be done in any ſort that good may come of it. The next thing is, how they did villanouſly abuſe her all the night long, whereby alſo they killed her; for when they had caſt her off in the morning, ſhe came to the dore of the houſe where her husband was, and falling downe there, lay dead.

This was an abomination not heard of before, that when the woman came into their hands, they did among them abuſe her all the night. Who would beleeue ſuch a thing, if it ſhould not be reported by them that are of credite? Oh therefore what vnknowne villanies and treacheries are committed on earth? And yet beſide them, the world ſwarmes with theſe
Note. that are knowne: what auaileth it to rehearſe them? yea, thoſe that be of this kind, the Scripture is full of them, the world is tainted with them, the common wealth is poiſoned, and the Church is moſt wofully annoyed with them: the which what a ſeemely thing were it, to ſee it void of them, but euen ſo as it might be, if Gods matters were but halfe ſo carefully regarded as mens owne that are priuate? But O times, oh daies. Let them that

that bewaile them in other, be at deadly hatred with them in themselues: for so farre (God be thanked) remedy may be had.

When they had got at their hands that which they sought, and had abused her all the night, they sent her away in the morning. A cleere glosse, 2
their example and practise is, to shewe the wickednes that is in them, who looke after nothing els but to serue their turne by other mens harmes; euery one for himselfe, beare it they as they can, who sustaine the losse. There is no regard of equity nor honesty among the greatest number. In so much as many couples, vse one another, but for their pleasure or profit, marke it well in all kindes of fellowship and dealings, euen to serue their turne by them, and otherwise care not one for another; nay shunne and are weary Note.
one of another; in so doing, little better then *Amon*, who when he had a- 2.Sam.13.14.15.
bused *Thaman*, could not abide her.

The fourth point followeth, what their treachery brought to passe, euen Vers.26.
the womans death. The Leuites concubine fell downe dead, and so lay with her hands on the threshold: and this befell her by meanes of the hurt that she took by those wicked men of Gibeah. So that with their whoredom they committed murther also. This is one of the fruits of it which many other very noysome and hurtfull accompany it, euen such as it selfe is: marke it who will; this with such like sinnes neuer goe alone, but as the Apostle saith, surfiting leadeth drunkennes as it were by the hand, and so Note.
doth strife leade enuy, and chambering wantonnes: which should be cause sufficient why we should abhorre them, yea and shut our eyes at all the allurements that may leade to them: and much more it should settle such as be religious, that they keepe themselues from all liking or lingring that way, I meane after any knowne sinne, for it hath other such that accompany it: for example, a tetchines of heart, conceitednes, and waywardnes, and such like, (that are sinnes of another kinde) which how many other noysome sins doe accompany them, and what cursed and fearefull fruit they bring forth, who doth not see.

But to leaue the sinne of the men of Gibeah, the holy story thus setting 2
downe the punishment vpon his concubine, doth call vs to the consideration of the reuenge which God tooke vpon her. She had committed adultery before, as we heard in the second verse, and she had not her due for the fact, which was death by the law, but was receiued againe of her husband, no repentance heard of for the same, and now behold, how she had it yet another way: so that time did not weare out the remembrance of her sinne, but a time came that punished it, and that in a more odious and grieuous manner. For we see, that she suffred death, and that not only for her Note.
adultery, but euen as it were in it. Whether she repented for it, and her other sinnes we can not gather, seeing the Scripture maketh no mention thereof. We see but that which is outward, how God hath made her an example, who searcheth the heart, but fearefull (we see) it was howsoeuer.

But suppose she did repent and had faith, then it is sure she escaped eternall death: but yet for all that, God will haue discipline and correction for grieuous crimes, to be obserued and executed in the common wealth vpon euill doers; which if they be meekely and patiently borne of them that are penitent, they are onely fatherly chastisements on Gods behalfe; but the

Magistrate

Magistrate ought not, to neglect his duty therein, as cause shall require, though the partie repent; and if he doe, God himselfe will be the auenger of the sinne. The which *Iosua* knowing, did stone *Achan* to death for the trouble that he wrought in Israel, although he gaue good signes of his repentance.

Iosu.7.25.

Thus as she had the reward of her whorish life, in that it brought her to a shamefull death: so they may cleerely see if they list, that they lay the foundation of the like iudgement, who sinne as she did, in whoredome or otherwise in the like manner. And let this be marked, that the sinne which most preuaileth in any, and is most embraced and delighted in, watcheth them the greatest mischiefe, and oft times God punisheth like with like, as we haue heard it was with *Adonibezek*. But yet for all this, men play with their sinne, and vse it as a baite to intice them, which should be counted their bane, that will if it can destroy and kill them. But a wise man will carefully marke what sinne sits neerest his heart, and watcheth his ouerthrow; and be so farre from nourishing it, that he will by all meanes decline and turne from that, yea and from all outward occasions that make way to it; and among all other temptations whereto he is subiect, and lieth open, he will most of all oppose himselfe euery way against the prouocations to that.

Note. Iudg.1.7. Note.

Vers.27. It followeth, how the men rising in the morning, and the Leuite ready to goe on his way, found his concubine laid dead on the threshold. Wherein we may see, that God would haue this to be knowne, which might many wayes and that easily haue bin otherwise, I meane hidden: and namely, that some of them might haue carried her from company aside, to satisfie their leaud lusts, and then if she had died vnder their hands, they might easily haue cast her into some secret place, so that it should not haue been knowne what had become of her: but she being thus found dead, both Gods punishment vpon her was apparently seene, and also thereby reuenge vpon the malefactors executed.

And thus doth God bring to light many horrible treacheries, as murders and adulteries, to the end the wickednes of the world may be knowne, and some of them punished, that many may bee warned, and made wary that they rush not into them; and Minister, and Magistrate, may more carefully doe their duties against them. For where such wickednes is not knowne, there can be but cold pursuing of it by either of them. But to let them passe, they may walke in sweete peace, who abhorre the least euill, that so they may be in no danger of falling into the greatest.

THE

THE NINETIE NINE SERMON ON THE XIX. CHAPTER OF THE BOOKE OF IVDGES.

The third part of the Chapter.

Verse 28. *And he said vnto her, Vp, and let vs goe: but she answered not. Then he tooke her vp vpon the asse: and the man rose vp and went to his place.*

29. *And when he was come to his house, he tooke a knife and laid hand on his concubine, and diuided her in peeces with her bones into twelue parts, and sent her through all the quarters of Israel.*

30. *And all that sawe it said, There was no such thing done or seene since the time that the children of Israel came vp from the land of Egypt vnto this day: consider the matter, consult and giue sentence.*

IN this last part of the Chapter is shewed, how the Leuite comming forth to goe on his way, and finding his concubine to lie dead; tooke her vp, and laid her on his asse and went home: and there cut her body into twelue peeces, and sent them to all the tribes of Israel, to euery one a part, to consider of the fact, seeing there was no chiefe Magistrate to complaine vnto. And all that sawe it said, there had bin no such example shewed, from their comming out of Egypt. With the sending of the parts of her body, we must vnderstand also, that he sent messengers with them to shew the matter that was done; for they could not otherwise haue knowne what it meant: and so he wished them to meete together, and consider of it. *The summe.*

By this that fell out thus here to the Leuite, we may see what sore casualties and heauy troubles may meete with vs, yea and that also when wee walke in our simplicity and innocency, while we are wandring here on the earth. For why? God is grieuously prouoked, and one way or other, he is constrained to shewe it, when through the hardnes of mens hearts, his word cannot reclaime them. And though it may be obiected, that such things doe seldome come to passe, yet I speake of such as may, and doe fall out oft. As he to haue his wife so abused, then to lose her in his trauaile, what an heauy calamity was it to the man? Not much vnlike was the affliction of *Naomi* in some respect, a good woman, who going from her dwelling in Bethlehē Ephratah into the land of Moab, by reason of a famine, did there bury her husband, and two sonnes which went thither with her, and she was left there a poore desolate widow, lamenting at her returne home in this manner: I went out full, but I returne empty, call me no more *Naomi*, (which name signified pleasantnes,) but call me *Morah*, for the almighty hath humbled Doct.ver.28. Ruth.1.21.

humbled me,and filled me with much bitternes, and brought my soule into aduersitie.

Gen 35.18. So *Iacob* buried his deare wife *Rachel*, as he came from *Laban* in Aram betwixt Bethel and Ephra in the land of Canaan going to his father *Isaac*. Thus the Lord hath seene good to exercise his seruants with bitter & smartie calamities,euen in this state of mariage, (who doth all things well) that when they are kindly matched together, and in like mindednes fitted to serue him in good sort,they are parted oft times in their greene and young, or middle yeeres;which is to ỹ remainders,as the cutting off a peece of their

Note. flesh,that they may not be taken vp too much with the delights of mariage, and other such innumerable and smarty afflictions befall them and others, and yet (a wonderfull thing to vtter) thus it must be, or else they be nestled and drowned here in this deceiueable and transitorie life, from the which and the baites thereof, they cannot be weaned, but by such bitter chastisements cast vpon them,to make them distaste the allurements of sinne, and to wearie them here, and cause them to long homeward. And this vse (to say no more) let vs all learne to make of them.

Vers.29. This strange act of the Leuites, that hee is here said to haue done,in that he cut his concubine in peeces, and sent them through the land, though it may seeme to sauour of an hard heart, wee must consider that the thing was weightie,and punishment was to be sought,as hee could, there being no Magistrate to repaire vnto for iustice. To his concubine he did no hurt,and though without speciall cause, it had not been meete to haue done such a thing,as that his cutting of her in peeces was ; yet all things well considered,that was a forcible meane,to stirre vp the heads of the people in euery tribe to seeke,consider of,and to punish so horrible a villanie, as they saw by this sending the parts of her body among them,the men of Gibeah had wrought.

Doct. That which we are to learne here,is this:that euill is to be pursued where it is committed,as there may helpe be obtained against it,and complaint is to be made to them that are in authoritie to procure the punishing of it: and as the crime and fault is more odious & grieuous,thereafter is reuenge (though without a reuenging minde) to be sought thereof; as this fact not being common,was noised not after a common manner.This is to be done according to the qualitie of the offence, whether it be open to the Magistrate,or priuate in a familie,because we know that otherwise sin gathereth

Note. head,and getteth strength by sufferance,till it be past amending : but yet regard must be had of such,as being otherwise more simple and harmelesse, and are knowne to be woond into bad fellowship by the bold and subtill, regard (I say) must be had of such,that they be more fauourably vsed.

Vers.30. In that it is recorded here,that when there came any rumour of it,they in all places wondred at it, and said, the like had not been heard of among them ; it teacheth that wee should, when wee heare of foule matters to be done in the countrey,or citie,we should be stricken in our hearts,and amazed at the hearing of them, bewaile them also, and report and speake of them to make them odious among all,and to strike a feare thereby into the wicked; and so we should doe about the punishments inflicted on the committers of such facts. For the hearing of them doth make the hearts of many ny to quake, who are readily enough disposed that way: and though they be themselues such as haue no great goodnesse in them, which (wee know) were able to hold them within holy bounds, yet it restraineth them from such lewdnes, as they might otherwise haue been like to haue falne into; as (no doubt) many are feared from murther, by the terrible spectacles that they behold, I meane of such malefactors to hang in chaines for their crueltie.

So by his willing and aduising the heads of Israel, to consider of the fact, 2.
by the manner of making it knowne to them, all in authoritie should know, that they ought to weigh duly, the faults that are brought before them, to consult, and speake about them, and censure them accordingly. Euen as also the gouernours of families should marke the reports that are made to them, of any dangerous or desperate parts, that are plaid by any in the house, and to what outrage they may be like to grow if they be suffered, that in time and wise manner, they may be staied and cut off from causing trouble to the whole house, yea and the Common-wealth also, as through sufferance such accidents fall out in both dally.

The end of the 19. Chapter.

THE TWENTIETH CHAPTER OF THE booke of Iudges.

Verse 1. *Then all the children of Israel went out, and the congregation was gathered together as one man, from Dan to Beer-sheba, with the land of Gilead vnto the Lord in Mizpeh.*

2. *And the chiefe of all the people, and all the tribes of Israel assembled in the congregation of the people of God, foure hundred thousand footmen that drew sword.*

3. *(Now the children of Beniamin heard that the children of Israel were gone vp to Mizpeh) Then the children of Israel said, How is this wickednesse committed?*

4. *And the same Leuite, the womans husband that was slaine, answered and said, I came vnto Gibeah that is in Beniamin with my concubine to lodge.*

5. *And the men of Gibeah arose against me, and beset the house round about vpon me by night, thinking to haue slaine me, and haue forced my concubine that she is dead.*

6. *Then I tooke my concubine, and cut her in pieces, and sent her thorowout all the countrey of the inheritance of Israel, for they haue committed abomination and villanie in Israel.*

7. *Behold, ye are all children of Israel, giue your aduice and counsell herein.*

The summe of the Chapter.

THE summe of this Chapter is thus much: that the Israelites hauing receiued the message from the Leuite, mentioned in the former Chapter, set a day of meeting with consent about this matter complained of vnto them, and they being come together, heare the accusation of the Leuite: after the which they require of them of *Beniamin*, that they bring forth the guiltie persons of Gibeah before them, that they might proceede against them according to their doings: but they yeelded not thereto, neither would hearken to their brethren the Iſraelites, but put themſelues in armor againſt them. Therefore they made warre with them, and the Iſraelites being chaced and ſmitten downe by them, renued their warre, and were againe ſlaine of the Beniamites, a great number of them: but they praying to God did at laſt ouercome, yea and vtterly deſtroy them, a few hundreds excepted.

The parts three. The parts of this Chapter are three. Firſt, the diſſenting and diſagreeing of the Beniamites with the Iſraelites, when in the meeting of the Iſraelites together at Mizpeh, they could not draw the Beniamites to them, to reaſon and debate of the matter: and this to verſe 17. The ſecond thing is the double warre betwixt them, in both which the Iſraelites were ſmitten downe by the men of Beniamin: to verſe 26. Laſtly, how the Iſraelites ouercame them, and this to the end.

The firſt part of the Chapter.

Foure things in part 1. IN the firſt part we are to conſider theſe foure things. The firſt, the meeting of the children of Iſrael together in Mizpeh, to the fourth verſe. Secondly, the Leuites opening of his cauſe before them, to verſe 8. Thirdly, the Iſraelites requiring of the men of Beniamin, to deliuer to them the malefactors of Gibeah to bee puniſhed, to the middeſt of the 13. verſe. The fourth, the Beniamites refuſing, and putting themſelues in armour againſt them, to verſe 17.

The ſumme of verſe 1. Now to begin with the firſt of theſe foure points, and namely in this firſt verſe: It is ſaid here that the whole company of the children of Iſrael were come forth out of their habitations, for they came from the vttermoſt borders of the land, from Dan in the North, and Beerſheba in the South, and from Gilead which is beyond Iordan in the Eaſt. They met (I ſay) in a place that was fitteſt, with one conſent, and they came together vnto the Lord, to make him of their counſell, and pray for his direction and bleſſing: for where a company of the godly is together, there God is preſent with them: as it is ſaid, God ſtood in the aſſemblie of the Gods: meaning that the Iudges ſo called when they conſult, iudge, and giue ſentence, ought not to thinke that they pleade their owne cauſe, but Gods, and to be faithfull, for they haue God among them, to behold their doings. (Pſal. 82. 1.)

Doct. This ſhould teach vs, that when men meete to good ends, they ſhould ſeeke to the Lord, as *Iehoſaphat* did in great danger: (2. Chro. 20. 3.) and hauing him preſent with them, they ſhould behaue themſelues as in his preſence, according to the end for which they come together, whether it be to prayer and hearing of the word, or to conſult and debate, as theſe did heere, about weightie and doubtfull caſes, which ſhould cauſe vs in all ſuch matters and dealings to be more religious then for the moſt part we are. For if God be preſent, oh how ought wee to draw neere to him, and euery way to behaue our ſelues before him, (who haue him the beholder of vs) as is meete for his greatnes: which the Fathers haue duly obſerued, when they knew God was among them, for they framed themſelues to ſhew all high reuerence in the place, as *Iacob* did at Bethel. (Gen. 28. 16. 17.) And therefore great is the ſinne of them who in their weightieſt affaires thinke leaſt of God, much leſſe behaue

themſelues

themselues reuerently in his presence, and least of all make him of their counsell,but are ashamed so to doe.

Againe,in their meeting with consent to so good an end,as to take order 2
against euill doers,we are taught that we all ought to be as one man,willing and ready to ioyne in good causes,as to pursue euill contrarily, for the vpholding of goodnesse. For dissenting and diuersitie of mindes in good attempts is a great hindrance thereof. It is said of the Apostles,that they were Act.2.1.
all of one minde who were appointed to be the builders vp of the Church
in one and the same truth: and so did *Paul* will the people to be of one mind Phil.2.2.
in the embracing of the doctrine of the Gospell. So were the people of Israel affected in the daies of *Iosua,* when they heard that the two tribes and halfe,had set vp an Altar after their departure from their brethren, they all
set against them, as fearing they had gone about to set vp a new religion. Iosh.22.16.
Rarely is this vnion and agreement in good things found in this age,as for many to embrace the Gospell heartily, but euen betwixt such as goe for Christians,there shall be hollownesse and dissembling, or at least through want of knowledge in some, or impotencie in affection: which causeth so little good to be done,and much more when they are implacable, and not to be drawne to any consent in good things, but rather of one minde in euill: and it is not a little to their reproch,when in good causes, as in prouiding for the poore, pursuing of disorders among them, and about their common rates making,for bearing charges in townes together,they cannot agree in one, but contend bitterly,and that is also among some, done euen on the Sabbath.

Here it is shewed,that the chiefe in the tribes,were the setters forward of Vers.2.
the rest,and assembled thus many,as are here spoken of,euen hundred thousands. To shew vs, what force it hath to draw on other, when the chiefest men in any societie are first in good matters, and begin themselues: which
S. *Paul* knowing,did first moue the Ministers and the ancient men and wo- Tit.2.1.2.
men to be examples to the rest in the doing of their duties. In euill the example of the ancient and the wealthie, doth very much harme,as wee may
reade in *Ezra:* and see in *Corah*; who despising *Moses,*whom God had set Ezra 9.2.
vp and honoured,drew many to be of his conspiracie: wherfore they haue Numb.16.2.
much to answere for to God,who being aboue other in place, and condi- Note.
tion, are not also before them in grace, innocencie and other fruites of the Spirit: for many shall curse them who haue fallen by their counsell or bad example.

The holy storie relateth,that the tribe of *Beniamin* heard that their bre- Vers.3.
thren the men of Israel were assembled: whereby it appeareth that they came not among them,who could not be ignorant of the fact, (for the Leuite sent the message to euery tribe) and therefore they shewed their ill conscience therein, and that they tooke part with the wicked men of Gibeah, who were of their tribe. For otherwise if they had bin vpright and indifferent,they would (as they had iust cause) haue come among the other tribes, to haue shewed themselues blamelesse and innocent in the matter,yea and further to haue brought forth the euill doers to punishment: whereas they now gaue vehement suspition that they did communicate with them in their wicked doings,and more then winke at their sinne.

Doct. vers. 3. By this we should learne, to be far from taking part with euill causes, or so much as to allow of them, it is a shrewde token that our hearts are euill, and that we incline too much to the sinne our selues, when we shew that we fauour it in others. *Paul* maketh that a greater fault, then to commit it, when he saith: Not onely they doe such things themselues, (meaning horrible facts) but also fauour them that doe them. If they see them in their deere friends, let them doe what they can, to reforme them, but in no wise sooth them vp therein. But the directest way to keep themselues from bearing with them in others, (what sinnes soeuer they be) is to haue them in hatred and detestation themselues.

Rom. 1. 31.

2 The wisdome and well aduised care of the men of Israel, is also set downe in this verse, in that they inquired of the matter further when they were met, and did not rush vpon them of Beniamin furiously, for the report of the Leuite, but shewed that they were carefull to doe without offence all that they did; for the men of Beniamin heard that they were come together about the matter, and yet met not with them, and for all this did not they of Israel therefore contend with them by and by, but friendly sent to them. So should we deale in all matters, and namely in controuersies with men: I meane considerately go to worke, and take them in hand, and without passion or perturbation of minde, as anger, rage, and desire of reuenge; and especially in our owne case, so that neither we be distracted, and that other may see our patience and good dealing. And the rather, for that the most doe vtterly disguise themselues in their disagreements and controuersies with their neighbours, not abiding to be crossed in the least manner, neither to heare any thing that liketh them not, neither keeping measure in their words, but breaking out furiosly, which is far off from procuring things honest in the sight of all men: which when it is not done, great is the offence that is committed against God.

Note.

1. Tim. 4. 16.

Vers. 1. 2. 3. And by the whole course of their dealings mentioned in these three verses, we may learne, how zealously and earnestly euery man ought to set himselfe against foule and notorious offences. They are in no wise to be coloured, couered, or defended, but with vprightnesse of heart, and iustice to be proceeded against: For so is euill taken out of the way in towne or house, as king *Salomon* said of *Ioab*, to *Benaiah*, Smite him that he may dye, that thou maiest take away the bloud that *Ioab* shed causelesse, from me and from the house of my father. And if many Tribes did thus carefully, goe against this fact of the men of Gibeah, how much more ought this, yea, and may also be done among a few in Townes and housholds?

1. King. 2. 31.

Vers. 4. 5. 6. Now the men of Israel, being there to heare the matter, giuing occasion to the Leuite to lay it out, saying: How is this wickednesse committed? The Leuite the womans husband being permitted to speake, began after this manner. I came to lodge (not to hurt any man) with my concubine in Gibeah, and the men of the place, who were the inhabitants thereof beset the house in the night, and threatned to kill me, (meaning, vnlesse I would be subiect to their vnnaturall and beastly lust; which rather then I would haue yeelded vnto, I would haue chosen to die,) yet my concubine I could not withhold from them, whom they so abused all night, that she dyed. Hereupon I sent the parts of her through the land, because the villanie

villanie was so horrible, and yee are they in whom it is, to redresse it, consider yee now therefore, and consult about it.

In this questioning and answere made on both sides, we may consider what a benefit speech and language is, without the which (as the like may be said of all weightie matters, concerning both Church and Common wealth,) how could they haue knowne one an others minde? Such a singular mercie of God we see it to be, that we may conuerse and deale together by the helpe of speech and language, as we doe, both good and bad about all things that we need both heauenly and earthly; and what a dead thing were it otherwise to liue together? as we see, how vncomfortable it is, to be in companie with the dumbe that cannot speake. Also we see, when by warre or persecution, one neighbour is separated from an other, so that they cannot meet or see one an other, what an vncomfortable thing it is, as we haue heard in this booke in the daies of *Shamgar* and *Iael*, the high waies were vnoccupied. Now if a little solitarinesse, when we want the companie one of an other but a while, be so wearisome and vncomfortable, how much more when we liue and dwell together, and yet can say nothing to any that can be vnderstood, nor any other to vs, how much more (I say, is that irksome and tedious? So that the greater is the benefite of language among vs; (as examples, daily experience, and common reason, euery where doe testifie.) And I speake of this, as I may of all the like ordinarie benefits of God, to bring them, if it may be, into greater account among vs, for that I obserue, that we inioy so many of these common blessings of God, and yet make so slight account and reckoning of them. To speake of some for example, in that we haue the spectacles to helpe the eye-sight (without the which the most of such as are aged, were almost no better then blinde,) and stilts for the lame, to helpe, vphold, and carrie themselues by, without which many must lye as bedred all the yeare, and more then halfe dead: these are singular mercies of God, as they may see, both who stand in need of them, and such as need them not also, when they behold what helpes they be to such as vse them. But I goe further: For what a benefit is health, foode, outward peace, kind neighbourhod, the freedom that we haue from many sore paines and diseases? Besides, the Sunne to shine, and the raine to fall vpon our grounds, all which are the common benefits of God. But as great blessings as all these are vnto vs, and the like, yet what thanks are yeelded to God for them, of the most, or how many haue euer thought them to be such mercies as they are, till they be driuen by the extreame want of them to acknowledge it? Nay, I say more, who doth not abuse them all in such a shamefull manner, as that they are more bold by hauing so many of his good blessings, to sinne the more boldly against him, and so to fight against him, as it were with his owne weapons? I except not this benefit of speech and language which is the occasion of that which I say of this matter; yet oh! who can reckon vp the vnrulinesse, disorders, and mischiefes of the tongue, as Saint *Iames* saith? And this is the fruit which for the most part we yeeld vnto the Lord for the benefit of it. But of this point hath been enough said in the 12. chapter, by occasion of *Shibboleth*.

Furthermore in this narration of the Leuite, we who haue heard the fact

Doct. Iudg. 5.6. Note. Note. Iam. 3.6. Doct. vers. 4. 5. 6.

fact laied out before, as it was done, doe see that it is reported to the heads of Israel, euen as it was set downe by the holie storie before to be done. By the which we are taught truly, simply, and nakedly to relate and vtter our complaints, accusations, and depositions, without subtiltie, lying, or additions to the truth: to aggrauate them, neither by intemperate and vnquiet
1.Cor.6.4. mindes to propound our cause, but to commit it to discreete persons to bee heard, and iudged of: by the comprimitting of wise men, if it may be, or otherwise as the quality of the matter doth require. And as we must submit our selues to the Magistrates sentence, if it come before him, so ought wee to doe, if it be put to men of vnderstanding by our choice or consent to bee determined, and not to dislike or flie backe from their agreement if it like vs not, which is meere dishonesty, and the greater; if discurtesie and hard measure be offred by vs vnto them, as falling out with them for their good will: yet this must be excepted, that the comprimittors haue giuen their answer, and set downe their conclusion corruptly, or at least without due hearing the cause; which if it can be proued, their iudgement may with good conscience be refused.

2 Of the foulenes of the fact here laid forth by the Leuite, and of his so sending of the parts of his concubine among the tribes, I haue spoken before in the 19. Chapter: here the thing to be noted is this: the diligence and trauaile that the man tooke to bring such an odious fact to punishment: especially it being so hard to bring to passe, for it is cleere that he sought not any recompence to himselfe, or benefit thereby, no he sought none, but punishment to the euill doers. And we see he so preuailed with the tribes, that he gathered all Israel together to determine about it: which how great a fruite it was of his labour, who doth not see? which is a strong incouragement to vs, to doe the like, and in the like cause to vse diligence proportionable though the matter be smaller, and in seeking the due punishment of sinne, let the desire of obtaining God set vs about it, rather then our owne will, or that our priuate benefit be sought thereby: and we shall not neede to feare, but we may assure our selues, that we please God in so doing, and that he will giue successe accordingly as he shall see best.

Verse 7. As the Leuite laid out the matter, so the heads of Israel were there of purpose to heare it, and before consultation or determination, asked how that wickednes was committed, and there they attended the Leuites answer. And by them we are taught, when we are called to heare any waightie matter, either openly or priuatly; how to deale and behaue our selues: and that is to heare it with attendance and marking, and much more if it be a question betwixt two or many, to vnderstand both parties so well, that we
1.King.3.23. are able to repeat their owne words, as *Salomon* in a doubtfull cause betwixt two women did, saying, this woman speaketh thus, and that woman otherwise, &c.

This I say is to be done before there be consulting and determining about it, and then to speake and doe, as there shall be cause. And this is to be practised of Iudges, comprimitters, or any other whose aduice shall be asked in waighty causes. And so in our owne, we are to deale betwixt God and our selues: we must doe as we reade of the prodigall, what did he? when he came to himselfe, he did as it were, speake to himselfe and demand, saying,
How

How many hired seruants in my fathers house haue bread enough, and I die for hunger, &c. And when he had seene thereby into his estate, that of necessity he must seeke to haue it relieued, then he consulted how that should be, and afterward resolued, that the best way that hee could take for it, was to goe and humble himselfe to his father, and so he did, and he preuailed and obtained much more, then he durst thinke of or looke for. Luk. 15. 17.

Verse 8. *Then all the people arose as one man, saying, There shall not a man of vs goe to his tent, neither any turne into his house.*

9. *But now this is that thing which we will doe to Gibeah : we will goe vp by lot against it.*

10. *And we will take ten men of the hundred throughout all the tribes of Israel, and an hundred of the thousand, and a thousand of ten thousand to bring victual for the people, that they may doe (when they come to Gibeah of Beniamin) according to all the villany that it hath done in Israel.*

11. *So all the men of Israel were gathered against the city, knit together as one man.*

12. *And the tribes of Israel sent men through all the tribes of Beniamin, saying, What wickednes is this, that is committed among you?*

13. *Now therefore deliuer vs, those wicked men which are in Gibeah, that wee may put them to death, and put away euill from Israel : but the children of Beniamin would not obey the voyce of their brethren, the children of Israel.*

14. *But the children of Beniamin gathered themselues together out of the cities vnto Gibeah, to come out and fight against the children of Israel.*

15. *And the children of Beniamin were numbred at that time of the cities, sixe and twenty thousand men that drew sword, besides the inhabitants of Gibeah which were numbred seuen hundred chosen men.*

16. *Of all this people, were seuen hundred chosen men being left handed: al these could sling stones, at an haires breadth and not faile.*

HOw the tribes heard the matter, we haue seene. In these verses is shewed what was done on both sides, I meane by Israel and Beniamin: the people of Israel hauing heard the matter by the Leuite, (who could proue it by his seruant, and the old man with whom he lodged;) after that they had considered of it, resolued to see the fact punished, and that before they went home to their houses. And to that end tooke order to goe against them by warre, but yet first to send word to the men of Beniamin to deliuer to them those wicked persons of Gibeah, to be dealt with by them, as they had giuen cause. And this they did, to the end that they might take no iust occasion to except against them for rash dealing and vnbrotherly. But as for the men of Beniamin, they sent backe such a message to them againe, that they would not hearken to them, nor receiue information of the matter from them, but most vnwisely and vnkindly, rather adressed themselues to warre against them. *The summe.*

Here therefore occasion is offred to speake of them both: and first of the men of Israel how they agreed among themselues what they would doe, and how they did accordingly send messengers to the other. They say they will not goe to their houses, till they had looked to the matter. Their speede Vers. 8.

they made in this busines is to be noted. For no man doubteth but that they had all cause enough to haue returned home, but they thought they had greater cause to looke to this disorder first, though it was to their owne hindrance. And so we should bee minded, to goe about weighty and necessa-
Iosh.10.6.7. ry affaires speedily, for we know delay to be dangerous. Thus did *Iosua* for the Gibeonites, their necessity requiring all possible speed against their neighbour cities, which came against them.

Gen.24.33. Thus *Abrahams* seruant would not eate nor refresh himselfe, before hee had done that which he went for, to wit, to doe his masters message, and receiue an answere thereof. Thus when *Naash* the Ammonite, had vantage ouer the men of Iabesh Gilead, and would not release them, vnles they would suffer him to put out the right eyes of them all, they complained to their brethren, and it was made knowne to *Saul*, who seeing they had but a short time to giue in their answere, he assembled all Israel with all expediti-
1.Sam.11.11. on, & thereby rescued them out of the hands of *Naash*, and slue the Ammonites with an exceeding great slaughter. And so we see what great good is done by following matters in season, and not to defer them. Lamentable it is to see, how slacknes and coldnes on the contrary hindreth good successe.
Lam 1.7. In the weightiest matters of all other, how oft doe we see it complained of in the Scriptures? Ierusalem remembred and regarded her Sabbaths, when they were taken from her, but made no reckoning of them before. And Christ our Sauiour bewailed the posterity of the same people, for that they
Luk.19.42. knew not the time of their visitation. Euen so in both these instances wee haue too wofull experience, how like our age is to theirs. And so we fare, for in many good motions and holy desires which God worketh in vs, how soone doe we quench and extinguish them, by slouth or some other corruption; which by following and nourishing of them, might haue broken out into a commendable measure of zeale and feruentnes to the doing of much good?

Vers.9.10. That they sought to remedy the euill speedily among themselues, we haue heard in the former verse: but in what manner this was to be effected and brought to passe, was no lesse necessary for them to goe about. For a great multitude were come together, and they resolued to goe to warre against the Beniamites their brethren, if they should refuse to deliuer those wicked men of Gibeah into their hands to bee punished. But first they would make triall and send to them about it. But if they should withstand them, and defend those wicked men, as they did; they purposed to goe to warre against them, and by casting of lots to appoint some to carry victual to the rest, that should be in armour against the Beniamites, because they knew not how long they should be held in warre there.

Doct. Their wisedome was commendable in considering of the best way that was to be taken, and it is to teach vs to follow them therein. For a good thing may possibly be, and is gone about some time I confesse, but it is marred by reason the ill manner it is done in: as if they had set vpon the men of Beniamin before they had sent messengers vnto them to know what they would doe, they had giuen them great aduantage, and had done very vniustly and vnwisely: so had the ten tribes done to the two tribes and an halfe when they had set vp an altar at their parting from them. So *Gedeon* did wisely,

wisely, who being commanded to cast downe the altar of *Baal* which his Iosh.22.19.
father had, and to cut downe the groue that was by it, did it in the night, lest if he had done it in the day light, the men of the citie should not onely haue hindred, but also haue killed him. Euen so, the auoiding of dangers, offences, and all inconueniences, as farre as wee can, in doing good things, shall well testifie that we doe wisely goe about, and take them in hand, and contrarily, if we doe otherwise.

Also more particularly, in that they would not iudge them of Beniamin 2
so wilfull, as to beare with and defend the wicked men of Gibeah: no, although they refused to come among them, till they had made triall, wee should be taught this: that no conceits of our owne, or reports by other, nor any likelihoods of our brethrens offending and guiltinesse, without cleere knowledge thereof, should cause vs to accuse, or breake out against them, and thinke hardly of them, and shew our selues strange toward them, (the countenance being a bewraier of the heart) but if wee see likelihoods of any displeasure, conceiued by them against vs, or euill intended; doe we
as our Sauiour aduiseth vs; that is, goe to them, and debate the matter with Matth.5.23.
them, if it be worth it; or if not, passe wee by it, and so keepe wee our selues from bitternes and reuenge; and though they be faultie, yet allay wee it in them also by the same meanes, as much as in vs lieth, or heap we hot coales vpon their heads by well doing. It commeth oft times to passe, that such vnlooked for preuentions of euill purposes in them by our friendly talking, Note.
and manifesting of our innocencie and vprightnes of heart toward them, whereas they thought hardly of vs, is a cutting off the euill that was in their hearts against vs, and maketh them ashamed that they were so ill minded toward vs, when they see that we haue giuen them so small cause.

Their casting of lots in so doubtfull a case, who should carrie victuall, and 3
who should hold weapon in hand, it was to shew that they purposed to offer wrong to none. As *Salomon* teacheth, saying: The lot maketh dissention Prou.18.18.
to cease, and taketh it away betwixt the mightie. The vse of it is in weightie causes to determine, but not to abuse Gods ordinance, to make it serue our pleasure in what we will. And generally in all things, the chiefe in all societies, must carefully foresee that they deale equally and indifferently, especially betwixt themselues and others in matters of profit, and that none bee burthened, as neere as may be, neither haue cause to complaine giuen vnto them, no not in rates making, nor such like doings, but that al good example be giuen to the rest.

Here is shewed how they did indeed that which they purposed, for they Vers.11.12.13.
sent messengers to the men of Beniamin, as they agreed among themselues to doe, that they might know what they were resolued to doe about the deliuering vp to them those wicked men of Gibeah, before they set vpon them by warre. So promises of lawfull things, and good purposes ought to bee performed and fulfilled. Stedfastnes and constancie is a goodly grace and gift of God, to shew our selues to bee the same in all good things that wee were, or at least that we purposed and professed to bee, and such as wee are willing men should take vs to be. And the like is to be said of our professing the Gospell, which doth, as our word, testifie our religious minde, vnlesse we dissemble. It is dishonestly to goe from our word, though it be a most Psal.15.4.
common

common practise in the world, and the time will come when it will bee
Note. somewhat to vs, when our conscience shall be awakned out of the sleepe of drowsinesse and darknes, wherein it hath long lien, howsoeuer in the meane while we will make all seeme good that we like, be it neuer so bad. More particularly, what promises are made at mariages betwixt couples, of great matters, as of loue and agreement together, and of such kinde vsage of the one by the other: but what commeth all vnto? All is meere dissimulation in the most, and in many of the rest, forgetfulnes of their word, and promise breaking. And so it is in bargaining, and in promises made to good vses, and to the poore; they goe from them that made them: there is no hold of their word, no, nor of their writing and witnesse, with a great many. But when at the comming to the Sacrament, or in sicknesse or any other calamity, men deale so with God, to goe from their word and promise that they made to him, what marueile if they deale so one with another? So that it may well bee said, that faithfulnes and stedfastnes in performance of our lawfull couenants and promises, is a commendable ornament, where it may be found.

Vers. 12. 13. In these verses it is further said, that the men of Israel sent to the Beniamites, because they came not among them at Mizpeh, (which was a sore token of their ill meaning and dissenting from their brethren) they sent (I say) to them, though they would not iudge them to maintaine them of Gibeah, laying before them the foulenes of the fact, and required of them to bring foorth and deliuer the committers of it to bee punished: but they would not, and so they sent them word againe. By this dealing of the Israelites with them refusing to come among them, that they doe now by their authoritie charge them vpon their perill to yeeld vp the offenders, wee see they are now commanded (which was their great reproch to deliuer the euill doers, who might haue been reckoned as brethren among them to iudge them, if they would haue been perswaded to come and ioyne with them against them, when they were intreated. So men lose their credit and account that they were in, by their wilfulnes and dishonestie.

Doct. Thus it commeth to passe oft times, that they who might sit on the bench, must after a sort stand at the barre; and well worthie: while they fall
Note. to bad courses, and forsaking the fellowship of the honest and wel disposed, doe linke themselues in with such as are of bad qualities and of ill report. As *Achan*, who was of a substantiall familie in the chiefe tribe, namely of Iu-
Iosh. 7. 18. dah, was, by stealing the execrable thing which God had forbiddē, brought foorth to execution among the people, to his vtter shame, and was stoned to death for his euill doing. And *Zimri* one of the chiefe among his bre-
Numb. 25. 8. thren, had the like reward, for bringing into his tent in the hoast, a strange woman, and for committing wickednesse with her. Euen so it is a iust recompence to men, to come into discredit, and to be brought into meane account for their dishonestie, who might haue liued in good estate both toward God and in the world, if they could haue knowne themselues, and haue been held within compasse. And we know how ill it went with *Rehoboam* when he refused the good counsell of the graue counsellors, and followed the aduice of the young heads, for ten tribes went from him.

2 The men of Israel did commendably to follow the matter so throughly, and

and to seeke the cutting off, of such lawlesse and vnruly persons: the reason is added, (as we haue heard the like before) that euill, to wit, the displeasure of God, and plagues thereby might be remoued, which their wickednes would haue caused and procured, as *Salomon* saith of *Ioab*. And who can deny but that it is a worthy worke of God, to pursue wickednes for the remouall of his iudgements? But such workes are rarely to be found among vs, but slouth and the shunning of cost and paine taking, and partiality in fauouring euill doers, one of these is in the way to hinder it, therefore so many iudgements are among vs. I may adde this, that some will haue no hand against such, because their owne deeds be as euill. 1.King.2.31.

This be said of the men of Israel; now lastly in these verses, it is said, that the men of *Beniamin*, (who are next to bee spoken of) would not deliuer those wicked men of Gibeah, but refused so to doe; and thereby bewraied their euill hearts in bearing with their sinne, and in keeping away from the meeting with the men of Israel their brethren. From whence we may note diuers things: as first this, that though we through charity, must hope the best of men suspected, whose name is brought into question, when there is no apparent proofe thereof vnto vs; for all this they are neuer the innocenter, nor freer from blame, but oft times are found as bad as they were thought and reported to be; and God in due time bringeth their guiltines to light against them. To the iust challenging and reproch of such as being conuicted of euill in their owne consciences, doe yet carry themselues the bolder in lying still in their sinne, because no pregnant proofes can as yet be brought forth to charge and condemne them: as we read of *Gehazi*, let such know they doe but walke in a net, they cannot so keepe their wickednes from the knowledge of men, but if the Lord bewray it not to their shame, as oft times he doth, yet beside the accusation of their owne hearts, they shall themselues be many times the bewrayers of it, either by confession therof, or the breaking out of it, as these men of *Beniamin* did now shew by their answere, that they tooke part with those wicked men. 3. 2.King.5.25. 26.

In these verses it appeareth, that not only they resisted their brethrens message, denying to yeeld the wicked men into their hands, but also they professe openly, that they will defend and stand with them, and therefore put themselues in armor against their brethren the Israelites. And by this they shewed that they were content to breake off fellowship and friendship with their brethren, and to ieopard the losse of their goods and liues also, rather then they would offer those wicked men of Gibeah to punishment, or that they should sustaine the least reproch: who would thinke that one of the chiefe tribes, and great among the rest, should heape so many sinnes together, and all for the maintenance of so great a sinne? Vers.14.15.16.

But by this it may be gathered, that the pride of mans heart is monstrous, who hauing great cause, (as these men of *Beniamin* had, for the foule fact done among them) great cause I say to be humbled, and who should cast themselues to the ground before God, for the corrupt poison that was in their hearts, and the manifold wickednesses of their liues, which haue made them guilty of damnation, as many times as they haue haires on their heads, doe yet through vnbeliefe and the darknesse that is in them, lift vp their bristles and proudly take vpon them, wilfully and stifneckedly to allow 2.

Note. low and defend sinne in other, yea and that which is most horrible. It is indeede time that the Lord should make such to know him by his iudgements: who doe boldly resist his word, and prouoke him in that manner that these did. And in these men as in a glasse, ye may see that which the
Rom.7.13. Apostle affirmeth, to wit, that sinne is out of measure sinfull.

Vers.15.16. To the aggrauating of their sinne, it is said, that they were many in number, euen sixe and twenty thousand and sixe hundred chosen men: and that they had excellent gifts in warlike manhood, and skill, which ought to haue made them more thankfull and fruitfull in all well-doing to the honouring of God: but it appeareth, that they were the prouder because of these gifts of God. And this is the vse that men commonly make of them, euen to lift vp their stomakes by meanes of them. It is said they were strong men for warre, and some hundreds of them could fling stones at an haires breadth: whereby is meant, that they had a gift that way whereby they went beyond other men. And we may see that this put stomacke into them, and caused them to swell and not to care for, but to set light by their brethren. Oh how much were it to be desired, that many had neuer had the excellent gifts which they enioy: for then should they neuer haue sinned as they haue done. For thereby they haue bin emboldned to the wickednesse that they haue wrought, as *Salomon* noteth of mens riches, that they are their
Prou.18.11. strong hold, Pro.18. And whereas they comming naked into the world, and which is more, being abiects and castawayes from the presence of God by their owne deseruings; whereas I say in these respects, they should with *Abraham* and other such, be meane and base in their owne eyes, and marueile that they liue at all, much more that they enioy many blessings from God, they yet are high minded, looke aloft, and dare more boldly doe much mischiefe, because they haue (they say) that which shall beare them out. This be said of the first part of the Chapter.

THE HVNDRED SERMON, ON THE XX. CHAPTER OF THE BOOKE OF IVDGES.

The second part of the Chapter.

Verse 17. *Also the men of Israel beside Beniamin, were numbred foure hundred thousand men that drew sword; and these were men of warre.*

18. *And the children of Israel arose and went vp to the house of God, and asked counsell of God, and said, Which of vs shall goe vp first to the battell against the children of Beniamin? And the Lord said, Iudah shall goe vp first.*

19. *And the children of Israel rose vp in the morning, and encamped against Gibeah.*

20. *And*

20. *And the men of Israel went out to battell against Beniamin, and the men of Israel put themselues in aray to fight against them at Gibeah.*

21. *And the children of Beniamin came forth out of Gibeah, and destroyed downe to the ground of the Israelites that day, twenty and two thousand men.*

22. *And the people of the men of Israel incouraged themselues, and set their battell againe in aray, in the place where they put themselues in aray the first day.*

23. (*And the children of Israel went vp and wept before the Lord vntill euen, and asked counsell of the Lord, saying, Shall I goe vp againe to battell against the children of Beniamin my brother? And the Lord said, Goe vp against him.*)

24. *And the children of Israel came neere against the children of Beniamin, the second day.*

25. *And Beniamin went forth against them out of Gibeah the second day, and destroyed downe to the ground of the children of Israel againe, eighteene thousand men; all these drew the sword.*

WHen the people of Israel heard the answere of the men of *Beniamin*, and further perceiued, that they would defend those wicked men of Gibeah by warre, they also addressed themselues thereto, and asked of the Lord, which Tribe among them should begin. And they came against them: but the men of *Beniamin* slew a great number of them. Then they renued the battel, and asked of the Lord, if they should goe againe to warre against them: and the Lord bad them goe. And going out against them, were slaine againe of the Beniamites, though they were skilfull warriours. Now we hauing heard the summe of these verses, let vs more particularly looke further into them. *The summe.*

And of these two warres, first of the formost. It is marueiled at, their cause being good, that they fell before them of Beniamin, and yet they counselled with the Lord, who should among them first begin the warre. Whereby they were answered, that he was pleased with their going against their brethren, and in the second attempt they were certified thereof more fully. And yet there were thousands of them slaine againe. But whatsoeuer men mutter or obiect, (for they will not sticke to be medling) the Lord might dispose of the issue and successe, as it pleased him, without any iniurie done to them that were ouercome. And hereby we may be taught, that it is free for the Lord, to afflict where it pleaseth him: he shall alwaies haue iust cause so to do; and the innocentest shall not be able iustly to say vnto him, Why hast thou done thus? The reason is, seeing he doth all things well: neither can euill dwell with the Almightie, but we are corrupt, and in our best actions defectiue. *The summe of all in generall.* *Doct.* Mark. 7. 37.

Therefore, when we will take vpon vs to iudge of Gods works, (which we like not of) after our owne pleasure, we must know, that Gods secrets are hidden from vs, so that we cannot alwaies see why he afflicteth: and yet there are euer causes enough of his so doing; the Lord being perfectly righteous and good: and though by meanes of our blindnesse and selfe-loue we cannot espie and find them out oft times, yet we knowing how corrupt and badly minded we are, yea, and blinde in his matters, and how many loose parts we play with him, for the which he doth not alwaies by and by chastise vs, why should we not thinke, and be perswaded, that when he correcteth vs, he hath iust cause to doe it, though he execute it not some good time afterward?

But not onely for such slips he correcteth vs, but to preuent such and greater in vs also, and to abate the strength of pride, or some other sinne whereunto we are most prone. To be sure, the sinne that our consciences doth most accuse vs of, should be first alleaged of vs, as the cause thereof, as *Iosephs* brethren did. And who doth not know that God will make triall what patience, faith, obedience, and thankfulnesse is in vs, which appeareth thereby most easily; and whether such grace be in vs or no.

Note.

Gen.42.21.

And it shall be a good proofe to vs, that we iustifie him in all his doings, when we can hold our peace while he crosseth vs; as in sending vnseasonable weather at and before sowing and reaping, and while he ioynteth vs in our attempts to our great disappointment, and by sicknesse, losses, displeasure of our betters, and with other aduersities followeth vs. And especially while the case is such with vs, that we thinke his word and deed doe hardly agree together, but iarre and iangle the one with other: as in many things it seemeth to vs at the first sight that they doe; And as there was some shew and likelihood thereof here, where they asked of the Lord, which of them should first goe to fight against Beniamin, and he answered, Iudah should first goe, and yet he deliuered them into the hands of the men of Beniamin, so that two and twentie thousand fell before them, as if he had not bidden them goe: or if he had, why should he not likewise blesse them, they doing as he bad them? The like was that which the Lord did to the Shunamite: that to the great ioy of her heart, he gaue her a sonne, who had no childe before, and when he grew vp to be able to run about, he tooke him from her againe: as if thereby he would mocke her; and yet she still beleeued in him, that she should receiue him againe from the dead. Therefore (as I said) it shall well proue, that we honour God highly, when we euer hold God to be righteous in all that he doth, yea, euen then, when he shall deale most strangely with vs, speaking yet in his word most kindly: so that his words and his deeds seeme not to agree together.

2.King.4.20. 28.37.

Vers.17. to 21. But as it is not expressed, what the cause was, why God gaue Israel the foile; whether this, that they did trust in their great armie, and therefore doubted not of the victorie, neither therefore did they aske of God in their going to him, whether they should preuaile ouer them or no; or whether it were, because they did not as well pursue the men of Dan for their Idolatrie, a little before, (it being so horrible a fact) as well as the iniurie offered to the Leuites concubine; both which were probable; though, I say, this be not expressed, yet it is cleere, that the Israelites did well in seeking to punish those wicked men of Gibeah, and their cause was good. It should teach vs alwaies to looke to that. For otherwise we may be sure to haue God against vs, though there were no other thing else to accuse vs.

Doct. from vers.17. to 21.

But innocencie and a good cause is a strong defence to vs, though we haue many things against vs. But when we haue also a good and an excusing conscience besides, through the certaintie of our saluation, and the vprightnesse of our heart; then haue we much more cause to reioice and be confi-

Prou.28.1.

1.Tim.1.4.

confident, then when we onely know that our cause is good, and that the thing which we take in hand, and goe about, is pleasing to God. And if it was so with the men of Israel, there was no cause of feare vnto them. But when one of these defences goe without the other, as the maintaining of a good cause without the other two; or the other without this, what can be looked for, but hard successe, as here this people of Israel had? And though all these concurre, yet outward prosperitie is not alwaies to be looked for, seeing Gods loue is not to be measured thereby. Note.

Their asking counsell of God, who should begin the battell, was commendable, and gaue them satisfaction about that doubt: but they should as well haue sued to the Lord by earnest prayer for blessing in that their attempt, & haue asked if they should preuaile: which it is not said here, that they did, as afterward in the third setting vpon the Beniamites, they did both. And by this we may take knowledge of our slight manner of dealing in Gods matters, and those that we are to be occupied about: as to instance in particular, when we goe about marriage; also in gouerning of our families, or any other waightie affaires; in all which we should be verie circumspect, that we be well perswaded of Gods will, and his approuing of the things we goe about, and shew that we depend vpon him for blessing therein, by our serious calling vpon him. Vers.18. Note.

In place whereof, we for the most part, goe to worke coldly, slightly, and looking but to some one thing; and loose, vnaduised, and carelesse in many other, which is not according to that which we are taught. And therefore the Lord oftimes plucketh vs by the eare, and by some crosse, and disappointing of vs, in that which we desire and hope for, sheweth that he is offended with vs for seruing him after such a loose manner. And when we haue smarted for our sinne, we see it, and then we can goe to the Lord more feruently, and both bewaile that which we haue done amisse, and take a better course afterward. And many of these broken dealings we offer vnto the Lord, no better then mortlings and vntimely sacrifices were in the time of the Law: so vnconstant wee are in the most of our good attempts and actions. Note.

For all the good cause that the people of Israel had, and the men of Beniamin as bad; yet did these preuaile against them. And why, thinke we? not so much for any thing that God respected in them of Beniamin, (whose doings he abhorred) as for that he disliked in the Israelites, as I haue said. And therefore wee must beware that wee iudge not of things nor persons by the euent that followeth their doings. *Ahab* preuailed twice against *Benhadad*, yet we know hee was an Idolater, and a wicked man. And so what is more common then the oppressor and offerer of wrong, to iustle and ouercome the innocent and righteous man? for he prospereth in his outward affaires, while the godly is holden vnder of wants and pouertie: as it is written, *Iudgement must begin at the house of God.* Vers.19.20.21. 1.Pet.4.17.

But what then? The Lord will haue a time to bridle and pull downe the one, as he did these Beniamites; and to shew that hee regardeth the other, I meane the vpright man, after hee hath corrected him in a fatherly manner, and in the meane while, let his word stablish our iudgement in the truth which I now teach: namely, that a man cannot know who is in the fauour Eccles.9.1.

Eccles.9.1. of God or out of it, by prosperitie or aduersitie, neither by good or ill successe in his earthly affaires. And this be said of the first betwixt Israel and the men of Beniamin.

Vers.22.23. 24.25. Now followeth the second betwixt Israel and Beniamin. In going about this, it is said, that the people of Israel did yet take heart, and incouraged themselues againe to warre, for all the losse that they sustained, to wit, of two and twentie thousand men. But first they asked of the Lord, whether they should go against them, they being their brethren. Shewing thereby, that they made some doubt of it by meanes of their ill successe, and therfore did not in any setled perswasion of faith goe about it before they had Gods answere, but looked onely to the goodnesse of their cause. They did also weepe before the Lord vntill euening, and worship him. Whereby what may we gather, but that they prayed vnto him? which being a chiefe part of his worship, was that which they had most need to doe, and cause to offer those their praiers vnto him. And the Lord answering them, bad them goe againe against them: which they doing the next day, were smitten downe by the Beniamites the second time, euen as many almost as at the first.

Doct. vers.22. Here wee may see how the Israelites heartened themselues to warre againe, and then asked of the Lord if they should goe: and though hee bad them goe, yet they fell againe before the Beniamites. Now what was that which did incourage them, when they saw before, how they were smitten downe by them? which (who seeth not) might haue been enough to dismay them? Truly the goodnesse of their cause, for which they fought, did chiefly incourage them. Which may teach vs, that we ought not to faint

Luk.18.1. Gal.6.9. and leaue off a good matter, though it succeed not by and by. I deny not, but there must goe other things with it, as I haue said, euen true repentance for former sinnes, and casting away all confidence in our selues: but so likewise we must looke still to goe forward in a good matter when wee haue begun it.

Doct. vers.23. Their asking counsell of God with weeping was commendable in them, in that they were touched with the affliction, and laid it to their heart; and more, if they did it for their sinne, which is not certaine, though they wept and prayed to the Lord, and so, as he answered them, and allowed them to goe forward against the Beniamites. All this is meete to be in vs also in our trouble. And what then (ye will say) shall follow? I answere, (no doubt) much good in respect thereof, if there be no other thing in the way to hinder, as I said euen now. But if they did these things, or if we doe the like, and yet doe them houerly, and because of our present need, and shall not search

Note. our selues throughly to cast out all that may lie secretly to waite vs a mischiefe, euen this may be sufficient to hold vs from attaining that which we seeke. So that the good duties which we shall doe to God in this or the like case, are not to be omitted, although they yeeld not present fruite, but yet we are to looke if any thing be wanting therein which we may see to be required, or whether wee haue not offered our duties in too slight a manner: both which being amended, there is no cause of feare to vs, howsoeuer it shall please the Lord to trie vs.

Now it is said, that for all that the Israelites did, which I haue mentioned,

ned, yet they failed of the victorie, and were slaine againe, as before, as Vers.24.25.
though God had not regarded thẽ for all that they did, and yet had bidden *Doct.*
them goe: which they tooke (no doubt) as a great token of their good successe. But I say to this, that he did not promise so much to them, neither did they aske that of the Lord, (as in the third attempt following, wee may gather they did, and God then answered, that hee would deliuer them into their hands) they little doubting (in deed) of the victorie, because of their great number, and the goodnesse of their cause, as I said before. But therein they failed, (as may appeare by that their asking of God afterward, if they should preuaile) as if the Lord would shew them thereby, that they were too confident in their owne strength; or at least did not as yet throughly search themselues.

This their ill successe when they looked for good, must teach vs, not to be bold to promise to our selues that which wee desire, and would haue, when God hath not giuen his word and promise for the same, which must shew vs what his minde and will is therein, as in things vncertaine. For the truth is, we are too readie to looke for much, if our likelihood be any at all; and if we haue a conceit, that God will grant it; as if wee pray for it, and be perswaded, (though without ground or good warrant) that our doings please him: all which is but froth, and as a dreame. And therein wee deale much
like to *Saul*, who would take vpon him in his good mood, to offer sacrifice 1.Sam.15.9.
to God before *Samuel* came, when yet he ought not to haue done so, but to rest on the word of God: and therefore it turned to his great hurt and damage. So that we may see what good intents doe helpe, when there is not knowledge to direct. Euen so doe wee oft times, that as hee looked to bee commended for that which he did, when hee was for the same sharply reproued; so wee are readie to thinke of the will-worship that we giue him, though it was neuer by him required. But seeing we haue a rule giuen vs of him to bee guided by, hee will shew vs our folly, yea boldnes to presume without him, and his allowance; as here hee did to the men of Israel, who thought themselues so sure of victorie against the Beniamites, through many likelihoods that they had thereof. And yet in neither of both their consultings with the Lord, did they aske this of him, whether they should preuaile against Beniamin, neither had they answere that they should; & therefore they could haue no assurance of it. But to leaue them and to come to our selues, it is true, that as sometime we doubt so deeply of Gods promise,
(though there be no iust cause so to doe) that nothing can stay and vphold Note.
vs: so at other times we conceiue such hope where yet wee haue no promise, that nothing can restraine nor hold vs backe from bold presuming, and looking for that which we desire. Thus by extremities wee are much led; but to liue by faith, which is the happie estate and the meane betwixt both; it is the hardest thing to attaine to, for which cause God is driuen to bring vs within compasse, as he did these here, by withholding from them that which they thought they had been sure of. And this be said of their second battaile.

The third part of the Chapter.

Verſe 26. *Then all the children of Iſrael, and all the people went vp, and came*
vnto the houſe of God, and wept, and ſate there before the Lord, and faſted that day
vntill Euen, and offered burnt offerings, and peace offerings before the Lord.
27. *And the children of Iſrael enquired of the Lord, (for the Arke of the Coue-*
nant of God was there in thoſe dayes.
28. *And Phinehas the ſonne of Eleazar, the ſonne of Aaron ſtood before it in*
thoſe dayes,) ſaying; Shall I yet againe goe out to battell againſt the children of Ben-
iamin my brother, or ſhall I ceaſe? And the Lord ſaid, Goe vp; for to morrow I will
deliuer them into thine hand.
29. *And Iſrael ſet liers in waite round about Gibeah.*
30. *And the children of Iſrael went vp againſt the children of Beniamin on the*
third day, and put themſelues in aray againſt Gibeah, as at other times.
31. *And the children of Beniamin went out againſt the people, and were drawne*
away from the city, and they began to ſmite of the people and kill as at other times, in
the high wayes, of which one goeth vp to the houſe of God, and the other to Gibeah in
the field, about thirty men of Iſrael.
32. *And the children of Beniamin ſaid, They are ſmitten downe before vs, as at*
the firſt: But the children of Iſrael ſaid, Let vs flee, and draw them from the city vn-
to the high wayes.
33. *And all the men of Iſrael roſe vp out of their place, and put themſelues in a-*
ray at Baal-Tamar: and the liers in waite of Iſrael came forth out of their places,
euen out of the medowes of Gibeah.
34. *And there came againſt Gibeah ten thouſand choſen men of all Iſrael, and*
the battell was ſore: but they knew not that euill was neere them.
35. *And the Lord ſmote Beniamin before Iſrael, and the children of Iſrael de-*
ſtroyed of the Beniamites that day, twenty and fiue thouſand, and an hundred men;
all theſe drew the ſword.
36. *So the children of Iſrael ſaw that they were ſmitten: for the men of Iſrael*
gaue place to the Beniamites, becauſe they truſted vnto the liers in waite, which they
had ſet beſide Gibeah.
37. *And the liers in waite haſted, and ruſhed vpon Gibeah, and the liers in*
waite drew themſelues along, and ſmote all the city with the edge of the ſword.
38. *Now there was an appointed ſigne betweene the men of Iſrael and the liers*
in waite, that they ſhould make a great flame with ſmoake, riſe vp out of the
city.
39. *And when the men of Iſrael retired in the battell, Beniamin began to ſmite*
and kill of the men of Iſrael about thirty perſons, for they ſaid, Surely they are ſmitten
downe before vs as in the firſt battell.
40. *But when the flame began to riſe vp out of the city, with a pillar of ſmoke,*
the Beniamites looked behind them, and behold; the flame of the city aſcended vp to
heauen.
41. *And when the men of Iſrael turned againe, the men of Beniamin were ama-*
ſed; for they ſaw that euill was come vpon them.
42. *Therefore they turned their backs before the men of Iſrael vnto the way of*
the

the wildernes, but the battell ouertooke them: and them which came out of the cities, they destroyed in the midst of them.

43. *Thus they inclosed the Beniamites round about, and chased them, and trod them downe with ease ouer against Gibeah toward the sun rising.*

44. *And there fell of Beniamin eighteene thousand men; all these were men of valour.*

45. *And they turned and fled toward the wildernes vnto the rocke of Rimmon: and they gleaned of them in the high wayes fiue thousand men: and pursued hard after them vnto Gidom, and slew two thousand men of them.*

46. *So that all which fell that day of Beniamin were twentie and fiue thousand men that drew the sword; all these were men of valour.*

NOw followeth the third attempt of the people of Israel, in the warre that they made with the men of *Beniamin*. But first how they sought the Lord by true repentance, and preuailed against them. And how the Beniamites being all well nigh slaine by them, the rest who were but few that escaped, fled away to saue their liues. *The summe of all these verses in generall.*

This battel, seeing it is laid forth at large, I will contract into a more narrow roome: know we therefore, that first the repentance of Israel is mentioned to verse 29. Then the warre is set downe in a generall manner, to verse 36. Thirdly, more particularly to verse 47. And fourthly, the flight of the men of *Beniamin*, and the further wasting of them, and destroying of their cities, is added in the two last verses. But first let vs come to the Israelites seeking to God, to the 29. verse, with the which I will begin before I proceed to the warre. *The parts 4.*

The signes and effects of their repentance were these: to wit, that they went solemnly together to Shiloh into the house of the Lord, where the Tabernacle and the Arke were at that time: and then that there they wept, and fasted all the day, and offered burnt sacrifices to the Lord, and asked counsell of him whether they should goe forward still against *Beniamin*, or desist; submitting themselues to his will, and receiued at that time an answere from him, which they had not before done, and that was, that hee would deliuer them into their hands. This they now did, for they saw that God accepted not their former seekings vnto him. *The summe of vers. 26, 27, 28.*

That which we haue to learne here is, that afflictions doe not by and by breake the hearts of Gods people, but they continue hardened if they intertained any sinne before vnrepented of, and lie in it still when the affliction commeth vpon them. For why? First they hope that it shall not long continue: and secondly, they hauing much corruption in them still, and it getting strength through selfeloue, and their weake and inconstant resisting and opposing it, they are sometime foiled with it, and the longer they haue suffered it, the faster hold it taketh on them, and windeth in, and draweth liking from them thereunto: so that they cannot easily iustle it out, and get hereby dislike against it; and therefore when God feareth them out of it by affliction, though they can doe no lesse, (except they be in a deepe sleepe) then remember and thinke of that sinne which doth most check their conscience; yet they doe not alwayes heartily, but sometime faintly confesse it, and renounce it, as their fathers did in the tenth Chapter of this *Doct.*

Iud.10.10. booke: or at least not constantly pursue it afterward, and pray against it, so farre as till they haue driuen it out of their loue and liking.

And so it commeth to passe, that affliction it selfe doth not alwayes breake the heart with remorse and turning from their sinne, (as neither it did at the first so worke in these men of Israel;) but God either continuing it, or sending some new calamity and correction to rowze and awake them, (as he did here the Israelites by this third battaile;) it preuaileth at length, and causeth them seriously to repent and turne vnto him. But before that, they being blinded with the sinne that is in them, they hold backe from repenting, as *Ionah* did for a time, especially if they haue any thing in them, that they may rest on, as their former perswasion of Gods loue, or some gifts of grace in them. Thereby I say it is, that they be not so soone brought vpon their knees, no not by affliction. And so *Dauid* speaketh of himselfe
Psa. 32.5. in the 32. Psalme, how hardly he ouercame himselfe, and what difficulty he found in submitting himselfe meekely and humbly to God in confessing his sinne. Oh therefore great is his patience and long suffering in bearing thus with his, and waiting their repentance, whereas affliction should at the first arresting of vs, make vs see, that God hath a controuersie against vs, yea
Note. we should serue God truly before it come. For the which cause sometime he scareth his children from the baites of sinne, which hold them in the deceiuablenes thereof in their prosperitie, before troubles come. True it is, as I haue said, this is not alway at the first entring of affliction, vnlesse there haue been a well keeping and framing of the heart before, and that it hath not bin farre gone in the liking of the sinne, although inticed and lightly moued thereto, then affliction may be a meane at the first to stay the sinne: and this is most commendable, when it is so. But the wicked are so farre from taking warning by their sinne at first, when God punisheth them, that the longer his roddes be vpon them, the more they storme and rage vnder them.

And by this which hath bin said, we may gather, that the children of Israel did not so throughly search, nor so seriously looke into themselues before, as now at this third attempt, but lamented chiefly for the calamity that had befallen them, and wept before the Lord for that their expectation was disappointed. But now they looked more earnestly, what should cause God to deny them helpe, for they saw they had prouoked him other wayes, though they fought in a good cause, and they bewailed their sinne, and turned to God from their hearts, and declared the same by signes and fruites. For though they were but outward, yet proceeding from a repentant heart in them, for otherwise God would not haue regarded them, they were in them true testimonies therof. Euen as we reade of the like to haue bin done
Iud.2.3. by their fathers at Bochim, and those that came long after them in the time
Hos.14.3.4. of the Prophet *Hosea*. But yet the like or the most of the same fruites and signes may be seene in men, and yet no repentance in them, if the heart repent not, which is to be marked. So that if we haue walked with God more loosely, (as this people had done,) or yet still doe; let vs call our selues to a reckoning from time to time, till we haue found it out: for deadnes and
Iam.5.16. drowsines in doing duty, is no fit seruice for him, who requireth feruency
2.Cor.9.7. and chearefulnes: and when we haue found it out, let vs make no long tariance

tariance nor delay, but ſpeedily, as this people here did, powre out our hearts at large with confeſſion of our ſinnes, accuſing our ſelues, feruent prayer for pardon and other grace, with couenants renewed for fruits of amendment, and thankeſgiuing for ſuch grace ſhewed vpon vs. And thus
did theſe men of Iſrael here, and they in *Hoſee*. And then returne wee to Hoſ.14.2.3.
what duety ſoeuer God layeth on vs to performe it, as they here did, and we Reuel.2.5.
ſhall proſper.

Of burnt offerings and peace offerings, what they were, and what was *Doct.2.*
ſignified by them for our inſtruction, reade notes on Chapter 2. verſe
3.4.5. 3

Their asking counſell of the Lord by the high Prieſt, who was then *Phinehas* the ſonne of *Eleazar*, the ſonne of *Aaron*, (for he was ſaid then to ſtand before the Lord,) and the anſwering of them againe; they doe both teach vs, in our doubtful caſes to doe the like, by the meanes that we haue, to wit,
to ſearch the canonicall Scriptures, and to repaire to his true Miniſters, and Ioh.5.37.
to truſt aſſuredly, that God will anſwere vs thereby to our good contentment, and that he will bee heard of vs, alſo we deſiring to bee ſatisfied in our doubtfull caſes: of both which I haue ſpoke before

And this fruit of their repentance, namely, that they ſhewed themſelues ready to be at Gods pleaſure and command, either in going to warre againe, although they might much haue bin diſcouraged therefrom by hard ſucceſſe, or in forbearing and deſiſting from it, they hauing been ſo ſore prouoked; this, I ſay, teacheth vs a good leſſon, that we ſhould euer be ready at Gods command, accordingly as we pray; *Thy will be done*, and to bee
ready to obey; euen before, as the Theſſalonians were, and to be diligent- 2.Theſ.3.4.
ly giuen to euery good worke, as *Paul* willed the widowes to be in his time, 1.Tim.5.10.
and to ſit cloſe thereto, and not to be flitting, off and on, and vnſetled, as many are, who yet would bee taken to be of the forwardeſt ſort. Remem-
bring that it is our wiſdome to obey God, as *Moſes* teacheth in Deutero- Deut.4.6.
nomy; and that it is good alwayes in a good thing to be conſtant. For it is the Gal.4.18.
one thing that is euer neceſſary, whatſoeuer we are occupied about, and Luk.10.42.
therefore our hearts ſhould euer be vpon it.

It is added that the Arke of God was there, (when it is ſaid that they aſ- *The clearing of a*
ked counſell;) that is, in Shiloh, not farre from Gibeah: as alſo it is ſaid in *doubt in ver.28.*
the next Chapter, that there was the houſe of God: & being ſo neere them, they might the eaſlier conſult with the Lord there. But the holy ſtory recordeth another thing, that may be marueiled at, to wit, that *Phineas* the ſonne of *Eleazar*, the ſonne of *Aaron*, was then high Prieſt, which (as I ſay) may be marueiled at, if this ſtory be ſet in the right place, as it ſtandeth in order. Alſo if it be granted, that the acts mentioned in it, were done after the death of *Samſon*: for then was *Phinehas* well toward foure hundred yeares old, whereas the age of a man at that time, was but foure ſcore, and that with paine.

He was a man for his courage, wiſdome and grace, meete to doe that Pſal.90.10.
worthy and memorable act againſt *Zimri* and *Cozbi*, mentioned in the Num.25.8.
booke of Numbers, and that whileſt the children of Iſrael were in the wildernes: at which time in all probability he could not be vnder thirty yeare
old, and *Eleazar* his father a little before made high Prieſt in *Aarons* roome, Num.20.28.
then

then lately deceased. After that act he remained with the people of God some space in the desert, *Moses* then being aliue. After their departure from thence, and the death of *Moses*, when *Iosua* entred into his place, from that time, to his death were betwixt 17. and 18. yeares. For so much time was taken vp in the acts mentioned in the booke of *Iosua*, from the beginning to the end. And the things mentioned in the booke of Iudges did take vp three hundred yeares, not aboue a yeare wanting.

Now all these things being considered, *Phinehas* must bee some three hundred and fifty yeares old at the least: which to be so, we haue no reason

Psal. 90. 10. to thinke, hauing nothing in the Scripture for proofe of it, seeing before this in *Moses* time, as I said, a man scarcely attained to one hundred. I therefore take this, that is said of *Phinehas*; that he was high Priest when this battell was fought, to bee a good argument to proue, that both the warre here spoken of, and the other acts mentioned in the last fiue Chapters of this booke, were not done after the death of *Samson*, according to the order in which they are set downe, but are to be referred to the time after the death of *Iosua*, and the good rulers that out liued him, when there arose another generation that knew not the Lord, and before the time of the Iudges, or there about, or a little after, as I haue had occasion to say in another place. This I haue set downe for the clearing of the story.

Doct. in ver. 28 Now that which remaineth in this 28. verse, is this: that now at last, the Lord promiseth victorie to Israel, who fighting in a good cause, had yet bin twice ouercome by the Beniamites before. Thus the Lord teacheth vs, that though he correct his owne deare children for a season, (hee seeing alwaies good cause thereof when he doth so) yet he will in due time deliuer them,

Hos. 6. 2. as he saith in *Hosea*: *After two daies, in the third hee will restore vs.* And *David*

Psal. 30. 5. speaketh not vnlike to this, when he saith: *Heauinesse may abide for a night, but ioy commeth in the morning*, meaning shortly; both of them setting down a certaine number for an vncertaine. Euen as it is in another place: *The*

Psal. 125. 3. *Lord will not suffer the rod of the wicked to lie alwaies on the lot of the righteous, lest they should reach out their hand to iniquitie.* This is more worth then all gold, where it is beleeued.

And it may the easilier be beleeued, seeing it is certaine, that when hee correcteth his for their sinne, he doth it with that minde that here hee did, to wit, to bring them neerer to him, I meane to repentance: the which though they hardly see for the time, and more hardly yeeld vnto at the first; yet whē by striuing they haue attained to it, they would not for any worldly benefit forgoe it againe. But though that sinne which they haue taken

Note. and drunken in, as mixed wine, must as lothsome vomit be cast vp againe, whereto they are hardly brought; yet let them labour to be contented to doe so, seeing the ease that will come thereby, shall be so great. And this be said of Israels repenting, and of Gods answering them. Now I will proceed to the warre.

Vers. 29 to 36. This is set downe first generally, as I said, to verse 36. The summe where-

The summe. of is this. The people of Israel went vp against Gibeah, where the men of Beniamin were, and prouoked them to come foorth, as they had done before: and in the meane while they had placed ten thousand strong men about Gibeah secretly, to enter the citie as soone as the other should goe out.

And

And when the Beniamites came out,and were drawne from the city,Israel went backe,and began againe to fall before them, about some thirtie men; which put them of Beniamin in hope,that they should smite them againe, as they had done before : but in the meane while,the two bands of the Israelites inclosed them ; the ten thousand,I meane, who had hidden themselues by the citie,and got into it,when they of Beniamin went out to follow the battaile, and the other who drew the Beniamites from the citie, who were not suspected : so that there were slaine of them fiue and twentie thousand,and an hundred,that were fit for warre.

Here first,in that the Israelites for all the discouragement that they had twice sustained before, did yet hold out in the good cause which they had taken in hand, and when they had repented, receiued new incouragement from God; herein (I say) their constancie is worthie to be followed of vs, namely that in ill successe wee search our selues better, and so turne to the Lord againe and be more feruent : for as much as wee are soone faint and wearie otherwise in any good worke that is enioyned vs of God, especially if we haue not good successe therein. For he will not allow any idle persons,slothfull, and vnprofitable, to dwell in his house, but will cast them out as vagabounds, but the other hee will blesse abundantly. This is that which we should looke to throughout our life,that wee hauing warrant for the thing we doe from God,and a good conscience toward him and men, we may feare none that shall set themselues against vs, but waite patiently vpon him. And much more in our generall calling to the profession and practise of Christianitie,we must be constant and vnwearied therein. Doct.v.29.30. Lam.3.40.

By the Beniamites hoping and promising themselues good successe, as they before had enioyed ; especially when there fell againe now the third time,about some thirtie men of Israel by their hard following the battaile, and yet they had nothing to encourage them but onely their good successe which they had in the two former battailes : by this (I say) we see,that the hope of wicked persons is, that they shall still be suffered to goe on in their bad course,and prosper and thriue in the world as they haue done. This is the chiefe thing that they minde,and which they set their hearts vpon;yea and that to the day of their death,they cannot awake out of their not drowzie but deadly sleepe ; nor by any meanes bee perswaded to looke to their end. If yee can tell them of any good, as it is in the Psalme ; or if yee will preach vnto them pleasant things,as the people of Anathoth said to *Ieremy*, then ye are for them. But doth it fall out as they hope ? for a while,I grant it may : but when it shall bee otherwise with them, so that they haue not their hearts desire granted them,but they are disappointed,and it hath not gone well with them in some of their attempts,but that they haue bin crossed ; yet doth this(thinke we) bring them to a better minde ? no, but they hope still they shall outgrow and wade out of such vnwelcome changes. And thus are their mindes occupied. Doct.v.31.32. Psal.4.7.

But what if they had all things to fall out to them according to their desire ? doth happinesse consist in the things which a man possesseth ? did not he that excelled other in the pleasures and glorie of this world (*Salomon* by name) leaue this behinde him confirmed by long experience and due obseruation in his life to all posteritie,that all is vanitie and vexation of spirit ? Luke 12.15. Eccles.2.11.

What

What is then their wisedome that set themselues to liue deliciously for a season, and to receiue the fruite of their worke, and their reward in perpetuall torment afterward; what is it, I say, but most grosse and palpable foo-
Psal.37.36. lishnes? For their state turneth as a wheele in a moment, and is changed, and the place where they were shall know them no more. For they shall be plucked out of their tabernacle, and rooted out, how sure soeuer they see-
Psal.52.7. med to be setled. Euen as the Psalmist bringeth in the righteous thus spea-
Psal.43.3. king of them: Behold the man that took not God for his strength, but tru-
& 27.1. sted vnto the multitude of his riches. But rest we on God, and make we him our stay, and wee shall stand safe and sure, when they shall crie out for feare and there shall be none to deliuer them. Psal.20.

Sense & Doct. out of vers.33. 34.35. But behold, while they were soothing vp themselues with the hope of the victorie, (for they said among themselues, when they saw some few slaine; Oh they fall before vs againe as in the former times) and while they were thus telling themselues of peace, behold, I say, while they were thus occupied, euen then euill and mischiefe was toward them, when they little thought of it, for the men of Israel had cooped and hedged them in, so that they could escape no way out of their hands: and fiue and twentie thousand of them were slaine that day.

Here is exemplified cleerely vnto vs that which I touched before, to wit, that the hope of vaine, profane, and vnbeleeuing persons is deceitfull, and their prosperous state flitting, euen when it seemeth to them to be most setled; For Gods thoughts are not as mens. They hoped they had God sure enough on their sides, and tyed to them, and why? because hee had giuen them successe before: but God had purposed another thing. And so hee doth others such as they are: for to speake as the truth is, if men were not senselesse, how should they looke to haue God at their becke and desire, who prouoke him to wrath against them continually by their many and boldly committed iniquities? Nay, if it were not that God is wonderfully patient, they might looke for no other but destruction euery day.

And therefore it is no marueile that Gods vengeance falles vpon one or other of them from time to time, as might easily be seene, if it were marked. Looke vpon *Pharaoh, Iezabel, Haman, Absolom*, with many more such, and among vs numbers, who in the top and middest of their flourishing, haue bin cut off, when it had been out of season, nay most harsh to them, as it was to
1.Sam.25.37. *Nabal*, to haue been told any such thing before, namely their abasement and ruine to haue been at hand, and most dangerous it would haue been to the persons, who should haue said; so shall it be to them. Therefore the hope
Iob 18.14. of all such is like the spiders web, that is suddenly swept downe, and like a broken tooth which deceiueth him that trusteth to it. And as *Samson* in an-
Note. swering the wicked woman, and in telling her at last where his strength lay; thought to do as he had done before, that is, to escape the Philistims hands, but he knew not that euill was neere to him, and that the Lord was gone from him; and therefore hee was taken and bound and carried away by them: So and much more these, whom the Lord was neuer with, trusting
Luke 1.51. to their former prosperitie, vanish away in their imaginations, and get nothing lesse then they dreame of; that is, not earthly felicitie. And by this we may see that the Lord meeteth with thē early or late, one time or other.

It

It is further to be marked which is said in this verse, that although Israel destroyed those Beniamites, yet the Lord is said to haue smote them, and it is attributed to him and said, and that they were slaine by him. To teach vs, that though God vse men as his instruments to bring his worke to passe, yet it is he that is all in all, and to him the glorie is to be ascribed in the deliuerance of his seruants, and the ouerthrow of his enemies. Euen as it is said to *Iehosaphat*, Thou shalt not neede to feare, God will be with thee, when hee was in great danger: so it is said of greater matters, Though men plant and water by preaching the Gospell, yet God is he who giueth the increase and blessing. And euen so in the most casuall matters the Lord ruleth: which I doe the rather vrge and stand vpon, seeing few marke it, or thinke so, but ascribe the euent of things to chance and fortune: so that howsoeuer vnruly and rebellious flesh iudgeth, as it pleaseth it, yet we shall finde this to be our wisedome, to submit our selues to him, and to depend vpon his prouidence in all things. For if he haue spoken the word, it is not wit nor power of man (who is but a worme of his making) that can alter or frustrate it; nor the gates of hell, nor any infernall rage or resistance that can in the least manner hinder, much lesse preuaile against it. And againe, if proud and bad men haue been met withall, and crossed by their enemies, or any other way, as the King of Aram was by *Elishah* the Prophet, let them know, that whosoeuer be the instrument of their sorrow, the Lord is the chiefe worker of it. And this be said of the slaughter of the men of Beniamin. Doct. vers. 35. 2. Chron. 20. 17 1. Cor. 3. 6. Matth. 16. 18. 2. King. 6.

Now in the verses following to the 47, it is in more particular manner set downe how the whole number of these fiue and twentie thousand was slaine. And that was thus: Eighteene thousand when the two armies of the Israelites inclosed the Beniamites in the first meeting of them both together. This is set downe to the 45 verse, then as the men of Beniamin fled to the wildernes to the rock of Rimmon, the Israelties gleaned (as it is called) fiue thousand, as they were scattered one from another, and pursuing them further, they slew two thousand more. The rest being but sixe hundred, fled and escaped: After all this is shewed how the Israelites returned and smote all that remained of Beniamin both man and beast, and destroyed their cities. Vers. 36. to the end. *The summe.*

Beside that which we haue heard alreadie, before the Beniamites were slaine, wee may see that Israel had appointed with the ten thousand to make a great smoake rise vp in the citie, and a mightie shoute or noise to be made, at the seeing and hearing whereof, their brethren in the battaile might know that they had entred the citie, that then they might turne backe vpon the Beniamites, and so betwixt both armies inclose them, and so they did: which made the men of Beniamin to quaile and be faint hearted. Vers. 36. to 42. *Doct.*

By this policie of the men of Israel to allure and draw foorth them of Beniamin out of the citie, and then the tenne thousand tha[t] lay in secret, to enter; I might, I say, by this shew that all policie is not vnlawfull, as neither was the like that was practised by *Ioshua*, but onely such as is wicked, but both these the Lord allowed. But I haue spoke of this before. Only here this may be noted, that as wee see it was here with the people of Beniamin, when men are drunke with confidence in themselues, and successe that they haue had in former times, they doe not commonly suspect danger and pre- Iosh. 8. 5. 6.

uent it, though they haue ſufficient cauſe to doe ſo. Theſe men of Beniamin thought all had been well with them, becauſe of their former victories. So it fareth with men: they take thought no further, but hope that it ſhall bee with them ſtill, as it hath been. So is it with the idle, with the gameſter, and other wicked: they looke not about them how neere euill is to them, till it take hold of them: neither doe they commonly goe about to preuent a miſchiefe, vntill they feele ſmart and hurt by it. Oh therefore how happie are they, who being vnder Gods protection haue no cauſe to feare any ſuch
Prou.6.21. thing, neither are they in danger thereof, ſeeing hee watcheth ouer them? And to this may be added that which followeth, to make of both one.

2 It is ſaid, when many of the Beniamites were ſlaine, the reſt who ranne away to ſaue their liues, were ſore purſued by Iſrael, and then they ſaw that euill was at hand againſt them. And this may be obſerued, that either men are cut off by death, or paſt hope of life commonly, before they can re-turne to God. No warning ſerues them. They haue euer one deluſion or o-ther to hold them from ſeeking after God, and fill their heads and hands with imployments, though they be as fond as his that ſaid, I will firſt goe
Matth.8. burie my father, and then I will follow thee. It were a wonder, if one ſhould take heed by the hurt and example of another. For though they ſee that
Note. they are neere a miſchiefe, yet they haue no heart to relent, and to humble themſelues to God, that is vtterly taken from them: but rather they harden their hearts againſt him: verifying the Scripture, As they loued not bleſ-
Pſal.109.17. ſing in their life, ſo at their death it is farre from them.

Doct. out of verſ.38. to 42. To the ouercomming of the Beniamites this did greatly helpe, that the men of Iſrael had agreed among themſelues, that the tenne thouſand that lay about the citie, ſhould enter when the Beniamites were drawne out po-litikely by that armie that lay on the foreſide of the citie, and by a great fire and the ſmoake of it appearing, they ſhould giue a ſigne to their brethren, that they were entred into the citie, that ſo the other might returne backe vpon the Beniamites. For they could not elſe haue knowne when to haue retired and gone backe againſt them. Now if they who were entred into the citie, had failed through vnfaithfulnes or careleſnes, then had the reſt loſt all. For before that, the Beniamites began to ſmite them down, as hath been ſaid before.

By this we may ſee how neceſſarie faithfulnes and truſtineſſe is in warre, as well as in peace; euen betwixt all that in honeſt and good cauſes repoſe truſt and confidence one in another. The reaſon is great: for men would neuer attempt great matters, as theſe of Iſrael did againſt Beniamin, if they had not ſome truſtie to them: for if they ſhould not be ſo, the other muſt be diſappointed in their greateſt neceſſitie. And if any will ſay, Why ſhould not theſe ſhew themſelues true and truſtie to their brethren, who were in the ſame caſe with them, to proſper or to be ſlaine? I anſwere, it was meete, I grant: but ſo it is alſo (ye will ſay) for husband and wife to be, and for ſer-uants to their maſters to ſhew the ſame faithfulnes: ſo partners one to the other, and executors to them that put them in truſt; and ſo I ſay of all o-ther. But yet euen theſe who are tyed with a neere bond one to the other, doe often faile, (from whence ariſe the infinit lamentable complaints euery where) and are vnfaithfull, though to their iuſt reproch, and to the high

com-

commendation of them that are faithfull and trusty : as why should they not be so, when both they haue pawned their credit by the promise they haue made, and the other trust in them.

THE HVNDRED AND ONE SERMON, ON THE XX. AND XXI. CHAPTERS OF THE BOOKE OF IVDGES.

ALthough the whole number of 25000. be generally set downe before, yet there were but 18000. slaine at the first : afterward in the chacing of them, 5000. fell at one time, and 2000. at another, as in these verses is to be seene. By all of them let this bee noted, what a vaine thing it is to put confidence in deceiuable helpes, like to broken staues; as these men of *Beniamin* did in their skill, cunning and might, and withall in the good successe that they had in the two former battels. Now neither these, nor the city, which had bin to them such a shelter, could bee any refuge vnto them : so that although they had skill, yet there was then no vse of it; God was all in all. So it hath bin with all such as haue made flesh their arme, but knew not the Lord, to put their confidence in him : *Corah, Benhadad* and other. So shall it be, and is daily with them that are caught with the deceitfulnes of sinne, and haue promised vnto themselues peace in transitory and vncertaine riches and pleasures. And for many of them, it may bee truly affirmed, that if a man were in presence with them, he might heare them cry out most fearefully, but too late, and say, they were deceiued: and the rest bewray their folly some other way, they looked for great matters here, and as for God, they neuer thought that he would disappoint them, such are the wise Politicians of this world : also in their braue mindes, both yong men and great persons, and such as begin the world at their solemne marriages, in such iollity, that all the corner ringeth of their doings; but how are the most of them disappointed and cut off from their hope, and some of them full soone? But they that trust in God, and sit close to his promises, though their simplicity be despised and scorned, shall be as mount Sion that cannot be remoued; and not cast from their hope, how contemptible soeuer they seeme to be in the eyes of other that doe flourish.

Vers.42.to 47.
Doct.
Psal.125.1.

Also it is to very good purpose, to note by the example of these men of *Beniamin* thus destroyed, what commeth of stomacke, wilfulnes, and of the pride of heart. They were vsed by their brethren the Israelites friendy, and kindely : and were called together with the other tribes, to aduise and determine against those wicked men of Gibeah; but they would not ioyne with their brethren, but defended those cursed men against them, euen by weapon and warre. Now we see what they haue gained thereby ; that at three sundry times they were slaine, euen 25000. persons.

2.King.3.21. 24.25. The Moabites being tributaries to the King of Israel, and refusing to pay their due to him ; when he with two other Kings came against them, they would not sue nor seeke to him for peace, when yet they saw there was cause; but wilfully went out to resist and fight against them, and were most miserably destroyed by the King of Israel and his assistants. And what gained

2.King.19.35. *Zenacherib* by his pride and stomacke against the kinde and good King *Ezekiah*? The Lord hath left his example extant to his perpetuall shame, so that after all his boastings and bragges, as that he would make Israel to eate their owne dung, and in like manner to drinke ; there was slaine of his army in one night by the Angel of God, an hundred fourescore and fiue thousand men. So hath the end bin of many wilfull persons, euen fearefull and lamentable, as we see daily in many of them ; and all to this end, that

1.Pet.5.5. we may regard that Scripture the more that saith, *God resisteth the proud*, yea euen he himselfe ; but he giueth grace to the humble. Particulars are infinit to instance in. For how many haue lost much by frowardnes and stomacke, beside the trouble and sorrow which they haue got thereby ? who were otherwise prouided to haue liued in good manner for their condition, if they had knowne themselues, and could haue walked humbly?

3. Another thing worthy our consideration, is, that God let these men see their destruction before it came, that thereby their punishment might bee made greater to them As if a man should see his children slaine before his face, and then be put to death himselfe. Oft times God doth thus, either to breake their hearts, and to bring them to repentance, as he did the penitent theefe ; or else that they may haue their sorrowes increased, who would take no warning against their sinne, and that other may be admonished thereby. And some are forced to vtter as much, that their punishment is

Gen.4.13. more then they can beare, as *Cain* : and some are loaden with the heare say of their trouble, when they know it before, as *Nabal* was with hearing of his

1.Sam.25.37. death. The vse of this is ; that we feare God, and waite on him patiently and confidently to auoid these, and especially in the greatest iudgements, to wit, the noysome sauor of eternall death, by terrors that cannot be borne, before it come.

4 And lastly, let all workers of iniquity learne by these, and know that their punishment is not remoued from them to whom it is deferred : As too many thinke that if God scourge not, neither plague them by and by after their wicked doings, as their consciences doe oft feare he will ; they thinke

1.Sam.15.32. with *Agag*, that the bitternes of death is past. As we may gather by the

Psal.50.21. speeches of them that are mentioned in the Psalme, as that the almighty taketh no knowledge of their doings ; and that he will doe neither good nor euill. But let the people of God say rather, that if they prouoke him ; the thing that they feare shal certainly come vpon them: and therefore let them make sure worke to be free from their feares, by preuenting of them through their shrouding themselues vnder Gods protection.

5 Now we haue heard the story of these battailes from the beginning to the end, we may the better see this one thing, namely what great proceedings in sinne, and calamity arise from such beginnings as we make light

matters

matters and little account of. What was the beginning of all these broiles betwixt the Israelites and the men of *Beniamin*, but the lewdnes and beastly behauiour of the vile men of *Gibeah* with the Leuites concubine? The abusing of whom in that villanous manner as they did, they made it but a sport and a pastime: but what was the end of it? and what came of it, but the troubling of the whole land, with the losse of many thousand mens liues? So what was the beginniug of *Iudas* his woe, but acquaintance with the Priests, professed and set enemies to his deare master? whereby he after that he was hired by them for money, betraied him into their hands. And what next? for he thought, (it is like enough) his master could easily escape their hands when he listed; as he had seene him to auoid danger after the like manner: and so hee might haue gotten the booty, and the offence might haue seemed the smaller. But when he saw that he was condemned, he fell into horrible astonishment, and forthwith cast the money backe againe to the Priests of whom he tooke it, hauing had no vse of it, nor bene- Matth.27.3.
fit by it, but onely that he had it in his hands, and to shew how little either it, or the Priests fauour could helpe him, who forsooke him in his greatest need; in a desperat mood he went a part, and hanged himselfe. So what is the beginning of our shame, great losse, and oft times of vtter vndoing, or sorrow our bellies full, to be sure in the meane season? As in particulars, the killing of a man, of what beginnings commeth it, but of anger, and displeasure taking against him, yea and sometime by iesting with him, whereby he being prouoked, quarrelling, contending, and hot broiles insue, whereof commeth murther. So the first step to shamelesse whoredom, and damnation thereby, what is it, but a lewd eye, and an vncleane heart? and yet what great matters are these made among men, but common and ordinary? So a small and secret lye, what a light and small thing is it counted? but we see that swearing, forswearing, cursing, deceiuing, and what not, doe insue thereof, as was found in *Peter* himselfe through frailty; and what Mark.14.71.
may then be looked for of other, whose whole life, or a great part of it, is sutable to such behauiour.

Verse 47. *But sixe hundred men turned and fled to the wildernesse, vnto the rocke Rimmon, and abode in the rocke Rimmon foure moneths.*

48. *And the men of Israel turned againe vpon the children of Beniamin, and smote them with the edge of the sword, as well the men of euery city, as the beast, and all that came to hand: also they set on fire all the cities that they came to.*

AFter this great slaughter of the Beniamites, it is said here, that sixe hun- Vers.47.
dred that had escaped the hands of the men of Israel, fled to the rocke *Doct.*
of Rimmon: there to get shelter for the sauing of their liues: and why God reserued these, it was (out of question) his singular mercy so to doe, (who deserued it no more then the rest,) that a tribe might not faile in Israel, when he might iustly haue made a riddance of them all vtterly. Thus God shewes mercy in iudgement: and when he punisheth mens offences, yet he doth not exercise that seuerity, (as we may see by the sauing of these) that he might iustly haue done. To teach vs, that men should meekely and contentedly beare his corrections, and not complaine that they are the greatest that

that could haue befallen them, when yet it is cleare to all that will see, that he hath spared them from many farre sorer, and borne with them when he might haue consumed them.

2. But then this must needs be a speciall fauour to these sixe hundred that they were suffered to liue, and were not pursued, as the other seuen thousand were, which were gleaned in the way, and slaine, (as the other 18000. were) who yet escaped in the former battailes: And thereafter let vs note, that it is a singular mercy of God, when in the desolation and affliction of many, he separates and freeth some. As in the great murthering of many of Gods Saints in time of persecution, he reserued some to be the seed of the Church for the time to come. So in punishing many for their whoredomes, robberies and other villanies, yet he sheweth mercy to many, and that for their amendment. All these are duely to be considered, that they who inioy them, may fare the better thereby, as well to the comfort of their soules, by the right vse of them, as they doe by their bodily preseruation. But how much more when he taketh away our companions in euill, so that they die in impenitency, and yet brings vs to repentance who haue sinned as grieuously as they.

Verse 48. And in that they were spoiled that remained in the city, euen vnto the beasts, and in that the men of Israel destroyed all the cities that they could come by, and set them on fire, we may see the lamentable desolation that ciuill warre brings, and how it wastes all; both man, woman and child, cattell, corne and houses. Which is to be marked, to the end we may be highly thankfull, that God hath so long preserued vs from it, and in the meane while, to teach vs, that we make precious vse of our peace. And as for the so doing to the cities and people of *Beniamin*, as wee haue heard Israel did to them, it was their rashnes and cruelty so to doe: for we must know that though God in Deuteronomy required it to be so done to Idolaters, who

Deut.13.16. were cursed nations; yet they had no commandement to deale so with these their brethren, for ought that we can see; (although the fact of these wicked men of Gibeah were very odious) and that the more appeareth to be so, for that in the next Chapter they acknowledge and bewaile it, that they had left them without wiues. And this be said of the whole Chapter.

The end of the 20. Chapter.

THE TWENTIE ONE CHAPTER.

Verse 1. *Now the men of Israel had sworne in Mizpeh, saying, There shall not any of vs giue his daughter vnto Beniamin to wife.*

2. *And the people came to the house of God, and abode there till Euen before God, and lift vp their voyces, and wept sore.*

3. *And said, O Lord God of Israel, why is this come to passe in Israel, that there should be to day one tribe lacking in Israel?*

4. *And it came to passe on the morrow, that the people rose early, and built there an Altar, and offered burnt offerings and peace offerings.*

5. *And the children of Israel said, Who is there among al the tribes of Israel, that came not vp with the congregation vnto the Lord? for they had made a great oath concerning*

concerning him that came not vp to the Lord to Mizpeh,saying,He shall surely be put to death.

6. *And the children of Israel repented them for Beniamin their brother, and said,There is one tribe cut off from Israel this day.*

7. *How shall wee doe for wiues for them that remaine,seeing wee haue sworne by the Lord,that we will not giue them of our daughters to wiues?*

8. *And they said,What one is here of the tribes of Israel that came not vp to Mizpeh to the Lord? And behold there came none to the campe from Iabesh Gilead to the assembly.*

9. *For the people were numbred,and behold,there were none of the inhabitants of Iabesh Gilead there.*

10. *And the congregation sent thither twelue thousand men of the valiantest, and commanded them,saying, Goe, and smite the inhabitants of Iabesh Gilead with the edge of the sword,with the women and children.*

11. *And this is the thing that ye shall doe,ye shall vtterly destroy euery male, and euery woman that hath lien by man.*

12. *And they found among the inhabitants of Iabesh Gilead,foure hundred yong virgins that had knowne no man, by lying with any male; and they brought them vnto the campe to Shiloh,which is in the land of Canaan.*

13. *And the whole congregation sent some to speake to the children of Beniamin that were in the rocke Rimmon,and to call peaceably vnto them.*

14. *And Beniamin came againe at that time,and they gaue them wiues which they had saued aliue of the women af Iabesh Gilead; and yet they sufficed them not.*

15. *And the people repented them for Beniamin,because that the Lord had made a breach in the tribes of Israel.*

THe summe of this Chapter is this. The Israelites after they had ended the warre with the men of Beniamin, and sworne not to giue wiues to them of their daughters, doe here now aske counsell of the Lord how to preserue a tribe in those few of them that remained. Also they destroy the men of Iabesh Gilead, from among the which they tooke foure hundred maides,and gaue them to the Beniamites for wiues: and for the rest that yet wanted,to wit,two hundred,they wish them to take them in Shiloh, at the yeerely meeting there,and promise to perswade their parents to be content, and so they both, I meane the eleuen tribes and the Beniamites, returne home. *The summe of the Chapter.*

The first part is their consulting with the Lord,to vers.8. Secondly, their giuing wiues to foure hundred of them out of Iabesh Gilead, to vers.16. Thirdly, they prouided for the rest at Shiloh, before they returned: and this to the end. *The parts 3.*

The first part of the Chapter.

TO begin with the first part,as it lieth in order,and so with the foure former verses,it appeares that the Israelites had shewed too much seuerity to the remainder of their brethren the Beniamites, and had not onely without warrant slaine the women and children of Beniamin, but also added thereto yet more stiffenes and seueritie against these sixe hundred afterwards.

wards. It may be thought that their desire was (in their heate of pursuite) to haue vtterly razed out the whole tribe, for a requitall of the great slaughter of their men, as well as the reuenge of the villanie of Gibeah. But seeing that (by the prouidence of God) this their purpose was crossed, (and it is like the sixe hundred men were so surely entrenched in this fort of Rimmon, that they were out of the Israelites reach) therefore they consented together, and (for the better prouision that there should be no repealing thereof) they bound themselues with an oath (as appeares in the first verse) not to giue their daughters to them to bee their wiues. Which was rashly done of them, when yet they had killed (as I said) the women with the children of them that remained, which was ouer cruell, beside their rashnesse. And therefore this first verse is to be vnderstood of the former time when they slew the Beniamites in warre: euen then, or by and by after, they vpon it in their heate, sware that none of them should giue them wiues of their daughters. And thus we are to vnderstand the first verse; and not to ioyne it with the other that follow, for the acts mentioned in them were done at another time and meeting afterwards. For it were against all sense that they should at the same time sweare thus to grieue and trouble them, and yet pitie them also and seeke helpe for them, in that wherein they hurt them. Therefore there was some time, lesse or more, of intermission betweene. So that we are to vnderstand this first verse thus: that they had before sworne, but not that they did it then. This was needfull to bee said for the cleering of that doubt, and for the right vnderstanding of the first verse. Now I will proceed to the second and third.

After all this was done by the Israelites, which I haue here set downe, at another time shortly following, when they had better weighed the matter, as that a tribe was like to be cut off and to faile, and then that they had taken their oath that they would not repaire and make it vp againe; they saw the case of the Beniamites to be very lamentable, and that themselues had not done as became them; and then they began to pitie them being their brethren. But seeing that which was done, could not bee vndone againe, therefore they purposed to goe to the Lord about it, and went together into the house of the Lord, and there bewailed it. For they saw that they must either speedily seeke the redresse of it, or else they must driue them to goe take them wiues of strangers, contrary to Gods commandement; and so doing, they themselues must haue chiefe part in the sinne, if any such thing should bee done: wherefore they wept for it before the Lord, and desired him to direct them what to doe in that behalfe.

Doct. 1. vers. 1. Now out of this verse let vs learne as followeth. First this: These men of Israel (for a great part of them) being well approued for their godlines, and besides other commendable parts in them, going into the house of the Lord to fast and pray, and accuse themselues, as they saw they had cause; before they attempted warre the third time; and yet presently after, to passe their bounds in rashnes and crueltie, and to sweare that no mercie should be shewed by them in giuing wiues to the comfortlesse Beniamites: these things, I say, hauing been thus done by the men of Israel; it teacheth, how soone we shake off the strength of grace, and quench it in vs, how well soeuer we were seasoned with it but a little before, and had fast setled our

selues

ſelues in a right good courſe. Whereas who would not thinke,but that we being once ſo well refreſhed with care,wiſedome,and conſcience, but that we might be like to walke in the ſtrength thereof many daies after? euen as *Elias* did trauaile fourtie daies in the ſtrength of his meate. But is it thus with vs? No: but as it was here with them. If we haue well brought our hearts in frame,and finde our ſelues readily diſpoſed to any good dutie to day,yet to morrow we ſhall begin to decline,and by degrees the longer we continue,the more cold we ſhall grow, and further off from the feruencie which was in vs before: euen as a ſtone heated in the Sunne doth in a little time after it is taken out, returne to the naturall coldnes that was in it before.Such is the corruption and badnes of our hearts,that as a candle goeth Note. out and ſpendeth it ſelfe,euen ſo doe we,euen of our ſelues,ſoone languiſh from a right good eſtate. Yea and that while we are buſily occupied at our callings,though lawfull,yet euen from thence our euill hearts take occaſion to quench the ſparkles of grace that were kindled in vs before. Take a proofe of that which I ſay from one or two inſtances: As when wee haue well paſſed the Sabbath,or kept a faſt vnto the Lord; yet commonly how ſoone decline we and waxe cold, who might haue bin like to haue walked in the ſtrength of thoſe times well paſſed before. And yet thus it is with vs, vnleſſe wee looke very carefully to our ſelues. And much more when wee walke among many prouocations to euill, and when wee be inticed by allurements which are many,and ſuch as ſtrongly draw vs from our ſtedfaſtnes in faith and knowledge; what marueile is it then,if we be ſoone vnſetled and diſtempered? euen as the candle violently blowne out,muſt needs be ſooner extinct then otherwiſe. This is the cauſe why Gods people doe labour euer and anone to haue recourſe to God,and why they be not negligent in other good meanes vſing,and eſpecially not to be long from him in feruent prayer, to the end they may keepe well, when they be well, and nouriſh their good beginnings, that ſo thereby they may put violence to their ſinnes,that as little as may be, they may grow and abide in their naturall force; but contrarily good beginnings may bee well continued. And though all this bee little enough, yet all may ſee, that it is more by a great deale then others thinke needes. When men haue ſometime clenſed their hearts commendably from their ſpeciall ſinnes,beſtowing good coſt thereon,(which is an high degree of grace) for a while it be well with them,but without faithfulnes,feruencie and conſtancie,they ſhall ſoone be diſguiſed, and change to an ill ſtate,as to dulnes,deadnes of ſpirit, yea and worſe,as if it had neuer been better with them. This I haue ſaid to reuiue the impreſſion of the ſame inſtruction ſo often vrged in the former Chapters, and laſt of all in chap.16.verſe 1.

Further in this verſe in that theſe men of Iſrael had offered ſuch hard 2
meaſure to them of Beniamin,as to kill their women and children, and to deſtroy their cattell and cities, and when they ſaw the ſixe hundred that eſcaped to bee without wiues, yet not onely to reſolue to giue them none, but for the making good their word,to ſweare to it alſo,and that raſhly and in their heate: this, I ſay,bewraieth another foule corruption and maladie of the heart, and that is this: when wee deſire to fulfill the luſt of the fleſh

in any euill which we are inticed vnto, we ſhall not conſult or inquire into it, what we haue againſt vs to diſcourage and driue vs from it (oh we cannot
Note. abide to heare of that:) but what doe we? wee make worke for the accompliſhing of our deſire, and follow it with tooth and naile, till wee haue fulfilled it, as theſe men of Iſrael did by taking their oath; for then they were ſure they could not goe backe any more. Thus when *Ionah* had ſet himſelfe to
Ionah 1.3. flye to Tarſus, that he might not goe to Niniue, as God had commanded him (for he was vtterly vnwilling to goe thither) what did he? he went to the hauen where he ſhould take ſhip; and there finding one that was going to Tarſhiſh, hee foorthwith paid the fare thereof, and went downe into the ſhip, and fell faſt aſleepe; and this he did to make ſure worke, that he might not be hindred from his deſired iourney. *Herod*, leſt his purpoſe might poſſibly be croſſed in giuing *Herodias* to the halfe of his kingdom, bound himſelfe hand and foote from ſhrinking, by taking an oath. And but for that oath, it is like he had gone back. But it is iuſt with God to make mens cords, wherewith they draw ſinne to themſelues with violence, whips to ſcourge themſelues, till they wiſh themſelues at more libertie againe. It was the practiſe of thoſe trecherous enemies of *Paul*, that they would binde themſelues to faſting by a vow, till they had ſlaine him. Their ſtomacke was as good to haue ſtood to the word, if neceſſitie had not reſiſted them. Oh how vnequall diuiders are we betweene God and our luſts? If we make God a promiſe; ſlight purpoſe of amendment or dutie, we thinke may ſerue, & to be a great matter: wheras if the diuell and we enter league, we preſently offer him bond, and put him in good ſecuritie. An inſtance or two I will ſet downe. If wee owe money, and are not willing to pay it, wee haue twentie waies to conuey our money, that we may ſay boldly, we cannot pay it, wee haue it not. If alſo we haue ſet our mind vpon vnlawfull mariage, or, which is a further degree of euill, to commit filthineſſe, or to bee reuenged vpon our enemie, or priuilie to deceiue our neighbour, or any ſuch like; wee will follow our deſires with ſecrecie and cunning, that wee may not be ioynted, nor broken off from that we deſire. And there may be no queſtioning nor debating what to doe, (for then there were hope that we might deſiſt:) but that wiſedome we vtterly ſhunne and auoide, till we haue done that which
Prou. 20.25. we would, according to that which *Salomon* ſaith, After the treſpaſſe we begin to inquire, but not before. Contrarily, if any good be required to bee done of vs, which we haue no liking to do, we will haue all ſhifts, and make all excuſes that we can, to the end we may auoid and ſhift it off. And if we be found fault with, for our ſo doing, (as moſt iuſtly we may) yet to be ſure,
Note. we haue had our deſire, euen that which we ſought: but if we cannot ſhift it, but wee muſt doe it, yet wee will goe about it ſo awkly and vntowardly, that it were as good it were vndone. Whereas wee ſhould in good things be forward (the Lord louing a cheerefull doer of dutie) and ready to one good thing as to another: and againſt the time of temptation to euill, wee ſhould ſtudy for all reaſons poſſible, to diſſwade and hold our ſelues backe from yeelding to it: duly and deeply weighing theſe reaſons, and often times to that purpoſe, as neede ſhall require, that they may diſſwade and alienate vs from the ſame. But if we cannot in ſo doing, be held back, then

to

to bewray our weakenes to some faithfull friend to strengthen vs against it: so that which by weaker meanes cannot bee effected, may be brought to passe by the stronger.

Now in that they swore to this, that they would not giue their daughters to be wiues to them of *Beniamin*; their sinne was the greater. For in that they had sworne to deny them their daughters, but saw their fault afterwards, that they had not bin well aduised in taking their oath, we should learne by this, that a great regard is to be had in taking of an oath. For as when we repaire to the house of God, we should take heed how we heare; so we should in this case, take heed how we sweare. For what doe we, when we take an oath, but call for a curse from God vpon vs, if wee sweare not truely? Therefore the heathen did vpon an oath taken to them, looke for faithfulnes from them that were their enemies, and had promised it, yea if it had concerned their goods or liues; as we reade of *Rahab*, who trusted the spies that couenanted with her at Iericho, when they had sworne to her. And *Ioshua* would not suffer the oath to be broken which was giuen to the Gibeonites. Therefore *Ieremy* the Prophet teacheth how an oath should be taken, when he sheweth, that it should be in righteousnes, in iudgement, and in truth: that is, truly, and in a good and righteous cause onely, and aduisedly and in a good manner. See that which hath bin said vpon the like occasion in Chapter 15. in *Samsons* words to the men of Iudah; and in Chapter 11. in *Iphtahs* demand of the Elders. 3.

Eccles 4.16. Luk. 8.18. Iosh 2.12. Iosh. 9.19. Ier. 4.2.

And by this that the men of Israel had bound themselues with an oath to be reuenged vpon the sinne of *Beniamin*, learne wee more particularly two things: the one from the affection in generall, the other from the particular action. Their affection against sinne wilfully committed was notable in the generall: for they were carried with indignation and detestation to see that any should be so farre gone in euill, as to defend the cursed acts of the wicked men of Gibeah, yea though both the principall and accessaries were of their owne flesh. And from this ground, that we abhorre sinne for it owne sake, and for that it is vnseemely yea and odious in it selfe; from this ground (I say) it should be, that we loath it in our selues and in other, and not onely for the cursed fruits thereof. For the which cause, it is that is said in the Psalme, that a vile person is contemptible in the eyes of the godly. So it is said by way of commendation of the Church of Ephesus, *Thou canst not abide them who are called Iewes and are not, but doe lie.* The like is said of the Church of Pergamus, hating the Nicolaitans. But we beare it wel enough that men are wicked, and are little troubled to see or heare of it, whereas the godly mourne for it. A signe therefore it is that we doe not greatly abhorre sinne, and all because we see that such as reproue it, are in odious account with men, and they that commit it in greatest fauour. This point might require larger insisting vpon, if it had not often before bin enlarged. See Chapter 19. 4.

Psal. 15.4. Reuel. 2.2. Reuel. 2.15. Ezek. 9.4.

Now touching the carriage of the action in the particular, and their manner of proceeding, they marueilously offended through the want of godly wisedome. For how could they iustifie this rash decree of theirs against their brethren, and the establishment thereof by an oath? Both which they added to the slaying of the women of *Beniamin* in Chapter 20. verse the last. 5.

By

By this therefore marke we here further, how true that is which Saint *Iames*
Iam.3.2. affirmeth, In many things we sin all. And more particularly, there is much mixture of our corruption in our best actions and duties, and many blemishes where yet we would doe well. Which howsoeuer the Lord couereth in his good seruants, when it is the fruit of that vnauoydable bondage vnder corruption, which we carry about vs, (and therefore priuily conueyeth it selfe into the duties of religion) yet must not be nourished or slightly neglected, as if our goodnes might outface the euill and beare vs out in it. Especially if it proceed from wilfulnes, or from a suppressing of our knowledge and vnprofitable vse of the grace which is giuen vs, yea or vnaduisednes, which is yet more pardonable. But whatsoeuer the cause be, the effect is
Gen.27.8.&c. common. As *Rebeccahs* lie in obeying Gods ordinance doth clearely testi-
2.Sam.17.20. fie: with the fact of the woman that concealed *Ahimaaz* and *Ionathan*. And wofull experience teacheth, that oft times out of that which we seeke to doe well, euill ariseth. For example: we rebuke oft times, and that iustly, and yet we breake into anger, and we doe not therein commonly labour after the good of the party: so likewise zeale turneth to choller; lawfull mirth, nay religious, into lightnes and wantonnes for want of heed taking, there-
1.Tim.5.2. fore *Paul* willeth *Timothy* to reproue yong women with chastnes: so wee promise well, but by occasion we disappoint and defraud: so praying turneth to lip-labour, and religion it selfe when it was intended, and begun, (through our inconstancy) into hypocrisie, which is worst of all. By all which, it appeares, that godly wisedom is a grace peculier and distinct from other gifts of the spirit: which is bestowed by God vpon all that seeke it, to the end it may be as an inward guide to frame the actions of our liues, in a beautifull and commendable manner.

Prou.4.23. This is the cause why the Lord so oft and earnestly chargeth vs to watch diligently both our hearts and tongues, that so it may goe well with our liues. And who seeth not, that we haue great need to doe thus? This is our commendation, and all is little enough, though all this while Popery denieth, and that most falsly and shamelessely, that corruption is mixed with our best actions. But further, though we doe not the good that wee would, let not the loose and vnreformed, (who are vtterly turned away from goodnes) thinke their state to be as good as the best, seeing the forwardest are not free from sinne; for they differ from the other as light from darknesse, when they be at the best, and euen as farre differing shall the reward of both be. But of this before also (especially of the vse of the doctrine) hath bin treated in the wise behauiour of *Iael*, and the practise of diuers other the seruants of God in this booke, exemplified by other Scriptures.

6 Lastly in this verse, by saying that they would not giue their daughters in marriage, they shew that parents haue this due owed to them at their childrens hands, and to be giuen and performed vnto them, that their consent be sought in their marriage: without the which they haue no power nor liberty giuen them of God to proceed therein, and to bestow themselues. This is a peece of the honour that they owe to them, and their shame and sore blemish, who professing to be guided by God, doe deny it them. But beside note this, that though neither God, nature, nor good lawes doe al-

low any other, but that they should doe so, yet popish superstition doth admit and allow the contrary. See notes vpon *Calebs* offer in the first Chapter of this booke.

Here therefore to passe to the second verse, by the consideration that the Israelites had of their former act against *Beniamin*, they disliked and did now bewaile it, as they did also the oath which they tooke: for the acts of the first verse and these following were not done all together, as I noted in the exposition of this verse. By this we may learne, that we may possibly doe many things that are euill, vnaduisedly, and in no sort as were meete, which afterwards when we thinke of them more considerately, we see our fault and bewaile it: our offence commeth from hence, for that wee doe not commonly weigh things so deeply at first, as after we are driuen to doe. We should by this be taught wisedom: to wit, that we beware of rashnes in the things we take in hand, yea though zeale be ioyned therewith, as *Saul* his action in offering sacrifice before *Samuel* came, doth well admonish. For as we may see more in time by well considering matters and by good obseruation, then we can at the first; so rashnes is euer euill, and doth nothing well. And who would be willing to come to take shame and sorrow afterward for that which he hastily and without regard went about? and yet this is the least inconuenience that commeth of such doings, that after we are weary and ashamed of them: according to that of the Apostle, generally spoken of all sinne, *What fruit had ye of those things, whereof you are now ashamed?*

Vers. 2. Doct. 1. Note. 1. Sam. 13. 13. Rom. 6. 21.

The other thing, that they came together into the house of the Lord, till euening, to lament their rashnes and cruelty, as I haue shewed they did, doth further teach vs, that not only we doe (as I haue said) oft bewaile that euill afterward, which we rashly committed; but also that repentance must come one time or other for such doings. And that if we cannot like to come oft to such bewailings thereof, we must beware of such offendings. And if it were not thus, that where men take in such sweete morsels of sin, as they count them, they did vomit and cast them vp as excrements, they must needs burst with the multitude of them, and be spoiled. Yea and the more faithfull and feruent they are, the sooner they will see how they haue prouoked God that way, and seeke to be at one with him, and not sleepe vpon their sinne, nor suffer the sun to goe downe ouer their heads, and they lie still in it. Yet in great and grieuous falles, the heart oft times is hardened after the committing of such facts, and doth not by and by relent as in smaller; the reason is, because men more grossely delight themselues in the one then in the other; as it was in that sinne of *Dauids*: and therefore he lay a sleepe in it so long, and was hardlier brought to any lamenting and melting for it, then he was for numbring the people, which was by a great deale a smaller offence. And though he worshipped God before *Nathan* came to him, and roused him vp out of his sinne; yet it was but houerly and slightly performed, and without any comfort. And the case so standing with *Dauid*, that he did with so much adoe come to acknowledge and cast vp his filthy gorge, and that he slept in it so long, it is a shrewd likelihood that many doe the same, nay farre worse, and are very hardly brought to grone vnder their burden at all, and heartily to renounce their sinnes, which yet cannot be vnknowne to them. But I will leaue them with this watch-word, that they

2. 2. Sam. 11. 6. 13. 2. Sam. 24. 14. 17. Psal. 32. 5. Note.

boldly tempt God who doe so, and shew great enmity to themselues, so long to debarre their liues of such comforts and communion as they might haue with God, and that for such base pleasures of sinne which are but for a short season. And who can tell in the meane while, they being thus long estranged from God, whether they euer repented at all, euen then when they made the fairest flourish and shew, or not? As I said in his due place by occasion of *Samsons* repentance.

3. And further let vs note, that as they went oft into the house of God to pray, confesse their sinnes, and enquire of God to know his will, so we must intend to doe the like duties in our commings thither, and therefore oft frequent such places. But beside the negligence of the common sort, it is lamentable, after so long continuing of them, to thinke how few of the better sort doe vse them aright: but sleeping, wandring, gasing, prating, and soone to be weary, and worse then all these are vsuall with both sorts, and a repairing to the place of Gods worship to meete their companions, and dispatch their busines, rather then learne and to be well moued; seeing it is but dull sitting at home. They know not that the assembling of the faithfull to heare and pray, is the house of God, and that he dwelleth there, to feede his people with the bread of life, and to season them with sauing knowledge and good gouernment, and comfor, for in that manner he is said to be with his. For if they did know and beleeue it, they should with our father *Iacob*, frame themselues to reuerence, as he did, when hee vnderstood so much, saying; oh, this is Gods house, I was not aware of it. And yet many come
Gen.28.16. thither willingly, and for all that, behaue themselues sometime thus vnseemely, as I haue said, when they come there.

Vers.3. Here it is shewed, how they complained, that a tribe was failing and missing, and how they besought the Lord for the repairing and making vp of it againe. And although they had wasted it by their owne fault, yet they now saw it, and did as became them, to sue to God for the recouering of it, and to sorrow deeply for their so great offence. Thus we are taught to doe: to pity the miserable and distressed estate of our brethren, yea though they suffer for their euill doings; as these did pity the Beniamites: and who seeth not that this affection and behauiour did much better become them, then their former want of compassion toward them, and cruelty? For although men receiue due punishment for their deserts, yet are they to be pitied, not
Iosh.7.19. mocked; neither is sorrow to be added to their sorrow, but as *Iosua* did to
1.Cor.5.5. *Achan*, and *Paul* to the incestuous Corinthian, a seeking of their returne to God. There must be an end of seuerity, and measure vsed, euen where
2.Cor.11.24. correction is due, as the Lords command: in limiting the number of stripes among the Iewes, proueth. But here I end.

THE

THE HVNDRED AND TWO SERMON ON THE XXI. CHAPTER OF THE BOOKE OF IVDGES.

Here in their ſeeking to God for direction to repaire a- Verſ.4.
gaine the tribe of *Beniamin*, the Lord gaue them anſwere, (as is moſt like) by that which followeth of the men of Iabeſh Gilead, to wit, that they ſhould ſlay them, and prouide wiues there for the men of *Beniamin*. The Iſraelites therefore, when they were certified of Gods minde, they aroſe the next morning, & built an altar, (it is like that the altar which was in the houſe of the Lord, was not able to receiue the ſacrifices that were to be offered) and thereon they offered peace offerings to the Lord, both for the victory, and for ſatisfying their deſire, in token of their thankfulnes, and alſo burnt offerings, to teſtifie their repentance which they had before profeſſed.

By both we gather inſtruction accordingly. For thanks (of which I haue Doct. 1.
ſpoken oft) this onely I will ſay at this time, that as they met in the houſe of the Lord with conſent together to offer peace offrings, for the cauſes before mentioned, which was common to them all: So we ſhould learne to doe, not euery man in priuate onely for the good things he hath receiued, but the whole congregation in publike. And they who haue deſired the prayers of their brethren in their ſicknes and diſeaſes, ſhould in like manner deſire in their recouery, that thankes ſhould be rendred to God for them: which ſhould be very auaileable afterward to moue them to their duties, and other, againſt they ſhould be viſited, to looke better to themſelues. But it is vtterly neglected: for where is any ſuch thing ſeene to be done?

For their repentance, they did before (as I ſaid) offer it to the Lord, be- 2
wailing their ſinne before him. Now they hauing receiued Gods anſwere for the recouering of the tribe of *Beniamin*, they were much heartened and enlarged, and they doe ſolemnly by their burnt offrings declare, that they gaue themſelues wholly to the Lord, they not hauing (perhaps) ſo fit opportunity to doe it before, nor their hearts ſo well ſetled, when as yet they had not receiued anſwere from God about this thing. It ſhould teach vs, when we will make profeſſion of our repentance to God, that wee doe it heartily and throughly, not houerly and ſlightly, as too many doe, thinking that any thing may ſerue in that caſe: a thing done by halues is neuer done; but when it is waightily performed, it is the next way ſo to continue it afterward.

For the building of an other altar, before the worſhip of God was ſtabli- 3
ſhed at Ieruſalem, it was not vnlawfull: for ſo did *Gedeon*, and *Salomon*.

Iosh.22.16. And yet if yee aske, why the two tribes and an halfe, when they returned home from their brethren, after the diuision of the land of Canaan, were challenged for doing so; I say, their brethren the ten tribes, thought they had done it to seuer themselues from them in the true worship of God, and to haue professed another religion; which they knew they ought not to haue done. But if they had knowne for what cause they had done so, and had been priuie thereto, they would haue said nothing: as appeareth by their allowing of it, and consenting to that which they did, after they had word from their brethren. Therefore, to returne, as the Israelites here builded another altar to inlarge and more set forward the worship of God, and
Ioh.15.9. more plentifully to serue and honour him; so wee should all endeuour to doe, to wit, to bring foorth much fruite, for therein God is honoured.

That God did answere them, we may gather by that they were satisfied, and gaue thankes: and if they had no answere from him, it would haue in-
1.Sam.28.15. creased their griefe, as *Sauls* was, when hee cried out, *The Lord speaketh no more to me*, &c. And what the Lords answere was to them, appeareth by this speech of the chiefe Elders of Israel to their brethren: to wit, that they should inquire what one of all the tribes was away, or what familie or city, when they appeared before the Lord in Mizpeh: for vpon Gods answere they did inquire, and (as they had couenanted) all that were found not to haue appeared there, those they put to death. Now those whom they found to haue been away were the men of Iabesh Gilead. Them therefore they slew, and reserued the virgins for the sixe hundred of the men of Beniamin, and then they peaceably called for them (who remained as yet in the rocke of Rimmon) to come forth to them, promising them that they should be without danger.

Doct.vers.5. By this that they made inquiry, who among the rest ioyned not nor consented to come together, and goe against the men of Gibeah; and now hauing consulted with the Lord, they found that the men of Iabesh were away; it teacheth, that diligent note should be taken, by such as are in authoritie, who are forward in good causes, and who are not, that accordingly they may be dealt with. And therefore (to come to particulars) note should be taken, who are aduancers of Gods true worship, and who are enemies, and in societies of men, who are builders vp with the Lord, and who are pluckers downe, that they may bee censured or preferred, as they deserue and giue cause. If yee aske how they shall be knowne and discerned to be such: I answer, If they stand not, goe not, hold not with, or at least tolerate not the good part, then they may be knowne to be against it: according to
Matth.12.30. our Sauiour Christs words, *He that is not with me, is against me*: and so on the contrary. This doctrine is very necessarie for these times. For men thinke, that their priuate actions & words, may be as they list & like, euen as they thinke thought to be free: but God will haue them trie all, the one as the other, by his word. And he that will well consider it, may see, that not only Scripture requireth it, but common reason teacheth, that wee should all agree, and be of one minde in good things, and against euill. How commen-
Iudg.1.3. dable was it in *Simeon* to ioyne himselfe to *Iudah* his brother, and the men of Mount Ephraim to assist *Micab* against the Danites that had spoiled him?
18.7. And how ill became it the men of Succoth and Penuel to doe the contra-

rie,

rie, as in the pursuite of Gods enemies to refuse to aide *Gedeon*? For denying the truth, this onely I will say, that some of the ancient Fathers of the Church, and *Augustine* by name, though for a time they held that heretikes were not to be compelled to embrace the faith; yet vpon better aduice, and weighing the publike scandall ensuing ineuitably thereupon, afterward retracted their opinion, and confirmed the point in hand as lawfull, for the Christian Magistrate to execute.

They say they agreed that such as came not vp to Mizpeh should bee slaine, and thereto they tooke an oath. Behold the streight equitie that was here obserued: and yet great reason there was thereof, as wee haue heard. But how rare is it to see the like in such a manner executed, as here it was, without partiality? That euen they who consent not to such iustice so executed, shall themselues haue part in the punishment. For why? Indeede slight correction is not meete for foule transgression: but woe be to them who make the peoples sin a matter of meere gaine, and cause them to loath the ordinances of God, when they see what course is taken for the censuring of this particular transgression. *Doct.*2.

And in that they had it brought freshly to their remembrance, by Gods answere to them, which they thought not of before: namely, of the couenant which they had made in Mizpeh; they had, I say, forgot it before, that all should be slaine that appeared not in Mizpeh, as may be gathered out of verse 5. Wee see in this one thing what benefit wee receiue by repairing to God in the congregation, beside knowledge and quickening of heart, euen this: that we be put in remembrance of many good things, which would otherwise slip out of minde: A necessarie point to be marked: for alas how slipperie are our memories? and how oft doe we heare many excellent instructions before they be our owne? Therefore God hath allowed vs oft and weekly recourses to heare sermons, as he seeth we haue need, and commanded preaching to be vsed in season and out of season, to the end wee may remember that which was forgotten. *Doct.*3. 2.Tim.4.2.

In this verse it is shewed, that the men of Israel repented them greatly for Beniamin, bewailing it much, that a tribe was cut off from Israel: so that with their triumph, and ioy that they had thereby, yet deepe sorrow was annexed and ioyned. So it is, when wee be not wise and watchfull, euen in the good things which we goe about: for although wee haue some good fruite thereof, yet wee may easily diminish our ioy by our owne folly, yea bring sorrow to our selues, as they did here, in stead thereof. As *Iphtah* after his victorie ouer the Ammonites, through his rash vow made, turned his great ioy into exceeding sorrow and mourning. Vers.6. Iudg.11.35.

And what marueile though it be thus, when such griefe is brought vpon vs through our owne procuring, and when the condition of all, euen the best, is such in this life, that though we doe not alwaies see cause, by reason of our blindnes, yet God seeing it meete that it should be so, trouble and calamitie will meete with vs, and allay our lawfullest reioycing: as wee see in *Iacobs* lamenting for *Ioseph*, crying out, *An euill beast hath deuoured him, Ioseph is rent in peeces:* and *Dauids* for *Absolom*, whose death when he heard of hee bewailed thus: *Would God I had died for thee, O Absolom, my sonne, my sonne.* But what then will ye say: Is it all one whether wee be circumspect in our Gen.37.33.34. 2.Sam.18.33.

 matters

matters or no? seeing trouble and sorrow meete with the good as well as the bad, and with the carefull as well as with the carelesse liuer? I answere: Farre be it from vs so to thinke. For though we be free from affliction in no estate of life, yet the trouble that commeth through our own folly and procuring, is bitter and smartie in a double respect: whereas that which God sendeth in his fauour, for whatsoeuer cause it seemeth good to him, though of it selfe it be distasting to vs, is gentle and tollerable, and farre more easily borne, though all be iust.

This latter kinde God doth indeed mixe with our pleasures and lawfull delights, as for other causes, so for this especially, that we should not be eaten vp of them, and so condemned with the world that doth so: for hee knoweth how neerely we are addicted to them, so that we haue need to be weaned from the excessiue delighting in them, by affliction and calamitie. And this is the worst that he meaneth, or intendeth to vs thereby. But those that we draw vpon our selues through our sinne, as negligence and anaduised dealing, but specially by wilfulnes, doe fret as a canker, and eate out the sweetnes which wee might enioy by our true seruing of God, and by the many commodities and priuiledges which wee haue thereby. So that our life yeeldeth vs not the hundreth part of comfort and contentment, that it might and would otherwise doe, but becommeth wearisome and tedious vnto vs thereby.

Note.

Vers. 7. In that great distresse of their brethren, they cast with themselues how to helpe them with wiues: and the rather to make amends both to the Lord for their rash oath, and their brethren for their crueltie. It teacheth vs, to

Iosh. 10. 10. take care for the supplying the wants of our brethren: as *Iosbua* was carefull to helpe the Gibeonites in the danger they were in by their neighbours. And it standeth vs in hand to looke to our selues in this case: for doubtlesse the more we enioy our selues, the more vnacquainted wee shall be with the wants of others, and carelesse of them, without speciall grace; if we proceed not to a worse degree, euen to mirke and grudge (like swine at the trough) that others should fare well with vs. As he who repined at the wages of his fellow, though he had his due. For which hee had this bitter reproofe; *Is*

Matth. 20. 15. *thine eye euill because I am good?* And this care should be shewed, either in outward calamities or inward distresses of minde, especially in sicknesse, as wee may: remembring that the Lord Iesus in that great day, shall call the neglect thereof into question, before many others: as by the finall sentence

Matth 25. 43. of condemnation (Matth. 25.) appeares. We should weigh others cases by our owne, and streine our selues in their great necessities to doe more then we are otherwise well able: and like our Sauiour, learne this dutie to pitie others, by experience of that in our selues, I meane desire to be pitied when

Act 4. 34, 35. wee are in distresse. How did they in the Primitiue Church sell their possessions to relieue the need of their brethren? knowing, that, to be little respected in our wants is a great affliction of it selfe. Oh, what good might many doe, if they had an heart, and were ready thereto? Well, when they would be glad themselues of mercie, they shall be left forsaken in miserie. But many crie out of this vile propertie in themselues, when they see how God meeteth with them. I handled this point a little before vpon the like occasion, where I brought foorth the example of an vnhappie woman, who ſmarted for this ſinne of incompaſſionatnes, aboue many. The Lord redreſſe it. All for the moſt part are for themſelues,and yet all too little that way. Thoſe lepers of whom we reade, 2.King.7. ſhall riſe vp in iudgement againſt the men of this age,and condemne it: for they hauing well filled and furniſhed themſelues with victuals and ſpoile in the forſaken tents of the Aramites,could not be at quiet, till they had communicated the ſame to the whole common behoofe of their brethren: whereas many of vs,ſo it may goe well with our ſelues,care but little for others whether they ſinke or ſwimme. Yea this diſeaſe may euen taint the beſt,and that in reſpect of the beſt things,or elſe would not *Paul* haue willed the Theſſalonians in the third chapter and firſt verſe of the ſecond Epiſtle,to pray for him and all his fellow Miniſters,that the Goſpell might haue free paſſage among others,as well as among themſelues. We ſhall not eaſily forgoe our right for another, and wiſh him well with our owne loſſe,as *Paul* did *Agrippa*,if we cannot beteame him a part with vs in our welfare.

2 King.7.9.

2.Theſ.3.1.

2 And here further marke the vnwiſe diſpoſition of men. If they ſee one flouriſh and proſper,they commonly enuie him: but if his eſtate be ouerthrowne,and he brought to miſerie,then they pitie him. Which argue two foule faults in them, to wit, enuie and follie. For what is it elſe but enuie, when they cannot reioyce,but fret at anothers welfare? and what leſſe then follie in them, to cauſe trouble to themſelues, by their neighbours hurt, which they haue ſmall need of: whereas it might before haue been remedied,as here it might haue been with theſe?

3. But whereas I ſaid in verſe 4. that it was very like that God gaue anſwere to them that they ſhould take wiues for the Beniamites from the men of Iabiſh Gilead; this verſe confirmeth it. In that they demand one of another, how they ſhould get wiues for them, it came of the anſwere that they receiued of God: for he bad them, by inquiring who were abſent, releeue them. And if he had not giuen them ſome anſwere as he had done in former times, though it be not expreſſed, they had returned heauy from him much more then they were before. And in that (I ſay) God anſwered them, it appeares by this,that the men of Iſrael had not found out, that they of Iabeſh had bin abſent before they lately ſought counſell of the Lord. So that it is moſt likely, that God either ſent them to Iabeſh particularly by name, or in generall bad them ſearch out who were away at Mizpeh, and take wiues from them for the Beniamites. And ſo they inquired among themſelues, and found that the men of Iabeſh had been abſent. And this that I haue laſt ſet downe, I take to be the Lords anſwere to them,as may be gathered by the 5. verſe. Whereby let vs learne,that God is ready to reſolue the doubts of ſuch as are troubled, and to ſatisfie their lawfull deſires, though it be ſometime without particular directing and appointing them the meanes for the bringing of it to paſſe: and all to this end, that they may take the more paine to aske after them, and ſo finde them out.

The ſecond part of the Chapter.

AS wee haue heard in the fifth verſe,ſo in this 8. it is repeated, that they inquired who had been away from Mizpeh, and they found that the men Verſ.8.9.

men of Iabesh Gilead had not bin there with their brethren: which was as much as to shew themselues enemies to their attempt, and to animate others by their example to doe the like. And though the fault of the Beniamites was very great, yet these seemed to fauour it, when they refused to ioyne with their brethren in the warre for so good a cause, and so weakened (as much as in them lay) the authority of the common wealth, for in view taking it was found that they had not bin there.

Doct. By this searching out and inquiring after such as did but fauour the wicked, it must teach vs, that such diligent inquiry should be made for offenders and malefactors, as mens places and callings will permit, and after their impiety and iniquity: for so the Lord inioyneth. As we see in the seeking
Iosh. 7.19. out of *Achan*, and in *Iacobs* seeking out of the Idols that were among his
Gen. 35.1.2. people, that came from Laban at Padana Aram. So Papists, traytors, whoremongers, drunkards, and masterlesse persons, with such idle caterpillers should be sought after, and ferrited out of their holes and dennes. I remember what I haue read of a certaine King (in ancient times) of England, who finding the land much annoyed with vermin, as wolues, foxes &c, appointed to euery man a certaine summe of money, for euery head he could shew of those beasts which he had destroyed: by which policy, the land in short time grew well purged of such noysome creatures. The Lord put the like minde into them, whom (vnder himselfe) it chiefly concerneth, to destroy betimes (with *Dauid*) all incorrigible workers of iniquity, from out of the Church, as being a farre greater bane to it, then the other to the Common wealth. And this should be done, lest the Philistim Idolaters should goe before vs in prouiding for the welfare of their common wealth, who with great trauaile and toile sought out and pursued *Samson*, when he had sore annoyed thẽ. And euen so ought euery priuat Christian to search, yea throughly to search out the seuerall corruptions of his heart, and dan-
Lament. 3.40. gerous qualities that are in this life, as the Prophet *Ieremy* willeth, which do waite him as great mischiefe, as open and grosse iniquities doe the Church and common wealth. This I haue thought good to adde, to that which I haue spoken hereof in the 5. verse, tending to the same purpose: this onely difference there is, that there they consented to decree against the fauourers of *Beniamin*, and here they execute the decree: without which it had bin to little purpose to haue consented in it.

2 Againe, if God wil haue men stand forth to ioyne with their neighbours for the benefit of the common wealth, (as these men of Iabesh for not doing so, were so dealt with as we heard) much lesse will he allow men to bee newters, or of no religion in the Church, seeing from true religion rightly
1. Kings 18.21. imbraced, all other duties should come. So *Elias* reproued the people that would shew themselues to be neither on Baals side, nor on the Lords, say-
Reuel. 3.15. ing: *How long will ye halt betwixt two opinions? if God be God, follow him; if Baal be God, then goe after him. And the people answered him not a word.* The Lord likewise reproued and threatned them in the Church of Laodicea, who were neither hot nor cold, but lukewarme, that he would vomit thẽ out of his mouth. So that we should know, that constancy and sincerity in our seuerall duties and particular actions of our life, is required of vs, and that we indeuour to serue God wholly and not in part.

And

And lastly, let it be marked, that if the men of Israel could draw out 3.
them of Iabesh from the rest, to punishment for their vnfaithfulnes, much more will the Lord doe so to them that halt and bee false hearted towards him; and especially in the latter day. For why? they redeeming their ease, pleasures, and profits with the losse of religion and christian walking, hee hath pronounced that he wil not know them, (that is for his) or that no such shall taste of his supper. Luk 13 27. Luk 14. 24.

In these verses is shewed, that the whole congregation of the men of Israel, sent out twelue thousand strong men to slay the inhabitants of Iabesh Gilead with women and children, if the women had lien by men. And there they had 400. virgins, and so they called those men that had fled to the rocke of Rimmon, that they might come peaceably to them, and gaue them wiues of those whom they saued aliue for them, but for all that they had not wiues enow for them all. Vers. 10.11.12. 13.14.

By this iudgement executed vpon the men of Iabesh, who would not come among their brethren against the malefactors of Gibeah when they were sent to by them, we may see that God will one time or other be auenged of such as beare with them that are euill, and are enemies of the common good of his people; whether through stomacke they doe it, or for their owne priuate wealth, and such as flesh and hold with the wicked to the weakening of the good. Also he will haue a day fit for all caterpillers and cormorants, that waste the meaner sort, raisers of prices by holding in their commodities, being but in few mens hands: likewise with them that vse their wealth, countenance and might to defend the bad, and discourage the good; these I say, and all other such that lie in the way to doe much mischiefe, he will meete with them, so as shall be little to their liking. Also the idle hacksters, and such as liue without callings in play, whoring, and robbing may be added vnto them: he will (I say) vndoubtedly haue a day for such (though they neither feare nor beleeue it) when he will call them to a reckoning and to iudgement. Doct: vers. 10. Reuel. 3. 17.

And much more then, they shall not goe vnpunished, who destroy the Church, and further not the flourishing estate of it by the weeding out, and cutting downe of noysome members, by nourishing the true Ministers of Christ, and the sincere preaching of the word. It shall not alwayes be summer with them, but the Lord will in his good time take them in hand, and declare by their punishment, what liking he euer had of them or their doings, when they were in their prime and applauded of those that were like minded vnto them. And to this must be added a remarkable circumstance, which layeth open the iustice and equity of the punishment, as well as the former doth declare Gods seuerity in punishing. By that speech of *Moses* to the congregation of Israel, Numb. 16, 29. If these men die the common death of men, or if they bee visited after the visitation of all men, the Lord hath not sent me: it appeareth, that the very manner of a iudgement is much for the enlarging of the hidiousnes thereof, and the hainousnes of the sinne that caused it. And so doth this heere: for we see that as, for the corrupt respect which these men of Iabesh had, they fauoured the cause of the Beniamites: so the Lord most iustly caused the Beniamites (for whose sake they had offended God) to be the occasion and meane of vtter ruine to

the

the men of Iabesh. And so commonly the obiect, matter, and occasion of mens boldnes in sinning, becomes the chiefe scourge and matter of punishment to the committer. As *Iudas* his money was his hangman, the Shechemites and *Abimelech* were each others executioners. But I note it onely, referring the reader now in the vpshot of this long worke to the places of the like former discourse. See chap. 9. and chap. 14. 15. compared with chap. 15. 6. and two or three other.

2 Though they gaue them a charge to destroy both men, women and children, yet we see no cōmandemēt of God that they should do so. But it may be they shewed too much seueritie in so doing: as they did indeed vnlesse they had God going before them therein. If it came of the Lord, we must know that hee saw cause of so doing, which they of themselues otherwise might not take vpon them to doe. As if the women had heartned and set forward their husbands to withstand their brethren, they then iustly suffred with them. But whether they did so or no, thereby all of that sexe may learne to take heed that they be not counsellers nor consenters to their husbands in euill, for God seeth it, and they shall smart and suffer with them. Act. 5. 10. As we reade that *Saphira* was partaker with her husband *Ananias* in his fact, and therefore was she also partaker with him in his punishment. And so I say of the children, if God bad them put them also to the sword, he saw cause euen to pursue them in whom the parents tooke their delight. And therefore God oft punisheth them with their gouernours, yea and the rest that are about them, oft times as hee did them that were of *Ahabs*, and *Ieroboams* house. So that it is danger (we see) to them that be linked in with the wicked, or to be seruants to, or in house with them, yea the very dogge that attendeth them, doth not escape in such a case, when God commands to destroy euery one that pisseth against the wall.

But if God did not commaund them of Israel, to destroy all except the virgins, then was it their sinne, and very crueltie. And so wee are to know, that all censure and hardnes inflicted vpon offenders that is more then their due punishment, it is no otherwise to be accounted of then crueltie. And this rigour in men to the which they are most prone, euen as too much lenitie and bearing with faults, on the other side, are extremities, in which yet men delight, and doe not for the most part rest in the meane betwixt both, but either passe ouer faults without punishment, or else exceed and goe too farre in executing of it: as the Reader hath alreadie seene in their like fact to them of Beniamin, where I haue spoken of this more at large.

Vers. 11. Here the holy storie telleth vs how the men of Israel expound their own commission contained in the former verse, to wit, what women are meant, when they commanded the messengers whō they sent to Iabish Gilead, to kill thē, namely all that had knowne man by lying with any. And it was set downe to good purpose that the messengers might not be deceiued: Therby we must learne, that we must labour for plainnesse, and to be vnderstood in our speeches, for misconceiuing breedeth much error. Therefore our Sauiour taught the Sadduces that they erred, because they knew not the scriptures. And so it is with vs in all our bargaines likewise, and contracts, want of plainnesse breeds much contention, though there be no ill meaning and purpose of deceiuing: therefore woe to them that practise subtiltie, and of

set

set purpose intend it. But almost euery chapter in this booke containes matter of this argument. See *Iphtahs* demaund expressely offered to the Ephramites, *Samsons* bargaine with his companions, &c.

By weighing these two verses we may see that not onely the maried wo- Vers.11 12.
men, but also such as had dishonested themselues by whoredome are taken into the number of them that were to be slaine. Whereby all of that kinde who heare it, are incouraged to virginitie and chastitie, and consequently to innocencie and honestie. For why? God hath threatned the workers of iniquitie, and therefore it can be no otherwise, but one time or other their sinne will finde them out. And wee see the same in this action: for where no man could see any thing amisse outwardly, or at least feare any danger, yet their sin setteth a marke vpon them, and draweth them foorth to iudgement, and it doth threaten to the committers, woe and sorrow, while the righteous is bold as a lion.

We haue heard before in this chapter how the men of Israel pitied and Vers.13.
wept for their brethren the Beniamites. In this verse it appeareth that when they had punished them sufficiently, their wrath was fully appeased towards them. For they sent to them that they might come foorth without feare or danger, and gaue them wiues, so many as they had for them, and prouided also for the rest afterwards. This dealing of theirs with their brethren giueth vs example what to doe in the like case: to wit, that when wee see wee haue wronged and hurt our brethren, (for such hard heartednes is too common) yet wee should so throughly weigh the euill that wee haue done against them, that we should seeke to make peace with them and be reconciled to them, and make them satisfaction, which is according to S. *James* his
words, that men should confesse their faults one to another. Oh men must Iam.5.16.
not be implacable, and vnappeaseable, nor keepe their displeasure: it is too
much that they haue conceiued any at all, which the Apostle oft reproueth. Rom.12.19.
An ill kinde of men it is, who cannot be brought to be reconciled to such as haue some way wronged them: For though they haue offended, yet after satisfaction made, offenders ought to be receiued againe, as both *Paul*
declared by willing that the excommunicate incestuous Corinthian should 2.Cor.2.7.
so be: and also by his intreating *Philemon* to receiue againe, *Onesimus* his ser- Philem.17.
uant that had runne away from him. Few such there are that doe relent, (it must be granted) to the end they may be pitied: therfore such as do, should not be repelled and other discouraged thereby. It is but the ouercomming of our euill hearts to bring this to passe, the which to crosse and subdue
should be our ioy, and honour: as they that doe so, shall most certainly find Prou.16.32.
it at the last. And of the three kinds of angrie men: 1. soone displeased, and soone pleased againe: 2. hardly displeased, and hardly appeased: this third sort is farre worst, who are displeased easily, but hardly or not at all pacified. But I repeate nothing of that I haue said.

The men of Israel did as they had promised to deale with that remnant Vers.14.
of Beniamin: for when they came to them to Shiloh, they gaue them foure hundred virgins for wiues, whom they had brought from Iabesh Gilead, and did not defraud them who trusted to their promise. Which commendeth truth and faithfulnes to vs toward them that relie vpon vs, not as *Abimelech* resembled by the bramble, who bad the men of Shechem put their trust

trust in him, but he deceiued them. It is one peece of good dealing, whereby a Christian man getteth and keepeth credit and good report with his brethren, (which is a precious treasure) and such looke for faithfulnes one to another: but they that doe otherwise, purchase much hurt to themselues
Prou. 20.6. thereby, and yet as the wise man complaineth, Where shall one find a faithfull man? And how apparant the necessitie hereof is, let the Heathen Philistims be iudges, chap. 16. compare verse 5. with 18. and see notes there-vpon.

Vers. 14.15. It is said in these two verses that they had not yet wiues enow for the men of Beniamin: so that the breach that was made in that tribe was a great griefe to Israel still, seeing many of the Beniamites were yet vnprouided of wiues. Here to say nothing of this that they might haue had wiues enow for them all in Iabesh, if they had suffered the women therein to liue, as they ought to haue done, for any thing we finde in the text of Gods commanding the contrary: to omit this, I say, we may learne by their dealing so rashly against their brethren which still lay vpon them and sore grieued
Note. them, that such breaches as we make by wilfulnes, and haste, are not easily made vp, neither doth the griefe that in repentance is conceiued for such doings end at once, nor in a short time, as the sinne is not intended, gone about, and committed at once, but it lieth heauily vpon the committers thereof, and long oppresseth their mindes many yeeres after.

So that it ought for good cause to make all that loue their peace (though there were no other cause) to be watchfull against such offences: for mens loose and slight dealings, doe cause sorrow and other trouble which are not easily remoued, when they be once bred and conceiued.

Doct. 2. in vers. 14.15. And further, in that they hauing receiued an answere from God, (as we haue heard) how they should prouide wiues for Beniamin, whereby there is no doubt but they might so haue done, if they had well looked vnto it, and considered of it, yet they going rashly to worke in their doings, they had not (as it is said here) wiues enow for them: hereby wee may learne how ill we prouide, when we heare Gods will deliuered and declared vnto vs, and yet we doe not labour to vnderstand it aright and marke it, to be acquainted with it, that so we may bee led thereby in our particular actions, which were no small ease and benefit vnto vs. But we receiue it by halfes, and therefore we are to seeke, and vncertaine about it, what to doe, and are as the most are, loose in our liues and vnreformed, and yet dislike it not; or else wee bee destitute of direction to guide our selues, and complaine oft times for the same, as these did here, who being told by the Lord how they should prouide wiues for the Beniamites, yet they said they had not yet enow, how shall we doe for wiues to the remnant that want? And this is the sinne and the complaint which is almost euery where: that people complaine they cannot tell what to doe, when they haue done amisse, neither know what the will of God is, when yet it is among them, and the Gospell which bringeth tidings of it, is preached vnto them. But the cause of this crying out is this, that men doe not giue their mindes to vnderstand and
Matth. 13.19. learne, nor set their hearts to follow that which they heare to bee taught them. And being thus, the euill one commeth and blindfoldeth them, that they be in no better case (if not in worse) then they who heare not at all. I

cannot

cannot better resemble the follie and shame of such persons, then by rash and hasty messengers, which are so eager vpon their iourney, that they leaue their errand behind them, or take it by halfes with them. So that when they be demaunded what it is, either they must to their shame say, They know not, (as *Abimaaz* to *Dauid*, 2.Sam.18.29) or else doe worse, euen answere of their owne head, they know not what. He is a good hearer who (like a wise messenger) mindeth his errand as well as his way, and can helpe himselfe when need requireth.

THE HVNDRED AND THREE AND LAST SERMON, ON THE XXI. CHAPTER OF THE BOOKE OF IVDGES.

The third part of the Chapter.

Verse 16. *Therefore the Elders of the congregation said, How shall we doe for wiues to the remnant? for the women of Beniamin are destroyed.*

17. *And they said, There must be an inheritance for them that be escaped of Beniamin, that a tribe be not destroyed out of Israel.*

18. *Howbeit we may not giue them wiues of our daughters. For the children of Israel haue sworne, saying, Cursed be he that giueth a wife to Beniamin.*

19. *Then they said, Behold, there is a feast of the Lord in Shiloh yeerely, in a place which is on the North side of Bethel, on the East side of the hie way that goeth vp from Bethel to Shechem, and on the South of Lebanon.*

20. *Therefore they commanded the children of Beniamin, saying, Goe and lie in waite in the vineyards.*

21. *And see, and behold if the daughters of Shiloh come out to daunce in dances, then come ye out of the vineyards, and catch you euery man his wife of the daughters of Shiloh, and goe to the land of Beniamin.*

22. *And it shall be when their fathers or their brethren come vnto vs to complaine, that we will say vnto them, Be fauourable vnto them for our sakes: because we reserued not to each man his wife in the warre: for ye did not giue vnto them at this time, that ye should be guilty.*

23. *And the children of Beniamin did so, and tooke them wiues according to their number, of them that had daunced, whom they caught: and they went and returned vnto their inheritance.*

24. *And the children of Israel departed thence at that time, euery man to his tribe, and to his family, and they went out from thence euery man to his inheritance.*

25. *In those dayes there was no King in Israel: euery man did that which was right in his owne eyes.*

The summe of these verses. WHen the men of Israel had not prouided wiues enough for the Beniamites out of Iabesh Gilead, they consulted together what to doe for them which yet wanted, and how they might get wiues for the rest, seeing the inheritance must remaine to that tribe, (as they said) and they had bound themselues with an oath, not to giue of their owne daughters vnto them, then they thought of a way how they might doe it, and that was at one of the common feasts yearely kept in Shilo. And thus they aduised the men of Beniamin: that when the maids that came to the feast should meete together to dance in open place according to the custome, where they might easily haue accesse to them, that they should come out of the vineyards vnawares to them, and catch vp euery man a maid, and carry her away to be his wife. And when the men of Shilo should complaine to them, they would take vpon them to answere the matter, and appease them. And so those two hundred of Beniamin did, and departed home with them, and after this, all the people of Israel went euery man to his owne inheritance. Now seeing many monstrous acts were wrought in those times, it is againe repeated in the last verse, to the end we should not maruaile that things were carried in so euill a manner, as we haue heard in these fiue last Chapters, that in those dayes there was no King in Israel: and therefore euery one did that which seemed good in his owne eies.

Doct. verse 16. Though it was the fault of the men of Israel that they were driuen to this trouble and care to seeke the repairing of the tribe of Beniamin, yet it was commendable in them that they ceased not to goe about to prouide for them which as yet wanted wiues: for it is said here by them, what shall we doe for wiues for the rest of them of *Beniamin*? And it teacheth according to the doctrine of the law of God, that when men see that they haue wronged their brethren, and done them hurt, though vnder a good pretence, yet when they in better aduisednes see their fault, they should shew by good testimony that they seeke to make them as they are able, some satisfaction, & that they are grieued for the iniury they did them. For such dealing doth as well comfort those that had the harme, when they see they are pitied by them that did it, as it giueth good shew of the repentance of them who haue done it.

And to teach vs who are vile and sinfull, the better to practise this doctrine; let vs consider how the Lord himselfe, who is righteous and bountifull to men, (so farre is hee off from doing them any wrong) doth pity them that offend him, when it repenteth them of the euill they wrought against him. How much more ought they who haue wronged other, to be sory for it, and desirous to make them amends? Herein *Saul*, if he had been as constant, as hee gaue great shew in words hereof to *Dauid*, he had been commendable; who when he pursued *Dauid* to kill him, and saw euen then that *Dauid* had saued his life when he could haue taken it from him, lift vp
1. Sam. 24. 17. his voyce and said, *Thou art more righteous then I, my sonne Dauid, come againe.* But I spare the reader in an argument so oft discussed.

2 Also by their care for these of Beniamin that yet wanted, wee should learne to goe forward with good attempts, and things well begun. If these had

had not ſo done,they had left their work halfe vndone,as if an houſe ſet vp, were left vncouered and vndawbed: So in all workes that are commendable, it doth much concerne them who attempt them,not to leaue them in the midway. But to goe forward with them till they be finiſhed; which I vrge rather,ſeeing many begin good matters,but few bring them to a good end: the reaſon is,that men are ſo fickle and inconſtant that they are ſoone wearie,and ſooneſt of all in that which is moſt excellent. When men come firſt to the place of preferment and to be aduanced,Miniſters or Magiſtrates I meane; many of them purpoſe to reforme much that is amiſſe,and to bring religion and preaching into account, thinking there is good cauſe ſo to doe: but when they ſee the backwardnes that is in other, how little incouragement they haue thereto, and finde that it is no pleaſure to the fleſh to be painfull in good doing, eſpecially if there goe no profit with it, they ſoone breake off their good beginnings, that I ſay no more. So in marriage there is good liking,and loue betwixt many couples at the firſt, as it is well beſeeming perſons in that condition: and yet as time commeth on, it is neglected and forgotten, and turned into the contrary. So ſeruants at the firſt, many of them I meane, are diligent and well gouerned, but beſide ill example and counſell,they of their own ill diſpoſition,become as the worſt ſort: And ſo I might inſtance infinitly, as in neighbours at their firſt meeting, and ſo foorth. But ſeeing they neither haue vpright hearts (for the moſt part) or if they haue, for that they doe not ſtrengthen their good beginnings with renuing their couenants daily, and looking carefully to the keeping of them with earneſt prayer that they may doe ſo,and arme themſelues againſt all diſcouragements and prouocations, they are changed and diſguiſed as if they had neuer well begun. And ſo I may ſay of the profeſſion of the Goſpell it ſelfe in the moſt that embrace it, as I haue laſt of all noted in the firſt verſe of this chapter. Looke into *Gedeon* his purſuite of the Midianites, whom he had in chace, notwithſtanding the diſcouragement of them of Succoth and Penuel.

Note.

Note.

Further Iſrael ſaid, the inheritance muſt be reſerued for them that eſcaped of Beniamin,& not be taken from them which was allotted vnto them, leſt a tribe ſhould faile in Iſrael: meaning thereby that they muſt ſeeke to preſerue it among them, and not be negligent in letting it faile,and a way laid open to other,to make an vniuſt claiming of it. Verſ.17.

And therein they haue left a moſt worthie example to poſteritie, that none ſhould dare lay claime to other mens lands or goods, when they ſee they are weake and ſimple,and haue ſmall power, and few friends to helpe them to their right,and they and their commodities lie open as a pray vnto the world,when they haue none to ſtand by them: For theſe men of Iſrael neither would, neither doe ſo themſelues, nor ſuffer other, as much as in them lay. Whereas (God helpe) it is a common practiſe in theſe daies for men to play the coſoners,and by euill meanes and ſhifts to inrich themſelues with the loſſe and diſcommoditie of other, and of ſuch eſpecially as are ſhiftleſſe. The kindes whereby they deceiue are innumerable: for they knowing how timerous many ſimple men are,either feare them with ſuits, and ſo make them take a little for all that is due vnto them, and to loſe the greateſt part, or with threats conſtraine them to leaue their dwelling and

Note.

Matth.23.14. occupyings. Some lie in waite to defeate sillie widowes by marrying them, and to make a pray of them: and which is much worse, when they haue wasted and made what they can of them, they cause them to liue in vtter miserie. And those who are neerest to such helplesse people, I meane in blood or affinitie, and might helpe them, yet to shunne trouble and charge are willing enough to leaue them as a bootie to their oppressors: as *Dauid* did *Mephibosheth* to *Ziba*. This and such like (for I cannot prosecute all) Gods faithfull seruants had need to abhorre, and not dare to meddle in, but helpe (as these men of Israel did) their brethren to their right.

2 Moreouer, by the care of the men of Israel in seeking to preserue a tribe, which otherwise had perished, we are taught to maintaine posteritie, which is a great blessing of God. For though our long continued peace and prosperitie in the land haue multiplied and increased the people, till one is wearie of another, yet it is the sinne of them that murmure at it, who should rather giue thankes for it, seeing it is God that prouideth food for them, and at his cost they liue all, and they helpe least the maintaining of the poore, who doe grudge most at the multitude of them. And who may murmur at other more then they at them? The multitude of the people is the glorie of
Prou.28.2. the King: and if they be religiously trained vp in their youth, as they ought to be, they are the honour of their parents also, and the godly mourne that are destitute of them. If Heathens, euen the Romanes, for a respect to a politique good, did so regard posteritie, that they fined such as wilfully liued single: and honoured marriage by granting sundrie immunities to their citizens who had begat three sonnes: which they called, *The prerogatiue of three Children*, &c. what a shame is it for vs Christians not to haue more speciall regard to the bodily and spirituall welfare of them whom we haue begot, not onely as a support of the Common-wealth, but also a Seminary of the Church?

Vers.18. But in that these men of Israel said, they could not helpe Beniamin with wiues themselues, seeing they had taken an oath to the contrary, they therein were deceiued. For though they had a good pretence to keep their oath vnbroken, seeing they counted an oath an holy and sacred thing, yet they should rather haue broken it, then to haue done as they did. For their oath was rash and vnlawfull, neither were they therefore bound to haue kept it,
Mark.6.20. but ought to haue broken it, as *Herods* should haue been, euen as it ought not at first to haue been taken at all. Euen so wee must take heed of the like swearing; and if we haue been ouerseene in taking our oath, yet let vs not increase sinne by keeping it: But of an oath I haue spoken before. Onely here I say, let not the pretence of a thing holy, make vs more prophane: as those hypocriticall Pharisies pretending the holines of the Sabbath, sought thereby to discredit the most holy actions of mercie performed by him that was Lord of the Sabbath. An oath is a good seruant when it serues to tye vs to a superiour dutie: but an euill master, when it forestals it.

Vers.19.20.21. We haue heard that the men of Israel consulted how they might prouide wiues for the remnant of Beniamin; now they lay downe their aduice to them how they should come by them, and they called the two hundred men of Beniamin to that end, and told them how they should lie in waite in the vineyards, and when the maides came out to daunce hard by, accor-

ding

ding to the custome at the feast, they should step foorth, and catch euery man one. And to that end they doe so diligently describe the place where they should haue them. Here diuers things are to be considered.

And first of the way that they found out to come by them, and what is to be thought of it, and that they of Beniamin did as they aduised them. Secondly, of the solemnitie and the feast that is said to haue been yeerely kept there, namely in Shiloh. Thirdly, of the maides comming foorth to daunce at the place here mentioned. And lastly, how the men of Israel promised to pacifie the parents of the maids (if need were) whom the Beniamites catched vp, as they were aduised. *Foure things to be considered in these verses.*

Concerning the first, that is, the way which they found out to prouide for the Beniamites, as is here set downe, it was vtterly vnlawfull, the counsel I meane that they gaue them. And so though their care and thought taking for them was commendable in the generall, yet in the particular aduising of them so as they did, their doing cannot be iustified. Much like to the fact of the vniust steward: who when he was warned to giue an account of his stewardship, and that he might be no longer in his place, he consulted what to doe, and therein he did well: but when hee stroke off his masters due in the tenants debt, and went to prouide for himselfe that way, hee did very badly. Euen thus many of the good seruants of God shew their weakenes this way exceedingly; as *David* may be one: who generally said well, that the offender mentioned by *Nathan* ought to dye: yet in particular, himself was the man. And it teacheth vs that generally we may possibly doe commendably, as these did heere who haue been spoken of, and yet particularly wee may faile much, and iustly bee reproued for many of our actions. For example, how many commend the Gospell as shewing themselues willing to be guided by it, but in their particular doings they walke so vnbeseeming it, that such as see them and know them not, aske whether they be professors of it, their liues be so vnlike the doctrine of it: so we say, we loue one another, but yet by a small, or no occasion we contend, fall out, and liue vncharitably and vnpeaceably: so we affirme, that men shall haue all good dealing at our hands, and we take scorne that we should not be taken and counted for honest men: yet we breake promise, euen then when it is to the great hindrance of our neighbour, and goe from our couenant and word, (making little conscience thereof) yea and against writing and witnes too, if we can. Which with the like dealings of men were the cause (such slipperie actions of men I meane) why the Lord speaketh as he doth in Deuteronomie, that the people had said well all that they had said, (when they readily offered themselues to heare *Moses* in all that God should say to them by him) but what addeth he? Oh (saith he) that there were such an heart in them, that they did feare me, and keepe all my Commandements alwaies, that it may goe well with them. Thereby declaring, that it is to little purpose to make good offers in generall, if wee be not prepared in the seuerall actions of our liues to performe them. And therefore God himselfe commended *Iob* for the feare of his name, and departing from euill; which he would not haue done, but for that he made conscience in and throughout his life, of his particular actions. And the more wee should feare our selues, because we see that the two sisters dearely beloued of

The first. Luk.16.3. 2.Sam.12.5.6. Deut.5.29. Iob.2.3.

of Christ, *Martha* and *Mary*, who would not haue done so, yet failed through
Ioh.11.39. infirmitie. For when they wept sore for their brother *Lazarus* death, Christ comming to them, they said in generall, that hee could doe all things, and therefore including this that hee could raise him againe from death; yet when he asked them where they had laid him, as going about to raise him, they then in particular bewraied this infirmitie to bee in them, that they thought he could not: answering to that end, O Lord he now stinketh, for he hath been dead foure daies.

These men of Israel therefore did ill, as we haue heard in their aduice to their brethren, for they ought not to seeke wiues for them against their parents consent, much lesse giue aduice to steale them: but beside both, did they not for all their oft alleaging that they could not breake their oath, and could not therefore giue their daughters to them for wiues; yet did they not (I say) for all this, aduise them such a way to come by wiues, that they did little better then breake their oath thereby? For whose daughters were they whom they willed the Beniamites to catch vp, when they came to Shiloh according to the custome? were they not theirs who dwelt in the land? yea were they not the daughters of the men of Shiloh, where the campe then was? who were of them (no doubt) that tooke the oath not to giue any: and therefore they belonged to one of the eleuen tribes. And if they were absent from the rest when the aduice was giuen, yet did not the rest aduise the two hundred to take them? Then although they did not breake their oath directly, yet indirectly they did.

2 But it will be obiected, they saw no other way, and they themselues could not giue wiues to them, because of the oath they had taken to the contrary. To the first I answere, that they might (but for their former rashnes) haue seene a way, I meane if they had saued the women of Iabesh aliue: and againe, I say, euill may not bee done, that good may come thereof. To the last, I say, that while they kept their oath, they did worse then if they had gone from it and broke it, and yet in some sort they broke it notwithstanding, (as I haue said) though (it is no doubt) they meant it not. More might be said to the like purpose.

But here let vs marke about this first point, that their error and needlesse trouble, which they caused to themselues, came both from hence that they asked not counsell of God: the case being so doubtfull as it was, that they did not aske counsell of him (I say) as they had done at diuers times before, and now they neglected to doe so, wee may see what came of it. And by it we may learne that when we take things in hand, not knowing Gods mind about them, we may take it for certaintie that euill shall come of it, and the further we goe, the more inconueniences we runne into; euen as one that ventring and going out of his way, for want of asking direction, goeth on he knoweth not whither, vntil he come back againe with shame & sorrow. So it is with vs, till wee repent of our first straying, for not asking direction and knowing Gods minde: as it is a true saying, If a man grant one absurditie in reasoning, he falleth into many. And this would soone appeare a greater matter to any, but that the most part of men make no conscience how they do things, neither seeke any knowledge whereby they may be guided aright. But in the meane while, this causeth to such much sorrow. So that

we

we ſee that the furtheſt way about, is (as the prouerbe ſaith) oft times the neereſt way home. And better it were to be aduiſed in our doings, then by raſhnes to be brought to vndoe all againe.

And may it not ſeeme ſtrange to vs that they who asked counſell foure or fiue times in this and the former chapter, ſhould yet now paſſe by it in ſuch a ſtreight as this was? They muſt not ſuffer a tribe to faile in Iſrael for want of wiues to the Beniamites, (they ſaid) and yet they had ſworne that they would giue them none. What? would they then compell them to goe marrie ſtrangers, which was an abomination? Was it not then high time for them to aske of the Lord (as they vſed) what they ſhould doe? but run on head? But what of this will ye ſay? I anſwere: that we may obſerue by this, that men who are willing and ready, for the moſt part of their actions, to take God with them, yet ſhall in ſome caſes and at ſome times bee ſo ſtrangely blinded, that they ſhall not ſeeke to bee reſolued of ſuch great doubts as trouble them, ſo that they can ſee no way to get out of them, but goe forward headlong: neither will they ſee how they bee ſnared and inbondaged, till they haue done that which they would, when it is too late.

And as I haue ſhewed the inconuenience of doing things without knowledge of Gods will, ſo the like may be ſaid of their binding themſelues by an oath not to giue them wiues of their daughters. For in ſo doing, they grounding themſelues vpon a falſe principle, and yet thinking that they ought not to breake their oath; what doe they but worſe, in counſelling them to ſteale wiues, and that alſo from among themſelues, who had ſworne to giue them none? Thus when we goe vpon an ill ground, marke how we are grauelled, and compelled to doe things abſurdly, vnconſcionably and diſhoneſtly, and yet we can doe no other; we can neither goe back, (becauſe we thinke we ſhould not doe otherwiſe then we haue done) neither can we goe forward, but wee muſt doe many things amiſſe, as wee haue heard theſe men of Iſrael to haue done. Oh therefore begin well, that anſwerably thereto wee may goe forward. Great danger there is in both, either in beginning amiſſe, when we take things in hand, or in not proceeding well when we haue well begun. Note.

Now for the men of Beniamin, to ſhew that they followed the aduice of Iſrael, as it appeareth in the 22. verſe they did, what marueile is it? For they were deeply plunged into miſerie by a kinde of baniſhment and many troubles and wants thereby, yea feare of their liues. And therefore by this one peece of kindneſſe of their brethren in prouiding them wiues, they were brought out of all. The thing to be obſerued here is this: that we haue great cauſe to pray God that wee be not caſt into ſore calamities and troubles and many: For wee are ready therein to take any conditions ſo we may be freed from them. Eſpecially pray we that we be not forſaken of him therein, for then wee will doe any thing to come out of them. For though theſe men of Beniamin had brought thoſe afflictions vpon themſelues, and therefore could not looke to be vnpurſued; yet wee, who are in good eſtate, and innocent, may be tried alſo, and in ſtreights may eaſily be to ſeeke what to doe. This be ſaid of the firſt of the foure things in theſe three verſes, namely of the way that Iſrael found out to get wiues for the Verſ.20 21.

two hundred Beniamites, and their following it, and what is to be thought of it.

The second. Vers.19. The second was of the solemne feast yeerely kept in Shiloh. It is said here that one of those yeerely feasts was now to be kept there. Wee know Deut.16.3.13. as we reade in Deuteronomie that there were many of those solemne feasts commanded of God to bee kept by the children of Israel after they came out of the desert, to the end they might hold and haue in minde Gods great workes done for them and their fathers there: and this feast here mentioned, was one of them, though it be hard to say which of them it was; the Passeouer, the feast of Pentecost, or of Tabernacles, or any other. These feasts were appointed of God to put the people in remembrance of some speciall benefit of God bestowed vpon them, and to praise him at the remembrance thereof with ioy. The signification thereof was that we should Prou.15.15. 1.Cor.5.8. keepe a continuall feast to the Lord all our life long in sinceritie, (for it is feasting to doe so) as 1.Cor.5. is to be seene. This may bee further laid out. And this of the feast or solemnitie as farre as this place giues occasion.

The third point in ver.19.20.21 The third thing is the maids comming foorth to daunce at the time of this solemnitie. In the first institution of this and the other feasts they were 1.Sam.18.7. Exod.15. kept and obserued of them in a seemly and goodly manner, as they did also at great victories gotten ouer their enemies, or other ouerthrowes of them. But at this time here spoken of, when there was no King in Israel, and therefore there was little regarding and looking to good order in any thing almost belonging to the worship of God, but the Leuites were neglected, as we haue seene chap.17. contrary to the law; it was marueile that there was any thing remaining and continued of it. But though it was in some sort kept of them that would; yet now that there was small regard had of the true worship of God among the Israelites, therefore this dauncing of the maids was but a remnant of the ancient solemnity that had sometime been, as the remainder of some building plucked downe, held by custome rather, then the first appointed and holy ordinance of God retained. And though I cannot say that the vsing of it betwixt themselues was turned to wanton and profane lightnes, in stirring vp one another to further sinne, (as vsually no better fruite proceedeth from such doings) because the text relates no such thing, yet it is againe as cleere, that they vsed it not as in times past it had been accustomed to be, to wit, with holy reioycing and praysing of God in many respects, as they had cause offered them, and with solemne assemblies in the congregation to that purpose; but for custome, as many vse the seruice of God at this day where they haue no sound preaching, which is farre from Gods ordinance and first institution.

Doct.1.out of all. From hence occasion is offered to obserue two things. The one, seeing it had been sometime in vse among them, what a pleasant thing it was at such times to the Fathers to frequent holy assemblies, which they did in those solemne meetings on the first day of their feast and on the last, God so prouiding for their comfort, and to reioyce together there as the Lord had appointed. By which we may learne, that it is the heauenliest point of our outward communion, and ioyfullest part of our life, as it was to them, to goe together into the house of the Lord, as the Prophet in the Psalme Psal.122.1. testifieth, saying: *I reioyced when I heard them say, Goe, let vs goe together into the*

the house of the Lord. And to what end? Euen to meete the Lord there, and to haue communion with him by the recording of his benefits with our selues, and stirring vp one another to the remembring and praysing of him for his many fauours, & to quicken our hope for such as he hath promised hereafter to grant vs. And as wee may haue our part herein, it shall be our wisedome to enioy it, and to make our whole liues sutable thereto, and more fruitfull and sauourie thereby to all our brethren: which otherwise will be tainted with the infection and sinne of the times that we liue in. And this of the first thing of the two.

The second thing to be noted here is this, how lamentable it was to see those holy solemnities (appointed by God, and sometime in high price with men) to haue at that time scarce any remainder left of them, (through the sin of all sorts) and that which was remaining, to be onely a retaining of the same by custome, rather then any honouring of God therein. For when all sorts had corrupted their waies, (who should haue maintained good order therein) what could the dancing of these maids be, but a ceremonious keeping of the custome, which had been sometime well obserued? 2

By the which may be gathered, that it is a heauie case to see the solemne and holy assemblies ordained by God, such as our Sabbaths are, to be so farre from that due regarding them, which ought to be, (I speake of many places) but neglected of the people, and they suffered to runne whither they will, and the Ministers who should draw them together by their heauenly instructions, to haue no words of exhortation and doctrine in their mouthes to reioice the peoples hearts, but to be as vnfit through their scandalous liues, to stand vp among them, as other of them are vnable or vnwilling to breake the bread of life to them. And when the Sabbath is passed without profit, or in more sinne committed then other daies are; what may we thinke of spending the rest of the weeke?

But in that these maids were the daughters of the Israelites, who consented as they all did to this, that they would not giue them for wiues to the Beniamites, I demaund: would they at the first consent that the oath should not be broken at all, as in verse 1 they did; and did they yet now thinke to keepe it by these meanes, to wit, by this aduice giuing to the Beniamites? Thus while they seeke to bee guiltlesse in not breaking the oath, they make themselues guiltie by breaking it, though indirectly. And this the Israelites did by the aduice they gaue the men of Beniamin to catch their daughters while they were dauncing together in Shiloh, and so they committed many sinnes while they went about to auoide one. For though the men of Shiloh were not priuie to the aduice giuen the Beniamites, as it appeareth; they had the more wrong offered them, and the other neuerthelesse caused the oath that had been taken to be broken. *Doct.3.* Iudg.21.1.

And the same thing many doe, while they seeke in speciall manner to be free from one sinne, and looke no further; in the meane while they runne into many, besides that they be not altogether free from that neither. More particularly we are to know, that such taking of wiues or seeking them is vtterly vnlawfull and euill, whatsoeuer necessitie may driue men to it. For else the fact of Shechem, the sonne of *Hamor* in catching vp *Dinah* and defiling her, but yet with desire and purpose to marrie her, might haue been lesse

lesse euill. But to returne, we must haue speciall regard, that as we labour to auoid one anoyance, so we doe another.

2 And from hence let vs further learne, that if in those lawfull meetings of those maids in Shiloh, so great an inconuenience fell out; then what may bee looked for in those that are vnlawfull altogether and needlesse? As young men and maids in dauncing together, and their vnseasonable company keepings to drinke and draw one another to sinne; night meetings also betwixt them, or ranging and running out of their gouernours houses for such ends & purposes to markets and faires. Wheras their going thither Note. euen for necessarie vses, should bee in the companie of sober and honest companions, who might both aduise them well, and be witnesses of their good carriage there, and they themselues should be armed against euill, as well as to minde and intend none. The same be said of women who must be no gadders, and men themselues must see iust cause of their going forth, or else let them looke for it, that their returning home shall bee in worse case then their going out, and also that one euill and danger or other shall meete with them.

Vers. 22. Now, to their words in the three former verses they adde in this verse, in way of preoccupation or preuenting an obiection which the men of Beniamin might haue put foorth, saying: How will the men of Shiloh take this? (for their daughters they were which they should catch vp.) They answere that when they shall come to them to complaine, they will desire them to be contented.

Now, for answering that which may be obiected, in that it is said in the common translation by the men of Israel, that the men of Shiloh had sinned for that they had not giuen them wiues before, there is no sense in their words to speake so to them, neither are they so to be vnderstood, but rather as in the purer translation appeares, they goe about to excuse the men of Shiloh, freeing them from blame and take it vpon themselues, as if they should say: You haue not giuen your daughters to the Beniamites, neither are guiltie of breaking your oath; but wee request it of you to bee content, and the fault that is, we take it vpon our selues.

We haue heard that the Israelites fell into many inconueniences, when they in so weightie a matter forgot or neglected to aske counsell of God, the thing so requiring as it did, that they should haue consulted with him for the men of Beniamin. Now there is no question to be made of them, though they did amisse in so doing, but that they would follow speedily their direction in getting them wiues, by catching vp euery man one of the maids as they were dauncing: for no man doubteth, but that they were glad to be prouided for, howsoeuer it were. But had it not been to be wished that they who counselled them so to doe, had done it vpon a better con- Doct. sideration? This was little better then the doing of them, whom *Salomon* speakes of in the Prouerbs, who would first commit euill, and afterward inquire of the lawfulnes of it: and so these counselled the men of Beniamin first to aduenture the catching vp of the maides for their wiues, and afterwards they would pacifie their parents as well as they could.

This is an vsuall manner of dealing among men, to worke that which their hearts leade them to, and then to make an end as they can. For example,

ample,to carrie away mens commodities when they stand in need of them, and make no agreement for them,and the prices rising in the meane while, when they come to reckon for them,they differ betwixt themselues sometimes almost halfe in halfe about the price with contention,and discontentment on one part at least. Thus youths (couples I meane) deale about their marriage,they make vp their match betwixt themselues by consent together,or doe worse,and then they force their parents to condescend to their contract or fornication; and if they doe not,they can make no mends but doe the like againe with other. And so I might say of many such doings: which should teach those that are wise,to begin their matters in good aduisednes, that so they may haue a good end of them,and not bee driuen through rashnes to salue them,when it is too late. Note.

The answere of the men of Israel had been good, in saying they would intreate them to be content for their sakes, if that about which they should haue intreated them had been but some small trespasse in their commodities,which they could haue made good againe: but being in a great and weighty matter in stealing away their children,in that they said they would take vpon them to pacifie them,and to cause them to breake their oath, neither of which they would themselues willingly haue yeelded vnto; it was their great sinne, and in no wise allowable in them, much lesse commendable. Whereby we may learne for what manner of trespasses we may take vpon vs to pacifie and intreate one another: and that is not for great faults, which are as the cutting off an arme or hand,or to perswade to put vp such damages and hurts as cannot bee recompenced, as here, the stealing away of our children, which is much more then the losse of our goods: but in small matters which may easily be borne, for them wee may seeke to pacifie one another: and for other to see that satisfaction be made,if it may be,and if it be expedient. Doct. 2.

Their faire speaking to the Beniamites had been commendable,if it had come from a good ground. Euen so learne wee,who are to aduise any, not to say that which will like the persons, (as they did here the Beniamites) (which thing is too commonly done in that case,especially to our superiours) but speake as *Michaiah* did: who professed boldly, that whatsoeuer the Lord said to him that he would speake. Euen so let vs bee afraid to goe on the left hand or on the right,for pleasing or displeasing of men (and yet let vs be farre from prouoking them iustly). For although we might seeme to get great fauour by speaking pleasingly to them at the first, yet when they shall see that they thriue not by the counsell giuen them, or come to consider better of the matter, that wee dealt not conscionably with them, they will hate vs as fast and as deeply, as at the first they seemed to loue vs, at least they will giue vs small thankes for our labour. And *Salomon* speaketh truly,he that dealeth plainly (as knowledge guideth him) shall finde more fauour at the last,then he that flattereth. Doct. 3. 1.King.22.14. Prou.28.23.

But howsoeuer the fact of the men of Beniamin is not to be excused in taking their offer,although they were in great necessitie,yet the sinne of the Israelites was by farre a grieuouser offence, who had of their owne heads perswaded them to it. Somewhat hath been said of both, and of the Beniamites,

iamites, that when men be in ſtreights, they are not their owne to conſider aduiſedly what they doe; but follow that which will helpe them out, howſoeuer God forbid it.

Verſe 23. Now we haue heard of the Beniamites accepting their brethrens aduice and offer of taking them wiues, the holy ſtorie here relates this to vs, that after they had ſmarted thus, as we haue heard, by the Lords ſore puniſhing of them, in the purſute of them, and alſo with feare of loſing their liues, and the loſſe of almoſt their whole tribe, and this for their horrible iniquitie; after this I ſay: it is heere added in the ſtorie, that they were exceedingly cooled and taken downe, in that they did readily hearken then to the counſell of their brethren the Iſraelites, who before would not; and returned to their inheritances quietly and ſpeedily, and were glad that they might ſo doe; and there they built and dwelt: whereas if they could haue been content to haue kept themſelues peaceable in their habitations and dwellings at firſt, and haue ioyned with the other tribes againſt the villany of the men of Gibeah, they might (we all ſee) haue auoided all thoſe and many other grieuous dangers, and might haue enioyed their peace and other commodities at their pleaſure.

Doct. But in them as in a glaſſe we may ſee our owne faces, and cleerely behold our ſelues by their example. For it is too common, that when we may liue at great libertie both in the partaking of theſe earthly bleſſings of God, and alſo in the enioying of ſpirituall, as theſe Beniamites might haue done; yet Note. they be oft times of ſmall account with vs, and little reckoning is made of them by vs, we being glutted with them, and become proud by meanes of them, neither can we be kept in any compaſſe to flye the ſinnes of the time, and to walke with God in vprightnes as we ought, (oh that is too ſtreight a curbing vp of vs) but wee breake out intemperatly and very offenſiuely, and ſo we draw many ſorrowes & miſeries vpon vs, which needed not elſe haue been, and when wee haue ſeene what commeth of our rebellious wilfulnes, and haue well ſmarted thereby, then many of vs crie out, and would Note. be glad to be in our former eſtate againe, though I deny not but that ſome harden their hearts vtterly, euen to their iuſt deſtruction. But had it not been farre better for vs, and the part of wiſe men to haue ſhifted off ſo many troubles? But oh, none of Gods benefits are ſauourie vnto vs when hee beſtoweth them freely vpon vs, vntill wee haue paid deare for the ill vſing Pſal. 55. 19. of them, as the Pſalmiſt ſaith, ſeeing they haue no changes in their liues, therefore they feare not God. But many when for their ſinne they haue been laden with many puniſhments, grow wiſer (as theſe did) in their outward carriage, to liue at home peaceably, and to keepe compaſſe in their liues; ſo it were to be wiſhed, that they did ſo from their hearts, who among vs haue ranged and gone out of the way; ſearching themſelues, and ſo Lament. 3. 40. turning againe (from the ſinnes which they finde out) vnto the Lord, for that were a thing in deed worthie, and to be reioyced for.

Verſ. 24. We haue heard in the former verſe that the men of Beniamin returned home to their inheritance: the ſame is ſaid of all Iſrael, when they had ended all this great buſineſſe about this foule fact of the men of Gibeah, and their three battailes with the Beniamites, and after that they had prouided wiues

wiues for them,I say, then they returned also to their inheritance. Whereby wee see that there is in these changeable things,a time of trouble, and a time of peace. It could bee no otherwise with them then it was. So that when we see that God will trie vs,and raise vp affliction against vs,we must arme our selues for it,and not shift it off indirectly, or seeke to come out of it vnlawfully: but let vs beware that wee bring it not vpon our selues, neither suffer as euill doers; and when hee will inlarge vs with his benefits, let vs vse them well also: and in trouble let vs waite, and God will send a time of peace againe,or of better peace where we shall not need it: and so let vs learne in euery estate to attend vpon him, which is to haue the right vse of our dwelling here below.

Note.

1.Pet.3.17.

2.

And as these men of Israel went home to their houses and enioyed the peaceable estate that they did before, after that they had met together about the sinne of the men of Gibeah and punished the same: Euen so after we haue laboured (as our callings doe require) in pursuing euill in others, or carefully gone about to purge it out of our selues, (there hauing been cause so to doe) or haue well and commendably gone through other troubles,we may boldly be much the quieter afterwards,not to be idle,but the better to be fitted to doe other duties.

Vers.25.

Now followeth the last verse,wherein after so much and great abomination,as we haue heard,to haue been committed in those times; it is added as a reason to the shutting vp of all,that there was no King or ordinary Magistrate in those daies, and therefore the confusion and disorder was so great,as we haue heard in these fiue last chapters, and there hath in all ages been too great proofe of it. So that if men were wise,they would not so vnprofitably both for their soules welfare,and for their bodily good, liue vnder the ciuill Magistrate, maintaining peace and the Gospell,as the most doe; to wit,to enioy the manifold liberties and commodities that God offereth thereby,to little or no good of their soules,if they be not much the worse for them. They would (no doubt) if they were destitute thereof, make great offers of the much good that the would doe,so as they might enioy them. Whereas now, few do so,I meane prize the time, and take that benefit by the Gospel,that they might in such daies of peace,but giue themselues to riot,profanenes,open disorder in their life,or (if all doe not so) yet of them that make not right profit of it,the most of them spend their daies in ignorance,and in vnprofitable trifling out of the time, in which nothing can be well done.

The Conclusion.

And thus I hauing said what I purposed of this chapter, (as God hath giuen abilitie) and so of the whole booke,as I could remember those things which I preached out of it,nothing so fully nor liuely (I confesse) as in the vttering of them was done; I haue now this one thing to adde,as a watch word to the reader, out of the whole. And that is this, that the principall thing to be noted throughout the booke, is, that the Lord doth shew his manner of gouerning and dealing with his people in it,and the nature and disposition of the people also; wherein he bewraieth our course and practise euen at this day,as it hath been in other ages,and will be vnto the end; to wit,that the people vsually by their sinne prouoke God euery one his

way:

way: then he puniſheth them as he ſeeth beſt, for their amendment. And in their tribulations they ſeeke him, either in the truth of their heart, or at leaſt they make great ſhew that they doe ſo: whereat the Lord is ſo moued
Note. with compaſſion and pitie toward them, that hee breaketh the bands of their affliction, according to the ſuites that they make to him in the depth of their ſorrowes, or elſe who ſhould remaine vpon the face of the earth? and ſo he ſetteth them againe at liberty. And wheras they ſhould after their deliuerance ſinne no more in ſuch manner as before, as alſo our Sauiour
Ioh.5.14. willed the man in the like caſe (that is mentioned in the Goſpell) yet they forget both Gods kindnes in remouing their afflictions, and their owne promiſe and couenant that they made with him of amendment, when they were in their anguiſh; and breake out of courſe againe moſt commonly, and are readie to doe worſe then they did before. And this is Gods dealing with them, and their manner of dealing with him againe from time to time. So that this booke is a moſt cleere glaſſe to behold our ſelues in.

But it is not our commendation to be like them herein: And to the end that we may not, two things would be amended of vs. The one, that wee ſhould be reſolute againſt offending God throughout our life, and hauing obtained ſuch mercie from him as to know that our ſinnes are forgiuen vs,
Pſal.119.9. we ſhould afterward aboue all things take heed to our waies, as Gods word
Deut.5.29. teacheth vs; that thus it might come to paſſe that though wee cannot but ſinne, yet wee might not willingly be carried after it. Which courſe, if it were well looked after, no ſmall fruite and comfort would inſue thereby:
Pſal.19.11. for in keeping of his Commandements there is great reward. The other is, that if we muſt needs breake out of compaſſe ſometime, (as we are not ignorant that the fleſh beareth a ſtrong hand in vs) yet we ſhould not lye in ſuch tranſgreſſion, no, nor ſo much ſleepe in it all night, and ſo prouoke our good God to awake and rouze vs vp by his corrections, but preuent them
Ierem.8.6. ſpeedily: by ſaying; *Oh, what haue we done?* &c. This were the onely way to haue God ſurely bound to vs, and to make our liues moſt happie, which is the chiefe vſe that wee ſhould make of this booke, and of the whole Scripture.

FINIS.

Gentle Reader, I entreate thee beare with and correct with thy pen these errors following: The Coppie being very badly written, and the Author farre off, and vnable to tend the presse.

Pag.3.line 33.reade,the which.p.4.l.23.r.case.p.14.l.5.r.strangenesse.p.35.l.2..r. should winne. p.44.l.34.r.place.p.48. l.41.r.neare p.63.l.9.r.one of.p 68.l.10.r.maintained.p 70.l.28. r. to endeuour that our. p.73.l.36.r.enioyed. p.79.l.10.r. are farre.p.82.l.45.put out [either].p.86.l.30.r.is it not lawfull.p.89.l.2.r. liue and die.p.106.l.6.put out [and] p.108.l.8.r. being such. p.119.l.44.r.the most grow. p.122.l.37.r.outward and inward. p.141.l.46.r. they cryed. p.142.l.3.r.remouing from them. p.158.l.33.r. before, doe testifie as much,and their many. p.159.l.7.r. preserued. p.164.l.25. put out [notwithstanding he].p.172 l.32.r.Let vs consider the first.p.189.l.9.r.way.p 190.l.16. put out [and]. p.194.l.8.put out [from the Lord].p 207.l.43.put out [and].p.208.l.20.r.they cast not their.p.211.l.3.put out [of].p.212.l.13. r.purposeth.p.219.l.12. r.enioyed.p.229.l.37.r.in all things.p.230.l.17.put out [that].p.231.l.26.r.thankes was for.p.235.l.44. r.haue.p.236.l.10. r.and the.p.238.l.36.r.behold in others.p.241.l.2.r.that they.p.246.l.42.r.burden of.p.247.l.8.r. day in lewd. p.251.l.33.r. they who ouercame.p.261.l.19.r.ill fauourednesse of it.p.262.l.30.r. haue lent.p.265.l.35.put out [in]. p.272.l 15.put out [but].p.284.l.2.r.now followes.p.287.l.41.r.they not preuenting. p.290.l.38.r. it shall. p.296.l.33.r. let them giue.p.301. last.r.but eagerly.p.302.l.13.r.answering.p.307.l.11.r.I answere.l.28.r.resolution.l.33.r.care are requisite.p 315.last.r. that he was.p.316.l.16.r.who doe not.p.320.l.32.r.for he.p.322.l.2.r.note this, that.p.324.l.25. put out [seeing]. p.331.l.43.r. assist him.p.339.l.8.r.a good man might.p.341.l.6.put out [that].l.7.put out [who going about the same,to].p.345.last.r. praying for Sodom and Gomorrah.p.346.l.2.put out [priuiledge].ibid.l.8.r. of this in the story. p.347.l.38.r. been foiled. p.352.l.12.r.sent them backe.p.372.l.24.r.another euen as the. p.377.l.32.put out [and].p.379.l 46.put out [not].p.380. l.2.put out [yet].p.396.l.31.put out [this].p.417.l.28. r.was so farre.p.425.l.45.r.goodliest.p.431.l.5.r by vncleanenesse. p.437.l.29.r.who crie before him,and say.p 449.l 8 r.much lesse.p.473.l. 16. r. another thus much. p.479.l.23.r.but when. p.486.l.11.r.looked for.p.509.l.8.r.permission.p.511.l.1.r.were so.p.530.l.39.r.true whether we. p.536.l.5.r.are as.p.539. l.10.r.and the other shall.l.25.r.in need of.p.556 l.48.r exceed him.p.586.l.15. r.set it on.p.600.l.39. r.are as. p.605.l.10. r.were generally.p.622.l.7.r.and yet again,if he l.40.r.hauing now.l.41.put out [But].p.653.l.38.r.change : but yesterday. p.684.l.47.r.not in anger.p.686.l.2.r.yea and.p.696.l.38.r.her father.p.701.l.5.r.which he.p.711.l.46.r wounds.p 715.l.30. r.it will be demanded whether.p.721.l.22.r.for such as S.*Iames*.p.723.l.31.r.haue fulfilled.p.742.l 40.r.is not as yet.p.747. l.1.r.all cases.p.758.l.2.r.much more.p.782.l.36.r.continue.p.783.l.17.r.lesse then.p.806.l.21.r.minister.l.38.like twinnes. p.814.l.38.r.beware.p.820 l.31.r.at least hard by.p.821.l 1.r.immoderate. p.822.l.1.r. these respects. l.19. put out [grieuous.].p.827.l.13.r.offended.p.835.l.19.r.from Laish.l.43.r.we had.l.44.r. farre meaner thing.p.836.l 43.r.they be : yea. p.865.l.27.r.as our.p.866.l.15.r.she did.p.872.l.14.put out [their].p.875.l.47.put out [and].p.900.l.22.r.herein it was the more.l.31.r.heire and Lord.p.905.l.4.r.cleare glasse.p.909.l.17.r.daily.p.914.l.29.r.obtaining honour to God.p.917.l.vlt. r.dishonesty.p.946.l.20.r.comfort.p.949.l.2.r.For auouching of which truth.p.968.l.37.r.As many.p.969.l.31.r.that they would.p.970.l.28.r.much as sleepe.